A CALENDAR OF SOVIET TREATIES

1917–1957

*The Hoover Institution on
War, Revolution, and Peace
Documentary Series, No. 4*

A CALENDAR OF SOVIET TREATIES 1917-1957

ROBERT M. SLUSSER

JAN F. TRISKA

with the assistance of
GEORGE GINSBURGS
WILFRED O. REINERS

STANFORD UNIVERSITY PRESS
STANFORD, CALIFORNIA
1959

STANFORD UNIVERSITY PRESS
STANFORD, CALIFORNIA

Library of Congress Catalog Card Number: 59-10638
PRINTED IN THE UNITED STATES OF AMERICA

PREFACE

In September 1956 the Hoover Institution on War, Revolution, and Peace of Stanford University commissioned us to undertake a documentary study of forty years of Soviet treaties. Recognizing that identification of the treaties was an essential part of our task, we set as our first goal the preparation of a Calendar of Soviet Treaties, in which would be listed every identified international agreement entered into by Soviet Russia during the period 1917–57, together with data bearing on its status and references to sources for its text or existence.

The present volume represents the attainment of this goal. Complete in itself, the *Calendar of Soviet Treaties* is intended to serve not only as the foundation for later volumes in our Study of Soviet Treaties but also as a basic reference work for all scholars in the field.

We have made the *Calendar* as complete, detailed, and accurate as the time and resources available to us permitted. We recognize, however, that we have not been able to consult all relevant sources of information and that new ones in a variety of languages are appearing continually. We recognize, furthermore, the presence of an irreducible minimum of error in a work of this character, bringing together as it does a huge mass of disparate factual data. We accordingly invite users of the *Calendar* to send us any additions, changes, or corrections which they may note in the course of their work with the volume. Materials of this kind should be addressed to A Study of Soviet Treaties, Hoover Institution, Stanford University, Stanford, California.

We take the present opportunity to thank Dr. C. Easton Rothwell, Director of the Hoover Institution from 1952 to 1959, for his unfailing support for our work. We are deeply grateful to the staff of the Hoover Institution for their help, and for the part they played in making our work a stimulating and enlightening experience. For research assistance we extend our thanks to Professor Masao Onoe, of Kobe University; Mr. Richard Hovanissian; Dr. Frank Houn; Mr. Victor Lee; Mr. Ray Smith; and Mr. Leo Vuosalo.

We acknowledge with particular thanks our indebtedness to officials of the Embassies and Foreign Ministries of a number of States who responded to our requests for assistance by providing us with official information about their countries' treaties with Soviet Russia. We also wish to thank the participants in two conferences held to discuss the Soviet Treaty Study in the Spring of 1958, at Stanford and at the University of California in Los Angeles, for their comments and advice on our plans.

Grateful as we are to those who have helped us, and much as we hope to have learned from them, we must take full responsibility for the *Calendar* as it now appears.

R. M. S.
J. F. T.

CONTENTS

Introduction   ix

CALENDAR OF SOVIET TREATIES   1

Appendixes

   1. *Unratified Treaties*   399

   2. *Secret Soviet-German*
       Military Agreements, 1921–1933   403

   3. *Nongovernmental Agreements*   413

   4. *Unverified Treaties*   427

   5. *Addenda*   431

List of Abbreviations   449

Short Title List   450

Index   461

INTRODUCTION

The purpose of this volume is simple: to identify the international agreements entered into by Soviet Russia during the first forty years of its existence, from its establishment on November 7, 1917, through the end of the year 1957. For the sake of simplicity and convenience we have called it *A Calendar of Soviet Treaties*. We have not, however, confined our material to those formal international agreements generally designated as "treaties" but have admitted into our text *all* verified international agreements to which Soviet Russia was a party, no matter what their form. To have drawn a more restricted line, we felt, would have meant simplifying our task at the cost of impoverishing our results.

It follows, therefore, that the term "treaty" as used here is even broader than the *descriptive* definition of the term employed by Soviet writers, which can be summarized as an agreement between two or more parties, usually States, usually embodied in a written document, establishing a relationship between the parties. In the Soviet view, the names given to the instrument—treaty, tractate, pact, convention, accord, declaration, exchange of notes, protocol, covenant, arrangement, resolution, compact, modification, supplement, regulations, etc.—are conventional rather than substantive denominations.*

Soviet specialists in international law have evolved not only a descriptive but also a *normative* definition of the term "treaty," reserving it for those international agreements which meet a selected group of criteria established by them as an ideological adjunct of Soviet foreign policy. The analysis of these criteria, useful as it is for an understanding of the motives and methods

---

* For Soviet discussions of the character and designation of treaties, see Ye. A. Korovin, *Mezhdunarodnoe pravo perekhodnogo vremeni*, Moscow, 1923; Ye. Pashukanis, "Dogovor mezhdunarodnyi," *Entsiklopediia gosudarstva i prava*, Moscow, 1925; Ye. A. Korovin, *Sovremënnoe mezhdunarodnoe publichnoe pravo*, Moscow, 1926, p. 92; Ye. Pashukanis, *Ocherki po mezhdunarodnomu pravu*, Moscow, 1935, p. 157; N. P. Kolchanovskii, "Organizatsionnye formy, mezhdunarodno-pravovye osnovy i tekhnika sovremënnoi diplomatii," in V. P. Potëmkin, ed., *Istoriia diplomatii*, Vol. 3, Moscow-Leningrad, 1945, pp. 803–5; Ye. A. Korovin, "Mezhdunarodnoe pravo na sovremënnom etape," *Bol'shevik*, No. 19 (Oct. 1946), p. 25; F. I. Kozhevnikov, "Sovetskoe gosudarstvo i mezhdunarodnye dogovory," in Ye. A. Korovin, ed., *SSSR i problemy mezhdunarodnogo prava*, Moscow, 1947, p. 80; F. I. Kozhevnikov, *Mezhdunarodnoe pravo*, Moscow, 1947, p. 369; F. I. Kozhevnikov, "Nekotorye voprosy teorii i praktiki mezhdunarodnogo dogovora," *Sovetskoe gosudarstvo i pravo*, No. 2 (1954), p. 65; V. I. Lisovskii, *Mezhdunarodnoe pravo*, Kiev, 1955, p. 230; and V. M. Shurshalov, *Osnovaniia deistvitel'nosti mezhdunarodnykh dogovorov*, Moscow, 1957.

For an authoritative Western treatment of the question of which international agreements are and which are not to be regarded as treaties, see Denis P. Myers, "The name and scope of treaties," *American Journal of International Law*, Vol. 51 (1957), pp. 574–605.

of Soviet foreign policy, would be irrelevant for our present purposes, and we have accordingly ignored Soviet ideological considerations in choosing our material.*

On the other hand, we have gone beyond the types of treaties recognized by both Soviet and Western international law specialists, and have included many quasi-agreements—joint communiqués, joint statements, memoranda, etc.—which Soviet foreign policy makers use to order and regulate Soviet relations with other States.

Finally, we have included a number of international agreements arrived at during international conferences. Often negotiated orally and frequently recorded only in unofficial documents such as memoirs, agreements of this type constitute an important aspect of contemporary international relations. To have omitted them from the *Calendar* would have meant to leave out a vital part of the historical record.

Those whose interest lies exclusively in traditional international treaties will find listed here all the relevant agreements of this type for which we have been able to find satisfactory evidence. Those whose concern is rather with the broad and complex problems of international relations and Soviet foreign policy will find it useful, we believe, to have as full a listing as possible, regardless of the form a particular agreement may take.

Since the organization of the *Calendar* may appear somewhat complex at first glance, a brief statement of the principles according to which the text has been compiled may prove useful.

The basic unit in the *Calendar* is the listing of an individual agreement. Each entry consists of the following elements: (1) a serial number, serving to identify the agreement, (2) a title or subject, (3) the main body of the entry, consisting of a précis of data concerning the agreement, followed by a list of (4) sources and/or (5) references.

The *serial number* serves as a brief identifying reference for the agreement. Basically it consists of two parts, a date in condensed numerical form, and an indication of the type of the agreement (bilateral, plurilateral, or multilateral). In the case of bilateral agreements, this indication takes the form of the name, in full or abbreviated, of the partner State. Thus 21/iii/16/T refers to a bilateral agreement between the RSFSR and Turkey signed on March 16, 1921. (For a list of the abbreviations used to identify partner States, see p. 449.)

For agreements between Soviet Russia and two or more States, the type-of-treaty designation may take one of several forms, as follows: (1) Agreements with a small number of States, or international agreements less than universal in scope or intention, are identified by the suffix "Pl," for "Plurilateral." Thus the serial numbers for the conventions of July 3 and 4, 1933,

* The evolution of the Soviet concept of treaties is traced in our article, "Treaties and other sources of order in international relations: the Soviet view," *American Journal of International Law,* Vol. 52 (1958), pp. 699–726.

are 33/vii/3/Pl and 33/vii/4/Pl. (2) General international agreements to which Soviet Russia is a party are identified either by the suffix "Mul," designating multilateral agreements to which Soviet Russia acceded on the date of original signature, or by the year of original signature, designating agreements to which Soviet Russia acceded only after an interval. In the latter case the first element of the serial number is determined by the date of Soviet accession, and the entry appears under that date, with a cross-reference under the date of original signature. Thus 25/viii/19/Mul identifies a multilateral convention of August 19, 1925, to which the Soviet Union was an original signatory, while 49/xii/6/1948 refers to a multilateral convention of 1948 to which the USSR acceded on December 6, 1949.

If an agreement was concluded over an interval of time (e.g., an exchange of notes sent on different dates, or an international conference which lasted longer than a single day), the date used for the serial number is the latest one concerned. Thus an exchange of notes between the USSR and Latvia of December 17, 1930, and January 14, 1931, has the serial number 31/i/14/Lat and is listed under January 14, 1931.

If more than one agreement was concluded with a given partner on a single day, or if it seems desirable in the interests of accuracy to differentiate between a number of components constituting a complex entity (e.g., a treaty accompanied by one or more exchanges of notes), a letter suffix is added to the serial number of each separate agreement or component. Thus 22/viii/12/Fin/a identifies the agreement between the RSFSR and Finland of August 12, 1922, concerning repatriation, while 22/viii/12/Fin/b refers to the agreement of the same date between the same partners concerning the return of ships.

The *title or subject*, set in boldface type, identifies the partners to the agreement (if it is a bilateral agreement) and indicates its subject. Wherever feasible the official title has been used, or the one under which the agreement is generally known; when the official or generally known title is unnecessarily cumbersome, uninformative, or ideologically loaded, however, we have substituted a shorter or more descriptive one. Parties to plurilateral agreements have been listed immediately below the title in most cases, but signatories to multilateral agreements have usually not been listed.

The *entry* brings together all relevant identified data on the juridical status of the agreement, including the date and place of signature and dates of ratification, entry into force, duration, modification or extension, and termination. Where information under any of these headings is not indicated, it is either not applicable or not known. References for factual data shown are to be found among the sources and references listed immediately below the entry. Individual citations for data shown are given only when conflicting evidence from several sources makes it desirable to give the reader the material from which to form his own conclusions. In general we have followed the information given in Soviet sources unless there appeared to be valid reason to reject it.

For treaties and agreements concluded up to 1940 we have limited our-
selves in most cases to a bare identification, believing that the history of the
first twenty-odd years of Soviet foreign relations is relatively well known and
its records relatively accessible in translation or summary. For treaties and
agreements concluded during 1940 and later, however, we have broadened
our treatment to include brief summaries of some or all of the principal provisions of a number of agreements, or relevant data on their history. These
summaries make no claim to completeness and are intended as a guide to
the full texts of the agreements concerned rather than as a substitute for them.
Where the text of an agreement is available in English translation in an easily
accessible authoritative source (e.g., the United Nations *Treaty Series*), we
have usually omitted any summary of provisions. We have followed the same
policy with secondary functional agreements (e.g., parcel post agreements),
the provisions of which are usually standardized and not of particular interest.

Below the entry are shown *sources and references*. By source we mean
a text of the agreement; by reference, any other identification, from a comprehensive summary to a bare mention. Sources are commonly listed in the following order: (1) official Soviet sources, including the central metropolitan
press; (2) other Soviet sources; (3) official sources of the treaty partner;
(4) other sources of the treaty partner; (5) official international sources,
particularly the *Treaty Series* of the League of Nations and the United Nations; and (6) any other sources. The language in which the text is printed
can be assumed to be the language of the source whenever the source gives
only a single version. When more than one version is given, language references follow the source citation (e.g., "R" indicates that the source gives the
Russian-language text, "E" the English-language text, and so forth, in accordance with the list of language abbreviations on p. 449).

Both sources and references are identified either in full or, more frequently, by short title or abbreviation, in accordance with the Short Title
List given on pp. 450–60. All sources and references listed without comment
have been checked directly; if it was not possible to check a primary source
mentioned in an available secondary source, we have listed both. Primary
source references from the official treaty series of a number of States which
were provided through the courtesy of the Embassies or Foreign Ministries
of those States, and which it was not possible to check directly, are identified
by an asterisk(*) preceding the listing.

Included in the main text of the *Calendar* are a relatively small number of
entries which are not agreements, even in a broad sense, but which are directly related to agreements and which we chose to bring to the reader's attention in direct association with the text. Other borderline documents have
been listed in the first four appendixes: 1, treaties subject to ratification but
not ratified; 2, secret Soviet-German military agreements; 3, nongovernmental
international agreements; and 4, agreements reported but not satisfactorily
verified. Agreements and data identified after completion of the main text
are given in Appendix 5.

A CALENDAR OF SOVIET TREATIES

1917–1957

1917

- 17/xii/4/Ger

Agreement between the Russian armies on the Western Front and the German armies opposing them concerning temporary suspension of hostilities

Signed Dec. 4, 1917 (Nov. 21, 1917, Old Style), in Soly.
Extends from Dec. 6 to 17, 1917, or until the signing of a general armistice; takes the place of earlier (unspecified) partial agreements on the cessation of hostilities.
Sources: *Izv.*, Dec. 8, 1917 (Nov. 25, 1917, Old Style).
DVP, 1, pp. 36–38.
Note: For discussion of sources, see note under 17/xii/15/CP/a.

- 17/xii/5/CP

Agreement between the Russian High Command and the High Command of the Central Powers (Germany, Austria-Hungary, Bulgaria, and Turkey) concerning temporary suspension of hostilities

Signed Dec. 5, 1917 (Nov. 22, 1917, Old Style), in Brest-Litovsk.
Extends from Dec. 7 to 17, 1917; supersedes all earlier partial agreements concerning suspension of hostilities. Superseded by armistice of Dec. 15, 1917.
Sources: *Izv.*, Dec. 7, 1917 (Nov. 24, 1917, Old Style).
Arkhiv russkoi revoliutsii, 20, pp. 54–55.
FRUS, 1918, Russia, 1, p. 307 (abridged and inaccurate).
STS, 1, p. 1, citing *FRUS, loc. cit.*
Note: For discussion of sources, see note under 17/xii/15/CP/a.

- 17/xii/15/CP/a

Armistice between Russia and the Central Powers

Signed Dec. 15, 1917 (Dec. 2, 1917, Old Style), in Brest-Litovsk.
Extends from Dec. 17, 1917, through Jan. 14, 1918, with automatic continuation until 7 days after denunciation by either side. Supersedes agreement concerning suspension of hostilities of Dec. 5, 1917 (see note below). Notice of termination given by German military headquarters Feb. 17, 1918.
Sources: *DVP*, 1, pp. 47–51.

TRP, pp. 1–7 (E, G), citing
  Deutscher Reichsanzeiger, Dec. 18, 1917.
STS, 1, p. 1.
Note on the agreement of Dec. 5, 1917, concerning temporary suspension of hostilities:

According to Art. 8 of the armistice of Dec. 15, 1917, the armistice superseded the agreement concerning suspension of hostilities of Dec. 5, 1917. It has been generally assumed that the agreement in question is the one here listed under 17/xii/5/CP. A recent Soviet documentary compilation, however (*DVP*, 1, p. 51), states that the text of the Dec. 15 armistice is inaccurate, and that the correct reference should be to the Dec. 4 agreement (here listed under 17/xii/4/Ger). *DVP*, 1, omits all mention of the Dec. 5 agreement.

There appears to be no question, however, that an agreement concerning the suspension of hostilities was in fact signed at Brest-Litovsk on Dec. 5, 1917, and that it is this agreement, rather than the agreement of Dec. 4, 1917, which is referred to in Art. 8 of the Dec. 15 armistice. Contemporary evidence for the existence of the Dec. 5 agreement is consistent and conclusive; it includes both Soviet and German sources. On the Soviet side, in addition to the *Izv.* reference cited under 17/xii/5/CP, see a statement by L. B. Kamenev, one of the members of the negotiating commission, summarizing the agreement, in *Izv.*, Dec. 9, 1917 (Nov. 26, 1917, Old Style), reprinted in Kamenev, *Bor'ba za mir*, p. 12; on the German side, see Max Hoffmann, *War diaries*, vol. 2, pp. 194–95, and *Die Friedensverhandlungen in Brest-Litowsk*, p. 13. In addition, a Russian émigré army officer, one of the negotiating commission on the Soviet side, has written a full account of the negotiations, including the Dec. 5 agreement: Fokke, D. G., "Na stsene i za kulisami Brestskoi tragikomedii," *Arkhiv russkoi revoliutsii*, 20, pp. 5–207; text of the Dec. 5 agreement, pp. 54–55.

There can be no doubt, therefore, that *DVP*, 1, is inaccurate in denying the existence of the Dec. 5 agreement and substituting for it that of Dec. 4.

● 17/xii/15/CP/b

Supplement to the armistice between Russia and the Central Powers

Signed Dec. 15, 1917 (Dec. 2, 1917, Old Style), in Brest-Litovsk.
Provides for establishment of a mixed commission in Petrograd to work out measures for re-establishment of postal and trade relations, transmission of books and newspapers, etc.
Sources: *DVP*, 1, p. 52.
  TRP, pp. 9–10 (E, G), citing
    Deutscher Reichsanzeiger, Dec. 18, 1917.
  STS, 1, p. 2.

● 17/xii/18/T/a

Armistice between the Russian and Turkish armies fighting on the Caucasian-Turkish front

Signed Dec. 18, 1917 (Dec. 5, 1917, Old Style), in Erzincan (Erzindzhan).
Entered into force on signature.
Source: *DVP*, 1, pp. 53–56.

● 17/xii/18/T/b

Act concerning demarcation lines, supplementing the Russo-Turkish armistice

Signed Dec. 18, 1917 (Dec. 5, 1917, Old Style), in Erzincan (Erzindzhan).
Source: *DVP*, 1, pp. 56–57.

1918

● 18/i/31/AH

Agreement between the RSFSR and Austria-Hungary concerning repatriation of civilians

Signed Jan. 31, 1918 (Jan. 18, 1918, Old Style), in Petrograd.
Enters into force on confirmation by governments of both signatories, to take place not later than 14 days after signature.
Protocol and supplement signed Feb. 10, 1918.
Source: *DVP*, 1, pp. 637–39.
Note: The text of this agreement, as well as that of the following 8 agreements listed, was evidently first published in *DVP*, 1, based on archival materials. All 9 agreements were signed in Petrograd by representatives of the mixed commission established under the armistice of Dec. 15, 1917. Although a number of the agreements call for confirmation by the governments of the signatories, no contemporary publication of the texts has been traced, nor any reference to their confirmation.

● 18/ii/7/CP

Agreement between the RSFSR and the Central Powers concerning repatriation of wounded and sick prisoners of war

Signed Feb. 7, 1918 (Jan. 25, 1918, Old Style), in Petrograd.
Enters into force on confirmation by the RSFSR and one other signatory.
Source: *DVP*, 1, pp. 639–43.

● 18/ii/9/Ger

Agreement between the RSFSR and Germany concerning repatriation of civilians, with supplementary protocol and final protocol

Signed Feb. 9, 1918 (Jan. 27, 1918, Old Style), in Petrograd.
Enters into force on confirmation by both governments.
Source: *DVP*, 1, pp. 644–47.

● 18/ii/10/AH

Protocol and supplement to the agreement between the RSFSR and Austria-Hungary of January 31, 1918, concerning repatriation of civilians

Signed Feb. 10, 1918 (Jan. 28, 1918, Old Style), in Petrograd.
Source: *DVP*, 1, p. 647.

● 18/ii/11/Bul

Agreement between the RSFSR and Bulgaria concerning repatriation of civilians, with protocol and supplementary protocol

Signed Feb. 11, 1918, in Petrograd.
Enters into force on confirmation by both governments, to take place within 15 days of signature.
Source: *DVP*, 1, pp. 648–51.

● 18/ii/13/AH

Agreement between the RSFSR and Aus-

tria-Hungary concerning treatment of prisoners of war

Signed Feb. 13, 1918 (Jan. 31, 1918, Old Style), in Petrograd.
Subject to confirmation.
Source: *DVP*, 1, pp. 651–52.

● 18/ii/14/AH

Agreement between the RSFSR and Austria-Hungary concerning temporary rules for postal, telegraph, and railroad communications, with final protocol

Signed Feb. 14, 1918, in Petrograd.
Enters into force on confirmation by both governments.
Source: *DVP*, 1, pp. 652–58.

● 18/ii/14/Bul

Agreement between the RSFSR and Bulgaria concerning postal, telegraph, and maritime service, with supplementary protocol

Signed Feb. 14, 1918, in Petrograd.
Subject to approval by both governments.
Source: *DVP*, 1, pp. 662–65.

● 18/ii/14/T

Agreement between the RSFSR and Turkey concerning temporary regulation of postal, telegraph, and maritime service

Signed Feb. 14, 1918, in Petrograd.
Subject to approval by both governments.
Source: *DVP*, 1, pp. 658–61.

● 18/iii/ /China

Border agreement between the Soviet regime in Siberia and Chinese border authorities

Signed during March 1918, at Matsievskaia.
References: *Izv.*, Mar. 19, 1918.
  Kennan, 2, p. 70.

● 18/iii/1/FSWR

Treaty of friendship and brotherhood between the RSFSR and the Finnish Socialist Workers' Republic

Signed Mar. 1, 1918, in Petrograd.
Sources: *Izv.*, Mar. 10, 1918.
  Texts of the Finland "peace," pp. 5–12.
  Krasnaia letopis', 1932, No. 5–6, pp. 87–92.

STS, 1, pp. 2–4.
Kliuchnikov, 2, pp. 120–21 (excerpts).

● 18/iii/3/CP

Peace treaty between the RSFSR and the Central Powers, with five appendices (Treaty of Brest-Litovsk)

Signed Mar. 3, 1918, in Brest-Litovsk (and in Bucharest on Mar. 7, 1918, by von Kühlmann, German Secretary of State for Foreign Affairs).
Ratified by the RSFSR Mar. 15, 1918; by Germany, Mar. 26, 1918. Entered into force Mar. 29, 1918, on exchange of acts of ratification in Berlin. Acts of ratification subsequently exchanged with Austria-Hungary (July 4, 1918, in Berlin); with Bulgaria (July 9, 1918, in Berlin); and with Turkey (July 12, 1918, in Berlin). Supplemented on date of signature by treaties concerning political and legal questions with Austria-Hungary, Bulgaria, Germany, and Turkey (next 4 documents), and on Aug. 27, 1918, by a treaty, two supplementary agreements, and an exchange of notes with Germany.
Annulled by Soviet decree of Nov. 13, 1918 (*SU*, 1918, No. 95, Art. 947, covering all supplementary treaties and agreements), and by Art. 116 of the Treaty of Versailles of June 28, 1919.

Sources:

(a) Text of the treaty: *Mirnyi dogovor*, pp. 3–8.
  TRP, pp. 13–21 (E, G), citing
    RGbl, No. 77, June 11, 1918.
  DVP, 1, pp. 119–24.
  STS, 1, pp. 4–5.

(b) Appendix 1 (map):
  Mirnyi dogovor, facing p. 9.
  DVP, 1, facing p. 124.
  TRP, pp. 22–24, citing
    Vorwärts, Mar. 5, 1918.
  STS, 1, p. 5 (summary).

(c) Appendix 2, concerning economic relations between Germany and Russia, with 2 sub-appendices and final protocol to sub-appendix 1:
  Mirnyi dogovor, pp. 11–70.
  DVP, 1, pp. 125–46.
  TRP, pp. 25–113 (E, G).
  STS, 1, pp. 5–11.

(d) Appendix 3, concerning economic relations between Russia and Austria-Hun-

gary, with sub-appendix and final proto-
col:
  Mirnyi dogovor, pp. 89–122.
  DVP, 1, pp. 148–64.
  TRP, pp. 141–42 (in part).
  STS, 1, pp. 11–12 (in part).
(e) Appendix 4, concerning economic re-
lations between Russia and Bulgaria:
  Mirnyi dogovor, p. 137.
  DVP, 1, pp. 164–65.
  TRP, pp. 159–60.
  STS, 1, p. 12.
(f) Appendix 5, concerning economic re-
lations between Russia and Turkey:
  Mirnyi dogovor, p. 142.
  DVP, 1, pp. 165–66.
  TRP, pp. 165–66.

● 18/iii/3/AH

**Treaty between the RSFSR and Austria-
Hungary concerning political and legal
matters, supplementing the peace treaty
between the RSFSR and the Central
Powers**

Signed Mar. 3, 1918, in Brest-Litovsk.
Entered into force Mar. 29, 1918. Acts of
ratification exchanged July 4, 1918, in
Berlin.
Sources: *Mirnyi dogovor*, pp. 123–36.
  DVP, 1, pp. 183–95.
  TRP, pp. 143–57 (E, G), citing
    Vienna *Fremden-Blatt*, Mar. 16, 1918,
    and *Pester Lloyd*, Mar. 16, 1918.
  STS, 1, pp. 17–19.

● 18/iii/3/Bul

**Treaty between the RSFSR and Bulgaria
concerning political and legal matters,
supplementing the peace treaty between
the RSFSR and the Central Powers**

Signed Mar. 3, 1918, in Brest-Litovsk.
Entered into force Mar. 29, 1918. Acts of
ratification exchanged July 9, 1918, in
Berlin.
Sources: *Mirnyi dogovor*, pp. 138–41.
  DVP, 1, pp. 195–98.
  TRP, pp. 161–63.
  STS, 1, pp. 19–20.

● 18/iii/3/Ger

**Treaty between the RSFSR and Germany
concerning political and legal matters,
supplementing the peace treaty between
the RSFSR and the Central Powers**

Signed Mar. 3, 1918, in Brest-Litovsk (and

by von Kühlmann Mar. 7, 1918, in Buch-
arest).
Entered into force Mar. 29, 1918, on ex-
change of acts of ratification in Berlin.
Supplementary protocols concerning (1)
the exchange of prisoners of war, signed
June 24, 1918; (2) commercial vessels
and cargoes, signed July 19, 1918.
Sources: *Mirnyi dogovor*, pp. 71–88.
  DVP, 1, pp. 166–83.
  TRP, pp. 115–37 (E, G), citing
    RGbl, No. 77, June 11, 1918.
  STS, 1, pp. 12–17.

● 18/iii/3/T

**Treaty between the RSFSR and Turkey
concerning political and legal matters,
supplementing the peace treaty between
the RSFSR and the Central Powers**

Signed Mar. 3, 1918, in Brest-Litovsk.
Entered into force Mar. 29, 1918. Acts of
ratification exchanged July 12, 1918, in
Berlin.
Sources: *Mirnyi dogovor*, pp. 143–49.
  DVP, 1, pp. 199–204.
  TRP, pp. 167–71.
  STS, 1, pp. 20–22.

● 18/iii/9/Rom/a

**Agreement between the RSFSR and Ro-
mania concerning political and military
matters**

Signed Mar. 5, 1918, in Jassy, and Mar. 9,
1918, in Odessa.
Repudiated by Romania later in Mar.
1918, with the incorporation of Bessarabia
into Romania.
Sources: *Izv.*, March 31, 1918.
  SDD RSFSR, 1, pp. 74–75.
  SDD, 1, p. 154.
  SDD, 1–2, 1928, pp. 113–14; *ibid.*, 1935,
    pp. 156–57.
  DVP, 1, pp. 210–11.
  STS, 1, p. 22.

● 18/iii/9/Rom/b

**Protocol between the RSFSR and Ro-
mania concerning exchange of prisoners**

Signed Mar. 5, 1918, in Odessa, and Mar.
9, 1918, in Jassy.
Source: *DVP*, 1, p. 209.

● 18/iii/9/Rom/c

Protocol between the RSFSR and Ro-

mania concerning the return of Russian soldiers in Romania

Signed Mar. 9, 1918.
References: *Izv.*, Mar. 31, 1918.
 SDFP, 1, p. 66.

● 18/iii/9/Rom/d

Protocol between the RSFSR and Romania concerning evacuation by Romania of the Akkerman district and a general political amnesty for Romanian political emigrants and deserters

Signed Mar. 9, 1918.
References: *Izv.*, Mar. 31, 1918.
 SDFP, 1, p. 66.

● 18/v/4/Ukraine. See Appendix 5.

● 18/vi/1/Sweden

Trade agreement between the RSFSR and the Swedish Trade Delegation

Signed June 1, 1918, in Moscow.
Source: *DVP*, 1, pp. 341–42.

● 18/vi/3/AH

Agreement between the RSFSR and Austria-Hungary concerning repatriation of prisoners of war

Signed June 3, 1918, in Moscow.
Entered into force on signature.
Source: *DVP*, 1, pp. 678–79.

● 18/vi/4/1904

Hague Convention concerning the exemption of hospital ships from port and other dues

Signed Dec. 21, 1904, at The Hague.
A decree published in *Izv.*, June 4, 1918, stated that the RSFSR recognized "the Geneva Convention . . . both in its original as well as in all later versions, and also all other international conventions and agreements concerning the Red Cross which were recognized by Russia before October 1917." The decree did not specify which conventions and agreements were referred to, but in the first official Soviet collection of treaties (*SDD RSFSR*, 1), 3 international Red Cross conventions were printed following the text of the June 4, 1918, decree: the present one and the 2 which follow. All 3 conventions were subsequently re-ratified by the USSR: see 25/vi/16/1904, /1906, and /1907.

Source: *SDD RSFSR*, 1, pp. 228–29.
Reference (decree): *Vestnik NKID*, 1919, No. 1, pp. 86–87.

● 18/vi/4/1906

Geneva Convention for the amelioration of the condition of sick and wounded soldiers in the field

Signed July 6, 1906, in Geneva.
For history, see 18/vi/4/1904.
Source: *SDD RSFSR*, 1, pp. 230–38.

● 18/vi/4/1907

Hague Convention for the adaptation to maritime warfare of the principles of the Geneva Convention of July 6, 1906

Signed Oct. 18, 1907, at The Hague.
For history, see 18/vi/4/1904.
Sources: *SDD RSFSR*, 1, pp. 239–46.
 Scott, pp. 163–81.

● 18/vi/12/Ukr

Armistice between the RSFSR and the Ukraine

Signed June 12, 1918, in Kiev.
Sources: Kliuchnikov, 2, pp. 142–44.
 TUP, p. 154 (summary).
 Svoboda Rossii, June 18, 1918.
 STS, 1, p. 23 (summary).

● 18/vi/17/Ger

Armistice between the Soviet army and the armies of Germany and the Ukraine

Signed June 17, 1918, in Khar'kov.
Signed on the basis of Art. 1 of the armistice of June 12, 1918.
Source: Kliuchnikov, 2, pp. 146–47.

● 18/vi/24/Ger

Protocol between the RSFSR and Germany concerning basic principles for the exchange of able-bodied prisoners of war

Signed June 24, 1918, in Berlin.
Constitutes a supplement to the treaty between the RSFSR and Germany of Mar. 3, 1918.
Source: *DVP*, 1, pp. 679–80.

● 18/vii/ /Ger

Exchange of notes between the RSFSR and Germany concerning the guard at the German embassy in Moscow

Sent during July 1918.
References: *VPSR*, p. 15.
  Carr, 3, p. 83.

● 18/vii/19/Ger

Protocol between the RSFSR and Germany concerning procedure for commercial vessels and cargoes which have fallen into the hands of the enemy

Signed July 19, 1918, in Berlin.
Constitutes a supplement to the treaty between the RSFSR and Germany of Mar. 3, 1918.
Source: *DVP*, 1, pp. 680–81.

● 18/vii/29/Fin

Agreement between the RSFSR and Finland concerning liberation and exchange of citizens arrested for political reasons

Signed July 29, 1918, in Moscow; on behalf of Finland, by representatives of the German embassy in Moscow.
Entered into force on signature.
Sources: *DVP*, 1, pp. 412–14.
  Texts of the Finland "peace," p. 53, based on *Daily review of the foreign press*, Aug. 1, 1918, from the Russian radio (incomplete and inaccurate, but with some details not given in *DVP*).
  STS, 1, p. 23 (same text as above).

● 18/viii/8/Ger

Agreement between the RSFSR and Germany concerning postal, telegraph, and railroad communications

Signed Aug. 8, 1918, in Moscow.
Enters into force on approval by both governments.
Source: *DVP*, 1, pp. 681–92.

● 18/viii/9/Pl

Agreement between the RSFSR and diplomatic representatives of Sweden, Denmark, and Switzerland, on behalf of the Entente Powers, concerning exchange of civilian and military personnel

Signed Aug. 9, 1918, in Moscow.
Source: *DVP*, 1, p. 422.

● 18/viii/27/Ger/a

Treaty between the RSFSR and Germany concerning political and territorial matters, supplementing the treaty of peace of March 3, 1918

Signed Aug. 27, 1918, in Berlin.
Entered into force Sept. 6, 1918, on exchange of acts of ratification in Berlin.
Supplemented by a financial agreement, a civil law agreement, and an exchange of notes of the same date (next 3 documents).
Abrogated, together with other agreements signed the same day, by the decree of Nov. 13, 1918, which annulled the peace treaty of Mar. 3, 1918.
Sources: *DVP*, 1, pp. 437–45.
  TRP, pp. 179–89 (G, E), citing
    Deutscher Reichsanzeiger, Sept. 7, 1918.
  STS, 1, pp. 23–25.

● 18/viii/27/Ger/b

Financial agreement between the RSFSR and Germany

Signed Aug. 27, 1918, in Berlin.
Entered into force Sept. 6, 1918, on exchange of acts of ratification in Berlin.
Supplements the treaty concerning political and territorial matters of the same date.
Annulled by decree of Nov. 13, 1918.
Sources: *DVP*, 1, pp. 445–53.
  TRP, pp. 121–202 (G, E), citing
    Deutscher Reichsanzeiger, Sept. 7, 1918.
  STS, 1, pp. 25–27.

● 18/viii/27/Ger/c

Civil law agreement between the RSFSR and Germany

Signed Aug. 27, 1918, in Berlin.
Entry into force: Arts. 1–12, Sept. 6, 1918, on exchange of acts of ratification in Berlin; Arts. 13–45 were to have been entered into force 2 months thereafter or later.
Supplements the treaty concerning political and territorial matters of the same date.
Annulled by decree of Nov. 13, 1918.
Sources: *DVP*, 1, pp. 692–703.
  TRP, pp. 203–19 (G, E), citing
    Deutscher Reichsanzeiger, Sept. 7, 1918.
  STS, 1, pp. 27–30.

● 18/viii/27/Ger/d

Exchange of notes between the RSFSR and Germany constituting a secret military protocol to the treaty of the same date

Signed Aug. 27, 1918, in Berlin.
Sources: *Europäische Gespräche* (Hamburg), 4, 1927, No. 3, pp. 148–53, citing the German Reichsarchiv;
    Poslednye novosti (Paris), Feb. 15, 1925; and
    Revue d'histoire de la guerre mondiale, Apr. 1925, pp. 150–53.
STS, 2, pp. 221–22.

● 18/ix/12/Ger

Agreement between the RSFSR and Germany concerning requisitioning in areas occupied by German troops

Signed Sept. 12, 1918, in Orsha.
Reference: *Pr.*, Oct. 24, 1918.

● 18/ix/15/Ger

Protocol of an agreement between the RSFSR and Germany concerning evacuation of the area occupied by German troops east of the Berezina River

Signed Sept. 15, 1918, in Vilna.
Based on Art. 3 of the treaty of Aug. 27, 1918 (18/viii/27/Ger/a). Supplemented by protocol of Oct. 10, 1918.
Source: *DVP*, 1, pp. 478–82.
Reference: *Izv.*, Sept. 17, 1918.

● 18/ix/21/Denmark

Trade and credit agreement between the RSFSR and the Danish Mission in Petrograd

Signed Sept. 21, 1918, in Petrograd.
Provides for delivery by Danish firms of vegetable seeds under contracts negotiated with the Department of Agriculture of the Government of Russia before November 1917.
Source: *DVP*, 1, pp. 493–94.

● 18/x/10/Ger

Protocol between the RSFSR and Germany supplementing the agreement of September 15, 1918, concerning evacuation of the area occupied by German troops east of the Berezina River

Signed Oct. 10, 1918, in Narva.
In accordance with Art. 3 of the agreement of Sept. 15, 1918, certain agreements, date unknown, concerning the transfer of railroads and equipment were reached between the German military authorities and the RSFSR Commissariat of Ways of Communication, and embodied in a 32-point protocol. This protocol reproduces point 30, on which agreement was not reached, together with the decision of the Russo-German border commission.
Source: *DVP*, 1, pp. 517–20.

● 18/x/28/Sweden

Trade agreement between the RSFSR and Sweden

Signed Oct. 28, 1918, in Petrograd.
Entered into force Oct. 31, 1918, under the agreement of Oct. 31, 1918.
Source: *DVP*, 1, pp. 704–705.
References: Shtein, 1925, pp. 11, 84, 85. Korolenko, p. 12.

● 18/x/31/Sweden

Agreement between the RSFSR and Sweden supplementing the trade agreement of October 28, 1918

Signed Oct. 31, 1918, in Petrograd.
Takes the place of the additional trade treaty called for in Arts. 5 and 6 of the agreement of Oct. 28, 1918, and provides for its immediate entry into force.
Source: *DVP*, 1, pp. 705–706.

1919

● 19/i/15/Fin. See Appendix 5.

● 19/iii/23/Bash

Agreement between the RSFSR and the Bashkir Government concerning establishment of the Autonomous Bashkir Republic within the RSFSR

Published Mar. 23, 1919. Confirmed by the RSFSR on or prior to publication.
Unilaterally abrogated by Soviet decree of May 19, 1920, concerning the governmental structure of the Autonomous Soviet Bashkir Republic (*SU*, 1920, No. 45, Art. 203); see Pipes, Richard E., *Formation of the Soviet Union*, pp. 166–67.

Sources: *Izv.*, Mar. 23, 1919.
    Vestnik NKID, 1919, No. 1, pp. 93–96.
    SU, 1919, No. 46, Art. 451.
    Obrazovanie SSSR, pp. 164–68 (emended text).

● 19/v/27/Af

Exchange of letters between the RSFSR and Afghanistan concerning reciprocal recognition

Sent Apr. 21, 1919, from Kabul and May 27, 1919, from Moscow.
Source: *DVP*, 2, pp. 174–75.
References: Fischer, p. 285.
  Eudin and North, p. 104.

June 1, 1919. Decree of the All-Russian Central Executive Committee concerning unification of the SSR's of Russia, the Ukraine, Latvia, Lithuania, and Belorussia

Sources: *SU*, 1919, No. 21, Art. 264.
  Obrazovanie SSSR, p. 126.
  SDFP, 1, pp. 157–58 (extract).

June 28, 1919. Treaty of Versailles

(1) Covenant of the League of Nations, see 34/ix/18/1919; (2) Charter of the International Labour Organisation, see 54/iv/26/1946.

● 19/xi/2/Pol

Agreement between the Red Cross Societies of the RSFSR and Poland concerning the final solution of the question of Polish hostages in the RSFSR

Signed Nov. 2, 1919, in Mikachevichi.
Entered into force on signature; not subject to ratification.
Implementing agreement signed Nov. 9, 1919 (next document).
Sources: *Krasnaia kniga*, pp. 72–75.
  Livre rouge, pp. 73–75.
  STS, 1, pp. 30–31.

● 19/xi/9/Pol

Agreement between the Red Cross Societies of the RSFSR and Poland concerning exchange of civilian prisoners

Signed Nov. 9, 1919, in Mikachevichi.
Entered into force on signature; not subject to ratification.
Implements agreement of Nov. 2, 1919.

Sources: *Krasnaia kniga*, pp. 75–80.
  Livre rouge, pp. 76–81.
  STS, 1, pp. 31–33.

● 19/xi/19/Est

Agreement between the RSFSR and Estonia concerning exchange of hostages and civilian prisoners

Signed Nov. 19, 1919, in Tartu (Yur'ev).
Reference: *Izv.*, Nov. 25, 1919.

● 19/xi/19/Lat

Agreement between the RSFSR and Latvia concerning exchange of hostages and civilian prisoners

Signed Nov. 19, 1919, in Tartu (Yur'ev).
Reference: *Izv.*, Nov. 25, 1919.

● 19/xi/19/Lith
Agreement between the RSFSR and Lithuania concerning exchange of hostages and civilian prisoners

Signed Nov. 19, 1919, in Tartu (Yur'ev).
Entered into force on signature.
Source: *DVP*, 2, pp. 291–93.
Reference: *Izv.*, Nov. 25, 1919.

● 19/xii/18/Denmark

Agreement between the RSFSR and Denmark concerning repatriation

Signed Dec. 18, 1919, in Copenhagen.
Sources: *SDD RSFSR*, 1, pp. 139–40.
  Vestnik NKID, 1920, No. 4–5, pp. 128–29 (R, G).
  STS, 1, p. 33.

● 19/xii/31/Est

Treaty between the RSFSR and Estonia concerning suspension of hostilities

Signed Dec. 31, 1919, in Tartu (Yur'ev).
Covers the period Jan. 3 to 10, 1920, and thereafter until 24 hours after notification by either side.
Sources: Kliuchnikov, 2, pp. 424–25.
  RT, No. 1, Jan. 5, 1920.
  STS, 1, pp. 33–34.

1920

● 20/i/30/Lat. See Appendix 5.

● 20/ii/1/Lat. See Appendix 5.

● 20/ii/2/Est

Peace treaty between the RSFSR and Estonia, with annexes and supplementary articles

Signed Feb. 2, 1920, at Tartu (Yur'ev).

Ratified by the RSFSR Feb. 4, 1920; by Estonia Feb. 13, 1920. Entered into force Mar. 29, 1920, on exchange of acts of ratification in Moscow. Reaffirmed by pact of mutual assistance of Sept. 28, 1939. Lost validity Aug. 6, 1940, with the incorporation of Estonia into the USSR.
Sources: *Izv.*, Feb. 8, 1920.
  Vestnik NKID, 1920, No. 3, pp. 86–97.
  SU, 1920, No. 7, Art. 44.
  SDD RSFSR, 1, pp. 100–16.
  SDD, 1, pp. 195–206.
  *RT, 1920, No. 24/25.
  LNTS, 11, pp. 30–71 (Est., R, F, E).
  STS, 1, pp. 34–38.

Feb. 9, 1920. Treaty on Spitsbergen
See 35/ii/27/1920.

● 20/ii/12/UK
Agreement between the RSFSR and the United Kingdom concerning exchange of military and civilian prisoners, with two annexes and two lists of names
Signed Feb. 12, 1920, in Copenhagen (except for the second annex, which was signed on Feb. 20, 1920, in Copenhagen; not listed separately).
Sources: *SDD RSFSR*, 1, pp. 120–24.
  Vestnik NKID, 1920, No. 3, pp. 83–85.
  *BPP, 1920, Russia No. 1, Cmd. 587.
  *BFSP, 113, p. 428.
  LNTS, 1, pp. 264–69 (E, F).
  STS, 1, pp. 38–39.

● 20/iii/10/Lith
Protocol between the RSFSR and the Red Cross Society of Lithuania concerning conditions for exchange of hostages and civilian prisoners
Signed Mar. 10, 1920.
Supplements the agreement of Nov. 19, 1919 (19/xi/19/Lith).
Reference: *DVP*, 2, p. 745.

● 20/iii/31/Est. See Appendix 5.

● 20/iv/6/Est
Agreement between the RSFSR and Estonia concerning procedure for choice of citizenship
Signed Apr. 6, 1920, in Moscow.
Confirmed by the RSFSR Apr. 6, 1920; entered into force for the RSFSR on confirmation, for Estonia on signature.
Sources: *SDD RSFSR*, 1, pp. 247–49.
  STS, 1, pp. 39–40.

● 20/iv/19/Ger
Agreement between the RSFSR and Germany concerning repatriation of prisoners of war and interned civilians
Signed Apr. 19, 1920, in Berlin.
Confirmed by the RSFSR Apr. 25, 1921.
Entered into force May 31, 1920, on exchange of acts of ratification.
Supplemented by agreements of July 7, 1920, Jan. 22, 1921, and May 6, 1921 (21/v/6/Ger/b).
Sources: *SU*, 1921, No. 10, Art. 70.
  Vestnik NKID, 1920, No. 6–7, pp. 125–27.
  SDD RSFSR, 1, pp. 128–30.
  SDD, 1, pp. 225–26.
  LNTS, 2, pp. 63–69 (G, E, F).
  STS, 1, pp. 40–41.

● 20/iv/20/Belgium/a
Agreement between the RSFSR and Belgium concerning political relations
Signed Apr. 20, 1920, in Copenhagen; on behalf of Belgium by the French consul. In return for a Belgian declaration that it will not interfere in internal Russian politics nor undertake any aggressive measures against the Soviet Republic, the RSFSR agrees to cancel judicial proceedings or decisions against Belgians in Russia and repatriate them under the repatriation agreement of the same date (20/iv/20/Belgium/b).
Sources: *SDD RSFSR*, 1, p. 119.
  SDD, 1, p. 218.
  SDD, 1–2, 1928, pp. 175–76.
  DVP, 2, pp. 467–68.
  STS, 1, p. 42.

● 20/iv/20/Belgium/b. See Appendix 5.

● 20/iv/20/France
Agreement between the RSFSR and the Ukrainian SSR on the one hand and France on the other concerning repatriation of prisoners of war and civilians, with supplementary articles, supplementary agreement, and declaration
Signed Apr. 20, 1920, in Copenhagen.
Declaration consists of a pledge by the French Government that it will not interfere in internal Russian politics, nor undertake any aggressive measures against the Russian and Ukrainian Soviet Republics.
Sources: *SDD RSFSR*, 1, pp. 156–62.
  Vestnik NKID, 1920, No. 4–5, pp. 129–34 (R, F).

SDD, 1, pp. 296–300.
STS, 1, pp. 41–42.

• 20/iv/23/Ger

Agreement between the RSFSR and Germany concerning repatriation of prisoners of war

Signed Apr. 23, 1920, in Tallinn (Reval).
Entered into force on signature.
Sources: *SU*, 1922, I, No. 7, Art. 85.
  SDD RSFSR, 1, pp. 131–32.
  SDD, 1, p. 227.
  STS, 1, p. 43.

• 20/iv/27/Italy/a

Agreement between the RSFSR and Italy concerning exchange of prisoners of war and interned civilians

Signed Apr. 27, 1920, in Copenhagen.
Supplemented by 2 exchanges of notes (see Appendix 5).
Sources: *SDD RSFSR*, 1, pp. 141–42.
  Vestnik NKID, 1920, No. 4–5, pp. 135–36 (R, F).
  TC, 26, p. 75.
  STS, 1, p. 43.

• 20/iv/27/Italy/b, c. See Appendix 5.

Apr. 29, 1920. Armistice agreement between Japanese military forces and the Provisional Government of the Maritime Province

Sources: *DVP*, 2, pp. 496–98.
  Soviet Russia, June 12, 1920, pp. 584–85.
  STS, 1, p. 44.

• 20/v/7/GrDR/a

Peace treaty between the RSFSR and the Georgian Democratic Republic

Signed May 7, 1920, in Moscow.
Entered into force on signature.
Supplemented by an agreement signed May 12, 1920.
Sources: *Izv.*, May 9, 1920.
  Vestnik NKID, 1920, No. 6–7, pp. 114–20.
  SU, 1920, No. 64, Art. 282.
  SDD RSFSR, 1, pp. 27–34.
  Mirnyi dogovor mezhdu Rossiei i Gruziei.
  RSFSR i GDR, pp. 8–16.
  STS, 1, pp. 44–46.

• 20/v/7/GrDR/b

Secret supplement to the peace treaty between the RSFSR and the Georgian Democratic Republic

Signed May 7, 1920, in Moscow.
Entered into force on signature. Provides that the Georgian Democratic Republic shall recognize the right of Communist organizations on its territory to free existence and activity, especially the right to hold meetings and to publish, including newspapers. Both this secret agreement and the peace treaty became invalid on the fall of the Georgian Government in 1921.
Sources: *SDD RSFSR*, 3, p. 295.
  STS, 1, p. 46.
  Batsell, pp. 253–54.

• 20/v/12/GrDR

Agreement between the RSFSR and the Georgian Democratic Republic concerning a border dispute between Georgia and Azerbaidzhan

Signed May 12, 1920, in Moscow.
Entered into force on signature.
Supplements the peace treaty of May 7, 1920.
Sources: *SDD RSFSR*, 1, pp. 33–34.
  SU, 1920, p. 303 (part of Art. 282).
  STS, 1, p. 46.

• 20/v/14/FER. See Appendix 5.

• 20/v/20/Persia

Exchange of notes between the RSFSR and Persia concerning sending a Persian diplomatic mission to Moscow

Sent May 20, 1920, from Teheran and Moscow.
Source: *Izv.*, May 22, 1920.
References: Eudin and North, p. 100.
  London *Times*, May 24, 1920.

• 20/v/21/H

Agreement between the RSFSR and the Ukrainian SSR on the one hand and Hungary on the other concerning repatriation of prisoners of war and civilians

Signed May 21, 1920, in Copenhagen.
Entered into force on approval by signatories. Listed in *SDD*, 1–2, 1928, as no longer valid.
Sources: *SU*, 1922, I, No. 7, Art. 86.
  SDD RSFSR, 1, pp. 125–27.
  SDD, 1, pp. 219–20.
  STS, 1, p. 47.

• 20/v/27/Sinkiang

Agreement between the RSFSR and Sinkiang concerning border trade and the return of Russian soldiers and refugees (Ili protocol)

Signed May 27, 1920, in Ili (Kul'dzha), Sinkiang.
To be confirmed within 10 days by authorities in Tashkent and Urumchi. According to Cheng, p. 101, approved by the Central Chinese Government in Sept. 1921.
Sources: *DVP*, 2, pp. 546–59.
  TA, pp. 23–25 (from the Chinese text).
  STS, 1, pp. 47–48 (same).
Note: A corrupt text, undated and without source reference, is given in Norins, *Gateway to Asia*, pp. 61–62; cited in *STS*, 1, p. 59, under date Sept. 4, 1920.

• 20/vi/2/T

Exchange of notes between the RSFSR and Turkey concerning establishment of diplomatic relations

Sent Apr. 26, 1920, from Angora and June 2, 1920, from Moscow.
Sources (Soviet note): Kliuchnikov, 3, I, pp. 26–27.
  Eudin and North, pp. 186–87.
  SDFP, 1, pp. 187–88.
Reference: Eudin and North, pp. 106–107.

• 20/vi/12/Lat

Treaty between the RSFSR and Latvia concerning re-evacuation of refugees

Signed June 12, 1920, in Moscow.
Entered into force on signature. Superseded by agreement of Nov. 6, 1921 (21/xi/6/Lat/a).
Sources: *Izv.*, June 22, 1920.
  Vestnik NKID, 1920, No. 4–5, pp. 136–39.
  SU, 1920, No. 58, Art. 262.
  SDD RSFSR, 1, pp. 143–47.
  LRR, pp. 67–70, citing
    VV, No. 134, June 16, 1920.
  STS, 1, pp. 48–49.

June 15, 1920. Supplementary armistice agreement between Soviet and Japanese military forces in the Far East

Supplements the armistice agreement of Apr. 29, 1920.
Reference: *DVP*, 2, p. 759.

June 21, 1920. Convention concerning

establishment of an International Institute of Refrigeration

See 24/vi/17/1920.

• 20/vi/30/Lith

Treaty between the RSFSR and Lithuania concerning re-evacuation of refugees

Signed June 30, 1920, in Moscow.
Entered into force on signature.
Sources: *SU*, 1921, No. 4, Art. 35.
  Vestnik NKID, 1920, No. 6–7, pp. 121–24.
  SDD RSFSR, 1, pp. 151–55.
  SDD, 1, pp. 248–51.
  *VŽ, No. 42, Art. 434.
  *LS, 1, pp. 24–29.
  STS, 1, p. 49.

• 20/vii/5/Austria

Agreement between the RSFSR and the Ukrainian SSR on the one hand and Austria on the other concerning repatriation of prisoners of war and interned civilians

Signed July 5, 1920, in Copenhagen.
Entered into force on signature. Ratified by the RSFSR July 9, 1920; by Austria, July 14, 1920. Extended by agreement of Dec. 7, 1921 (21/xii/7/Austria/b).
Sources: *SDD RSFSR*, 1, pp. 117–18.
  SDD, 1, pp. 213–14.
  STS, 1, pp. 49–50.

• 20/vii/7/Ger

Agreement between the RSFSR and Germany concerning repatriation of prisoners of war and interned civilians

Signed July 7, 1920, in Berlin.
Entered into force on signature.
Supplements the agreement of Apr. 19, 1920.
Sources: *SU*, 1922, I, No. 7, Art. 83.
  Vestnik NKID, 1920, No. 8, pp. 171–72.
  SDD RSFSR, 1, pp. 133–34.
  SDD, 1, pp. 227–28.
  LNTS, 2, pp. 85–90 (G, E, F).
  STS, 1, p. 50.

• 20/vii/7/UK. See Appendix 5.

• 20/vii/10/Lith. See Appendix 5.

• 20/vii/12/Lith

Peace treaty between the RSFSR and Lithuania

Signed July 12, 1920, in Moscow.
Ratified by Lithuania Aug. 6, 1920; by the
RSFSR Sept. 9, 1920.
Entered into force Oct. 14, 1920, on ex-
change of acts of ratification in Moscow.
Reaffirmed by treaties of Sept. 28, 1926,
and Oct. 10, 1939. Modified by protocol
of Oct. 27, 1939.
Sources: *SU*, 1920, No. 96, Art. 515.
  Izv., Sept. 21, 1920.
  Vestnik NKID, 1920, No. 8, pp. 159–70.
  SDD RSFSR, 1, pp. 50–62.
  SDD, 1, pp. 97–106.
  SDD, 1–2, 1928, pp. 59–68.
  *VŽ, No. 53, Art. 509.
  *LS, 1, pp. 30–52.
  LNTS, 3, pp. 105–37 (R, Lith., E, F).
  STS, 1, pp. 50–54.

● 20/vii/14/Lith

**Exchange of notes between the RSFSR
and Lithuania concerning the passage of
Soviet troops through Lithuanian territory**

Sent July 14, 1920.
References: Chronology in Lenin, *Soch.*,
  1st ed., 17, p. 473.
  Eudin and Fisher, p. 10, citing
    London *Times*, Aug. 5, 1920.

● 20/vii/15/J

**Armistice agreement between the Far
Eastern Republic and Japan**

Signed July 15, 1920, in Gongota.
Entered into force July 18, 1920.
Source: Kliuchnikov, 3, I, pp. 38–39
  (summarized in part).
Note: Shishkin, p. 163, mentions two ear-
lier armistice agreements between the Far
Eastern Republic and Japan. The first,
concluded July 2, 1920, covered the right
bank of the river Shilka; the second, on
July 10, 1920, the left bank.

● 20/vii/16/J

**Joint declaration by representatives of
the Far Eastern Republic and Japan concerning establishment of a buffer state
and associated matters**

Signed July 16, 1920, in Gongota.
Source: Kliuchnikov, 3, I, pp. 40–41.

● 20/viii/10/Arm

**Military agreement between the RSFSR
and Armenia**

Signed Aug. 10, 1920, in Tbilisi.
References: Cited in treaty of Dec. 2,
  1920.
  Vratzian, p. 410.
  Navasardian, p. 173.

● 20/viii/11/Lat

**Peace treaty between the RSFSR and
Latvia**

Signed Aug. 11, 1920, in Riga.
Ratified by the RSFSR Sept. 11, 1920; by
Latvia, Sept. 25, 1920. Entered into force
Oct. 4, 1920, on exchange of acts of rati-
fication in Moscow. Reaffirmed by the
pact of mutual assistance of Oct. 5, 1939.
Sources: *SU*, 1920, No. 95, Art. 514.
  Izv., Sept. 21, 1920.
  Vestnik NKID, 1920, No. 8, pp. 144–58.
  *Mirnyi dogovor mezhdu Rossiei i Lat-
    viei.*
  SDD RSFSR, 1, pp. 35–49.
  SDD, 1, pp. 75–86.
  SDD, 1–2, 1928, pp. 37–48.
  LRR, pp. 70–80.
  LNTS, 2, pp. 195–231 (R, Lat., E, F).
  STS, 1, pp. 54–58.

● 20/viii/13/Fin

**Armistice agreement between the RSFSR
and Finland**

Signed Aug. 13, 1920, in Tartu (Yur'ev).
Entered into force Aug. 15, 1920.
Sources: Kliuchnikov, 3, I, pp. 46–47.
  *SS, 1918–1920, No. 21 (Finnish, R).
  STS, 1, pp. 58–59.

● 20/viii/19/Est

**Agreement between the RSFSR and Es-
tonia concerning repatriation of prisoners of war, refugees, hostages, and others**

Signed Aug. 19, 1920, in Tallinn. En-
tered into force, retroactively, from Apr. 1,
1920.
Sources: *SU*, 1921, No. 4, Art. 34.
  Vestnik NKID, 1921, No. 1–2, pp. 184–
    85.
  SDD RSFSR, 1, pp. 163–64.
  SDD, 1, pp. 300–301.
  STS, 1, p. 59.

● 20/ix/13/Af

**Provisional treaty between the RSFSR
and Afghanistan**

Initialed Sept. 13, 1920, in Kabul.

Reference: Teplinskii, pp. 10, 13.

● 20/ix/13/Kh/a

Treaty of alliance between the RSFSR and the Khorezm Soviet People's Republic

Signed Sept. 13, 1920, in Moscow.
Acts of ratification exchanged Mar. 9, 1921, in Moscow.
Sources: *SU*, 1921, No. 29, Art. 161.
    SDD RSFSR, 1, pp. 17–22.
    SDD, 1, pp. 184–88.
    STS, 1, pp. 59–60.

● 20/ix/13/Kh/b

Economic agreement between the RSFSR and the Khorezm Soviet People's Republic

Signed Sept. 13, 1920, in Moscow.
Replaced by agreement of June 29, 1922.
Sources: *SU*, 1921, No. 35, Art. 187.
    SDD RSFSR, 1, pp. 23–26.
    STS, 1, pp. 60–61.

● 20/ix/17/Est/a

Convention between the RSFSR and Estonia concerning direct rail communications for passengers and freight

Signed Sept. 17, 1920, in Tallinn.
Ratified by Estonia Apr. 12, 1921; by the RSFSR June 24, 1921. Entered into force provisionally on signature; definitively Jan. 19, 1922, on exchange of acts of ratification in Tallinn. Duration 3 years, with automatic extension if not denounced 6 months before expiration. Supplemented on the same day by the following 4 documents. Continued by convention of July 5, 1923 (23/vii/5/Est/a). Listed in *SDD*, 1–2, 1928, p. 339, as no longer valid.
Sources: *SDD RSFSR*, 1, pp. 174–80.
    SDD, 1, pp. 418–22.
    RT, 1921, No. 51/52.
    STS, 1, pp. 61–63.

● 20/ix/17/Est/b

Protocol of a conference of representatives of the RSFSR and Estonia for conclusion of a convention concerning direct rail communications for passengers and freight

Signed Sept. 17, 1920, in Tallinn.
Supplements the convention of the same date. Modified by 2 protocols of July 5,
1923 (23/vii/5/Est/b and /c).
Source: *SDD RSFSR*, 1, pp. 180–89.

● 20/ix/17/Est/c

Agreement between the railroad authorities of the RSFSR and Estonia concerning movement of through trains

Signed Sept. 17, 1920, in Tallinn.
Supplements the convention of the same date.
Source: *SDD RSFSR*, 1, pp. 189–93.

● 20/ix/17/Est/d

Regulations concerning the transportation of passengers and their baggage and freight in direct rail communications between the RSFSR and Estonia

Signed Sept. 17, 1920, in Tallinn.
Constitutes an annex to Art. 2 of the convention of the same date. Modified by protocol of July 5, 1923 (23/vii/5/Est/b).
Source: *SDD RSFSR*, 1, pp. 193–214.

● 20/ix/17/Est/e

Agreement between the railroad authorities of the RSFSR and Estonia concerning direct rail communications and the exchange of freight cars

Signed Sept. 17, 1920, in Tallinn.
Constitutes an annex to Art. 3 of the convention of the same date.
Source: *SDD RSFSR*, 1, pp. 215–25.

Sept. 24, 1920. Agreement between Japanese military forces and the Provisional Government of the Maritime Province concerning establishment of a neutral zone south of the river Iman after withdrawal of Japanese forces from Khabarovsk

Supplements the armistice agreement of Apr. 29, 1920.
Sources: *Soviet Russia*, Dec. 11, 1920, p. 593.
    STS, 1, p. 63.

● 20/ix/25/Lith

Agreement between the Azerbaidzhan SSR and Lithuania concerning legal guarantees

Signed Sept. 25, 1920, in Tbilisi.
Entered into force on signature.
Sources: *STS*, 1, p. 63, citing
    LS, 1 (1st ed.), pp. 53–54.
    VŽ, No. 58, Art. 542.

● 20/ix/30/Az/a

Treaty of military and economic alliance between the RSFSR and the Azerbaidzhan SSR

Signed Sept. 30, 1920, in Moscow.
Entered into force on signature; not subject to ratification.
Sources: *SU*, 1920, No. 85, Art. 426.
  Vestnik NKID, 1920, No. 8, p. 143.
  Izv., Oct. 30, 1920.
  SDD RSFSR, 1, pp. 1–2.
  STS, 1, p. 64.

● 20/ix/30/Az/b

Agreement between the RSFSR and the Azerbaidzhan SSR concerning coordination of food policies

Signed Sept. 30, 1920, in Moscow.
Sources: *SU*, 1920, No. 85, Art. 426.
  Vestnik NKID, 1920, No. 9–10, pp. 155–56.
  SDD RSFSR, 1, pp. 3–4.
  STS, 1, p. 64.

● 20/ix/30/Az/c

Agreement between the RSFSR and the Azerbaidzhan SSR concerning unification of the administration of posts, telegraph, telephone, and radio-telegraph

Signed Sept. 30, 1920, in Moscow.
Replaces earlier, unspecified agreements between communications authorities of the signatories.
Sources: *SU*, 1920, No. 85, Art. 426.
  Vestnik NKID, 1920, No. 9–10, pp. 156–57.
  SDD RSFSR, 1, pp. 5–6.
  STS, 1, p. 65.

● 20/ix/30/Az/d

Agreement between the RSFSR and the Azerbaidzhan SSR concerning financial matters

Signed Sept. 30, 1920, in Moscow.
Sources: *SU*, 1920, No. 85, Art. 426.
  Vestnik NKID, 1920, No. 9–10, pp. 153–55.
  SDD RSFSR, 1, pp. 7–8.
  STS, 1, pp. 64–65.

● 20/ix/30/Az/e

Agreement between the RSFSR and the Azerbaidzhan SSR concerning foreign trade

Signed Sept. 30, 1920, in Moscow.
Sources: *SU*, 1920, No. 85, Art. 426.
  Vestnik NKID, 1920, No. 9–10, p. 153.
  SDD RSFSR, 1, pp. 9–10.
  STS, 1, p. 65.

● 20/ix/30/Az/f

Agreement between the RSFSR and the Azerbaidzhan SSR concerning conduct of a unified economic policy

Signed Sept. 30, 1920, in Moscow.
Sources: *SU*, 1920, No. 85, Art. 426.
  Vestnik NKID, 1920, No. 9–10, p. 152.
  SDD RSFSR, 1, pp. 11–12.
  STS, 1, pp. 65–66.

● 20/x/2/Hei

Agreement between the Far Eastern Republic and Heilungkiang Province concerning border trade

Signed Oct. 2, 1920, in Manchuli.
Source: *Reference material on the Sino-Soviet conference*, 3, pp. 11a–13b.

● 20/x/5/Pol

Agreement (procès-verbal) between the RSFSR and Poland to conclude an armistice not later than October 8, 1920

Signed Oct. 5, 1920.
Reference: *Izv.*, Oct. 6, 1920.
  LNTS, 4, pp. 8, 32 (F, E).

● 20/x/12/Pol/a

Agreement between the RSFSR and the Ukrainian SSR on the one hand and Poland on the other concerning preliminary conditions of peace, with two annexes (Preliminary peace treaty)

Signed Oct. 12, 1920, in Riga.
Ratified by the RSFSR Oct. 23, 1920; by Poland, Oct. 26, 1920. Entered into force Nov. 2, 1920, on exchange of acts of ratification in Libau.
Supplemented by protocol and agreement of Feb. 24, 1921 (21/ii/24/Pol/b and /c).
Annexes: (1) map, not included in the sources listed; (2) armistice agreement (next document).
Sources: *SU*, 1920, No. 97, Art. 516.
  Izv., Oct. 17, 1920.
  Vestnik NKID, 1920, No. 9–10, pp. 162–71.
  SDD RSFSR, 1, pp. 63–73.
  SDD, 1, pp. 265–76.

DURP, 1921, No. 28, Arts. 161, 162.
LNTS, 4, pp. 7–45 (R, U, P, E, F).
STS, 1, pp. 67–69.

● 20/x/12/Pol/b

Armistice agreement between the RSFSR and the Ukrainian SSR on the one hand and Poland on the other

Signed Oct. 12, 1920, in Riga.
Data on ratification and entry into force identical with those for the preliminary peace treaty (20/x/12/Pol/a). Duration 21 days, with automatic prolongation if not denounced, until ratification of a final peace treaty.
Extended by protocol of Feb. 24, 1921 (21/ii/24/Pol/a). Concluded in accordance with Art. 13 of the preliminary peace treaty and constitutes Annex 2 to that agreement.
Sources: Text included with those shown for 20/x/12/Pol/a.

● 20/x/14/Fin

Peace treaty between the RSFSR and Finland, with note, five declarations, and an annex (Treaty of Dorpat)

Signed Oct. 14, 1920, in Tartu (Dorpat).
Ratified by the RSFSR Oct. 23, 1920; by Finland Dec. 11, 1920. Entered into force Dec. 31, 1920, on exchange of acts of ratification in Moscow.
Modified by agreement of July 7, 1922.
Sources: *SU*, 1921, No. 71, Art. 573.
   Vestnik NKID, 1921, No. 7–8, pp. 124–40.
   SDD RSFSR, 1, pp. 76–99.
   SDD, 1, pp. 171–84.
   SDD, 1–2, 1928, pp. 130–42.
   SS, 1921, No. 1 (Finnish, R).
   LNTS, 3, pp. 5–79 (R, Finnish, Sw., E, F).
   STS, 1, pp. 69–75.

● 20/xi/ /Bukh

Temporary military-political agreement between the RSFSR and the Bukhara Soviet Republic

Signed during Nov. 1920.
Mentioned in Art. 2 of the treaty of alliance of Mar. 4, 1921 (21/iii/4/Bukh/a), in accordance with which it remains in force until conclusion of a military-political agreement.

● 20/xi/14/GrDR

Agreement between the RSFSR and the Azerbaidzhan SSR on the one hand and the Georgian Democratic Republic on the other concerning trade and transit, with secret supplement concerning storage of oil

Signed Nov. 14, 1920, in Tbilisi.
Sources: *SDD RSFSR*, 1, pp. 165–71.
   RSFSR i GDR, pp. 42–49.
   STS, 1, pp. 75–77.

● 20/xi/15/FER

Agreement between the RSFSR and the Far Eastern Republic concerning establishment of zoological farm reservations in the region of Lake Baikal

Signed Nov. 15, 1920, in Moscow and Verkhne-Udinsk.
Entered into force on signature. Duration 25 years, but declared invalid by decree of Dec. 22, 1922 (*SU*, 1923, I, No. 1, Art. 3), as a result of the incorporation of the Far Eastern Republic into the RSFSR.
Sources: *SU*, 1922, I, No. 8, Art. 88.
   Izv., Mar. 3, 1921.
   SDD RSFSR, 1, pp. 172–73.
   STS, 1, pp. 77–78.

● 20/xi/16/Lat

Agreement between the RSFSR and Latvia concerning repatriation of prisoners of war

Signed Nov. 16, 1920, in Riga.
Sources: *SDD RSFSR*, 1, pp. 148–50.
   Vestnik NKID, 1921, No. 3–4, pp. 135–36.
   STS, 1, p. 78.

● 20/xi/30/FER/a

Convention between the RSFSR and the Far Eastern Republic concerning direct rail communications

Signed Nov. 30, 1920.
Ratified by the RSFSR June 18, 1921. Declared invalid by decree of Dec. 22, 1922 (see 20/xi/15/FER).
Sources: *SDD RSFSR*, 2, pp. 129–32.
   STS, 1, pp. 78–80.

● 20/xi/30/FER/b

Convention between the RSFSR and the Far Eastern Republic concerning condi-

tions of navigation on internal border waterways

Signed Nov. 30, 1920, in Chita.
Ratified by the RSFSR June 18, 1921. Declared invalid by decree of Dec. 22, 1922 (see 20/xi/15/FER).
Sources: *SDD RSFSR*, 2, pp. 133–37.
　STS, 1, pp. 80–81.

● 20/xii/2/Arm

Agreement between the RSFSR and the Armenian Republic concerning recognition of the independence of Armenia

Signed Dec. 2, 1920.
Sources: *SDD RSFSR*, 3, pp. 14–15.
　Terterian, "The Levon Chanth Mission to Moscow," *Armenian Review*, 8, 1955, No. 3, p. 101.
　STS, 1, p. 82.
　Eudin and North, p. 109.

Dec. 2, 1920. Temporary postal agreement between the RSFSR and Estonia
See 21/i/25/Est.

● 20/xii/9/GrDR

Agreement between the RSFSR and the Georgian Democratic Republic concerning procedure for the choice of Georgian citizenship

Signed Dec. 9, 1920, in Moscow.
Entered into force Dec. 23, 1920.
Sources: *Izv.*, Dec. 23, 1920.
　Vestnik NKID, 1920, No. 9–10, pp. 157–60.
　SU, 1921, No. 4, Art. 36.
　SDD RSFSR, 1, pp. 135–38.
　STS, 1, pp. 82–83.

● 20/xii/16/GrDR

Agreement between the RSFSR and the Georgian Democratic Republic concerning ships of the RSFSR in Georgian ports

Signed Dec. 16, 1920, in Moscow.
Sources: *RSFSR i GDR*, p. 77 (extracts).
　STS, 1, p. 83.

● 20/xii/28/Ukr

Treaty of workers' and peasants' alliance between the RSFSR and the Ukrainian SSR, with supplementary decree and five annexes

Signed Dec. 28, 1920, in Moscow.
Ratified by the RSFSR Dec. 29, 1920; approved by the Fifth All-Ukrainian Congress of Soviets in Feb. 1921.
Sources: *SU*, 1921, No. 1, Art. 13.
　Vestnik NKID, 1921, No. 3–4, pp. 137–38.
　Izv., Jan. 1, 1921.
　SDD RSFSR, 1, pp. 15–16.
　STS, 1, pp. 83–84.

● 20/xii/30/FER

Treaty between the RSFSR and the Far Eastern Republic concerning boundaries

Signed Dec. 15, 1920, in Moscow, and Dec. 30, 1920, in Chita.
Ratified by the Far Eastern Republic Jan. 4, 1921; by the RSFSR Apr. 14, 1921. Entered into force Dec. 30, 1920. Declared invalid by decree of Dec. 22, 1922 (see 20/xi/15/FER).
Sources: *SDD RSFSR*, 2, pp. 78–79.
　STS, 1, p. 84.

1921

● 21/i/6/CER

Agreement between the Far Eastern Republic and the Chinese administration of the Chinese Eastern Railway concerning the disarming and evacuation of White Russian troops

Signed Jan. 6, 1921; carried out by Chang Tso-lin Jan. 7, 1921, although not signed by the central Chinese authorities.
Source: Parfenov, pp. 281–83.

● 21/i/16/BSSR

Military-economic alliance between the RSFSR and the Belorussian SSR

Signed Jan. 16, 1921, in Moscow.
Sources: *Izv.*, Apr. 6, 1921.
　SDD RSFSR, 1, pp. 13–14.
　STS, 1, p. 84.

● 21/i/17/Austria

Agreement between the Ukrainian SSR and Austria concerning redemption of

treasury bills deposited with the Austro-Hungarian Bank in favor of the Ukrainian State

Signed Jan. 17, 1921, in Vienna.
Entered into force on signature; not subject to ratification.
Source: *Not published in Austria, but registered in the Austrian Haus-, Hof- und Staatsarchiv under Zl. 214/21.

• 21/i/22/Ger/a

Agreement between the RSFSR and Germany concerning repatriation of prisoners of war and interned civilians, supplementing the agreement of April 19, 1920, with declaration by the Central Administration for Affairs of Military and Civilian Prisoners, in Berlin

Signed Jan. 22, 1921, in Riga.
Entered into force on signature.
Modified by agreement of May 6, 1921 (21/v/6/Ger/b).
Sources: *SU*, 1922, I, No. 7, Art. 84.
    Vestnik NKID, 1921, No. 3–4, pp. 138–39.
    SDD RSFSR, 2, pp. 89–90.
    SDD, 1, pp. 229–30.
    STS, 1, pp. 84–85.

• 21/i/22/Ger/b

Agreement between the RSFSR and Germany concerning repatriation of Red Army soldiers

Signed Jan. 22, 1921, in Riga.
Source: *Vestnik NKID*, 1921, No. 3–4, p. 140.

• 21/i/25/Est

Temporary postal agreement between the RSFSR and Estonia

Signed Dec. 2, 1920, in Moscow, and Jan. 25, 1921, in Tallinn.
Ratified by Estonia Apr. 18, 1921; by the RSFSR May 18, 1921.
Superseded by convention of June 27, 1924 (24/vi/27/Est/a).
Sources: *SDD RSFSR*, 2, pp. 149–51.
    SDD, 1, pp. 369–71.
    *RT, 1921, No. 27.
    LNTS, 11, pp. 73–85 (R, Est., F, E).
    STS, 1, pp. 81–82.

• 21/i/28/Lith/a

Agreement between the Ukrainian SSR and Lithuania concerning procedure for choosing Lithuanian citizenship

Signed Jan. 28, 1921, in Moscow.
Not subject to ratification; entered into force Oct. 26, 1922, on ratification of the peace treaty between the Ukrainian SSR and Lithuania. Modified by supplementary treaty of Apr. 5, 1922 (22/iv/5/Lith/b).
Sources: *Mirnyi dogovor mezhdu Ukrainoi i Litvoi*, pp. 8–10.
    SDD, 1, pp. 256–59.
    *LS, 1, pp. 67–72.
    STS, 1, pp. 85–86.

• 21/i/28/Lith/b

Agreement between the Ukrainian SSR and Lithuania concerning provisional regulations for transportation of Lithuanian refugees on their re-evacuation from the Ukrainian SSR

Signed Jan. 28, 1921, in Moscow.
Entered into force Feb. 14, 1921.
Source: *Mirnyi dogovor mezhdu Ukrainoi i Litvoi*, pp. 11–12.
References: **LS*, p. 73.
    STS, 1, p. 86.

• 21/ii/14/Lith/a

Peace treaty between the Ukrainian SSR and Lithuania

Signed Feb. 14, 1921, in Moscow.
Ratified by the Ukrainian SSR Mar. 3, 1921; entered into force Oct. 26, 1922, on exchange of acts of ratification in Khar'-kov. Supplemented by treaty of Apr. 5, 1922 (22/iv/5/Lith/b).
Sources: *Mirnyi dogovor mezhdu Ukrainoi i Litvoi*, pp. 3–7.
    SDD, 1, pp. 106–110.
    SDD, 1–2, 1928, pp. 68–72, citing Ukrainian collection of laws, 1921, No. 8, Arts. 226, 227.
    STS, 1, pp. 86–87.

• 21/ii/14/Lith/b

Treaty between the Ukrainian SSR and Lithuania concerning re-evacuation of refugees

Signed Feb. 14, 1921, in Moscow.
Sources: *Mirnyi dogovor mezhdu Ukrainoi i Litvoi*, pp. 13–15.
    SDD, 1, pp. 260–61.
    STS, 1, p. 87.

● 21/ii/24/Pol/a

Protocol concerning extension of the armistice agreement of October 12, 1920, between the RSFSR and the Ukrainian SSR on the one hand and Poland on the other

Signed Feb. 24, 1921, in Riga.
Entered into force on signature.
Extends the armistice (20/x/12/Pol/b) until exchange of acts of ratification of the peace treaty with Poland, or until 42 days after denunciation.
Sources: *SDD RSFSR*, 2, p. 42.
  Vestnik NKID, 1921, No. 3–4, p. 140.
  STS, 1, p. 92.

● 21/ii/24/Pol/b

Protocol between the RSFSR and the Ukrainian SSR on the one hand and Poland on the other concerning establishment of a mixed border commission

Signed Feb. 24, 1921, in Riga.
Entered into force on signature. Carries out a provision of the preliminary peace treaty of Oct. 12, 1920 (20/x/12/Pol/a).
Sources: *SDD RSFSR*, 2, pp. 80–82.
  Vestnik NKID, 1921, No. 3–4, pp. 141–43.
  STS, 1, pp. 87–88.

● 21/ii/24/Pol/c

Agreement between the RSFSR and the Ukrainian SSR on the one hand and Poland on the other concerning repatriation, with supplementary protocol

Signed Feb. 24, 1921, in Riga.
Entered into force on signature. Extends Art. 7 of the preliminary peace treaty of Oct. 12, 1920 (20/x/12/Pol/a). Completion of repatriation marked by protocol of Dec. 27, 1927.
Sources: *Izv.*, Apr. 9, 1921.
  Vestnik NKID, 1921, No. 5–6, pp. 181–92.
  SU, 1921, No. 43, Art. 220.
  SDD RSFSR, 2, pp. 108–20.
  SDD, 1–2, 1928, pp. 180–91.
  Monitor Polski, 1921, No. 100.
  LNTS, 4, pp. 141–99 (R, P, U, E, F).
  STS, 1, pp. 88–92.

● 21/ii/26/Lat/a

Convention between the RSFSR and Latvia concerning direct rail communications for passengers and freight

Signed Feb. 26, 1921, in Riga.

Enters into force on exchange of acts of ratification. Duration 3 years; if not denounced 6 months before expiration, extended for 3-year periods.
Supplemented on the same day by the following 3 documents.
Listed in *SDD*, 1–2, 1928, p. 329, as no longer valid.
Sources: *SDD RSFSR*, 2, pp. 138–42 (without supplements).
  Ibid., 3, pp. 146–51.
  SDD, 1, pp. 372–76.
  STS, 1, pp. 95–96.

● 21/ii/26/Lat/b

Protocol of a conference of representatives of the Governments of the RSFSR and Latvia for conclusion of a convention concerning direct rail communications for passengers and freight

Signed Feb. 26, 1921, in Riga.
Supplements the convention of the same date.
Source: *SDD RSFSR*, 3, pp. 152–60.

● 21/ii/26/Lat/c

Regulations concerning transportation of passengers and their baggage and freight in direct rail communications between the RSFSR and Latvia

Signed (presumably) Feb. 26, 1921, in Riga.
Supplements the convention of the same date.
Source: *SDD RSFSR*, 3, pp. 160–81.

● 21/ii/26/Lat/d

Agreement between the railroad authorities of the RSFSR and Latvia concerning direct rail communications and the use of freight cars, with annex

Signed (presumably) Feb. 26, 1921, in Riga.
Supplements the convention of the same date.
Source: *SDD RSFSR*, 3, pp. 181–244.

● 21/ii/26/Persia

Treaty of friendship between the RSFSR and Persia

Signed Feb. 26, 1921, in Moscow.
Ratified by the RSFSR Mar. 20, 1921; by Persia Dec. 15, 1921. Acts of ratification exchanged Feb. 26, 1922, in Teheran. Entered into force on signature. Significance

of articles 3, 5, 6, 13 and 20 further defined in exchange of notes dated Dec. 12, 1921.
Reaffirmed by treaty of Oct. 1, 1927 (27/x/1/Persia/a).
Invoked in Soviet declaration of Aug. 25, 1941, concerning entry of Soviet troops into Iran (see 41/ix/8/Iran).
See further Appendix 5.
Sources: *SU*, 1921, No. 73, Art. 597.
  Vestnik NKID, 1922, No. 1–3, pp. 158–64.
  SDD RSFSR, 2, pp. 36–41.
  SDD, 1, pp. 148–53.
  SDD, 1–2, 1928, pp. 107–13.
  LNTS, 9, pp. 383–413 (R, Per., E, F).
  STS, 1, pp. 92–94.

● 21/ii/28/Af

Treaty of friendship between the RSFSR and Afghanistan

Signed Feb. 28, 1921, in Moscow.
Ratified by the RSFSR Apr. 20, 1921; by Afghanistan Aug. 13, 1921. Entered into force on ratification by signatories. Acts of ratification exchanged Sept. 14, 1921, in Kabul. Reaffirmed by final protocol of treaty of Aug. 31, 1926.
Arts. 9 and 10 were considered to have expired under the protocol to the border agreement of June 13, 1946 (46/vi/13/Af/a). (Art. 9 calls for the signing of a separate agreement on the basis of a plebiscite to be held in the border lands which had belonged to Afghanistan in the 19th century, carrying out a promise made by Lenin to the Afghanistan Government. Art. 10 calls for material and financial assistance to Afghanistan by the RSFSR.)
Sources: *SU*, 1924, I, No. 36, Art. 343.
  SDD RSFSR, 2, pp. 15–17.
  SDD, 1, pp. 40–42.
  SDD, 1–2, 1928, pp. 10–12.
  STS, 1, pp. 96–97.

● 21/iii/3/Lat

Temporary agreement between the RSFSR and Latvia concerning postal and telegraph communications

Signed Mar. 3, 1921, in Riga.
Confirmed by the RSFSR Mar. 23, 1921. Entered into force Mar. 27, 1921, on exchange of documents of confirmation in Riga.
Sources: *SDD RSFSR*, 2, pp. 143–46.

SDD, 1, pp. 343–46.
SDD, 1–2, 1928, pp. 276–79.
STS, 1, pp. 97–98.

● 21/iii/4/Bukh/a

Treaty of alliance between the RSFSR and the Bukhara Soviet Republic

Signed Mar. 4, 1921, in Moscow.
Ratified by the RSFSR Mar. 20, 1921. Enters into force on exchange of acts of ratification.
Sources: *SU*, 1921, No. 73, Art. 595.
  SDD RSFSR, 2, pp. 7–11.
  SDD, 1, pp. 42–46.
  STS, 1, pp. 98–100.

● 21/iii/4/Bukh/b

Economic agreement between the RSFSR and the Bukhara Soviet Republic

Signed Mar. 4, 1921, in Moscow.
Ratified by the RSFSR Mar. 20, 1921. Enters into force on exchange of acts of ratification.
Superseded by agreement of Aug. 9, 1922.
Sources: *SU*, 1921, No. 73, Art. 596.
  SDD RSFSR, 2, pp. 12–14.
  STS, 1, p. 100.

● 21/iii/7/Hei

Agreement between the Far Eastern Republic and Heilungkiang Province concerning direct rail communications between the Chinese Eastern Railway and Chita Railway

Signed Mar. 7, 1921, in Manchuli.
Entered into force Mar. 8, 1921.
Source: *Reference material on the Sino-Soviet Conference*, 3, pp. 11a–13b.

● 21/iii/16/Est

Temporary agreement between the RSFSR and Estonia concerning telegraph communications

Signed Mar. 16, 1921, in Tallinn.
Entered into force Apr. 2, 1921, on exchange of acts of ratification in Riga.
Valid until 3 months after denunciation.
Superseded by convention of June 27, 1924 (24/vi/27/Est/c).
Sources: *SDD RSFSR*, 2, pp. 147–48.
  SDD, 1, pp. 367–68.
  STS, 1, pp. 104–105.

● 21/iii/16/T

Treaty of friendship between the RSFSR and Turkey, with three annexes

Signed Mar. 16, 1921, in Moscow.
Ratified by the RSFSR Mar. 20, 1921; by Turkey July 21, 1921. Entered into force Sept. 22, 1921, on exchange of acts of ratification in Kars. Modified by protocol of May 31, 1926.
Reaffirmed by protocol of June 29, 1926.
Sources: *SU*, 1921, No. 73, Art. 598.
  Izv., Mar. 22, 1921.
  Vestnik NKID, 1922, No. 1–3, pp. 164–69.
  SDD RSFSR, 2, pp. 72–77.
  SDD, 1, pp. 155–60.
  *Düstur, 2, p. 102.
  STS, 1, pp. 100–102.
  BFSP, 118, pp. 990–96.

● 21/iii/16/UK

Trade agreement between the RSFSR and the United Kingdom, with declaration concerning recognition of claims

Signed Mar. 16, 1921, in London.
Entered into force on signature. Extended to Canada by exchange of notes dated July 3, 1922. Denounced by the United Kingdom, with immediate effect, on May 27, 1927, on the grounds of Soviet subversive activity in the United Kingdom.
Sources: *SU*, 1921, No. 74, Arts. 600, 601.
  Vestnik NKID, 1921, No. 9–10, pp. 173–77.
  Izv., Mar. 31, 1921.
  SDD RSFSR, 2, pp. 18–23.
  SDD, 1, pp. 47–52.
  **Cmd. 1207.
  *BFSP, 114, p. 373.
  LNTS, 4, pp. 127–36 (E, F).
Reference: *SU*, 1921, No. 34, Art. 182 (internal measures to carry out the agreement).

● 21/iii/18/GrDR

Agreement between the RSFSR and the Georgian Democratic Republic concerning cessation of hostilities

Signed Mar. 18, 1921, in Kutais.
Entered into force on signature.
Sources: *RSFSR i GDR*, pp. 99–100.
  STS, 1, p. 105.

● 21/iii/18/Pol

Peace treaty between the RSFSR and Poland, with five annexes

Signed Mar. 18, 1921, in Riga (the RSFSR signing also for the Belorussian and Ukrainian SSR's).
Ratified by the RSFSR Apr. 14, 1921; by Poland Apr. 16, 1921. Entered into force Apr. 27, 1921, on exchange of acts of ratification in Minsk. Reaffirmed by protocol of May 5, 1934. Unilaterally abrogated by the USSR Sept. 17, 1939, following the entry of Soviet troops into Poland.
Sources: *SU*, 1921, No. 41–42, Art. 219; *ibid.*, No. 43, Art. 220.
  Vestnik NKID, 1921, No. 5–6, pp. 157–80.
  SDD RSFSR, 2, pp. 43–71.
  SDD, 1, pp. 121–48.
  SDD, 1–2, 1928, citing Ukrainian collection of laws, 1921, No. 8, Arts. 223–225.
  *DURP, 1921, No. 49, Arts. 300, 301.
  LNTS, 6, pp. 51–169 (R, P, U, E, F).
  STS, 1, pp. 105–16.

● 21/iii/28/T

Convention between the RSFSR and Turkey concerning repatriation of military and civilian prisoners

Signed Mar. 28, 1921, in Moscow.
Entered into force on signature. Ratified by Turkey July 21, 1921. Supplements Art. 13 of the treaty of Mar. 16, 1921 (21/iii/16/T). Listed in *SDD*, 1–2, 1928, p. 197, as no longer valid.
Sources: *SU*, 1921, No. 43, Art. 221.
  Vestnik NKID, 1921, No. 3–4, pp. 144–46.
  SDD RSFSR, 2, pp. 121–23.
  SDD, 1, pp. 279–81.
  *Düstur, 2, p. 118.
  STS, 1, p. 116.

● 21/iv/16/Pl

Agreement between the RSFSR and the Armenian, Azerbaidzhan, and Georgian SSR's concerning administration of railroad communications in the Transcaucasus

Signed Apr. 16, 1921, in Baku and Tbilisi.
Confirmed Aug. 8, 1921, and Jan. 14, 1922.
Sources: *SDD RSFSR*, 3, pp. 9–11.
  STS, 1, pp. 116–17.

Apr. 20, 1921. Declaration recognizing the right to a flag of states having no seacoast

See 35/iv/7/1921.

- 21/iv/23/Ger

Treaty between the Ukrainian SSR and Germany concerning repatriation

Signed Apr. 23, 1921, in Berlin.
Entered into force on signature.
Source: *SDD*, 1, pp. 236–37.

- 21/v/6/Ger/a

Temporary agreement between the RSFSR and Germany concerning extension of the sphere of activity of delegations engaged in care of prisoners of war, with protocol

Signed May 6, 1921, in Berlin.
Entered into force on signature. Valid until 3 months after denunciation. Supplemented by protocol of June 29, 1924. Superseded by treaty of Oct. 12, 1925 (25/x/12/Ger/a). In effect, a temporary commercial agreement.
Sources: *Izv.*, July 3, 1921.
Vestnik NKID, 1921, No. 9–10, pp. 178–81.
SU, 1921, No. 68, Art. 542.
SDD RSFSR, 2, pp. 24–28.
SDD, 1, pp. 54–58.
*RGbl, 1921, No. 75, p. 929.
LNTS, 6, pp. 267–83 (R, G, E, F).
STS, 1, pp. 119–20.

- 21/v/6/Ger/b

Agreement between the RSFSR and Germany concerning repatriation of prisoners of war and interned civilians, with protocol

Signed May 6, 1921, in Berlin.
Ratified by the RSFSR July 30, 1921. Entered into force on signature, except for Arts. 2, 4 and 9, which entered into force on exchange of acts of ratification, Aug. 30, 1921, in Berlin. Modifies the agreement of Jan. 22, 1921 (21/i/22/Ger).
Sources: *Izv.*, Oct. 11, 1921.
Vestnik NKID, 1921, No. 9–10, pp. 181–84.
SU, 1922, I, No. 7, Art. 82.
SDD RSFSR, 2, pp. 91–94.
SDD, 1, pp. 230–33.
*RGbl, 1921, No. 84, p. 1161.
LNTS, 12, pp. 177–89 (G, E, F).
STS, 1, pp. 118–19.

- 21/v/21/GrSSR/a

Treaty of alliance between the RSFSR and the Georgian SSR

Signed May 21, 1921, in Moscow.
Entered into force on signature.
Sources: *SDD RSFSR*, 3, pp. 18–19.
STS, 1, p. 120.

- 21/v/21/GrSSR/b

Agreement between the RSFSR and the Georgian SSR concerning financial matters

Signed May 21, 1921, in Moscow.
Entered into force on signature.
Sources: *SDD RSFSR*, 3, pp. 20–22.
STS, 1, p. 121.

- 21/v/25/Ger

Exchange of notes between the RSFSR and Germany concerning courier service

Sent May 6, 17 and 25, 1921, in Berlin.
Sources: *SDD RSFSR*, 2, pp. 95–97.
Vestnik NKID, 1921, No. 9–10, pp. 184–86.
STS, 1, pp. 117–18.

- 21/vi/1/Pol

Protocol between the RSFSR and the Belorussian and Ukrainian SSR's on the one hand and Poland on the other concerning instructions for arbitration commissions to deal with border incidents

Signed June 1, 1921, in Minsk.
Entered into force on signature. Supplemented by protocol of Jan. 24, 1922.
Sources: *SDD RSFSR*, 2, pp. 83–85.
STS, 1, pp. 121–22.

- 21/vi/12/Lat

Provisional agreement between the RSFSR and Latvia concerning transportation of passengers, baggage and freight between the railroads of Latvia and the rail network Orël-Vitebsk

Signed June 12, 1921.
References: *LS, p. 513; *ibid.*, 2d ed., p. 734.

- 21/vi/28/Lith

Agreement between the RSFSR and Lithuania concerning procedure for choice of Lithuanian citizenship, with annex

Signed June 28, 1921, in Moscow.
Entered into force July 14, 1921; not subject to ratification. Listed in *SDD*, 1–2, 1928, p. 178, as no longer valid.

Sources: *Izv.*, July 14 and 15, 1921.
  SU, 1922, I, No. 7, Arts. 80, 81.
  SDD RSFSR, 2, pp. 102–107.
  SDD, 1, pp. 251–55.
  *LS, 1, pp. 98–103.
  STS, 1, pp. 122–23.

● 21/vii/22/Lat

Agreement between the RSFSR and Latvia concerning procedure for choice of citizenship

Signed July 22, 1921, in Riga.
Entered into force Aug. 2, 1921. Constitutes Part I of a Soviet-Latvian agreement on political and legal matters; Part II, concerning repatriation, and Part III, concerning export and destruction of property, signed Nov. 6, 1921.
Sources: *Izv.*, Aug. 2, 1921.
  SDD RSFSR, 2, pp. 98–101.
  LRR, pp. 96–100.
  STS, 1, pp. 123–24.

● 21/vii/26/BSSR

Agreement between the RSFSR and the Belorussian SSR concerning financial matters

Signed July 26, 1921, in Moscow.
Entered into force on signature.
Sources: *SDD RSFSR*, 2, pp. 5–6.
  STS, 1, pp. 124–25.

● 21/vii/28/H

Agreement between the RSFSR and the Ukrainian SSR on the one hand and Hungary on the other concerning exchange of prisoners of war and interned civilians

Signed July 28, 1921, in Riga.
Ratified by the RSFSR July 29, 1921; by Hungary Aug. 12, 1921. Entered into force Aug. 12, 1921. Listed in *SDD*, 1–2, 1928, p. 176, as no longer valid.
Sources: *Izv.*, Sept. 4, 1921.
  SU, 1922, I, No. 11, Art. 94.
  SDD RSFSR, 2, pp. 86–88.
  SDD, 1, pp. 220–22.
  STS, 1, pp. 125–26.

● 21/viii/3/Lat/a

Treaty between the Ukrainian SSR and Latvia concerning future relations, with annex

Signed Aug. 3, 1921, in Moscow.
Entered into force Mar. 16, 1923, on ex-change of acts of ratification in Khar'kov. Makarov, 1925, states that the treaty was ratified by the Ukrainian SSR in 1921 and promulgated on June 19, 1922 (citing Ukrainian collection of laws, 1922, No. 31, Art. 483), and re-enacted on Mar. 16, 1923 (citing *ibid.*, 1923, No. 15, Arts. 259–261). Supplemented by protocol dated Nov. 10, 1922.
Sources: *SDD*, 1, pp. 86–97.
  SDD, 1–2, 1928, pp. 48–59.
  LRR, pp. 86–96.
  LNTS, 17, pp. 317–63 (R, Lat., U, E, F).
  STS, 1, pp. 126–29.

● 21/viii/3/Lat/b

Convention between the Ukrainian SSR and Latvia concerning repatriation of Latvian refugees from the Ukrainian SSR

Signed Aug. 3, 1921, in Moscow.
Entered into force on signature. Listed in *SDD*, 1–2, 1928, p. 178, as no longer valid.
Sources: *SDD*, 1, pp. 244–48.
  LRR, pp. 82–86.
  LNTS, 17, pp. 295–315 (R, Lat., E, F).
  STS, 1, pp. 129–30.

● 21/viii/10/Mongolia

Exchange of telegrams between the RSFSR and the People's Revolutionary Government of Outer Mongolia concerning Soviet military aid

Mongolian request sent during July 1921; Soviet reply, agreeing to keep Soviet forces in Mongolia "until defeat of the common enemy," sent Aug. 10, 1921.
For a Soviet note of Jan. 24, 1925, announcing withdrawal of Soviet forces, see *SDFP*, 2, pp. 7–8.
Sources (Soviet telegram): *Izv.*, Aug. 10 and 12, 1921.
  Eudin and North, pp. 204–205.
  SDFP, 1, pp. 252–53.
Reference: *Ibid.*, 2, p. 7.
Note: For earlier Soviet agreements on aid to the Mongolian revolutionaries in 1920 and 1921, see Eudin and North, pp. 122, 125.

● 21/viii/16/UK

Agreement between the RSFSR and the United Kingdom concerning the Anglo-Russian submarine cable

Signed Aug. 16, 1921, in London. Not subject to ratification.

Provides for continuation in force, with modifications, of provisions of the agreements between the British and Russian Postal and Telegraph Administrations of Nov. 14, 1916, and June 10/23, 1916. Modified by exchange of notes dated Dec. 1 and 6, 1921 (21/xii/6/UK).
Sources: *SDD RSFSR*, 3, 279–80.
  SDD, 1, pp. 342–43.
  SDD, 1–2, 1928, pp. 275–76.
  BFSP, 117, pp. 350–51.
  LNTS, 31, pp. 85–88 (E, F).
  STS, 1, p. 131.

• 21/viii/20/Pr

Agreement between the RSFSR and the American Relief Administration concerning procedure for famine relief

Signed Aug. 20, 1921, in Riga.
Chronologically the first, and substantively the most important, of the agreements concerning famine relief concluded during 1921 and subsequently between the Soviet Government and private philanthropic organizations abroad. For an analysis showing the agreements to be international treaties even though one of the partners in each case is not a State, see Korovin, 1925, pp. 95–103, and the same author's article, "Inostrannaia filantropicheskaia deiatel'nost' v RSFSR i eë pravovye formy," *Sovetskoe pravo*, 1922, No. 1. For an agreement terminating the work of the ARA, see 23/vi/15/Pr.
Sources: *SDD RSFSR*, 2, pp. 152–55.
  Vestnik NKID, 1922, No. 4–5, pp. 236–40.
  VPSS, 2, pp. 149–52.
  Kliuchnikov, 3, I, pp. 109–11.
  Fisher, pp. 507–10.
  Hiebert, pp. 441–46.
References: Korovin, 1925, pp. 96–97.
  Itogi bor'by, p. 332.

• 21/viii/23/Fin

Agreement between the RSFSR and Finland concerning establishment of border trading posts

Signed Aug. 23, 1921.
Reference: Chronology in Lenin, *Soch.*, 1st ed., 18, II, p. 246.

• 21/viii/27/Pr/a

Agreement between the RSFSR and Fridtjof Nansen, High Commissioner of the Geneva Conference for Aid to the Famine Victims in Russia, concerning famine relief, with annex (Chicherin-Nansen agreement)

Signed Aug. 27, 1921, in Moscow.
Provides for negotiations concerning a credit to the RSFSR of 10 million pounds sterling. For an agreement between the RSFSR and Norway based on this agreement, see 22/xi/15/Norway.
Annexes: (A) An agreement of the same date between Chicherin and Nansen concerning principles for European voluntary relief to Russia; (B) official information provided by the Soviet Government on relief requirements.
Sources: *Vestnik NKID*, 1922, No. 4–5, pp. 240–43 (omits Annex B).
  Soviet Russia, Jan. 1922, pp. 22–23 (same).
  Kliuchnikov, 3, I, pp. 111–12 (shortened and without the annexes).

• 21/viii/27/Pr/b

Supplementary agreement between the RSFSR and Fridtjof Nansen concerning famine relief operations of the International Russian Relief Executive

Signed Aug. 27, 1921, in Moscow.
Source: *Vestnik NKID*, 1922, No. 4–5, pp. 243–45.

• 21/viii/29/Pr

Agreement between the RSFSR and the German Red Cross concerning medical aid to famine victims

Signed Aug. 29, 1921.
Reference: Korovin, 1925, pp. 99–100.

• 21/ix/2/Norway

Temporary agreement between the RSFSR and Norway concerning political and economic relations

Signed Sept. 2, 1921, in Christiania (Oslo).
Ratified by the RSFSR Sept. 19, 1921; by Norway Oct. 1, 1921. Entered into force Oct. 1, 1921. Superseded by treaty of Dec. 15, 1925.
Sources: *SU*, 1921, No. 75, Art. 612.
  Vestnik NKID, 1921, No. 9–10, pp. 186–89.
  SDD RSFSR, 2, pp. 32–35.
  SDD, 1, pp. 117–20.
  LNTS, 7, pp. 293–301 (E, F).

• 21/ix/7/Fin

Temporary agreement between the RSFSR and the Administration of Finnish State Railroads concerning transfer of railroad rolling stock

Signed Sept. 7, 1921.
Superseded by temporary agreement of Dec. 14, 1921.
Reference: Mentioned in Art. 76 of 21/xii/14/Fin.

● 21/ix/16/Pr

Agreement between the RSFSR and representatives of the Society of Friends (Quakers) concerning famine relief

Signed Sept. 16, 1921.
An earlier agreement, concluded in Dec. 1920 between the RSFSR Commissariat of Supplies and English and American Quakers, is mentioned in Forbes, John, "American Friends and Russian relief," *Bulletin of Friends Historical Association*, Autumn 1952, p. 125; not listed separately here.
Source: *God bor'by*, pp. 121–22.
Reference: *Itogi bor'by*, p. 332.

● 21/ix/17/T

Convention between the Ukrainian SSR and Turkey concerning repatriation of military and civilian prisoners

Signed Sept. 17, 1921, in Moscow.
Source: *SDD*, 1, pp. 281–85.

● 21/ix/19/Pl

Agreement between the RSFSR, Finland, and Norway concerning telegraph communications

Signed Sept. 19, 1921, in Riga.
Approved by the RSFSR Sept. 30, 1921; by Finland Nov. 4, 1921; and by Norway Nov. 5, 1921.
Sources: *LNTS*, 15, pp. 191–93 (E, F). *BFSP*, 116, pp. 733–34 (F).

● 21/ix/21/Pl

Agreement between the RSFSR and the Bukhara and Khorezm People's Soviet Republics concerning administration of the Amu-Darya flotilla

Signed Sept. 21, 1921.
Mentioned in and amended by the agreement of Apr. 30, 1923.

● 21/ix/27/Fin

Temporary agreement between the RSFSR and Finland concerning rafting timber in the Minalanioki and Tulemanioki Rivers

Signed Sept. 27, 1921, in Helsinki.
Entered into force on signature. Covers the period Autumn 1921–Spring 1922; valid until conclusion of the permanent agreement called for in the peace treaty of Oct. 14, 1920.
Sources: *SU*, 1922, I, No. 7, Art. 78. *Vestnik NKID*, 1921, No. 9–10, pp. 189–91. *SDD RSFSR*, 2, pp. 124–26. *STS*, 1, pp. 133–34.

● 21/ix/30/Arm

Agreement between the RSFSR and the Armenian SSR concerning financial matters

Signed Sept. 30, 1921, in Moscow.
Entered into force on signature.
Sources: *SDD RSFSR*, 2, pp. 3–4 (misnumbered 5–6). *SU*, 1921, No. 72, Art. 588. *STS*, 1, p. 134.

Sept. 30, 1921. International convention for suppression of the traffic in women and children

See 47/xii/18/1921, 47/xii/18/1947/a, and 54/viii/11/1950.

● 21/x/1/Persia

Temporary railroad agreement between the Transcaucasian SSR's and Persia

Signed Oct. 1, 1921.
Mentioned in and superseded by the railroad agreement of Sept. 13, 1940 (40/ix/13/Iran/a).

● 21/x/1/Pr

Agreement between the RSFSR and the Ukrainian SSR on the one hand and the American Mennonite Relief on the other concerning famine relief, with annex

Signed Oct. 1, 1921, in Moscow.
Provides for provision of supplies to a minimum value of $50 thousand. Annex provides for participation of Holland Mennonite Relief, to a value of $75 thousand.
Source: Hiebert, pp. 446–52.
References: Korovin, 1925, p. 100. *Itogy bor'by*, p. 332. Hiebert, pp. 150–51.

● 21/x/3/H

Protocol between the RSFSR and the Ukrainian SSR on the one hand and

Hungary on the other concerning exchange of prisoners of war through the mediation of Latvia and the International Red Cross

Signed Oct. 3, 1921, in Riga.
Entered into force on signature. Listed in *SDD*, 1–2, 1928, as no longer valid.
Sources: *SDD RSFSR*, 3, pp. 80–83.
    SDD, 1, pp. 222–24.
    STS, 1, pp. 134–35.

Oct. 6, 1921. International Metric Convention
See 25/vi/16/1921.

• 21/x/7/Pol

Agreement between the RSFSR and Poland concerning the expulsion from Poland of the "Russian Political Committee" headed by Boris Savinkov

Signed Oct. 7, 1921, in Warsaw.
Reference: *MP RSFSR, 1922*, p. 42.

• 21/x/11/Fin

Agreement between the RSFSR and Finland concerning rafting timber in the Repola and Porosozero volosts

Signed Oct. 11, 1921, in Helsinki.
Entered into force on signature.
Sources: *SU*, 1922, I, No. 7, Art. 79.
    SDD RSFSR, 2, pp. 127–28.
    STS, 1, pp. 135–36.

• 21/x/13/T

Treaty of friendship between the Azerbaidzhan, Armenian, and Georgian SSR's on the one hand, with the participation of the RSFSR; and Turkey on the other

Signed Oct. 13, 1921, in Kars.
Ratified by the RSFSR and Turkey Mar. 16, 1922. Arts. 6, 14, 15, 16, 18, and 19 entered into force on signature; remainder of the treaty entered into force Sept. 11, 1922, on exchange of acts of ratification in Erivan.
Modified by protocol of May 31, 1926.
Sources: *SDD RSFSR*, 3, pp. 49–57.
    SDD, 1, pp. 160–67.
    SDD, 1–2, 1928, pp. 120–26.
    *Düstur, 3, p. 24.
    STS, 1, pp. 136–37.

• 21/x/18/Pr

Agreement between the RSFSR and the International Trade Union Alliance concerning famine relief

Signed Oct. 18, 1921, in Berlin.
Source: *Soviet Russia*, Jan. 1922, p. 23.
References: Korovin, 1925, p. 100.
    Itogi bor'by, p. 332.

• 21/x/19/Pr

Agreement between the RSFSR and the American Relief Administration concerning food remittances

Signed Oct. 19, 1921, in Moscow.
Sale of remittances under this agreement was terminated by Apr. 1, 1923.
Sources: Hiebert, pp. 457–60.
    Fisher, pp. 514–16.
References: *Itogi bor'by*, p. 332.
    Fisher, p. 121.

• 21/x/20/Pr/a

Agreement between the Ukrainian SSR and the American Mennonite Relief concerning famine relief, with annex

Signed Oct. 20, 1921, in Khar'kov.
Provides for provision of supplies to a minimum value of $25 thousand. Annex provides for sending provisions to the Ukraine against drafts purchased by individuals outside the Ukraine or Russia.
Source: Hiebert, pp. 452–56.
Reference: *Ibid.*, pp. 161–62.

• 21/x/20/Pr/b

Agreement between the Ukrainian SSR and Holland Mennonite Relief concerning famine relief

Signed Oct. 20, 1921, in Khar'kov.
Reference: Hiebert, p. 162.

• 21/x/28/Mongolia

Exchange of notes between the RSFSR and the People's Revolutionary Government of Outer Mongolia concerning Soviet military aid to wipe out resistance in western Mongolia

Sent Oct. 17 and 28, 1921.
References: *SDFP*, 2, p. 7, citing
    Tikhii okean, 1936, 3, p. 73.

• 21/x/31/Fin

Act regulating the functions of the Central Russian-Finnish Mixed Commission, established under Art. 37 of the peace treaty of October 14, 1920

Signed Oct. 31, 1921, in Helsinki.
Source: **SS*, 1921, No. 14 (Finnish, R).

● 21/xi/5/MPR

Agreement between the RSFSR and the Mongolian People's Republic concerning establishment of friendly relations

Signed Nov. 5, 1921, in Moscow.
Entered into force on signature. According to Korolenko, p. 22, still valid in 1953.
Sources: *SU*, 1921, No. 77, Art. 655.
   SDD RSFSR, 2, pp. 29–31.
   SDD, 1, pp. 114–16.
   SDD, 1–2, 1928, pp. 77–79.
   STS, 1, pp. 137–38.

● 21/xi/6/Lat/a

Agreement between the RSFSR and Latvia concerning repatriation

Signed Nov. 6, 1921, in Riga.
Enters into force on publication in *Izv.*, to take place not later than 14 days after signature; publication in *Izv.* took place June 23, 1922.
Constitutes Part II of a Soviet-Latvian agreement on political and legal matters. For Part I, concerning repatriation, see 21/vii/22/Lat; for Part III, concerning export and destruction of property, see 21/xi/6/Lat/b.
Sources: *Izv.*, June 23, 1922.
   Vestnik NKID, 1922, No. 6, pp. 167–69.
   SDD RSFSR, 3, pp. 84–87.
   SDD, 1, pp. 237–39.
   LRR, pp. 100–102.
   LNTS, 17, pp. 259–63, 278–85 (R, Lat., E, F).

● 21/xi/6/Lat/b

Agreement between the RSFSR and Latvia concerning export and destruction of property

Signed Nov. 6, 1921, in Riga.
Enters into force on publication in *Izv.*, to take place not later than 14 days after signature; publication in *Izv.* took place June 23, 1922.
Constitutes Part III of a Soviet-Latvian agreement on political and legal matters. For Part I, concerning repatriation, see 21/vii/22/Lat; for Part II, concerning repatriation, see 21/xi/6/Lat/a.
Sources: *Izv.*, June 23, 1922.
   Vestnik NKID, 1922, No. 6, pp. 169–73.
   SDD RSFSR, 3, pp. 88–94.
   SDD, 1, pp. 239–43.
   LRR, pp. 102–106.
   LNTS, 17, pp. 263–71, 285–93 (R, Lat., E, F).

● 21/xi/8/Pr

Agreement between the RSFSR and a group of Swedish trade and industrial enterprises concerning famine relief

Signed Nov. 8, 1921.
References: Korovin, 1925, p. 100.
   Itogi bor'by, p. 332 (dates the agreement Oct. 30, 1921).

● 21/xi/14/Pr

Agreement between the RSFSR and Fridtjof Nansen concerning relief parcels

Signed Nov. 14, 1921.
Reference: *Itogi bor'by*, p. 333.

Nov. 11–16, 1921. International Labour Organisation Conventions Nos. 10, 11, 15, and 16

See 56/vii/6/1921/a through /d.

● 21/xi/25/Est/a

Treaty between the Ukrainian SSR and Estonia concerning future relations

Signed Nov. 25, 1921, in Moscow.
Ratified by Estonia Dec. 16, 1921; by the Ukrainian SSR Apr. 7, 1923. Entered into force Oct. 27, 1923, on exchange of acts of ratification in Moscow. Modified by protocols of May 27, 1922, and Feb. 17, 1923.
Sources: *SDD*, 1, pp. 207–11.
   SDD, 1–2, 1928, pp. 166–70.
   RT, 1922, No. 9/10.
   LNTS, 11, pp. 121–42 (U, Est., R, E, F).

● 21/xi/25/Est/b

Agreement between the Ukrainian SSR and Estonia concerning procedure for choosing Estonian or Ukrainian citizenship, with annex

Signed Nov. 25, 1921, in Moscow.
Entered into force Oct. 27, 1923. Listed in *SDD*, 1–2, 1928, p. 209, as no longer valid.
Sources: *SDD*, 1, pp. 301–306.
   RT, 1922, No. 9/10.
   LNTS, 11, pp. 143–66 (U, Est., R, E, F).
   STS, 1, pp. 142–44.

● 21/xi/27/Pol

Temporary agreement between the RSFSR and Poland concerning railroad traffic between Stolbce and Negoreloe

Signed Nov. 27, 1921, in Negoreloe.
Enters into force on confirmation.
Listed in *SDD*, 1–2, 1928, p. 329, as no
longer valid.
Sources: *SDD RSFSR*, 3, pp. 245–52.
  SDD, 1, pp. 376–82.
  STS, 1, pp. 144–46.

● 21/xii/6/UK

**Exchange of notes between the RSFSR
and the United Kingdom concerning
cable rates**

Sent Dec. 1 and 6, 1921, in London.
Incorporates recommendations of a Telegraph Conference of the Baltic States,
held in Riga on Sept. 10, 1921. Modifies
agreement of Aug. 16, 1921. Not subject
to confirmation, but revised rates were
confirmed by Soviet Commissariat of Posts
and Telegraph in exchange of telegrams
on Nov. 14 and 15, 1921 (not listed separately).
Sources: *BFSP*, 117, pp. 351–53.
  LNTS, 31, pp. 88–89 (E, F).
  STS, 1, pp. 146–47.

● 21/xii/7/Austria/a

**Temporary agreement between the
RSFSR and the Ukrainian SSR on the
one hand and Austria on the other concerning future relations**

Signed Dec. 7, 1921, in Vienna.
Ratified by the RSFSR Jan. 12, 1922; by
the Ukrainian SSR Jan. 14, 1922. Entered
into force Feb. 14, 1922, on exchange of
acts of ratification in Vienna. Extended
to the USSR by exchange of notes dated
Sept. 8, 1923.
Sources: *SU*, 1922, I, No. 3, Art. 39.
  SDD RSFSR, 3, pp. 29–35.
  SDD, 1, pp. 35–39.
  SDD, 1–2, 1928, pp. 4–8.
  BGbl, 147/22
  LNTS, 20, pp. 153–81 (R, U, G, E, F).

● 21/xii/7/Austria/b

**Agreement between the RSFSR and the
Ukrainian SSR on the one hand and
Austria on the other extending the agreement of July 5, 1920, concerning repatriation of prisoners of war and interned civilians**

Signed Dec. 7, 1921, in Vienna.
Ratified by the RSFSR Jan. 12, 1922.
Entered into force Feb. 14, 1922, on ex-
change of acts of ratification in Vienna.

Listed in *SDD*, 1–2, 1928, p. 173, as no
longer valid.
Sources: *SU*, 1922, I, No. 3, Art. 39.
  Vestnik NKID, 1922, No. 6, pp. 163–66.
  SDD RSFSR, 3, pp. 73–79.
  SDD, 1, pp. 214–18.
  BGbl, 148/22.
  STS, 1, pp. 148–50.

● 21/xii/10/Ger

**Agreement between the RSFSR and Ger-
many concerning return of merchant
ships**

Signed Dec. 10, 1921.
Mentioned in and replaced by agreement
of Apr. 23, 1923.

● 21/xii/12/Persia

**Exchange of notes between the RSFSR
and Persia concerning Arts. 3, 5, 6, 13,
and 20 of the treaty of friendship of
February 26, 1921**

Sent Dec. 12, 1921, in Teheran.
Concerns foreign trade and internal pol-
icy.
Sources: *LNTS*, 9, pp. 410–13 (E, F).
  STS, 1, pp. 150–51, citing
    BFSP, 114, pp. 907–909.

● 21/xii/14/Fin

**Temporary agreement between the
RSFSR and Finland concerning rail
transportation of passengers, baggage
and freight from Finland to Russia and
vice versa, via the frontier stations of
Rajajoki and Valeasaari (Beloostrov)**

Signed Dec. 14, 1921, in Helsinki.
Entered into force Dec. 24, 1921. Super-
sedes temporary agreement of Sept. 7,
1921.
Listed in *SDD*, 1–2, 1928, p. 330, as no
longer valid.
Sources: *SU*, 1922, I, No. 8, Art. 87.
  SDD RSFSR, 3, pp. 253–78.
  SDD, 1, pp. 402–17.
  SS, 1921, No. 15 (Finnish, R).
  LNTS, 16, pp. 221–315 (Finnish, R, E,
    F).

● 21/xii/17/Pol

**Temporary agreement between the
Ukrainian SSR and Poland concerning
rail transportation between Szepietovka
and Zdolbunowo**

Signed Dec. 17, 1921, in Warsaw.
Ratified by the Ukrainian SSR Jan. 27, 1922; by Poland Jan. 25, 1922. Listed in *SDD*, 1–2, 1928, p. 330, as no longer valid.
Source: *SDD*, 1, pp. 382–91.

● 21/xii/23/Lat

Temporary agreement between the RSFSR and Latvia concerning parcel post

Signed Dec. 23, 1921, in Riga.
Confirmed by the RSFSR Jan. 12, 1922.
Sources: *SDD*, 1, pp. 346–50.
    SDD, 1–2, 1928, pp. 279–83.
    STS, 1, pp. 157–58.

● 21/xii/25/Pr

Agreement between the RSFSR and Fridtjof Nansen concerning a loan from Norway for famine relief

Signed Dec. 25, 1921.
Reference: *Itogi bor'by*, p. 333.

● 21/xii/26/Italy/a

Preliminary agreement between the RSFSR and Italy concerning political and economic matters, with declaration concerning recognition of claims

Signed Dec. 26, 1921, in Rome.
Entered into force on signature. Under Art. 13, a trade convention was signed in Genoa on May 24, 1922; it was not ratified, however, by the RSFSR. Instead, this preliminary agreement was extended by exchange of notes dated June 22, 1922. Listed in *SDD*, 1–2, 1928, p. 29, as no longer valid.
Sources: *SU*, 1922, I, No. 11, Art. 95.
    Vestnik NKID, 1922, No. 1–3, pp. 170–74.
    SDD RSFSR, 3, pp. 39–46.
    SDD, 1, pp. 69–75.
    *TC, 27, p. 428.
    STS, 1, pp. 158–59.

● 21/xii/26/Italy/b

Preliminary agreement between the Ukrainian SSR and Italy concerning political and economic matters, with declaration concerning recognition of claims

Signed Dec. 26, 1921, in Rome.
Listed in *SDD*, 1–2, 1928, p. 29, as no longer valid.
Source: **TC*, 27, pp. 438–48.
References: *SDD*, 1, p. 75.
    STS, 1, p. 160.

● 21/xii/27/Pr. See Appendix 5.

● 21/xii/30/Pr/a

Agreement between the RSFSR and the American Relief Administration concerning famine relief to adults

Signed Dec. 30, 1921.
Source: Fisher, p. 524.
Reference: *Itogi bor'by*, p. 333.

● 21/xii/30/Pr/b

Agreement between the RSFSR and the American Relief Administration concerning purchase by the RSFSR of food supplies and seed in America for famine relief

Signed Dec. 30, 1921.
Provides for purchase by the RSFSR of materials to a value of $10 million.
Source: Fisher, pp. 526–27.
References: *Itogi bor'by*, p. 333.
    Fisher, p. 157.

● 21/xii/31/Pr

Agreement between the Ukrainian SSR and Fridtjof Nansen concerning famine relief

Signed Dec. 31, 1921.
References: *Itogi bor'by*, p. 333.
    Korovin, 1925, p. 98.

1922

● 22/i/10/Pr

Agreement between the Ukrainian SSR and the American Relief Administration concerning provision of food for famine relief

Signed Jan. 10, 1922, in Moscow.
Source: Fisher, pp. 528–31.
References: *Itogi bor'by*, p. 333.

Hiebert, p. 163.
Fisher, pp. 251–53.

● 22/i/19/BSSR

Agreement between the RSFSR and the Belorussian SSR concerning entry of the Belorussian SSR into the Federal Committee on Agricultural Affairs

Signed Jan. 19, 1922, in Moscow.
Entered into force on signature.
Sources: *SDD RSFSR*, 3, pp. 16–17.
   STS, 1, p. 161.

• 22/i/21/T

Treaty of friendship between the Ukrainian SSR and Turkey

Signed Jan. 21, 1922, in Angora (according to Turkish records and some Soviet sources, Jan. 2, 1922).
Ratified by Turkey Mar. 16, 1922; by the Ukrainian SSR Mar. 23, 1922. Entered into force June 23, 1922, on exchange of acts of ratification in Khar'kov. Provisions similar to those of the RSFSR-Turkish treaty of Mar. 16, 1921.
Sources: *SDD*, 1, pp. 167–71.
   SDD, 1–2, 1928, pp. 126–30.
   *Düstur, 3, p. 14.
   STS, 1, pp. 160–61, citing
     BFSP, 120, pp. 953–57.

• 22/i/24/Pol

Protocol between the RSFSR and the Belorussian and Ukrainian SSR's on the one hand and Poland on the other supplementing the agreement of June 1, 1921, concerning instructions for arbitration commissions to deal with border incidents

Signed Jan. 24, 1922, in Warsaw.
Entered into force on signature.
Sources: *SDD RSFSR*, 3, pp. 58–59.
   STS, 1, p. 161.

• 22/ii/1/Pr

Agreement between the Ukrainian SSR and the American Relief Administration concerning purchase of food and seed for famine relief

Signed Feb. 1, 1922.
Provides for purchase by the Ukrainian SSR of supplies to a value of approximately $2 million.
Reference: Fisher, pp. 157–58.

Feb. 1, 1922. Temporary commercial agreement between the RSFSR and Sweden

See Appendix 1.

• 22/ii/13/Pr

Agreement between the RSFSR and the Central Committee of the organization "Pro Russia" under the Italian Socialist Party concerning famine relief

Signed Feb. 13, 1922.
Reference: *Itogy bor'by*, p. 333.
Note: *MP RSFSR, 1922*, p. 37, mentions an agreement concerning repatriation of former Italian prisoners-of-war and other Italian citizens, signed by the Soviet mission in Italy and the Central Committee of "Pro Russia," probably early in 1922. Not otherwise identified and not listed separately.

• 22/ii/17/FER

Treaty of economic alliance between the RSFSR and the Far Eastern Republic

Signed Feb. 17, 1922, in Moscow.
Entered into force on signature. Declared invalid by decree of Dec. 22, 1922 (see 20/xi/15/FER).
Sources: *Izv.*, Apr. 23, 1922.
   Vestnik NKID, 1922, No. 6, pp. 174–78.
   SDD RSFSR, 3, pp. 23–28.
   STS, 1, pp. 161–62.

• 22/ii/22/Pl

Protocol between the RSFSR and the Armenian SSR, the Azerbaidzhan SSR, the Belorussian SSR, the Bukhara People's Soviet Republic, the Georgian SSR, the Far Eastern Republic, the Ukrainian SSR, and the Khorezm Soviet Republic concerning the transfer to the RSFSR of the representation of the various republics to the European Economic Conference, with declaration

Signed Feb. 22, 1922, in Moscow.
Sources: *Izv.*, Feb. 25, 1922.
   SDD RSFSR, 3, pp. 1–3.
   STS, 1, p. 163.

• 22/ii/27/Pr

Agreement between the RSFSR and the Lithuanian Red Cross concerning food parcels for famine relief

Signed Feb. 27, 1922.
Reference: *Itogi bor'by*, p. 333.
Note: Source cited, under the same date, lists an agreement concerning food parcels concluded with the NDVK; meaning of the abbreviation is not known.

• 22/iii/ /Persia/a

Agreement between the RSFSR and Persia concerning lease of fishing vessels for the spring season

Signed during the spring, 1922, in Teheran.
Reference: *MP RSFSR, 1922*, p. 62.

● 22/iii/ /Persia/b

Temporary agreement between the RSFSR and Persia concerning the water supply to the Tejen region

Signed during the spring, 1922, in Teheran.
Reference: *MP RSFSR, 1922,* p. 62.

● 22/iii/ /Pr

Agreement between the RSFSR and the Student Friendship Fund concerning provision of food for students

Signed during Mar. 1922.
Reference: Fisher, p. 465.

Mar. 1, 1922. Temporary commercial treaty between the RSFSR and Sweden

See Appendix 1.

● 22/iii/12/Pl

Treaty of alliance between the Azerbaidzhan, Armenian, and Georgian SSR's, establishing the Federative Union of Socialist Soviet Republics of the Transcaucasus

Signed Mar. 12, 1922.
Sources: *Zhizn' natsional'nostei,* Apr. 14, 1922, No. 6–7, p. 16.
   Istoriia sovetskoi konstitutsii, pp. 358–59 (incomplete).

● 22/iii/12/VC

Agreement between the RSFSR and the Vatican concerning famine relief

Signed Mar. 12, 1922, in the Vatican City.
References: *MP RSFSR, 1922,* p. 27.
   Korovin, 1925, p. 101.
   Itogy bor'by, p. 18.

● 22/iii/16/Pr

Agreement between the RSFSR and the French Red Cross concerning famine relief

Signed Mar. 16, 1922, in Berlin.
References: *Itogi bor'by,* p. 333.
   Korovin, 1925, pp. 100–101.
   Rubinshtein, p. 244.

● 22/iii/20/T/a

Convention between the Georgian SSR and Turkey concerning the use by citizens of both countries of pastures lying on the opposite side of the border, with three annexes

Signed Mar. 20, 1922, in Tbilisi.
Ratified by Turkey Apr. 13, 1925; by the USSR May 12, 1926. Acts of ratification exchanged Feb. 13, 1928, in Angora. Entered into force Apr. 15, 1922. Duration 5 years; if not denounced 6 months before expiration, remains in force until 1 year after withdrawal or request for modification by either signatory.
Extended by exchange of notes dated Sept. 18 and Dec. 15, 1927 (27/xii/15/T), and by protocol of May 17, 1928.
Sources: *SDD,* 1, pp. 321–25.
   SDD, 1–2, 1928, pp. 244–48.
   SZ, 1928, II, No. 34, Art. 143 (R, F).
   *Düstur, 6, p. 244.
   STS, 1, pp. 163–64.

● 22/iii/20/T/b

Convention between the Georgian SSR and Turkey concerning crossing the border by inhabitants of border regions

Signed Mar. 20, 1922, in Tbilisi.
Ratified by Turkey Feb. 23, 1925; by the USSR Jan. 8, 1926. Acts of ratification exchanged Mar. 11, 1927, in Angora. Entered into force Apr. 15, 1922; duration 5 years. If not denounced 6 months before expiration, remains in force until 1 year after withdrawal or request for modification by either signatory.
Extended by exchange of notes dated Nov. 17 and Dec. 14, 1927 (27/xii/14/T).
Sources: *SZ,* 1927, II, No. 32, Art. 171.
   SDD, 1, pp. 276–79.
   SDD, 1–2, 1928, pp. 194–97.
   *Düstur, 6, p. 235.
   STS, 1, pp. 164–65.

● 22/iii/21/Fin

Agreement between the RSFSR and Finland transferring the solution of border incidents to the Central Mixed Russo-Finnish Commission

Signed Mar. 21, 1922, in Moscow.
Superseded by the border agreement of June 1, 1922.
Sources: *SDD RSFSR,* 3, p. 60.
   *SS, 1922, No. 7.
   STS, 1, p. 165.

● 22/iii/30/Pl

Final protocol between the RSFSR, Estonia, Latvia, and Poland concerning economic problems and the consolidation of

peace in Eastern Europe, in preparation for the European Conference at Genoa

Signed Mar. 30, 1922, in Riga.
Sources: *SDD RSFSR*, 3, pp. 4–6.
  SDFP, 1, pp. 296–98, citing
    Materialy Genuezskoi konferentsii
    (M., 1922), p. 78.
  STS, 1, pp. 165–66.

• 22/iv/5/Lith/a

Agreement between the Ukrainian SSR and Lithuania concerning temporary rules for the transportation by rail of the property of persons choosing Lithuanian citizenship

Signed Apr. 5, 1922, in Khar'kov.
Listed in *SDD*, 1–2, 1928, p. 178, as no longer valid.
Source: *SDD*, 1, pp. 262–64.

• 22/iv/5/Lith/b

Supplementary treaty between the Ukrainian SSR and Lithuania to the peace treaty of February 14, 1921, with supplementary protocol

Signed Apr. 5, 1922, in Khar'kov.
Entered into force Oct. 26, 1922, on exchange of acts of ratification in Khar'kov. Modifies both the peace treaty and the agreement of Jan. 28, 1921, concerning choice of citizenship (21/i/28/Lith/a).
Sources: *SDD*, 1, pp. 110–14.
  SDD, 1–2, 1928, pp. 72–76.
  STS, 1, pp. 166–67.

• 22/iv/11/Pl

Agreement between the RSFSR and the Armenian, Azerbaidzhan, and Georgian SSR's concerning financial relations, with two annexes

Signed Apr. 11, 1922, in Moscow.
Entered into force July 8, 1922, on confirmation.
Sources: *SU*, 1922, Appendix II.
  SDD RSFSR, 4, pp. 5–8.
  STS, 1, pp. 167–68.

• 22/iv/16/Ger

Treaty between the RSFSR and Germany (Treaty of Rapallo)

Signed Apr. 16, 1922, in Rapallo.
Ratified by the RSFSR May 16, 1922; by Germany July 4, 1922. Entered into force

on signature, except Arts. 1-c and 4, which entered into force Jan. 31, 1923, on exchange of acts of ratification in Berlin. Extended to the Union Republics by an agreement of Nov. 5, 1922. Reaffirmed by the treaties of Oct. 12, 1925 (25/x/12/Ger/a), and Apr. 24, 1926 (26/iv/24/Ger). Annulled June 22, 1941 (Rönnefarth-Euler, p. 73). For a denial by Commissar of Foreign Affairs G. V. Chicherin that the treaty contained any secret clauses, dated Apr. 29, 1922, see *SDFP*, 1, pp. 304–305, and Eudin and Fisher, p. 202. For a discussion of evidence on Soviet-German clandestine military agreements, see Appendix 2.
Sources: *Izv.*, May 10, 1922.
  SU, 1923, I, No. 33, Art. 374.
  SDD RSFSR, 3, pp. 36–38.
  SDD, 1, pp. 58–59.
  SDD, 1–2, 1928, pp. 15–17.
  *RGbl, 1922, II, No. 18, p. 677.
  LNTS, 19, pp. 247–52 (G, E, F).
  STS, 1, pp. 168–69.
  BFSP, 118, pp. 586–87.
  PV, 1, pp. 107–109.

Apr. 20, 1922. Agreement between the Ukrainian Red Cross and the Nansen Commission

Reference: *Itogy bor'by*, p. 333.

• 22/v/9/Est

Treaty between the RSFSR and Estonia concerning rafting timber

Signed May 9, 1922, in Tallinn.
Ratified by the RSFSR June 22, 1922. Entered into force provisionally on signature; definitively on Oct. 2, 1922, on exchange of acts of ratification in Tallinn.
Sources: *SDD RSFSR*, 3, pp. 117–22.
  SDD, 1, pp. 337–41.
  SDD, 1–2, 1928, pp. 271–74.
  *RT, 1922, No. 95.
  STS, 1, pp. 169–70.

• 22/v/10/Pl

Agreement between the RSFSR and the Belorussian and Ukrainian SSR's on the one hand, and the League of Nations' Commission for Combating Epidemics on the other, concerning aid to the People's Commissariats of Health of the signatory republics

Signed May 10, 1922, in Santa Margarita; signed by the representative of the RSFSR

on behalf not only of the Belorussian and Ukrainian SSR's but also of "all other Union Governments which constitute part of the geographical concept of Russia."
Sources: *SDD RSFSR*, 3, pp. 290–94.
  SDD, 1, pp. 433–35.
  SDD, 1–2, 1928, pp. 357–59.

May 19, 1922. Genoa Conference
See Appendix 1.

• 22/v/24/Pl

Agreement between the RSFSR and the Azerbaidzhan, Armenian, and Georgian SSR's concerning unification of the administrations of posts, telegraph, telephone, and radio-telegraph

Signed May 24, 1922, in Moscow.
Sources: *SDD RSFSR*, 3, pp. 12–13.
  STS, 1, p. 170.

May 24, 1922. Temporary commercial treaty between the RSFSR and Italy
See Appendix 1.

• 22/v/27/Est

Supplementary protocol between the Ukrainian SSR and Estonia to the treaty of November 25, 1921, concerning future relations

Signed May 27, 1922, in Moscow.
Acts of ratification exchanged Oct. 27, 1923, in Moscow.
Sources: *SDD*, 1, pp. 211–12.
  SDD, 1–2, 1928, pp. 170–71.
  *RT, 1922, No. 159.
  STS, 1, pp. 170–71.

• 22/v/31/MPR

Protocol between the RSFSR and the Mongolian People's Republic concerning ownership of various property

Signed May 31, 1922, in Urga.
Sources: *SU*, 1922, Appendix II.
  SDD RSFSR, 4, pp. 25–26.
  SDD, 1–2, 1928, pp. 178–79.
  TA, pp. 102–103.
  STS, 1, p. 171.

• 22/vi/1/Fin

Agreement between the RSFSR and Finland concerning measures for ensuring security of the border, with protocol

Signed June 1, 1922, in Helsinki.
Evidently entered into force on signature, without ratification. Duration 1 year, with automatic extension unless denounced with 3 months' notice. Supersedes the agreement of Mar. 21, 1922.
Sources: *SU*, 1922, Appendix II.
  SDD RSFSR, 3, pp. 61–72.
  SDD, 1, pp. 307–15.
  SDD, 1–2, 1928, pp. 210–18.
  *SS, 1922, No. 8 (R, Finnish).
  LNTS, 16, pp. 317–47 (R, Finnish, Sw., E, F).
  STS, 1, pp. 171–73.

• 22/vi/5/Cz

Temporary treaty between the RSFSR and Czechoslovakia concerning trade and commerce and the maintenance of neutrality

Signed June 5, 1922, in Prague.
Ratified by the RSFSR June 22, 1922; by Czechoslovakia July 14, 1922. Notes concerning confirmation sent by the RSFSR July 5, 1922; by Czechoslovakia Aug. 9, 1922.
Entered into force Aug. 9, 1922. Valid until 6 months after denunciation.
Sources: *SU*, 1922, Appendix II; *ibid.*, I, No. 48, Art. 608 (ratification).
  SDD RSFSR, 4, pp. 17–21.
  SDD, 1, pp. 188–91.
  SDD, 1–2, 1928, pp. 145–49.
  STS, 1, pp. 173–74.

• 22/vi/6/Cz

Temporary treaty between the Ukrainian SSR and Czechoslovakia concerning trade and commerce and the maintenance of neutrality

Signed June 6, 1922, in Prague.
Ratified by Czechoslovakia July 14, 1922; by the Ukrainian SSR July 19, 1922.
Text is a translation, with appropriate modifications, of 22/vi/5/Cz.
Sources: *SDD*, 1, pp. 192–95.
  SDD, 1–2, 1928, pp. 149–52 (U), citing *Visti VUTsIK*, 1922, No. 31, Art. 483.
  STS, 1, p. 175.

• 22/vi/7/Ger

Protocol between the RSFSR and Germany concerning reciprocal transfer of the embassies in Berlin and Petrograd
Signed June 7, 1922.
Reference: *MP RSFSR*, *1922*, p. 30.

• 22/vi/8/Pr

Agreement between the RSFSR and

Fridtjof Nansen concerning relief parcels to Russian professors

Signed June 18, 1922.
Reference: *Itogi bor'by*, p. 333.

● 22/vi/13/Fin

Temporary agreement between the RSFSR and Finland concerning establishment of telegraph communications

Signed June 13, 1922, in Helsinki.
Entered into force June 23, 1922. Superseded by convention of June 18, 1924 (24/vi/18/Fin/c).
Sources: *SU*, 1922, Appendix II.
   SDD RSFSR, 3, pp. 287–90.
   SDD, 1, pp. 362–64.
   *SS, 1922, No. 9 (R, Finnish, F).
   LNTS, 16, pp. 349–60 (R, Finnish, Sw., E, F).
   STS, 1, p. 175.
   BFSP, 116, pp. 727–29 (F).

● 22/vi/19/Pol

Temporary agreement between the Ukrainian SSR and Poland concerning rail transportation between Volochisk and Podvolochisk

Signed June 19, 1922, in Warsaw.
Ratified by the Ukrainian SSR Aug. 18, 1922; by Poland Aug. 25, 1922. Listed in *SDD*, 1–2, 1928, p. 330, as no longer valid.
Source: *SDD*, 1, pp. 392–401.

● 22/vi/22/Fin

Temporary agreement between the RSFSR and Finland concerning establishment of postal communications

Signed June 22, 1922, in Helsinki.
Entered into force July 7, 1922. Superseded by the convention of June 18, 1924 (24/vi/18/Fin/b).
Sources: *SU*, 1922, Appendix II.
   SDD RSFSR, 4, pp. 42–45.
   SDD, 1, pp. 364–67.
   *SS, 1922, No. 10 (R, Finnish).
   LNTS, 16, pp. 361–77 (R, Finnish, Sw., E, F).
   STS, 1, pp. 176–77.
   BFSP, 116, pp. 730–33 (F).

● 22/vi/22/Italy

Exchange of notes between the RSFSR and Italy concerning extension of the preliminary agreement of Dec. 26, 1921

Signed June 22, 1922, in Rome. For history, see 21/xii/26/Italy/a.
Sources: *SDD RSFSR*, 3, pp. 46–48.
   STS, 1, p. 176.

● 22/vi/24/Lat

Sanitary convention between the RSFSR and the Belorussian and Ukrainian SSR's on the one hand and Latvia on the other

Signed June 24, 1922, in Tartu.
Ratified by the RSFSR July 31, 1922. Entered into force Oct. 18, 1923, on exchange of acts of ratification in Moscow.
Sources: *SDD*, 1, pp. 423–32 (misdated 1923).
   SDD, 1–2, 1928, pp. 340–49 (same).
   LRR, pp. 114–23.
   LNTS, 38, pp. 9–55 (R, G, E, F).
   STS, I, pp. 177–80; cf. *ibid.*, pp. 219–22.

● 22/vi/25/Est

Sanitary convention between the RSFSR and the Belorussian and Ukrainian SSR's on the one hand and Estonia on the other

Signed June 25, 1922, in Tartu.
Ratified by the RSFSR July 31, 1922; by Estonia Feb. 13, 1923. Entered into force Oct. 27, 1923, on exchange of acts of ratification in Moscow.
Sources: *SDD*, 1, pp. 432–33.
   SDD, 1–2, 1928, p. 356.
   *RT, 1923, No. 30.
   STS, 1, p. 180.

● 22/vi/29/Kh

Economic agreement between the RSFSR and the Khorezm Soviet People's Republic

Signed June 29, 1922, in Tashkent.
Ratified by the RSFSR Sept. 25, 1922; by Khorezm Oct. 12, 1922. Entered into force on signature. Replaces agreement of Sept. 13, 1920 (20/ix/13/Kh/b).
Sources: *SDD RSFSR*, 4, pp. 13–14.
   SDD, 1, pp. 336–37.
   STS, 1, pp. 180–81.

● 22/vii/3/UK

Exchange of notes between the RSFSR and the United Kingdom concerning extension of the trade agreement of March 16, 1921, to Canada

Sent July 3, 1922, in London.
Entered into force July 3, 1922. De-

nounced by Canada in a note of June 2, 1927, following denunciation by the United Kingdom of the basic agreement (see 21/iii/16/UK).

Sources: *SU*, 1924, I, No. 36, Art. 344.
  SDD RSFSR, 4, pp. 15–16.
  SDD, 1, p. 53.
  LNTS, 13, pp. 37–39 (E, F).
  STS, 1, p. 181.

● 22/vii/4/Pol

Regulations on the settlement of border disputes between the RSFSR and Poland

Signed July 4, 1922, in Nesvizh, by a Soviet-Polish border commission.
Reference: *MP RSFSR, 1922*, p. 43.

● 22/vii/7/Fin

Agreement between the RSFSR and Finland concerning former government property

Signed July 7, 1922, in Moscow.
Modifies Art. 22 of the peace treaty of Oct. 14, 1920.
Sources: *SU*, 1922, Appendix II.
  SDD RSFSR, 4, p. 27.
  SDD, 1, p. 285.
  SDD, 1–2, 1928, p. 198.
  SS, 1922, No. 27 (R, Finnish).
  LNTS, 19, pp. 99–103 (R, Finnish, E, F).
  STS, 1, p. 181.

● 22/vii/9/T/a

Postal-telegraph convention between the RSFSR and the Armenian, Azerbaidzhan, and Georgian SSR's on the one hand and Turkey on the other

Signed July 9, 1922, in Tbilisi.
Ratified by the USSR July 27, 1923. Enters into force on exchange of acts of ratification, except for some of the provisions concerning posts, which come into force one month after signature.
Sources: *SDD*, 1, pp. 355–62.
  SDD, 1–2, 1928, pp. 291–98.
  STS, 1, pp. 181–84.

● 22/vii/9/T/b

Railroad convention between the RSFSR and the Armenian, Azerbaidzhan, and Georgian SSR's on the one hand and Turkey on the other

Signed July 9, 1922, in Tbilisi.

Ratified by Turkey Apr. 13, 1925; by the USSR July 20, 1927. Entered into force Dec. 23, 1928, on exchange of acts of ratification in Angora. Modified by protocol of Dec. 23, 1928, and by agreements of Oct. 20, 1936, and June 5, 1939 (39/vi/5/T/b).

Sources: *SZ*, 1929, II, No. 14, Art. 83.
  SDD, 5, pp. 138–45.
  Düstur, 6, p. 276.
  STS, 1, pp. 184–85.

August 1922. Exchange of letters between the RSFSR and the American Relief Administration, acting for the American Mennonite Relief, concerning validation of an undated agreement between the RSFSR and the American Mennonite Relief concerning aid for agricultural reconstruction

Text of the agreement in Hiebert, pp. 460–62.

● 22/viii/9/Bukh

Economic agreement between the RSFSR and the Bukhara People's Soviet Republic

Signed Aug. 9, 1922, in Moscow.
Ratified by the RSFSR Aug. 24, 1922; by Bukhara Sept. 17, 1922. Entered into force on signature. Supersedes agreement of Mar. 4, 1921 (21/iii/4/Bukh/b). Supplemented by customs agreement of May 31, 1923.
Sources: *SDD RSFSR*, 4, pp. 9–10.
  SDD, 1, pp. 316–17.
  STS, 1, p. 186.

● 22/viii/12/Fin/a

Agreement between the RSFSR and Finland concerning repatriation, with three declarations

Signed Aug. 12, 1922, in Helsinki.
Entered into force on signature.
Sources: *SU*, 1922, I, No. 50, Art. 634.
  SDD RSFSR, 4, pp. 28–36.
  SDD, 1, pp. 286–93.
  SS, 1922, No. 11 (Finnish, R).
  LNTS, 19, pp. 105–42 (R, Finnish, Sw., E, F).
  STS, 1, pp. 186–89.

● 22/viii/12/Fin/b

Agreement between the RSFSR and Finland concerning the return of ships

Signed Aug. 12, 1922, in Helsinki.
Entered into force on signature. Carries
out a provision of the peace treaty of Oct.
14, 1920.
Sources: *SU*, 1923, I, No. 52, Art. 516.
  SDD RSFSR, 5, pp. 24–27.
  SS, 1922, No. 26 (R, Finnish).
  STS, 1, pp. 189–90.

● 22/viii/16/Lat

**Protocol of an agreement between the
RSFSR and Latvia concerning exchange
of arrested and imprisoned persons**

Signed Aug. 16, 1922, in Riga. Ratified
by the RSFSR Oct. 2, 1922. Exchange to
be completed by Dec. 1, 1922.
Sources: *SDD RSFSR*, 4, pp. 22–24.
  STS, 1, p. 190.
Reference: *MP RSFSR, 1922*, pp. 40–41.

● 22/ix/20/FER

**Agreement between the RSFSR and the
Far Eastern Republic concerning passport matters**

Signed Sept. 20, 1922, in Moscow.
Entered into force on signature. Declared
invalid by decree of Dec. 22, 1922 (see
20/xi/15/FER).
Sources: *SDD RSFSR*, 4, pp. 11–12.
  STS, 1, pp. 191–92.

● 22/ix/20/Fin

**Agreement between the RSFSR and Fin-
land concerning fishing regulations in
the Gulf of Finland**

Signed Sept. 20, 1922, in Helsinki. En-
tered into force Nov. 20, 1922. Duration
10 years, with automatic extension for 10
years if not denounced.
Sources: *SU*, 1924, I, No. 36, Art. 345.
  SDD RSFSR, 4, pp. 39–41.
  SDD, 1, pp. 325–27.
  SDD, 1–2, 1928, pp. 248–50.
  SS, 1922, No. 16 (R, Finnish).
  LNTS, 19, pp. 143–52 (R, Finnish, Sw.,
    E, F).
  STS, 1, p. 191.

● 22/x/ /Pol

**Temporary agreement between the
RSFSR and Poland concerning border
railroad traffic**

Signed during Oct. 1922.

Subject to confirmation.
Reference: *MP RSFSR, 1922*, p. 47.

● 22/x/21/Fin

**Convention between the RSFSR and Fin-
land concerning fishing and seal hunting in territorial waters of the Arctic
Ocean**

Signed Oct. 21, 1922, in Helsinki. Ratified
by the RSFSR Nov. 9, 1922.
Entered into force July 2, 1924, on ex-
change of acts of ratification in Moscow.
Duration 10 years; if not denounced 1
year before expiration, extended for 10-
year periods.
Modified by protocol of July 31, 1923.
Sources: *SZ*, 1925, I, No. 12, Art. 97.
  SDD, 2, pp. 60–63.
  SDD, 1–2, 1928, pp. 259–62.
  SS, 1924, No. 16 (R, Finnish).
  LNTS, 29, pp. 197–209 (R, Finnish,
    Sw., E, F).
  STS, 1, p. 192.

● 22/x/24/J

**Agreement between the armies of the Far
Eastern Republic and Japan concerning
evacuation of Vladivostok by Japanese
troops**

Signed Oct. 24, 1922, at Sedanka siding.
Evacuation to be completed by Oct. 25,
1922.
References: *MP RSFSR, 1922*, p. 76.
  Shishkin, p. 258.

● 22/x/26/Pr

**Agreement between the RSFSR and the
American Relief Administration concerning clothing remittances**

Signed Oct. 26, 1922.
Action under the agreement terminated by
Apr. 1923.
Reference: Fisher, p. 424.

● 22/x/28/Fin/a

**Agreement between the RSFSR and Fin-
land concerning maintenance of the
main channel and fishing in the border
water systems between Russia and Finland**

Signed Oct. 28, 1922, in Helsinki.
Ratified by the RSFSR Dec. 7, 1922; by
Finland May 11, 1923. Entered into force
May 18, 1923, on exchange of acts of rati-

fication in Helsinki. Duration 5 years; if not denounced 6 months before expiration, extended for 5-year periods. Revived by the USSR under Art. 12 of the peace treaty of Feb. 10, 1947, by notification of Mar. 13, 1948 (see 48/iii/16/Fin).
Sources: *SU*, 1923, I, No. 52, Art. 515.
  SDD RSFSR, 5, pp. 13–16.
  SDD, 1, pp. 327–29.
  SDD, 1–2, 1928, pp. 250–53.
  *SS, 1923, No. 9 (R, Finnish).
  LNTS, 19, pp. 183–97 (R, Finnish, Sw., E, F).
  STS, 1, pp. 197–98.

• 22/x/28/Fin/b

Convention between the RSFSR and Finland concerning floating of timber in water courses running from the territory of Russia into the territory of Finland and vice versa

Signed Oct. 28, 1922, in Helsinki. Ratified by the RSFSR Dec. 7, 1922; by Finland Mar. 11, 1923. Entered into force May 18, 1923, on exchange of acts of ratification in Helsinki. Valid until 2 years after denunciation.
Modified by convention of Oct. 15, 1933. Revived by the USSR under Art. 12 of the peace treaty of Feb. 10, 1947, by notification of Mar. 13, 1948 (see 48/iii/16/Fin) ; re-entered into force Mar. 13, 1948.
Sources: *SU*, 1923, I, No. 53, Art. 515.
  SDD RSFSR, 5, pp. 16–23.
  SDD, 1, pp. 330–36.
  *SS, 1923, No. 8 (R, Finnish).
  LNTS, 19, pp. 153–81 (R, Finnish, Sw., E, F).
  STS, 1, pp. 193–96.

• 22/x/28/Fin/c

Agreement between the RSFSR and Finland concerning the conditions under which the RSFSR and its citizens shall be entitled to free transit through the district of Petsamo (Pechenga)

Signed Oct. 28, 1922, in Helsinki. Entered into force Dec. 28, 1922. Duration 5 years; if not denounced 1 year before expiration, extended for 5-year periods.
Sources: *SU*, 1922, Appendix II.
  SDD RSFSR, 5, pp. 9–12.
  SDD, 1, pp. 293–96.
  *SS, 1922, No. 18 (R, Finnish).

  LNTS, 19, pp. 200–212 (R, Finnish, Sw., E, F).
  STS, 1, pp. 192–93.

• 22/x/28/Fin/d

Convention between the RSFSR and Finland concerning fishing and seal hunting on Lake Ladoga

Signed Oct. 28, 1922, in Helsinki. Ratified by the RSFSR Nov. 30, 1922 (decree of ratification dated Jan. 31, 1924). Entered into force July 2, 1924, on exchange of acts of ratification in Moscow. Duration 10 years; if not denounced 1 year before expiration, extended for 10-year periods.
Modified by protocol of July 12, 1924. Terminated by Soviet decree of June 27, 1933 (*SZ*, 1933, II, No. 19, Art. 191) ; Finnish Government notified of termination June 29, 1933; convention expired July 2, 1934.
Sources: *SZ*, I, 1925, No. 12, Art. 98.
  SDD, 2, pp. 63–67.
  SDD, 1–2, 1928, pp. 262–67.
  *SS, 1924, No. 15 (R, Finnish).
  LNTS, 29, pp. 211–28 (R, Finnish, Sw., E, F).
  STS, 1, pp. 196–97.

• 22/xi/5/Ger

Agreement between the RSFSR and the Ukrainian SSR on the one hand and Germany on the other extending the Treaty of Rapallo of April 16, 1922, to the Union Republics

Signed Nov. 5, 1922, in Berlin. The Soviet signatories signed also on behalf of the Belorussian, Armenian, Azerbaidzhan, and Georgian SSR's and the Far Eastern Republic.
Ratified by the Belorussian SSR Dec. 1, 1922; by the Georgian SSR Feb. 12, 1922; by the Azerbaidzhan SSR Jan. 12, 1923; by the Ukrainian SSR Dec. 14, 1922; and by the Armenian SSR Feb. 1, 1923. Entered into force Oct. 25, 1923, on exchange of acts of ratification in Berlin. Arts. 2–9 superseded by treaty of Oct. 12, 1925 (25/x/12/Ger/a).
Sources: *SDD*, 1, pp. 60–63.
  SDD, 1–2, 1928, pp. 17–18.
  *RGbl, 1923, II, No. 27, p. 315.
  LNTS, 26, pp. 387–94 (G, E, F).
  STS, 1, pp. 198–99.
  BFSP, 118, pp. 587–90 (F).

• 22/xi/10/Lat

Protocol between the Ukrainian SSR and Latvia concerning responsibility for requisitions and military actions on Ukrainian territory before July 26, 1922

Signed Nov. 10, 1922, in Moscow. Supplements the treaty of Aug. 3, 1921 (21/viii/3/Lat/a).
Source: *SDD*, 1–2, 1928, p. 59.

• 22/xi/15/Norway

Agreement between the RSFSR and Norway concerning conditions of a loan offered by Norway to the RSFSR

Signed Nov. 15, 1922, in Moscow.
Entered into force on signature. Based on the Chicherin-Nansen agreement of Aug. 27, 1921 (21/viii/27/Pr).
Sources: *SU*, 1922, I, No. 80, Art. 1005.
   SDD RSFSR, 4, pp. 37–38.
   SDD, 1, pp. 320–21.
   SDD, 1–2, 1928, pp. 243–44.
   STS, 1, p. 199.

• 22/xii/11/Pr

Agreement between the RSFSR and the American Jewish Joint Distribution Committee concerning aid for agricultural and other reconstruction

Signed Dec. 11, 1922.
Reference: Fisher, p. 460.

• 22/xii/30/Pl

Treaty concerning the establishment of the Union of Soviet Socialist Republics

Signed Dec. 30, 1922, in Moscow, by the RSFSR, the Ukrainian and Belorussian SSR's, and the Transcaucasian SFSR (including the Armenian, Azerbaidzhan, and Georgian SSR's).
Confirmed by the 1st Congress of Soviets of the USSR Dec. 30, 1922. Ratified by the USSR July 6, 1923, and entered into force on that date. Definitively ratified, in expanded form, by the 2d Congress of Soviets of the USSR on Jan. 31, 1924, as the second section of the Constitution of the USSR (see *MPID*, 1, p. 38).

Sources: *Izv.*, Dec. 31, 1922.
   Obrazovanie SSSR, pp. 333–37, citing Stalin, *Soch.*, 5, appendix II, pp. 396–401;
   Pravda, Dec. 31, 1922;
   Konstitutsii i konstitutsionnye akty Soiuza SSR (1922–1936), M., 1940, pp. 19–22;
   S"ezdy Sovetov SSSR v postanovleniiakh i rezoliutsiiakh, M., 1939, pp. 20–24;
   Pervaia konstitutsiia Soiuza SSR, M., 1948, pp. 341–45.
   STS, 1, pp. 199–201, citing Dept. of State translation of text as published in Riga, Jan. 10, 1923.

1923

• 23/i/4/Fin

Exchange of notes between the RSFSR and Finland concerning consular matters

Sent Jan. 2 and 4, 1923, in Helsinki.
Sources: *SZ*, 1925, I, No. 59, Art. 442.
   MZh, 1925, No. 3, pp. 157–58.
   SDD, 3, 1927, pp. 61–63; *ibid.*, 1932, pp. 48–49.
   STS, 1, p. 201.

• 23/ii/7/Pol

Sanitary convention between the RSFSR and the Belorussian and Ukrainian SSR's on the one hand and Poland on the other

Signed Feb. 7, 1923, in Warsaw.
Ratified by the Belorussian SSR Mar. 2, 1923; by the RSFSR Mar. 8, 1923; by the Ukrainian SSR Apr. 10, 1923; and by Poland Aug. 22, 1923. Entered into force Jan. 28, 1924, 20 days after the exchange of acts of ratification in Warsaw. Duration 3 years, with automatic extension thereafter until denounced with 1 year's notice. According to a letter from the Polish delegation to the League of Nations dated Feb. 7, 1927, the convention was extended by tacit consent.
Sources: *SDD*, 2, pp. 118–24.
   SDD, 1–2, 1928, pp. 349–56.
   DURP, 1924, No. 13, Arts. 111, 112.
   LNTS, 49, pp. 286–314 (P, R, U, E, F).
   STS, 1, pp. 201–204.

• 23/ii/17/Est

Supplementary protocol between the Ukrainian SSR and Estonia to the treaty

of November 25, 1921, concerning future relations

Signed Feb. 17, 1923, in Khar'kov.
Entered into force Oct. 27, 1923, on exchange of acts of ratification in Moscow.
Sources: *SDD*, 1, p. 212.
  SDD, 1–2, 1928, pp. 171–72.
  *RT, 1923, No. 109/110.
  STS, 1, pp. 204–205.

● 23/ii/20/MPR. See Appendix 5.

● 23/ii/21/Fin

Exchange of notes between the RSFSR and Finland concerning exemption of certain urban property from stamp duty and all other charges on the occasion of its homologation or registration

Sent Feb. 12, 14 and 21, 1923, in Helsinki.
Sources: **SS*, 1923, No. 3 (Finnish, F).
  LNTS, 19, pp. 220–23 (E, F).
  STS, 1, p. 204.

● 23/iv/23/Denmark

Preliminary agreement between the RSFSR and Denmark concerning political and economic relations, with protocol and declaration concerning claims

Signed Apr. 23, 1923, in Moscow.
Ratified by the RSFSR June 13, 1923; by Denmark June 8, 1923. Entered into force June 15, 1923, on exchange of acts of ratification in Moscow. Extended by exchange of notes of June 18, 1924 (24/vi/18/Denmark/c). Superseded by the treaty of commerce and navigation of Aug. 17, 1946 (46/viii/17/Denmark/a).
Sources: *SU*, 1923, I, No. 45, Art. 477 (E, R).
  MZh, 1923, No. 2, pp. 143–49.
  SDD, 1, pp. 63–68.
  SDD, 1–2, 1928, pp. 20–26.
  *DT, 1923.
  *Lovtidende A 1923, p. 1601.
  LNTS, 18, pp. 15–27 (E, F).
  STS, 1, pp. 205–206.

● 23/iv/23/Ger

Agreement between the RSFSR and Germany concerning merchant vessels which have fallen under the authority of the other party, with exchange of notes

Signed Apr. 23, 1923, in Moscow.
Entered into force on signature. Signed in fulfillment of Art. 1–b of the Treaty of Rapallo of Apr. 16, 1922. Replaces agreement of Dec. 10, 1921. Listed in *SDD*,

1–2, 1928, p. 177, as no longer valid.
Sources: *SU*, 1923, I, No. 33, Art. 375.
  MZh, 1923, No. 2, pp. 137–40.
  SDD RSFSR, 5, pp. 6–9.
  SDD, 1, pp. 233–36.
  STS, 1, p. 207.

● 23/iv/25/Persia

Postal convention between the RSFSR and Persia, with declaration

Signed Apr. 25, 1923, in Moscow. Extended to the Transcaucasian SFSR by the declaration of the same date.
Ratified by the RSFSR May 9, 1923; by the USSR June 21, 1927; acts of ratification exchanged Dec. 14, 1927, in Moscow. Entered into force July 25, 1923 (3 months after signature); definitive entry into force Feb. 3, 1925. Valid until 1 year after denunciation. Supplementary protocol concerning official language and entry into force signed Oct. 7, 1924. Supplemented by protocol of Nov. 23, 1927, concerning air communications.
Sources: *SZ*, 1928, II, No. 24, Art. 109.
  SDD, 1, pp. 350–52.
  SDD, 1–2, 1928, pp. 285–88.
  LNTS, 110, pp. 323–31 (E, F).
  STS, 1, p. 208.
  BFSP, 118, pp. 953–56 (F).

● 23/iv/27/Persia

Telegraph convention between the RSFSR and Persia, with declaration

Signed Apr. 27, 1923, in Moscow. Extended to the Transcaucasian SFSR by the declaration of the same date.
Ratified by the RSFSR May 9, 1923; by the USSR June 21, 1927; acts of ratification exchanged Dec. 14, 1927, in Moscow. Entered into force July 27, 1923 (3 months after signature); definitive entry into force Jan. 27, 1925. Supplementary protocol concerning official language and entry into force signed Oct. 7, 1924.
Sources: *SZ*, 1928, II, No. 24, Art. 110.
  SDD, 1, pp. 352–55.
  SDD, 1–2, 1928, pp. 288–91.
  LNTS, 110, pp. 333–39 (E, F).
  STS, 1, p. 209.
  BFSP, 118, pp. 957–60 (F).

● 23/iv/30/Pl

Agreement between the RSFSR and the Bukhara and Khorezm People's Soviet Republics concerning administration of the Amu-Darya flotilla

Signed Apr. 30, 1923, in Moscow.
Entered into force on signature. Amends the agreement of Sept. 21, 1921.
Sources: *SU*, 1923, I, No. 40, Art. 435.
   SDD RSFSR, 5, p. 5.
   SDD, 1, p. 372.
   STS, 1, pp. 209–210.

• 23/v/24/Pol

Postal and telegraph convention between the RSFSR and the Belorussian and Ukrainian SSR's on the one hand and Poland on the other, with final protocol and supplementary protocol

Signed May 24, 1923, in Moscow. Extended to the Transcaucasian SFSR by final protocol. Ratified by the USSR Feb. 27, 1925; by Poland Feb. 28, 1925. Entered into force Mar. 2, 1925, on exchange of acts of ratification in Warsaw. Valid until 3 months after denunciation. Denounced by the USSR Oct. 11, 1930, with effect from Jan. 11, 1931.
Sources: *SZ*, 1928, II, No. 10, Art. 42 (R, P).
   SDD, 4, 1928, pp. 141–59.
   MZh, 1925, No. 2, pp. 186–205.
   *DURP, 1925, No. 26, Arts. 174, 175.
   LNTS, 50, pp. 341–413 (R, P, E, F).
   STS, 1, pp. 210–16.

• 23/v/31/Bukh

Customs agreement between the RSFSR and the Bukhara People's Soviet Republic, with supplementary protocol

Signed May 31, 1923, in Moscow.
Entered into force on signature. Supplements economic agreement of Aug. 9, 1922.
Sources: *SU*, 1923, I, No. 52, Art. 517.
   MZh, 1923, No. 2, pp. 140–43.
   SDD, 1, pp. 317–20.
   STS, 1, pp. 216–17.

• 23/vi/5/Fin

Agreement between the RSFSR and Finland concerning navigation by Finnish merchant and cargo vessels of the Neva between Lake Ladoga and the Gulf of Finland, with protocol

Signed June 5, 1923, in Moscow.
Ratified by the USSR July 11, 1924. Entered into force provisionally June 18, 1923; definitively July 12, 1924, on exchange of acts of ratification in Moscow. Valid until 9 months after denunciation.

Art. 7, giving regulations for Finnish merchant and cargo vessels, was amended by exchange of notes dated Sept. 2, 1927, and was revised by agreement of Mar. 17, 1928.
Sources: *SZ*, 1924, I, No. 16, Art. 157.
   SDD, 2, pp. 104–109.
   SDD, 1–2, 1928, pp. 330–35.
   *SS, 1923, No. 17 (R, Finnish).
   LNTS, 18, pp. 203–25 (R, Finnish, Sw., E, F).
   STS, 1, pp. 217–18.

• 23/vi/15/Pr

Agreement between the RSFSR and the American Relief Administration concerning termination of the ARA's operations

Signed June 15, 1923.
For the agreement establishing procedure for the ARA's famine relief operations, see 21/viii/20/Pr.
Source: Fisher, pp. 551–52.

• 23/vii/5/Est/a

Convention between the USSR and Estonia concerning direct rail communications for passengers and freight

Signed July 5, 1923, in Tallinn.
Ratified by Estonia Aug. 4, 1923; by the USSR Oct. 10, 1923. Acts of ratification exchanged June 12, 1924, in Moscow.
Continues the convention of Sept. 17, 1920 (20/ix/17/Est/a). Supplemented by the following 3 documents. Listed in *SDD*, 1–2, 1928, p. 339, as no longer valid.
Sources: *SZ*, 1925, I, No. 20, Art. 133.
   SDD, 2, pp. 113–17.
   *RT, 1923, No. 111.
   STS, 1, pp. 222–23.

• 23/vii/5/Est/b

Protocol between the USSR and Estonia concerning rail communications

Signed July 5, 1923, in Tallinn.
Supplements the convention of the same date, and modifies the protocol of Sept. 17, 1920 (20/ix/17/Est/b), as well as the Regulations of the same date (20/ix/17/Est/d).
Sources: *SZ*, 1925, I, pp. 244–46.
   SDD, 2, pp. 115–17.

• 23/vii/5/Est/c

Protocol between the USSR and Estonia concerning rail communications

Signed July 5, 1923, in Tallinn.

Supplements the convention of the same
date, and modifies the protocol of Sept. 17,
1920 (20/ix/17/Est/b).
Sources: *SZ*, 1925, I, pp. 246–47.
    SDD, 2, p. 117.

**July 24, 1923. Convention concerning
the regime of the Black Sea Straits (Lausanne Convention)**

See Appendix 1.

● 23/vii/28/Austria

**Agreement between the USSR and Aus-
tria concerning embassy buildings**

Signed July 28, 1923.
Entered into force on signature. Imple-
mented by agreement of July 16, 1927.
Reference: *Included in Austrian Haus-,
    Hof- und Staatsarchiv under Zl. 1396/
    23; not published in Austria.

● 23/vii/28/Fin

**Agreement between the USSR and Fin-
land concerning maintenance of order in
the parts of the Gulf of Finland situated
outside territorial waters, the upkeep of
maritime installations, and pilotage service in the Gulf**

Signed July 28, 1923, in Helsinki.
Ratified by the USSR Sept. 7, 1923. Entered into force Dec. 19, 1924, on exchange
of acts of ratification in Helsinki. Valid
until 1 year after denunciation. Amended
by protocol of Apr. 13, 1929 (29/iv/13/
Fin/b).
Sources: *SZ*, 1925, I, No. 20, Art. 134 (R,
    Finnish).
    SDD, 2, pp. 110–13.
    SDD, 1–2, 1928, pp. 335–39.
    **SS*, 1924, No. 42 (R, Sw.).
    LNTS, 32, pp. 101–17 (R, Finnish, Sw.,
    E, F).
    STS, 1, pp. 223–24.

● 23/vii/31/Fin

Protocol between the USSR and Finland

modifying the convention of October 21,
**1922, concerning fishing and seal hunt-
ing**

Signed July 31, 1923, in Helsinki.
Sources: *SZ*, 1925, I, p. 163.
    SDD, 1–2, 1928, p. 262.
    STS, 1, p. 224.

● 23/ix/8/Austria

**Exchange of notes between the USSR
and Austria extending to the USSR the
temporary agreement of December 7,
1921, concerning future relations**

Signed Sept. 8, 1923, in Vienna.
Entered into force on signature; not sub-
ject to ratification.
Sources: *SDD*, 1, pp. 34–35.
    SDD, 1–2, 1928, pp. 3–4.
    **BGbl*, 525/23.
    LNTS, 20, pp. 167–68, 178–81 (G, E,
    F).
    STS, 1, p. 225.

**Sept. 12, 1923. Convention for suppres-
sion of the circulation of and traffic in
obscene publications**

See 35/vii/8/1923 and 47/xii/18/1947/b.

● 23/xi/20/Rom

**Regulations concerning measures to pre-
vent and settle conflicts which might
arise along the Dniester River**

Signed by the USSR and Romania Nov.
20, 1923, in Tiraspol.
Confirmed by the USSR Jan. 8, 1924.
Enters into force after confirmation by
both signatories.
Sources: *SDD*, 2, pp. 28–31, citing
    Vestnik TsIK, SNK i STO SSSR,
    1924, No. 1.
    SDD, 1–2, 1928, pp. 191–94.
    STS, 1, pp. 225–26.

● 23/xii/4/Rom. See Appendix 5.

● 23/xii/8/Cz. See Appendix 5.

1924

**Jan. 25, 1924. International agreement
for the creation at Paris of an international office for dealing with contagious
diseases of animals**

See 27/x/20/1924.

● 24/ii/7/Italy/a

**Treaty of commerce and navigation be-
tween the USSR and Italy, with annex
and final protocol**

Signed Feb. 7, 1924, in Rome.

Ratified by the USSR Mar. 7, 1924. Entered into force Mar. 22, 1924 (15 days after exchange of acts of ratification, which took place Mar. 7, 1924, in Rome). Duration (except for general political provisions) 3 years; if not denounced 6 months before expiration, valid until 1 year after denunciation. Modified by exchange of notes of Feb. 7, 1939 (39/ii/7/Italy/c).
Sources: *SDD*, 2, pp. 35–48.
    MZh, 1924, No. 2–3, pp. 276–89.
    SDD, 1–2, 1928, pp. 219–32.
    *TC, 31, p. 95.
    STS, 1, pp. 227–31.

• 24/ii/7/Italy/b

Customs agreement between the USSR and Italy, with five annexes

Signed Feb. 7, 1924, in Rome.
Ratified by the USSR Mar. 7, 1924. Entered into force Mar. 22, 1924 (15 days after exchange of acts of ratification, which took place Mar. 7, 1924, in Rome). Duration 3 years. Superseded by customs convention of May 6, 1933 (33/v/6/Italy/a).
Sources: *SDD*, 1–2, 1928, pp. 232–43.
    *TC, 31, p. 120.
    STS, 1, pp. 231–32 (omits annexes).

• 24/ii/8/UK

Exchange of notes between the USSR and the United Kingdom concerning recognition of the USSR *de jure* and the settlement of outstanding questions

Sent Feb. 2, 1924, from Moscow, and Feb. 8, 1924, from London.
Sources: *SDD*, 2, pp. 6–9 (including Soviet decree of Feb. 2, 1924, on recognition).
    STS, 1, pp. 226–27.

• 24/ii/13/Italy

Exchange of notes between the USSR and Italy concerning recognition of the USSR *de jure*

Sent Feb. 7, 1924, from Rome, and Feb. 13, 1924, from Moscow.
Sources: *SDD*, 2, pp. 15–16.
    SDD, 1–2, 1928, pp. 29–30.
    STS, 1, pp. 232–33.

• 24/ii/26/Austria

Exchange of notes between the USSR and Austria concerning recognition of the USSR *de jure*

Sent Feb. 25, 1924, from Moscow, and Feb. 26, 1924, from Vienna (Austrian records give date of second note as Feb. 29, 1924).
Sources: *SDD*, 2, pp. 5–6.
    SDD, 1–2, 1928, p. 9.
    *Registered in Austrian Haus-, Hof- und Staatsarchiv, neues politisches Archiv, Kart. 337.
    STS, 1, p. 234.

• 24/iii/8/Greece

Exchange of notes between the USSR and Greece concerning recognition of the USSR *de jure*

Sent Mar. 8, 1924, in Berlin.
Sources: *SDD*, 2, p. 11.
    STS, 1, p. 234.

• 24/iii/10/Norway

Exchange of notes between the USSR and Norway concerning recognition of the USSR *de jure*

Sent Feb. 15 and Mar. 10, 1924, in Oslo.
Sources: *SDD*, 2, pp. 24–25.
    SDD, 1–2, 1928, pp. 80–81.
    STS, 1, p. 233.

Mar. 14, 1924. General agreement between the USSR and China
See Appendix 1.

• 24/iii/15/Sweden/a

Commercial agreement between the USSR and Sweden

Signed Mar. 15, 1924, in Stockholm.
Ratified by the USSR and Sweden May 9, 1924. Entered into force May 10, 1924, on exchange of acts of ratification in Stockholm. Valid until 6 months after denunciation. Listed in Korolenko, p. 104, as still in force as of Nov. 25, 1953.
Provides that pending conclusion of an agreement on reciprocal recognition of tonnage measurement certificates, the Russo-Swedish declaration on this subject of June 14/27, 1907, is to continue in force.
On signing, the Soviet representative made 2 unilateral declarations, (1) concerning Swedish diplomatic property in the USSR, and (2) concerning ships of the former Russian navy or commercial fleet. These

were in addition to the declaration concerning claims (next document).
Sources: *SZ*, 1924, I, No. 16, Art. 158 (R, E).
  SDD, 2, pp. 68–70.
  SDD, 1–2, 1928, pp. 267–71.
  Sö, 1924, No. 7, pp. 43–49.
  LNTS, 25, pp. 251–59 (E, F).
  STS, 1, pp. 235–36.

● 24/iii/15/Sweden/b
Declaration by the USSR and Sweden concerning claims

Signed Mar. 15, 1924, in Stockholm.
Not subject to ratification.
Sources: *Sö*, 1924, No. 8, p. 51 (Sw., E).
  LNTS, 25, pp. 258–59 (E, F).
  STS, 1, p. 236.

● 24/iii/18/Sweden
Exchange of notes between the USSR and Sweden concerning recognition of the USSR *de jure*

Sent Mar. 15 and 18, 1924, in Stockholm.
Sources: *SDD*, 2, p. 27.
  SDD, 1–2, 1928, p. 153.
  STS, 1, pp. 234–35.

● 24/iii/24/Canada
Exchange of notes between the USSR and Canada concerning recognition of the USSR *de jure*

Sent Mar. 24, 1924.
Reference: Eudin and Fisher, p. 416.

● 24/iv/6/Japan
Temporary agreement between the USSR and Japan concerning fisheries

Signed Apr. 6, 1924.
Reference: Rubinshtein, p. 506.

● 24/iv/24/Pol/a
Convention between the USSR and Poland concerning direct rail transportation of passengers and freight, with supplementary protocol and two annexes

Signed Apr. 24, 1924, in Warsaw.
Ratified by the USSR Apr. 24, 1924; by Poland Mar. 4, 1925. Entered into force May 22, 1925 (15 days after exchange of acts of ratification, which took place May 7, 1925, in Warsaw). Valid until 6 months

after denunciation. For the annexes, see the following 2 documents. Modified and supplemented by protocol of July 26, 1934 (34/vii/26/Pol/a).
Sources: *SZ*, 1928, II, No. 68, Art. 280 (R, P).
  MZh, 1925, No. 3, pp. 140–48.
  SDD, 5, pp. 123–31.
  DURP, 1925, No. 50, Arts. 344, 345.
  LNTS, 37, pp. 33–52, 66–81 (R, P, E, F).
  STS, 1, pp. 236–39.

● 24/iv/24/Pol/b
Regulations concerning direct transportation of passengers and baggage between the USSR and Poland

Undated; constitutes Annex 1 to the Soviet-Polish rail convention of Apr. 24, 1924 (preceding document). Under protocol of July 26, 1934, to remain in force until the drawing up of special regulations for transportation of passengers and baggage.
Sources: *SZ*, 1928, II, No. 68, Art. 280, pp. 1652–63 (R, P).
  MZh, 1925, No. 3, pp. 148–53.
  SDD, 5, pp. 131–35.
  LNTS, 37, pp. 52–59, 82–89 (R, P, E, F).
  STS, 1, pp. 239–41.

● 24/iv/24/Pol/c
Amendments and additions to the International Berne Convention on the transportation of goods by rail

Undated; constitutes Annex 2 to the Soviet-Polish rail convention of Apr. 24, 1924. The Berne Convention, originally dated Oct. 14, 1890, is cited in the edition of Dec. 22, 1908.
Superseded by protocol of July 26, 1934 (34/vii/26/Pol/a).
Sources: *SZ*, 1928, II, No. 68, Art. 280, pp. 1663–68 (R, P).
  MZh, 1925, No. 3, pp. 153–56.
  SDD, 5, pp. 136–38.
  LNTS, 37, pp. 60–65, 90–95 (R, P, E, F).
  STS, 2, pp. 241–42.

● 24/v/28/Pr
Agreement between the USSR and the American Mennonite Relief concerning aid for agricultural reconstruction

Signed May 28, 1924, in Moscow.

Entered into force on signature; valid until Dec. 31, 1924.
Source: Hiebert, pp. 462–65.

• 24/v/31/China/a

Agreement between the USSR and China concerning general principles for the settlement of problems, with seven declarations and an exchange of notes

Signed May 31, 1924, in Peking.
Ratified by the USSR Aug. 8, 1924. Entered into force on signature.
Declarations concern (1) transfer of real estate, (2) property of the Russian Orthodox Mission, (3) treaties concerning China, (4) transfer by China to a third party of rights and privileges renounced by the USSR, (5) Russian share of the Boxer Indemnity, (6) rights of extraterritoriality and consular jurisdiction, and (7) personnel policies on the Chinese Eastern Railway. Exchange of notes concerns service by former Russian subjects in the Chinese army and police. Supplemented by the following 2 documents.
Effectiveness interrupted by rupture of diplomatic relations between the USSR and China on July 17, 1929.
Sources: *SZ*, 1925, I, No. 18, Art. 131 (R, E).
　　SDD, 2, pp. 16–23.
　　SDD, 1–2, 1928, pp. 30–37.
　　TA, pp. 133–40.
　　LNTS, 37, pp. 175–91 (E, F).
　　STS, 1, pp. 242–44.

• 24/v/31/China/b

Agreement between the USSR and China concerning provisional management of the Chinese Eastern Railway

Signed May 31, 1924, in Peking.
Confirmed by the USSR Aug. 8, 1924; by China, date unknown. Entered into force on signature.
Declaration 7 accompanying the agreement on general principles of the same date (preceding document), which deals with personnel policies on the Chinese Eastern Railway, actually relates to this agreement and is sometimes printed with it.
Sources: *SZ*, 1925, I, No. 19, Art. 132 (R, E).
　　SDD, 2, pp. 102–104.
　　SDD, 1–2, 1928, pp. 327–29.
　　TA, pp. 141–44.

LNTS, 37, pp. 193–201 (E, F).
STS, 1, p. 244.

• 24/v/31/China/c

Exchange of notes between the USSR and China concerning establishment of diplomatic relations

Signed May 31, 1924, in Peking.
Entered into force on signature.
Diplomatic relations were broken off on July 17, 1929, following Soviet-Chinese hostilities arising in part from disputes over the administration of the Chinese Eastern Railway; relations were re-established by exchange of notes of Dec. 12, 1932.
Sources: *Izv.*, June 1, 1924.
　　VP, 2, p. 898.

• 24/vi/17/1920

Convention concerning establishment at Paris of an International Institute of Refrigeration

Signed June 21, 1920, in Paris.
Ratified by the USSR June 17, 1924. Soviet entry into the Institute approved at a General Conference on July 9, 1926; approval communicated to the Soviet Government by the French Ambassador in note of Aug. 20, 1926. Enters into force for each signatory on deposit of its act of ratification. Duration 10 years, with automatic renewal for 5-year periods unless a signatory withdraws or changes its category, with 1 year's notice.
Modified by revision of Nov. 23, 1934 (see 34/xi/23/Mul), and convention of May 31, 1937, which the USSR signed but evidently did not ratify (see Appendix 1). The USSR withdrew as of June 21, 1945, but on Mar. 25, 1955, signed a new international convention on the International Institute of Refrigeration (see 55/iii/25/Mul).
Sources: *SZ*, 1927, II, No. 37, Arts. 201, 202 (R, F).
　　SDD, 4, 1928, pp. 115–22; *ibid.*, 1936, pp. 54–60.
　　LNTS, 8, pp. 66–77 (E, F).

• 24/vi/18/Denmark/a

Note from Denmark extending recognition *de jure* to the USSR

Sent June 18, 1924, in London.
Soviet acknowledgment, of the same day,

is incorporated in the exchange of notes constituting an agreement on commerce and navigation (next document).
Sources: *SDD*, 2, p. 12.
   SDD, 1–2, 1928, p. 25.
   STS, 1, p. 262.

● 24/vi/18/Denmark/b

Exchange of notes between the USSR and Denmark constituting an agreement on commerce and navigation, with declaration concerning claims

Signed June 18, 1924, in London.
Extends the preliminary agreement of Apr. 23, 1923, pending conclusion of a final treaty of commerce and navigation. Superseded by treaty of commerce and navigation of Aug. 17, 1946 (46/viii/17/Denmark/a).
Sources: *SDD*, 2, pp. 12–14.
   SDD, 1–2, 1928, pp. 26–29.
   *DT, 1924.
   *Lovtidende A, 1924, p. 1075.
   LNTS, 27, pp. 149–55 (E, F).
   STS, 1, pp. 262–63.

● 24/vi/18/Fin/a

Convention between the USSR and Finland concerning telephone communications, with final protocol

Signed June 18, 1924, in Helsinki.
Confirmed by the USSR Aug. 16, 1924; diplomatic declarations concerning confirmation exchanged the same day in Moscow. Entered into force Aug. 26, 1924 (10 days after exchange of diplomatic declarations). Valid until 3 months after denunciation.
Denounced by Finland June 30, 1936, on the grounds that it was superseded by the International Telecommunication Convention of Dec. 9, 1932, which both the USSR and Finland had signed (see 32/xii/9/Mul/a). The Soviet Commissar of Foreign Affairs accordingly declared the convention abrogated as of Sept. 30, 1936.
Sources: *SZ*, 1924, I, No. 30, Art. 265.
   SDD, 2, pp. 95–98.
   SDD, 1–2, 1928, pp. 318–22.
   *SS, 1924, No. 20 (R, Finnish).
   LNTS, 29, pp. 295–312 (R, Finnish, Sw., E, F).
   STS, 1, pp. 257–58.

● 24/vi/18/Fin/b

Convention between the USSR and Fin-

land concerning postal communications, with supplementary protocol

Signed June 18, 1924, in Helsinki.
Confirmed by the USSR Aug. 16, 1924; diplomatic declarations concerning confirmation exchanged the same day in Moscow. Entered into force Sept. 15, 1924 (30 days after exchange of diplomatic declarations). Valid until 3 months after denunciation.
Supersedes the temporary agreement of June 22, 1922. Modified by protocol of Oct. 7, 1929.
Sources: *SZ*, 1924, I, No. 30, Art. 263 (R, F).
   SDD, 2, pp. 74–88.
   SDD, 1–2, 1928, pp. 298–312.
   *SS, 1924, No. 21 (Finnish, F).
   LNTS, 29, pp. 313–75 (R, Finnish, Sw., E, F).
   STS, 1, pp. 252–57.

● 24/vi/18/Fin/c

Convention between the USSR and Finland concerning telegraph communications, with supplementary protocol and annex

Signed June 18, 1924, in Helsinki.
Confirmed by the USSR Aug. 16, 1924; diplomatic declarations concerning confirmation exchanged the same day in Moscow. Entered into force Aug. 26, 1924 (10 days after exchange of diplomatic declarations). Valid until 3 months after denunciation. Supersedes the temporary agreement of June 13, 1922.
Sources: *SZ*, 1924, I, No. 30, Art. 264 (R, F).
   SDD, 2, pp. 89–94.
   SDD, 1–2, 1928, pp. 312–18.
   *SS, 1924, No. 19 (Finnish, F).
   LNTS, 29, pp. 265–94 (R, Finnish, Sw., E, F).
   STS, 1, pp. 258–60.

● 24/vi/18/Fin/d

Convention between the USSR and Finland concerning direct transportation of passengers and freight by rail

Signed June 18, 1924, in Helsinki.
Ratified by the USSR Apr. 10, 1925; by Finland Jan. 23, 1925. Acts of ratification exchanged July 14, 1925, in Moscow. Entered into force Sept. 12, 1925 (60 days after exchange of acts of ratification). Valid until 6 months after denunciation.

Supplemented by Regulations of the same date (next document). Revised by convention of Jan. 5, 1933. Further modified by protocol of Feb. 11, 1936.
Sources: *SZ*, 1926, I, No. 49, Art. 359 (R, Finnish, Sw.).
  SDD, 3, 1927, pp. 238–44; *ibid.*, 1932, pp. 144–64.
  *SS, 1925, No. 16 (R, Finnish).
  LNTS, 47, pp. 153–239 (R, Finnish, Sw., E, F).
  STS, 1, pp. 245–52.

• 24/vi/18/Fin/e

Regulations concerning direct transportation of passengers and freight by rail between the USSR and Finland

Signed June 18, 1924, in Helsinki.
Supplements the rail convention of the same date. Modified by agreement of Mar. 29, 1927, and exchange of notes dated Nov. 17, 1928. Declared no longer valid by protocol of Feb. 11, 1936.
Sources: Included with sources shown for 24/vi/18/Fin/d.

• 24/vi/18/Fin/f

Agreement between the USSR and Finland concerning reciprocal return of archives and documents of public institutions, with protocol and annex

Signed June 18, 1924, in Helsinki.
Ratified by Finland July 11, 1924; by the USSR Apr. 10, 1925. Entered into force July 15, 1925, on exchange of acts of ratification in Helsinki. Listed in *SDD*, 3, 1932, p. 48, as no longer valid.
Sources: *SZ*, 1926, I, No. 16, Art. 111 (R, Finnish, Sw.).
  SDD, 3, 1927, pp. 50–61.
  *SS, 1925, No. 17 (R, Finnish).
  LNTS, 47, pp. 241–70 (R, Finnish, Sw., E, F).
  STS, 1, pp. 260–62.

• 24/vi/27/Est/a

Convention between the USSR and Estonia concerning postal communications, with final protocol and supplementary protocol

Signed June 27, 1924, in Tallinn.
Ratified by the USSR July 3, 1925; by Estonia Nov. 25, 1924. Entered into force provisionally on signature, under the final protocol; definitively Nov. 19, 1925, on

exchange of acts of ratification in Moscow (which was to have taken place not later than Dec. 31, 1924). Valid until 6 months after denunciation. Supersedes temporary postal agreement of Dec. 2, 1920, and Jan. 25, 1921 (21/i/25/Est).
Sources: *SZ*, 1927, II, No. 1, Art. 1, pp. 1–29 (R, Est.).
  SDD, 3, 1927, pp. 138–52; *ibid.*, 1932, pp. 115–29.
  *RT, 1924, No. 146.
  STS, 1, pp. 263–67.

• 24/vi/27/Est/b

Convention between the USSR and Estonia concerning telephone communications, with final protocol and supplementary protocol

Signed June 27, 1924, in Tallinn.
Ratified by Estonia Nov. 25, 1924; by the USSR July 3, 1925. Entered into force provisionally on signature, under the final protocol; definitively Nov. 19, 1925, on exchange of acts of ratification in Moscow (which was to have taken place not later than Dec. 31, 1924). Valid until 6 months after denunciation.
Sources: *SZ*, 1927, II, No. 1, Art. 1, pp. 39–49 (R, Est.).
  SDD, 3, 1927, pp. 158–63; *ibid.*, 1932, pp. 134–39.
  *RT, 1924, No. 146.
  STS, 1, pp. 267–68.

• 24/vi/27/Est/c

Convention between the USSR and Estonia concerning telegraph and radio-telegraph communications, with final protocol and supplementary protocol

Signed June 27, 1924, in Tallinn.
Ratified by the USSR July 3, 1925; by Estonia Nov. 25, 1924. Entered into force provisionally on signature, under the final protocol; definitively Nov. 19, 1925, on exchange of acts of ratification in Moscow (which was to have taken place not later than Dec. 31, 1924). Valid until 6 months after denunciation. Supersedes temporary agreement of Mar. 16, 1921.
Sources: *SZ*, 1927, II, No. 1, Art. 1, pp. 30–39 (R, Est.).
  SDD, 3, 1927, pp. 153–58; *ibid.*, 1932, pp. 129–34.
  *RT, 1924, No. 146.
  STS, 1, pp. 269–70.

• 24/vi/27/Est/d

Agreement between the USSR and Estonia concerning exchange of postal money orders, with final protocol

Signed June 27, 1924, in Tallinn.
Ratified by Estonia Nov. 25, 1924; by the USSR July 3, 1925. Entered into force provisionally on signature, under the final protocol; definitively Nov. 19, 1925, on exchange of acts of ratification in Moscow (which was to have taken place not later than Dec. 31, 1924). Valid until 6 months after denunciation. Supplemented by Regulations of the same date (next document). According to *SDD*, 3, 1932, p. 139, "temporarily not being applied."
Sources: *SZ*, 1927, II, No. 1, Art. 1, pp. 49–59 (R, Est.).
      SDD, 3, 1927, pp. 163–68 (R, Est.).
      *RT, 1924, No. 146.
      STS, 1, pp. 270–72.

• 24/vi/27/Est/e

Regulations concerning exchange of postal money orders between the USSR and Estonia

Signed June 27, 1924, in Tallinn.
Supplements the agreement of the same date (24/vi/27/Est/d); enters into and remains in force for the same period.
Sources: *SZ*, 1927, II, No. 1, Art. 1, pp. 59–63 (R, Est.).
      SDD, 3, 1927, pp. 169–71.

July 3, 1924. Trade treaty between the USSR and Persia
See Appendix 1.

• 24/vii/12/Fin

Protocol between the USSR and Finland concerning identification papers of citizens engaged in fishing and seal hunting on Lake Ladoga, with annex

Signed July 12, 1924, in Moscow.
Modifies the convention of Oct. 28, 1922 (22/x/28/Fin/d).
Sources: *SZ*, 1925, I, No. 12, Art. 98, p. 172.
      SDD, 1–2, 1928, pp. 266–67.
      STS, 1, p. 272.

• 24/vii/18/Pol

Consular convention between the USSR and Poland, with two supplementary protocols and exchange of notes

Signed July 18, 1924, in Moscow.
Ratified by the USSR Mar. 19, 1926; by Poland Mar. 27, 1926. Entered into force Apr. 22, 1926 (21 days after exchange of acts of ratification, which took place Apr. 1, 1926, in Warsaw). Valid until 6 months after denunciation.
Sources: *SZ*, 1926, I, No. 38, Art. 282 (R, P).
      SDD, 3, 1927, pp. 38–50; *ibid.*, 1932, pp. 37–48.
      *DURP, 1926, No. 35, Arts. 210, 211.
      LNTS, 49, pp. 201–49 (R, P, E, F).
      STS, 1, pp. 273–77.

• 24/vii/29/Ger

Protocol between the USSR and Germany concerning settlement of the dispute over the Soviet Trade Mission in Germany, with annex

Signed July 29, 1924, in Berlin.
Supplements and remains in force as long as the temporary agreement of May 6, 1921 (21/v/6/Ger/a).
Sources: *Izv.*, July 30, 1924.
      SDD, 2, pp. 9–10.
      SDD, 1–2, 1928, pp. 18–19.
      STS, 1, p. 277.
Reference: Eudin and Fisher, pp. 277–78.
Note: Sources listed do not include the annex (floor plan of the quarters of the Soviet Trade Mission in Germany).

• 24/vii/31/Pol

General final protocol of the Mixed Soviet-Polish Border Demarcation Commission, with annexes

Signed July 31, 1924.
Included as Annex 1 to the agreement of Apr. 10, 1932, concerning legal relations in the border zone.
Sources: *SZ*, 1933, No. 26, Art. 245, pp. 186–216 (R, P).
      SDD, 8, pp. 60–78.
      LNTS, 141, pp. 370–98, 426–61 (R, P, E, F).

• 24/viii/4/Mexico

Declaration (aide-mémoire) by Mexico concerning recognition of the USSR *de jure*

Published Aug. 4, 1924, in Berlin.
According to *Istoriia diplomatii*, 3, p. 301, diplomatic relations between the USSR and Mexico were established Aug. 1, 1924. For a Soviet statement dated Feb. 1, 1930,

on the rupture of diplomatic relations with Mexico, see *SDFP*, 2, pp. 437–38.
Sources: *SDD*, 2, p. 23.
  SDD, 1–2, 1928, p. 77.
  STS, 1, p. 277.

● 24/viii/6/Hejaz

Agreement between the USSR and Hejaz concerning establishment of diplomatic and economic relations

Dated Aug. 6, 1924.
Reference: *Istoriia diplomatii*, 3, p. 301.

Aug. 8, 1924. (1) General political treaty and (2) Treaty of commerce and navigation between the USSR and the United Kingdom

See Appendix 1.

● 24/viii/28/Mul/a

Universal Postal Convention, with related documents

Signed Aug. 28, 1924, in Stockholm.
Ratified by the USSR Aug. 31, 1925. Entered into force Oct. 1, 1925; duration indefinite. Supersedes the convention of Nov. 30, 1920 (not signed by the RSFSR); superseded by the convention of June 28, 1929.
Full contents (as given in *LNTS*, 40): text, pp. 19–85; final protocol, pp. 86–91; regulations for execution, pp. 92–165; final protocol to the regulations, pp. 164–67; annexes to the regulations, pp. 169–237; and supplement to the final protocol to the convention, pp. 238–47.
Sources: *SZ*, 1927, II, No. 13, Art. 85 (R, F).
  SDD, 3, 1927, pp. 172–208.
  LNTS, 40, as listed above (E, F).

● 24/viii/28/Mul/b

Agreement of the Universal Postal Union concerning insured letters and boxes, with related documents

Signed Aug. 28, 1924, in Stockholm.
Ratified by the USSR Aug. 31, 1925. Entered into force Oct. 1, 1925; duration indefinite. Superseded by the agreement of June 28, 1929 (29/vi/28/Mul/b). Supplements the Universal Postal Convention of the same date.
Full contents (as given in *LNTS*, 40): text, pp. 249–83; final protocol, pp. 282–83; regulations for execution, pp. 284–97;

and annexes to the regulations, pp. 299–305.
Sources: *SZ*, 1927, II, No. 13, Art. 87.
  SDD, 3, 1927, pp. 208–25.
  LNTS, 40, as listed above (E, F).

● 24/viii/28/Mul/c

Agreement of the Universal Postal Union concerning money orders, with related documents

Signed Aug. 28, 1924, in Stockholm.
Ratified by the USSR Aug. 31, 1925. Entered into force Oct. 1, 1925; duration indefinite. Superseded by agreement of June 28, 1929, which the USSR did not sign. Supplements the Universal Postal Convention of the same date.
Full contents (as given in *LNTS*, 40): text, pp. 437–67; regulations, pp. 468–85; and annexes to the regulations, pp. 487–99.
Sources: *SZ*, 1927, II, No. 13, Art. 86.
  SDD, 3, 1927, pp. 226–34.
  LNTS, 40, as listed above (E, F).

● 24/ix/4/Alb

Exchange of notes between the USSR and Albania concerning establishment of diplomatic relations

Sent July 4, 1924, from Tirana, and Sept. 4, 1924, from Moscow.
Sources: Kliuchnikov, 3, I, p. 313 (extracts).
  VP, 2, p. 907.
  STS, 1, p. 272.

Sept. 5, 1924. Treaty between the USSR and Hungary concerning establishment of diplomatic and consular relations

See Appendix 1.

● 24/ix/12/Sweden

Agreement between the USSR and Sweden concerning exchange of parcel post and insured letters

Signed Sept. 12, 1924, in Stockholm.
Confirmed by the USSR Nov. 24, 1924. Declarations concerning confirmation exchanged Nov. 11, 1924, in Stockholm. Entered into force Oct. 1, 1924; remains in force until entry into force of the Universal Postal Union agreements on parcel post and insured letters (i.e., Oct. 1, 1925; the USSR did not sign the agreement on parcel post).

Sources: *SZ*, 1925, I, No. 22, Art. 146.
   SDD, 2, pp. 98–101.
   SDD, 1–2, 1928, pp. 322–25.
   LNTS, 31, pp. 75–83 (E, F).

● 24/ix/19/Austria

Agreement between the USSR and Austria concerning legal assistance in civil cases

Signed Sept. 19, 1924, in Moscow.
Ratified by the USSR Nov. 14, 1924; by Austria Dec. 18, 1924. Entered into force Feb. 12, 1925 (1 month after exchange of acts of ratification, which took place Jan. 12, 1925, in Vienna). Valid until 6 months after denunciation. Modified by exchange of notes dated Apr. 6, 1927.
Sources: *SZ*, 1925, I, No. 22, Art. 145.
   SDD, 2, 1925, pp. 32–34.
   SDD, 1–2, 1928, pp. 173–75.
   *BGbl, 1925, No. 45.
   STS, 1, p. 279.

● 24/ix/20/China

Agreement between the USSR and the Government of the Three Autonomous Eastern Provinces of China (Mukden Government) concerning mutual rights and privileges

Signed Sept. 20, 1924, in Mukden.
Ratified by the Peking government Mar. 12, 1925, as a supplement to the agreement on general principles of May 31, 1924.
Sources: *SZ*, 1927, II, No. 32, Art. 172 (R, E).
   SDD, 5, pp. 118–23.
   TA, pp. 148–52.
   STS, 1, pp. 279–81.
References: Wei, pp. 56 (protest by the Peking government against signing) and 174 (Chinese ratification).

● 24/x/ /Sinkiang

Exchange of notes between the USSR and Sinkiang concerning consulates

Sent during Oct. 1924.
Provides for establishment of Soviet consulates at Urumchi (Tihwa), Tarbagatai, Ili, Altai, and Kashgar, and Chinese consulates at Tashkent, Andijan, Alma Ata, Zaisan, and Semipalatinsk.
References: Cheng, p. 168.
   Whiting, p. 9.

Note: According to V. Conolly, *Soviet economic policy in the East* (London, Oxford University Press, 1933), p. 129, the Soviet-Sinkiang agreement on consulates was part of a general commercial agreement concluded in 1925.

● 24/x/3/MPR

Agreement between the USSR and the Mongolian People's Republic concerning telegraph communications, with supplementary protocol

Signed Oct. 3, 1924, in Urga.
Confirmed by the USSR July 2, 1923 (*sic*, as given in *SDD*, 2, p. 74; error for 1925?)
Valid until Jan. 1, 1927. Extended to Jan. 1, 1929, and modified by protocol of Feb. 22, 1927.
Sources: *SZ*, 1925, I, No. 20, Art. 135.
   SDD, 2, pp. 72–74.
   SDD, 1–2, 1928, pp. 283–85.
   STS, 1, p. 281.
Note: Two other agreements between the USSR and the Mongolian People's Republic were signed and ratified in 1924, according to Eudin and North, p. 257: an agreement for the establishment of a Soviet-Mongolian Bank, and a Soviet-Mongolian convention. For other reported Soviet-Mongolian agreements, see Appendix 4.

● 24/x/7/Persia

Protocol between the USSR and Persia concerning official language and entry into force of the postal convention of April 25, 1923, and the telegraph convention of April 27, 1923

Signed Oct. 7, 1924, in Teheran.
Sources: *LNTS*, 110, pp. 339–41 (Persian, R, E, F).
   STS, 1, p. 282.

● 24/x/28/France

Exchange of telegrams between the USSR and France concerning establishment of diplomatic relations

Sent Oct. 28, 1924, from Paris and Moscow.
Sources: *SZ*, 1924, I, No. 19, Art. 188 (Soviet reply).
   SDD, 1–2, 1928, pp. 143–45.
   STS, 1, p. 282.

1925

• 25/i/20/J/a

Convention between the USSR and Japan concerning general principles of mutual relations

Signed Jan. 20, 1925, in Peking.
Ratified by the USSR Feb. 20, 1925; by Japan Feb. 25, 1925. Entered into force Apr. 15, 1925, on exchange of acts of ratification in Peking. Supplemented by the following 6 documents.
Sources: *SZ*, 1925, I, No. 46, Art. 342 (E, R).
    MZh, 1925, No. 2, pp. 206–208.
    SDD, 3, 1927, pp. 10–12; *ibid.*, 1932, pp. 7–9.
    CDT, No. 39.
    LNTS, 34, pp. 31–37 (E, F).
    STS, 1, pp. 283–84.
Note 1: Art. 2 provides for continuance in force of the Treaty of Portsmouth between Russia and Japan of Sept. 5, 1905. It further provides that all other treaties, conventions and agreements between Russia and Japan prior to Nov. 7, 1917, are to be re-examined at a conference for possible revision or annulment. No conference for this purpose was ever held, but according to a communication from the Japanese Foreign Ministry in Sept. 1957, the following treaties between Russia and Japan were considered to be in force between the USSR and Japan at the time of the outbreak of hostilities in 1945: (1) Treaty concerning the exchange of Sakhalin Island for the Kurile Islands, with related documents, dated May 7, 1875; (2) Treaty of Portsmouth, dated Sept. 5, 1905; (3) Exchange of notes concerning the reciprocal waiver of consular fees on certificates of origin, dated Jan. 12, 1910; (4) Agreement concerning the exchange of money orders, dated Feb. 28, 1910, and Dec. 18, 1912; (5) Treaty of extradition, with supplementary declaration, dated June 1, 1911; (6) Agreement concerning reciprocal recognition of companies, dated June 23, 1911; (7) Convention concerning reciprocal protection of industrial property, dated June 23, 1911; and (8) Convention concerning reciprocal protection of industrial property in China, dated June 23, 1911.
Note 2: For a possible secret protocol to the convention, see Nicolaevsky, Boris, "Russia, Japan and the Pan-Asiatic Move-

ment to 1925," *Far Eastern Quarterly*, Vol. 8, No. 3, May 1949, pp. 270–71.

• 25/i/20/J/b

Protocol between the USSR and Japan concerning governmental diplomatic property, debts owed to Japan by the former Russian Government, evacuation of Japanese troops from Northern Sakhalin, and agreements with third parties

Signed Jan. 20, 1925, in Peking.
Constitutes Protocol A to the convention of the same date, and to be considered ratified with it.
Sources: *SZ*, 1925, I, No. 46, Art. 342, pp. 683–84, 687–88 (E, R).
    MZh, 1925, No. 2, pp. 208–210.
    SDD, 3, 1927, pp. 13–14; *ibid.*, 1932, pp. 9–11.
    LNTS, 34, pp. 36–39 (E, F).
    STS, 1, p. 284.

• 25/i/20/J/c

Protocol between the USSR and Japan concerning concessions in Northern Sakhalin

Signed Jan. 20, 1925, in Peking.
Constitutes Protocol B to the convention of the same date, and to be considered ratified with it.
Sources: *SZ*, 1925, I, No. 46, Art. 342, pp. 685–86, 689–90 (E, R).
    MZh, 1925, No. 2, pp. 210–12.
    SDD, 3, 1927, pp. 14–16; *ibid.*, 1932, pp. 11–12.
    LNTS, 34, pp. 40–43 (E, R).
    STS, 1, pp. 284–85.

• 25/i/20/J/d

Declaration by the USSR disavowing responsibility for the conclusion of the Treaty of Portsmouth between Russia and Japan of September 5, 1905

Signed Jan. 20, 1925, in Peking.
Annexed to the convention of the same date.
Sources: *SZ*, 1925, I, No. 46, Art. 342, pp. 691, 693 (E, R).
    MZh, 1925, No. 2, p. 212.
    SDD, 3, 1927, p. 16; *ibid.*, 1932, p. 12.
    LNTS, 34, pp. 42, 43 (E, F).
    STS, 1, 285.

● 25/i/20/J/e

Exchange of notes between the USSR and Japan concerning Japanese industrial operations in Northern Sakhalin

Sent Jan. 20, 1925, in Peking.
Annexed to the convention of the same date.
Sources: *SZ*, 1925, I, No. 46, Art. 342, pp. 691–94 (F, R).
  MZh, 1925, No. 2, pp. 212–13.
  SDD, 3, 1927, pp. 16–18; *ibid.*, 1932, pp. 13–14.
  LNTS, 34, pp. 44–47 (E, F).
  STS, 1, p. 285.

● 25/i/20/J/f

Note expressing the regret of the USSR to Japan for the Nikolaevsk incident of 1920

Sent Jan. 20, 1925, in Peking.
Annexed to the convention of the same date. For background of the Nikolaevsk incident, see Eudin and North, pp. 133–34.
Sources: *LNTS*, 34, pp. 46–47 (E, F).
  MZh, 1925, No. 2, p. 214.
  STS, 1, p. 285.

● 25/i/20/J/g

Protocol of signature to the convention of January 20, 1925, between the USSR and Japan

Signed Jan. 20, 1925, in Peking.
Incorporates a memorandum by the Japanese Plenipotentiary to the Plenipotentiary of the USSR dated Aug. 29, 1924, concerning conditions of oil and coal fields worked by the Japanese in Northern Sakhalin.
Source: *LNTS*, 34, pp. 46–53 (E, F).

Feb. 19, 1925

(1) International opium convention; see 35/x/31/1925/a and 46/xii/11/Mul.
(2) Final Act of the Second International Opium Conference; see 35/x/31/1925/b.

● 25/ii/20/Fin

Agreement between the USSR and Finland concerning exchange of postal money orders

Signed Feb. 20, 1925, in Helsinki.
Ratified by the USSR Feb. 10, 1925. Entered into force Apr. 14, 1925 (1 month after exchange of diplomatic declarations concerning ratification, which took place Mar. 14, 1925, in Moscow). Valid until

entry into force of the Stockholm International Agreement concerning exchange of postal money orders (24/viii/28/Mul/c), i.e., Oct. 1, 1925. According to *SDD*, 3, 1932, p. 115, "temporarily not being applied."
Sources: *SZ*, 1925, I, No. 47, Art. 343 (R, Finnish).
  MZh, 1925, No. 2, pp. 215–18.
  SDD, 3, 1927, pp. 134–37.
  *SS, 1925, No. 5 (R, Finnish).
  LNTS, 34, pp. 153–67 (R, Finnish, Sw., E, F).
  STS, 1, pp. 285–86.

● 25/iii/19/Lat

Exchange of declarations between the USSR and Latvia concerning reciprocal recognition of tonnage measurement certificates

Signed Mar. 19, 1925, in Riga.
Entered into force on signature. Valid until 6 months after denunciation. According to *SDD*, 3, 1927, p. 236, confirmed by the USSR Nov. 15, 1924 (*sic*: error for 1925?).
Sources: *SZ*, 1925, I, No. 59, Art. 443 (R, Lat.).
  MZh, 1925, No. 3, pp. 156–57.
  SDD, 3, 1927, pp. 236–37; *ibid.*, 1932, pp. 142–43.
  LRR, pp. 124–25.
  LNTS, 38, pp. 141–45 (R, Lat., E, F).
  STS, 1, p. 287.

● 25/iv/4/J. See Appendix 5.

● 25/iv/11/1875

International Telegraph Convention

Signed July 22, 1875 (July 10, 1875, Old Style), in St. Petersburg.
Recognized as valid for the USSR Apr. 11, 1925. For annexed International Service Regulations, see 25/x/29/Mul. Superseded by International Telecommunication Convention of Dec. 9, 1932 (32/xii/9/Mul/a).
Sources: *SZ*, 1928, II, No. 6, Art. 28.
  LNTS, 57, pp. 212–19 (E, F).
Reference: *SDD*, 6, p. 89 (Soviet adherence).

● 25/vi/16/1904

Hague Convention concerning the exemption of hospital ships from port and other dues

Signed Dec. 21, 1904, at The Hague.
Ratified by the USSR June 16, 1925, with
immediate effect. Previously accepted by
the RSFSR: see 18/vi/4/1904.
Sources: *SZ*, 1926, II, No. 38, Arts. 226,
227 (R, F).
SDD, 4, 1936, pp. 97–98.

• 25/vi/16/1906

**Geneva Convention for the amelioration
of the condition of sick and wounded
soldiers in the field**

Signed July 6, 1906, in Geneva.
Ratified by the USSR June 16, 1925, with
immediate effect. Previously accepted by
the RSFSR: see 18/vi/4/1904 and /1906.
Superseded by the convention of July 27,
1929 (see 31/viii/25/1929).
Source: *SZ*, 1926, II, No. 38, Arts. 226,
228 (R, F).

• 25/vi/16/1907

**Hague Convention for the adaptation to
maritime warfare of the principles of the
Geneva Convention of July 6, 1906**

Signed Oct. 18, 1907, at The Hague.
Ratified by the USSR June 16, 1925, with
immediate effect. Previously accepted by
the RSFSR: see 18/vi/4/1904 and /1907.
Superseded by the convention of Aug. 12,
1949 (see 49/xii/12/1949/b).
Sources: *SZ*, 1926, II, No. 38, Arts. 226,
229 (R, F).
SDD, 4, 1936, pp. 98–105.

• 25/vi/16/1921

**International convention introducing
changes into the International Metric
Convention signed May 20, 1875, in
Paris, and the Statute annexed to it**

Signed Oct. 6, 1921, in Sèvres.
Soviet adherence by decree of June 16,
1925. French Government notified of Soviet adherence by note of Aug. 12, 1925;
acknowledgment of notification sent Aug.
28, 1925. For Soviet adherence to the 1875
convention, see 25/vii/21/1875.
Source: *SZ*, 1927, II, No. 19, Arts. 109,
110, and 111.
SDD, 4, 1928, pp. 131–36.

**June 17, 1925. Protocol concerning pro-
hibition of the use in war of asphyxiating, poisonous or other gases, and of
bacteriological methods of warfare**

See 27/xii/2/1925.

• 25/vi/25/Italy

**Exchange of notes between the USSR
and Italy concerning import and export
of samples**

Sent June 16 and 25, 1925, in Moscow.
Sources: **TC*, 34, pp. 377–80.
STS, 1, p. 287.

• 25/vi/29/Denmark

**Exchange of notes between the USSR
and Denmark constituting an agreement
concerning reciprocal recognition of tonnage measurement certificates**

Sent Dec. 13, 1924, and June 23 and 29,
1925, in Copenhagen. (Soviet sources give
the date of the third note as July 29, 1925,
but internal evidence, together with Dan-
ish official records, supported by *LNTS*,
loc. cit., indicates June 29, 1925.)
Entered into force July 1, 1925. Extended
by exchange of notes dated Jan. 24, 1929.
Superseded by treaty of commerce and
navigation of Aug. 17, 1946 (46/viii/17/
Denmark/a).
Sources: *SZ*, 1926, I, No. 16, Art. 112
(F, R).
SDD, 3, 1927, pp. 235–36; *ibid.*, 1932,
pp. 141–42.
*DT, 1925.
LNTS, 36, pp. 251–57 (E, F).
STS, 1, pp. 282–83.

• 25/vii/21/1875

**International Metric Convention, with
Statute**

Signed May 20, 1875, in Paris; modified
by convention of Oct. 6, 1921.
Soviet adherence by decree of July 21,
1925. For Soviet adherence to the convention of Oct. 6, 1921, see 25/vi/16/1921.
Sources: *SZ*, 1926, II, No. 32, Arts. 191,
192 (R, F).
SDD, 4, 1928, pp. 122–30.

• 25/viii/3/Pol

**Agreement between the USSR and Po-
land concerning settlement of border disputes**

Signed Aug. 3, 1925, in Moscow.
Confirmed by the USSR and Poland Sept.
1, 1925. Enters into force 1 month after
exchange of information concerning confirmation. Valid until 3 months after denunciation. Superseded by convention of
June 3, 1933 (33/vi/3/Pol/a). Repro-

duced as annex 2 to the agreement of Apr.
10, 1932, concerning legal relations in the
border zone.
Sources: *SZ*, 1926, I, No. 17, Art. 113.
　SDD, 3, 1927, pp. 70–73; *ibid.*, 1932, pp.
　55–58.
　STS, 1, pp. 287–88.

• 25/viii/19/Mul

**Convention concerning suppression of
the contraband traffic in alcoholic products, with final protocol**

Signed Aug. 19, 1925, in Helsinki.
Ratified by the USSR July 10, 1929; act
of ratification deposited Sept. 10, 1929;
entered into force for the USSR Oct. 10,
1929 (30 days after deposit of act of ratification). Valid until 1 year after denunciation. Supplemented by agreement of
the same date (next document) and by
protocol of Apr. 22, 1926.
Sources: *SZ*, 1929, II, No. 45, Art. 254
　(F, R).
　SDD, 5, pp. 46–53.
　LNTS, 42, pp. 73–89 (E, F).

• 25/viii/19/Pl

**Agreement between the USSR, Estonia,
and Finland defining areas subject to
control under the convention of August
19, 1925, concerning suppression of the
contraband traffic in alcoholic products**

Signed Aug. 19, 1925, in Helsinki.
Ratified, act of ratification deposited, and
entered into force together with the con-
vention of the same date (preceding docu-
ment); duration the same. Supplemented
by protocol of Apr. 22, 1926.
Sources: *SZ*, 1929, II, pp. 967–68, 975–76
　(F, R).
　SDD, 5, pp. 53–54.
　LNTS, 42, pp. 88–91 (E, F).

• 25/x/12/Ger/a

**Treaty between the USSR and Germany
comprising (1) an agreement concerning conditions of residence and business
and legal protection, (2) an economic
agreement, (3) a railway agreement, (4)
an agreement concerning navigation, (5)
a fiscal agreement, (6) an agreement
concerning commercial courts of arbitration, and (7) an agreement concern-**

**ing legal protection of industrial prop-
erty, with final protocol**

Signed Oct. 12, 1925, in Moscow.
Ratified by the USSR Dec. 18, 1925. Entered into force Mar. 11, 1926 (1 month
after exchange of acts of ratification,
which took place Feb. 11, 1926, in Berlin).
Duration of agreements 1–5, 2 years; of
agreements 6 and 7, 4 years; thereafter
until 6 months following denunciation.
Supersedes the temporary agreement of
May 6, 1921 (21/v/6/Ger/a), and Arts.
2–9 of the agreement of Nov. 5, 1922. Re-
affirms the treaty of Apr. 16, 1922 (Treaty
of Rapallo). Supplemented by protocol
of Dec. 21, 1928. Economic agreement
modified by exchange of notes of Aug. 23,
1935.
Sources: *SZ*, 1926, I, No. 28, Art. 181
　(G, R).
　MZh, 1926, No. 1, pp. 152–87; *ibid.*,
　No. 2, pp. 182–89.
　SDD, 3, 1927, pp. 74–114; *ibid.*, 1932,
　pp. 59–96.
　*RGbl, 1926, II, No. 1, pp. 1–59.
　LNTS, 53, pp. 7–161 (R, G, E, F).
　STS, 1, pp. 288–302.
Note: Under Art. 7 of the General
Clauses, the following pre-1917 treaties
were to be regarded as in force between
the signatories: (1) Convention for the
redemption of Sound and Belts duties,
signed Mar. 14, 1857, in Copenhagen; (2)
Convention concerning unification and improvement of the metric system, signed
May 20, 1875, in Paris; (3) Telegraph
Convention signed July 22, 1875, in St.
Petersburg, and Regulations for its execution, as revised at Lisbon, June 11, 1908;
(4) Convention concerning the protection
of underwater telegraph cables, signed
Mar. 14, 1884, in Paris, with additional
articles of the same date and of Dec. 1,
1886, and Mar. 23, 1887, and final protocol
of July 7, 1887; (5) Convention concerning the exemption of hospital ships from
port and other duties, signed Dec. 21,
1904, at The Hague; (6) Convention concerning the international circulation of automobiles, signed Oct. 11, 1909, in Paris;
(7) Convention concerning the unification
of certain regulations concerning collisions and salvage at sea, signed Sept. 23,
1910, in Brussels; (8) International radio-
telegraph convention, signed July 5, 1912,
in London; and (9) International sanitary convention, signed Jan. 17, 1912, in
Paris.

- 25/x/12/Ger/b

Consular treaty between the USSR and Germany, with annex and final protocol

Signed Oct. 12, 1925, in Moscow.
Ratified by the USSR Dec. 18, 1925. Entered into force Mar. 11, 1926 (1 month after exchange of acts of ratification, which took place Feb. 11, 1926, in Berlin). Duration 5 years; thereafter until 1 year following denunciation. Supplemented by protocol of Dec. 21, 1928.
Sources: *SZ*, 1926, I, No. 28, Art. 181, pp. 469–502 (R, G).
MZh, 1926, No. 2, pp. 192–210.
SDD, 3, 1927, pp. 19–35; *ibid.*, 1932, pp. 19–37.
*RGbl, 1926, II, pp. 60–83.
LNTS, 53, pp. 164–225 (R, G, E, F).
STS, 1, pp. 303–308.

- 25/x/12/Ger/c

Agreement between the USSR and Germany concerning legal aid in civil cases

Signed Oct. 12, 1925, in Moscow.
Ratified by the USSR Dec. 18, 1925. Entered into force Mar. 11, 1926 (1 month after exchange of acts of ratification, which took place Feb. 11, 1926, in Berlin). Duration 5 years; thereafter until 1 year following denunciation. Supplemented by protocol of Dec. 21, 1928. Modified by exchange of notes dated Feb. 7 and Mar. 20, 1931 (31/iii/20/Ger).
Sources: *SZ*, 1926, I, No. 28, Art. 181, pp. 503–509 (R, G).
MZh, 1926, No. 2, pp. 210–13.
SDD, 3, 1927, pp. 35–38; *ibid.*, 1932, pp. 34–37.
*RGbl, 1926, II, pp. 84–88.
LNTS, 53, pp. 227–39 (R, G, E, F).
STS, 1, pp. 302–303.

- 25/x/27/1907

International agreement concerning establishment of an International Office of Public Health, with Statute

Signed Dec. 9, 1907, in Rome.
Soviet adherence by decree of Oct. 27, 1925. Signed in Rome by a Soviet representative Nov. 17, 1925. An exchange of notes between the Italian Government and the USSR dated Nov. 30, 1925, and Jan. 8 and 19, 1926, dealt with Soviet adherence and notification of other signatories. The USSR withdrew with effect from Nov. 15, 1950 (*BTS*, 1949, No. 78, Cmd. 7873).

Sources: *SZ*, 1926, I, No. 69, Arts. 528, 529 (R, F).
SDD, 4, 1936, pp. 92–96.

- 25/x/27/1912

International sanitary convention, with two annexes and protocol

Signed Jan. 17, 1912, in Paris.
Soviet adherence by decree of Oct. 27, 1925. Note to this effect signed Nov. 6, 1925, in Paris; acknowledged in French reply Nov. 21, 1925. Entered into force for the USSR Nov. 2, 1926 (date of publication in *SZ*). Enforced internally within the USSR by decree of Apr. 30, 1926 (*SZ*, 1926, I, No. 69, Arts. 531, 532). Superseded by convention of June 21, 1926.
Source: *SZ*, 1926, I, No. 69, Arts. 528, 530.

- 25/x/29/Mul

International Service Regulations annexed to the International Telegraph Convention of July 22, 1875, as revised at Paris, October 29, 1925

Signed Oct. 29, 1925, in Paris.
Date of Soviet ratification unknown, but prior to Nov. 30, 1929 (*LNTS*, 92, p. 396). Entered into force Nov. 1, 1926. For protocol making changes and additions to the regulations, signed Sept. 22, 1928, in Brussels, see 29/x/8/1928.
Source: *LNTS*, 57, pp. 201–435 (E, F).

- 25/x/29/Pl

Convention between the USSR, Estonia, and Latvia concerning through passenger and freight communications by rail, with related documents

Signed Oct. 29, 1925, in Riga.
Soviet decree of ratification dated Sept. 13, 1926. Acts of ratification exchanged Aug. 31, 1927, in Riga. Entered into force Dec. 1, 1925, under final protocol. Valid until 6 months after denunciation. Abrogated by agreement of Apr. 21, 1933, with effect from Feb. 1, 1934.
Full contents (*LNTS*, 66): (1) Text of the convention, pp. 225–31; (2) Traffic regulations governing the through carriage of passengers and baggage by rail between the USSR, Latvia, and Estonia, pp. 233–69; (3) Annex 1, pp. 271–73; (4) Regulations concerning transport of goods in through traffic on the railroads

of the USSR, Latvia, and Estonia, pp. 275–334; (5) Annexes 2–5, pp. 335–47; (6) Temporary provisions concerning modifications in and addenda to (2) above; (7) Temporary provisions concerning modifications in and addenda to (4) above; and (8) Final protocol, pp. 347–58.

Sources: *SZ*, 1928, II, No. 8, Art. 34.
 SDD, 4, 1928, pp. 162–233.
 LNTS, 66, pp. 147–358 (R, E, F).

Nov. 27, 1925. Convention concerning measurement of vessels employed in inland navigation

See Appendix 1.

● 25/xii/15/Norway

Treaty of commerce and navigation between the USSR and Norway, with final protocol

Signed Dec. 15, 1925, in Moscow.
Ratified by the USSR Jan. 29, 1926. Entered into force Mar. 3, 1926, on exchange of acts of ratification in Oslo. Duration 3 years; thereafter until 1 year following denunciation. Supersedes temporary agreement of Sept. 2, 1921. Listed in Korolenko, p. 104, as still valid as of Nov. 25, 1953.

Sources: *SZ*, 1926, I, No. 26, Art. 163, (R, F).
 MZh, 1926, No. 4, pp. 120–36.
 SDD, 3, 1927, pp. 114–29; *ibid.*, 1932, pp. 96–110.
 LNTS, 47, pp. 9–37 (E, F).
 STS, 1, pp. 308–13.

● 25/xii/17/T

Treaty of friendship and neutrality between the USSR and Turkey, with three protocols

Signed Dec. 17, 1925, in Paris.

Ratified by the USSR Jan. 8, 1926; by Turkey Feb. 11, 1926. Entered into force June 29, 1926, on exchange of acts of ratification in Istanbul. Duration 3 years; thereafter, if not denounced with 6 months' notice, extended for 1-year periods. Protocol concerning exchange of acts of ratification signed June 29, 1926. Extended by protocols of Dec. 17, 1929, Oct. 30, 1931, and Nov. 7, 1935, and by exchange of notes dated June 5, 1939. Denounced by the USSR Mar. 19, 1945: "In view of the profound changes which have taken place during the course of World War II, this treaty does not correspond any longer to the new circumstances and requires serious improvement" (*Izv.*, Mar. 21, 1945).

For an official Soviet denial, published on Dec. 24, 1925, that the treaty contains any secret clauses or protocols, see *SDFP*, 2, pp. 79–80; Eudin and Fisher, pp. 323–24.

Sources: *SZ*, 1926, II, No. 26, Art. 170.
 MZh, 1926, No. 1, pp. 188–89.
 SDD, 3, 1927, pp. 9–10; *ibid.*, 1932, pp. 5–7.
 *Kanunlarimiz, 5, p. 295.
 *RG, No. 306.
 LNTS, 157, pp. 353–57 (E, F).
 STS, 1, p. 313.

● 25/xii/29/1909

Convention on the international circulation of automobiles

Signed Oct. 11, 1909, in Paris.
Soviet adherence by decree of Dec. 29, 1925. Superseded by convention of Apr. 24, 1926 (26/iv/24/Mul).

Sources: *SZ*, 1926, I, No. 23, Arts. 152, 153.
 SDD, 3, 1927, pp. 261–76.

Dec. 31, 1925. Baltic Geodetic Convention

See 29/ii/9/1925.

1926

● 26/ / /J

Exchange of notes between the USSR and Japan concerning consular relations

Sent during 1926.
Mentioned in a Soviet note published Sept. 14, 1937, concerning closing of the Japanese consulates in Novosibirsk and Odessa (*SDFP*, 3, p. 255, citing *Izv.*).

● 26/i/24/China

Agreement between the USSR and the Mukden Government concerning settlement of the dispute over the Chinese Eastern Railway

Signed Jan. 24, 1926, in Mukden, by the Soviet Consul-General in Mukden and an official of the Government of the Three

Autonomous Eastern Provinces.
Sources: *Izv.*, Jan. 27, 1926.
   SDFP, 1, pp. 82–83.

● 26/ii/1/Af. See Appendix 5.

● 26/ii/2/1884

International convention concerning protection of underwater telegraph cables, with declaration and final protocol

Signed Mar. 14, 1884, in Paris; declaration signed Dec. 1, 1886, and final protocol July 7, 1887.
Soviet adherence by decree of Feb. 2, 1926.
Sources: *SZ*, 1926, II, No. 31, Arts. 187, 190.
   SDD, 4, 1936, pp. 74–80.
Reference: *SZ*, 1926, I, No. 22, Art. 145 (Soviet decree of Mar. 5, 1926, concerning internal legislation related to the convention).

● 26/ii/2/1910/a

Convention for unification of certain rules concerning collisions between vessels at sea

Signed Sept. 23, 1910, in Brussels.
Soviet adherence by decree of Feb. 2, 1926.
Sources: *SZ*, 1926, II, No. 31, Arts. 187, 188 (R, F).
   SDD, 4, 1936, pp. 82–85.
Reference: *SZ*, 1926, I, No. 22, Art. 145 (Soviet decree of Mar. 5, 1926, concerning internal legislation related to the convention).

● 26/ii/2/1910/b

Convention for unification of rules concerning assistance and salvage at sea

Signed Sept. 23, 1910, in Brussels.
Soviet adherence by decree of Feb. 2, 1926.
Source: *SZ*, 1926, II, No. 31, Arts. 187, 189 (R, F).
Reference: *SZ*, 1926, I, No. 22, Art. 145 (Soviet decree of Mar. 5, 1926, concerning internal legislation related to the convention).

● 26/ii/2/1911

Convention concerning protection of fur seals

Signed July 7, 1911, in Washington.
Soviet adherence by decree of Feb. 2, 1926.

Sources: *SZ*, 1926, I, No. 24, Arts. 154, 155 (E, R).
   SDD, 3, 1927, pp. 129–34; *ibid.*, 1932, pp. 110–14.

● 26/ii/19/Hejaz

Exchange of notes between the USSR and the King of Hejaz and Sultan of Nejd and Associated Territories concerning recognition and establishment of diplomatic relations

Sent Feb. 16 and 19, 1926.
Sources: *SDD*, 4, p. 14.
   SDFP, 2, p. 88 (Soviet note).
   STS, 1, p. 313.

● 26/ii/20/Persia

Agreement between the USSR and Persia concerning use of border rivers and waters from the river Geri-Rud (Tejen) to the Caspian Sea

Signed Feb. 20, 1926, in Askhabad (Poltoratsk).
Confirmed by Persia Aug. 18, 1926; by the USSR Aug. 20, 1926. Acts of ratification exchanged Sept. 24, 1926, in Teheran. Entered into force on signature.
Sources: *SZ*, 1927, II, No. 33, Art. 176 (R, Persian).
   SDD, 3, 1927, pp. 64–70; *ibid.*, 1932, pp. 50–55.
   STS, 1, pp. 314–16.
   SDFP, 2, pp. 88–92 (extracts).

● 26/iii/4/Est

Exchange of notes between the USSR and Estonia constituting a provisional agreement concerning reciprocal recognition of tonnage measurement certificates

Sent Mar. 4, 1926, in Tallinn.
Entered into force on signature. Six months' notice required for alteration.
Sources: *SZ*, 1927, II, No. 1, Art. 2 (R, Est.).
   SDD, 3, 1927, pp. 260–61; *ibid.*, 1932, pp. 164–65.
   *RT, 1926, No. 29.
   LNTS, 62, pp. 77–83 (R, Est., E, F).
   STS, 1, pp. 316–17.

● 26/iv/9/Norway

Declaration by the USSR and Norway concerning reciprocal recognition of tonnage measurement certificates

Signed Apr. 9, 1926, in Oslo.
Entered into force on signature. Six
months' notice required for termination.
Sources: *SZ*, 1926, I, No. 35, Art. 249 (R,
F).
    SDD, 3, 1927, pp. 237–38; *ibid.*, 1932,
pp. 143–44.
    LNTS, 48, pp. 185–89 (E, F).
    STS, 1, p. 317.

**Apr. 21, 1926. Protocol amending Art.
10 of the convention of June 7, 1905,
concerning establishment of a permanent International Institute of Agriculture**
See 36/iv/4/1926.

● 26/iv/22/Pl

**Protocol between the USSR, Estonia, and
Finland defining state borders under the
agreement of August 19, 1925, supplementary to the convention of the same
date concerning suppression of the contraband traffic in alcoholic products, with
final protocol**

Signed Apr. 22, 1926, in Moscow.
Ratified, deposited and entered into force
together with the agreement and convention of Aug. 19, 1925. Constitutes an integral part of the convention of Aug. 19,
1925.
Sources: *SZ*, 1929, II, No. 45, Art. 245,
pp. 968–70 (R, F).
    SDD, 5, pp. 54–55.
    RT, 1927, No. 6.
    LNTS, 45, pp. 183–88 (E, F).

● 26/iv/24/Ger

**Treaty of neutrality and nonaggression
between the USSR and Germany, with
exchange of notes**

Signed Apr. 24, 1926, in Berlin.
Ratified by the USSR June 22, 1926. En-
tered into force June 29, 1926, on ex-
change of acts of ratification in Berlin.
Duration 5 years. Extended by protocol
of June 24, 1931.
Reaffirms validity of the Treaty of Rapallo
(22/iv/16/Ger).
Exchange of notes concerns Germany's
entry into the League of Nations.
Sources: *SZ*, 1926, II, No. 27, Art. 171
(R, G).
    MZh, 1926, No. 5, pp. 109–12.
    SDD, 4, 1928, pp. 16–18.
    RGbl, 1926, II, No. 30, pp. 359–63.

LNTS, 53, pp. 387–96 (R, G, E, F).
STS, 1, pp. 317–18.
Reference: Eudin and Fisher, pp. 279–80.

● 26/iv/24/Mul

**International convention concerning
motor traffic, with six annexes**

Signed Apr. 24, 1926, in Paris.
Ratified by the USSR Sept. 14, 1927 (de-
cree of ratification dated Dec. 1, 1927);
act of ratification deposited Oct. 24, 1929.
Entered into force for the USSR Oct. 24,
1930 (1 year after deposit of ratification).
Supersedes convention of Oct. 11, 1909
(25/xii/29/1909).
Sources: *SZ*, 1929, II, No. 49, Art. 283
(R, F).
    SDD, 6, pp. 150–76.
    LNTS, 108, pp. 123–63 (E, F).

● 26/v/31/T

**Protocol between the USSR and Turkey
concerning establishment of a one-year
limit for persons wishing to exercise the
right to change their citizenship by moving from one country to the other**

Signed May 31, 1926, in Moscow.
Ratified by the USSR Oct. 5, 1926. En-
tered into force Mar. 11, 1927, on ex-
change of acts of ratification in Ankara.
Modifies provisions of Art. 12 of the treaty
of Mar. 16, 1921 (21/iii/16/T), and of
Art. 13 of the treaty of Oct. 13, 1921.
Sources: *SZ*, 1927, II, No. 32, Art. 173 (R,
F).
    SDD, 4, 1928, pp. 34–35.
    STS, 1, p. 318.
    SDFP, 2, pp. 117–18.

● 26/vi/21/Mul

**International sanitary convention, with
annex and protocol of signature**

Signed June 21, 1926, in Paris.
Ratified by the USSR July 19, 1928; Soviet act of ratification deposited Feb. 26,
1929, with immediate effect. Soviet reservations on signature incorporated in the
final protocol and repeated in the protocol
of deposit of the act of ratification, dated
Feb. 26, 1929 (*SZ*, 1929, II, pp. 495–96).
Replaces the Sanitary Conventions of
Jan. 17, 1912 (see 25/x/27/1912), and
Dec. 3, 1903, for signatories. Modified by
conventions of Oct. 31, 1938, and Dec. 15,
1944, which the USSR did not sign.

Under a protocol of July 22, 1946 (46/vii/22/Mul/d), the duties and functions conferred by this convention on the Office International d'Hygiène Publique were transferred to the World Health Organization or its Interim Commission.
Sources: *SZ*, 1929, II, No. 19, Art. 106 (R, F).
  SDD, 5, pp. 148–204.
  LNTS, 78, pp. 229–349 (E, F).

June 23, 1926. Customs agreement between the USSR and Greece
See Appendix 1.

● 26/vi/24/Iceland

Exchange of notes between the USSR and Iceland concerning recognition of the USSR *de jure* and establishment of diplomatic relations

Sent June 22 and 24, 1926, in Moscow.
Sources: *SDD*, 5, pp. 12–13.
  Kliuchnikov, 3, I, p. 346.
  STS, 1, p. 319.

● 26/vi/29/T

Protocol between the USSR and Turkey concerning exchange of acts of ratification of the treaty of friendship and neutrality of December 17, 1925

Signed June 29, 1926, in Istanbul.
Reaffirms principles of the treaties of Mar. 16, 1921, and Dec. 17, 1925.
Sources: *SZ*, 1926, II, No. 26, pp. 429–31.
  SDD, 3, 1932, pp. 6–7.
  LNTS, 157, pp. 358–59 (E, F).

● 26/vii/2/Ger

Exchange of notes between the USSR and Germany constituting an agreement concerning courier service

Sent June 7 and July 2, 1926, in Moscow.
Entered into force July 2, 1926.
Reference: *VVerz.*, p. 193.

● 26/vii/19/Lat

Agreement between the USSR and Latvia concerning consideration and settlement of border disputes, with protocol

Signed July 19, 1926, in Riga.
Confirmed by the USSR Aug. 10, 1926.
Entered into force Aug. 19, 1926 (1 month after signature, on condition of confirma-

tion by signatories). Valid until 3 months after denunciation. Modified by exchange of notes dated Apr. 9, 1937.
Sources: *SZ*, 1927, II, No. 17, Art. 102 (R, Lat.)
  SDD, 4, 1928, pp. 38–42.
  LRR, pp. 144–48.
  LNTS, 54, pp. 155–75 (R, Lat., E, F).
  STS, 1, pp. 320–22.

● 26/vii/21/Sweden

Exchange of notes between the USSR and Sweden concerning reciprocal protection of trade-marks

Sent July 21, 1926, in Moscow.
Entered into force July 21, 1926.
Sources: *SDD*, 4, 1928, p. 144.
  Sö, 1926, No. 24 (F, Sw.).
  LNTS, 57, pp. 9–11 (E, F).

● 26/viii/ /TT

Treaty of friendship between the USSR and Tannu-Tuva

Signed during Aug. 1926.
Modeled on the agreement of Nov. 5, 1921, between the USSR and the Mongolian People's Republic. Includes agreements on reciprocal recognition of independence and exchange of diplomatic representatives. In 1945 the USSR annexed Tannu-Tuva.
Reference: Friters, p. 131, citing
  V. Durdenevski, "Narodni respubliki Tsentralnoi Asii (Mongolska ta Tuvinska)," *Skidny svit*, 1929, No. 3, p. 114.

● 26/viii/18/Af. See Appendix 5.

● 26/viii/22/Uruguay

Exchange of telegrams between the USSR and Uruguay concerning recognition of the USSR *de jure* and establishment of diplomatic relations

Sent Aug. 21, 1926, from Montevideo and Aug. 22, 1926, from Moscow.
Sources: *Izv.*, Aug. 24, 1926.
  SDD, 5, p. 13.
  STS, 1, p. 322.

● 26/viii/31/Af

Treaty of neutrality and nonaggression between the USSR and Afghanistan, with final protocol

Signed Aug. 31, 1926, in Paghman.

Ratified by the USSR Nov. 9, 1926. Entered into force Apr. 10, 1927, on exchange of acts of ratification in Kabul. Duration 3 years; thereafter extended for 1 year unless denounced with 6 months' notice. Final protocol reaffirms the treaty of Feb. 28, 1921. Expired in 1931; replaced by the treaty of June 24, 1931.
Sources: *SZ*, 1928, II, No. 3, Art. 16 (R, Persian).
    SDD, 4, 1928, pp. 11–14.
    STS, 1, pp. 322–23.
    SDFP, 2, pp. 130–33.

• 26/viii/31/Ger

Agreement between the USSR and Germany concerning inheritance rights

Signed Aug. 31, 1926.
References: *Russian Review*, Sept. 1926, p. 167.
    Frankfurter Zeitung, Sept. 1, 1926 (cited in Degras, p. 108).

Sept. 25, 1926. Convention concerning slavery

See 56/viii/ /1926.

• 26/ix/28/Lith

Treaty of nonaggression between the USSR and Lithuania, with two exchanges of notes

Signed Sept. 28, 1926, in Moscow.
Ratified by the USSR and Lithuania Nov. 5, 1926. Entered into force Nov. 9, 1926, on exchange of acts of ratification in Kaunas. Duration 5 years, except Arts. 1 (re-

affirming the peace treaty of July 12, 1920), and 2 (binding the signatories to "respect in all circumstances each other's sovereignty and territorial integrity and inviolability"), which are of indefinite duration; thereafter extended for 1-year periods until denounced with 6 months' notice. Extended by protocols of May 6, 1931, and Apr. 4, 1934. Reaffirmed by treaty of Oct. 10, 1939.
First exchange of notes concerns Lithuania's membership in the League of Nations; second concerns a Lithuanian-Polish territorial dispute.
Sources: *Izv.*, Sept. 30, 1926.
    MZh, 1926, No. 11, pp. 121–24.
    SZ, 1927, II, No. 1, Art. 3 (R, Lith.).
    SDD, 4, 1928, pp. 19–22.
    *$VŽ$, 1926, No. 241, Art. 1568.
    LNTS, 60, pp. 145–59 (R, Lith., E, F).
    STS, 1, pp. 323–24.
Reference: Eudin and Fisher, p. 282.
Note: With regard to the territorial provisions of the treaty Poland sent the USSR a note on Oct. 23, 1926, reaffirming its claim to Vilna; the Soviet reply of Nov. 19, 1926, denied any intention to alter the Soviet-Polish boundary. Text, *MZh*, 1926, No. 12, pp. 90–91.

• 26/xi/14/T

Joint communiqué by the USSR and Turkey concerning strengthening of political relations

Issued Nov. 14, 1926.
Sources: *Izv.*, Nov. 16, 1926.
    SDFP, 2, pp. 141–42.

1927

• 27/i/8/T/a

Convention between the USSR and Turkey concerning use of water from border rivers and streams

Signed Jan. 8, 1927, in Kars.
Ratified by the USSR Mar. 4, 1927. Entered into force June 26, 1928, on exchange of acts of ratification in Angora. Duration 5 years; thereafter extended for 1-year periods until annulled or amended. Supplemented by a protocol of the same date (next document). Reaffirmed by exchange of notes of July 15, 1937 (37/vii/15/T/e).

Sources: *SZ*, 1928, II, No. 53, Art. 207 (R, F).
    SDD, 5, pp. 26–31.
    *$Kanunlarimiz$, 5, p. 325.
    *RG, No. 649.
    STS, 1, pp. 324–25.
    BFSP, 127, pp. 926–30 (F).
    SDFP, 2, pp. 147–50.

• 27/i/8/T/b

Protocol between the USSR and Turkey concerning construction of a dam for the Sardarabad Canal, with annex

Signed Jan. 8, 1927, in Kars.

Supplements the convention of the same date. Data on ratification and entry into force identical with those for the convention.

Provides for joint use of water from the dam; both states to share expense of construction. Annex (not reproduced in sources cited) consists of a sketch plan of the dam. The dam was built by the USSR on the Soviet side of the border, but because the 2 States were unable to agree on payment, Turkey did not receive any of the water (see *NYT*, Aug. 10, 1953). A new agreement on the use of water from the dam was signed on Sept. 15, 1953.

Sources: *SZ*, 1928, II, No. 53, Art. 207.
    SDD, 5, pp. 30–31.
    BFSP, 127, pp. 930–32 (F).
    SDFP, 2, pp. 150–52.

• 27/ii/2/Sweden

Exchange of notes between the USSR and Sweden constituting an agreement on rights and immunities of consuls

Sent Feb. 2, 1927, in Moscow.
Entered into force on signature. Valid until 3 months' after denunciation.
Sources: *SZ*, 1927, II, No. 19, Art. 112 (R, F).
    SDD, 4, 1928, pp. 35–37.
    Sö, 1927, No. 2 (F, Sw.)
    STS, 1, pp. 325–26.
    SDFP, 2, pp. 153–54.

• 27/ii/22/MPR

Protocol between the USSR and the Mongolian People's Republic extending and modifying the agreement of October 3, 1924, concerning telegraph communications

Signed Feb. 22, 1927, in Ulan Bator.
Validity of 1924 agreement extended to Jan. 1, 1929.
Sources: *SZ*, 1927, II, No. 37, Art. 203 (including revised text of 1924 agreement).
    SDD, 4, 1928, pp. 137–40 (same).
    STS, 1, p. 326.

Mar. 9, 1927. Treaty of nonaggression and neutrality between the USSR and Latvia

See Appendix 1.

• 27/iii/11/T

Treaty of commerce and navigation between the USSR and Turkey, with annex and final protocol

Signed Mar. 11, 1927, in Angora.
Ratified by the USSR Apr. 6, 1927. Entered into force July 4, 1927 (1 month after exchange of acts of ratification, which took place June 4, 1927, in Angora). Duration 1 year; thereafter until 6 months following denunciation. According to Korolenko, p. 52, expired during Oct. 1930; superseded by treaty of Mar. 16, 1931.
Sources: *SZ*, 1927, II, No. 39, Art. 213 (R, F).
    SDD, 4, 1928, pp. 100–13.
    Düstur, 8, p. 1315.
    STS, 1, pp. 326–29.
    SDFP, 2, pp. 164–77.

• 27/iii/29/Fin

Agreement between the USSR and Finland modifying the Regulations of June 18, 1924, concerning direct transportation of passengers and freight by rail

Signed Mar. 29, 1927, in Helsinki.
Ratified by Finland May 14, 1927; by the USSR July 6, 1927. Entered into force Dec. 23, 1927 (60 days after exchange of acts of ratification, which took place Oct. 24, 1927, in Moscow). Duration same as that of the convention of June 18, 1924 (24/vi/18/Fin/d).
Sources: *SZ*, 1927, II, No. 45, Art. 267 (R, Finnish, Sw.).
    SDD, 4, 1928, pp. 234–36.
    SS, 1927, No. 26 (R, Finnish).
    LNTS, 71, pp. 11–23 (R, Finnish, Sw., E, F).
    STS, 1, pp. 329–30.

• 27/iv/6/Austria

Exchange of notes between the USSR and Austria concerning suspension of Art. 8 of the agreement of September 19, 1924, concerning legal assistance in civil cases

Sent Apr. 6, 1927, in Vienna.
Ratified by Austria Apr. 22, 1927. Entered into force on signature.
Concerns reciprocal waiver of quarterly transfer of fees.
Sources: *BGbl*, 1927, No. 156.
    STS, 1, pp. 330–31, citing
        Martens, 3d series, 31, pp. 431–32.

● 27/iv/14/Switz

Exchange of notes between the USSR and Switzerland concerning settlement of the dispute over the assassination of V. V. Vorovsky

Sent Apr. 14, 1927, in Berlin.
Notes incorporate a declaration by the signatories concerning settlement of the dispute.
Sources: *SDD*, 4, 1928, pp. 27–30 (including decrees of the USSR, Ukrainian SSR, Transcaucasian SFSR, and Belorussian SSR ending the economic boycott of Switzerland).
  STS, 1, p. 331.
  SDFP, 2, pp. 180–81 (declaration).
References: *Izv.*, Apr. 16, 1927, reprinted *VP*, 3, pp. 111–12.
  Eudin and Fisher, p. 349.

● 27/iv/19/Hejaz

Exchange of notes between the USSR and the Kingdom of Hejaz, Nejd, and Associated Territories concerning recognition and maintenance of diplomatic relations

Sent Apr. 3, 15, and 19, 1927, in Hejaz.
Sources: *SDD*, 4, 1928, p. 15.
  STS, 1, pp. 313–14.
  SDFP, 2, p. 181 (Soviet note).

● 27/iv/26/Austria

Exchange of notes between the USSR and Austria concerning reciprocal registration of trade-marks

Sent Apr. 26, 1927, in Moscow.
Entered into force Apr. 26, 1927.
Sources: *SDD*, 4, 1928, pp. 56–57.
  STS, 1, p. 331.
Reference: **BGbl*, 1927, No. 185.

● 27/v/25/Iceland

Exchange of notes between the USSR and Iceland concerning the regime of most-favored-nation in trade relations

Sent May 25, 1927, in Moscow; signed on behalf of Iceland by the Danish diplomatic representative in Moscow.
Entered into force on signature; valid until 6 months after denunciation. According to Korolenko, p. 47, still valid as of Nov. 25, 1953.

Constitutes in effect a commercial agreement, and takes the place of the extension to Iceland of the Soviet-Danish preliminary agreement of Apr. 23, 1923, provided for in that agreement.
Sources: *SZ*, 1927, II, No. 32, Art. 174 (E, R).
  SDD, 4, 1928, pp. 59–61.
  LNTS, 63, pp. 105–109 (E, F).
  STS, 1, pp. 331–32.

● 27/vi/2/Lat/a

Agreement between the USSR and Latvia concerning legal aid in civil cases

Signed June 2, 1927, in Moscow.
Ratified by the USSR Oct. 31, 1927. Entered into force Jan. 12, 1928 (1 month after exchange of acts of ratification, which took place Dec. 12, 1927, in Riga). Duration 5 years; thereafter valid until 1 year following denunciation. Modified by exchange of notes dated Dec. 17, 1930, and Jan. 14, 1931 (31/i/14/Lat).
Sources: *SZ*, 1928, II, No. 19, Art. 89 (R, Lat.).
  SDD, 4, 1928, pp. 31–34.
  STS, 1, pp. 332–33.
  SDFP, 2, pp. 217–20.
Reference: *SZ*, 1928, II, No. 42, Art. 230 (ratification).

● 27/vi/2/Lat/b

Commercial treaty between the USSR and Latvia, with final protocol

Signed June 2, 1927, in Moscow.
Ratified by the USSR Oct. 31, 1927. Entered into force Nov. 5, 1927, on exchange of acts of ratification in Riga. Duration 5 years; if not denounced 6 months before expiration, extended for 1-year periods, or until denounced with 3 months' notice. Abrogated by Soviet decree of Apr. 29, 1932; Latvian Government notified May 4, 1932; treaty invalid after Nov. 5, 1932 (*SZ*, 1932, II, No. 24, Art. 252). Supplemented by a customs convention of the same date (next document).
Sources: *Izv.*, June 4, 1927.
  SZ, 1928, II, No. 15, Art. 66 (R, Lat.).
  SDD, 4, 1928, pp. 61–72.
  LRR, pp. 148–55.
  LNTS, 68, pp. 321–39, 348–63 (R, Lat., E, F).
  STS, 1, pp. 333–36.

• 27/vi/2/Lat/c

Customs convention between the USSR and Latvia, with related documents

Signed June 2, 1927, in Moscow.
Data on ratification, entry into force and extension same as for the commercial treaty of the same date (preceding document).
Related documents: final protocol, 2 annexes, and final protocol to the annexes.
Sources: *SZ*, 1928, II, No. 15, Art. 66.
  SDD, 4, 1928, pp. 68–72.
  LRR, pp. 155–59.
  LNTS, 68, pp. 339–47, 362–71 (R, Lat., E, F).
  STS, 1, pp. 335–36.

• 27/vi/15/Italy

Exchange of notes between the USSR and Italy concerning reciprocal registration of trade-marks

Sent June 19, 1926, and June 15, 1927, in Moscow.
Sources: *SDD*, 4, 1928, pp. 58–59.
  STS, 1, pp. 318–19.

• 27/vii/16/Austria

Agreement between the USSR and Austria concerning execution of the agreement of July 28, 1923, concerning embassy buildings

Signed July 16, 1927.
Reference: *Haus-, Hof- und Staatsarchiv under Zl.2147/27.

• 27/viii/8/Est

Agreement between the USSR and Estonia concerning procedure for settlement of border disputes, with protocol

Signed Aug. 8, 1927, in Tallinn.
Ratified by the USSR Oct. 26, 1927; by Estonia Nov. 1, 1927. Entered into force Jan. 20, 1928, on exchange of acts of ratification in Moscow. Valid until 3 months after denunciation. Protocol, which defines sectors of the border, modified by protocol of Oct. 22, 1931.
Sources: *SZ*, 1928, II, No. 21, Art. 93 (R, Est.).
  SDD, 4, 1928, pp. 49–55.
  RT, 1927, No. 104.

LNTS, 70, pp. 401–25 (R, Est., E, F).
STS, 1, pp. 336–38.

• 27/viii/14/Persia

Exchange of notes between the USSR and Persia concerning establishment of the position of border commissioners

Sent Aug. 14, 1927, in Teheran.
Sources: *SZ*, 1928, II, No. 30, Art. 132 (R, Persian).
  SDD, 4, 1928, pp. 43–46.
  STS, 1, pp. 338–39.
  SDFP, 2, pp. 244–47.

• 27/ix/2/Fin

Exchange of notes between the USSR and Finland concerning regulations for Finnish merchant and cargo vessels navigating the Neva

Sent Sept. 2, 1927, in Helsinki.
Entered into force provisionally Sept. 15, 1927. Modifies Art. 7 of the agreement of June 5, 1923; Art. 7 further revised by agreement of Mar. 17, 1928.
Sources: *SS*, 1927, No. 22 (Finnish, F).
  LNTS, 69, pp. 76–78 (E, F).
  STS, 1, pp. 339–40.

• 27/x/1/Persia/a

Treaty of nonaggression and neutrality between the USSR and Persia, with two protocols and an exchange of notes

Signed Oct. 1, 1927, in Moscow.
Ratified by the USSR Nov. 2, 1927. Entered into force Jan. 31, 1928, on exchange of acts of ratification in Teheran. Duration 3 years; thereafter extended for 1-year periods, or until 6 months following denunciation. Reaffirms provisions of the treaty of Feb. 26, 1921.
Exchange of notes concerns Persia's position as a member of the League of Nations.
Sources: *Izv.*, Oct. 2, 1927.
  SZ, 1928, II, No. 41, Art. 160 (R, Persian).
  SDD, 4, 1928, pp. 23–26.
  LNTS, 112, pp. 275–95 (R, Pers., E, F).
  STS, 1, pp. 340–41.

• 27/x/1/Persia/b

Agreement between the USSR and Persia concerning exploitation of fisheries

on the southern shore of the Caspian Sea, with related documents

Signed Oct. 1, 1927, in Moscow.
Ratified by the USSR Nov. 2, 1927. Entered into force Jan. 31, 1928, on exchange of acts of ratification in Teheran.
Provides for establishment of a mixed Soviet-Persian company, to be organized by the Soviet and Persian Governments, with a 25-year concession to catch and prepare fish within the area covered by the agreement. Under this provision a mixed company, "Iranryba," was set up. Its charter expired Jan. 31, 1953, and a Soviet proposal to renew it was declined by the Iranian Government. Iran did, however, agree to honor the provision of this agreement not to grant the fishing rights to any third government or individual for an additional 25 years (see *Izv.*, Feb. 3, 1953, and *DIA, 1953*, pp. 348–49). Related documents: Protocol (1) concerns definition of term "Persian nationals." (2) concerns property purchased by the Soviet Government from Martin Lianozov, under an agreement of Aug. 10, 1923 (see Appendix 3), and includes an extract from this agreement. (3) concerns rights and claims of Martin Lianozov against the Persian Government. (4) concerns fishing quotas. (5) concerns passport and visa formalities for Soviet citizens. Exchanges of notes: (1) concerns methods of fishing. (2) concerns claims of Martin Lianozov. (3) concerns political propaganda and agitation by Soviet citizens in Persia and the organization of trade unions. (4) concerns claims by Persian citizens against Martin Lianozov. (5) concerns chairmanship of the mixed company and procedure for voting. Persian text of protocol (2) amended by protocol of Jan. 31, 1928.
Sources: (1) Text and 5 protocols: *SZ*, 1928, II, No. 41, Art. 161, pp. 1062–78 (R, F).
SDD, 5, pp. 74–82.
LNTS, 112, pp. 297–356 (R, Persian, E, F).
STS, 1, pp. 348–51.
(2) Exchange of notes (1):
SZ, 1928, II, pp. 1078–80.
SDD, 5, pp. 82–83.
LNTS, 112, pp. 314–17, 357.
STS, 1, p. 351.
(3) Exchange of notes (2):
SZ, 1928, II, pp. 1080–82.
SDD, 5, p. 83.

LNTS, 112, pp. 316–19, 357–58.
STS, 1, p. 351.
(4) Exchange of notes (3):
LNTS, 112, pp. 318–21, 358–59.
STS, 1, p. 351.
(5) Exchange of notes (4):
SZ, 1928, II, pp. 1082–83.
SDD, 5, p. 84.
LNTS, 112, pp. 320–23, 359.
STS, 1, pp. 351–52.
(6) Exchange of notes (5):
SDD, 5, pp. 84–85.
LNTS, 112, pp. 322, 360.
STS, 1, p. 352.

● 27/x/1/Persia/c

Exchange of notes between the USSR and Persia concerning Port Pehlevi

Sent Oct. 1, 1927, in Moscow.
Sources: *SZ*, 1928, II, No. 42, Art. 163.
SDD, 4, 1928, pp. 95–100.
STS, 1, pp. 347–48.
SDFP, 2, pp. 266–69.

● 27/x/1/Persia/d

Customs convention between the USSR and Persia, with final protocol, exchange of notes, and three lists

Signed Oct. 1, 1927, in Moscow.
Ratified by the USSR Dec. 16, 1927. Entered into force Feb. 29, 1928 (1 month after exchange of acts of ratification, which took place Jan. 31, 1928, in Teheran). Abrogated by exchange of notes dated May 10 and 18, 1928 (28/v/18/Persia), following adoption by Persia of an autonomous customs tariff on May 3, 1928. Replaced by customs convention of Mar. 10, 1929.
Sources: *SZ*, 1928, II, No. 17, Art. 73 (R, F) (omits the exchange of notes).
STS, 1, pp. 345–47 (omits the lists).

● 27/x/1/Persia/e

Exchange of notes between the USSR and Persia constituting a temporary trade agreement, with related documents

Sent Oct. 1, 1927, in Moscow.
Duration 2 years; expired Oct. 1, 1929.
Related documents: 2 annexes, 4 supplementary exchanges of notes, and 2 protocols. Second protocol, concerning transit of munitions, omitted from Soviet sources cited.

Sources: *SZ*, 1928, II, No. 42, Art. 162.
 SDD, 4, 1928, pp. 72–95.
 STS, 1, pp. 342–45, citing
  Childs, pp. 134–54.
 SDFP, 2, pp. 255–66.

• 27/x/9/Sweden

Convention between the USSR and Sweden concerning the legal status of the Soviet Trade Mission in Sweden, with final protocol

Signed Oct. 9, 1927, in Moscow.
Ratified by the USSR Feb. 15, 1928; by Sweden Mar. 31, 1928. Entered into force Mar. 31, 1928, on exchange of acts of ratification in Stockholm. Valid until 6 months after denunciation. Duration not to exceed that of the commercial agreement of Mar. 15, 1924. Listed in Korolenko, p. 47, as still valid as of Nov. 25, 1953.
Sources: *SZ*, 1928, II, No. 30, Art. 131
  (R, F).
 SDD, 5, pp. 85–88.
 Sö, 1928, No. 8 (Sw., F).
 LNTS, 71, pp. 411–17 (E, F).
 STS, 1, pp. 352–53.

• 27/x/10/Lat

Convention between the USSR and Latvia concerning arbitration tribunals in commercial and civil cases, with final protocol

Signed Oct. 10, 1927, in Riga.
Ratified by the USSR Oct. 31, 1927. Entered into force Aug. 29, 1928, on exchange of acts of ratification in Riga. Duration 5 years; if not denounced 6 months before expiration, extended for 1-year periods.
Latvian text of the convention amended by protocol of May 18, 1928 (28/v/18/Lat).
Sources: *SZ*, 1929, II, No. 1, Art. 1.
 SDD, 5, pp. 14–19.
 LRR, pp. 159–65.
 LNTS, 84, pp. 47–75 (R, Lat., E, F).
 STS, 1, pp. 353–55.
Reference: *SZ*, 1928, II, No. 42, Art. 230
  (ratification).

• 27/x/20/1924

International agreement for the creation at Paris of an international office for dealing with contagious diseases of animals, with Statute

Signed Jan. 25, 1924, in Paris.
Soviet adherence by declaration of Oct. 20, 1927; acknowledged by French Government Mar. 5, 1928. Entered into force for the USSR Oct. 20, 1927. Duration 7 years, with automatic extension for 7-year periods for signatories which have not denounced it 1 year before expiration.
Sources: *SZ*, 1928, II, No. 57, Arts. 226, 227 (R, F).
 SDD, 5, pp. 110–17.
 LNTS, 57, pp. 135–46 (E, F).

• 27/x/29/Mul

Convention for the creation at Paris of an International Office of Chemistry, with Regulations

Signed Oct. 29, 1927, in Paris.
Soviet ratification deposited by Oct. 14, 1931. Duration 6 years; thereafter automatically extended for 6-year periods, unless denounced with 2 years' notice.
Sources: *LNTS*, 127, pp. 27–39 (E, F).
 Hudson, 4, pp. 3205–3207.

• 27/xi/23/Persia

Protocol between the USSR and Persia concerning establishment of a link between the airlines of the USSR and those of Persia

Signed Nov. 23, 1927, in Teheran.
Entered into force on signature. Supplements the postal convention of Apr. 25, 1923.
Sources: *SZ*, 1928, II, No. 23, Art. 111
  (R, Persian).
 SDD, 4, 1928, pp. 233–34.
 STS, 1, p. 356, citing
  Droit aerien, 13, 1929, p. 528.
 SDFP, 2, pp. 280–82.

• 27/xi/28/Af

Agreement between the USSR and Afghanistan concerning the airline Kabul-Tashkent

Signed Nov. 28, 1927, in Kabul.
Entered into force on signature. Valid until Jan. 1, 1929.
Sources: *SZ*, 1928, II, No. 21, Art. 94 (R, Persian).
 SDD, 4, 1928, pp. 160–62.
 STS, 1, pp. 356–57, citing
  Droit aerien, 13, 1929, pp. 440–42.
 SDFP, 2, pp. 283–86.

● 27/xii/2/1925

Protocol concerning prohibition of the use in war of asphyxiating, poisonous or other gases, and of bacteriological methods of warfare

Signed June 17, 1925, in Geneva.
Soviet adherence by declaration of Dec. 2, 1927. Ratified by the USSR Mar. 7, 1928.
Protocol of ratification signed in Paris, Apr. 5, 1928, with reservations: (1) that the protocol is binding on the USSR only with respect to those states which signed and ratified, or definitely adhered to, the protocol; and (2) that it ceases to be binding on the USSR with respect to those states, the armed forces of which, as well as the formal or actual allies of which, do not respect the provisions of the protocol.
Sources: *SZ*, 1928, II, No. 35, Art. 145 (E, F).
    MZh, 1928, No. 4, pp. 102–103.
    SDD, 5, pp. 3–5.
    LNTS, 94, pp. 65–74 (E, F).
Note: For an analysis of the significance of the Soviet reservations on signing, see Ernest A. Gross, "U.S. proposes investigation of bacteriological warfare charges," *DSB*, 27, 1952, pp. 32–37.

● 27/xii/14/T

Exchange of notes between the USSR and Turkey modifying and extending the convention of March 20, 1922, concerning border crossing

Sent Nov. 17 and Dec. 14, 1927, in Angora.
The Soviet note of Nov. 17, 1927, includes a request for modification of the 1922 convention (22/iii/20/T/b), and thus fixes its termination at Nov. 17, 1928.
By decree of Sept. 27, 1927, the USSR Council of People's Commissars approved the draft of a new convention on border crossing (for the convention, see 28/viii/6/T/c).
Sources: *SZ*, 1928, II, No. 34, Art. 144 (R, F).

SDD, 4, 1928, pp. 48–49.
STS, 1, pp. 355–56.

● 27/xii/15/T

Exchange of notes between the USSR and Turkey modifying and extending the convention of March 20, 1922, concerning the use of pastures

Sent Sept. 18 and Dec. 15, 1927, in Angora.
The Soviet note of Sept. 18, 1927, includes a request for modification of the convention (22/iii/20/T/a), and thus fixes its termination at Sept. 18, 1928. For a further extension, see 28/v/17/T.
By decree of July 5, 1927, the USSR Council of People's Commissars approved the draft of a new convention concerning use of pastures (for the convention, see 28/viii/6/T/a).
Sources: *SZ*, 1928, II, No. 42, Arts. 164, 165 (E, F).
    SDD, 4, 1928, pp. 46–48.
    STS, 1, p. 340.

● 27/xii/23/Denmark

Exchange of notes between the USSR and Denmark concerning reciprocal registration of trade-marks

Sent Dec. 23, 1927, in Moscow.
Sources: *SDD*, 4, 1928, pp. 57–58.
    DT, 1, p. 357.
    Lovtidende A, 1928, p. 17.
    LNTS, 70, pp. 245–49 (E, F).
    STS, 1, p. 357.

● 27/xii/27/Pol

Protocol between the USSR and Poland concerning exchange of political prisoners

Signed Dec. 27, 1927.
Completes action under the repatriation agreement of Feb. 24, 1921 (21/ii/24/Pol/c). For a further agreement on the exchange of prisoners, see 32/viii/3/Pol.
Reference: *Izv.*, Jan. 4, 1928.

1928

● 28/i/16/Norway

Exchange of notes between the USSR and Norway concerning mutual notification in the case of nationals of either country being arrested in the other

Sent June 9 and Oct. 26, 1927, and Jan. 16, 1928, in Moscow.
Sources: *LNTS*, 70, pp. 239–43 (omits the note of June 9, 1927) (E, F).
    STS, 1, p. 355.

• 28/i/23/J

Fishery convention between the USSR and Japan, with related documents

Signed Jan. 23, 1928, in Moscow.
Ratified by the USSR May 7, 1928; by Japan May 22, 1928. Entered into force May 28, 1928 (5 days after exchange of acts of ratification, which took place May 23, 1928, in Tokyo). Duration 8 years; thereafter to be revised or renewed, and then revised or renewed at the end of every 12 years; notice of desire to revise may be given 1 year before termination; if notice is not given, extended for an additional 12 years.
Supplemented by agreement of Aug. 13, 1932. Expired in Dec. 1936 and denounced by Japan (*Izv.*, Apr. 4, 1939; *SDFP*, 3, p. 326). Extended by protocols of May 25, 1936; Dec. 28, 1936; Dec. 29, 1937; Apr. 2, 1939; Dec. 31, 1939; Jan. 20, 1941; Mar. 20, 1942; Mar. 25, 1943; and Mar. 30, 1944.
Related documents: Protocols A, B, and C; final protocol; exchanges of notes, (1) concerning taxes and fees; (2) concerning auction of fishery lots; (3) concerning fishing by Tsentrosoiuz; and (4) concerning lease of fishery lots. Annexes and exchanges of notes are not included in the Soviet sources listed below, or in *STS*, 1.
Sources: *SZ*, 1928, II, No. 52, Art. 206 (E, R).
  SDD, 5, pp. 89–106.
  *CDT, No. 104.
  LNTS, 80, pp. 341–99 (E, F).
  STS, 1, pp. 357–63.

• 28/i/31/Persia

Protocol between the USSR and Persia concerning amendment of the Persian text of the second protocol to the agreement of October 1, 1927, concerning exploitation of fisheries on the southern shore of the Caspian Sea

Signed Jan. 31, 1928, in Teheran.
Sources: *SZ*, 1929, II, No. 14, Art. 84 (R, F).
  STS, 1, p. 363.

• 28/ii/24/Norway

Convention between the USSR and Norway concerning reciprocal protection of industrial property rights, with final protocol

Signed Feb. 24, 1928, in Moscow.

Ratified by the USSR May 26, 1928. Entered into force Sept. 5, 1928 (2 months after exchange of acts of ratification, which took place July 5, 1928, in Oslo). Valid until 6 months after denunciation.
Sources: *SZ*, 1928, II, No. 62, Art. 252 (R, F).
  SDD, 5, pp. 72–74.
  LNTS, 79, pp. 9–15 (E, F).
  STS, 1, pp. 363–64.

• 28/iii/3/Est

Agreement between the USSR and Estonia concerning reciprocal protection of trade and commercial marks

Signed Mar. 3, 1928, in Tallinn.
Ratified by Estonia May 25, 1928; by the USSR June 20, 1928. Entered into force Aug. 30, 1928, on exchange of acts of ratification in Moscow. Valid until 3 months after denunciation.
Sources: *SZ*, 1928, II, No. 66, Art. 268 (R, F).
  SDD, 5, pp. 88–89.
  *RT, 1925, No. 52.
  LNTS, 80, pp. 401–405 (E, F).
  STS, 1, p. 364.

• 28/iii/17/Fin

Agreement between the USSR and Finland concerning regulations for Finnish merchant and cargo vessels navigating the Neva

Signed Mar. 17, 1928, in Helsinki.
Ratified by the USSR May 26, 1928; by Finland June 27, 1928. Entered into force July 31, 1928, on exchange of acts of ratification in Moscow. Revises Art. 7 of the agreement of June 5, 1923; duration the same.
Sources: *SZ*, 1928, II, No. 56, Art. 225 (R, Finnish).
  SDD, 5, pp. 145–47.
  *SS, 1928, No. 21.
  LNTS, 80, pp. 151–63 (R, Finnish, Sw., E, F).
  STS, 1, pp. 364–65.

• 28/v/17/T

Protocol between the USSR and Turkey extending the convention of March 20, 1922, concerning the use of pastures

Signed May 17, 1928, in Angora.
Ratified by Turkey May 24, 1928; confirmed by the USSR July 31, 1928. Dura-

tion of the 1922 convention (22/iii/30/T/a) extended for 4 months beyond expiration date of Sept. 17, 1928.
Sources: *SZ*, 1929, II, No. 3, Art. 11 (R, F).
*Düstur, 9, p. 1076.
STS, 1, pp. 365–66.

- 28/v/18/Lat

Protocol between the USSR and Latvia concerning amendments in the Latvian text of the convention of October 10, 1927, concerning arbitration tribunals

Signed May 18, 1928, in Riga. Ratified by the USSR July 18, 1928. Enters into force at the same time as the convention which it supplements (i.e., Aug. 29, 1928); acts of ratification exchanged on that date in Riga.
Sources: *SZ*, 1929, II, No. 1, Art. 2 (R, Lat.).
SDD, 5, pp. 19–20.
LNTS, 84, pp. 60–63, 74–77 (R, Lat., E, F).

- 28/v/18/Persia

Exchange of notes between the USSR and Persia abrogating the customs convention of October 1, 1927

Sent May 10 and 18, 1928, in Teheran.
For the 1927 convention, see 27/x/1/Persia/d.
Sources: *SZ*, 1928, II, No. 66, Arts. 269, 270 (pp. 1615–18; R, F).
STS, 1, p. 365.

- 28/v/31/Persia

Convention between the USSR and Persia concerning border crossing by inhabitants of border regions, with annex and supplementary protocol

Signed May 31, 1928, in Teheran.
Ratified by the USSR July 25, 1928. Entered into force Nov. 1, 1929, on exchange of acts of ratification in Moscow. Duration 3 years; thereafter until 1 year following denunciation. Terminated as of July 24, 1938, by Soviet note of July 24, 1937 (*SZ*, 1937, II, No. 35, Art. 297).
Sources: *SZ*, 1929, II, No. 50, Art. 284 (R, F).
SDD, 6, pp. 19–24.
LNTS, 110, pp. 343–55 (E, F).
STS, 1, pp. 366–67.

- 28/vi/ /Af. See Appendix 5.

- 28/viii/6/T/a

Convention between the USSR and Turkey concerning use of pastures across the border by citizens of both states, with three annexes

Signed Aug. 6, 1928, in Angora.
Ratified by the USSR Jan. 2, 1929; by Turkey Feb. 23, 1929. Entered into force May 2, 1929, on exchange of acts of ratification in Angora. Duration 5 years; if not denounced 6 months before expiration, extended until 1 year following denunciation.
Replaces the convention of Mar. 20, 1922 (22/iii/20/T/a).
Sources: *SZ*, 1929, II, No. 26, Art. 147 (R, F).
SDD, 5, pp. 32–38.
Düstur, 9, p. 1076.
STS, 1, pp. 368–70.

- 28/viii/6/T/b

Convention between the USSR and Turkey concerning prevention of the spread of animal diseases across the border between the Georgian SSR and Turkey, with protocol and four annexes

Signed Aug. 6, 1928, in Angora.
Ratified by Turkey Feb. 23, 1929; by the USSR Mar. 27, 1929. Entered into force Apr. 3, 1929, on exchange of acts of ratification in Angora. Duration 5 years; conditions for validity same as those for convention of the same date concerning pastures (preceding document); becomes invalid on denunciation of that convention.
Sources: *SZ*, 1929, II, No. 26, Art. 147 (R, F).
SDD, 5, pp. 32–38.
*Düstur, 10, p. 451.
STS, 1, pp. 368–70.

- 28/viii/6/T/c

Convention between the USSR and Turkey concerning border crossing by inhabitants of border zones

Signed Aug. 6, 1928, in Angora.
Ratified by the USSR Jan. 2, 1929; by Turkey Feb. 23, 1929. Entered into force Dec. 2, 1929, on exchange of acts of ratification in Angora. Duration 5 years; if neither party denounces it or requests its modification 6 months before expiration, extended until 1 year following denunciation.

1928   67

Replaces the convention of Mar. 20, 1922
(22/iii/20/T/b).
Sources: *SZ*, 1930, II, No. 23, Art. 141
   (R, F).
   SDD, 6, pp. 24–29.
   *Düstur, 10 (I), p. 410.
   STS, 1, pp. 372–73.
   SDFP, 2, pp. 328–33.

● 28/viii/6/T/d

**Convention between the USSR and Tur-
key concerning procedure for consideration and settlement of border disputes,
with protocol**

Signed Aug. 6, 1928, in Angora.
Ratified by the USSR Jan. 2, 1929; by
Turkey Feb. 23, 1929. Entered into force
Sept. 10, 1929 (1 month after exchange
of acts of ratification, which took place
Aug. 10, 1929, in Angora). Duration 3
years. Extended by protocols of Oct. 10,
1932; Mar. 28, 1933; Nov. 29, 1933; Apr.
12, 1934; Oct. 6, 1934; and by exchange
of notes of June 9, 1936. Superseded by
convention of July 15, 1937.
Sources: *SZ*, 1930, II, No. 49, Art. 300
   (R, T, F).
   SDD, 6, pp. 29–36.
   Düstur, 10 (I), p. 429.
   STS, 1, pp. 367–68 (omits the protocol).
   SDFP, 2, pp. 325–28 (same).

● 28/viii/14/Persia

**Exchange of notes between the USSR
and Persia concerning establishment of
the position of border commissioners**

Sent Aug. 14, 1928, in Teheran.
Supplemented by exchange of notes dated
Oct. 15 and Nov. 20, 1928 (28/xi/20/Per-
sia).
Sources: *SZ*, 1928, II, No. 30, Art. 132
   (R, Per.).
   SDD, 5, pp. 21–24.
   STS, 1, pp. 338–39.

● 28/viii/27/Mul

**General Treaty for renunciation of war
as an instrument of national policy
(Kellogg-Briand Pact; Treaty of Paris)**

Signed Aug. 27, 1928, in Paris.
Adherence of the USSR by decree of Aug.
29, 1928. Declaration of adherence signed
Sept. 6, 1928, and given to the French Ambassador in Moscow the same day. Soviet
act of ratification deposited Sept. 27, 1928,
with immediate effect. Entered into force

July 24, 1929. Protocol concerning entry
into force signed Feb. 9, 1929.
Sources: *SZ*, 1929, II, No. 41, Art. 234
   (R, F).
   SDD, 5, pp. 5–8.
   LNTS, 94, pp. 57–64 (E, F).

**Sept. 22, 1928. Protocol concerning
changes and additions to the International Service Regulations annexed to the
International Telegraph Convention of
1875, as revised in 1925**
See 29/x/8/1928.

● 28/ix/24/Fin

**Exchange of notes between the RSFSR
and Finland constituting an agreement
concerning appointment of border commissioners on the Karelian Isthmus**

Sent Sept. 24, 1928, in Helsinki.
Entered into force Nov. 1, 1928. Duration
1 year; thereafter extended from year to
year, unless either party, with 3 months'
notice, declares its wish to change or de-
nounce it.
Sources: *SDD*, 5, pp. 38–41.
   *SS, 1928, No. 28 (Finnish, F).
   LNTS, 82, pp. 63–69 (E, F).
   STS, 1, pp. 374–75.

● 28/ix/24/Lith

**Exchange of notes between the USSR and
Lithuania constituting a trade agreement**

Sent Sept. 24, 1928, in Kaunas.
Valid until 6 months after denunciation.
Sources: *SZ*, 1929, II, No. 14, Art. 85 (R,
   Lith.).
   SDD, 5, pp. 70–71.
   *VŽ, 1928, No. 285, Art. 1848.
   STS, 1, p. 374.
   SDFP, 2, pp. 339–40.

● 28/xi/1/Yemen

**Treaty of friendship and commerce be-
tween the USSR and Yemen (Treaty of
Sanaa)**

Signed Nov. 1, 1928, in Sanaa.
Ratified by the USSR Jan. 23, 1929. Entered into force June 24, 1929, on exchange of acts of ratification in Sanaa.
Duration 10 years. Extended for 10 years
by exchange of notes in Feb. 1939 (39/
ii/ /Yemen). Lapsed in 1949, but revived under treaty of Oct. 31, 1955.

Sources: *SZ*, 1929, II, No. 53, Art. 318
   (R, A).
SDD, 6, pp. 6–8.
STS, 1, pp. 375–76.
SDFP, 2, pp. 340–42.
BFSP, 129, p. 949.

● 28/xi/17/Fin

**Exchange of notes between the USSR
and Finland modifying the Regulations
of June 18, 1924, concerning direct
transportation of passengers and freight**

Sent Nov. 17, 1928, in Helsinki.
For the 1924 regulations, see 24/vi/18/
Fin/e.
Sources: *SZ*, 1930, II, No. 23, Art. 143
   (R, F).
SDD, 6, pp. 147–48.
SS, 1928, No. 36 (Finnish, F).
LNTS, 78, pp. 472–75 (E, F).

● 28/xi/20/Persia

**Exchange of notes between the USSR
and Persia concerning border commissioners**

Sent Oct. 15 and Nov. 20, 1928, in Te-
heran.
Supplements the exchange of notes of
Aug. 14, 1928.
Sources: *SDD*, 5, pp. 24–26.
STS, 1, p. 375.

● 28/xi/22/Mul

**Convention concerning international ex-
hibitions, with protocol and protocol of
signature**

Signed Nov. 22, 1928, in Paris.
Ratified by the USSR Oct. 17, 1935; act
of ratification deposited in Paris Nov. 2,
1935; entered into force for the USSR
Dec. 2, 1935, 1 month after deposit of act
of ratification.
Protocol of signature incorporates a declaration by the USSR that, with regard to
the provision that an interval of at least
5 years must elapse between 2 special exhibitions of the same kind organized in
the same country, it reserves the right to
regard as separate countries the 6 constituent members of the USSR — the
RSFSR, the Ukraine, the Transcaucasian
Federation, Belorussia, Turkmenistan, and
Uzbekistan.
Denounced by the United Kingdom vis-à-
vis the USSR Aug. 8, 1945. Denounced
by the USSR Jan. 20, 1949, with immediate effect.
Sources: *LNTS*, 111, pp. 343–85 (E, F).
SZ, 1936, II, No. 16, Art. 139.
SDD, 9, pp. 181–96.

● 28/xii/21/Ger

**Protocol between the USSR and Ger-
many concerning commercial and economic relations, with eight annexes**

Signed Dec. 21, 1928, in Moscow.
Confirmed by the USSR Jan. 8, 1929. Sup-
plements the treaties of Oct. 12, 1925.
Sources: *SZ*, 1929, II, No. 7, Art. 36
   (R, G).
SDD, 5, pp. 56–70.
RGbl, 1929, II, No. 5, p. 53.
STS, 1, pp. 376–80 (incomplete).

● 28/xii/23/T

**Protocol between the USSR and Turkey
concerning exchange of acts of ratification of the railroad convention of July
9, 1922**

Signed Dec. 23, 1928, in Angora.
Calls for convocation of a railroad confer-
ence. For the 1922 convention, see 22/vii/
9/T/b.
Sources: *SZ*, 1929, II, No. 14, Art. 83,
   pp. 306–307 (R, F).
STS, 1, p. 380, citing
   BFSP, 132, p. 877.

1929

● 29/ / /MPR. See Appendix 5.

● 29/i/24/Denmark

**Exchange of notes between the USSR
and Denmark extending the agreement
of June 29, 1925, concerning reciprocal
recognition of tonnage measurement certificates**

Sent Jan. 15 and 24, 1929, in Copenhagen.
Initiated by a Soviet *note verbale* of June
27, 1928, informing the Danish Government that the Registration Office of the
USSR had drawn up new regulations for
tonnage measurement of ships.
Superseded by the treaty of commerce and
navigation of Aug. 17, 1946.

Sources: *DT, 1929.
  *Lovtidende A, 1929, p. 358.
  LNTS, 88, pp. 325–27 (E, F).
  STS, 2, p. 1.

• 29/i/25/Ger

Convention between the USSR and Germany concerning conciliation procedure

Signed Jan. 25, 1929, in Moscow.
Ratified by the USSR Mar. 20, 1929. Entered into force Apr. 12, 1929, on exchange of acts of ratification in Berlin. Duration 3 years. Extended by protocol of June 24, 1931.
Establishes a conciliation commission.
Sources: SZ, 1929, II, No. 21, Art. 114
  (R, G).
  SDD, 5, pp. 10–13.
  *RGbl, 1929, II, No. 20, p. 179.
  LNTS, 90, pp. 219–31 (R, G, E, F).
  STS, 2, pp. 1–2.

• 29/ii/9/Pl

Protocol concerning entry into force of the General Treaty of August 27, 1928, for renunciation of war as an instrument of national policy (Litvinov Protocol)

Signed Feb. 9, 1929, in Moscow, by the USSR, Estonia, Latvia, Poland, and Romania. Subsequently adhered to by Lithuania, Danzig, and Persia.
Ratified by the USSR Feb. 13, 1929; act of ratification deposited Mar. 5, 1929, together with that of Latvia. Act of ratification of Estonia deposited Mar. 16, 1929; of Romania Mar. 30, 1929; of Lithuania Apr. 5, 1929. Turkey acceded Apr. 1, 1929; Danzig, Apr. 30, 1929; Persia, July 4, 1929. Enters into force between ratifying signatories on deposit of acts of ratification.
Includes the text of the 1928 treaty as an annex.
Sources: SZ, 1929, II, No. 15, Art. 87 (R,
  F).
  MZh, 1929, No. 2, pp. 97–99.
  SDD, 5, pp. 8–10.
  LNTS, 89, pp. 369–75 (E, F).
  STS, 2, p. 2.

• 29/ii/9/1925

Baltic Geodetic Convention

Signed Dec. 31, 1925, in Helsinki.
Soviet adherence by declaration of Feb. 9, 1929; entered into force for the USSR on

that date. Duration 12 years from date of original entry into force, Jan. 1, 1925. Extended for an additional 12 years by protocol of June 22, 1936.
The USSR on Mar. 14, 1938, gave notice of intention to withdraw, with effect from Dec. 31, 1939.
Sources: SZ, 1929, II, No. 21, Art. 113 (R,
  G, F).
  SDD, 5, pp. 106–10.
  LNTS, 79, pp. 167–77 (E, F, G).

• 29/iii/10/Persia

Customs convention between the USSR and Persia, with supplementary protocol

Signed Mar. 10, 1929, in Teheran.
Not subject to ratification. Entered into force Mar. 24, 1929 (14 days after signature). Valid until May 10, 1936; if not denounced 1 month before expiration, valid until 6 months after denunciation. Replaces customs convention of Oct. 1, 1927 (27/x/1/Persia/d).
Sources: SZ, 1929, II, No. 37, Art. 216
  (R, F; includes extract from Persian tariff).
  SDD, 6, pp. 52–59.
  LNTS, 107, pp. 419–25 (E, F).
  STS, 2, p. 3.

• 29/iv/13/Fin/a

Convention between the USSR and Finland concerning customs supervision in the Gulf of Finland, with final protocol

Signed Apr. 13, 1929, in Moscow.
Ratified by Finland June 13, 1929; by the USSR July 3, 1929. Entered into force Oct. 10, 1929 (1 month after exchange of acts of ratification, which took place Sept. 10, 1929, in Helsinki). Valid until 1 year after denunciation.
Provisions extended by protocol of the same date (next document) to the agreement of July 28, 1923 (23/vii/28/Fin).
Sources: SZ, 1929, II, No. 45, Art. 255
  (R, Finnish, Sw.).
  SDD, 5, pp. 41–45.
  *SS, 1929, No. 32 (R, Finnish).
  LNTS, 96, pp. 93–99, 102–106, 108–14
  (R, Finnish, Sw., E, F).
  STS, 2, pp. 4–5.

• 29/iv/13/Fin/b

Protocol between the USSR and Finland amending the agreement of July 28, 1923, concerning maintenance of order

in the Gulf of Finland, in accordance
with the convention of April 13, 1929,
concerning customs supervision in the
Gulf of Finland

Signed Apr. 13, 1929, in Moscow.
Ratified by Finland June 13, 1929; by the
USSR July 3, 1929. Entered into force
Oct. 10, 1929 (1 month after exchange of
acts of ratification, which took place Sept.
10, 1929, in Helsinki). Remains in force
as long as the convention of the same date
(preceding document).
Sources: *SZ*, 1929, II, No. 45, Art. 256
(R, Finnish, Sw.).
SDD, 5, pp. 45–46.
**SS, 1929, No. 32 (R, Finnish).
LNTS, 96, pp. 100–101, 106–107, 114–
15 (R, Finnish, Sw., E, F).
STS, 2, p. 5.

• 29/iv/16/Ger

**Exchange of notes between the USSR and
Germany constituting an agreement concerning reciprocal recognition of tonnage measurement certificates**

Sent Apr. 16, 1929, in Moscow.
Entered into force Apr. 16, 1929.
Sources: *SZ*, 1929, II, No. 26, Art. 148
(R, G).
SDD, 6, pp. 146–47.
*RMbl, No. 27, July 5, 1929, p. 425.
LNTS, 109, pp. 327–31 (E, G, F).
STS, 2, p. 5.

**Apr. 16, 1929. International convention
for the protection of plants**
See 35/ix/26/1929.

• 29/iv/20/Mul

**International convention for suppression
of counterfeiting currency, with protocol**

Signed Apr. 20, 1929, in Geneva.
Ratified by the USSR May 3, 1931; act of
ratification deposited July 13, 1931. Entered into force for the USSR Jan. 17,
1932 (90 days after deposit of act of ratification). Valid for any signatory until 1
year following denunciation.
Protocol includes a declaration by the
USSR that it does not intend to have re-
course to the jurisdiction of the Permanent Court of International Justice.
Sources: *SZ*, 1932, II, No. 6, Art. 62 (R,
F).
SDD, 7, pp. 40–53.
LNTS, 112, pp. 371–93 (E, F).

• 29/v/17/Est/a

**Commercial treaty between the USSR
and Estonia, with final protocol**

Signed May 17, 1929, in Tallinn.
Ratified by Estonia July 26, 1929; by the
USSR Aug. 7, 1929. Entered into force
Sept. 19, 1929 (15 days after exchange of
acts of ratification, which took place Sept.
4, 1929, in Moscow). Duration 3 years;
thereafter until 6 months following de-
nunciation. Supplemented by 2 exchanges
of notes on the same day (next 2 docu-
ments), and by trade agreements of Oct.
31, 1934, and Sept. 28, 1939 (39/ix/28/
Est/b).
Sources: *SZ*, 1929, II, No. 42, Art. 235
(R, F).
SDD, 6, pp. 69–79.
*RT, 1929, No. 71.
LNTS, 94, pp. 323–43 (E, F).
STS, II, pp. 5–9.

• 29/v/17/Est/b

**Exchange of notes between the USSR and
Estonia concerning most-favored-nation
regime in trade treaties**

Sent May 17, 1929, in Tallinn.
Supplements the commercial treaty of the
same date.
Sources: *LNTS*, 94, pp. 342–45 (E, F).
STS, 2, p. 9.

• 29/v/17/Est/c

**Exchange of notes between the USSR
and Estonia concerning certificates of
origin of goods**

Sent May 17, 1929, in Tallinn.
Supplements the commercial treaty of the
same date.
Sources: *LNTS*, 94, pp. 346–47 (E, F).
STS, 2, p. 9.

• 29/v/31/Mul/a

**International convention for the safety
of life at sea, with regulations**

Signed May 31, 1929, in London.
Ratified by the USSR June 3, 1935. Entered into force for the USSR Oct. 2, 1935
(3 months after deposit of act of ratification, which took place July 2, 1935). Duration for each signatory 5 years after
entry into force for that signatory; thereafter until 1 year following denunciation.
Denounced by the USSR by decree of

Sept. 8, 1955, with effect from Oct. 3, 1956, in connection with ratification of the successor convention of June 10, 1948 (54/v/10/1948).
Sources: *SZ*, 1936, II, No. 38, Art. 324 (R, E, F).
SDD, 9, pp. 327–421.
LNTS, 136, pp. 81–205 (E, F).

• 29/v/31/Mul/b

Final Act of the International Conference on Safety of Life at Sea

Signed May 31, 1929, in London.
Supplements the convention of the same date.
Source: *SZ*, 1936, II, No. 38, Art. 324, pp. 928–58, 1048–62 (R, E, F).

• 29/vi/11/Greece

Convention of commerce and navigation between the USSR and Greece

Signed June 11, 1929, in Athens.
Ratified by the USSR June 13, 1930; by Greece Oct. 5, 1929. Entered into force Nov. 17, 1930, on exchange of acts of ratification in Moscow. Duration 1 year; if not denounced 3 months before expiration, valid until 3 months after denunciation. Listed in Korolenko, p. 104, as still valid as of Nov. 25, 1953.
Sources: *SZ*, 1929, II, No. 54, Art. 322 (R, F).
SDD, 6, pp. 45–50.
*Greek official gazette, 1929, A, No. 368.
STS, 2, pp. 9–11.

• 29/vi/28/Mul/a

Universal Postal Convention, with related documents

Signed June 28, 1929, in London.
Ratified by the USSR July 2, 1930; act of ratification deposited July 22, 1930. Entered into force July 1, 1930. Duration indefinite. Supersedes the convention of Aug. 28, 1924; superseded by the convention of Mar. 20, 1934.
Full contents (as given in *LNTS*, 102): text, pp. 252–311; final protocol, pp. 312–27; regulations for execution, pp. 328–413; final protocol to the regulations, pp. 414–21; annexes to the regulations, pp. 424–503; provisions concerning air mail, pp. 504–35; final protocol to the provisions concerning air mail, pp. 534–43; an-

nexes to the provisions concerning air mail, pp. 546–53.
Of the accompanying agreements, the USSR signed only the agreement concerning insured letters and boxes (next document). It did not sign the agreements concerning parcel post, money orders, transfers to and from postal checking accounts, collection of bills and drafts, and newspaper subscriptions.
Sources: *SZ*, 1931, II, No. 1, Art. 1 (R, F).
SDD, 6, pp. 92–145.
LNTS, 102, as listed above (E, F).

• 29/vi/28/Mul/b

Agreement of the Universal Postal Union concerning insured letters and boxes, with related documents

Signed June 28, 1929, in London.
Data on ratification and entry into force same as for the convention of the same date, which it supplements (preceding document). Superseded by agreement of Mar. 20, 1934 (34/iii/20/Mul/b).
Full contents (*LNTS*, 103): text, pp. 10–39; final protocol, pp. 40–47; regulations for execution, pp. 48–65; annexes to the regulations, pp. 68–71.
Sources: *SZ*, 1931, II, No. 1, Art. 1, pp. 310–53 (R, F).
SDD, 6, pp. 136–45.
LNTS, 103, pp. 5–71 (E, F).

July 27, 1929. Geneva Convention for the amelioration of the condition of sick and wounded in armies in the field

See 31/viii/25/1929.

• 29/viii/2/Persia

Parcel post agreement between the USSR and Persia, with supplementary protocol

Signed Aug. 2, 1929, in Moscow.
Ratified by the USSR Oct. 27, 1929. Entered into force Dec. 31, 1929, on exchange of acts of ratification in Moscow. (Date given in *LNTS*, 109, p. 101, as Dec. 13, 1929). Duration 1 year; if not denounced 3 months before expiration, extended indefinitely.
Sources: *SZ*, 1929, II, No. 53, Art. 321 (R, F).
SDD, 6, pp. 80–86.
LNTS, 109, pp. 99–113 (E, F).
STS, 2, p. 11.

● 29/viii/17/J

Exchange of notes between the USSR and Japan constituting an agreement concerning reciprocal recognition of tonnage measurement certificates

Sent Aug. 17, 1929, in Tokyo.
Entered into force Sept. 15, 1929.
Sources: *SZ*, 1929, II, No. 53, Art. 285 (R, F).
   SDD, 6, pp. 148–50.
   STS, 2, pp. 13–14.

● 29/x/3/UK

Protocol between the USSR and the United Kingdom concerning procedure for settlement of outstanding questions

Signed Oct. 3, 1929, in London.
Confirmed by the USSR Oct. 11, 1929; approved by the House of Commons Nov. 5, 1929.
Sources: *SZ*, 1929, II, No. 50, Art. 286 (R, E).
   SDD, 6, pp. 5–6.
   *Cmd. 3418.
   STS, 2, p. 14.
   SDFP, 2, pp. 398–99.

● 29/x/7/Fin

Protocol between the USSR and Finland modifying the postal convention of June 18, 1924, with supplementary protocol

Signed Oct. 7, 1929, in Helsinki.
Ratified by the USSR Oct. 27, 1929. Entered into force Nov. 14, 1929 (15 days after exchange of acts of ratification, which took place Oct. 30, 1929, in Moscow).
Supplementary protocol modifies the supplementary protocol to the 1924 convention (24/vi/18/Fin/b).
Sources: *SZ*, 1929, II, No. 53, Art. 320 (R, Finnish, Sw., F).
   SDD, 6, pp. 87–88.
   SS, 1929, No. 41 (Finnish, F).
   LNTS, 96, pp. 349–63 (R, Finnish, Sw., E, F).
   STS, 2, pp. 14–15.

● 29/x/8/1928

Protocol concerning changes and additions to the International Service Regulations annexed to the International Telegraph Convention of 1875, as revised 1925 in Paris

Signed Sept. 22, 1928, in Brussels.

Ratified by the USSR Oct. 8, 1929, with effect from Oct. 1, 1929. For the 1875 convention, see 25/iv/11/1875. For the International Service Regulations, see 25/x/29/Mul.
Sources: *SZ*, 1929, II, No. 53, Art. 319.
   SDD, 6, pp. 89–92.
   LNTS, 88, pp. 347–52 (E, F).

● 29/x/12/Mul/a

Convention for the unification of certain rules concerning international air transport, with supplementary protocol

Signed Oct. 12, 1929, in Warsaw.
Ratified by the USSR July 7, 1934. Entered into force for the USSR Nov. 18, 1934 (90 days after deposit of act of ratification, which took place Aug. 20, 1934, in Warsaw). Amended by protocol of Sept. 28, 1955.
Sources: *SZ*, 1934, II, No. 20, Art. 176 (R, F).
   SDD, 8, pp. 326–39.
   LNTS, 137, pp. 11–43 (E, F).

● 29/x/12/Mul/b

Final protocol of the Second International Conference on private law affecting air questions

Signed Oct. 12, 1929, in Warsaw.
Supplements the convention of the same date.
Source: *LNTS*, 137, pp. 44–59 (E, F).

● 29/x/19/Af

Exchange of telegrams between the USSR and Afghanistan concerning recognition of a new regime in Afghanistan

Sent Oct. 15, 17, and 19, 1929.
In answer to 2 telegrams from Afghanistan announcing the seizure of power by Marshal Muhammad Nadir Khan, the USSR on Oct. 19 acknowledged receipt of the announcement and declared its willingness to continue and develop good neighborly relations with Afghanistan on the basis of existing agreements.
Sources: *Izv.*, Oct. 20, 1929.
   Sabanin, 1929, pp. 195–96.
   SDFP, 2, pp. 400–401 (Soviet telegram only).

● 29/xii/3/China

Protocol between the USSR and the Mukden Government concerning settlement of the conflict over the Chinese Eastern Railway

Signed Dec. 3, 1929, in Nikol'sk-Ussuriisk.
Superseded by protocol of Dec. 22, 1929.
Sources: *Izv.*, Dec. 4, 1929.
  MZh, 1930, No. 1, p. 116.
  SZ, 1930, II, No. 30, Art. 174 (R, C).
  SDD, 6, pp. 8–9.
  STS, 2, p. 15.
  SDFP, 2, pp. 405–406.

● 29/xii/17/T

Protocol between the USSR and Turkey extending the treaty of friendship and neutrality of December 17, 1925 (Karakhan Protocol)

Signed Dec. 17, 1929, in Ankara.
Ratified by the USSR Jan. 26, 1930; by Turkey Feb. 20, 1930. Entered into force July 28, 1930, on exchange of acts of ratification in Moscow (see 30/vii/28/T). Supplemented by protocol of Mar. 7, 1931. Extended by protocols of Oct. 30, 1931, and Nov. 7, 1935.
Extends the 1925 treaty for 2 years; if not denounced 6 months before expiration, extended for an additional year. Constitutes an integral part of the 1925 treaty, and to have the same duration.
Sources: *SZ*, 1930, II, No. 56, Art. 345 (R, F).
  SDD, 6, pp. 11–13.
  Düstur, 11 (I), p. 132.
  STS, 2, pp. 15–16.

● 29/xii/21/UK

Exchange of notes between the USSR and the United Kingdom and the British Dominions on the occasion of the resumption of diplomatic relations

Sent Dec. 20 and 21, 1929, in London and Moscow.
Incorporates a pledge by the USSR to refrain from hostile propaganda which originally formed part of the General Treaty of Aug. 8, 1924 (unratified; see Appendix 1). The pledge was considered applicable also to the British Dominions— Canada, Australia, New Zealand, Union of South Africa, Irish Free State, and Newfoundland, as well as to the Government of India.
Sources: *Izv.*, Dec. 22, 1929.
  BTS, 1930, No. 2 (Cmd. 3467).
  LNTS, 99, pp. 61–69 (E, F).
  STS, 2, pp. 16–17.

● 29/xii/22/China

Protocol between the USSR and the Mukden Government concerning settlement of the conflict over the Chinese Eastern Railway

Signed Dec. 22, 1929, in Khabarovsk.
Entered into force on signature. Supersedes the protocol of Dec. 3, 1929.
On Feb. 8, 1930, the Foreign Ministry of the central Chinese Government issued a manifesto disavowing provisions of the protocol not directly related to the CER and calling for a Sino-Soviet conference.
Sources: *Izv.*, Dec. 23, 1929.
  MZh, 1930, No. 1, pp. 118–20.
  SZ, 1930, II, No. 30, Art. 175 (R, C).
  SDD, 6, pp. 9–11.
  STS, 2, pp. 17–18.
  SDFP, 2, pp. 434–36.

1930

● 30/i/20/Est

Agreement between the USSR and Estonia concerning legal aid in civil cases, with final protocol

Signed Jan. 20, 1930, in Tallinn.
Ratified by the USSR Feb. 16, 1930; by Estonia Apr. 9, 1930. Entered into force June 28, 1930 (1 month after exchange of acts of ratification, which took place May 28, 1930, in Moscow). Duration 5 years; thereafter until 1 year following denunciation. Amended by exchange of notes dated Dec. 22, 1930, and Jan. 8, 1931 (31/i/8/Est).
Sources: *SZ*, 1930, II, No. 38, Art. 215 (R, F).
  SDD, 6, pp. 15–18.
  RT, 1930, No. 33.
  LNTS, 103, pp. 225–31 (E, F).
  STS, 2, pp. 18–19.

● 30/iii/21/Italy

Exchange of notes between the USSR and Italy constituting an agreement concerning exemption of certificates of origin from consular visas

Sent Mar. 21, 1930, in Moscow.
Entered into force May 15, 1930, under exchange of notes of Sept. 11, 1931. Modified by exchanges of notes of June 2, 1931, and of Aug. 7, Sept. 20, and Oct. 23, 1932 (32/x/23/Italy).

Sources: *SZ*, 1930, II, No. 32, Art. 183 (R, F).
　　SDD, 6, pp. 50–52.
　　*TC, 41, p. 343.
　　STS, 2, pp. 19–20.

● 30/iv/16/UK

Temporary commercial agreement between the USSR and the United Kingdom, with related documents

Signed Apr. 16, 1930, in London.
Entered into force on signature. Valid until replaced by a commercial treaty, or until 6 months after denunciation. Extended to certain British colonies by exchange of notes dated Dec. 1, 1930, and Jan. 19, 1931 (31/i/19/UK). Denounced by the United Kingdom Oct. 17, 1932, with effect from Apr. 16, 1933.
Related documents: protocol; supplementary protocol; declaration by the British Government excluding the Union of South Africa and the Irish Free State from provisions of the agreement; and declaration by the USSR concerning vessels of the former Russian fleet.
Sources: *SZ*, 1930, II, No. 56, Art. 346 (R, E).
　　SDD, 6, pp. 37–43.
　　*BTS, 1930, No. 19, Cmd. 3352.
　　*BFSP, 132, p. 125.
　　LNTS, 101, pp. 409–21 (E, F).
　　STS, 2, pp. 20–21.

● 30/v/19/Lith

Exchange of notes between the USSR and Lithuania concerning reciprocal recognition of trade-marks

Sent May 17 and 19, 1930, in Kaunas.
Entered into force May 19, 1930.
Sources: **VŽ*, No. 329, Art. 2258.
　　STS, 2, p. 22, citing
　　　LS, 2, pp. 34–37.

● 30/v/20/MPR

Agreement between the USSR and the Mongolian People's Republic concerning questions of citizenship

Signed May 20, 1930.
Expired Feb. 28, 1934. Mentioned in and replaced by the agreement of Apr. 24, 1937.

● 30/v/22/UK

Temporary agreement between the USSR and the United Kingdom concerning

regulation of the fisheries in waters contiguous to the northern coasts of the USSR, with two protocols

Signed May 22, 1930, in London.
Entered into force on signature. Valid until replaced by a formal convention, or until 6 months after denunciation. Denounced by the USSR Jan. 5, 1953, but extended for 1 year by note of June 24, 1953.
Sources: *SZ*, 1930, II, No. 56, Art. 347 (R, E).
　　SDD, 6, pp. 43–45.
　　*BTS, 1930, No. 22, Cmd. 3583.
　　*BFSP, 132, p. 332.
　　LNTS, 102, pp. 103–107 (E, F).
　　STS, 2, p. 22.

● 30/vi/　/MPR/a

Agreement between the USSR and the Mongolian People's Republic concerning sanitation

Probably signed during June 1930, in Ulan Bator.
Ratified by the USSR.
Reference: *SUR*, Nov. 1930, p. 174.

● 30/vi/　/MPR/b

Agreement between the USSR and the Mongolian People's Republic concerning eradication of animal diseases

Probably signed during June 1930, in Ulan Bator
Ratified by the USSR.
Reference: *SUR*, Nov. 1930, p. 174.

● 30/vi/　/MPR/c

Agreement between the USSR and the Mongolian People's Republic concerning border crossing

Probably signed during June 1930, in Ulan Bator.
Ratified by the USSR.
Reference: *SUR*, Nov. 1930, p. 174.

June 7, 1930

(1) Convention providing a uniform law for bills of exchange and promissory notes; see 36/xi/25/1930/a.
(2) Convention concerning settlement of certain conflicts of laws in connection with bills of exchange and promissory notes; see 36/xi/25/1930/b.
(3) Convention concerning stamp laws in

connection with bills of exchange and promissory notes; see 36/xi/25/1930/c.

● 30/vi/13/Ger

Joint statement by the USSR and Germany concerning mutual relations

Issued June 13, 1930.
Sources: *SUR*, 8, 1930, No. 7–8, p. 111.
SDFP, 2, p. 440.
Reference: Hilger and Meyer, pp. 233–35.

● 30/vi/28/MPR. See Appendix 5.

June 28, 1930. Convention on forced labor
See 56/vi/4/1930.

● 30/vii/5/Mul/a

International Load Line Convention, with final protocol and four annexes

Signed July 5, 1930, in London.
Ratified by the USSR May 17, 1932. Entered into force for the USSR Jan. 1, 1933 (3 months after deposit of act of ratification, which took place Oct. 1, 1932). Duration 5 years; thereafter until 1 year following denunciation.
Sources: *SZ*, 1933, II, No. 15, Art. 150 (R, E, F).
SDD, 7, pp. 124–86.
UST, No. 858.
LNTS, 135, pp. 303–423 (E, F).

● 30/vii/5/Mul/b

Final Act of the international conference on load lines

Signed July 5, 1930, in London.
Supplements the convention of the same date.
Sources: *SZ*, 1933, II, No. 15, Art. 150, pp. 156–83, 260–74 (R, E, F).
SDD, 6, pp. 186–98.

● 30/vii/26/Italy

Exchange of notes between the USSR and Italy concerning immunity of property belonging to a foreign state

Sent July 26, 1930, in Rome.
Sources: *SZ*, 1930, II, No. 56, Art. 348 (R, I).
SDD, 6, pp. 14–15.
*TC, 42, p. 259.
STS, 2, p. 23.
SDFP, 2, pp. 451–52.
BFSP, 132, p. 713.

● 30/vii/28/T

Protocol between the USSR and Turkey concerning exchange of acts of ratification of the protocol of December 17, 1929, extending the treaty of friendship and neutrality of December 17, 1925

Signed July 28, 1930, in Moscow.
Sources: *SZ*, 1930, II, No. 56, Art. 345, pp. 950–51 (R, F).
SDD, 6, pp. 12–13.
LNTS, 157, pp. 362–63 (E, F).
STS, 2, p. 23.

● 30/viii/1/Mul

Convention concerning anti-diphtheria serum

Signed Aug. 1, 1930, in Paris.
Ratified by the USSR June 15, 1931. Entered into force for the USSR Apr. 1, 1932 (4 months after deposit of act of ratification, which took place Nov. 30, 1931, in Paris). Valid for each signatory until 1 year following denunciation.
Under a protocol of July 22, 1946 (46/vii/22/Mul/d), the duties and functions conferred by this convention on the Office Internationale d'Hygiène Publique were transferred to the World Health Organization or its Interim Commission.
Sources: *SZ*, 1932, II, No. 8, Art. 84 (R, F).
SDD, 7, pp. 199–203.
LNTS, 128, pp. 9–19 (E, F).

● 30/viii/2/Italy

Credit agreement between the USSR and Italy, with three annexes

Signed Aug. 2, 1930, in Rome.
Entered into force July 1, 1930; valid to June 30, 1931; thereafter extended from year to year, until denounced 3 months before expiration. Superseded by agreement of Apr. 27, 1931.
Sources: *TC, 42, pp. 277–83.
STS, 2, p. 24.

● 30/x/3/T

Joint communiqué by the USSR and Turkey reaffirming friendship

Issued Oct. 3, 1930.
Source: *SDFP*, 2, pp. 456–57, citing *MP*, 1930, p. 241.

Oct. 23, 1930
(1) Agreement concerning manned lightships not on their stations; see 31/iv/27/1930/a.
(2) Agreement concerning maritime signals; see 31/iv/27/1930/b.

● 30/xii/25/T

Exchange of notes between the USSR and Turkey concerning provisions for visits of warships

Sent Nov. 25 and Dec. 25, 1930, in Ankara.
Entered into force Dec. 25, 1930.
Sources: *SZ*, 1931, II, No. 4, Art. 53 (R, F).
  SDD, 7, pp. 19–20.
  STS, 2, pp. 24–25.
  SDFP, 2, pp. 461–62.

1931

● 31/i/8/Est

Exchange of notes between the USSR and Estonia modifying the agreement of January 20, 1930, concerning legal aid in civil cases

Sent Dec. 22, 1930, and Jan. 8, 1931, in Tallinn.
Entered into force Jan. 8, 1931. Provides for modifications in accordance with Soviet administrative abolition of guberniia and okrug courts.
Sources: *SZ*, 1931, II, No. 9, Art. 116 (R, Est.).
  SDD, 7, pp. 39–40.
  STS, 2, p. 26.

● 31/i/14/Lat

Exchange of notes between the USSR and Latvia modifying the agreement of June 2, 1927, concerning legal aid in civil cases

Sent Dec. 17, 1930, and Jan. 14, 1931, in Riga.
Entered into force Jan. 14, 1931. For background see 31/i/8/Est.
Sources: *SZ*, 1931, II, No. 9, Art. 115 (R, Lat.).
  SDD, 7, pp. 38–39.
  STS, 2, pp. 25–26.

● 31/i/19/UK

Exchange of notes between the USSR and the United Kingdom extending the temporary commercial agreement of April 16, 1930, to certain British colonies

Sent Dec. 1, 1930, and Jan. 19, 1931, in Moscow.
Entered into force Dec. 1, 1930. Agreement extended to the following colonies: Bermuda, British Guiana, Falkland Islands, Jamaica, Malta, Seychelles, Trinidad and Tobago, and Windward Islands.

Sources: *SZ*, 1931, II, No. 4, Art. 52 (E, R).
  LNTS, 107, pp. 548–51 (E, R, F).
  STS, 2, p. 25.

● 31/ii/28/MPR

Exchange of notes between the USSR and the Mongolian People's Republic constituting an agreement concerning questions relating to extradition of criminals

Sent Feb. 28, 1931.
Mentioned in an exchange of notes of Aug. 25, 1958, between the USSR and the MPR, as being superseded by the treaty of the same date concerning reciprocal legal aid in civil, family and marriage, and criminal cases (*VVS*, 1958, No. 35, Art. 424, p. 956).

● 31/iii/7/T

Protocol between the USSR and Turkey concerning naval armament in the Black Sea, with protocol of signature

Signed Mar. 7, 1931, in Ankara.
Ratified by the USSR May 23, 1931; by Turkey July 22, 1931. Entered into force Aug. 10, 1931 (*SDD*, 8, p. 20; according to *LNTS*, 157, p. 365, the Turkish Government had requested entry into force from date of Turkish ratification). Supplements Art. 2 of the protocol of Dec. 17, 1929, extending the treaty of friendship and neutrality of Dec. 17, 1925, and on ratification becomes an integral part of that protocol. Extended by protocols of Oct. 30, 1931 (31/x/30/T/b), and Nov. 7, 1935.
Sources: *SZ*, 1931, II, No. 16, Art. 232 (R, F).
  SDD, 8, p. 20.
  LNTS, 157, pp. 365–67 (E, F).
  STS, 2, p. 27.

● 31/iii/16/T

Treaty of commerce and navigation between the USSR and Turkey, with final protocol

Signed Mar. 16, 1931, in Moscow.
Ratified by Turkey July 22, 1931; by the USSR Aug. 3, 1931. Entered into force Sept. 9, 1931. Acts of ratification exchanged Sept. 15, 1931, in Ankara. (Treaty provides for entry into force 1 month after exchange of acts of ratification, but according to *SDD*, 7, p. 107, the earlier date was agreed upon.) Duration 1 year; thereafter until 6 months after denunciation. Supplemented by trade agreement of Apr. 17, 1932. Expired Jan. 1, 1937, but prolonged by mutual agreement until conclusion of the treaty of commerce and navigation of Oct. 8, 1937 (*Pr.*, Oct. 11, 1937). Supersedes the treaty of Mar. 11, 1927.
Sources: *SZ*, 1931, II, No. 18, Art. 247 (R, F).
  SDD, 7, pp. 95–107.
  *RG, No. 1865, Aug. 5, 1931.
  STS, 2, pp. 27–31.
  SDFP, 2, pp. 479–90.

● 31/iii/20/Ger

Exchange of notes between the USSR and Germany amending the agreement of October 12, 1925, concerning legal aid in civil cases

Sent Feb. 7 and Mar. 20, 1931, in Berlin. Entered into force Mar. 20, 1931. For background see 31/i/8/Est. For the 1925 agreement, see 25/x/12/Ger/c.
Sources: *SZ*, 1931, II, No. 9, Art. 114 (R, G).
  SDD, 7, pp. 37–38.
  STS, 2, pp. 26–27.

● 31/iii/24/J

Agreement between the USSR and Japan concerning a provisional rate for payments by Japanese firms for lease of fishing lots

Negotiated Apr. 24, 1931.
In Soviet interpretation, no longer valid from Mar. 2, 1934 (see *Izv.*, Mar. 9, 1934; *SDFP*, 3, pp. 76–77).
Reference: *Izv.*, Apr. 28, 1931.

Mar. 28, 1931. Agreement concerning procedure in case of undischarged or lost triptychs

See 35/ix/6/1931.

Mar. 30, 1931. (1) Convention concerning unification of road signals
See 36/i/23/1931.

(2) Convention concerning taxation of foreign motor vehicles
See 35/vii/23/1931.

● 31/iv/16/MPR

Agreement between the USSR and the Mongolian People's Republic concerning execution of judgments in civil cases

Date of signing unknown; entered into force Apr. 16, 1931.
Reference: *Yezhenedel'nik sovetskoi yustitsii*, 1931, No. 14, p. 31, cited in *AJIL*, 31, pp. 63–65.

● 31/iv/27/Italy

Credit agreement between the USSR and Italy, with two annexes

Signed Apr. 27, 1931, in Rome.
Duration 1 year (1931); thereafter extended for 1 year, unless denounced 3 months before expiration. Supersedes agreement of Aug. 2, 1930; superseded by agreement of May 6, 1933 (33/v/6/Italy/b).
Sources: *SUR*, May 1931, p. 116.
  *TC, 43, pp. 167–72.
  STS, 2, p. 32.
Reference: *SDFP*, 2, pp. 495–97 (summary).

● 31/iv/27/1930/a

Agreement concerning manned lightships not on their stations, with regulations

Signed Oct. 23, 1930, in Lisbon.
Signed by the USSR Apr. 27, 1931, without reservation as to the necessity for subsequent ratification. Entered into force for the USSR July 26, 1931 (90 days after signature). Duration 7 years; thereafter until 1 year following denunciation.
Sources: *SZ*, 1931, II, No. 20, Art. 270 (R, E, F).
  SDD, 7, pp. 113–17.
  LNTS, 112, pp. 22–28 (E, F).

● 31/iv/27/1930/b

Agreement concerning maritime signals, with regulations

Signed Oct. 23, 1930, in Lisbon.
Signed by the USSR Apr. 27, 1931, without reservation as to the necessity for subsequent ratification. Entered into force for the USSR Nov. 22, 1931 (date of general entry into force). Duration 7 years; thereafter until 1 year following denunciation for each signatory.
Sources: *SZ*, 1931, II, No. 21, Art. 272 (R, E, F).
  SDD, 7, pp. 117–24.
  LNTS, 125, pp. 95–111 (E, F).

● 31/v/6/Lith

Protocol between the USSR and Lithuania extending for five years the treaty of nonaggression of September 28, 1926

Signed May 6, 1931, in Moscow.
Ratified by the USSR June 23, 1931. Entered into force Aug. 29, 1931, on exchange of acts of ratification in Kaunas. Extends the 1926 treaty for 5 years; if not denounced 6 months before expiration, extended for 1-year periods. For further extension, see 34/iv/4/Lith.
Sources: *SZ*, 1931, II, No. 16, Art. 231 (R, Lith.).
  SDD, 7, pp. 11–12.
  *VŽ, 1931, No. 371, Art. 2536.
  *LS, 2, pp. 181–83.
  LNTS, 125, pp. 255–63 (R, Lith., E, F).
  STS, 2, pp. 32–33.

● 31/vi/2/Italy

Exchange of notes between the USSR and Italy modifying the agreement of March 21, 1930, concerning certificates of origin

Sent June 2, 1931, in Moscow.
Entered into force June 2, 1931. Agreement further modified by exchange of notes of Aug. 7, Sept. 20, and Oct. 23, 1932 (32/x/23/Italy).
Sources: *SZ*, 1931, II, No. 20, Art. 271 (R, F).
  SDD, 7, pp. 68–69.
  *TC, 43, p. 311.
  STS, 2, p. 33.

● 31/vi/13/T

Agreement between the USSR and Turkey concerning direct rail communications

Signed June 13, 1931, in Ankara.
Reference: *ERSU*, July 15, 1931, p. 334.

● 31/vi/24/Af

Treaty of neutrality and nonaggression between the USSR and Afghanistan

Signed June 24, 1931, in Kabul.
Soviet decree of ratification dated Sept. 5, 1931. Entered into force Oct. 15, 1931, on exchange of acts of ratification in Kabul. Duration 5 years; thereafter until 6 months following denunciation. Extended for 10 years by protocol of Mar. 29, 1936; re-extended for 10 years by protocol of Dec. 18, 1955 (55/xii/18/Af/a).
Sources: *SZ*, 1932, II, No. 5, Art. 61 (R, Persian).
  SDD, 7, pp. 3–5.
  LNTS, 157, pp. 372–81 (R, Persian, E, F).
  STS, 2, pp. 33–34.

● 31/vi/24/Ger

Protocol between the USSR and Germany extending the treaty of neutrality and nonaggression of April 24, 1926, and the convention of January 25, 1929, concerning conciliation procedure

Signed June 24, 1931, in Moscow.
Ratified by the USSR Apr. 29, 1933; by Germany May 5, 1933. Acts of ratification exchanged May 5, 1933, in Moscow. Extends the 1926 treaty until June 30, 1933, thereafter until 1 year following denunciation. Validity of the 1929 convention to extend as long as the 1926 treaty.
Sources: *SZ*, 1933, II, No. 12, Art. 134 (R, G).
  SDD, 8, pp. 7–8.
  *RGbl, 1933, II, No. 21, p. 311.
  LNTS, 157, pp. 383–91 (R, G, E, F).
  STS, 2, p. 34.

July 13, 1931. Convention for limiting the manufacture and regulating the distribution of narcotic drugs

See 35/x/31/1931 and 46/xii/11/Mul.

● 31/vii/17/Greece

Exchange of notes between the USSR and Greece constituting an agreement concerning reciprocal recognition of trade and commercial marks

Sent July 14 and 17, 1931, in Athens.
Ratified by Greece July 22, 1931. Entered into force July 17, 1931.
Sources: **Greek official gazette, 1931, A, No. 264.

STS, 2, p. 34, citing
  BL, 47, Nov. 1931, pp. 1813–14.
Reference: *ERSU*, Dec. 1, 1931, p. 544.

● 31/viii/25/1929

Geneva Convention for the amelioration of the condition of the wounded and sick in armies in the field

Signed July 27, 1929, in Geneva.
The USSR adhered by declaration of Aug. 25, 1931; in accordance with a decree of May 12, 1930, the declaration was final and did not require ratification. Entered into force for the USSR Mar. 26, 1932 (6 months after deposit of declaration of adherence, Sept. 29, 1931).
Supersedes the conventions of Aug. 22, 1864, and July 6, 1906 (see 18/vi/4/1906 and 25/vi/16/1906). Superseded by convention of Aug. 12, 1949 (see 49/xii/12/1949/a).
Sources: *SZ*, 1932, II, No. 4, Art. 60.
  SDD, 7, pp. 204–20.
  LNTS, 118, pp. 303–41 (E, F).

● 31/viii/29/Lith

Protocol between the USSR and Lithuania concerning the legal status of the Soviet Trade Mission in Lithuania, with two exchanges of notes

Signed Aug. 29, 1931, in Kaunas.
Entered into force on signature. Valid until 6 months after denunciation. Exchanges of notes concern transit through Lithuania and most-favored-nation treatment with regard to such transit.
Sources: *SZ*, 1932, II, No. 10, Art. 105 (R, Lith.).
  SDD, 7, pp. 71–75.
  VŽ, 1931, No. 366, Art. 2499.
  LS, 2, pp. 191–96.
  STS, 2, p. 35.

● 31/ix/11/Italy

Exchange of notes between the USSR and Italy concerning entry into force of the agreement of March 21, 1930, concerning certificates of origin

Sent Sept. 11, 1931, in Moscow.
Establishes May 15, 1930, as date of entry into force of the 1930 agreement.
Sources: *SZ*, 1931, II, No. 20, Art. 271 (R, F).
  SDD, 7, pp. 69–70.
  TC, 43, p. 465.
  STS, 2, p. 36.

● 31/x/1/Sinkiang

Provisional trade agreement between the USSR and Sinkiang, with four annexes

Signed Oct. 1, 1931, in Tihwa (Urumchi), Sinkiang.
Entered into force on signature.
History: Signed on behalf of the Provisional Government of Sinkiang without the knowledge or approval of the central Chinese Government. Contents revealed in June 1933, after the downfall of Gen. Chin Shu-jen, Governor of Sinkiang; the agreement was thereupon declared null and void by the central Government in Nanking. For a suggestion that the agreement may have been accompanied by secret annexes concerning Soviet military assistance to Sinkiang, see Whiting, pp. 9–10.
Sources and references: Wu, pp. 376–79.
  STS, 2, pp. 36–37, citing Wu, *loc. cit.*, and
    Journal of the Royal Central Asian Society, Oct. 20, 1933, pp. 541–42.
  North-China Herald, Sept. 20, 1933, p. 452 (gives date as Oct. 31, 1931).
  SDFP, 2, pp. 507–10.
Chinese sources:
  The Soviet Union's economic invasion of Sinkiang, pp. 26–29.
  Records of an inspection tour in Sinkiang, pp. 81–87 (cited in Wei, p. 126).

● 31/x/22/Est

Protocol between the USSR and Estonia modifying the protocol to the agreement of August 8, 1927, concerning procedure for settlement of border disputes

Signed Oct. 22, 1931, in Tallinn.
Ratified by the USSR Dec. 7, 1931; by Estonia Dec. 18, 1931. Entered into force May 26, 1932, on exchange of acts of ratification in Moscow.
Sources: *SZ*, 1932, II, No. 15, Art. 159 (R, Est.).
  SDD, 7, pp. 62–64.
  RT, 1931, No. 112.
  LNTS, 122, pp. 349–54 (R, Est., E, F).
  STS, 2, p. 37.

● 31/x/27/Persia

Convention between the USSR and Persia concerning settlement, commerce, and navigation, with related documents

Signed Oct. 27, 1931, in Teheran.
Ratified by Persia Mar. 1, 1932; by the

USSR Mar. 15, 1932. Entered into force
June 22, 1932, on exchange of acts of ratification in Moscow. Duration 3 years.
Modified by exchange of notes of Dec. 11,
1933.
Related documents: final protocol; annex; and 11 exchanges of notes concerning (1) concessions; (2) representation
of Soviet economic organizations in Persian courts; (3) price of petroleum products and derivatives; (4) export of car-
pets; (5) contracts with Soviet economic
organizations; (6) import of opium and
its derivatives; (7) use of the Caspian Sea
by nationals of third countries; (8) ownership of former Russian commercial and
naval vessels; (9) lease by the USSR of
land in the port of Bandar Shah; (10)
maintenance of border roads; and (11)
construction of a bridge and other installations in Pehlevi.
Sources: *SZ*, 1932, II, No. 17, Art. 186
    (R, F).
    SDD, 7, pp. 75–95.
    Childs, pp. 211–47.
    STS, 2, pp. 37–45.

● 31/x/30/T/a

**Communiqué concerning negotiations
between the USSR and Turkey**

Issued Oct. 30, 1931.
Sources: *Izv.*, Nov. 2, 1931.
    SDFP, 2, p. 513.

● 31/x/30/T/b

**Protocol between the USSR and Turkey
extending the treaty of friendship and
neutrality of December 17, 1925, and
related protocols**

Signed Oct. 30, 1931, in Ankara.
Ratified by the USSR Jan. 3, 1932; by
Turkey June 25, 1932. Entered into force
July 21, 1932, on exchange of notes concerning ratification in Ankara. In addition to the 1925 treaty, extends the protocols of Dec. 17, 1929, and Mar. 7, 1931,
5 years from date of expiration; thereafter if not denounced 6 months before expiration, extended for an additional year.
Further extended by protocol of Nov. 7,
1935.
Sources: *SZ*, 1932, II, No. 19, Art. 209 (R,
    F).
    SDD, 7, pp. 20–21.
    Düstur, 13, p. 732.

LNTS, 157, pp. 366–69.
STS, 2, p. 45.

● 31/xi/23/J/a

**Parcel post agreement between the USSR
and Japan**

Signed Nov. 23, 1931, in Moscow.
Ratified by the USSR May 17, 1932; by
Japan June 6, 1932. Entered into force
Aug. 25, 1932 (1 month after exchange of
acts of ratification, which took place July
25, 1932, in Tokyo). Valid until 3 months
after denunciation. Supplemented by
Regulations of the same date (next docu-
ment).
Sources: *SZ*, 1932, II, No. 19, Art. 208
    (R, F).
    SDD, 7, pp. 108–12.
    CDT, No. 177.
    LNTS, 132, pp. 133–41 (E, F).
    STS, 2, pp. 45–46.

● 31/xi/23/J/b

**Regulations for execution of the parcel
post agreement of November 23, 1931,
between the USSR and Japan**

Signed Nov. 23, 1931, in Moscow.
Entry into force and validity the same as
those for the agreement of the same date.
Source: *LNTS*, 132, pp. 142–45 (E, F).

● 31/xii/22/Ger/a

**Joint statement by the USSR and Ger-
many concerning development of economic relations**

Issued Dec. 22, 1931.
Sources: *Izv.*, Dec. 24, 1931.
    SDFP, 2, p. 521.

● 31/xii/22/Ger/b

**Protocol between the USSR and Ger-
many concerning development of economic relations**

Signed Dec. 22, 1931, in Berlin.
Entered into force May 7, 1932, on exchange of notes for this purpose (not
listed separately).
References: *Izv.*, Dec. 24, 1931.
    STS, 2, p. 46 (summary), citing *Izv.*,
        loc. cit., and
        Private sources.

1932

● 32/i/21/Fin

Treaty between the USSR and Finland concerning nonaggression and the peaceful settlement of disputes, with protocol of signature

Signed Jan. 21, 1932, in Helsinki.
Ratified by the USSR July 11, 1932. Entered into force Aug. 9, 1932, on exchange of acts of ratification in Moscow. Duration 3 years; if not denounced 6 months before expiration, renewed for an additional 2 years. Extended to Dec. 31, 1945, by protocol of Apr. 7, 1934. Supplemented by convention on conciliation procedure of Apr. 22, 1932.
Under the protocol of signature, signatories agree that denunciation of the treaty shall "neither cancel nor restrict the undertakings arising from the Pact for the renunciation of war signed at Paris on Aug. 27, 1928." Denounced by the USSR Nov. 28, 1939 (text of Soviet denunciation in *SDFP*, 3, pp. 402–403).
Sources: *SZ*, 1932, II, No. 23, Art. 250, pp. 314–18 (R, F).
   SDD, 7, pp. 21–24.
   SS, 1932, No. 13, (F, Finnish).
   LNTS, 157, pp. 393–99 (E, F).
   STS, 2, pp. 46–47.

● 32/ii/5/Lat

Treaty of nonaggression between the USSR and Latvia

Signed Feb. 5, 1932, in Riga.
Ratified by the USSR July 11, 1932. Entered into force July 28, 1932, on exchange of acts of ratification in Moscow. Duration 3 years; may be denounced 6 months before expiration by either party, or without notice if the other party commits an aggression upon any third state. If not denounced, automatically extended for 2-year periods. Extended to Dec. 31, 1945, by protocol of Apr. 4, 1934. Supplemented by convention concerning conciliation procedure of June 18, 1932. Reaffirmed by pact of mutual assistance of Oct. 5, 1939.
Sources: *SZ*, 1932, II. No. 23, Art. 248 (R, Lat.).
   SDD, 7, pp. 6–8.
   LRR, pp. 170–71.

LNTS, 148, pp. 114–19, 122–25 (R, Lat., E, F).
STS, 2 pp. 47–48.

● 32/iii/12/Norway. See Appendix 5.

● 32/iv/3/Af/a, b. See Appendix 5.

● 32/iv/10/Pol

Agreement between the USSR and Poland concerning legal relations in the border zone, with related documents

Signed Apr. 10, 1932, in Moscow.
Ratified by the USSR July 17, 1933; by Poland July 25, 1933. Entered into force Oct. 4, 1933 (30 days after exchange of acts of ratification, which took place Sept. 4, 1933, in Warsaw). Duration 5 years; if not denounced 6 months before expiration, extended for further 5-year periods. Contents (*LNTS*, 141): Text, pp. 350–67, 408–23; final protocol, pp. 366–69, 422–25; Annex 1, General final protocol of July 31, 1924, of the Mixed Soviet-Polish Border Demarcation Commission, pp. 370–99, 426–59; annexes to the General final protocol (protocols of the commission, maps and sketches; listed but not reproduced), pp. 398–401, 460–61; Annex 2, Agreement of Aug. 3, 1925, concerning settlement of border conflicts, pp. 400–407, 462–67.
Sources: *SZ*, 1933, II, No. 26, Art. 245 (R, P).
   SDD, 8, pp. 49–78.
   DURP, 1933, No. 73, Arts. 541, 542.
   LNTS, 141, pp. 349–417 (R, P, E, F).
   STS, 2, pp. 48–51.

● 32/iv/17/T

Trade agreement between the USSR and Turkey

Signed Apr. 17, 1932.
Supplements the treaty of commerce and navigation of Mar. 16, 1931. According to Korolenko, p. 53, twice extended, expiring on Jan. 1, 1937, together with the treaty of 1931. Dates of extension not known; possibly Korolenko refers to the trade agreements of June 29, 1934, and June 24, 1935.
References: Korolenko, *loc. cit.*
   Smirnov, p. 80.

● 32/iv/22/Est

Agreement between the USSR and Estonia concerning direct freight shipments to and from Leningrad and transit through Estonia

Negotiated at a conference in Leningrad which ended Apr. 22, 1932.
Enters into force on ratification.
Reference: *ERSU*, May 15, 1932, p. 238.

● 32/iv/22/Fin

Convention between the USSR and Finland concerning conciliation procedure

Signed Apr. 22, 1932, in Helsinki.
Ratified by the USSR July 11, 1932. Entered into force Aug. 9, 1932, on exchange of acts of ratification in Moscow. Becomes an integral part of the treaty of nonaggression of Jan. 21, 1932; duration the same.
Sources: *SZ*, 1932, II, No. 23, Art. 250, pp. 319–25 (R, F).
SDD, 7, pp. 24–27.
SS, 1932, No. 13 (Finnish, F).
LNTS, 157, pp. 401–409 (E, F).
STS, 2, pp. 51–52.

● 32/v/3/Ger

Agreement between the USSR and Germany concerning grain

Signed May 3, 1932, in Berlin.
Entered into force on signature. On the same day an agreement was signed between the Soviet Trade Mission in Germany and the German Reichsbank concerning use of the Reichsmark in all trade between Germany and the USSR and establishing a legal exchange rate (see Appendix 3).
Reference: *VVerz.*, p. 353.

● 32/v/4/Est

Treaty between the USSR and Estonia concerning nonaggression and the peaceful settlement of disputes

Signed May 4, 1932, in Moscow.
Ratified by Estonia, July 29, 1932; by the USSR Aug. 5, 1932. Entered into force Aug. 18, 1932, on exchange of acts of ratification in Tallinn. Duration 3 years; may be denounced 6 months before expiration, or by either party at any time without notice in the event of an act of aggression by the other party

against any third State. If not denounced, extended indefinitely for 2-year periods. Extended to Dec. 31, 1945, by protocol of April 4, 1934. Supplemented by convention of June 16, 1932, concerning conciliation procedure. Reaffirmed by pact of mutual assistance of Sept. 28, 1939.
Sources: *SZ*, 1932, II, No. 23, Art. 251, pp. 325–29 (R, Est.).
SDD, 7, pp. 32–34.
RT, 1932, No. 62.
LNTS, 131, pp. 297–307 (R, Est., E, F).
STS, 2, pp. 52–53.

● 32/v/8/T

Informal agreement between the USSR and Turkey concerning a Soviet long-term credit to Turkey of eight million dollars

Announced May 8, 1932, in a TASS communiqué concerning the visit to Moscow of the Turkish premier and foreign minister.
Also mentioned in the communiqué were continuation of close political collaboration and strengthening of economic and cultural intercourse between the 2 States. For a protocol embodying the agreement on credit, see 34/i/21/T.
References: *Izv.*, May 8, 1932.
SDFP, 2, pp. 531–32.
Smirnov, pp. 80–81.

● 32/v/28/Ger

Protocol between the USSR and Germany concerning customs duties and reciprocal recognition of certificates of origin, with annex

Signed May 28, 1932, in Berlin.
Entered into force provisionally June 10, 1932, under an exchange of notes of the same date (not listed separately). Valid until Mar. 11, 1933; if not denounced 6 months before expiration, extended for 6-month periods until denounced with 6 months' notice. Annex lists goods and applicable customs duties.
Sources: *SZ*, 1932, II, No. 20, Art. 211 (misnumbered 209; R, G).
QR, July–Sept. 1932, pp. 29–31.
SDD, 7, pp. 65–67.
RGBl, 1932, II, No. 15, p. 143.
STS, 2, p. 53 (omits the annex).

• 32/vi/16/Est

Convention between the USSR and Estonia concerning conciliation procedure

Signed June 16, 1932, in Moscow.
Ratified by the USSR Aug. 5, 1932; by Estonia July 29, 1932. Entered into force Aug. 18, 1932, on exchange of acts of ratification in Tallinn. Becomes an integral part of the treaty of nonaggression of May 4, 1932; duration the same.
Sources: *SZ*, 1932, II, No. 23, Art. 251, pp. 329–33 (R, Est.).
  SDD, 7, pp. 34–36.
  *RT, 1932, No. 62.
  LNTS, 131, pp. 310–21 (R, Est., E, F).
  STS, 2, p. 54.

• 32/vi/17/Fin

Agreement between the USSR and Finland concerning navigation in the Gulf of Finland

Signed June 17, 1932, in Helsinki.
Possibly not formalized in a written document: *Pravda*, June 18, 1932, states that "agreement was reached" at a Soviet-Finnish maritime conference which ended on June 17, 1932, on a number of "very important matters concerning navigation between Finland and Leningrad and on communications in winter between the islands of the Gulf of Finland and the mainland."
Reference: *Pravda, loc. cit.*

• 32/vi/18/Lat

Convention between the USSR and Latvia concerning conciliation procedure

Signed June 18, 1932, in Riga.
Ratified by the USSR July 11, 1932. Entered into force July 28, 1932, on exchange of acts of ratification in Moscow. Becomes an integral part of the treaty of nonaggression of Feb. 5, 1932; duration the same.
Sources: *SZ*, 1932, II, No. 23, Art. 249 (R, Lat.).
  SDD, 7, pp. 8–11.
  LRR, pp. 172–75.
  LNTS, 148, pp. 130–43 (R, Lat., E, F).
  STS, 2, pp. 54–55.

• 32/vii/25/Pol

Treaty of nonaggression between the USSR and Poland, with two protocols of signature

Signed July 25, 1932, in Moscow.

Ratified by Poland Nov. 26, 1932; by the USSR Nov. 27, 1932. Entered into force Dec. 23, 1932, on exchange of acts of ratification in Warsaw. Duration 3 years; if not denounced 6 months before expiration, extended for 2 years. Supplemented by convention concerning conciliation procedure of Nov. 23, 1932. Extended to Dec. 31, 1945, by protocol of May 5, 1934. Re-affirmed by exchange of notes of Sept. 10, 1934, and by joint communiqué of Nov. 26, 1938.
First protocol of signature declares that expiration or denunciation of this treaty would not limit or cancel the obligations of the signatories arising under the General Treaty of Aug. 27, 1928, for the renunciation of war as an instrument of national policy. Second protocol of signature concerns draft of a convention on conciliation procedure (see 32/xi/23/Pol).
Sources: *SZ*, 1933, II, No. 6, Art. 98 (R, P).
  SDD, 7, pp. 12–15.
  *DURP, 1932, No. 115, Arts. 951, 952.
  LNTS, 136, pp. 41–53 (R, P, E, F).
  STS, 2, pp. 55–56.
Reference: *Izv.*, Jan. 26, 1932 (text of agreement as initialed Jan. 25, 1932).

• 32/viii/3/Pol

Protocol between the USSR and Poland concerning exchange of political prisoners

Signed Aug. 3, 1932, in Moscow.
References: *Izv.*, Sept. 10, 1932.
  STS, 2, p. 56, citing *Izv., loc. cit.*, and Private sources.

• 32/viii/13/J

Provisional agreement between the USSR and Japan concerning fisheries

Signed Aug. 13, 1932, in Moscow.
Supplements the fishery convention of Jan. 23, 1928.
Sources: *Izv.*, Aug. 22, 1932 (summary).
  STS, 2, p. 57.
Reference: *SDFP*, 2, pp. 534–35.

• 32/ix/13/Af

Exchange of notes between the USSR and Afghanistan constituting an agreement concerning settlement of border incidents

Sent Sept. 13, 1932, in Kabul.

Presumably entered into force Sept. 13, 1932. Duration 3 years; thereafter until 6 months following denunciation.
Sources: *SZ*, 1932, II, No. 24, Art. 254 (R, Persian).
   SDD, 7, pp. 54–62.
   STS, 2, pp. 57–59.
   SDFP, 2, pp. 535–41.

● 32/x/10/T

Protocol between the USSR and Turkey extending for six months the convention of August 6, 1928, concerning procedure for consideration and settlement of border disputes

Signed Oct. 10, 1932, in Ankara.
The 1928 convention (28/viii/6/T/d) was further extended by protocol of Mar. 28, 1933, and subsequently.
Reference: Mentioned in protocol of Mar. 28, 1933.

● 32/x/23/Italy

Exchange of notes between the USSR and Italy modifying the agreement of March 21, 1930, concerning certificates of origin

Sent Aug. 7, Sept. 20, and Oct. 23, 1932, in Moscow.
Sources: *SZ*, 1932, II, No. 24, Art. 253 (R, I).
   SDD, 7, pp. 70–71.
   STS, 2, pp. 56–57.

● 32/xi/23/Pol

Convention between the USSR and Poland concerning conciliation procedure

Signed Nov. 23, 1932, in Moscow.
Ratified by Poland Nov. 26, 1932; by the USSR Nov. 27, 1932. Entered into force Dec. 23, 1932, on exchange of acts of ratification in Warsaw. Becomes an integral part of the nonaggression treaty of July 25, 1932; duration the same.
A draft of the convention was considered at the time of signing of the nonaggression treaty, under the 2nd protocol of signature of that treaty.
Sources: *SZ*, 1933, II, No. 6, Art. 99 (R, P).
   SDD, 7, pp. 15–18.

DURP, 1932, No. 115, Arts. 952, 953.
LNTS, 136, pp. 55–71 (R, P, E, F).
STS, 2, pp. 59–60.

● 32/xi/29/France/a

Treaty of nonaggression between the USSR and France

Signed Nov. 29, 1932, in Paris.
Ratified by the USSR Feb. 13, 1933. Entered into force Feb. 15, 1933, on exchange of acts of ratification in Moscow. Duration 2 years; thereafter until 1 year following denunciation.
Supplemented by convention regarding conciliation procedure of the same date (next document). Confirms provision of the General Treaty of Aug. 27, 1928, for the renunciation of war as an instrument of policy that "the settlement or solution of all disputes or conflicts . . . which may arise among [the signatories] shall never be sought except by pacific means . . ."
Sources: *Izv.*, Nov. 30, 1932.
   SZ, 1933, II, No. 8, Art. 118 (R, F).
   SDD, 7, pp. 27–29.
   *JO, Feb. 17, July 28, 1933.
   LNTS, 157, pp. 411–19 (R, E, F).
   STS, 2, pp. 60–61.

● 32/xi/29/France/b

Convention between the USSR and France concerning conciliation procedure

Signed Nov. 29, 1932, in Paris.
Ratified by the USSR Feb. 13, 1933. Entered into force Feb. 15, 1933, on exchange of acts of ratification in Moscow. Supplements the treaty of nonaggression of the same date; duration the same.
Sources: *SZ*, 1933, II, No. 8, Art. 119 (R, F).
   SDD, 7, pp. 29–32.
   *JO, Feb. 17, 1933.
   LNTS, 157, pp. 421–30 (R, E, F).
   STS, 2, p. 61.

● 32/xi/30/Fin

Exchange of notes between the USSR and Finland concerning reciprocal recognition of trade-marks

Sent Nov. 30, 1932, in Moscow.

Sources: *SDD*, 7, p. 107.
SS, 1932, No. 20 (Finnish, F).
STS, 3, pp. 61–62.

● 32/xii/9/Mul/a

International Telecommunication Convention, with annex

Signed Dec. 9, 1932, in Madrid.
Ratified by the USSR Apr. 7, 1935; Soviet act of ratification deposited June 6, 1935. General entry into force Jan. 1, 1934; no special provision was made for subsequent entry into force. May be denounced with 1 year's notice.
Establishes the International Telecommunications Union. Replaces the International Telegraph Conventions of Paris, 1865; of Vienna, 1868; of Rome, 1872; and of St. Petersburg, 1875, and the Regulations annexed to them, and the International Radiotelegraph Conventions of Berlin, 1906, London, 1912, and Washington, 1927, and the Regulations annexed to them. Of these, the USSR acceded only to that of 1875 (see 25/iv/11/1875). Abrogated by the convention of Oct. 2, 1947 (47/x/2/Mul/a). Annex comprises a glossary of terms.
Supplemented by the following 5 documents.
Sources: *SDD*, 8, 1935, pp. 202–27.
LNTS, 151, pp. 4–49 (E, F).
USTS, 1934, No. 867.

● 32/xii/9/Mul/b

General radio regulations annexed to the International Telecommunication Convention, with fourteen annexes and final protocol

Signed Dec. 9, 1932, in Madrid.
Soviet act of ratification deposited Apr. 23, 1935. General entry into force Jan. 1, 1934. Supplement the International Telecommunication Convention of the same date. Revised at Cairo Apr. 8, 1938. (The USSR signed, but apparently did not ratify, the Cairo revision. See Appendix 1.) Superseded by regulations of Oct. 2, 1947 (47/x/2/Mul/b).
Source: *LNTS*, 151, pp. 278–447 (E, F).

● 32/xii/9/Mul/c

Additional radio regulations annexed to the International Telecommunication Convention

Signed Dec. 9, 1932, in Madrid.
Soviet act of ratification deposited Apr. 23, 1935. General entry into force Jan. 1, 1934.
Supplement the International Telecommunication Convention of the same date.
Source: *LNTS*, 151, pp. 448–65 (E, F).

● 32/xii/9/Mul/d

Additional protocol to the acts of the International Radiotelegraph Conference of Madrid signed by the Governments of the European Region, with annex

Signed Dec. 9, 1932, in Madrid. Presumably ratified by the USSR together with the convention of the same date. Entered into force on signature. Calls for a conference of the Governments of the European Region, to meet before entry into force of the General Radiocommunication Regulations of Madrid (i.e., Jan. 1, 1934), for the purpose of allocating broadcasting frequencies (see 33/vi/19/Mul/a). Special position of the USSR recognized under provisions of Chapter 4 of the protocol.
Source: *LNTS*, 151, pp. 466–79 (E, F).

● 32/xii/10/Mul/a

Telegraph regulations annexed to the International Telecommunication Convention, with two annexes and final protocol

Signed Dec. 10, 1932, in Madrid.
Soviet act of ratification deposited Apr. 23, 1935. General entry into force Jan. 1, 1934. Supplement the International Telecommunication Convention of Dec. 9, 1932. Revised at Cairo, Apr. 4, 1938 (the USSR did not accede to the revised regulations).
Source: *LNTS*, 151, pp. 50–225 (E, F).

● 32/xii/10/Mul/b

Telephone regulations annexed to the International Telecommunication Convention, with annex

Signed Dec. 10, 1932, in Madrid.
Soviet act of ratification deposited Apr. 23, 1935. General entry into force Jan 1, 1934. Supplement the International Telecommunication Convention of Dec. 9,

1932. Revised at Cairo, Apr. 4, 1938 (the USSR did not accede to the revised regulations).
Source: *LNTS*, 151, pp. 227–77 (E, F).

● 32/xii/12/China

Exchange of notes between the USSR and China concerning re-establishment of diplomatic and consular relations

Sent Dec. 12, 1932, in Geneva.
Entered into force Dec. 12, 1932. Re-establishes relations which had been interrupted on July 17, 1929 (see 24/v/31/China/c).
Sources: *Izv.*, Dec. 13, 1932.
   SDD, 7, pp. 5–6.
   Chen, p. 88.
   STS, 2, p. 62.
Reference: *SDFP*, 2, pp. 550–51.

1933

● 33/ / /Ger

Agreement between the USSR and Germany concerning postponement of payments on the Soviet debt to Germany

Signed in 1933.
Reference: *STS*, 2, p. 62, citing
   Private sources.

● 33/i/5/Fin

Convention between the USSR and Finland revising the convention of June 18, 1924, concerning direct transportation of passengers and freight by rail

Signed Jan. 5, 1933, in Helsinki.
Ratified by the USSR Feb. 23, 1933. Entered into force May 8, 1933 (60 days after exchange of acts of ratification, which took place Mar. 10, 1933, in Moscow). Duration the same as that of the convention which it revises (24/vi/18/Fin/d). Convention further modified by protocol of Feb. 11, 1936.
Sources: *SZ*, 1933, II, No. 9, Art. 120 (R, Finnish, Sw.).
   SDD, 8, pp. 322–25.
   SS, 1933, No. 6 (Finnish, R).
   STS, 2, pp. 62–63.

● 33/iii/28/T

Protocol between the USSR and Turkey extending for an additional six months the convention of August 6, 1928, concerning procedure for consideration and settlement of border disputes

Signed Mar. 28, 1933, in Ankara.
Ratified by Turkey June 12, 1933. The 1928 convention (28/viii/6/T/d) was further extended by protocol of Nov. 29, 1933, and subsequently.
Sources: *Düstur*, 14 (II), p. 1616.

STS, 2, p. 63, citing
   LT, 11, pp. 646–47.

● 33/iv/21/Pl

Agreement between the USSR, Estonia, and Latvia abrogating the convention of October 29, 1925, concerning through passenger and freight communications by rail, and the annexed regulations

Signed Apr. 21, 1933, in Riga.
Ratified by the USSR June 27, 1933. Entered into force (i.e., convention of 1925 became invalid) on Feb. 1, 1934 (1st day of 2nd month following month in which acts of ratification are deposited, which took place Dec. 16, 1933, in Riga).
Sources: *SZ*, 1934, II, No. 4, Art. 43 (R, Lat., Est.).
   SDD, 8, pp. 339–40.

● 33/iv/22/Greece

Agreement between the USSR and Greece concerning reciprocal abolition of consular visas on bills of health of merchant ships

Signed Apr. 22, 1933, in Athens.
Reference: Greek Embassy, 1957.

● 33/v/6/Italy/a

Customs convention between the USSR and Italy, with final protocol

Signed May 6, 1933, in Rome.
Ratified by the USSR Aug. 17, 1933. Entered into force provisionally June 12, 1933, in accordance with exchange of notes dated June 10, 1933; definitively Feb. 8, 1934, on exchange of acts of ratification in Rome. Valid until 6 months after denunciation, which may not, how-

ever, take place before Jan. 1, 1934.
Supersedes customs convention of Feb. 7,
1924 (24/ii/7/Italy/b). Reaffirmed for
1939 by the 1st secret protocol to the trade
and payments agreement of Feb 7, 1939
(39/ii/7/Italy/b).
Sources: *SZ*, 1934, II, No. 6, Art. 47
   (R, I).
   SDD, 8, pp. 113–16.
   TC, 46, p. 71.
   LNTS, 158, pp. 51–58 (I, E, F).
   STS, 2, p. 64.

● 33/v/6/Italy/b

Credit agreement between the USSR and Italy, with two annexes

Signed May 6, 1933, in Rome.
Entered into force on signature; valid
through Dec. 31, 1933. Supersedes agree-
ment of Apr. 27, 1931.
Sources: *TC*, 46, pp. 76–81.
   STS, 2, pp. 64–65.
Reference: *SUR*, June 1933, pp. 136–37.

● 33/v/29/Norway

Trade agreement for 1933 between the USSR and Norway

Signed May 29, 1933, in Oslo.
References: *Izv.*, June 6, 1933.
   STS, 2, p. 65.

● 33/vi/3/Pol/a

Convention between the USSR and Poland concerning procedure for investigating and settling border incidents and disputes, with final protocol and protocol of signature

Signed June 3, 1933, in Moscow.
Ratified by the USSR July 7, 1933; by
Poland Sept. 13, 1933. Entered into force
Nov. 4, 1933 (45 days after exchange of
acts of ratification, which took place Sept.
20, 1933, in Warsaw). Duration 5 years;
if not denounced 6 months before expira-
tion, extended for an additional 5 years.
Supplemented by protocol of the same
date (next document). Supersedes the
agreement of Aug. 3, 1925.
Sources: *SZ*, 1933, II, No. 28, Art. 252
   (R, P).
   SDD, 8, pp. 79–87.
   DURP, 1933, No. 90, Arts. 698, 699.
   LNTS, 142, pp. 265–301, 306–307 (R,
   P, E, F).
   STS, 2, pp. 65–67.

● 33/vi/3/Pol/b

Protocol between the USSR and Poland concerning appointment of representatives for border affairs

Signed June 3, 1933, in Moscow.
Supplements the convention of the same
date. Modified by exchange of notes
dated Nov. 12 and 13, 1936 (36/xi/13/
Pol).
Sources: *SZ*, 1933, II, No. 28, Art. 252,
   pp. 243–49 (R, P).
   SDD, 8, pp. 88–91.
   LNTS, 142, pp. 280–87, 300–305 (R,
   P, E, F).

● 33/vi/3/J

Exchange of notes between the USSR and Japan concerning negotiations between the USSR and Manchukuo for the sale of the Chinese Eastern Railway

Sent June 3, 1933.
Sources: *Izv.*, June 4, 1933.
   SDFP, 3, p. 21.

● 33/vi/10/Italy

Exchange of notes between the USSR and Italy concerning provisional entry into force of the customs convention of May 6, 1933

Sent June 10, 1933, in Rome.
References: *SZ*, 1934, II, p. 72.
   Italian Embassy, 1957.

● 33/vi/19/Mul/a

European Broadcasting Convention, with final protocol

Signed June 19, 1933, in Lucerne.
Subject to ratification; evidence of Soviet
ratification has not been found. Entered
into force Jan. 15, 1934. Signed in accordance with the Additional protocol to
the acts of the International Radiotelegraph Conference of Madrid (32/xii/9/
Mul/d). Supplemented by the Lucerne
Plan (next document).
Source: *LNTS*, 154, pp. 133–39, 170–73
   (E, F).

● 33/vi/19/Mul/b

Lucerne Plan for the allocation of radio broadcasting frequencies

Signed June 19, 1933, in Lucerne.
Annexed to the European Broadcasting

Convention of the same date (preceding document).
Source: *LNTS*, 154, pp. 148–69 (E, F).

● 33/vi/19/Pol

Convention between the USSR and Poland concerning floating timber in border rivers, with final protocol

Signed June 19, 1933, in Warsaw.
Ratified by the USSR Sept. 27, 1933; by Poland May 12, 1934. Entered into force July 5, 1934 (30 days after exchange of acts of ratification, which took place June 5, 1934, in Moscow). Under provisions of the final protocol, signatories are to exchange notes upon signature of the convention providing for its immediate entry into force provisionally, pending exchange of acts of ratification. Duration 5 years; if not denounced 6 months before expiration, extended for additional 5-year periods.
Supplemented by protocol of July 9, 1933.
Sources: *SZ*, 1934, II, No. 15, Art. 138 (R, P).
SDD, 8, pp. 125–32.
DURP, 1934, No. 58, Arts. 506, 508.
STS, 2, pp. 67–69.

● 33/vii/3/Pl

Convention concerning the definition of aggression, with annex and protocol of signature

Signed July 3, 1933, in London.
Original signatories: USSR, Afghanistan, Estonia, Latvia, Persia, Poland, Romania, Turkey. Acceded to by Finland Jan. 31, 1934.
Ratified by the USSR Aug. 17, 1933. Acts of ratification deposited in Moscow as follows: USSR, Poland, and Romania, Oct. 16, 1933; Afghanistan, Oct. 20, 1933; Persia, Nov. 16, 1933; Latvia and Estonia, Dec. 4, 1933; Turkey, Mar. 23, 1934. Enters into force between signatories on deposit of their acts of ratification. Valid indefinitely.
Sources: *Izv.*, July 5, 1933.
SZ, 1933, II, No. 24, Art. 241 (R, F).
SDD, 8, pp. 31–34.
LNTS, 147, pp. 67–77 (E, F).
STS, 2, pp. 69–70.

● 33/vii/4/Fin

Convention between the USSR and Fin-

land concerning reindeer, with final protocol

Signed July 4, 1933, in Helsinki.
Ratified by the USSR Jan. 17, 1934. Entered into force Mar. 3, 1934 (30 days after exchange of acts of ratification, which took place Jan. 31, 1934, in Moscow). Valid until 2 years after denunciation.
Sources: *SZ*, 1934, II, No. 7, Art. 48 (R, Finnish, Sw.).
SDD, 8, pp. 91–102.
SS, 1934, No. 7 (Finnish, R).
LNTS, 149, pp. 83–129 (R, Finnish, Sw., E, F).
STS, 2, pp. 71–74.

● 33/vii/4/Pl

Convention concerning the definition of aggression, with annex

Signed July 4, 1933, in London. Signatories: USSR, Czechoslovakia, Romania, Turkey, Yugoslavia.
Ratified by the USSR Aug. 17, 1933. Acts of ratification deposited in Moscow as follows: USSR, Czechoslovakia, Romania, and Yugoslavia, Feb. 17, 1934; Turkey, Mar. 23, 1934. Enters into force between signatories on deposit of their acts of ratification. Valid indefinitely.
Text virtually identical with that of the convention of July 3, 1933, with the exception that this convention makes specific provision (Art. 4) for subsequent accession; in the July 3 convention, this provision is contained in the protocol of signature.
Sources: *SZ*, 1934, II, No. 6, Art. 46 (R, F).
SDD, 8, pp. 31–34.
LNTS, 148, pp. 211–19 (E, F).
STS, 2, pp. 70–71.

● 33/vii/5/Lith

Convention between the USSR and Lithuania concerning the definition of aggression, with annex

Signed July 5, 1933, in London.
Ratified by the USSR Aug. 17, 1933. Entered into force Dec. 14, 1933, on exchange of acts of ratification in Moscow. Valid indefinitely.
Text virtually identical with that of the convention of July 3, 1933.
Sources: *SZ*, 1933, II, No. 30, Art. 260 (R, F).

SDD, 8, pp. 12–15.
*VŽ, 1933, No. 433, Art. 3017.
*LS, 2, pp. 252–55.
LNTS, 148, pp. 79–85 (E, F).
STS, 2, p. 74.

● 33/vii/9/Pol

Protocol between the USSR and Poland concerning floating timber on the border canal during the spring floods

Signed July 9, 1933, in Moscow.
Ratified by the USSR Sept. 27, 1933; by Poland May 12, 1934. Entered into force July 5, 1934 (30 days after exchange of acts of ratification, which took place June 5, 1934, in Moscow). Supplements the convention of June 19, 1933, concerning floating timber in border rivers; duration the same.
Sources: *SZ*, 1934, II, No. 15, Art. 139 (R, P).
SDD, 8, pp. 131–32.
*DURP, 1934, No. 58, Arts. 507, 508.
STS, 2, pp. 74–75.

● 33/vii/28/Spain

Exchange of telegrams between the USSR and Spain concerning establishment of diplomatic relations

Sent July 28, 1933, from Madrid and Moscow.
Sources: *Izv.*, July 29, 1939.
SDD, 9, pp. 39–40.
STS, 2, p. 75.

● 33/viii/13/Uruguay

Exchange of telegrams between the USSR and Uruguay concerning establishment of permanent diplomatic missions

Sent Aug. 11, 1933, from Montevideo, and Aug. 13, 1933, from Moscow.
On Dec. 28, 1935, Uruguay announced its decision to break off relations with the USSR.
For a Soviet letter of Dec. 30, 1935, to the League of Nations commenting on the action, see *SDFP*, 3, pp. 150–51 and 159–64.
Sources: *SUR*, Sept. 1933, p. 192.
STS, 2, p. 75.

● 33/viii/25/Mul

Final Act of the Conference of Wheat Importing and Exporting Countries, with related documents

Signed Aug. 25, 1933, in London.
Entered into force on signature. Soviet export quota for 1933–34 and 1934–35 to be negotiated subsequently.
Contents (*LNTS*, 141): Text, pp 72–81; Annex A (definitions and standards), pp. 80–81; Annex B, Report of the sub-committee on the constitution of a Wheat Advisory Committee, with Annex, Basis of contributions to Advisory Committee, pp. 80–85; and Minutes of final meeting, pp. 86–89.
Source: *LNTS*, 141, pp. 72–89 (E, F).
References: *VT*, 1943, No. 12, pp. 8–9.
   LNOJ, Special supplement No. 193, p. 158.

● 33/ix/2/Italy

Treaty of friendship, nonaggression and neutrality between the USSR and Italy

Signed Sept. 2, 1933, in Rome.
Ratified by the USSR Oct. 7, 1933; by Italy Sept. 21, 1933. Entered into force Dec. 15, 1933, on exchange of acts of ratification in Moscow. Duration 5 years; thereafter until 1 year following denunciation.
Sources: *SZ*, 1933, II, No. 30, Art. 261 (R, I).
   SDD, 8, pp. 8–10.
   *TC, 46, p. 304.
   LNTS, 148, pp. 319–29 (R, I, E, F).
   STS, 2, pp. 75–76.

● 33/ix/8/Greece

Trade and clearing agreement between the USSR and Greece, with three exchanges of notes

Signed Sept. 8, 1933, in Athens.
Entered into force Sept. 11, 1933; duration 6 months, unless renewed by an exchange of notes. Superseded by agreement of June 8, 1934.
Exchanges of notes concern (1) import of Soviet agricultural machinery; (2) chartering of Greek ships on behalf of Soviet commercial organizations; and (3) validity of contracts between the Soviet Trade Mission and Greek merchants concluded prior to this agreement which had been denounced by the Mission following a ministerial decree of the Greek Government of June 28, 1933.
Sources: **Greek official gazette, 1933, A, No. 331.

STS, 2, pp. 76–78, citing
SSSkS, 1933, No. 12.

● 33/x/3/T

Barter agreement between the USSR and Turkey

Signed Oct. 3, 1933, in Ankara.
Source: *STS*, 2, p. 78 (summary), citing
Private sources.

● 33/x/9/Pol

Exchange of notes between the USSR and Poland constituting a temporary customs agreement, with list of duty reductions

Sent Sept. 18 and Oct. 9, 1933, in Warsaw.
Ratified by Poland May 12, 1934. Valid
through Mar. 31, 1934.
Sources: **DURP*, 1934, No. 78, Art. 725.
STS, 2, p. 78.

Oct. 11, 1933. International convention for suppression of the traffic in women of full age

See 47/xii/18/1933, 47/xii/18/1947/a,
and 54/viii/11/1950.

● 33/x/15/Fin

Convention between the USSR and Finland modifying the convention of October 28, 1922, concerning floating of timber in border water courses, with final protocol

Signed Oct. 15, 1933, in Moscow.
Ratified by the USSR Jan. 13, 1934. Entered into force Feb. 7, 1934, on exchange of acts of ratification in Helsinki. Constitutes an integral part of the convention of 1922 (22/x/28/Fin/b). Renewed under an exchange of notes in Mar. 1948 (48/iii/16/Fin).
Sources: *SZ*, 1934, II, No. 10, Art. 80
(R, Finnish).
SDD, 8, pp. 139–50.
*SS, 1934, No. 10 (Finnish, R).
LNTS, 149, pp. 243–83 (R, Finnish, E, F).
STS, 2, pp. 79–82.

● 33/xi/14/Af. See Appendix 5.

● 33/xi/15/US

Gentlemen's agreement between the USSR and the United States of America concerning a payment to the United States on pre-Soviet Russian debts

Initialed Nov. 15, 1933, in Washington, D.C.
Provides for payment by the USSR of not less than $75 million nor more than $150 million on account of the debt of the Provisional Government of Russia or otherwise, in the form of a percentage above the ordinary rate of interest on a loan to be granted by the United States, all other claims of both Governments and their nationals to be regarded as eliminated.
Sources: *FRUS*, 1933, II, p. 804.
FRUS, SU 1933–1939, pp. 26–27.

● 33/xi/16/US

Exchange of notes between the USSR and the United States of America concerning establishment of diplomatic relations, with related documents

Sent Nov. 16, 1933, in Washington, D.C.
Preceded by an exchange of Oct. 10 and 17, 1933, concerning discussion of outstanding questions (*STS*, 2, pp. 78–79). Related documents include exchanges of notes dated Nov. 16, 1933, as follows: (1) a pledge by the USSR not to interfere in the internal affairs of the United States, not to commit any act endangering the security of the United States, not to permit the formation or residence on its territory of any group aiming at the overthrow of or change in the political or social order of the United States; (2) a guarantee by the USSR of the rights of freedom of conscience and religion on the part of citizens of the United States in the USSR; (3) a statement by the USSR concerning its willingness to conclude a consular convention; (4) an agreement by the USSR temporarily not to press certain of its claims as successor government against the United States and its nationals; (5) an agreement by the USSR to waive all claims arising out of activity of United States forces in Siberia subsequent to Jan. 1, 1918; and (6) a joint statement concerning methods for settling outstanding questions of indebtedness and claims.
In 1955 the United States offered to make the guarantee of religious freedom reciprocal, following Soviet expulsion of an American Roman Catholic priest resident in Moscow, an action which the United States protested as a violation of the 1933 agreement (see *DSB*, 32, 1955, pp. 424–

26; *ibid.*, 33, pp. 102–104, 784–85). The USSR, in a reply of Nov. 10, 1955, rejected the proposal under the terms in which it was made (see *ibid.*, p. 888).
Sources: *FRUS, 1933*, 2, pp. 805–14.
 FRUS, SU 1933–1939, pp. 27–37.
 SDD, 8, pp. 4–5 (exchange of notes only).
 AJIL, 28, 1934, No. 1, supplement, pp. 1–11.
 STS, 2, pp. 82–86.

● 33/xi/29/T

Protocol between the USSR and Turkey extending for an additional six months the convention of August 6, 1928, concerning procedure for consideration and settlement of border disputes

Signed Nov. 29, 1933, in Ankara.
Ratified by Turkey Apr. 7, 1934. The 1928 convention (28/viii/6/T/d) was further extended by protocol of Apr. 12, 1934, and subsequently.
Sources: **Düstur*, 15, p. 331.
 STS, 2, p. 86, citing
  LT, 12, pp. 259–60.

● 33/xii/4/Lat/a

Treaty of commerce between the USSR and Latvia, with final protocol

Signed Dec. 4, 1933, in Moscow.
Ratified by the USSR Dec. 17, 1933. Entered into force Dec. 31, 1933, on exchange of acts of ratification in Riga. Duration 2 years; if not denounced 6 months before expiration, extended for successive 1-year periods; under the final protocol, 2 additional months added to final year of validity.
Sources: *SZ*, 1934, II, No. 4, Art. 44 (R, Lat.).

SDD, 8, pp. 116–25.
LRR, pp. 178–84.
LNTS, 148, pp. 145–75 (R, Lat., E, F).
STS, 2, pp. 86–88.

● 33/xii/4/Lat/b

Economic agreement between the USSR and Latvia, with final protocol

Signed Dec. 4, 1933, in Moscow.
Entered into force Jan. 1, 1934. Duration the same as that of the treaty of commerce of the same date (preceding document). Modified by protocol of June 21, 1937.
Sources: *LRR*, pp. 184–86.
 LNTS, 148, pp. 177–87 (R, Lat., E, F).
 STS, 2, pp. 88–89.

● 33/xii/5/Italy

Protocol between the USSR and Italy extending existing economic and commercial agreements through December 31, 1934

Signed Dec. 5, 1933, in Rome.
For subsequent extension, see 34/xii/31/Italy.
Reference: *STS*, 2, p. 89, citing
 BL, 51, Jan. 1934, supplement, pp. 38–39.

● 33/xii/11/Persia

Exchange of notes between the USSR and Persia concerning settlement of commercial disputes

Sent Dec. 11, 1933, in Teheran.
Modifies the convention of Oct. 27, 1931; duration the same.
Source: *STS*, 2, p. 89 (summary) citing Private sources.

● 33/xii/30/Lat. See Appendix 5.

1934

● 34/i/11/France

Temporary commercial agreement between the USSR and France, with three protocols

Signed Jan. 11, 1934, in Paris.
Ratified by the USSR Jan. 17, 1935. Entered into force Jan. 24, 1934. Acts of ratification exchanged Nov. 12, 1935, in Paris. Valid through Dec. 31, 1934, except for Art. 3 (concerning the status of the Soviet Trade Mission in France),

which remains valid through Dec. 31, 1935. Extended and modified by protocol of Dec. 9, 1934, and by agreements of Jan. 6, 1936; Jan. 21, 1936; Dec. 17, 1936; Dec. 31, 1937; and Dec. 30, 1938. Expired Jan. 1, 1940 (Korolenko, pp. 80–81).
Sources: *SZ*, 1936, II, No. 4, Art. 43 (R, F).
 SDD, 8, pp. 158–72.
 *JO, Jan. 24, 1934.
 LNTS, 167, pp. 349–84 (R, E, F).
 STS, 2, pp. 90–92.

● 34/i/21/T

Protocol between the USSR and Turkey concerning realization of a credit of eight million dollars, with supplementary protocol and annex

Signed Jan. 21, 1934, in Ankara.
Ratified by the USSR Apr. 27, 1934; by Turkey May 17, 1934. Entered into force May 28, 1934, on exchange of acts of ratification in Ankara. Carries out provisions of agreement in principle which was reached in May 1932 (see 32/v/8/T).
Sources: *SZ*, 1934, II, No. 420, pp. 92–94 (R, F).
   SDD, 8, pp. 133–39.
   *Düstur, 15 (I), p. 475.
   STS, 2, pp. 92–94.
   SDFP, 3, pp. 61–65.

● 34/ii/4/H

Exchange of notes between the USSR and Hungary concerning establishment of diplomatic relations

Sent Feb. 4, 1934, in Rome.
Entered into force Feb. 4, 1934.
Sources: *Izv.*, Feb. 7, 1934.
   SDD, 8, pp. 6–7.
   AD, 1935, pp. 253–54 (F).
   STS, 2, p. 94.

● 34/ii/6/H

Protocol between the USSR and Hungary concerning establishment of a Soviet legation in Budapest

Signed on or about Feb. 6, 1934.
Sources: *STS*, 2, p. 94 (summary), citing *Pester Lloyd* (Budapest), Feb. 13, 1934.

● 34/ii/16/Pol

Communiqué concerning negotiations between the USSR and Poland

Issued Feb. 16, 1934.
Reaffirms the nonaggression pact and the convention for definition of aggression (32/vii/25/Pol and 33/vii/3/Pl), and mentions agreement to raise diplomatic missions to the status of embassies.
Sources: *Pr.*, Feb. 16, 1934.
   SDFP, 3, p. 75.

● 34/ii/16/UK

Temporary commercial agreement between the USSR and the United Kingdom, with annex concerning balance of payments

Signed Feb. 16, 1934, in London.
Ratified by the United Kingdom Mar. 1, 1934; by the USSR Mar. 13, 1934. Entered into force Mar. 21, 1934, on exchange of acts of ratification in Moscow. Valid until 6 months after denunciation. Listed by Korolenko, p. 104, as still in force as of Nov. 25, 1953.
Sources: *SZ*, 1934, II, No. 15, Art. 136 (R, E).
   SDD, 8, pp. 103–13.
   SDTD, 1, pp. 241–51.
   *BTS, 1934, No. 11, Cmd. 4567.
   *BFSP, 137, p. 188.
   LNTS, 149, pp. 445–70 (R, E, F).
   STS, 2, pp. 94–97.

Mar. 16, 1934. Agreement between the USSR and Sweden concerning a loan by Sweden of one hundred million Swedish crowns

See Appendix 1.

● 34/iii/20/Ger

Economic protocol between the USSR and Germany

Signed Mar. 20, 1934, in Berlin.
Details in Appendix 5.

● 34/iii/20/Mul/a

Universal Postal Convention, with related documents

Signed Mar. 20, 1934, in Cairo.
Ratified by the USSR Mar. 17, 1935; act of ratification deposited Apr. 26, 1935 (May 7, 1935, according to *LNTS*, 174, p. 177). General entry into force Jan. 1, 1935. Duration indefinite; signatories may withdraw with 1 year's notice. Supersedes the convention of June 28, 1929; superseded by convention of May 23, 1939.
   Full contents (*LNTS*, 174): text, pp. 176–237; final protocol, pp. 238–51; regulations for execution, pp. 252–349; annexes to the regulations, pp. 351–431; provisions concerning air mail, pp. 432–49; final protocol to the provisions concerning air mail, pp. 460–67; annexes to the provisions concerning air mail, pp. 469–77.
   The USSR also signed the agreement

concerning insured letters and boxes (next document). It did not sign the agreements concerning parcel post, money orders, postal checking accounts, payments on delivery, and newspaper subscriptions.

Sources: *SZ*, 1935, II, No. 19–30, Art. 167 (R, F).
SDD, 8, pp. 227–87.
LNTS, 174, as listed above (E, F).

● 34/iii/20/Mul/b

Agreement of the Universal Postal Union concerning insured letters and boxes, with related documents

Signed Mar. 20, 1934, in Cairo.
Ratified by the USSR Mar. 17, 1935; act of ratification deposited Apr. 26, 1935 (May 7, 1935, according to *LNTS*, 175, p. 9). Entered into force Jan. 1, 1935. Duration indefinite. Superseded by the agreement of May 23, 1939, which the USSR is not known to have signed.
Full contents (*LNTS*, 175): text, pp. 8–37; final protocol, pp. 38–45; regulations for execution, pp. 46–65; annexes to the regulations, pp. 68–71.

Sources: *SZ*, 1935, II, No. 19–30, Art. 167, pp. 626–78 (R, F).
SDD, 9, pp. 304–17.
LNTS, 175, pp. 5–71.

● 34/iv/4/Est

Protocol between the USSR and Estonia extending the treaty of May 4, 1932, concerning nonaggression and the peaceful settlement of disputes

Signed Apr. 4, 1934, in Moscow.
Ratified by the USSR Apr. 27, 1934; by Estonia June 11, 1934. Entered into force June 26, 1934, on exchange of acts of ratification in Tallinn. Extends the 1932 treaty to Dec. 31, 1945.

Sources: *SZ*, 1934, II, No. 16, Art. 143 (R, Est.).
SDD, 8, pp. 25–27.
*RT, 1934, No. 53.
LNTS, 150, pp. 87–93 (R, Est., E, F).
STS, 2, pp. 97–98.

● 34/iv/4/Lat

Protocol between the USSR and Latvia extending the nonaggression treaty of February 5, 1932

Signed Apr. 4, 1934, in Moscow.

Ratified by the USSR Apr. 27, 1934. Entered into force June 2, 1934, on exchange of acts of ratification in Riga. Extends the 1932 treaty through Dec. 31, 1945.

Sources: *SZ*, 1934, II, No. 16, Art. 140 (R, Lat.).
SDD, 8, pp. 11–12.
LRR, p. 172.
LNTS, 148, pp. 118–21, 126–27 (R, Lat., E, F).
STS, 2, p. 97.

● 34/iv/4/Lith

Protocol between the USSR and Lithuania extending the treaty of nonaggression of September 28, 1926

Signed Apr. 4, 1934, in Moscow.
Ratified by the USSR Apr. 27, 1934. Entered into force June 4, 1934, on exchange of acts of ratification in Kaunas. Extends the 1926 treaty through Dec. 31, 1945.

Sources: *SZ*, 1934, II, No. 16, Art. 141 (R, Lith.).
SDD, 8, pp. 15–16.
*VŽ, No. 445, Art. 3110.
*LS, 2, pp. 308–10.
LNTS, 186, pp. 267–75 (R, Lith., E, F).
STS, 2, p. 97.

● 34/iv/7/Fin

Protocol between the USSR and Finland extending the treaty of January 21, 1932, concerning nonaggression and the peaceful settlement of disputes

Signed Apr. 7, 1934, in Moscow.
Ratified by the USSR Apr. 27, 1934. Entered into force Dec. 19, 1934, on exchange of acts of ratification in Helsinki. Extends the 1932 treaty through Dec. 31, 1945. For denunciation by the USSR, see 32/i/21/Fin.

Sources: *SZ*, 1934, II, No. 22, Art. 197 (R, Finnish).
SDD, 8, pp. 21–22.
*SS, 1934, No. 58 (Finnish, F).
LNTS, 155, pp. 325–29 (E, F).
STS, 2, p. 98.

● 34/iv/12/T

Protocol between the USSR and Turkey extending for an additional six months the convention of August 6, 1928, concerning procedure for consideration and settlement of border disputes

Signed Apr. 12, 1934, in Ankara.
Ratified by Turkey July 4, 1934. The 1928
convention (28/viii/6/T/d) was further
extended by protocol of Oct. 6, 1934, and
subsequently.
Sources: *Düstur, 15, p. 1403.
  STS, 2, p. 98, citing
    RG, No. 2750, July 12, 1934, pp.
    4125–26.

• 34/iv/19/UK/a

**Parcel post convention between the
USSR and the United Kingdom**

Signed Apr. 19, 1934, in London.
Ratified by the USSR Dec. 17, 1934. Acts
of ratification exchanged Dec. 28, 1934, in
Moscow. To come into force on a date
fixed by agreement between the postal authorities of the signatories; thereafter
valid until 6 months following denunciation.
Supplemented by regulations of the same
date (next document). Notes concerning
interpretation of certain provisions were
exchanged on Apr. 19 and May 28, 1934
(see 34/v/28/UK), and on Jan. 21, Mar.
9, and Mar. 11, 1935 (see 35/iii/11/UK).
Sources: SZ, 1935, II, No. 2, Art. 10
  (R, E).
  SDD, 8, pp. 189–202.
  *Cmd. 4669, 1934.
  LNTS, 158, pp. 331–50, 360–69 (R,
  E, F).
  STS, 2, pp. 98–102.

• 34/iv/19/UK/b

**Regulations concerning parcel post be-
tween the USSR and the United Kingdom**

Signed Apr. 19, 1934, in London.
Entry into force and duration same as for
the convention of the same date (preced-
ing document).
Source: LNTS, 158, pp. 350–57, 369–75
  (R, E, F).

• 34/v/5/Pol

**Protocol between the USSR and Poland
extending the treaty of nonaggression of
July 25, 1932, with final protocol**

Signed May 5, 1934, in Moscow.
Ratified by the USSR May 25, 1934; by
Poland June 15, 1934. Entered into force
June 16, 1934, on exchange of acts of rati-
fication in Warsaw. Extends the 1932

treaty through Dec. 31, 1945. If not denounced 6 months before expiration, the
1932 treaty is extended for further 2-year
periods.
Final protocol reaffirms validity of the
peace treaty of Mar. 18, 1921, as constituting the basis of mutual relations between the signatories, and disavows any
intention on the part of the USSR of interfering in the territorial dispute between
Poland and Lithuania.
Sources: SZ, 1934, II, No. 16, Art. 142
  (R, P).
  SDD, 8, pp. 16–18.
  *DURP, 1934, No. 53, Arts. 487, 488.
  LNTS, 157, pp. 431–39 (R, P, E, F).
  STS, 2, pp. 102–103.

• 34/v/19/Norway

**Trade agreement between the USSR and
Norway**

Signed May 19, 1934, in Oslo.
Duration 1 year.
References: STS, 2, p. 103 (summary),
  citing
    Morgenbladet (Oslo), May 20, 1934.

• 34/v/25/Fin

**Convention between the USSR and Fin-
land concerning fishing and seal hunting in Lake Ladoga, with protocol and
two annexes**

Signed May 25, 1934, in Moscow.
Ratified by the USSR Nov. 17, 1934. En-
tered into force Nov. 21, 1934, on ex-
change of acts of ratification in Helsinki.
Valid until 1 year after denunciation.
Sources: SZ, 1934, II, No. 22, Art. 196
  (R, Finnish).
  SDD, 8, pp. 150–58.
  *SS, 1934, No. 53 (Finnish, R).
  LNTS, 155, pp. 207–35 (R, Finnish,
  E, F).
  STS, 2, pp. 103–104.

• 34/v/28/UK

**Exchange of notes between the USSR and
the United Kingdom concerning interpretation of Articles 3 and 33 of the parcel post convention of April 19, 1934**

Sent Apr. 19 and May 28, 1934, in London.
Sources: LNTS, 158, pp. 357–58, 375–76
  (E, F).
  *Cmd. 4669, 1934.
  STS, 2, p. 102.

● 34/vi/7/Mul

Exchange of telegrams between the USSR and the League of Nations concerning Soviet accession to an embargo on arms shipments to Bolivia and Paraguay

Sent June 4 and 7, 1934.
Source: *SDFP*, 3, p. 83 (Soviet reply), citing
    LNOJ, 1934, p. 835.
Reference: *SIA, 1933*, p. 436.

● 34/vi/8/Greece

Trade and clearing agreement between the USSR and Greece

Signed June 8, 1934, in Athens.
Ratified by Greece June 9, 1934. Entered into force retroactively from Apr. 12, 1934; valid through Dec. 31, 1934. Supersedes the agreement of Sept. 8, 1933.
Sources: *Greek official gazette, 1934, A, No. 235.
    STS, 2, pp. 104–106, citing
        SSSkS, 1934, No. 14.

● 34/vi/9/Cz

Exchange of notes between the USSR and Czechoslovakia concerning establishment of diplomatic relations

Sent June 9, 1934, in Geneva.
Sources: *SDD*, 8, pp. 23–24.
    AD, 1935, pp. 255–56 (F).
    STS, 2, p. 106.

● 34/vi/9/Rom/a

Exchange of notes between the USSR and Romania concerning establishment of diplomatic relations

Sent June 9, 1934, in Geneva.
Sources: *Izv.*, June 10, 1934.
    SDD, 8, pp. 19–20.
    AD, 1935, pp. 254–55 (F).
    STS, 2, pp. 106–107.

● 34/vi/9/Rom/b

Exchange of notes between the USSR and Romania constituting an agreement concerning non-interference in each other's internal affairs

Sent June 9, 1934, in Geneva.
No limit set for validity.
Sources: *SUR*, July 1934, pp. 163–64.
    STS, 2, p. 107.

● 34/vi/11/Denmark

Trade agreement between the USSR and Denmark

Signed June 11, 1934, in Copenhagen.
Reference: Danish Embassy, 1957.

● 34/vi/22/Pol

Exchange of notes between the USSR and Poland constituting a temporary customs agreement, with list of duty reductions

Sent June 22, 1934, in Warsaw.
Valid through Dec. 31, 1934. Extended through Dec. 31, 1935, by exchange of notes of Dec. 1, 1934.
Sources: *DURP*, 1935, No. 53, Art. 345.
    STS, 2, p. 107.

● 34/vi/29/T

Trade agreement between the USSR and Turkey

Signed June 29, 1934, in Ankara.
Entered into force July 1, 1934; valid until Jan. 1, 1935.
Sources: *STS*, 2, p. 107 (summary), citing
    Private sources.
Reference: *Pr.*, July 1, 1934.

● 34/vii/13/Greece

Agreement between the USSR and Greece concerning consular fees on passports

Signed July 13, 1934, in Moscow.
Reference: Greek Embassy, 1957.

● 34/vii/23/Bul/a

Exchange of telegrams between the USSR and Bulgaria concerning establishment of diplomatic relations

Sent July 23, 1934, from Sofia and Moscow.
Relations were formally broken off by a Soviet note of Sept. 5, 1944 (*VPSS VP*, 2, pp. 181–83), and were re-established by an exchange of notes of Aug. 14 and 16, 1945 (45/viii/16/Bul).
Sources: *Izv.*, July 24, 1934.
    SDD, 8, pp. 5–6.
    AD, 1935, pp. 256–57 (F).
    STS, 2, p. 108.

• 34/vii/23/Bul/b

Protocol between the USSR and Bulgaria concerning non-interference in each other's internal affairs

Signed July 23, 1934, in Istanbul.
No limit set for validity.
Sources: *STS*, 2, p. 108, citing
    Martens, 3rd series, 30, pp. 49–50.

• 34/vii/25/Mul

International convention for protection against dengue fever

Signed July 25, 1934, in Athens.
Ratified by the USSR May 13, 1936; Soviet act of ratification deposited in Athens June 23, 1936. Entered into force for the USSR July 23, 1936 (1 month after deposit of act of ratification). Duration 5 years; thereafter until 6 months following withdrawal for any signatory.
Under a protocol of July 22, 1946 (46/vii/22/Mul/d), the duties and functions conferred by this convention on the Office Internationale d'Hygiène Publique were transferred to the World Health Organization or its Interim Commission.
Sources: *SZ*, 1936, II, No. 37, Art. 322
    (R, F).
    SDD, 9, pp. 446–50.
    LNTS, 177, pp. 59–69 (F, E).

• 34/vii/26/Pol/a

Protocol between the USSR and Poland modifying certain provisions of the convention of April 24, 1924, concerning direct rail transportation, with final protocol

Signed July 26, 1934, in Moscow.
Ratified by the USSR Jan. 28, 1935; by Poland May 10, 1935. Entered into force July 21, 1935 (30 days after exchange of acts of ratification, which took place June 21, 1935, in Warsaw). Constitutes an integral part of the convention of Apr. 24, 1924 (24/iv/24/Pol/a); duration the same.
Supplemented by regulations concerning border crossing (next document).
Sources: *SZ*, 1935, II, No. 16, Art. 134
    (R, P).
    SDD, 8, pp. 311–16.
    DURP, 1935, No. 56, Arts. 358, 359.
    LNTS, 164, pp. 301–11, 320–27 (R, P, E, F).
    STS, 2, pp. 108–109.

• 34/vii/26/Pol/b

Regulations between the USSR and Poland concerning crossing the border by railroad, postal, and other employees and their stay in the territory of the other party, with two annexes

Undated; annexed to the protocol signed July 26, 1934, in Moscow (preceding document).
Sources: *SZ*, 1935, II, No. 16, Art. 134,
    pp. 246–54 (R, P).
    SDD, 8, pp. 316–21.
    LNTS, 164, pp. 310–19, 326–33 (R, P, E, F).

• 34/vii/30/Est

Communiqué concerning political negotiations between the USSR and Estonia

Issued July 30, 1934.
Calls for conclusion of an Eastern European pact of mutual assistance.
Sources: *Izv.*, July 30, 1934.
    SDFP, 3, pp. 86–87.

• 34/viii/3/Lat

Communiqué concerning political negotiations between the USSR and Latvia

Issued Aug. 3, 1934.
Mentions Lithuanian support for the conclusion of an Eastern European pact of mutual assistance.
Sources: *Izv.*, Aug. 3, 1934.
    SDFP, 3, pp. 87–88.

• 34/viii/8/Ger

Trade protocol between the USSR and Germany

Signed Aug. 8, 1934, in Berlin.
Entered into force on signature.
References: *VVerz.*, p. 438.
    Ostwirtschaft, July–Aug., 1934, pp. 101–102.

• 34/ix/10/Pol

Exchange of notes between the USSR and Poland reaffirming existing treaties, on the occasion of the entry of the USSR into the League of Nations

Sent Sept. 10, 1934, in Moscow.
Specifically includes, among the existing Soviet-Polish treaties reaffirmed, the treaty of nonaggression (32/vii/25/Pol) and the convention concerning the definition of aggression (33/vii/3/Pl).

Sources: *Polish White Book*, pp. 180–81.
  STS, 2, p. 110, citing
    BFSP, 137, pp. 627–28.
  SDFP, 3, p. 89 (Soviet note).

• 34/ix/15/Mul

Documents concerning entry of the USSR into the League of Nations

Signed Sept. 15, 1934, in Geneva.
The documents include (1) a telegram to the Soviet Commissar of Foreign Affairs from the delegates of 30 States to the 15th Assembly of the League of Nations inviting the USSR to join the League; (2) a letter to the League Council from the First Delegate of Sweden stating that the Governments of Denmark, Finland, Norway, and Sweden have confirmed to the USSR their intention of voting in favor of the entry of the USSR into the League; (3) a letter to the President of the Assembly from the Soviet Commissar of Foreign Affairs accepting the invitation to join the League; and (4) a resolution adopted by the Council of the League appointing the USSR a permanent member of the Council as soon as its admission into the League has been approved by the Assembly. For Soviet entry into the League, see 34/ix/18/1919.
Sources: *SDD*, 8, pp. 35–37 (omitting (4) above).
  DIA, 1934, pp. 99–101, citing
    Verbatim record of the 15th League Assembly, Sept. 17, 1934.

• 34/ix/17/Alb

Exchange of notes between the USSR and Albania concerning establishment of diplomatic relations

Sent Sept. 17, 1934, in Rome.
Entered into force Sept. 17, 1934.
Sources: *SDD*, 8, pp. 3–4.
  STS, 2, p. 111.

• 34/ix/18/1919

Resolution concerning entry of the USSR into the League of Nations

Adopted by the Assembly of the League of Nations Sept. 18, 1934.
Soviet entry into the League of Nations followed earlier negotiations, which included an exchange of notes with Poland of Sept. 10, 1934, and diplomatic correspondence of Sept. 15, 1934. Soviet entry entailed acceptance of the Covenant of the League of Nations, originally adopted as part of the Treaty of Versailles of June 28, 1919. The USSR was expelled from the League of Nations on Dec. 14, 1939, following condemnation of its attack on Finland.
Sources: (1) Resolution of Sept. 18, 1934:
  SDD, 8, p. 37.
  DIA, 1934, p. 101, citing
    Verbatim record of the 15th League Assembly, Sept. 18, 1934.
(2) Covenant of the League of Nations:
  SDD, 8, pp. 37–48.

• 34/x/6/T

Protocol between the USSR and Turkey extending for an additional six months the convention of August 6, 1928, concerning procedure for consideration and settlement of border disputes

Signed Oct. 6, 1934, in Ankara.
Ratified by Turkey Nov. 24, 1934. The 1928 convention (28/viii/6/T/d) was further extended by exchange of notes of June 9, 1936.
Sources: *Düstur*, 16, p. 4.
  STS, 2, p. 111, citing
    RG, No. 2866, Nov. 28, 1934, p. 4499.

• 34/x/31/Est

Trade agreement between the USSR and Estonia

Signed Oct. 31, 1934, in Moscow.
Entered into force Jan. 1, 1935. Duration 2 years, through Dec. 31, 1937. Supplements the commercial treaty of May 17, 1929 (29/v/17/Est/a).
Sources: *RT*, 1935, No. 14.
  STS, 2, pp. 111–12, citing
    ELV, 12, pp. 323–27.

• 34/xi/23/Mul

Revision of the convention of June 21, 1920, concerning establishment of an International Institute of Refrigeration

Adopted at a general conference of the International Institute of Refrigeration on Nov. 23, 1934.
Ratified by the USSR Apr. 17, 1935. For the 1920 convention, see 24/vi/17/1920.
Source: *SZ*, 1935, II, No. 17, Art. 136 (R, F).

● 34/xi/27/MPR

Gentlemen's agreement between the USSR and the Mongolian People's Republic concerning mutual aid in case of attack by a third party

Concluded Nov. 27, 1934.
Replaced by protocol of mutual assistance of Mar. 12, 1936.
Reference: S. Avarzed, "The foreign policy of the Mongolian People's Republic," *Int. aff.*, 1958, No. 10, p. 39.

● 34/xii/1/MPR/a

Trade agreement between the USSR and the Mongolian People's Republic

Signed Dec. 1, 1934, in Moscow.
Reference: *Pr.*, Dec. 2, 1934.

● 34/xii/1/MPR/b

Agreement between the USSR and the Mongolian People's Republic concerning payments

Signed Dec. 1, 1934, in Moscow.
Reference: *Pr.*, Dec. 2, 1934.

● 34/xii/1/MPR/c

Agreement between the USSR and the Mongolian People's Republic concerning currency exchange rates

Date of signature unknown, but possibly Dec. 1, 1934.
Reference: *Tikhii okean*, No. 1 (3), Jan.–Mar. 1935, p. 266 (report of the Mongolian Prime Minister to the Seventh Great Hural on Dec. 24, 1934).

● 34/xii/1/MPR/d

Agreement between the USSR and the Mongolian People's Republic concerning mixed Soviet-Mongolian companies

Date of signature unknown, but possibly Dec. 1, 1934.
Provides for Mongolian ownership of the mixed companies "Mongoltrans," "Mongolsherst'," "Mongsovbuner'," and "Promkombinat." Accompanied by an informal agreement concerning conditions of employment of Soviet workers.
Reference: same as for 34/xii/1/MPR/c.

● 34/xii/1/Pol

Exchange of notes between the USSR and Poland constituting a temporary customs agreement

Sent Dec. 1, 1934, in Warsaw.
Ratified by Poland Apr. 12, 1935. Extends the temporary customs agreement of June 22, 1934, through Dec. 31, 1935.
Sources: *DURP*, 1935, No. 53, Art. 346.
STS, 2, p. 112.

● 34/xii/5/France

Protocol between the USSR and France concerning conclusion of an Eastern Pact

Signed Dec. 5, 1934, in Geneva.
Czechoslovakia adhered to the protocol by exchange of notes dated Dec. 7, 1934.
Sources: *SDD*, 8, pp. 22–23.
STS, 2, p. 112.
SDFP, 3, pp. 96–97.

● 34/xii/7/Cz

Exchange of notes between the USSR and Czechoslovakia concerning Czechoslovakia's adherence to the Franco-Soviet protocol of December 5, 1934, concerning conclusion of an Eastern Pact

Sent Dec. 7, 1934, in Geneva.
Sources: *SDD*, 8, pp. 24–25.
STS, 2, p. 113.
SDFP, 3, p. 97 (Soviet note).

● 34/xii/9/France

Protocol between the USSR and France concerning commercial relations

Signed Dec. 9, 1934, in Moscow.
Entered into force on signature. Extends the temporary commercial treaty of Jan. 11, 1934, until conclusion of a new trade agreement, or throughout 1935. Further extended and modified by agreement of Jan. 6, 1936, and subsequently.
Sources: *Izv.*, Dec. 20, 1934.
STS, 2, p. 113.
SDFP, 3, pp. 99–100.

● 34/xii/14/Pl

Protocol between the USSR, Poland, and Germany concerning regulation of the export of rye and rye flour, with final protocol

Signed Dec. 14, 1934, in Moscow.
Initialed on Sept. 26, 1934, and approved by the signatories. Entered into force Jan. 1, 1935; valid through July 31, 1935.
References: *VVerz.*, p. 444.
Ostwirtschaft, Sept. 1934, p. 142; *ibid.*, Dec. 1934, p. 190.

● 34/xii/22/Mul/a

Agreement for dispensing with bills of health

Signed Dec. 22, 1934, in Paris.
Ratification not required. Entered into force Apr. 1, 1935. Duration 5 years from signature; thereafter until 6 months following denunciation.
For modification, see 46/vii/22/Mul/d.
Sources: *SZ*, 1935, II, No. 7, Art. 52 (R, F).
  SDD, 8, pp. 341–43.
  LNTS, 183, pp. 153–59 (E, F).
  Hudson, 6, pp. 958–61.

● 34/xii/22/Mul/b

Agreement for dispensing with consular visas on bills of health

Signed Dec. 22, 1934, in Paris.
Ratification not required. Entered into force Apr. 1, 1935. Duration 5 years from signature; thereafter until 6 months following denunciation.
For modification, see 46/vii/22/Mul/d.
Sources: *SZ*, 1935, II, No. 7, Art. 53 (R, F).
  SDD, 8, pp. 343–46.
  LNTS, 183, pp. 145–51 (E, F).
  Hudson, 6, pp. 962–65.

● 34/xii/31/Italy

Protocol between the USSR and Italy extending existing economic and commercial agreements

Signed Dec. 31, 1934, in Rome.
Extends unspecified agreements until conclusion of commercial negotiations currently being conducted.
Sources: *STS*, 2, p. 113, citing
  BL, 52, Jan. 1935, supplement, pp. 34–35.

1935

● 35/ii/8/Rom/a

Agreement between the USSR and Romania concerning establishment of direct rail communications

Signed Feb. 8, 1935, in Moscow.
Traffic to start Aug. 1, 1935, on completion of a bridge over the Dnestr (see next document). The conference at which this agreement was adopted also agreed on exchange of railroad cars between the railroads of the USSR and Romania.
Reference: *Izv.*, Feb. 10, 1935.

● 35/ii/8/Rom/b

Agreement between the USSR and Romania concerning reconstruction of a railroad bridge across the Dniester

Signed Feb. 8, 1935, in Moscow.
Reconstruction to be completed by Aug. 1, 1935.
Reference: *Izv.*, Feb. 10, 1935.

● 35/ii/20/Mul/a

International convention for the campaign against contagious diseases of animals, with declaration

Signed Feb. 20, 1935, in Geneva.
Ratified by the USSR May 16, 1937; act of ratification deposited Sept. 20, 1937.

Entered into force Mar. 23, 1938. Duration 2 years; thereafter, if not denounced with 6 months' notice, extended for 4 years; thereafter valid until denounced with 6 months' notice.
Sources: *SZ*, 1937, II, No. 37, Art. 328 (R, E, F).
  SDD, 10, pp. 109–19.
  LNTS, 186, pp. 173–90 (E, F).

● 35/ii/20/Mul/b

International convention concerning the transit of animals, meat, and other products of animal origin, with annex

Signed Feb. 20, 1935, in Geneva.
Ratified by the USSR May 16, 1937; act of ratification deposited Sept. 20, 1937.
Entered into force Dec. 6, 1938. Duration 2 years; thereafter extended for 4 years, and subsequently, if not denounced 6 months before expiration.
Sources: *SZ*, 1937, II, No. 37, Art. 329 (R, E, F).
  SDD, 10, pp. 120–33.
  LNTS, 193, pp. 37–57 (E, F).

● 35/ii/20/Mul/c

International convention concerning export and import of animal products, other than meat, meat preparations,

fresh animal products, milk, and milk products, with annex

Signed Feb. 20, 1935, in Geneva.
Ratified by the USSR May 16, 1937; act of ratification deposited Sept. 20, 1937. Entered into force Dec. 6, 1938. Duration 2 years; thereafter extended for 4 years, and subsequently, if not denounced 6 months before expiration.
Sources: *SZ*, 1937, II, No. 37, Art. 330 (R, E, F).
  SDD, 10, pp. 133–43.
  LNTS, 193, pp. 59–77 (E, F).

● 35/ii/27/1920

Treaty concerning the Archipelago of Spitsbergen, with annex

Signed Feb. 9, 1920, in Paris.
Soviet adherence by decree of Feb. 27, 1935. Entered into force for the USSR May 7, 1935.
Sources: *SZ*, 1935, II, No. 17, Art. 138 (R, E, F).
  SDD, 9, pp. 53–61.
  LNTS, 2, pp. 7–19 (E, F).

● 35/iii/5/Greece

Trade and clearing agreement between the USSR and Greece

Signed Mar. 5, 1935, in Athens.
Ratified by Greece Mar. 8, 1935. Entered into force on signature; applied retroactively from Feb. 10, 1935. Valid through Dec. 31, 1935.
Sources: *Greek official gazette, 1935, A, No. 154.
  STS, 2, pp. 114–15, citing *SSSkS*, 1935, No. 3.

● 35/iii/7/Ger

Parcel post agreement between the USSR and Germany, with final protocol

Signed Mar. 7, 1935, in Moscow.
Ratified by the USSR July 13, 1935. Entered into force Sept. 7, 1935 (1 month after exchange of acts of ratification, which took place Aug. 7, 1935, in Berlin). Duration the same as that of the treaty of Oct. 12, 1925 (25/x/12/Ger/a).
Sources: *SZ*, 1936, II, No. 11, Art. 111 (R, G).
  SDD, 9, pp. 268–77.
  RGbl, 1935, II, No. 38, p. 508.

LNTS, 169, pp. 7–21 (E, F).
STS, 2, pp. 115–17.

● 35/iii/11/UK

Exchange of notes between the USSR and the United Kingdom concerning the Russian text of the parcel post convention of April 19, 1934

Sent Jan. 21, Mar. 9 and 11, 1935, in London.
Sources: *LNTS*, 158, pp. 358–59, 377–78 (E, F).
  STS, 2, pp. 113–14.

● 35/iii/23/Manchukuo

Agreement between the USSR and Manchukuo concerning transfer to Manchukuo of the rights of the USSR to the Chinese Eastern Railway, with final protocol

Signed Mar. 23, 1935, in Tokyo.
Entered into force on signature. Supplemented by a protocol and 3 exchanges of notes between the USSR and Japan (next 2 items).
Sources: *SZ*, 1935, II, No. 11, Art. 89, pp. 127–52 (R, E).
  SDD, 8, pp. 288–303.
  STS, 2, pp. 118–22.

● 35/iii/23/Pl

Protocol between the USSR, Japan, and Manchukuo concerning payments to be made by Manchukuo to the USSR for the Chinese Eastern Railway

Signed Mar. 23, 1935, in Tokyo.
Supplements the Soviet-Manchukuo protocol (preceding document); supplemented by 3 exchanges of notes between the USSR and Japan (following item).
Sources: *SZ*, 1935, II, No. 11, Art. 89, pp. 152–58 (R, E).
  SDD, 8, pp. 303–307.
  CDT, No. 283.
  STS, 2, pp. 122–23, citing *BFSP*, 139, pp. 611–13.

● 35/iii/23/J

Exchange of notes between the USSR and Japan concerning guarantee of payments by Manchukuo to the USSR for the Chinese Eastern Railway

Sent Mar. 23, 1935, in Tokyo.
Supplements the Soviet-Manchukuo agreement and the Soviet-Manchukuo-Japan

protocol of the same date (two preceding documents). Three exchanges of notes are involved: (1) Japan guarantees payment by Manchukuo to the USSR within the time limit set; (2) Japan confirms the conclusion of a loan contract between Manchukuo and a Japanese banking syndicate; and (3) Japan guarantees payment by Manchukuo to the USSR notwithstanding any difficulties which may arise.
Sources: *SZ*, 1935, II, No. 11, Art. 89, pp. 158–64 (R, E).
SDD, 8, pp. 307–11.
STS, 2, p. 123 (omitting the 2nd exchange), citing
BFSP, 139.

• 35/iii/23/Lith

Trade protocol for 1935 between the USSR and Lithuania

Signed Mar. 23, 1935, in Moscow.
Source: *STS*, 2, p. 118 (summary), citing Private sources.
Reference: *Izv.*, Mar. 27, 1935.

• 35/iii/25/Cz/a

Treaty of commerce and navigation between the USSR and Czechoslovakia, with annex and final protocol

Signed Mar. 25, 1935, in Prague.
Ratified by the USSR Apr. 27, 1935. Entered into force provisionally Apr. 15, 1935; definitively June 23, 1935 (15 days after exchange of acts of ratification, which took place June 8, 1935). Valid until 1 year after denunciation. Superseded by the treaty of commerce and navigation of Dec. 11, 1947.
Sources: *SZ*, 1935, II, No. 14–15, Art. 131 (R, Cz.).
SDD, 8, pp. 172–86.
SZN, 1935, No. 61.
LNTS, 161, pp. 257–307 (R, Cz., E, F).
STS, 2, pp. 124–27.
Reference: *SZ*, 1935, II, No. 9, Art. 64 (decree concerning provisional entry into force).

• 35/iii/25/Cz/b

Agreement between the USSR and Czechoslovakia concerning reciprocal protection of rights to industrial property, with final protocol

Signed Mar. 25, 1935, in Prague.

Ratified by the USSR Apr. 27, 1935. Entered into force provisionally Apr. 22, 1935; definitively June 23, 1935 (15 days after exchange of acts of ratification, which took place June 8, 1935, in Moscow). Valid until 1 year after denunciation.
Sources: *SZ*, 1935, II, No. 14–15, Art. 132 (R, Cz.).
SDD, 8, pp. 187–88.
SZN, 1935, No. 62.
LNTS, 161, pp. 309–18 (R, Cz., E, F).
STS, 2, p. 127.

• 35/iv/7/1921

Declaration recognizing the right to a flag of states having no seacoast

Signed Apr. 20, 1921, in Barcelona.
Adherence of the USSR approved Apr. 7, 1935; entered into force for the USSR May 16, 1935.
Sources: *SZ*, 1935, II, No. 17, Art. 137 (E, F, R).
SDD, 9, p. 421.
LNTS, 7, pp. 73–75 (E, F); *ibid.*, 156, p. 177 (Soviet accession).

• 35/iv/9/Ger/a

Trade agreement between the USSR and Germany

Signed Apr. 9, 1935, in Berlin.
Covers settlement of Soviet debts due during 1935, Soviet exports to Germany, and current Soviet orders in Germany. The German Embassy, 1958, mentions "several" supplementary exchanges of notes.
References: *Pr.*, *Izv.*, Apr. 10, 1935.
Ostwirtschaft, Apr.–May, 1935, p. 62.
Hoeffding, p. 478.

• 35/iv/9/Ger/b

Credit agreement between the USSR and Germany

Signed Apr. 9, 1935, in Berlin.
Provides for a German credit of 2 million Reichsmarks, to be repaid in 5 years at 2 per cent, for Soviet purchases in Germany supplementary to those covered by the trade agreement of the same date. After several extensions, the period for utilization of the credit expired June 30, 1937 (*Ostwirtschaft*, Aug.–Sept., 1937, p. 105).
References: *Pr.*, *Izv.*, Apr. 10, 1935.
Ostwirtschaft, Apr.–May, 1935, pp. 62–

63; *ibid.*, June–July, 1935, pp. 90–92 (summary).
STS, 2, pp. 127–28, based partly on Private sources.
Hoeffding, p. 478.

● 35/v/ /Uruguay

Trade agreement between the USSR and Uruguay

Signed during May 1935, in Montevideo.
Sources: STS, 2, p. 128 (summary), citing *El pueblo* (Montevideo), June 27, 1935.

● 35/v/2/France

Treaty of mutual assistance between the USSR and France, with protocol of signature

Signed May 2, 1935, in Paris.
Soviet decree of ratification dated Mar. 8, 1936. Ratified by France Mar. 12, 1936. Entered into force Mar. 27, 1936, on exchange of acts of ratification in Paris (under Art. 5, exchange was to have taken place in Moscow, but Paris was substituted by mutual agreement). Duration 5 years; if not denounced 1 year before expiration, valid until 1 year after denunciation.
Sources: *Pr.*, May 4, 1935.
　SZ, 1936, II, No. 7, Art. 72 (R, F).
　SDD, 9, pp. 45–49.
　AD, 1936, pp. 152–55 (F).
　*JO, May 17, 1936.
　LNTS, 167, pp. 395–406 (R, F, E).
　STS, 2, pp. 128–29.

● 35/v/6/Af

Agreement between the USSR and Afghanistan concerning the campaign against locusts

Signed May 6, 1935, in Kabul.
Entered into force on signature. Duration 3 years; if not denounced 1 year before expiration, extended for additional 3-year periods.
Sources: SZ, 1935, II, No. 16, Art. 135 (R, Persian).
　SDD, 9, pp. 118–21.
　LNTS, 164, pp. 335–49 (R, Persian, E, F).
　STS, 2, p. 129.

● 35/v/16/Cz/a

Treaty of mutual assistance between the USSR and Czechoslovakia, with protocol of signature

Signed May 16, 1935, in Prague.
Soviet decree of ratification dated June 7, 1935. Entered into force June 8, 1935, on exchange of acts of ratification in Moscow. Duration 5 years; if not denounced 1 year before expiration, valid until 1 year following denunciation.
Sources: *Pr.*, May 18, 1935.
　SZ, 1935, II, No. 14–15, Art. 130 (R, Cz.).
　SDD, 9, pp. 49–52.
　LNTS, 159, pp. 347–61 (R, Cz., E, F).
　STS, 2, pp. 130–31.

● 35/v/16/Cz/b

Agreement between the USSR and Czechoslovakia concerning establishment of regular air service between Moscow and Prague

Signed May 16, 1935, in Moscow.
References: *Pr., MDN*, May 17, 1935.

● 35/v/16/France

Communiqué concerning negotiations between the USSR and France

Issued May 16, 1935.
Mentions agreement to continue joint efforts on behalf of an Eastern European security pact.
Sources: *MKh*, 1935, No. 5, p. 143.
　SDFP, 3, pp. 131–32.

● 35/v/16/Sinkiang

Loan agreement between Sovsintorg and Sinkiang

Signed May 16, 1935, in Tihwa.
Provides for a 5-year loan to Sinkiang of 5 million rubles, to be repaid in produce at 4 per cent interest. Signed by Sinkiang without the approval of the Central Chinese Government.
References: Cheng, p. 174.
　Soviet Union's economic invasion of Sinkiang, pp. 32–38.
　Whiting, pp. 28–30.

● 35/v/30/Iran

Exchange of notes between the USSR

and Iran concerning transfer to Iran of lighthouses situated on the Iranian coast of the Caspian Sea

Sent May 30, 1935, in Teheran.
Sources: *SDD*, 9, pp. 318–19.
  STS, 2, p. 131.

● 35/vi/3/Cz

Credit agreement between the USSR and a consortium of banks in Czechoslovakia

Signed June 3, 1935, in Prague.
Entered into force on signature; remains in force until discharge of all obligations assumed therein. Despite the fact that the signatory on the Czech side is not the Czechoslovak Government, the agreement has the effect and substance, if not the form, of a state treaty. Evidently extended in Jan. 1936 (see *Pr.*, Jan. 26, 1936).
Source: *STS*, 2, pp. 132–33, citing Private sources.
References: *Pr.*, June 4, 1935.
  Ostwirtschaft, June–July, 1935, pp. 96–97.

● 35/vi/8/Cz

Parcel post agreement between the USSR and Czechoslovakia

Signed June 8, 1935, in Moscow.
Ratified by the USSR Jan. 25, 1936. Entered into force Mar. 1, 1936 (1 month after exchange of acts of ratification, which took place Jan. 31, 1936, in Prague). Valid until 1 year after denunciation. Annulled by protocol to the parcel post agreement of Aug. 8, 1951.
Sources: *SZ*, 1936, II, No. 14, Art. 127 (R, F).
  SDD, 9, pp. 295–304.
  LNTS, 167, pp. 181–95 (E, F).
  STS, 2, pp. 133–35.

● 35/vi/11/Cz

Communiqué concerning negotiations between the USSR and Czechoslovakia

Issued June 11, 1935.
Mentions satisfaction of both States with existing treaties and agreements between them, and need for increased collaboration in the fields of science, literature and art. Both States to strive for effective realization of a comprehensive collective organization of security.
Sources: *MKh*, 1935, No. 6, p. 143.
  SDFP, 3, pp. 135–36.

● 35/vi/15/Italy

Credit agreement between the USSR and Italy, with two annexes

Signed June 15, 1935, in Rome.
Entered into force on signature. Valid until June 30, 1936.
Note: *Ostwirtschaft*, June–July, 1935, p. 97, mentions 2 additional Soviet-Italian agreements signed on this date: (1) concerning settlement of the trade balance, and (2) extending through June 30, 1936, the concession of the mixed Italian-Soviet company "Irtrans" for goods transit to Iran.
Sources: *SDTD*, 1, pp. 214–17.
  *TC, 49, pp. 276–81.
  STS, 2, pp. 135–36.

● 35/vi/17/Denmark

Trade agreement for 1935 between the USSR and Denmark

Signed June 17, 1935, in Copenhagen. (NB: exact date of signature is not certain. *STS*, 2, p. 135, gives date as June 11, 1935, citing *Pravda*, June 18, 1935, and private sources. *Pravda, loc. cit.*, in a TASS dispatch datelined Stockholm, June 17, 1935, reports the agreement but without specifying the date. As reprinted in *VP*, 4, p. 49, however, the *Pravda* account gives the date as June 17, 1935. Finally, the Danish Embassy, 1957, dates the agreement June 7, 1935).
References: *Pravda*, June 18, 1935; reprinted *VP*, 4, p. 49.
  STS, 2, p. 135, as indicated.

June 22, 1935. International Labour Organisation Convention No. 47

See 56/vi/4/1935.

● 35/vi/24/T

Trade agreement between the USSR and Turkey

Signed June 24, 1935, in Ankara.
Duration 6 months.
Reference: *Pravda*, June 30, 1935.

● 35/vi/25/Colombia

Exchange of notes between the USSR and Colombia concerning establishment of diplomatic relations

Sent June 25, 1935, in Rome.

Sources: *SDD*, 9, p. 4.
  AD, 10, p. 203 (F).
  STS, 2, p. 136.

● 35/vii/8/1910

Agreement for suppression of the circulation of obscene publications

Signed May 4, 1910, in Paris.
Soviet adherence July 8, 1935, as a consequence of adherence to the convention for suppression of the circulation of and traffic in obscene publications of 1923 (next document).
Enters into force for each signatory 6 months after deposit of act of ratification. Valid until 1 year following denunciation. Modified by protocol of May 4, 1949 (see 49/v/14/1949/a and /b).
Sources: *SZ*, 1936, II, No. 21, Art. 179, pp. 450–53 (R, F).
  SDD, 9, pp. 105–107.
  BFSP, 103, p. 251.

● 35/vii/8/1923

International convention for suppression of the circulation of and traffic in obscene publications

Signed Sept. 12, 1923, in Paris.
Soviet adherence July 8, 1935. Enters into force for each signatory 30 days after deposit of act of ratification. Valid until 1 year after denunciation. Adherence to this convention automatically involves adherence to the agreement of May 4, 1910 (preceding document). Modified by protocol of Nov. 12, 1947 (see 47/xii/18/1947/b).
Sources: *SZ*, 1936, II, No. 21, Art. 179 (R, E, F).
  SDD, 9, pp. 100–105.
  LNTS, 27, pp. 213–33 (E, F).

● 35/vii/10/Bul

Parcel post agreement between the USSR and Bulgaria

Signed July 10, 1935, in Moscow.
Soviet decree of ratification dated Jan. 9, 1936. Entered into force May 29, 1936 (1 month after exchange of acts of ratification, which took place Apr. 29, 1936, in Sofia). Duration 2 years; if not denounced 3 months before expiration, valid until 3 months after denunciation.
Sources: *SZ*, 1936, II, No. 19, Art. 177 (R, F).

SDD, 9, pp. 262–68.
LNTS, 168, pp. 275–85 (E, F).
STS, 2, pp. 136–38.

● 35/vii/12/Belgium

Exchange of notes between the USSR and Belgium concerning establishment of diplomatic relations

Sent July 12, 1935, in Paris.
Sources: *Izv.*, July 14, 1935.
  AD, 1936, p. 204 (F).
  SDD, 9, pp. 38–39.
  STS, 2, p. 139.

● 35/vii/13/US

Exchange of notes between the USSR and the United States of America constituting a commercial agreement

Sent July 13, 1935, in Moscow.
Entered into force July 13, 1935. Valid for 1 year. Extended by exchange of notes of July 11, 1936.
Sources: *SZ*, 1935, II, No. 14–15, Art. 133 (E, R).
  SDTD, 1, pp. 269–71.
  EAS, 81, pp. 1–2.
  LNTS, 162, pp. 91–95 (E, F).
  STS, 2, pp. 138–39.
  SDFP, 3, pp. 137–38.

● 35/vii/15/US

Exchange of notes between the USSR and the United States of America concerning purchases to be made by the USSR in the United States during the coming year

Sent July 11 and 15, 1935, in Moscow.
Sources: *EAS*, 81, p. 3.
  LNTS, 162, pp. 96–97 (E, F).
  STS, 2, p. 138.

● 35/vii/23/1931

Convention concerning taxation of foreign motor vehicles, with annex and protocol

Signed Mar. 30, 1931, in Geneva.
Soviet accession dated July 23, 1935, with effect from Jan. 23, 1936. Original entry into force Feb. 6, 1933. Duration 2 years after entry into force; thereafter may be denounced with 1 year's notice.
Sources: *SZ*, 1936, II, No. 33, Art. 317 (R, E, F).
  SDD, 9, pp. 434–45.
  LNTS, 138, pp. 149–77 (E, F).

● 35/viii/23/Ger

Exchange of notes between the USSR and Germany concerning the address of the Soviet Trade Mission in Berlin

Sent Aug. 23, 1935, in Berlin.
Modifies Art. 5 of the economic agreement of Oct. 12, 1925 (part 2 of 25/x/12/Ger/a).
Sources: *RGbl*, 1935, II, No. 41, pp. 641–42.
  STS, 2, pp. 139–40.

● 35/viii/26/Lux

Exchange of notes between the USSR and Luxembourg concerning establishment of diplomatic relations

Sent Aug. 26, 1935, in Paris.
Entered into force Aug. 26, 1935.
Sources: *SDD*, 9, p. 42.
  AD, 10, p. 205 (F).
  STS, 2, p. 140.

● 35/viii/27/Iran/a

Treaty between the USSR and Iran concerning settlement, commerce, and navigation, with related documents

Signed Aug. 27, 1935, in Teheran.
Soviet decree of ratification dated Feb. 17, 1936. Acts of ratification exchanged June 8, 1936, in Moscow. Entered into force June 22, 1936. Duration 3 years; if not denounced 1 year before expiration, valid until 1 year after denunciation. Terminated June 22, 1938, under an exchange of notes between the USSR and Iran (*SP*, 1939, Art. 158); date of exchange unknown, but presumably June 22, 1937.
Related documents include final protocol; list of USSR import quotas for 1935–1936; and 4 exchanges of notes, concerning (1) warships and merchant vessels belonging to the former Russian Government; (2) reciprocal recognition of trademarks; (3) nationals of third countries in ports of the Caspian Sea; and (4) lease of land in the ports of Bandar-Shah and Bandar Nov-Shah for Soviet agencies.
Sources: *SZ*, 1937, II, No. 7, Art. 36, pp. 73–95, 108–30 (R, F).
  AD, 1936, pp. 157–79 (F).
  SDD, 9, pp. 129–50.
  LNTS, 176, pp. 299–333 (E, F).
  STS, 2, pp. 140–46.

● 35/viii/27/Iran/b

Convention between the USSR and Iran concerning the campaign against locusts in border districts

Signed Aug. 27, 1935, in Teheran.
Soviet decree of ratification dated Feb. 17, 1936. Entered into force June 8, 1936, on exchange of acts of ratification in Moscow. Duration 3 years; if not denounced 1 year before expiration, valid until 1 year after denunciation.
Sources: *SZ*, 1936, II, No. 7, Art. 36, pp. 95–97, 130–32 (R, F).
  SDD, 9, pp. 153–55.
  LNTS, 176, pp. 335–41 (E, F).
  STS, 2, p. 146.

● 35/viii/27/Iran/c

Convention between the USSR and Iran concerning the campaign against plant diseases and parasites

Signed Aug. 27, 1935, in Teheran.
Soviet decree of ratification dated Feb. 17, 1936. Entered into force June 8, 1936, on exchange of acts of ratification in Moscow. Duration 3 years; if not denounced 1 year before expiration, valid until 1 year after denunciation. Supplemented by protocol of Oct. 3, 1945.
Sources: *SZ*, 1937, II, No. 7, Art. 36, pp. 98–99, 132–34 (R, F).
  SDD, 9, pp. 151–53.
  LNTS, 176, pp. 343–47 (E, F).
  STS, 2, p. 147.

● 35/viii/27/Iran/d

Veterinary sanitary convention between the USSR and Iran, with three annexes

Signed Aug. 27, 1935, in Teheran.
Soviet decree of ratification dated Feb. 17, 1936. Entered into force June 8, 1936, on exchange of acts of ratification. Annex 3, Form of Veterinarian Certificate, was not included in the original notes of ratification, but was separately put into force by an exchange of notes dated Aug. 3, 1936. Duration 3 years; if not denounced 1 year before expiration, valid until 1 year after denunciation.
Sources: *SZ*, 1937, II, No. 7, Art. 36, pp. 100–107, 135–43 (R, F).
  SDD, 9, pp. 156–64.
  LNTS, 176, pp. 349–63 (E, F).
  STS, 2, pp. 147–48.

● 35/viii/27/Iran/e

**Exchange of notes between the USSR and
Iran concerning entry into force of railroad conventions for direct and transit
communications**

Sent Aug. 27, 1935, in Teheran.
No details are available on the railroad
conventions.
Reference: *Izv.*, Aug. 30, 1935.

● 35/viii/27/Iran/f

**Agreement between the USSR and Iran
concerning loading and unloading in
Iranian ports of the Caspian Sea**

Signed Aug. 27, 1935, in Teheran.
Accompanied by a note from the Iranian
Foreign Minister concerning plans for im-
provement of loading facilities at Caspian
ports.
Reference. *Izv.*, Aug. 30, 1935.

● 35/ix/5/BL

**Temporary commercial convention be-
tween the USSR and the Belgium-Luxembourg Economic Union**

Signed Sept. 5, 1935, in Paris.
Soviet ratification decree dated Aug. 21,
1936. Arts. 1–6 entered into force provisionally from Oct. 1, 1935; definitive
entry into force Aug. 21, 1936, on exchange of acts of ratification in Moscow.
Duration 3 years; thereafter until denounced with 3 months' notice. Arts. 1–6,
however, invalid from Oct. 1, 1937; these
articles were extended to Aug. 21, 1939,
however, by an exchange of notes of Nov.
5, 1937. Extended to Dec. 31, 1939, by
exchange of notes of Aug. 21 and Oct. 1,
1939. Arts. 1, 3, 4, and 5 revived by exchange of notes of Feb. 18, 1948 (48/ii/
18/BL/a). Listed by Korolenko, p. 104,
as still valid as of Nov. 25, 1953.
Sources: *SZ*, 1937, II, No. 2, Art. 10
    (R, F).
SDD, 9, pp. 121–29.
Memorial, 1935, p. 1046.
LNTS, 173, pp. 169–86 (R, F, E).
STS, 2, p. 148.

● 35/ix/6/1931

**Agreement concerning procedure in case
of undischarged or lost triptychs**

Signed Mar. 28, 1931, in Geneva.
Soviet adherence dated Sept. 6, 1935, with

effect from Dec. 5, 1935. After 1 year's
operation for any signatory, may be de-
nounced with 6 months' notice.
Sources: *SZ*, 1936, II, No. 4, Art. 45 (R,
    E, F).
SDD, 9, pp. 422–23.
LNTS, 119, pp. 47–51 (E, F).

● 35/ix/26/1929

**International convention for the protec-
tion of plants, with annex**

Signed Apr. 16, 1929, in Rome.
Soviet adherence dated Sept. 26, 1935,
with effect from Mar. 26, 1936. Duration
indefinite; may be denounced with 1 year's
notice. Enforced within the USSR by decree of the People's Commissariat of Agriculture dated June 2, 1936, to which are
annexed (1) Regulations for external
quarantine of plants, and (2) List of
plant diseases and parasites subject to
external quarantine for the USSR (*SZ*,
1936, II, No. 30, Art. 300, pp. 607–46).
Replaced by convention of Dec. 6, 1951
(see 56/iv/24/1951).
Sources: *SZ*, 1936, II, No. 30, Art. 300
    (R, F).
SDD, 9, pp. 204–13.
LNTS, 126, pp. 305–31 (E, F).

● 35/x/31/1925/a

**International opium convention, with an-
nex and protocol**

Signed Feb. 19, 1925, in Geneva.
Soviet adherence Oct. 31, 1935, with effect
from Jan. 29, 1936. May be denounced
by any signatory with 1 year's notice.
Title varies: also referred to as "Convention relating to dangerous drugs" and "International convention adopted by the Second Opium Conference (League of Nations)." Supplemented by the Final Act
of the Second International Opium Conference (next document) and by the convention on narcotic drugs of July 13, 1931
(35/x/31/1931/a). Under a protocol of
July 22, 1946 (46/vii/22/Mul/d), the
duties and functions conferred by this
convention on the Office Internationale
d'Hygiène Publique were transferred to
the World Health Organization or its Interim Commission. See also 46/xii/11/
Mul.
Sources: *SZ*, 1937, II, No. 17, Art. 106 (R,
    E, F).

SDD, 9, pp. 450–72.
LNTS, 81, pp. 317–58 (E, F).

• 35/x/31/1925/b

Final Act of the Second International Opium Conference

Signed Feb. 19, 1925, in Geneva.
Soviet adherence to the convention of the same date (preceding document) included this document.
Source: *SZ*, 1937, II, No. 17, Art. 106, pp. 280–302, 326–35 (R, E, F).

• 35/x/31/1931/a

Convention for limiting the manufacture and regulating the distribution of narcotic drugs, with protocol of signature

Signed July 13, 1931, in Geneva.
Soviet adherence dated Oct. 31, 1935, with effect from Jan. 29, 1936. Duration 5 years; thereafter may be denounced with approximately 6 months' notice. Supplements the International Opium Convention of Feb. 19, 1925 (35/x/31/1925/a). Supplemented by the Final Act of the conference at which the convention was adopted (next document). Under a protocol of July 22, 1946 (46/vii/22/Mul/d), the duties and functions conferred by this convention on the Office Internationale d'Hygiène Publique were transferred to the World Health Organization or its Interim Commission. See also 46/xii/11/Mul.
Sources: *SZ*, 1937, II, No. 17, Art. 107 (R, E, F).
    SDD, 9, pp. 472–96.
    LNTS, 139, pp. 301–49 (E, F).

• 35/x/31/1931/b

Final Act of the conference to study a draft convention for limiting the manufacture and regulating the distribution of narcotic drugs

Signed July 13, 1931, in Geneva.
Soviet adherence to the convention of the same date included this document.
Source: *SZ*, 1937, II, No. 17, Art. 107, pp. 386–418, 446–62 (R, E, F).

• 35/xi/7/T

Protocol between the USSR and Turkey extending the treaty of friendship and neutrality of December 17, 1925, and related protocols

Signed Nov. 7, 1935, in Ankara.
Soviet decree of ratification dated Feb. 16, 1936. Ratified by Turkey Dec. 20, 1935.
Entered into force Mar. 16, 1936, on exchange of acts of ratification in Moscow. In addition to the 1925 treaty, the protocol concerns the related protocols of Dec. 17, 1929, Mar. 7, 1931, and Oct. 30, 1931, and the naval protocol of Mar. 7, 1931; all extended to Nov. 7, 1945; thereafter unless denounced 6 months before expiration, extended for successive 2-year periods. For denunciation by the USSR on Mar. 19, 1945, see 25/xii/17/T.
Sources: *SZ*, 1936, II, No. 17, Art. 140 (R, F).
    SDD, 9, pp. 44–45.
    Düstur, 17, p. 115.
    LNTS, 179, pp. 127–29 (E, F).
    STS, 2, p. 150.

• 35/xi/15/Pl. See Appendix 5.

• 35/xi/16/Cz

Consular convention between the USSR and Czechoslovakia, with final protocol

Signed Nov. 16, 1935, in Moscow.
Ratified by the USSR May 10, 1936.
Entered into force June 7, 1936 (15 days after exchange of acts of ratification, which took place May 23, 1936, in Prague). Valid until 1 year after denunciation. Superseded by convention of Oct. 5, 1957 (57/x/5/Cz/b).
Sources: *SZ*, 1936, II, No. 35, Art. 319 (R, F).
    AD, 1936, pp. 180–89.
    SDD, 9, pp. 89–99.
    LNTS, 169, pp. 143–59 (E, F).
    STS, 2, pp. 150–53.

• 35/xi/22/US

Exchange of notes between the USSR and the United States of America concerning execution of letters rogatory, with annex

Sent Nov. 22, 1935, in Moscow.
Sources: *SZ*, 1936, II, No. 4, Art. 44 (R, E).
    SDD, 9, pp. 79–84.
    EAS, No. 83.
    LNTS, 167, pp. 303–11 (E, F).
    STS, 2, pp. 153–54.
Reference: *DSB*, 37, 1957, p. 810.

• 35/xii/21/1890

Convention concerning establishment of

an International Union for the Publication of Customs Tariffs, with Regulations and protocol of signature

Signed July 5, 1890, in Brussels.
Soviet adherence dated Dec. 21, 1935. Original entry into force Apr. 1, 1891. Duration 7 years, with automatic extension thereafter for successive 7-year periods. May be denounced by any signatory 1 year before expiration. Revised by protocol of Dec. 16, 1949 (see 54/viii/27/1949).
Sources: *SZ*, 1936, II, No. 29, Art. 298 (R, F).
SDD, 9, pp. 196–203.

1936

● 36/i/6/France

Agreement between the USSR and France modifying and extending the temporary commercial agreement of January 11, 1934, with three annexes and protocol of signature

Signed Jan. 6, 1936, in Paris.
Confirmed by the USSR Jan. 25, 1936, with temporary effect from date of signature, pending ratification. Extends the agreement of 1934 through Dec. 31, 1936. Modified by agreement of Jan. 21, 1936. Extended and modified by agreements of Dec. 17, 1936, and subsequently.
Annexes: (1) list of products of Soviet origin subject to minimum tariff; (2) list of products of Soviet origin subject to reduction in general tariff; and (3) list of products of Soviet origin subject to minimum tariff, to be imported during 1936 under quota.
Sources: *SDD*, 9, pp. 164–70.
AD, 1936, pp. 189–96 (F).
*JO, Jan. 7, 1936.
STS, 2, p. 155.
Reference: *SZ*, 1936, II, No. 2, Art. 20 (temporary entry into force).

● 36/i/11/Greece

Trade and clearing agreement between the USSR and Greece

Signed Jan. 11, 1936, in Athens.
Ratified by Greece Jan. 21, 1936. Entered into force on signature; applied retroactively from Jan. 1, 1936. Valid through Dec. 31, 1936.
Sources: **Greek official gazette, 1936, A, No. 135.
STS, 2, p. 156, citing
SSSkS, 1936, No. 3.

● 36/i/15/Lith

Trade agreement for 1936 between the USSR and Lithuania

Signed Jan. 15, 1936, in Moscow (according to *Izv.*, Jan. 16, 1936, this was an oral agreement).
References: *Izv.*, Jan. 16, 1936.
STS, 2, p. 157, citing
Private sources.

● 36/1/21/France

Agreement between the USSR and France modifying the commercial agreement of January 6, 1936, with three annexes

Signed Jan. 21, 1936, in Paris.
Confirmed by the USSR Feb. 25, 1936, with temporary effect from date of signature, pending ratification. Modifies and completes the three lists annexed to the agreement of Jan. 6, 1936. Extended and modified by agreement of Dec. 17, 1936, and subsequently.
Sources: *SDD*, 9, pp. 170–76.
AD, 1936, pp. 196–99 (F).
*JO, Jan. 23, 1936.
STS, 2, p. 157.
Reference: *SZ*, 1936, II, No. 6, Art. 60 (temporary entry into force).

● 36/i/23/1931

Convention concerning unification of road signals, with annex and three tables

Signed Mar. 30, 1931, in Geneva.
Adherence of the USSR became valid Jan. 23, 1936 (6 months after deposit of act of ratification). Soviet act of ratification was therefore deposited on or about July 23, 1935, and Soviet ratification must have taken place before that date. Duration 8 years after entry into force; thereafter may be denounced with 1 year's notice.
Sources: *SZ*, 1936, II, No. 33, Art. 316 (R, E, F).
SDD, 9, pp. 423–34.
LNTS, 150, pp. 247–68 (E, F).

● 36/ii/ /Iran. See Appendix 5.

• 36/ii/4/France

Agreement between the USSR and France concerning removal of import duties on Soviet products and the transit of French merchandise through the territory of the USSR

Signed Feb. 4, 1936, in Paris.
Confirmed by the USSR Apr. 7, 1936, with temporary effect from Apr. 1, 1936, pending ratification. Extends through Dec. 31, 1938, most-favored-nation treatment for goods of one party in transit through the territory of the other.
Sources: *SDD*, 9, pp. 176–77.
  AD, 1936, pp. 199–200 (F).
  *JO, Mar. 13, 1936, p. 2862.
  STS, 2, pp. 157–58.

• 36/ii/11/Fin

Protocol between the USSR and Finland modifying the convention of June 18, 1924, concerning direct transportation of passengers and freight by rail

Signed Feb. 11, 1936, in Helsinki.
Soviet decree of ratification dated Apr. 7, 1936. Entered into force June 12, 1936 (60 days after exchange of acts of ratification, which took place Apr. 13, 1936, in Moscow). Duration same as that of the convention of 1924 (24/vi/18/Fin/d). Abrogates the Regulations of June 18, 1924 (24/vi/18/Fin/e).
Sources: *SZ*, 1936, II, No. 17, Art. 141 (R, Finnish).
  SDD, 9, pp. 324–27.
  *SS, 1936, No. 24 (Finnish, R).
  LNTS, 172, pp. 403–10 (R, Finnish, E, F).
  STS, 2, p. 158.

• 36/ii/17/Rom

Payments agreement between the USSR and Romania, with protocol

Signed Feb. 17, 1936, in Bucharest.
Entered into force Mar. 1, 1936 (15 days after signature). Valid for 9 months; if not denounced 1 month before expiration, valid until 1 month after denunciation. Remaining balance terminated by protocol of May 8, 1945 (45/v/8/Rom/d).
Source: *STS*, 2, pp. 158–59, citing
  MO, Mar. 16, 1936, pp. 2174–75.
Reference: *Izv.*, Feb. 18, 1936.

• 36/iii/3/Pol

Exchange of notes between the USSR and Poland constituting a temporary customs agreement, with list of duty reductions

Sent Mar. 3, 1936, in Warsaw.
Ratified by Poland Nov. 9, 1936. Entered into force provisionally Mar. 18, 1936. Valid through Dec. 31, 1936.
Sources: **DURP*, 1936, No. 21, Art. 171.
  STS, 2, p. 159, citing
  ZT, 1936, 4, pp. 17–19.

• 36/iii/9/France

Parcel post agreement between the USSR and France, with final protocol

Signed Mar. 9, 1936, in Moscow.
Soviet decree of ratification dated July 15, 1936. Entered into force Aug. 14, 1936 (15 days after exchange of acts of ratification, which took place July 30, 1936, in Paris). Valid through Dec. 31, 1940, but may be denounced with 6 months' notice from Dec. 31, 1938. If not denounced by June 30, 1940, extended for 3-year periods until denounced 3 months before expiration. Protocol concerns transit through the USSR of French goods to Iran.
Sources: *SZ*, 1936, II, No. 36, Art. 321 (R, F).
  SDD, 9, pp. 286–95.
  *JO, Aug. 18, 1936.
  LNTS, 179, pp. 131–45 (F, E).
  STS, 2, pp. 159–62.

• 36/iii/12/MPR

Protocol of mutual assistance between the USSR and the Mongolian People's Republic

Signed Mar. 12, 1936, in Ulan Bator.
Entered into force on signature. Duration 10 years. Replaces the gentlemen's agreement of Nov. 27, 1934. Just before expiration in 1946, converted into the treaty of friendship and mutual assistance of Feb. 27, 1946 (46/ii/27/MPR/a).
Protested by China as a violation of Art. 5 of the treaty of May 31, 1924, in a note of Apr. 7, 1936; answered by a Soviet note of Apr. 8, 1936 (*Pravda*, Apr. 9, 1936, reprinted *VP*, 4, pp. 125–27).
Sources: *Pravda*, Apr. 8, 1936.
  SZ, 1936, II, No. 23, Art. 213 (R, M).
  SDD, 9, pp. 43–44.
  STS, 2, p. 162.
  SDFP, 3, pp. 168–70.

• 36/iii/29/Af

Protocol between the USSR and Afghanistan extending the treaty of neutrality and nonaggression of June 24, 1931

Signed Mar. 29, 1936, in Moscow.
Soviet decree of ratification dated Aug. 8, 1936. Entered into force Sept. 3, 1936, on exchange of acts of ratification in Kabul. Extends the 1931 treaty through Mar. 29, 1946, and thereafter until 1 year following denunciation.
Sources: *SZ*, 1937, II, No. 8, Art. 37 (R, Persian).
    SDD, 9, pp. 37–38.
    LNTS, 177, pp. 467–71 (R, Persian, E, F).
    STS, 2, p. 162.

• 36/iii/31/Pol/a

Exchange of notes between the USSR and Poland constituting an agreement concerning reciprocal recognition of tonnage measurement certificates

Sent Mar. 31, 1936, in Moscow.
Ratified by Poland Nov. 17, 1936. Entered into force Jan. 3, 1937 (30 days after exchange of notes concerning ratification, which took place Dec. 4, 1936, in Warsaw). Valid until 6 months after denunciation. Extended to Danzig by exchange of notes of Feb. 23, 1937.
Sources: *SZ*, 1937, II, No. 23, Art. 157 (R, P).
    SDD, 9, pp. 320–22.
    DURP, 1937, No. 3, Arts. 23, 24.
    LNTS, 186, pp. 203–10.
    STS, 2, pp. 162–63.

• 36/iii/31/Pol/b

Exchange of notes between the USSR and Poland constituting an agreement concerning most-favored-nation treatment with regard to dues paid by merchant ships

Sent Mar. 31, 1936, in Moscow.
Ratified by Poland Nov. 17, 1936. Entered into force Jan. 3, 1937 (30 days after exchange of notes concerning ratification, which took place Dec. 4, 1936, in Warsaw). Valid until 6 months after denunciation. Extended to Danzig by exchange of notes of Feb. 23, 1937.
Sources: *SZ*, 1937, II, No. 23, Art. 158 (R, P).
    SDD, 9, pp. 322–24.
    DURP, 1937, No. 3, Arts. 25, 26.

LNTS, 186, pp. 211–18 (R, P, E, F).
STS, 2, p. 163.

• 36/iv/4/1905

Convention concerning establishment of a permanent International Institute of Agriculture

Signed June 7, 1905, in Rome.
Adherence of the USSR dated Apr. 4, 1936. Modified by protocol of Apr. 21, 1926 (next document). The USSR withdrew from the convention on Feb. 12, 1938.
Sources: *SZ*, 1936, II, No. 34, Art. 318 (R, F).
    SDD, 9, pp. 214–17.

• 36/iv/4/1926

Protocol modifying the convention of June 7, 1905, concerning establishment of a permanent International Institute of Agriculture

Signed Apr. 21, 1926, in Rome.
Adhered to by the USSR Apr. 4, 1936, together with the 1905 convention (preceding document).
Sources: *SZ*, 1936, II, No. 34, Art. 318, pp. 718–20, 723–25 (R, F).
    SDD, 9, pp. 217–18.
    LNTS, 88, p. 410 (E, F).

• 36/iv/16/T

Exchange of notes between the USSR and Turkey concerning negotiations for a revision of the Lausanne Convention on the Black Sea Straits

Sent Apr. 11 and 16, 1936.
The USSR was not a signatory to the Lausanne Convention of July 24, 1923 (see Appendix 1).
Sources: *MKh*, 1936, No. 5, p. 163.
    SDFP, 3, pp. 188–89 (Soviet note).

• 36/iv/29/Ger

Agreement between the USSR and Germany concerning trade and payments in 1936

Signed Apr. 29, 1936, in Berlin.
Entered into force on signature. Valid through Dec. 31, 1936 (or until Feb. 28, 1937, for use of export permits by the USSR; this date was subsequently extended by German action to June 30, 1937

—see *Ostwirtschaft*, Aug. 1936, p. 107).
According to the German Embassy, 1958,
the agreement was accompanied by sev-
eral exchanges of notes. Extended through
Dec. 31, 1937, by exchange of notes dated
Dec. 24, 1936.
References: *Ostwirtschaft*, Apr./May
 1936, pp. 57–58 (summary).
 STS, 2, p. 164 (summary).
 Izv., May 1, 1936.

**May 13, 1936. Agreement for a uniform
system of maritime buoyage, with annexed regulations**
See Appendix 1.

● 36/v/25/J
**Protocol between the USSR and Japan
extending the fishery convention of January 23, 1928**

Signed May 25, 1936, in Moscow.
Entered into force on signature. Extends
the convention of 1928 through Dec. 31,
1936. Re-extended by protocol of Dec.
28, 1936, and subsequently.
Sources: *SZ*, 1936, II, No. 37, Art. 323
 (R, E).
 SDD, 9, p. 180.
 CDT, No. 386.
 STS, 2, p. 164.

● 36/vi/9/T
**Exchange of notes between the USSR
and Turkey extending the convention of
August 6, 1928, concerning procedure
for consideration and settlement of border disputes**

Sent June 9, 1936, in Moscow.
Ratified by Turkey Dec. 22, 1936. Extends
the 1928 convention (28/viii/6/T/d) until
entry into force of the new convention currently being negotiated (presumably 37/
vii/15/T/a).
Sources: *STS*, 2, pp. 164–65, citing
 LT, 15, p. 103.

● 36/vi/14/Pol
**Agreement between the USSR and Po-
land concerning the legal status of the
Soviet Trade Mission in Poland, with
final protocol**

Signed June 14, 1936, in Warsaw.
Ratified by the USSR June 1, 1939. Law
on ratification was passed by the Polish
Sejm June 16, 1939, but was not promulgated by the President of Poland. Entered
into force provisionally Mar. 27, 1939;
definitive entry into force was to have
taken place 15 days after exchange of acts
of ratification. Duration 2 years; if not
denounced 6 months before expiration, extended for 1-year periods indefinitely. For
exchange of notes concerning exchange of
acts of ratification, see 39/ii/19/Pol/e.
Sources: *VT*, 1939, No. 5–6, pp. 17–21.
 DURP, 1939, No. 24, Art. 154.
 STS, 2, pp. 165–66.

● 36/vi/22/Mul
**Protocol concerning renewal of the Bal-
tic Geodetic Convention of December 31,
1925**

Signed June 22, 1936, in Helsinki, by the
USSR, Denmark, Finland, Latvia, Estonia,
Germany, Danzig, and Poland; on July 9,
1936, by Sweden; and on Sept. 15, 1936,
by Lithuania.
Soviet decree of ratification dated Feb. 28,
1937. Entered into force Mar. 9, 1937 (on
deposit of the final act of ratification, that
of the USSR). Extends validity of 1925
convention for an additional 12 years, beginning Jan. 1, 1937. For the 1925 convention, see 29/ii/9/1925.
Sources: *SZ*, 1937, II, No. 25, Art. 171
 (R, G, F).
 RGbl, 1937, II, No. 18, p. 141.
 LNTS, 178, pp. 439–43 (E, F, G).

**June 24, 1936. International Labour Or-
ganisation Convention No. 52**
See 56/vii/6/1936/a.

● 36/vi/26/Mul
**Procès-verbal to alter the latest date of
issue of the annual statement of the estimated world requirement of dangerous
drugs**

Signed June 26, 1936, in Geneva.
Drawn up by the supervisory body, as provided for by the International Convention
of July 13, 1931, for limiting the manufacture and regulating the distribution of
narcotic drugs. Had not entered into
force as of July 10, 1944 (requires signature by all States parties to the convention of July 13, 1931).
Source: League of Nations Document
 C.286(a).M.174(a).1936.XI, cited in

LNOJ, Special supplement No. 193, p. 129.

June 26, 1936. Convention for suppression of the illicit traffic in dangerous drugs

See 46/xii/11/Mul and Appendix 1.

• 36/vi/29/Denmark

Parcel post agreement between the USSR and Denmark

Signed June 29, 1936, in Moscow.
Soviet decree of ratification dated Oct. 31, 1936. Entered into force Jan. 7, 1937 (1 month after exchange of acts of ratification, which took place Dec. 7, 1936, in Copenhagen). Valid until 6 months after denunciation.
Sources: *SZ*, 1937, II, No. 14, Art. 72 (R, F).
  SDD, 9, pp. 277–85.
  *Lovtidende C, Danmarks Traktater, 1937, p. 4.
  LNTS, 174, pp. 93–107 (E, F).
  STS, 2, pp. 166–68.

• 36/vii/7/Denmark

Trade agreement between the USSR and Denmark

Signed July 7, 1936, in Copenhagen.
Modified by agreement of July 22, 1936.
Reference: Danish Embassy, 1957.

• 36/vii/11/US

Exchange of notes between the USSR and the United States of America extending the commercial agreement of July 13, 1935

Sent July 11, 1936, in Moscow.
Extends the agreement of 1935 to July 13, 1937.
Sources: *SZ*, 1936, II, No. 35, Art. 320 (R, E).
  SDD, 9, pp. 117–18.
  EAS, No. 96, pp. 1–2.
  STS, 2, p. 169.

• 36/vii/13/US

Exchange of notes between the USSR and the United States of America concerning purchases to be made by the USSR in the United States during the coming year

Sent July 9 and 13, 1936, in Moscow.
Sources: *EAS*, No. 96, pp. 2–3.
  STS, 2, p. 168.

July 17, 1936. Agreement between the USSR and the United Kingdom concerning a naval treaty

See 37/vii/17/UK.

• 36/vii/20/Pl

Convention concerning the regime of the Black Sea Straits, with four annexes and a protocol (Montreux Convention)

Signed July 20, 1936, in Montreux.
Soviet decree of ratification dated July 31, 1936; act of ratification deposited Nov. 9, 1936. Provisional entry into force Aug. 15, 1936; definitive entry into force Nov. 9, 1936. Duration 20 years; if not denounced 2 years before expiration, valid until 2 years after denunciation. Replaces the Lausanne Convention of July 24, 1923 (not adhered to by the USSR; see Appendix 1).
Reaffirmed by the USSR in a declaration dated Aug. 10, 1941 (*VPSS VP*, 1, p. 129).
For a proposal at the Potsdam Conference to revise the Convention, see 45/viii/1/ (16). For an exchange of notes between the USSR and the United States concerning revision, see 46/viii/19/US.
Sources: *SZ*, 1937, II, No. 13, Art. 71 (R, F).
  SDD, 9, pp. 61–78.
  LNTS, 173, pp. 213–41 (E, F).

• 36/vii/22/Denmark

Agreement between the USSR and Denmark modifying the trade agreement of July 7, 1936

Signed July 22, 1936, in Copenhagen.
Reference: Danish Embassy, 1957.

• 36/vii/28/UK

Exchange of notes between the USSR and the United Kingdom constituting an agreement on trade credits, with annex

Sent July 28, 1936, in London.
Covers Soviet orders from Aug. 1, 1936, through Sept. 30, 1937. Credit of £10 million to be repaid in 5 years.
Sources: **Cmd. 5253, 1936.
  STS, 2, pp. 169–70.
Reference: *Pravda*, July 31, 1936.

● 36/viii/3/Iran

Exchange of notes between the USSR and Iran concerning confirmation of the third annex of the veterinary sanitary convention of August 27, 1935

Sent Aug. 3, 1936.
For the convention, see 35/viii/27/Iran/d.
Reference: *SZ*, 1937, II, p. 106.

● 36/viii/5/France

Exchange of notes between the USSR and France concerning Soviet adherence to the principle of nonintervention in the Spanish civil war

Sent Aug. 5, 1936, in Moscow.
For a Soviet statement of Aug. 23, 1936, on the same subject, see *SDFP*, 3, pp. 203–204.
References: *Izv.*, Aug. 6, 1936.
SDFP, 3, p. 203.

● 36/viii/11/France

Agreement between the USSR and France concerning transmission of legal and notarial documents and the execution of letters rogatory in civil and commercial matters

Signed Aug. 11, 1936, in Paris.
Soviet decree of ratification dated Sept. 29, 1936. Entered into force Nov. 8, 1936, under an exchange of notes dated Oct. 8, 1936 (not listed separately). Acts of ratification exchanged Oct. 8, 1936, in Moscow. Valid until 6 months after denunciation.
Sources: *SZ*, 1937, II, No. 3, Art. 11 (R, F).
SDD, 9, pp. 85–89.
*JO, Oct. 1936.
LNTS, 176, pp. 365–71 (E, F).
STS, 2, pp. 170–71.

Sept. 23, 1936. Convention concerning the use of broadcasting in the cause of peace
See Appendix 1.

● 36/x/ /Spain

Agreement between the USSR and Spain concerning transfer of part of the Spanish gold reserve to the Soviet State Bank

Signed during Oct. 1936, in Madrid.
Ratified by both signatories. For estimates of the amount involved, ranging from $3 to $5 hundred million, see Allen, 1952, pp. 304–305.
Reference: Alvarez del Vayo, pp. 284–87.

● 36/x/20/T

Agreement between the USSR and Turkey modifying the railroad convention of July 9, 1922

Signed Oct. 20, 1936, in Moscow.
Ratified by the USSR Feb. 17, 1937; by Turkey May 7, 1937. Entered into force July 3, 1937, on exchange of acts of ratification in Ankara. Duration the same as that of the convention of 1922 (22/vii/9/T/b).
Sources: *SZ*, 1937, II, No. 35, Art. 295 (R, F).
*Düstur, 18, p. 622.
STS, 2, p. 171.

Oct. 24, 1936. International Labour Organisation Convention No. 58
See 56/vii/6/1936/b.

● 36/x/28/Est

Exchange of notes between the USSR and Estonia concerning repair of border markers

Sent Oct. 28, 1936, in Tallinn.
Sources: *SDD*, 9, pp. 112–14.
STS, 2, p. 172.

Nov. 6, 1936. Procès-verbal concerning the rules of submarine warfare
See 37/ii/3/1936.

● 36/xi/13/Pol

Exchange of notes between the USSR and Poland concerning Soviet representatives for border affairs

Sent Nov. 12 and 13, 1936, in Warsaw.
Entered into force Nov. 23, 1936. Modifies the protocol of June 6, 1933, concerning appointment of representatives for border affairs (33/vi/3/Pol/b).
Sources: *SDD*, 9, pp. 108–12.
STS, 2, p. 172 (omits detailed list of representatives).

● 36/xi/20/China

Parcel post agreement between the USSR and China

Signed Nov. 20, 1936, in Nanking.
Entered into force Jan. 1, 1937. Super-

seded by agreement of Feb. 7, 1950 (50/
ii/7/CPR/a).
Reference: *Izv.*, Nov. 22, 1936.

● 36/xi/25/1930/a

**Convention providing a uniform law for
bills of exchange and promissory notes,
with two annexes and a protocol**
Signed June 7, 1930, in Geneva.
Soviet accession dated Nov. 25, 1936 (with
technical reservation provided for in Annex 2). Entered into force Jan. 1, 1934;
for the USSR, Feb. 23, 1937 (90 days
after deposit of act of accession). Duration 2 years; thereafter may be denounced
with 90 days' notice (or in urgent cases,
2 days' notice).
Annex 1 is a "Uniform law on bills of
exchange and promissory notes"; Annex
2 lists reservations which may be made
by signatories.
Sources: *SZ*, 1937, II, No. 18, Art. 108
    (R, F, E).
    SDD, 9, pp. 218–50.
    LNTS, 143, pp. 257–315 (E, F).

● 36/xi/25/1930/b

**Convention concerning settlement of cer-
tain conflicts of laws in connection with
bills of exchange and promissory notes,
with protocol**
Signed June 7, 1930, in Geneva.
Soviet accession dated Nov. 25, 1936. Entered into force Jan. 1, 1934; for the
USSR, Feb. 23, 1937 (90 days after deposit of act of accession). Duration for
each signatory 2 years from date of entry
into force for that signatory; thereafter
may be denounced with 90 days' notice.
Sources: *SZ*, 1937, II, No. 18, Art. 109
    (R, F, E).
    SDD, 9, pp. 250–56.
    LNTS, 143, pp. 317–35 (E, F).

● 36/xi/25/1930/c

**Convention concerning stamp laws in
connection with bills of exchange and
promissory notes, with protocol**
Signed June 7, 1930, in Geneva.
Soviet accession dated Nov. 25, 1936. Entered into force Jan. 1, 1934; for the
USSR, Feb. 23, 1937 (90 days after deposit of act of accession). Duration for
each signatory 2 years from date of entry
into force for that signatory; thereafter
may be denounced with 90 days' notice.

Sources: *SZ*, 1937, II, No. 18, Art. 110
    (R, F, E).
    SDD, 9, pp. 256–61.
    LNTS, 143, pp. 337–53 (E, F).

● 36/xii/17/France

**Agreement between the USSR and
France extending the temporary commercial agreement of January 11, 1934,
and the supplementary agreements of
January 6 and 21, 1936, with two annexes**
Signed Dec. 17, 1936, in Paris.
Subject to ratification. Provisional entry
into force Jan. 1, 1937. Extends basic
agreements through Dec. 31, 1937. Further extensions by agreements of Dec. 31,
1937, and subsequently.
Sources: *SDD*, 9, pp. 177–79.
    STS, 2, p. 173, citing
    JO, Dec. 31, 1936.
Reference: *Pravda*, Dec. 19, 1936.

● 36/xii/24/Ger

**Exchange of notes between the USSR and
Germany constituting a protocol extend-
ing the agreement of April 29, 1936,
concerning trade and payments**
Sent Dec. 24, 1936, in Berlin.
Extends the earlier agreement through
Dec. 31, 1937. Further extended in part by
agreement of Dec. 16, 1937. The German
Embassy, 1958, mentions a supplementary
exchange of notes, but without giving
details.
References: *Ostwirtschaft*, Jan. 1937, pp.
    1–2.
    STS, 2, p. 173, citing *Ostwirtschaft, loc.
    cit.*, and
    Wirtschaftsnachrichten, D e c. 2 8,
    1936.

● 36/xii/28/J

**Protocol between the USSR and Japan
extending the fishery convention of January 23, 1928**
Signed Dec. 28, 1936, in Moscow.
Entered into force on signature. Extends
the convention of 1928 through Dec. 31,
1937. Re-extended by protocol of Dec. 29,
1937, and subsequently.
Sources: *SZ*, 1937, II, No. 14, Art. 73
    (R, E).
    SDD, 9, pp. 180–81.
    CDT, No. 416.
    STS, 2, p. 173.

1937

• 37/i/7/US

Exchange of notes between the USSR and the United States of America concerning claims in regard to debts and nationalized property

Sent Jan. 7, 1937, in Moscow.
Source: *SDD*, 10, pp. 23–25.

• 37/i/23/Lith

Trade agreement for 1937 between the USSR and Lithuania

Concluded orally Jan. 23, 1937, in Moscow.
References: *Izv.*, Jan. 24, 1937.
  STS, 2, p. 173.

• 37/ii/3/Spain. See Appendix 5.

• 37/ii/3/1936

Rules of submarine warfare

Signed Nov. 6, 1936, in London, as part of a "Procès-verbal concerning the rules of submarine warfare set forth in Part IV of the Treaty of London, April 22, 1930."
Soviet adherence by declaration of Feb. 3, 1937, in Moscow. Soviet instrument of accession deposited Feb. 16, 1937; receipt acknowledged Feb. 26, 1937. (According to *UNTS*, 122, p. 349, however, a Soviet instrument of accession to the procès-verbal of Nov. 6, 1936, was deposited with the British Government on Dec. 27, 1936; this would indicate that the USSR signed or acceded to that document. This information, however, appears to be incompatible with both the contemporary information from British sources in *LNTS*, 173, and the official Soviet references).
Sources: *SZ*, 1937, II, No. 25, Art. 170 (R, E, F).
  SDD, 9, pp. 497–98.
  LNTS, 173, pp. 353–57 (the procès-verbal of Nov. 6, 1936).
  Hudson, 7, pp. 490–92.

• 37/ii/11/Fin

Communiqué concerning negotiations between the USSR and Finland

Issued Feb. 11, 1937.
States that existing agreements between the 2 States provide the framework for uninterrupted friendly and good-neighborly relations.
Sources: *Izv.*, Feb. 11, 1937.
  SDFP, 3, p. 234.

• 37/ii/23/Pol

Exchange of notes between the USSR and Poland concerning extension to Danzig of the agreements of March 31, 1936, concerning reciprocal recognition of tonnage measurement certificates and dues paid by merchant ships

Sent Feb. 23, 1937.
References: *SZ*, 1937, II, pp. 644, 647.
  SDD, 9, p. 324.

• 37/ii/27/Greece

Trade and clearing agreement between the USSR and Greece

Signed Feb. 27, 1937, in Athens.
Ratified by Greece Apr. 17, 1937. Entered into force on signature; applied retroactively from Jan. 1, 1937. Expires Dec. 31, 1937. Extended by agreement of Apr. 18, 1938.
Sources: *Greek official gazette, 1937, A, No. 180.
  STS, 2, p. 173, citing
  SSSkS, 1937, No. 9.

• 37/iv/9/Lat

Exchange of notes between the USSR and Latvia constituting an agreement concerning repair and restoration of boundary marks

Sent Apr. 9, 1937, in Riga.
Entered into force Apr. 15, 1937. Valid as long as the agreement of July 19, 1926, concerning consideration and settlement of border disputes, which it modifies.
Sources: *LNTS*, 185, pp. 384–87 (R, Lat., E, F).
  LRR, pp. 187–88.
  STS, 2, pp. 174–75.

• 37/iv/24/MPR

Agreement between the USSR and the Mongolian People's Republic concerning questions of citizenship

Signed Apr. 24, 1937, in Ulan Bator.

Entered into force Nov. 6, 1937, on exchange of acts of ratification in Ulan Bator. Valid until 6 months after denunciation. Replaces the agreement of May 20, 1930.
Source: *SDD*, 10, pp. 20–22.

May 31, 1937. Convention modifying the convention of June 21, 1920, concerning the establishment at Paris of an International Institute of Refrigeration
See Appendix 1.

● 37/v/6/Mul

Agreement concerning regulation of the production and marketing of sugar, with protocol

Signed May 6, 1937, in London.
Ratified by the USSR Jan. 7, 1938; act of ratification deposited Feb. 26, 1938. Entered into force provisionally Sept. 1, 1937, under protocol of July 22, 1942. Duration 5 years; thereafter may be denounced with 3 months' notice. Extended for 2 years by protocol of July 22, 1942, and subsequently by protocols of Aug. 31, 1944; Aug. 31, 1945; Aug. 30, 1946; Aug. 29, 1947; and Aug. 31, 1948. The USSR signed those of 1942, 1944, 1945, and 1946, but evidently not those of 1947 and 1948. Listed in *SDD*, 10, p. 238, as no longer in force.
Sources: *VVS*, Dec. 20, 1938.
　USTS, 990, pp. 2–27.
　Hudson, 7, pp. 651–84 (E, F).

June 8, 1937. International agreement for the regulation of whaling
See 46/xi/25/1937.

● 37/vi/18/Lat

Communiqué concerning negotiations between the USSR and Latvia

Issued June 18, 1937.
Mentions agreement on collaboration to strengthen peace on the basis of collective security and the League of Nations principles.
Sources: *MKh*, 1937, No. 8, p. 169.
　SDFP, 3, p. 241.

● 37/vi/21/Lat

Protocol between the USSR and Latvia modifying the economic agreement of December 4, 1933

Signed June 21, 1937, in Moscow.
Ratified by the USSR Apr. 16, 1938. Entered into force June 1, 1938, on exchange of acts of ratification in Riga. Valid as long as the 1933 agreement (33/xii/4/Lat/b).
Sources: *VVS*, Aug. 9, 1938.
　LRR, pp. 186–87.
　LNTS, 189, pp. 131–37 (R, Lat., E, F).
　STS, 2, p. 175.

June 22, 1937. International Labour Organisation Conventions Nos. 59 and 60
See 56/vii/7/1937/a and /b.

● 37/vii/2/J

Agreement between the USSR and Japan concerning withdrawal of military forces from the Amur River islands

Negotiated orally July 2, 1937, in Moscow.
References: *Izv.*, July 3, 1937.
　SDFP, 3, p. 243.

● 37/vii/3/Af. See Appendix 5.

● 37/vii/14/UK

Exchange of notes between the USSR and the United Kingdom concerning reciprocal notification of arrests and imprisonments

Sent July 14, 1937, in Moscow.
Reference: British Embassy, 1958.

● 37/vii/15/T/a

Convention between the USSR and Turkey concerning procedure for considering and settling border incidents and disputes, with final protocol

Signed July 15, 1937, in Moscow.
Ratified by the USSR Jan. 10, 1938; by Turkey, June 20, 1938. Entered into force May 20, 1939 (45 days after exchange of acts of ratification, which took place Apr. 5, 1939, in Ankara). Duration 5 years; if not denounced 6 months before expiration, extended for further 5-year terms. Supplemented by 2 protocols and 2 exchanges of notes (following 4 documents).
Sources: *VVS*, Sept. 29, 1939, No. 33.
　SDD, 10, pp. 32–46.
　Düstur, 19, p. 1351.
　STS, 2, pp. 175–79, citing
　　RG, No. 3955, July 9, 1938, pp. 10192–97.

• 37/vii/15/T/b

Protocol between the USSR and Turkey concerning appointment of border commissioners

Signed July 15, 1937, in Moscow.
Constitutes an integral part of the border convention of the same date. Modified by exchange of notes dated July 5, 1939.
Sources: *VVS*, Sept. 29, 1939, No. 33.
   SDD, 10, pp. 46–50.

• 37/vii/15/T/c

Protocol between the USSR and Turkey concerning border contact points

Signed July 15, 1937, in Moscow.
Constitutes an integral part of the border convention of the same date.
Sources: *VVS*, Sept. 29, 1939, No. 33.
   SDD, 10, pp. 50–51.

• 37/vii/15/T/d

Exchange of notes between the USSR and Turkey constituting an agreement concerning restitution for damages caused by border incidents and disputes

Sent July 15, 1937, in Moscow.
Valid for the first year of operation of the border convention of the same date. If neither party wishes to alter the conditions agreed upon for the coming year 1 month before expiration, extended for an additional year.
Sources: *VVS*, Sept. 29, 1939, No. 33.
   SDD, 10, pp. 51–54.
   STS, 2, p. 178.

• 37/vii/15/T/e

Exchange of notes between the USSR and Turkey concerning use of water from border rivers and streams

Sent July 15, 1937, in Moscow.
Reaffirms validity of the convention on the same subject of Jan. 8, 1927 (27/i/8/T/a), in connection with signing of the border convention of July 15, 1937.
Sources: *VVS*, Sept. 29, 1939, No. 33.
   SDD, 10, pp. 54–55.
   STS, 2, pp. 178–79.

• 37/vii/16/T

Communiqué concerning negotiations between the USSR and Turkey

Issued July 16, 1937.
Reaffirms friendship between the 2 States, reinforced by existing bilateral and multilateral treaties and agreements.
Sources: *MKh*, 1937, No. 8, p. 175.
   SDFP, 3, pp. 246–47.

• 37/vii/17/UK

Agreement between the USSR and the United Kingdom providing for limitation of naval armament and exchange of information concerning naval construction, with protocol of signature

Signed July 17, 1937, in London.
Ratified by the USSR Sept. 14, 1937. Entered into force Nov. 4, 1937 (entry into force was to take place simultaneously with that of the companion naval treaty between the United Kingdom and Germany, and while the naval treaty signed in London on Mar. 25, 1936, was in force. The British-German naval treaty concerned also entered into force Nov. 4, 1937, with the exchange of acts of ratification in London). Valid through Dec. 31, 1942, but may be suspended by either party if it becomes engaged in war.
Exchange of notes concerning the Russian text of the agreement sent Nov. 12 and 19, 1937 (see 37/xi/19/UK). Modified by protocol of July 6, 1938. Suspended by the United Kingdom by a communication received in the Secretariat of the League of Nations Nov. 16, 1939.
For an announcement of agreement reached during negotiations from May 13 through July 30, 1936, see *Pravda*, Aug. 2, 1936, reprinted *VP*, 4, pp. 179–80. See also Beloff, 1, p. 134.
Sources: *VVS*, June 5, 1938, No. 6.
   *BTS, 17, 1938, Cmd. 5679.
   LNTS, 187, pp. 93–138 (R, E, F).
   STS, 2, pp. 179–83.

• 37/viii/4/US/a

Exchange of notes between the USSR and the United States of America constituting a commercial agreement

Sent Aug. 4, 1937, in Moscow.
Entered into force Aug. 6, 1937. Duration 1 year. Extended by exchange of notes dated Aug 5, 1938; Aug. 2, 1939; Aug. 6, 1940; July 31–Aug. 2, 1941; and July 31, 1942. Denounced, with 6 months' notice, by the United States in a note of June 23, 1951 (*DSB*, 25, 1951, p. 95).
Sources: *SZ*, 1937, II, No. 35, Art. 296 (E, R).
   EAS, No. 105, pp. 1–5.

LNTS, 182, pp. 114–21 (E, F).
STS, 2, p. 184.

● 37/viii/4/US/b

**Exchange of notes between the USSR
and the United States of America concerning exemption from excise tax of
coal, coke, and coal or coke briquettes
imported into the United States from
the USSR**

Sent Aug. 4, 1937, in Moscow.
Sources: *EAS*, No. 105, pp. 7–8.
   LNTS, 182, pp. 122–25 (E, F).
   STS, 2, p. 185.

● 37/viii/5/US

**Exchange of notes between the USSR
and the United States of America concerning purchases to be made by the
USSR in the United States during the
coming year**

Sent Aug. 2 and 5, 1937, in Moscow.
Sources: *EAS*, No. 105, pp. 6–7.
   LNTS, 182, pp. 120–22 (E, F).
   STS, 2, pp. 183–84.

● 37/viii/9/Iran

**Exchange of notes between the USSR
and Iran concerning transfer to Iran of
the floating lighthouse "Ashur-Ade"**

Sent Aug. 4 and 9, 1937, in Teheran.
Source: *SDD*, 10, pp. 26–28.

● 37/viii/21/China

**Treaty of nonaggression between the
USSR and China**

Signed Aug. 21, 1937, in Nanking.
Entered into force on signature. Duration
5 years; if not denounced 6 months before
expiration, extended for successive 2-year
periods. Confirms "in a more precise
manner the obligations mutually undertaken under the Treaty for the renunciation of war signed in Paris on Aug. 27,
1928" (28/viii/27/Mul). According to
NT, 1948, No. 9, p. 32, automatically extended for 2 years on Feb. 20, 1948.
Sources: *Izv.*, Aug. 30, 1937.
   VVS, June 15, 1938, No. 7.
   Chen, pp. 113–14.
   LNTS, 181, pp. 101–105.
   STS, 2, p. 185.
Note: Whiting, p. 49, mentions "secret
pledges of Soviet economic and military

assistance" as additions to the treaty; no
source cited.

● 37/ix/14/Mul

**Agreement concerning piracy by subma-
rines in the Mediterranean, with two annexes and a map (Nyon Arrangement)**

Signed Sept. 14, 1937, in Nyon.
Entered into force on signature. Supple-
mented by agreement of Sept. 17, 1937.
Sources: *SZ*, 1938, No. 16, Art. 108 (E,
   F, R).
   LNTS, 181, pp. 135–48 (E, F).
   Hudson, 7, pp. 831–39 (E, F).

● 37/ix/17/Mul

**Agreement concerning attacks by aircraft
and surface vessels on merchant ships in
the Mediterranean**

Signed Sept. 17, 1937, in Geneva.
Entered into force on signature. Supple-
ments the agreement of Sept. 14, 1937.
Sources: *SZ*, 1938, No. 16, Art. 109 (E,
   F, R).
   LNTS, 181, pp. 149–52 (E, F).
   Hudson, 7, pp. 839–41 (E, F).

● 37/x/8/T/a

**Treaty of commerce and navigation be-
tween the USSR and Turkey, with final
protocol**

Signed Oct. 8, 1937, in Ankara.
Ratified by Turkey May 6, 1938; by the
USSR Aug. 25, 1938. Entered into force
provisionally on signature; definitive entry
into force was to be on exchange of acts
of ratification, but according to Korolenko, p. 253, the exchange did not take
place. Nevertheless the treaty was considered still in force as of Nov. 25, 1953
(*ibid.*, p. 104). Duration 3 years from
date of signature; if not denounced 3
months before expiration, extended for
1-year periods. Supersedes the treaty of
Mar. 16, 1931. Modified by exchange of
notes dated Mar. 31, 1938.
Sources: *SDD*, 10, pp. 78–93.
   Korolenko, pp. 244–53.
   STS, 2, pp. 185–88, citing
     RG, May 13, 1938, pp. 9841–46, and
     BL, 55, Apr. 1938, pp. 718–30.

● 37/x/8/T/b

Exchange of notes between the USSR

and Turkey concerning tax assessment of the Soviet Trade Mission in Turkey

Sent Oct. 8, 1937, in Ankara.
Source: *STS*, 2, pp. 188–89.

• 37/x/8/T/c

Trade and clearing agreement between the USSR and Turkey, with three annexes and an exchange of notes

Signed Oct. 8, 1937, in Ankara.
Ratified by Turkey May 13, 1938. Entered into force on signature. Valid until Jan. 1, 1939; if not denounced 3 months before expiration, extended for 1-year periods.
Annexes consist of tariff numbers and lists of products which may be imported into Turkey from the USSR with or without quotas, and forms of certificates of origin. Exchange of notes concerns exclusion from the account mentioned in the agreement of the salaries and operating expenses of Soviet diplomatic and commercial representatives in Turkey. Annex 1 modified by exchange of notes dated May 18, 1938. Does not affect Soviet imports into Turkey under the agreement of Jan. 21, 1934 (presumably refers to the credit protocol of that date).
Sources: *STS*, 2, p. 189, citing
    RG, May 13, 1938, No. 3906, pp. 9845–46.

• 37/xi/5/BL

Exchange of notes between the USSR and the Belgium-Luxembourg Economic Union extending and modifying the temporary commercial treaty of September 5, 1935

Sent Nov. 5, 1937, in Brussels.
Extends validity of Arts. 1 to 6 of the agreement through Aug. 21, 1939. Further extension by exchange of notes dated Aug. 21 and Oct. 1, 1939 (39/x/1/BL).
Sources: *SZ*, 1938, No. 25, Art. 174 (F, R).
    Memorial, 1937, p. 856.
    STS, 2, p. 190, citing
        MB, Dec. 3, 1937, pp. 7360–61.

• 37/xi/15/Ger

Agreement between the USSR and Germany concerning closing of German consulates in the USSR

Reached during negotiations which ended Nov. 15, 1937. Provides for closing of

German consulates-general at Leningrad and Tbilisi and consulates at Khar'kov, Vladivostok and Odessa by Jan. 15, 1938. For an agreement concerning reopening of some German consulates, see 40/vii/5/Ger.
References: *SDFP*, 3, pp. 265–66, citing
    Journal de Moscou, Nov. 23, 1937.

Nov. 16, 1937. (1) Convention for creation of an International Criminal Court and (2) Convention for prevention and punishment of terrorism
See Appendix 1.

• 37/xi/19/UK

Exchange of notes between the USSR and the United Kingdom concerning the Russian text of the naval agreement of July 17, 1937

Sent Nov. 12 and 19, 1937.
Sources: **BTS*, 1938, No. 17, Cmd. 5679.
    LNTS, 187, pp. 124, 137 (E, F).
    STS, 2, p. 190.

• 37/xi/20/Italy

Agreement between the USSR and Italy concerning closing of Italian consulates in the USSR

Reached during negotiations which ended Nov. 20, 1937. Provides for closing of Italian consulate-general at Kiev, consulates at Leningrad and Tbilisi, and vice-consulates at Novorossiisk and Batum by Jan. 20, 1938.
References: *SDFP*, 3, p. 266, citing
    Journal de Moscou, Nov. 23, 1937.

• 37/xii/15/Pol

Exchange of notes between the USSR and Poland constituting a temporary customs agreement, with list of duty reductions

Sent Dec. 15, 1937, in Warsaw.
Temporary entry into force for Poland Dec. 29, 1937. Valid until Mar. 31, 1938.
Sources: **DURP*, 1937, No. 90, Art. 645.
    STS, 2, pp. 190–91.

• 37/xii/16/Ger

Agreement between the USSR and Germany extending the deadline for payments under the protocol of December 24, 1936

Signed Dec. 16, 1937, in Berlin.
Extends deadline for payments resulting
from transactions concluded up to Dec.
31, 1937.
Sources: *STS*, 2, p. 191, citing
    DD, Dec. 23, 1937.

● 37/xii/23/Lith

**Trade agreement for 1938 between the
USSR and Lithuania**

Signed Dec. 23, 1937, in Moscow.
Reference: *Izv.*, Dec. 24, 1937.

● 37/xii/29/J

**Protocol between the USSR and Japan
extending the fishery convention of January 23, 1928**

Signed Dec. 29, 1937, in Moscow.
Entered into force on signature. Convention of 1928 extended to Dec. 31, 1938.

Re-extended by protocol of Apr. 2, 1939,
and subsequently.
Sources: *SZ*, 1938, No. 12, Art. 79 (E, R).
    *CDT, No. 452.
    STS, 2, p. 191.

● 37/xii/31/France

**Agreement between the USSR and France
extending the temporary commercial
agreement of January 11, 1934, and related documents**

Signed Dec. 31, 1937, in Paris.
Subject to ratification. Provisional entry
into force Jan. 1, 1938. Extends the agreements of Jan. 11, 1934, Jan. 6, 1936, Jan.
21, 1936, and Dec. 17, 1936, through Dec.
31, 1938. Modifies the first list annexed
to the agreement of Jan. 6, 1936, as modified by the agreement of Jan. 21, 1936.
Extended by agreement of Dec. 30, 1938.
Sources: *STS*, 2, p. 191, citing
    JO, Jan. 1, 1938, p. 156.

1938

● 38/ii/26/Est

**Trade agreement for 1938 between the
USSR and Estonia**

Signed Feb. 26, 1938, in Moscow.
Superseded by agreement of Sept. 28,
1939 (39/ix/28/Est/b).
Reference: *Pravda*, Feb. 28, 1938.

Mar. 1938. Loan to China of $50 million
See 38/v/ /China.

● 38/iii/1/Ger

**Trade and clearing agreement between
the USSR and Germany**

Signed Mar. 1, 1938, in Berlin.
Applied retroactively from Jan. 1, 1938;
covers the year 1938. Extended by ex-
changes of notes of Dec. 19, 1938, Dec.
31, 1939, and Dec. 31, 1940. Extended to
Austria by agreement of Sept. 1, 1938.
Source: *STS*, 2, p. 192 (summary), citing
Deutsche Devisenerlasse, Mar. 3, 1938.

● 38/iii/31/T

**Exchange of notes between the USSR
and Turkey concerning branches of the
Soviet Trade Mission in Turkey**

Sent Mar. 31, 1938, in Moscow.
Ratified by Turkey June 26, 1938. Modifies Art. 15 of the treaty of commerce and
navigation of Oct. 8, 1937 (37/x/8/T/a).
Under that agreement the Soviet Trade
Mission was to have the right to open
branches in Istanbul, Trebizond, Mersin,
Kars, Konia, and Eskisehir, as well as
other branches to be agreed on subsequently. Under the present exchange of
notes the right to open branches is restricted to Istanbul and Kars.
Sources: *SDD*, 10, pp. 93–94.
    STS, 2, p. 192, citing
        RG, May 17, 1938, No. 3909, pp.
        9861–62.

**Apr. 8, 1938. General Radio Regulations
(Cairo Revision, 1938) annexed to the
International Telecommunication Con-
vention of December 9, 1932**
See Appendix 1.

● 38/iv/11/Fin

**Parcel post agreement between the USSR
and Finland**

Signed Apr. 11, 1938, in Moscow.
Ratified by the USSR Dec. 19, 1938. En-

tered into force Apr. 1, 1939 (1st day of the 3rd month after exchange of acts of ratification, which took place Jan. 25, 1939). Valid until 3 months after denunciation.

Sources: *VVS*, Apr. 22, 1939, No. 12.
*SS, 1939, No. 5 (Finnish, F).
STS, 2, pp. 192–94.

● 38/iv/16/Belgium

Parcel post agreement between the USSR and Belgium

Signed Apr. 16, 1938, in Moscow.
Ratified by the USSR June 10, 1939. Entered into force Aug. 11, 1939 (1 month after exchange of acts of ratification, which took place July 11, 1939, in Brussels). Valid as long as the temporary commercial treaty of Sept. 5, 1935, between the USSR and the Belgium-Luxembourg Economic Union, or until 6 months after denunciation. Modified by exchanges of notes of Feb. 12 and June 28, 1951 (51/vi/28/Belgium); Nov. 21, 1951, and Feb. 5, 1952 (52/ii/5/Belgium); and Aug. 26 and Sept. 11, 1953 (53/ix/11/Belgium).

Sources: *VVS*, Nov. 13, 1939, No. 35.
SDD, 10, pp. 144–54.

● 38/iv/18/Greece

Agreement between the USSR and Greece extending the trade and clearing agreement of February 27, 1937

Signed Apr. 18, 1938, in Athens.
Applied retroactively from Dec. 31, 1937; extends the original agreement through Dec. 31, 1938.

Sources: *Greek official gazette, 1938, A, No. 199.
STS, 2, p. 194, citing
SSSkS, 1938, No. 16.

● 38/iv/28/Fin

Protocol between the USSR and Finland concerning demarcation of the border, with maps and protocol of border marks

Signed Apr. 28, 1938, by a mixed Soviet-Finnish border commission.
Confirmed by and mentioned in the border treaty of Dec. 9, 1948.

● 38/v/ /China

Agreement between the USSR and China

concerning two loans to China each of fifty million dollars

Signed during May 1938 in Moscow.
The evidence for this agreement is fragmentary and inconsistent, but it seems probable that some loan agreement was made about this time.

References: Wu, p. 268.
Wei, pp. 140, 141 (calls the first loan a credit and barter agreement, signed "shortly after the Munich settlement"; dates the second loan Feb. 1939. Wei's source is Chinese News Service, *Contemporary China*, May 25, 1941, p. 5).
McLane, p. 129, dates the two loans in Mar. and July 1938, citing *China Handbook, 1937–1945* (rev. ed., 1947), p. 209.

● 38/v/18/T

Exchange of notes between the USSR and Turkey modifying annex 1 of the trade and clearing agreement of October 8, 1937

Sent May 18, 1938, in Ankara.
Ratified by Turkey July 3, 1938.
Source: *RG*, July 13, 1938, No. 3958, p. 10253, cited in *STS*, 2, p. 194.

● 38/v/26/Af

Agreement between the USSR and Afghanistan concerning the campaign against parasites and diseases of the cotton plant

Signed May 26, 1938, in Kabul.
Entered into force on signature. Duration 3 years; if not denounced 1 year before expiration, extended for 3-year periods.
Source: *SDD*, 10, pp. 105–109.
Reference: *Izv.*, May 28, 1938.

June 24, 1938. Protocol amending the international agreement of June 8, 1937, for the regulation of whaling

See 46/xi/25/1938.

● 38/vii/6/UK

Protocol between the USSR and the United Kingdom modifying the agreement of July 17, 1937, providing for limitation of naval armament and exchange of information concerning naval construction

Signed July 6, 1938, in London.
Entered into force on signature. An ex-

change of notes dated Jan. 11 and Feb. 10, 1939 (not listed here) made a minor correction in the Russian text of the protocol (*LNTS*, 197, pp. 398, 399).
Sources: *SZ*, 1939, No. 24, Art. 156.
　BTS, 1939, No. 39, Cmd. 6074.
　LNTS, 197, pp. 396–99 (E, F).

● 38/viii/4/US

Exchange of notes between the USSR and the United States of America concerning purchases to be made by the USSR in the United States during the coming year

Sent Aug. 2 and 4, 1938, in Moscow.
Sources: *SZ*, 1939, No. 24, Art. 157.
　EAS, No. 132, pp. 3–4.
　LNTS, 193, pp. 308–309 (E, F).
　STS, 2, p. 195.

● 38/viii/5/US/a

Exchange of notes between the USSR and the United States of America extending the commercial agreement of August 4, 1937, for one year

Sent Aug. 5, 1938, in Moscow.
Entered into force Aug. 5, 1938. Extends the agreement of 1937 to Aug. 6, 1939. Further extended by exchange of notes dated Aug. 2, 1939, and subsequently.
Sources: *SZ*, 1939, No. 24, Art. 157, pp. 378–79.
　EAS, No. 132, pp. 1–2.
　LNTS, 193, pp. 306–307 (E, F).
　STS, 2, pp. 195–96.

● 38/viii/5/US/b

Exchange of notes between the USSR and the United States of America concerning exemption from excise tax of coal, coke, and coal or coke briquettes imported into the U.S. from the USSR

Sent Aug. 5, 1938, in Moscow.
Valid for the duration of the 1937 commercial agreement.
Sources: *EAS*, No. 132, pp. 4–5.
　LNTS, 193, pp. 309–10 (E, F).
　STS, 2, p. 196.

● 38/viii/10/J

Agreement between the USSR and Japan concerning settlement of the dispute on the Soviet-Manchurian border

Negotiated orally Aug. 10, 1938, in Moscow.
Provides for establishment of a mixed commission to re-demarcate the border.
References: *MKh*, 1938, No. 9, p. 211.
　SDFP, 3, pp. 298–99.

● 38/ix/1/Ger. See Appendix 5.

● 38/xi/26/Pol

Joint communiqué by the USSR and Poland concerning diplomatic and commercial relations

Signed Nov. 26, 1938, in Moscow.
Confirms existing treaties between the USSR and Poland, including specifically the treaty of nonaggression of July 25, 1932. Abrogated, together with all other valid treaties between the USSR and Poland, by a Soviet note of Sept. 17, 1939 (39/ix/17/Pol).
Sources: *Izv.*, Nov. 27, 1938.
　PV, 3, I, pp. 982–83 (F), citing
　　Monitor Polski, Nov. 28, 1938.
　STS, 2, p. 196.
　SDFP, 3, p. 312.

● 38/xi/30/Denmark

Exchange of notes between the USSR and Denmark concerning payment for goods supplied to the USSR during 1937

Sent Nov. 29 and 30, 1938, in Copenhagen.
Reference: Danish Embassy, 1957.

● 38/xii/19/Ger

Exchange of notes between the USSR and Germany extending the trade and clearing agreement of March 1, 1938

Sent Dec. 19, 1938, in Berlin.
Entered into force Dec. 19, 1938. Extends the agreement of March 1938 through Dec. 31, 1939. Re-extended by exchange of notes dated Dec. 31, 1939, and subsequently.
References: *Izv.*, Dec. 23, 1938.
　VVerz., p. 601.

● 38/xii/21/Pol

Statement concerning commercial negotiations between the USSR and Poland

Published Dec. 21, 1938; summarizes negotiations held from Dec. 16 to 19, 1938, in Moscow.
Calls for signing of a commercial treaty,

an agreement on trade for 1939, and a clearing agreement.
Sources: *MKh*, 1939, No. 1, p. 144.
  SDFP, 3, p. 314.

● 38/xii/23/Fin

Exchange of notes between the USSR and Finland confirming documents and maps defining the state border

Signed Dec. 23, 1938, in Moscow.
The documents hereby confirmed were prepared by a Soviet-Finnish commission for demarcation of the border. Date of the documents unknown.
Reference: *Izv.*, Dec. 27, 1938.

● 38/xii/30/France

Agreement between the USSR and France extending the temporary commercial agreement of January 11, 1934, and related documents

Signed Dec. 30, 1938, in Paris
Subject to ratification. Provisional entry into force Jan. 1, 1939. Extends the agreements of Jan. 11, 1934, Jan. 6, 1936, Jan. 21, 1936, Dec. 17, 1936, and Dec. 11, 1937, through Dec. 31, 1939.

Sources: *STS*, 2, pp. 196–97, citing
  JO, Dec. 31, 1938, p. 14858.
Reference: *Izv.*, Jan. 3, 1939.

1939

● 39/ii/ /Yemen

Exchange of notes between the USSR and Yemen extending the treaty of friendship and commerce of November 1, 1928

Sent during Feb. 1939.
Extends the 1928 treaty to June 25, 1949.
Reference: *Izv.*, Feb. 6, 1939.

● 39/ii/7/Italy/a

Trade and payments agreement between the USSR and Italy

Signed Feb. 7, 1939, in Rome.
Entered into force on signature. Valid through Dec. 31, 1939. Supplemented by 6 secret protocols (next item).
Sources: **TC*, 54, pp. 18–21.
  STS, 2, pp. 197–98.
Reference: Korolenko, p. 63.

● 39/ii/7/Italy/b

Secret protocols between the USSR and Italy supplementing the trade and payments agreement of February 7, 1939

Signed Feb. 7, 1939, in Rome.
Subjects: (1) Validity of the customs convention of May 6, 1933, reaffirmed for duration of the agreement. (2) Construction and delivery of a destroyer for the USSR. (3) Renewal of the 1932 contract for supplying the Italian Navy with oil (for the original contract, see Appendix 3). (4) Payment of claims. (5) Opening of a special clearing account in a Rome

bank for "certain specified purchases" by the Soviet Government. (6) Lists of items (industrial and military) which Italian firms may sell to the Soviet Government, and of other items (raw materials, metals and grain) which they may purchase.
Source: *STS*, 2, p. 198, citing
  Private sources.

● 39/ii/7/Italy/c

Exchange of notes between the USSR and Italy concerning commercial transactions between Italian firms and Soviet economic organizations

Sent Feb. 7, 1939, in Rome.
Two exchanges are involved: (1) concerning guarantees of commercial transactions by the Soviet Trade Mission in Italy, and (2) concerning the appointment by the Soviet Trade Mission in Italy of a resident agent in Italy authorized to represent Soviet agencies in court. The first agreement enters into force May 1, 1939. Supplements Art. 3 of the treaty of commerce and navigation of Feb. 7, 1924 (24/ii/7/Italy/a).
Sources: *STS*, 2, p. 199, citing
  TC, 54, pp. 22–27.

● 39/ii/11/Lat

Trade agreement for 1939 between the USSR and Latvia

Signed Feb. 11, 1939, in Moscow.
References: *Izv.*, Feb. 14, 1939.
  STS, 2, p. 199, citing *Izv.*, *loc. cit.*, and
  Private sources.

● 39/ii/14/Lith

Trade agreement for 1939 between the USSR and Lithuania

Signed Feb. 14, 1939, in Kaunas.
Reference: *Izv.*, Feb. 15, 1939.

● 39/ii/19/Pol/a

Commercial treaty between the USSR and Poland, with final protocol, supplementary protocol, and two annexes

Signed Feb. 19, 1939, in Moscow.
Ratified by the USSR June 1, 1939. Ratification decree passed by the Polish Sejm June 29, 1939, but decree of ratification was not promulgated by the President of Poland. Was to have entered into force 15 days after exchange of acts of ratification. Provisional entry into force for Poland Mar. 27, 1939. Duration indefinite, but may be denounced during any yearly period not later than 3 months before the end of the year.
Annexes give forms for certificates of origin. Final protocol (not given in Soviet source cited) concerns negotiations for an agreement concerning arbitration in commercial disputes. For related documents, see the following 4 items.
Sources: *VT*, 1939, No. 5–6, pp. 10–15.
 DURP, 1939, No. 24, Art. 153.
 STS, 2, pp. 200–201.
Reference: *Izv.*, Feb. 20, 1939.

● 39/ii/19/Pol/b

Clearing agreement between the USSR and Poland

Signed Feb. 19, 1939, in Moscow.
Supplements the commercial treaty of the same date.
References: *Izv.*, Feb. 20, 1939.
 Korolenko, p. 63.
 STS, 2, p. 201 (gives summary of a "confidential clearing agreement," presumably the same document).

● 39/ii/19/Pol/c

Trade agreement between the USSR and Poland

Signed Feb. 19, 1939, in Moscow.
References: *Izv.*, Feb. 20, 1939.
 STS, 2, p. 201 (lists a "confidential quota agreement" with two lists of goods for Soviet-Polish trade; presumably the same document).

● 39/ii/19/Pol/d

Exchange of notes between the USSR and Poland concerning temporary entry into force of the commercial treaty of February 19, 1939, with protocol

Sent Feb. 19, 1939, in Moscow.
Provides that the commercial treaty and protocol shall temporarily enter into force by mutual agreement, at a date to be set in a further exchange of notes, in advance of the formal entry into force.
Sources: *VT*, 1939, No. 5–6, p. 22.
 STS, 2, pp. 201–202.

● 39/ii/19/Pol/e

Exchange of notes between the USSR and Poland concerning exchange of acts of ratification of the commercial treaty of February 19, 1939, and the agreement of June 14, 1936, concerning the legal status of the Soviet Trade Mission in Poland

Sent Feb. 19, 1939, in Moscow.
Provides for both exchanges to take place on the same, unspecified, day. As far as is known, the exchange was never carried out.
Source: *STS*, 2, p. 202.

● 39/ii/25/US/a

Parcel post agreement between the USSR and the United States of America

Signed Feb. 25, 1939, in Washington, D.C. Entered into force Apr. 16, 1939. Valid until 6 months after denunciation. Supplemented by Regulations of the same date (next document).
Source: *SDD*, 10, pp. 164–78.

● 39/ii/25/US/b

Regulations for execution of the parcel post agreement of February 25, 1939, between the USSR and the United States of America

Signed Feb. 25, 1939, in Washington, D.C. Entry into force and validity same as for the parcel post agreement of the same date.
Source: *SDD*, 10, pp. 179–87.

● 39/iv/2/J/a

Protocol between the USSR and Japan

extending the fishery convention of January 23, 1928

Signed Apr. 2, 1939, in Moscow.
Entered into force on signature. Extends the 1928 convention through Dec. 31, 1939. Re-extended by protocol of Dec. 31, 1939, and subsequently. Supplemented by 2 exchanges of notes (next item).
Sources: *Izv.*, Apr. 4, 1939.
    SP, 1939, No. 27, Art. 181.
    *CDT, No. 497.
    STS, 2, p. 202.
    SDFP, 3, pp. 327–28.

• 39/iv/2/J/b

Exchange of notes between the USSR and Japan concerning auction of fishery lots

Sent Apr. 2, 1939, in Moscow.
Two exchanges are involved: (1) modifies Protocol A of the convention of Jan. 23, 1928. Supplements the protocol of the same date.
Sources: *SP*, 1939, No. 27, Art. 181, pp. 420–23.
    STS, 2, pp. 202–203.

• 39/v/23/Mul

Universal Postal Convention, with related documents

Signed May 23, 1939, in Buenos Aires.
Date of Soviet ratification unknown. According to Hudson, 8, p. 304, the USSR was not among those states which had deposited their act of ratification by Jan. 1, 1947. The Soviet Government did, however, sign and ratify the 1947 convention (47/vii/5/Mul/a), and evidently regarded itself as a member of the Universal Postal Union in December 1940, when it notified the International Bureau of the Union that mail and parcel post for Latvia, Lithuania, and Estonia, as the result of their incorporation into the USSR, was subject to the postal agreements in force between the USSR and other countries, including agreements of the Union (see *DSB*, 4, 1941, p. 676).
Entered into force July 1, 1940. Duration indefinite. Supersedes convention of Mar. 20, 1934; superseded by convention of July 5, 1947 (47/vii/5/Mul/a).
Full contents (*LNTS*, 202): Text, pp. 168–213; final protocol, pp. 214–23; regulations for execution, pp. 224–302; an-

nexes to the regulations, pp. 303–43; provisions concerning air mail, pp. 344–63; final protocol to the provisions concerning air mail, pp. 364–68; annexes to the provisions concerning air mail, pp. 369–72; interpretation of certain articles of the convention, pp. 373–80.
It is possible that the USSR also signed the agreement concerning insured letters and boxes, as it did in 1934 and 1947; the USSR was not, however, among the states which had deposited an act of ratification of that document by Jan. 1, 1947 (Hudson, 8, p. 350). It is probable that, as in 1934 and 1947, the USSR did not sign the agreements concerning parcel post, money orders, postal checking accounts, payments on delivery, and newspaper and periodical subscriptions.
Sources: *LNTS*, 202, as listed above (E, F).
    Hudson, 8, pp. 303–50.

• 39/vi/5/T/a

Exchange of notes between the USSR and Turkey extending the treaty of friendship and neutrality of December 17, 1925

Sent June 5, 1939.
Extends the 1925 treaty to Nov. 7, 1945. Note: This exchange is known only from an entry in *SDD*, 10, p. 237. It appears to be merely a confirmation of the protocol of Nov. 7, 1935, which also extended the 1925 treaty and related documents to Nov. 7, 1945.

• 39/vi/5/T/b

Agreement between the USSR and Turkey modifying the railroad convention of July 9, 1922, with protocol

Signed June 5, 1939, in Ankara.
Ratified by Turkey Apr. 16, 1940. Entered into force provisionally on signature; definitively, on exchange of acts of ratification. Duration same as that of the convention of July 9, 1922 (22/vii/9/T/b).
Sources: *SDD*, 10, pp. 221–22.
    STS, 2, p. 203, citing
      RG, Apr. 16, 1940, No. 4486, pp. 13654–55.

• 39/vi/16/China/a

Commercial treaty between the USSR and China, with annex concerning the Soviet Trade Mission in China

Signed June 16, 1939, in Moscow.
Ratified by the USSR Jan. 5, 1940. Entered into force Mar. 16, 1940, on exchange of acts of ratification in Chungking. Duration 3 years; if not denounced 3 months before expiration, extended for 1-year periods. Supplemented by an exchange of notes (next item).
Sources: *VVS*, June 15, 1940, No. 16.
   VT, 1940, No. 2, pp. 2–9.
   STS, 2, pp. 203–205.
   SDFP, 3, pp. 341–48.

● 39/vi/16/China/b

Exchange of notes between the USSR and China supplementing the commercial treaty of June 16, 1939

Sent June 16, 1939, in Moscow.
Glosses the expression "third countries" as used in the treaty.
Sources: *VVS*, June 15, 1940, No. 16.
   VT, 1940, No. 2, pp. 9–10.
   STS, 2, pp. 205–206.
   SDFP, 3, pp. 348–49.

● 39/vii/5/T

Exchange of notes between the USSR and Turkey modifying the protocol of July 15, 1937, concerning appointment of border commissioners

Sent July 5, 1939, in Ankara.
Ratified by Turkey July 12, 1939.
References: *STS*, 2, p. 206 (summary), citing
   RG, July 12, 1939, No. 4256, p. 12232.

● 39/vii/10/China

Agreement between the USSR and China concerning a loan to China of 150 million dollars

Signed, presumably, July 10, 1939 (but cf. note below).
Note: The date of this agreement is not definitely established. The date given is that in Zhukov, p. 494. Chinese sources, however, give other dates. Wu, p. 269, gives a circumstantial account of the signing of the agreement, based on an interview with the Chinese negotiator, Dr. Sun Fo, in 1941, according to which the agreement was signed in June 1939. Wei, p. 143, places the agreement in Aug. 1939, citing Chinese News Service, *Contempo-*

rary China, May 25, 1941, p. 5 (no source cited). Kapitsa, p. 114, agrees with Wu in giving the date as June 1939. Compare the loan agreement of May 1938 (38/v/ /China).

● 39/viii/2/US/a

Exchange of notes between the USSR and the United States of America extending the commercial agreement of August 4, 1937, for one year

Sent Aug. 2, 1939, in Moscow.
Extends the agreement of 1937 to Aug. 6, 1940. Further extended by exchange of notes of Aug. 6, 1940, and subsequently.
Sources: *VT*, 1939, No. 8, pp. 11–12.
   EAS, No. 151, pp. 1–3.
   LNTS, 200, pp. 541–43 (R, E, F).
   STS, 2, p. 206.

● 39/viii/2/US/b

Exchange of notes between the USSR and the United States of America concerning purchases to be made by the USSR in the United States during the coming year

Sent Aug. 2, 1939, in Moscow.
Sources: *VT*, 1939, No. 8, pp. 11–12.
   SP, 1939, No. 50, Art. 424, pp. 767–68.
   EAS, No. 151, pp. 4–5.
   LNTS, 200, pp. 543–45 (E, R, F).
   STS, 2, p. 206.

● 39/viii/2/US/c

Exchange of notes between the USSR and the United States of America concerning exemption from excise tax of coal, coke, and coal or coke briquettes imported into the United States from the USSR

Sent Aug. 2, 1939, in Moscow.
Valid for the duration of the 1937 commercial agreement.
Sources: *VT*, 1939, No. 8, p. 13 (US note only).
   SP, 1939, No. 50, Art. 424, p. 768 (same).
   EAS, No. 151, pp. 5–6.
   LNTS, 200, pp. 545–46 (E, R, F).
   STS, 2, p. 207.

● 39/viii/19/Ger

Trade and credit agreement between the

USSR and Germany, with three annexes and a secret final protocol

Signed Aug. 19, 1939, in Berlin.
Duration 2 years. German Embassy, 1958, mentions a related exchange of notes, but gives no details. Supplemented by protocol of Aug. 26, 1939.
Secret final protocol provides for a refunding of one-half per cent of the interest rate charged on the credit (200 million Reichsmarks), reducing the interest rate to 4½ per cent.
Sources: *NSR*, pp. 83–85 (summary).
   Seidl, pp. 97–99.
   STS, 2, pp. 207–208.
References: *Izv.*, Aug. 21, 1939.
   MKh, 1939, No. 9, p. 246.
   SDFP, 3, p. 359.

• 39/viii/23/Ger/a

Treaty of nonaggression between the USSR and Germany

Signed Aug. 23, 1939, in Moscow.
Ratified by the USSR Aug. 31, 1939. Acts of ratification exchanged Sept. 24, 1939, in Berlin. Entered into force on signature. Duration 10 years; if not denounced 1 year before expiration, extended for an additional 5 years. Terminated by the German attack on the USSR, June 21, 1941.
Supplemented by a secret protocol of the same date (next document). Violation of this treaty by Germany was made one of the counts in the indictment of certain German leaders brought before the International Military Tribunal at Nuremberg in Nov. 1945 (see *Trial of war criminals*, p. 89).
Sources: *Izv.*, Aug. 24, 1939.
   VVS, Dec. 13, 1939, No. 37.
   RGbl, 1939, II, No. 38.
   NSR, pp. 76–77.
   STS, 2, p. 208.
   SDFP, 3, pp. 359–60, citing
      MKh, 1939, No. 9, p. 10.

• 39/viii/23/Ger/b

Secret protocol between the USSR and Germany concerning spheres of influence in Eastern Europe

Signed Aug. 23, 1939, in Moscow.
Supplements the nonaggression treaty of the same date. Modified by a secret protocol of Sept. 28, 1939, concerning the division of Lithuania (39/ix/28/Ger/c). Principal provisions: (1) The Baltic States and Finland to be divided between the Soviet and German spheres of influence, the boundary to coincide with the northern boundary of Lithuania. (2) The boundary between the Soviet and German spheres of influence in Poland to be the line of the rivers Narew, Vistula, and San. (3) The question of whether or not to maintain an independent Polish state to be decided by a "friendly agreement" between the 2 States. (4) With regard to Southeastern Europe, the USSR stresses its interest in Bessarabia; Germany declares its complete political disinterestedness in these areas.
Sources: *NSR*, p. 78.
   Seidl, pp. 90–91.
   DGFP, 7, pp. 246–47.
   STS, 2, p. 208.
   SDFP, 3 pp. 360–61.

• 39/viii/26/Ger

Confidential protocol between the USSR and Germany concerning the exchange rate of the Reichsmark in Soviet-German trade

Signed Aug. 26, 1939, in Berlin.
Supplements the trade and credit agreement of Aug. 19, 1939. Known only from a reference to it in the confidential summary of the negotiations concerning that agreement by an official of the German Foreign Office on Aug. 29, 1939 (*NSR*, p. 84; reprinted *STS*, 2, p. 208).

• 39/ix/9/China

Agreement between the USSR and China concerning establishment of regular air communications between Alma-Ata and Hami

Signed Sept. 9, 1939.
Mentioned in *SDD*, 10 (1955), p. 237, as no longer valid. For a possible extension, see 49/v/11/China.
Reference: Summary of provisions in
   Whiting, p. 65, citing
      A record of Soviet plundering in Sinkiang, 2, pp. 77 ff.

• 39/ix/15/J

Armistice agreement between the USSR and Japan, acting for the Mongolian

People's Republic and Manchukuo respectively

Signed on or about Sept. 15, 1939, in Moscow.

In addition to the armistice agreement, an understanding was reached on establishment of a mixed commission to determine the Manchurian-Mongolian border; for an agreement on this subject, see 39/xi/19/J.

References: *Pr.*, Sept. 16, 1939 (summary).

    STS, 2, p. 208.
    SDFP, 3, pp. 373–74, citing
      MKh, 1939, No. 9, p. 248.

Sept. 17, 1939. Note from the USSR to Poland abrogating existing treaties between the USSR and Poland

On the same day a copy of the note was sent to the diplomatic representatives of all states with which the USSR maintained diplomatic relations, assuring them that the USSR intended to conduct a policy of neutrality in its relations with their government.

Sources: *Izv.*, Sept. 18, 1939; *SDFP*, 3, pp. 374, 376.

● 39/ix/18/Ger

Joint communiqué by the USSR and Germany concerning military actions in Poland by the armies of the two States

Signed Sept. 18, 1939.

Text as issued is Stalin's draft, substituted by him for the original German draft which he criticized for presenting the facts "all too frankly."

Sources: *Izv.*, Sept. 20, 1939.
    NSR, p. 100.
    Seidl, p. 118.
    DGFP, D, 8, p. 97.

● 39/ix/22/Ger

Agreement between the armies of the USSR and Germany concerning a demarcation line in occupied Poland

Concluded on or about Sept. 22, 1939; embodied in a joint communiqué of Sept. 22, 1939.

The boundary agreed on was somewhat modified by the treaty of Sept. 28, 1939 (39/ix/28/Ger/a), and by a protocol of Oct. 4, 1939.

Reference: *Izv.*, Sept. 23, 1939 (communiqué).

● 39/ix/23/H

Agreement between the USSR and Hungary concerning resumption of diplomatic relations

Concluded on or before Sept. 23, 1939.

Possibly not embodied in a formal document. Relations had been broken off by the USSR in early Feb. 1939, following Hungary's accession to the Anti-Comintern Pact.

Reference: *NYT*, Sept. 24, 1939, p. 40.

● 39/ix/28/Est/a

Pact of mutual assistance between the USSR and Estonia

Signed Sept. 28, 1939, in Moscow.

Ratified by the USSR Sept. 29, 1939; by Estonia Oct. 2, 1939. Entered into force Oct. 4, 1939, on exchange of acts of ratification in Tallinn. Duration 10 years; if not denounced 1 year before expiration, extended for 5 years. Reaffirms the peace treaty of Feb. 2, 1920, and the treaty concerning nonaggression and the peaceful settlement of disputes of May 4, 1932.

On June 16, 1940, V. M. Molotov, Chairman of the Council of People's Commissars of the USSR, sent a note to the Estonian Government alleging violation of the pact by Estonia and demanding the establishment of a new government in Estonia and the entrance of Soviet troops into key cities (see 40/vi/16/Est).

Sources: *Izv.*, Sept. 29, 1939.
    VVS, Dec. 13, 1939, No. 37.
    RT, 1939, No. 15.
    LNTS, 198, pp. 223–29 (R, Est., E, F).
    DSB, 1, 1939, pp. 543–44.
    STS, 2, p. 210.

Note: *STS*, 2, *loc. cit.*, gives 2 secret supplementary clauses, concerning (1) size of Soviet forces in Estonia, and (2) use of the harbor of Tallinn by the USSR, citing *DSB*, *loc. cit. DSB*, however, gives only the published text of the treaty.

● 39/ix/28/Est/b

Trade agreement between the USSR and Estonia

Signed Sept. 28, 1939, in Moscow.

Ratified by Estonia Oct. 7, 1939. Entered into force Oct. 1, 1939. Valid through Dec. 31, 1940. Based on the commercial treaty

of May 17, 1929. Supersedes the agreement of Feb. 26, 1938.
Sources: *RT, Oct. 13, 1939, No. 16.
  STS, 2, p. 211, citing RT, loc. cit.
Reference: Izv., Sept. 29, 1939.
Note: STS, 2, loc. cit., gives a summary of a secret supplementary protocol, which is not included in the source cited (RT, loc. cit.). The protocol concerns trade items, repairs to Estonian ships and rail facilities, and transit rights for Estonian trade. In part the contents of the protocol are covered in the Izv. report cited above.

• 39/ix/28/Ger/a

Friendship and border treaty between the USSR and Germany, with map

Signed Sept. 28, 1939, in Moscow.
Acts of ratification exchanged Dec. 15, 1939, in Berlin. Entered into force on signature. Supplemented by a confidential protocol and 2 secret protocols (next 3 documents), and by a protocol of Oct. 4, 1939. Under a treaty of July 30, 1941, between the USSR and the Polish Government-in-Exile, the USSR declared invalid its agreement with Germany in 1939 concerning the partition of Poland (see 41/vii/30/Pol/a).
Sources: Izv., Sept. 29, 1939.
  VVS, Mar. 29, 1940, No. 10.
  PV, 3, II, pp. 1102–1104 (R, G), citing RGbl, 1940, II, No. 1, p. 4.
  NSR, pp. 105–106.
  Seidl, pp. 124–25.
  DGFP, D, 8, pp. 164–65 (map included as appendix).
  STS, 2, p. 209.
  SDFP, 3, p. 377.

• 39/ix/28/Ger/b

Confidential protocol between the USSR and Germany concerning transfer to the USSR or Germany of persons of German, Ukrainian, or Belorussian origin from occupied areas in Poland

Signed Sept. 28, 1939, in Moscow.
Supplements the friendship and border treaty of the same date. Implemented by agreement of Nov. 16, 1939.
Sources: NSR, p. 106.
  Seidl, p. 126.
  DGFP, D, 8, p. 165.
  STS, 2, p. 209.
  SDFP, 3, p. 378.

• 39/ix/28/Ger/c

Secret protocol between the USSR and Germany concerning the division of Lithuania between Soviet and German spheres of influence

Signed Sept. 28, 1939, in Moscow.
Supplements the friendship and border treaty of the same date. Modifies the secret protocol of Aug. 23, 1939 (39/viii/23/Ger/b). Supplemented by an exchange of notes of Oct. 8, 1939.
Provides that the territory of the Lithuanian State shall fall to the Soviet sphere of influence, while the province of Lublin and part of the province of Warsaw fall to that of Germany.
Sources: NSR, p. 107.
  Seidl, p. 125.
  DGFP, D, 8, p. 166.
  STS, 2, p. 209.
  SDFP, 3, p. 378.

• 39/ix/28/Ger/d

Secret protocol between the USSR and Germany concerning suppression of resistance in occupied Poland

Signed Sept. 28, 1939, in Moscow.
Supplements the friendship and border treaty of the same date.
Sources: NSR, p. 107.
  Seidl, p. 126.
  DGFP, D, 8, p. 166.
  STS, 2, p. 209.
  SDFP, 3, p. 379.

• 39/ix/28/Ger/e

Declaration by the USSR and Germany calling for an end to the war between Germany on the one hand and Great Britain and France on the other

Signed Sept. 28, 1939, in Moscow.
Sources: Izv., Sept. 28, 1939.
  NSR, p. 108.
  PV, 3, II, p. 1111.
  DGFP, D, 8, p. 167.
  STS, 2, p. 209.
  SDFP, 3, pp. 379–80.

• 39/ix/28/Ger/f

Exchange of notes between the USSR and Germany concerning trade

Sent Sept. 28, 1939, in Moscow.
Supplemented by a 2nd exchange of notes

(next item). Implemented by agreement of Feb. 11, 1940.
Sources: *NSR*, pp. 108–109.
  DGFP, D, 8, pp. 167–68.
  Seidl, pp. 127–28.
  PV, 3, II, pp. 1112–13.
  STS, 2, pp. 209–10.
  SDFP, 3, p. 379.

● 39/ix/28/Ger/g

Exchange of notes between the USSR and Germany concerning (1) railroad communications between Germany and Romania, Iran, Afghanistan, and the countries of the Far East, and (2) trade of Soviet oil for German coal and steel

Sent Sept. 28, 1939.
Supplements the exchange of notes of the same date concerning trade (preceding item).
Sources: *NSR*, 109.
  DGFP, D, 8, pp. 168–69.
  Seidl, pp. 128–29.
  STS, 2, p. 210.

● 39/x/1/Belgium

Exchange of notes between the USSR and Belgium extending the temporary commercial treaty of September 5, 1935

Sent Aug. 21 and Oct. 1, 1939.
Extends the 1935 treaty through Dec. 31, 1939.
Source: **Memorial*, 1939, p. 1027.

● 39/x/4/Ger

Protocol between the USSR and Germany concerning demarcation of the Soviet-German border in occupied Poland, with map

Signed Oct. 4, 1939, in Moscow.
Acts of ratification exchanged Dec. 15, 1939, in Berlin. Entered into force on signature. Supplements the friendship and border treaty of Sept. 28, 1939.
Provides for demarcation of the border by a mixed Soviet-German commission, to begin its work Oct. 9, 1939. Task completed on Dec. 12, 1940 (*PV*, 3, II, p. 1110).
Sources: *VVS*, 1940, No. 14.
  PV, 3, II, pp. 1104–10.
  *RGbl, 1940, II, No. 1, p. 3.
  STS, 2, pp. 211–12.

● 39/x/5/Lat

Pact of mutual assistance between the USSR and Latvia

Signed Oct. 5, 1939, in Moscow.
Ratified by the USSR Oct. 8, 1939. Entered into force Oct. 11, 1939, on exchange of acts of ratification in Riga. Duration 10 years; if not denounced 1 year before expiration, extended for an additional 10 years.
Reaffirms the peace treaty of Aug. 11, 1920, and the treaty of nonaggression of Feb. 5, 1932. Supplemented by a military agreement of Oct. 23, 1939.
On June 16, 1940, V. M. Molotov, Chairman of the Council of People's Commissars of the USSR, sent a note to the Latvian Government alleging violation of the pact by Latvia and demanding the establishment of a new government in Latvia and the entrance of Soviet troops into key cities (see 40/vi/16/Lat).
Sources: *Izv.*, Oct. 6, 1939.
  VVS, Dec. 13, 1939, No. 37.
  LRR, pp. 198–99.
  LNTS, 198, pp. 381–87.
  STS, 2, p. 213.

● 39/x/8/Ger

Secret exchange of notes between the USSR and Germany confirming an understanding concerning procedure for the division of Lithuania

Sent Oct. 8, 1939, in Moscow.
Supplements the secret protocol of Sept. 28, 1939, concerning the division of Lithuania (39/ix/28/Ger/c).
Sources: *NSR*, pp. 118–19.
  DGFP, D, 8, p. 244.
  STS, 2, p. 213.

● 39/x/10/Lith

Treaty between the USSR and Lithuania concerning mutual assistance and the transfer of the city of Vilna and Vilna Province to Lithuania, with map

Signed Oct. 10, 1939, in Moscow.
Ratified by the USSR Oct. 12, 1939; by Lithuania Oct. 16, 1939. Entered into force Oct. 16, 1939, on exchange of acts of ratification in Kaunas. Duration of those portions of the treaty concerning mutual assistance 15 years; if not denounced 1 year before expiration, extended for an

additional 10 years. Reaffirms the peace treaty of July 12, 1920, and the nonaggression treaty of Sept. 28, 1926. Transfer of Vilna provided for in protocol of Oct. 27, 1939.

On June 14, 1940, V. M. Molotov, Chairman of the Council of People's Commissars of the USSR, sent a note to the Lithuanian Government alleging violation of the treaty by Lithuania and demanding the establishment of a new government in Lithuania and the entrance of Soviet troops into key cities (see 40/vi/15/Lith). See also the secret protocols with Germany of Sept. 28, 1939 (39/ix/28/Ger/c) and Oct. 8, 1939.

Sources: *Izv.*, Oct. 11, 1939.
VVS, Dec. 13, 1939, No. 37.
*VŽ, No. 669, Art. 4916.
STS, 2, pp. 213–14.
DSB, 1, 1939, pp. 705–707.
SDFP, 3, pp. 380–82.

● 39/x/11/UK. See Appendix 5.

● 39/x/15/Lith

Trade agreement for 1939–1940 between the USSR and Lithuania

Signed Oct. 15, 1939, in Moscow.
References: *VT*, 1939, No. 10, p. 1.
    STS, 2, p. 214, citing *VT*, *loc. cit.*, and Private sources.

● 39/x/18/Lat

Trade agreement for 1939–1940 between the USSR and Latvia, with protocol

Signed Oct. 18, 1939, in Moscow.
Entered into force Nov. 1, 1939. Valid until Dec. 31, 1940.
References: *VT*, 1939, No. 10, p. 1.
    STS, 2, pp. 214–15 (summary), citing *VT*, *loc. cit.*, and Private sources.

● 39/x/18/T

Statement on negotiations between the USSR and Turkey

Published Oct. 18, 1939.
Sources: *SDFP*, 3, pp. 384–85, citing *MKh*, 1939, No. 10, p. 174.

● 39/x/23/Lat

Agreement between the USSR and Latvia

concerning establishment of Soviet military bases in Latvia

Signed Oct. 23, 1939, in Riga.
Implements the mutual assistance treaty of Oct. 5, 1939. Signed by a mixed Soviet-Latvian military commission.
Reference: London *Times*, Oct. 25, 1939.

● 39/x/24/Ger

Agreement between the USSR and Germany concerning Soviet grain exports to Germany

Signed on or about Oct. 24, 1939, in Moscow.
Provides for exports of 1 million tons of grain and cereal.
Reference: *NYT*, Oct. 25, 1939.

● 39/x/27/Lith

Protocol between the USSR and Lithuania concerning redefinition of the border as the result of the transfer to Lithuania of the city and province of Vilna, with map

Signed Oct. 27, 1939, in Moscow.
Ratified by Lithuania Nov. 3, 1939. Entered into force on signature. Replaces Art. 2 of the peace treaty of July 12, 1920. Carries out provisions of the treaty of Oct. 10, 1939.
Sources: *STS*, 2, pp. 215–16, citing *VŽ*, Oct. 27, 1939.

Nov. 1 and Nov. 2, 1939
See Appendix 5.

● 39/xi/16/Ger

Agreement between the USSR and Germany concerning repatriation of persons of German origin from the parts of Poland occupied by the USSR and of persons of Ukrainian and Belorussian origin from the parts of Poland occupied by Germany, with protocol and supplementary protocol

Signed Nov. 16, 1939, in Moscow.
Implements the confidential protocol of Sept. 28, 1939 (39/ix/28/Ger/b).
References: *Izv.*, Nov. 20, 1939.
    VVerz., p. 643.
    DGFP, D, 8, p. 165.
    SDFP, 3, pp. 400–401.
Note: *STS*, 2, pp. 216–17, prints a summary of an agreement on this subject,

dated Nov. 3, 1939, citing the *Frankfurter Zeitung* of Nov. 5, 1939; possibly an unofficial advance text.

● 39/xi/19/J

Agreement between the USSR and Japan concerning establishment of a mixed commission for demarcation of the border between the Mongolian People's Republic and Manchukuo

Signed Nov. 19, 1939, in Moscow.
For negotiation of the agreement, see 39/ix/15/J. For border agreements, see 40/vi/9/J and 40/vii/18/J.
References: *Pr., Izv.*, Nov. 20, 1939.
  SDFP, 3, p. 400.

● 39/xii/1/FDR

Exchange of notes between the USSR and the Finnish Democratic Republic concerning recognition and establishment of diplomatic relations

Sent Dec. 1, 1939.
References: *Pr., Izv.*, Dec. 2, 1939.
  SDFP, 3, p. 406.

● 39/xii/2/FDR

Treaty of mutual assistance and friendship between the USSR and the Finnish Democratic Republic

Signed Dec. 2, 1939, in Moscow.
Subject to ratification. Exchange of acts of ratification was to have taken place in Helsinki. Entered into force on signature. Duration (for parts concerned with mutual assistance, Arts. 3–5) 25 years; if not denounced 1 year before expiration, extended for a further 25 years.
Tacitly ignored in the peace treaty between the USSR and Finland of Mar. 12, 1940.
Sources: *Izv.*, Dec. 3, 1939.
  STS, 2, pp. 217–18.
  Mazour, pp. 238–40.
  SDFP, 3, pp. 407–409.

● 39/xii/11/Bul

Convention between the USSR and Bulgaria concerning establishment of air communications between Moscow and Sofia

Signed Dec. 11, 1939, in Sofia.
Ratified by Bulgaria May 2, 1940.
Reference: *Pravda*, Dec. 12, 1939.

● 39/xii/23/Ger/a

Agreement between the USSR and Germany concerning establishment of regular air communications

Signed Dec. 23, 1939, in Moscow.
Was to have entered into force on exchange of acts of ratification. *VVerz.*, p. 647, mentions a technical protocol (*Zeichnungsprotokoll*) and supplementary agreement; no details given.
References: *Izv.*, Dec. 28, 1939.
  VVerz., p. 647.
  STS, 2, p. 217, citing
    Frankfurter Zeitung, Dec. 29, 1939
    (summary).

● 39/xii/23/Ger/b

Agreement between the USSR and Germany concerning rail communications

Signed Dec. 23, 1939, in Moscow.
Entered into force on signature. *VVerz.*, p. 648, indicates that several railroad agreements were concluded on this date. The summary given in *STS*, 2, p. 218, based on the *Frankfurter Zeitung* for Dec. 27/28, 1939, mentions agreements on freight tariffs; on routing railroad traffic to border freight transfer terminals; and on the use of freight cars.

● 39/xii/31/Ger

Exchange of notes between the USSR and Germany extending the trade and clearing agreement of March 1, 1938

Sent Dec. 31, 1939, in Moscow.
Entered into force Dec. 31, 1939. Extends agreement of March 1938 through Dec. 31, 1940. Re-extended by exchange of notes dated Dec. 31, 1940.
References: *VT*, 1940, No. 1, p. 19.
  VVerz., p. 649.

● 39/xii/31/J/a

Agreement between the USSR and Japan concerning payment of the final installment due the USSR from Manchukuo for the Chinese Eastern Railway and settlement of claims

Signed Dec. 31, 1939, in Moscow.
Sources: *Pr., Izv.*, Jan. 1, 1940.
  AQSU, Apr. 1940, pp. 55–56.
  STS, 2, pp. 219–20.
  SDFP, 3, pp. 415–16.

● 39/xii/31/J/b

Protocol between the USSR and Japan extending the fishery convention of January 23, 1928

Signed Dec. 31, 1939, in Moscow.
Extends the convention of 1928 through Dec. 31, 1940. Re-extended by a protocol of Jan. 20, 1941, and subsequently. Supplemented by exchange of notes (next item).
Sources: *Pravda, Izv.,* Jan. 1, 1940.

CDT, No. 526.
STS, 2, p. 219.

● 39/xii/31/J/c

Exchange of notes between the USSR and Japan concerning fishery lots

Sent Dec. 31, 1939, in Moscow.
Supplements the protocol of the same date.
Sources: *Izv.,* Jan. 1, 1940.
   STS, 2, p. 219.

1940

● 40/i/5/Bul/a

Treaty of commerce and navigation between the USSR and Bulgaria, with annex concerning the Soviet Trade Mission in Bulgaria

Signed Jan. 5, 1940, in Moscow.
Ratified by the USSR Feb. 3, 1940. Entered into force provisionally Feb. 5, 1940 (1 month after signature), definitively Feb. 13, 1940, on exchange of acts of ratification in Sofia. Duration 3 years, or until 3 months after denunciation. Listed in *SDD*, 10 (1955), p. 236, as no longer valid.
Sources: *VT*, 1940, No. 3, pp. 9–20.
   BFSP, 144, pp. 261–74, citing
      Bulgarian State Gazette, No. 25, Feb.
      3, 1940.
References: *Pravda, Izv.,* Jan. 6, 1940.
   DSB, 12, 1945, p. 895.

● 40/i/5/Bul/b

Agreement between the USSR and Bulgaria concerning trade and payments during 1940

Signed Jan. 5, 1940, in Moscow.
Total trade for 1940 to amount to 920 million leva. Soviet agricultural machinery, ferrous metals, oil products, fertilizers, chemicals, cellulose, cotton, etc., in exchange for Bulgarian hogs, rice, leather goods, tobacco, rose oil, etc.
References: *Pravda, Izv.,* Jan. 6, 1940.
   VT, 1940, No. 3, p. 30.

● 40/ii/11/Ger

Economic agreement between the USSR and Germany, with a protocol and several exchanges of notes

Signed Feb. 11, 1940, in Moscow.
Entered into force on signature. Soviet industrial materials and foodstuffs in exchange for German manufactured goods and armaments. Carries out agreement contained in exchange of notes of Sept. 28, 1939 (39/ix/28/Ger/f). Supplemented by agreement of Jan. 10, 1941 (41/i/10/Ger/a), and protocol of Apr. 18, 1941.
References: *Izv.,* Feb. 14, 1940.
   VT, 1940, No. 3, pp. 1, 5.
   VVerz., p. 651.
   SDFP, 3, pp. 420–21.

● 40/iii/12/Fin

Peace treaty between the USSR and Finland, with map and protocol concerning an armistice

Signed Mar. 12, 1940, in Moscow.
Ratified by Finland Mar. 15, 1940; by the USSR Mar. 19, 1940. Entered into force on signature. Acts of ratification exchanged Mar. 20, 1940, in Moscow.
Supplemented by exchange of notes dated Apr. 8, 1940, concerning procedure for exchange of prisoners of war; by act of transfer of Petsamo to Finland, dated Apr. 9, 1940; and by border protocol of Apr. 29, 1940. Annulled by Finland June 26, 1941.
Revived by the armistice of Sept. 19, 1944, and the peace treaty of Feb. 10, 1947, except for Art. 4 (concerning the Hangö Peninsula), Art. 5 (concerning Soviet troop withdrawal from Petsamo), and Art. 6 (concerning transit through Petsamo district), which were replaced by new provisions.
Sources: *Izv.,* Mar. 14, 1940.
   VVS, 1940, No. 14.
   SDD, 10, pp. 11–17.
   SS, 1940, No. 3 (Finnish, R).

DSB, 2, 1940, pp. 453–56.
BFSP, 144, pp. 383–88.
SDFP, 3, pp. 421–23, citing
    MKh, 1940, No. 3, p. 17.

● 40/iii/25/Iran/a

**Treaty of commerce and navigation be-
tween the USSR and Iran**

Signed Mar. 25, 1940, in Teheran.
Ratified by Iran Apr. 4, 1940; by the
USSR Apr. 7, 1940. Entered into force
provisionally on signature; definitive
entry into force on exchange of acts of
ratification. Duration 3 years; if not denounced 6 months before expiration, valid
until 6 months after denunciation. Renewed by an exchange of notes dated Nov.
4, 1950. Listed by Korolenko, p. 104, as
still valid as of Nov. 25, 1953. Provisions
of Art. 10 concerning goods transit modified by agreement of Apr. 27, 1957.
Supplemented by 5 exchanges of notes
sent the same day (following 5 items).
Sources: *VT*, 1940, No. 5, pp. 18–28.
    SDD, 10, pp. 56–71.
    BFSP, 144, pp. 419–31, citing
        Iranian official gazette, Apr. 6, 1940.
    SDFP, 3, pp. 424–34.
Reference: *Izv.*, Mar. 12, 1940 (draft ini-
    tialed Mar. 10, 1940).

● 40/iii/25/Iran/b

**Exchange of notes between the USSR
and Iran concerning nationals of third
States employed on the Caspian Sea**

Sent Mar. 25, 1940, in Teheran.
Sources: *VT*, 1940, No. 5, pp. 28–29.
    SDD, 10, pp. 71–72.
    BFSP, 144, p. 431.
    SDFP, 3, p. 434.

● 40/iii/25/Iran/c

**Exchange of notes between the USSR
and Iran concerning reciprocal protection of trade-marks**

Sent Mar. 25, 1940, in Teheran.
Sources: *VT*, 1940, No. 5, pp. 30–31.
    SDD, 10, pp. 72–74.
    BFSP, 144, pp. 432–33.
    SDFP, 3, p. 435.

● 40/iii/25/Iran/d

**Exchange of notes between the USSR
and Iran concerning representation of
Soviet commercial organizations in Iranian courts**

Sent Mar. 25, 1940.
Supplements Art. 8 of the treaty of com-
merce and navigation of the same date.
Sources: *VT*, 1940, No. 5, p. 29.
    SDD, 10, pp. 74–75.
    BFSP, 144, p. 432.
    SDFP, 3, p. 434.

● 40/iii/25/Iran/e

**Exchange of notes between the USSR
and Iran concerning procedure for registration of passports of employees of the
Soviet Trade Mission in Iran**

Sent Mar. 25, 1940, in Teheran.
Valid for the duration of the treaty of
commerce and navigation of the same
date.
Source: *SDD*, 10, pp. 76–77.

● 40/iii/25/Iran/f

**Exchange of notes between the USSR
and Iran concerning technical conditions
for railroad freight transportation and
payment for reciprocal services**

Sent Mar. 25, 1940, in Teheran.
Calls for convocation of a Soviet-Iranian
railroad conference in Moscow within 3
months.
Sources: *VT*, 1940, No. 5, pp. 31–32.
    BFSP, 144, pp. 433–34.
    SDFP, 3, p. 435.

● 40/iv/ /Ger

**Understanding between the USSR and
Germany concerning maintenance of
Sweden's independence**

Negotiated during Apr. 1940, in Moscow.
Mentioned in a TASS statement of May 4,
1940.
References: *SDFP*, 3, pp. 449–50, citing
    MKh, 1940, No. 4–5, p. 270.

● 40/iv/ /Sweden

**Agreement between the USSR and Swe-
den concerning regular air communications during the summer of 1940**

Signed shortly before Apr. 26, 1940.
Negotiated and signed by the Soviet Main
Administration of Civil Aviation and the
Swedish company "Aerotransport." Pro-
vides for daily flights Moscow-Stockholm
from May 3 to Nov. 2, 1940.
Reference: *Izv.*, Apr. 26, 1940.

● 40/iv/8/Fin

Exchange of notes between the USSR and Finland concerning procedure for exchange of prisoners of war

Sent Apr. 8, 1940.
Supplements the peace treaty of Mar. 12, 1940.
Reference: *SDD*, 10, p. 237.

● 40/iv/9/Fin

Act of transfer of Petsamo to Finland

Signed Apr. 9, 1940, in Petsamo.
Carried out in accordance with the peace treaty of Mar. 12, 1940.
Sources: *Pravda*, Apr. 13, 1940.
   Izv., Apr. 14, 1940.

● 40/iv/9/Ger

Agreement between the USSR and Germany concerning use by Germany of a naval base on the Murman Coast

Negotiated Apr. 9, 1940, in Moscow.
Reference: *NSR*, pp. 139, 185.

● 40/iv/19/Fin

Exchange of notes between the USSR and Finland concerning establishment of temporary direct telephone and telegraph communications between Moscow and Helsinki

Sent Apr. 19, 1940.
Listed as no longer valid in *SDD*, 10 (1955), p. 237.

● 40/iv/29/Fin

Protocol between the USSR and Finland concerning demarcation of the border

Signed Apr. 29, 1940, in Moscow.
Signed in accordance with Art. 2 of the peace treaty of Mar. 12, 1940.
References: *Pravda*, Apr. 30, 1940.
   Izv., May 1, 1940.

● 40/v/11/Yug/a

Treaty of commerce and navigation between the USSR and Yugoslavia, with supplementary protocol concerning the Soviet Trade Mission in Yugoslavia and the Temporary Yugoslav Trade Mission in the USSR

Signed May 11, 1940, in Moscow.
Ratified by the USSR May 23, 1940. En-tered into force May 31, 1940, on exchange of acts of ratification in Belgrade. Duration 3 years; if not denounced 3 months before expiration, valid until 3 months after denunciation.
Sources: *VVS*, 1940, No. 23.
   SDD, 10, pp. 94–104.
   BFSP, 144, pp. 529–37, citing
      Yugoslav official gazette, May 25, 1940.

● 40/v/11/Yug/b

Agreement between the USSR and Yugoslavia concerning trade and payments for 1940–1941

Signed May 11, 1940, in Moscow.
Provides for total trade of 176 million dinars. Yugoslav metals and metal ores, bacon fat and other products in exchange for Soviet agricultural and other machinery, kerosene, cotton, etc.
Reference: *Izv.*, May 12, 1940.

● 40/vi/ /Yug. See Appendix 5.

● 40/vi/9/J

Agreement between the USSR and Japan concerning the border between Manchukuo and the Mongolian People's Republic

Signed June 9, 1940.
Supplemented by an agreement of July 18, 1940.
Reference: *Izv.*, June 10, 1940.

● 40/vi/10/Ger

Convention between the USSR and Germany concerning procedure for settlement of border disputes and incidents

Signed June 10, 1940, in Moscow.
Reference: *Pravda*, June 16, 1940.

June 11, 1941

See Appendix 1.

● 40/vi/12/Ger

Agreement between the USSR and Germany concerning direct telephone and telegraph communications between the USSR and Germany

Signed June 12, 1940, in Berlin.
References: *SDD*, 10, p. 236.
   Izv., July 3, 1940.

• 40/vi/15/Lith

Soviet ultimatum to Lithuania demanding formation of a new government in Lithuania and the entrance of Soviet troops into major cities in Lithuania

Sent June 14, 1940; accepted by Lithuania June 15, 1940.
Sources: *Izv.*, June 16, 1940.
  SDFP, 3, pp. 453–55.

• 40/vi/16/Est

Soviet ultimatum to Estonia demanding formation of a new government in Estonia and the entrance of Soviet troops into major cities in Estonia

Sent and accepted June 16, 1940.
References: *Izv.*, June 17, 1940.
  SDFP, 3, p. 456.

• 40/vi/16/Lat

Soviet ultimatum to Latvia demanding formation of a new government in Latvia and the entrance of Soviet troops into major cities in Latvia

Sent and accepted June 16, 1940.
Sources: *Pr.*, *Izv.*, June 17, 1940.
  SDFP, 3, pp. 455–56.

• 40/vi/25/Yug

Agreement between the USSR and Yugoslavia concerning establishment of diplomatic relations

Concluded on or before June 25, 1940.
Reference: *Izv.*, June 26, 1940 (TASS announcement dated June 25, 1940).

• 40/vi/28/Fin/a

Commercial treaty between the USSR and Finland, with annex concerning the Soviet Trade Mission in Finland

Signed June 28, 1940, in Moscow.
Ratified by the USSR July 10, 1940. Entered into force Aug. 12, 1940, on exchange of acts of ratification in Helsinki. Valid until Dec. 31, 1940; thereafter may be denounced with 6 months' notice.
Sources: *VT*, 1940, No. 7, pp. 6–12.
  VVS, Sept. 12, 1940, No. 30.
  SS, 1940, No. 14 (Finnish, R).
  BFSP, 144, pp. 388–95.

• 40/vi/28/Fin/b

Agreement between the USSR and Finland concerning payments

Signed June 28, 1940, in Moscow.
Entered into force July 1, 1940. Valid until Dec. 31, 1940; thereafter may be denounced with 3 months' notice.
Source: *VT*, 1940, No. 7, pp. 12–14.
References: *Izv.*, June 29, 1940.
  Korolenko, p. 63.

• 40/vi/28/Rom

Exchange of notes between the USSR and Romania constituting an agreement concerning cession to the USSR of Bessarabia and Eastern Bukovina, with map

Sent June 26, 27, and 28, 1940.
Soviet title: "Exchange of notes concerning peaceful solution of the dispute concerning Bessarabia and Eastern Bukovina." Four notes are involved: (1) A Soviet ultimatum of June 26, 1940; (2) Romanian reply of June 27, 1940; (3) 2nd Soviet note, dated June 27, 1940, setting forth precise conditions for evacuation of the areas by Romania; and (4) 2nd Romanian note, dated June 28, 1940, accepting the Soviet demands.
Annulled by the entry of Romania into the war against the USSR on June 22, 1941, but re-established under the armistice conditions of August 1944 (44/viii/25/Rom), the armistice agreement of Sept. 12, 1944 (44/ix/12/Rom/a), and the peace treaty of Feb. 10, 1947.
Sources: *Izv.*, June 29, 1940.
  SDD, 10, pp. 28–31.
  PV, 3, II, pp. 1276–79 (F).
  SDFP, 3, pp. 458–61, citing
    MKh, 1940, No. 6, p. 8.

• 40/vii/5/Ger

Agreement between the USSR and Germany concerning reopening of consulates

Concluded on or before July 5, 1940.
Provides for reopening of the German consulate at Leningrad and the opening of new consulates at Vladivostok and elsewhere. For closing of the Leningrad consulate, see 37/xi/15/Ger.
Reference: *NYT*, July 6, 1940.

• 40/vii/18/J

Agreement between the USSR and Japan

concerning the boundary between Manchukuo and the Mongolian People's Republic

Signed July 18, 1940.
On the same date a Mongolian-Manchurian border commission signed an agreement on the basis of this agreement and the earlier one of June 9, 1940.
References: *Izv.*, Aug. 8 and 27, 1940.
Japan Chronicle, Aug. 29, 1940, p. 262 (summary), cited by Degras, p. 235.

● 40/vii/27/Af

Trade agreement between the USSR and Afghanistan

Signed July 27, 1940, by Vostokintorg (Sovafgantorg) and the National Bank of Afghanistan.
Afghan wool, cotton, opium, and other goods in exchange for Soviet cotton fabrics, sugar, petroleum products, factory equipment, and motor vehicles. According to Korolenko, pp. 96–97, preceded by earlier, unspecified, agreements.
References: *VT*, 1940, No. 8, p. 10, citing *Pravda*, July 28, 1940 (Kabul report citing *al-Islah*).

● 40/vii/27/China

Trade agreement between the USSR and China

Signed on or before July 27, 1940.
Based on the commercial treaty of 1939 (39/vi/16/China/a).
Reference: *NYT*, July 27, 1940 (report from Chungking).

● 40/vii/29/Ger

Exchange of notes between the USSR and Germany concerning appointment of a diplomatic representative to negotiate the transfer of persons of German origin from Bessarabia and Northern Bukovina to Germany

Sent July 29, 1940.
Mentioned in the agreement on the same subject of Sept. 5, 1940.

● 40/viii/6/US/a

Exchange of notes between the USSR and the United States of America extending the commercial agreement of August 4, 1937, for an additional year

Sent Aug. 6, 1940, in Moscow.
Entered into force Aug. 7, 1940. Extends the 1937 agreement to Aug. 6, 1941. Further extended by exchange of notes dated Aug. 2, 1941, and subsequently. Supplemented by an exchange of notes of the same date (not listed) confirming the equal authenticity of the Russian and English texts of the exchange (*VT*, 1940, No. 9, pp. 16–17).
Sources: *VT*, 1940, No. 9, pp. 12–14 (R, E).
EAS, No. 179, pp. 1–2.
LNTS, 200, pp. 547–49 (R, E, F).

● 40/viii/6/US/b

Exchange of notes between the USSR and the United States of America concerning purchases to be made by the USSR in the United States during the coming year

Sent Aug. 6, 1940, in Moscow.
Sources: *VT*, 1940, No. 9, pp. 14–16 (R, E).
EAS, No. 179, pp. 3–4.
LNTS, 200, pp. 549–51 (R, E, F).

● 40/viii/6/US/c

Exchange of notes between the USSR and the United States of America concerning exemption from excise tax of coal, coke, and coal or coke briquettes imported into the United States from the USSR

Sent Aug. 6, 1940, in Moscow.
Valid for the duration of the 1937 agreement.
Sources: *EAS*, No. 179, pp. 4–5.
LNTS, 200, pp. 551–52 (R, E, F).

● 40/viii/31/Ger

Treaty between the USSR and Germany concerning legal relations on the border, with protocol and final protocol

Signed Aug. 31, 1940, in Berlin.
Ratified by the USSR and Germany Dec. 5, 1940. Entered into force Dec. 5, 1940. Acts of ratification exchanged Jan. 30, 1941, in Moscow.
Sources: *VVS*, Apr. 8, 1941, No. 41.
RGbl, 1941, II, No. 8, p. 41.
References: *Pravda*, Sept. 3, 1940.
SDD, 10, p. 237.

● 40/ix/ /Sweden. See Appendix 5.

● 40/ix/3/H/a

Treaty of commerce and navigation between the USSR and Hungary, with protocol and two annexes

Signed Sept. 3, 1940, in Moscow.
Ratified by the USSR Nov. 30, 1940. Provisional entry into force Sept. 15, 1940, under an exchange of notes of the same date (next item); definitive entry into force Jan. 11, 1941 (30 days after exchange of acts of ratification, which took place Dec. 12, 1940, in Budapest). Valid until 3 months after denunciation. Listed in *SDD*, 10 (1955), p. 236, as no longer valid.
Protocol provides for prohibition of export, import, or transit of war matériel under certain conditions. Annex 1 concerns the legal position of the Soviet Trade Mission in Hungary. Annex 2 concerns arbitration.
Sources: *VVS*, Feb. 21, 1941, No. 9.
    VT, 1940, No. 10, pp. 5–15.
References: *Pravda, Izv.*, Sept. 4, 1940.
    DSB, 12, 1945, pp. 893–94 (annex concerning arbitration).

● 40/ix/3/H/b

Exchange of notes between the USSR and Hungary concerning date of entry into force of the treaty of commerce and navigation of September 3, 1940

Sent Sept. 3, 1940, in Moscow.
Source: *VT*, 1940, No. 10, p. 18.

● 40/ix/3/H/c

Trade and payments agreement between the USSR and Hungary, with two annexes

Signed Sept. 3, 1940, in Moscow.
Entered into force Sept. 15, 1940. Duration 1 year; if not denounced 1 month before expiration, extended for further 1-year periods until denounced.
For first year of operation, provides for exchange of trade valued at $3.7 million each. Soviet timber, cotton, magnesium and chrome ores, etc., in exchange for Hungarian railroad rolling stock, pipes, vessels, electric motors, and other equipment. Annexes contain lists of goods.
Source: *VT*, 1940, No. 10, pp. 15–18 (omits the annexes).
Reference: *Izv.*, Sept. 4, 1940.

● 40/ix/5/Ger

Agreement between the USSR and Germany concerning transfer of persons of German origin from Bessarabia and Northern Bukovina to Germany, with protocol and supplementary protocol

Signed Sept. 5, 1940, in Moscow.
Entered into force on signature. Appointment of a diplomatic representative to negotiate the transfer was provided for under an exchange of notes of July 29, 1940.
References: *Pr., Izv.*, Sept. 7, 1940.
    VVerz, p. 677.
    Schechtmann, pp. 180–91, 505–506.

● 40/ix/6/Fin

Agreement between the USSR and Finland concerning direct railroad freight traffic

Signed Sept. 6, 1940, in Moscow.
Entered into force Oct. 1, 1940. Listed in *SDD*, 10 (1955), p. 237, as no longer valid.
Source: **SS*, 1940, No. 19 (Finnish, G).
Reference: *Pravda*, Sept. 15, 1940.

● 40/ix/7/Sweden/a

Trade and payments agreement between the USSR and Sweden

Signed Sept. 7, 1940, in Moscow.
Entered into force on signature. Duration 5 years; if not denounced 6 months before expiration, extended for 1-year periods. Extended for 5 years by protocol of Oct. 7, 1946 (46/x/7/Sweden/a). Listed in Korolenko, p. 107, as still valid as of Nov. 25, 1953.
Supplemented by agreements on an arbitration court, trade during 1940–41, and credit (next 3 documents).
Source: *Sö*, 1946, No. 22 (R, Sw.).
Reference: *Izv.*, Sept. 8, 1940.

● 40/ix/7/Sweden/b

Agreement between the USSR and Sweden concerning an arbitration court

Signed Sept. 7, 1940, in Moscow.
Constitutes an annex to Art. 14 of the trade and payments agreement of the same date. Listed in Korolenko, p. 150, as still valid as of Nov. 25, 1953.
Source: *Sö*, 1946, No. 22, pp. 267–71 (Sw., R).
Reference: Korolenko, pp. 64, 150–51.

- 40/ix/7/Sweden/c

Trade agreement for 1940–1941 between the USSR and Sweden

Signed Sept. 7, 1940, in Moscow.
Covers trade during the first year of operation of the trade and payments agreement of the same date. Mentioned in and superseded by protocol of Oct. 7, 1946 (46/x/7/Sweden/a).

- 40/ix/7/Sweden/d

Credit agreement between the USSR and Sweden, with protocol

Signed Sept. 7, 1940, in Moscow.
Provides for a credit to the USSR of 100 million Swedish crowns, to be used in 2 years, repayable in 5 at 4½ per cent interest, for purchase of machinery and equipment supplementary to that covered by the trade agreement of the same date. Remained in force until Dec. 7, 1946, date of the entry into force of the credit agreement of Oct. 7, 1946 (46/x/7/Sweden/b).
References: *Izv.*, Sept. 8, 1940.
  Korolenko, pp. 85–86.

- 40/ix/13/Iran/a

Agreement between the USSR and Iran concerning railroad communications

Signed Sept. 13, 1940, in Moscow.
Enters into force on the date of entry into force of the decisions of the 3rd Soviet-Iranian railroad conference. Valid until 6 months after denunciation. Supersedes the temporary agreement of Oct. 1, 1921. Supplemented by regulations for conferences (next document).
Source: *SDD*, 10, pp. 188–93.

- 40/ix/13/Iran/b

Regulations for conferences concerned with Soviet-Iranian railroad communications

Constitutes an annex to the agreement concerning railroad communications of Sept. 13, 1940.
Source: *SDD*, 10, pp. 193–96.

- 40/ix/13/Iran/c

Border railroad agreement between the USSR and Iran, with thirteen annexes

Signed Sept. 13, 1940, in Moscow.
Enters into force on entry into force of the railroad agreement of the same date (40/ix/13/Iran/a). Valid until 6 months after denunciation.
Source: *SDD*, 10, pp. 196–219 (does not include the technical annexes).

- 40/ix/18/Denmark

Trade and payments agreement between the USSR and Denmark

Signed Sept. 18, 1940, in Moscow.
Provides for total exchange during first 6 months of operation to a value of 14.4 million Danish crowns. Danish ships, diesels, electric motors, compressors, presses, and other equipment in exchange for Soviet cotton, kerosene, benzine, apatites, etc. Supplemented by protocol of May 21, 1941.
References: *Pravda, Izv.*, Sept. 19, 1940.

- 40/x/1/Ger/a

Agreement between the USSR and Germany concerning direct railroad freight communications

Signed Oct. 1, 1940, in Berlin.
Entered into force on signature.
References: *SDD*, 10, p. 237.
  Pravda, Oct. 5, 1940.
  VVerz., p. 682.

- 40/x/1/Ger/b

Agreement between the USSR and Germany concerning border railroad communications

Signed Oct. 1, 1940, in Berlin.
Entered into force on signature.
References: *SDD*, 10, p. 237.
  VVerz., p. 682.

- 40/x/1/Ger/c

Agreement between the USSR and Germany concerning direct railroad passenger communications

Signed Oct. 1, 1940, in Berlin.
Entered into force on signature.
References: *SDD*, 10, p. 237.
  Pravda, Oct. 5, 1940.
  VVerz., p. 682.

- 40/x/11/Fin

Agreement between the USSR and Finland concerning demilitarization of the Aaland Islands

Signed Oct. 11, 1940, in Moscow.
Ratified by the USSR Oct. 18, 1940; by
Finland Oct. 19, 1940. Entered into force
on signature. Acts of ratification exchanged Oct. 21, 1940, in Helsinki. Based
on an oral agreement reported from Berlin
July 26, 1940 (*NYT*, July 27, 1940). Renewed under the armistice of Sept. 19,
1944, and the exchange of notes dated
Mar. 13 and 16, 1948, with effect from
Mar. 13, 1948 (see 48/iii/16/Fin).
On Jan. 21, 1939, the Finnish and Swed-
ish Governments had notified the USSR
and the signatories of the convention of
Oct. 20, 1921, concerning the non-fortifi-
cation and neutralization of the Aaland
Islands (not signed by the RSFSR), of
their intention to remilitarize the islands.
The USSR did not reply to this communi-
cation (see *PV*, 3, II, p. 1017).
Sources: *Izv.*, Oct. 12, 1940.
  SDD, 10, pp. 17–19.
  SS, 1940, No. 24 (Finnish, R).
  PV, 3, II, pp. 1364–68.
  UNTS, 67, pp. 140–51 (R, Finnish,
  E, F).

● 40/x/25/Ger

**Communiqué concerning formation of a
United Danube Commission, to replace
the International Danube Commission
and the European Danube Commission**

Issued Oct. 25, 1940.
Reflects agreement between the USSR and
Germany, with the assent of Italy, to form
a United Danube Commission composed
of representatives of the USSR, Germany,
Italy, Romania, Bulgaria, Hungary, Slo-
vakia, and Yugoslavia. Protested by the
United Kingdom on Oct. 29, 1940, as a
violation of Soviet neutrality; Soviet reply
denying the charge dated Nov. 2, 1940
(*Izv.*, Nov. 5, 1940; *SDFP*, 3, p. 476).
Sources: *Pr.*, *Izv.*, Oct. 26, 1940.
  SDFP, 3, p. 475.
Reference: Beloff, 2, p. 341.

● 40/xi/5/US

**Agreement between the USSR and the
United States of America concerning
opening of a United States consulate in
Vladivostok**

On Sept. 27, 1940, in Moscow, the United
States requested establishment of the consulate. On Nov. 5, 1940, the USSR agreed

to opening the consulate after Nov. 20,
1940. For its closing, see 47/vi/16/US.
Source: *FRUS, 1940*, 3, p. 462.

● 40/xi/18/Fin

**Protocol between the USSR and Finland
concerning demarcation of the border,
with maps and protocols of border marks**

Signed Nov. 18, 1940, in Imatra, by a
mixed Soviet-Finnish border commission.
Validated by exchange of notes dated May
10, 1941.
Mentioned in the border treaty of Dec. 9,
1948.

● 40/xi/26/Sinkiang

**Agreement between the USSR and Sin-
kiang concerning prospecting, exploration, and exploitation of tin mines and
associated minerals**

Signed Nov. 26, 1940, in Tihwa.
Entered into force on signature. Duration
50 years.
Sources: *The Soviet Union's economic
  invasion of Sinkiang*, pp. 39–45 (C,
  E, R).
  Whiting, pp. 280–86.
Reference: *Ibid.*, pp. 66–68.

● 40/xii/6/Slovakia/a

**Treaty of commerce and navigation be-
tween the USSR and Slovakia, with annex concerning the Soviet Trade Mission
in the Slovak Republic**

Signed Dec. 6, 1940, in Moscow.
Ratified by the USSR Jan. 25, 1941. En-
tered into force Feb. 4, 1941, on exchange
of acts of ratification in Bratislava.
Source: *VVS*, Apr. 25, 1941, No. 17.
Reference: *Izv.*, Dec. 7, 1940.

● 40/xii/6/Slovakia/b

**Trade and payments agreement between
the USSR and Slovakia**

Signed Dec. 6, 1940, in Moscow.
Provides for trade to a value of $4.8 mil-
lion during first year of operation. Soviet
cotton, grain cultures, phosphates, etc., in
exchange for Slovakian cables, electric
motors, steel pipes, yarn, etc.
References: *Izv.*, Dec. 7, 1940.
  MKh, 1941, No. 1, p. 131.

- 40/xii/11/China

Trade agreement between the USSR and China

Signing announced Dec. 11, 1940.
Provides for trade, including tea, to the amount of $100 million Chinese. Constitutes Part 1 of a trade agreement completed in January 1941 (see 41/i/3/China and 41/i/12/China).
Reference: *NYT*, Jan. 5, 1941.

- 40/xii/31/Ger

Exchange of notes between the USSR and Germany constituting an agreement extending the trade and clearing agreement of March 1, 1938

Sent Dec. 31, 1940, in Moscow.
Entered into force Dec. 31, 1940. Extends the agreement of March 1938 to Aug. 1, 1942.
Reference: *VVerz.*, pp. 691–92.

1941

- 41/i/3/China

Trade agreement between the USSR and China

Signed Jan. 3, 1941.
Chinese wool in exchange for Soviet machinery and military supplies. Constitutes Part 2 of a trade agreement begun in Dec. 1940 and completed later in Jan. 1941. (see 40/xii/11/China and 41/i/12/China).
Reference: *NYT*, Jan. 5, 1941.

- 41/i/10/Ger/a

Economic agreement between the USSR and Germany

Signed Jan. 10, 1941, in Moscow.
Entered into force on signature. Valid until Aug. 1, 1942. Based on the agreement of Feb. 11, 1940. Supplemented by exchange of notes concerning payments (next document). Provides for exchange of Soviet oil products, industrial raw materials, foodstuffs, and grains for German industrial equipment.
References: *Pravda*, Jan. 11, 1941.
    VVerz., p. 692.
    SDFP, 3, pp. 481–82.

- 41/i/10/Ger/b

Exchange of notes between the USSR and Germany concerning payments

Sent Jan. 10, 1941, in Moscow.
Supplements the economic agreement of the same date.
References: *VVerz.*, p. 692.
    NSR, p. 268.

- 41/i/10/Ger/c

Protocol between the USSR and Germany

concerning termination of business activities in the Baltic States

Signed Jan. 10, 1941, in Moscow.
Entered into force on signature.
Reference: *VVerz.*, p. 692.

- 41/i/10/Ger/d

Agreement between the USSR and Germany concerning transfer of persons of German citizenship or national origin from the Lithuanian SSR to Germany, and of persons of Lithuanian citizenship or Lithuanian, Belorussian, or Russian national origin from those portions of Lithuania (the Memel and Suwalki areas) incorporated into Germany to the Lithuanian SSR, with supplementary protocol

Signed Jan. 10, 1941, in Kaunas.
Entered into force on signature.
References: *Izv.*, Jan. 11, 1941.
    VVerz., p. 692.

- 41/i/10/Ger/e

Agreement between the USSR and Germany concerning transfer of persons of German citizenship or national origin from the Latvian and Estonian SSR's to Germany, with supplementary protocol and final protocol

Signed Jan. 10, 1941, in Riga.
References: *Izv.*, Jan. 11, 1941.
    VVerz., p. 693.

- 41/i/10/Ger/f

Agreement between the USSR and Germany concerning property claims arising out of population transfers in the Baltic States

Signed Jan. 10, 1941, in Moscow.
Entered into force on signature.
References: *Izv.*, Jan. 11, 1941.
    VVerz., p. 693.

● 41/i/10/Ger/g

**Treaty between the USSR and Germany
concerning the border between the Lithuanian SSR and Germany, with exchange
of notes**

Signed Jan. 10, 1941, in Moscow.
Subject to ratification. Entered into force
on signature. Protested on behalf of Lat-
via by the Latvian Ambassador to the
United States in a note of Jan. 12, 1941
(*LRR*, p. 226).
Sources: *Pr.*, Jan. 11, 1941 (omits the ex-
    change of notes).
    SDFP, 3, pp. 479–81.
Reference: *VVerz.*, pp. 692–93.

● 41/i/10/Ger/h

**Secret protocol between the USSR and
Germany concerning the sale by Germany to the USSR of that part of Lithuania allocated to Germany by the secret
protocol of September 28, 1939**

Signed Jan. 10, 1941, in Moscow.
For the protocol of Sept. 28, 1939, see
39/ix/28/Ger/c.
Sources: *NSR*, pp. 267–68.
    Seidl, pp. 308–309.

● 41/i/12/China

**Trade agreement between the USSR and
China**

Announced Jan. 12, 1941, in Chungking.
Chinese minerals in exchange for Soviet
military machinery and supplies, to the
value of $100 million U.S. Completes the
trade agreement begun in Dec. 1940 and
continued in early Jan. 1941 (see 40/xii/
11/China and 41/i/3/China).
Reference: *NYT*, Jan. 13, 1941.

● 41/i/20/J/a

**Protocol between the USSR and Japan
extending the fishery convention of January 23, 1928**

Signed Jan. 20, 1941, in Moscow.
Signed by Japan ad referendum; notification of Japan's approval made Jan. 29,
1941.

Entered into force on signature. Extends
the convention of 1928 to Dec. 31, 1941.
Re-extended by protocol of Mar. 20, 1942,
and subsequently. Supplemented by exchange of notes (next document).
Sources: *MKh*, 1941, No. 2, p. 95.
    Izv., Jan. 21, 1941.
    *CDT, No. 548.

● 41/i/20/J/b

**Exchange of notes between the USSR
and Japan concerning auction of fishery
lots**

Sent Jan. 20, 1941, in Moscow.
Sources: *MKh*, 1941, No. 2, pp. 95–96.
    Izv., Jan. 21, 1941.

● 41/i/20/J/c

**Agreement between the USSR and Japan
concerning establishment of a mixed
commission to prepare a new fishery
convention**

Concluded on or about Jan. 20, 1941.
References: *Izv.*, Jan. 21, 1941.
    MKh, 1941, No. 2, p. 97.

● 41/ii/24/Switz

**Trade agreement between the USSR and
Switzerland**

Signed Feb. 24, 1941, in Moscow.
Entered into force Mar. 1, 1941, on ratification by signatories. Provides for exchange during first year of trade to a value
of 112.4 million francs for each party;
during second year, 150 million francs.
Swiss machine tools, electrical equipment,
turbines, generators, electric motors,
steam boilers, hydraulic presses, precision
instruments, etc., in exchange for Soviet
grain products, timber, oil products, cotton, etc.
Expired, according to the Swiss view, June
22, 1941, on outbreak of war between the
USSR and Germany. According to Korolenko, p. 92, violated by Switzerland and
not renewed. Superseded by trade agreement of Mar. 17, 1948 (48/iii/17/
Switz/c).
Source: **RO*, 1941, No. 57, p. 266.
Reference: *Izv.*, Feb. 25, 1941.

● 41/ii/25/Ger

**Exchange of notes between the USSR
and Germany concerning exchange of re-**

ports on the water level and ice conditions on the Memel

Sent Dec. 31, 1940, and Feb. 25, 1941, in Moscow.
Entered into force Feb. 25, 1941. Supplemented by a note of Mar. 3, 1941 (not listed separately), correcting the note of Feb. 25, 1941.
Reference: *VVerz.*, p. 695.

● 41/ii/26/Rom/a

Treaty of commerce and navigation between the USSR and Romania, with annex concerning the Soviet Trade Mission in Romania

Signed Feb. 26, 1941, in Moscow.
Ratified by the USSR Apr. 11, 1941. Entered into force Apr. 28, 1941, on exchange of acts of ratification in Bucharest.
Source: *VVS*, 1941, No. 25.
References: *Izv.*, Feb. 27, 1941.
  MKh, 1941, No. 4, p. 191.

● 41/ii/26/Rom/b

Trade and payments agreement between the USSR and Romania

Signed Feb. 26, 1941, in Moscow.
Provides for total trade during first year of operation to a value of $8 million U.S. Expenditure of balance of the account provided for in a protocol of May 8, 1945 (45/v/8/Rom/d).
References: *Izv.*, Feb. 27, 1941.
  MKh, 1941, No. 4, p. 191.

● 41/iii/ /H/a

Agreement between the USSR and Hungary concerning telegraph communications

Signed on or about Mar. 2, 1941.
Reference: *Izv.*, Mar. 2, 1941.

● 41/iii/ /H/b

Agreement between the USSR and Hungary concerning railroad communications

Signed on or about Mar. 2, 1941.
Reference: *Izv.*, Mar. 2, 1941.

● 41/iii/12/Thailand

Exchange of notes between the USSR and Thailand concerning establishment

of diplomatic, consular, and commercial relations

Sent Mar. 12, 1941, in Moscow.
Source: *Izv.*, Mar. 13, 1941.

● 41/iii/25/T

Joint statement by the USSR and Turkey concerning neutrality

Published Mar. 25, 1941.
Sources: *Izv.*, Mar. 25, 1941.
  SDFP, 3, p. 484, citing
    MKh, 1941, No. 4, p. 195.

● 41/iv/4/Belgium

Trade and payments agreement between the USSR and Belgium

Signed Apr. 4, 1941, in Moscow.
Reference: *Izv.*, Apr. 5, 1941.

● 41/iv/5/Yug

Treaty of friendship and nonaggression between the USSR and Yugoslavia

Signed Apr. 5, 1941, in Moscow.
Subject to ratification. Entered into force on signature. Duration 5 years; if not denounced 1 year before expiration, extended for an additional 5 years.
Sources: *Pr.*, *Izv.*, Apr. 6, 1941.
  MKh, 1941, No. 5, pp. 135–56.
  BFSP, 144, pp. 878–79.
  SDFP, 3, pp. 484–85.

● 41/iv/10/Norway

Trade and payments agreement between the USSR and Norway

Signed Apr. 10, 1941, in Moscow.
References: *Pravda, Izv.*, Apr. 11, 1941.

● 41/iv/13/J/a

Pact of neutrality between the USSR and Japan

Signed Apr. 13, 1941, in Moscow.
Ratified by the USSR and Japan Apr. 25, 1941. Entered into force Apr. 25, 1941, on ratification by both parties. Acts of ratification exchanged May 20, 1941, in Tokyo. Duration 5 years; if not denounced 1 year before expiration, extended for an additional 5 years. Denounced by the USSR Apr. 5, 1945 (*Izv.*, Apr. 6, 1945). Supplemented by a joint declaration of

the same date (next document). Accompanied by an informal agreement in principle that Japan would terminate its oil and coal concessions in North Sakhalin (see *VPSS VP*, 2, pp. 94–95). For implementation, see 44/iii/30/J/a.
Sources: *VVS*, 1941, No. 24.
  Izv., Apr. 15, 1941.
  *CDT, No. 563.
  BFSP, 144, p. 839.
  SDFP, 3, pp. 486–87, citing
    MKh, 1941, No. 5, p. 139.

● 41/iv/13/J/b

Joint declaration by the USSR and Japan pledging respect for the territorial integrity and inviolability of Manchukuo and the Mongolian People's Republic

Signed Apr. 13, 1941, in Moscow.
Supplements the pact of neutrality of the same date.
Sources: *Izv.*, Apr. 15, 1941.
  VVS, 1941, No. 24.
  BFSP, 144, p. 840.
  SDFP, 3, p. 487.

● 41/iv/18/Ger

Protocol between the USSR and Germany concerning fulfillment of the economic agreement of February 11, 1940, with exchange of notes

Signed Apr. 18, 1941, in Berlin.
Entered into force on signature.
Reference: *VVerz.*, p. 700.

● 41/v/10/Fin

Exchange of notes between the USSR and Finland validating the protocol of November 18, 1940, concerning demarcation of the border

Signed May 10, 1941, in Moscow.
Source: **SS*, 1941, No. 12 (Finnish, R).

● 41/v/16/Iraq

Exchange of notes between the USSR and Iraq concerning establishment of diplomatic, commercial, and consular relations

Sent May 16, 1941, in Ankara.
Background as given in *Pravda*, May 12, 1941: Negotiations began at the end of 1940, with a proposal by Iraq for the establishment of diplomatic relations, to be accompanied by a Soviet statement recognizing the independence of the Arabic

countries, including Iraq. The USSR agreed to the establishment of diplomatic relations, but refused to issue the declaration requested. Negotiations were broken off, but were resumed on May 3, 1941, when Iraq sent a note proposing establishment of relations without the declaration; this proposal was agreed to by the USSR on May 13, 1941.
References: *Pr.*, *Izv.*, May 18, 1941.
  SDFP, 3, p. 488.

● 41/v/21/Denmark

Trade protocol between the USSR and Denmark

Signed May 21, 1941, in Moscow.
Covers the period from Mar. 18, 1941, through Apr. 30, 1942. Total value of trade for each party to be 28.5 million Danish crowns. Danish cranes, diesels, steamship machinery, equipment for cement factories, and other machinery and equipment, in exchange for Soviet cotton, petroleum products, phosphates, chemicals, tobacco, timber, etc. Supplements the trade and payments agreement of Sept. 18, 1940.
Reference: *Izv.*, May 22, 1941.

● 41/v/30/Sweden

Agreement between the USSR and Sweden concerning settlement of property claims relating to the Baltic States

Signed May 30, 1941, in Moscow.
Reference: *Izv.*, May 31, 1941.

● 41/vii/12/UK

Agreement between the USSR and the United Kingdom concerning joint action in the war against Germany, with protocol

Signed July 12, 1941, in Moscow.
Valid for the duration of the war. Protocol provides that the agreement enters into force on signature and is not subject to ratification. Replaced by treaty of alliance of May 26, 1942.
Sources: *VVS*, 1941, No. 32.
  VPSS VP, 1, pp. 131–32.
  *BTS, 1941, No. 15, Cmd. 6304.
  BFSP, 144, pp. 643–44.
  LNTS, 204, pp. 277–82 (R, E, F).
  DSB, 5, 1941, pp. 240–41.

● 41/vii/18/Cz

Agreement between the USSR and the

Czechoslovak Government-in-Exile concerning resumption of diplomatic relations and mutual aid in the war against Germany

Signed July 18, 1941, in London.
Not subject to ratification; entered into force on signature. Provides for establishment on Soviet territory of Czech military units, under the Soviet High Command. Supplemented by military agreement of Sept. 27, 1941.
Sources: *VVS*, 1941, No. 33.
  VPSS VP, 1, p. 134.
  BFSP, 144, p. 754.

● 41/vii/22/MPR

Agreement between the USSR and the Mongolian People's Republic concerning compensation to the USSR for expenditures for the maintenance and education of Mongolian citizens in educational institutions of the USSR

Signed July 22, 1941.
Listed in *SDD*, 11 (1955), p. 198, as no longer valid; presumably replaced by the agreement of May 12, 1948.

● 41/vii/30/Pol/a

Agreement between the USSR and the Polish Government-in-Exile concerning resumption of diplomatic relations and mutual aid in the war against Germany, with secret protocol

Signed July 30, 1941, in London.
Not subject to ratification; entered into force on signature. Provides for the establishment of a Polish army on Soviet territory, under the Soviet High Command. Secret protocol provides that all claims are to be considered in future negotiations.
Diplomatic relations were broken off by the USSR by a note of Apr. 25, 1943, following the controversy over the discovery of mass graves of Polish officers in Katyń Forest near Smolensk (text of the Soviet note in *VPSS VP*, 1, pp. 301–303).
Sources: *VVS*, 1941, No. 24.
  VPSS VP, 1, p. 128.
  BFSP, 144, p. 869.
  Rozek, p. 62.

● 41/vii/30/Pol/b

Protocol between the USSR and the Polish Government-in-Exile concerning an amnesty for Polish citizens imprisoned in the USSR

Signed July 30, 1941, in London.
Enters into force on re-establishment of diplomatic relations. Carried out in the USSR by a decree of Aug. 12, 1941 (*VVS*, 1941, No. 37).
Sources: *VVS*, 1941, No. 24.
  VPSS VP, 1, p. 122.
  BFSP, 144, p. 869.

● 41/viii/ /France. See Appendix 5.

● 41/viii/2/US/a

Exchange of notes between the USSR and the United States of America extending the commercial agreement of August 4, 1937, for one year

Sent Aug. 2, 1941, in Washington, D.C.
Confirmed by the USSR Aug. 4, 1941; proclaimed in force by the United States Aug. 6, 1941.
Entered into force Aug. 6, 1941. Extends the 1937 agreement to Aug. 6, 1942. Further extended by exchange of notes dated July 31, 1942.
Sources: *VPSS VP*, 1, p. 123.
  EAS, No. 215.
  DSB, 5, 1941, p. 116.
  UNTS, 102, pp. 269–73 (E, F).

● 41/viii/2/US/b. See Appendix 5.

● 41/viii/5/Greece

Agreement between the USSR and the Greek Government-in-Exile concerning establishment of diplomatic relations

Concluded Aug. 5, 1941.
Reference: Greek Embassy, 1957.

● 41/viii/5/Norway

Exchange of notes between the USSR and the Norwegian Government-in-Exile concerning re-establishment of diplomatic relations

Sent Aug. 5, 1941, in London.
References: *Izv.*, Aug. 9, 1941.
  VPSS VP, 1, p. 128.
  SDD, 11, p. 38.

● 41/viii/7/Belgium

Agreement between the USSR and the Belgian Government-in-Exile concerning re-establishment of diplomatic relations

Signed Aug. 7, 1941, in London.
References: *Izv.*, Aug. 9, 1941.

VPSS VP, 1, p. 128.
SDD, 11, p. 35.

Aug. 12, 1941. Atlantic Charter

See 41/ix/24/1941.

• 41/viii/14/Pol

Agreement between the Soviet High Command and the Polish High Command concerning formation of a Polish army in the USSR

Signed Aug. 14, 1941, in Moscow.
Implements military provisions of the agreement of July 30, 1941 (41/vii/30/Pol/a).
Supplemented by a loan agreement of Jan. 22, 1942.
Source: *BFSP*, 144, pp. 870–72.
References: *VPSS VP*, 1, pp. 129–30.
Anders, p. 53.

• 41/viii/16/UK

Agreement between the USSR and the United Kingdom concerning mutual deliveries, credit, and methods of payment

Signed Aug. 16, 1941, in Moscow.
Entered into force on signature. Valid for the period of utilization of the credits and effecting of deliveries provided for in the agreement. Supplemented by a bank agreement of Sept. 7, 1941.
Provides for a total credit of £10 million. On the exhaustion of this credit the British Government in June 1942 advanced an additional £25 million credit on the same terms (*VPSS VP*, 1, p. 265). Credit provisions revised by agreement of June 27, 1942. Further modified by protocol of Dec. 27, 1947 (47/xii/27/UK/a).
Sources: *BTS*, 1948, No. 34, Cmd. 7439.
BFSP, 147, pp. 1040–44.
UNTS, 91, pp. 341–53 (E, R, F).
References: Korolenko, pp. 66–68.
VPSS VP, 1, p. 132.

Aug. 25, 1941. Declaration by the USSR to Iran concerning the entry of Soviet troops into Iran

See 41/ix/8/Iran.

• 41/ix/7/UK

Agreement between the State Bank of the USSR and the Bank of England regulating methods of payment and exchange

Signed Sept. 7, 1941.
Supplements the agreement of Aug. 16, 1941.
Reference: British Embassy, 1958.

• 41/ix/8/Iran

Exchange of notes between the USSR and Iran concerning entry of Soviet troops into Iran

Sent Aug. 25, 26, 28, and 30, and Sept. 1, 6, and 8, 1941.
Exchange began with a Soviet declaration submitted to the Government of Iran on Aug. 25, 1941, setting forth the reasons in consequence of which the Soviet Government had decided to "exercise the right belonging to the Soviet Union under Art. 6 of the treaty of 1921 [21/ii/26/Persia] of temporarily sending its troops into Iranian territory in the interests of self-defense." The declaration pledged withdrawal of Soviet troops from Iran "as soon as [the] danger threatening the interests of Iran and of the USSR has been removed." On the same date the British Government made a statement justifying the entry of British forces into southern Iran (text in *DAFR*, 4, pp. 674–76). Relations between Iran and the occupying Powers were subsequently regulated in the treaty of Jan. 29, 1942.
Sources (declaration of Aug. 25, 1941):
VPSS VP, 1, pp. 134–38.
DAFR, 4, pp. 676–81, citing
Moscow news, Aug. 25, 1941.
Reference: *SDD*, 11 (1955), p. 197, lists the correspondence among treaties no longer valid.

• 41/ix/20/France

Exchange of notes between the USSR and the Government of Free France concerning joint action in the war against Germany

Sent Sept. 20, 1941.
Mentioned in the preamble to the treaty of alliance and mutual assistance of Dec. 10, 1944.

• 41/ix/24/1941

Atlantic Charter

Signed Aug. 12, 1941, by the Heads of Government of the United States of America and the United Kingdom; published Aug. 14, 1941. Soviet adherence by declaration of Sept. 24, 1941, in London.

Reaffirmed in the United Nations declaration of Jan. 1, 1942.
Sources: *EAS*, 1942, No. 236, p. 4.
VPSS VP, 1, pp. 144–47 (Soviet declaration); 147–48 (Charter).
Izv., Sept. 26, 1941.
SDD, 11, pp. 41–44.
LNTS, 204, pp. 384–87 (E, F).
Hudson, 9, pp. 3–5 (E, F).
Axis in defeat, pp. 1–2.

● 41/ix/24/Mul

Inter-Allied agreement concerning rehabilitation principles

Signed Sept. 24, 1941, in London.
Provides for establishment of a bureau by the United Kingdom with which the Allied Governments and authorities should collaborate in framing estimates of their requirements.
Source: *United Nations agreements*, pp. 15–16, citing Cmd. 6315.

● 41/ix/27/Cz

Military agreement between the Soviet High Command and the High Command of Czechoslovakia

Signed Sept. 27, 1941, in Moscow.
Implements military provisions of the agreement of July 18, 1941. Supplemented by a loan agreement of Jan. 22, 1942 (42/i/22/Cz).
Reference: *VPSS VP*, 1, p. 149.

● 41/ix/27/France

Exchange of notes between the USSR and the Government of Free France concerning recognition and mutual assistance in the war against Germany

Sent Sept. 27, 1941, in London.
Sources: *VPSS VP*, 1, pp. 148–49.
JO, Dec. 30, 1941.

● 41/ix/28/Pol. See Appendix 5.

● 41/x/1/Pl

Confidential protocol concerning provision of military and other supplies for the USSR, with three annexes (First Lend-Lease Protocol)

Signed Oct. 1, 1941, in Moscow, by the USSR, the United Kingdom, and the United States of America. Canada, which was not a signatory of the first 2 protocols, made deliveries through the United States or the United Kingdom; it was a signatory of the 3rd and 4th protocols. Covers the period Oct. 1, 1941, through June 30, 1942. Followed by protocols of Oct. 6, 1942, Oct. 19, 1943, and Apr. 17, 1945. Supplemented by exchange of notes dated Oct. 30 and Nov. 4, 1941 (41/xi/4/US).
Source: *DSES*, 22, pp. 3–12.
References: Korolenko, p. 75.
SIA, ABR, p. 23.
Feis, pp. 16–17.

● 41/x/16/Af. See Appendix 5.

● 41/xi/4/Sweden

Protocol between the USSR and Sweden concerning regulation of questions concerning trade under wartime conditions

Signed Nov. 4, 1941, in Kuibyshev.
Entered into force on signature.
Reference: Swedish Embassy, 1957.

● 41/xi/4/US

Exchange of notes between the USSR and the United States of America concerning conditions for Lend-Lease shipments

Sent Oct. 30 and Nov. 4, 1941.
Provides for shipments to the USSR of materials to a value of up to $1 billion. Soviet indebtedness to be repaid in 10 years, starting 5 years after the end of the war, without interest. Supplemented by exchange of notes in Feb. 1942 (42/ii/23/US). Modified by agreement of June 11, 1942.
Sources: *DAFR*, 4, pp. 605–607.
Correspondence, 2, pp. 14–15.
VPSS VP, 1, pp. 156–57.
Reference: *SIA, ABR*, pp. 23–24.

● 41/xi/14/US

Exchange of letters between the USSR and the United States of America concerning organizational forms of cooperation between the Red Cross societies of the two States

Sent Nov. 6, 1941, from Washington, D.C., and Nov. 14, 1941, from Kuibyshev.
Provides for provision to the USSR of medical supplies up to ca. $5 million, as a gift from the American people.
Source: *Correspondence*, 2, pp. 16–17.

● 41/xii/4/Pol

Joint declaration of friendship and mutual aid by the USSR and the Polish Government-in-Exile

Signed Dec. 4, 1941, in Moscow.
Sources: *VPSS VP*, 1, pp. 168–69.
  BFSP, 144, p. 873, citing
    Dziennik Polski, Dec. 6, 1941.

● 41/xii/31/Pol

Agreement between the USSR and the Polish Government-in-Exile concerning a loan to Poland for assistance to Polish citizens in the USSR

Signed Dec. 31, 1941, in Kuibyshev.
Provides for a loan of 100 million rubles.
Reference: *VPSS VP*, 1, p. 170.

1942

● 42/i/1/Mul

Declaration of the United Nations

Signed Jan. 1, 1942, in Washington, D.C.
Reaffirms the purposes and principles of the Atlantic Charter of Aug. 14, 1941 (see 41/ix/24/1941).
Sources: *Izv.*, Jan. 3, 1942.
  VPSS VP, 1, pp. 170–71.
  SDD, 11, pp. 44–45.
  EAS, 236, pp. 1–3.
  BFSP, 144, pp. 1070–72.
  LNTS, 204, pp. 382–85 (E, F).
Reference: *DS GFPS*, 15, p. 62.

● 42/i/22/Cz

Agreement between the USSR and the Czechoslovak Government-in-Exile concerning a loan for maintenance of a Czech brigade in Soviet territory

Signed Jan. 22, 1942, in Kuibyshev.
Supplements the military agreement of Sept. 27, 1941.
Reference: *VPSS VP*, p. 190.

● 42/i/22/Pol

Agreement between the USSR and the Polish Government-in-Exile concerning a loan to Poland for maintenance of the Polish Army in Soviet territory

Signed Jan. 22, 1942, in Kuibyshev.
Supplements the military agreement of Aug. 14, 1941. Provides for a loan of 300 million rubles.
Reference: *VPSS VP*, 1, p. 189.

● 42/i/29/Iran

Treaty of alliance between the USSR and the United Kingdom on the one hand and Iran on the other, with three annexes

Signed Jan. 29, 1942, in Teheran.
Ratified by the USSR Jan. 27, 1943 (although not subject to ratification). According to Hudson, 9, p. 7, the Iranian Parliament approved a draft of the treaty Jan. 26, 1942. Entered into force on signature. Valid until the date fixed for withdrawal of Allied forces from Iranian territory (not later than 6 months after conclusion of an armistice or peace between the Allied Powers and Germany and her associates; date of expiration on Mar. 2, 1946 [*BFSP*, 151, p. 212], was based on date of surrender by Japan, Sept. 2, 1945).
Regulates relations between Iran and the occupying Powers (for correspondence concerning entry of Soviet troops into Iran, see 41/ix/8/Iran). Annexes consist of three notes: (1) to Iran from the USSR and the United Kingdom pledging their support for Iranian territorial integrity, sovereignty, and political independence at any peace conferences at the end of the war or other general international conferences; (2) from Iran to the USSR and the United Kingdom pledging not to maintain diplomatic relations with any state not in diplomatic relations with either the USSR or the United Kingdom; and (3) from the USSR and the United Kingdom to Iran stating that (a) Iran shall not be required to participate in any war or military action against a foreign Power or Powers, (b) Iran shall not bear the costs of works carried out by the USSR and the United Kingdom for military purposes in Iran, and (c) the provisions of Annex 1 shall remain in force even if the treaty becomes invalid before the conclusion of peace.
Sources: *VPSS VP*, 1, pp. 190–96.
  BFSP, 144, pp. 1017–21, citing
    Cmd. 6335.

DSB, 6, 1942, pp. 249–52.
UNTS, 93, pp. 279–301 (R, E, Pers., F).
Hudson, 9, pp. 7–11.

● 42/ii/5/Canada

Agreement between the USSR and Canada concerning establishment of consular relations

Signed Feb. 5, 1942, in London.
Not subject to ratification; entered into force on signature.
Sources: *SDD*, 11, p. 140.
 BFSP, 144, pp. 1092–93, citing
  CTS, 1942, No. 9.

● 42/ii/21/SA

Agreement between the USSR and the Union of South Africa concerning establishment of consular relations

Signed Feb. 21, 1942, in London.
Not subject to ratification; entered into force on signature. No longer valid, according to the Embassy of the Union of South Africa, 1957.
Sources: *SDD*, 11, pp. 140–41.
 *Union of South Africa, Treaty Series,
  1942, No. 2.

● 42/ii/23/US

Exchange of communications between the USSR and the United States of America concerning the grant to the USSR of an additional one billion dollars' Lend-Lease aid and methods of delivery

Sent Feb. 13, 18, and 23, 1942, from Washington, D.C., and Moscow.
Supplements the agreement reached in Nov. 1941 (see 41/xi/4/US). Superseded by agreement of June 11, 1942.
Source: *Correspondence*, 2, pp. 19–22.

● 42/iii/8/Pol. See Appendix 5.

● 42/iii/20/J/a

Protocol between the USSR and Japan extending the fishery convention of January 23, 1928

Signed Mar. 20, 1942, in Kuibyshev.
Signed by Japan ad referendum; notification of Japan's approval made Mar. 28, 1942. Entered into force on signature. Extends the 1928 convention through Dec. 31, 1942. Re-extended by protocol of Mar. 25, 1943, and subsequently. Supple-

mented by exchange of notes (next document).
Source: *CDT*, No. 602.
Reference: *VPSS VP*, 1, p. 198.

● 42/iii/20/J/b

Exchange of notes between the USSR and Japan concerning fishery lots

Sent Mar. 20, 1942, in Kuibyshev.
Supplements protocol of same date.
Reference: *VPSS VP*, 1, p. 198.

● 42/v/26/UK

Treaty between the USSR and the United Kingdom concerning alliance in the war against Germany and collaboration and mutual assistance after the war

Signed May 26, 1942, in London.
Ratified by the USSR June 18, 1942; by the United Kingdom June 24, 1942. Entered into force July 4, 1942, on exchange of acts of ratification in Moscow. Part 1 valid until the defeat of Germany; Part 2 valid for 20 years; unless denounced 1 year before expiration, valid until 1 year after denunciation. Replaces the agreement of July 12, 1941. On Mar. 24, 1947, agreement was reached on desirability of revising the treaty (see 47/iii/24/UK). Annulled by the USSR May 7, 1955.
Full title, as given in *LNTS*, 204, p. 353: "Treaty for an alliance in the war against Hitlerite Germany and her associates in Europe, and providing also for collaboration and mutual assistance thereafter."
Sources: *VVS*, 1942, No. 38.
 Izv., June 12, 1942.
 VPSS VP, 1, pp. 270–73.
 BFSP, 144, pp. 1038–41, citing
  BTS, 1942, No. 2, Cmd. 6376.
 LNTS, 204, pp. 353–62 (E, R, F).
 DSB, 7, 1942, pp. 781–83.
Reference: *VVS*, 1955, No. 7, Art. 169 (decree of annulment).

● 42/vi/11/US

Agreement between the USSR and the United States of America concerning principles applicable to mutual aid in the conduct of the war against aggression, with exchange of notes (Lend-Lease agreement)

Signed June 11, 1942, in Washington, D.C. Entered into force on signature. Valid

until a date to be agreed upon by the signatories. Exchange of notes provides that the agreement supersedes two earlier agreements on the same subject, the most recent being the exchange of notes in Feb. 1942 (see 42/ii/23/US) ; the earlier, unspecified, agreement was presumably that of Oct. 30 and Nov. 4, 1941 (41/xi/4/US). Sources: *SDD*, 11, pp. 24–28, citing
　　Izv., June 13, 1942.
　VPSS VP, 1, pp. 242–46.
　DSB, 6, 1942, pp. 532–34.
　Twentieth report to Congress on Lend-Lease operations, pp. 60–63.
　EAS, No. 253, pp. 1–6.
　UNTS, 105, pp. 285–95 (E, F).

● 42/vi/12/Canada

Agreement between the USSR and Canada concerning establishment of diplomatic relations

Signed June 12, 1942, in London.
Not subject to ratification; entered into force on signature.
Sources: *Izv.*, June 13, 1942.
　VPSS VP, 1, p. 251.
　BFSP, 144, p. 1093, citing
　　CTS, 1942, No. 12.

● 42/vi/12/UK

Joint communiqué by the USSR and the United Kingdom concerning the visit of the Soviet Commissar of Foreign Affairs to London

Published June 12, 1942.
Accompanies and comments on the published text of the treaty of May 26, 1942. Refers to "full agreement [dogovorennost'] with regard to the urgent task of creating a second front in Europe in 1942."
Source: *Izv.*, June 12, 1942.
Reference: *Correspondence*, 1, p. 57.

● 42/vi/22/UK

Exchange of letters between the USSR and the United Kingdom constituting an agreement concerning ships' expenses and freights, with memorandum

Sent June 22, 1942, in Kuibyshev.
Applied retroactively from June 22, 1941. Valid until 3 months after denunciation.
Sources: *BFSP*, 147, pp. 1044–47, citing
　　BTS, 1948, No. 34, Cmd. 7439.
　UNTS, 91, pp. 355–65 (E, F).

● 42/vi/27/UK

Agreement between the USSR and the United Kingdom concerning financing of British military deliveries and other aid

Signed June 27, 1942, in Moscow.
Applied retroactively from June 22, 1941. Modifies the credit agreement of Aug. 16, 1941, but is distinct from the extension of that credit by an additional £25 million shortly before the signing of this agreement.
References: *VPSS VP*, 1, pp. 264–65.
　VT, 1944, No. 6. p. 28.

● 42/vii/7/Pl

Exchanges of notes between the USSR and (1) the United States of America and (2) the United Kingdom concerning approval of the proposed Second Lend-Lease Protocol

Sent May 29 and July 7, 1942, in Washington, D.C., and London.
On May 29, 1942, President Roosevelt sent Soviet Commissar of Foreign Affairs V. M. Molotov the text of a Proposed Second Protocol covering the period July 1, 1942, through June 30, 1943. On July 7, 1942, the USSR in identic notes to the United States and the United Kingdom accepted the protocol, which became part of Annex 1 to the Second Lend-Lease Protocol (42/x/6/Pl). The Soviet letter of July 7, 1942 became Annex 2.
Source: *DSES*, 22, pp. 16, 46–47.

● 42/vii/10/Neth

Agreement between the USSR and the Netherlands Government-in-Exile concerning establishment of diplomatic relations

Signed July 10, 1942, in London.
Not subject to ratification; entered into force on signature.
Sources: *Izv.*, July 12, 1942.
　VPSS VP, 1, p. 266.
　BFSP, 144, p. 1227.
　UNTS, 241, pp. 475–79 (R, Dutch, E, F).

● 42/vii/22/Mul

Protocol providing for entry into force and extension of the agreement of May

6, 1937, concerning regulation of the production and marketing of sugar

Signed July 22, 1942, in London.
Provides that the 1937 agreement shall be considered in force as of Sept. 1, 1937, between governments which have ratified it, and that it shall continue in force for 2 years after Aug. 31, 1942. Agreement further extended by protocol of Aug. 31, 1944, and subsequently.
Sources: Hudson, 9, pp. 24–25.
  BFSP, 144, pp. 1074–76, citing Cmd. 6395.
  USTS, 1945, No. 990.
Reference: *VT*, 1943, No. 9, pp. 28–29.

• 42/vii/31/Pol. See Appendix 5.

• 42/vii/31/US

Exchange of notes between the USSR and the United States of America extending the commercial agreement of August 4, 1937

Sent July 31, 1942, in Washington, D.C. Entered into force Aug. 1, 1942, on approval by the USSR and proclamation by the President of the United States. Extends the 1937 agreement to Aug. 6, 1943, and thereafter, unless superseded by a more comprehensive commercial agreement, until 6 months after denunciation. The 1937 agreement was denounced by the United States in a note of June 23, 1951 (*DSB*, 25, 1951, p. 95).
Sources: *VPSS VP*, 1, p. 267.
  EAS, 265, pp. 1–2.
  DSB, 7, 1942, p. 663.
  UNTS, 102, pp. 274–77 (E, F).

• 42/viii/1/Norway

Exchange of notes between the USSR and the Norwegian Government-in-Exile concerning reorganization of diplomatic missions into embassies

Sent Aug. 1, 1942, in London.
Reference: *SDD*, 11, p. 40.

• 42/viii/17/UK

Joint communiqué concerning a conference between the USSR and the United Kingdom

Published Aug. 17, 1942, following negotiations between military and governmental officials of the USSR and the

United Kingdom in Moscow, from Aug. 12 to 15, 1942. The United States of America was represented by its Ambassador in Moscow, Mr. Harriman.
Mentions "a number of decisions" which were reached in regard to the war against Germany and her allies and reaffirms "the existence of close friendship and understanding between the Soviet Union, Great Britain, and the United States of America. . ."
Sources: USSR Embassy, *Information Bulletin*, Aug. 20, 1942.
  DAFR, 5, pp. 249–50.

• 42/ix/8/Canada

Credit agreement between the USSR and Canada

Signed Sept. 8, 1942, in London.
Provides for a credit of $10 million Canadian for Soviet purchases of wheat and flour.
References: *VT*, 1944, No. 6, p. 29, citing *Izv.*, June 11, 1944.
  Korolenko, p. 73.

• 42/ix/14/Yug

Exchange of notes between the USSR and the Yugoslav Government-in-Exile concerning reorganization of diplomatic missions into embassies

Signed Sept. 14, 1942, in London.
Reference: *SDD*, 11, p. 41.

• 42/ix/28/Cz

Exchange of notes between the USSR and the Czechoslovak Government-in-Exile concerning reorganization of diplomatic missions into embassies

Sent Sept. 28, 1942, in London.
Reference: *SDD*, 11, p. 40.

• 42/ix/28/France

Joint communiqué by the USSR and the French National Committee concerning recognition of the Committee as the representative of France

Published Sept. 28, 1942.
Source: *VPSS VP*, 1, pp. 271–72.

• 42/ix/30/UK

Exchange of notes between the USSR and the United Kingdom concerning ex-

change of information on military weapons

Sent Sept. 30, 1942, in Moscow.
Reference: British Embassy, 1958.

• 42/x/5/Cuba

**Exchange of notes between the USSR
and Cuba concerning establishment of
diplomatic and consular relations**

Sent Oct. 5, 1942.
On Apr. 3, 1952, the USSR suspended
diplomatic relations with Cuba, following
Cuba's refusal on Mar. 21, 1952, to allow
Soviet diplomatic representatives to enter
the country (*NT*, 1952, No. 15, p. 32).
Listed in *SDD*, 11 (1955), p. 198, as no
longer in force.

• 42/x/6/Pl

**Protocol concerning provision of mili-
tary and other supplies for the USSR,
with three annexes (Second Lend-Lease
Protocol)**

Signed Oct. 6, 1942, in Washington, D.C.,
by the USSR, the United Kingdom, and
the United States of America.
Covers the period July 1, 1942, through
June 30, 1943. Continues the agreement
begun with protocol of Oct. 1, 1941; followed by protocol of Oct. 19, 1943. For
negotiation of the protocol, see 42/vii/
7/Pl.
Source: *DSES*, 22, pp. 15–48.
References: *VT*, 1943, No. 10–11, pp.
   36–37.
 VPSS VP, 1, p. 272.
 Korolenko, p. 75.

• 42/x/10/Australia

**Exchange of notes between the USSR
and Australia concerning establishment
of diplomatic relations**

Sent Oct. 10, 1942, in Moscow.
Not a formal agreement; the Australian
note proposed publication of an announcement that both Governments had decided
to exchange ambassadors, and the Soviet
reply concurred in the suggestion. The
announcement was made on Oct. 13, 1942.
On Apr. 23, 1954, the USSR informed
the Australian Government that it was re-
calling its ambassador, and demanded the

withdrawal of the Australian Ambassador
in Moscow, following the revelation of
Soviet espionage in Australia. In Mar.
1959, an agreement was reached on re-es-
tablishment of diplomatic relations (*Prav-
da*, Mar. 17, 1959).
References: *Izv.*, Oct. 13, 1942; *ibid.*,
   Apr. 24, 1954.
 VPSS VP, 1, p. 273.
 SDD, 11, p. 34.
 Australian Embassy, 1957.

• 42/x/13/Lux. See Appendix 5.

• 42/xi/4/Neth

**Oral agreement between the USSR and
the Netherlands Government-in-Exile
concerning reorganization of diplomatic
missions into embassies**

Negotiated Oct. 22 and Nov. 4, 1942, in
London.
Reference: *SDD*, 11, p. 40.

• 42/xi/12/Mexico

**Exchange of notes between the USSR
and Mexico concerning re-establishment
of diplomatic relations**

Sent Nov. 10 and 12, 1942, in Washington,
D.C.
Preceded by an informal oral agreement.
Sources: *Izv.*, Nov. 20, 1942.
 VT, 1943, No. 1–2 pp. 7–8.
 BFSP, 144, pp. 1178–79.
Reference: *SDD*, 11, p. 37.

• 42/xii/ /France. See Appendix 5.

• 42/xii/17/Mul

**Joint declaration concerning extermina-
tion of the Jewish population of Europe
by Hitlerite forces**

Issued Dec. 17, 1942, by the USSR, the
United Kingdom, the United States of
America, the French National Committee,
and the Governments-in-Exile of Belgium,
Czechoslovakia, Greece, Luxembourg, The
Netherlands, Norway, Poland, and Yugo-
slavia.
Sources: *Izv.*, Dec. 18, 1942.
 SDD, 11, pp. 45–46.
 VPSS VP, 1, pp. 286–87.
 United Nations agreements, pp. 13–14.

1943

- 43/i/5/Mul

Inter-Allied declaration condemning acts of dispossession committed in territories under enemy occupation or control

Signed Jan. 5, 1943, in London, by the USSR and 17 other States; subsequently adhered to by 15 additional States.
Denounces German seizures of property in Europe and declares them to be null and void. Accepted as a basis for action in the peace treaties of Feb. 10, 1947, with Italy, Bulgaria, Hungary, Finland, and Romania.
Sources: *Izv.*, Jan. 6, 1943.
  VT, 1943, No. 1–2, p. 7.
  VPSS VP, 1, pp. 294–95.
  SDD, 11, p. 162.
  BFSP, 151, pp. 217–21, citing Cmd. 6418.
  DSB, 8, 1943, p. 21.
  Hudson, 9, pp. 49–50.

- 43/i/21/Belgium

Exchange of notes between the USSR and the Belgian Government-in-Exile concerning reorganization of diplomatic missions into embassies

Sent Dec. 26, 1942, and Jan. 21, 1943, in Kuibyshev.
References: *Izv.*, Apr. 18, 1943.
  VT, 1943, No. 3–4, p. 7.
  VPSS VP, pp. 299–300.
  SDD, 11, p. 39.

- 43/i/27/Uruguay

Exchange of notes between the USSR and Uruguay concerning re-establishment of diplomatic and commercial relations

Sent Jan. 27, 1943, in Washington, D.C.
Preceded by an informal oral agreement on Jan. 25, 1943.
Sources: *Pravda, Izv.*, Jan. 30, 1943.
  VT, 1943, No. 1–2, p. 9.
  VPSS VP, 1, pp. 295–96.
  BFSP, 145, pp. 312–13.
Reference: *SDD*, 11, p. 38.

- 43/ii/4/Colombia

Exchange of notes between the USSR and Colombia concerning exchange of ambassadors

Sent Feb. 3 and 4, 1943, in Washington, D.C.
Develops the relations initiated by the agreement of June 25, 1935.
Diplomatic relations were broken off by Colombia on May 3, 1948, following charges of Soviet aid to the revolutionary movement in Colombia (see *SIA, 1947–1948*, pp. 479–80).
Sources: *Izv.*, Feb. 9, 1943.
  VPSS VP, 1, pp. 297–98.
  VT, 1943, No. 1–2, p. 10.
Reference: *SDD*, 11, p. 198.

- 43/iii/18/Iran

Payments agreement between the USSR and Iran

Signed Mar. 18, 1943.
Referred to in Art. 4 of the agreement of Dec. 2, 1954, concerning settlement of border and financial questions, which provides for settlement of all claims under this agreement.

- 43/iii/25/J/a

Protocol between the USSR and Japan extending the fishery convention of January 23, 1928

Signed Mar. 25, 1943, in Kuibyshev.
Signed by Japan ad referendum; notification of Japan's approval made Apr. 6, 1943. Entered into force on signature. Extends the convention of 1928 through Dec. 31, 1943. Re-extended by protocol of Mar. 30, 1944 (44/iii/30/J/b). Supplemented by exchange of notes (next document).
References: *VT*, 1943, No. 3–4, p. 7.
  VPSS VP, 1, p. 342.

- 43/iii/25/J/b

Exchange of notes between the USSR and Japan concerning fishery lots

Sent Mar. 25, 1943, in Kuibyshev.
Supplements the protocol of the same date.
References: *VT*, 1943, No. 3–4, p. 7.
  VPSS VP, 1, p. 342.

- 43/iv/14/Greece

Exchange of notes between the USSR and the Greek Government-in-Exile concern-

ing reorganization of diplomatic missions into embassies

Sent Apr. 14, 1943, in London.
References: *Izv.*, Apr. 17, 1943.
    VT, 1943, No. 3–4, p. 7.
    SDD, 11, p. 40.

• 43/iv/21/Ethiopia

Exchange of notes between the USSR and Ethiopia concerning establishment of diplomatic relations

Sent Apr. 21, 1943, in London.
References: *Izv.*, July 1, 1943.
    VT, 1943, No. 7–8, p. 8.
    SDD, 11, p. 39.

• 43/v/28/Cz

Agreement between the USSR and the Czechoslovak Government-in-Exile concerning a grant of funds, materials, and services for maintenance of the Czech Brigade on Soviet territory for the duration of the war

Signed May 28, 1943.
References: *VT*, 1943, No. 6, p. 11.
    VPSS VP, 1, p. 333.

• 43/vi/3/Mul

Final Act of the United Nations conference on food and agriculture, with declaration, resolutions, and recommendations

Signed June 3, 1943, in Hot Springs, Virginia.
Sources: *DSB*, 8, 1943, pp. 546–72.
    DSCS, 52, pp. 5–59.
    United Nations agreements, pp. 45–77.
Reference: *VT*, 1943, No. 6, pp. 11–17.

• 43/vi/14/Mexico

Exchange of notes between the USSR and Mexico concerning reorganization of diplomatic missions into embassies

Sent June 7 and 14, 1943, in Moscow.
References: *Izv.*, June 17, 1943.
    VPSS VP, 1, pp. 344–45.
    VT, 1943, No. 7–8, p. 9.
    SDD, 11, p. 40.

• 43/vii/26/Egypt

Exchange of notes between the USSR and Egypt concerning establishment of diplomatic relations

Sent July 6, 1943, from Cairo, and July 26, 1943, from London.
Entered into force Aug. 26, 1943.
References: *Izv.*, Sept. 9, 1943.
    VPSS VP, 1, p. 349.
    VT, 1943, No. 9, p. 17.
    SDD, 11, p. 36.

• 43/viii/26/France

Declaration by the USSR concerning its decision to recognize the French Committee of National Liberation as the representative of the governmental interests of France, and to establish diplomatic relations with the Committee

Issued Aug. 26, 1943, in Moscow.
On June 3, 1943, the French Committee of National Liberation was established and issued a declaration, which it sent, together with a request for recognition, to the Soviet Government on June 17, 1943. This declaration is the Soviet reply. The Soviet declaration was acknowledged for the Committee by Generals de Gaulle and Giraud on Aug. 31, 1943 (texts in *Izv.*, Aug. 31, 1943).
Sources: *Izv.*, Aug. 27, 1943.
    VT, 1943, No. 9, p. 13.
    VPSS VP, 1, p. 349.

• 43/ix/1/US

Exchange of notes between the USSR and the United States of America concerning modification of shipments under the Third Lend-Lease Protocol

Soviet reply sent Sept. 1, 1943, in answer to an undated United States proposed schedule of supplies and shipments. Included in the annexes to the Third Lend-Lease protocol (43/x/19/Pl).
Source: *DSES*, 22, pp. 52–56.

• 43/ix/3/Italy

Armistice agreement between the United Nations and Italy

Signed Sept. 3, 1943, at Allied Headquarters in Sicily (Fairfield Camp). Signed by General Eisenhower on behalf of the United Nations.
Entered into force Sept. 8, 1943. Supplemented by the "long" armistice agreement of Sept. 29, 1943 (43/ix/29/Italy).

Approved in advance by the USSR Sept. 2, 1943.
Sources: *United States and Italy*, pp. 51–52.
Cmd. 6693.
VPSS VP, 1, pp. 350–52.
Hudson, 9, pp. 50–52.
References: *SIA, ABR*, pp. 306–307.
Correspondence, 1, p. 389.

• 43/ix/29/Italy

Instrument of surrender of Italy (Additional conditions of the armistice with Italy)

Signed Sept. 29, 1943, in Malta.
Entered into force on signature. Supplements the armistice agreement of Sept. 3, 1943 (the "short" armistice). Agreed to in advance by the USSR Aug. 27, 1943.
As originally signed, the preamble to the document spoke of an armistice agreement between the United States and the United Kingdom on the one hand and Italy on the other. By a protocol of Nov. 9, 1943 (43/xi/9/Italy), the preamble was amended to state that (1) the Governments of the United States and the United Kingdom were acting on behalf of all the United Nations in regard to the armistice of Sept. 3, 1943, and (2) the terms of this instrument were those on which the Soviet Government, as well as the Governments of the United States and the United Kingdom, were prepared to suspend hostilities with Italy.
Sources: *United States and Italy*, pp. 55–64.
Cmd. 6693.
Hudson, 9, pp. 52–59.
Reference: *Correspondence*, 1, p. 389.

• 43/x/4/Iceland

Exchange of telegrams between the USSR and Iceland concerning establishment of diplomatic relations

Sent July 27, 1943, from Reykjavik, Sept. 21, 1943, from Moscow, and Oct. 4, 1943, from Reykjavik.
Reference: *SDD*, 11, p. 36.

• 43/x/13/Pl

Joint declaration by the USSR, the United Kingdom and the United States

of America recognizing Italy as a co-belligerent

Issued Oct. 13, 1943.
On the same day the Italian Government declared war on Germany.
Sources: *VPSS VP*, 1, pp. 353–54.
VT, 1943, No. 10–11, p. 36.
United States and Italy, p. 71.
Reference: *Correspondence*, 1, pp. 169–70.

• 43/x/19/Pl

Protocol concerning provision of military and other supplies for the USSR, with annexes (Third Lend-Lease Protocol)

Signed Oct. 19, 1943, in London, by the USSR, the United Kingdom, the United States of America, and Canada.
Covers the period July 1, 1943, through June 30, 1944. Continues the agreement begun with protocols of Oct. 1, 1941, and Oct. 6, 1942; followed by protocol of Apr. 17, 1945. Annexes include schedules of supplies and shipments by the 3 Western Powers. For an exchange of notes concerning modification of proposed shipments by the United States, see 43/ix/1/US.
Source: *DSES*, 22, pp. 51–85.
References: *VT*, 1943, No. 10–11, pp. 36–37.
VPSS VP, 1, p. 355.

• 43/x/30/Pl/a

Joint communiqué concerning the conference of Foreign Ministers in Moscow

Signed Oct. 30, 1943, in Moscow, at the end of a conference which began Oct. 19, 1943, by the Foreign Ministers of the USSR, the United Kingdom, and the United States of America; published Nov. 1, 1943.
Provides for establishment of a European Advisory Commission in London to deal with European problems arising out of the war (terms and powers of the Commission defined in a protocol of Nov. 1, 1943), and for establishment of an Advisory Council for Italy, to consist of representatives of the Three Powers and the French Committee of National Liberation, with provision for subsequent admission of Greece and Yugoslavia. Supplemented by declarations on general security, Italy,

Austria, and German atrocities (next 4 documents).
Sources: *Izv.*, Nov. 2, 1943.
VPSS VP, 1, pp. 411–14.
SDD, 11, pp. 46–48.
DSB, 9, 1943, pp. 307–308.

• 43/x/30/Pl/b

Declaration on general security

Signed Oct. 30, 1943, in Moscow, by the Foreign Ministers of the USSR, the United Kingdom, and the United States of America, and the Ambassador of China to the USSR. Calls for establishment of "a general international organization . . . for the maintenance of international peace and security."
Sources: *Izv.*, Nov. 2, 1943.
VPSS VP, 1, pp. 414–15.
SDD, 11, pp. 48–49.
DSB, 9, 1943, pp. 308–309.
Hudson, 9, pp. 82–83.
Axis in defeat, pp. 2–3.

• 43/x/30/Pl/c

Declaration concerning Italy

Signed Oct. 30, 1943, in Moscow, by the Foreign Ministers of the USSR, the United Kingdom, and the United States of America.
Defines the bases of Allied policy towards Italy and for re-establishment by the Italian people of "governmental and other institutions based upon democratic principles . . ."
Sources: *Izv.*, Nov. 2, 1943.
VPSS VP, 1, pp. 416–17.
SDD, 11, pp. 50–51.
DSB, 9, 1943, pp. 309–10.

• 43/x/30/Pl/d

Declaration concerning Austria

Signed Oct. 30, 1943, in Moscow, by the Foreign Ministers of the USSR, the United Kingdom, and the United States of America.
Declares null and void the annexation of Austria by Germany of Mar. 15, 1938, and calls for re-establishment of a free and independent Austria.
Sources: *Izv.*, Nov. 2, 1943.
VPSS VP, 1, p. 417.
SDD, 11, p. 51.
DSB, 9, 1943, p. 310.

• 43/x/30/Pl/e

Declaration concerning German atrocities

Signed Oct. 30, 1943, in Moscow, by the Heads of Government of the USSR, the United Kingdom, and the United States of America; published Nov. 1, 1943.
For an agreement concerning the trial of major German war criminals based on this declaration, see 45/viii/8/Pl/a.
Sources: *Izv.*, Nov. 2, 1943.
VPSS VP, 1, pp. 418–19.
SDD, 11, pp. 51–52.
DSB, 9, 1943, pp. 310–11.
Axis in defeat, pp. 3–4.

• 43/xi/1/Pl

Protocol concerning establishment of a European Advisory Commission

Signed Nov. 1, 1943, in Moscow, by the Foreign Ministers of the USSR, the United Kingdom, and the United States of America.
Defines tasks and powers of the Commission, establishment of which was mentioned in the joint communiqué of Oct. 30, 1943 (43/x/30/Pl/a).
Reference: Mosely, 1950, pp. 581, 582.

• 43/xi/9/Italy

Protocol between the Allied High Command and Italy concerning modifications in the text of the instrument of surrender of September 29, 1943

Signed Nov. 9, 1943, in Brindisi.
For summary of provisions affecting the USSR, see 43/ix/29/Italy.
Sources: Hudson, 9, pp. 60–61, citing
TIAS, No. 1604, p. 23, and
Cmd. 6693, p. 11.
United States and Italy, pp. 65–66.

• 43/xi/9/Mul

Agreement establishing the United Nations Relief and Rehabilitation Administration (UNRRA)

Signed Nov. 9, 1943, in Washington, D.C. The USSR was among the original signatories; the Ukrainian and Belorussian SSR's acceded during 1945. Signature of the agreement was preceded by the preparation and circulation of two drafts, on June 10 and Sept. 20, 1943. "The ac-

tivities of the Administration were discontinued in 1947, its functions being transferred to various specialized agencies of the United Nations" (Hudson, 9, p. 84). Residual assets transferred to the UN by an agreement of Sept. 27, 1948 (not listed here).
Sources: *DSCS*, 53, pp. 7–20.
  EAS, 352, pp. 1–8.
  BFSP, 145, pp. 159–67, citing
    BTS, 1943, No. 3, Cmd. 6491.
References: *VT*, 1943, No. 12, pp. 37–39.
  SDD, 11, p. 199.

Nov. 10, 1943. Order establishing the Allied Control Commission for Italy
See 44/i/ /Pl.

• 43/xi/17/Canada

Exchange of notes between the USSR and Canada concerning reorganization of diplomatic missions into embassies

Sent Nov. 13 and 17, 1943, in Moscow.
References: *Izv.*, Dec. 11, 1943.
  SDD, 11, p. 40.

• 43/xii/1/Pl/a

Declaration concerning coordinated action in the war against Germany and postwar cooperation

Signed Dec. 1, 1943, in Teheran, by the Heads of Government of the USSR, the United Kingdom, and the United States of America, at the conclusion of a conference which began Nov. 28, 1943.
In regard to "plans for the destruction of the German forces," affirms "complete agreement as to the scope and timing of the operations to be undertaken . . ." In regard to peace, signatories "recognize fully the supreme responsibility resting on us and all the United Nations to make a peace which will command the goodwill of the overwhelming mass of the peoples of the world . . ."
Sources: *Izv.*, Dec. 7, 1943.
  VPSS VP, 1, pp. 369–70.
  SDD, 11, pp. 53–54.
  DSB, 9, 1943, p. 409.
  Axis in defeat, pp. 5–6.
  DAFR, 6, p. 235.

• 43/xii/1/Pl/b

Declaration concerning Iran

Signed Dec. 1, 1943, in Teheran, by the Heads of Government of the USSR, the United Kingdom, and the United States of America.
Provides for economic assistance to Iran during the war and expresses the desire of the signatories "for the maintenance of the independence, sovereignty, and territorial integrity of Iran."
Sources: *Izv.*, Dec. 7, 1943.
  VPSS VP, 1, pp. 370–71.
  SDD, 11, p. 54.
  DSB, 9, 1943, pp. 409–10.
  DAFR, 6, pp. 235–36.

• 43/xii/1/Pl/c

Military conclusions of the Teheran Conference

Initialed Dec. 1, 1943, in Teheran, by the Heads of Government of the USSR, the United Kingdom, and the United States of America.
Agreements: (1) The Partisans in Yugoslavia to be supported with supplies and equipment and by commando operations. (2) From the military point of view, most desirable that Turkey should enter the war on the side of the Allies before the end of the year. (3) Military staffs of the 3 Powers to keep in close touch in regard to impending operations in Europe; a cover plan to be prepared. The conference took note of (1) a statement by Stalin that if Turkey were at war with Germany and were attacked by Bulgaria, the USSR would immediately be at war with Bulgaria; (2) that Operation "Overlord" would be launched during May 1944, in conjunction with an operation against France, and that Soviet forces would launch an offensive at about the same time.
Sources: *BFSP*, 148, pp. 19–20, citing
  BPP, 1947, Misc. No. 8, Cmd. 7092.
  Decade of American foreign policy, pp. 24–25.

• 43/xii/1/Pl/d

Agreement concerning transfer of Italian naval vessels to the USSR

Negotiated on or about Dec. 1, 1943, in Teheran, by the Heads of Government of the USSR, the United Kingdom, and the United States of America.
Reference: *Correspondence*, 1, pp. 186–88, 190–91, 197–98, 208–209.

● 43/xii/1/Pl/e

Understanding concerning the postwar boundaries of Poland

Reached on Dec. 1, 1943, in Teheran, by the Heads of Government of the USSR, the United Kingdom, and the United States of America.
References: *Correspondence*, 1, pp. 212, 267.
Churchill, 5, pp. 394–97.

● 43/xii/12/Cz

Treaty of friendship, mutual assistance, and postwar collaboration between the USSR and the Czechoslovak Government-in-Exile, with protocol

Signed Dec. 12, 1943, in Moscow.

Ratified by the USSR and Czechoslovakia Dec. 20, 1943. Acts of ratification exchanged Dec. 22, 1943, in Moscow. Entered into force on signature. Duration 20 years; if not denounced 1 year before expiration, extended for an additional 5 years.
Protocol provides for adherence to the treaty of other States bordering the USSR or Czechoslovakia which were the victims of aggression by Germany.
Sources: *VVS*, 1944, No. 2.
VPSS VP, 1, pp. 373–76.
VT, 1944, No. 1, pp. 11–13.
SDD, 11, pp. 28–31.
BFSP, 145, pp. 238–40.
DSP, 1, 1948, pp. 228–29.

● 43/xii/31/US. See Appendix 5.

1944

● 44/ / /US

Agreement between the USSR and the United States of America concerning distribution in the USSR of *Amerika*, a Russian-language magazine published in the United States

Negotiated during 1944.
Provides for distribution of 10,000 copies. For an agreement authorizing an increase to 50,000 copies, see 46/iv/23/US.
Reference: *DSB*, 27, 1952, pp. 127–28.

● 44/i/ /Pl

Agreement concerning appointment of Soviet and French representatives as observers on the Allied Control Commission for Italy

Negotiated during Jan. 1944.
Background: The armistice agreement with Italy of Sept. 29, 1943, provided for establishment of a Control Commission representative of the United Nations to regulate and execute the terms of the armistice under the direction of the Supreme Allied Commander. The Commission, as established by an order of the Supreme Allied Commander on Nov. 10, 1943, consisted exclusively of British and American personnel, in about equal numbers. Meanwhile, at the Moscow Conference of Foreign Ministers in Oct. 1943, agreement was reached on the establishment of an Advisory Council for Italy, which was to include representatives of

the USSR, the United Kingdom, the United States, and the French Committee of National Liberation (see 43/x/30/Pl/a). Not satisfied with their membership on the Advisory Council, however, in the light of their exclusion from the Allied Control Commission, the Soviets and the French asked for participation in the Commission, and in Jan. 1944 the British and Americans agreed to the appointment of Soviet and French representatives to the Commission as observers.
Abolition of the Commission was agreed on at the conference of Foreign Ministers in Apr.–May 1946 (see 46/v/16/Pl).
Reference: *SIA, ABR*, pp. 309–10.
Note: A Department of State summary on the organization of the Allied Control Commission for Italy issued in Aug. 1944 states that the personnel of the Commission is "roughly 50 per cent American and 50 per cent British, the only exceptions being a Soviet and a French representative . . . attached to the staff of the chief commissioner." The date on which the Soviet and French representatives were added is not indicated.
DSB, 11, 1944, pp. 137–38, reprinted in *United States and Italy*, pp. 76–78.

● 44/ii/2/US. See Appendix 5.

● 44/ii/11/Canada

Agreement between the USSR and Canada concerning principles relating to the

provision by Canada of military supplies for the USSR

Signed Feb. 11, 1944, in Ottawa.
Entered into force on signature; valid until date of termination to be agreed on by signatories. Based on a Canadian law of May 14, 1943, concerning military supplies for the United Nations. Listed in *SDD*, 11 (1955), p. 197, as no longer valid.
Sources: *MKh*, 1944, No. 3–4, pp. 76–78.
VT, 1944, No. 2–3, pp. 12–15.
VPSS VP, 2, pp. 80–84.
SFP PW, 2, pp. 51–53.
CTS, 1944, No. 4.
Reference: Korolenko, pp. 73–74.

● 44/ii/16/China

Agreement between the USSR and China concerning the purchase by China of the Wu-su Hsien oil field installations and equipment from the USSR

Signed Feb. 16, 1944, in Tihwa, Sinkiang.
Entered into force on signature. Concluded by the central Chinese Government in an effort to remedy the situation created by the oral promise of Sheng Shih-tsai, former governor of Sinkiang, permitting the USSR to dig oil wells and refine oil in Wu-su Hsien.
Source: *The Soviet Union's economic invasion of Sinkiang*, pp. 124–25.
Reference: Whiting, p. 86.

● 44/ii/23/Pl

Joint declaration concerning purchase of gold from countries not constituting part of the United Nations

Issued Feb. 23, 1944, by the USSR, the United Kingdom, and the United States of America.
Based on the Inter-Allied declaration of Jan. 5, 1943.
Source: *SFP PW*, 2, p. 55.

● 44/iii/10/J

Agreement between the USSR and Japan concerning procedure for transfer to the Soviet Government of the property of Japanese oil and coal concessions in North Sakhalin

Signed Mar. 10, 1944, in Moscow.
Signed on the same day that a protocol on the transfer was initialed; for the protocol, see 44/iii/30/J/a. Provides that an act of transfer shall be signed on North Sakhalin on the receipt of word from Moscow that the protocol of transfer and the protocol extending the fishery convention (see 44/iii/30/J/b) have been signed.
Sources: *VT*, 1944, No. 4–5, p. 38.
VPSS VP, 2, pp. 98–99.
SFP PW, 2, p. 62.

● 44/iii/11/Italy

Exchange of notes between the USSR and Italy (Government of Marshal Badoglio) concerning establishment of diplomatic relations

Sent Mar. 7 and 11, 1944.
References: *VT*, 1944, No. 2–3, p. 35 (TASS dispatch of Mar. 13, 1944, from Algiers).
VPSS VP, 2, p. 91.
SFP PW, 2, p. 57.
SIA, RE, p. 425.

● 44/iii/30/J/a

Protocol between the USSR and Japan concerning transfer to the USSR of Japanese oil and coal concessions in North Sakhalin, with annex

Signed Mar. 30, 1944, in Moscow; initialed Mar. 12, 1944 (see 44/iii/10/J).
Entered into force on signature. Terminates the concessionary agreements of Dec. 14, 1925 (see Appendix 3), and all subsequent treaties and agreements on the subject. Carries out an informal agreement reached at the time of signature of the neutrality pact of Apr. 13, 1941 (see 41/iv/13/J/a). Annex (not reproduced in sources cited) consists of Conditions for application of the protocol.
Sources: *Izv.*, Mar. 31, 1944.
VT, 1944, No. 4–5, pp. 37–38.
VPSS VP, 2, pp. 96–98.
CDT, No. 688.
Moore, pp. 202–204.

● 44/iii/30/J/b

Protocol between the USSR and Japan extending the fishery convention of January 23, 1928

Signed Mar. 30, 1944, in Moscow.
Entered into force on signature. Extends the 1928 convention for 5 years from Jan. 1, 1944. Modifies protocol A and the first exchange of notes annexed to the con-

vention. Supplemented by 2 exchanges of notes (next item).
Sources: *Izv.*, Mar. 31, 1944.
   VT, 1944, No. 4–5, pp. 38–41.
   VPSS VP, 2, pp. 99–102.
   SFP PW, 2, pp. 62–64.
   CDT, No. 687.
   Moore, pp. 205–207.

● 44/iii/30/J/c

Exchange of notes between the USSR and Japan concerning fishery lots

Sent Mar. 30, 1944, in Moscow.
Two exchanges were sent concerning (1) rent of fishery lots, and (2) a guarantee by Japan that fishery lots located on the eastern shore of Kamchatka and the Oliutorsky raion (Koriak National Okrug) would not be exploited by the concessionaires for the duration of the war in the Pacific. First exchange of notes extends for 5 years, from Jan. 1, 1944, the special concessionary agreements of Nov. 3, 1928, with accompanying documents and supplementary agreements (see Appendix 3).
Sources: *Izv.*, Mar. 31, 1944.
   VT, 1944, No. 4–5, pp. 40–41.
   VPSS VP, 2, pp. 102–104.
   SFP PW, 2, pp. 64–65.
   Moore, pp. 208–10.

● 44/iii/30/J/d

Exchange of notes between the USSR and Japan concerning closing of consulates

Sent Mar. 30, 1944.
Provides for closing of the Japanese Consulate-General in Aleksandrovsk and Vice-Consulate in Okha in North Sakhalin, and the Soviet consulates in Hakodate and Tsuruga.
References: *Izv.*, Mar. 31, 1944.
   VT, 1944, No. 4–5, p. 37.
   VPSS VP, 2, p. 96.
   SFP PW, 2, p. 60.

● 44/iv/13/NZ

Exchange of notes between the USSR and New Zealand concerning establishment of diplomatic relations

Sent Apr. 13, 1944, in London.
Not subject to ratification; entered into force Apr. 13, 1944.
References: *Izv.*, Apr. 14, 1944.

VT, 1944, No. 4–5, p. 41.
VPSS VP, 2, p. 107.
SFP PW, 2, p. 67.
Note: In commenting on treaty relations between New Zealand and the USSR, the Embassy of New Zealand stated in a letter of Aug. 7, 1957, "It is possible that the New Zealand Government may also be bound by bilateral agreements concluded between the Government of the United Kingdom and the Government of the Soviet Union during the period before the Government of New Zealand became fully responsible for the conduct of its own foreign relations. The question would in each case depend on the terms of the particular agreement."

● 44/iv/23/Denmark

Exchange of notes between the USSR and the Danish Freedom Council ("Fighting Denmark") concerning establishment of diplomatic relations

Sent Apr. 18 and 23, 1944.
Denmark had broken off relations with the USSR in 1941, under German pressure.
References: *Izv.*, July 11, 1944.
   VT, 1944, No. 7–8, pp. 33–34.
   VPSS VP, 2, pp. 152–53.
   SFP PW, 2, pp. 91–92.

● 44/v/8/CR

Exchange of notes between the USSR and Costa Rica concerning establishment of diplomatic and consular relations

Sent May 8, 1944, in Mexico City.
Preceded by an informal understanding. In June 1948 Costa Rica informally allowed her relations with the USSR to lapse (see *SIA, 1947–1948*, p. 482).
References: *Izv.*, May 12, 1944.
   VT, 1944, No. 6, p. 30.
   VPSS VP, 2, p. 122.
   SDD, 11, p. 36.

● 44/v/8/Cz

Agreement between the USSR and the Czechoslovak Government-in-Exile concerning relations between the Soviet High Command and Czechoslovak administrative authorities after the entry of Soviet troops into Czechoslovak territory

Signed May 8, 1944, in London.

Entered into force on signature. Listed in *SDD*, 11 (1955), p. 199, as no longer valid.

Conclusion of the a g r e e m e n t was announced at a Soviet press conference on Apr. 30, 1944, and an advance copy of the text of the agreement was produced at the conference.

Sources: *MKh*, 1944, No. 5, pp. 85–86.
　VPSS VP, 2, pp. 116–22 (press conference); 123–25 (text).
　SFP PW, 2, pp. 72–77.

May 10, 1944. Declaration of the International Labour Organisation

See 54/iv/26/1946.

● **44/v/13/Pl**

Joint statement addressed to Hungary, Romania, Bulgaria, and Finland, urging their withdrawal from collaboration with Germany

Issued May 13, 1944, by the USSR, the United Kingdom, and the United States of America.

Source: *SFP PW*, 2, pp. 80–81.

● **44/v/16/Norway**

Agreement between the USSR and the Norwegian Government-in-Exile concerning civil administration and jurisdiction in Norwegian territory after its liberation by Allied expeditionary forces

Signed May 16, 1944, in London.

Similar agreements were signed by Norway on the same day with the United Kingdom and the United States of America.

References: *VT*, 1944, No. 6, p. 30.
　VPSS VP, 2, p. 135.
　SDD, 11, p. 198.
　SFP PW, 2, p. 82.

● **44/v/18/UK**

Informal agreement between the USSR and the United Kingdom concerning a temporary division of the Balkans into operational spheres of influence

Proposed by the United Kingdom May 5, 1944; accepted by the USSR May 18, 1944. Assigns Bulgaria and Romania to the Soviet sphere of operations, Yugoslavia and Greece to the British. Accepted on a 3-months' basis by the United States of America June 11, 1944, with the under-standing that at the end of that time it would be reviewed by the 3 Powers and that no postwar spheres of influence were being established. Extended by an informal agreement of Oct. 9, 1944 (44/x/9/UK).

References: Hull, 2, pp. 1451–58.
　SIA, ABR, p. 422.

● **44/vii/　/US**

Informal agreement between the USSR and the United States of America concerning an exchange of views of technical experts on questions of the coordination of technical measures in the field of international civil aviation

Reached during exploratory negotiations held during June and July, 1944, in Washington, D.C.

Continuing its efforts to work out regulations for international civil aviation, the United States sponsored a conference of 52 nations at Chicago from Nov. 1 to Dec. 7, 1944, which drew up 4 conventions (texts in *DAFR*, 7, pp. 572–614). The USSR refused to attend the conference, on the ground that Switzerland, Portugal, and Spain had been invited (TASS communiqué of Oct. 30, 1944, in *SFP PW*, 2, p. 210).

References: *VPSS VP*, 2, pp. 168–69.
　SFP PW, 2, p. 101.

● **44/vii/22/Mul**

Final Act of the United Nations Monetary and Financial Conference, with three annexes

Signed July 22, 1944, at Bretton Woods, New Hampshire.

Annexes: A, Articles of agreement of the International Monetary Fund; B, Articles of agreement of the International Bank for Reconstruction and Development; C, Summary of agreements of the Bretton Woods Conference.

On the same date the chairman of the Soviet delegation stated that the USSR would contribute 1.2 billion dollars to the capital of the International Bank for Reconstruction and Development.

Sources: *DSCS*, 55, pp. 11–99.
　DS, IOCS, 1.3, vol. 1, pp. 927–1015; *ibid.*, vol. 2, pp. 1244–45, for Soviet statement.
　DAFR, 6, pp. 331–98.

● 44/vii/22/Syria

Exchange of telegrams between the USSR and Syria concerning establishment of diplomatic relations

Sent July 21, 1944, from Damascus, and July 22, 1944, from Moscow.
Sources: *Izv.*, July 25, 1944.
 VPSS VP, 2, pp. 153–54.
 VT, 1944, No. 7–8, p. 34.
 SFP PW, 2, pp. 92–93.
Reference: *SDD*, 11, p. 38.

● 44/vii/25/Pl

Agreement concerning an Instrument of Unconditional Surrender by Germany

Signed July 25, 1944, in London, by representatives of the USSR, the United Kingdom, and the United States of America in the European Advisory Commission. Supplemented by protocol of Sept. 12, 1944, concerning occupation zones in Germany and the administration of Greater Berlin. Modified by an agreement at the Yalta Conference (see 45/ii/11/Pl/b, Part 3) and by a protocol of May 1, 1945 (45/v/1/Pl/b) concerning inclusion of the French Provisional Government as a signatory. The surrender instrument was not used in the surrender of Germany, and did not come into force (for Germany's surrender, see 45/v/7, 8/Ger).
Reference: Mosely, 1950, p. 494.

● 44/vii/26/Pol

Agreement between the USSR and the Polish Committee of National Liberation concerning relations between the Soviet High Command and Polish administrative authorities after the entry of Soviet troops into Polish territory

Signed July 26, 1944, in Moscow.
Entered into force on signature. Establishes the eastern boundaries of postwar Poland. This is the first agreement between the USSR and the "Lublin Committee"; it was accompanied by an exchange of diplomatic representatives, constituting *de facto* recognition. For *de jure* recognition, see 45/i/5/Pol.
Sources: *Izv.*, July 27, 1944.
 VT, 1944, No. 7–8, pp. 32–33.
 VPSS VP, 2, pp. 157–59.
 SFP PW, 2, pp. 94–96.
References: *SDD*, 11, p. 198.
 SIA, RE, p. 191.
 Rozek, p. 419.

● 44/viii/3/Lebanon

Exchange of telegrams between the USSR and Lebanon concerning establishment of diplomatic relations

Sent July 31, 1944, from Beirut, and Aug. 3, 1944, from Moscow.
Sources: *Izv.*, Aug. 5, 1944.
 VT, 1944, No. 9, p. 31.
 VPSS VP, 2, pp. 162–63.
 SFP PW, 2, pp. 97–98.
Reference: *SDD*, 11, p. 37.

● 44/viii/11/Pl

Agreement concerning preliminary unofficial negotiations between the USSR, the United Kingdom, and the United States of America for establishment of an international organization for maintenance of peace and security

Announced Aug. 11, 1944.
Provides for negotiations to begin Aug. 21, 1944, in Washington, D.C.
Reference: *SFP PW*, pp. 100–101.

● 44/viii/23/Rom

Conditions for an armistice with Romania

Proposed by the USSR Apr. 12, 1944; accepted by Romania Aug. 23, 1944.
Provides for re-establishment of the Soviet-Romanian border according to the agreement of 1940 (40/vi/28/Rom). Romania declared war on Germany on Aug. 24, 1944. For the armistice agreement with Romania, see 44/ix/12/Rom.
Source: *VPSS VP*, 2, pp. 174–75.
Reference: *SIA, HE*, pp. 626–27.

● 44/viii/31/Mul

Protocol extending the agreement of May 6, 1937, concerning regulation of the production and marketing of sugar

Signed Aug. 31, 1944, in London.
Extends the 1937 agreement through Aug. 31, 1945. Further extended by protocol of Aug. 31, 1945, and subsequently.
Sources: *USTS*, 990, 1945, pp. 33–34.
 BFSP, 145, pp. 504–506, citing
  BTS, 1946, No. 45, Cmd. 6949.
 Hudson, 9, pp. 25–27.

● 44/ix/ /Pl. See Appendix 5.

● 44/ix/3/Fin

Cease-fire agreement between the USSR and Finland

Negotiated during the period Aug. 25–
Sept. 3, 1944.
Entered into force Sept. 4, 1944. For the
armistice agreement with Finland, see 44/
ix/19/Fin.
References: *VPSS VP*, 2, pp. 177–79.
  SIA, RE, pp. 268–70.

• 44/ix/9/Bul

**Cease-fire agreement between the USSR
and Bulgaria**

Negotiated between Sept 6 and 9, 1944.
Entered into force Sept. 9, 1944.
The USSR had broken off relations with
Bulgaria and announced the existence of
a state of war in a note of Sept. 5, 1944
(*VPSS VP*, 2, pp. 181–83). On Sept. 6,
1944, the Bulgarian Government requested an armistice with the USSR; on
the 7th, it announced that it had broken
off relations with Germany, and on the
8th declared war on Germany. On Sept.
9, according to an official Soviet announcement, Soviet forces ceased military operations against Bulgaria (*VPSS VP*, 2, pp.
200–201). For the armistice agreement
with Bulgaria, see 44/x/28/Bul.

• 44/ix/9/Iraq

**Exchange of telegrams between the
USSR and Iraq concerning establishment
of diplomatic relations**

Sent Aug. 25, 1944, from Baghdad, and
Sept. 9, 1944, from Moscow.
Sources: *Izv.*, Sept. 13, 1944.
  VT, 1944, No. 9, pp. 31–32.
  VPSS VP, 2, pp. 212–13.
  SFP PW, 2, p. 127.
Reference: *SDD*, 11, p. 36.

• 44/ix/9/Pol/a

**Agreement between the Ukrainian SSR
and the Polish Committee of National
Liberation concerning evacuation of
Ukrainian population from Polish territory and Polish population from the territory of the Ukrainian SSR**

Signed Sept. 9, 1944, in Lublin.
Completion of the operation marked by
protocol of May 6, 1947. Possibly the first
Soviet treaty signed by N. S. Khrushchev.
References: *VPSS VP*, 2, pp. 202–204.
  MKh, 1944, No. 9, p. 81.
  SFP PW, 2, pp. 121–22.

• 44/ix/9/Pol/b

**Agreement between the Belorussian SSR
and the Polish Committee of National
Liberation concerning evacuation of Belorussian population from Polish territory
and Polish population from the territory
of the Belorussian SSR**

Signed Sept. 9, 1944, in Lublin.
References: *VPSS VP*, 2, pp. 202–204.
  MKh, 1944, No. 9, p. 81.
  SFP PW, 2, pp. 121–22.

• 44/ix/12/Pl/a

**Protocol of agreement concerning occu-
pation zones in Germany and the administration of Greater Berlin, with two maps**

Signed Sept. 12, 1944, by representatives
of the USSR, the United Kingdom, and
the United States of America in the European Advisory Commission.
Approved by the United Kingdom Dec.
5, 1944; by the United States Feb. 2,
1945; and by the USSR Feb. 6, 1945. Entered into force Feb. 6, 1945, on approval
by signatories.
Specifies the areas provided for in Art. 11
of the Instrument of Unconditional Surrender by Germany prepared on July 25,
1944 (44/vii/25/Pl). Leaves for further
negotiation the final demarcation of the
northwest and southwest occupation zones,
and the northwest and southern sectors of
Greater Berlin. Modified by agreement of
Nov. 14, 1944 (44/xi/14/Pl/a), and protocol of July 26, 1945 (45/vii/26/Pl/a).
Denounced by the USSR, together with
associated supplementary agreements, in
a note of Nov. 27, 1958 (*NYT*, Nov. 28,
1958).
Sources: *SDD*, 11, pp. 55–57.
  UST, 5, pp. 2078–86, citing
    TIAS, 3071.
  UNTS, 227, pp. 279–85, 292–94 (R, E,
    F).

• 44/ix/12/Rom

**Armistice agreement with Romania, with
annex**

Signed Sept. 12, 1944, in Moscow, by the
USSR and Romania. The Soviet represen-
tative, Marshal R. Ya. Malinovski, signed
on behalf of the United Kingdom and the
United States of America as well as the
USSR. A note of the same date author-

ized him to sign for the United States (see *EAS*, 490).

Entered into force on signature. Restores the boundary between the USSR and Romania established by the agreement of June 28, 1940 (40/vi/28/Rom), and restores Transylvania to Romania. Provides for payment to the USSR by Romania of $300 million in reparations, over 6 years, and for the establishment of an Allied Control Commission under the chairmanship of the USSR to regulate and control execution of the terms of the agreement until conclusion of peace. Supplemented by a protocol of the same date (next document), and by a reparations agreement of Jan. 16, 1945. Modified by agreements of Sept. 1945 (see 45/ix/13/Rom/b, /c, and /d).

Sources: *VT*, 1944, No. 9, pp. 1–5.
   VPSS VP, 2, pp. 205–10.
   SFP PW, 2, pp. 123–27.
   EAS, 490, 1946, pp. 1–15.
   DSB, 11, 1944, pp. 289–92.
   BFSP, 145, pp. 506–12.
   Hudson, 9, pp. 139–43.

● 44/ix/12/Pl/b

Protocol to the armistice agreement with Romania

Signed Sept. 12, 1944, in Moscow, by the USSR, the United Kingdom, and the United States of America.

Concerns (1) repatriation of Allied prisoners of war and internees, (2) definition of the term "war material" as used in the armistice, and (3) use of Allied vessels returned by Romania.

Sources: *EAS*, 490, 1946, p. 15.
   Hudson, 9, pp. 143–44, citing
     Cmd. 6585, p. 6.

● 44/ix/19/Fin

Armistice agreement with Finland, with annex and two maps

Signed Sept. 19, 1944, in Moscow, by the USSR and Finland. The representative of the USSR (Andrei Zhdanov) signed also on behalf of the United Kingdom, and of all the United Nations at war with Finland.

Not subject to ratification; entered into force on signature. Re-establishes (1) the peace treaty of Mar. 12, 1940, with modifications, and (2) the agreement concern-

ing demilitarization of the Aaland Islands of Oct. 11, 1940. Provides for establishment of an Allied Control Commission in Helsinki under the chairmanship of the USSR to supervise execution of provisions. Finland returns Petsamo (Pechenga) oblast to the USSR; the USSR renounces its rights to the lease of the Hangö Peninsula; and Finland agrees to lease to the USSR territory for establishment of a naval base at Porkkala-Udd. Finland to pay the USSR $300 million in reparations over 6 years. Supplemented by a protocol of the same date (next document) and a reparations agreement of Dec. 17, 1944.

Modified by decision of the Allied Control Commission in late July 1945 (see 45/viii/5/Fin). Agreement on lease to the USSR of Porkkala-Udd terminated by agreement of Sept. 19, 1955 (55/ix/19/Fin/a). Superseded by the peace treaty of Feb. 10, 1947.

Sources: *VT*, 1944, No. 9, pp. 6–14.
   VPSS VP, 2, pp. 215–20.
   SFP PW, 2, pp. 128–37.
   BFSP, 145, pp. 513–25, citing
     Cmd. 6586.
   SS, 1944, No. 4 (R, Finnish).
   Hudson, 9, pp. 144–51.
   DSB, 12, 1945, pp. 261–67.

● 44/ix/19/UK

Protocol to the armistice agreement with Finland

Signed Sept. 19, 1944, in Moscow, by the USSR and the United Kingdom.

Concerns (1) repatriation of Allied prisoners of war and internees, (2) definition of the term "war material" as used in the armistice, and (3) use of Allied vessels returned by Finland.

Sources: Hudson, 9, pp. 151–52.
   BFSP, 145, pp. 524–25, citing
     Cmd. 6586, p. 10.

● 44/ix/22/Pol

Agreement between the Lithuanian SSR and the Polish Committee of National Liberation concerning evacuation of Lithuanian population from Polish territory and Polish population from the territory of the Lithuanian SSR

Signed Sept. 22, 1944, in Lublin.
References: *VPSS VP*, 2, pp. 230–32.
   SFP PW, 2, pp. 138–39.

• 44/ix/23/UK

Agreement between the USSR and the United Kingdom concerning establishment of direct radio-telephone service

Signed Sept. 23, 1944, in Moscow.
Entered into force on signature. Valid until 6 months after denunciation. Modified by an exchange of notes dated Apr. 19 and July 9, 1946 (46/vii/9/UK).
Sources: *SDD*, 11, pp. 177–85.
  BFSP, 145, pp. 485–90, citing
    BTS, 1947, No. 2, Cmd. 7028 (modified text of 1946).
  UNTS, 10, pp. 171–92 (E, R, F; modified text).

• 44/ix/28/Pl

Joint statement concerning conversations on an international peace and security organization

Signed Sept. 28, 1944, at Dumbarton Oaks, Washington, D.C., by the heads of delegations of the USSR, the United Kingdom, and the United States of America; issued to the press Sept. 29, 1944.
The USSR was represented at the first phase of the conversations, which lasted from Aug. 27 to Sept. 28, 1944, but not at the second and concluding phase, from Sept. 29 to Oct. 7, 1944. The USSR did, however, publish the "Proposals for the establishment of a general international organization" which were issued at the end of the conference (see 44/x/7/Pl and 44/x/9/Pl).
Sources: *VPSS VP*, 2, p. 237.
  SFP PW, 2, p. 142.
  DSB, 11, 1944, p. 342.
Reference: *DS GFPS*, *15*, pp. 327–28.

• 44/ix/28/Yug/a

Press communiqué concerning an agreement between the USSR and the Yugoslav National Committee of Liberation concerning joint military operations in Yugoslavia

Published Sept. 28, 1944, following negotiations in Moscow between Stalin and Tito.
Calls for Soviet military support for Yugoslav forces fighting the Germans. On completion of military operations, Soviet forces to be withdrawn from Yugoslavia. In Yugoslav territories occupied by Soviet forces, civil administration to be carried out by the National Committee of Liberation.
Sources: *Izv.*, Sept. 29, 1944.
  Dedijer, pp. 231–32.

• 44/ix/28/Yug/b

Agreement between the USSR and the Yugoslav National Committee of Liberation concerning a Soviet loan

Negotiated during 1944, possibly during the talks in Sept. between Tito and Stalin. Yugoslav indebtedness under this loan, to the amount of $945,000 US, was to be settled under the protocol of Dec. 27, 1948.

• 44/x/7/Pl

Proposals for establishment of a general international security organization

Signed Oct. 7, 1944, at Dumbarton Oaks, Washington D.C.
Drawn up in conversations held from Aug. 27 to Oct. 7, 1944, attended by representatives of the United States of America, the United Kingdom, the USSR, and China. Accompanied and introduced by a statement of the participating governments (44/x/9/Pl). The procedure for voting in the Security Council of the proposed organization was subsequently agreed to at the Yalta Conference, where it was incorporated in the Protocol of Proceedings (45/ii/11/Pl/b). See also *DAFR*, 7, p. 360, and *DSB*, 12, 1945, p. 394.
Sources: *VPSS VP*, 2, pp. 243–59.
  SFP PW, 2, pp. 146–54.
  DSB, 11, 1944, pp. 368–74.
  DSCS, 56, pp. 8–22.
  DSCS, 60, pp. 5–22.

• 44/x/8/Pl

Protocol to the armistice agreement with Finland concerning compensation to Canada for nickel mines in former Finnish territory

Signed Oct. 8, 1944, in Moscow, by the USSR, the United Kingdom, and Canada. Entered into force on signature. Provides for payment by the USSR of $20 million US over 6 years. Modified by protocol of Sept. 29, 1947.
Sources: *Izv.*, Oct. 20, 1944.
  VT, 1944, No. 10, p. 15.
  VPSS VP, 2, p. 270.

SFP PW, 2, p. 161.
CTS, 1944, No. 29.
BFSP, 145, p. 525.
UNTS, 45, pp. 311–15 (E, R, F).
Hudson, 9, pp. 152–53.

● 44/x/9/Pl

Statement by the participating governments in the conversations on an international peace and security organization

Published Oct. 9, 1944, to accompany and introduce the "Proposals for establishment of a general international security organization" (44/x/7/Pl). Issued more or less simultaneously by the governments represented at the conversations (the United States of America, the United Kingdom, the USSR, and China).
Sources: *VPSS VP*, 2, p. 243.
  SFP PW, 2, p. 146.
  DSB, 11, 1944, p. 367.

● 44/x/9/UK

Informal agreement between the USSR and the United Kingdom concerning spheres of influence in the Balkans

Negotiated Oct. 9, 1944, in Moscow.
Consists of an informal proposal by Churchill, accepted by Stalin, for allocation of Soviet, British, and other interests in Romania, Greece, Yugoslavia, Hungary, and Bulgaria.
Source: Churchill, 6, p. 227 (U.S. edition) ; p. 198 (British edition).

● 44/x/10/MPR

Agreement between the USSR and the Mongolian People's Republic concerning exchange of mail and packages

Signed Oct. 10, 1944, in Ulan Bator.
Entered into force on signature. Valid until 6 months after denunciation.
Source: *SDD*, 11, pp. 185–93.

● 44/x/11/Bul

Agreement concerning preliminary conditions for an armistice with Bulgaria

Negotiated Oct. 11, 1944.
In answer to a request by Bulgaria for an armistice, made at the time of the cease-fire agreement (44/ix/9/Bul), the USSR, the United Kingdom, and the United States of America on Oct. 11, 1944, sent Bulgaria a note stating that negotiations

for an armistice could be started only after Bulgaria had agreed to withdraw its forces and officials from Greece and Yugoslavia within 15 days; to supervise the withdrawal, representatives of the three governments would be sent to Bulgaria as an Allied Military Mission. Bulgaria accepted these conditions on the same day. For the armistice, see 44/x/28/Bul.
Sources: *VPSS VP*, 2, pp. 261–63.
  SFP PW, 2, p. 156.
Reference: *SIA, ABR*, p. 471.

● 44/x/18/US. See Appendix 5.

● 44/x/20/Pol

Economic agreement between the USSR and the Polish Committee of National Liberation

Signed Oct. 20, 1944.
Provides for Soviet deliveries during Oct. and Nov. 1944, on credit without interest, of coal, flour, oil products, automobiles, salt, and other goods, and for Soviet assistance in rebuilding Warsaw. Polish exports in payment to begin in June 1945, but on Poland's request, deferred until mid-1946.
References: *VT*, 1950, No. 5, pp. 4–5.
  VT SSSR, p. 66.

● 44/x/21/UK

Joint communiqué by the USSR and the United Kingdom concerning political negotiations

Issued Oct. 21, 1944, in Moscow.
Covers talks held from Oct. 9 to 18, 1944. Mentions agreements reached in regard to (1) the Polish question, (2) an armistice with Bulgaria, and (3) conduct of a joint policy in Yugoslavia. States that talks were conducted with the knowledge and approval of the United States, which was represented by its Ambassador, Mr. Harriman, as observer.
Sources: *VPSS VP*, 2, pp. 271–72.
  SFP PW, 2, p. 162.
  DAFR, 7, pp. 347–48.

● 44/x/23/France

Declaration by the USSR concerning recognition of the French Provisional Government

Signed Oct. 23, 1944, in Paris.
Similar declarations were made on the

same day by the United States of America
and the United Kingdom.
Sources: *Izv.*, Oct. 24, 1944.
   VPSS VP, 2, p. 274.
   SFP PW, pp. 163–64.
References: *SDD*, 11, p. 39.
   Churchill, 6, pp. 244–49; British ed.,
     pp. 213–17.
   SIA, ABR, p. 493.

● 44/x/25/Italy

**Declaration by the USSR concerning es-
tablishment of full diplomatic relations
with Italy**

Made Oct. 25, 1944, in Rome.
The USSR had already established diplomatic relations with the Badoglio regime
(see 44/iii/11/Italy). In the present declaration they requested the Italian Government to agree to the designation of
their representative, M. A. Kostylev, as
ambassador. The United States announced its decision to renew relations
with Italy on Oct. 26, 1944 (*DSB*, 11,
1944, p. 491).
References: *Izv.*, Oct. 26, 1944.
   VPSS VP, 2, p. 280.
   SFP PW, p. 167.
   SDD, 11, p. 36.

● 44/x/28/Bul

Armistice agreement with Bulgaria

Signed Oct. 28, 1944, in Moscow, by the
USSR and the United Kingdom, acting
on behalf of all the United Nations at war
with Bulgaria. Both the Soviet representative, Marshal F. I. Tolbukhin, and the
British representative, Lt. Gen. J. A. H.
Gammell, signed also on behalf of the
United States, in accordance with notes
of the same date (*UNTS*, 123, p. 238).
Entered into force on signature. Provides
for establishment of an Allied Control
Commission under the chairmanship of
the USSR to supervise execution of pro-
visions. Reparations by Bulgaria to the
United Nations to be decided later. Sup-
plemented by a protocol of the same date
(next document).
Sources: *Izv.*, Oct. 31, 1944.
   VT, 1944, No. 10, pp. 1–4.
   VPSS VP, 2, pp. 286–91.
   SFP PW, 2, pp. 170–73.
   EAS, 437, pp. 1–16 (E, R, B).
   DSB, 11, 1944, pp. 492–94.

BFSP, 145, pp. 526–30, citing
   Cmd. 6587.
UNTS, 123, pp. 223–34, 239–42 (E, R,
   F, B).

● 44/x/28/Pl

**Protocol to the armistice agreement with
Bulgaria**

Signed Oct. 28, 1944, in Moscow, by the
USSR, the United States of America, and
the United Kingdom.
Concerns (1) relief of the population of
Greek and Yugoslav territories, (2) defi-
nition of the term "war material" as used
in the armistice agreement, (3) use of
Allied vessels returned by Bulgaria, and
(4) provision by Bulgaria for needs of
representatives of the United States and
the United Kingdom.
Sources: *Izv.*, Oct. 31, 1944.
   VT, 1944, No. 10, p. 4.
   VPSS VP, 2, pp. 291–92.
   SFP PW, 2, p. 173.
   DSB, 11, 1944, p. 494.
   UNTS, 123, pp. 236–37, 243 (E, R, F).

● 44/xi/11/Pl

**Joint communiqué concerning an invita-
tion to the French Provisional Government to become a member of the European Advisory Commission**

Issued Nov. 11, 1944, by the USSR, the
United Kingdom, and the United States
of America. France became a member on
Nov. 27, 1944.
Sources: *DSB*, 11, 1944, p. 583.
   SFP PW, 2, pp. 177–78.
References: *VPSS VP*, 2, p. 299.
   SIA, ABR, p. 477.
   Mosely, 1950, p. 598.

● 44/xi/14/Pl/a

**Agreement modifying the protocol of
September 12, 1944, concerning occupation zones in Germany and the administration of Greater Berlin, with map**

Signed Nov. 14, 1944, in London, by representatives of the USSR, the United Kingdom, and the United States of America in
the European Advisory Committee.
Approved by the United Kingdom Dec.
5, 1944; by the United States Feb. 2,
1945; and by the USSR Feb. 6, 1945.

Entered into force Feb. 6, 1945, on approval by signatories. Defines southwestern and northwestern occupation zones and allocates northwestern sector of Berlin to the United Kingdom, southern sector to the United States.
Modified by protocol of July 26, 1945.
Sources: *SDD*, 11, pp. 57–59.
  UST, 5, pp. 2087–92.
  UNTS, 227, pp. 286–91, 295–96 (R, E, F).
Reference: Mosely, 1950, p. 599.

● 44/xi/14/Pl/b

Agreement concerning control machinery in Germany

Signed Nov. 14, 1944, in London, by representatives of the USSR, the United Kingdom, and the United States of America in the European Advisory Committee. Confirmed by the United Kingdom Dec. 5, 1944; by the United States Jan. 24, 1945; and by the USSR Feb. 6, 1945. Entered into force Feb. 6, 1945, on confirmation by signatories.
Provides for establishment of a Control Council to direct the administration of occupied Germany. Modified by agreement of May 1, 1945, providing for inclusion of the French Provisional Government in the Control Council (45/v/1/Pl/a).
Sources: *SDD*, 11, pp. 62–65.
  UST, 5, pp. 2063–71.
  UNTS, 236, pp. 359–71 (R, E, F).

● 44/xi/25/Yug

Joint communiqué by the USSR and Yugoslavia concerning establishment of a unified Yugoslav Government

Issued Nov. 25, 1944, in Moscow, following conversations held from Nov. 20 to 23, 1944.
Calls for formation of a united Yugoslav Government on the basis of agreements concluded between Tito (President of the National Committee of Liberation of Yugoslavia) and Dr. I. Šubašić (Prime Minister of the Royal Yugoslav Government). The Tito-Šubašić agreement of Nov. 1, 1944, was subsequently made the basis for a Big Three agreement on Yugoslavia (see 45/ii/9/Pl).
Sources: *VPSS VP*, 2, pp. 311–12.
  SFP PW, 2, pp. 184–85.

● 44/xii/10/France

Treaty of alliance and mutual assistance between the USSR and the French Provisional Government

Signed Dec. 10, 1944, in Moscow.
Ratified by France, Dec. 22, 1944; by the USSR Dec. 25, 1944. Entered into force Feb. 15, 1945, on exchange of acts of ratification in Paris. Duration 20 years; if not denounced 1 year prior to expiration, extended until 1 year following denunciation. Annulled by the Presidium of the Supreme Soviet May 7, 1955 (*VVS*, 1955, No. 7, Art. 170).
On Mar. 28, 1945, TASS denied a newspaper report that the treaty contained a secret clause giving France freedom of action in the West and the USSR freedom of action in Eastern Europe, and stated that the treaty contained no secret clauses.
Sources: *Izv.*, Dec. 19, 1944.
  VT, 1944, No. 11–12, pp. 13–14.
  MKh, 1944, No. 12, pp. 82–83.
  VPSS VP, 2, pp. 327–30.
  SFP PW, 2, pp. 194–95.
  VVS, 1945, No. 36.
  *JO, Mar. 7, 1945.
  BFSP, 149, pp. 632–35.
  DSP, 1, 1948, p. 230.
  DSB, 12, 1945, pp. 39–40.
Reference: Churchill, 6, pp. 256–60; British ed., pp. 225–27.

● 44/xii/11/Chile

Exchange of notes between the USSR and Chile concerning establishment of diplomatic and consular relations

Sent Dec. 11, 1944, in Washington, D.C. Preceded by an informal understanding. Diplomatic relations were broken off by Chile on Oct. 21, 1947, on charges of subversive activities by the Soviet diplomatic mission in Chile (text of the Chilean note in *DIA, 1947–1948*, p. 788).
Sources: *Izv.*, Dec. 13, 1944.
  VT, 1944, No. 11–12, pp. 16–17.
  VPSS VP, 2, pp. 321–22.
  SFP PW, 2, pp. 190–91.
  *Chile, Report of the Ministry of Foreign Affairs, 1944, p. 121.

● 44/xii/11/France

Joint communiqué by the USSR and France concerning the visit of General Charles de Gaulle to Moscow

Issued Dec. 11, 1944, following negotiations in Moscow from Dec. 2 to 10, 1944.
Source: *SFP PW*, 2, p. 190.

● 44/xii/12/Nicaragua

**Exchange of notes between the USSR
and Nicaragua concerning establishment
of diplomatic and consular relations**

Sent Nov. 10 and Dec. 12, 1944, in Mexico
City.
Preceded by an informal understanding.
References: *Izv.*, Dec. 17, 1944.
VT, 1944, No. 11–12, p. 17.
VPSS VP, 2, pp. 322–23.
SFP PW, 2, p. 191.
SDD, 11, p. 37.

● 44/xii/16/Fin

**Protocol concerning demarcation of the
border between the USSR and Finland
in the Porkkala-Udd region, with annex,
maps, and protocol of border marks**

Prepared by a mixed Soviet-Finnish commission Dec. 16, 1944.
Put into effect by exchange of notes on
Mar. 14, 1945. Modified by agreement of
Sept. 19, 1955 concerning transfer of
Porkkala-Udd to Finland (55/ix/19/Fin/
a). For the annex, see 45/x/26/Fin. Mentioned in the border treaty of Dec. 9,
1948.

● 44/xii/17/Fin

**Agreement between the USSR and Fin-
land concerning reparations deliveries by
Finland**

Signed Dec. 17, 1944, in Helsinki.
Carries out provisions of armistice agreement of Sept. 19, 1944. Provides for a
total of $300 million US in Finnish goods,
in equal yearly installments for 6 years,
from Sept. 19, 1944, to Sept. 19, 1950.
Term for delivery extended by agreement
of Dec. 31, 1945. Amount of payments
reduced under Soviet declaration of June
3, 1948 (48/vi/3/Fin).
References: *Izv.*, Dec. 20, 1944.
VT, 1944, No. 11–12, p. 15.
VPSS VP, 2, pp. 325–26.
SFP PW, 2, pp. 192–93.
SIA, RE, p. 279.

● 44/xii/30/Bul

**Agreement between the USSR and Bul-
garia concerning handing over to Bulgaria of eleven individuals accused as
war criminals**

Soviet agreement, with the consent of the
United Kingdom and the United States of
America, announced Dec. 30, 1944, in
answer to a request by Bulgaria.
Reference: *SFP PW*, 2, p. 198 (TASS
communiqué).

1945

● 45/ / /Norway

**Agreement between the USSR and Nor-
way concerning establishment of a mixed
Soviet-Norwegian commission to investi-
gate living and working conditions of
Soviet citizens in German captivity in
Norway**

Concluded during 1945.
Mentioned in the communiqué of Apr. 28,
1948, concerning work of the commission.

● 45/i/5/Pol

**Exchange of letters between the USSR
and the Provisional Government of Poland concerning establishment of diplomatic relations**

Sent Jan. 2, 1945, from Lublin, and Jan.
5, 1945, from Moscow.

For Soviet *de facto* recognition of the Polish Committee of National Liberation, the
predecessor of this regime, see 44/vii/26/
Pol. The Committee transformed itself
into a Provisional Government on Dec. 31,
1944 (see *SIA, RE*, p. 192).
References: *Izv.*, Jan. 6, 1945.
VT, 1945, No. 1–2, p. 23.
SDD, 11, p. 38.

● 45/i/16/Rom

**Reparations agreement b e t w e e n the
USSR and Romania**

Signed Jan. 16, 1945, in Bucharest.
Based on Art. 11 of the armistice agreement of Sept. 12, 1944. Provides for total
reparations from Romania to a value of
$300 million, to be delivered in 6 equal
annual installments b e t w e e n Sept. 12,

1944, and Sept. 12, 1950. Modified by agreements of Sept. 1945 (45/ix/13/Rom/ b) and Apr. 1946 (46/iv/15/Rom), and by the peace treaty of Feb. 10, 1947. Amount of reparations payments reduced under an exchange of notes in June 1948 (48/vi/7/Rom).
References: *Izv.*, Jan. 18, 1945.
  VPSS VP, 3, pp. 65–66.
  VT, 1945, No. 1–2, p. 24.
  DSB, 15, 1946, p. 396.

● 45/i/20/H

Armistice agreement with Hungary, with annex

Signed Jan. 20, 1945, in Moscow, by the USSR and the Provisional National Government of Hungary. The Soviet representative, Marshal K. Ye. Voroshilov, signed also on behalf of the United Kingdom, the United States of America, and all the United Nations at war with Hungary. A note of the same date authorized him to sign for the United States (*EAS*, No. 456, p. 32).
Entered into force on signature. Provides for establishment of an Allied Control Commission in Budapest under the chairmanship of the USSR. Procedure for work of the Allied Control Commission modified by Soviet letter of July 12, 1945: see 45/viii/1/(11). Nullifies the Vienna Awards of Nov. 2, 1938, and Aug. 30, 1940, under which Hungary acquired Northern Transylvania and part of Slovakia. Hungary to pay $300 million in reparations over 6 years, of which $200 million to be paid to the USSR.
Supplemented by a protocol of the same date (next document), and by a reparations agreement of June 15, 1945.
Sources: *Izv.*, Jan. 22, 1945.
  VT, 1945, No. 1–2, pp. 17–22.
  VPSS VP, 3, pp. 76–84.
  EAS, No. 456, pp. 1–28 (R, E, H).
  DSB, 12, 1945, pp. 83–86.
  BFSP, 145, pp. 788–95, citing Cmd. 7280.
  OT, Sept, 16, 1945, pp. 7–22.
  UNTS, 140, pp. 397–425 (R, E, F, H).
  Hudson, 9, pp. 276–81.

● 45/i/20/Pl

Protocol to the armistice agreement with Hungary

Signed Jan. 20, 1945, in Moscow, by the USSR, the United Kingdom, and the United States of America.
Concerns (1) definition of the term "war material" as used in the armistice and (2) use of Allied vessels returned by Hungary.
Sources: *VPSS VP*, 3, pp. 84–85.
  BFSP, 145, p. 795.
  EAS, No. 456, pp. 30–31 (R, E).
  DSB, 12, 1945, p. 86.
  UNTS, 140, pp. 405, 418–19 (R, E, F).
  Hudson, 9, pp. 281–82.

● 45/i/31/Fin

Trade agreement between the USSR and Finland

Signed Jan. 31, 1945, probably in Helsinki.
USSR to supply before June 1, 1945, 30,000 tons of food grains, 1,000 tons of sugar, and 300 tons of confectionery products, in exchange for Finnish nickel, cobalt, pyrites, armaments, and repairs to Soviet military vessels in Finnish harbors, by the end of 1945.
References: *Izv.*, Feb. 2, 1945.
  VT, 1945, No. 1–2, p. 23; *ibid.*, 1956, No. 12, p. 1.
  VPSS VP, 3, p. 96.
  DSB, 15, 1946, p. 393.

● 45/ii/8/US

Oral agreement between the USSR and the United States of America concerning use of air bases in Soviet territory

Negotiated Feb. 8, 1945, at Yalta.
Provides for use by United States planes of bases in the Maritime Province and in liberated areas in Southeastern Europe, and for a survey by United States experts of the effects of bombing in Eastern and Southeastern Europe.
References: *FRUS, CMY*, pp. 766–67.
  SIA, ABR, p. 543.

● 45/ii/9/Pl

Oral agreement concerning formation of a Yugoslav Government

Concluded Feb. 9, 1945, at Yalta, by the USSR, the United Kingdom, and the United States of America.
Provides for enforcement of the Tito-Šubašić agreement of Nov. 1, 1944, with recommended amendments. (For text of

the Tito-Šubašić agreement, see *FRUS, CMY*, pp. 251–53; see also 44/xi/25/ Yug.) The agreement on Yugoslavia was subsequently embodied in the Report (45/ ii/11/Pl/a) and the Protocol of the proceedings of the Crimea Conference (45/ii/ 11/Pl/b).
References: *FRUS, CMY*, pp. 845–46.
SIA, ABR, p. 560.

● 45/ii/11/Pl/a

Report of the Crimea Conference

Signed Feb. 11, 1945, at Yalta, by the Heads of Government of the USSR, the United Kingdom, and the United States of America.
Includes a statement on the results of the conference covering the following agreements:
(1) *The defeat of Germany*: Military measures have been "fully agreed and planned in detail"; meetings of the 3 military staffs to continue as necessary.
(2) *Occupation and control of Germany*: Germany to be divided into 3 occupation zones; a central Control Commission to be established in Berlin; France to be invited to take over a zone of occupation and join the Control Commission; limits of the French Zone to be fixed by the European Advisory Commission. German militarism and Nazism to be destroyed.
(3) *Reparation by Germany*: Germany to make compensation in kind to the United Nations in the war; a commission for the compensation of damage to be established in Moscow.
(4) *United Nations Conference*: A conference of the United Nations to be called in San Francisco on Apr. 25, 1945, to prepare the charter of a general international organization to maintain peace and security. China and the French Provisional Government to be invited to share in sponsoring invitations to the conference.
(5) *Declaration on liberated Europe*: Signatories agree jointly "to assist the people in any liberated state or former Axis satellite state in Europe where in their judgment conditions require (a) to establish conditions of internal peace; (b) to carry out emergency measures for the relief of distressed peoples; (c) to form interim governmental authorities broadly representative of all democratic elements in the population and pledged to the earliest possible establishment through free elections of governments responsible to the will of the people; and (d) to facilitate where necessary the holding of such elections."
(6) *Poland*: The Polish Provisional Government to be reorganized "on a broader democratic basis" and redesignated the Polish Provisional Government of National Unity. A commission composed of representatives of the 3 Powers to consult with members of the Provisional Government and with "other Polish democratic leaders" with a view to the reorganization. The Polish Provisional Government of National Unity to be "pledged to the holding of free and unfettered elections as soon as possible, on the basis of universal suffrage and universal ballot." Diplomatic relations to be established with the new Polish Government by the 3 Powers. The eastern frontier of Poland to follow the Curzon Line with minor digressions in favor of Poland; Poland to receive "substantial accessions of territory in the north and west," but "final delimitation of the western frontier of Poland" to await the peace conference.
(7) *Yugoslavia*: The agreement between Marshal Tito and Dr. Šubašić to be put into effect immediately and a new government formed on that basis (see 45/ii/9/ Pl). A temporary parliament to be formed in Yugoslavia, and legislative acts passed by the Anti-Fascist Assembly of National Liberation to be reviewed by a constituent assembly.
(8) *Meetings of Foreign Secretaries*: "Permanent machinery" to be set up for regular consultation; meetings to be held about every 3 or 4 months, in the 3 capitals in rotation, the first to be held in London.
(9) *Unity for peace as for war*: The signatories reaffirm their "common determination to maintain and strengthen in the peace to come that unity of purpose and of action which has made victory possible and certain for the United Nations in this war."
Note: A number of the provisions of the Report of the conference are repeated, either verbatim or in closely similar terms, in the Protocol of the proceedings of the conference (next document).
Sources: *Izv.*, Feb. 13, 1945.
SDD, 11, pp. 67–74.
VPSS VP, 3, pp. 100–109.

BFSP, 148, pp. 80–88, citing
Cmd. 7088.
FRUS, CMY, pp. 968–75.
DAFR, 7, pp. 348–55.
DSB, 12, 1945, pp. 213–16.

• 45/ii/11/Pl/b

Protocol of the proceedings of the Crimea Conference

Signed Feb. 11, 1945, at Yalta, by the Foreign Secretaries (Ministers) of the USSR, the United Kingdom, and the United States of America. Released to the press Mar. 24, 1947.
Covers the following topics: (1) *World organization*: Provides for convocation of a conference of the United Nations in the United States on Apr. 25, 1945. Defines nations to be invited to the conference; the United Kingdom and the United States to support the admission of the Belorussian and Ukrainian SSR's. Draft text of the invitation given, including provisions for voting in the Security Council (supplementing the proposals of Oct. 7, 1944 —see 44/x/7/Pl). The 5 nations with permanent seats on the Security Council to consult each other prior to the United Nations conference on the question of territorial trusteeship. (Partially repeats material given in Part IV of the Report of the conference.)
(2) *Declaration on liberated Europe*: Repeats verbatim Part V of the Report of the conference.
(3) *Dismemberment of Germany*: Art. 12 (a) of the Surrender Terms for Germany (see 44/vii/25/Pl) modified to give the 3 Powers "supreme authority with respect to Germany," with authority to take such steps, "including the complete disarmament, demilitarization, and the dismemberment of Germany as they deem requisite for future peace and security." Study of procedure for dismemberment referred to a 3-Power committee, with provision for addition of a French representative.
(4) *Zone of occupation in Germany for the French, and Control Council for Germany*: French zone of occupation to be formed out of the British and American zones. The French Provisional Government to be invited to become a member of the Allied Control Council for Germany. Summarizes material from Part II of the Report of the conference.

(5) *Reparation*: Repeats verbatim the protocol concerning reparations in kind from Germany, which was also issued separately (see 45/ii/11/Pl/c).
(6) *Major war criminals*: The subject to be investigated by the 3 Foreign Secretaries for report after the close of the conference.
(7) *Poland*: Repeats verbatim Part VI of the Report of the conference, but without the preamble in which the signatories reaffirm their "common desire to see established a strong, free, independent, and democratic Poland."
(8) *Yugoslavia*: Repeats, with minor changes, Part VII of the Report of the conference.
(9) *The boundaries between Italy and Yugoslavia and between Italy* [*sic*; possibly an error for Yugoslavia—see *FRUS, CMY*, note, p. 981] *and Austria*: Proposals made by the British delegation, to be considered by the American and Soviet delegations, for later expression of views.
(10) *Yugoslav-Bulgarian relations*: The 3 Foreign Secretaries to discuss a proposal for a Yugoslav-Bulgarian pact of alliance.
(11) *Southeastern Europe*: Notes have been submitted by the British delegation, for consideration by the American and Soviet delegations, concerning the Control Commission in Bulgaria, Greek claims on Bulgaria, and oil equipment in Romania.
(12) *Iran*: Views on the situation in Iran to be "pursued through the diplomatic channel."
(13) *Meetings of the 3 Foreign Secretaries*: Summarizes Part VIII of the Report of the conference.
(14) *The Montreux Convention and the Straits*: The next meeting of the 3 Foreign Secretaries to consider proposals by the USSR for revision of the Montreux Convention (see 36/vii/20/Pl); Turkey to be informed "at the appropriate moment."
Sources: *SDD*, 11, pp. 74–80.
FRUS, CMY, pp. 975–82.

• 45/ii/11/Pl/c

Protocol concerning reparations in kind from Germany

Signed Feb. 11, 1945, at Yalta, by the Heads of Government of the USSR, the United Kingdom, and the United States of America. Released to the press Mar. 24, 1947.

Provides for payment by Germany of reparations in kind consisting of (a) removals of German property, (b) annual deliveries of goods from current production, and (c) use of German labor. An Allied Reparation Commission to be established in Moscow representing the 3 Powers. With regard to the total sum and distribution of the reparation, the Soviet and United States delegations agree that the Reparations Commission "should take in its initial studies as a basis for discussion" the Soviet proposal that Germany should pay a total of $20 billion, one-half to go to the USSR. The British delegation dissociated itself from naming any figure on reparations.

Incorporated verbatim into the Protocol of the proceedings of the conference (preceding document).

By a protocol of Aug. 22, 1953, between the USSR and the German Democratic Republic, the USSR agreed to terminate reparations payments from the GDR as of Jan. 1, 1954 (see 53/viii/22/GDR/a). Sources: *SDD*, 11, pp. 80–81.
  FRUS, CMY, pp. 982–83.

● 45/ii/11/Pl/d

Secret agreement concerning entry of the USSR into the war against Japan

Signed Feb. 11, 1945, at Yalta, by the Heads of Government of the USSR, the United Kingdom, and the United States of America. Released to the press Feb. 11, 1946.

Provides for (1) maintenance of the *status quo* in Outer Mongolia (the Mongolian People's Republic); (2) Soviet acquisition of southern Sakhalin; (3) internationalization of Dairen and lease of Port Arthur as a naval base to the USSR; (4) establishment of a joint Soviet-Chinese company to operate the Chinese Eastern Railway and the South Manchurian Railway; (5) retention by China of sovereignty in Manchuria; and (6) cession of the Kurile Islands to the USSR. Assent of Generalissimo Chiang Kai-shek to be obtained to measures concerning Outer Mongolia and the ports and railroads. The USSR indicates its readiness to conclude a treaty of friendship and alliance with the National Government of China (carried out in Aug. 1945: see 45/viii/

China/a). For the Soviet declaration calling on Japan to surrender, see 45/viii/8/J. Sources: *Izv.*, Feb. 12, 1946; *Pr.*, Feb. 13, 1946.
  VT, 1946, No. 1–2, p. 10.
  VPSS VP, 3, pp. 111–12.
  VPSS, 1946, pp. 90–91.
  BFSP, 148, pp. 88–89, citing Cmd. 6735, 1946.
  EAS, No. 498, 1946.
  FRUS, CMY, p. 984.
  DAFR, 7, p. 356.
  DSB, 14, 1946, p. 282.
  Hudson, 9, pp. 282–83.
  Chen, pp. 194–95.

● 45/ii/11/UK/a

Agreement between the USSR and the United Kingdom concerning repatriation of liberated Soviet citizens in the United Kingdom, with two annexes

Signed Feb. 11, 1945, at Yalta.
Entered into force on signature. Annexes concern (1) jurisdiction over Soviet citizens and members of Soviet groups in the United Kingdom; (2) financial measures in regard to loans to liberated Soviet citizens. Supplemented by an exchange of notes of the same date (next document).
Source: *SDD*, 11, pp. 143–47.

● 45/ii/11/UK/b

Exchange of notes between the USSR and the United Kingdom concerning the status of liberated Soviet citizens in the United Kingdom

Sent Feb. 11, 1945, at Yalta.
Provides that liberated Soviet citizens in the United Kingdom should be subordinated to Soviet military law pending their repatriation. Supplements the agreement of the same date (preceding document). Source: *SDD*, 11, pp. 148–49.

● 45/ii/11/UK/c

Agreement between the USSR and the United Kingdom concerning treatment and repatriation of Soviet citizens liberated by forces operating under British command, and of British citizens liberated by forces operating under Soviet command

Signed Feb. 11, 1945, at Yalta. Signed by the United Kingdom on behalf of the

Governments of Canada, Australia, New Zealand, the Union of South Africa, and India.
Entered into force on signature. Supplemented by 2 exchanges of notes (next item). A similar agreement was signed on the same date with the United States (45/ii/11/US/a).
Sources: *SDD*, 11, pp. 149–54.
  BFSP, 147, pp. 1047–51, citing
    Daily Telegraph (London), Feb. 13, 1945.

● 45/ii/11/UK/d

Exchange of notes between the USSR and the United Kingdom modifying the agreement of the same date concerning treatment and repatriation of liberated Soviet and British citizens

Sent Feb. 11, 1945, at Yalta.
Comprises 2 exchanges of notes: (1) Provides that the Government of Australia is not bound by provisions of Art. 6 of the basic agreement (45/ii/11/UK/c), concerning conditions of work by liberated citizens pending their repatriation; (2) question of reimbursement of loans advanced to liberated citizens in Italy, Romania, and Bulgaria to be negotiated later.
Source: *SDD*, 11, pp. 152–54.

● 45/ii/11/US/a

Agreement between the USSR and the United States of America concerning treatment and repatriation of Soviet citizens liberated by forces operating under American command, and of American citizens liberated by forces operating under Soviet command

Signed Feb. 11, 1945, at Yalta.
Entered into force on signature. A similar agreement was signed on the same date with the United Kingdom (45/ii/11/UK/c). For termination on June 8, 1951, of the activities of the Soviet repatriation mission in the United States Zone of Austria, construed by the USSR as a violation of this agreement, see *DSB*, 24, 1951, pp. 1019–20.
Sources: *SDD*, 11, pp. 154–57.
  DSB, 14, 1946, pp. 444–45.
  EAS, No. 505, 1946, pp. 1–9.
  UNTS, 68, pp. 175–87 (E, R, F).
Reference: Deane, 1951, pp. 9–19.

● 45/ii/11/US/b

Exchange of notes between the USSR and the United States of America concerning voting procedure in the General Assembly of the United Nations

Sent Feb. 10 and 11, 1945, at Yalta.
In reply to a note from President Roosevelt, Marshal Stalin agreed to support, if desired, an increase in the number of votes for the United States from 1 to 3. President Roosevelt noted that agreement had been reached to support at the forthcoming UN conference the admission of the Belorussian and Ukrainian SSR's as members of the General Assembly.
Sources: *FRUS, CMY*, pp. 966–68.
  Correspondence, 2, pp. 191–92.

Feb. 27, 1945
See Appendix 5.

● 45/iii/8/DR

Exchange of notes between the USSR and the Dominican Republic concerning establishment of diplomatic and consular relations

Sent Mar. 7 and 8, 1945, in Mexico City.
References: *Izv.*, Mar. 13, 1945.
  VT, 1945, No. 3, p. 43.
  VPSS VP, 3, p. 132.
  SDD, 11, p. 35.

● 45/iii/9/Rom

Exchange of notes between the USSR and Romania concerning establishment of Romanian administration in Transylvania

Sent Mar. 8, 1945, from Bucharest and Mar. 9, 1945, from Moscow.
Sources: *Izv.*, Mar. 10, 1945.
  VT, 1945, No. 3, p. 42.
  VPSS VP, 3, pp. 132–34.

● 45/iii/13/Belgium

Agreement between the USSR and Belgium concerning repatriation of citizens displaced as a result of the war

Signed Mar. 13, 1945, in Brussels.
Entered into force on signature. Duration 3 months; if not denounced 1 month before expiration, renewed for further 3-month periods until denounced. For a

report on execution of the agreement, see *Pravda*, Jan. 16, 1946.
Sources: *SDD*, 11, pp. 141–43.
UNTS, 19, pp. 235–41 (E, F).

• 45/iii/14/Bul

Trade agreement between the USSR and Bulgaria, with five annexes

Signed Mar. 14, 1945, in Moscow.
Includes list of goods to be traded. Soviet metals, petroleum products, cotton, rubber, industrial and agricultural machinery, chemicals, paper, cellulose, hay, oats, medicines, in exchange for Bulgarian tobacco, agricultural products, vegetable oils, ores, and cotton goods.
Supplemented by a trade agreement of Dec. 15, 1945, and by a protocol of Apr. 1946 (see 46/iv/27/Bul/b).
References: *VT SSSR*, p. 11.
  Economic treaties, p. 1, citing
  DV, 1945, Nos. 127 and 240.
DSB, 15, 1946, p. 392.

• 45/iii/14/Fin

Exchange of notes between the USSR and Finland concerning entry into force of the border protocol of Dec. 16, 1944, describing the border in the region of Porkkala-Udd, with annexes

Sent Mar. 14, 1945, in Helsinki.
Source: **SS*, 1945, No. 1 (Finnish, R).

• 45/iii/14/Venezuela

Exchange of notes between the USSR and Venezuela concerning establishment of diplomatic and consular relations

Sent Mar. 14, 1945, in Washington, D.C.
On June 19, 1952, the USSR suspended diplomatic relations with Venezuela following a raid on the Soviet Embassy by the Venezuelan police (*NT*, 1952, No. 25, p. 32).
Sources: *Izv.*, Mar. 16, 1945.
VT, 1945, No. 3, p. 43.
VPSS VP, 3, pp. 141–42.
Reference: *SDD*, 11, p. 197.

• 45/iii/31/Cz. See Appendix 5.

• 45/iv/2/Brazil. See Appendix 5.

• 45/iv/11/Yug

Treaty of friendship, mutual assistance, and postwar collaboration between the USSR and Yugoslavia

Signed Apr. 11, 1945, in Moscow.
Ratified by Yugoslavia June 10, 1945; by the USSR June 15, 1945; acts of ratification exchanged Aug. 25, 1945, in Belgrade. Entered into force on signature. Duration 20 years; if not denounced 1 year before expiration, extended for successive 5-year periods.
Denounced by the USSR Sept. 28, 1949, on the grounds that evidence produced in the trial of László Rajk, earlier that month, had shown that Yugoslavia had been working against the USSR and had thereby ended the treaty *de facto*. In a reply of Oct. 1, 1949, Yugoslavia rejected the charge and accused the USSR of having broken the treaty (see *Yugoslav White Book*, pp. 140–45; *DIA, 1949–1950*, pp. 473–80).
Sources: *Pr., Izv.*, Apr. 12, 1945.
VVS, 1946, No. 3.
VT, 1945, No. 4–5, pp. 8–9.
VPSS VP, 3, pp. 175–78.
BFSP, 145, pp. 1177–78.
DSB, 12, 1945, pp. 774–75.
DSP, 1, 1948, p. 231.
Reference: *VVS*, 1945, No. 35 (ratification).

• 45/iv/13/Yug

Trade agreement between the USSR and Yugoslavia, with protocol

Signed Apr. 13, 1945, in Moscow.
Protocol concerns prices; mentioned in Art. 3 of the agreement of Nov. 30, 1945, concerning deliveries of petroleum products.
References: *Izv.*, Apr. 17, 1945.
VT, 1945, No. 4–5, p. 42.
VPSS VP, 3, p. 185.

• 45/iv/17/Pl

Protocol concerning provision of military and other supplies to the USSR, with annexes (Fourth Lend-Lease Protocol)

Signed Apr. 17, 1945, in Ottawa, by the USSR, the United Kingdom, the United States of America, and Canada.
Covers the period from July 1, 1944 (retroactively), through June 30, 1945. Continues the agreement begun with pro-

tocol of Oct. 1, 1941, and continued with those of Oct. 6, 1942, and Oct. 19, 1943. Lend-Lease operations were terminated by a presidential order of Aug. 21, 1945 (*SIA, ABR*, p. 674) ; a terminal agreement was signed between the United States and the USSR on Oct. 15, 1945.
Source: *DSES*, 22, pp. 89–156.
References: *Izv.*, Apr. 21, 1945.
  VT, 1945, No. 4–5, p. 42.
  VPSS VP, 3, pp. 189–90.
  Korolenko, p. 75.
  SIA, ABR, p. 515.

• 45/iv/18/Bolivia

Exchange of notes between the USSR and Bolivia concerning establishment of diplomatic and consular relations

Sent Apr. 18, 1945, in Washington, D.C.
References: *Izv.*, Apr. 20, 1945.
  VT, 1945, No. 4–5, p. 41.
  VPSS VP, 3, p. 661.
  SDD, 11, p. 35.

• 45/iv/19/Guatemala

Exchange of notes between the USSR and Guatemala concerning establishment of diplomatic relations

Sent Apr. 19, 1945, in Washington, D.C.
References: *Izv.*, Apr. 21, 1945.
  VT, 1945, No. 4–5, p. 41.
  VPSS VP, 3, pp. 194–95.
  SDD, 11, p. 35.

• 45/iv/21/Pol

Treaty of friendship, mutual assistance, and postwar collaboration between the USSR and the Polish People's Republic

Signed Apr. 21, 1945, in Moscow.
Ratified by the USSR May 11, 1945; by Poland Sept. 19, 1945; acts of ratification exchanged Sept. 20, 1945, in Warsaw. Entered into force on signature. Duration 20 years; if not denounced 1 year before expiration, extended for 5-year periods.
Sources: *Izv.*, Apr. 22, 1945.
  VT, 1945, No. 4–5, pp. 10–12.
  VPSS VP, 3, pp. 197–201.
  VVS, 1946, No. 3.
  SDD, 11, pp. 21–24.
  *DURP, 1945, No. 47, Arts. 268, 269.
  UNTS, 12, pp. 391–403 (R, P, E, F).
  BFSP, 145, pp. 1166–68.
  DSB, 14, 1946, pp. 340–41.

Note: At some time between the Yalta Conference (Feb. 4–11, 1945), and the Potsdam Conference (July 16–Aug. 2, 1945), the USSR turned over to the Polish People's Republic that part of its assigned zone of occupation in Germany lying east of the Oder and Neisse Rivers. Although no agreement covering the transfer has been published, or even reported, it is highly probable that one was concluded, and it is reasonable to suppose that it was signed at about the time of this first major treaty between the USSR and the new Polish Government. For approval of the transfer pending the peace settlement, see 45/viii/1/(9).

• 45/iv/29/Austria

Announcement of recognition by the USSR of the Provisional Government of Austria

Broadcast Apr. 29, 1945, by Radio Moscow.
For re-establishment of diplomatic relations between the USSR and Austria, see 45/x/24/Austria.
Reference: *SIA, ABR*, pp. 581–82.

• 45/iv/29/Pl

Instrument of surrender of German and Italian forces in Italy

Signed Apr. 29, 1945, in Caserta, by plenipotentiaries of the German Army in Italy and Lt. Gen. W. D. Morgan, chief of staff of Allied Force Headquarters.
Entered into force May 2, 1945.
Source: *DAFR*, 7, pp. 183–84.
Reference: *VPSS VP*, 3, p. 674.

• 45/v/1/Pl/a

Agreement modifying the agreement of November 14, 1944, concerning control machinery in Germany to provide for inclusion of the French Provisional Government in the Control Council

Signed May 1, 1945, in London, by representatives of the USSR, the United Kingdom, the United States of America, and the French Provisional Government in the European Advisory Commission.
Approved by the United States May 14, 1945; by the United Kingdom May 17, 1945; by the French Provisional Government May 18, 1945; and by the USSR May 25, 1945. Entered into force May

25, 1945, on approval by signatories. Denounced by the USSR in a note of Nov. 27, 1958 (*NYT*, Nov. 28, 1958).
Sources: *SDD*, 11, pp. 66–67.
  UST, 5, pp. 2072–77 (*TIAS* 3070).
  UNTS, 236, pp. 400–405 (R, E, F).

● 45/v/1/Pl/b

Protocol concerning inclusion of the French Provisional Government as a signatory to the Instrument of Unconditional Surrender by Germany

Signed May 1, 1945, by representatives of the USSR, the United Kingdom, the United States of America, and the French Provisional Government in the European Advisory Commission.
Modifies the agreement of July 25, 1944.
Reference: Mosely, 1950, p. 494.

● 45/v/6/Pl

Exchange of messages between the High Commands of the Red Army and the Western Allies concerning military operations in Czechoslovakia

Sent Apr. 25 and 30 and May 4, 5, and 6, 1945, between General Eisenhower's headquarters (SHAEF) and the United States Military Mission in Moscow for transmission to the Soviet High Command. In a message transmitted Apr. 25, 1945, replying to a request from SHAEF for information on Soviet plans, the Soviet High Command stated that it planned to conduct operations for the clearing of German forces from the east bank of the Elbe River north and south of Berlin and from the Vltava River valley. In his message of May 4, 1945, General Eisenhower stated that Allied forces planned to advance to the line Karlsbad-Pilsen-Budweis, and after capture of these points, would be ready to continue their advance into Czechoslovakia to the Elbe and Vltava to clear the west bank of these rivers. In its reply, transmitted May 5, 1945, the Soviet High Command stated that the reference to clearing operations in its message of Apr. 25 referred to both east and west banks of the Vltava (i.e., included the city of Prague), and requested that Allied forces in Czechoslovakia halt at the line Karlsbad-Pilsen-Budweis. The Soviet request was agreed to in General Eisenhower's telegram of May 6, 1945.
Source: *DSB*, 20, 1949, pp. 665–67.

● 45/v/7/Ger

Act of military surrender of the German High Command

Signed May 7, 1945, at Rheims, by a representative of the German High Command in the presence of Gen. Walter Bedell Smith for the Supreme Commander, Allied Expeditionary Force; Gen. Susloparov for the Soviet High Command; and Maj. Gen. F. Sevez, as witness, for the French Army.
Entered into force on signature. Preceded by surrender of German and Italian forces in Italy on Apr. 29, 1945 (45/iv/29/Pl), and of German armed forces in Holland, Northwest Germany, and Denmark on May 4, 1945 (not listed here, since the USSR was not directly associated with the surrender, which in any case was superseded by this general act of surrender). Confirmed by an act of surrender of the following day (45/v/8/Ger).
Sources: *DSB*, 13, 1945, p. 106.
  EAS, 502, 1946, pp. 1–2.
  DAFR, 7, pp. 185–86.
Reference: *VPSS VP*, 3, p. 683.

● 45/v/8/Fin

Trade agreement for 1945 between the USSR and Finland

Signed May 8, 1945, in Moscow.
USSR to supply 5,000 tons of wheat and 25,000 tons of rye, as well as fuel and lubricating oils, kerosene, salt, apatite, leather products, and tobacco, in exchange for Finnish paper, cellulose, and prefabricated houses. Total trade volume to be $17 million US.
References: Korolenko, p. 88.
  DSB, 15, 1946, p. 393.

● 45/v/8/Ger

Act of military surrender of the German High Command

Signed May 8, 1945, in Berlin, by representatives of the German High Command in the presence of Air Chief Marshal A. W. Tedder for the Supreme Commander, Allied Expeditionary Force; Marshal G. K. Zhukov on behalf of the Supreme Command of the Red Army; Gen. F. de Lattre de Tassigny for the French Army; and Gen. Carl Spaatz, Commander of United States Strategic Air Forces. Confirms and replaces the act of surrender of May 7, 1945 (45/v/7/Ger).

Entered into force on signature.
Sources: *Izv.*, May 9, 1945.
  VT, 1945, No. 4–5, p. 3.
  VPSS VP, 3, pp. 261–62.
  SDD, 11, pp. 82–83.
  EAS, No. 502, 1946, pp. 3–5.
  DSB, 13, 1945, pp. 106–107.
  DAFR, 7, pp. 186–87.
  Hudson, 9, pp. 312–14.

● 45/v/8/Rom/a

Agreement between the USSR and Romania concerning economic collaboration

Signed May 8, 1945, in Moscow.
Entered into force July 16, 1945, on exchange of acts of ratification in Bucharest. Duration 5 years; if not denounced 1 year before expiration, extended indefinitely, or until 1 year after denunciation.
Provides for establishment of Soviet-Romanian joint-stock companies for oil production (see 45/vii/17/Rom); river and maritime navigation (see 45/vii/19/Rom); air transport and civil aviation (see 45/viii/8/Rom); lumber (see 46/iii/20/Rom); and for joint development of the Romanian glass, mining, and metallurgical industries, as well as for establishment of a joint Soviet-Romanian bank in Bucharest (see 45/viii/15/Rom). See also entries under Mar. 9, 1949, and Aug. 20, 1949. Supplemented by a protocol (next document).
Agreements of 1954 provided for the transfer and sale to Romania of Soviet shares in 12 Soviet-Romanian joint-stock companies (see 54/iii/31/Rom/b and 54/ix/18/Rom). See also 55/xii/13/Rom and 56/x/22/Rom.
Sources: *BFSP*, 149, pp. 876–80.
  Roumania at the Peace Conference, pp. 134–36.
  Economic treaties, pp. 18–23.
Reference: *DSB*, 15, 1946, pp. 396–97.

● 45/v/8/Rom/b

Protocol between the USSR and Romania concerning the content and form of organization of the collaboration of Romania and the USSR in certain fields of the Romanian economy

Signed May 8, 1945, in Moscow.
Supplements the agreement of the same date concerning economic collaboration.

Sources: *BFSP*, 149, pp. 880–84.
  Roumania at the Peace Conference, pp. 137–40.

● 45/v/8/Rom/c

Trade agreement between the USSR and Romania, with two annexes

Signed May 8, 1945, in Moscow.
Source: *Economic treaties*, pp. 73–75 (omits the annexes), citing *MO*, 1945, No. 133.
References: *VT*, 1949, No. 11, p. 12; *ibid.*, 1950, No. 5, p. 7.
  DSB, 15, 1946, pp. 396, 397.

● 45/v/8/Rom/d

Protocol between the USSR and Romania concerning liquidation of the balance of the account of the State Bank of the USSR in the Romanian National Bank

Signed May 8, 1945, presumably in Moscow.
Terminates balance remaining under the agreement of Feb. 15, 1936, and transfers it to the account established by agreement of Feb. 26, 1941.
Source: *Economic treaties*, p. 72, citing *MO*, 1945, No. 133.

● 45/v/16/Denmark

Exchange of notes between the USSR and Denmark concerning re-establishment of diplomatic relations

Sent May 10 and 16, 1945, in Moscow.
In its note the Soviet Government stated that it considered the Danish request for re-establishment of diplomatic relations to be a condemnation of the act of the former Danish Government, under German pressure, breaking off diplomatic relations with the USSR on June 21, 1941.
References: *Izv.*, May 22, 1945.
  VT, 1945, No. 6, p. 38.
  VPSS VP, 3, pp. 688, 696.
  SDD, 11, p. 35.

● 45/v/23/Pl. See Appendix 5.

● 45/v/31/Pl

Informal agreement concerning establishment of a Control Council for Germany

Negotiated shortly before May 31, 1945,

by the USSR, the United Kingdom, the United States of America, and France.
Reference: *Izv.*, May 31, 1945.

● 45/vi/5/Pl/a

Declaration concerning the defeat of Germany and the assumption of supreme authority with respect to Germany

Signed June 5, 1945, in Berlin, by the USSR, the United Kingdom, the United States of America, and the French Provisional Government.
Entered into force on signature. Supplemented by agreements of July 25 and Sept. 20, 1945.
Sources: *Izv.*, June 6, 1945.
VT, 1945, No. 6, pp. 3–7.
VPSS VP, 3, pp. 273–81.
SDD, 11, pp. 84–90.
DSB, 12, 1945, pp. 1051–55.
TIAS, 1520, 1946.
Cmd. 6648, 1945.
UNTS, 68, pp. 189–211 (E, F, R).
Hudson, 9, pp. 314–19.
DAFR, 7, pp. 217–22.

● 45/vi/5/Pl/b

Statement concerning zones of occupation in Germany

Issued June 5, 1945, in Berlin, by the USSR, the United Kingdom, the United States of America, and the French Provisional Government.
Sources: *VT*, 1945, No. 6, p. 9.
VPSS VP, 3, p. 284.
DSB, 12, 1945, p. 1052.
BFSP, 145, p. 802.
DAFR, 7, pp. 222–23.
Reference: *Izv.*, June 6, 1945.

● 45/vi/5/Pl/c

Statement concerning consultation with the governments of other nations in connection with the exercise of supreme authority with respect to Germany

Issued June 5, 1945, in Berlin, by the USSR, the United Kingdom, the United States of America, and the French Provisional Government.
Sources: *Izv.*, June 6, 1945.
VT, 1945, No. 6, p. 9.
VPSS VP, 3, pp. 272–73.
DSB, 12, 1945, p. 1053.
BFSP, 145, p. 804.
DAFR, 7, p. 222.

● 45/vi/5/Pl/d

Statement concerning control machinery in Germany

Issued June 5, 1945, in Berlin, by the USSR, the United Kingdom, the United States of America, and the French Provisional Government.
Sources: *VT*, 1945, No. 6, pp. 8–9.
VPSS VP, 3, pp. 282–83.
DSB, 12, 1945, p. 1054.
BFSP, 145, pp. 803–804.
DAFR, 7, pp. 223–24.
Reference: *Izv.*, June 6, 1945.

● 45/vi/6/US

Negotiations between the USSR and the United States of America

From May 26 to June 6, 1945, negotiations were conducted in Moscow between Marshal Stalin and Harry Hopkins, representing the President of the United States. No formal agreements were reached, but the negotiations led to a number of understandings which underlay later written agreements. Subjects discussed included the following: (1) designation of a place and time for a meeting of the Heads of Government of the USSR, the United Kingdom, and the United States; (2) appointment of a Soviet representative (Marshal G. K. Zhukov) to the Allied Control Council for Germany; (3) disposal of the German fleet; (4) reorganization of the Provisional Polish Government, and recognition of it by the United States; (5) date of the Soviet planned attack in Manchuria; (6) plans for negotiations between Stalin and a representative of the National Government of China; (7) Soviet assurances of support to the National Government of China in its efforts for unification of the country; (8) postwar control of Manchuria by China; (9) establishment of a trusteeship for Korea including representatives of the USSR, the United States, the United Kingdom, and China; (10) voting procedure in the Security Council of the United Nations—Stalin accepted the American position that the Big Power right of veto applied only to questions involving enforcement action, not to the right of any member to bring before the Council any situation for discussion; and (11) American relief supplies for Poland through the Red Cross.

Source: Hopkins' notes of the negotiations, as given in Sherwood, pp. 891–911.
Reference: *SIA, ABR*, pp. 585–88.

● 45/vi/7/Pl

Statement concerning voting procedure in the Security Council

Issued June 7, 1945, by the USSR, the United Kingdom, the United States of America, and China.
Concerns the question of unanimity of permanent members in the decisions of the Security Council of the United Nations.
Sources: *DSB*, 12, 1945, p. 1047.
United Nations documents, pp. 267–71.

● 45/vi/12/Pl

Statement concerning an invitation to Polish leaders to come to Moscow for a conference on the formation of a Provisional Polish Government of National Unity

Issued June 12, 1945, in Washington, London, and Moscow. Signed by the Ambassadors of the United Kingdom and the United States to the USSR and the Soviet Commissar of Foreign Affairs.
Issued in accordance with a decision of the Yalta Conference (see 45/ii/11/Pl/a), as modified during the Stalin-Hopkins negotiations (45/vi/6/US).
Sources: *VPSS VP*, 3, p. 294.
DSB, 12, 1945, p. 1095.
DAFR, 7, pp. 902–903.

● 45/vi/15/H

Agreement between the USSR and the Provisional National Government of Hungary concerning payment of reparations by Hungary, with annexes

Signed June 15, 1945, in Budapest.
Provides for reparations deliveries to a total value of $200 million US, in six equal annual installments between Jan. 20, 1945, and Jan. 20, 1951. To include machinery, ships, grain, cattle, and other goods. Annexes provide a detailed list of articles to be delivered and a schedule for their delivery. Carries out provisions of Art. 12 of the armistice agreement of Jan. 20, 1945. Terms of payment extended to 8 years by agreement of Apr. 1946 (46/iv/18/H). Amount of payments reduced under an exchange of notes in June 1948 (48/vi/7/H).

References: *Izv.*, June 21, 1945.
VT, 1945, No. 6, p. 38.
VPSS VP, 3, p. 297.
DSB, 15, 1946, p. 394.

● 45/vi/16/Ecuador

Exchange of notes between the USSR and Ecuador concerning establishment of diplomatic and consular relations

Sent June 12 and 16, 1945, in Mexico City.
According to the Embassy of Ecuador, 1957, the agreement did not become effective.
References: *Izv.*, June 28, 1945.
VT, 1945, No. 6, p. 38.
VPSS VP, 3, pp. 298–99.
SDD, 11, p. 39.

● 45/vi/16/US

Exchange of telegrams between the USSR and the United States of America concerning entry of United States troops into Berlin and Vienna and withdrawal of United States forces in Germany to the zonal boundary

Sent June 14, 1945, from Washington, D.C., and June 16, 1945, from Moscow.
Withdrawal by the United States made conditional on conclusion of a military agreement providing access to Berlin. For the military agreement, see 45/vi/29/Pl. A similar exchange of telegrams took place between the USSR and the United Kingdom.
Reference: Mosely, 1950, p. 604.
Mentioned in a note of July 6, 1948, from the United States, the United Kingdom, and France to the USSR protesting the Soviet blockade of Berlin (text in *Germany, 1947–1949*, p. 205; *DAFR*, 10, pp. 84–85). See also the Soviet reply of July 14, 1948, *ibid.*, pp. 86–88.

● 45/vi/23/Mul. See Appendix 5.

● 45/vi/26/Mul/a

Charter of the United Nations

Signed June 26, 1945, in San Francisco.
Ratified by the USSR Aug. 20, 1945; by the Ukrainian SSR Aug. 22, 1945; and by the Belorussian SSR Aug. 30, 1945. Acts of ratification of the USSR and the Ukrainian and Belorussian SSR's deposited Oct. 24, 1945, with immediate effect.

Supplemented by the Statute of the International Court of Justice (next document).

Note: Hudson, 9, prints the following technical documents relating to administration of the United Nations: (1) Rules of procedure of the General Assembly, adopted Nov. 17, 1947; (2) Provisional rules of procedure of the Security Council, adopted Jan. 17, 1946; (3) Rules of procedure of the Economic and Social Council, adopted Mar. 18, 1949; (4) Rules of procedure of the Trusteeship Council, adopted Apr. 23, 1947; (5) Regulations concerning registration and publication of treaties, adopted Dec. 14, 1946; (6) Provisional financial regulations of the United Nations, adopted Nov. 20, 1947, revising earlier regulations of Feb. 13, 1946, and Dec. 11, 1946; (7) Staff rules of the United Nations, codified May 13, 1948; and (8) Convention on the privileges and immunities of the United Nations, signed Feb. 13, 1946. The last-named was ratified by the USSR and is listed under 53/ix/22/1946; the others are not listed separately.

Sources: *Izv.*, June 27, 1945.
VPSS VP, 3, pp. 397–435.
SDD, 12, pp. 14–47.
USTS, 993, 1946 (E, F, R, S, C).
BTS, 1946, No. 67, Cmd. 7015 (E, F, R, S, C).
Hudson, 9, pp. 327–36 (E, F).
DSB, 12, 1945, pp. 1119–42.

• 45/vi/26/Mul/b

Statute of the International Court of Justice

Annexed to the Charter of the United Nations, signed June 26, 1945, in San Francisco.
Ratified together with the Charter; entered into force Oct. 24, 1945. Supplemented by Rules of the International Court of Justice dated May 6, 1946 (Hudson, 9, pp. 529–58; not listed here).
Sources: *VPSS VP*, 3, pp. 435–55.
SDD, 12, pp. 47–63.
USTS, 993, 1946 (E, F, R, S, C).
BTS, 1946, No. 67, Cmd. 7015 (E, F, R, S, C).
DSB, 12, 1945, pp. 1134–42.
Hudson, 9, pp. 510–29 (E, F).

• 45/vi/26/Mul/c

Interim arrangements of the United Nations

Signed June 26, 1945, in San Francisco.
Sources: *EAS*, No. 461 (E, F, R, S, C).
DSB, 12, 1945, pp. 1142–43.
Hudson, 9, pp. 366–69 (E, F).
Reference: *SDD*, 11, p. 199.

• 45/vi/29/Cz

Treaty between the USSR and Czechoslovakia concerning the incorporation of Sub-Carpathian Ruthenia (Transcarpathian Ukraine) into the Ukrainian SSR, with protocol and map

Signed June 29, 1945, in Moscow.
Ratified by Czechoslovakia Nov. 22, 1945; by the USSR Nov. 27, 1945. Acts of ratification exchanged Jan. 30, 1946, in Prague.
Protocol provides for (1) establishment of a mixed demarcation commission to mark the new border; (2) choice of Soviet or Czech citizenship by inhabitants of the transferred area; and (3) establishment of a mixed liquidation commission to supervise juridical and financial aspects of the transfer, including transfer of governmental property from Czechoslovakia to the USSR. Work of the liquidation commission to be completed within 18 months from ratification.
Sources: *Pravda, Izv.*, June 30, 1945.
MKh, 1945, No. 8, pp. 67–70.
VPSS VP, 3, pp. 309–12.
SDD, 11, pp. 31–34.
BFSP, 145, pp. 1096–98.
References: *VVS*, 1945, No. 79 (Soviet ratification).
DSB, 15, 1946, p. 392 (summary).

• 45/vi/29/France

Agreement between the USSR and the French Provisional Government concerning treatment and repatriation of Soviet citizens under the control of French authorities and of French citizens under the control of Soviet authorities, with protocol

Signed June 29, 1945, in Moscow.
Entered into force on signature. Provisions closely similar to those of earlier agreements with the United Kingdom (45/ii/11/UK/c) and the United States (45/ii/11/US/a). Protocol provides that (1) citizens subject to repatriation include those guilty of crimes, including crimes committed on the territory of the other contracting party, and (2) the agreement extends to citizens of French protectorates and possessions.

On Dec. 9, 1947, the Soviet Government sent a note to the French Government charging violation of the agreement by France and announcing termination of activities of the Soviet and French repatriation missions (*Izv.*, Dec. 10, 1947).
Source: *SDD*, 11, pp. 158–61.
Reference: *Izv.*, June 30, 1945.

● 45/vi/29/Pl

Oral agreement on the entry of American and British troops into Berlin

Negotiated June 29, 1945, in Berlin by military representatives of the USSR, the United Kingdom, and the United States of America.
Covers (1) size of garrison of each of the forces to occupy Berlin, (2) period for entry, (3) movement of liaison representatives and reconnaissance parties, (4) transfer of wounded Germans and displaced persons, (5) assignment of ground and air routes of access to Berlin from Western Germany, and (6) freedom of all traffic to Berlin from border search or control by customs or military authorities. For a Soviet interpretation of the agreement, in a letter of June 9, 1952, see *DSB*, 27, 1952, p. 314.
Reference: Clay, pp. 24–26.

● 45/vii/4/Pl

Agreement concerning control machinery in Austria

Signed July 4, 1945, in London by representatives of the USSR, the United Kingdom, the United States of America, and the French Provisional Government in the European Advisory Commission. First published in summary form Aug. 8, 1945. Establishes a Four-Power Allied Commission for Austria. Superseded by agreement of June 28, 1946.
Sources: Hudson, 9, pp. 558–63 (E, F), citing
   BTS, 1946, No. 49, Cmd. 6958.
References (summary of Aug. 8, 1945):
   DSB, 13, 1945, p. 221.
   VPSS VP, 3, pp. 370–72.

● 45/vii/6/Pol

Agreement between the USSR and the Provisional Government of National Unity of Poland concerning the right to relinquish Soviet citizenship on the part of persons of Polish and Jewish nationality [*sic*] living in the USSR and their removal into Poland, and the right to relinquish Polish citizenship on the part of persons of Russian, Ukrainian, Belorussian, Ruthenian, and Lithuanian nationality living in Polish territory and their removal into the USSR, with protocol

Signed July 6, 1945, in Moscow.
Provides for establishment of a mixed Soviet-Polish commission to coordinate the agreement. Transfers to be completed by Dec. 31, 1945. Protocol concerns technical details of the transfer. Does not affect provisions of the agreements of Sept. 9 and 22, 1944.
References: *Izv.*, July 7, 1945.
   DSB, 15, 1946, p. 395.

● 45/vii/7/Pl

Agreement concerning establishment of a Four-Power governing body (Kommandatura) in Berlin

Negotiated July 7, 1945, in Berlin, by military representatives of the USSR, the United Kingdom, and the United States of America. Entered into force on signature. The Four-Power Kommandatura established under this agreement functioned until its meeting of June 16, 1948, when it was broken up by Soviet withdrawal.
Source: *DGO*, p. 39.
Reference: Clay, pp. 31, 363.

● 45/vii/7/Pol/a

Treaty of commerce and navigation between the USSR and the Polish People's Republic, with annex concerning the Soviet Trade Mission in Poland

Signed July 7, 1945, in Moscow.
Ratified by Poland July 23, 1945; by the USSR Aug. 7, 1945. Entered into force Dec. 29, 1945, on exchange of acts of ratification in Warsaw. Duration indefinite; may be denounced 3 months before expiration of any yearly period, with effect at the end of that year. Listed in Korolenko, p. 104, as still in force as of Nov. 25, 1953.
Sources: *VT*, 1945, No. 7–8, pp. 15–19.
   SDD, 12, pp. 97–103.
   Korolenko, pp. 261–65.
References: *VVS*, 1945, No. 48 (ratification).
   DSB, 15, 1946, pp. 395–96.

- 45/vii/7/Pol/b

Trade protocol between the USSR and the Polish People's Republic

Signed July 7, 1945, in Moscow.
Regulates trade during the second half of 1945. Total value of trade $120 million U.S.
References: *Izv.*, July 10, 1945.
　VT, 1945, No. 7–8, pp. 14–15.
　DSB, 15, 1946, p. 396.

- 45/vii/9/Pl

Agreement concerning zones of occupation in Austria and administration of the city of Vienna, with two maps

Signed July 9, 1945, in London, by representatives of the USSR, the United Kingdom, the United States of America, and the French Provisional Government in the European Advisory Commission. First published in summary form Aug. 8, 1945. Approved by the United Kingdom July 12, 1945; by France July 16, 1945; by the USSR July 21, 1945; and by the United States July 24, 1945. Entered into force July 24, 1945, on approval by signatories. Supplemented by a protocol of July 26, 1945 (45/vii/26/Pl/b). Terminated on completion of the withdrawal from Austria of the forces of the Allied and Associated Powers in accordance with Art. 20 of the State Treaty for Austria of May 15, 1955.
Sources: *TIAS*, No. 1600, 1947.
　BFSP, 145, pp. 850–52, citing
　　BTS, 1946, No. 49, Cmd. 6958.
　UNTS, 160, pp. 359–68 (E, F).
　Hudson, 9, pp. 564–67 (E, F).
References: *VPSS VP*, 3, p. 372.
　DSB, 13, pp. 221–22.

- 45/vii/11/Pol

Agreement between the USSR and the Polish People's Republic concerning changes in the administration of Polish railroads

Signed July 11, 1945, in Moscow.
Provides for transfer of the Polish railroads from the Soviet authorities which administered them during the war to the Polish Ministry of Communications, beginning Aug. 1, 1945.
References: *Izv.*, July 18, 1945.
　VPSS VP, 3, pp. 329–30.
　DSB, 15, 1946, p. 396.

July 11, 1945. Agreement concerning evacuation of Soviet forces from Chinese territory after the capitulation of Japan
See 45/viii/14/China/g.

- 45/vii/14/China. See Appendix 5.

- 45/vii/17/Rom

Agreement between the USSR and Romania concerning establishment of a joint-stock Soviet-Romanian company for exploration, extraction, refining, and marketing of oil and oil products, "Sovrompetrol," with three annexes

Signed July 17, 1945, in Bucharest.
Ratified by the USSR and Romania Aug. 17, 1945. Entered into force on signature. Annexes give lists of companies, the shares and assets of which are to be contributed by each party, and of state oil lands to be leased to the company. Carries out a provision of the agreement of May 8, 1945, concerning economic collaboration (45/v/8/Rom/a). Statutes of the company and enacting legislation passed Oct. 24, 1945 (*MO*, 1945, No. 243, cited in *Economic treaties*, p. 16). Soviet shares to be sold to Romania by agreement of Dec. 13, 1955 (55/xii/13/Rom).
Sources: *Roumania at the Peace Conference*, pp. 140–45.
　Economic treaties, pp. 24–30.
References: *VVS*, 1945, No. 64.
　DSB, 15, 1946, p. 397.
　Economic treaties, pp. 15–16, citing
　　MO, 1945, No. 186.

- 45/vii/19/Rom

Agreement between the USSR and Romania concerning establishment of a joint-stock Soviet-Romanian navigation company, "Sovromtransport," with protocol and annex

Signed July 19, 1945, in Bucharest.
Ratified by the USSR and Romania Aug. 19, 1945. Statutes and enacting legislation passed Aug. 19, 1945 (*MO*, 1945, No. 188, cited in *Economic treaties*, p. 16). Soviet shares to be sold to Romania under a 1954 agreement (see 54/iii/31/Rom/b).
References: *VVS*, 1945, No. 64 (ratification).
　MO, 1945, No. 188, cited in *Economic treaties*, p. 16.
　DSB, 15, 1946, p. 397.

● 45/vii/25/Pl

Agreement concerning certain additional requirements to be imposed on Germany

Signed July 25, 1945, in London, by representatives of the USSR, the United Kingdom, the United States of America, and the French Provisional Government in the European Advisory Commission. The same agreement was signed Sept. 20, 1945, in Berlin, by the Commanders-in-Chief of the occupation forces in Germany of the USSR, the United Kingdom, the United States of America, and France.

Confirmed by the USSR Sept. 4, 1945. Supplements the declaration of June 5, 1945, concerning the defeat of Germany (45/vi/5/Pl/a).

Sources: *SDD*, 11, pp. 91–104.
  DSB, 13, 1945, pp. 515–21.
  Hudson, 9, pp. 319–27.

July 21 and 25, 1945. Military agreements reached at the Potsdam Conference

See 45/viii/1/(19).

● 45/vii/26/Pl/a

Agreement concerning changes in the occupation zones in Germany and the administration of Greater Berlin, with map

Signed July 26, 1945, in London, by representatives of the USSR, the United Kingdom, the United States of America, and the French Provisional Government in the European Advisory Commission.

Approved by the United States July 29, 1945; by the United Kingdom Aug. 2, 1945; by the French Provisional Government Aug. 7, 1945; and by the USSR Aug. 13, 1945. Approved by the Allied Control Council for Germany July 30, 1945. Entered into force Aug. 13, 1945, on approval by signatories. Modifies the protocol of Sept. 12, 1944 (44/ix/12/Pl/a) and the agreement of Nov. 14, 1944 (44/xi/14/Pl/a), to provide for inclusion of France among the occupying Powers.

Sources: *SDD*, 11, pp. 59–62.
  UST, 5, pp. 2093–2109 (*TIAS*, 3071).
  UNTS, 227, pp. 297–309 (R, E, F).

● 45/vii/26/Pl/b

Protocol concerning military conditions for the occupation of Vienna

Signed July 26, 1945, in Vienna, by military representatives of the USSR, the United Kingdom, the United States of America, and the French Provisional Government.

Implements the agreement of July 9, 1945, concerning occupation zones and the administration of Vienna.

Reference: *SIA, FPC GA*, p. 308.

July 26, 1945. Potsdam Declaration concerning terms of surrender by Japan

See 45/viii/8/J.

● 45/viii/1/Pl/a

Communiqué concerning the Three-Power Conference at Berlin (Potsdam communiqué)

Signed Aug. 1, 1945, at the end of a conference between the USSR, the United Kingdom, and the United States of America, held in Potsdam from July 17, to Aug. 2, 1945; published Aug. 2, 1945. For contents, see note following next document.

Sources: *Izv.*, Aug. 3, 1945.
  SDD, 11, pp. 107–22.
  VPSS VP, 3, pp. 336–57.
  DSB, 13, 1945, pp. 153–61.

● 45/viii/1/Pl/b

Protocol of the Three-Power Conference at Berlin, with two annexes (Potsdam protocol)

Prepared Aug. 1, 1945, during a conference held in Potsdam from July 17 to Aug. 2, 1945; published Mar. 24, 1947. For contents, see note below.

Sources: *SDD*, 11, pp. 122–36.
  DAFR, 8, pp. 925–38, citing
  NYT, Mar. 25, 1947.

Note: Some of the agreements reached at the Potsdam Conference were incorporated either wholly or in part into both the Protocol and the Communiqué (preceding document); others were summarized or referred to in only one of these documents; still others were not referred to in either. Both Communiqué and Protocol mention a number of issues on which no agreement was reached.

No official text of the proceedings of the Conference has been published so far by any of the participating Governments, and the record of agreements reached must therefore be pieced together from the two official documents and from memoirs published subsequently by participants. Particularly valuable for this purpose are the following books: Byrnes, James F., *Speaking frankly* (1947); Deane, John R., *The strange alliance* (1947); and Leahy, William D., *I was there* (1950). A useful summary of the Conference is provided in *SIA, ABR*, pp. 606–29 (1950). Combining information from these sources, it appears that the following agreements were reached at the Potsdam Conference:

• 45/viii/1/(1)

Agreement on establishment of a Council of Foreign Ministers

Negotiated at the Potsdam Conference, July 18 and 20, 1945.
Provides for establishment of a Council of Foreign Ministers of the USSR, the United Kingdom, the United States of America, France, and China. First meeting to be held in London not later than Sept. 1, 1945. First task to be drafting of peace treaties with Italy, Romania, Hungary, Bulgaria, and Finland, and preparation of proposals for settlement of outstanding territorial questions. Subsequently a peace settlement for Germany to be prepared. For first session of the Council, see 45/x/2/Pl.
Sources: Incorporated into both the Communiqué (Part II) and the Protocol (Part I), but with significant differences: (1) the Protocol gives the full text of the draft invitation to be sent to France and China; (2) following the text of the agreement as given in the Communiqué it is stated that in connection with the establishment of the Council of Foreign Ministers the Conference decided to recommend the dissolution of the European Advisory Commission (for establishment of this body see 43/x/30/Pl/a) and the transfer of its responsibilities for coordination of Allied policy for the control of Germany and Austria to the Allied Control Council in Berlin and the Allied Commission in Vienna.
Given as a separate agreement in Hudson, 9, pp. 577–79, citing Cmd. 7087, 1947.

• 45/viii/1/(2)

Agreement concerning the political and economic principles to govern the treatment of Germany in the initial control period

Negotiated at the Potsdam Conference, July 19 and 30, 1945.
Provides political and economic principles to guide the Allied Control Council in the occupation of Germany. The German population throughout Germany to be treated uniformly, "so far as is practicable." Germany to be treated as a single economic unit. "For the time being," no central German Government to be established.
Sources: Identical texts given in the Communiqué (Part III) and the Protocol (Part II). Given as a separate agreement in Hudson, 9, pp. 580–83, citing Cmd. 7087, 1947, p. 4.

• 45/viii/1/(3)

Agreement concerning reparations from Germany

Negotiated at the Potsdam Conference, July 30 and Aug. 1, 1945.
Provisions: (1) Soviet reparations claims from Germany to be met from the Soviet occupation zone of Germany and from appropriate German external assets. (2) Poland's reparations claims to be met by the USSR from its own share. (3) Reparations claims of the United States, the United Kingdom, and other countries entitled to reparations to be met from the Western occupation zones of Germany and from appropriate German external assets. (4) The USSR to receive a total of 25 per cent of such industrial capital equipment from the Western zones of Germany as is unnecessary for the German peace economy. Of this, 15 per cent to be primarily from the metallurgical, chemical, and machine construction industries, and to be exchanged for an equivalent value of foodstuffs and industrial products; 10 per cent to be transferred without payment of any kind in return. (5) The USSR renounces all claims for reparations from other German enterprises located in the Western zones of Germany and to German foreign assets in all countries except Bulgaria, Finland, Hungary, Romania, and Eastern Austria. (6) The United States and the United Kingdom renounce all claims for reparations from German assets in Bulgaria, Finland, Hungary, Romania, and Eastern Austria. (7) The USSR

makes no claim to gold captured by Allied troops in Germany.

For a treaty between the USSR and Poland concerning reparations, see 45/viii/16/Pol/a.

Sources: Identical texts given in the Communiqué (Part IV) and the Protocol (Part III). Given as a separate agreement in Hudson, 9, pp. 583–85, citing Cmd. 7087, 1947, p. 7.

● 45/viii/1/(4)

Agreement concerning principles to govern distribution of the German Navy and merchant marine

Negotiated at the Potsdam Conference, July 29 and Aug. 1, 1945.

Provides for distribution of the German Navy and merchant marine between the USSR, the United Kingdom, and the United States, and for establishment of 2 tripartite commissions to handle technical details of the distribution. For a joint communiqué concerning execution of the agreement, see 46/i/22/Pl.

Source: Full text given in the Protocol (Part IV); summary only given in the Communiqué (Part V).

● 45/viii/1/(5)

Agreement concerning transfer to the USSR of the City of Koenigsberg and the adjacent area

Negotiated at the Potsdam Conference, on or about Aug. 1, 1945.

The Prime Minister of the United Kingdom and the President of the United States agree to support at the "forthcoming peace settlement" the Soviet proposal for the "ultimate transfer" of Koenigsberg to the Soviet Union, which was agreed to "in principle" at the conference.

References: Summarized in identical terms in the Communiqué (Part VI) and the Protocol (Part V).

● 45/viii/1/(6)

Agreement to examine a proposal by the USSR concerning extension of the authority of the Austrian Provisional Government to all of Austria

Negotiated at the Potsdam Conference,

on or about Aug. 1, 1945. For Soviet recognition of the Provisional Government of Austria, see 45/iv/29/Austria.

References: Summarized in the Communiqué (Part VIII) and the Protocol (Part VII) in identical terms except that the Protocol includes an agreement concerning reparations (next item).

● 45/viii/1/(7)

Agreement not to exact reparations from Austria

Negotiated at the Potsdam Conference, Aug. 1, 1945.

Reference: Summarized in Part VII of the Protocol.

● 45/viii/1/(8)

Statement concerning the Polish Provisional Government of National Unity

Drawn up at the Potsdam Conference, on or about July 21, 1945.

Records decision of the United Kingdom and the United States of America to recognize the Polish Provisional Government of National Unity and to withdraw recognition from the Polish Government-in-Exile in London.

Sources: Identical texts given in the Communiqué (section A of Part IX) and the Protocol (section A of Part VIII).

● 45/viii/1/(9)

Agreement concerning the western border of Poland

Negotiated at the Potsdam Conference, July 30 and 31, 1945.

Provides that pending final determination of Poland's western border in the peace settlement with Germany, Poland shall administer the "former German territories" east of the Oder-Neisse line, including the City of Danzig. For transfer by the USSR of administrative responsibilities in these areas to Poland, see the note following 45/iv/21/Pol. On July 6, 1950, an agreement was signed between Poland and the German Democratic Republic making the Oder-Neisse line the official boundary between the two States.

Sources: Identical texts given in the Communiqué (section B of Part IX) and the Protocol (section B of Part VIII).

• 45/viii/1/(10)

Statement concerning common policy for establishing the conditions of lasting peace in Europe

Drawn up at the Potsdam Conference, on or about July 31, 1945.
Concerns peace treaties with and recognition of Italy, Finland, Bulgaria, Hungary, and Romania; freedom of access by the press to Romania, Bulgaria, Hungary, and Finland; and admission of additional states to the United Nations (but not including the Spanish Government).
Sources: Identical texts given in the Communiqué (Part X) and the Protocol (Part IX).

• 45/viii/1/(11)

Agreement concerning revision of procedure of the Allied Control Commissions in Romania, Bulgaria, and Hungary, with annex

Negotiated at the Potsdam Conference, on or about July 31, 1945.
Provides for regular consultation between the Soviet and other members of the Commissions and for free movement of persons and mail in the three States. Annex is a letter dated July 12, 1945, from the Soviet Government to the representatives of the United States and the United Kingdom on the Allied Control Commission in Hungary specifying procedure for the Commission. The letter was accepted at the Conference as the basis for work of all three Allied Control Commissions.
References: Summarized in the Communiqué (Part XII) and the Protocol (Part XI). Soviet letter of July 12 included in the Protocol as Annex 1.

• 45/viii/1/(12)

Agreement concerning the removal of Germans from Poland, Czechoslovakia, and Hungary

Negotiated at the Potsdam Conference, on or about Aug. 1, 1945.
Sources: Identical texts given in the Communiqué (Part XIII) and the Protocol (Part XII).

• 45/viii/1/(13)

Agreement concerning establishment of
two bilateral commissions to investigate questions arising from the removal of oil equipment in Romania

Negotiated at the Potsdam Conference, probably on or about Aug. 1, 1945.
Provides for establishment of a Soviet-British and a Soviet-American commission of experts. The Soviet-American commission was terminated as of June 12, 1947, the United States delegation having been unable to secure Soviet recognition of the validity of their data on Soviet-seized oil property owned by United States firms in Romania.
Reference: Summarized in Part XIII of the Protocol.

• 45/viii/1/(14)

Agreement concerning withdrawal of troops from Teheran

Negotiated at the Potsdam Conference, on or about Aug. 1, 1945.
Provides for immediate withdrawal of Allied troops from Teheran and for consideration by the Council of Foreign Ministers at its meeting in Sept. 1945 of further stages in the withdrawal of troops from Iran.
Reference: Summarized in Part XIV of the Protocol.

• 45/viii/1/(15)

Agreement that the Zone of Tangier is to remain international

Negotiated at the Potsdam Conference, probably on or about Aug. 1, 1945.
For the Final Act of an international conference on the re-establishment of the international regime in Tangier, see 45/viii/31/Pl.
Reference: Summarized in Part XV of the Protocol.

• 45/viii/1/(16)

Agreement concerning revision of the Montreux Convention on the Black Sea Straits

Negotiated at the Potsdam Conference, probably on or about Aug. 1, 1945.
Provides for direct conversations between each of the three Governments represented at the Conference and Turkey. For the Montreux Convention, see 36/vii/20/Pl. A Soviet proposal at the Yalta Conference to revise the Montreux Con-

vention was approved by Roosevelt and Churchill (*SIA, ABR*, p. 561); see the Protocol of proceedings of the Crimea Conference (45/ii/11/Pl/b), Part XIV.
Reference: Summarized in Part XVI of the Protocol.

● 45/viii/1/(17)

Agreement concerning directives to military commanders on the Allied Control Council for Germany

Negotiated at the Potsdam Conference, probably on or about Aug. 1, 1945.
Directives to be sent covering all decisions of the Conference affecting matters within the scope of the commanders' duties.
Reference: Summarized in Part XIX of the Protocol.

● 45/viii/1/(18)

Agreement concerning the inclusion of a representative of France on the Allied Reparations Commission

Negotiated at the Potsdam Conference, July 31, 1945.
References: Leahy, p. 423.
SIA, ABR, p. 625.
Note: Not mentioned in either the Communiqué or the Protocol.

● 45/viii/1/(19)

Agreement concerning military collaboration in the Far East

Negotiated at the Potsdam Conference, July 21 and 25, 1945, by military representatives of the USSR and the United States of America.
Provides for (1) installation of weather stations at Khabarovsk and Petropavlovsk, with American personnel; (2) establishment of operational boundaries between American and Soviet air and naval operations in the Far East, evidently including demarcation of Korea along the 38th parallel; (3) exchange of liaison detachments; and (4) reciprocal use of air and naval bases for repairs and safe haven.
References: Deane, pp. 272–74.
Leahy, pp. 415–16, 418.
Correspondence, 2, p. 253.
SIA, ABR, p. 633.
Note: (1) The Communiqué contains a reference (Part XIV) to military talks at the Conference, which is repeated ver-

batim in the Protocol (Part XXI). Neither gives the substance of the agreements reached. (2) In addition to the texts or summaries of agreements reached at the Conference, the Communiqué and Protocol include references to the following issues on which no agreement was reached: (a) trial of war criminals (Communiqué, Part VII; Protocol, Part VI); (b) disposition of former Italian territories (Communiqué, Part XI; Protocol, Part X); (c) international inland waterways (Protocol, Part XVII); (d) convening of a European inland transport conference (Protocol, Part XVIII); and (e) use of Allied property for satellite reparations (Protocol, Part XX, with Annex 2).

● 45/viii/5/Fin

Communiqué by the Allied Control Commission for Finland concerning modification of the conditions of the armistice

Published Aug. 5, 1945, based on a decision taken in late July 1945.
Modifies the armistice agreement of Sept. 19, 1944. Permits Finland greater freedom in movement of ships and airplanes; use of telegraph, post and telephone communications freed for representatives of the United Nations and neutral governments. Compare the agreement of the Potsdam Conference concerning revision of procedure of the Allied Control Commissions in Romania, Bulgaria, and Hungary (45/viii/1/(11)).
Source: *VPSS VP*, 3, p. 358.

● 45/viii/6/Fin

Exchange of declarations between the USSR and Finland concerning re-establishment of diplomatic relations

Made on Aug. 6, 1945, in Helsinki.
References: *Izv.*, Aug. 7, 1945.
SDD, 11, p. 39.
VT, 1945, No. 7–8, p. 40.
VPSS VP, 3, pp. 358–59.

● 45/viii/6/Rom

Exchange of declaration between the USSR and Romania concerning re-establishment of diplomatic relations

Sent Aug. 6, 1945, in Bucharest.
References: *Izv.*, Aug. 7, 1945.
SDD, 11, p. 38.
VT, 1945, No. 7–8, p. 40.
DSB, 15, 1946, p. 398.

● 45/viii/8/J

Declaration by the USSR to Japan calling for Japanese surrender

Sent Aug. 8, 1945.
States that the USSR will consider itself at war with Japan from Aug. 9, 1945. Background: On July 26, 1945, at the Potsdam Conference, President Truman for the United States and Prime Minister Churchill for the United Kingdom, with the assent of Generalissimo Chiang Kaishek for China, issued a declaration (known as the Potsdam Declaration) calling on Japan to surrender. Stalin, who was present at the conference, was informed of the contents of the declaration, but the USSR was not asked to sign it on the grounds that it was not yet at war with Japan. Nevertheless in issuing its own declaration to Japan on Aug. 8, the USSR announced its "adherence" to the declaration of July 26. It is noteworthy that in the official Soviet treaty series (*SDD*, 11), the declaration of July 26 is given as a regular entry, while that of Aug. 8 is included as a footnote.
Carries out a pledge made by the USSR at the Yalta Conference (see 45/ii/11/Pl/d). For the Japanese response to the two declarations, see 45/viii/11/J and 45/viii/14/J. For the Japanese surrender, see 45/ix/2/J.
Sources: (1) Declaration of July 26, 1945:
   SDD, 11, pp. 104–106 (includes both the Declaration of Aug. 8, 1945, and the earlier Declaration by the United States, China, and the United Kingdom, issued at the Cairo Conference on Dec. 1, 1943).
   DSB, 13, 1945, pp. 137–38.
   DAFR, 8, pp. 105–106.
   (2) Declaration of Aug. 8, 1945:
   Pravda, Aug. 9, 1945.
   SDD, 11, p. 104.

● 45/viii/8/Pl/a

Agreement concerning prosecution and punishment of the major war criminals of the European Axis

Signed Aug. 8, 1945, in London, by the USSR, the United Kingdom, the United States of America, and the French Provisional Government. Subsequently adhered to by a number of other States.
Drafted at a conference held in London from June 26 to Aug. 8, 1945. Based on the Declaration concerning German atrocities issued at Moscow on Oct. 30, 1943 (43/x/30/Pl/e). Entered into force on signature; for States which adhered subsequently, on notification of adherence to the Government of the United Kingdom. Duration 1 year; thereafter indefinitely, or until 1 month following notice by any signatory of intention to terminate. Supplemented by the annexed Charter of the International Military Tribunal (next document).
Sources: *SDD*, 11, pp. 163–65.
   DSB, 13, 1945, pp. 222–23.
   EAS, No. 472, 1946 (including the Charter; R, E, F).
   BFSP, 145, pp. 872–81, citing *BTS*, 1946, No. 27, Cmd. 6903.
   UNTS, 82, pp. 279–85, 302–304 (E, F, R).
   Hudson, 9, pp. 632–36 (E, F).
   DAFR, 8, pp. 341–44.

● 45/viii/8/Pl/b

Charter of the International Military Tribunal

Annexed to the Agreement concerning prosecution and punishment of the major war criminals of the European Axis, signed August 8, 1945, in London, by the USSR, the United Kingdom, the United States of America, and the French Provisional Government.
The Tribunal established under this Charter conducted a trial of accused persons and organizations at Nuremberg from Nov. 14, 1945, to Oct. 1, 1946. For an announcement concerning the first list of defendants, see 45/viii/29/Pl. Verbal changes were made in the Russian and French texts of the Charter by a protocol of Oct. 6, 1945, signed in London (*EAS*, No. 472, 1946, pp. 45–47; E, F, R; not listed here). Rules of procedure of the Tribunal were adopted at Nuremberg, Oct. 29, 1945 (Hudson, 9, pp. 647–53; not listed here).
Sources: *SDD*, 11, pp. 165–72.
   DSB, 13, 1945, pp. 223–26.
   UNTS, 82, pp. 284–301, 304–11 (E, F, R).
   Hudson, 9, pp. 637–47 (E, F).

● 45/viii/8/Rom

Agreement between the USSR and Ro-

mania concerning establishment of a Soviet-Romanian joint-stock civil aviation company, "T. A. R. S."

Signed Aug. 8, 1945, in Bucharest.
Ratified by the USSR Sept. 7, 1945; by Romania Feb. 14, 1946. Based on the protocol of May 8, 1945 (45/v/8/Rom/a). Statutes and enacting legislation passed Oct. 24, 1945 (*MO*, 1945, No. 245, cited in *Economic treaties*, p. 16). Supplementary protocol signed Feb. 18, 1948 (48/ii/18/Rom/b). Soviet shares to be sold to Romania under a 1954 agreement (see 54/iii/31/Rom/b).
References: *VVS*, 1945, No. 67.
VPSS, 1945, p. 14.
DSB, 15, 1945, p. 397.

● 45/viii/10/Pl

Organization plan of the Allied Control Council for Germany

Approved Aug. 10, 1945, in Berlin, by the Four-Power Allied Control Council, including representatives of the USSR, the United Kingdom, the United States of America, and the French Provisional Government.
The Control Council established under this plan functioned until its meeting of Mar. 20, 1948, when it was broken up by Soviet withdrawal.
Reference: Clay, pp. 35, 355–57.

● 45/viii/11/Fin

Supplementary trade agreement between the USSR and Finland

Signed Aug. 11, 1945, in Moscow.
Covers trade through June 1946. Soviet cereals, salt, coal, coke, fuel and lubricating oils, apatite, sugar, tobacco, fodder cakes, etc., in exchange for Finnish cellulose, paper, cardboard, and paper products.
Reference: *DSB*, 15, 1946, p. 393.

● 45/viii/11/J

Exchange of notes concerning surrender by Japan

Sent Aug. 10, 1945, by the Swiss Chargé d'Affaires ad interim in Washington, D.C., transmitting a message of the Japanese Government, and Aug. 11, 1945, by the Secretary of State of the United States of America, on behalf of the Governments of the United States, the United Kingdom, the USSR, and China. Concerns the form of government of Japan after surrender and the position of the Emperor. Japan announced its readiness to accept the terms set forth in the joint declaration of July 26, 1945 (see 45/viii/8/J). For the Allied reply, see 45/viii/14/J.
Sources: *VPSS VP*, 3, pp. 376–79.
Pravda, Aug. 11, 1945.
MKh, 1945, No. 10, supplement, p. 25.
DSB, 13, 1945, pp. 205–206.
DAFR, 8, pp. 106–108.
Axis in defeat, pp. 29–31.

● 45/viii/12/US

Exchange of communications between the USSR and the United States of America concerning conditions for surrender by Japan

Sent Aug. 11 (probably) and 12, 1945.
Provides for designation of General of the Army Douglas MacArthur as Supreme Commander for the Allied Powers to accept, coordinate, and carry into effect the general surrender of the Japanese armed forces. Japanese forces in the Soviet area of operations to surrender to Lt. Gen. Derevianko as representative of the Soviet Military High Command.
Source: *Correspondence*, 2, pp. 260–61.

● 45/viii/14/China/a

Treaty of friendship and alliance between the USSR and China

Signed Aug. 14, 1945, in Moscow.
Ratified by the USSR and China Aug. 24, 1945. Entered into force Aug. 24, 1945, on exchange of acts of ratification in Chungking. Duration 30 years; if not denounced 1 year before expiration, extended indefinitely, or until 1 year after denunciation. Supplemented by 2 exchanges of notes (next 2 items) and 5 agreements (following 5 items). Annulled by exchange of notes of Feb. 14, 1950, between the USSR and the Chinese People's Republic (see 50/ii/14/CPR/c). Declared null and void by the Government of the Republic of China Feb. 25, 1953. On Feb. 1, 1952, at its 6th regular session, the General Assembly of the United Nations adopted a resolution which stated *inter alia* "that the USSR obstructed the efforts of the National Government of China in re-establishing Chinese national

authority in the Three Eastern Provinces after the surrender of Japan and gave military and economic aid to the Chinese Communists against the National Government of China; that the USSR, in its relations with China since the surrender of Japan, has failed to carry out the Treaty of Friendship and Alliance . . . of 14 August 1945."

Sources: *Izv.*, Aug. 28, 1945; *Pr.*, Aug. 27, 1945.
   VVS, 1945, No. 59.
   VPSS VP, 3, pp. 458–61.
   MKh, 1945, No. 10, supplement, pp. 16–17.
   VT, 1945, No. 9, pp. 4–6.
   Chen, pp. 218–20.
   UNTS, 10, pp. 319–21 (R), 318–16 (C), 334–39 (E, F).
   DSB, 14, 1946, pp. 201, 204.
   Moore, pp. 265–67, citing
      NYT, Aug. 27, 1945 (from Moscow radio).

● 45/viii/14/China/b

Exchange of notes between the USSR and China concerning relations between the USSR and China

Sent Aug. 14, 1945, in Moscow.
Supplements and constitutes a part of the treaty of friendship and alliance of the same date. Provides that (1) the USSR will support China morally and with military and material assistance, to be rendered exclusively to the National Government as the Central Government of China; (2) the USSR reaffirms its respect for the complete sovereignty of China over the Three Eastern Provinces and its recognition of their territorial and administrative integrity; and (3) with regard to Sinkiang, the USSR confirms that it has no intention of interfering in the internal affairs of China.

Sources: *Izv.*, Aug. 28, 1945; *Pravda*, Aug. 27, 1945.
   VVS, 1945, No. 59.
   VPSS VP, 3, pp. 473–74.
   MKh, 1945, No. 10, supplement, p. 22.
   VT, 1945, No. 9, pp. 14–15.
   Chen, pp. 220–21.
   UNTS, 10, pp. 321–22 (R), 326–24 (C), 340–43 (E, F).
   DSB, 14, 1946, p. 204.
   Moore, p. 276, citing
      NYT, Aug. 27, 1945 (from Moscow radio).

● 45/viii/14/China/c

Exchange of notes between the USSR and China concerning Outer Mongolia

Sent Aug. 14, 1945, in Moscow.
Supplements the treaty of friendship and alliance of the same date. Entered into force Aug. 24, 1945, together with the treaty. Provides that China will recognize the independence of Outer Mongolia (the Mongolian People's Republic) if its desire for independence is indicated by a plebiscite after the defeat of Japan.

Sources: *Izv.*, Aug. 28, 1945; *Pravda*, Aug. 27, 1945.
   VVS, 1945, No. 59.
   VPSS VP, 3, pp. 475–76.
   MKh, 1945, No. 10, supplement.
   VT, 1945, No. 9, p. 15.
   Chen, p. 222.
   UNTS, 10, pp. 322–23 (R), 314–13 (C), 342–44 (E, F).
   DSB, 14, 1946, pp. 204–205.
   Moore, p. 277.

● 45/viii/14/China/d

Agreement between the USSR and China concerning the port of Dairen, with protocol

Signed Aug. 14, 1945, in Moscow.
Entered into force Aug. 24, 1945, on ratification by signatories. Duration 30 years. Protocol provides (1) for a 30-year lease by the USSR of half the harbor installations and equipment and (2) that sections of the Chinese Changchun Railway located within the boundaries of the Port Arthur naval base area and connecting Dairen with Mukden will not be subject to military supervision or control. Abrogated by the USSR Feb. 14, 1950; by China Feb. 25, 1953, together with the treaty of friendship and alliance.

Sources: *Izv.*, Aug. 28, 1945; *Pravda*, Aug. 27, 1945 (protocol not included).
   VVS, 1945, No. 59.
   VPSS VP, 3, pp. 469–71.
   MKh, 1945, No. 10, supplement, pp. 20–21 (omits the protocol).
   VT, 1945, No. 9, p. 12 (same).
   Chen, pp. 226–28.
   UNTS, 10, pp. 327–29 (R), 308–307 (C), 354–59 (E, F).
   DSB, 14, 1946, p. 205.
   Moore, pp. 273–74 (omits the protocol).

● 45/viii/14/China/e

Agreement between the USSR and China concerning Port Arthur, with annex and map

Signed Aug. 14, 1945, in Moscow.
Entered into force Aug. 24, 1945, on ratification by the signatories. Duration 30 years. Supplements the treaty of friendship and alliance of the same date. Provides for joint occupation of the Port Arthur naval base by China and the USSR, and for establishment of a Sino-Soviet Military Commission to deal with questions arising in consequence of the joint use of the base. Annex constitutes a detailed description of the naval base zone, and provides for demarcation of the border by a mixed Soviet-Chinese Commission. Abrogated by the USSR Feb. 14, 1950; by China Feb. 25, 1953, together with the treaty of friendship and alliance.
Sources: *Izv.*, Aug. 28, 1945; *Pravda*,
    Aug. 27, 1945.
VVS, 1945, No. 59.
VPSS VP, 3, pp. 467–69.
MKh, 1945, No. 10, supplement, pp.
    19–20.
VT, 1945, No. 9, pp. 9–11.
Chen, pp. 228–31.
UNTS, 10, pp. 329–31 (R), 306–304
    (C), 358–63 (E, F).
DSB, 14, 1946, pp. 205–206.
Moore, pp. 272–73 (omits the annex).

● 45/viii/14/China/f

Agreement between the USSR and China concerning relations between the Soviet commander-in-chief and the Chinese administration following the entry of Soviet forces into the territory of the Three Eastern Provinces in connection with the war against Japan, with annexed protocol

Signed Aug. 14, 1945, in Moscow.
Entered into force Aug. 24, 1945, on ratification of the treaty of friendship and alliance of the same date. Abrogated by the USSR Feb. 14, 1950; by China Feb. 25, 1953, together with the treaty of friendship and alliance. For the annexed protocol, see next item.
Sources: *Izv.*, Aug. 28, 1945; *Pravda*,
    Aug. 27, 1945.
VVS, 1945, No. 59.
VPSS VP, 3, pp. 471–73.
MKh, 1945, No. 10, supplement, pp.
    21–22.

VT, 1945, No. 9, pp. 13–14.
Chen, pp. 231–33.
UNTS, 10, pp. 331–33 (R), 303–302
    (C).
DSB, 14, 1946, pp. 206–207.
Moore, pp. 274–76.

● 45/viii/14/China/g

Protocol between the USSR and China concerning evacuation of Soviet forces from Chinese territory after the capitulation of Japan

Annexed to the agreement of Aug. 14, 1945, concerning relations between the Soviet commander-in-chief and the Chinese administration (preceding document).
Formally, an extract from the minutes of a meeting on July 11, 1945, between Marshal Stalin and Dr. T. V. Soong, President of the Executive Yuan of the Chinese Republic, at which Stalin, in answer to a question by Dr. Soong, stated that "three months would be a maximum period sufficient for the completion of the withdrawal of troops." Stalin, according to the minutes, declined to include any provision for the evacuation of Soviet troops within 3 months following the defeat of Japan in the agreement which was being negotiated; however, this extract was signed by the Chinese and Soviet diplomats who signed the agreement (Wang Shih-chieh and V. M. Molotov), and annexed to it. It appears to be omitted from all published Soviet texts of the agreement.
Sources: *DSB*, 14, 1946, p. 201.
    Chen, p. 233.
    UNTS, 10, p. 333 (R), 302 (C) 368–
        69 (E, F).

● 45/viii/14/China/h

Agreement between the USSR and China concerning the Chinese Changchun Railway

Signed Aug. 14, 1945, in Moscow.
Entered into force Aug. 24, 1945, on ratification by the signatories. Duration 30 years, after which the full ownership of the railway and its assets reverts to China. Abrogated by the USSR Feb. 14, 1950; by China Feb. 25, 1953, together with the treaty of friendship and alliance of the same date.
Sources: *Izv.*, Aug. 28, 1945; *Pravda*,
    Aug. 27, 1945.

VVS, 1945, No. 59.
VPSS VP, 3, pp. 458–61.
MKh, 1945, No. 10, supplement, pp. 17–19.
VT, 1945, No. 9, pp. 6–9.
Chen, pp. 223–26.
UNTS, 10, pp. 323–27 (R), 312–309 (C), 346–55 (E, F).
DSB, 14, 1946, pp. 207–208.
Moore, pp. 267–71.

● 45/viii/14/J

Exchange of communications concerning surrender by Japan

Sent Aug. 14, 1945. Comprises (1) a note from the Swiss Chargé d'Affaires ad interim in Washington, D.C., to the Secretary of State of the United States of America transmitting (2) a communication from the Japanese Government to the Governments of the United States, the United Kingdom, the USSR, and China signifying Japan's acceptance of the conditions of the Potsdam Declaration of July 26, 1945 (see 45/viii/8/J), and (3) a note from the Secretary of State to the Swiss Chargé d'Affaires ad interim enclosing for transmission to the Japanese Government a message from the United States Government concerning procedure for surrender.
For the Instrument of Surrender by Japan, see 45/ix/2/J.
Sources: *Pravda*, Aug. 15, 1945 (Japanese communication).
  MKh, 1945, No. 10, pp. 25–26.
  VPSS VP, 3, p. 380.
  DSB, 13, 1945, pp. 255–56.
  Axis in defeat, pp. 31–33.

● 45/viii/15/Rom

Agreement between the USSR and Romania concerning establishment of a joint-stock Soviet-Romanian bank, "Sovrombank," in Bucharest

Signed Aug. 15, 1945.
Carries out a provision of the agreement concerning economic collaboration of May 8, 1945 (45/v/8/Rom/a). Statutes of the bank enacted Oct. 26, 1945 (*MO*, 1945, No. 245, cited in *Economic treaties*, p. 16). Enacting legislation passed Dec. 7, 1945 (*MO*, 1945, No. 281, cited *ibid.*). Soviet shares to be sold to Romania under a 1954 agreement (see 54/iii/31/Rom/b).
Reference: *DSB*, 15, 1946, p. 396.

Aug. 15, 1945

General Order No. 1, issued by the Supreme Commander of the Allied Powers (SCAP), concerning surrender of Japanese forces
Provides *inter alia* for surrender of Japanese forces in Manchuria to the Soviet Army.
References: McLane, pp. 199–200; Feis, *The China Tangle*, pp. 358–59.

● 45/viii/16/Bul

Exchange of notes between the USSR and Bulgaria concerning re-establishment of diplomatic relations

Sent Aug. 14 and 16, 1945, in Sofia.
References: *Pravda, Izv.*, Aug. 15, 1945.
  MKh, 1945, No. 10, supplement, p. 30.
  VT, 1945, No. 7–8, p. 40.
  VPSS VP, 3, p. 381.
  SDD, 11, p. 35.

● 45/viii/16/Pol/a

Agreement between the USSR and the Provisional Government of National Unity of Poland concerning reparations for damages caused by the German occupation

Signed Aug. 16, 1945, in Moscow.
Not subject to ratification; entered into force on signature. The USSR to satisfy Poland's reparations claims out of its own share of German reparations deliveries, in accordance with an agreement reached at the Potsdam Conference (see 45/viii/1/(3)). In exchange, starting in 1946, Poland to deliver annually to the USSR, for the duration of the occupation of Germany, 8 million tons of coal during the first year of deliveries, 13 million tons annually in the next 4 years, and 12 million tons each subsequent year, at a special agreed price. Conditions for delivery by Poland modified by agreement of Mar. 5, 1947 (47/iii/5/Pol/d); deliveries terminated under protocol of Nov. 1953 (53/xi/ /Pol); Poland's remaining debt under the agreement cancelled in Nov. 1956 (see 56/xi/18/Pol).
Sources: *Pravda, Izv.*, Aug. 17, 1945.
  MKh, 1945, No. 10, supplement, pp. 11–12.
  VT, 1945, No. 9, pp. 18–20.
  VPSS VP, 3, pp. 388–91.
  Economic treaties, pp. 33–34, citing

Odbudowa Panstwa Polskiego, Aug.
16, 1945, p. 52.
DSB, 14, 1946, pp. 343–44.
BFSP, 145, pp. 1168–70.

● 45/viii/16/Pol/b

Treaty between the USSR and the Polish People's Republic concerning the Soviet-Polish state border, with map

Signed Aug. 16, 1945, in Moscow.
Ratified by Poland Dec. 31, 1945; by the USSR Jan. 13, 1946. Entered into force Feb. 5, 1946, on exchange of acts of ratification in Warsaw.
Provides for establishment of a mixed Soviet-Polish commission to carry out demarcation of the border. For establishment of the commission, see *Pravda,* Mar. 11, 1946. For documents signed on completion of the commission's work, see 47/iv/30/Pol. Modified by agreement of Feb. 15, 1951.
Sources: *Pravda, Izv.,* Aug. 17, 1945.
    MKh, 1945, No. 10, supplement, pp. 10–11.
    VT, 1945, No. 9, pp. 16–18, 20.
    SDD, 12, pp. 76–77.
    *DURP, 1947, No. 35, Arts. 167, 168.
    UNTS, 10, pp. 193–201 (R, P, E, F).
    DSB, 14, pp. 341–43.
    BFSP, 145, pp. 1170–72.

● 45/viii/20/Rom

Exchange of notes between the USSR and Romania concerning reorganization of diplomatic missions into embassies

Sent Aug. 20 and 24, 1945, in Bucharest.
References: *Izv.,* Aug. 28, 1945.
    SDD, 11, p. 40.

● 45/viii/21/H

Temporary agreement between the USSR and Hungary concerning organization of postal and telephone-telegraph communications

Signed Aug. 21, 1945.
Superseded by agreement of Sept 22, 1947 (47/ix/22/H/a); no longer valid after Oct. 15, 1947.
Mentioned in the final protocol to the agreement of Sept. 22, 1947.

Aug. 21, 1945. Proposal for establishment of a Far Eastern Advisory Commission

See 45/ix/29/Pl.

● 45/viii/27/H/a

Agreement between the USSR and Hungary concerning economic collaboration

Signed Aug. 27, 1945, in Moscow.
Ratified by the USSR Dec. 26, 1945; by Hungary Dec. 20, 1945. Duration 5 years. Provides for establishment of joint-stock Soviet-Hungarian companies for prospecting of bauxite and its manufacture into aluminum (see 46/iv/8/H/b); prospecting and refining oil (see 46/iv/8/H/a); coal production; development of power plants; development of the chemical industry; development of the manufacture of electrical and agricultural machinery; development of river, motor, and air transport (see 46/iii/29/H/a and /b); establishment of a bank to finance transportation development; and establishment of an agricultural research center and a mechanization center. For a secret protocol concerning conversion of the Soviet-Hungarian companies to Soviet monopolies, see 47/xii/9/H/b. For an agreement on the sale to Hungary of Soviet shares in some of the Soviet-Hungarian companies, see 54/xi/6/H.
References: *Izv.,* Aug. 29, 1945.
    VVS, 1946, No. 1.
    DSB, 15, 1946, pp. 394–95.

● 45/viii/27/H/b

Trade agreement between the USSR and Hungary

Signed Aug. 27, 1945, in Moscow.
Covers the period Sept. 1945–Dec. 31, 1946. Provides for exchange of goods to a total value of $30 million US. Soviet coke, iron ore, pig iron, etc., for Hungary; Hungary to manufacture Soviet raw fibres into yarn for the USSR. Supplemented by a final protocol July 15, 1947 (47/vii/5/H/c).
References: *Izv.,* Aug. 29, 1945.
    VT, 1945, No. 7–8, p. 41.
    VPSS VP, 3, pp. 476–77.
    DSB, 15, 1946, p. 394.

● 45/viii/27/US. See Appendix 5.

● 45/viii/29/Pl

Joint communiqué listing major war criminals to be tried by the International Military Tribunal

Issued Aug. 29, 1945, by the Committee of Chief Prosecutors for the investigation and prosecution of major war criminals, composed of representatives of the USSR, the United Kingdom, the United States of America, and the French Provisional Government.

Names 24 individuals included in the first list of defendants. For the agreement establishing the International Military Tribunal, see 45/viii/8/Pl/a.

At the Potsdam Conference Stalin had pressed for an agreement on including a list of war criminals in the final communiqué. This proposal was not accepted by the United States and the United Kingdom, although references to the subject were included in the communiqué and protocol of the Conference (see Note 2 to 45/viii/1/(19)).

Sources: *Pravda*, Aug. 30, 1945.
  MKh, 1945, No. 10, supplement, p. 14.
  DSB, 13, 1945, p. 301.

• 45/viii/30/Pl

Proclamation concerning establishment of the Control Council for Germany

Issued Aug. 30, 1945, in Berlin, by the Control Council for Germany, including representatives of the USSR, the United Kingdom, the United States of America, and the French Provisional Government.

Source: *DGO*, pp. 58–59, citing
  Control Council, *Official Gazette*, No. 1, p. 4.

• 45/viii/30/US

Exchange of communications between the USSR and the United States of America concerning conditions of surrender of Japanese armed forces

Sent Aug. 15, 16, 17, 22, 26, and 30, 1945, between Washington, D.C., and Moscow (dates in some cases approximate).

Following agreements reached: (1) General Order No. 1 covering details of the surrender of Japanese armed forces modified to include the Kurile Islands in the area to be surrendered to the commander-in-chief of Soviet Forces in the Far East. (2) The United States to be granted the right to land on Soviet airfields on one of the Kurile Islands in emergency cases during the period of occupation of Japan. Commercial air-

craft of the United States to be granted landing rights on a Soviet airfield on one of the Kuriles.

A Soviet request that the area to be surrendered to Soviet troops should include the northern half of the Island of Hokkaido was not accepted. Apparently no decision was taken on a Soviet request for the right of Soviet commercial planes to land on a United States airfield on one of the Aleutian Islands.

Source: *Correspondence*, 2, pp. 261–69.

• 45/viii/31/Mul

Protocol extending the agreement of May 6, 1937, concerning regulation of the production and marketing of sugar

Signed Aug. 31, 1945, in London.

Extends the 1937 agreement through Aug. 31, 1946. Further extended by protocol of Aug. 30, 1946, and subsequently.

Sources: *VT*, 1946, No. 3, pp. 35–36.
  BFSP, 145, pp. 886–88, citing
    BTS, 1946, No. 45, Cmd. 6949.
  USTS, 1945, No. 990.
  TIAS, 1946, No. 1523.

• 45/viii/31/Pl

Final Act of the conference concerning re-establishment of the international regime in Tangier

Signed Aug. 31, 1945, in Paris, by the USSR, the United Kingdom, the United States of America, and the French Provisional Government.

Background: The international regime in Tangier was established by a convention dated Dec. 18, 1923, amended by a protocol of July 25, 1928. The USSR was not a party to either of these documents, although Tsarist Russia had signed the Act of Algeciras of Apr. 7, 1906, which provided for the internationalization of Tangier. During World War II Spain occupied Tangier, dissolved most of the international administration, and, in January 1943, proclaimed the incorporation of Tangier into Spanish Morocco.

The question of restoring international controls in Tangier was taken up by representatives of the United States, the United Kingdom, and France at a conference in July 1945. At the Potsdam

Conference, later in the same month, Stalin advanced a claim for Soviet participation in the international administration, but in the absence of France at the conference, no agreement was reached. Shortly thereafter, however, the French Government convened a conference on the subject, with representatives of the 4 Powers listed above. The conference, which met from Aug. 10 to 31, 1945, prepared two documents: the Final Act, and an Anglo-French agreement on re-establishment of international controls. The Final Act, which the USSR signed, recommended *inter alia* that (1) a conference should be convened in Paris within 6 months after establishment of a provisional regime for the Tangier Zone based on the 1923 Statute, to consider amendments to conventions in force, and (2) that the USSR and the United States should be invited to participate in the provisional regime. In the accompanying Anglo-French agreement, provision was made for the inclusion of the USSR and the United States as members of the international administration. The Final Act also included a declaration by the Soviet delegation calling for replacement of the Franco regime in Spain by a democratic government as a condition to Spanish participation in the administration of the international zone.

On Oct. 11, 1945, the Spanish military occupation of Tangier came to an end and the provisional international regime was established; a representative of the United States was included, but the USSR did not avail itself of the invitation to participate, presumably because of its dislike for the Franco regime. The conference to consider amendments to the 1923 Statute, as called for in the Final Act of the conference of August 1945, was never held; instead, the provisional regime was continued, although modifications in the Anglo-French agreement of Aug. 31, 1945, on which it was based, were negotiated in Nov. 1952.

Sources (Final Act): *SDD*, 11, pp. 172–76.
  BFSP, 145, pp. 881–85, citing Cmd. 6678, 1945.
  DSB, 13, 1945, pp. 613–16.
References (background): *SIA, WN*, pp. 313–16.
  SIA, 1952, pp. 53–54.
  EB, 21, p. 785.

● 45/ix/2/J

Instrument of surrender by Japan

Signed Sept. 2, 1945, at Tokyo Bay, on behalf of the Japanese Emperor and the Japanese Government; accepted by General Douglas MacArthur, Supreme Commander for the Allied Powers, for the United States of America, China, the United Kingdom, and the USSR, and in the interests of the other United Nations at war with Japan (Australia, Canada, the French Provisional Government, the Netherlands, and New Zealand).
Constitutes full acceptance of the terms of the Potsdam Declaration of July 26, 1945 (see 45/viii/8/J).
Sources: *Izv.*, Sept. 4, 1945.
  SDD, 11, pp. 137–39.
  VPSS VP, 3, pp. 479–83.
  MKh, 1945, No. 10, supplement, pp. 26–27.
  UNTS, 139, pp. 387–93 (E, F).
  EAS, 493, 1946, pp. 1–3.
  DSB, 13, 1945, pp. 364–65.

● 45/ix/8/Cz

Preliminary trade agreement between the USSR and Czechoslovakia

Signed Sept. 8, 1945, in Moscow.
Covers the remaining period of 1945, but possibly extended until conclusion of the trade agreement of Apr. 12, 1946. Soviet iron ore, manganese, chrome ore, cotton, rice, fats and other foodstuffs, flax, wool, coal, petroleum and other oil products, pyrites and rock salt, in exchange for Czech machine tools, electrotechnical products, rolling mills, harvesting and other light machinery, locomotives, and electric motors.
Reference: *DSB*, 15, 1946, p. 393.

● 45/ix/10/Switz

Final procès-verbal of the commission to examine the living conditions of Soviet citizens who had escaped from German captivity and taken refuge in Switzerland

Signed Sept. 10, 1945, in Berne, by the chiefs of the Soviet and Swiss delegations on the commission.
References: Swiss Consulate, San Francisco, 1957.
  Izv., Oct. 2, 1945.

- 45/ix/13/Rom/a

Agreement between the USSR and Romania concerning deliveries of grain to Romania

Signed during negotiations from Sept. 4 to 13, 1945, in Moscow.

Provides for Soviet deliveries of 150,000 tons each of wheat and corn, to be repaid by Romanian deliveries of equal amounts, plus 5 per cent, in 1946–1947.

References: *Izv.*, Sept. 13, 1945.
VT, 1945, No. 10, pp. 1–2.
VPSS VP, 1945, pp. 32–34.
DSB, 15, 1946, p. 398.

- 45/ix/13/Rom/b

Agreement between the USSR and Romania concerning substitution of other goods for grain in reparation deliveries, and deferment of part of the grain delivery until the following harvest year

Signed during negotiations in Moscow from Sept. 4 to 13, 1945.

Concerns reparations deliveries under the armistice agreement of Sept. 12, 1944. Provides for oil deliveries of equivalent value in place of 24,000 tons of barley, 20,000 tons of wheat, and 40,000 tons of corn, representing arrears on reparations deliveries for 1944 and 1945; delivery of 20,000 tons of wheat and 40,000 tons of corn, representing the balance of the deliveries for 1945, to be postponed until the next harvest.

References: Same as for 45/ix/13/Rom/a.

- 45/ix/13/Rom/c

Agreement between the USSR and Romania concerning a reduction in deliveries by Romania of food and fodder for use of the Soviet troops in Romania and of material and financial payments as required by the Allied High Command in Romania

Signed during negotiations in Moscow from Sept. 4 to 13, 1945.

References: Same as for 45/ix/13/Rom/a.

- 45/ix/13/Rom/d

Agreement between the USSR and Romania concerning a reduction of Romania's indebtedness under the armistice agreement of September 12, 1944

Signed during negotiations in Moscow from Sept. 4 to 13, 1945.

Concerns Art. 12 of the armistice agreement, which provides that Romania shall return to the USSR all valuables and materials removed from Soviet territory during the war. Provides for acceptance by Romania of a valuation of 948 billion lei to cover her indebtedness under Art. 12 of the armistice agreement; signatories agree that goods to the value of 348 billion lei have already been restored to the USSR; remaining indebtedness reduced to 300 billion lei, to be paid by instalments within 3 years, in view of Romania's participation in the war against Germany and the supply of Romanian goods to Soviet occupation troops.

References: Same as for 45/ix/13/Rom/a.

- 45/ix/13/Rom/e

Agreement between the USSR and Romania concerning transportation

Signed during negotiations in Moscow from Sept. 4 to 13, 1945.

Provisions: (1) Soviet military control over Romanian railroads to be abolished and the railroads returned to control of the Romanian Government by Dec. 1945; (2) 15,000 railroad cars and 115 locomotives, taken as war booty, to be returned by the USSR; (3) the USSR agrees to pay the cost of changing the cars from Soviet broad gauge to European standard gauge; (4) 6,398 captured German railroad cars to be leased to Romania for 2 years; (5) tracks converted to Soviet gauge to be changed back to European standard gauge; (6) the USSR to lease 2,000 motor trucks to Romania; and (7) 18 naval vessels, 23 harbor vessels, and a portion of the Romanian merchant marine, taken as war booty by Soviet forces, to be returned to Romania.

References: Same as for 45/ix/13/Rom/a.

- 45/ix/13/Rom/f

Agreement between the USSR and Romania concerning repatriation

Signed during negotiations in Moscow from Sept. 4 to 13, 1945.

Provides for repatriation of Romanian

prisoners held by Soviet forces, including 83,000 already en route, and for repatriation on a voluntary basis of Bessarabian and Bukovinian citizens of the USSR residing in Romania.
References: Same as for 45/ix/13/ Rom/a.

• 45/ix/13/Rom/g

Agreement between the USSR and Romania concerning collaboration in the fields of culture and education

Signed during negotiations in Moscow from Sept. 4 to 13, 1945.
Possibly the first of the postwar agreements between the USSR and the occupied States of Eastern Europe concerning cultural collaboration.
References: *Izv.*, Sept. 13, 1945.
    VT, 1945, No. 10, p. 2.
    VPSS VP, 1945, p. 34.

• 45/ix/17/US

Agreement between the USSR and the United States of America concerning boundary changes between the Soviet and American zones of occupation in Germany

Signed Sept. 17, 1945, in Wanfried, Saxony.
Sources: *UST*, 5, pp. 2177–81 (*TIAS* 3081).
    UNTS, 235, pp. 345–49 (R, E, F).

Sept. 20, 1945. Agreement concerning certain additional requirements to be imposed on Germany

See 45/vii/25/Pl.

• 45/ix/25/H

Exchange of notes between the USSR and Hungary concerning re-establishment of diplomatic relations

Sent Sept. 25, 1945, in Budapest.
References: *SDD*, 12, p. 13.
    Izv., Sept. 27, 1945.
    DSB, 15, 1946, p. 395.

• 45/ix/27/Mul/a

Agreement concerning establishment of a European Central Inland Transport Organization, with protocol

Signed Sept. 27, 1945, in London, by the USSR and 12 other States.
Entered into force on signature. Dura-

tion 2 years; thereafter indefinitely, although after 18 months after signature any member may give notice of intention to withdraw, to take effect after 6 months. The protocol provides for various technical matters relating to the work of the organization established by the agreement. Entry into force and duration same as for the agreement.
Not all the Governments which signed the agreement also signed the protocol; the USSR, however, signed both. Supplemented by a protocol of the same date concerning transfer from the Provisional Organization for European Inland Transport (next document).
For background, see Hudson, 9, pp. 666–67.
Sources: *UNTS*, 4, pp. 327–63, 368–86 (E, F, R).
    EAS, No. 494, 1946, pp. 1–18.
    BFSP, 145, pp. 888–908, citing *BTS*, 1946, No. 34, Cmd. 6919.
    Hudson, 9, pp. 666–90 (E, F).

• 45/ix/27/Mul/b

Protocol concerning transfer from the Provisional Organization for European Inland Transport to the European Central Inland Transport Organization

Signed Sept. 27, 1945, in London, by the USSR and 12 other States.
Background: Under an agreement of May 8, 1945 (not signed by the USSR and not listed here) there was established a Provisional Organization for European Inland Transport. This protocol provides for transfer of the records, assets, and liabilities of the Provisional Organization to the European Central Inland Transport Organization established by the agreement of Sept. 27, 1945 (preceding document).
Sources: *UNTS*, 5, pp. 362–67, 386–88 (E, F).
    EAS, 494, 1946, pp. 16–18.
    BFSP, 145, pp. 905–908.

• 45/ix/29/Pl

Agreement on establishment of a Far Eastern Advisory Commission

Announced in a statement by the Secretary of State of the United States of America on Sept. 29, 1945, in London; the statement was released to the press Oct. 1, 1945.

Background: On Aug. 21, 1945, the United States proposed to China, the United Kingdom, and the USSR the establishment of the Commission, in a paper setting forth its proposed terms of reference (text in *DSB*, 13, 1945, pp. 561, 580). The proposal was accepted "promptly" by the USSR and China (*SIA, ABR*, p. 641), but establishment was delayed until the assent of the British Government had been received. The Commission held its first meeting Oct. 30, 1945 (*DSB*, 13, 1945, pp. 643, 728); the USSR was not represented, nor did it send a representative to subsequent meetings during Nov. and Dec. 1945 (*ibid.*, pp. 769, 967). By an agreement of the Conference of Foreign Ministers in Moscow during December 1945, the Commission was replaced by a Far Eastern Commission (see 45/xii/27/(2)).
Reference (statement of Sept. 29, 1945): *DSB*, 13, 1945, p. 545.

● 45/x/ /Neth

Exchange of notes between the USSR and The Netherlands concerning establishment of a Soviet Trade Mission in The Netherlands

Sent during Oct. 1945.
Reference: Korolenko, p. 94.

● 45/x/2/Pl

First meeting of the Council of Foreign Ministers

Held Sept. 11 to Oct. 2, 1945, in London, by the Foreign Ministers of the USSR, the United Kingdom, the United States of America, the French Provisional Government, and China.
The major task of the meeting was to prepare draft peace treaties with Italy, Finland, Romania, Bulgaria, and Hungary, in accordance with a decision of the Potsdam Conference (see 45/viii/1/(1)). Preliminary agreements were reached on the following questions: (1) Each of the 5 peace treaties to include a Bill of Rights guaranteeing the citizens of the country in question freedom of speech, religious worship, political belief, and public meeting. (2) Italian sovereignty to be restored on signature of the peace treaty. (3) The Dodecanese Islands to be ceded to Greece (final Soviet assent to the proposal was withheld

pending further study). (4) Italy's former African colonies to be administered under the trusteeship provisions of the United Nations. (5) The boundary between Italy and Yugoslavia to be based mainly on ethnic considerations (for appointment of a commission of experts to prepare a report on the Italy-Yugoslavia boundary, see 46/ii/28/Pl). (6) No changes to be made in the boundary between Italy and Austria. (7) Only minor changes to be made in the boundary between Italy and France. (8) A free port under international control to be established in the Trieste area. (9) Italy to have no substantial armaments industry. No agreements were reached at the conference on (1) the holding of a general peace conference, and (2) the question of reparations from Italy.
References: The communiqués issued during the meeting are given in *DSB*, 13, 1945, pp. 392–93, 564–66. See also *DSB*, 13, 1945, pp. 507–12 (report by Secretary of State James F. Byrnes; also published separately, Washington, D.C., 1945).
DSES, 24, pp. 16–18.
SIA, RE, p. 455.

● 45/x/2/UK

Exchange of notes between the USSR and the United Kingdom concerning the time of withdrawal of Allied troops from Iran

Sent during the first session of the Council of Foreign Ministers, Sept. 11 to Oct. 2, 1945. According to a Soviet note to the United States of Nov. 29, 1945 (text in *DSB*, 13, 1945, pp. 934–35), the exchange was brought to the attention of the Council of Foreign Ministers in their London meeting in Sept. 1945, and "did not find objection in any quarters." For Soviet withdrawal from Iran, see 46/iii/26/Iran.
Reference: *DSB*, 13, *loc. cit.*

● 45/x/3/Iran

Protocol between the USSR and Iran supplementing the convention of August 27, 1935, concerning the campaign against plant diseases and parasites

Signed Oct. 3, 1945, in Teheran.
Subject to ratification. Entered into force on signature. Constitutes an integral part

of the 1935 convention (35/viii/27/ Iran/c). Supplements the list of plant diseases and parasites to be combatted, and provides for technical details of quarantine and border controls. Calls for annual Soviet-Iranian conferences to combat agricultural diseases and parasites, including locusts in the border regions.
Source: *SDD*, 12, pp. 104–107.

Oct. 6, 1945. Protocol correcting an error in the Russian text of the Statute of the International Military Tribunal

See 45/viii/8/Pl/b.

● 45/x/15/US

Agreement between the USSR and the United States of America concerning disposition of Lend-Lease supplies in inventory or procurement in the United States, with two schedules

Signed Oct. 15, 1945, in Washington, D.C.
Entered into force on signature. Provides for Soviet purchase of Lend-Lease supplies after the presidential order of Aug. 21, 1945, terminating Lend-Lease. Soviet sources maintain that the United States violated the agreement by ending deliveries at the end of 1946 (*VT*, 1948, No. 5, p. 2; Korolenko, p. 76). For background see *SIA, ABR*, pp. 674–75, 690–93.
Annexes comprise Schedules I-A and I-B, containing detailed information with regard to materials and equipment to be supplied under the agreement, and Schedule II, setting forth the terms and conditions under which articles are to be transferred and shipped.
Sources: *UST*, 7, pp. 2819–27 (omits text of Schedules I-A and I-B, which "are deposited with the Agreement in the archives of the Department of State, where they are available for reference").
Twenty-first report to Congress on Lend-Lease operations, pp. 48–53 (omits Schedules I-A and I-B).
UNTS, 278, pp. 151–65 (E, F; omits Schedules I-A and I-B, which are to be published in *UNTS*, 315, Annex B).
DAFR, 8, pp. 127–32 (omits Schedules I-A and I-B).

● 45/x/22/Cz

Agreement between the USSR and Czechoslovakia concerning establishment of mail and telephone-telegraph communications, with final protocol

Signed Oct. 22, 1945, in Moscow.
Entered into force on signature. Valid until abrogation by mutual agreement, or until 6 months after denunciation. Various technical details of the agreement and final protocol were modified as of Aug. 8, 1951. Date of the agreement establishing these changes, if any, is unknown.
Source: *SDD*, 12, pp. 167–78.
References: *DSB*, 15, 1946, p. 393.
Izv., Oct. 23, 1945.

● 45/x/24/Austria

Exchange of notes between the USSR and the Provisional Government of Austria concerning re-establishment of diplomatic relations

Sent Oct. 20 and 24, 1945, in Vienna.
Reference: *SDD*, 12, p. 13.

● 45/x/26/Fin

Protocol between the USSR and Finland concerning the boundary between the USSR and Finland in the Pechenga (Petsamo) area, with annexes and maps

Signed Oct. 26, 1945, by a joint Soviet-Finnish border commission. Confirmed by an exchange of notes of Feb. 19, 1946. Establishes the course of the boundary provided for in the armistice agreement of Sept. 19, 1944. Annexes, together with that of the border protocol of Dec. 16, 1944, include regulations for maintenance and supervision of border marks and clearings.
References: *Izv.*, Oct. 30, 1945.
DSB, 15, 1946, p. 393.
Mentioned in the border treaty of Dec. 9, 1948.

● 45/x/26/Pl

Protocol defining the junction point of the borders of the USSR, Finland, and Norway

Signed Oct. 26, 1945, by a joint Soviet-Finnish commission for demarcation of the border between the USSR and Finland, sitting in joint committee with a Norwegian representative.

References: *Izv.*, Oct. 30, 1945.
  DSB, 15, 1946, p. 393.

Oct. 29, 1945. Rules of procedure of the International Military Tribunal

See 45/viii/8/Pl/b.

• 45/xi/ /China

Informal agreement between the USSR and China concerning a delay in evacuation of Soviet troops from Manchuria

A TASS communiqué of Nov. 30, 1945, announced that the USSR had agreed to retain its troops in Manchuria "for a certain time" on the request of the Chinese Nationalist Government. The status of the agreement and its form are obscure; for analysis, see McLane, pp. 208–209.
Reference: *Pravda*, Nov. 30, 1945 (communiqué).

• 45/xi/7/US

Exchange of communications between the USSR and the United States of America concerning withdrawal of Soviet and American troops from Czechoslovakia

Sent on or about Nov. 1, 1945, from Washington, D.C., and Nov. 7, 1945, from Moscow.
Provides that troop withdrawal shall be completed by Dec. 1, 1945.
Source: *Correspondence*, 2, pp. 276–78.

• 45/xi/10/Alb

Exchange of notes between the USSR and the Provisional Government of Albania concerning establishment of diplomatic relations

Sent Nov. 10, 1945, in Tirana.
References: *Izv.*, Nov. 11, 1945.
  VT, 1945, No. 11–12, p. 24.
  SDD, 12, p. 3.

• 45/xi/13/Yug

Agreement between the USSR and Yugoslavia concerning conditions of work of Soviet experts assigned to Yugoslavia

Signed Nov. 13, 1945, in Moscow.
Entered into force on signature. Registered with the UN by Yugoslavia Nov. 27, 1951. Experts to be employed for one year from the date of their arrival in Yugoslavia.

Source: *UNTS*, 116, pp. 139–51 (R, SC, E, F).

Nov. 16, 1945. Constitution of the United Nations Educational, Scientific, and Cultural Organization (UNESCO)

See 54/iv/21/1945.

• 45/xi/23/Pol

Agreement between the USSR and the Polish Provisional Government of National Unity concerning establishment of direct rail communications

Signed Nov. 23, 1945, in Moscow.
Regulates conditions of freight transportation, tariffs, conditions of use of railroad equipment, payments, responsibility for the safety of transports, and conditions for transports between the Soviet Zone of Occupation in Germany and the USSR passing through Poland. Superseded by agreement of 1950 concerning transportation of freight by rail (50/ / /Pl).
References: *Izv.*, Nov. 27, 1945.
  VT, 1945, No. 11–12, p. 24.
  DSB, 15, 1946, p. 396.

Nov. 26, 1945. Protocol amending the international agreement of June 8, 1937, concerning the regulation of whaling, and the protocol of June 24, 1938, on the same subject

See 46/xi/25/1945.

• 45/xi/27/China

Agreement between the USSR and China concerning withdrawal of Chinese Communist forces from Changchun and Mukden and their occupation by Chinese Nationalist forces

Announced Nov. 27, 1945.
References: McLane, p. 212, citing
  NYT, Nov. 28, 1945, p. 1.

Nov. 30, 1945. Agreement by the Allied Control Council for Germany concerning establishment of 3 corridors for air travel between Berlin and Western Germany

See Appendix 3.

• 45/xi/30/Yug

Agreement between the USSR and Yugoslavia concerning deliveries of petroleum products

Signed Nov. 30, 1945, in Belgrade.
Entered into force on signature. Valid
until 1 month after denunciation.
Provides for monthly Soviet deliveries
of petroleum products starting Dec. 1,
1945, in addition to deliveries for the
Yugoslav national economy, to be repaid
by Yugoslav deliveries of goods of corresponding value. Prices to be fixed in
accordance with the protocol concerning
prices attached to the trade agreement
of Apr. 13, 1945. Registered with the
UN by Yugoslavia Nov. 27, 1951.
Source: *UNTS*, 116, pp. 153–59 (R, SC,
E, F).

• 45/xii/7/Pl

**Recommendation of a tripartite commis-
sion on distribution of the German merchant fleet between the USSR, the United
Kingdom, and the United States of
America**

Prepared by a tripartite commission representing the 3 Powers, at the end of
meetings from Sept. 1 to Dec. 7, 1945.
For agreement at the Potsdam Conference on establishment of the commission,
see 45/viii/1/(4).
Reference: *Pr.*, Mar. 8, 1946 (com-
        muniqué by the commission con-
        cerning distribution).

• 45/xii/15/Bul

**Supplementary trade agreement between
the USSR and Bulgaria**

Signed Dec. 15, 1945, in Sofia.
Supplements the trade agreement of Mar.
10, 1945. USSR to supply 30,000 metric
tons of wheat by Apr. 1, 1946, to be repaid by Bulgaria by Apr. 1, 1947. According to a press report from Sofia of
June 8, 1946, the USSR released Bulgaria from the obligation to repay the
50,000 [*sic*] tons of wheat loaned in
1945 (*DSB*, 15, 1946, p. 392).
Reference: *DSB, loc cit.*

• 45/xii/27/Pl

**Communiqué concerning a meeting of
the Foreign Ministers**

Signed Dec. 27, 1945, in Moscow; released to the press the same day. The
meeting of the Foreign Ministers of the
USSR, the United Kingdom, and the

United States of America was held Dec.
16 to 26, 1945, in Moscow.
Note on the form of the document: The
communiqué proper consists of a short
paragraph giving the dates and site of
the conference and relating it to the decisions of the Yalta and Berlin (Potsdam) conferences. It is signed by the
three Foreign Ministers and dated Dec.
27, 1945. The communiqué leads directly to the Report of the Meeting,
which constitutes the major document
prepared by the conference (for contents, see below). The Report, in turn,
has a short introductory paragraph similar to the communiqué but omitting the
reference to the Yalta and Berlin conferences; it is also signed by the three
Foreign Ministers and dated Dec. 27,
1945. In most sources the Report is
either undated or given the same date as
the other documents; in the English and
French versions in *UNTS*, 20, however,
the Report is dated Dec. 26, 1945. All
the sources listed below give the text
of the Report, but some introduce it by
the text of the communiqué, others by
the shorter introductory paragraph.
There appears to be no significance in
these variations, and they have not been
mentioned in the sources listed below.
Both communiqué and introductory
paragraph are given in *DSB*, 13, and
UNTS, 20.
Contents of the report: Seven separate
agreements are incorporated in the report. As in the case of the agreements
reached at the Potsdam Conference, it
will be convenient to list these separately
below, following the list of sources. In
some cases it has been necessary to supplement the agreements listed in the report by evidence from other sources.
Sources: *Izv.*, Dec. 28, 1945.
    VT, 1945, No. 11–12, pp. 2–10.
    VPSS 1945, pp. 153–66.
    SDD, 12, pp. 64–75.
    TIAS, 1555 (1946).
    DSB, 13, 1945, pp. 1027–32.
    DSCS, 79, pp. 9–18.
    UNTS, 20, pp. 259–93 (R, E, F).

• 45/xii/27/(1)

**Agreement concerning preparation of
peace treaties with Italy, Romania, Bulgaria, Hungary, and Finland**

Negotiated during the conference of Foreign Ministers of the USSR, the United Kingdom, and the United States of America Dec. 16 to 26, 1945, in Moscow. In part, announced by the conference on Dec. 24, 1945 (so indicated in the preamble to the Report of the conference; see also Byrnes, pp. 114–15).

Establishes the following procedure for preparation of the 5 peace treaties: (1) Drafts of the peace treaties to be prepared by members of the Council of Foreign Ministers. (Modifying the procedure agreed on at the Potsdam Conference —see 45/viii/1/(1)—it was agreed to drop China entirely as a participant and to limit France's participation to the peace treaty with Italy.) (2) A general peace conference, composed of representatives of all those States which had actively waged war with substantial forces against the European members of the Axis, to be convoked not later than May 1, 1946, for the purpose of reviewing the draft peace treaties and drawing up recommendations for their modification or extension. (The conference was actually convened on July 29, 1946; for its recommendations, see 46/x/15/Pl.) At the conference, representatives of the 5 defeated States to be given an opportunity to present their views. (3) The Council of Foreign Ministers to prepare final texts of the peace treaties in the light of the recommendations of the conference. (4) The final text of each treaty to be signed by all the States which had actively waged war against the State concerned.

Source: Part I of the Report of the conference (45/xii/27/Pl, above).

Reference: SIA, ABR, pp. 704–705.

Note: In its account of the procedure for drafting the peace treaties, DSES, 24, p. 20, states that it was agreed by the Foreign Ministers at this conference "that the signing of the peace treaties with Italy, the three Balkan nations and Finland would make it possible to withdraw from these countries forces of occupation, excepting some troops of the Soviet Union in Romania and Hungary, through which the Soviet Union maintained its lines of communication with its occupation forces in Austria." As the source for this supplementary agreement, DSES 24 cites Secretary of State Byrnes' radio report on the conference made Dec. 30, 1945. In the text of the address as

given in DSB, 13, 1945, pp. 1033–36, 1047, however, there is only a passing reference to the withdrawal of troops from Romania and Bulgaria, with no specific indication of any agreement reached. In the same radio talk, Mr. Byrnes stated, "There was no subject as to which an agreement was reached that was not covered in the communiqué published Friday [Dec. 28, 1945], apart from instructions to the representatives of the three Governments to facilitate agreements in the field." There is no reference to the troop agreement in Mr. Byrnes' account of the conference in Speaking Frankly (pp. 110–22).

● 45/xii/27/(2)

Agreement concerning establishment of a Far Eastern Commission and an Allied Council for Japan

Negotiated during the conference of Foreign Ministers of the USSR, the United Kingdom, and the United States in Moscow, Dec. 16 to 26, 1945. China concurred in the agreement.

(1) Provides for establishment of a Far Eastern Commission, composed of representatives of the USSR, the United Kingdom, the United States of America, China, France, The Netherlands, Canada, Australia, New Zealand, India, and the Philippine Commonwealth, and defines its organization and functions; and (2) provides for establishment of an Allied Council for Japan, composed of a chairman in the person of the Supreme Commander for the Allied Powers in Japan or his deputy to serve as United States member, and members for the USSR, China, and, jointly, the United Kingdom, Australia, New Zealand, and India, and defines its operating procedure and functions. The Far Eastern Commission takes the place of the Far Eastern Advisory Commission, establishment of which was announced Sept. 29, 1945 (see 45/ix/29/Pl). The USSR was represented from its first meeting, Feb. 26, 1946, in Washington, D.C. (DSB, 14, 1946, p. 375). For a Soviet note of protest dated Apr. 28, 1952, on dissolution of the commission, see DIA, 1952, pp. 480–82.

Sources: Part II of the Report of the conference (45/xii/27/Pl, above).

Hudson, 9, pp. 663–66, citing
  TIAS, 1555.
DAFR, 8, pp. 275–78.
Chen, pp. 241–45.

• 45/xii/27/(3)

**Agreement concerning establishment of
a provisional Korean government**

Negotiated during the conference of Foreign Ministers of the USSR, the United
Kingdom, and the United States in Moscow, Dec. 16 to 26, 1945.
Provides for establishment of a Joint
Commission to assist in formation of a
provisional Korean Government, composed of representatives of the United
States Command in southern Korea and
the Soviet Command in northern Korea,
and for convening a Soviet-American
conference in Korea within two weeks
(see 46/ii/5/US/a and /b). For earlier
Soviet-American discussion of postwar
controls in Korea, see 45/vi/6/US (i).
For the division of Korea into Soviet
and American zones, see 45/viii/1/(19).
For work of the Joint Commission, see
47/v/12/US.
Source: Part III of the Report of the
  conference (45/xii/27/Pl, above).

• 45/xii/27/(4)

Agreement concerning policy in China

Negotiated during the conference of Foreign Ministers of the USSR, the United
Kingdom, and the United States in Moscow, Dec. 16 to 26, 1945.
Covers (1) agreement on "the need for
a unified and democratic China under
the National Government, for broad participation by democratic elements in all
branches of the National Government,
and for a cessation of civil strife"; (2)
reaffirmation of adherence to the policy
of "non-interference in the internal affairs of China"; and (3) agreement between the Foreign Ministers of the USSR
and the United States "as to the desirability of withdrawal of Soviet and American forces from China at the earliest
practicable moment consistent with the
discharge of their obligations and responsibilities."
Sources: Part IV of the Report of the
  conference (45/xii/27/Pl, above).
  Chen, p. 241.

• 45/xii/27/(5)

**Agreement concerning policy in Ro-
mania**

Negotiated during the conference of Foreign Ministers of the USSR, the United
Kingdom, and the United States in Moscow, Dec. 16 to 26, 1945.
Covers (1) "broadening" of the Romanian Government; (2) holding of "free
and unfettered elections . . . as soon as
possible on the basis of universal and
secret ballot," during which the reorganized government is to "give assurances
concerning the grant of freedom of the
press, speech, religion, and association";
and (3) recognition of the Government of
Romania by the United States and the
United Kingdom. A commission representing the 3 Powers to be sent to Romania to supervise the reorganization of
the government.
Source: Part V of the Report of the
  conference (45/xii/27/Pl, above).

• 45/xii/27/(6)

Agreement concerning policy in Bulgaria

Negotiated during the conference of Foreign Ministers of the USSR, the United
Kingdom, and the United States in Moscow, Dec. 16 to 26, 1945.
Concerns (1) a Soviet undertaking to
"advise" the Bulgarian Government of
the Fatherland Front with regard to the
desirability of the inclusion of two representatives of "other democratic groups,"
and (2) recognition of the Government
of Bulgaria by the United States and the
United Kingdom.
Source: Part VI of the Report of the
  conference (45/xii/27/Pl, above).

• 45/xii/27/(7)

**Agreement concerning establishment by
the United Nations of a commission for
the control of atomic energy**

Negotiated during the conference of Foreign Ministers of the USSR, the United
Kingdom, and the United States in Moscow, Dec. 16 to 26, 1945.
The 3 Powers represented at the conference agree (1) to recommend establishment of a commission "to consider problems arising from the discovery of atomic
energy and related matters," and (2) to
invite France and China, together with

Canada, to sponsor a resolution on the subject at the first session of the General Assembly of the United Nations in Jan. 1946. The original proposal to establish a commission on atomic energy under the United Nations was made in a declaration by the United States, the United Kingdom, and Canada on Nov. 15, 1945 (text in Hudson, 9, pp. 783–86). The United Nations Atomic Energy Commission was established on Jan. 24, 1946 (*ibid.*)

Source: Part VII of the Report of the conference (45/xii/27/Pl, above); includes the draft resolution on the commission.
DAFR, 8, pp. 548–50.

● 45/xii/29/France

Commercial agreement between the USSR and the French Provisional Government, with protocol

Signed Dec. 29, 1945, in Moscow.
Ratified by the USSR Apr. 30, 1946; by France May 2, 1946. Entered into force May 2, 1946, on exchange of acts of ratification in Paris. Duration 5 years; may be denounced not later than Sept. 30 of any year, to take effect Dec. 31 of that year. Expired at the end of 5 years; succeeded by the agreement of Sept. 3,

1951. Concluded on the basis of the treaty of alliance and mutual assistance of Dec. 10, 1944.
Incorporates provisions governing the legal status of the Soviet Trade Mission in France. Protocol provides (1) that the commercial attaché of the French Embassy in Moscow shall enjoy diplomatic privileges and immunities, and (2) that an agreement will be reached on the number of staff personnel of the Soviet Trade Mission in France.

Sources: *VT*, 1946, No. 1–2, pp. 11–15.
*JO, June 20, 1946.
DSB, 15, 1946, pp. 553–55.
References: *Izv.*, Dec. 30, 1945.
VT, 1945, No. 11–12, p. 24.

● 45/xii/31/Fin

Agreement between the USSR and Finland concerning extension of the period of reparations payments and reduction of annual instalments, with protocol

Signed Dec. 31, 1945, in Helsinki.
Modifies the agreement of Dec. 17, 1944. Modified by agreement of July 28, 1948. Period of reparations payments extended from 6 to 8 years. Reduction in payments for 1946 approximately $15 million US.
Reference: *DSB*, 15, 1946, pp. 393–94.

1946

● 46/ / /Cz

Agreement between the USSR and Czechoslovakia concerning direct railroad freight communications

Signed during 1946.
Superseded by the agreement concerning transportation of freight by rail of 1950 (50/ / /Pl).
Reference: Genkin, p. 130.

● 46/i/8/Pl. See Appendix 5.

Jan. 17, 1946. Provisional rules of procedure of the Security Council of the United Nations

See Note to 45/vi/26/Mul/a.

● 46/i/19/Mul/a

Proclamation concerning establishment

of an International Military Tribunal for the Far East

Issued Jan. 19, 1946, in Tokyo, by Gen. Douglas MacArthur, Supreme Commander for the Allied Powers.
Constitution, jurisdiction and functions of the Tribunal are set forth in the Charter, approved on the same day (next document).

Sources: *SDD*, 12, pp. 85–86.
DSB, 14, 1946, p. 361.
DAFR, 8, pp. 353–54.

● 46/i/19/Mul/b

Charter of the International Military Tribunal for the Far East

Promulgated Jan. 19, 1946, in Tokyo, together with a proclamation by the Supreme Commander for the Allied Powers (preceding document). Amended by

order of Apr. 26, 1946 (see 46/iv/26/
Mul). As amended, provides for not
less than 6 nor more than 11 members
for the Tribunal, to be appointed by the
Supreme Commander from names submitted by the signatories to the Instrument of Surrender of Japan (45/ix/2/J),
together with India and the Philippines.
As established, the Tribunal consisted of
representatives from Australia, Canada,
China, the United Kingdom, The Netherlands, New Zealand, the USSR, the
United States of America, France, India,
and the Philippines (*DAFR*, 8, p. 352).
For the indictment of 28 military and
political wartime leaders of Japan, presented on Apr. 29, 1946, see *Trial of
Japanese war criminals*, pp. 45–63, summarized in *DSB*, 14, 1946, pp. 846–48,
853.

Sources: *SDD*, 12, pp. 79–85 (text as
amended Apr. 26, 1946).
DAFR, 8, pp. 354–58 (same).
DSB, 14, 1946, pp. 361–64 (original
text).

• 46/i/22/Pl

**Joint communiqué concerning disposal
of the German Navy**

Issued Jan. 22, 1946, by the USSR, the
United Kingdom, and the United States
of America.
For an agreement at the Potsdam Conference on disposal of the German Navy,
see 45/viii/1/(4).

Sources: *Pr.*, Jan. 23, 1946.
DSB, 14, 1946, p. 173.
DAFR, 8, p. 244.

• 46/ii/5/US/a

**Joint communiqué concerning military
administration in Korea**

Signed Feb. 5, 1946, in Seoul, by representatives of the Soviet and United States
military commands in Korea, at the end
of a conference which began Jan. 16.
1946.
Mentions agreements concerning (1) establishment of economic, administrative
and transport subcommissions; (2) railroad, highway and maritime transport;
(3) movement of Korean citizens between the 2 occupation zones; (4) postal
exchange between the 2 zones; (5) distribution of radio channels among the
radio stations of Korea; (6) measures
for further coordination between the 2

commands in respect to administrative
and economic questions; and (7) formation of a joint commission (see next
document).
Source: *Pr.*, Feb. 8, 1946.
Reference: *DAFR*, 8, p. 835.

• 46/ii/5/US/b

**Joint communiqué concerning establish-
ment of a Joint Commission for Korea**

Signed Feb. 5, 1946, in Seoul, by representatives of the Soviet and United States
military commands in Korea.
Task of the commission to be assistance
in the formation of a Provisional Government for Korea. Establishment of the
commission carries out an agreement of
the Foreign Ministers in Dec. 1945 (see
45/xii/27/(3)). For press communiqués
of the commission, see *Pravda*, Mar. 24
and 28 and Apr. 4 and 20, 1946.
Source: *Pravda*, Feb. 7, 1946.

• 46/ii/8/Pol

**Agreement between the USSR and the
Polish Provisional Government of National Unity concerning grain deliveries
to Poland**

Signed Feb. 8, 1946.
Provides for deliveries by the USSR of
200,000 tons of grain on credit during the
period ending Mar. 31, 1946, to be repaid
by Poland by the end of 1946.
Reference: *VT SSSR*, p. 73.

**Feb. 13, 1946. (1) Financial regulations
of the United Nations**

See Note to 45/vi/26/Mul/a.

**(2) Convention concerning privileges
and immunities of the United Nations**

See 53/ix/22/1946.

• 46/ii/15/Rom/a

**Payments agreement between the USSR
and Romania**

Signed Feb. 15, 1946.
Reference: *VT*, 1949, No. 11, p. 12.

• 46/ii/15/Rom/b

**Protocol between the USSR and Ro-
mania concerning the most-favored-nation principle**

Signed Feb. 15, 1946.
Reference: *VT*, 1949, No. 11, p. 12.

• 46/ii/19/Fin

Exchange of notes between the USSR and Finland confirming the protocol of October 26, 1945, concerning the boundary between the USSR and Finland in the Pechenga (Petsamo) area

Sent Feb. 19, 1946.
Source: *SS, 1946, No. 5 (Finnish, R).
References: *Pr., Izv.*, Feb. 21, 1946.
 VPSS, 1946, p. 93.

• 46/ii/27/MPR/a

Treaty of friendship and mutual assistance between the USSR and the Mongolian People's Republic

Signed Feb. 27, 1946, in Moscow.
Ratified by the USSR Apr. 23, 1946. Entered into force June 7, 1946, on exchange of acts of ratification in Ulan Bator (*UNTS*, 48, p. 184, however, gives Apr. 26, 1946, as date of exchange of acts of ratification and entry into force). Based on the protocol of mutual assistance of Mar. 12, 1936, which it incorporates verbatim and extends for 10 years; thereafter, if not denounced 1 year before expiration, extended for an additional 10 years.
Sources: *VVS*, 1946, No. 13.
 VT, 1946, No. 3, pp. 7–8.
 VPSS, 1946, pp. 100–102.
 SDD, 12, pp. 11–13.
 UNTS, 48, pp. 177–87 (R, M, E, F).
 DSB, 14, 1946, p. 968.

• 46/ii/27/MPR/b

Agreement between the USSR and the Mongolian People's Republic concerning economic and cultural collaboration

Signed Feb. 27, 1946, in Moscow.
Entered into force on signature. Duration 10 years; if not denounced 1 year before expiration, extended for an additional 10 years.
Sources: *Izv.*, Feb. 28, 1946.
 VT, 1946, No. 3, p. 9.
 VPSS, 1946, pp. 103–104.
 SDD, 12, pp. 96–97.
 UNTS, 216, pp. 221–29 (R, M, E, F).
 DSB, 14, 1946, pp. 968–69.

• 46/ii/28/Pl

Joint communiqué concerning appointment of a commission of experts to prepare a report on the Italy-Yugoslavia boundary

Signed Feb. 28, 1946, by the Council of Foreign Ministers' Deputies, representing the USSR, the United Kingdom, the United States of America, and France.
Carries out a decision of the Council of Foreign Ministers in Sept. 1945 (see 45/x/2/Pl).
Source: *DSB*, 14, 1946, p. 391.

• 46/iii/ /Pol

Agreement between the USSR and the Polish Provisional Government of National Unity concerning organization of air communications

Signed during Mar. 1946, probably shortly before the 24th, in Moscow.
Provides for transportation over the routes Moscow-Warsaw, Moscow-Warsaw-Berlin, and Warsaw-Berlin, and for technical assistance to the Polish Civil Air Fleet.
References: *Pr., Izv.*, Mar. 24, 1946.
 VT, 1946, No. 3, p. 34.

• 46/iii/6/Iran

Joint communiqué by the USSR and Iran concerning negotiations on matters of common interest

Published Mar. 8, 1946, following negotiations from Feb. 19 to Mar. 6, 1946, in Moscow.
No specific agreements mentioned.
Source: *Pravda*, Mar. 8, 1946.

• 46/iii/8/Pl. See Appendix 5.

• 46/iii/18/Switz

Exchange of notes between the USSR and Switzerland concerning re-establishment of diplomatic relations

Sent Mar. 18, 1946, in Belgrade.
On Nov. 1, 1944, the USSR rejected a request by Switzerland for re-establishment of diplomatic relations (*VPSS VP*, 2, pp. 294–95). Subsequently the USSR, in response to a proposal by Switzerland, sent a military mission to Switzerland (date of request unknown).
References: *Pr., Izv.*, Mar. 20, 1946.
 VT, 1946, No. 3, p. 33.
 VPSS, 1946, pp. 108–109.
 SDD, 12, p. 13.
 *Swiss official communiqué dated Mar. 19, 1946, published in the Swiss press.

• 46/iii/20/Pol

Agreement between the USSR and the

Polish Provisional Government of National Unity concerning establishment of postal and telephone and telegraph communications, with final protocol

Signed Mar. 20, 1946, in Moscow.
Entered into force on signature. Valid until 6 months after denunciation.
Final protocol concerns technical details. Certain provisions of the agreement and the final protocol concerning telephone and telegraph communications were subsequently modified or abolished with effect from Oct. 10, 1949; date of the supplementary agreement, if any, not known. (Text of changes in *SDD*, 12, pp. 126–27, 130.)
Source: *SDD*, 12, pp. 120–33.

● 46/iii/20/Rom

Agreement between the USSR and Romania concerning establishment of a Soviet-Romanian joint-stock lumber company, "Sovromles"

Signed Mar. 20, 1946.
Ratified by Romania May 1, 1946. Carries out a provision of the agreement of May 8, 1945, concerning economic collaboration (45/v/8/Rom/a). Statute of the company promulgated July 2, 1946; enacting legislation July 6, 1946. Supplementary protocol signed Feb. 18, 1948 (48/ii/18/Rom/a).
Reference: *Economic treaties*, p. 16, citing *MO*, 1946, Nos. 101, 150, 154.

Mar. 20, 1946

Announcement of beginning of evacuation of Soviet military units from the island of Bornholm, in accordance with an informal agreement between the USSR and Denmark. Calls for completion of evacuation within 1 month.
Sources: *Pr., Izv.*, Mar. 20, 1946.
　VPSS, 1946, p. 110.
Reference: *SIA, RE*, p. 575.

Mar. 23, 1946

Announcement that withdrawal of Soviet forces from Manchuria, except Port Arthur and Dairen, would be completed by the end of April 1946.
Source: *Pravda*, Mar. 24, 1946.
Reference: McLane, p. 228.

Mar. 23, 1946

Bulgarian law establishing a Soviet-Bulgarian mining company: *DV*, 1946, No. 71, cited in *Economic treaties*, p. 12. Presumably based on an agreement between the USSR and Bulgaria concerning establishment of joint-stock companies, similar to the agreements concerning economic collaboration with Romania (45/v/8/Rom/a) and Hungary (45/viii/27/H/a). See Sipkov, Ivan, "Postwar nationalizations and alien property in Bulgaria," *AJIL*, July 1958, p. 489, citing *Otechestven Front*, Oct. 13, 1954, for a Bulgarian decree of Oct. 9, 1954, concerning dissolution of the company. See also 55/xi/26/Bul for an agreement concerning transfer to Bulgaria of Soviet shares in the joint-stock mining company "Gorubso."

● 46/iii/24/Iran

Informal understanding between the USSR and Iran concerning withdrawal of Soviet troops from Iran

Negotiated Mar. 24, 1946; announced Mar. 26, 1946.
Background: On Mar. 2, 1946, the Anglo-Soviet-Iranian treaty of alliance of Jan. 29, 1942, under which Soviet troops were stationed in northern Iran, expired. Even before that date, in Jan. 1946, Iran had submitted to the Security Council of the United Nations a complaint against "interference of the Soviet Union, through the medium of their officials and armed forces, in the internal affairs of Iran." On Mar. 24, 1946, the Soviet Ambassador to Iran delivered a memorandum to the Prime Minister of Iran announcing that evacuation of the Red Army would begin on Mar. 24 and would last from 5 to 6 weeks; on Mar. 26, TASS announced completion of the withdrawal of Soviet troops from certain districts, which the announcement stated had begun on Mar. 2.
References (TASS announcement of Mar. 26, 1946): *Pr.*, Mar. 25, 1946; *Izv.*, Mar. 26, 1946.
　VPSS, 1946, p. 111.

● 46/iii/29/H/a

Agreement between the USSR and Hungary concerning establishment of a Soviet-Hungarian joint-stock civil aviation company

Signed Mar. 29, 1946, in Budapest.
Carries out a provision of the agreement concerning economic collaboration of

Aug. 27, 1945 (45/viii/27/H/a). Statute of the company promulgated by Hungarian law of May 4, 1946 (*Economic treaties*, p. 13, citing *MK*, 1946, No. 100).
References: *Pravda*, Apr. 8, 1946.
  DSB, 15, 1946, p. 395.

● 46/iii/29/H/b

Agreement between the USSR and Hungary concerning establishment of a Soviet-Hungarian joint-stock navigation company

Signed Mar. 29, 1946, in Budapest.
Carries out a provision of the agreement concerning economic collaboration of Aug. 27, 1945 (45/viii/27/H/a). Statutes of the company promulgated by Hungarian law of May 4, 1946 (*Economic treaties*, p. 13, citing *MK*, 1946, No. 100). By a Hungarian decree of Apr. 12, 1947, the Soviet-Hungarian Navigation Company "Meszhart" was exempted from taxes and duties (*ibid.*, p. 14, citing *MK*, 1947, No. 82).
References: *Pravda*, Apr. 8, 1946.
  DSB, 15, 1946, p. 395.

● 46/iv/4/Iran

Joint communiqué concerning negotiations between the USSR and Iran

Signed Apr. 4, 1946, in Moscow.
Provisions: (1) Soviet troops to evacuate Iranian territory completely, within a month and a half from Mar. 24, 1946. (2) Agreement on establishment of a mixed Soviet-Iranian oil company to be submitted to the Iranian Mejlis for confirmation within 7 months after Mar. 24, 1946. (3) Iranian Azerbaidzhan recognized as an internal concern of Iran.
The agreement on establishment of the mixed Soviet-Iranian oil company, embodied in an exchange of notes, was rejected by the Mejlis on Oct. 22, 1946. For provisions of the agreement, see *Pravda*, Apr. 8, 1946.
Sources: *Pr., Izv.*, Apr. 6, 1946.
  VT, 1946, No. 4–5, p. 1.
  VPSS, 1946, p. 113.

● 46/iv/6/France

Agreement between the USSR and the French Provisional Government concerning delivery of grain to France

Signed Apr. 6, 1946, in Moscow.
Provides for Soviet deliveries of 400,000 tons of wheat and 100,000 tons of barley during the period April–June 1946.
References: *Pr.*, Apr. 8, 1946; *Izv.*, Apr. 9, 1946.
  VT, 1946, No. 4–5, p. 39.
  VPSS, 1946, p. 117.

● 46/iv/8/H/a

Agreement between the USSR and Hungary concerning establishment of a Soviet-Hungarian joint-stock company for exploration and extraction of oil and gas, refinement of oil and sale of oil products

Signed Apr. 8, 1946, in Budapest.
Carries out a provision of the agreement concerning economic collaboration of Aug. 27, 1945 (45/viii/27/H/a). Actually 3 Soviet-Hungarian oil companies were established: (1) On July 23, 1946, a Hungarian decree promulgated the statutes of the Soviet-Hungarian crude oil company "Maszovol" (*MK*, 1946, No. 164, cited in *Economic treaties*, p. 13). Under a Hungarian decree of Apr. 12, 1947, the company was exempted from taxes and duties. (*MK*, 1947, No. 82, cited *ibid.*) (2) On July 25, 1946, a Hungarian decree promulgated the statutes of the Hungarian-Soviet crude oil company "Molaj" (*MK*, 1946, No. 166, cited *ibid.*). By a decree of Apr. 12, 1947, the company was exempted from taxes and duties (*MK*, 1947, No. 82, cited *ibid.*, p. 14). (3) On Jan. 21, 1950, a Hungarian decree promulgated the statutes of the Hungarian-Soviet Oil Company, and exempted it from taxes and duties (*MK*, 1950, No. 13, cited *ibid.*, p. 15).
References: *Pr., Izv.*, Apr. 13, 1946.
  VT, 1946, No. 4–5, p. 40.
  DSB, 15, 1946, p. 394.

● 46/iv/8/H/b

Agreement between the USSR and Hungary concerning establishment of a Soviet-Hungarian joint-stock company for bauxite-aluminum

Signed Apr. 8, 1946, in Budapest.
Carries out a provision of the agreement of Aug. 27, 1945, concerning economic collaboration (45/viii/27/H/a). Actually 4 Soviet-Hungarian bauxite-aluminum companies were established: (1) On July 25, 1946, a Hungarian decree promulgated the statutes of the Soviet-Hungarian

bauxite-aluminum company "Danube Valley Aluminum Industry" (*MK*, 1946, No. 166, cited in *Economic treaties*, p. 13). (2) On Aug. 6, 1946, a Hungarian decree promulgated the statutes of the Soviet-Hungarian bauxite-aluminum company "Magyar Bauxitbanya" (*MK*, 1946, No. 177, cited *ibid.*; translation of the decree, *ibid.*, pp. 35–50). On Apr. 12, 1947, a Hungarian decree exempted the Soviet-Hungarian bauxite-aluminum companies from taxes and duties (*MK*, 1947, No. 82, cited *ibid.*, p. 14). (3) On Aug. 31, 1948, a Hungarian decree promulgated the statutes of the Soviet-Hungarian bauxite-aluminum company "Aluminum ore-mines and industry" (*MK*, 1948, No. 196, cited *ibid.*, p. 15). (4) A Hungarian decree of Jan. 21, 1950, promulgated the statutes of the Soviet-Hungarian Bauxite-Aluminum Company and exempted it from taxes and duties (*MK*, 1950, No. 13, cited *ibid.*).
References: *Pr., Izv.*, Apr. 13, 1946.
VT, 1946, No. 4–5, p. 40.
DSB, 15, 1946, p. 394.
Ibid., 25, 1951, pp. 323–24.

● 46/iv/12/Cz/a

Trade agreement between the USSR and Czechoslovakia, with protocols

Signed Apr. 12, 1946, in Moscow.
Ratified by Czechoslovakia May 28, 1946.
Duration 1 year, subject to extension.
References: *Pr., Izv.*, Apr. 16, 1946; *Pr.*, June 2, 1946.
VT, 1946, No. 4–5, p. 40.
VPSS, 1946, pp. 118–19.

● 46/iv/12/Cz/b

Protocol between the USSR and Czechoslovakia concerning settlement of unfinished accounts remaining from prewar trade operations

Signed Apr. 12, 1946, in Moscow.
References: Same as for 46/iv/12/Cz/a.

● 46/iv/12/Pol

Trade agreement between the USSR and the Polish Provisional Government of National Unity

Signed Apr. 12, 1946, in Moscow.
Not subject to ratification. Covers the period Apr. 1, 1946–Apr. 1, 1947; value of trade $96 million US each.
References: *Pr., Izv.*, Apr. 14, 1946.

VT, 1946, No. 4–5, p. 39.
VPSS, 1946, pp. 117–18.

● 46/iv/15/Rom

Agreement between the USSR and Romania concerning extension from six to eight years of the term of payment of reparations by Romania

Negotiated shortly before Apr. 15, 1946, probably in the form of an exchange of notes. Modifies the reparations agreement of Jan. 16, 1945.
References: *Pr.*, Apr. 15, 1946; *Izv.*, Apr. 16, 1946.
VT, 1946, No. 4–5, p. 39.
VPSS, 1946, p. 118.

● 46/iv/18/H

Joint communiqué by the USSR and Hungary concerning extension from six to eight years of the term of payment of reparations by Hungary

Issued at the end of negotiations held from Apr. 9 to 18, 1946, in Moscow.
Modifies the reparations agreement of June 15, 1945.
Sources: *Pr., Izv.*, Apr. 19, 1946.
VT, 1946, No. 4–5, p. 40.

● 46/iv/18/US

Communiqué concerning political reconstruction in Korea

Issued Apr. 18, 1946, in Seoul, by the USSR–United States Joint Commission for Korea.
Covers agreement on "the first point of the joint program of work covering the conditions of the consultation with democratic parties and social organizations." For establishment of the Joint Commission, see 45/xii/27/(3).
Sources: *DAFR*, 8, pp. 837–38.
DSB, 16, 1947, p. 173.

● 46/iv/23/US

Exchange of notes between the USSR and the United States of America concerning an increase in the circulation of *Amerika* in the USSR

In answer to 3 notes and an oral request from the United States in 1946, the USSR in a note of Apr. 23, 1946, stated that the distributing agency in the USSR could "undertake the distribution of 50,000

copies of *Amerika,* starting June 1, 1946."
In a note of June 20, 1950, the USSR
denied that any agreement existed to dis-
tribute 50,000 copies. On July 15, 1952,
the United States in a note to the USSR,
stated that publication of *Amerika* was
being suspended immediately because of
progressive restriction by the Soviet Government on its distribution and sale in the
USSR, and requested the USSR to suspend immediately the publication and distribution in the United States of the USSR
Information bulletin (DSB, 27, 1952, p.
127).
Reference: *DSB,* 27, 1952, p. 128.

● 46/iv/24/Fin

**Joint communiqué concerning negotia-
tions between the USSR and Finland**

Issued at the end of negotiations held from
Apr. 17 to 24, 1946, in Moscow.
Provisions: (1) The USSR agrees to
waive further compensation for property
removed by Finland from the USSR; (2)
the USSR to sell Finland 100,000 tons
of grain and supply Finland with fertilizers; (3) Finland to lease to the USSR
a power station for the Petsamo nickel
mines (for an agreement carrying out
this provision, see 46/iv/30/Fin/b); and
(4) the USSR agrees to consider the improvement of Finland's transportation system.
Reference: *SIA, RE,* p.·282, citing
   Soviet news, Apr. 26, 1946, and
   London *Times,* Apr. 26, 1946.

● 46/iv/26/Mul

**Order amending the Charter of the In-
ternational Military Tribunal for the Far
East**

Promulgated Apr. 26, 1946, in Tokyo, by
General Headquarters, Supreme Commander for the Allied Powers.
Modifies the constitution of the Tribunal,
the procedure for trial, and provisions for
power of the Tribunal and conduct of
the trial. For the charter, see 46/i/19/
Mul/b.
Source: *DSB,* 14, 1946, pp. 890, 907.

● 46/iv/26/Yug

**Agreement between the USSR and Yugo-
slavia concerning delivery of grain and
pulse to Yugoslavia**

Signed Apr. 26, 1946, in Belgrade.
Entered into force on signature. Provides
for Soviet deliveries of 60,000 tons of
wheat and 5,000 tons of peas and beans
not later than July 15, 1946, to be repaid
by Yugoslav deliveries of 65,000 tons of
corn not later than Sept. 1, 1946, and
other goods before the end of 1946. Registered with the UN by Yugoslavia Nov.
27, 1951.
Source: *UNTS,* 116, pp. 161–69 (R, SC,
   E, F).

● 46/iv/27/Bul/a

**Trade agreement for 1946 between the
USSR and Bulgaria**

Signed Apr. 27, 1946, in Moscow.
References: *Izv.,* Apr. 28, 1946.
   VT, 1946, No. 4–5, p. 41.
   VPSS, 1946, p. 121.

● 46/iv/27/Bul/b

**Protocol between the USSR and Bulgaria
concerning completion of Soviet deliveries under the trade agreement of March
14, 1945**

Signed during Apr. 1946, probably in the
course of negotiations for the 1946 trade
agreement (preceding document).
Provides for delivery of 13,250 tons of oil
products, 22,650 tons of ferrous metals,
250 tons of light metals, 9,903 tons of
chemicals, 22,000 tons of fertilizer, 12,400
tons of cellulose paper, and an electric-
power station of 12,000 watts.
Reference: *DSB,* 15, 1946, p. 392.

● 46/iv/30/Fin/a

**Trade agreement for 1946 between the
USSR and Finland**

Signed Apr. 30, 1946, in Moscow.
References: *Pr.,* May 3, 1946; *Izv.,* May
   4, 1946.
   VT, 1946, No. 4–5, p. 41.
   VPSS, 1946, p. 122.
   Korolenko, p. 88.

● 46/iv/30/Fin/b

**Agreement between the USSR and Fin-
land concerning lease to the Soviet combine Pechenga-Nikel' of a concession for
a power station on the Patso-Yoki, with
protocol**

Signed Apr. 30, 1946, in Moscow.

Superseded by a protocol of Feb. 3, 1947 (47/ii/3/Fin/d).

References: *Pr.*, May 3, 1946; *Izv.*, May 4, 1946.
VT, 1946, No. 4–5, p. 41.
SIA, RE, p. 282.

May 4, 1946. (1) Hungarian decree promulgating the statute of a Soviet-Hungarian civil aviation company

See 46/iii/29/H/a.

(2) Hungarian decree promulgating the statute of a Soviet-Hungarian navigation company

See 46/iii/29/H/b.

● 46/v/11/Belgium

Exchange of notes between the USSR and Belgium concerning execution of judicial instructions

Sent Nov. 27, 1945, Apr. 18, May 3, and May 11, 1946.
Source: *SDD*, 12, pp. 78–79.

● 46/v/16/Pl

Second meeting of the Council of Foreign Ministers (first half)

Held Apr. 25 through May 16, 1946, in Paris, by the Foreign Ministers of the USSR, the United Kingdom, the United States of America, and France.
Agreements were reached on the following subjects: (1) Delegations of all 4 Powers to participate in discussion of the peace treaties with Italy, Romania, Bulgaria, Hungary, and Finland. (2) The Italian Navy to be limited and "surplus naval units" to be disposed of. (3) Minor changes to be made in the French-Italian boundary. (4) A committee to be appointed to study a proposed change in the French-Italian boundary in the Tenda-Briga area. (5) The armistice agreement with Italy (43/ix/29/Italy) to be revised and the Control Commission for Italy to be abolished (for establishment of the Commission, Nov. 10, 1943, see 44/i/ / Pl).
The Council discussed, but did not reach agreement on, the following topics among others: (1) reparations from Italy; (2) the form of trusteeship for former Italian colonies in Africa; (3) the Italy-Yugoslavia boundary; (4) freedom of navigation on the Danube; (5) a peace treaty for Austria; (6) a peace treaty with Germany.
On May 16, 1946, the Council recessed, to reassemble on June 15, 1946 (for the second half of the meeting, see 46/vii/12/ Pl).

References: Byrnes, pp. 124–29.
SIA, ABR, p. 719.

● 46/v/24/US

Agreement between the USSR and the United States of America concerning organization of commercial radio teletype communication channels

Signed May 24, 1946, in Moscow.
Entered into force on signature. Valid until 6 months after denunciation.
Sources: *SDD*, 12, pp. 134–37.
TIAS, 1527, 1946.
UNTS, 4, pp. 201–13 (R, E, F).

● 46/v/27/Pol

Joint communiqué concerning negotiations between the USSR and Poland

Published May 27, 1946, at the end of negotiations which began May 23, 1946, in Moscow.
Covers agreements on the following points: (1) annulment of all financial obligations incurred during the war for armament and maintenance of the Polish Army, including obligations of the former Polish Government-in-Exile, and of obligations resulting from deliveries by the Polish Government for the Red Army; (2) provision by the USSR of armaments and ammunition for the Polish Army on long-term credits; (3) provision by the USSR of a credit to Poland based on Soviet gold reserves, to enable Poland to meet its most pressing needs; (4) the USSR to speed up deliveries of supplies to Poland under previously concluded agreements. Mentions discussion of trade; exchange of cultural treasures; repatriation of Polish citizens from the USSR and of Russian, Ukrainian, Belorussian, and Lithuanian citizens from Poland; questions concerning Germany; and "other questions of interest to both Governments."
Sources: *Pr.*, May 27, 1946; *Izv.*, May 28, 1946.
VT, 1946, No. 6–7, pp. 1–2.

● 46/vi/5/Argentina

Exchange of notes between the USSR

and Argentina concerning establishment of diplomatic, consular, and commercial relations

Sent June 5, 1946, in Buenos Aires; announced in a joint communiqué of June 6, 1946.

References: *SDD*, 12, p. 13.

Izv., June 7, 1946 (joint communiqué).

VT, 1946, No. 6–7, p. 32 (same).

● 46/vi/8/Yug/a

Joint communiqué concerning negotiations between the USSR and Yugoslavia

Prepared on or about June 8, 1946, in Moscow; published June 11, 1946.

Refers to "full agreement on all questions concerning economic collaboration, trade, material supply to the Yugoslav Army, and close cultural and political collaboration." The USSR to supply the Yugoslav Army with armaments, ammunition, etc., on long-term credit, and to assist Yugoslavia in the re-establishment of its armament industry. Mentions the trade agreement signed during the negotiations (see 46/vi/8/Yug/a), and adds that "decisions were taken in regard to close economic collaboration" between the two governments (see 46/vi/8/Yug/c).

Sources: *Izv.*, June 11, 1946; *Pr.*, June 12, 1946.

VT, 1946, No. 6–7, p. 3.

● 46/vi/8/Yug/b

Trade agreement between the USSR and Yugoslavia

Signed during negotiations in Moscow which ended June 8, 1946.

Provides for Soviet deliveries of raw materials and technical and other goods.

Reference: Mentioned in the joint communiqué of June 8, 1946.

● 46/vi/8/Yug/c

Agreement between the USSR and Yugoslavia concerning economic collaboration

Signed June 8, 1946, in Moscow.

Mentioned in the agreements of Feb. 4, 1947, concerning establishment of the Soviet-Yugoslav joint-stock Danube steamship company "Juspad" and the civil aviation company "Justa" (47/ii/4/Yug/a and /b).

June 8, 1946. Press report concerning release of Bulgaria from obligation to repay 50,000 tons of wheat borrowed in 1945

See 45/xii/15/Bul.

● 46/vi/13/Af/a

Agreement between the USSR and Afghanistan concerning demarcation of the Soviet-Afghanistan border, with protocol

Signed June 13, 1946, in Moscow.

Ratified by Afghanistan Sept. 16, 1946; by the USSR Nov. 28, 1946. Entered into force Jan. 12, 1947, on exchange of acts of ratification in Kabul.

Provides for establishment of a mixed commission to map the border; work to begin within 3 months from date of entry into force of the agreement. Protocols of the commission to be ratified. (For work of the commission, see *Izv.*, Apr. 26, 1947; for a protocol signed on completion of its work, see 48/ix/29/Af.)

Protocol provides that Arts. 9 and 10 of the treaty of friendship of Feb. 28, 1921, have expired. Supplemented by 2 exchanges of notes (next 2 items).

Sources (including the exchanges of notes):

VVS, 1947, No. 6.

VPSS, 1946, pp. 141–46.

SDD, 13, pp. 262–66.

BFSP, 146, pp. 564–66, citing *al-Islah*, Sept. 19, 1946.

UNTS, 31, pp. 147–67 (R, Persian, E, F).

Reference: *Pr.*, June 14, 1946.

● 46/vi/13/Af/b

Exchange of notes between the USSR and Afghanistan concerning demarcation of a sector of the Soviet-Afghanistan border

Sent June 13, 1946, in Moscow.

Supplements the border agreement of the same date (preceding document). Provides for establishment of a mixed commission to redefine a sector of the border on the basis of the documents and maps of the Anglo-Russian Demarcation Commission of 1885–1888.

Sources: See those listed for 46/vi/13/Af/a.

● 46/vi/13/Af/c

Exchange of notes between the USSR

and Afghanistan concerning use of water
from the Kushka River

Sent June 13, 1946, in Moscow.
Supplements the border agreement of the
same date.
Sources: See those listed for 46/vi/13/
   Af/a.

• 46/vi/19/France

**Treaty between the USSR and France
concerning establishment of postal and
telephone-telegraph communications,
with final protocol**

Signed June 19, 1946, in Moscow.
Entered into force July 1, 1946. Valid
until 6 months after denunciation. Protocol concerns technical details of communications.
Source: SDD, 12, pp. 156–67.

• 46/vi/28/Pl

**Agreement concerning machinery of con-
trol in Austria, with annex**

Signed June 28, 1946, in Vienna, by the
USSR, the United Kingdom, the United
States of America, and France. Released
to the press July 19, 1946.
Entered into force on signature. Valid
until revised or abrogated by agreement
between the signatories. Defines the
authority of the Austrian Government and
the composition and powers of the Allied
Commission for Austria. Replaces the
agreement of July 4, 1945. Abrogated by
Art. 20 of the State Treaty with Austria
of May 15, 1955, with effect from entry
into force of that treaty (July 27, 1955).
Annex provides a list of the divisions of
the Allied Commission.
Sources: DSB, 15, 1946, pp. 175–78.
   TIAS, 2097, 1951.
   BFSP, 146, pp. 504–11, citing
      BTS, 1946, No. 49, Cmd. 6958.
   UNTS, 138, pp. 85–109 (R, E, F).
   Hudson, 9, pp. 567–76.
Reference: SIA, FPC GA, pp. 324–31.

• 46/vii/8/Denmark/a

**Commercial agreement between the
USSR and Denmark**

Signed July 8, 1946, in Moscow.
Entered into force on signature. Duration 2 years. If not denounced 1 month
before expiration, extended for 1-year pe-

riods. Extended to July 8, 1950, by protocol of July 8, 1948 (48/vii/8/Denmark/
a), and thereafter for 1-year periods until
denounced 1 month before expiration.
Quantities and types of merchandise exchanged under this agreement were defined in protocols, the first of which was
concluded on the same day (next document). A second protocol was signed
July 8, 1948 (48/vii/8/Denmark/b), covering trade through Dec. 31, 1949; thereafter, none was signed until July 17, 1953,
covering trade through June 30, 1954;
during the period 1950 through the first
half of 1953, trade was carried on without protocols (Korolenko, pp. 84–85).
Sources: VT, 1946, No. 12, pp. 7–9.
   *Lovtidende C, Danmarks Traktater,
      1946, p. 259.
References: VT, 1946, No. 6–7, p. 33.
   Izv., July 10, 1946.

• 46/vii/8/Denmark/b

**Trade protocol between the USSR and
Denmark**

Signed July 8, 1946, in Moscow.
Covers trade during the period July 1,
1946, through Dec. 31, 1947. Danish but-
ter and meat in return for Soviet raw ma-
terials and industrial commodities.
References: Izv., July 10, 1946.
   VT, 1946, No. 6–7, p. 33.
   Korolenko, p. 84.

• 46/vii/9/UK

**Exchange of notes between the USSR
and the United Kingdom modifying the
agreement of September 23, 1944, concerning establishment of direct radio-
telephone service between the two countries**

Sent Apr. 19 and July 9, 1946.
The modified agreement was put into force
under a further exchange of notes of July
24, Aug. 17, and Sept. 7, 1946 (see 46/
ix/7/UK), with effect from Aug. 25, 1946.
Source: SDD, 12, pp. 108–109.
Reference: SDD, 11, p. 177 (summary).

• 46/vii/10/Cz

**Agreement between the USSR and Czech-
oslovakia concerning choice of citizenship and resettlement**

Signed July 10, 1946, in Moscow.
Provisions: Soviet citizens of Czech or

Slovak nationality residing in the former Volynskaia *guberniia*, and Czech citizens of Russian, Ukrainian, and Belorussian nationality residing in Czechoslovakia, are given the right to petition for choice of citizenship, to be submitted not later than Sept. 15, 1946. Repatriation to be concluded not later than Nov. 15, 1946. A mixed Soviet-Czech commission to be established in Moscow to carry out provisions.

By a subsequent agreement (46/x/25/Cz), the deadline for petitions was extended to Nov. 15, 1946, and for resettlement to Mar. 15, 1947.

References: *Izv.*, July 11, 1946.
VT, 1946, No. 6–7, p. 34.

● 46/vii/12/Pl

Second meeting of the Council of Foreign Ministers (second half)

Held June 15 through July 12, 1946, in Paris, by the Foreign Ministers of the USSR, the United Kingdom, the United States of America, and France.

Agreements were reached on the following subjects: (1) Trieste to be made a Free Territory under the United Nations. (2) The Italy-Yugoslavia boundary proposed by France to be accepted. (3) The Dodecanese Islands to be ceded to Greece and demilitarized. (4) The question of disposition of former Italian colonies in Africa to be postponed until 1 year after signature of the peace treaty with Italy, and the colonies meanwhile to be left under British military administration. (5) Italy to pay the USSR $100 million over 7 years in reparations, to come from specialized armament machinery, Italian-owned assets in the satellite states, and current production. (6) A general conference to consider the draft peace treaties with Finland, Romania, Bulgaria, Hungary, and Italy, which the Council had prepared, to be held in Paris starting July 29, 1946. For the peace conference, see 46/x/15/Mul.

References: Byrnes, pp. 131–37.
SIA, ABR, pp. 719–20.
DSB, 15, 1946, pp. 167–72.
DSES, 24, pp. 27–29.

● 46/vii/16/Austria

Communication from the USSR to Aus-

tria concerning Soviet claims on German assets in Austria

Sent July 16, 1946, in reply to an oral request on July 15, 1946.
For background, see *DAFR*, 8, p. 286.
Source: *DAFR*, 8, pp. 287–88, citing *NYT*, July 21, 1946.

● 46/vii/22/Mul/a

Final Act of the International Health Conference for establishment of an international health organization

Signed July 22, 1946, in New York. Signed by the USSR subject to ratification and by the Belorussian and Ukrainian SSR's without reservation.

The conference, convened by the Economic and Social Council of the United Nations under a resolution of Feb. 15, 1946, met in New York from June 19 to July 22, 1946.

For documents drawn up at the conference, see the next 3 items.
Sources: *DSCS*, 91, pp. 35–42.
UNTS, 9, pp. 3–32 (R, E, F, C, S).

● 46/vii/22/Mul/b

Constitution of the World Health Organization

Signed July 22, 1946, in New York. The USSR and Belorussian and Ukrainian SSR's signed, subject to ratification.

Acts of acceptance deposited by the USSR Mar. 24, 1948; by the Ukrainian SSR Apr. 3, 1948; and by the Belorussian SSR Apr. 7, 1948. Entered into force Apr. 7, 1948.

On July 24, 1948, the First World Health Assembly adopted World Health Organization Regulations No. 1, concerning nomenclature (including the compilation and publication of statistics), with respect to diseases and causes of death. The regulations entered into force Jan. 1, 1950, for 52 states, including the USSR and the Belorussian and Ukrainian SSR's (*UST*, 7, pp. 79–84, 125–26; *TIAS* 3482). Supplementary regulations were adopted at the Second World Health Assembly on June 30, 1949, which entered into force Oct. 24, 1949; the USSR and Belorussian and Ukrainian SSR's signed (*UST*, 7, pp. 85–86, 127–28).

On Feb. 16, 1949, the USSR and Ukrainian and Belorussian SSR's withdrew from the WHO, criticizing its expenditures on control of disease and dissemination of medical knowledge; a TASS dispatch of Feb. 19 charged that the staff of the organization had too many British and United States members. WHO officials, meanwhile, reported that the USSR had not paid its assessments for 1948 and 1949. On July 8, 1955, at the 20th session of UNESCO, the Soviet delegate announced that the USSR would rejoin; it did so on Jan. 27, 1956.

Sources: Durdenevski and Krylov, pp. 299–317.
BFSP, 148, pp. 145–65, citing
BTS, 1948, No. 43, Cmd. 7458.
DSCS, 91, pp. 43–67.
TIAS, 1808 (1949).
UNTS, 14, pp. 185–267 (R, E, F, C, S).
DSB, 15, 1946, pp. 211–19.

• 46/vii/22/Mul/c

Arrangement establishing an Interim Commission of the World Health Organization

Signed July 22, 1946, in New York; the USSR and Belorussian and Ukrainian SSR's signed.
Entered into force on signature. The Interim Commission established under this agreement held its first meeting during the International Health Conference, on July 19, 20, and 23, 1946, electing the Soviet representative, Dr. F. G. Krotkov, as temporary chairman (DSCS, 91, pp. 30–31).

Sources: BFSP, 148, pp. 165–71, citing
BTS, 1948, No. 43, Cmd. 7458.
TIAS, 1561 (1947).
DSCS, 91, pp. 68–77.
UNTS, 9, pp. 33–65 (R, E, F, C, S).

• 46/vii/22/Mul/d

Protocol concerning the Office Internationale d'Hygiène Publique, with annex

Signed July 22, 1946, in New York; the USSR and Belorussian and Ukrainian SSR's signed.
Entered into force Oct. 20, 1947. Provides for transfer of the duties and functions of the Office Internationale d'Hygiène Publique, as between signatories, to the World Health Organization or its Interim Commission; the agreement of Dec. 9, 1907, which defined the duties and functions of the Office to be terminated and the Office dissolved when all signatories

of the agreement have agreed to its termination (Russia was a signatory).
Annex lists 15 international conventions and agreements conferring duties and functions on the Office Internationale d'Hygiène Publique which are modified by this protocol. Of these the USSR had adhered to the following: (1) International sanitary convention of June 21, 1926 (26/vi/21/Mul); (2) International Opium Convention of Feb. 19, 1925 (35/x/31/1925/a); (3) Convention for limiting the manufacture and regulating the distribution of narcotic drugs of July 13, 1931 (35/x/31/1931/a); (4) Convention concerning anti-diphtheria serum of Aug. 1, 1930 (30/viii/1/Mul); (5) International convention for protection against dengue fever of July 25, 1934 (34/vii/25/Mul); (6) Agreement for dispensing with bills of health of Dec. 22, 1934 (34/xii/22/Mul/a); and (7) Agreement for dispensing with consular visas on bills of health of Dec. 22, 1934 (34/xii/22/Mul/b).

Sources: BFSP, 148, pp. 171–75, citing
BTS, 1948, No. 43, Cmd. 7458.
TIAS, 1754.
UNTS, 9, pp. 66–89 (R, E, F, C, S).
DSCS, 91, pp. 78–85.

July 23, 1946. Hungarian decree promulgating the statutes of the Soviet-Hungarian crude oil company "Maszovol"

See 46/iv/8/H/a.

• 46/vii/25/Cz/a

Agreement between the USSR and Czechoslovakia concerning establishment of air services, with protocol

Signed July 25, 1946, in Moscow.
Entered into force on signature. Duration 5 years; thereafter automatically renewed for 5-year periods until denunciation 6 months before expiration. Provisions include the right of Czechoslovak aircraft with Czechoslovak crews to fly over the Soviet Zone of Occupation of Germany. Protocol specifies the routes to be flown.

Source: UNTS, 27, pp. 232–49 (R, Cz., E, F).

• 46/vii/25/Cz/b. See Appendix 5.

July 25, 1946. Hungarian decrees promulgating the statutes of (1) the Soviet-Hungarian crude oil company "Molaj"

See 46/iv/8/H/a.

(2) the Soviet-Hungarian bauxite-aluminum company "Danube Valley Aluminum Industry"

See 46/iv/8/H/b.

Aug. 6, 1946. Hungarian decree promulgating the statutes of the Soviet-Hungarian bauxite-aluminum company "Magyar Bauxitbanya"

See 46/iv/8/H/b.

● 46/viii/8/Denmark

Agreement between the USSR and Denmark concerning establishment of telegraph communications, with annex

Signed Aug. 8, 1946, in Moscow.
Entered into force on signature. Duration 10 years, although either party may withdraw before that time with 1 year's notice. Art. 19 provides that at the end of 10 years the agreement may be extended; according to a note in *SDD*, 12 (1956), p. 119, the agreement was so extended, for an additional 10 years; date of agreement to extend not indicated. Annex lists rates for certain telegraph routes.
Source: *SDD*, 12, pp. 110–20.

Aug. 9, 1946. Treaty of friendship, commerce and navigation between the USSR and Uruguay

See Appendix 1.

● 46/viii/17/Denmark/a

Treaty of commerce and navigation between the USSR and Denmark, with annex concerning the Soviet Trade Mission in Denmark

Signed Aug. 17, 1946, in Moscow.
Ratified by Denmark Nov. 5, 1946; by the USSR Dec. 1, 1946. Entered into force Dec. 31, 1946, on exchange of acts of ratification in Copenhagen. Duration 5 years; if not denounced 6 months before expiration, extended for 1-year periods. Supersedes the preliminary agreement of Apr. 23, 1923; the exchange of notes constituting an agreement on commerce and navigation of June 18, 1924 (24/vi/18/Denmark/b); and the exchange of notes of 1924, 1925, and 1929 concerning reciprocal recognition of tonnage measurement certificates (25/vi/29/Denmark and 29/i/24/Denmark). Listed in Korolenko, p.

104, as still valid as of Nov. 25, 1953. Supplemented by a protocol on arbitration (next item).
Sources: *VVS*, 1947, No. 11.
　VT, 1946, No. 12, pp. 1–7.
　SDD, 12, pp. 87–95.
　Korolenko, pp. 265–70.
　VPSS, 1946, pp. 171–81.
　*Lovtidende C, Danmarks Traktater, 1946, p. 307.
　UNTS, 8, pp. 201–33 (R, D, E, F).
　BFSP, 146, pp. 717–23.

● 46/viii/17/Denmark/b

Protocol between the USSR and Denmark concerning temporary principles of arbitration

Signed Aug. 17, 1946, in Moscow.
Entered into force Dec. 31, 1946, together with the treaty of commerce and navigation of the same date. Duration 1 year, but may be extended if at the end of that time the agreement on arbitration called for in Art. 14 of the treaty of commerce and navigation has not been concluded. Extended by protocol of July 8, 1948 (48/vii/8/Denmark/a); listed in Korolenko, p. 85, as still valid as of Nov. 25, 1953.
Source: *SDD*, 12, pp. 95–96.

● 46/viii/19/Fin/a

Agreement between the USSR and Finland concerning telegraph and telephone communications

Signed Aug. 19, 1946, in Moscow.
Entered into force on signature. Valid until 1 year after denunciation. Changes in tariff rates were made by a supplementary protocol of June 17, 1955 (55/vi/17/Fin/a), which was made an integral part of this agreement.
Sources: *SDD*, 12, pp. 137–44.
　*SS, 1946, No. 14 (R, Finnish).

● 46/viii/19/Fin/b

Agreement between the USSR and Finland concerning postal exchange

Signed Aug. 19, 1946, in Moscow.
Entered into force on signature. Valid until 1 year after denunciation. Modified by a supplementary protocol of June 17, 1955 (55/vi/17/Fin/b), which was made an integral part of this agreement, and by an exchange of notes of June 1 and Aug. 26, 1953 (53/viii/26/Fin).

Sources: *SDD*, 12, pp. 144–56.
    *SS, 1946, No. 15 (R, Finnish).

• 46/viii/19/US

Exchange of notes between the USSR and the United States of America concerning revision of the regime of the Black Sea Straits established by the Montreux Convention of July 20, 1936

Sent Aug. 7 and 19, 1946, in Washington, D.C. The Soviet note incorporates a note of the same date to Turkey setting forth the substance of the Soviet proposals.
In its reply the United States reaffirms its willingness to participate in a conference to revise the Montreux Convention, and expresses its general agreement with a number of the Soviet proposals, but rejects the Soviet proposals that (1) a new regime for the Straits should be established which would be confined to Turkey and other Black Sea Powers, and (2) Turkey and the USSR should organize joint means of defense of the Straits.
Sources: *DSB*, 15, 1946, pp. 420–22.
    Hurewitz, 2, pp. 268–71.

• 46/viii/30/Mul

Protocol extending the agreement of May 6, 1937, concerning regulation of the production and marketing of sugar

Signed Aug. 30, 1946, in London.
Extends the 1937 agreement through Aug. 31, 1947. The agreement was further extended by protocols of Aug. 29, 1947, and Aug. 31, 1948, but the USSR evidently did not sign these.
Sources: *BFSP*, 146, pp. 511–513, citing *BTS*, 1946, No. 45, Cmd. 6949.
    TIAS, 1614 (1947).

• 46/ix/7/UK

Exchange of notes between the USSR and the United Kingdom concerning entry into force of the agreement of September 23, 1944, concerning establishment of direct radio-telephone service, as modified by an exchange of notes of April 19 and July 9, 1946

Sent July 24, Aug. 17, and Sept. 7, 1946, in Moscow.
Fixes Aug. 25, 1946, as the date on which the amended agreement will be considered in force. For the earlier exchange of notes, see 46/vii/9/UK.
Source: *SDD*, 12, p. 110.

Reference: *SDD*, 11, p. 177.

• 46/ix/25/Pl. See Appendix 5.

Oct. 2, 1946. Final Articles Revision Convention, 1946, of the International Labour Organisation
See 54/iv/26/1946.

• 46/x/7/Sweden/a

Protocol between the USSR and Sweden modifying and extending the trade and payments agreement of September 7, 1940, with two lists

Signed Oct. 7, 1946, in Moscow.
Entered into force Dec. 10, 1946, under an exchange of notes in Stockholm. Extends the 1940 agreement by 5 years, and thereafter for successive 1-year periods, until denounced with 6 months' notice. Lists specify types and quantities of materials to be traded by each party, to a value of 1 million Swedish crowns each, from date of entry into force until Dec. 31, 1947. Supersedes the trade lists established under the trade agreement of Sept. 7, 1940.
Sources: *VT*, 1946, No. 10–11, pp. 25–26 (omits the lists).
    Sö, 1946, No. 23, pp. 272–79 (R, Sw.).

• 46/x/7/Sweden/b

Credit agreement between the USSR and Sweden, with annex, list, and protocol

Signed Oct. 7, 1946, in Moscow.
Ratified by Sweden Nov. 15, 1946; by the USSR Nov. 26, 1946. Entered into force Dec. 10, 1946, on exchange of acts of ratification in Stockholm.
Provides for a Swedish credit to the USSR of 1 billion Swedish crowns, to be used within 5 years in approximately equal annual instalments, and repaid within 15 years, nominally at 3 per cent, actually at approximately 2⅜ per cent. Credit to be used for Soviet purchases in Sweden of industrial machinery and equipment. Annex provides a sample form for Soviet orders. List specifies types and quantities of equipment to be purchased. Protocol provides that unused credits remaining under the credit agreement of Sept. 7, 1940 (40/ix/7/Sweden/d), should be applied to the new credit, and that on entry into force of the protocol, the credit agreement of Sept. 7, 1940, together with its protocol, will cease to be valid.
Sources: *VVS*, Feb. 5, 1947, No. 5.

VT, 1946, No. 10–11, pp. 19–24.
VPSS, 1946, pp. 203–13.
Sö, 1946, No. 24, pp. 281–93 (R, Sw.).

● 46/x/7/Sweden/c

Exchange of notes between the USSR and Sweden concerning an increase in trade

Sent Oct. 7, 1946, in Moscow.
Calls for increase in trade over the volume established under the lists annexed to the protocol of the same date (46/x/7/Sweden/a).
Sources: *VT*, 1946, No. 10–11, p. 27.
Sö, 1946, No. 23, p. 280 (R, Sw.).

● 46/x/7/Sweden/d

Exchange of notes between the USSR and Sweden concerning prices for goods purchased in Sweden by the USSR

Sent Oct. 7, 1946, in Moscow.
Provides that Sweden shall take measures to ensure that prices charged the USSR for equipment purchased in Sweden do not exceed those charged other countries for analogous goods at the time the Soviet orders were placed.
Sources: *VT*, 1946, No. 10–11, pp. 24–25.
Sö, 1946, No. 24, p. 294 (R, Sw.).

● 46/x/7/Sweden/e

Informal agreement between the USSR and Sweden concerning settlement of certain property claims arising out of the war

Negotiated during trade conversations in Moscow which ended Oct. 7, 1946.
Reference: Mentioned in the TASS dispatch concerning the conversations: *Izv.*, Oct. 9, 1946.

Oct. 9, 1946. (1) Charter of the International Labour Organisation, as amended at Montreal
See 54/iv/26/1946.

(2) International Labour Organisation Conventions Nos. 77, 78, and 79
See 56/vii/6/1946/a, /b, and /c.

● 46/x/15/Mul

Conference to consider the draft peace treaties with Finland, Romania, Hungary, Bulgaria, and Italy

Held July 29 to Oct. 15, 1946, in Paris, under the sponsorship of the USSR, the United Kingdom, the United States, and France, by representatives of the following States: the USSR, the United Kingdom, the United States, France, China, Australia, Belgium, the Belorussian SSR, Brazil, Canada, Czechoslovakia, Ethiopia, Greece, India, The Netherlands, Norway, New Zealand, Poland, the Ukrainian SSR, the Union of South Africa, and Yugoslavia.
To carry out its tasks, the Conference established a number of committees, including a General Commission (which never met), a Military Commission, and a Legal and Drafting Commission, on each of which were represented all 21 nations represented at the Conference; five Political and Territorial Commissions for each of the 5 States with which a peace treaty was to be concluded; and two Economic Commissions, one for Italy, the other for the 3 Balkan States and Finland. The USSR, the Belorussian SSR, and the Ukrainian SSR were represented on all the political and economic commissions. The Conference adopted recommendations for consideration of the Council of Foreign Ministers on the following substantive matters: (1) The boundary of Trieste and the Italy-Yugoslavia boundary to be those agreed upon by the Council of Foreign Ministers; (2) general principles for administration of the Free Territory of Trieste; (3) territorial adjustments provided for in the draft peace treaties with Romania and Finland to be accepted; (4) Italy to pay $325 million reparations to the USSR, Yugoslavia, Greece, and Ethiopia; (5) Romania to pay $300 million reparations to the USSR; (6) Bulgaria to pay $125 million reparations to Yugoslavia and Greece; (7) Hungary to pay $300 million reparations, of which $200 million to be paid to the USSR; (8) Finland to pay $300 million reparations to the USSR; (9) claims against the defeated nations arising out of the war to be compensated at 75%; (10) restitution or compensation to be made in the case of objects of artistic, historical, or archeological value removed during the war; (11) special provisions to be included in the Romanian and Hungarian treaties for restitution or compensation to people of Jewish faith or ancestry; (12) the Ambassadors or Ministers of the Council Powers to represent the Allies for 18 months in all matters concerning

execution and interpretation of the treaties; (13) procedures established for settling disputes arising out of execution of
the treaties on which the Council of Foreign Ministers had not reached agreement; (14) in regard to general commercial relations of the 5 defeated States,
(a) the principle of most-favored-nation
treatment to be applicable in branches
of economic activity in which state monopolies exist, and (b) nations bordering on the three Balkan States not to be
exempted from the commercial provisions
of the treaties with those States; (15) in
regard to international commercial aviation rights in the 5 defeated States, (a)
equality of opportunity and nondiscrimi-
natory treatment to be granted, and (b)
the first 2 "freedoms of the air" to be
granted on a reciprocal basis; (16) a
provision for re-establishment of freedom
of navigation on the Danube to be included in the treaties with the 3 Balkan
States; (17) a new international organization to be formed to safeguard freedom
of navigation on the Danube, to be established at an international conference to
be held within 6 months after the entry
into force of the treaties with the 3 Balkan States (for the conference, see 48/
viii/18/Pl).
The conference discussed, but did not
reach agreement on, the following subjects, among others: (1) Bulgarian claims
against Greece, and Greek claims against
Bulgaria; (2) a reduction in the figure
for Hungarian reparations; (3) a reduction in the figure for Finnish reparations;
(4) Italian reparations to Albania; and
(5) the economic situation in Hungary.
At the end of the conference, the Council
of Foreign Ministers decided to meet
next in New York, starting Nov. 4, 1946,
to consider recommendations of the conference and to begin discussion of a peace
treaty with Germany (see 46/xii/12/Pl).
References: An extensive selection of
documents prepared by the conference is given in DSCS, 103.
There are summaries in the following:
DSES, 24, pp. 36–51; SIA, RE, pp. 340–
42; Byrnes, pp. 138–49.

● 46/x/21/Pl. See Appendix 5.

● 46/x/25/Cz

Informal agreement between the USSR

**and Czechoslovakia modifying the agree-
ment of July 10, 1946, concerning choice
of citizenship and resettlement**

Announced Oct. 25, 1946.
Extends deadline for presentation of applications to Nov. 15, 1946, and for resettlement to Mar. 15, 1947.
Reference: Izv., Oct. 25, 1945.

● 46/x/25/Sweden/a

**Agreement between the USSR and Swe-
den concerning establishment of regular
air communications**

Signed Oct. 25, 1946, in Moscow.
Entered into force on signature. Duration 5 years; thereafter extended from
year to year, until denounced 6 months
before expiration. Provides for flights on
the line Moscow-Helsinki-Stockholm.
Agreement of Finland to use of Finnish air
facilities to be obtained. Supplemented
by a protocol and a technical agreement
(next 2 documents). Modified by protocol of Jan. 23, 1954 (54/i/23/Sweden);
superseded by agreement of Mar. 31,
1956 (56/iii/31/Sweden).
Sources: SDD, 12, pp. 189–92.
    Sö, 1946, No. 35, pp. 339–40 (R, Sw.).
References: Izv., Oct. 29, 1946 (gives
    date as Oct. 26, 1946).
    VT, 1946, No. 10–11, p. 38.

● 46/x/25/Sweden/b

**Protocol between the USSR and Sweden
concerning flights using air facilities in
Finland**

Signed Oct. 25, 1946, in Moscow.
Entered into force on signature. Duration the same as that of the agreement
of the same date concerning establishment
of regular air communications (preceding
document), which it supplements. Calls
for negotiations with Finland to obtain
permission for use of an airport near
Helsinki. The USSR undertakes to obtain
the assent of the Allied (Soviet) High
Command in Finland for such use.
Source: SDD, 12, 1956, p. 192.

Oct. 25, 1946

Technical agreement between the Main
Administration of Civil Aviation under the
Council of Ministers of the USSR and the
Swedish corporation "Aerotransport" con-
cerning servicing of the air line between
Moscow and Stockholm.

References: *Izv.*, Oct. 29, 1956.
   VT, 1946, No. 10–11, p. 38.

● 46/x/31/Pl

Preliminary telecommunication conference

Held Sept. 28 to Oct. 31, 1946, in Moscow, by the USSR, the United Kingdom, the United States of America, France, and China.
Agreements were reached on the following subjects: (1) Next World Telecommunications Conference to convene July 1, 1947, to revise the Telecommunications Convention of Madrid (see 32/xii/9/Mul/a). (2) The International Telecommunications Union to be reorganized to include an Administrative Council, a Secretariat, and a Central Frequency Registration Board. (3) A World High-Frequency Broadcasting Conference to be called in the autumn of 1947 to assign frequencies to short wave stations throughout the world and to establish a new World High-Frequency Broadcasting Organization.
References: *DSB*, 15, 1946, pp. 943–46 (report by United States representative).
   DAFR, 8, pp. 694–96.

● 46/xi/5/Sweden

Parcel post agreement between the USSR and Sweden

Signed Nov. 5, 1946, in Moscow.
Entered into force on signature. Duration indefinite, but may be denounced with 6 months' notice. Modified by exchanges of notes of June 29 and Aug. 26, 1953 (53/viii/26/Sweden), and Nov. 24 and Dec. 4, 1954 (54/xii/4/Sweden).
Source: *SDD*, 12, pp. 179–88.
References: *Izv.*, Nov. 7, 1946.
   VT, 1946, No. 10–11, p. 38.

● 46/xi/25/1937

International agreement for the regulation of whaling

Signed June 8, 1937, in London. Soviet accession Nov. 25, 1946.
Original entry into force May 7, 1938. For the USSR, entered into force on accession. Originally valid until June 30, 1938; extended by declaration of the British Foreign Secretary dated June 29, 1938. Modified by protocol of June 24, 1938

(for Soviet accession, see next document). Further modified by protocol of Feb. 7, 1944, to which the USSR did not accede. Modified and extended to the 1946–1947 season by protocol of Nov. 26, 1945 (46/xi/25/1945), and to the 1947–1948 season by protocol of Dec. 2, 1946 (46/xii/2/Mul/d). Supplemented by the International Convention for the Regulation of Whaling of Dec. 2, 1946 (46/xii/2/Mul/a). Listed in *SDD*, 10 (1955), p. 238, as no longer valid.
Sources (text): *BTS*, 1938, No. 37, Cmd. 5757.
   LNTS, 190, pp. 79–91 (E, F).
   Hudson, 7, pp. 754–62, citing *USTS*, 933.
Reference (Soviet accession): *BTS*, 1946, No. 72, Cmd. 7016, p. 10.

● 46/xi/25/1938

Protocol amending the international agreement of June 8, 1937, for the regulation of whaling

Signed June 24, 1938, in London. Soviet accession Nov. 25, 1946.
Entered into force provisionally July 1, 1938; definitively, Dec. 30, 1938. For the USSR, entered into force on accession.
Sources (text): *BPP*, Misc. No. 6, 1938, Cmd. 5827.
   LNTS, 196, pp. 132–36 (E, F).
   Hudson, 7, pp. 762–65.
Reference (Soviet accession): *BTS*, 1946, No. 72, Cmd. 7016, p. 10.

● 46/xi/25/1945

Protocol for the regulation of whaling during the 1946–1947 season

Signed Nov. 26, 1945, in London. Soviet accession Nov. 25, 1946.
Modifies the international agreement of June 8, 1937 (46/xi/25/1937), as modified by the protocol of June 24, 1938 (46/xi/25/1938), and extends it to the 1946–1947 season. Entered into force Mar. 3, 1947, under a protocol of that date (47/iii/3/Mul). Extended for the 1947–1948 season by protocol of Dec. 2, 1946 (46/xii/2/Mul/d).
Sources (text): *BTS*, 1946, No. 70, Cmd. 7009.
   BFSP, 145, pp. 936–40.
   UNTS, 11, pp. 43–53 (E, F).
   Hudson, 9, pp. 114–17.

References (Soviet accession) : *BTS, loc. cit.*
UNTS, 11, p. 50.

● 46/xii/2/Mul/a

International convention for the regulation of whaling

Signed Dec. 2, 1946, in Washington, D.C. Ratified by the USSR July 15, 1948; act of ratification deposited Sept. 11, 1948. Entered into force Nov. 10, 1948. Supplemented by an annexed schedule (next document), and by a protocol of Nov. 19, 1956 (56/xi/19/Mul). Establishes an International Whaling Commission, with one member from each signatory.
Sources: *VVS*, 1949, No. 16.
 SDD, 13, pp. 370–77.
 BPP, Misc. No. 3, 1946, Cmd. 7043, pp. 16–20.
 BTS, 1949, No. 5, Cmd. 7604.
 UNTS, 161, pp. 72–89 (E, F).
 Hudson, 9, pp. 117–21, citing *TIAS*, No. 1849.

● 46/xii/2/Mul/b

Schedule annexed to the international convention for the regulation of whaling

Incorporated in the convention signed Dec. 2, 1946, in Washington, D.C.
Sets technical standards and limits for whaling. Modified at meetings of the International Whaling Commission in 1949 (see 49/vi/7/Mul), 1950 (50/vii/21/Mul), 1951 (51/vii/30/Mul), 1952 (52/vi/6/Mul), 1953 (53/vi/26/Mul), 1954 (54/vii/23/Mul) and 1955 (55/vii/23/Mul).
Sources: *BPP*, Misc. No. 3, 1947, Cmd. 7043, pp. 20–23.
 UNTS, 161, pp. 90–99 (E, F).
 Hudson, 9, pp. 121–24.

● 46/xii/2/Mul/c

Final Act of the International Whaling Conference, with annex and addendum

Signed Dec. 2, 1946, in Washington, D.C., at the conclusion of a conference held from Nov. 20 to Dec. 2, 1946.
Annex gives nomenclature of whales. Addendum concerns a proposal by The Netherlands dealing with the conservation and development of whale stocks.
Source: *BPP*, Misc. No. 3, 1947, Cmd. 7043, pp. 3–15.

● 46/xii/2/Mul/d

Protocol for the regulation of whaling during the 1947–1948 season

Signed Dec. 2, 1946, in Washington, D.C. Entered into force Feb. 5, 1948. Soviet acceptance notified Dec. 11, 1947. Extends the protocol of Nov. 26, 1945 (46/xi/25/1945).
Sources: *BPP*, Misc. No. 3, 1947, Cmd. 7043, p. 24.
 BFSP, 146, pp. 531–32.
 BTS, 1948, No. 14, Cmd. 7354.
 TIAS, No. 1708.
 UNTS, 161, pp. 361–63 (E, F).

● 46/xii/5/Fin/a

Trade and payments agreement between the USSR and Finland

Signed Dec. 5, 1946, in Moscow.
Entered into force on signature. Duration 2 years; if not denounced 3 months before expiration, extended for 1-year periods. Establishes a commission to supervise execution, to meet every 3 months alternately in Moscow and Helsinki. Types and quantities of commodities to be determined by supplementary protocols (for the first such protocol, see next document). Superseded by the trade agreement of June 13, 1950 (50/vi/13/Fin/a).
Sources: *VT*, 1947, No. 1, pp. 4–6.
 *SS, 1946, No. 1 (Finnish, R).
References: *Izv.*, Dec. 7, 1946.
 Korolenko, p. 88.

● 46/xii/5/Fin/b

Trade protocol for 1947 between the USSR and Finland, with annex

Signed Dec. 5, 1946, in Moscow.
Concluded on the basis of the trade and payments agreement of the same date (preceding document). Annex lists goods to be traded during 1947.
References: *Izv.*, Dec. 7, 1946.
 VT, 1946, No. 10–11, p. 28.
 Korolenko, p. 88.

● 46/xii/10/Sweden

Exchange of notes between the USSR and Sweden concerning entry into force of the trade protocol of Oct. 7, 1946

Sent Dec. 10, 1946, in Stockholm. For the protocol, see 46/x/7/Sweden/a.

References: *Izv.*, Dec. 11, 1946.
  VT, 1946, No. 10–11, p. 39.

● 46/xii/11/Mul

Protocol amending the agreements, conventions, and protocols on narcotic drugs concluded at The Hague on January 23, 1912; at Geneva on February 11, 1925, February 19, 1925, and July 13, 1931; at Bangkok on November 27, 1931; and at Geneva on June 26, 1936, with annex

Signed Dec. 11, 1946, at Lake Success, New York. The USSR and Ukrainian SSR signed subject to ratification, the Belorussian SSR without reservation.
Accepted by the USSR Oct. 25, 1947; by the Ukrainian SSR Jan. 8, 1948. Provides for transfer from the League of Nations to the United Nations and the World Health Organization or its Interim Commission of certain duties and functions in connection with control of narcotic drugs. Annex lists five international agreements modified by the protocol. Of these the USSR acceded to 2: (1) the International Opium Convention (Convention relating to dangerous drugs) of Feb. 19, 1925 (see 35/x/31/1925/a); and (2) the Convention for limiting the manufacture and regulating the distribution of narcotic drugs of July 13, 1931 (see 35/x/31/1931/a). It signed, but apparently did not ratify, the Convention for suppression of the illicit traffic in dangerous drugs of June 26, 1936: see Appendix 1.
Sources: *SDD*, 13, pp. 480–87.
  BFSP, 148, pp. 230–39, citing
    BTS, No. 35, 1947, Cmd. 7135.
  TIAS, 1671 (1948).
  UNTS, 12, pp. 179–239 (R, E, F, C, S).

Dec. 11, 1946. Financial regulations of the United Nations

See Note to 46/vi/26/Mul/a.

● 46/xii/12/Pl/a

Third meeting of the Council of Foreign Ministers

Held Nov. 4 through Dec. 12, 1946, in New York, by the Foreign Ministers of the USSR, the United Kingdom, the United States of America, and France.
Agreements were reached on the following subjects: (1) Trieste: More than 20 separate agreements were reached on principles for the permanent statute and provisional regime of the Free Territory of Trieste, including powers of the governors; reduction of occupation troops; provisions for elections; citizenship; and boundaries. Establishment of a 4-Power commission to investigate financial matters was agreed on, and of an international port commission, to include a Soviet representative. Statute to be included as an annex to the peace treaty with Italy. For a protocol on appointment of a governor for Trieste, see next item. For modification of the agreements on Trieste, see 54/x/12/Pl. (2) Procedure established for settling disputes arising out of the peace treaties. (3) Treaties with the 3 Balkan States to include a provision on freedom of navigation of the Danube. An international conference to establish a Danube navigation authority to be convoked within 6 months after signing the peace treaties. (4) Peace treaties to include provisions on commercial relations. (5) Peace treaties to provide for recognition of civil aviation rights. (6) Reparations: (a) Italy to pay $360 million over 7 years, of which $100 million to be paid to the USSR, the remainder to Yugoslavia, Greece, Ethiopia, and Albania. (b) Romania to pay $300 million over 8 years to the USSR. Procedure established for settling disputes over prices to be paid by Romania for goods acquired from Allied nationals and delivered as reparations. (c) Hungary to pay $300 million over 8 years, of which $200 million to be paid to the USSR, the remainder to Czechoslovakia and Yugoslavia. (d) Bulgaria to pay $70 million over 8 years to Greece and Yugoslavia. (e) Finland to pay $300 million over 8 years to the USSR. (7) Compensation at the rate of 66⅔ per cent to be paid to nationals of the United Nations for wartime damage to or destruction of their property in the 5 treaty States. (8) No change to be made in the Greece-Bulgaria boundary. The Bulgarian side of the boundary to be demilitarized. (9) Provisions of an Austria-Italy agreement on the South Tyrol of Sept. 5, 1946, to be included as an annex to the peace treaty with Italy. (10) The peace treaties with Italy, Romania, Hungary, Bulgaria, and Finland to be signed Feb. 10, 1947, in Paris. (11) The next meeting of the Council of Foreign Ministers (CFM) to take place in Moscow Mar. 10, 1947. (12) Agenda for the next meeting of the CFM

to include a report from the Allied Control Authority for Germany; establishment of a provisional government for Germany; drafting of a German peace treaty; disarmament and demilitarization of Germany; and the coal situation in Europe. (13) Special deputies of the Foreign Ministers to be appointed for preparation of draft treaties with Germany and Austria, to begin work in Jan. 1947.
References: *DSES*, 24, pp. 52–62.
  DSCS, 93.
  Byrnes, pp. 150–55.
  SIA, ABR, pp. 721–23, 729.

● 46/xii/12/Pl/b

Protocol concerning appointment of a governor for the Free Territory of Trieste

Signed Dec. 12, 1946, in New York, by the Foreign Ministers of the USSR, the United Kingdom, the United States of America, and France.
Provides that the 4 signatory Powers will endeavor to assure appointment of a governor by the date of entry into force of the peace treaty with Italy (i.e., Sept. 15, 1947). For agreements of the Council of Foreign Ministers on Trieste, see the preceding item, (1).
References: Quoted in notes sent Apr. 20, 1950, by the USSR to the United Kingdom, the United States, and France demanding changes in their policies towards Trieste. Text of the notes in *Izv.*, Apr. 21, 1950, and *VPSS, 1950*, pp. 143–50.

Dec. 14, 1946. United Nations regulations concerning registration and publication of treaties

See Note to 46/vi/26/Mul/a.

● 46/xii/19/J

Agreement concerning repatriation of Japanese prisoners of war and civilians from the USSR and from territories under Soviet control, as well as Korean nationals from Japan to Soviet-occupied North Korea, with two annexes

Signed Dec. 19, 1946, in Tokyo, by the Soviet representative on the Allied Control Council for Japan and the Headquarters of the Supreme Commander for the Allied Powers in Japan.
Included as an annex to notes addressed to the Secretary-General of the United Na-

tions from representatives of Australia, the United Kingdom, and the United States of America on Aug. 25, 1950, in support of an item to be placed on the provisional agenda of the Fifth Session of the General Assembly concerning "Failure of the USSR to repatriate or otherwise account for prisoners of war detained in Soviet territory." Annex 1 concerns procedure for harboring ships in Soviet ports and ports under Soviet control; Annex 2 concerns navigation communications.
Source: *DSB*, 23, 1950, pp. 431–33.
References: *Izv.*, May 20, 1949 (Soviet declaration claiming completion of repatriation except for those under trial as war criminals).
  VPSS, 1949, p 101.

● 46/xii/27/Norway/a

Trade and payments agreement between the USSR and Norway

Signed Dec. 27, 1946, in Moscow.
Entered into force on signature. Duration 2 years; if not denounced 3 months before expiration, extended for 1-year periods. Still valid as of Nov. 25, 1953 (Korolenko, p. 107).
Provides for conclusion of trade protocols stipulating quantity and value of goods to be delivered. Trade contracts to be concluded within the scope of these protocols. The first such protocol was signed at the same time (see next document); subsequent protocols were signed Jan. 6, 1948, and Jan. 10, 1949. From 1949 to 1953, trade was carried out on the basis of trade contracts between Eksportkhleb and the Norwegian state grain monopoly (Korolenko, p. 87); see entries under Feb. 15, 1949, May 7, 1952, and Apr. 29, 1953, Appendix 3.
Sources: *VT*, 1947, No. 2, pp. 2–4.
  UNTS, 17, pp. 283–301 (R, N, E, F).
References: *Izv.*, Dec. 31, 1946.
  VT, 1946, No. 12, p. 29.

● 46/xii/27/Norway/b

Trade protocol for 1947 between the USSR and Norway

Signed Dec. 27, 1946, in Moscow.
The USSR to supply industrial raw materials and other goods. Concluded on the basis of the trade and payments agreement of the same date (preceding document).

References: *Izv.*, Dec. 31, 1946.
VT, 1946, No. 12, p. 29.

● 46/xii/31/Thailand
Exchange of notes between the USSR

and Thailand concerning re-establishment of diplomatic relations

Sent Dec. 28 and 31, 1946, in Stockholm.
References: *SDD*, 12, p. 14.
  SIA, 1947–1948, p. 367.

1947

● 47/i/30/Sweden
Agreement between the USSR and Sweden concerning general conditions for delivery of goods to the USSR, with annex

Signed Jan. 30, 1947, in Stockholm, by the Soviet Trade Mission in Sweden and the Swedish General Export Union.
Valid until 6 months after denunciation. Listed in Korolenko, p. 109, as still valid as of Nov. 25, 1953. Based on the credit agreement and protocol of Oct. 7, 1946 (46/x/7/Sweden/a and /b). Includes as an annex "General conditions of deliveries from Sweden to the USSR."
Source: *VT*, 1947, No. 2, pp. 6–15.
Reference: Korolenko, pp. 87, 109.

● 47/ii/3/Fin/a
Treaty between the USSR and Finland concerning transfer to the USSR of part of the state territory of Finland in the region of the Jäniskoski hydroelectric station and the Niskakoski control dam, with annex and map

Signed Feb. 3, 1947, in Helsinki.
Ratified by Finland Feb. 21, 1947; by the USSR Mar. 3, 1947. Entered into force Apr. 18, 1947, on exchange of acts of ratification in Moscow. Establishes a mixed Soviet-Finnish border commission to determine the new state frontier; to complete work by Oct. 1, 1947. For a protocol signed on completion of the commission's work, see 47/xii/7/Fin.
The USSR to pay 700 million Finnish Marks in one payment for the transferred territory and installations. Annex describes the territory to be transferred.
Sources: *VVS*, 1947, No. 19.
  VT, 1947, No. 4, pp. 42–44.
  SDD, 13, pp. 268–70.
  VPSS, 1947, I, pp. 51–54.
  UNTS, 216, pp. 231–45 (R, Finnish, E, F).
  BFSP, 149, pp. 571–72.

Reference: *Izv.*, Feb. 5, 1947; *ibid.*, Apr. 19, 1947.

● 47/ii/3/Fin/b
Agreement between the USSR and Finland concerning use by the USSR of former German funds in Finland transferred to the USSR, with annex and two protocols

Signed Feb. 3, 1947, in Helsinki.
Ratified by Finland Feb. 21, 1947; by the USSR Mar. 3, 1947. Entered into force Apr. 18, 1947, on exchange of acts of ratification in Moscow.
Provides for use by the USSR of 600 million Finnish Marks for expenses of the Soviet combine Pechenga-Nikel' on the basis of an agreement of Jan. 25, 1947, between that organization and the Finnish company Imatra-Voima. Annex lists goods to be supplied by Finland to the USSR during 1947 and 1948, to the value of 3.02 million Finnish Marks. For the protocols, see next 2 documents.
Sources: *VVS*, 1947, No. 19.
  VT, 1947, No. 4, pp. 35–42.
  VPSS, 1947, I, pp. 39–51.
  *SS, 1948, No. 24 (Finnish, R).
Reference: *Izv.*, Feb. 5, 1947; *ibid.*, Apr. 19, 1947.

● 47/ii/3/Fin/c
Protocol between the USSR and Finland concerning establishment of a Soviet-Finnish joint-stock company for production of artificial fibers

Signed Feb. 3, 1947, in Helsinki.
Annexed to the agreement of the same date concerning use by the USSR of former German funds (preceding document). Calls for signature of a separate agreement, within 1 month, covering legal, financial, and technical conditions for organization and operation of the company.
Sources: See those listed for 47/ii/3/Fin/b.

• 47/ii/3/Fin/d

Protocol between the USSR and Finland concerning work of the Soviet combine Pechenga-Nikel' in Finland

Signed Feb. 3, 1947, in Helsinki.
Annexed to the agreement of the same date concerning use by the USSR of former German funds (47/ii/3/Fin/c). Supersedes the agreement and protocol of Apr. 30, 1946 (46/iv/30/Fin/b).
Sources: See those listed for 47/ii/3/ Fin/b.

• 47/ii/4/Yug/a

Agreement between the USSR and Yugoslavia concerning establishment of a Soviet-Yugoslav joint-stock Danube steamship company, "Juspad," with five annexes

Signed Feb. 4, 1947, in Belgrade.
Entered into force on signature. Duration 30 years; if on expiration Yugoslavia does not exercise its option to buy the Soviet shares, continues until terminated by mutual agreement. Abrogated by a protocol of Aug. 31, 1949. Based on the agreement of June 8, 1946, concerning economic collaboration (46/vi/8/Yug/b).
Annexes: (1) Statute of the company; (2) list of equipment delivered by the USSR in payment of its share in the company; (3) list of vessels transferred to the company by Yugoslavia; (4) evaluation of vessels transferred to the company by Yugoslavia; (5) schedule of ports and port equipment leased to the company by Yugoslavia.
Source: *UNTS*, 116, pp. 171–279 (R, SC, E, F).
Reference: Dedijer, pp. 284–85.

• 47/ii/4/Yug/b

Agreement between the USSR and Yugoslavia concerning establishment of a Soviet-Yugoslav joint-stock civil aviation company, "Justa," with four annexes

Signed Feb. 4, 1947, in Belgrade.
Entered into force on signature. Duration 30 years; if on expiration Yugoslavia does not exercise its option to buy the Soviet shares, continues until terminated by mutual agreement. Abrogated by protocol of Aug. 31, 1949. Based on the agreement of June 8, 1946, concerning economic collaboration (46/vi/8/Yug/b).

Annexes: (1) Statute of the company; (2) list of property to be invested in the company by Yugoslavia; (3) list of property to be invested in the company by the USSR; (4) list of property to be leased to the company by Yugoslavia (with 8 maps).
Source: *UNTS*, 130, pp. 235–313 (R, SC, E, F).
Reference: Dedijer, pp. 282–84.

• 47/ii/10/Bul

Treaty of peace with Bulgaria, with six annexes

Signed Feb. 10, 1947, in Paris, by the USSR, the United Kingdom, the United States of America, Australia, the Belorussian SSR, Czechoslovakia, Greece, India, New Zealand, the Ukrainian SSR, the Union of South Africa, Yugoslavia, and Bulgaria. (Note: the peace treaties with Bulgaria, Finland, Hungary, Italy, and Romania were signed by Soviet Foreign Minister V. M. Molotov on Jan. 29, 1947, in New York, in advance of the formal signing. See *Izv.*, Jan. 30, 1947). Ratified by the USSR Aug. 29, 1947. Entered into force Sept. 15, 1947, on deposit of acts of ratification of the USSR, the United Kingdom, and the United States. A protocol concerning entry into force was signed by the 3 Powers on that date (*BFSP*, 148, pp. 338–39; not listed separately).
For background and analysis of provisions, see Leiss and Dennett, pp. 85–93.
Annexes: (1) Map showing Bulgarian frontiers; (2) definition of military, military air, and naval training; (3) definition and list of war material; (4) rights in industrial, literary and artistic property; (5) contracts, prescription and negotiable instruments; (6) provisions for review of judgments by Bulgarian courts.
Sources: *Izv.*, Feb. 20, 1947.
  VPSS, 1947, I, pp. 290–326.
  SDD, 13, pp. 26–54.
  BFSP, 148, pp. 313–37, citing
    BTS, 1948, No. 52, Cmd. 7483.
  TIAS, 1650 (1947).
  UNTS, 41, pp. 21–133 (R, E, F, B).
  Leiss and Dennett, pp. 251–72.

• 47/ii/10/Fin

Treaty of peace with Finland, with six annexes

Signed Feb. 10, 1947, in Paris, by the USSR, the United Kingdom, Australia, the Belorussian SSR, Canada, Czechoslovakia, India, New Zealand, the Ukrainian SSR, the Union of South Africa, and Finland.
Ratified by the USSR Aug. 29, 1947. Entered into force Sept. 15, 1947, on deposit of acts of ratification of the USSR and the United Kingdom. A protocol concerning entry into force was signed by the 2 Powers on that date (*BFSP*, 148, pp. 361–63; not listed separately).
For background and analysis of provisions, see Leiss and Dennett, pp. 153–59.
Annexes: (1) Map showing the frontiers of Finland and the areas of Pechenga (Petsamo) and Porkkala-Udd; (2) definition of military, military air and naval training; (3) definition and list of war material; (4) special provisions relating to industrial, literary, and artistic property, and to insurance; (5) contracts, prescription, and negotiable instruments; (6) provisions for review of judgments by Finnish prize courts and courts.
Sources: *Izv.*, Feb. 20, 1947.
   VPSS, 1947, I, pp. 327–60.
   SDD, 13, pp. 235–61.
   BFSP, 148, pp. 339–61, citing
      BTS, 1948, No. 53, Cmd. 7484.
   *SS, 1947, No. 20 (Finnish, R, E, F).
   UNTS, 48, pp. 203–303 (R, E, F, Finnish).
   Leiss and Dennett, pp. 322–41.
   Mazour, pp. 260–79.

● 47/ii/10/H

Treaty of peace with Hungary, with six annexes

Signed Feb. 10, 1947, in Paris, by the USSR, the United Kingdom, the United States of America, Australia, the Belorussian SSR, Canada, Czechoslovakia, India, New Zealand, the Ukrainian SSR, the Union of South Africa, Yugoslavia, and Hungary.
Ratified by the USSR Aug. 29, 1947. Entered into force Sept. 15, 1947, on deposit of acts of ratification of the USSR, the United Kingdom, and the United States. A protocol concerning entry into force was signed by the 3 Powers on that date (*BFSP*, 148, pp. 392–94; not listed separately).
For background and analysis of provisions, see Leiss and Dennett, pp. 93–101.

Annexes: (1) Maps showing (a) Hungarian frontiers and (b) Hungarian-Czechoslovak frontier; (2) definition of military and military air training; (3) definition and list of war material; (4) special provisions relating to industrial, literary, and artistic property, and to insurance; (5) contracts, prescription, and negotiable instruments; (6) provisions for review of judgments by Hungarian courts.
Sources: *Izv.*, Feb. 19, 1947.
   VPSS, 1947, I, pp. 248–89.
   SDD, 13, pp. 54–88.
   BFSP, 148, pp. 363–92, citing
      BTS, 1948, No. 54, Cmd. 7485.
   TIAS, 1651 (1947).
   *OT, July 25, 1947, pp. 177–237.
   UNTS, 41, pp. 136–262 (R, E, F, H).
   Leiss and Dennett, pp. 273–97.

● 47/ii/10/Italy

Treaty of peace with Italy, with seventeen annexes

Signed Feb. 10, 1947, in Paris, by the USSR, the United Kingdom, the United States of America, China, France, Australia, Belgium, the Belorussian SSR, Brazil, Canada, Czechoslovakia, Ethiopia, Greece, India, The Netherlands, New Zealand, Poland, the Ukrainian SSR, the Union of South Africa, Yugoslavia, and Italy.
Ratified by the USSR Aug. 29, 1947. Entered into force Sept. 15, 1947, on deposit of the acts of ratification of the USSR, the United Kingdom, the United States, and France. A procès verbal concerning entry into force was signed by the 4 Powers on that date (*BFSP*, 148, pp. 481–82; not listed separately).
For background and analysis of provisions, see Leiss and Dennett, pp. 16–79.
Annexes: (1) Maps showing (a) the Italian frontiers, (b) the French-Italian boundary, (c) the Yugoslav-Italian boundary, (d) boundaries of the Free Territory of Trieste, and (e) sea areas defined in Art. 11 of the treaty; (2) detailed description of the French-Italian boundary; (3) guarantees in connection with Mont Cenis and the Tenda-Briga district; (4) provisions agreed on by the Austrian and Italian Governments on Sept. 5, 1946, concerning administrative measures in the South Tyrol; (5) provisions for the water supply for Gorizia and vicinity; (6) permanent Statute of the

Free Territory of Trieste; (7) instrument for the Provisional Regime of the Free Territory of Trieste; (8) instrument for the Free Port of Trieste; (9) technical dispositions concerning the Free Territory of Trieste; (10) economic and financial provisions relating to the Free Territory of Trieste; (11) Joint Declaration by the USSR, the United Kingdom, the United States of America, and France concerning Italian territorial possessions in Africa; (12) lists of naval vessels (a) to be retained by Italy and (b) to be placed at the disposal of the Governments of the USSR, the United Kingdom, the United States of America, and France; (13) definitions of (a) naval terms, (b) military, military air and naval training, (c) war material, with list, and (d) the terms "demilitarization" and "demilitarized"; (14) economic and financial provisions relating to ceded territories; (15) special provisions relating to industrial, literary, and artistic property, and to insurance; (16) contracts, prescription, and negotiable instruments; (17) provisions for review of decisions and judgments of Italian prize courts and courts.

Sources: *Izv.*, Feb. 16, 1947.
VPSS, 1947, I, pp. 64–207.
SDD, 13, pp. 88–203.
BFSP, 148, pp. 394–481, citing
   BTS, 1948, No. 50, Cmd. 7481.
TIAS, 1648 (1947).
UNTS, 49, pp. 3–507 (R, E, F, I);
   50 (maps).
Leiss and Dennett, pp. 163–250.

• 47/ii/10/Rom

Treaty of peace with Romania, with six annexes

Signed Feb. 10, 1947, in Paris, by the USSR, the United Kingdom, the United States of America, Australia, the Belorussian SSR, Canada, Czechoslovakia, India, New Zealand, the Ukrainian SSR, the Union of South Africa, and Romania. Ratified by the USSR Aug. 29, 1947. Entered into force Sept. 15, 1947, on deposit of the acts of ratification of the USSR, the United Kingdom, and the United States. A protocol concerning entry into force was signed by the 3 Powers on that date (*BFSP*, 148, pp. 509–11; not listed separately).

For background and analysis of provisions, see Leiss and Dennett, pp. 101–107.

Annexes: (1) Map showing the Romanian frontiers; (2) definition of military, military air, and naval training; (3) definition and list of war material; (4) special provisions relating to industrial, literary, and artistic property, and to insurance; (5) contracts, prescription, and negotiable instruments; (6) provisions for review of decisions and orders by Romanian prize courts and of judgments by Romanian courts.

Sources: *Izv.*, Feb. 18, 1947.
VPSS, 1947, I, pp. 208–47.
SDD, 13, pp. 203–34.
BFSP, 148, pp. 482–509, citing
   BTS, 1948, No. 55, Cmd. 7486.
TIAS, 1649 (1947).
UNTS, 42, pp. 3–124 (R, E, F, Romanian).
Leiss and Dennett, pp. 298–321.

• 47/ii/10/Pl

Protocol concerning establishment of a Four-Power Naval Commission, disposal of excess units of the Italian fleet, and return by the USSR of warships on loan, with annex

Signed Feb. 10, 1947, in Paris, by the USSR, the United Kingdom, the United States of America, and France.
Entered into force on signature. Provides for distribution of naval vessels listed in Annex 12(b) of the peace treaty with Italy (47/ii/10/Italy). Annex lists distribution of the vessels among the USSR, the United Kingdom, the United States, France, Greece, Yugoslavia, and Albania. Later in 1947 the United States renounced its share of the Italian vessels, and the United Kingdom did likewise, with minor exceptions (see *SIA, 1947–1948*, p. 115).

Sources: *DSB*, 16, 1947, pp. 815–16
   (omits the annex).
TIAS, 1733 (1948).
Decade of American foreign policy, pp. 467–70.
BFSP, 148, pp. 306–12, citing
   BTS, 1948, No. 13, Cmd. 7353.
UNTS, 140, pp. 111–27 (R, E, F).

• 47/ii/11/Norway/a

Agreement between the USSR and Norway concerning establishment of telegraph and telephone communications

Signed Feb. 11, 1947, in Moscow.

Entered into force Apr. 1, 1947. Valid until 6 months after denunciation.
Source: *SDD*, 13, pp. 434–38.

● 47/ii/11/Norway/b

Parcel post agreement between the USSR and Norway, with final protocol

Signed Feb. 11, 1947, in Moscow.
Entered into force Mar. 11, 1947 (1 month after signature). Valid until 6 months after denunciation.
By an exchange of notes of Aug. 26 and Sept. 7, 1953 (53/ix/7/Norway), the minimum unit for insured parcels was reduced from 300 to 200 francs.
Final protocol concerns technical details of postal communications. Entry into force and duration the same as for the agreement.
Source: *SDD* 13, pp. 438–48.

Feb. 19, 1947. Agreement between the Soviet Military Administration in Germany and Norway concerning trade, with protocol

See Appendix 3.

● 47/ii/20/Rom/a

Treaty of commerce and navigation between the USSR and Romania, with annex concerning the Soviet Trade Mission in Romania

Signed Feb. 20, 1947, in Moscow.
Ratified by the USSR Apr. 26, 1946. Entered into force May 16, 1947, on exchange of acts of ratification in Bucharest. Duration 2 years; if not denounced 6 months before expiration, extended for an additional 12 months. Listed in Korolenko, p. 104, as still valid as of Nov. 25, 1953.
Sources: *VT*, 1947, No. 4, pp. 29–34.
  VPSS, 1947, I, pp. 361–70.
  SDD, 13, pp. 336–44.
  Korolenko, pp. 270–75.
  UNTS, 226, pp. 79–107 (R, Romanian, E, F).
References: *Izv.*, Feb. 21, 1947.
  MO, No. 85, Apr. 11, 1947, cited in *Economic treaties*, p. 4.

● 47/ii/20/Rom/b

Trade and payments agreement for 1947 between the USSR and Romania

Signed Feb. 20, 1947, in Moscow.

The USSR to provide raw materials for the Romanian metallurgical and textile industries as well as industrial materials and equipment, in exchange for Romanian oil products, construction materials, etc.
References: *Izv.*, Feb. 21, 1947.
  VT, 1947, No. 2, p. 38.

● 47/ii/25/Pl

Decree of the Allied Control Council for Germany concerning abolition of the state of Prussia

Signed Feb. 25, 1947, by representatives of the USSR, the United Kingdom, the United States of America, and France on the Allied Control Council for Germany. Endorsed by the Council of Foreign Ministers at their 4th meeting (see 47/iv/24/Pl).
Sources: *DIA, 1947–1948*, pp. 412–13.
  Germany, 1947–1949, p. 151.

Jan. 14 – Feb. 25, 1947

Conference of Foreign Ministers' Deputies of the USSR, the United Kingdom, the United States of America, and France, to consider preparation of a peace treaty with Germany and hear the views of other countries. No agreements were reached, but the conference prepared a final report incorporating the memoranda submitted by Belgium, The Netherlands, Luxembourg, Yugoslavia, Greece, Norway, Czechoslovakia, Poland, Brazil, Australia, the Union of South Africa, Canada, the Belorussian SSR, and Denmark. Text in *Documentation française, Notes documentaires et études*, No. 569, Mar. 12, 1947.

● 47/iii/3/Mul

Supplementary protocol concerning entry into force of the whaling protocol of November 26, 1945

Signed Mar. 3, 1947, in London; the signature of the USSR was not subject to ratification or approval.
For signatories, brings the protocol of 1945 (46/xi/25/1945) into force immediately.
Sources: *BFSP*, 148, pp. 511–12, citing *BTS*, 1947, No. 28, Cmd. 7107.
  TIAS, 1634 (1947).

● 47/iii/5/Pol/a

Joint communiqué by the USSR and Po-

land concerning political and economic negotiations

Issued at the end of negotiations held from Feb. 25 to Mar. 5, 1947, in Moscow. Lists 6 specific agreements (next 6 items) and then mentions agreements on (1) conversion of the railroad line Cracow-Katowice-Przemyzl to European gauge before Nov. 1, 1947; (2) transfer to Poland before May 15, 1947, of its share of the German fleet; and (3) acceleration of the return to Poland of Polish citizens in the USSR as a result of the war, including former German citizens. It is not clear whether the latter 3 agreements were embodied in separate instruments or not.
Sources: *Izv.*, Mar. 6, 1947.
    VT, 1947, No. 2, p. 1.
    VPSS, 1947, I, pp. 371–72.

● 47/iii/5/Pol/b

Agreement between the USSR and Poland on a loan to Poland

Signed during negotiations in Moscow from Feb. 25 to Mar. 5, 1947.
Not subject to ratification. Provides for a Soviet loan of $28,855,000 in gold.
References: See those listed for 47/iii/5/Pol/a.

● 47/iii/5/Pol/c

Agreement between the USSR and Poland concerning settlement of reciprocal financial obligations outstanding on January 1, 1947, and the establishment of principles for financial payments in the future

Signed during negotiations in Moscow from Feb. 25 to Mar. 5, 1947.
Not subject to ratification.
References: See those listed for 47/iii/5/Pol/a.

● 47/iii/5/Pol/d

Agreement between the USSR and Poland concerning reduction of Polish coal deliveries to the USSR

Signed during negotiations in Moscow from Feb. 25 to Mar. 5, 1947.
Not subject to ratification. Provides for reduction by 50 per cent of deliveries under the agreement of Aug. 16, 1945, concerning reparations (45/viii/16/Pol/a).

References: See those listed for 47/iii/5/Pol/a.

● 47/iii/5/Pol/e

Agreement between the USSR and Poland concerning transfer to Poland of railroad rolling stock seized by the USSR as war booty

Signed during negotiations in Moscow from Feb. 25 to Mar. 5, 1947.
Not subject to ratification.
References: See those listed for 47/iii/5/Pol/a.

● 47/iii/5/Pol/f

Agreement between the USSR and Poland concerning scientific and technical collaboration in the field of industrial production

Signed Mar. 5, 1947, in Moscow.
Not subject to ratification. Entered into force on signature. Duration 5 years; if not denounced 1 year before expiration, extended for 5 years more.
Based on the treaty of friendship, mutual aid, and postwar collaboration of Apr. 21, 1945. Establishes a Polish-Soviet commission, to meet twice annually, in Moscow and Warsaw.
Source: *SDD*, 13, pp. 335–36.
References: See those listed for 45/iii/5/Pol/a.

● 47/iii/5/Pol/g

Agreement between the USSR and Poland concerning provision to Poland of armaments and military equipment on credit

Signed during negotiations in Moscow from Feb. 25 to Mar. 5, 1947.
Not subject to ratification.
References: See those listed for 47/iii/5/Pol/a.

● 47/iii/24/UK

Negotiations between the USSR and the United Kingdom

On Mar. 24, 1947, Marshal Stalin conferred with British Foreign Secretary Ernest Bevin in Moscow. Agreements were reached on (1) desirability of revising the Soviet-British treaty of alliance of May 26, 1942, to meet peacetime condi-

tions, and (2) need for expansion of trade between the two countries.
References: *DIA, 1947–1948*, pp. 271–72, citing *H.C. Deb.*, 5th ser., Vol. 437, col. 1740; *ibid.*, Vol. 436, col. 34.

• 47/iv/7/India

Exchange of notes between the USSR and India concerning establishment of diplomatic relations

Sent Apr. 2 and 7, 1947, in Nanking.
References: *Izv.*, Apr. 15, 1947.
  SDD, 13, p. 25.

Apr. 12, 1947. Hungarian decrees exempting Soviet-Hungarian joint-stock companies from taxes and duties

See 46/iv/8/H/a and /b, and *DSB*, 25, 1951, p. 325.

• 47/iv/13/Af

Agreement between the USSR and Afghanistan concerning establishment of radio-telegraph communications

Signed Apr. 13, 1947, in Kabul.
Entered into force July 13, 1947 (3 months after signature). Duration 3 years; if not denounced 6 months before expiration, extended for successive 1-year periods.
Provides for establishment of communications between Tashkent and Kabul; other terminal points may be designated by subsequent exchange of notes.
Source: *SDD*, 13, pp. 394–97.
Reference: *Izv.*, Apr. 20, 1947.

• 47/iv/15/US. See Appendix 5.

Apr. 23, 1947. Rules of procedure of the Trusteeship Council of the United Nations

See Note to 46/vi/26/Mul/a.

• 47/iv/24/Fin/a

Agreement between the USSR and Finland concerning regulation of Lake Inari by means of the regulating dam at Niskakoski, with four annexes

Signed Apr. 24, 1947, in Moscow.
Entered into force on signature. Based on the agreement of Feb. 3, 1947, concerning use by the USSR of former German funds in Finland (47/ii/3/Fin/b).

Defines the rights and powers of the Soviet combine Pechenga-Nikel' in regard to the regulation of Lake Inari. Modified by 2 protocols signed Apr. 29, 1954, the 1st concerning execution of the agreement, the 2nd modifying the annexed rules (next document).
Annexes: (1) Map showing the border area in the region of Lake Inari; (2) map showing location of bench mark for the regulation of Lake Inari (the map, incidentally, is dated Helsinki, Oct. 26, 1943); (3) Rules . . . (see next document); (4) blank form for personnel pass for technical observers.
Sources: *SDD*, 13, pp. 272–79.
  SS, 1947, No. 10 (Finnish, R).

• 47/iv/24/Fin/b

Rules for regulating the water level on Lake Inari in connection with operation of the Niskakoski dam

Annexed to the agreement of Apr. 24, 1947, between the USSR and Finland, concerning regulation of Lake Inari.
Under a protocol of Apr. 29, 1954 (54/iv/29/Fin/b), changes were made in the technical procedure for allowing water to escape from Lake Inari. Further modified by protocol of Feb. 24, 1956 (56/ii/24/Pl).
Sources: Same as for 47/iv/24/Fin/a.

• 47/iv/24/Pl

Fourth meeting of the Council of Foreign Ministers

Held Mar. 10 through Apr. 24, 1947, in Moscow, by the Foreign Ministers of the USSR, the United Kingdom, the United States of America, and France.
Agreements were reached on the following subjects: (1) The Council endorsed the decree of the Allied Control Council for Germany of Feb. 25, 1947, abolishing the Prussian State. (2) Repatriation of all German prisoners-of-war held by the 4 Powers to be completed by the end of 1948. (3) Yugoslavia given the right to seize Austrian property in Yugoslavia. (4) Next session of the CFM to be held in London in Nov. 1947. (5) An Austrian Treaty Commission to be established to examine disagreed questions of the Austrian treaty.
References: *SIA, 1947–1948*, pp. 228–36; *ibid., 1949–1950*, p. 287.

DAFR, 9, p. 91.
DSCS, 98.
DIA, 1947–1948, pp. 412–510.

● 47/iv/30/Pol

Protocol between the USSR and Poland concerning demarcation of the state border, with maps and related documents

Signed Apr. 30, 1947, in Warsaw, by the mixed Soviet-Polish border commission established by the agreement of Aug. 16, 1945 (45/viii/16/Pol/b).
Reaffirmed by an agreement of July 8, 1948 (48/vii/8/Pol/a).
Reference: *Izv.*, May 7, 1947.

May 3, 1947

First meeting of the Working Groups of the USSR and the United States of America to negotiate a Lend-Lease settlement, see entry under Mar. 21, 1951. The Groups prepared an "Outline of Main Points of Settlement Proposed by the United States Side."

● 47/v/6/Pol

Protocol between the Ukrainian SSR and Poland concerning completion of the evacuation of Ukrainian citizens from Polish territory to the Ukrainian SSR and of Polish citizens from the Ukrainian SSR to Poland

Signed May 6, 1947, in Warsaw.
Marks completion of the operation provided for in the agreement of Sept. 9, 1944 (44/ix/9/Pol/a).
References: *Izv.*, May 8, 1947.
VPSS, 1947, I, pp. 383–84.

● 47/v/12/US

Exchange of notes between the USSR and the United States of America concerning resumption of the work of the Joint Commission for Korea

Sent Apr. 8 and 19 and May 2, 7, and 12, 1947.
The Joint Commission, established by an agreement of the Council of Foreign Ministers in Dec. 1945 (see 45/xii/27/(3)), convened on Mar. 20, 1946, but adjourned *sine die* May 8, 1946, following failure to agree on the definition of the word "democratic." For further correspondence on the Joint Commission, see 47/viii/23/US. Sources: *Sovetskii Soiuz i koreiskii vo-*

pros, pp. 13–29 (omits the letter of May 12, 1947).
Korea, pp. 33–42.
References: *SIA, 1947–1948*, p. 312.
DAFR, 9, pp. 114–15.

● 47/v/24/Fin

Agreement between the USSR and Finland granting Finland the right of railroad transit for freight and passengers through the area of the Soviet naval base at Porkkala-Udd

Signed May 24, 1947, in Moscow.
Entered into force on signature. Duration 1 year. If not denounced 1 month before expiration, extended for 1-year periods.
Listed in *SDD*, 13 (1956), p. 495, as no longer valid.
Sources: *SS, 1947, No. 11 (Finnish, R).
BFSP, 149, pp. 572–74.

● 47/vi/12/Rom

Agreement between the USSR and Romania concerning direct rail communications

Signed June 12, 1947, in Moscow.
Listed in *SDD*, 13 (1956), p. 495, as no longer valid. Superseded by the agreement of 1950 concerning transportation of freight by rail (50/ / /Pl).
Reference: *Izv.*, June 20, 1947.

● 47/vi/16/US

Agreement between the USSR and the United States of America concerning opening of an American consular office in Leningrad

Announced June 16, 1947, by the Department of State.
The consulate in Leningrad was never opened; negotiations between the 2 countries during 1947 and the first half of 1948 were unsuccessful, and in Aug. 1948 the USSR, in a note to the United States, claimed that the agreement on a consulate in Leningrad "had lost its validity." The note added that the USSR had decided to close its consulates in New York and San Francisco, and to ask for immediate closing of the American consulate in Vladivostok (text of Soviet note, *NYT*, Aug. 25, 1948).
Reference: *DSB*, 16, 1947, p. 1307.

● 47/vi/19/Pl

Directive concerning basic post-surrender policy for Japan

Adopted June 19, 1947, by the Far Eastern Commission, composed of representatives of the USSR, the United States of America, the United Kingdom, Australia, Canada, China, France, India, The Netherlands, New Zealand, and the Philippines. Closely modeled on the statement of United States initial post-surrender policy for Japan dated Sept. 6, 1945 (text in *DSB*, 13, 1945, pp. 423–27).
Sources: *DSB*, 17, 1947, pp. 216–21.
  Decade of American foreign policy, pp. 652–59.

● 47/vi/22/Pl

Exchange of notes between the USSR and the United Kingdom and France concerning convocation of a conference to discuss plans for American aid to Europe

Sent by the United Kingdom and France June 19, 1947; Soviet reply June 22, 1947. For the conference, see 47/vii/2/Pl.
Source: *DIA, 1947–1948*, pp. 30–32 (F).
Reference: *SIA, 1947–1948*, p. 33.

● 47/vi/30/Pl

Documents concerning the border mark at the junction of the borders of the USSR, Afghanistan, and Iran

Signed June 30, 1947, in Serakhsa.
Mentioned in the treaty of Jan. 18, 1958, between the USSR and Afghanistan concerning the regime on the Soviet-Afghanistan state border (*VVS*, 1958, No. 28, Art. 374).

July 2, 1947. Conference to consider plans for American aid to Europe

Held June 27 through July 2, 1947, in Paris, by the Foreign Ministers of the USSR, the United Kingdom, and France. The conference agreed only on publication of documents submitted to it.
Reference: *SIA, 1947–1948*, pp. 33–37.

July 4, 1947. Agreement between the United Nations and the Universal Postal Union

See (1) 47/vii/5/Mul/a and (2) 52/vii/11/Mul/a.

● 47/vii/5/Bul

Trade and payments agreement between the USSR and Bulgaria

Signed July 5, 1947, in Moscow.
Entered into force on signature. Valid through Dec. 31, 1948; if not denounced 1 month before expiration, extended for 1-year periods. Listed in Korolenko, p. 107, as still valid as of Nov. 25, 1953.
Sources: *VT*, 1947, No. 10, pp. 30–31.
  Dewar, pp. 108–11.

● 47/vii/5/Mul/a

Universal Postal Convention, with related documents

Signed July 5, 1947, in Paris. The USSR and Belorussian and Ukrainian SSR's signed.
Ratified by the USSR Feb. 15, 1949; by the Ukrainian SSR Apr. 28, 1949. Entered into force July 1, 1948. Duration indefinite; signatories may withdraw with 1 year's notice. Supersedes the convention of May 23, 1939; superseded by the convention of July 11, 1952 (52/vii/11/Mul/a).
Full contents (*BFSP*, 148): Text, pp. 521–37; final protocol, pp. 537–62; Annex: Agreement between the United Nations and the Universal Postal Union of July 4, 1947, pp. 562–65; provisions concerning air mail, pp. 567–83; final protocol to the provisions concerning air mail, pp. 583–84; and annexes to the provisions concerning air mail, pp. 585–91. The USSR and the Belorussian and Ukrainian SSR's also signed the agreement concerning insured letters and boxes (next document), but not the agreement concerning parcel post.
Sources: *BFSP*, 148, as listed above, citing
    BTS, 1949, No. 57, Cmd. 7794.
  TIAS, 1850 (1949).
Reference: Listed in *SDD*, 13 (1956), p. 495, as no longer valid (dated July 3, 1947).

● 47/vii/5/Mul/b

Agreement concerning insured letters and boxes, with final protocol

Signed July 5, 1947, in Paris. The USSR and Belorussian and Ukrainian SSR's signed.
Ratified by the USSR Feb. 15, 1949. En-

tered into force July 1, 1948. Duration
indefinite. Supersedes the agreement of
May 23, 1939 (see 39/v/23/Mul) ; superseded by the agreement of July 11, 1952
(52/vii/11/Mul/b).
Sources: *BFSP*, 148, pp. 591–605, citing
    BTS, 1949, No. 58, Cmd. 7795.
Reference: Listed in *SDD*, 13 (1956), p.
    495, as no longer valid (dated July
    3, 1947).

● 47/vii/5/Yug/a

**Trade and payments agreement between
the USSR and Yugoslavia, with protocol**

Signed July 5, 1947, in Moscow.
Entered into force on signature. Duration 2 years; if not denounced 3 months
before expiration, extended for 1-year periods. Protocol specifies prices and conditions for payments. For the protocol for
1949, see 48/xii/27/Yug. Omitted from
the list in Korolenko, p. 107, of trade
treaties still valid as of Nov. 25, 1953.
Source: *VT*, 1947, No. 9, pp. 32–33 (omits
    the protocol).
Reference: *Izv.*, July 29, 1947.

● 47/vii/5/Yug/b

**Agreement between the USSR and Yugo-
slavia concerning reciprocal provision of
funds for maintenance of diplomatic
missions and other non-commercial payments**

Signed July 5, 1947, probably in Moscow.
Mentioned in the trade protocol of Dec.
27, 1948, which provides for settlement
of a debt of $5.1 million US under this
agreement.

● 47/vii/12/Cz

**Joint communiqué by the USSR and
Czechoslovakia concerning trade relations**

Signed at the end of negotiations from
July 9 to 12, 1947, in Moscow; published
July 13, 1947.
Following agreements included: (1) A
5-year trade agreement to be negotiated;
annual trade contingents to be established
by separate agreements. (2) Deliveries
for 1948 to be agreed upon before signature of the 5-year agreement. (3) In
1948, the USSR to deliver 200,000 tons
of wheat, 200,000 tons of fodder grain
and maize, 60,000 tons of calcic fertilizer,

5,000 tons of nitrogen fertilizer, 20,000
tons of cotton, and oil seeds, peas, wool,
iron, manganese, and chrome ores, ferrous alloys, etc., in exchange for Czech
rails, locomotives, oil pipes, equipment for
footwear and sugar industries, lathes,
electric motors, etc. For the 5-year trade
agreement, see 47/xii/11/Cz/b.
According to unofficial reports, the most
important decision taken during the negotiations was that Czechoslovakia, in accordance with a Soviet demand, should
withdraw its acceptance of an invitation
to take part in a conference in Paris on
American aid to Europe (see Schmidt,
pp. 100–102).
Sources: *Izv.*, July 13, 1947.
    VPSS, 1947, II, pp. 17–18.

● 47/vii/15/Australia

**Exchange of notes between the USSR
and Australia concerning transformation
of diplomatic missions into embassies**

Sent July 15, 1947, in Moscow.
Reference: *SDD*, 13, p. 25.

● 47/vii/15/H/a

**Treaty of commerce and navigation be-
tween the USSR and Hungary, with annex concerning the Soviet Trade Mission
in Hungary**

Signed July 15, 1947, in Moscow.
Ratified by Hungary Nov. 22, 1947; by
the USSR Dec. 26, 1947. Entered into
force Jan. 19, 1948, on exchange of acts of
ratification in Budapest. Valid until 6
months after denunciation. Listed in Korolenko, p. 104, as still valid as of Nov. 25,
1953.
Sources: *VVS*, 1948, No. 10.
    VT, 1948, No. 1, pp. 29–33.
    VPSS, 1947, II, pp. 19–30.
    SDD, 13, pp. 324–33.
    Korolenko, pp. 276–81.
    *OT, 1947, No. 23, pp. 285–92.
    UNTS, 216, pp. 247–83 (R, E, F, H).
Reference: *Economic treaties*, pp. 68–71.

● 47/vii/15/H/b

**Trade and payments agreement between
the USSR and Hungary, with two annexes**

Signed July 15, 1947, in Moscow. Entered
into force on signature, but applied retroactively from June 1, 1947. Valid through

July 31, 1948; if not denounced 1 month before expiration, extended for successive 1-year periods. By a protocol of Oct. 2, 1948 (48/x/2/H/b), extended to Dec. 31, 1949.
Sources: *VT*, 1947, No. 10, pp. 32–33.
VPSS, 1947, II, pp. 30–34.
Dewar, pp. 111–13 (text as amended by protocol of Oct. 2, 1948).
Note: Sources listed omit the annexes.

• 47/vii/15/H/c

Final protocol, concerning financial payments, to the trade agreement between the USSR and Hungary of August 27, 1945

Signed July 15, 1947, in Moscow.
Provides for transfer of financial surpluses under the 1945 agreement to trade accounts under the trade and payments agreement of July 15, 1947 (preceding document).
Reference: Mentioned in Art. 11 of the trade and payments agreement.

• 47/vii/25/Yug/a

Agreement between the USSR and Yugoslavia concerning deliveries of industrial equipment to Yugoslavia on credit, with two annexes

Signed July 25, 1947, in Moscow.
Entered into force on signature. Abrogated by the USSR in 1949. Registered with the UN by Yugoslavia May 9, 1952. Provides for delivery during 1948–1953 of equipment for ferrous and non-ferrous metal plants, oil processing, chemical and cement enterprises, and other equipment and materials for the oil, coal, timber, and other industries, and for Soviet technical aid in establishing the enterprises. Total credit granted approximately $135 million, to be repaid in 7 years after Jan. 1, 1950; exact total to be determined by a supplementary protocol not later than Dec. 31, 1948.
Annexes: (1) List of plants and equipment to be delivered on credit from the USSR to Yugoslavia; (2) specimen form for bonds to be used in repayment of the credit.
Source: *UNTS*, 130, pp. 315–413 (R, SC, E, F).
References: *VT*, 1947, No. 10, p. 35.
Dedijer, pp. 288–89.

• 47/vii/25/Yug/b

Trade agreement between the USSR and Yugoslavia

Signed July 25, 1947, in Moscow.
Possibly in the form of a protocol with lists of goods to be delivered. Covers period from June 1, 1947, through May 31, 1948.
Reference: *Izv.*, July 29, 1947.

• 47/vii/26/Alb/a

Joint communiqué by the USSR and Albania concerning economic and cultural relations

Signed at the end of negotiations from July 14 to 26, 1947, in Moscow.
Mentions agreement on credit (next document) and "exchange of opinion on other questions."
Sources: *Izv.*, July 27, 1947.
VPSS, 1947, II, pp. 34–35.
VT, 1948, No. 1, p. 28.

• 47/vii/26/Alb/b

Credit agreement between the USSR and Albania

Signed on or about July 26, 1947, in Moscow.
Provides for a "small" Soviet loan to Albania, to be used for purchase of equipment for light industry and agricultural machinery.
Mentioned in the communiqué of the same date (preceding document).

• 47/viii/ /Pol

Agreement between the USSR and Poland concerning supplementary delivery of grain to Poland

Concluded during or earlier than Aug. 1947.
Provides for deliveries of 300,000 tons of grain. For an earlier agreement on grain deliveries, see 46/ii/8/Pol.
Reference: *VT SSSR*, p. 73.

• 47/viii/4/Pol

Trade agreement between the USSR and Poland

Signed Aug. 4, 1947, in Moscow.
Duration 1 year. Soviet ores, aluminum,

cotton, asbestos, apatites, benzine, etc., in exchange for Polish coal, zinc, coke, soda, woolen materials, etc.

References: *Izv.*, Aug. 5, 1947.
VT, 1947, No. 10, p. 35; *ibid.*, 1955, No. 4, p. 2.

Aug. 14, 1947

Agreement between the United Nations and the International Telecommunication Union, drafted Aug. 12–14, 1947, included as Annex 5 to the International Telecommunication Convention of Oct. 2, 1947 (47/x/2/Mul/a), and as Annex 6 to the convention of Dec. 22, 1952 (52/xii/22/Mul). Entered into force Jan. 1, 1949, under a protocol of Apr. 26, 1949. Text in *UNTS*, 30, pp. 316–31 (E, F); text of the protocol, *ibid.*, pp. 330–35.

• 47/viii/23/Bul

Agreement between the USSR and Bulgaria concerning deliveries of industrial equipment to Bulgaria on credit

Signed Aug. 23, 1947.
Provides for delivery of equipment for a mineral fertilizer factory and an electrostation, for transforming coal into semi-coke, and for Soviet technical aid.
References: *Izv.*, Sept. 2, 1947.
VT, 1947, No. 10, p. 35; *ibid.*, 1951, No. 9, p. 17.
VT SSSR, p. 150.

• 47/viii/23/US

Exchange of notes between the USSR and the United States of America concerning work of the Joint Commission for Korea

Sent Aug. 11 and 23, 1947.
For earlier communications on the Joint Commission, see 47/v/12/US. The Commission, which resumed work on May 22, 1947, was deadlocked again by mid-July; under this exchange of notes it was instructed to prepare a report on its work.
Sources: *Sovetskii Soiuz i koreiskii vopros*, pp. 30–32, 38–40.
DSB, 17, 1947, pp. 398–99, 475–76.
DIA, 1947–1948, pp. 688–90.

• 47/viii/23/Yug

Agreement between the USSR and Yugoslavia concerning the sale to Yugoslavia

of railroad rolling stock, with three annexes and a protocol

Signed Aug. 23, 1947, in Moscow.
Entered into force on signature. Registered with the UN by Yugoslavia Nov. 27, 1951.
Provides for the sale to Yugoslavia of 100 locomotives and 7,000 freight cars, to be delivered by Dec. 1, 1947. Repayment to be in goods over 5 years, beginning July 1, 1948. A special agreement to be drawn up covering quantity, price, and quality of the goods.
Annexes: (1) Blank list of rolling stock; (2) blank record of delivery of locomotives; (3) blank record of delivery of freight cars. Protocol concerns return to Yugoslavia of Yugoslav rolling stock seized by the Soviet Army elsewhere, and return from Yugoslavia to other countries and occupation zones of non-Yugoslav rolling stock.
Source: *UNTS*, 116, pp. 281–311 (R, SC, E, F).

Aug. 29, 1947. Protocol extending the agreement of May 6, 1937, concerning regulation of the production and marketing of sugar

See 46/viii/30/Mul.

• 47/ix/15/H

Agreement between the USSR and Hungary concerning direct rail communications

Signed Sept. 15, 1947.
Listed in *SDD*, 13 (1956), p. 494, as no longer valid. Superseded by the agreement of 1950 concerning transportation of freight by rail (50/ / /Pl).

Sept. 15, 1947. Protocols (in one case a procès verbal) concerning entry into force of the peace treaties with Bulgaria, Finland, Hungary, Italy, and Romania

See 47/ii/10/Bul, /Fin, /H, /Italy, and /Rom.

• 47/ix/22/H/a

Agreement between the USSR and Hungary concerning establishment of postal and telephone-telegraph communications, with final protocol

Signed Sept. 22, 1947, in Moscow.
Entered into force on signature. Valid

until 6 months after denunciation. Protocol (1) provides that the temporary agreement of Aug. 21, 1945 shall lose validity from Oct. 15, 1947, and (2) regulates postal relations between Hungary and the Soviet Army of Occupation.
Source: *SDD*, 13, pp. 416–24.

• 47/ix/22/H/b
Parcel post agreement between the USSR and Hungary

Signed Sept. 22, 1947, in Moscow.
Entered into force Nov. 22, 1947 (2 months after signature). Valid until 6 months after denunciation. Under subsequent agreements, certain technical details were modified with effect from July 1, 1948, July 1, 1951, and July 1, 1952. The date of these agreements is known only in the case of the 1953 changes (see 53/viii/27/H).
Source: *SDD*, 13, pp. 425–33.

Sept. 22, 1947. Conference of directors of the International Meteorological Organization

See 48/iv/2/1947.

• 47/ix/27/Mul
Report on the proceedings of the International High Frequency Broadcasting Conference

Prepared at the end of the conference, which met from Aug. 16, 1947, through Sept. 27, 1947, in Atlantic City, New Jersey.
The USSR and the Belorussian and Ukrainian SSR's took part in the conference.
Includes recommendations, an agenda for the next High Frequency Broadcasting Conference, to be held in Mexico City, and resolutions.
Source: *DS IOCS*, I, 4, pp. 184–92.

• 47/ix/29/Pl
Protocol concerning modification in the method of payment by the USSR to Canada under the protocol of October 8, 1944, to the armistice agreement with Finland

Signed Sept. 29, 1947, in Ottawa, by the USSR and Canada; concurrence of the United Kingdom given in a dispatch of Nov. 19, 1947, annexed to the protocol.

Entered into force on signature. Provides that the remaining sum to be paid, $11,666,500 US, shall be paid in 10 equal instalments, ending Dec. 31, 1951.
Sources: *CTS*, 1947, No. 24.
UNTS, 45, pp. 125–31 (E, F).
Reference: *Izv.*, Oct. 1, 1947.

• 47/x/1/Pol
Parcel post agreement between the USSR and Poland

Signed Oct. 1, 1947, in Moscow. Entered into force Nov. 1, 1947 (1 month after signature).
Valid until 6 months after denunciation. Under subsequent agreements, certain technical details were modified with effect from July 1, 1953, Feb. 7, 1956, and Feb. 7, 1957. The date of these agreements is known only in the case of the 1953 changes (see 53/ix/17/Pol).
Source: *SDD*, 13, pp. 448–59.

• 47/x/2/Mul/a
International Telecommunication Convention, with related documents

Signed Oct. 2, 1947, in Atlantic City, New Jersey, at the end of a conference from July 2 to Oct. 2, 1947. The USSR and Belorussian and Ukrainian SSR's signed. Acts of ratification of the Belorussian and Ukrainian SSR's deposited Jan. 3, 1949; of the USSR, July 1, 1949. Entered into force Jan. 1, 1949, for signatories whose act of ratification or accession had been deposited before that date. May be denounced with 1 year's notice.
Defines the composition, functions, and structure of the International Telecommunication Union. Supersedes the conventions of 1865, 1868, 1872, 1875, 1906, 1912, 1927, and 1932 (see 32/xii/9/Mul/a). Superseded by convention of Dec. 22, 1952 (52/xii/22/Mul).
Related documents consist of 5 annexes, final protocol, and 10 additional protocols. Annexes: (1) List of members of the Union; (2) definition of terms used in the convention; (3) provisions for arbitration; (4) general regulations annexed to the convention; (5) agreement between the United Nations and the International Telecommunication Union, drawn up during Aug. 1947 (see entry under Aug. 14, 1947). Final protocol lists reservations

and declarations by signatories, including those of the USSR with regard to provisions for membership in the Union. None of the additional protocols directly concerns the USSR. Following the protocols are given resolutions, recommendations, and opinions of the conference; none of these directly concerns the USSR. Supplemented by radio regulations (next document) and telegraph regulations (49/viii/5/Mul).

Sources: *International Telecommunication Convention*, 1947 (E, F).
   BFSP, 148, pp. 684–741, citing
      BTS, 1950, No. 76, Cmd. 8124.
   TIAS, 1901 (1950).
References: Listed in *SDD*, 14 (1957), p. 356, as no longer valid.
   DS, IOCS, I, 4, pp. 49–80.

● 47/x/2/Mul/b

Radio regulations annexed to the International Telecommunication Convention, with related documents

Signed Oct. 2, 1947, in Atlantic City, New Jersey, at the end of a conference from May 16 to Oct. 2, 1947. The USSR and Belorussian and Ukrainian SSR's signed. General entry into force Jan. 1, 1949. Supersedes the regulations of 1932 (32/xii/9/Mul/b), as amended Apr. 8, 1938 (see Appendix 1). Superseded by regulations of Dec. 22, 1952, which the USSR did not sign (see 52/xii/22/Mul).
Related documents: (1) Appendices, 16 in the first series, 3 in the second. These are technical and do not directly concern the USSR. (2) Additional radio regulations. (3) Additional protocol to the acts of the International Radio Conference, signed by delegates of the European Region, establishing an 8-nation Committee, including the USSR, to prepare a preliminary draft plan for the allocation of frequencies by Mar. 15, 1948. (4) Directives for the European Regional Broadcasting Conference scheduled to meet July 1, 1948, in Copenhagen. (5) Reservation by the USSR concerning limitation of the proposed conference to signatories of the International Telecommunication Convention, thus excluding several of the European SSR's (the Baltic States).
For the Work of the Copenhagen convention, see 48/ix/15/Mul.
Source: *Radio regulations*, 1947.
Reference: *DS, IOCS*, I, 4, pp. 8–48.

Oct. 11, 1947. Convention of the World Meteorological Organization

See 48/iv/2/1947.

● 47/x/13/Pl/a, b. See Appendix 5.

● 47/x/14/Fin

Agreement between the USSR and Finland concerning direct rail transportation of passengers and freight between Helsinki and Leningrad

Signed Oct. 14, 1947.
Reference: Finnish Embassy, 1957.

Oct. 20, 1947

Protocol amending the convention of Sept. 30, 1921, for suppression of the traffic in women and children and the convention of Oct. 11, 1933, for suppression of the traffic in women of full age

See 47/xii/18/1947/a and 54/viii/11/1950.

Nov. 12, 1947

(1) Convention of Sept. 30, 1921, for suppression of the traffic in women and children, as amended by the protocol of Oct. 20, 1947

See 47/xii/18/1921.

(2) Convention of Oct. 11, 1933, for suppression of the traffic in women of full age, as amended by the protocol of Oct. 20, 1947

See 47/xii/18/1933.

(3) Protocol to amend the convention of Sept. 12, 1923, for suppression of the traffic in and circulation of obscene publications

See 47/xii/18/1947/b.

● 47/xi/15/Bul

Agreement between the USSR and Bulgaria concerning training of Bulgarian citizens in civic institutions of higher learning in the USSR and their maintenance

Signed Nov. 15, 1947.
Replaced by agreement of Mar. 7, 1952.
Listed in *SDD*, 13 (1956), p. 494, as no longer valid.

● 47/xi/16/Fin. See Appendix 5.

Nov. 17, 1947. Rules of procedure of the General Assembly of the United Nations

See Note to 45/vi/26/Mul/a.

Nov. 20, 1947. Provisional financial regulations of the United Nations

See Note to 45/vi/26/Mul/a.

• **47/xi/28/Cz**

Convention between the USSR and Czechoslovakia concerning quarantine of agricultural plants and their protection from parasites and diseases

Signed Nov. 28, 1947, in Prague.
Ratified by the USSR June 5, 1948. Entered into force Sept. 4, 1948, on exchange of acts of ratification in Moscow. Duration 5 years; if not denounced 1 year before expiration, extended for 5-year periods.
List of parasites supplemented under agreement of June 16, 1953.
Sources: *VVS*, 1949, No. 14.
    SDD, 13, pp. 382–86.
    UNTS, 216, pp. 285–301 (R, Cz., E, F).

• **47/xii/1/Fin/a**

Treaty of commerce between the USSR and Finland, with annex concerning the Soviet Trade Mission in Finland

Signed Dec. 1, 1947, in Moscow.
Ratified by Finland Mar. 12, 1948; by the USSR Mar. 30, 1948. Entered into force Apr. 26, 1948, on exchange of acts of ratification in Helsinki. Duration 5 years; thereafter, until 12 months after denunciation. Listed by Korolenko, p. 104, as still valid as of Nov. 25, 1953.
Sources: *VVS*, 1949, No. 8.
    VT, 1948, No. 4, pp. 37–41.
    VPSS, 1947, II, pp. 84–94.
    Korolenko, pp. 282–87.
    SS, 1948, No. 12–13 (Finnish, R).
    UNTS, 217, pp. 3–33 (R, Finnish, E, F).
Reference: *Izv.*, Dec. 3, 1947.

• **47/xii/1/Fin/b**

Trade protocol for 1948 between the USSR and Finland

Signed Dec. 1, 1947, in Moscow.
Soviet grains and fodder, metals, and fertilizers, in exchange for Finnish timber, prefabricated houses, cellulose, paper, etc.

References: *Izv.*, Dec. 3, 1947.
    VT, 1948, No. 6, pp. 13–14.

• **47/xii/3/Pl**

Documents concerning the frontier mark erected at Muotkavaara (Krokfjellet) at the junction point of the state frontiers of the USSR, Norway, and Finland

Signed Dec. 3, 1947, in Helsinki, by Norway and the joint Soviet-Finnish commission for demarcation of the border in the area of the Jäniskoski hydroelectric station and the Niskakoski control dam.
Mentioned in the protocol of Feb. 7, 1953, concerning maintenance of the border mark.

• **47/xii/7/Fin**

Protocol between the USSR and Finland concerning demarcation of the border in the area of the Jäniskoski hydroelectric station and the Niskakoski control dam, with eight appendices

Signed Dec. 7, 1947, in Helsinki, by the mixed commission established under the treaty of Feb. 3, 1947 (47/ii/3/Fin/a). Entered into force Aug. 21, 1950, under an exchange of notes of May 29 and July 18, 1950 (50/vii/18/Fin). Confirmed by the border treaty of Dec. 9, 1948. Appendices give technical data, maps, and drawings.
Sources: *BFSP*, 1948, pp. 575–96 (omits the appendices), citing
    SS, 1950, No. 34.
Reference: *Izv.*, Dec. 16, 1947.

• **47/xii/9/H/a**

Communiqué concerning negotiations between the USSR and Hungary on economic matters

Issued Dec. 9, 1947, in Moscow.
Mentions signing, on Dec. 9, 1947, of 3 protocols, with annexes, and an exchange of notes (see next 4 documents). States that negotiations dealt with (1) payment by Hungary to the USSR under indebtedness by Hungarian physical and legal persons to German physical and legal persons; (2) settlement of matters related to activities of the Soviet-Hungarian joint-stock companies; and (3) activities of enterprises transferred to the USSR under the Potsdam agreement of Aug. 1945. Agreement also reached on the

question of German assets in Hungary and "other questions."
Sources: *Izv.*, Dec. 10, 1947.
    VPSS, 1947, II, pp. 101–102.

● 47/xii/9/H/b

Secret protocol between the USSR and Hungary concerning conversion of the Soviet-Hungarian joint-stock companies into Soviet monopolies

Signed Dec. 9, 1947, in Moscow.
Mentioned in the communiqué on negotiations (preceding document). For the agreement under which the companies were established, see 45/viii/27/H/a.
Reference: *DSB*, 25, 1951, p. 327.

● 47/xii/9/H/c

Secret protocol between the USSR and Hungary concerning payment by Hungary to the USSR of a Soviet claim based on debts of Hungarian nationals to German nationals

Signed Dec. 9, 1947, in Moscow.
Provides for payment of $45 million, ⅔ of which is to be invested in approximately 200 Hungarian enterprises in which the USSR has an interest, the remainder to be paid for in goods over 4 years. Mentioned in the communiqué on negotiations (47/xii/9/H/a).
Reference: *DSB*, 25, 1951, p. 327.

● 47/xii/9/H/d

Secret protocol between the USSR and Hungary authorizing transfer to the USSR of former German assets in Hungary without assuming their liabilities

Signed Dec. 9, 1947, in Moscow.
Mentioned in the communiqué on negotiations.
Reference: *DSB*, 25, 1951, p. 327.

● 47/xii/9/H/e

Exchange of notes between the USSR and Hungary

Sent Dec. 9, 1947, in Moscow.
Subject unknown. Mentioned in the communiqué on negotiations (47/xii/9/H/a).

● 47/xii/11/Cz/a

Treaty of commerce and navigation between the USSR and Czechoslovakia, with annex concerning the Soviet Trade Mission in Czechoslovakia

Signed Dec. 11, 1947, in Moscow.
Ratified by Czechoslovakia Apr. 8, 1948; by the USSR, Apr. 28, 1948. Entered into force June 15, 1948, on exchange of acts of ratification in Prague. Valid until 1 year after denunciation. Listed in Korolenko, p. 104, as still valid as of Nov. 25, 1953. Supersedes the treaty of commerce and navigation of Mar. 25, 1935 (35/iii/25/Cz/a).
Sources: *VVS*, 1949, No. 9.
    VT, 1948, No. 6, pp. 26–30.
    VPSS, 1947, II, pp. 102–13.
    SDD, 13, pp. 352–62.
    Korolenko, pp. 287–93.
    UNTS, 217, pp. 35–71 (R, Cz., E, F).
    Dewar, pp. 100–106.
    Economic treaties, pp. 54–67.

● 47/xii/11/Cz/b

Trade and payments agreement between the USSR and Czechoslovakia

Signed Dec. 11, 1947, in Moscow.
Covers the period 1948–1952. Annual exchange of goods to total 5 billion Czech crowns for each party. Signed in accordance with the joint communiqué of July 12, 1947.
Reference: *VT*, 1948, No. 4, p. 12; *ibid.*, No. 11, p. 2.

● 47/xii/11/Cz/c

Agreement between the USSR and Czechoslovakia concerning a short-term credit for Czechoslovakia

Signed Dec. 11, 1947, in Moscow.
Reference: *VT*, 1948, No. 4, p. 12.

● 47/xii/11/Cz/d

Agreement between the USSR and Czechoslovakia concerning scientific and technical collaboration

Signed Dec. 11, 1947, in Moscow.
Entered into force on signature. Duration 5 years; if not denounced 12 months before expiration, extended for an additional 5 years. Establishes a Soviet-Czech commission, to meet at least twice annually, in Moscow and Prague.
Source: *SDD*, 13, pp. 362–63.
Reference: *Izv.*, Dec. 13, 1947.

- 47/xii/15/Alb

Agreement between the USSR and Albania concerning training of Albanian citizens in civic institutions of higher learning in the USSR and their maintenance

Signed Dec. 15, 1947.
Supplemented by protocol of Jan. 16, 1951. Superseded by agreement of July 5, 1952. Mentioned in *SDD*, 13 (1956), p. 494, as no longer valid.

- 47/xii/15/Pl

Fifth meeting of the Council of Foreign Ministers

Held Nov. 25 through Dec. 15, 1947, in London, by the Foreign Ministers of the USSR, the United Kingdom, the United States of America, and France.
Discussion concerned Germany's frontiers; establishment of a central German government; and reparations from Germany. An agreement was reached (on Dec. 11) to set Germany's annual production of steel at 11½ million tons. The USSR accepted in principle a percentage reduction of its claims on German assets in eastern Austria.
References: *SIA, 1947–1948*, pp. 238–41; *ibid., 1949–1950*, pp. 282–83.
Marshall, 1947.

- 47/xii/15/Rom

Agreement between the USSR and Romania concerning training of Romanian citizens in civic institutions of higher learning in the USSR and their maintenance

Signed Dec. 15, 1947.
Superseded by agreement of Mar. 20, 1952.
Mentioned in *SDD*, 13 (1956), p. 495, as no longer valid.

- 47/xii/15/Yug

Agreement between the USSR and Yugoslavia concerning training of Yugoslav citizens in civic institutions of higher learning in the USSR and their maintenance

Signed Dec. 15, 1947, in Moscow.
Entered into force on signature. Valid for the academic year 1947–1948. Covers the education of 250 persons. Registered with the UN by Yugoslavia Nov. 27, 1951. For provisions to settle Yugoslav indebtedness under this agreement, see 48/xii/27/Yug.
Source: *UNTS*, 116, pp. 313–25 (R, SC, E, F).

- 47/xii/17/Bul/a

Agreement between the USSR and Bulgaria concerning establishment of postal and telephone-telegraph communications, with final protocol

Signed Dec. 17, 1947, in Moscow.
Entered into force on signature. Valid until 6 months after denunciation. Final protocol concerns details of communications.
Source: *SDD*, 13, pp. 398–407.

- 47/xii/17/Bul/b

Parcel post agreement between the USSR and Bulgaria

Signed Dec. 17, 1947, in Moscow.
Entered into force Jan. 17, 1948 (1 month after signature). Valid until 6 months after denunciation. Under subsequent agreements, certain technical details were modified with effect from July 1, 1948, July 1, 1951, and July 1, 1953. The date of these agreements is known only for the 1953 changes (see 53/ix/17/Bul).
Source: *SDD*, 13, pp. 407–16.

- 47/xii/18/Norway

Final protocol of the mixed Soviet-Norwegian border commission, with related documents, constituting an agreement for demarcation of the state border between the USSR and Norway

Signed Dec. 18, 1947, in Moscow.
Approved by both governments and entered into force May 23, 1949, under an exchange of notes of that date. Reaffirmed in the border treaty of Dec. 29, 1949. Related documents: (1) Descriptive protocol; (2) annexes to the descriptive protocol, consisting of 415 protocols describing the boundary marks and an album of maps and triangulation diagrams.
Source: *UNTS*, 52, pp. 3–434 (R, N, E, F).
Note: The annexes to the descriptive protocol are omitted from *UNTS, loc cit.*, but a certified copy of them has been deposited with the UN Secretariat.
Reference: *Izv.*, Dec. 23, 1947.

● 47/xii/18/1921

**International convention for suppression
of the traffic in women and children**

Signed Sept. 30, 1921, in Geneva;
amended by a protocol of Nov. 12, 1947
(see 47/xii/18/1947/a).
Soviet act of accession deposited Dec. 18,
1947; that of the Belorussian SSR May
21, 1948. (Note: According to the *UNTS*
references, 11, p. 424, and 15, p. 450, the
accessions of the USSR and Belorussian
SSR were to the unrevised 1921 convention. Since the date of Soviet accession,
however, was that on which the USSR
acceded to the 1947 protocol revising the
1921 convention (see 47/xii/18/1947/a),
it is probable that the accessions were in
fact to the revised convention.) The revised convention entered into force Apr.
24, 1950. Superseded by the convention
of Mar. 21, 1950 (see 54/viii/11/1950).
Sources: (1) text of 1921: *LNTS*, 9, pp.
415–33 (E, F).
(2) text of 1947: *UNTS*, 53, pp. 40–
47 (E, F).

● 47/xii/18/1933

**International convention for suppression
of the traffic in women of full age**

Signed Oct. 11, 1933, in Geneva; amended
by a protocol of Nov. 12, 1947 (see 47/
xii/18/1947/a).
Soviet act of accession deposited Dec. 18,
1947; that of the Belorussian SSR May
21, 1948, effective July 21, 1948. (Note:
In both cases the *UNTS* references, 11, p.
425, and 15, p. 425, refer to the unrevised
1933 convention. It is probable, however,
that the accessions were in fact to the
revised conventions. See note to preceding document.) The revised convention
entered into force Apr. 24, 1950. Superseded by the convention of Mar. 21, 1950
(see 54/viii/11/1950).
Sources: (1) text of 1933: *LNTS*, 150,
pp. 431–43 (E, F).
(2) text of 1947: *UNTS*, 53, pp. 49–
57 (E, F).

● 47/xii/18/1947/a

**Protocol to amend the convention for
suppression of the traffic in women and
children of September 30, 1921, and
the convention for suppression of the
traffic in women of full age of October
11, 1933, with annex**

Approved by the General Assembly of
the UN Oct. 20, 1947. Opened for signature Nov. 12, 1947, at Lake Success, N.Y.;
signed by the USSR, Dec. 18, 1947.
Entered into force Nov. 12, 1947. Annex
gives textual amendments to the 1921 and
1933 conventions. For these conventions,
see the 2 preceding documents.
Sources: *UNTS*, 53, pp. 13–38 (R, E, F,
C, S).
BFSP, 148, pp. 871–79.
Listed in *SDD*, 13 (1956), p. 495, as no
longer valid.

● 47/xii/18/1947/b

**Protocol to amend the convention for
suppression of the circulation of and
traffic in obscene publications of September 12, 1923, with annex**

Signed Nov. 12, 1947, at Lake Success,
N.Y.; by the USSR, Dec. 18, 1947.
For the USSR, entered into force Dec. 18,
1947. Annex, modifying the text of the
1923 agreement, entered into force Feb.
2, 1950. For the 1923 agreement, see 35/
vii/8/1923.
Sources: *SDD*, 13, pp. 307–10.
BFSP, 148, pp. 824–28, citing
BTS, 1952, No. 2, Cmd. 8438.
UNTS, 46, pp. 169–200 (R, E, F, C, S).

● 47/xii/19/Fin

**Agreement between the USSR and Fin-
land concerning direct rail communications, with annex**

Signed Dec. 19, 1947, in Moscow.
Entered into force on signature. Valid
until 6 months after denunciation. Subsequently modified, with effect from Jan. 1,
1953; date of agreement on modification
unknown. Annex gives Regulations concerning conferences on Soviet-Finnish direct rail communications.
Sources: *SDD*, 13, pp. 387–93 (incorporating 1953 changes).
SS, 1948, No. 1 (Finnish, R).
Reference: *Izv.*, Dec. 27, 1947.

● 47/xii/22/Norway

**Informal agreement between the USSR
and Norway concerning trade in 1948**

Reached during negotiations in Moscow
which ended Dec. 22, 1947.
For a protocol embodying the agreement,
see 48/i/6/Norway.
Reference: *Izv.*, Dec. 23, 1947.

● 47/xii/27/UK/a

Protocol of agreement between the USSR and the United Kingdom on questions of trade and finance, with annex and two schedules

Signed Dec. 27, 1947, in Moscow.
Entered into force on signature. Listed by Korolenko, p. 107, as still valid as of Nov. 23, 1953.
Annex covers the following agreements: (1) short-term arrangements; (2) long-term arrangements; (3) financial arrangements; and (4) transport arrangements. The 2 schedules list equipment for delivery from the United Kingdom to the USSR. The financial agreement (part 3 of the annex) modifies the agreement of Aug. 16, 1941.
Sources: *BFSP*, 147, pp. 1051–57, citing *BTS*, 1948, No. 34, Cmd. 7439.
UNTS, 91, pp. 113–35 (R, E, F).

References: *Izv.*, Dec. 28, 1947.
VT, 1948, No. 4, p. 13.
SIA, 1947–1948, pp. 102–103.

● 47/xii/27/UK/b

Exchange of notes between the USSR and the United Kingdom constituting a payments agreement

Sent Dec. 27, 1947, in Moscow.
Entered into force Jan. 15, 1948.
Sources: **BTS*, 1948, No. 32, Cmd. 7431.
UNTS, 82, pp. 251–57.

● 47/xii/31/Sweden

Trade protocol for 1948 between the USSR and Sweden

Signed Dec. 31, 1947, in Moscow.
References: *VT*, 1948, No. 3, p. 29.
Izv., Jan. 1, 1948.

1948

● 48/i/ /US

Informal agreement between the USSR and the United States of America concerning the return of eight Lend-Lease vessels

Reached during Jan. 1948.
Covers return of 7 tankers and 1 dry-cargo freighter; transfer completed by Mar. 27, according to a TASS statement published Apr. 10, 1948.
References: *Izv.*, Apr. 10, 1948.
VPSS, 1948, I, pp. 187–88.

● 48/i/6/Bul. See Appendix 5.

● 48/i/6/Norway

Trade protocol for 1948 between the USSR and Norway

Signed Jan. 6, 1948, in Moscow.
References: *Izv.*, Jan. 7, 1948.
VT, 1948, No. 3, p. 29.
VPSS, 1948, I, p. 44.

● 48/i/10/Bul/a and /b

Two protocols between the USSR and Bulgaria concerning regulation of certain questions connected with the transfer of former German assets in Bulgaria to Soviet possession

Signed Jan. 10, 1948, in Moscow.

References listed provide no information on content of the protocols, nor basis for distinguishing between them.
References: *Izv.*, Jan. 13, 1948.
VPSS, 1948, I, p. 44.

● 48/i/26/Pol/a

Joint communiqué by the USSR and Poland concerning economic negotiations

Signed Jan. 26, 1948, in Moscow, at the end of negotiations which began Jan. 15, 1948.
Mentions long-term trade agreement and agreement on delivery of Soviet industrial equipment to Poland on credit (next two documents). Mentions further (1) Soviet agreement to sell Poland 200,000 tons of grain on credit, to be delivered within 3 months, and discussion during the negotiations of (2) fulfillment of the agreement of Mar. 5, 1947, on technical collaboration and (3) questions concerned with deliveries during 1948 of Poland's share of German reparations. For the agreement of Mar. 5, 1947, see 47/iii/5/Pol/f.
Sources: *Izv.*, Jan. 27, 1948.
VPSS, 1948, I, pp. 49–50.

● 48/i/26/Pol/b

Long-term trade agreement between the USSR and Poland

Signed Jan. 26, 1948, in Moscow.
Not subject to ratification. Covers the
period 1948–1952. Reciprocal deliveries
to total 5.3 billion rubles. Soviet iron,
chrome, and manganese ores, oil products,
cotton, aluminum, asbestos, automobiles,
tractors, etc., in exchange for Polish coal,
coke, textiles, sugar, zinc, steel products,
railroad rolling stock, etc. Volume of
trade increased under protocols of Jan.
15, 1950, and June 29, 1950 (50/vi/29/
Pol/c).
References: *VT*, 1948, No. 11, p. 2; *ibid.*,
    1955, No. 4, p. 2.
    See also sources listed for 48/i/26/Pol/
    a.

• 48/i/26/Pol/c

**Agreement between the USSR and Po-
land concerning delivery of Soviet industrial equipment to Poland on credit**

Signed Jan. 26, 1948, in Moscow.
USSR to deliver equipment for a metallurgical factory, electrical and chemical
equipment, metal-working, textile, and
other industrial equipment, and machinery for rebuilding cities and ports, over
the period 1948–1956.
References: *VT*, 1955, No. 4, p. 2.
    Sources cited for 48/i/26/Pol/a.

• 48/ii/4/Rom/a

**Treaty of friendship, collaboration and
mutual assistance between the USSR and
Romania**

Signed Feb. 4, 1948, in Moscow.
Ratified by Romania Feb. 13, 1948; by the
USSR Feb. 19, 1948. Acts of ratification
exchanged Mar. 10, 1948, in Bucharest.
Entered into force on signature. Duration
20 years; if not denounced 1 year before
expiration, extended for 5-year periods
until denounced.
Sources: *Izv.*, Feb. 5, 1948.
    VVS, 1949, No. 5.
    VPSS, 1948, I, pp. 52–55.
    SDD, 13, pp. 20–22.
    UNTS, 48, pp. 189–201 (R, Rom., E,
    F).
    BFSP, 152, pp. 801–803
    DSP, 1, 1948, pp. 234–35.

• 48/ii/4/Rom/b

**Protocol between the USSR and Ro-
mania concerning demarcation of the
border, with two maps**

Signed Feb. 4, 1948, in Moscow.

Entered into force on signature. Defines
the boundary between the 2 States as provided for in Art. 1 of the peace treaty
with Romania (47/ii/10/Rom). Calls for
establishment of a mixed Soviet-Romanian border commission to carry out demarcation of the boundary. For completion of the commission's work, see 49/ix/
27/Rom.
Source: *SDD*, 13, pp. 266–67.

• 48/ii/9/Cz

**Agreement between the USSR and Czech-
oslovakia concerning general conditions
of deliveries from Czechoslovakia to the
USSR, with protocol**

Signed Feb. 9, 1948, in Prague.
Entered into force Feb. 20, 1948, under
the protocol.
Source: *VT*, 1948, No. 4, pp. 41–45.

• 48/ii/12/Yug

**Joint statement by the USSR and Yugo-
slavia concerning mutual consultation
on questions of foreign policy**

Signed Feb. 12, 1948, in Moscow.
Reference: Dedijer, pp. 323–24.

• 48/ii/18/BL/a

**Exchange of notes between the USSR
and Belgium concerning application of
the active provisions of the temporary
commercial convention of Sept. 5, 1935**

Sent Feb. 18, 1948, in Moscow.
Provides for revival of Arts. 1, 3, 4 and
5 of the 1935 convention (35/ix/5/BL).
Convention to remain in force until the
conclusion of a treaty on commerce and
navigation; negotiations to begin in the
near future for such a treaty.
Sources: *VT*, 1948, No. 6, p. 33.
    SDD, 13, pp. 313–14.

• 48/ii/18/BL/b

**Commercial agreement between the
USSR and the Belgium-Luxembourg
Economic Union, with two annexes**

Signed Feb. 18, 1948, in Moscow; by the
Belgian Ambassador to the USSR on behalf of the Belgium-Luxembourg Economic Union. Initialled Jan. 21, 1948
(*Izv.*, Jan. 22, 1948).
Entered into force on signature. Valid
until 6 months after denunciation. Listed
in Korolenko, p. 107, as still valid as of
Nov. 25, 1953.

Annexes list deliveries for 1948 and, in part, 1949; thereafter, deliveries to be determined by separate protocols. First such protocol signed Nov. 14, 1950, second Jan. 30, 1954, and third Aug. 2, 1956.
During 1948–1949, the USSR to export grains, lumber, cellulose, apatites, calcic soda, manganese ores, asbestos, furs, etc., in return for steel, nonferrous metals, excavators and crane equipment, cables, leather, coffee, etc., from Belgium-Luxembourg.
Sources: *VT*, 1948, No. 6, p. 31 (omits the annexes).
  SDD, 13, pp. 311–12 (same).
  Bulletin commercial Belge, No. 6, Mar. 15, 1948, supplement.
Reference: *Izv.*, Feb. 19, 1948.

● 48/ii/18/BL/c

Payments agreement between the USSR and the Belgium-Luxembourg Economic Union

Signed Feb. 18, 1948, in Moscow; initialled Jan. 21, 1948 (*Izv.*, Jan. 22, 1948). Entered into force on signature. Duration the same as that of the commercial agreement of the same date (preceding document).
Source: *VT*, 1948, No. 6, pp. 31–33.
References: Korolenko, pp. 91–92.
  Izv., Feb. 19, 1948.

● 48/ii/18/Burma

Exchange of notes between the USSR and Burma concerning establishment of diplomatic and consular relations

Sent Feb. 18, 1948, in London.
References: *Izv.*, Feb. 25, 1948.
  VPSS 1948, I, pp. 134–35.
  SDD, 13, p. 25.
  SIA, 1947–1948, p. 456.

● 48/ii/18/H

Treaty of friendship, collaboration and mutual assistance between the USSR and Hungary

Signed Feb. 18, 1948, in Moscow.
Ratified by Hungary Mar. 12, 1948; by the USSR Mar. 30, 1948. Entered into force Apr. 22, 1948, on exchange of acts of ratification in Budapest. Duration 20 years; if not denounced 1 year before expiration, extended for 5-year periods.
Sources: *Izv.*, Feb. 19, 1948.

VVS, 1949, No. 5.
VPSS, 1948, I, pp. 127–30.
SDD, 13, pp. 17–19.
OT, May 7, 1948.
UNTS, 48, pp. 163–75 (R, H, E, F).
DSP, 1, 1948, pp. 235–36.

● 48/ii/18/Rom/a

Trade and payments agreement for 1948 between the USSR and Romania

Signed Feb. 18, 1948, in Moscow.
References: *Izv.*, Feb. 20, 1948.
  VT, 1948, No. 6, p. 34.
  VPSS, 1948, I, p. 134.

● 48/ii/18/Rom/b

Supplementary protocol between the USSR and Romania concerning the Soviet-Romanian joint-stock lumber company

Signed Feb. 18, 1948.
For establishment of the company, see 46/iii/20/Rom.
Reference: *Economic treaties*, p. 16, citing *MO*, 1948, No. 65.

● 48/ii/18/Rom/c

Supplementary protocol between the USSR and Romania concerning the Soviet-Romanian joint-stock civil aviation company

Signed Feb. 18, 1948.
For establishment of the company, see 45/viii/8/Rom.
Reference: *Economic treaties*, p. 16, citing *MO*, 1948, No. 65.

Feb. 27, 1948. United States note to the USSR concerning Lend-Lease negotiations

See entry under Mar. 21, 1951.

● 48/iii/ /Italy. See Appendix 5.

● 48/iii/1/H. See Appendix 5.

● 48/iii/3/Egypt/a
Trade agreement between the USSR and Egypt

Signed Mar. 3, 1948, in Cairo.
Provides for exchange of Egyptian cotton for Soviet grain, lumber, ammonium sulfate, etc. Supplemented by a protocol (next document).

References: *Izv.*, Mar. 7, 1948.
VPSS, 1948, I, p. 147.
VT, 1948, No. 6, p. 34; *ibid.*, No. 7, p. 30.

• 48/iii/3/Egypt/b

Protocol between the USSR and Egypt concerning commercial relations

Signed Mar. 3, 1948, in Cairo.
Provides for application of most-favored-nation principle in regard to customs duties, navigation, and the legal position of legal and physical persons of one party on the territory of the other.
References: *VT*, 1948, No. 7, p. 30; *ibid.*, 1955, No. 1, p. 20.
Korolenko, pp. 80, 128.

• 48/iii/16/Fin

Exchange of notes between the USSR and Finland concerning renewal of prewar treaties

Sent Mar. 13 and 16, 1948, in Helsinki.
Renews the following prewar treaties: (1) Agreement of Oct. 11, 1940, concerning demilitarization of the Aaland Islands (40/x/11/Fin). (2) Agreement of Oct. 28, 1922, concerning maintenance of the main channel and fishing in the border water systems between Russia and Finland (22/x/28/Fin/a). (3) Convention of Oct. 28, 1922, concerning floating of timber in border water courses (22/x/28/Fin/b). (4) Convention of Oct. 15, 1933, modifying (3) (33/x/15/Fin).
Source: *SDD*, 13, pp. 306–307.

• 48/iii/17/Switz/a

Commercial treaty between the USSR and Switzerland

Signed Mar. 17, 1948, in Moscow.
Ratified by Switzerland July 1, 1948; by the USSR July 13, 1948. Entered into force Aug. 31, 1948 (20 days after exchange of acts of ratification, which took place, Aug. 11, 1948, in Berne). Duration 1 year; if not denounced 3 months before expiration, valid until 6 months after denunciation. Listed in Korolenko, p. 104, as still valid as of Nov. 25, 1953. Valid for Liechtenstein for the duration of the Swiss-Liechtenstein customs union.
Sources: *VVS*, 1949, No. 13.
VT, 1948, No. 7, pp. 25–27.
SDD, 13, pp. 363–67.
Korolenko, pp. 293–95.

RO, 1948, p. 869.
UNTS, 217, pp. 73–85 (R, F, E).
BFSP, 152, pp. 820–24 (F).

• 48/iii/17/Switz/b

Agreement between the USSR and Switzerland concerning the Soviet Trade Mission in Switzerland

Signed Mar. 17, 1948, in Moscow.
Approved by Switzerland Mar. 31, 1948; approval notified to the USSR Apr. 7, 1948. Approval of the USSR notified to Switzerland Apr. 9, 1948. Entered into force Apr. 1, 1948. Duration 2 years; if not denounced 3 months before expiration, valid until 6 months after denunciation. Valid for Liechtenstein for the duration of the Swiss-Liechtenstein customs union.
Sources: *VVS*, 1949, No. 13.
VT, 1948, No. 7, pp. 27–28.
SDD, 13, pp. 368–70.
Korolenko, pp. 296–97.
RO, 1948, p. 360.
UNTS, 217, pp. 87–96 (R, F, E).
BFSP, 152, pp. 824–26 (F).
Reference: *Izv.*, Mar. 19, 1948.

• 48/iii/17/Switz/c

Trade agreement between the USSR and Switzerland, with annexes

Signed Mar. 17, 1948, in Moscow.
Approved by Switzerland Mar. 31, 1948; approval notified to the USSR Apr. 7, 1948. Approval of the USSR notified to Switzerland Apr. 9, 1948. Entered into force Apr. 1, 1948. Duration 2 years; if not denounced 3 months before expiration, extended indefinitely, or until 6 months after denunciation. Valid for Liechtenstein for the duration of the Swiss-Liechtenstein customs union. Supersedes the trade agreement of Feb. 24, 1941.
Provides for exchange of Soviet grains, lumber, etc., for Swiss power machinery, machine tools, and electrotechnical equipment. Payments to be in Swiss francs or other convertible currency. Annexes list goods to be exchanged.
Sources: *VT*, 1948, No. 7, pp. 29–30.
RO, 1948, p. 363.
References: *Izv.*, Mar. 19, 1948.
VPSS, 1948, I, pp. 163–64.

• 48/iii/18/Bul

Treaty of friendship, cooperation, and

mutual assistance between the USSR and Bulgaria

Signed Mar. 18, 1948, in Moscow.
Ratified by Bulgaria Apr. 1, 1948; by the USSR Apr. 7, 1948. Acts of ratification exchanged May 11, 1948, in Sofia. Entered into force on signature. Duration 20 years; if not denounced 1 year before expiration, extended for 5-year periods.
Sources: *VVS*, 1949, No. 6.
  Izv., Mar. 19, 1948.
  VPSS, 1948, I, pp. 158–61.
  SDD, 13, pp. 15–17.
  UNTS, 48, pp. 135–47 (R, B, E, F).
  DSP, 1, 1948, pp. 236–37.

• 48/iv/1/Bul/a

Treaty of commerce and navigation between the USSR and Bulgaria, with annex concerning the Soviet Trade Mission in Bulgaria

Signed Apr. 1, 1948, in Moscow.
Ratified by the USSR July 13, 1948. Entered into force Aug. 7, 1948, on exchange of acts of ratification in Sofia. Duration 5 years; if not denounced 1 year before expiration, extended until 1 year after denunciation. Listed in Korolenko, p. 104, as still valid as of Nov. 25, 1953.
Sources: *VVS*, 1949, No. 10.
  VT, 1948, No. 7, pp. 20–25.
  VPSS, 1948, I, pp. 165–76.
  SDD, 13, pp. 314–23.
  Korolenko, pp. 297–303.
  UNTS, 217, pp. 97–133 (R, B, E, F).

• 48/iv/1/Bul/b

Trade agreement for 1948 between the USSR and Bulgaria

Signed Apr. 1, 1948, in Moscow.
References: *Izv.*, Apr. 3, 1948.
  VPSS, 1948, I, p. 178.
  VT, 1948, No. 6, p. 34.

• 48/iv/2/1947

Convention of the World Meteorological Organization, with two annexes and a protocol

Signed Oct. 11, 1947, in Washington, D.C. Act of accession of the USSR deposited Apr. 2, 1948; acts of accession of the Belorussian and Ukrainian SSR's deposited Apr. 12, 1948. Entered into force Mar. 23, 1950.
Establishes the World Meteorological Or-

ganization and defines its composition and functions. Members may withdraw with 12 months' notice.
Annexes list (1) States represented at the conference of directors of the International Meteorological Organization convened at Washington, D.C., Sept. 22, 1947 (including the USSR), and (2) territories or groups of territories represented at the same conference. Protocol provides for eventual admission of Spain.
Sources: *SDD*, 14, pp. 231–46 (omits the protocol).
  BFSP, 148, pp. 741–59, citing
    BTS, 1950, No. 36, Cmd. 7989.
  UST, 1, pp. 281–355, citing
    TIAS, 2052 (1947).
  UNTS, 77, pp. 143–81 (E, F).
  Durdenevski and Krylov, pp. 318–31,

• 48/iv/6/Fin

Treaty of friendship, cooperation, and mutual assistance between the USSR and Finland

Signed Apr. 6, 1948, in Moscow.
Ratified by Finland Apr. 30, 1948; by the USSR May 11, 1948. Entered into force May 31, 1948, on exchange of acts of ratification in Helsinki. Duration 10 years; if not denounced 1 year before expiration, extended for 5-year periods. Extended for 20 years by protocol of Sept. 19, 1955 (55/ix/19/Fin/b).
Sources: *VVS*, 1949, No. 6.
  VPSS, 1948, I, pp. 183–85.
  SDD, 13, pp. 22–24.
  SS, 1948, No. 17 (Finnish, R).
  UNTS, 48, pp. 149–61 (R, Finnish, E, F).
  BFSP, 152, pp. 356–58.
  DSP, 1, 1948, pp. 237–38.
  Mazour, pp. 280–82.

• 48/iv/8/Pol

Convention between the USSR and Poland concerning quarantine of agricultural plants and their protection from parasites and diseases

Signed Apr. 8, 1948, in Warsaw.
Ratified by Poland Aug. 2, 1948; by the USSR Aug. 18, 1948. Entered into force Oct. 22, 1948, on exchange of acts of ratification in Moscow. Duration 5 years; if not denounced 1 year before expiration, extended for 5-year periods.
Sources: *VVS*, 1949, No. 14.
  SDD, 13, pp. 378–82.

DURP, 1949, No. 2, Arts. 4, 5.
UNTS, 26, pp. 191–211 (R, P, E, F).

• 48/iv/28/Norway/a and/b

Communiqué and protocol between the USSR and Norway concerning work of a mixed Soviet-Norwegian commission to investigate living and working conditions of Soviet citizens in German captivity in Norway

The communiqué was published Apr. 28, 1948.
The commission, which was established in 1945 (see 45/ / /Norway), investigated prisoner-of-war camps during 1946 and 1947. It found that approximately 100,000 Soviet prisoners had been held by the Germans in Norway, of whom 10,000 died during captivity and 90,000 were repatriated. On completion of its work the commission prepared a protocol.
Source (communiqué): *Pravda*, Apr. 28, 1948.

• 48/v/1/Pakistan

Exchange of notes between the USSR and Pakistan concerning establishment of diplomatic relations

Sent. Apr. 27, 1948, from New York, and May 1, 1948, from Moscow.
Preceded by an informal understanding, initiated by Pakistan on Apr. 13, 1948.
Sources: *Izv.*, May 4, 1948.
VPSS, 1948, I, pp. 191–92.
Reference: *SDD*, 13, p. 26.

Feb. 20–May 6, 1948

Conference of the Deputy Foreign Ministers of the USSR, the United Kingdom, the United States of America, and France. Discussions concerned preparations for an Austrian peace treaty and included consideration of Soviet claims on German assets in Austria, the Austrian borders, and Yugoslav claims against Austria for reparations. No agreements were reached. See *DAFR*, 10, pp. 150–51; *DSB*, 18, 1948, pp. 746–47; and *SIA, 1949–1950*, pp. 283–85.

• 48/v/12/MPR

Agreement between the USSR and the Mongolian People's Republic concerning training of Mongolian citizens in civic institutions of higher learning in the USSR and their maintenance

Signed May 12, 1948.
Listed in *SDD*, 13 (1956), p. 494, as no longer valid. Replaced by the agreement of Apr. 30, 1952; presumably replaced the agreement of July 22, 1941.
Reference: *Izv.*, May 2, 1948.

• 48/v/13/Pol. See Appendix 5.

May 13, 1948. Staff rules of the United Nations

See Note to 45/vi/26/Mul/a.

• 48/v/18/Israel

Exchange of telegrams between the USSR and the Provisional Government of Israel concerning recognition of Israel by the USSR

Sent May 15, 1948, from Tel Aviv and May 18, 1948, from Moscow.
For an agreement to establish diplomatic missions, see 48/v/26/Israel.
Sources: *Izv.*, May 18, 1948 (Soviet note).
VPSS, 1948, I, p. 203 (same).
Reference: *SDD*, 13, p. 25.

• 48/v/22/Indonesia

Exchange of notes between the USSR and Indonesia concerning establishment of consular relations

Sent May 22, 1948, in Prague.
References: *Pr.*, *Izv.*, May 26, 1948.
VPSS, 1948, I, p. 215.

• 48/v/26/Israel

Exchange of telegrams between the USSR and Israel concerning establishment of diplomatic missions in Moscow and Tel Aviv

Sent May 24, 1948, from Tel Aviv and May 26, 1948, from Moscow.
For Soviet recognition of Israel, see 48/v/18/Israel. Diplomatic relations between the 2 states were ended by a Soviet note of Feb. 11, 1953, following explosion of a bomb on the premises of the Soviet diplomatic mission in Israel. Relations were re-established by an exchange of notes dated July 6 and 15, 1953 (53/vii/15/Israel).
Sources: *Izv.*, May 26, 1948.
VPSS, 1948, I, pp. 215–16.
Reference: *SDD*, 13, p. 25.

• 48/v/28/Pol

Agreement between the USSR and Po-

land concerning training of Polish citizens in civic institutions of higher learning in the USSR and their maintenance

Signed May 28, 1948.
Replaced by an agreement of May 19, 1952 (52/v/19/Pol). Listed in *SDD*, 13 (1956), p. 495, as no longer valid.

● 48/vi/3/Fin

Decision by the Soviet Government to reduce reparations payments by Finland

Announced June 3, 1948.
The decision was formally in answer to a request of May 19, 1948, by 3 Communist members of the Finnish cabinet; there appears to have been no official request for a reduction by the Finnish Government, but following the Soviet declaration, letters of thanks were sent to Stalin by Finnish officials. Provides for a reduction of reparations payments by 50 per cent starting July 1, 1948. For the agreement establishing Finland's reparations obligations, see 44/xii/17/Fin.
Sources: *Izv.*, June 4, 1948, p. 4.
VPSS, 1948, I, p. 217.

● 48/vi/7/H

Exchange of notes between the USSR and Hungary concerning reduction in reparations payments by Hungary

Sent June 5 and 7, 1948, in Budapest.
Provides for reduction of reparations payments by 50 per cent starting July 1, 1948. For the agreement establishing Hungary's reparations obligations, see 45/vi/15/H.
Sources: *Izv.*, June 11, 1948.
VPSS, 1948, I, pp. 221–22.

● 48/vi/7/Rom

Exchange of notes between the USSR and Romania concerning reduction in reparations payments by Romania

Sent June 4 and 7, 1948.
Provides for reduction of reparations payments by 50 per cent starting July 1, 1948. For the agreement establishing Romania's reparations obligations, see 45/vi/16/Rom.
Sources: *Izv.*, June 9, 1948 (Soviet note).
VPSS, 1948, I, p. 220 (same).

June 10, 1948. Final Act of the International Conference on Safety of Life at Sea

See 54/iv/19/1948.

● 48/vi/11/Cz

Agreement between the USSR and Czechoslovakia concerning training of Czechoslovak citizens in civic institutions of higher education in the USSR and their maintenance

Signed June 11, 1948.
Superseded by the agreement of Apr. 11, 1952 (52/iv/11/Cz). Listed in *SDD*, 13 (1956), p. 495, as no longer valid.

● 48/vi/19/Fin

Convention between the USSR and Finland concerning procedure for settling border disputes and incidents, with related documents

Signed June 19, 1948, in Moscow.
Entered into force July 19, 1948 (30 days after signature). Duration 5 years; if not denounced 6 months before expiration, extended for 5 years.
Provides for appointment of Border Commissars by both states to deal with disputes. Related documents consist of 4 annexed blank forms for personal identification in connection with border relations; a protocol specifying the officials to be named by both states as Border Commissars; and a final protocol, concerning clarification of various provisions of the convention.
Sources: *SDD*, 13, pp. 281–305.
SS, 1948, No. 19 (Finnish, R).
BFSP, 152, pp. 358–66 (text of convention only).
References: *Izv.*, June 22, 1948.
VPSS, 1948, I, p. 228.

● 48/vi/24/Pl

Statement concerning the decisions of the London Conference on Germany

Signed June 24, 1948, in Warsaw, by the Foreign Ministers of the USSR, Albania, Bulgaria, Czechoslovakia, Yugoslavia, Poland, Romania, and Hungary.
From Feb. to June, 1948, a Six-Power conference on Germany met in London (see *SIA, 1947–1948*, pp. 261–63). The Warsaw statement of June 24 sharply criticized the decisions announced by the London conference and called for the following steps: (1) adoption of measures by agreement between the USSR, the United Kingdom, the United States of America, and France to guarantee completion of the demilitarization of Germany; (2) estab-

lishment of Four-Power control over the heavy industry of the Ruhr for a definite period; (3) formation by Four-Power agreement of a "provisional democratic and peaceable all-German government"; (4) conclusion of a peace treaty with Germany "in conformity with the Potsdam decisions" and withdrawal of occupation forces from Germany within a year after conclusion of the peace treaty; and (5) adoption of "measures to ensure the discharge by Germany of her reparations obligations toward the countries which suffered from German aggression."

Sources: *The Soviet Union and the Berlin question*, pp. 32–41.
DIA, 1947–1948, pp. 566–74.

July 1, 1948

Changes in parcel post agreements of (1) Sept. 22, 1947, between the USSR and Hungary.
See 47/ix/22/H/b.
(2) Dec. 17, 1947, between the USSR and Bulgaria.
See 47/xii/17/Bul/b.

● 48/vii/2/Neth

Trade and payments agreement between the USSR and The Netherlands, with two annexes

Signed July 2, 1948, in Moscow.
Entered into force on signature, but applied retroactively from June 10, 1946. Valid until 3 months after denunciation. Listed in Korolenko, p. 107, as still valid as of Nov. 25, 1953. Supplemented by protocols of Apr. 28, 1954, and June 27, 1956. Establishes a joint commission on implementation, to meet alternately in The Hague and Moscow.
Annexes list commodities to be traded during the 1st year and, in some cases, later. Soviet grains, lumber, apatites, calcium salt, ferromanganese, asbestos, coal tar, etc., in exchange for Dutch vessels, equipment, rubber, cables, dyes, quinine, herring, etc. Supplemented by protocols of Apr. 28, 1954, and June 27, 1956.
Source: *VT*, 1948, No. 8, pp. 25–27 (omits annexes).
References: *Izv.*, July 4, 1948.
VPSS, 1948, II, p. 15.
Korolenko, pp. 84–85.

● 48/vii/8/Denmark/a

Protocol between the USSR and Den-

mark modifying and extending the commercial agreement of July 8, 1946, and extending the arbitration protocol of August 17, 1946

Signed July 8, 1948, in Moscow.
Extends the commercial agreement of 1946 (46/vii/8/Denmark/a) to July 8, 1950, and provides for interest payment at 2 per cent on trade balances exceeding 2 million Danish crowns, subject to modification if the exchange value of the crown is altered. Extends the arbitration protocol of 1946 (46/viii/17/Denmark/b) for duration of the commercial agreement.
Sources: *VT*, 1948, No. 8, p. 27.
Lovtidende C, Danmarks Traktater, 1948, p. 343.

● 48/vii/8/Denmark/b

Trade protocol between the USSR and Denmark

Signed July 8, 1948, in Moscow.
Covers the period July 1, 1948, through Dec. 31, 1949. Concluded on the basis of the commercial agreement of July 8, 1946 (46/vii/8/Denmark/a).
Reference: Korolenko, p. 84.

● 48/vii/8/Pol/a

Treaty between the USSR and Poland concerning the regime on the Soviet-Polish state border, with final protocol

Signed July 8, 1948, in Moscow.
Ratified by Poland Dec. 23, 1948; by the USSR Jan. 20, 1949. Entered into force Jan. 20, 1949, on ratification by both parties. Acts of ratification exchanged Feb. 15, 1949, in Warsaw. Duration 5 years; if not denounced 6 months before expiration, extended for 5 years.
Modified by protocol of Dec. 8, 1951. Reaffirms the boundary established under the border treaty of Aug. 16, 1945 (45/viii/16/Pol/b), as defined in the protocol of Apr. 30, 1947. Final protocol provides clarification of various points in the treaty.
Sources: *VVS*, 1949, No. 53.
SDD, 14, pp. 112–31.
DURP, 1949, No. 43, Arts. 323, 324.
UNTS, 37, pp. 25–105 (R, P, E, F).
References: *Izv.*, July 9, 1948.
VPSS, 1948, II, p. 16.

● 48/vii/8/Pol/b

Convention between the USSR and Po-

land concerning procedure for settling border disputes and incidents, with related documents

Signed July 8, 1948, in Moscow.
Ratified by Poland Dec. 23, 1948; confirmed by the USSR Feb. 9, 1949. Entered into force Mar. 15, 1949, on exchange of reports of confirmation. Duration 5 years; if not denounced 6 months before expiration, extended for 5 years. Modified by protocol of Dec. 8, 1951.
Provides for appointment of Border Commissioners by both states to deal with disputes and incidents. Related documents consist of (1) 4 annexed blank forms for personal identification in connection with border relations; (2) a protocol specifying the officials to be named by both states as Border Commissioners; and (3) a final protocol, providing clarification of various provisions of the convention.
Sources: *SDD*, 14, pp. 132–52.
DURP, 1949, No. 3, Arts. 325, 326.
References: *Izv.*, July 9, 1948.
VPSS, 1948, II, p. 16.

July 9 and 10, 1948. International Labour Organisation Conventions Nos. 87 and 90

See 56/vii/6/1948/a and /b.

July 6 and 16, 1948. Exchange of letters between the USSR and the United States of America concerning access to Berlin by the Western Powers

See 45/vi/16/US.

July 24, 1948. World Health Organization Regulations No. 1, concerning nomenclature with respect to diseases and causes of death

See 46/vii/22/Mul/b.

● **48/viii/4/NK**

Agreement between the USSR and the People's Committee of Northern Korea concerning training of North Korean students in civic institutions of higher education in the USSR and their maintenance, with protocol

Signed Aug. 4, 1948.
Expired Sept. 1, 1952, on entry into force of the agreement of May 6, 1952.
Apparently the first agreement between the USSR and the provisional regime of the Soviet-occupied zone of Korea. The Korean People's Democratic Republic

was proclaimed in Sept. 1948, and was recognized by the USSR in Oct. (see 48/x/12/KPDR).
References: Listed in *SDD*, 13 (1956), p. 494, as no longer valid.
Mentioned in the agreement of May 6, 1952.

● **48/viii/9/Bul**

Credit agreement between the USSR and Bulgaria

Signed Aug. 9, 1948.
Together with the agreement of Aug. 23, 1947, gives Bulgaria a credit of $65 million for Soviet assistance in building electrostations, plants for the production of synthetic fertilizer, ferrous and nonferrous metallurgy, plants for refining nonferrous ores, machine-building factories, etc.
Reference: *VT SSSR*, p. 150.

● **48/viii/18/Pl**

Convention concerning the regime of navigation on the Danube, with two annexes and a supplementary protocol

Signed Aug. 18, 1948, in Belgrade, by the USSR, Bulgaria, Czechoslovakia, Hungary, Romania, the Ukrainian SSR, and Yugoslavia, at the end of a conference which began July 30, 1948. The United States of America, the United Kingdom, and France were represented at the conference, but refused to sign the convention on the grounds that it failed to conform to the decision of the Paris peace conference of 1946 (see 46/x/14/Mul(17)) and was inconsistent with the spirit of the United Nations Charter.
Ratified by the USSR Apr. 15, 1949; Soviet act of ratification deposited May 11, 1949. Act of ratification of the Ukrainian SSR deposited May 14, 1949.
Provides for establishment of a Danube Commission at Galatz, with 1 representative from each "Danubian state," and a Special River Administration for the lower Danube and the Iron Gates section. Annex 1 provides for admission of Austria to the Danube Commission after settlement of the question of an Austrian peace treaty. Annex 2 concerns works necessary to ensure normal conditions of navigation in the Gabčikovo-Gönyü sector. Supplementary protocol provides that the Danube Convention of July 23, 1921, is no longer in force, and cancels obligations of the former European Danube Commission.

In Dec. 1953 it was agreed to change the site of the Danube Commission to Budapest (see 53/xii/17/Pl). For a Soviet-Romanian agreement on establishment of a Special River Administration for the mouth of the Danube, see 53/xii/5/Rom/a to /c.

Following the first meeting on Nov. 11, 1949, of the Danube Commission established by the convention, the United States, the United Kingdom, and France sent notes to members of the Commission stating that they considered the convention to be invalid because it violated established concepts of international waterways, negated the provisions of the peace treaties with the 3 Balkan States of Feb. 10, 1947, failed to carry out decisions of the Council of Foreign Ministers, deprived a number of European States of their treaty rights, denied Austria representation on the Commission, and made no provision for German participation (text of U.S. note in *DSB*, 21, 1950, p. 832).

Sources: *VVS*, 1949, No. 61.
    SDD, 14, pp. 336–49.
    UNTS, 33, pp. 181–225 (R, E, F).
References: *Izv.*, Aug. 19, 1948.
    VPSS, 1948, II, p. 29.
    SIA, 1947–1948, pp. 172–73.

● 48/viii/20/Rom/a

Agreement between the USSR and Romania concerning establishment of postal and telephone-telegraph communications

Signed Aug. 20, 1948, in Moscow.
Entered into force on signature. Valid until 6 months after denunciation.
Source: *SDD*, 13, pp. 459–67.

● 48/viii/20/Rom/b

Parcel post agreement between the USSR and Romania

Signed Aug. 20, 1948, in Moscow.
Entered into force Sept. 20, 1948 (1 month after signature). Valid until 6 months after denunciation. Modified by protocol of Jan. 7, 1952, and exchange of notes of Aug. 26–Sept. 10, 1953 (53/ix/10/Rom).
Source: *SDD*, 13, pp. 468–79.

● 48/viii/30/Pl

Four-Power directive on implementation of general principles for ending the Berlin crisis

Sent Aug. 30, 1948, to the 4 Military Governors of Berlin, following agreement between the USSR, the United Kingdom, the United States of America, and France, in Moscow.
Provides that subject to agreement on implementation being reached among the 4 Military Governors, (1) restrictions on communications, transport, and commerce between Berlin and the Western Zones of Germany and to and from the Soviet Zone shall be lifted, and (2) that the German currency of the Soviet Zone shall be introduced as the sole currency for Berlin.
Sources: *VPSS, 1948*, II, pp. 30–31.
    The Soviet Union and the Berlin Question, pp. 47–48.
    DAFR, 10, pp. 96–97.

Aug. 31, 1948. Hungarian decree promulgating the statute of the Soviet-Hungarian bauxite-aluminum company "Aluminum ore-mines and industry"

See 46/iv/8/H/b.

● 48/ix/3/Alb/a

Trade agreement between the USSR and Albania

Signed Sept. 3, 1948.
Reference: *VT*, 1949, No. 8, p. 5.

● 48/ix/3/Alb/b

Agreement between the USSR and Albania concerning a Soviet trade credit for Albania

Signed Sept. 3, 1948.
Reference: *VT*, 1949, No. 8, p. 5.

Sept. 3, 1948. United States note to the USSR concerning Lend-Lease negotiations

See entry under Mar. 21, 1951.

● 48/ix/15/Mul/a

European broadcasting convention, with related documents

Signed Sept. 15, 1948, in Copenhagen. The USSR and Belorussian and Ukrainian SSR's signed.
Ratified by the USSR Jan. 25, 1950. Soviet act of ratification deposited Mar. 4, 1950; acts of ratification of the Belorussian and Ukrainian SSR's deposited July 20, 1950. Entered into force Mar. 15, 1950. May be denounced with 1 year's notice.

Related documents: (1) Plan for distribution of frequencies (see next document); (2) final protocol, concerning objections and reservations of Portugal to the convention; (3) protocol, being an agreement between Norway and Romania concerning frequency allocations. In addition, statements were made at the conference by a number of states, including the USSR and the Belorussian and Ukrainian SSR's (texts in *BTS, loc. cit.*).
Sources: *SDD*, 14, pp. 326–32 (text of the convention only).
BTS, 1950, No. 30, Cmd. 7946 (E, F, R).
BFSP, 151, pp. 551–61.
References: *Izv.*, Mar. 14, 1950.
VPSS, 1950, p. 121.

● 48/ix/15/Mul/b

Copenhagen Plan for distribution of frequencies between the broadcasting stations of the European Broadcasting Area

Signed Sept. 15, 1948, in Copenhagen, as an annex to the European broadcasting convention (preceding document). The USSR and the Belorussian and Ukrainian SSR's signed.
Entered into force Mar. 15, 1950.
Source: *BTS*, 1950, No. 30, Cmd. 7946, pp. 8–24.

● 48/ix/18/NK

Exchange of notes between the USSR and the "Supreme National Assembly" of Korea concerning withdrawal of Soviet troops from Korea

Sent Sept. 10, 1948, from North Korea, and Sept. 18, 1948, from Moscow.
The "Supreme National Assembly," established in Aug. 1948, in Soviet-occupied North Korea, appealed to the Governments of the USSR and the United States of America on Sept. 10 to withdraw their forces from Korea. In its reply the USSR stated that Soviet forces would begin withdrawal not later than the 2nd half of Oct., completing the movement by the end of Dec. 1948.
Source: *Sovetskii Soiuz i koreiskii vopros*, pp. 94–101.
References: *SIA, 1947–1948*, pp. 322–23, citing
Soviet news, Sept. 20, 1948.
DIA, 1947–1948, pp. 703–704.
DSB, 19, 1948, p. 456.

Sept. 27, 1948. Agreement transferring residual assets of UNRRA to the United Nations
See 43/xi/9/Mul.

● 48/ix/29/Af

Protocol between the USSR and Afghanistan concerning demarcation of the border, with maps and annexes

Signed Sept. 29, 1948, in Tashkent.
Prepared by the mixed commission established under the agreement of June 13, 1946 (46/vi/13/Af/a).
Reaffirmed by a treaty of Jan. 18, 1958, concerning the regime on the Soviet-Afghanistan state border (text in *VVS*, 1958, No. 28, Art. 374).
Reference: *Izv.*, Oct. 1, 1948.

● 48/x/2/H/a

Trade protocol between the USSR and Hungary

Signed Oct. 2, 1948, in Moscow.
Covers the period Aug. 1, 1948 through Dec. 31, 1949.
Mentioned in the preamble to the companion protocol of the same date (next document).

● 48/x/2/H/b

Protocol between the USSR and Hungary modifying and extending the trade and payments agreement of July 15, 1947

Signed Oct. 2, 1948, in Moscow.
Extends the 1947 agreement (47/vii/15/H/b) to Dec. 31, 1949; thereafter, if not denounced 1 month before expiration, extended for successive 1-year periods. Modifications concern (1) provision that all payments should be entered in the trade balance without delay, and (2) method of settlement of trade indebtedness by either party after expiration of the agreement.
Source: *VT*, 1948, No. 12, p. 20.

● 48/x/12/KPDR

Exchange of notes between the USSR and the Korean People's Democratic Republic concerning establishment of diplomatic and commercial relations

Sent Oct. 8, 1948, from Pyongyang and Oct. 12, 1948, from Moscow.

Sources: *Izv.*, Oct. 13, 1948.
VPSS, 1948, I, pp. 30–31.
Sovetskii Soiuz i koreiskii vopros, pp. 106–109.
References: *SDD*, 13, p. 26.
SIA, 1947–1948, p. 323.

● 48/x/28/H

Agreement between the USSR and Hungary concerning training of Hungarian citizens in civic institutions of higher education in the USSR and their support

Signed Oct. 28, 1948.
Superseded by the agreement of May 19, 1952 (52/v/19/H). Listed in *SDD*, 13 (1956), p. 494, as no longer valid.

● 48/xi/6/Italy

Preliminary agreement between the USSR and Italy concerning reparations deliveries by Italy

Signed Nov. 6, 1948, in Moscow.
Provides for transfer to the USSR of 33 Italian vessels, in 5 groups, starting Jan. 15, 1949. The USSR accepts as a basis for a reparations settlement Italian proposals made on Sept. 11, 1948. For the final agreement on reparations, see 48/xii/11/Italy/b.
Reference: Mentioned in the communiqué of Dec. 11, 1948 (48/xii/11/Italy/a).

● 48/xi/19/Mul

Protocol bringing under international control drugs outside the scope of the convention of July 13, 1931, for limiting the manufacture and regulating the distribution of narcotic drugs, as amended by the protocol of December 11, 1946

Signed Nov. 19, 1948, in Paris. The USSR and Belorussian SSR signed without reservation, the Ukrainian SSR subject to ratification. Entered into force Dec. 1, 1949. May be denounced before the 1st of July of any year with effect from the beginning of the following year.
At the time of signature the USSR and Belorussian and Ukrainian SSR's made a declaration concerning their disagreement with Art. 8, providing for extension of the protocol to territories (*UST*, 2, pp. 1660, 1666, and 1667).
Sources: *SDD*, 14, pp. 350–54.

BTS, 1950, No. 4, Cmd. 7874 (E, F, R, C, S).
BFSP, 151, pp. 593–99.
UST, 2, pp. 1629–76 (*TIAS*, 2308).
Reference: *DAFR*, 10, pp. 450–51.

Dec. 3, 1948

Letter from the Soviet Kommandatura in Berlin to the Vice-Chairman of the Berlin City Parliament recognizing the Provisional Democratic Magistrat as the only legal administration of Berlin.
Source: *DGO*, p. 348 (extract).

● 48/xii/9/Fin

Treaty between the USSR and Finland concerning the regime on the Soviet-Finnish state border, with final protocol

Signed Dec. 9, 1948, in Moscow.
Ratified by Finland Jan. 27, 1949; by the USSR Feb. 14, 1949. Entered into force Apr. 8, 1949, on exchange of acts of ratification in Helsinki. Duration 5 years; if not denounced 6 months before expiration, extended for 5 years.
Reaffirms the border established in documents of Apr. 28, 1938, Nov. 18, 1940, Dec. 16, 1944, Oct. 26, 1945, and Dec. 7, 1947. Modified by agreement of Sept. 19, 1955, concerning transfer of Porkkala-Udd to Finland (55/ix/19/Fin/a). Final protocol provides clarification of various points in the treaty.
Sources: *VVS*, 1949, No. 54.
SDD, 14, pp. 198–209.
SS, 1949, No. 10 (Finnish, R).
UNTS, 217, pp. 135–79 (R, Finnish, E, F).

Dec. 9, 1948. Convention on the prevention and punishment of the crime of genocide

See 49/xii/16/1948.

● 48/xii/11/Italy/a

Joint communiqué by the USSR and Italy concerning economic relations

Signed Dec. 11, 1948, in Moscow.
Concerns negotiations from Aug. 12, 1948, to Dec. 11, 1948, on reparations and trade. Mentions the following agreements: (1) Preliminary agreement concerning reparations deliveries (see (48/xi/6/Italy); (2) final agreement on reparations; (3) trade agreement; (4) payments agreement; and (5) treaty of com-

merce and navigation (next 4 documents).
Sources: *Izv.*, Dec. 14, 1948.
  VPSS, 1948, II, pp. 128–29.

• 48/xii/11/Italy/b

Agreement between the USSR and Italy concerning reparations payments by Italy, with annex

Signed Dec. 11, 1948, in Moscow.
Entered into force on signature. Provides for payment by Italy of reparations to a total value of $100 million US, in accordance with the peace treaty (47/ii/10/Italy), to be effected by transfer of Italian assets in Romania, Bulgaria, and Hungary, and delivery of commodities, a list of which constitutes the annex. Transfer of assets to be completed within 8 months. Separate mixed commissions to be established for each country in which property is to be transferred. Delivery of commodities to be carried out in 5 years, starting Sept. 15, 1949. For a preliminary agreement on reparations, see 48/xi/6/Italy.
References: *VT*, 1949, No. 1, pp. 1–2.
  Korolenko, p. 95.
  See also 48/xii/11/Italy/a.

• 48/xii/11/Italy/c

Trade agreement between the USSR and Italy, with four annexes

Signed Dec. 11, 1948, in Moscow.
Entered into force on signature. Duration 3 years; thereafter until 6 months after denunciation. Listed in Korolenko, p. 107, as still valid as of Nov. 25, 1953. Annexes list goods to be traded, the first 2 within 1 year, the 3rd and 4th within 3. Further lists of trade contingents to be signed subsequently.
Establishes a mixed commission to oversee execution of the agreement and the payments agreement of the same date (next document).
Sources: *VT*, 1949, No. 3, pp. 21–22 (omits the annexes).
  SDD, 13, pp. 333–35 (same).

• 48/xii/11/Italy/d

Payments agreement between the USSR and Italy

Signed Dec. 11, 1948, in Moscow.
Entered into force on signature. Duration

same as that of the trade agreement of the same date (preceding document). Listed in Korolenko, p. 96, as still valid as of Nov. 25, 1953.
Source: *VT*, 1949, No. 3, pp. 22–24.
Reference: *VT*, 1949, No. 1, p. 3.

• 48/xii/11/Italy/e

Treaty of commerce and navigation between the USSR and Italy, with annex concerning the Soviet Trade Mission in Italy and protocol

Signed Dec. 11, 1948, in Moscow.
Ratified by Italy Feb. 5, 1952; by the USSR Feb. 19, 1952. Entered into force Mar. 28, 1952, on exchange of acts of ratification in Rome. Duration 5 years; thereafter, valid until 1 year after denunciation. Listed in Korolenko, p. 104, as still valid as of Nov. 25, 1953.
Protocol concerns quantitative restrictions on import and export and privileges with regard to payment of dues and charges.
Sources: *VVS*, 1952, No. 16.
  SDD, 15, pp. 65–75.
  Korolenko, pp. 303–10.
  UNTS, 217, pp. 181–221 (R, I, E, F).

• 48/xii/15/Cz

Joint communiqué by the USSR and Czechoslovakia concerning economic relations

Signed Dec. 15, 1948, in Moscow.
Concerns negotiations from Dec. 7 to 15, 1948, which dealt with political as well as economic questions. Mentions decisions by the USSR to assist Czechoslovakia by provision of raw materials for industry, industrial equipment, machinery for heavy machine construction, building, lumbering, mining, etc.; extension of technical collaboration; and provision of a loan to Czechoslovakia in gold and free currency. Czechoslovakia to provide oil and railroad equipment and manufactured goods.
Note: It is possible that two formal agreements—a trade protocol for 1949 and an agreement on a Soviet loan—were signed at this time. An agreement on freight transportation by rail may also have been signed: see 50/ / /Pl.
Sources: *Izv.*, Dec. 16, 1948.
  VPSS, 1948, II, pp. 131–32.
Reference: Korolenko, p. 196.

● 48/xii/17/Fin

Trade agreement for 1949 between the USSR and Finland

Signed Dec. 17, 1948, in Moscow.
References: *Izv.*, Dec. 19, 1948.
 VPSS, 1948, II, p. 132.
 VT, 1949, No. 3, p. 25.

● 48/xii/22/Pl/a, b. See Appendix 5.

● 48/xii/27/Yug

Trade protocol for 1949 between the USSR and Yugoslavia, with three annexes

Signed Dec. 27, 1948, in Moscow.
Entered into force on signature. Covers the period Jan. 1 to Dec. 31, 1949. Based on the trade and payments agreement of July 5, 1947. Provides for settlement of Yugoslav debts under the agreement of July 5, 1947 (47/vii/5/Yug/b), costs of education of Yugoslav citizens in the USSR during the 2nd half of 1947 and the 1st half of 1948 (for an agreement on this subject, see 47/xii/15/Yug), and the 1944 Soviet loan to the Yugoslav National Liberation Committee (44/ix/28/Yug/b). Registered with the UN by Yugoslavia Nov. 27, 1951.
First 2 annexes list goods to be traded during 1949; annex 3 lists goods to be delivered by Yugoslavia during 1949 in payment of debts listed above.
Provides for a reduction of the volume of Soviet-Yugoslav trade by 8 times as compared with 1948, "in view of the unfriendly policies of the Yugoslav Government towards the Soviet Union" (*Izv.*, Dec. 31, 1948).
Source: *UNTS*, 116, pp. 327–43 (R, SC, E, F).
References: *Izv.*, Dec. 31, 1948.
 VPSS, 1948, II, p. 139.
 VT, 1949, No. 3, p. 25.
 Dedijer, pp. 326–27, 390.

1949

● 49/i/10/Norway. See Appendix 5.

● 49/i/15/Pol

Trade protocol for 1949 between the USSR and Poland

Signed Jan. 15, 1949, in Moscow.
Provides for increase of 35 per cent in trade over annual average under 5-year trade agreement of Jan. 26, 1948 (48/i/26/Pol/b); to reach 715 million rubles each, not counting equipment to be delivered under the credit agreement (48/i/26/Pol/c). Soviet cotton, iron, manganese, and chrome ores, automobiles, tractors, agricultural machinery, oil products, chemicals, etc., for Polish coal, railroad equipment, ferrous and nonferrous metals, textiles, sugar, etc.
References: *Izv.*, Jan. 18, 1949.
 VPSS, 1949, p. 39.
 VT, 1949, No. 3, p. 25.

● 49/i/18/Bul

Trade protocol for 1949 between the USSR and Bulgaria

Signed Jan. 18, 1949, in Moscow.
Provides for 20 per cent rise in volume of trade over 1948. Soviet oil products, cotton, ferrous and nonferrous metals, lathes, tractors, automobiles, artificial fertilizer, etc., for Bulgarian tobacco, lead and zinc concentrates, copper ore, cement, etc.
References: *Izv.*, Jan. 19, 1949.
 VPSS, 1949, p. 40.
 VT, 1949, No. 3, p. 25.

● 49/i/24/Pl

Secret protocol concerning establishment of the Council of Mutual Economic Aid

Signed Jan. 24, 1949, in Moscow, by the USSR, Bulgaria, Czechoslovakia, Hungary, Poland, and Romania. Albania joined the Council in Feb. 1949, the German Democratic Republic in Sept. 1950. Provisions: (1) Council to operate for 20 years, to coordinate the economy of the member States, standardize their industrial production, and provide mutual aid through trade, exchange of experience, loans, and investments. (2) Permanent Secretariat of the Council to be established in Moscow. (3) Council is entitled to full and detailed information from members. It is authorized to send observers and advisers to member States,

which are obligated to accept their advice.
(4) Council to develop a general plan for
economic coordination of member States.
(5) A fund of 100 million rubles to be
made available to the Secretariat, 50 million from the USSR and 10 million from
each of the other member States. (6)
Mixed companies to be set up between
member States to facilitate objectives of
the Council.
Title of the Council is abbreviated SEV
in Russian (for *Sovet ekonomicheskoi
vzaimopomoshchi*), CEMA, CMEA or
Comecon in English. For a communiqué announcing establishment of the
Council, see 49/i/25/Pl.
Reference (summary): *NYT*, June 4,
1949.

● 49/i/24/Rom/a

**Agreement between the USSR and Ro-
mania concerning technical aid to Romania**

Signed Jan. 24, 1949, in Moscow.
References: *Izv.*, Jan. 27, 1949.
VPSS, 1949, p. 44.
VT, 1949, No. 3, p. 25.

● 49/i/24/Rom/b

**Trade and payments agreement for 1949
between the USSR and Romania, with
two annexes**

Signed Jan. 24, 1949, in Moscow.
Entered into force on signature. Valid
through Dec. 31, 1949.
Provides for increase of 2½ times over
trade for 1948, to a total of 465 million
rubles each. Soviet industrial equipment,
automobiles, metals, agricultural machinery, iron ore, coke, cotton, grain, etc.,
for Romanian oil products, lumber, locomotives, wagons, barges, chemicals, meat
products, mass consumption goods, etc.
Annexes list goods to be delivered.
Sources (omitting lists): *VT*, 1949, No. 3,
pp. 20–21.
Economic treaties, pp. 76–79.
Dewar, pp. 114–16.
References: *Izv.*, Jan. 27, 1949.
VPSS, 1949, p. 44.

● 49/i/25/Pl

**Communiqué announcing establishment
of the Council of Mutual Economic Aid**

Published Jan. 25, 1949.
For establishment of the Council, see 49/
i/24/Pl.
Sources: *Izv.*, Jan. 25, 1949.
VPSS, 1949, pp. 44–45.
Int. org., 3, 1949, p. 407, citing
USSR Information bulletin, Feb. 11,
1949.

**Feb. 8, 1949. International convention
for the Northwest Atlantic fisheries**

Act of ratification of the USSR deposited
Apr. 10, 1958 (*DSB*, 38, 1958, p. 981).
Source: *TIAS*, 2089.

**Feb. 8, 1949. Meeting of the Deputy
Foreign Ministers**

See 49/xii/14/Pl.

● 49/ii/24/MPR. See Appendix 5.

Mar. 9, 1949

Romanian decree establishing the "Sovromgaz" company: *BO*, 1949, No. 5, cited
in *Economic treaties*, p. 16. For the basic
agreement providing for establishment of
Soviet-Romanian joint-stock companies,
see 45/v/8/Rom/a.

● 49/iii/12/MPR. See Appendix 5.

● 49/iii/17/KPDR/a

**Joint communiqué by the USSR and
the Korean People's Democratic Republic concerning economic relations**

Signed during negotiations from Mar. 3
to 20, 1949, in Moscow.
Mentions agreements on economic and
cultural collaboration; trade and payments; credit; and technical aid (next 4
documents).
Sources: *Izv.*, Mar. 22, 1949.
VPSS, 1949, p. 85.

● 49/iii/17/KPDR/b

**Agreement between the USSR and the
Korean People's Democratic Republic
concerning economic and cultural collaboration**

Signed Mar. 17, 1949, in Moscow.
Ratified by the Korean PDR Apr. 26,
1949; by the USSR May 17, 1949. Entered into force July 7, 1949, on exchange
of acts of ratification in Pyongyang. Duration 10 years; if not denounced 1 year

before expiration, extended until 1 year after denunciation.
Sources: *VPSS, 1949*, pp. 86–88.
Izv., Mar. 22, 1949.
SDD, 14, pp. 228–30.
UNTS, 221, pp. 3–11 (R, K, E, F).

● 49/iii/17/KPDR/c

Trade and payments agreement between the USSR and the Korean People's Democratic Republic

Signed Mar. 17, 1949, in Moscow.
Provides for "significant increase" in trade during 1949 and 1950. Listed in Korolenko, p. 107, as still valid as of Nov. 25, 1953.
References: Mentioned in the joint communiqué (49/iii/17/KPDR/a).
VT, 1955, No. 5, p. 1.

● 49/iii/17/KPDR/d

Agreement between the USSR and the Korean People's Democratic Republic concerning a Soviet credit

Signed Mar. 17, 1949, in Moscow.
Provides for a Soviet credit for purchase of goods in excess of the trade agreement of the same date (preceding document).
References: Mentioned in the joint communiqué (49/iii/17/KPDR/a).
VT, 1955, No. 5, p. 1.

● 49/iii/17/KPDR/e

Agreement between the USSR and the Korean People's Democratic Republic concerning Soviet technical aid

Signed Mar. 17, 1949, in Moscow.
References: Mentioned in the joint communiqué (49/iii/17/KPDR/a).
VT, 1955, No. 5, p. 1.

Mar. 18, 1949. Rules of procedure of the Economic and Social Council

See Note to 45/vi/26/Mul/a.

● 49/iv/2/Sweden

Trade protocol for 1949 between the USSR and Sweden

Signed Apr. 2, 1949, in Moscow.
Swedish ball bearings, high-quality steel and steel products, etc., in exchange for Soviet mineral fertilizer, asbestos, lubricating oils, etc.
References: *Izv.*, Apr. 6, 1949.

VPSS, 1949, pp. 95–96.
VT, 1949, No. 7, p. 33.

● 49/iv/10/Alb/a

Joint communiqué by the USSR and Albania concerning economic relations

Signed Apr. 10, 1949, in Moscow, at the end of negotiations which began Mar. 21, 1949. Mentions an agreement concerning delivery of industrial equipment to Albania on credit and a trade protocol for 1949 (next 2 documents).
Sources: *Izv.*, Apr. 12, 1949.
VPSS, 1949, p. 97.

● 49/iv/10/Alb/b

Agreement between the USSR and Albania concerning delivery of industrial equipment to Albania on credit

Signed on or about Apr. 10, 1949, in Moscow.
References: See 49/iv/10/Alb/a.

● 49/iv/10/Alb/c

Trade protocol for 1949 between the USSR and Albania

Signed on or about Apr. 10, 1949, in Moscow.
References: See 49/iv/10/Alb/a.

Apr. 26, 1949. Protocol concerning entry into force of the agreement between the United Nations and the International Telecommunication Union

See entry under Aug. 14, 1947.

● 49/iv/27/Rom

Agreement between the USSR and Romania concerning collaboration in the field of radio broadcasting

Signed Apr. 27, 1949.
Entered into force on signature. Duration 1 year; if not denounced 3 months before expiration, extended for 1-year periods. Under a supplementary protocol of Aug. 17, 1953, the 2 States agreed to prepare and exchange radio programs.
Source: *SDD*, 14, pp. 313–16.
Note: This appears to be the first agreement of its type, and as such served as a model for the later agreements with Poland (49/x/22/Pol), Hungary (50/iv/12/H), Albania (50/vi/27/Alb), the Mongolian People's Republic (53/ix/11/

MPR), and the Chinese People's Republic (54/viii/21/CPR).
According to Arno G. Huth, "Cooperative radio agreements," *Int. org.*, 6, 1952, pp. 396–406, the USSR also concluded agreements of this type with Czechoslovakia in 1949, and with Bulgaria in 1950. These agreements have not been further identified, and are not listed here.

• 49/v/4/Pl

Agreement concerning removal of restrictions on communications, transportation, and trade between Berlin and the Eastern and Western Zones of Germany

Initialled May 4, 1949, in New York, by the Deputy Foreign Ministers of the USSR, the United Kingdom, the United States of America, and France; incorporated in a communiqué published May 5, 1949.
Entered into force May 4, 1949. Provides for removal by May 12, 1949, of restrictions imposed by the USSR since Mar. 1, 1948, and for convening of a meeting of the Council of Foreign Ministers in Paris on May 23, 1949. Reaffirmed by the Council of Foreign Ministers in June 1949 (see 49/vi/20/Pl).
Sources: *Izv.*, May 6, 1949.
  VPSS, 1949, p. 99.
  UNTS, 138, pp. 123–26 (E, F, R).
  TIAS, No. 1915 (1949).
  DSB, 20, 1949, p. 631.
  DGO, pp. 389–90.

• 49/v/11/China

Agreement between the USSR and China concerning civil aviation

Signed during May 1949; exact date unknown, but given as May 11 in Wei, p. 233.
Extends an earlier Chinese-Soviet agreement on air rights in Sinkiang for 5 years (probably 39/ix/9/China). Possibly the last agreement concluded between the USSR and the Nationalist Government of China.
References: Wei, p. 233.
  Lattimore, *Pivot of Asia*, pp. 101–102.
  Whiting, p. 117.
  DSB, 22, 1950, pp. 218–19 (dates the agreement June 1949).

• 49/v/14/1949/a

Protocol amending the agreement for suppression of the circulation of obscene publications signed May 4, 1910, in Paris, with annex

Signed May 4, 1949, at Lake Success, New York; by the USSR, May 14, 1949, without reservations. On signing the USSR declared that it was not in agreement with Art. 7 of the annex, which provides for enforcement of the agreement in colonies, possessions, or areas under consular jurisdiction of signatories.
Entered into force for the USSR May 14, 1949. Annex entered into force Mar. 1, 1950. Provides for transfer to the United Nations of functions assigned to the French Government under the 1910 agreement. Annex lists textual amendments to the 1910 agreement (for the amended agreement, see the next document).
Sources: *SDD*, 14, pp. 211–15.
  UNTS, 30, pp. 3–22 (R, E, F, C, S) ;
  Soviet accession, p. 366.
  BTS, 1951, No. 13, Cmd. 8152 (R, E, F, C, S).

• 49/v/14/1949/b

Agreement for suppression of the circulation of obscene publications

Signed May 4, 1910, in Paris; amended by the protocol signed at Lake Success, New York, May 4, 1949, which the USSR signed May 14, 1949 (preceding document).
Entered into force Mar. 1, 1950.
For Soviet adherence, on July 8, 1935, to the 1910 convention, see 35/vii/8/1910.
Sources: *UNTS*, 47, pp. 159–65 (E, F).
  UST, 1, pp. 849–83 (*TIAS* 2164).

• 49/v/23/Norway

Exchange of notes between the USSR and Norway concerning approval and entry into force of the border protocol of December 18, 1947

Sent May 23, 1949, in Moscow.
Provides for entry into force of the 1947 protocol and related documents (47/xii/18/Norway) on May 23, 1949. Specifies the documents annexed to the 1947 protocol.
Source: *UNTS*, 52, pp. 92–93 (N), 210 (R), 318–20 (E), 435–36 (F).

May 28, 1949

Bulgarian law establishing a Soviet-Bulgarian civil aviation company: *DV*, May 28, 1949, No. 120, cited in *Economic treaties*, p. 12. For an agreement on transfer to Bulgaria of Soviet shares in the company, see 54/x/9/Bul.

• 49/vi/6/MPR/a

Agreement between the USSR and the Mongolian People's Republic concerning establishment of a Soviet-Mongolian joint-stock railroad company, "Ulan-Batorskaia zheleznaia doroga"

Signed June 6, 1949.
Mentioned in protocol of Apr. 16, 1957.

• 49/vi/6/MPR/b. See Appendix 5.

• 49/vi/7/Mul

Amendments to the schedule to the international convention for the regulation of whaling

Adopted at the first meeting of the International Whaling Commission, May 30–June 7, 1949, in London.
Entered into force Oct. 11, 1949, and Jan. 11, 1950.
For the convention and the annexed schedule, see 46/xii/2/Mul/a and /b.
Sources: *VVS*, 1950, No. 21.
    UNTS, 161, pp. 100–107 (E, F).

• 49/vi/20/Pl

Communiqué concerning the sixth meeting of the Council of Foreign Ministers

Signed at the end of a conference from May 23 to June 20, 1949, in Paris, by the Foreign Ministers of the USSR, the United Kingdom, the United States of America, and France.
Records the following agreements reached on Germany and Austria:
With regard to Germany: (1) During the 4th session of the General Assembly of the UN, starting in September 1949, the 4 governments will "exchange views" concerning the next meeting of the Council of Foreign Ministers on the German question. (2) The occupation authorities in Germany are to "consult together in Berlin on a quadripartite basis," for the purpose of mitigating the effects of the division of Germany and Berlin in regard to trade, movement of persons and goods, and exchange of information between the

Western Zones and the Eastern Zone and between Berlin and the Zones, and in regard to the administration of Berlin. (3) The Four-Power agreement on Berlin of May 4, 1949 (49/v/4/Pl), is reaffirmed. Occupation authorities are to have the obligation to ensure "normal functioning and utilization" of rail, water, and road transport for movement of persons and goods, as well as communications by post, telephone, and telegraph, between the Eastern Zone and the Western Zones and between the Zones and Berlin. (4) Occupation authorities to recommend to "the leading German economic bodies" of the Eastern and Western Zones establishment of closer economic ties between the Zones and "more effective implementation of trade and other economic agreements." With regard to Austria: (5) Austria's frontiers to be those of Jan. 1, 1938. (6) The treaty for Austria to provide for guarantees by Austria of protection of rights of the Slovene and Croatian minorities in Austria. (7) No reparations to be exacted from Austria (see the similar agreement at the Potsdam Conference, 45/viii/1/(7)), but Yugoslavia to have the right to seize Austrian property, rights and interests in Yugoslavia. (8) Austria to pay the USSR $150 million in freely convertible currency over 6 years. (9) "Definitive" settlement with Austria to include (a) relinquishment to Austria of all property, rights, or interests held or claimed as German assets, and immovable property in Austria held or claimed as war booty, with the exception of oil assets and Danube Shipping Company properties transferred to the USSR; and (b) provision that transfer to the USSR of rights, properties, and interests, and cession by the USSR to Austria of rights, properties, and interests, shall be without charges or claims on either part. (10) All former German assets which have become the property of the USSR shall not be subject to alienation without the consent of the USSR. (11) Deputy Foreign Ministers to resume their work in order to reach an agreement not later than Sept. 1, 1949, on the draft treaty for Austria. (For work of the Deputy Foreign Ministers during 1949, see 49/xii/14/Pl.)
Sources: *Izv.*, June 21, 1949.
    VPSS, 1949, pp. 111–14.
    DSB, 21, 1949, pp. 857–58.

Germany, 1947–1949, pp. 69–70.
DAFR, 11, pp. 103–104, 168.
DIA, 1949–1950, pp. 160–61, 507–508.
Note: Communiqués issued during the conference and Soviet materials presented there are given in *VPSS, 1949*, pp. 366–440.

● 49/vi/29/Pl/a

Three-way trade and payments agreement between the USSR, Finland, and Czechoslovakia

Signed June 29, 1949, in Moscow.
Each partner to deliver 20 million rubles' worth of goods: Finland, prefabricated houses, lumber, small vessels, etc., to the USSR; the USSR, foodstuffs to Czechoslovakia; and Czechoslovakia, sugar, machinery, and industrial goods to Finland.
References: *Pr., Izv.*, July 5, 1949.
  VT, 1949, No. 7, p. 34; *ibid.*, 1956, No. 12, p. 2.
  Genkin, p. 166.
Note: According to *VT*, 1956, No. 12, p. 2, similar agreements were concluded "in the following years" with the participation of the German Democratic Republic, Hungary, and Romania. These agreements, which have not been otherwise identified, have not been listed here. For later three-way agreements with Czechoslovakia and Finland, see 50/vi/ /Pl and references listed there.

● 49/vi/29/Pl/b

Three-way trade and payments agreement between the USSR, Finland, and Poland

Signed June 29, 1949, in Moscow.
Each partner to deliver 80 million rubles' worth of goods: Finland, prefabricated houses, lumber, small vessels, etc., to the USSR; the USSR, foodstuffs to Poland; and Poland, coal to Finland.
References: *Pr.*, July 5, 1949.
  VT, 1949, No. 7, p. 34; *ibid.*, 1956, No. 12, p. 2.
  Genkin, p. 166.

June 30, 1949. Supplementary regulations to World Health Organization Regulations No. 1

See 46/vii/22/Mul/b.

● 49/vii/26/H

Agreement between the USSR and Hungary concerning scientific and technical collaboration

Signed July 26, 1949, in Moscow.
Entered into force on signature. Duration 5 years; if not denounced 12 months before expiration, extended for 5 years. Provides for establishment of a Soviet-Hungarian commission to work out measures for collaboration, to meet not less than twice yearly. Based on the treaty of friendship, collaboration, and mutual assistance of Feb. 18, 1948.
Source: *SDD*, 14, pp. 220–21.

July 1, 1949. International Labour Organisation Convention No. 98

See 56/vii/6/1949.

● 49/vii/26/Pl

Agreement concerning procedure for quadripartite consultation among the Occupying Powers in Germany

Confirmed July 26, 1949, in Berlin, by a conference of the deputy commanders of occupation forces of the USSR, the United Kingdom, the United States of America, and France.
Provides for conferences of (1) commanders and their deputies, with responsibility for carrying out the decisions pertaining to Germany of the Council of Foreign Ministers in June 1949 (see 49/vi/20/Pl); and (2) specialist experts.
Source: *Izv.*, July 27, 1949.

● 49/vii/30/H

Protocol between the USSR and Hungary concerning redemarcation of the state border, with related documents

Signed July 30, 1949, in Moscow, by a mixed Soviet-Hungarian border commission.
Terminates the work of border redemarcation, carried out in accordance with Art. 1 of the peace treaty with Hungary (47/ii/10/H). Related documents include maps and other documents.
References: *Izv.*, Aug. 2, 1949.
  VPSS, 1949, p. 125.

● 49/vii/30/Manchuria

Trade agreement between the USSR and a Communist regime in Manchuria

Signed during July 1949, in Moscow, in

the course of negotiations which ended July 30.
Duration 1 year. Manchurian soy beans, plant oil, corn, rice, etc., in exchange for Soviet industrial equipment, vehicles, oil products, textiles, paper, medicines, etc.
References: *Izv.*, July 31, 1949.
   VT, 1949, No. 9, p. 32.
   VPSS, 1949, p. 124.
   SIA, 1949–1950, p. 332.

• 49/viii/4/Pl. See Appendix 5.

• 49/viii/5/Mul

Telegraph regulations (Paris revision, 1949), with three annexes and final protocol

Signed Aug. 5, 1949, in Paris. The USSR and the Belorussian and Ukrainian SSR's signed. A n n e x e d to the International Telecommunication Convention signed in Atlantic City, Oct. 2, 1947.
Entered into force July 1, 1950.
Annexes: (1) code to be used in service advices and in working; (2) payment of balances; and (3) s t a t e m e n t by the United States of America on signing. Final protocol lists statements by various governments on signing, not including the USSR or the two SSR's.
Sources: *TIAS*, 2175.
   UST, 2, I, pp. 17–381 (E, F).

Aug. 8, 1949. United States note to the USSR concerning Lend-Lease negotiations

See entry under Mar 21, 1951.

• 49/viii/12/Mul

Final Act of the diplomatic conference for revision of the Geneva Conventions, with eleven resolutions

Signed Aug. 12, 1949, in Geneva, at the end of a conference which began Apr. 21, 1949. The USSR and Belorussian and Ukrainian SSR's signed, with reservations. The conference revised or prepared 4 conventions which were signed by the USSR Dec. 12, 1949 (see 49/xii/12/1949/a to /d). The Belorussian and Ukrainian SSRs' reservations expressed regret that the resolution submitted by the Soviet delegation condemning the use of methods of mass extermination was rejected by the conference. The Soviet reservation repeated this statement and added that the

Soviet delegation considered that the problem of Protecting Powers had been satisfactorily solved by the conventions established at the conference. (The 2nd resolution annexed to the final act called for establishment of an international body to replace the Protecting Powers.) None of the other annexed resolutions directly concerns the USSR.
Sources: *UNTS*, 75, pp. 5–19 (E, F).
   BPP, Misc. No. 4, 1950, Cmd. 8033.

Aug. 20, 1949

Romanian decrees establishing the Soviet-Romanian joint-stock companies "Sovrommetal," "Sovromsig" (insurance), "Sovromcarbune" (c o a l), "Sovromconstructio," "Sovromchim" (chemicals), "Sovromtractor."
Reference: *BO*, 1949, No. 54, cited in *Economic treaties*, pp. 16–17. For the basic agreement providing for e s t a b l i s h m e n t of Soviet-Romanian joint-stock companies, see 45/v/8/Rom/a.

• 49/viii/27/Pl

Meeting of the Council of Mutual Economic Aid

Held Aug. 25–27, 1949, in Sofia, by the USSR, Albania, Bulgaria, Czechoslovakia, Hungary, Poland, and Romania.
The agreements reached were not published.
References: *Izv.*, Aug. 30, 1949.
   VPSS, 1949, p. 159.

• 49/viii/31/Yug

Protocol between the USSR and Yugoslavia concerning liquidation of the Soviet-Yugoslav joint-stock Danube steamship company "Juspad" and the Soviet-Yugoslav joint-stock civil aviation company "Justa," with four annexes

Signed Aug. 31, 1949, in Belgrade.
Entered into force on signature. Abrogates the agreements of Feb. 4, 1947, establishing the companies.
Annexes: (1) List of Soviet property to be exported to Yugoslavia. (2) List of Soviet property sold to Yugoslavia. (3) List of expended and scrapped Soviet property for which Yugoslavia is to pay compensation. (4) List of goods to be supplied to the USSR by Yugoslavia through clearing account.

Source: *UNTS*, 116, pp. 345–99 (R, SC, E, F).
Reference: *SIA, 1949–1950*, p. 260.

● 49/ix/27/Rom

Protocol between the USSR and Romania concerning demarcation of the state border, with related documents

Signed Sept. 27, 1949, in Bucharest, by a mixed Soviet-Romanian border commission.
Terminates the work of border demarcation, carried out in accordance with Art. 1 of the peace treaty with Romania (47/ii/10/Rom). For establishment of the border commission, see 48/ii/4/Rom/b. Related documents include maps and other documents.
References: *Izv.*, Sept. 28, 1949.
    VPSS, 1949, p. 163.

● 49/ix/27/US

Agreement between the USSR and the United States of America concerning return of Lend-Lease vessels, with annex

Signed Sept. 27, 1949, in Washington, D.C.
Entered into force on signature. Provides for return by Dec. 1, 1949, of 3 icebreakers and 27 frigates. Annex gives form for deed of delivery and receipt. For a report of a Soviet note of Nov. 16, 1951, promising to return 2 icebreakers by Dec. 1, 1951 (1 having been returned in 1949), see *NYT*, Nov. 17, 1951; *DAFR*, 13, p. 326. For a summary of negotiations to June 1952, see *DSB*, 26, 1952, pp. 879–81.
Sources: *TIAS*, 2060.
    UNTS, 149, pp. 23–33 (R, E, F).
Reference: (press communiqué): *DSB*, 21, 1949, p. 558.

● 49/x/2/CPR

Exchange of telegrams between the USSR and the Chinese People's Republic concerning establishment of diplomatic relations

Sent Oct. 1, 1949, from Peking, and Oct. 2, 1949, from Moscow.
On the same day that the Soviet telegram was sent, the USSR informed the chargé d'affaires of the Nationalist Government of China in Moscow that in view of the formation of the CPR the USSR

considered his Government to be a provincial one representing only Canton and no longer able to maintain diplomatic relations in the name of China. The USSR therefore considered its diplomatic relations with "Canton" ended, and had decided to recall its representatives (*Izv.*, Oct. 4, 1949).
Sources: *Izv.*, Oct. 2 and 4, 1949.
    VPSS, 1949, pp. 171–72.
Reference: *SDD*, 14, p. 28.

Oct. 10, 1949

Modifications in the agreement of Mar. 20, 1946, between the USSR and the Polish Provisional Government of National Unity concerning postal and telephone-telegraph communications.
See 46/iii/20/Pol.

● 49/x/16/GDR

Establishment of diplomatic relations between the USSR and the Provisional Government of the German Democratic Republic

Soviet decision announced Oct. 16, 1949. Background: The German Democratic Republic was established in the Soviet Zone of Germany Oct. 7, 1949. In a statement on Oct. 10, 1949, Gen. Chuikov, head of the Soviet Military Administration in Germany, announced that the USSR had decided to transfer to the "Provisional Government of the German Democratic Republic" the functions of administration previously carried out by the Soviet Military Administration (text in *DIA, 1949–1950*, pp. 380–82). On the 13th Stalin sent a message of congratulation to GDR President Wilhelm Pieck (*ibid.*, pp. 383–84), which Pieck answered on the 14th (*ibid.*, pp. 384–85).
Source (announcement of Oct. 16): *Izv.*, Oct. 16, 1949.
    VPSS, 1949, p. 174.

● 49/x/22/Pol

Agreement between the USSR and Poland concerning collaboration in the field of radio broadcasting

Signed Oct. 22, 1949, in Warsaw.
Entered into force on signature. Duration 1 year; if not denounced 3 months before expiration, extended for 1-year periods. Under a supplementary protocol of Sept.

5, 1953, the 2 States agreed to prepare
and exchange radio programs.
Source: *SDD*, 14, pp. 310–13.

• 49/xi/7/Pol

**Agreement between the USSR and Po-
land concerning transfer of Soviet Marshal K. K. Rokossovsky to the Polish
Army**

Transfer announced Nov. 7, 1949, in answer to a request by Poland.
In Nov. 1956, following a Soviet declaration of Oct. 30, 1956, concerning the
readiness of the USSR to negotiate agreements concerning stationing of Soviet
troops on the territory of other States
(see 56/x/30/H), Marshal Rokossovsky
was relieved of his duties as Polish Minister of National Defence and returned to
the USSR (*Izv.*, Nov. 20, 1956).
Reference: *Pravda*, Nov. 7, 1949.

**Nov. 11, 1949. Soviet statement concern-
ing establishment of a Soviet Control
Commission for Germany, replacing the
Soviet Military Administration in Germany**

Source: *DGO*, pp. 435–36.

• 49/xi/17/Pl

First meeting of the Danube Commission

Held Nov. 12–17, 1949, in Galatz, with
representatives of Bulgaria, Hungary, Romania, the USSR, Czechoslovakia, and
Yugoslavia.
Adopted the following documents: (1)
Rules of procedure; (2) statutes of organization of the secretariat and working
apparatus of the Danube Commission. For
establishment of the commission, see 48/
viii/18/Pl.
Source: *PDK*, 1 (R, F).
Reference: *Izv.*, Nov. 13, 19, 1949.

• 49/xi/19/GDR

**Exchange of notes between the USSR
and the German Democratic Republic
concerning establishment of a Soviet
Trade Mission in Berlin**

Sent Nov. 19, 1949, in Berlin.
Reference: *VT*, 1950, No. 2, p. 34.

• 49/xi/25/Rom/a

**Treaty between the USSR and Romania
concerning the regime on the Soviet-**

**Romanian state border, with final pro-
tocol**

Signed Nov. 25, 1949, in Moscow.
Ratified by Romania Feb. 13, 1950; by
the USSR June 3, 1950. Entered into
force June 3, 1950, on ratification by both
parties. Acts of ratification exchanged
June 20, 1950, in Bucharest. Duration 5
years; if not denounced 6 months before
expiration, extended for 5 years.
Reaffirms the boundary established under
the peace treaty (47/ii/10/Rom) and the
border protocol of Feb. 4, 1948 (48/ii/
4/Rom/b), as defined in the border documents of Sept. 27, 1949. Final protocol
provides clarification of various points in
the treaty.
Source: *SDD*, 14, pp. 157–76.
Reference: *Izv.*, Nov. 26, 1949.

• 49/xi/25/Rom/b

**Convention between the USSR and Ro-
mania concerning procedure for settling border disputes and incidents, with
related documents**

Signed Nov. 25, 1949, in Moscow.
Confirmed by the USSR May 30, 1950.
Entered into force June 6, 1950, on exchange of reports of confirmation. Duration 5 years; if not denounced 6 months
before expiration, extended for 5 years.
Provides for appointment of Border Commissioners by both states to deal with
disputes and incidents. Related documents consist of (1) 4 annexed blank
forms for personal identification in connection with border relations; (2) a protocol specifying the officials to be named
by both states as Border Commissioners;
and (3) a final protocol, providing clarification of various provisions of the convention.
Source: *SDD*, 14, pp. 177–97.
Reference: *Izv.*, Nov. 26, 1949.

• 49/xii/ /Bul

**Agreement between the USSR and Bul-
garia concerning direct rail communications**

Signed during Dec. 1949.
Superseded by the agreement of 1950 concerning transportation of freight by rail
(50/ / /Mul).
References: Genkin, p. 129.
        VT, 1954, No. 2, p. 30.

• 49/xii/9/MPR/a

Trade agreement for the period 1950–1954 between the USSR and the Mongolian People's Republic

Signed Dec. 9, 1949.
Followed by a trade agreement for the period 1955–1957 (54/xi/19/MPR/a).
Reference: Korolenko, p. 108.

• 49/xii/9/MPR/b. See Appendix 5.

• 49/xii/12/1949/a

Geneva Convention for the amelioration of the condition of the wounded and sick in armed forces in the field, with two annexes

Signed Aug. 12, 1949, in Geneva; by the USSR and Belorussian and Ukrainian SSR's Dec. 12, 1949, in Berne. All 3 signatures were with reservations (see below). Ratified by the USSR Apr. 17, 1954; act of ratification deposited May 10, 1954. Entered into force Oct. 21, 1950; for the USSR Nov. 10, 1954 (6 months after deposit). Acts of ratification of the Belorussian and Ukrainian SSR's deposited Aug. 3, 1954, with effect from Feb. 3, 1955. May be denounced with 1 year's notice in peacetime. Supersedes the convention of July 27, 1929 (see 31/viii/25/1929).
On signature, the Soviet delegation made the following reservation with regard to Art. 10: "The USSR will not recognize the validity of requests by the Detaining Power to a neutral State or to a humanitarian organization, to undertake the functions performed by a Protecting Power, unless the consent of the Government of the country of which the protected persons are nationals has been obtained." Similar reservations were made by the Belorussian and Ukrainian delegations.
Annexes: (1) Draft agreement concerning hospital zones and localities; (2) specimen identity card for members of medical and religious personnel attached to the armed forces.
Sources: *SDD*, 16, pp. 71–100.
  UNTS, 75, pp. 31–83 (E, F).
  BPP, 1950, Misc. No. 4, Cmd. 8033, pp. 8–27.
  UST, 6, pp. 3114–65 (*TIAS* 3362).
References: *SZ, 1938–1956*, pp. 160–61 (Soviet ratification).
  Izv., Dec. 14, 1949.

Note: (1) For analyses of Soviet reservations, see Brockhaus, Andreas, "Sowjetunion und Genfer Kriegsgefangenenkonvention von 1949," *Osteuropa-Recht*, 2, 1956, No. 2, pp. 286–94, and Latyshev, A., "Zhenevskie konventsii 1949 g. o zashchite zhertv voiny," *Sovetskoe gosudarstvo i pravo*, 1954, No. 7, pp. 121–25. Text of the reservations is given in *SDD*, 16, pp. 279–80.
(2) Texts of the 4 Geneva Conventions of 1949, with extended commentaries, are given in Jean S. Pictet, *Les conventions de Genève du 12 août 1949*, Geneva, 1956, 4 v.

• 49/xii/12/1949/b

Geneva Convention for the amelioration of the condition of wounded, sick, and shipwrecked members of armed forces at sea, with annex

Data on signature, ratification, and entry into force identical with those for 49/xii/12/1949/a.
Supersedes the Hague Convention of Oct. 18, 1907, for adaptation to maritime warfare of the principles of the Geneva Convention of July 6, 1906 (for Soviet adherence, see 18/vi/4/1907 and 25/vi/16/1907).
On signature the USSR and Belorussian and Ukrainian SSR's made reservations identical with those made with regard to 49/xii/12/1949/a.
Annex gives a specimen identity card for members of medical and religious personnel attached to the armed forces at sea.
Sources: *SDD*, 16, pp. 101–24.
  UNTS, 75, pp. 85–133 (E, F).
  BPP, 1950, Misc. No. 4, Cmd. 8033, pp. 27–43.
  UST, 6, pp. 3217–3315 (*TIAS* 3363).

• 49/xii/12/1949/c

Geneva Convention concerning the treatment of prisoners of war, with five annexes

Data on signature, ratification and entry into force identical with those for 49/xii/12/1949/a.
Supersedes the Geneva Convention of July 27, 1929, concerning the treatment of prisoners of war, to which the USSR did not accede.
On signature, the Soviet delegation made 3 reservations: (1) identical with that

made with regard to 49/xii/12/1949/a. (2) With regard to Art. 12, "The USSR does not consider as valid the freeing of a Detaining Power, which has transferred prisoners of war to another Power, from responsibility for the application of the Convention to such prisoners of war while the latter are in the custody of the Power accepting them." (3) With regard to Art. 85, "The USSR does not consider itself bound by the obligation, which follows from Art. 85, to extend the application of the Convention to prisoners of war who have been convicted under the law of the Detaining Power, in accordance with the principles of the Nuremberg trial, for war crimes and crimes against humanity, it being understood that persons convicted of such crimes must be subject to the conditions obtaining in the country in question for those who undergo their punishment." The Belorussian and Ukrainian delegations made similar reservations.
Annexes: (1) Model agreement concerning direct repatriation and accommodation in neutral countries of wounded and sick prisoners of war. (2) Regulations concerning mixed medical commissions. (3) Regulations concerning collective relief. (4) Specimen documents. (5) Model regulations concerning payments sent by prisoners to their own country.
Sources: *SDD*, 16, pp. 125–204.
   UNTS, 75, pp. 135–285 (E, F).
   BPP, 1950, Misc. No. 4, Cmd. 8033, pp. 44–98.
   UST, 6, pp. 3316–3515 (*TIAS* 3364).

● 49/xii/12/1949/d

Geneva Convention concerning the protection of civilian persons in time of war, with three annexes

Data on signature, ratification, and entry into force identical with those for 49/xii/12/1949/a.
On signature, the Soviet delegation made the following declaration: "Although the present Convention does not cover the civilian population in territory not occupied by the enemy and does not, therefore, completely meet humanitarian requirements, the Soviet delegation, recognizing that the said Convention makes satisfactory provision for the protection of the civilian population in occupied territory and in certain other cases, declares that it is authorized by the Government of

the USSR to sign the present Convention with the following reservations:" (1), identical with that made with regard to 49/xii/12/1949/a. (2), "The USSR will not consider as valid the freeing of a Detaining Power, which has transferred protected persons to another Power, from responsibility for the application of the Convention to the persons transferred, while the latter are in the custody of the Power accepting them." Similar statements and reservations were made by the Belorussian and Ukrainian delegations.
Annexes: (1) Draft agreement concerning hospital and safety zones and localities. (2) Draft regulations concerning collective relief. (3) Specimen documents.
Sources: *SDD*, 16, pp. 204–78.
   UNTS, 75, pp. 287–417 (E, F).
   BPP, 1950, Misc. No. 4, Cmd. 8033, pp. 99–147.
   UST, 6, pp. 3516–3695 (*TIAS*, 3365).

● 49/xii/14/Pl

Negotiations by the Deputy Foreign Ministers on a draft treaty for Austria

During 1949 the Deputy Foreign Ministers of the USSR, the United Kingdom, the United States of America, and France, met from Feb. 8 to Apr. 8, from Apr. 25 to May 10, and from June 30 to Sept. 1 in London, and on Sept. 23 and from Oct. 14 to Dec. 15 in New York (*DAFR*, 11, p. 167).
Agreements were reached, but not published, on 13 articles of the draft treaty for Austria, leaving 9 still in dispute.
References: *DAFR*, 11, pp. 167–68.
   Int. org., 3, 1949, pp. 178, 377–79; *ibid.*, 4, 1950, pp. 159–60.
   SIA, 1949–1950, pp. 285–88.
Note: Negotiations on the Austrian treaty up to 1950 are analyzed in Mosely, Philip E., "The treaty with Austria," *Int. org.*, 4, 1950, pp. 219–35.

● 49/xii/16/1948

Convention on the prevention and punishment of the crime of genocide

Signed Dec. 9, 1948, in Paris. Signed, with reservations, by the USSR and Belorussian and Ukrainian SSR's Dec. 16, 1949.

Ratified by the USSR Mar. 18, 1954; Soviet act of ratification deposited May 3, 1954, with effect from Aug. 1, 1954 (90 days after deposit). Acts of ratification of the Belorussian SSR deposited Aug. 11, 1954; of the Ukrainian SSR Nov. 15, 1954. General entry into force Jan. 12, 1951. Duration 10 years; thereafter for 5-year periods for signatories which have not denounced it 6 months before expiration.

Reservations by the USSR: (1) The USSR does not consider as binding upon itself the provision that disputes between signatories concerning interpretation, application, and implementation of the convention shall be referred for examination to the International Court of Justice at the request of any party to the dispute, and maintains that in each particular case the agreement of all parties to the dispute is essential for its submission to the International Court for decision. (2) The USSR considers that all provisions of the convention should extend to non-self-governing territories, including trust territories. The Belorussian and Ukrainian SSR's made similar reservations.

Sources: *VVS*, 1954, No. 12, Art. 244.
   SDD, 16, pp. 66–71.
   UNTS, 78, pp. 277–323 (E, F, R, C, S).
   BFSP, 151, pp. 682–87.
References: *SZ, 1938–1956*, p. 160 (Soviet ratification).
   UNTS, 196, p. 345 (Belorussian ratification).

DAFR, 10, pp. 429–30 (background).

Dec. 16, 1949. Protocol modifying the customs tariff convention of 1890

See 54/viii/27/1949.

● 49/xii/29/Norway

Treaty between the USSR and Norway concerning the regime on the Soviet-Norwegian state border and procedure for settling border disputes and incidents, with related documents

Signed Dec. 29, 1949, in Oslo.
Ratified by Norway June 30, 1950; by the USSR Oct. 23, 1950. Entered into force Oct. 30, 1950, on exchange of acts of ratification in Moscow. Duration 5 years; if not denounced 6 months before expiration, extended for 5-year periods.
Reaffirms the boundary established by the demarcation documents of Dec. 18, 1947 (47/xii/18/Norway). Provides for appointment by both states of Border Commissars, with deputies and assistants, to deal with disputes and incidents.
Related documents consist of (1) a protocol specifying the officials to be named by both states as Border Commissars; (2) a final protocol, concerning clarification of various provisions of the convention; and (3) 4 annexed blank forms for personal identification in connection with border relations.

Sources: *SDD*, 14, pp. 82–111.
   UNTS, 83, pp. 291–393 (R, N, E, F).
Reference: *Izv.*, Dec. 31, 1949.

1950

● 50/ / /Pl*

Agreement concerning transportation of freight by rail in direct international communications

Signed during 1950,* by the USSR, Albania, Bulgaria, Czechoslovakia, the German Democratic Republic, Hungary, Poland, and Romania.
Entered into force Nov. 1, 1951. As between signatories, supersedes the International Convention on Railway Freight Traffic, signed at Berne Oct. 14, 1890. Also supersedes bilateral rail freight

* Date of signature Dec. 6, 1950. See Appendix 5 under 50/xii/6/Pl/a.

agreements between the USSR and Poland (45/xi/23/Pol); Romania (47/vi/12/Rom); Hungary (47/ix/15/H); Bulgaria (49/xii/ /Bul); Czechoslovakia (46/ / /Cz); and the GDR (not identified, but signed either in 1949 or 1950; not listed here).
Russian title: Soglashenie o perevozke gruzov po zheleznym dorogam v priamom mezhdunarodnom soobshchenii, abbreviated MGS. Members of the MGS are the railroads of the signatory states, represented by their transportation ministries. Establishes a Unified transit tariff (Yedinyi transitnyi tarif, abbreviated YeTT). Modified and superseded by the agree-

ment on international freight communication of July 31, 1953. YeTT amended by agreement of Jan. 1955 (55/i/ /Pl).
References: *VT*, 1954, No. 2, pp. 30–31.
   Genkin, p. 129.

Jan. 21, 1950

Hungarian decrees promulgating the statutes of (1) the Soviet-Hungarian Bauxite-Aluminum Company.
See 46/iv/8/H/b.

(2) the Soviet-Hungarian Oil Company.
See 46/iv/8/H/a.

● 50/i/25/Pol/a

Trade protocol for 1950 between the USSR and Poland

Signed Jan. 25, 1950, in Moscow.
Provides for 34 per cent increase in volume of trade over 1949. Soviet cotton, iron, chrome and manganese ores, automobiles, tractors, agricultural and polygraphic machinery, oil products, chemicals, foodstuffs, etc., in exchange for Polish coal, railroad rolling stock, ferrous and nonferrous metals, textiles, sugar, etc.
References: *Izv.*, Jan. 28, 1950.
   VPSS, 1950, pp. 40–41.
   VT, 1950, No. 4, p. 33.

● 50/i/25/Pol/b

Protocol between the USSR and Poland concerning working conditions for Soviet specialists sent to Poland to give technical assistance, with annex

Signed Jan. 25, 1950.
Cited in the atomic energy agreement of Apr. 23, 1955 (55/iv/23/Pol), as the basis for the work of Soviet atomic specialists sent to Poland.

● 50/i/25/Pol/c

Agreement between the USSR and Poland concerning technical training of Polish specialists in the USSR

Signed Jan. 25, 1950.
Cited in the atomic energy agreement of Apr. 23, 1955 (55/iv/23/Pol), as the basis for the training of Polish atomic specialists in the USSR.

● 50/i/30/DRV

Exchange of notes between the USSR

and the Democratic Republic of Vietnam concerning establishment of diplomatic relations

On Jan. 14, 1950, the regime of Ho Chi-Minh in Northern Vietnam (Viet Minh) issued a declaration calling for recognition by other states. A copy was given to the Soviet Ambassador to Thailand in Bangkok on Jan. 19, and the USSR replied affirmatively on Jan. 30, 1950. For reports of Soviet military aid to the Viet Minh, see *SIA, 1949–1950*, p. 434.
Sources: *Izv.*, Jan. 31, 1950.
   VPSS, 1950, pp. 41–43.
References: *SDD*, 14, p. 27.
   SIA, 1949–1950, p. 429.

● 50/ii/3/Indonesia

Exchange of telegrams between the USSR and Indonesia concerning Soviet recognition of Indonesia and establishment of diplomatic relations

On Dec. 24 the Ambassador of The Netherlands to the USSR informed the USSR that Indonesia would formally be granted sovereignty Dec. 27, 1949, under an agreement of Nov. 2, 1949, and asked for Soviet recognition of the new State. The USSR replied affirmatively on Jan. 25, 1950, and on Jan. 26 sent a telegram to Indonesia announcing its recognition and intention to establish diplomatic relations. Indonesia replied Feb. 3, 1950.
Sources (Soviet telegram of Jan. 26):
   Izv., Jan. 26, 1950.
   VPSS, 1950, p. 40.
References: *VPSS, 1950*, pp. 38–39.
   SDD, 14, p. 28.

● 50/ii/7/CPR/a

Agreement between the USSR and the Chinese People's Republic concerning exchange of mail and parcel post

Signed Feb. 7, 1950, in Moscow.
Entered into force Mar. 1, 1950. Valid until 6 months after denunciation. Supersedes the agreement of Nov. 20, 1936. Modified by exchange of notes of Aug. 26 and Oct. 31, 1953, and by an unidentified agreement, probably in 1955, with effect from Jan. 1, 1956.
Source: *SDD*, 14, pp. 290–304.

● 50/ii/7/CPR/b

Agreement between the USSR and the

Chinese People's Republic concerning establishment of telephone and telegraph communications, with protocol

Signed Feb. 7, 1950, in Moscow.
Entered into force Mar. 1, 1950. Valid until 6 months after denunciation. Protocol provides for establishment of telegraph lines between Voroshilov and Dairen.
Source: *SDD*, 14, pp. 304–10.

• 50/ii/14/CPR/a

Joint communiqué by the USSR and the Chinese People's Republic concerning conclusion of political and economic treaties and agreements

Signed Feb. 14, 1950, in Moscow.
Mentions 1 treaty, 2 agreements, and 3 exchanges of notes (next 6 documents).
Sources: *Izv.*, Feb. 15, 1950.
VPSS, 1950, pp. 56–58.

• 50/ii/14/CPR/b

Treaty of friendship, alliance, and mutual assistance between the USSR and the Chinese People's Republic

Signed Feb. 14, 1950, in Moscow.
Ratified by both States Apr. 11, 1950. Entered into force Apr. 11, 1950, on ratification. Duration 30 years; if not denounced 1 year before expiration, extended for 5-year periods. Supplemented by an exchange of notes (next item).
Sources: *Izv.*, Feb. 15, 1950.
VVS, 1950, No. 36.
VPSS, 1950, pp. 58–60.
SDD, 14, pp. 15–17.
NT, 1950, No. 8.
Sino-Soviet treaty, pp. 5–8.
USSR Information bulletin, 10, 1950, No. 4, p. 108.
Hsin-hua Yueh-pao, 1, 1949, No. 5, pp. 1085–86.
UNTS, 226, pp. 5–9 (R, C), 12–17 (E, F).
AJIL, 44, 1950, No. 3, supplement, pp. 84–86.
Reference: Wei, pp. 266–78.

• 50/ii/14/CPR/c

Exchange of notes between the USSR and the Chinese People's Republic concerning political relations

Sent Feb. 14, 1950, in Moscow.
Provides for (1) annulment of the treaty of friendship and alliance of Aug. 14, 1945, between the USSR and China, as well as the agreements of the same date on the Chinese Changchun Railway, Port Arthur, and Dairen; and (2) recognition of the independence of the Mongolian People's Republic. Forms part of the treaty of friendship, alliance, and mutual aid of the same date (preceding document).
Sources: *VVS*, 1950, No. 36.
SDD, 14, pp. 17–19.
UNTS, 226, pp. 10–11 (R, C), 16–19 (E, F).
CDSP, 2, 1950, No. 45, p. 25.

• 50/ii/14/CPR/d

Agreement between the USSR and the Chinese People's Republic concerning the Chinese Changchun Railway, Port Arthur, and Dairen

Signed Feb. 14, 1950, in Moscow.
Ratified by both States and entered into force Apr. 11, 1950. Acts of ratification exchanged Sept. 30, 1950, in Peking.
Provisions: (1) The Chinese Changchun Railway to be transferred to the CPR after conclusion of a peace treaty with Japan, or not later than the end of 1952. Until transfer, joint USSR-CPR administration of the railroad to continue, with modifications. (2) Soviet troops to be withdrawn from Port Arthur after conclusion of a peace treaty with Japan, or not later than the end of 1952. Until withdrawal, civil administration of Port Arthur to be carried out by the CPR; military administration to be carried out by a joint USSR-CPR military commission. (3) Question of Dairen to be reviewed after conclusion of a peace treaty with Japan; administration meanwhile to be carried out by the CPR. A joint commission to be set up to arrange transfer of property in Dairen to the CPR, to be carried out during 1950.
History: (1) Chinese Changchun Railway: A joint communiqué of Sept. 15, 1952 (52/ix/15/CPR/b), announced creation of a mixed commission on transfer; transfer completed under a protocol of Dec. 31, 1952 (52/xii/31/CPR/a). For reconstitution of the company in Apr. 1950, see entry under Apr. 25, 1950. (2) Port Arthur: Presence of Soviet troops extended by exchange of notes of Sept. 15, 1952 (52/ix/15/CPR/c). A joint communiqué of Oct. 12, 1954 (54/x/12/CPR/d), announced that withdrawal would be completed by May 31, 1955. Final proto-

col on withdrawal signed May 24, 1955.
(3) Dairen: Completion of transfer of property reported in Jan. 1951 (*Izv.*, Jan. 18, 1951; *Soviet news*, Jan. 19, 1951).
Sources: *Izv.*, Feb. 15, 1950.
  VVS, 1950, No. 36.
  VPSS, *1950*, pp. 61–63.
  SDD, 14, pp. 19–24.
  Sino-Soviet treaty, pp. 9–13.
  USSR Information bulletin, 10, 1950, No. 4, p. 109.
  Hsin-hua Yueh-pao, 1, 1949, No. 5, pp. 1086–87.
  UNTS, 226, pp. 31–43 (R, C, E, F).
  AJIL, 44, 1950, No. 3, supplement, pp. 86–88.

● 50/ii/14/CPR/e
Credit agreement between the USSR and the Chinese People's Republic
Signed Feb. 14, 1950, in Moscow.
Ratified by both States Apr. 11, 1950. Entered into force on signature. Acts of ratification exchanged Sept. 30, 1950, in Peking.
Provides for a Soviet credit to the CPR of $300 million US, in 5 equal annual installments, starting Jan. 1, 1950, at 1 per cent per annum; to be repaid in 10 years, the 1st payment not later than Dec. 31, 1954. Credit to be used for purchase of Soviet equipment and materials, including equipment for power stations, metallurgical and engineering plants, coal and ore mines, railroad and other transport equipment, rails, etc. Nomenclature, quantities, prices, and delivery dates to be fixed by a special agreement. Annual protocols concerning delivery signed in 1950 (50/iv/19/CPR/c); 1951 (51/vi/15/CPR/b); 1952 (52/iv/12/CPR/b); 1953 (53/iii/21/CPR/b); and 1954 (54/i/23/CPR/b).
Sources: *Izv.*, Feb. 15, 1950.
  VVS, 1950, No. 36.
  VPSS, *1950*, pp. 64–66.
  SDD, 14, pp. 223–24.
  Sino-Soviet treaty, pp. 15–17.
  USSR Information bulletin, 10, 1950, No. 4, p. 110.
  Hsin-hua Yueh-pao, 1, 1949, No. 5, p. 1087.
  UNTS, 226, pp. 21–29 (R, C, E, F).
  AJIL, 44, 1950, No. 3, supplement, pp. 89–90.

● 50/ii/14/CPR/f
Exchange of notes between the USSR and the Chinese People's Republic concerning transfer to the CPR of industrial and commercial enterprises and other property acquired by Soviet organizations from Japanese owners in 1945
Sent Feb. 14, 1950, in Moscow.
Provides for establishment of a mixed commission to carry out the transfer, to be completed within 3 months. Completion of transfer marked by a protocol on Aug. 28, 1950. See also 50/viii/7/CPR.
Source: *SDD*, 14, pp. 26–27.

● 50/ii/14/CPR/g
Exchange of notes between the USSR and the Chinese People's Republic concerning transfer to the CPR of Soviet buildings in the military compound of Peking, with map and annex
Sent Feb. 14, 1950, in Moscow.
Provides for establishment of a mixed commission to carry out the transfer, to be completed within 1 month. Completion of transfer marked by a protocol on July 20, 1950.
Source: *SDD*, 14, pp. 24–25.

● 50/ii/17/Rom/a
Agreement between the USSR and Romania concerning scientific and technical collaboration
Signed Feb. 17, 1950, in Moscow.
Entered into force on signature. Duration 5 years; if not denounced 12 months before expiration, extended for 5 years. Provides for establishment of a Soviet-Romanian commission to implement the agreement, to meet not less than twice yearly, alternately in Moscow and Bucharest.
Source: *SDD*, 14, pp. 230–31.
Note: The atomic energy agreement of Apr. 22, 1955, cites an agreement of Feb. 17, 1950, as the basis for the technical training of Romanian atomic specialists in the USSR. Since there is nothing in the published text of the present agreement specifically covering such training, it is possible that there exists a separate USSR-Romania agreement of this date concerning technical training of Romanian specialists in the USSR.

● 50/ii/17/Rom/b
Trade and payments agreement for 1950 between the USSR and Romania

Signed Feb. 17, 1950, in Moscow.
Provides for increase in trade of more
than 30 per cent over 1949. Soviet cotton,
metals, iron ore, coke, automobiles, industrial and agricultural machinery, etc.,
in exchange for Romanian oil products,
wood products, wagons, chemicals, meat
products, etc.
References: *Pr., Izv.*, Feb. 22, 1950.
VPSS, 1950, pp. 70–71.
VT, 1950, No. 4, p. 33.
CDSP, 2, 1950, No. 9, p. 36.

● 50/ii/18/Bul/a

**Agreement between the USSR and Bul-
garia concerning scientific and technical
collaboration**

Signed Feb. 18, 1950, in Moscow.
Entered into force on signature. Duration
5 years; if not denounced 12 months before expiration, extended for 5 years. Provides for establishment of a Soviet-Bulgarian commission to implement the
agreement, to meet not less than twice
yearly, alternately in Moscow and Sofia.
Source: *SDD*, 14, pp. 216–17.

● 50/ii/18/Bul/b

**Trade protocol for 1950 between the
USSR and Bulgaria**

Signed Feb. 18, 1950, in Moscow.
Provides for increase in trade of more
than 20 per cent over 1949. Soviet cotton,
metals, oil products, industrial equipment, agricultural machinery, fertilizers,
etc., in exchange for Bulgarian lead and
zinc concentrates, tobacco, cement, etc.
References: *Pr., Izv.*, Feb. 21, 1950.
VPSS, 1950, p. 70.
VT, 1950, No. 4, p. 33.
CDSP, 2, 1950, No. 9, p. 32.

● 50/ii/22/Cz/a

**Trade protocol for 1950 between the
USSR and Czechoslovakia**

Signed Feb. 22, 1950, in Moscow.
Soviet grain, cotton, wool, iron and manganese ores, ferrous alloys, nonferrous metals, oil products, industrial equipment,
etc., in exchange for Czech pipes, rails,
cable, locomotives, power and other equipment, sugar, footwear, textiles, etc.
References: *Izv.*, Feb. 25, 1950.
VPSS, 1950, p. 72.

VT, 1950, No. 4, p. 34.
Schmidt, pp. 369–71.

● 50/ii/22/Cz/b

**Agreement between the USSR and Czech-
oslovakia concerning technical training
of Czechoslovak specialists in the USSR**

Signed Feb. 22, 1950.
Cited in the atomic energy agreement of
Apr. 23, 1950 (50/iv/23/Cz), as the basis
for the training of Czechoslovak atomic
specialists in the USSR.

● 50/ii/24/H/a

**Treaty between the USSR and Hungary
concerning the regime on the Soviet-
Hungarian state border, with final protocol**

Signed Feb. 24, 1950, in Moscow.
Ratified by Hungary May 22, 1950; by the
USSR June 3, 1950. Entered into force
June 22, 1950, on exchange of acts of rati-
fication in Budapest. Duration 5 years;
if not denounced 6 months before expira-
tion, extended for 5 years.
Reaffirms the boundary established under
the peace treaty (47/ii/10/H), and the
protocol of July 30, 1949.
Final protocol provides clarification of
various points in the treaty.
Source: *SDD*, 14, pp. 29–48.
References: *Izv.*, Feb. 25, 1950.
VPSS, 1950, p. 71.

● 50/ii/24/H/b

**Convention between the USSR and Hun-
gary concerning procedure for settling
border disputes and incidents, with related documents**

Signed Feb. 24, 1950, in Moscow.
Confirmed by the USSR May 31, 1950.
Entered into force May 31, 1950, on exchange of reports of confirmation. Duration 5 years; if not denounced 6 months
before expiration, extended for 5 years.
Provides for appointment of Border Commissioners by both States to deal with disputes and incidents. Related documents
consist of (1) 4 annexed blank forms for
personal identification in connection with
border relations; (2) a protocol specifying the administrative headquarters of
Border Commissioners; and (3) a final
protocol, concerning clarification of various provisions of the convention.

Source: *SDD*, 14, pp. 48–71.
References: *Izv.*, Feb. 25, 1950.
  VPSS, 1950, p. 71.

● 50/iii/1/H/a

Trade protocol for 1950 between the USSR and Hungary

Signed Mar. 1, 1950, in Moscow.
Provides for increase in trade of more than 20 per cent over 1949. Soviet cotton, iron ore, coke, metals, industrial equipment, agricultural machinery, wood products, etc., in exchange for Hungarian industrial equipment, locomotives, wagons, barges, textiles, etc.
References: *Pr., Izv.*, Mar. 4, 1950.
  VPSS, 1950, p. 80.
  VT, 1950, No. 4, p. 34.
  CDSP, 2, 1950, No. 10, p. 24.

● 50/iii/1/H/b

Agreement between the USSR and Hungary concerning technical production work by Hungarian specialists in the USSR

Signed Mar. 1, 1950.
Cited in the atomic energy agreement of June 13, 1955, as the basis for the work of Hungarian atomic specialists in the USSR.

Mar. 21, 1950. Convention for suppression of the traffic in persons and of the exploitation of the prostitution of others

See 54/viii/11/1950.

● 50/iii/27/CPR/a

Agreement between the USSR and the Chinese People's Republic concerning establishment of a Soviet-CPR joint-stock oil company, "Sovkitneft' "

Signed Mar. 27, 1950, in Moscow.
Ratified by the CPR Apr. 21, 1950; by the USSR June 3, 1950. Acts of ratification exchanged Sept. 30, 1950, in Peking. Duration 30 years. Soviet shares transferred to the CPR under a joint communiqué of Oct. 12, 1954 (54/x/12/CPR/e); the company ceased its activities as of Jan. 1, 1955 (*Izv.*, Jan. 1, 1955).
Provides for joint administration and sharing of profits and expenses. Purpose of the company to prospect, extract and refine oil and gas in Sinkiang.
References: *Izv.*, Mar. 29, 1950.

VPSS, 1950, pp. 122–23.
VT, 1950, No. 4, p. 34; *ibid.*, 1954, No. 2, p. 2.
Korolenko, p. 205.
VT SSSR, p. 43.

● 50/iii/27/CPR/b

Agreement between the USSR and the Chinese People's Republic concerning establishment of a Soviet-CPR joint-stock company for production of non-ferrous metals, "Sovkitmetall"

Data on signature, ratification, duration, and termination identical with those for 50/iii/27/CPR/a.
Purpose of the company to prospect for and extract nonferrous metals in Sinkiang.
References: Identical with those for 50/iii/27/CPR/a.

● 50/iii/27/CPR/c

Agreement between the USSR and the Chinese People's Republic concerning establishment of a Soviet-CPR joint-stock civil aviation company, "SKOGA"

Data on signature, ratification, and termination identical with those for 50/iii/27/CPR/a. Duration 10 years.
Provides for organization and use of routes terminating at Peking—Chita; Peking—Irkutsk; and Peking—Alma-Ata.
References: *Izv.*, Apr. 2, 1950.
  VPSS, 1950, pp. 123–24.
  VT, 1950, No. 4, p. 34; *ibid.*, 1954, No. 2, p. 2.
  VT SSSR, p. 43.

● 50/iii/27/CPR/d

Agreement between the USSR and the Chinese People's Republic concerning working conditions of Soviet specialists sent to the CPR as instructors and advisers in Chinese organizations

Signed Mar. 27, 1950.
Reference: *VT SSSR*, p. 44.

● 50/iii/27/Pl

Second meeting of the Danube Commission

Held Mar. 23–27, 1950, in Galatz, with representatives of Bulgaria, Hungary, Romania, the USSR, Czechoslovakia, and Yugoslavia.
Adopted the following documents: (1)

Plan of work for 1950; (2) table of organization of the secretariat and working apparatus; (3) decree on budget for 1950; (4) budget for 1950; (5) decree on navigation in the sector Gabčikovo-Gönyü; (6) decree on disposition of property of the former International Danube Commission.
Source: *PDK*, 2 (R, F).

● 50/iv/ /MPR

Agreement between the USSR and the Mongolian People's Republic concerning transformation of diplomatic missions into embassies

Negotiated on or before Apr. 4, 1950.
References: *Izv.*, Apr. 4, 1950.
　VPSS, 1950, p. 136.

● 50/iv/12/GDR

Trade and payments agreement for 1950 between the USSR and the German Democratic Republic

Signed Apr. 12, 1950, in Moscow.
Provides for increase in trade of more than 35 per cent over 1949. Soviet grains, fats, ferrous and nonferrous metals, trucks, apatite concentrate, manganese ore, oil products, coke, cotton, etc., in exchange for GDR industrial equipment, machines, cement, potassium salt, chemicals, coal briquettes, etc. Soviet deliveries during the 2nd half of 1950 increased under a protocol of July 21, 1950.
References: *Izv.*, Apr. 14, 1950.
　VPSS, 1950, p. 142.
　VT, 1950, No. 5, p. 15; *ibid.*, No. 6, p. 36.

● 50/iv/12/H

Agreement between the USSR and Hungary concerning collaboration in the field of radio broadcasting, with supplementary protocol

Signed Apr. 12, 1950, in Budapest.
Entered into force on signature. Duration 1 year; if not denounced 3 months before expiration, extended for 1-year periods. Supplementary protocol amplifies various provisions of the agreement.
Under a supplementary protocol of Aug. 28, 1953, the 2 States agreed to prepare and exchange radio programs. A supplementary protocol of June 14, 1956, (56/vi/14/H), provided for increased collaboration in the fields of radio and television.
Source: *SDD*, 14, pp. 265–70.

● 50/iv/19/CPR/a

Commercial agreement between the USSR and the Chinese People's Republic, with two annexes

Signed Apr. 19, 1950, in Moscow.
Ratified by the CPR May 12, 1950; by the USSR June 3, 1950. Entered into force, retroactively, from Jan. 1, 1950. Valid until Dec. 31, 1950. Acts of ratification exchanged Sept. 30, 1950, in Peking. Listed in Korolenko, p. 107, as still valid as of Nov. 25, 1953. Extended to Dec. 31, 1956, by the trade protocol for 1956 (55/xii/27/CPR).
Annexes, listing goods to be exchanged, to be drawn up in a separate protocol.
Source: *SDD*, 14, pp. 225–28 (omits annexes).
References: *Pr.*, *Izv.*, Apr. 21, 1950.
　VPSS, 1950, pp. 150, 219.

● 50/iv/19/CPR/b

Trade agreement for 1950 between the USSR and the Chinese People's Republic

Signed Apr. 19, 1950, in Moscow.
Soviet equipment in exchange for Chinese raw materials.
References: *Pr.*, *Izv.*, Apr. 21, 1950.
　VT, 1950, No. 6, p. 36.
　Korolenko, p. 198.

● 50/iv/19/CPR/c

Protocol between the USSR and the Chinese People's Republic concerning delivery by the USSR of equipment and goods under the credit agreement of February 14, 1950

Signed Apr. 19, 1950, in Moscow.
Covers deliveries during 1950–1952. This is the 1st annual protocol under the credit agreement (50/ii/14/CPR/e).
References: *Pr.*, *Izv.*, Apr. 21, 1950.
　VPSS, 1950, p. 150.
　Korolenko, p. 198.

Apr. 25, 1950

The USSR and the Chinese People's Republic formally reconstituted the Chinese Changchun Railway Company, after agreement on a new set of conditions to regulate the railroad's administration, following negotiations in Peking during Apr.

to implement the agreement on the railroad (50/ii/14/CPR/d). See *Current
background*, No. 62, Mar. 5, 1951, pp.
14–15.

● 50/v/15/GDR

**Exchange of letters between the USSR
and the German Democratic Republic
concerning reduction of reparations payments to the USSR**

Sent May 11, 1950, from Berlin, and May
15, 1950, from Moscow; the Soviet reply
had the approval of Poland.
Provides for reduction of reparations payments by 50 per cent, from a total of $10
billion, of which $3,658 million would be
paid by the end of 1950, to a total of
$3,171 million, to be paid in 15 years start-
ing in 1951, by goods from current production. Payment of reparations by the GDR
to end Jan. 1, 1954, under a protocol of
Aug. 22, 1953 (53/viii/22/GDR/b).
Sources: *Izv.*, May 16, 1950.
    VPSS, 1950, pp. 24–26.

● 50/v/19/GDR

**Communiqué announcing transfer to the
German Democratic Republic of twenty-
three enterprises appropriated by the
USSR as reparations**

Published May 19, 1950.
Source: *DGO*, pp. 492–93.
Reference: *SIA, 1949–1950*, p. 194.

● 50/v/24/Bul

**Exchange of notes between the USSR
and Bulgaria concerning execution of
letters rogatory**

Sent May 20 and 24, 1950, in Moscow.
Source: *SDD*, 14, pp. 210–11.

● 50/v/27/Rom

**Convention between the USSR and Ro-
mania concerning quarantine of agricultural plants and their protection from
parasites and diseases**

Signed May 27, 1950, in Bucharest.
Ratified by Romania July 10, 1950; by
the USSR Apr. 7, 1951. Entered into
force Apr. 21, 1951, on exchange of acts
of ratification in Moscow. Duration 5
years; if not denounced 1 year before
expiration, extended for 5-year periods.
Sources: *VVS*, 1951, No. 13.

SDD, 14, pp. 256–60.
UNTS, 221, pp. 13–33 (R, Romanian,
    E, F).

● 50/vi/   /Pl

**Protocol concerning three-way trade and
payments between the USSR, Czechoslovakia, and Finland**

Concluded during 1950, probably in June,
a year after the first such agreement (49/
vi/29/Pl/a).
Provides for delivery of goods from the
USSR to Czechoslovakia, from Czechoslovakia to Finland, and from Finland to
the USSR; goods to be delivered specified
in separate bilateral agreements. Deliveries balanced monthly in special accounts opened in Gosbank, the Czechoslovak State Bank, and the Bank of Finland.
For later agreements, see 51/   / /Pl,
52/ / /Pl, 53/ / /Pl, 54/ / /Pl,
55/ / /Pl, and 56/ / /Pl.
Reference: *VT SSSR*, pp. 86–87.

● 50/vi/   /Fin

**Agreement between the USSR and Fin-
land defining trade contingents for three-
way trade between the USSR, Czechoslovakia, and Finland**

For signature, provisions, and reference,
see preceding document.

● 50/vi/   /Cz

**Agreement between the USSR and Czech-
oslovakia defining trade contingents for
three-way trade between the USSR,
Czechoslovakia, and Finland**

For signature, provisions, and reference,
see 50/vi/   /Pl.

● 50/vi/9/H

**Convention between the USSR and Hun-
gary concerning measures for preventing
floods and regulating the water system
on the Soviet-Hungarian border in the
area of the Tisza River, with two annexes**

Signed June 9, 1950, in Uzhgorod.
Entered into force on signature. Duration
10 years; if not denounced 1 year before
expiration, extended for 10-year periods.
Provides for appointment by each state of
a commissioner with two deputies to carry
out terms. Annexes give specimen forms
for identification of commissioners and

deputies and for experts and technical personnel.
Source: *SDD*, 14, pp. 71–75.

● 50/vi/13/Fin/a

Trade agreement for the period 1951–1955 between the USSR and Finland

Signed June 13, 1950, in Moscow.
Ratified by Finland June 27, 1950; by the USSR Aug. 12, 1950. Entered into force Jan. 1, 1951. Acts of ratification exchanged Aug. 24, 1950, in Helsinki. Covers the period Jan. 1, 1951 through Dec. 31, 1955. Provides for trade to a value of 230 million rubles in 1951, rising to 320 million rubles in 1955. Details of deliveries to be defined annually in separate protocols. For the first protocol, for 1951, see 50/xii/2/Fin; for 1952, 51/xii/21/Fin; for 1953, 53/ii/23/Fin; for 1954, 53/xi/25/Fin. Supersedes the trade and payments agreement of Dec. 5, 1946 (46/xii/5/Fin/a). Supplementary deliveries provided for under protocols of Sept. 23, 1952, and Nov. 25, 1953.
Source: *SS*, 1950, No. 36 (Finnish, R).
References: *Pr., Izv.*, June 15, 1950.
  VPSS, 1950, pp. 178–79, 211.
  VT, 1950, No. 7, p. 36; *ibid.*, 1954, No. 1, p. 8.
  SIA, 1949–1950, p. 253.

● 50/vi/13/Fin/b

Trade protocol for 1950 between the USSR and Finland

Signed June 13, 1950, in Moscow.
Provides for trade during remaining 6 months of 1950 to a value of approximately $30 million.
References: *Pr., Izv.*, June 15, 1950.
  VPSS, 1950, pp. 178–79.
  VT, 1950, No. 7, p. 36.
  SIA, 1949–1950, p. 253.

● 50/vi/27/Alb

Agreement between the USSR and Albania concerning collaboration in the field of radio broadcasting, with supplementary protocol

Signed June 27, 1950, in Tirana.
Entered into force on signature. Duration 1 year; if not denounced 3 months before expiration, extended for 1-year periods.
Source: *SDD*, 14, pp. 261–65.

● 50/vi/29/Pol/a

Trade agreement for the period 1953–1958 between the USSR and Poland

Signed June 29, 1950, in Moscow.
Together with the companion protocol on trade during 1951–1952 (next document), provides for an increase of more than 60 per cent in annual volume of trade compared with 1948–1950.
References: *Pr., Izv.*, July 2, 1950.
  VPSS, 1950, p. 194.
  VT, 1950, No. 7, p. 38; *ibid.*, 1953, No. 7, p. 5; *ibid.*, 1955, No. 4, p. 2.

● 50/vi/29/Pol/b

Trade protocol for the period 1951–1952 between the USSR and Poland

Signed June 29, 1950, in Moscow.
References: Same as those cited for 50/vi/29/Pol/a.

● 50/vi/29/Pol/c

Agreement between the USSR and Poland concerning delivery of industrial equipment to Poland on credit during the period 1951–1958

Signed June 29, 1950, in Moscow.
Provides for a Soviet credit to Poland of 400 million rubles.
References: Same as those cited for 50/vi/29/Pol/a.

● 50/vii/1/GDR/a

Agreement between the USSR and the German Democratic Republic concerning establishment of postal communications

Signed July 1, 1950, in Moscow.
Entered into force on signature. Valid until 6 months after denunciation.
Sources: *SDD*, 14, pp. 270–75.
  Dokumente DDR, 4, pp. 11–16.

● 50/vii/1/GDR/b

Parcel post agreement between the USSR and the German Democratic Republic

Signed July 1, 1950, in Moscow.
Entered into force on signature. Valid until 6 months after denunciation.
Sources: *SDD*, 14, pp. 275–84.
  Dokumente DDR, 4, pp. 16–27.

● 50/vii/1/GDR/c

Agreement between the USSR and the German Democratic Republic concerning establishment of telegraph and telephone communications

Signed July 1, 1950, in Moscow.
Entered into force on signature. Valid until 6 months after signature.
Sources: *SDD*, 14, pp. 285–90.
   Dokumente DDR, 4, pp. 27–32.

● 50/vii/13/H

Convention between the USSR and Hungary concerning quarantine of agricultural plants and their protection from parasites and diseases

Signed July 13, 1950, in Budapest.
Ratified by the USSR Dec. 16, 1950. Entered into force Dec. 26, 1950, on exchange of acts of ratification, in Moscow.
Duration 5 years; if not denounced 1 year before expiration, extended for 5-year periods.
Sources: *VVS*, 1951, No. 3.
   SDD, 14, pp. 252–56.
   UNTS, 221, pp. 35–55 (R, H, E, F).
   CDSP, 3, 1951, No. 9, pp. 17–18.

● 50/vii/17/Af

Trade and payments agreement between the USSR and Afghanistan

Signed July 17, 1950.
Duration 4 years; thereafter extended (probably for 4-year periods) if not denounced. Includes trade specifications for the period July 1, 1950, through June 30, 1951; for later years of validity, trade contingents and prices to be defined annually. Each year's list to include as Soviet exports oil products and cotton textiles, as those of Afghanistan wool and cotton. Provides for conclusion of trade contracts both within and beyond the limits established in the annual lists. Payments to be cleared through the state banks of both States. Provides for arbitration of disputes.
References: *VT*, 1954, No. 5, p. 4; *ibid.*, 1957, No. 2, p. 8.
   Korolenko, pp. 97, 107.

● 50/vii/18/Fin

Exchange of notes between the USSR

and Finland concerning entry into force of the border protocol of Dec. 7, 1947

Sent May 29 and July 18, 1950.
Source: *BFSP*, 149, p. 597, citing
   SS, 1950, No. 34.

● 50/vii/20/CPR

Protocol between the USSR and the Chinese People's Republic concerning transfer to the CPR of Soviet buildings in the military compound of Peking

Signed July 20, 1950.
Marks completion of the transfer provided for in exchange of notes of Feb. 14, 1950 (50/ii/14/CPR/g).
Reference: *SDD*, 14, p. 25.

● 50/vii/21/Mul

Amendments to the schedule to the international convention for the regulation of whaling

Adopted at the second meeting of the International Whaling Commission, July 8–21, 1950, in Oslo.
Entered into force Nov. 1, 1950. For the convention and the annexed schedule, see 46/xii/2/Mul/a and /b.
Sources: *VVS*, 1950, No. 39.
   UNTS, 161, pp. 108–11 (E, F).

● 50/vii/21/GDR

Supplementary trade protocol for 1950 between the USSR and the German Democratic Republic

Signed July 21, 1950.
Provides for delivery by the USSR during the 2nd half of 1950 of 20,000 tons of animal and vegetable fats, 20,000 tons of meat, 17,000 tons of fish, and 8,000 tons of cotton, in addition to quantities called for under the agreement of Apr. 12, 1950. Deliveries on credit, to be repaid by deliveries of goods.
Reference: *VT SSSR*, p. 106.

● 50/viii/7/CPR

Agreement between the USSR and the Chinese People's Republic concerning measures for the transfer to the CPR of industrial and commercial properties acquired by Soviet organizations from Japanese owners in 1945

Signed Aug. 7, 1950, by a mixed Sino-Soviet property transfer commission, at

the end of negotiations which began July 8, 1950, under an exchange of notes of Feb. 14, 1950 (50/ii/14/CPR/f).
Actual transfer began Aug. 9, 1950, following ratification of the agreement. For completion, see 50/viii/28/CPR.
Reference: *Current background*, No. 62, Mar. 5, 1951, pp. 16–18.

● 50/viii/25/Bul

Convention between the USSR and Bulgaria concerning quarantine of agricultural plants and their protection from parasites and diseases

Signed Aug. 25, 1950, in Sofia.
Ratified by Bulgaria Jan. 2, 1951; by the USSR Feb. 10, 1951. Entered into force Feb. 26, 1951, on exchange of acts of ratification in Moscow. Duration 5 years; if not denounced 1 year before expiration, extended for 5-year periods.
Sources: *VVS*, 1951, No. 6.
  SDD, 14, pp. 247–51.
  UNTS, 221, pp. 57–77 (R, B, E, F).

● 50/viii/28/CPR

Agreement between the USSR and the Chinese People's Republic concerning completion of the transfer to the CPR of industrial and commercial properties acquired by Soviet organizations from Japanese owners in 1945, with related documents

Signed Aug. 28, 1950, in Mukden.
Marks completion of the transfer provided for under an exchange of notes of Feb. 14, 1950 (50/ii/14/CPR/f). Transfers completed Aug. 12, 15, and 17 at Mukden, Harbin, and Changchun. The full agreement consists of (1) a general agreement, (2) 4 subordinate agreements covering transferred properties, and (3) 2 volumes of documentary evidence. The whole transaction is designated a protocol in the Soviet source cited below.
References: *SDD*, 14, p. 26.
  Current background, No. 62, Mar. 5, 1951.

● 50/ix/26/Rom

Protocol between the USSR and Romania concerning working conditions for Soviet specialists sent to Romania to give technical assistance

Signed Sept. 26, 1950.

Cited in the atomic energy agreement of Apr. 22, 1955, as the basis for the work of Soviet atomic specialists sent to Romania.

● 50/ix/29/Canada

Exchange of notes between the USSR and Canada constituting an agreement concerning payment by the USSR for supplies delivered by Canada in 1945–1946

Sent Sept. 29, 1950, in Moscow.
Entered into force Sept. 29, 1950. Provides for payment in 5 equal instalments at 9-month intervals of $8,992,488.79 Canadian, covering wheat, flour, and cereals delivered to the USSR in 1945–1946.
Sources: *CTS*, 1950, No. 18.
  UNTS, 230, pp. 371–75 (E, F, R).

● 50/x/5/KPDR

Agreement between the USSR and the Korean People's Democratic Republic concerning conditions of trade deliveries

Signed Oct. 5, 1950.
Mentioned in Korolenko, p. 109, as still valid as of Nov. 25, 1953.

● 50/x/20/Pl

Joint declaration concerning the remilitarization of Western Germany

Signed Oct. 20, 1950, in Prague, by the USSR, Albania, Bulgaria, Czechoslovakia, the German Democratic Republic, Hungary, Poland, and Romania.
Attacks the decision of the United Kingdom, the United States of America, and France, announced Sept. 19, 1950, to end their state of war with Germany and to give West German authorities increased powers under a revised Occupation Statute, and the communiqués of the North Atlantic Council of Sept. 18 and 20, 1950, announcing its decision to establish a force to ensure the defence of Western Europe to which Western Germany would contribute. Calls instead for (1) publication of a proclamation by the USSR, the United Kingdom, the United States, and France stating that they will not allow the remilitarization of Germany; (2) removal of all obstacles to the development of Germany's "peaceful economy" and prevention of a revival of German military potential; (3) conclusion of a peace

treaty with Germany, to be followed by withdrawal of occupation forces; and (4) establishment of an all-German Constituent Council on the basis of equal representation of Eastern and Western Germany, to prepare for establishment of an "all-German, sovereign, democratic, peace-loving provisional government." Used as the basis of a Soviet proposal Nov. 3, 1950, in the Council of Foreign Ministers.
Sources: *Izv.*, Oct. 22, 1950.
   VPSS, 1950, pp. 223–31.
   DIA, 1949–1950, pp. 167–68 (conclusion only).
Reference: *SIA, 1949–1950,* pp. 78–79.

• 50/x/25/CPR

Agreement between the USSR and the Chinese People's Republic concerning working conditions for Soviet specialists sent to the CPR to give technical assistance in the installation and operation of Soviet equipment

Signed Oct. 25, 1950.
This is the 2nd such agreement concluded in 1950. For the first, see 50/iii/27/CPR/d.
Reference: *VT SSSR,* p. 44.

• 50/x/28/MPR. See Appendix 5.

• 50/xi/1/MPR. See Appendix 5.

• 50/xi/3/Cz

Five-year economic agreement between the USSR and Czechoslovakia

Signed Nov. 3, 1950, in Moscow.
Provides for increased economic collaboration in the period 1951–1955. During negotiations the parties agreed on an increase of trade, to reach an annual average volume 50 per cent higher than during 1948–1950. Deliveries for 1951 increased under a protocol of Mar. 13, 1951.
References: *Pr., Izv.,* Nov. 5, 1950, p. 2;
   Izv., Nov. 16, 1950.
   VPSS, 1950, pp. 233–34.
   VT, 1950, No. 12, p. 44; *ibid.,* 1952, No. 3, p. 15.
   CDSP, 2, 1950, No. 45, p. 26.
   Schmidt, pp. 350, 386.

• 50/xi/4/Iran

Exchange of letters between the USSR and Iran constituting an agreement for the renewal of trade on the basis of the treaty of commerce and navigation of March 25, 1940, with annex

Signed Nov. 4, 1950, in Teheran.
Covers the period Nov. 10, 1950, to Nov. 10, 1951. Listed in Korolenko, p. 107, as still valid as of Nov. 25, 1953. Annex lists goods to be exchanged. Subsequent deliveries provided for in agreement of May 1952 (52/v/ /Iran), and exchanges of notes of June 10 and Sept. 3, 1953. For the 1940 treaty, see 40/iii/25/Iran/a.
References: *Pr.,* Nov. 6, 1950; *Izv.,* Nov. 7, 1950.
   VPSS, 1950, p. 233.
   VT, 1954, No. 9, p. 4.

• 50/xi/14/BL

Trade protocol between the USSR and the Belgium-Luxembourg Economic Union

Signed Nov. 14, 1950, in Brussels.
Covers the period May 1, 1950 to May 1, 1951. Supplements the commercial agreement of Feb. 18, 1948 (48/ii/18/BL/b). Following expiration, no further protocols signed until Jan. 30, 1954; in the interim, trade contracts were concluded within the framework of the agreement of Feb. 18, 1948.
Source: **Informations commerciales,* No. 225, Nov. 24, 1950, supplement.
Reference: Korolenko, p. 91.

• 50/xi/29/Cz

Protocol between the USSR and Czechoslovakia concerning working conditions for Soviet specialists sent to Czechoslovakia to give technical assistance

Signed Nov. 29, 1950.
Cited in the atomic energy agreement of Apr. 23, 1955 (55/iv/23/Cz), as the basis for the work of Soviet atomic specialists sent to Czechoslovakia.

• 50/xii/2/Fin

Trade protocol for 1951 between the USSR and Finland

Signed Dec. 2, 1950, in Moscow.
Based on the 5-year trade agreement of June 13, 1950 (50/vi/13/Fin/a).
References: *Izv.,* Dec. 5, 1950, p. 4.
   VT, 1951, No. 2, p. 40.

• 50/xii/6/Pl/a, b. See Appendix 5.

• 50/xii/15/Pl

Third meeting of the Danube Commission

Held Dec. 10–15, 1950, in Galatz, with representatives of the USSR, Bulgaria, Czechoslovakia, Hungary, Romania, and Yugoslavia.

Adopted the following documents, among others: (1) Decree on establishment of a special river administration for the sector Rajka-Gönyü; (2) decree on clearing the Danube of sunken vessels; (3) decree on publication of new maps and charts for the Danube; (4) plan of work for 1951; (5) budget for 1951; (6) de-

cree on the flag and seal of the Danube Commission.
Source: *PDK*, 3 (R, F).

Dec. 15, 1950. Meetings of the Deputy Foreign Ministers

During the year 1950 the Deputy Foreign Ministers of the USSR, the United Kingdom, the United States of America, and France met on Jan. 9, Mar. 1, Apr. 26, May 2, 4, 23, and 26, July 10, Sept. 7, and Dec. 15, to negotiate a draft treaty for Austria. No agreements were reached.
References: *SIA, 1949–1950*, pp. 288–89; *DAFR*, 12, pp. 536–37; *Int. org.*, 1950, pp. 342, 538–39, 706.

1951

• 51/ / /Pl

Protocol concerning three-way trade and payments between the USSR, Czechoslovakia, and Finland

Concluded during 1951.
Accompanied by bilateral trade protocols between the 3 States (not listed separately).
For terms and reference, see 50/vi/ /Pl.

• 51/i/2/CPR

Agreement between the USSR and the Chinese People's Republic concerning navigation procedure on the border rivers Amur, Ussuri, Argun, and Sungacha and on Lake Hanka, and the establishment of conditions for navigation on these waterways

Signed Jan. 2, 1951, in Harbin.
Entered into force on signature. Provides for establishment of a mixed commission to carry out provisions.
Source: *SDD*, 14, pp. 333–36.

Jan. 15, 1951. Resumption of negotiations between the USSR and the United States of America concerning a Lend-Lease settlement

See entry under Mar. 21, 1951.

• 51/i/16/Alb

Protocol between the USSR and Albania supplementing the agreement of December 15, 1947, concerning training of Albanian citizens in the USSR

Signed Jan. 16, 1951.
Provisions unknown. Together with the basic agreement, superseded by the agreement of July 5, 1952; mentioned in Art. 8 of that agreement (*SDD*, 15, p. 261).

• 51/i/16/CPR

Agreement between the USSR and the Chinese People's Republic concerning direct rail communications

Signed Jan. 16, 1951.
Listed in *SDD*, 14 (1957), p. 356, as no longer valid. *VT*, 1954, No. 2, p. 30, mentions conclusion of such agreement in 1950; not otherwise identified. Cf. the agreement of Mar. 14, 1951, by which it was possibly superseded.

• 51/ii/15/Pol

Treaty between the USSR and Poland concerning exchange of territories, with protocol, two annexes, and a map

Signed Feb. 15, 1951, in Moscow.
Ratified by Poland May 28, 1951; by the USSR, May 31, 1951. Entered into force June 5, 1951, on exchange of acts of ratification in Moscow.
Modifies and supplements the border treaty of Aug. 16, 1945 (45/viii/16/Pol/ b). Provides for exchange of 2 areas, each of 480 sq. km., on the Soviet-Polish border. A mixed commission to begin work of demarcation within 3 months of entry into force; for the protocol marking completion of its work, see 51/x/23/Pol. For a protocol modifying the border treaty

and convention of July 8, 1948, in accordance with this treaty, see 51/xii/8/Pol. Protocol specifies measures to be taken on transfer, and provides for establishment of a mixed commission for the task. Annexes describe boundaries of areas transferred.

Sources: *VVS*, 1951, No. 23.
   SDD, 14, pp. 152–57.
   *DURP, 1952, No. 11, Arts. 63, 64.
References: *Izv.*, May 22 and June 6, 1951.
   SIA, 1951, p. 154.

● 51/ii/17/Alb/a

Agreement between the USSR and Albania concerning delivery to Albania on credit of industrial equipment during the period 1951–1955, together with technical assistance to Albania

Signed during negotiations which ended Feb. 17, 1951, in Moscow.
References: *Izv.*, Feb. 18, 1951.
   VT, 1951, No. 2, pp. 11, 40.

● 51/ii/17/Alb/b

Trade agreement for 1951 between the USSR and Albania

Signed during negotiations which ended Feb. 17, 1951, in Moscow.
References: *Izv.*, Feb. 18, 1951.
   VT, 1951, No. 2, pp. 11, 40.

● 51/iii/ /GDR

Protocol between the USSR and the German Democratic Republic concerning general conditions of trade deliveries

Signed during Mar. 1951.
Listed in Korolenko, p. 109, as still valid as of Nov. 25, 1953.
References: Korolenko, *loc. cit.*
   Liubimov, p. 22.

● 51/iii/9/Pol

Trade protocol for 1951 between the USSR and Poland

Signed Mar. 9, 1951, in Moscow.
References: *Izv.*, Mar. 13, 1951.
   VT, 1951, No. 6, p. 43.

● 51/iii/13/Cz

Protocol between the USSR and Czech-oslovakia concerning supplementary commodity deliveries during 1951

Signed Mar. 13, 1951, in Moscow.
Supplements the agreement of Nov. 3, 1950.
References: *Izv.*, Mar. 16, 1951.
   VT, 1951, No. 6, p. 43.
   Schmidt, pp. 350, 399–400.

● 51/iii/14/Bul

Trade protocol for 1951 between the USSR and Bulgaria

Signed Mar. 14, 1951, in Moscow.
References: *Izv.*, Mar. 17, 1951.
   VT, 1951, No. 4, p. 12; *ibid.*, No. 6, p. 43.

● 51/iii/14/CPR

Agreement between the USSR and the Chinese People's Republic concerning direct rail communications, with related documents

Signed Mar. 14, 1951, in Peking.
Provides for start of direct service for passengers, baggage, and freight Apr. 1, 1951. Related documents include regulations for transportation of passengers, baggage and freight, for railroad lines on the state border, and for settlement of accounts and handling of tables and reports. Possibly supersedes the agreement of Jan. 16, 1951.
References: *Izv.*, Mar. 30, 1951.
   VT, 1951, No. 6, p. 43.
   SCMP, 1951, No. 89, p. 9.

● 51/iii/14/Cz

Protocol between the USSR and Czechoslovakia concerning general conditions of deliveries

Signed Mar. 14, 1951.
Superseded by the agreement of Apr. 5, 1952 (52/iv/5/Cz/b).
Reference: *VT SSSR*, p. 86.

● 51/iii/15/Rom

Trade and payments agreement for 1951 between the USSR and Romania

Signed Mar. 15, 1951, in Moscow.
References: *Izv.*, Mar. 20, 1951.
   VT, 1951, No. 6, p. 43.

• 51/iii/16/GDR

Trade and payments agreement for 1951 between the USSR and the German Democratic Republic

Signed Mar. 16, 1951, in Moscow.
References: *Izv.*, Mar. 18, 1951.
  VT, 1951, No. 5, p. 5; *ibid.*, No. 6, p. 43.

• 51/iii/19/H/a

Trade protocol for 1951 between the USSR and Hungary

Signed Mar. 19, 1951, in Moscow.
References: *Izv.*, Mar. 22, 1951.
  VT, 1951, No. 4, p. 5; *ibid.*, No. 6, p. 43.

• 51/iii/19/H/b

Protocol between the USSR and Hungary concerning working conditions for Soviet specialists sent to Hungary to give technical assistance

Signed Mar. 19, 1950.
Cited in the atomic energy agreement of June 13, 1955, as the basis for work of Soviet atomic specialists sent to Hungary.

Mar. 21, 1951. Soviet note to the United States of America concerning a Lend-Lease settlement

Negotiations in 1951 for a settlement began Jan. 15 (*DSB*, 24, 1951, pp. 93–94). A United States note of Feb. 7, 1951, listed the vessels to be returned (*ibid.*, pp. 302–303). The Soviet note of Mar. 21, 1951 (*ibid.*, pp. 647–48), alleged violation by the United States of unspecified agreements on the sale of merchant ships and some naval ships to the USSR. In its reply of Apr. 6, 1951 (*ibid.*, pp. 646–47), the United States suggested that the alleged agreements were proposals made in United States notes of Feb. 27, 1948, Sept. 3, 1948, and Aug. 8, 1949, concerning disposition of Lend-Lease vessels; acceptance of these proposals, however, was conditional on conclusion of an over-all Lend-Lease settlement, as was stated by the United States representatives at the first meeting of the Working Groups on May 3, 1947. For further correspondence on the subject, see *DSB*, 25, 1951, p. 145; *ibid.*, 26, 1952, pp. 86–88; *ibid.*, 27, 1952, pp. 820–21.

• 51/iv/10/Bul

Agreement between the USSR and Bul-

garia concerning scientific research on the biology of commercial fishes of the Black Sea and exchange of experience on the technique of fishing

Signed Apr. 10, 1951, in Moscow.
Entered into force on signature. Duration 5 years; if not denounced 6 months before expiration, extended for 5-year periods. Provides for annual exchange of reports, the 1st by Aug. 1, 1951, thereafter by Apr. 1 of each year. Publications and specialists to be exchanged; details on employment of specialists to be determined by agreements each time.
Source: *SDD*, 14, pp. 217–20.

• 51/iv/14/Pl. See Appendix 5.

• 51/vi/3/Pl

Fourth meeting of the Danube Commission

Held May 23–June 3, 1951, in Galatz, with representatives of the USSR, Bulgaria, Czechoslovakia, Hungary, Romania, and Yugoslavia.
Adopted the following documents among others: (1) Basic statute for navigation of the Danube; (2) decree on rules for river inspection on the Danube; (3) decree on special collections on the Danube. In a note of Aug. 23, 1951, Yugoslavia stated that it considered the new rules for navigation null and void, as being contrary to the spirit and letter of the 1948 convention establishing the commission (48/viii/18/Pl).
Source: *PDK*, 4 (R, F).
Reference: *Int. org.*, 5, 1951, pp. 845–46.

• 51/vi/15/CPR/a

Trade protocol for 1951 between the USSR and the Chinese People's Republic

Signed June 15, 1951.
References: *Izv.*, June 21, 1951, p. 2.
  Korolenko, p. 198.
  SIA, 1951, p. 368.

• 51/vi/15/CPR/b

Protocol between the USSR and the Chinese People's Republic concerning delivery by the USSR of equipment and goods under the credit agreement of February 14, 1950

Signed June 15, 1951, in Moscow.

This is the 2nd annual protocol under the credit agreement (50/ii/14/CPR/e).
Reference: *Izv.*, June 21, 1951.

June 21, 1951. Meeting of the Deputy Foreign Ministers

Held Mar. 5–June 21, 1951, in Paris, by the Deputy Foreign Ministers of the USSR, the United Kingdom, the United States of America, and France. Purpose to draw up an agenda for a meeting of the Council of Foreign Ministers. No agreement reached, no agenda prepared.
References: *Int. org.*, 5, 1951, pp. 413–15, 646–50.
SIA, 1951, pp. 131–38.

● 51/vi/27/US

Interview concerning the possibility of a truce in Korea

Held June 27, 1951, in Moscow, between Soviet Deputy Foreign Minister A. A. Gromyko and United States Ambassador Admiral Alan Kirk.
Purpose to clarify implications of a speech delivered June 23, 1951, by Soviet representative to the UN Ya. A. Malik calling for discussions between the belligerents in Korea for a cease-fire and armistice. In his comments Mr. Gromyko explained that the USSR had in mind discussions on purely military matters between the military commanders rather than on political or territorial questions. Followed by negotiations in Korea for an armistice.
References: *DSB*, 25, 1951, p. 45.
DIA, 1951, pp. 633–34.

● 51/vi/28/Belgium

Exchange of notes between the USSR and Belgium concerning tariff duties and weight categories under the parcel post agreement of April 16, 1938

Sent Feb. 12 and June 28, 1951.
Reference: *SDD*, 10, pp. 148, 150.

June 29, 1951. International Labour Organisation Convention No. 100

See 56/iv/4/1951.

July 1, 1951. Changes in parcel post agreements of (1) Sept. 22, 1947, between the USSR and Hungary, and (2) Dec. 17, 1947, between the USSR and Bulgaria

See (1) 47/ix/22/H/b, and (2) 47/xii/17/Bul/b.

July 10, 1951
See Appendix 5.

● 51/vii/28/CPR

Agreement between the USSR and the Chinese People's Republic concerning establishment of a USSR-CPR joint-stock company for ship building and repair, "Sovkitsudostroi"

Signed July 28, 1951, in Peking.
Created on the basis of the Dal'dok factory, originally built by the Russians in 1903 on completion of the Chinese Eastern Railway, and rehabilitated by the Soviet Military Administration in 1946. Soviet shares transferred to the CPR under a joint communiqué of Oct. 12, 1954 (54/x/12/CPR/c).
Reference: *VT SSSR*, p. 43.

● 51/vii/30/Mul

Amendments to the schedule to the international convention for the regulation of whaling

Adopted at the third meeting of the International Whaling Commission, July 23–30, 1951, in Capetown.
For the convention and annexed schedule, see 46/xii/2/Mul/a and /b.
Source: *VVS*, 1952, No. 15.

● 51/viii/8/Cz

Parcel post agreement between the USSR and Czechoslovakia, with protocol

Signed Aug. 8, 1951, in Prague.
Entered into force on signature. Valid until 6 months after denunciation. Protocol annuls the agreement of June 8, 1935.
Source: *SDD*, 14, pp. 316–26.

Aug. 8, 1951. Changes in the agreement of Oct. 22, 1945, between the USSR and Czechoslovakia concerning establishment of mail and telephone-telegraph communications

See 45/x/22/Cz.

● 51/viii/24/Rom

Long-term agreement between the USSR and Romania concerning delivery of in-

dustrial equipment and technical aid to Romania and development of trade

Signed Aug. 24, 1951, in Moscow.
Covers trade for the period 1952–1955. Average annual volume to exceed by 50 per cent that of the period 1948–1951.
References: *Izv.*, Aug. 28, 1951.
   VT, 1951, No. 9, p. 38.
   Korolenko, p. 108.

● 51/ix/3/France

Agreement between the USSR and France concerning reciprocal trade relations and the status of the Soviet Trade Mission in France, with protocol

Signed Sept. 3, 1951, in Paris.
Ratified by France July 19, 1952; by the USSR Oct. 31, 1952. Entered into force Nov. 28, 1952, on exchange of acts of ratification in Moscow. Duration 5 years. May be denounced not later than Sept. 30 of any year, with effect from Dec. 31 of that year. Supersedes the agreement of Dec. 29, 1945. Extended by a protocol signed Nov. 14, 1958, ratified Feb. 17, 1959 (*VVS*, 1959, No. 8, Art. 63).
Protocol provides (1) that the commercial attaché of the French Embassy in Moscow shall enjoy diplomatic privileges and immunities, and (2) that an agreement will be reached on the number of staff personnel of the Soviet Trade Mission in France.
For an analysis of the differences between this agreement and that of Dec. 1945, see Korolenko, pp. 82–83.
Sources: *VVS*, 1953, No. 5.
   SDD, 15, pp. 75–81.
   Korolenko, pp. 310–14.
   *JO, Feb. 27, 1953, p. 1960.
   UNTS, 221, pp. 79–97 (F, R, E).
References: *Izv.*, Sept. 4, 1951.
   VT, 1951, No. 9, pp. 38–39.

Sept. 4–8, 1951. Conference in San Francisco for the conclusion and signature of a treaty of peace with Japan

The USSR was represented at the conference but did not sign the treaty.
See *SIA, 1951*, pp. 407–15.

● 51/ix/27/GDR/a

Agreement between the USSR and the German Democratic Republic concerning scientific and technical collaboration

Signed Sept. 27, 1951, in Moscow.

Entered into force on signature. Duration 5 years; if not denounced 12 months before expiration, extended for 5 years.
Provides for establishment of a USSR-GDR commission to carry out measures, to meet not less than twice yearly in Moscow and Berlin alternately.
Sources: *SDD*, 14, pp. 222–23.
   Dokumente DDR, 4, pp. 33–34.
Reference: *VT*, 1951, No. 10, p. 14.

● 51/ix/27/GDR/b

Trade agreement for the period 1952–1955 between the USSR and the German Democratic Republic

Signed Sept. 27, 1951, in Moscow.
Volume of trade for 1952 increased under a protocol of Apr. 11, 1952 (52/iv/11/GDR); for 1953 under a protocol of Apr. 26, 1953.
References: *Izv.*, Oct. 2, 1951.
   VT, 1951, No. 10, pp. 13–14, 44.
   Korolenko, p. 108.
   ND, Sept. 29, 1951.

● 51/x/23/Pol

Documents concerning demarcation of the state border between the USSR and Poland

Signed Oct. 23, 1951, in Warsaw, by the mixed Soviet-Polish border commission established by the border treaty of Feb. 15, 1951.
Documents define that part of the border modified by the Feb. 1951 treaty (51/ii/15/Pol).
Mentioned in and reaffirmed by a protocol of Dec. 8, 1951.

● 51/xii/6/CPR

Agreement between the USSR and the Chinese People's Republic concerning technical training of CPR specialists in the USSR

Signed Dec. 6, 1951.
Cited in the atomic energy agreement of Apr. 27, 1955 (55/iv/27/CPR), as the basis for the training of CPR atomic specialists in the USSR.

Dec. 6, 1951. International Plant Protection Convention

See 56/iv/24/1951.

● 51/xii/8/Pol

Protocol between the USSR and Poland concerning amendment of the treaty concerning the regime on the Soviet-Polish state border and the convention concerning procedure for settling border disputes and incidents, both of July 8, 1948, in accordance with the provisions of the treaty concerning exchange of territories of February 15, 1951

Signed Dec. 8, 1951, in Moscow.
Ratified by Poland Feb. 9, 1952; by the USSR Mar. 17, 1952. Entered into force Mar. 17, 1952, on ratification by both parties. Acts of ratification exchanged Mar. 28, 1952, in Warsaw. Constitutes an integral part of the 1948 treaty and convention, and is valid for the same duration.
Sources: *VVS*, 1952, No. 14.
   SDD, 14, pp. 112–13, 132–33.
   SDD, 15, pp. 17–21.
   *DURP, 1952, No. 23, Arts. 145 and 146.
   UNTS, 221, pp. 410–27 (R, P, E, F).

● 51/xii/17/Pl. See Appendix 5.

● 51/xii/19/Pl

Fifth meeting of the Danube Commission

Held Dec. 10–19, 1951, in Galatz, with representatives of the USSR, Bulgaria, Czechoslovakia, Hungary, Romania, and Yugoslavia.
Adopted the following documents, among others: (1) Plan of work for 1952; (2) decree on establishment of a single system of navigational conditions on the Danube; (3) decree on questions of tariff and sanitary inspection; (4) budget for 1952; and (5) rules of river inspection.
Source: *PDK*, 5 (R, F).
Reference: *Int. org.*, 7, 1953, pp. 300–301.

● 51/xii/21/MPR. See Appendix 5.

● 51/xii/21/Fin

Trade protocol for 1952 between the USSR and Finland

Signed Dec. 21, 1951.
Based on the 5-year trade agreement of June 13, 1950 (50/vi/13/Fin/a).
Reference: Korolenko, p. 89.

● 51/xii/26/MPR. See Appendix 5.

● 51/xii/29/MPR. See Appendix 5.

1952

● 52/ / /Pl. See Appendix 5.

● 52/ / /Pol. See Appendix 5.

● 52/i/7/Rom

Protocol between the USSR and Romania modifying the parcel post agreement of August 20, 1948

Signed Jan. 7, 1952.
Entered into force on signature. Provides for changes in certain payment rates and weight limits and in settling accounts.
Reference: *SDD*, 13, pp. 468–70.

● 52/i/23/H/a

Trade agreement for the period 1952–1955 between the USSR and Hungary

Signed Jan. 23, 1952, in Moscow.
Increase in trade for 1953 provided for by protocol of Mar. 24, 1953.

References: *Izv.*, Jan. 29, 1952.
   VT, 1952, No. 5, p. 36.
   Korolenko, p. 108.

● 52/i/23/H/b

Agreement between the USSR and Hungary concerning delivery of industrial equipment and technical assistance to Hungary

Signed Jan. 23, 1952, in Moscow.
References: Same as those for 52/i/23/H/a.

● 52/ii/5/Belgium

Exchange of notes between the USSR and Belgium concerning an alteration in tax rates under the parcel post agreement of April 16, 1938

Sent Nov. 21, 1951, and Feb. 5, 1952.
Reference: *SDD*, 10, p. 147.

• 52/ii/9/Bul

Trade protocol for 1952 between the USSR and Bulgaria

Signed Feb. 9, 1952, in Moscow.
References: *Pr., Izv.,* Feb. 14, 1952.
VT, 1952, No. 5, p. 36.
CDSP, 4, 1952, No. 7, p. 14.

• 52/ii/23/Egypt

Barter agreement between the USSR and Egypt

Signed Feb. 23, 1952.
Provides for exchange of Egyptian cotton for Soviet wheat.
Reference: *SIA, 1951,* p. 286.

• 52/ii/29/Pol

Agreement between the USSR and Poland concerning conditions of trade deliveries

Signed Feb. 29, 1952.
Listed in Korolenko, p. 109, as still valid as of Nov. 25, 1953.

• 52/iii/7/Bul

Agreement between the USSR and Bulgaria concerning training of Bulgarian citizens in civic institutions of higher learning in the USSR

Signed Mar. 7, 1952, in Moscow.
Entered into force Sept. 1, 1952. Number and specialties of persons to be determined by agreement between the USSR Ministry of Higher Education and the Committee for Affairs of Science, Art, and Culture under the Council of Ministers of Bulgaria not later than 4 months before start of the academic year. Supersedes the agreement of Nov. 15, 1947.
Source: *SDD,* 15, pp. 262–64.

• 52/iii/11/Italy

Trade protocol for 1952 between the USSR and Italy, with two annexes

Signed Mar. 11, 1952, in Rome.
Concluded under the trade agreement of Dec. 11, 1948 (48/xii/11/Italy/c). Annexes, listing goods to be traded, replace those of the 1948 agreement.
Reference: Korolenko, p. 96.

• 52/iii/20/Rom

Agreement between the USSR and Ro-
mania concerning training of Romanian citizens in civic institutions of higher education in the USSR

Signed Mar. 20, 1952, in Moscow.
Entered into force Sept. 1, 1952. Number and specialties of persons to be determined by agreement between the USSR Ministry of Higher Education and the Committee for Affairs of Higher Education under the Council of Ministers of Romania not later than 4 months before start of the academic year.
Supersedes the agreement of Dec. 15, 1947.
Source: *SDD,* 15, pp. 283–86.

• 52/iii/29/CPR

Agreement between the USSR and the Chinese People's Republic concerning conditions of trade deliveries

Signed Mar. 29, 1952.
Listed in Korolenko, p. 109, as still valid as of Nov. 25, 1953.
Reference: Korolenko, p. 194.

• 52/iv/5/Cz/a

Trade agreement between the USSR and Czechoslovakia

Signed Apr. 5, 1952.
Soviet raw materials, minerals, fertilizers, meat, butter, fats, rice, tea, grain, and oilseeds, in exchange for Czech textiles, leather goods, hops, paper, furniture, chemicals, and glass.
Reference: *SIA, 1952,* p. 158, citing
    B.B.C. Monitoring reports, II A, 1952, Nos. 303 and 304.

• 52/iv/5/Cz/b

Agreement between the USSR and Czechoslovakia concerning general conditions of deliveries

Signed Apr. 5, 1952.
Listed in Korolenko, p. 109, as still valid as of Nov. 25, 1953. Supersedes the protocol of Mar. 14, 1951.
References: Liubimov, p. 17.
    VT SSSR, p. 86.

• 52/iv/5/Pol

Agreement between the USSR and Poland concerning construction of a Palace of Culture and Science in Warsaw

Signed Apr. 5, 1952, in Warsaw.
References: *Izv.*, Apr. 6, 1952.
VT, 1955, No. 4, p. 3.

● 52/iv/11/Cz

Agreement between the USSR and Czechoslovakia concerning training of Czechoslovak citizens in civic institutions of higher learning in the USSR

Signed Apr. 11, 1952, in Moscow.
Entered into force Sept. 1, 1952. Number and specialties of persons to be determined by agreement between the USSR Ministry of Higher Education and the Ministry of Schools, Sciences and Arts of Czechoslovakia not later than 4 months before start of the academic year.
Supersedes the agreement of June 11, 1948.
Source: *SDD*, 15, pp. 286–89.

● 52/iv/11/GDR

Protocol between the USSR and the German Democratic Republic concerning supplementary deliveries of commodities during 1952

Signed Apr. 11, 1952, in Moscow.
Supplements the trade agreement of Sept. 27, 1951 (51/ix/27/GDR/b).
Reference: *VT*, 1952, No. 9, p. 11.

● 52/iv/12/CPR/a

Trade protocol for 1952 between the USSR and the Chinese People's Republic

Signed Apr. 12, 1952, in Moscow.
References: *Izv.*, Apr. 16, 1952.
VT, 1952, No. 5, p. 37.

● 52/iv/12/CPR/b

Protocol between the USSR and the Chinese People's Republic concerning delivery by the USSR of equipment and goods under the credit agreement of February 14, 1950

Signed Apr. 12, 1952, in Moscow.
This is the 3rd annual protocol under the credit agreement (50/ii/14/CPR/e).
References: *Izv.*, Apr. 16, 1952.
VT, 1952, No. 5, p. 37.
Korolenko, p. 198.

April 12, 1952

Communiqué issued at the end of the International Economic Conference held Apr. 3–12, 1952, in Moscow. Although persons from 49 States attended, they did so as individuals, not as official representatives of their governments. Text of the communiqué in *DIA, 1952*, pp. 249–51.

● 52/iv/19/Alb/a

Agreement between the USSR and Albania concerning conditions of trade deliveries

Signed Apr. 19, 1952.
Listed in Korolenko, p. 109, as still valid as of Nov. 25, 1953.

● 52/iv/19/Alb/b

Agreement between the USSR and Albania concerning scientific and technical collaboration

Signed Apr. 19, 1952, in Moscow.
Entered into force on signature. Duration 5 years; if not denounced 12 months before expiration, extended for 5 years.
Provides for establishment of a Soviet-Albanian commission of implementation, to meet not less than twice yearly in Moscow and Tirana alternately.
Source: *SDD*, 15, p. 84.
Reference: Korolenko, p. 202.

Apr. 29, 1952. Communiqué concerning transfer to the German Democratic Republic of sixty-six joint-stock companies

The joint-stock companies in the GDR (Sowjetische Aktiengesellschaften, abbreviated SAG), unlike those in other satellite States, were apparently not set up on the basis of a treaty of economic collaboration. For an agreement releasing the GDR from repayment for the companies, see 53/viii/22/GDR/b.
Source: *ND*, Apr. 29, 1952.
Reference: *Pravda*, May 3, 1952.

● 52/iv/30/MPR

Agreement between the USSR and the Mongolian People's Republic concerning training of Mongolian citizens in civic institutions of higher education in the USSR

Signed Apr. 30, 1952, in Moscow.
Entered into force Sept. 1, 1952. Number and specialties of persons to be determined by agreement between the USSR Ministry of Higher Education and the

MPR Ministry of Education not later than 4 months before start of the academic year. Supersedes the agreement of May 12, 1948.
Source: *SDD*, 15, pp. 278–80.

• 52/v/ /Iran

Trade agreement between the USSR and Iran

Signed during May 1952.
Reference: *VT*, 1954, No. 9, p. 4.

• 52/v/6/KPDR

Agreement between the USSR and the Korean People's Democratic Republic concerning training of KPDR citizens in civic institutions of higher education in the USSR

Signed May 6, 1952, in Moscow.
Entered into force Sept. 1, 1952. Number and specialties of persons to be determined by agreement between the USSR Ministry of Higher Education and the KPDR Ministry of Education not later than 4 months before start of the academic year. Supersedes the agreement and protocol of Aug. 4, 1948 (48/viii/4/NK).
Source: *SDD*, 15, pp. 275–78.

• 52/v/12/GDR/a

Agreement between the USSR and the German Democratic Republic concerning training of GDR citizens in civic institutions of higher education in the USSR

Signed May 12, 1952, in Moscow.
Entered into force Sept. 1, 1952. Number and specialties of persons to be determined by agreement between the USSR Ministry of Higher Education and the GDR State Secretariat for Higher Education not later than 4 months before start of the academic year. Supplemented by an exchange of notes of the same date (next document).
Source: *SDD*, 15, pp. 267–70.

• 52/v/12/GDR/b

Exchange of notes between the USSR and the German Democratic Republic concerning training of GDR citizens in the USSR

Sent May 12, 1952, in Moscow.
Provides for extension of the provisions of the agreement of the same date (preceding document) to GDR citizens who were accepted in institutions of higher education in the USSR during Oct. 1951.
Source: *SDD*, 15, pp. 270–71.

• 52/v/19/H

Agreement between the USSR and Hungary concerning training of Hungarian citizens in civic institutions of higher education in the USSR

Signed May 19, 1952, in Moscow.
Entered into force Sept. 1, 1952. Number and specialties of persons to be determined by agreement between the USSR Ministry of Higher Education and the Hungarian Ministry of Education not later than 4 months before start of the academic year. Supersedes the agreement of Oct. 28, 1948.
Source: *SDD*, 15, pp. 265–67.

• 52/v/19/Pol

Agreement between the USSR and Poland concerning training of Polish citizens in civic institutions of higher education in the USSR

Signed May 19, 1952, in Moscow.
Entered into force Sept. 1, 1952. Number and specialties of persons to be determined by agreement between the USSR Ministry of Higher Education and the Polish Ministry of Higher Education not later than 4 months before start of the academic year. Supersedes the agreement of May 28, 1948.
Source: *SDD*, 15, pp. 281–83.

• 52/vi/6/Mul

Amendments to the schedule to the international convention for the regulation of whaling

Adopted at the fourth meeting of the International Whaling Commission, June 3–6, 1952, in London.
For the convention and annexed schedule, see 46/xii/2/Mul/a and /b.
Source: *VVS*, 1952, No. 65.

• 52/vi/13/MPR. See Appendix 5.

• 52/vi/16/Bul

Agreement between the USSR and Bul-

garia concerning conditions of trade deliveries

Signed June 16, 1952.
Listed in Korolenko, p. 109, as still valid as of Nov. 25, 1953.

• 52/vi/25/Rom

Agreement between the USSR and Romania concerning conditions of trade deliveries

Signed June 25, 1952.
Listed in Korolenko, p. 109, as still valid as of Nov. 25, 1953.

June 28, 1952. International Labour Organisation Convention No. 103

See 56/vii/6/1952.

• 52/vi/30/H

Agreement between the USSR and Hungary concerning conditions of trade deliveries

Signed June 30, 1952.
Listed in Korolenko, p. 109, as still valid as of Nov. 25, 1953.
Note: Liubimov, p. 18, mentions a Soviet-Hungarian protocol on general conditions of trade deliveries signed at the end of Apr. 1952. Presumably an error for this agreement.

• 52/vii/1/GDR

Agreement between the USSR and the German Democratic Republic concerning working conditions of Soviet specialists sent to the GDR to give technical assistance

Signed July 1, 1952.
Cited in the atomic energy agreement of Apr. 28, 1955, as the basis for work of Soviet atomic specialists sent to the GDR.

• 52/vii/1/Pl

Sixth meeting of the Danube Commission

Held June 23–July 1, 1952, in Galatz, with representatives of the USSR, Bulgaria, Czechoslovakia, Hungary, Romania, and Yugoslavia.
Adopted the following documents among others: (1) Decree on coordination of the hydrometeorological service and observations on the Danube; and (2) decree on

review of the rules of procedure and statute of organization of the secretariat and working apparatus (the latter in answer to a Yugoslav proposal).
Source: *PDK*, 6 (R, F).
Reference: *Int. org.*, 7, 1953, p. 301.

• 52/vii/5/Alb

Agreement between the USSR and Albania concerning training of Albanian citizens in civic institutions of higher education in the USSR

Signed July 5, 1952, in Moscow.
Entered into force Sept. 1, 1952. Number and specialties of persons to be determined by agreement between the USSR Ministry of Higher Education and the Albanian Ministry of Education not later than 4 months before start of the academic year. Supersedes the agreement of Dec. 15, 1947 (47/xii/15/Alb), and the protocol of Jan. 16, 1951 (51/i/16/Alb).
Source: *SDD*, 15, pp. 259–61.

• 52/vii/11/Mul/a

Universal Postal Convention, with related documents

Signed July 11, 1952, in Brussels. The USSR and Belorussian and Ukrainian SSR's signed, with reservations (see below).
Ratified by the USSR July 24, 1953; by the Belorussian and Ukrainian SSR's Oct. 22, 1953. Entered into force July 1, 1953; for the USSR, July 24, 1953, on deposit of act of ratification. Duration indefinite; signatories may withdraw with 1 year's notice. Supersedes the convention of July 5, 1947 (47/vii/5/Mul/a); superseded by the convention of 1957 (57/x/3/Mul/a).
Full contents (*UNTS*, 169): (1) Text, pp. 14–101; (2) final protocol, pp. 102–17; (3) declaration on signature by the USSR and Belorussian and Ukrainian SSR's, and counter-declaration by China, pp. 112–15 (see below); (4) Annex: Agreement between the United Nations and the Universal Postal Union of July 4, 1947 (*UNTS*, 19, p. 219), with supplementary agreement of July 13, 1947 (*ibid.*, 43, p. 344); (5) detailed regulations for implementation, pp. 121–241; (6) annexes to the regulations (blank forms), pp. 242–305; (7) provisions con-

cerning air mail, pp. 306–41; (8) final protocol to the provisions concerning air mail, pp. 342–43; (9) annexes to the provisions concerning air mail (blank forms), pp. 344–59.

On signing the final protocol the delegations of the USSR and Belorussian and Ukrainian SSR's made a declaration stating that they (1) considered illegal the action of the congress in according to the representatives of the Nationalist Government of China (designated "the Kuomintang") the right to sign the convention in the name of China and maintained that only the representatives of the Central Government of the Chinese People's Republic had the right to sign the convention in the name of China; (2) considered unjustified the fact that the German Democratic Republic and the Korean People's Democratic Republic were not allowed to participate in the work of the congress and sign the convention; and (3) understood the term "Allemagne" in the preamble and final protocol to mean a unified Germany with a government for all Germany. In reply to the first part of the Soviet declaration the Government of the Republic of China asserted its right to sign the convention and related documents on behalf of China, and protested the inclusion of the Soviet declaration in the official text of the convention. Both the Federal Republic of Germany and the German Democratic Republic were later admitted to the Universal Postal Union (see O. Irinin, "Democratic Germany—A full-fledged member of the Universal Postal Union," *Int. aff.*, 1958, No. 11, pp. 104–105).

In addition to protesting the signature of Nationalist China, the USSR, at the 13th Universal Postal Congress which adopted the convention, declared that it did not recognize as a member of the Universal Postal Union the Bao-Dai regime of Vietnam, considering it to be illegal.

The USSR and Belorussian and Ukrainian SSR's also signed the agreement concerning insured letters and boxes (next document).

Sources: *SDD*, 15, pp. 91–227.
UNTS, 169, as listed above (E, F).
BTS, 1954, No. 28, Cmd. 9190, pp. 8–156.
UST, 4, pp. 1118–1436 (*TIAS* 2800).
Durdenevski and Krylov, pp. 227–44.

• 52/vii/11/Mul/b

Agreement of the Universal Postal Union concerning insured letters and boxes, with related documents

Signed July 11, 1952, in Brussels. The USSR and Belorussian and Ukrainian SSR's signed

Ratified by the USSR June 24, 1953; by the Belorussian and Ukrainian SSR's Oct. 22, 1953. Entered into force July 1, 1953; for the USSR, July 24, 1953 on deposit of act of ratification. Duration indefinite. Supersedes the agreement of July 5, 1947 (47/vii/5/Mul/b); superseded by the agreement of 1957 (57/x/3/Mul/b).
Related documents: (1) final protocol; (2) regulations for implementation; (3) annexes (blank forms).
Sources: *SDD*, 15, pp. 228–48 (omits the annexes).
BTS, 1954, No. 29, Cmd. 9189, pp. 4–44.

• 52/viii/ /Pl

Military conference

Held during Aug. 1952, in Prague, by the USSR, the Chinese People's Republic, Bulgaria, Czechoslovakia, Hungary, Poland, and Romania.
Purpose to assess progress in the reorganization of the armies of the Soviet satellite States and their further expansion and equipment with Soviet material. The conference was reported to have established a military coordinating committee under Marshal N. A. Bulganin.
Reference: *SIA, 1952*, p. 152, citing reports in the Western press.

• 52/viii/9/CPR/a

Agreement between the USSR and the Chinese People's Republic concerning training of CPR citizens in civic institutions of higher education in the USSR

Signed Aug. 9, 1952, in Moscow.
Entered into force Sept. 1, 1952. Number and specialties of persons to be determined by agreement between the USSR Ministry of Higher Education and the CPR Ministry of Education not later than 4 months before start of the academic year. Supplemented by an exchange of notes of the same date (next document).
Source: *SDD*, 15, pp. 271–74.

● 52/viii/9/CPR/b

Exchange of notes between the USSR and the Chinese People's Republic concerning training of CPR citizens in the USSR

Sent Aug. 9, 1952, in Moscow.
Provides for extension of the provisions of the agreement of the same date (preceding document) to citizens of the CPR who were studying in institutions of higher education in the USSR before entry into force of the agreement.
Source: *SDD*, 15, pp. 274–75.

● 52/viii/20/Pl

Agreement concerning establishment of a regular steamship line between the Black Sea ports of the USSR, Bulgaria, and Romania, and the ports of Albania, with two annexes

Signed Aug. 20, 1952, in Moscow, by the USSR, Albania, Bulgaria, and Romania. Entered into force on signature. Valid until 3 months after denunciation by any signatory.
Annexes: (1) regulations for loading and unloading operations: (2) tariff schedule and classification of cargoes.
The agency designated for the Romanian Government to coordinate questions arising under the agreement was the Soviet-Romanian joint-stock company "Sovrom-transport" (for establishment of the company, see 45/vii/19/Rom). A note in *SDD*, 15, p. 258, points out that under agreements in 1954 (see 54/iii/31/Rom/b), Soviet shares in the company were sold to Romania.
Source: *SDD*, 15, pp. 256–58 (omits the annexes).

● 52/ix/ /Af

Agreement between the USSR and Afghanistan concerning the showing of Soviet films in Afghanistan

Signed during Sept. 1952.
Reference: *Int. aff.*, 1956, No. 1, p. 48.

● 52/ix/15/CPR/a

Joint communiqué on negotiations between the USSR and the Chinese People's Republic

Issued Sept. 15, 1952, at the end of nego-tiations which began in mid-August, in Moscow.
Mentions discussion of "important political and economic questions" concerning relations between the USSR and the CPR, and agreements reached concerning the Chinese Changchun Railway and Port Arthur (next 2 documents).
Source: *Izv.*, Sept. 16, 1952.
   VT, 1952, No. 9, pp. 42–43.
   DIA, 1952, pp. 470–71.
   DAFR, 1952, pp. 293–94.
   SCMP, No. 417, Sept. 17, 1952, pp. 1–2.

● 52/ix/15/CPR/b

Joint communiqué by the USSR and the Chinese People's Republic concerning transfer of the Chinese Changchun Railway to the CPR

Issued Sept. 15, 1952, in Moscow.
Provides for establishment of a mixed USSR-CPR commission to carry out the transfer, by the end of 1952, under the agreement of Feb. 14, 1950 (50/ii/14/CPR/d). For a protocol marking completion of the transfer, see 52/xii/31/CPR/a.
Sources: *Izv.*, Sept. 16, 1952.
   VT, 1952, No. 9, p. 43.
   SDD, 14, p. 20; *ibid.*, 15, p. 15.
   DIA, 1952, p. 471.
   DAFR, 1952, p. 294.

● 52/ix/15/CPR/c

Exchange of notes between the USSR and the Chinese People's Republic concerning extension of the stay of Soviet troops in Port Arthur

Sent Sept. 15, 1952, in Moscow.
Under an agreement of Feb. 14, 1950 (50/ii/14/CPR/d), Soviet troops were to be withdrawn from Port Arthur after conclusion of a peace treaty with Japan, or not later than the end of 1952. The peace treaty with Japan of Sept. 8, 1951, was not signed by either the USSR or the CPR. By the present exchange of notes, which was made an integral part of the agreement of Feb. 14, 1950, the stay of Soviet troops in Port Arthur was extended until conclusion of a peace treaty between Japan and the USSR and CPR. Soviet troops were, however, evacuated by May 24, 1955 (see 54/x/12/CPR/f and 55/v/24/CPR).
Sources: *Izv.*, Sept. 16, 1952.
   VT, 1952, No. 9, pp. 43–44.

CDSP, 4, 1952, No. 37, pp. 6–7.
SCMP, No. 417, Sept. 17, 1952, pp. 2–3.
UNTS, 226, pp. 45–49 (R, C, E, F).
DIA, 1952, pp. 472–73.
DAFR, 1952, p. 295.

● 52/ix/15/Pl

Agreement concerning construction of a railroad from Tsinin to Ulan Bator and establishment of direct rail communications between the USSR, the Chinese People's Republic, and the Mongolian People's Republic

Signed Sept. 15, 1952, by the USSR, the CPR, and the MPR.
Provides for construction of the section Tsinin-Erlian-CPR frontier by the CPR; from Ulan Bator to the MPR frontier jointly by the USSR and the MPR. To be completed by 1955.
A joint communiqué published Jan. 4, 1956, marked completion of construction of the section from Ulan Bator to Tsinin and opening of direct rail communications between the 3 States (see 56/i/4/Pl).
References: Mentioned in the joint communiqué of Oct. 12, 1954 (54/x/12/Pl).

● 52/ix/21/Pl

Three-way trade and payments agreement between the USSR, Finland, and the Chinese People's Republic, with two annexes

Signed Sept. 21, 1952, in Moscow.
Entered into force on signature; valid until Dec. 31, 1952.
Provides for trade to the value of 34 million rubles for each party. The CPR to make deliveries to the USSR, the USSR to Finland, and Finland to the CPR. Details to be determined in separate bilateral agreements (see the next 2 documents).
Payments to be handled by Gosbank for the USSR, the Bank of Finland, and the Bank of the CPR.
References: *VT*, 1956, No. 12, p. 2.
    Private sources.

● 52/ix/21/CPR

Trade agreement between the USSR and the Chinese People's Republic

Signed Sept. 21, 1952, in Moscow.
Entered into force on signature; valid until Dec. 31, 1952. Specifies goods to be delivered by the CPR to the USSR

under the 3-way trade and payments agreement of the same date (preceding document).
Reference: Private sources.

● 52/ix/21/Fin

Trade agreement between the USSR and Finland

Signed Sept. 21, 1952, in Moscow.
Entered into force on signature; valid until Dec. 31, 1952.
Specifies goods to be delivered by the USSR to Finland under the 3-way trade and payments agreement of the same date (see 2 preceding documents).
Reference: Private sources.

● 52/ix/23/Fin

Agreement between the USSR and Finland concerning supplementary trade during 1952–1955

Signed Sept. 23, 1952.
Finland to export tankers, tugs, diesel ships, cranes, excavators, industrial equipment, prefabricated houses, lumber, in exchange for Soviet grains, sugar, cotton, oil products, industrial equipment, vehicles, chemicals, etc. Modifies the 5-year agreement of June 13, 1950 (50/vi/13/Fin/a).
References: *Izv.*, Sept. 24, 1952.
    VT, 1952, No. 9, p. 46; *ibid.*, 1954, No. 1, p. 8; *ibid.*, 1956, No. 12, p. 3.

● 52/ix/30/H

Agreement between the USSR and Hungary concerning transfer to Hungary of sixty-nine Soviet enterprises in Hungary

Signed Sept. 30, 1952.
The enterprises in question were acquired by the USSR under the Potsdam agreement awarding appropriate German external assets to the USSR as reparations (see 45/viii/1/(3)).
References: *VT*, 1953, No. 11, p. 20.
    SIA, 1952, p. 160.

Dec. 20, 1952. Convention on the political rights of women
See 53/iii/31/Mul.

● 52/xii/22/Mul

International Telecommunication Convention, with related documents

Signed Dec. 22, 1952, in Buenos Aires.

The USSR and Belorussian and Ukrainian SSR's signed. Ratified by the USSR Dec. 14, 1955; act of ratification deposited Jan. 12, 1956. Act of ratification of the Ukrainian SSR deposited Jan. 16, 1956; of the Belorussian SSR Feb. 21, 1956. Entered into force Dec. 22, 1952, for signatories whose act of ratification or accession had been deposited before that date. May be denounced with 1 year's notice. Defines the composition, functions, and structure of the International Telecommunication Union. Supersedes the convention of 1947 (47/x/2/Mul/a).

Related documents consist of 6 annexes and a final protocol. Annexes: (1) List of members of the Union. (2) List of associate members. (3) Definition of terms used in the convention. (4) Provisions for arbitration. (5) General regulations annexed to the convention. (6) Agreement between the United Nations and the International Telecommunication Union, drafted during Aug. 1947 (see entry under Aug. 14, 1947).

Final protocol lists reservations and declarations by signatories, including 2 by the USSR and Belorussian and Ukrainian SSR's stating (1) that they leave open the question of accepting the provisions of the convention concerning the International Frequency Registration Board and the radio regulations, and (2) that they consider illegal the decision taken by the conference to grant the representatives of (a) Nationalist China (designated "the Kuomintang representatives") the right to sign the convention on behalf of China, (b) the representatives of Southern Vietnam (designated "Bao-Dai Vietnam") and the Republic of Korea (designated "South Korea") the right to sign on behalf of Vietnam and Korea, and (c) the representatives of the Federal Republic of Germany (designated "the Bonn authorities") the right to sign on behalf of Germany.

Supplemented by radio regulations, which the USSR did not sign.

Sources: Durdenevski and Krylov, pp. 244–65, citing
   Mezhdunarodnaia konventsiia elektrosviazi, 1954, pp. 1–47.
UST, 6, pp. 1213–2021 (E, F, S, R, C).
References: *VVS*, 1955, No. 24, Art. 473 (Soviet ratification).
   DSB, 34, 1956, p. 356 (deposit of act of ratification).

● 52/xii/25/Rom

Convention between the USSR and Romania concerning measures for prevention of floods and regulation of the water level on the River Prut, with two annexes

Signed Dec. 25, 1952, in Kishinev.
Entered into force on signature. Duration 10 years; if not denounced 1 year before expiration, extended for 10-year periods. Calls for appointment by each party of commissioners, with deputies, to carry out provisions. Annexes give blank forms for identification of commissioners and experts.
Source: *SDD*, 15, pp. 21–31.

● 52/xii/26/Pl

Seventh meeting of the Danube Commission

Held Dec. 15–26, 1952, in Galatz, with representatives of the USSR, Bulgaria, Czechoslovakia, Hungary, Romania, and Yugoslavia.
Adopted the following documents, among others: (1) Plan of work for 1953; (2) budget for 1953; (3) decree on establishment of a single system of navigational conditions on the Danube; and (4) decree on the "unilateral actions" of the Yugoslav authorities in the Iron Gates sector.
Source: *PDK*, 7 (R, F).
Reference: *Int. org.*, 8, 1954, pp. 416–17.

● 52/xii/31/CPR/a

Protocol between the USSR and the Chinese People's Republic concerning transfer to the CPR of the Chinese Changchun Railway

Signed Dec. 31, 1952, in Harbin, by the joint commission set up in Sept. 1952 (see 52/ix/15/CPR/b).
Marks completion of the transfer agreed on in Feb. 1950 (see 50/ii/14/CPR/d).
References: *Izv.*, Jan. 1, 1953.
   CDSP, 5, 1953, No. 1, p. 19.
   SCMP, No. 483, Jan. 1–3, 1953, pp. 14–15.

● 52/xii/31/CPR/b

Documents concerning transfer of assets and operations of the Soviet Foreign Insurance Administration in Northeast China (Manchuria) to the China People's Insurance Company

Signed Dec. 31, 1952, at Port Arthur, by

representatives of the 2 insurance agencies.

The company which was set up in Dairen in 1946, handled chiefly fire insurance for Soviet enterprises, with some insurance business also for Chinese enterprises.

Reference: *SCMP*, No. 489, Jan. 10–12, 1953, p. 8.

1953

• 53/ / /Pl

Protocol concerning three-way trade and payments between the USSR, Czechoslovakia, and Finland

Concluded during 1953.

Accompanied by bilateral trade protocols between the 3 States (not listed separately).

For terms and reference, see 50/vi/ /Pl.

• 53/i/ /Bul. See Appendix 5.

Jan. 1, 1953. Changes in the agreement of Dec. 19, 1947, between the USSR and Finland concerning direct railroad communications

See 47/xii/19/Fin.

• 53/i/13/GDR

Agreement between the USSR and the German Democratic Republic concerning collaboration in the field of radio broadcasting, with supplementary protocol

Signed Jan. 13, 1953, in Moscow.

Entered into force on signature. Duration 1 year; if not denounced 3 months before expiration, extended for 1 year. Superseded by the agreement of Oct. 12, 1956.

Source: *Dokumente DDR*, 4, pp. 34–36.

• 53/ii/ /Cz

Long-term trade agreement between the USSR and Czechoslovakia

Concluded during Feb. 1953.

Covers the period 1951–1955. Details of trade to be specified in annual protocols.

Reference: *VT*, 1955, No. 2, p. 9.

Note: Soviet-Czechoslovak trade during all or part of the period covered by this agreement was already provided for under 2 earlier agreements, of 1947 (47/xii/11/Cz/b), and 1950 (50/xi/3/Cz). The 1947 agreement ran from 1948 through 1952; trade was to be increased under the 1950 economic agreement, which ran from 1951 through 1955, although it was not

explicitly stated in Soviet publications that it covered trade for that period. It is possible that the reference cited above is in error as to the scope of this agreement, and that its term of validity should read 1953 through 1958. It would then follow on expiration of the 1947 agreement and be followed by the 3-year agreement of Dec. 1957 (57/xii/13/Cz).

• 53/ii/7/Pl

Protocol concerning maintenance of the border mark erected at Muotkavaara (Krokfjellet) at the junction point of the state frontiers of the USSR, Norway, and Finland

Signed Feb. 7, 1953, in Helsinki, by the USSR, Norway, and Finland.

Entered into force July 1, 1953. Duration 15 years; if not denounced 6 months before expiration, extended for 15-year periods.

Provides for maintenance of the border mark by each of the 3 States in rotation, for 5-year periods, beginning Aug. 1, 1953. Maintenance to be in accordance with the border documents signed Dec. 3, 1947 (47/xii/3/Pl).

Source: *UNTS*, 173, pp. 143–61 (R, Finnish, N, E, F).

Reference: *Izv.*, Feb. 10, 1953.

• 53/ii/23/Fin

Trade protocol for 1953 between the USSR and Finland

Signed Feb. 23, 1953.

Based on the 5-year trade agreement of June 13, 1950 (50/vi/13/Fin/a).

References: *VT*, 1953, No. 11, p. 32.
Korolenko, p. 89.

• 53/ii/23/MPR. See Appendix 5.

• 53/iii/19/UK

Exchange of communications between the USSR and the United Kingdom concerning release of British civilians interned in North Korea

On Feb. 17, 1953, the United Kingdom asked the USSR if it would be willing to use its good offices to secure the release of a number of British citizens, including the British Minister at Seoul in 1950, from imprisonment in North Korea; on Mar. 19 the USSR agreed, and 10 days later provided information on the prisoners and stated that it was consulting with authorities of the Korean People's Democratic Republic concerning the method of repatriation.

Reference: *SIA, 1953,* p. 193, citing
> H.C. Deb., Apr. 2, 1953, 5th ser., Vol. 513, col. 1372–74.

- 53/iii/21/CPR/a

Trade protocol for 1953 between the USSR and the Chinese People's Republic

Signed Mar. 21, 1953, in Moscow.
Soviet metallurgical, mining, machine-building, chemical, power, transportation, and other equipment, agricultural machinery, pedigree cattle, seeds, in exchange for CPR nonferrous ores, rice, plant oil, oil-seeds, meat, tobacco, tea, fruits, wool, jute, raw silk, silk materials, leather, etc.
References: *Izv.,* Mar. 26, 1953.
> *VT,* 1953, No. 3, p. 39.
> *VT SSSR,* p. 49.
> *SCMP,* No. 540, Mar. 27, 1953, p. 1.

- 53/iii/21/CPR/b

Protocol between the USSR and the Chinese People's Republic concerning delivery by the USSR of equipment and goods under the credit agreement of February 14, 1950

Signed Mar. 21, 1953, in Moscow.
This is the 4th annual protocol under the credit agreement (50/ii/14/CPR/e).
References: *Pr., Izv.,* Mar. 26, 1953.
> *VT,* 1953, No. 3, p. 39.
> *CDSP,* 5, 1953, No. 12, p. 11.
> Korolenko, p. 198.

- 53/iii/21/CPR/c

Agreement between the USSR and the Chinese People's Republic concerning aid to the CPR in enlarging electro-stations already in operation and construction of new ones

Signed Mar. 21, 1953, in Moscow.

References: *Izv.,* Mar. 26, 1953.
VT, 1953, No. 3, p. 39.
VT SSSR, p. 49.
SIA, 1953, p. 238.
Note: *SIA, 1953,* p. 237, gives details of a reported agreement of the same date under which the USSR was to loan the CPR 5 billion rubles, repayable at 3 per cent interest over 10 years. If the report is valid, this was presumably a separate agreement.

- 53/iii/24/H

Trade protocol for 1953 between the USSR and Hungary

Signed Mar. 24, 1953, in Moscow.
Soviet metallurgical, mining, and other industrial equipment, cotton, iron ore, coke, agricultural equipment, etc., in exchange for Hungarian sea and river vessels, cranes, industrial equipment, locomobiles, locomotives, consumer goods, etc. Provides for an increase in volume of trade over that called for under the long-term agreement of Jan. 23, 1952 (52/i/23/H/a).
References: *Pr., Izv.,* Mar. 25, 1953.
> *VT,* 1953, No. 3, p. 39.
> *CDSP,* 5, 1953, No. 12,. p. 12.

- 53/iii/24/UK

Agreement between the USSR and the United Kingdom concerning convocation of a conference on air safety

Following the shooting down of a British aircraft en route to Berlin on Mar. 12, 1953, and attacks on 2 other British planes on Mar. 13, the United Kingdom protested in notes of Mar. 13 and 14 to Gen. V. I. Chuikov, Soviet Commander-in-Chief in Germany. In his reply of Mar. 18 Gen. Chuikov proposed holding a conference on air safety, a proposal accepted by the United Kingdom, according to a statement by the Prime Minister in the House of Commons on Mar. 24.
Source: *DIA, 1953,* pp. 40–42.

- 53/iii/31/Bul

Trade protocol for 1953 between the USSR and Bulgaria

Signed Mar. 31, 1953, in Moscow.
Soviet industrial equipment, agricultural machines, rolled ferrous metal, cotton, oil products, chemicals, etc., in exchange for

Bulgarian mining products, tobacco, meat, wines, fresh and dried fruit, tomato products, and other consumer goods.
References: *Izv.*, Apr. 1, 1953.
　　VT, 1953, No. 4, p. 46.

● 53/iii/31/Mul

Convention on the political rights of women

Opened for signature Mar. 31, 1953, in New York. Signed by the USSR and Belorussian and Ukrainian SSR's, with reservations (see below).
Ratified by the USSR Mar. 18, 1954; act of ratification deposited May 3, 1954, with effect from July 7, 1954. Acts of ratification of the Belorussian SSR deposited Aug. 11, 1954; of the Ukrainian SSR Nov. 15, 1954. General entry into force July 7, 1954. May be denounced with 1 year's notice.
Reservations by the USSR and Belorussian and Ukrainian SSR's on signature: (1) The 3 States declare their disagreement with the provision of Art. 7 that the juridical effect of a reservation to the convention is to make the convention inoperative as between the State making the reservation and any State which does not accept it; instead they maintain that a reservation affects only part of the convention, leaving the remainder operative between States parties to the convention. (2) The 3 States declare that they do not consider themselves bound by the provision that disputes between parties concerning interpretation or application of the convention shall be referred to the International Court of Justice for decision on request of any of the parties to the dispute, and declare that agreement of all parties to the dispute shall be necessary in each case. Five States (China, Denmark, Israel, the Dominican Republic, and Sweden) notified the Secretary-General of the UN that they did not accept these reservations, and the convention accordingly did not come into force between them and the USSR.
Sources: *VVS*, 1954, No. 12, Art. 243.
　　SDD, 16, pp. 290–94.
　　MZh, 1955, No. 10, pp. 158–59.
　　UNTS, 193, pp. 135–73 (R, E, F, S, C).
References: *SZ, 1938–1956*, p. 160 (Soviet ratification).
　　Int. org., 7, 1953, pp. 85–86 (approval of the draft in the UN, Dec. 1952).

● 53/iv/8/Alb

Trade protocol for 1953 between the USSR and Albania

Signed Apr. 8, 1953, in Moscow.
Soviet grain, equipment for the oil industry and for mechanization of construction, agricultural machines, fertilizer, rolled ferrous and nonferrous metals, chemicals, etc., in exchange for Albanian oil, bitumen, copper, leather goods, wool, tobacco, citrus fruits, etc.
References: *Izv.*, Apr. 9, 1953.
　　VT, 1953, No. 4, p. 46.
　　Korolenko, p. 107.

● 53/iv/8/MPR/a, b. See Appendix 5.

● 53/iv/9/Sweden

Trade protocol for 1953 between the USSR and Sweden

Signed Apr. 9, 1953, in Moscow.
Provides for a smaller volume of trade than in earlier years; expiration of the period for use of credits under the agreement of Oct. 7, 1946 (46/x/7/Sweden/b), a factor, according to *VT*, 1954, No. 4, p. 2.
References: *Pr.*, *Izv.*, Apr. 12, 1953.
　　VT, 1953, No. 4, p. 47.

● 53/iv/22/Pol

Trade protocol for 1953 between the USSR and Poland

Signed Apr. 22, 1953, in Moscow.
Soviet machines and equipment, cotton, iron, manganese, and chrome ores, oil and oil products, copper, aluminum, chemicals, etc., in exchange for Polish sea vessels, railroad rolling stock, coal, coke, zinc, cement, textiles, furniture, etc. Volume of trade to be greater than that provided for by long-term agreement of June 29, 1950 (50/vi/29/Pol/a).
References: *Pr.*, *Izv.*, Apr. 23, 1953.
　　VT, 1953, No. 4, pp. 46–47.
　　CDSP, 5, 1953, No. 16, p. 37.

● 53/iv/26/GDR

Trade protocol for 1953 between the USSR and the German Democratic Republic

Signed Apr. 26, 1953, in Moscow.
Soviet grains, cotton, wool, ferrous and nonferrous metals, iron and manganese ores, industrial and road-building equipment, vehicles, agricultural machinery,

etc., in exchange for GDR electro-techni-
cal and mining equipment, metal-working
lathes, equipment for the construction
material industry, experimental instruments, chemicals, consumer goods, etc.
Volume of trade to be greater than that
provided for by long-term agreement of
Sept. 27, 1951 (51/ix/27/GDR/b).
References: *Pr., Izv.*, Apr. 28, 1953.
 VT, 1953, No. 4, p. 47.
 CDSP, 5, 1953, No. 17, p. 26.

● 53/vi/ /CPR

**Agreement between the USSR and the
Chinese People's Republic concerning
Soviet material and technical aid**

Signed during the summer of 1953.
Provides for Soviet aid for 141 major
economic projects in the CPR and for
repayment by the CPR.
Reference: Private sources.

● 53/vi/10/Iran

**Exchange of notes between the USSR and
Iran constituting a trade agreement for
the current year**

Sent June 10, 1953, in Teheran.
Covers the period Apr. 1, 1953, through
Mar. 31, 1954. Volume of trade increased
under an exchange of notes of Sept. 3,
1953.
References: *Izv.*, June 13, 1953.
 VT, 1953, No. 6, p. 46; *ibid.*, 1954, No.
 9, p. 4.
 Korolenko, p. 98.

● 53/vi/12/Austria

**Verbal agreement between the USSR and
Austria concerning transformation of
diplomatic missions into embassies**

Negotiated June 9 and 12, 1953, in Mos-
cow.
References: *Pr., Izv.*, June 12, 1953.
 VVS, 1953, No. 6.
 SDD, 15, p. 16.
 CDSP, 5, 1953, No. 24, p. 51.

● 53/vi/14/Yug

**Agreement between the USSR and Yugo-
slavia concerning resumption of diplomatic relations**

Announced June 14, 1953, by Yugoslav

President Tito, referring to a Soviet request.
Following the break between Yugoslavia
and the Cominform in 1949, diplomatic
representatives of Yugoslavia in the USSR
and of the USSR in Yugoslavia were withdrawn during Oct. and Nov. 1949 (see
SIA, 1949–1950, pp. 265–66).
Reference: *SIA, 1953*, p. 126.

● 53/vi/16/Cz

**Agreement between the USSR and Czech-
oslovakia supplementing the convention
of November 28, 1947, concerning quarantine of agricultural plants**

Negotiated June 16, 1953, in Prague; possibly not embodied in a written document.
Adds 1 parasite to the list given in the
convention.
Reference: *SDD*, 13, p. 383.

● 53/vi/24/UK

**Exchange of notes between the USSR and
the United Kingdom extending for one
year the temporary fisheries agreement
of May 22, 1930**

Sent June 24, 1953.
On Jan. 5, 1953, the USSR denounced
the 1930 agreement, with effect from July
5, 1953. By a note of June 24, 1953, the
agreement was renewed for 1 year, dating
from July 6, 1953.
Reference: British Embassy, 1957.

**June 25, 1953. Instrument for the
amendment of the constitution of the
International Labour Organisation**

See 54/x/7/1953.

● 53/vi/26/Mul

**Amendments to the schedule to the in-
ternational convention for the regulation
of whaling**

Adopted at the 5th meeting of the International Whaling Commission, June
22–26, 1953, in London.
For the convention and annexed schedule,
see 46/xii/2/Mul/a and /b.
Source: *UNTS*, 252, pp. 316–23 (E, F).
Reference: *Int. org.*, 8, 1954, p. 424, citing
 FAO Fisheries Bulletin, 6, pp. 240–
 43.

● 53/vii/2/Norway. See Appendix 5.

● 53/vii/3/Pl

Eighth meeting of the Danube Commission

Held June 26–July 3, 1953, in Galatz, with representatives of the 6 member States. The meeting accepted a Soviet proposal for reorganization of the Commission.
Source: *PDK*, 8 (R, F).
Reference: *Int. org.*, 8, 1954, p. 417.

● 53/vii/15/France/a

Trade agreement between the USSR and France, with two annexes

Signed July 15, 1953, in Paris.
Entered into force on signature. Duration 3 years; if not denounced 6 months before expiration, valid until 6 months after denunciation. Even after expiration, provisions valid until final settlement of all obligations arising from trade deals concluded during validity. Extended through Dec. 31, 1959, by agreement of Feb. 11, 1957 (57/ii/11/France/a). Based on the agreement of Sept. 3, 1951.
Total trade during 1st year of operation to be valued at 12 billion francs for each party. Increase in 1st year's trade provided for by a protocol of Jan. 28, 1954. Annexes list goods, orders for which are to be placed during first year by each party. Trade contingents for later years of operation of the agreement to be defined in annual protocols. Provides for establishment of a mixed commission on implementation, to meet every 6 months alternately in Moscow and Paris.
Sources: *VT*, 1953, No. 9, pp. 43–45.
    SDD, 15, pp. 81–83 (omits the annexes).
    MOCI, No. 1566, p. 1941.
References: *Izv.*, July 17, 1953.
    VT, 1953, No. 7, p. 45; *ibid.*, 1954, No. 1, pp. 25, 30.
    Korolenko, pp. 82–83.

● 53/vii/15/France/b

Payments agreement between the USSR and France

Signed July 15, 1953, in Paris.
Entered into force on signature. Valid for the duration of the trade agreement of the same date (preceding document).
References: *Izv.*, July 17, 1953.
    VT, 1953, No. 7, p. 45; *ibid.*, 1954, No. 1, p. 25.

● 53/vii/15/Israel

Exchange of notes between the USSR and Israel concerning re-establishment of diplomatic relations

Sent July 6, 1953, from Tel Aviv, and July 15, 1953, from Moscow.
For earlier developments in Soviet-Israeli relations, see 48/v/26/Israel.
Source: *Izv.*, July 21, 1953.
References: *SDD*, 13, p. 25.
    SDD, 15, p. 16.
    SIA, 1953, p. 148.

July 15, 1953. Admission of the USSR to the United Nations Technical Assistance Program

The Soviet delegate at the 16th session of the UN Economic and Social Council (ECOSOC) announced that the USSR was "prepared to take part in the implementation of the UN Technical Assistance Program" and to appropriate 4 million rubles as its contribution to the Fund for 1953. See *Int. org.*, 7, 1953, p. 533; *ibid.*, 11, 1957, pp. 618–20. The Ukrainian and Belorussian SSR's joined the Fund in 1954 (*ibid.*)

● 53/vii/17/Austria

Agreement between the USSR and Austria concerning transfer to Austria of assets of the hydroelectric station at Ybbs-Persenbeug

Signed July 17, 1953, in Vienna, by the Administration of Soviet Property in Austria (Upravlenie sovetskim imushchestvom v Avstrii, abbreviated USIA), and the Austrian Ministry of Transport and Nationalized Enterprises.
Reference: *Izv.*, July 19, 1953.

● 53/vii/17/Den

Trade protocol between the USSR and Denmark, with two annexes

Signed July 17, 1953, in Copenhagen.
Entered into force on signature. Regulates trade from July 1, 1953, through June 30, 1954. Annexes list goods to be supplied by both parties.
During negotiations in June 1954 for renewal of the agreement, the USSR denied that there had been Soviet demands for

political concessions, as claimed by Denmark (*Izv.*, Aug. 1, 1954).
Sources: *Lovtidende C, Danmarks Traktater*, 1953, p. 239.
UNTS, 175, pp. 3–11 (R, D, E, F).
References: *Izv.*, July 19, 1953.
VT, 1953, No. 8, p. 42; *ibid.*, 1954, No. 8, p. 34.
Korolenko, p. 85.

• 53/vii/18/T

Exchange of notes between the USSR and Turkey concerning Soviet claims on Turkish territory and regulation of the Black Sea Straits

On May 30, 1953, the USSR sent Turkey a declaration renouncing claims made by the Armenian and Georgian SSR's in 1945 to Turkish territory and stating that the USSR considered it possible to reach a settlement on the problem of the Straits which would be acceptable to both States. In its reply of July 17, 1953, Turkey noted the declaration concerning renunciation of territorial claims and reminded the USSR that the question of the Straits was regulated by the Montreux Convention (see 36/vii/20/Pl).
Sources: *Izv.*, July 19, 1953.
DIA, 1953, pp. 277–78.

• 53/vii/28/Greece

Trade and payments agreement between the USSR and Greece, with two annexes

Signed July 28, 1953, in Athens.
Ratified by Greece Nov. 13, 1953. Entered into force on signature. Valid until July 28, 1954. If not denounced 1 month before expiration, extended until 3 months after denunciation.
Establishes a trade balance limit of $1 million US for each party. By a protocol of Jan. 19, 1957, this limit was raised to $2.5 million US. Annexes list goods to be exchanged.
Sources: *SDD*, 15, pp. 48–51 (omits annexes).
*Greek official gazette, Part A, 1953, No. 335.
References: *Izv.*, July 30, 1953.
VT, 1953, No. 8, p. 42; *ibid.*, 1954, No. 1, p. 25; *ibid.*, No. 11, p. 44.
Korolenko, pp. 98, 107.

• 53/vii/30/Austria

Exchange of notes between the USSR and Austria concerning occupation costs

In a note of July 30, 1953, the USSR, in answer to a request from the Austrian Government, agreed to take over all costs of the upkeep of Soviet occupation troops in Austria.
Source (Soviet note): *DIA, 1953*, p. 149, citing
Soviet news, Aug. 6, 1953.

• 53/vii/31/Pl

Agreement concerning international freight communication

Signed July 31, 1953, in Moscow, by the USSR, Albania, Bulgaria, the Chinese People's Republic, Czechoslovakia, the German Democratic Republic, Hungary, the Korean People's Democratic Republic, the Mongolian People's Republic, Poland, and Romania. The Viet-Nam Democratic Republic joined as of July 1956 (*VT*, 1957, No. 9, p. 3). Drawn up at a conference in Moscow July 2–23, 1953. Entered into force Jan. 1, 1954. Duration indefinite; may be denounced with 6 months' notice. Questions of implementation, amendment, or supplement to be examined at conferences of member States, to meet not less than once every 2 years. Modifies and replaces the agreement concerning transportation of freight by rail in direct international communications of 1950 (50/ / /Pl). Russian title: Soglashenie o mezhdunarodnom gruzovom soobshchenii, abbreviated SMGS.
References: *VT*, 1954, No. 2, pp. 32–33.
Genkin, pp. 129–30.
See further Appendix 5.

• 53/viii/1/Iceland

Trade and payments agreement between the USSR and Iceland, with two annexes

Signed Aug. 1, 1953, in Moscow.
Entered into force on signature. Duration 2 years; if not denounced, extended until 3 months after denunciation. Extended by protocols of June 19, 1954, Sept. 23, 1955, and Sept. 27, 1956. Supplemented by a loan agreement of Aug. 18, 1958.
Establishes a trade balance limit of 10 million Icelandic crowns for each party. By an exchange of notes of Sept. 23, 1955 (55/ix/23/Iceland/b), this limit was raised to 20 million Icelandic crowns. Trade limit to be altered proportionally to any change in the gold value of the Icelandic crown; such an alteration was ef-

fected by exchange of notes of Jan. 30 and Feb. 5, 1954 (54/ii/5/Iceland).

Annexes list goods to be exchanged: Soviet oil products, flour, cement, metallurgical products, etc., in exchange for Icelandic fish.

Source: *SDD*, 15, pp. 61–64 (omits the annexes).
References: *Izv.*, Aug. 4, 1953.
  VT, 1953, No. 8, p. 42; *ibid.*, 1954, No. 11, p. 8; *ibid.*, 1957, No. 1, p. 17.
  Korolenko, p. 99.

● 53/viii/3/Alb

Verbal agreement between the USSR and Albania concerning transformation of diplomatic missions into embassies

Negotiated Aug. 3, 1953, in Tirana.
References: *Izv.*, Aug. 4, 1953.
  VVS, 1953, No. 7.
  SDD, 15, p. 16.

● 53/viii/5/Argentina

Trade and payments agreement between the USSR and Argentina, with two annexes

Signed Aug. 5, 1953, in Buenos Aires.
Entered into force Aug. 15, 1953 (10 days after signature). Duration 1 year. If not denounced 90 days before expiration, extended for 1-year periods. Validity of annexes (listing goods to be exchanged) extended for 60 days by exchange of notes of Aug. 15, 1954. Supplemented by trade protocol for 1955 of May 19, 1955.

In addition to goods to be traded, as listed in the annexes, provides for purchases by Argentina during the first year of validity of machinery and equipment in the USSR to a value of $30 million US; the USSR to facilitate financing of the purchases. A mixed consultative committee to be set up in Buenos Aires to supervise execution of provisions.

Sources: *VT*, 1953, No. 10, pp. 36–39.
  SDD, 15, pp. 41–46 (omits annexes).
  Spanish-language official text, Argentine Embassy, Sept. 1957.
  UNTS, 221, pp. 99–127 (R, S, E, F).
References: *Izv.*, Aug. 6, 1953.
  VT, 1953, No. 8, p. 43; *ibid.*, 1955, No. 7, p. 13.
  Korolenko, pp. 99–100.
  SIA, 1953, p. 334.
  Allen, 1957, p. 444.

● 53/viii/10/Iran

Agreement between the USSR and Iran concerning convocation in Teheran of a mixed Soviet-Iranian commission to settle disagreements on financial, border, and other questions

Announced Aug. 10, 1953.
References: *Izv.*, Aug. 11, 1953.
  SIA, 1953, p. 185.

● 53/viii/17/Rom

Protocol between the USSR and Romania concerning preparation and exchange of radio programs

Signed Aug. 17, 1953, in Bucharest.
Entered into force Sept. 15, 1953.
Supplements the agreement of Apr. 27, 1949, concerning collaboration in the field of radio broadcasting.
Sources: *SDD*, 14, p. 315.
  SDD, 15, p. 90.

● 53/viii/18/Egypt

Payments agreement between the USSR and Egypt

Signed Aug. 18, 1953, in Cairo.
Entered into force on signature. Duration 1 year; if not denounced 3 months before expiration, extended from year to year. Establishes a credit limit of 1 million Egyptian pounds, subject to alteration proportional to any alteration in the value of the Egyptian pound.
Source: *SDD*, 15, pp. 52–54.
Reference: Korolenko, p. 100.

● 53/viii/22/GDR/a

Joint communiqué concerning negotiations between the USSR and the German Democratic Republic

Issued Aug. 22, 1953, following talks in Moscow which began Aug. 20, 1953.
Mentions the following agreements: (1) A peace conference on Germany must be called in the immediate future, with participation of the German people; further, an All-German Provisional Government must be formed by direct agreement between "Eastern and Western Germany," with the primary task of preparing and carrying out "free all-German elections" on the basis of which the German people, "without interference from foreign states," will decide the social and political struc-

ture of a "united, democratic and peace-loving Germany." (2) Various economic measures to aid the GDR (see next document). (3) The USSR to deliver to the GDR during 1953 goods to a value of approximately 590 million rubles, in addition to trade under the existing agreement, including foodstuffs, rolled ferrous metals, coal, copper, lead, aluminum, cotton, etc. (4) The USSR grants the GDR a credit of 485 million rubles, of which 135 million is to be in convertible foreign currency, to be repaid in 2 years, starting in 1955, at 2 per cent interest. (5) The USSR to free German prisoners-of-war imprisoned for war crimes, except those sentenced for particularly serious crimes. (6) Diplomatic missions of the 2 States to be raised to embassies (see 53/viii/22/GDR/c).
Sources: *Izv.*, Aug. 23, 1953.
　　VT, 1953, No. 9, pp. 2–3.
　　Itogi peregovorov, pp. 3–6.
　　DIA, 1953, pp. 168–70.
　　Dokumente DDR, 1, pp. 283–86.

● 53/viii/22/GDR/b

Protocol between the USSR and the German Democratic Republic concerning discontinuance of reparations payments by the GDR and other measures to alleviate the financial and economic obligations of the GDR arising out of the war

Signed Aug. 22, 1953, in Moscow.
Provisions: (1) The USSR, in agreement with Poland, to cease from Jan. 1, 1954, requiring payment of reparations by the GDR. Based on the Soviet statement of May 15, 1950, remaining total estimated at $2,537 million at 1938 world prices. (2) The USSR transfers to the GDR as of Jan. 1, 1954, 33 machine, chemical, metallurgical, and other works located in Germany and acquired by the USSR as reparations. A mixed commission to be established to carry out the transfer. The USSR releases the GDR from a debt of 430 million Marks for 66 Soviet industrial plants transferred to the GDR in 1952 (see entry under Apr. 29, 1952). (3) Costs of maintenance of Soviet armed forces in Germany to be reduced; for 1954 to total 1,600 million Marks, as against 1,950 million Marks in 1953 and 2,182 million Marks in 1949. (4) The USSR releases the GDR from payment of debts in foreign currencies represent-

ing occupation costs incurred since 1945, and from payment of national postwar debts to the USSR.
For a protocol concerning procedure for transfer of the 33 enterprises to the GDR, see 53/xii/1/GDR; see also 54/i/1/GDR. For a protocol signed on completion of the transfer, see 54/ii/15/GDR.
Sources: *Izv.*, Aug. 23, 1953.
　　VT, 1953, No. 9, pp. 3–4.
　　SDD, 15, pp. 46–48.
　　Itogi peregovorov, pp. 7–9.
　　Dokumente DDR, 4, pp. 39–41; *ibid.*, 1, pp. 286–88.
　　UNTS, 221, pp. 129–41 (R, G, E, F).
　　DGO, pp. 594–96.

● 53/viii/22/GDR/c

Verbal agreement between the USSR and the German Democratic Republic concerning transformation of diplomatic missions into embassies

Negotiated Aug. 22, 1953, in Moscow.
References: *SDD*, 15, p. 16.
　　Mentioned in the joint communiqué (53/viii/22/GDR/a).

● 53/viii/26/Sweden

Exchange of notes between the USSR and Sweden modifying the parcel post agreement of November 5, 1946

Sent June 29 and Aug. 26, 1953.
Entered into force July 1, 1953. Lowers the unit of insurance per parcel from 300 to 200 francs.
Reference: *SDD*, 12, p. 179.

● 53/viii/26/Fin

Exchange of notes between the USSR and Finland modifying the agreement of August 19, 1946, concerning postal exchange

Sent June 1 and Aug. 26, 1953.
Entered into force July 1, 1953. Lowers the unit of insurance per parcel from 300 to 200 francs.
Reference: *SDD*, 12, p. 151.

● 53/viii/27/H

Exchange of notes between the USSR and Hungary modifying the parcel post agreement of September 22, 1947

Sent June 16 and Aug. 27, 1953.

Entered into force July 1, 1953. Lowers the unit of insurance per parcel from 300 to 200 francs.
Reference: *SDD*, 13, p. 429.

● 53/viii/28/H

Protocol between the USSR and Hungary concerning preparation and exchange of radio programs

Signed Aug. 28, 1953, in Budapest.
Entered into force Sept. 15, 1953.
Supplements the agreement of Apr. 12, 1950, concerning collaboration in the field of radio broadcasting.
Source: *SDD*, 15, pp. 85–86.

● 53/ix/3/Iran

Exchange of notes between the USSR and Iran concerning an increase in trade for the current year

Sent Sept. 3, 1953, in Teheran.
Supplements the agreement of June 10, 1953.
References: *Pr.*, *Izv.*, Sept. 6, 1953.
VT, 1953, No. 9, p. 46; *ibid.*, 1954, No. 9, p. 4.
Korolenko, p. 98.
CDSP, 5, 1953, No. 36, p. 13.

● 53/ix/5/Pol

Protocol between the USSR and Poland concerning preparation and exchange of radio programs

Signed Sept. 5, 1953, in Warsaw.
Entered into force Sept. 20, 1953.
Supplements the agreement of Oct. 22, 1949, concerning collaboration in the field of radio broadcasting.
Sources: *SDD*, 14, pp. 312–13.
SDD, 15, p. 89.

● 53/ix/7/Norway

Exchange of notes between the USSR and Norway modifying the parcel post agreement of February 11, 1947

Sent Aug. 26 and Sept. 7, 1953.
Entered into force July 1, 1953. Lowers the unit of insurance per parcel from 300 to 200 francs.
Reference: *SDD*, 13, p. 443.

● 53/ix/10/Rom

Exchange of notes between the USSR

and Romania modifying the parcel post agreement of August 20, 1948

Sent Aug. 26 and Sept. 10, 1953.
Entered into force July 1, 1953. Lowers the unit of insurance per parcel from 300 to 200 francs .
Reference: *SDD*, 13, p. 474.

● 53/ix/11/Belgium

Exchange of notes between the USSR and Belgium modifying the parcel post agreement of April 16, 1938

Sent Aug. 26 and Sept. 11, 1953.
Lowers the unit of insurance per parcel from 300 to 200 francs.
Reference: *SDD*, 10, p. 144.

● 53/ix/11/MPR

Agreement between the USSR and the Mongolian People's Republic concerning collaboration in the field of radio broadcasting

Signed Sept. 11, 1953, in Moscow.
Entered into force on signature. Duration 1 year; if not denounced 3 months before expiration, extended for 1-year periods.
Source: *SDD*, 15, pp. 86–88.

● 53/ix/15/T

Agreement between the USSR and Turkey concerning irrigation of the Igdir plain, with three protocols

Signed Sept. 15, 1953, possibly in the form of an exchange of notes.
Provides for joint use of the waters of the Oktemberyan (Serderabad) dam and other matters concerning irrigation of the Igdir plain in northeastern Turkey and Soviet Armenia. Turkey to pay the USSR $413,748 for use of half the dam's yearly output. Protocols: (1) concerns installation of additional pumps along the river and joint use of the pumping station at Igdir; (2) provides for cooperative construction of levees along the banks of the Aras; (3) concerns repair of jetties on the river at Baskoy. For the 1927 agreement under which the Oktemberyan dam was built, see 27/i/8/T/b.
Reference: *NYT*, Sept. 16, 1953.

● 53/ix/17/Bul

Exchange of notes between the USSR and

Bulgaria modifying the parcel post agreement of December 17, 1947

Sent Aug. 27 and Sept. 17, 1953.
Entered into force July 1, 1953. Lowers the unit of insurance per parcel from 300 to 200 francs.
Reference: *SDD*, 13, p. 412.

● 53/ix/17/Pol

Exchange of notes between the USSR and Poland modifying the parcel post agreement of October 1, 1947

Sent Aug. 26 and Sept. 17, 1953.
Entered into force July 1, 1953. Lowers the unit of insurance per parcel from 300 to 200 francs.
Reference: *SDD*, 13, p. 454.

● 53/ix/19/KPDR

Joint communiqué concerning conversations between the USSR and the Korean People's Democratic Republic

Issued Sept. 19, 1953, in Moscow, at the end of talks which began Sept. 11. The Ambassador of the Chinese People's Republic to the USSR also took part in the talks.
Mentions the following agreements: (1) The 2 States express readiness to cooperate with all States concerned to achieve peaceful settlement of the Korean question on the basis of national unification of Korea and of giving the Korean people themselves the opportunity to settle the questions of the state system of Korea. (2) A Soviet gift of 1 billion rubles (offered during Aug. 1953), to restore the national economy of the KPDR, to be used for restoration of the Supun hydro-electric station on the Yalu River; the restoration and construction of ferrous and nonferrous metallurgical plants; chemical and cement works; and construction of enterprises in the textile and food industries. The USSR to give material and technical assistance and train KPDR specialists. (3) The USSR to supply equipment and materials for restoration of rail transport and communications, agriculture and stock-breeding, fishing, housing, hospitals, and schools. (4) The USSR to supply consumer goods. (5) Payments on previous Soviet credits to be deferred and new, more favorable terms for repayment granted.
Sources: *Izv.*, Sept. 20, 1953.

VT, 1953, No. 10, pp. 1–2.
DIA, 1953, pp. 424–25 (shortened).

● 53/ix/22/1946

Convention concerning privileges and immunities of the United Nations

Signed Feb. 13, 1946.
Act of accession of the USSR deposited Sept. 22, 1953; of the Belorussian SSR Oct. 22, 1953; of the Ukrainian SSR Nov. 23, 1953. All 3 States acceded with a reservation (see below). Entered into force for each signatory on deposit of act of accession. Valid for each signatory as long as it remains a member of the UN, or until revision.
Reservations of the USSR and Belorussian and Ukrainian SSR's concern the provision that (1) disputes arising out of the interpretation and application of the convention shall be referred to the International Court of Justice, unless the parties agree on another mode of settlement, and (2) in case of differences between the UN and a member, the Court shall be asked for an advisory opinion on any legal question involved, and its opinion shall be accepted as decisive. The 3 States maintained that the consent of all parties to a dispute to submit the dispute to the Court is required in every individual case.
Sources: *UNTS*, 1, pp. 15–33 (E, F).
　　SDD, 15, pp. 32–40.
　　Durdenevski and Krylov, pp. 335–42.
　　BTS, 1950, No. 10, Cmd. 7891.
　　Hudson, 9, pp. 499–510 (E, F).
References: *Pr.*, Sept. 25, 1953.
　　UNTS, 177, pp. 324–25 (Belorussian SSR accession).
　　UNTS, 180, pp. 296–97 (Ukrainian SSR accession).

Oct. 1, 1953. International agreement for regulation of the production and marketing of sugar

See 53/x/29/1953.

Oct. 20, 1953. Agreement between the USSR and the United States of America concerning return of Lend-Lease vessels

See 53/xii/26/US.

● 53/x/27/Italy

Trade protocol between the USSR and Italy, with exchange of notes

Signed Oct. 27, 1953, in Rome.

Entered into force on signature. Covers trade for 1 year, through Oct. 26, 1954. Soviet grain, oil, manganese and chrome ores, lumber, anthracite, asbestos, fur, paraffin, bristles, etc., in exchange for Italian oranges and lemons, artificial silk thread, silk materials, staple fibers, electric cables, equipment for the light and food industries, forge and press equipment, etc. Exchange of notes concerns delivery by Italy of freighters, diesel refrigerator vessels, tugs, cranes, and electrostations.
References: *Izv.*, Oct. 28, 1953.
    VT, 1953, No. 10, p. 42; *ibid.*, 1954, No. 1, p. 25.

● 53/x/29/1953

International agreement for regulation of the production and marketing of sugar (International sugar agreement)

Signed Oct. 1, 1953, in London; by the USSR Oct. 29, 1953, with reservations (see below).
Ratified by the USSR Jan. 9, 1954; act of ratification deposited Mar. 22, 1954, with immediate effect. Establishes an International Sugar Council, with 1 member from each participating State.
Soviet reservations: (1) "In view of the social and economic structure of the USSR and its planned economy," provisions of the convention concerning limitation of production and stocks of sugar and subsidization of exports of sugar are not applicable to the USSR. (2) Signing of the convention by the USSR does not signify recognition of the Nationalist Chinese Government as the legal and competent government of China.
Amended by a protocol of Dec. 1956 (56/xii/15/Mul). For Soviet accession to the 1937 agreement, see 37/v/6/Mul.
Sources: *SDD*, 16, pp. 313–49.
    UST, 6, pp. 203–432 (E, F, R, C, S).
    BPP, 1953, Misc. No. 10, Cmd. 9004.
References: *VT*, 1955, No. 2, p. 26.
    DSB, 29, 1953, pp. 542–47.

● 53/x/31/CPR

Exchange of notes between the USSR and the Chinese People's Republic modifying the parcel post agreement of February 7, 1950

Sent Aug. 26 and Oct. 31, 1953.
Entered into force July 1, 1953. Lowers the unit of insurance per parcel from 300 to 200 francs. For the 1950 agreement see 50/ii/7/CPR/a.
Reference: *SDD*, 14, p. 300.

● 53/xi/ /Pol

Protocol between the USSR and Poland concerning termination of coal deliveries by Poland to the USSR at special prices

Signed during Nov. 1953.
Delivery of coal at special prices was provided for by an agreement of Aug. 14, 1945 (45/viii/16/Pol/a), with modifications under an agreement of Mar. 1947 (47/iii/5/Pol/d).
Reference: *VT SSSR*, p. 76.

● 53/xi/5/Pol

Communiqué concerning a meeting of the Soviet-Polish commission for scientific and technical collaboration

Published Nov. 5, 1953; the meeting took place a few days earlier, in Warsaw.
Sources: *Izv.*, Nov. 5, 1953.
    VT, 1953, No. 11, p. 39.

● 53/xi/10/Alb

Joint communiqué concerning a meeting of the Soviet-Albanian commission for scientific and technical collaboration

Published Nov. 10, 1953; the meeting took place during Oct. 1953, in Moscow.
Sources: *Izv.*, Nov. 10, 1953.
    VT, 1953, No. 11, p. 40.

Nov. 19, 1953. Joint communiqué concerning negotiations between (1) the Red Cross and Red Crescent Societies of the USSR and (2) the Red Cross Society of Japan concerning repatriation of Japanese prisoners-of-war and civilians from the USSR

References: *NT*, 1953, No. 48, p. 32.
    SIA, 1953, p. 275.

● 53/xi/25/Fin

Trade protocol for 1954 between the USSR and Finland

Signed Nov. 25, 1953, in Moscow.
Provides for an increase in trade above 1954 quotas established in the agreement of June 13, 1950 (50/vi/13/Fin/a), as modified by the supplementary agreement of Sept. 23, 1952. Finland to provide vessels, floating cranes, equipment for the

wood-pulp industry, prefabricated houses, timber, paper, cartons, cellulose, staple fibers, etc., in exchange for Soviet grains, sugar, rice, oil products, cotton, fertilizer, rolled steel, ferrous alloys, anthracite, coke, asbestos, automobiles, chemicals, dyes, ores, etc. Consumer goods to be traded at a volume twice that of preceding year.
References: *Izv.*, Nov. 26, 1953. *VT*, 1953, No. 12, p. 31; *ibid.*, 1954, No. 1, p. 8.

● 53/xii/ /Israel. See Appendix 5.

● 53/xii/1/GDR

Protocol between the USSR and the German Democratic Republic concerning procedure for transfer to the GDR of thirty-three Soviet industrial enterprises in the GDR, with annex

Signed Dec. 1, 1953, in Berlin.
Annex lists enterprises to be transferred. For the protocol providing for the transfer, see 53/viii/22/GDR/b.
Source: *Dokumente DDR*, 1, pp. 298–99.
Reference: *Izv.*, Dec. 3, 1953.

● 53/xii/2/India/a

Commercial agreement between the USSR and India, with two annexes

Signed Dec. 2, 1953, in New Delhi.
Entered into force on signature. Duration 5 years; may be extended or renewed by negotiations begun 3 months before expiration. Followed by a 2nd 5-year agreement signed Nov. 16, 1958 (*Pravda*, Nov. 17, 1958). Covers payments and navigation as well as trade. Annexes list types of goods to be exchanged during 1st year of operation; lists to be revised annually. Validity of lists extended for 1 year by an exchange of notes of Dec. 23, 1954.
Sources: *VT*, 1954, No. 1, pp. 26–28. *SDD*, 15, pp. 54–57 (omits the annexes).
References: *Izv.*, Dec. 3, 1953 (joint communiqué). *VT*, 1955, No. 2, p. 19; *ibid.*, 1956, No. 10, p. 6.

● 53/xii/2/India/b

Exchange of notes between the USSR and

India concerning the Soviet Trade Mission in India
Sent Dec. 2, 1953, in New Delhi.
Source: *SDD*, 15, pp. 58–60.

● 53/xii/5/Rom/a

Agreement between the USSR and Romania concerning a special river administration for the mouth of the Danube, with protocol

Signed Dec. 5, 1953, in Bucharest.
Entered into force on signature. Duration 10 years; if not denounced 6 months before expiration, extended for 10-year periods.
Provides for establishment of the administration in Galatz and defines its structure and functions. Based on the convention of Aug. 18, 1948. Protocol provides that the 2 States shall cover any deficit incurred by the administration. Supplemented by an exchange of notes (next item). Modified by protocol of July 18, 1957.
Source: *SDD*, 15, pp. 249–54.

● 53/xii/5/Rom/b

Exchange of notes between the USSR and Romania concerning transfer to the special river administration for the mouth of the Danube of property necessary for maintenance of conditions for navigation on the Danube

Sent Dec. 5, 1953, in Bucharest.
Supplements the agreement of the same date (preceding document).
Source: *SDD*, 15, pp. 255–56.

Dec. 7, 1953. Protocol modifying the convention concerning slavery of Sept. 25, 1926

See 56/viii/ /1926.

● 53/xii/17/Indonesia

Exchange of notes between the USSR and Indonesia concerning establishment of embassies in Moscow and Djakarta

Sent Nov. 30, 1953, from Djakarta, and Dec. 17, 1953, from Moscow.
References: *Izv.*, Dec. 23, 1953. *SDD*, 15, p. 16.

- 53/xii/17/Pl

Ninth meeting of the Danube Commission

Held Dec. 9–17, 1953, in Galatz, with representatives of the 6 member States. The meeting agreed on change of the site of the Commission from Galatz to Budapest.
Source: *PDK*, 9 (R, F).
References: *MPID*, 1, p. 254.
  Int. org., 8, 1954, p. 417.

- 53/xii/24/Af

Trade protocol for 1954 between the USSR and Afghanistan

Signed Dec. 24, 1953, in Kabul.
Soviet oil products, metals, sugar, chemicals, medicine, cotton goods, automobiles, equipment, in exchange for Afghan wool, cotton, hides, dried fruit, oil seeds.
References: *Izv.*, Dec. 26, 1953.
  VT, 1954, No. 1, pp. 29–30.

- 53/xii/26/MPR

Trade protocol for 1954 between the USSR and the Mongolian People's Republic

Signed Dec. 26, 1953.
Soviet cotton, silk and woolen goods, sugar, flour, oil products, automobiles, and equipment, for Mongolian cattle, butter, wool, and other animal products.
References: *Izv.*, Dec. 27, 1953.
  VT, 1954, No. 1, p. 31.

- 53/xii/26/US

Exchange of notes between the USSR and the United States of America concerning return of Lend-Lease naval craft

Sent between Sept. 11 and Dec. 26, 1953. In answer to a United States aide-memoire of Sept. 11, 1953, requesting the return of 186 naval craft, the USSR on Oct. 20 expressed its willingness to negotiate for return of the craft. Further exchanges on Nov. 24, Dec. 3, and Dec. 24 led to an agreement in the Soviet note of Dec. 26 to meet with representatives of the United States on Dec. 28 to discuss technical questions concerned with return of the craft. For agreements on return of part of the number, see 54/iii/26/US, 54/xii/22/US, and 55/v/26/US.
Source: *DSB*, 30, 1954, pp. 44–47.

- 53/xii/31/GDR

Communiqué concerning completion of the transfer to the German Democratic Republic of thirty-three industrial enterprises in the GDR

Issued Dec. 31, 1953, by the mixed commission established in accordance with the protocol of Aug. 22, 1953 (53/viii/22/GDR/b). For the final protocol on transfer, see 54/ii/15/GDR.
Sources: *DGO*, pp. 596–97.
  Dokumente DDR, 1, pp. 299–300.

1954

- 54/ / /Pl

Protocol concerning three-way trade and payments between the USSR, Czechoslovakia, and Finland

Concluded during 1954.
Accompanied by bilateral trade protocols between the 3 States (not listed separately).
For terms and reference, see 50/vi/ /Pl.
  Also mentioned in *Highlights*, 3, 1955, No. 1, p. 12, citing *ZO*, 1954, No. 10.

- 54/i/ /Pl

Agreement concerning through goods and passenger railroad traffic between the Chinese People's Republic, the USSR, and Eastern Europe

Signed during Jan. 1954.
Reference: *SIA, 1954*, p. 238, citing *NCNA*, Jan. 15, 1954.

- 54/i/6/US. See Appendix 5.

- 54/i/8/Cz

Joint communiqué concerning the fifth meeting of the Soviet-Czechoslovak commission for scientific and technical collaboration

Published Jan. 8, 1954; the meeting took place during Dec. 1953, in Moscow.
Sources: *Izv.*, Jan. 8, 1954.
  VT, 1954, No. 1, p. 31.

- 54/i/16/Austria. See Appendix 5.

- 54/i/17/Bul

Communiqué concerning the f o u r t h meeting of the Soviet-Bulgarian commission for scientific and technical collaboration

Published Jan. 17, 1954; the meeting

took place a few days earlier, in Sofia.
Sources: *Izv.*, Jan. 17, 1954.
VT, 1954, No. 1, p. 32.

• 54/i/23/CPR/a

Trade protocol for 1954 between the USSR and the Chinese People's Republic

Signed Jan. 23, 1954, in Moscow.
Soviet metallurgical, mining, and power equipment, automobiles, tractors, agricultural, highway and construction machines, ferrous and nonferrous rolled metals, oil products, and chemicals, in exchange for CPR nonferrous metals, soybeans, peanuts, rice, plant oil, meat, tea, tobacco, fruits, wool, raw silk, silk goods, leather, etc.
References: *Izv.*, Jan. 26, 1954.
VT, 1954, No. 1, p. 32.
SCMP, No. 734, Jan. 23–25, 1954, p. 21.

• 54/i/23/CPR/b

Protocol between the USSR and the Chinese People's Republic concerning delivery by the USSR of equipment and goods under the credit agreement of February 14, 1950

Signed Jan. 23, 1954, in Moscow.
This is the 5th and final annual protocol under the credit agreement (50/ii/14/CPR/e).
References: *Izv.*, Jan. 26, 1954.
VT, 1954, No. 1, p. 32.
SIA, 1954, p. 238.

• 54/i/23/Sweden

Protocol between the USSR and Sweden modifying the agreement of October 25, 1946, concerning establishment of regular air communications

Signed Jan. 23, 1954, in Moscow.
Entered into force Jan. 23, 1954. Valid for the duration of the 1946 agreement (46/x/25/Sweden/a); superseded by agreement of Mar. 31, 1956 (56/iii/31/Sweden). Provides, *inter alia*, that Swedish flights may be made by Scandinavian Air Lines System (SAS), which includes Danish and Norwegian organizations.
Sources: *SDD*, 12, pp. 189–90.
Sö, 1954, No. 1 (R, Sw.).

• 54/i/25/Norway

Trade protocol for 1954 between the USSR and Norway

Signed Jan. 25, 1954, in Oslo.
Soviet grains, manganese and chrome ores, automobiles, etc., in exchange for Norwegian whale oil, herring, staple fiber, aluminum, etc.
References: *Izv.*, Jan. 26, 1954.
VT, 1954, No. 1, pp. 25, 32–33.

• 54/i/27/Af

Credit agreement between the USSR and Afghanistan

Signed Jan. 27, 1954, in Kabul.
Ratified by Afghanistan July 19, 1954.
Provides for a Soviet credit of $3.5 million US, to be used in construction of 2 grain elevators, a mill, and a mechanical bakery. The USSR to provide technical aid in construction of the works. To be repaid by annual delivery of goods, starting Jan. 1957, for 5 years. Supplemented by a protocol of Oct. 5, 1954 (see note to 54/x/5/Af).
References: *Pr.*, *Izv.*, Jan. 29, 1954.
VT, 1954, No. 1, p. 33; *ibid.*, 1955, No. 8, p. 2; *ibid.*, 1957, No. 2, p. 8.

• 54/i/28/France

Supplementary trade agreement between the USSR and France

Negotiated by the mixed commission established by the trade agreement of July 15, 1953 (53/vii/15/France/a), meeting Jan. 19 through 28, 1954, in Moscow.
Provides for increased trade during 1st year of operation of the 1953 agreement.
References: *Izv.*, Feb. 3, 1954.
VT, 1954, No. 2, p. 40.

• 54/i/30/BL

Trade protocol for 1954 between the USSR and the Belgium-Luxembourg Economic Union

Signed Jan. 30, 1954, in Brussels.
Based on the commercial agreement of Feb. 18, 1948 (48/ii/18/BL/b). Soviet grains, lumber, cellulose, automobiles, ferromanganese, manganese and chrome ores, anthracite, asbestos, pig iron, apatite concentrate, furs, canned goods, tobacco, etc., in exchange for staple fibers, artificial silk, woolen goods, herring, fats, meat, plant oil, leather, lead, rolled ferrous metals, etc., from Belgium-Luxembourg. Belgium to build for the USSR and deliver during 1954–1957 cargo steam-

ers, refrigerator ships, floating cranes, steam boilers, and other equipment. Volume of trade to be more than twice that of 1953.
References: *Izv.*, Jan. 31, 1954.
VT, 1954, No. 1, p. 25.

• 54/ii/2/Sweden

Trade protocol for 1954 between the USSR and Sweden

Signed Feb. 2, 1954, in Moscow.
Soviet oil and oil products, manganese and chrome ore, asbestos, oil cakes, furs, automobiles, etc., in exchange for Swedish staple fiber, paper, fishing vessels, equipment for the light, food, and lumber industries, electrical equipment, boring lathes, butter, high-grade rolled metal, etc. Vessels to be delivered 1955–1956.
References: *Izv.*, Feb. 3, 1954.
VT, 1954, No. 2, pp. 40–41; *ibid.*, No. 4, pp. 2–3.

• 54/ii/5/Iceland

Exchange of notes between the USSR and Iceland modifying the trade and payments agreement of August 1, 1953

Sent Jan. 30 and Feb. 5, 1954, in Moscow.
Revises the value of the Icelandic crown from 0.0951359 to 0.0545676 grams of fine gold.
Reference: *SDD*, 15, p. 63.

• 54/ii/6/Fin

Agreement between the USSR and Finland concerning a loan to Finland

Signed Feb. 6, 1954, in Moscow.
Ratified by the USSR May 11, 1954. Entered into force May 26, 1954, on exchange of acts of ratification in Helsinki. Provides for a loan to Finland of 40 million rubles, to be repaid within 10 years at 2½ per cent interest.
See further Appendix 5.
Sources: *VVS*, 1954, No. 13.
SDD, 16, pp. 311–13.
UNTS, 221, pp. 143–51 (R, Finnish, E, F).
References: *Izv.*, Feb. 9, 1954.
SZ, 1938–1956, p. 161.

• 54/ii/11/Bul

Trade protocol for 1954 between the USSR and Bulgaria

Signed Feb. 11, 1954, in Sofia.

Soviet industrial equipment, tractors, combines, and other agricultural machines, automobiles, rolled ferrous metal, rubber, paper, cotton, superphosphates, chemicals, pedigree cattle, etc., in exchange for Bulgarian nonferrous metals, tobacco, meat, canned vegetables, fresh and dried fruits, wines, fur coats, furniture, etc.
References: *Izv.*, Feb. 12, 1954.
VT, 1954, No. 2, p. 39.

• 54/ii/11/Pol

Trade protocol for 1954 between the USSR and Poland

Signed Feb. 11, 1954, in Moscow.
Soviet industrial equipment, tractors, combines, and other agricultural machines, automobiles, ball bearings, grain, cotton, wool, iron, manganese, and chrome ores, oil and oil products, apatite concentrate, copper, aluminum, ferrous alloys, etc., in exchange for Polish freighters and fishing vessels, locomotives, passenger and freight cars, coal, coke, zinc, cotton, woolen, linen, and silk materials, sugar, furniture, porcelain and glassware, etc.
References: *Izv.*, Feb. 12, 1954.
VT, 1954, No. 2, p. 39.

• 54/ii/13/GDR

Trade protocol for 1954 between the USSR and the German Democratic Republic

Signed Feb. 13, 1954, in Moscow.
Soviet grain and other foodstuffs, cotton, wool, ferrous and nonferrous metals, etc., in exchange for GDR vessels, freight cars, merchandise, and goods previously exported as reparations.
References: *Izv.*, Feb. 14, 1954.
VT, 1954, No. 2, p. 40.

• 54/ii/15/GDR

Protocol between the USSR and the German Democratic Republic concerning completion of the transfer to the GDR of thirty-three Soviet enterprises in the GDR

Signed Feb. 15, 1954, by the mixed commission established under the protocol of Aug. 22, 1953 (53/viii/22/GDR/b).
Transfer completed Dec. 31, 1953. For a communiqué marking completion, see 53/xii/31/GDR.
Reference: *SDD*, 15, p. 47.

● 54/ii/18/Pl

Four-Power communiqué concerning a meeting of the Foreign Ministers of the USSR, the United Kingdom, the United States of America, and France

Issued Feb. 18, 1954, in Berlin, at the end of a meeting which began Jan. 25, 1954.
Provisions: (1) The 4 Powers propose holding of a conference in Geneva, Apr. 26, 1954, for the purpose of reaching a peaceful solution of the Korean question; the problem of restoring peace in Indo-China also to be discussed at the conference, to which the 4 Powers, the Chinese People's Republic, and other interested States are to be invited. (2) The 4 Powers agree to hold an exchange of views subsequently to promote a successful solution of the problem of disarmament or the reduction of armaments.
The communiqué notes failure to agree on the German question, problems of European security, and the Austrian question, despite a full exchange of views on these matters. For the Geneva Conference on Korea and Indo-China, see 54/vii/21/Mul.
Sources: *Izv.*, Feb. 19, 1954.
     SDD, 16, pp. 19–20.
     DSB, 30, 1954, pp. 317–18.
     DS, IOCS, I, 26, pp. 217–18.
     BPP, 1954, Misc. No. 5, Cmd. 9080, p. 180.
     DIA, 1954, pp. 78–79.

● 54/iii/6/Alb

Trade protocol for 1954 between the USSR and Albania

Signed Mar. 6, 1954, in Moscow.
Albanian oil, bitumen, copper, plywood, tobacco, etc., in exchange for customary articles of Soviet export to Albania.
References: *Izv.*, Mar. 7, 1954.
     VT, 1954, No. 3, p. 43.

● 54/iii/15/KPDR

Trade protocol for 1954 between the USSR and the Korean People's Democratic Republic

Signed Mar. 15, 1954, in Moscow.
Soviet equipment, instruments, ferrous and nonferrous metals, oil products, rubber implements, chemical goods, etc., in exchange for KPDR nonferrous metals, fruit, etc.
References: *Izv.*, Mar. 18, 1954.
     VT, 1954, No. 3, pp. 4, 44.

● 54/iii/23/Egypt

Agreement between the USSR and Egypt concerning transformation of diplomatic missions into embassies

Announced Mar. 23, 1954.
Reference: *Izv.*, Mar. 23, 1954.

Mar. 25, 1954. Declaration by the USSR concerning relations between the USSR and the German Democratic Republic

Provisions: (1) The USSR establishes with the GDR the same relations as with other States. The GDR to have the freedom to decide on internal and external affairs, including the question of relations with the Federal Republic of Germany. (2) The USSR to maintain in the GDR functions connected with guaranteeing security and those resulting out of Four-Power agreements. It takes note of a declaration of the GDR that it acknowledges the duties arising for it from the Potsdam Agreement and those connected with temporary stationing of Soviet troops on GDR territory. (3) Supervision of the activities of state organs of the GDR by the Soviet High Commissioner for Germany to cease. Existence of the Occupation Statute for the Federal Republic of Germany denounced as incompatible with the national rights of the German people and as one of the main obstacles on the road to German national reunion.
Sources: *Izv.*, Mar. 26, 1954.
     DIA, 1954, pp. 88–89.
     Dokumente DDR, 1, pp. 303–304.
On Apr. 8, 1954, the Allied High Commission, representing the United Kingdom, the United States of America, and France, issued a declaration stating that the 3 Powers did not recognize the sovereignty of the GDR and did not intend to deal with it as a government (text, *DIA, 1954*, p. 89).

● 54/iii/26/US

Agreement between the USSR and the United States of America concerning return to the United States of thirty-eight small naval craft received by the USSR under Lend-Lease, with annex

Signed Mar. 26, 1954, in Washington, D.C.
Entered into force on signature. Return
to be carried out at Istanbul during May
and June 1954. The 38 naval craft are
part of the 186 concerning which the
USSR and the United States negotiated
in 1953 (see 53/xii/26/US). Annex is a
blank deed of delivery and receipt.
Sources: *UST*, 5, pp. 1067–77 (*TIAS*
    2990) (E, R).
    UNTS, 247, pp. 263–72 (R, E, F).
References: *DSB*, 30, 1954, pp. 563, 613.

● 54/iii/27/Egypt/a

Commercial agreement between the USSR and Egypt, with two annexes

Signed Mar. 27, 1954, in Cairo.
Duration 1 year; extended annually if not
denounced with 3 months' notice. Includes most-favored-nation provision for
trade and navigation. Annexes list goods
to be traded during 1st year: Soviet industrial equipment, tractors and agricultural machines, automobiles, ferrous products, oil products, lumber, grain, medicine, etc., in exchange for Egyptian rice,
cotton, artificial silk, hides, etc. Annexes
extended by protocol of May 12, 1955.
Supplemented by 2 exchanges of notes
(next items).
Source: *SDD*, 16, pp. 295–97 (omits the
    annexes).
References: *Pr., Izv.*, Mar. 30, 1954.
    VT, 1954, No. 4, p. 46.

● 54/iii/27/Egypt/b

Exchange of notes between the USSR and Egypt concerning transportation of trade shipments

Sent Mar. 27, 1954, in Cairo.
Provides that 50 per cent of Soviet-Egyp-
tian trade shall be transported in Egyptian ships whenever possible.
Source: *SDD*, 16, pp. 297–98.

● 54/iii/27/Egypt/c

Exchange of notes between the USSR and Egypt concerning Soviet trade represent-atives in Egypt

Sent Mar. 27, 1954, in Cairo.
Provides that only Soviet or Egyptian
citizens shall be hired as Soviet trade
agents or representatives in Egypt.
Source: *SDD*, 16, pp. 298–99.

● 54/iii/27/Pl

Meeting of the Council for Mutual Economic Aid

Held Mar. 26 and 27, 1954, in Moscow, by
Albania, Bulgaria, Czechoslovakia, the
German Democratic Republic, Hungary,
Poland, Romania, and the USSR.
Topics discussed included increase in pro-
duction of consumer goods, exchange of
experience in the field of agricultural
planning, and trade.
Reference: *Pr., Izv.*, Mar. 28, 1954.

● 54/iii/31/Rom/a

Trade protocol for 1954 between the USSR and Romania

Signed Mar. 31, 1954, in Moscow.
Soviet cotton, coke, iron ore, ferrous and
nonferrous metals, fertilizer, industrial
equipment, agricultural machinery, automobiles, etc., in exchange for Romanian
oil products, lumber, cement, chemical
products, fishing vessels, barges, etc.
References: *Izv.*, Apr. 2, 1954.
    VT, 1954, No. 5, p. 41.

● 54/iii/31/Rom/b

Agreement between the USSR and Romania concerning transfer and sale to Romania of Soviet shares in Soviet-Romanian joint-stock companies

Signed Mar. 31, 1954, in Moscow.
This agreement, together with a companion agreement of Sept. 18, 1954, provides
for transfer of Soviet shares in the following joint-stock companies: "Sovrom-
metall," "Sovromugol'," "Sovromtransport," "Sovromneftemash," "Sovromsu-
dostroi," "Sovromtraktor," "Sovrom-
khim," "Sovromgaz," "Sovromles," "Sov-
romstroi," "Sovrombank," and "T.A.R.S."
Available information does not provide
a basis for differentiating between the
content of the 2 agreements. For the
agreement under which the Soviet-Romanian joint-stock companies were established, see 45/v/8/Rom/a.
References: *Pr., Izv.*, Sept. 25, 1954.
    VT, 1954, No. 11, pp. 45–46.
    SDD, 15, p. 258.
    CDSP, 6, 1954, No. 39, pp. 16–17.
    SIA, 1954, p. 164.

● 54/iii/31/Rom/c

Credit agreement between the USSR and Romania

Signed Mar. 31, 1954, probably in Moscow.

Provides for a credit to Romania of 200 million rubles, of which 105 million is to be used for purchase of goods from the USSR in 1954, the remainder for repayment by Romania of the trade deficit for 1953. To be repaid within 3 years, beginning Jan. 1, 1956, at 2 per cent interest.
Reference: *VT SSSR*, p. 137.

● 54/iv/7/H

Trade protocol for 1954 between the USSR and Hungary

Signed Apr. 7, 1954, in Moscow.
Soviet cotton, coke, iron ore, ferrous alloys, lumber, fertilizer, industrial equipment, agricultural machinery, automobiles, ball bearings, etc., in exchange for Hungarian sea and river vessels, transport cranes, industrial equipment, hogs, cloth, etc.
References: *Izv.*, Apr. 8, 1954.
VT, 1954, No. 5, p. 41.

● 54/iv/15/Cz

Trade protocol for 1954 between the USSR and Czechoslovakia

Signed Apr. 15, 1954, in Moscow.
Soviet grain, industrial goods, cotton, wool, nonferrous metals, iron and manganese ores, mineral fertilizers, agricultural machinery and tractors, industrial equipment, etc., in exchange for Czech diesel passenger trains, river tugs, electrostations, electric trains, diesel motors, cranes, metal-working lathes, metallurgical machinery, equipment for the chemical, food, and light industries, woolen and cotton materials, leather footwear, sugar, etc.
References: *Izv.*, Apr. 16, 1954.
VT, 1954, No. 5, p. 42.

● 54/iv/19/1948

Final Act of the International Conference on Safety of Life at Sea, with related documents

Signed June 10, 1948, in London.
Soviet accession Apr. 19, 1954; act of

accession deposited May 10, 1954, with effect from Aug. 10, 1954.
Related documents (as given in *SDD*, 16; designation and numbering differ in other sources): Annex A, International convention for the safety of life at sea, 1948, with regulations and annexes (see 54/v/10/1948). Annex B, Regulations for preventing collisions at sea (ratified separately by the USSR: see 54/vii/14/1948). Annex C, Resolutions. Annex D, Recommendations.
Sources: *SDD*, 16, pp. 401–503.
BFSP, 151, pp. 483–503.
UST, 4, pp. 2956–76.
DS, IOCS, I, 6, pp. 49–194.

● 54/iv/21/1945

Constitution of the United Nations Educational, Scientific, and Cultural Organization (UNESCO)

Signed Nov. 16, 1945, in London. Signed by the USSR Apr. 21, 1954; by the Belorussian and Ukrainian SSR's May 12, 1954.
Original entry into force Nov. 4, 1946; subsequent accessions to take effect on deposit of the instrument of accession; for the USSR and Belorussian and Ukrainian SSR's, the date is the same as that of signature.
Sources: *SDD*, 16, pp. 583–95.
UNTS, 4, pp. 275–301 (E, F).
BTS, 1946, No. 50, Cmd. 6963.
References: *DSB*, 30, 1954, p. 884 (Soviet signature).
UNTS, 191, p. 358 (signature by the Belorussian and Ukrainian SSR's).

● 54/iv/26/1946

Final Articles Revision Convention, 1946, of the International Labour Organisation, with annex

Drafted at the Paris session of the International Labour Organisation (ILO) in Oct. 1945; approved at the ILO conference in Montreal Oct. 2, 1946, and by the General Assembly of the UN Dec. 14, 1946. Revised June 25, 1953 (see 54/x/7/1953). The original charter of the ILO formed part of the Treaty of Versailles of June 28, 1919.
The USSR joined the ILO Apr. 26, 1954, the Belorussian and Ukrainian SSR's May 13, 1954. Annex is a declaration on the aims and purposes of the ILO, adopted

May 10, 1944, in Philadelphia.
Sources: *SDD*, 16, pp. 351–73 (charter as amended through 1953).
Durdenevski and Krylov, pp. 267–87 (charter as amended to May 20, 1954).
DAFR, 10, pp. 423–26.
References: *Int. org.*, 1, 1947, pp. 117–18 (background and analysis).
Ibid., 8, 1954, p. 143 (Soviet intention to join the ILO, with reservations concerning compulsory submission of disputes to the International Court of Justice).

● 54/iv/28/Neth

Trade protocol for 1954 between the USSR and The Netherlands

Signed Apr. 28, 1954, at The Hague.
Soviet grains, lumber, cellulose, coal-tar, anthracite, apatite concentrates, asbestos, automobiles, furs, canned goods, etc., in exchange for Dutch staple fiber, butter, meats, herring, leather and leather goods, medicines, etc. Freight ships, refrigerator ships, pumps and dredges, floating cranes to be delivered by The Netherlands during 1954–1956. Constitutes the 1st supplementary protocol to the trade and payments agreement of July 2, 1948.
Source: *Trb.*, 1954, No. 49.
References: *Izv.*, Apr. 29, 1954.
VT, 1954, No. 5, p. 42.

● 54/iv/29/Fin/a

Protocol between the USSR and Finland concerning execution of the agreement of April 24, 1947, concerning regulation of Lake Inari

Signed Apr. 29, 1954, in Helsinki.
Entered into force on signature. For the 1947 agreement, see 47/iv/24/Fin/a.
Source: *SS*, 1954, No. 26 (Finnish, R).

● 54/iv/29/Fin/b

Protocol between the USSR and Finland modifying the rules of April 24, 1947, for regulating the water level on Lake Inari

Signed Apr. 29, 1954, in Helsinki.
Entered into force on signature. For the 1947 rules, see 47/iv/24/Fin/b. Further modified by protocol of Feb. 24, 1956 (56/ii/24/Pl).

Sources: *SDD*, 13, p. 277.
SS, 1954, No. 26 (Finnish, R).

● 54/iv/30/GDR

Protocol between the USSR and the German Democratic Republic concerning transfer to the GDR of the film archive of "Soveksportfilm" in the GDR, with list

Signed Apr. 30, 1954, in Berlin.
Source: *Dokumente DDR*, 4, pp. 41–42 (omits list).

● 54/iv/30/Lebanon/a

Trade and payments agreement between the USSR and Lebanon, with two annexes

Signed Apr. 30, 1954, in Beirut.
Ratified by Lebanon July 13, 1954; by the USSR July 29, 1954. Entered into force Sept. 11, 1954, 5 days after exchange of acts of ratification, which took place Sept. 6, 1954, in Beirut. Duration 1 year; if not denounced 3 months before expiration, extended from year to year. Annexes list types of goods to be exchanged. Lists extended for 1 year by exchange of notes of Oct. 1, 1955. Trade protocol for 1957 (56/x/13/Lebanon) based on and modifies this agreement. Supplemented by 2 exchanges of notes (next 2 items).
Sources: *VVS*, 1954, No. 23, Art. 446, pp. 803–809.
SDD, 16, pp. 299–306.
UNTS, 226, pp. 109–16 (R), 124–17 (A), 130–45 (E, F).
References: *Izv.*, May 1, 1954.
VT, 1945, No. 5, p. 42; *ibid.*, No. 11, pp. 44–45.

● 54/iv/30/Lebanon/b

Exchange of notes between the USSR and Lebanon concerning the value of trade between the two states

Sent Apr. 30, 1954, in Beirut.
Provides that the total value of Soviet imports from and exports to Lebanon for the first year of the trade and payments agreement of the same date (preceding document) shall be 10 million Lebanese pounds and an equivalent sum in rubles respectively, not including transit operations. Citrus fruits, apples, and bananas to constitute not less than 60 per cent of the total value of Lebanese exports.

Sources: *VVS*, 1954, No. 23, Art. 446, pp. 809–10.
UNTS, 226, pp. 125–26 (R, A), 144–47 (E, F).

● 54/iv/30/Lebanon/c

Exchange of notes between the USSR and Lebanon concerning the Soviet Trade Mission in Lebanon

Sent Apr. 30, 1954, in Beirut.
Sources: *VVS*, 1954, No. 23, Art. 446, pp. 810–12.
SDD, 16, pp. 306–309.
UNTS, 226, pp. 126–29 (R, A), 148–51 (E, F).

● 54/v/5/Cz

Communiqué concerning the sixth meeting of the Soviet-Czechoslovak commission for scientific and technical collaboration

Published May 5, 1954; the meeting took place during Apr. 1954, in Prague.
Sources: *Izv.*, May 5, 1954.
VT, 1954, No. 5, p. 43.

● 54/v/9/H

Communiqué concerning the fifth meeting of the Soviet-Hungarian commission for scientific and technical collaboration

Published May 9, 1954; the meeting took place during Apr. 1954, in Moscow.
Sources: *Izv.*, May 9, 1954.
VT, 1954, No. 5, p. 43.

● 54/v/10/1948

International convention for the safety of life at sea, 1948, with regulations and annex

Signed June 10, 1948, in London, as Annex A to the Final Act of the International Conference on Safety of Life at Sea, 1948. The USSR was represented at the conference but did not sign the Final Act; subsequently it acceded both to this convention and to the Final Act (see 54/iv/19/1948) and to the Regulations for preventing collisions at sea (see 54/vii/14/1948).
Act of ratification of the USSR deposited May 10, 1954, with effect from Aug. 10, 1954. General entry into force Nov. 19, 1952. May be denounced by any signatory 5 years after entry into force, with 1 year's notice. Supersedes the convention of May 31, 1929 (29/v/31/Mul/a), which the

USSR denounced by a decree of Sept. 8, 1955 (*VVS*, 1955, No. 16, Art. 316). Annex provides forms of various certificates.
Sources: *UNTS*, 164, pp. 113–357 (E, F).
BTS, 1953, No. 1, Cmd. 8720.
References: *UNTS*, 193, p. 361 (Soviet accession).
BTS, 1954, No. 78, Cmd. 9401 (same).

● 54/v/12/Mul

Final Act of the international conference on pollution of the sea by oil, with related documents

Signed May 12, 1954, in London. The USSR signed the Final Act of the conference; for Soviet signature of the convention prepared by the conference, see 54/viii/11/1954. Related documents: (1) Annex, consisting of 8 resolutions; (2) text of the convention; (3) Annex A, concerning prohibited zones; and (4) Annex B, form of oil record book.
Source: Cmd. 9197.

● 54/v/13/Israel

Exchange of notes between the USSR and Israel concerning transformation of diplomatic missions into embassies

Sent Apr. 29 and May 13, 1954, in Tel Aviv.
References: *Izv.*, June 17, 1954.
SDD, 13, p. 25; *ibid.*, 16, p. 18.

● 54/v/14/Mul

Convention for protection of cultural property in the event of armed conflict, with regulations and protocol

Signed May 14, 1954, at The Hague; drawn up by a UNESCO conference which met from Apr. 21 to May 12, 1954.
Ratified by the USSR Dec. 12, 1956; act of ratification deposited Jan. 4, 1957, with effect from Apr. 4, 1957 (3 months after deposit). Acts of ratification of the Ukrainian SSR deposited Feb. 6, 1957, with effect from May 6, 1957; of the Belorussian SSR deposited May 7, 1957, with effect from Aug. 7, 1957. General entry into force Aug. 7, 1956. May be denounced with 1 year's notice, unless the denouncing party is involved in armed conflict, in which case the convention continues in force until end of the conflict or return of the property in question.
Source: *VVS*, 1957, No. 3, Art. 54.
References: *VVS*, 1956, No. 24, Art. 527.
Int. org., 8, 1954, p. 393.
DSB, 36, 1957, p. 289.

- 54/v/24/Af

Credit agreement between the USSR and Afghanistan

Signed May 24, 1954.
Cited as the basis for contracts concluded during or before July 1956 providing for instruction by Soviet specialists of Afghan workers in the operation of grain combines (*Izv.*, July 25, 1956).

- 54/v/29/CPR. See Appendix 5.

- 54/vi/7/Bul

Trade agreement for the period 1955–1957 between the USSR and Bulgaria

Signed June 7, 1954.
Includes provision for delivery to Bulgaria of complex industrial equipment.
References: *VT*, 1953, No. 12, p. 8; *ibid.*, 1955, No. 11, p. 5.

- 54/vi/15/Pl. See Appendix 5.

- 54/vi/17/Iran

Exchange of notes between the USSR and Iran concerning trade for the current year

Sent June 17, 1954, in Teheran.
References: *Izv.*, June 19, 1954.
    VT, 1954, No. 9, p. 1.

- 54/vi/19/Iceland

Trade protocol between the USSR and Iceland

Signed June 19, 1954, in Moscow.
Covers the period July 1, 1954, through Dec. 31, 1955. Concluded under the trade and payments agreement of Aug. 1, 1953. Soviet oil products, grain and flour, cement, metal products, anthracite, etc., in exchange for fish.
References: *Izv.*, June 20, 1954.
    VT, 1954, No. 7, p. 44; *ibid.*, No. 11, p. 19.

- 54/vi/22/GDR

Supplementary trade protocol for 1954 between the USSR and the German Democratic Republic

Signed June 22, 1954, in Berlin.
Soviet rolled ferrous metals, coal, coke, wool, chemical products, etc., in exchange for GDR industrial equipment, electrotechnical products, precision instruments, optical equipment, etc.

References: *Izv.*, June 25, 1954.
    VT, 1954, No. 7, p. 44.
    Dokumenty GDR, pp. 258–59.

May 13–June 22, 1954

See Appendix 5.

June 22, 1954

Soviet accession to the protocol of Dec. 16, 1949, modifying the convention of July 6, 1890, concerning creation of an International Union for the Publication of Customs Tariffs.
See 54/viii/27/1949.

- 54/vi/25/Pl. See Appendix 5.

- 54/vi/29/France

Agreement between the USSR and France concerning establishment of regular air service between Moscow and Paris

Signed June 29, 1954, in Moscow.
Provides for Soviet flights Moscow–Prague and French flights Paris–Prague. Approval of Czechoslovakia for flights over her territory obtained.
Source: *SDD*, 16, pp. 398–400.
Reference: *Izv.*, July 1, 1954.

- 54/vii/ /Pol. See Appendix 5.

- 54/vii/10/Rom

Communiqué concerning the fourth meeting of the Soviet-Romanian commission for scientific and technical collaboration

Published July 10, 1954; the meeting took place during June 1954, in Bucharest.
Sources: *Izv.*, July 10, 1954.
    VT, 1954, No. 8, p. 37.

- 54/vii/14/1948

Regulations for preventing collisions at sea

Adopted June 10, 1948, in London, as Annex B to the Final Act of the International Conference on Safety of Life at Sea. Soviet accession July 14, 1954; notification of accession sent July 19, 1954. Entered into force Jan. 1, 1954. Supersede the regulations of 1889, which the RSFSR accepted in 1922 (Keilin, p. 16). For Soviet accession to the Final Act of 1948, see 54/iv/19/1948.
Sources: *SDD*, 16, pp. 552–71.
    DS, IOCS, I, 6, pp. 173–86.

• 54/vii/17/Fin/a

Joint communiqué concerning negotiations between the Foreign Ministers of the USSR and Finland

Issued July 17, 1954, in Moscow.
Covers general principles of international relations. Mentions agreement reached on the transformation of diplomatic missions into embassies.
Sources: *Izv.*, July 18, 1954.
   SDD, 16, pp. 16–17.
   Deklaratsii, 1957, pp. 246–47.

• 54/vii/17/Fin/b

Trade agreement for the period 1956–1960 between the USSR and Finland

Signed July 17, 1954, in Moscow.
Ratified by Finland Dec. 10, 1954; by the USSR Jan. 29, 1955. Entered into force Mar. 11, 1955, on exchange of acts of ratification in Helsinki.
Provides that Soviet imports from Finland, which for 1954 were valued at approximately 580 million rubles, are to increase as follows (in millions of rubles): 1956, 590; 1957, 595; 1958, 630; 1959, 640; and 1960, 655. Soviet exports, valued at not less than 425 million rubles for 1954, are to increase as follows (in millions of rubles): 1956, 430; 1957, 435; 1958, 470; 1959, 480; and 1960, 495. Trade imbalance, equaling 160 million rubles annually, to be covered to a value of 120 million rubles a year by agreements with 3rd States, and to a value of 40 million rubles by transfer of foreign exchange to Finland.
Soviet grains, sugar, fodder, artificial fertilizers, liquid and solid fuel, metals, castings, cotton, chemicals, furs, industrial equipment, automobiles, etc., in exchange for Finnish products of the shipbuilding, machine-building, cable, and other metalworking industries, prefabricated houses, lumber, pulpwood, cellulose, paper cartons, and paper products.
Sources: *VVS*, 1955, No. 12.
   *SS, 1955, No. 5 (Finnish, R).
References: *Izv.*, July 18, 1954.
   VT, 1954, No. 8, p. 37; *ibid.*, 1956, No. 1, p. 18; *ibid.*, No. 12, p. 4.

• 54/vii/21/Mul

Final declaration of the Geneva Confer-

ence on the problem of restoring peace in Indo-China

Drawn up July 21, 1954, in Geneva, at the end of a conference which began Apr. 26, 1954, with representatives of the USSR, the United Kingdom, the United States of America, France, Cambodia, the Democratic Republic of Vietnam, Laos, the Chinese People's Republic, and Vietnam. The United States and Vietnam did not sign the final declarations; the United States issued a separate declaration.
The conference was held in accordance with an agreement of the Foreign Ministers of the USSR, the United Kingdom, the United States, and France (see 54/ii/18/Mul). Its work fell into 2 phases, the 1st concerned with Korea, the 2nd with Indo-China. On Korea it was unable to reach any agreements; instead, the delegations of 16 States represented at the conference drew up a declaration on June 15, 1954, stating that further consideration by the conference of the Korean question would serve no useful purpose "so long as the Communist delegations reject the two fundamental principles" of (1) respect for and acceptance of the authority of the United Nations and (2) impartial and effective supervision of free elections in Korea (text of declaration in *DSB*, 31, 1954, pp. 16–17; *DIA, 1954*, pp. 350–51; *DS, IOCS*, II, 4, pp. 191–93).
The declaration on Indo-China took note of and was based on armistice agreements for Laos, Vietnam, and Cambodia which were signed June 20, 1954. Analysis in *SIA, 1954*, pp. 65–73.
Sources: *SDD*, 16, pp. 20–21. (*Ibid.*, pp. 22–34, armistice agreements for Vietnam; pp. 34–45, for Laos; pp. 45–51, for Cambodia; pp. 51–53, accompanying statements by Laos, Cambodia, France, and the United States.)
   DSB, 31, 1954, p. 164.
   DIA, 1954, pp. 138–40.

• 54/vii/23/Mul

Amendments to the schedule to the international convention for the regulation of whaling

Adopted at the sixth meeting of the International Whaling Commission, July 19–23, 1954, in Tokyo.
For the convention and annexed schedule, see 46/xii/2/Mul/a and /b.
Source: *UNTS*, 252, pp. 324–29 (E, F).

• 54/vii/28/Uruguay/a

Payments agreement between the State Banks of the USSR and Uruguay

Signed July 28, 1954, in Montevideo.
Duration 2 years, subject to extension.
Reference: *Pravda*, Aug. 1, 1954.

• 54/vii/28/Uruguay/b. See Appendix 5.

• 54/viii/11/1950

Convention for suppression of the traffic in persons and of the exploitation of the prostitution of others, with final protocol

Opened for signature Mar. 21, 1950, at Lake Success, N.Y.
Act of ratification of the USSR deposited Aug. 11, 1954, with effect from Nov. 9, 1954 (90 days after deposit). Act of ratification of the Ukrainian SSR deposited Nov. 15, 1954, with effect from Feb. 13, 1955. For Soviet declaration and reservation, see below. General entry into force July 25, 1951.
Consolidates the following international instruments: (1) International agreement of May 18, 1904, for suppression of the white slave traffic, as amended by the protocol of Dec. 3, 1948; (2) International convention of May 4, 1910, for suppression of the white slave traffic, as amended by the same protocol; (3) International convention of Sept. 30, 1921, for suppression of the traffic in women and children, as amended by the protocol of Oct. 20, 1947 (see 47/xii/18/1921); (4) International convention of Oct. 11, 1933, for suppression of the traffic in women of full age, as amended by the same protocol (see 47/xii/18/1933).
The Soviet declaration states that although the social conditions which give rise to the offense covered by the convention have been "eliminated" in the USSR, the USSR has decided to accede to the convention in view of the international importance of suppressing these offenses. The Soviet reservation states that the USSR does not consider itself bound by the provision that any dispute between parties to the convention concerning its interpretation or application shall, at the request of any one of the parties to the dispute, be referred to the International Court of Justice.
Sources: *SDD*, 16, pp. 280–90.
   UNTS, 96, pp. 271–319 (E, F, R, C, S).
Reference: *UNTS*, 196, pp. 349–50.

• 54/viii/11/1954

International convention for prevention of pollution of the sea by oil

Signed May 12, 1954, in London; by the USSR, Aug. 11, 1954, subject to ratification.
For the conference, see 54/v/12/Mul.
Reference: *Pravda*, Aug. 13, 1954.

• 54/viii/15/Argentina

Exchange of notes between the USSR and Argentina concerning extension of the validity of the annexes to the trade and payments agreement of August 5, 1953

Sent Aug. 15, 1954, in Buenos Aires.
Entered into force Aug. 15, 1954. Extends validity of the trade lists for 60 days.
Source: Spanish-language official text, Argentine Embassy, Sept. 1957.

• 54/viii/21/CPR

Agreement between the USSR and the Chinese People's Republic concerning collaboration in the field of radio broadcasting

Signed Aug. 21, 1954, in Moscow.
Source: *SDD*, 16, pp. 373–76.

• 54/viii/27/1949

Protocol modifying the Convention of July 5, 1890, concerning creation of an International Union for the Publication of Customs Tariffs, the Regulations for execution of the convention, and the protocol of signature

Signed Dec. 16, 1949, in Brussels.
Act of accession of the USSR deposited Aug. 27, 1954, with effect from Sept. 26, 1954 (30 days after deposit). Original entry into force May 5, 1950. For Soviet adherence to the original convention, see 35/xii/21/1890.
Source: *BTS*, 1950, No. 59, Cmd. 8050 (E, F).
Reference: *BTS*, 1954, No. 78, Cmd. 9401, p. 5 (Soviet accession).
Note: *DSB*, 31, 1954, p. 283, gives June 22, 1954, as date of deposit of the Soviet act of accession; possibly an error for date of accession.

• 54/ix/2/Greece

Exchange of notes between the USSR and Greece constituting a trade agreement, with two annexes

Sent Sept. 2, 1954, in Athens.
Ratified by Greece Mar. 14, 1955. Covers
the period July 28, 1954, to July 28, 1955.
Based on the trade and payments agree-
ment of July 28, 1953. Annexes list goods
to be exchanged, to a total value for each
party of $5 million.
Sources: *Greek official gazette, 1955, A,
   No. 119.
   UNTS, 230, pp. 34–39 (R, Greek, E, F).
References: Izv., Sept. 4, 1954.
   VT, 1954, No. 11, p. 44.

● 54/ix/3/Argentina

**Exchange of notes between the USSR and
Argentina constituting an agreement on
the exchange of motion pictures**

Sent Sept. 3, 1954, in Buenos Aires.
Entered into force Sept. 4, 1954. Duration
1 year; if not denounced 90 days before
expiration, extended from year to year.
Source: Spanish-language official text,
   Argentine Embassy, Sept. 1957.
Reference: Izv., Sept. 14, 1954.

● 54/ix/18/Pol

**Communiqué concerning the seventh
meeting of the Soviet-Polish commission
for scientific and technical collaboration**

Published Sept. 18, 1954; the meeting took
place a few days earlier, in Moscow.
Sources: Izv., Sept. 18, 1954.
   VT, 1954, No. 11, p. 45.

● 54/ix/18/Rom

**Agreement between the USSR and Ro-
mania concerning transfer and sale to
Romania of Soviet shares in Soviet-Romanian joint-stock companies**

Signed Sept. 18, 1954, in Moscow.
For provisions and references, see the companion agreement (54/iii/31/Rom/b).

● 54/ix/29/Sweden

**Agreement between the USSR and Swe-
den concerning cooperation for rescue in
the Baltic Sea**

Signed Sept. 29, 1954, in Moscow; initialed Sept. 4, 1954, following negotiations
which began Aug. 20, 1954 (Izv., Sept. 8,
1954).
Entered into force Jan. 1, 1955. Duration
3 years; if not denounced 6 months before
expiration, extended from year to year.

Sources: Sö, 1954, No. 46, pp. 479–82
   (R, Sw.).
   UNTS, 202, pp. 259–71 (R, Sw., E, F).

● 54/ix/30/Bul

**Communiqué concerning the fifth meet-
ing of the Soviet-Bulgarian commission
for scientific and technical collaboration**

Published Sept. 30, 1954; the meeting
took place during the 1st half of Sept. in
Moscow.
References: Izv., Sept. 30, 1954.
   VT, 1954, No. 11, p. 46.

● 54/ix/30/GDR

**Agreement between the USSR and the
German Democratic Republic concerning noncommercial payments**

Signed Sept. 30, 1954, in Moscow.
Entered into force on signature. Valid
until 3 months after denunciation.
Source: Dokumente DDR, 4, pp. 42–44.
References: Izv., Oct. 2, 1954.
   VT, 1954, No. 12, p. 41.
   Dokumenty GDR, pp. 260–61.

● 54/x/1/Yug

**Barter agreement between the USSR and
Yugoslavia, with annexes**

Signed Oct. 1, 1954, in Belgrade.
Covers deliveries during 1954 and through
Mar. 31, 1955. Annexes list goods to be
exchanged, to a total value for each party
of approximately 10 million rubles.
Marks the re-establishment of trade rela-
tions between the 2 States following the
break in 1948.
References: Izv., Oct. 2, 1954.
   VT, 1954, No. 11, pp. 21–22; ibid., 1955,
   No. 10, pp. 2–3.

● 54/x/5/Af

**Agreement between the USSR and Af-
ghanistan concerning Soviet credit and
technical aid for paving the streets of
Kabul and vicinity**

Signed Oct. 5, 1954, in Kabul.
Ratified by Afghanistan Feb. 7, 1955.
Soviet materials, equipment, vehicles, and
machinery to be provided on credit, to a
value of more than $2 million.
References: Izv., Oct. 10, 1954.
   VT, 1954, No. 12, p. 41; ibid., 1955,
   No. 8, p. 2.
Note: According to VT, 1957, No. 2, p. 8,

a protocol to the credit agreement of Jan. 27, 1954, was signed on Oct. 5, 1954. It is not clear whether the protocol is identical with or separate from this agreement.

• 54/x/5/GDR

Agreement between the USSR and the German Democratic Republic concerning establishment of consulates

Announced Oct. 5, 1954.
Reference: *Dokumenty GDR*, p. 261.

• 54/x/7/1953

Instrument for the amendment of the constitution of the International Labour Organisation

Adopted June 25, 1953, by the General Conference of the ILO, in Geneva.
Acts of ratification of the USSR and Belorussian and Ukrainian SSR's deposited Oct. 7, 1954. General entry into force May 20, 1954. For the constitution (charter), see 54/iv/26/1946.
Source: *UNTS*, 191, pp. 143–49 (E, F).
Reference: *Ibid.*, 200, p. 338 (ratification).

• 54/x/9/Bul

Agreement between the USSR and Bulgaria concerning transfer and sale to Bulgaria of Soviet shares in Soviet-Bulgarian joint-stock companies

Signed Oct. 9, 1954, in Sofia.
Provides for transfer of Soviet shares in the following joint - stock companies: "Korbso" (shipbuilding), "Sovbolstroi" (construction materials), and "Tabso" (civil aviation). To be paid for over a period of years. For establishment of the civil aviation company, see entry under May 28, 1949. For an agreement on sale to Bulgaria of shares in the Soviet-Bulgarian mining company "Gorubso," see 55/xi/26/Bul.
References: *Pr., Izv.*, Oct. 12, 1954.
VT, 1954, No. 12, pp. 9, 42.
CDSP, 6, 1954, No. 41, p. 7.
SIA, 1954, p. 164.

• 54/x/12/CPR/a

Communiqué on negotiations between the USSR and the Chinese People's Republic

Issued Oct. 12, 1954, in Peking, at the end of negotiations which began Sept. 29, 1954.

Mentions 8 agreements or joint statements (next 8 documents).
Sources: *Izv.*, Oct. 12, 1954.
VT, 1954, 10, pp. 1–2.
DIA, 1954, p. 321.

• 54/x/12/CPR/b

Joint declaration by the USSR and the Chinese People's Republic concerning Soviet-CPR relations and the international situation

Signed Oct. 12, 1954, in Peking.
Sources: *Izv.*, Oct. 12, 1954.
VT, 1954, No. 10, pp. 2–3.
SDD, 16, pp. 12–14.
Deklaratsii, 1957, pp. 182–84.
PC, Nov. 1, 1955, supplement, pp. 4–5.
UNTS, 226, pp. 57–67 (R, C, E, F).
DIA, 1954, pp. 322–23.

• 54/x/12/CPR/c

Joint declaration by the USSR and the Chinese People's Republic concerning relations with Japan

Signed Oct. 12, 1954, in Peking.
Sources: *Izv.*, Oct. 12, 1954.
VT, 1954, No. 10, p. 4.
SDD, 16, pp. 14–15.
Deklaratsii, 1957, pp. 184–86.
PC, Nov. 1, 1954, supplement, p. 6.
UNTS, 226, pp. 69–77 (R, C, E, F).
DIA, 1954, pp. 323–25.

• 54/x/12/CPR/d

Joint communiqué by the USSR and the Chinese People's Republic concerning withdrawal of Soviet troops from the naval base at Port Arthur and transfer of the naval base to the CPR

Issued Oct. 12, 1954, in Peking.
Withdrawal and transfer to be completed by May 31, 1955; to be carried out by the joint Soviet-CPR military commission established by the agreement of Feb. 14, 1950 (50/ii/14/CPR/d). Final protocol on withdrawal signed May 24, 1955.
Sources: *Izv.*, Oct. 12, 1954.
VT, 1954, No. 10, p. 5.
SDD, 14, pp. 21–23; *ibid.*, 16, pp. 15–16.
Deklaratsii, 1957, pp. 186–87.
PC, Nov. 1, 1954, supplement, p. 7.
UNTS, 226, pp. 51–55 (R, C, E, F).
DIA, 1954, pp. 327–28.

• 54/x/12/CPR/e

Joint communiqué by the USSR and the

Chinese People's Republic concerning transfer to the CPR of Soviet shares in Soviet-CPR joint-stock companies

Issued Oct. 12, 1954, in Peking.
Transfer to be completed by Jan. 1, 1955. Covers the following companies: (1) extraction of nonferrous and rare metals in Sinkiang; (2) production and refinement of oil in Sinkiang; (3) construction and repair of ships in Dairen; and (4) organization and operation of civil air lines. For establishment of (1), (2), and (4), see 50/iii/27/CPR/a through /c; for establishment of (3) see 51/vii/28/CPR. Payment by the CPR to be in goods over a period of years.
For a TASS communiqué on completion of transfer of (1), (2), and (3), see *Izv.*, Jan. 1, 1955; of (4), *ibid.*, Dec. 31, 1954.
Sources: *Izv.*, Oct. 12, 1954.
VT, 1954, No. 10, pp. 5–6.
PC, Nov. 1, 1954, supplement, pp. 7–8.
DIA, 1954, p. 325.

• 54/x/12/CPR/f

Agreement between the USSR and the Chinese People's Republic concerning scientific and technical collaboration

Signed Oct. 12, 1954, in Peking; summarized in a joint communiqué of the same date (not listed separately).
Duration 5 years; if not denounced 1 year before expiration, extended for 5 years. Provides for exchange of technical documentation and specialists. Establishes a Soviet-CPR commission for implementation, to meet not less than twice yearly, alternately in Moscow and Peking.
Source: *SDD*, 16, pp. 349–50.
References (joint communiqué text):
    Izv., Oct. 12, 1954.
    VT, 1954, No. 10, pp. 6–7.
    PC, Nov. 1, 1954, supplement, p. 8.
    DIA, 1954, pp. 326–27.

• 54/x/12/CPR/g

Joint communiqué by the USSR and the Chinese People's Republic concerning construction of a railroad, Lanchow–Urumchi–Alma-Ata, and the organization of direct communications

Issued Oct. 12, 1954, in Peking.
Each party to build the section of the railroad in its territory. The USSR grants the CPR technical assistance. Carried out in part under an agreement of Apr. 7, 1956 (56/iv/7/CPR/c).

Sources: *Izv.*, Oct. 12, 1954.
VT, 1954, No. 10, p. 7.
PC, Nov. 1, 1954, supplement, p. 9.
DIA, 1954, pp. 325–26.

• 54/x/12/CPR/h

Credit agreement between the USSR and the Chinese People's Republic

Signed Oct. 12, 1954, in Peking.
The USSR grants the CPR a long-term credit of 520 million rubles.
References: Mentioned in the communiqué on negotiations (54/x/12/CPR/a).

• 54/x/12/CPR/i

Protocol between the USSR and the Chinese People's Republic concerning Soviet technical aid

Signed Oct. 12, 1954, in Peking.
Provides for Soviet aid in construction of 15 industrial enterprises in addition to those agreed on earlier and increased deliveries for construction of 141 enterprises previously agreed on. Total value of aid to exceed 400 million rubles.
References: Mentioned in the communiqué on negotiations (54/x/12/CPR/a).

• 54/x/12/Pl

Joint communiqué by the USSR, the Chinese People's Republic, and the Mongolian People's Republic concerning construction of a railroad from Tsinin to Ulan-Bator and the organization of direct communications

Issued Oct. 12, 1954.
Mentions conclusion of an agreement between the 3 States on Sept. 15, 1952, concerning construction of the railroad. Construction to be shared by the 3 States and completed in 1955.
Sources: *Pr.*, Oct. 12, 1954.
VT, 1954, No. 10, p. 7.
DIA, 1954, p. 326.

Oct. 12, 1954. Letter from the USSR recognizing an agreement between Italy and Yugoslavia of October 5, 1954, concerning division of the territory of Trieste

Sent Oct. 12, 1954, to the Security Council of the United Nations.
The Italy-Yugoslavia agreement modifies the decisions concerning Trieste reached by the Council of Foreign Ministers in Dec. 1946 (see 46/xii/12/Pl/a), annexed

to the peace treaty with Italy (47/ii/10/ Italy). For background, see *SIA, 1947–1948*, pp. 120–21; *ibid., 1949–1950*, pp. 272–78; *ibid., 1953*, pp. 131–35.
Reference: *SIA, 1954*, p. 169.

• 54/x/28/GDR. See Appendix 5.

• 54/xi/3/Cz. See Appendix 5.

• 54/xi/6/H
Agreement between the USSR and Hungary concerning transfer and sale to Hungary of Soviet shares in Soviet-Hungarian joint-stock companies

Signed Nov. 6, 1954, in Moscow.
Provides for transfer of Soviet shares in the following joint-stock companies: "Masolai" (oil), "Masobal" (bauxite-aluminum), "Dunavel'di Timfel'd Ipar" (blueprinting, construction, and operation of bauxite - aluminum plants), "Meskhart" (shipping), "Masovlet" (civil aviation), and the Soviet Trade-Industrial Bank. To be paid for over a period of years. For the agreement under which the Soviet-Hungarian companies were established, see 45/viii/27/H/a.
References: *Izv.*, Nov. 10, 1954.
    VT, 1954, No. 12, p. 43.
    SIA, 1954, p. 164.

• 54/xi/10/France
Trade protocol between the USSR and France

Signed Nov. 10, 1954, in Paris.
Covers the period July 1, 1954, through Dec. 31, 1955. Soviet oil and oil products, coal, coal tar, lumber, cellulose, manganese ore, cotton, etc., in exchange for French ferrous metals, lead, cable, artificial silk, silk and woolen materials, meat, cocoa-beans, citrus fruits, etc. France to build freighters, diesel boilers, and other equipment for the USSR.
References: *Izv.*, Nov. 12, 1954.
    VT, 1954, No. 12, p. 43.

• 54/xi/19/MPR/a
Trade agreement for the period 1955–1957 between the USSR and the Mongolian People's Republic

Signed Nov. 19, 1954, in Moscow.
Signed on expiration of the trade agreement for 1950–1954 (49/xii/9/MPR). Supplemented by a protocol on trade for

1955 (next document). Soviet consumption goods, agricultural machinery and supplies, automobiles, and equipment for development of the stock-breeding, transportation, and other industries, in exchange for Mongolian wool, furs, cattle and meat, butter, and other products of animal husbandry.
References: *Izv.*, Nov. 20, 1954.
    VT, 1954, No. 12, p. 44.

• 54/xi/19/MPR/b
Trade protocol for 1955 between the USSR and the Mongolian People's Republic

Signed Nov. 19, 1954, in Moscow.
References: *Izv.*, Nov. 20, 1954.
    VT, 1954, No. 12, p. 44.

• 54/xi/28/Af
Trade protocol for 1955 between the USSR and Afghanistan

Signed Nov. 28, 1954, in Kabul.
Goods to be exchanged nearly identical with those provided for in the protocol for 1954 (53/xii/24/Af).
References: *Izv.*, Nov. 30, 1954.
    VT, 1954, No. 12, p. 44.
Note: According to *Pravda*, Jan. 6, 1955, Radio Karachi had just announced ratification by Afghanistan of a Soviet-Afghan trade agreement signed in Kabul Dec. 5, 1954. An agreement of this date has not been identified; the reference may be an error for the present agreement.

• 54/xii/ /Af. See Appendix 5.

• 54/xii/1/Fin
Communiqué concerning a visit to Finland of A. I. Mikoyan, Deputy Chairman of the Council of Ministers of the USSR

Issued Dec. 1, 1954, at the end of a visit which began Nov. 26, 1954.
Mentions (1) agreement by the USSR to grant Finland a loan, negotiations for which are to be undertaken; (2) agreement on increase in scientific and technical collaboration; and (3) agreement on the need to establish a system of security and the strengthening of peace for all Europe.
Sources: *Izv.*, Dec. 2, 1954.
    SDD, 16, pp. 17–18.
    Deklaratsii, 1957, pp. 247–48.

● 54/xii/2/Iran/a

Agreement between the USSR and Iran concerning settlement of border and financial questions, with related documents

Signed Dec. 2, 1954, in Teheran.
Ratified by Iran Mar. 20, 1955; by the USSR Apr. 25, 1955. Entered into force May 20, 1955, on exchange of acts of ratification in Moscow.
Provisions: (1) General course of the state border defined; both parties declare that they have no territorial claims on each other. (2) A mixed Soviet-Iranian border commission to be established to re-demarcate the state border; work to be completed within 1½ years from formation of the commission. (3) All financial claims and counterclaims arising out of World War II to be settled as follows: (a) the USSR to pay Iran 11,196,070.3 grams of gold for discharge of Iranian claims arising out of the payments agreement of Mar. 18, 1943; (b) the USSR to deliver to Iran goods to a value of $8,648,619.07 U.S. in discharge of claims under the same agreement; all claims and counterclaims of the 2 parties set forth during negotiations in 1950–1951 to be considered discharged.
Related documents: (1) 5 annexed maps. (2) Protocol concerning border adjustments. (3) 2 exchanges of notes (next 2 documents).
For an unofficial Iranian announcement of agreement on settlement of the financial claims, reached during negotiations, see *NYT*, July 2, 1954. For an article by the chairman of the Soviet delegation to the Soviet-Iranian border commission, on completion of the work of re-demarcating the border, see *Izv.*, Mar. 1, 1957; *CDSP*, 9, 1957, No. 9, p. 26; see also 57/ii/27/Iran.
Sources: *VVS*, 1955, No. 8, Art. 195 (text and protocol).
　MZh, 1955, No. 5, pp. 139–42 (text and maps).
　Hurewitz, 2, pp. 385–90 (text, abridged, and protocol).

● 54/xii/2/Iran/b

Exchange of notes between the USSR and Iran concerning a payment by the USSR to Iran

Sent Dec. 2, 1954, in Teheran.
Provides for delivery by the USSR of goods to a value of 10 million rials within 1 year from entry into force of the agreement of the same date.

Reference: Hurewitz, 2, p. 385 (based on Persian text, through the Dept. of State).

● 54/xii/2/Iran/c

Exchange of notes between the USSR and Iran concerning a border rectification

Sent Dec. 2, 1954, in Teheran.
Supplements the agreement of the same date.
Reference: Hurewitz, 2, p. 385.

● 54/xii/2/Pl

Joint declaration concerning policies of the Western Powers in regard to Germany

Signed Dec. 2, 1954, in Moscow, by the USSR, Albania, Bulgaria, Czechoslovakia, the German Democratic Republic, Hungary, Poland, and Romania.
Attacks the decisions taken Oct. 23, 1954, at a 9-Power conference in Paris.
Sources: *Izv.*, Dec. 3, 1954.
　SDD, 16, pp. 53–65.
　UNTS, 226, pp. 153–86 (R, E, F).
　DIA, 1954, pp. 64–70 (extracts).

● 54/xii/4/Sweden

Exchange of notes between the USSR and Sweden modifying the parcel post agreement of November 5, 1946

Sent Nov. 24 and Dec. 4, 1954.
Provides for increase in minimum weight for parcels for 3rd States from 5 to 10 kg.
Reference: *SDD*, 12, p. 181.

● 54/xii/15/Pl. See Appendix 5.

● 54/xii/22/US

Agreement between the USSR and the United States of America concerning return of twenty-seven Lend-Lease naval craft, with annex

Signed Dec. 22, 1954, in Washington, D.C.
Entered into force on signature. Provides for delivery of the vessels to the Japanese port of Maidzura during June and July 1955. The craft are part of the 186 concerning which the USSR and the United States negotiated in 1953 (see 53/xii/26/US). Annex is a blank deed of delivery and receipt.
Sources: *UST*, 6, pp. 51–60 (E, R).
　UNTS, 251, pp. 41–47 (R, E, F).
References: *Izv.*, Dec. 25, 1954.

DSB, 32, 1955, pp. 52, 113.

● 54/xii/23/India

Exchange of notes between the USSR and India concerning trade

Sent Dec. 23, 1954, in New Delhi.
Extends for 1 year the validity of the lists annexed to the commercial agreement of Dec. 2, 1953.
Reference: *VT*, 1955, No. 2, p. 19.

● 54/xii/28/CPR

Protocol concerning the first meeting of the USSR–Chinese People's Republic commission for scientific and technical collaboration

Signed Dec. 28, 1954, in Moscow.
Regulations for the commission's work were adopted at the meeting.
References: *Izv.*, Jan. 18, 1955.
   VT, 1955, No. 2, p. 28.
   SCMP, No. 959, Jan. 1–3, 1955, p. 30.

● 54/xii/28/KPDR/a

Agreement between the USSR and the Korean People's Democratic Republic concerning exchange of mail and parcel post

Signed Dec. 28, 1954, in Moscow.
Source: *SDD*, 16, pp. 376–89.

● 54/xii/28/KPDR/b

Agreement between the USSR and the Korean People's Democratic Republic concerning establishment of telephone and telegraph communications

Signed Dec. 28, 1954, in Moscow.
Source: *SDD*, 16, pp. 389–95.

● 54/xii/30/CPR/a

Agreement between the USSR and the Chinese People's Republic concerning establishment of regular air communications

Signed Dec. 30, 1954, in Peking.
Source: *SDD*, 16, pp. 396–98.
Reference: *SCMP*, No. 958, Dec. 31, 1954, p. 1.

● 54/xii/30/CPR/b

Protocol between the USSR and the Chinese People's Republic concerning termination of the USSR-CPR joint-stock civil aviation company and transfer of Soviet shares in the company to the CPR

Signed Dec. 30, 1954, in Peking.
Reference: Private source.

● 54/xii/30/CPR/c

Protocol between the USSR and the Chinese People's Republic concerning termination of the USSR-CPR joint-stock company for nonferrous and rare metals and transfer of Soviet shares in the company to the CPR

Signed Dec. 30, 1954, in Urumchi.
Reference: Private source.

● 54/xii/31/CPR/a

Protocol between the USSR and the Chinese People's Republic concerning termination of the USSR-CPR joint-stock oil company and transfer of Soviet shares in the company to the CPR

Signed Dec. 31, 1954, in Urumchi.
Reference: Private source.

● 54/xii/31/CPR/b

Protocol between the USSR and the Chinese People's Republic concerning termination of the USSR-CPR joint-stock company for shipbuilding and repair and transfer of Soviet shares in the company to the CPR

Signed Dec. 31, 1954, in Port Arthur.
Reference: Private source.

1955

● 55/ / /Pl

Protocol concerning three-way trade and payments between the USSR, Czechoslovakia, and Finland

Signed during 1955.
Accompanied by bilateral trade protocols between the 3 States (not listed separately).

For terms and reference, see 50/vi/ /Pl.

● 55/i/ /Pl

Amendments to the United Transit Tariff

Adopted during Jan. 1955 at a meeting in Bucharest of railroad authorities of the USSR, Albania, Bulgaria, the Chinese People's Republic, Czechoslovakia, the

German Democratic Republic, Hungary, the Korean People's Republic, the Mongolian People's Republic, Poland, and Romania.
Amendment of the United Transit Tariff (YeTT) was decided on at a railroad conference held during July 1953 in Moscow (see 53/vii/31/Pl). For establishment of the Tariff, see 50/ / /Pl.
Reference: VT, 1955, No. 3, p. 24.

• 55/i/5/Yug/a

Commercial agreement between the USSR and Yugoslavia, with two annexes

Signed Jan. 5, 1955, in Moscow.
Ratified by the USSR June 18, 1955; by Yugoslavia July 12, 1955. Entered into force provisionally on signature, under an exchange of notes of the same date (55/i/5/Yug/c), definitively July 23, 1955, on exchange of acts of ratification in Belgrade. Covers trade for the period Jan. 1–Dec. 31, 1955. If not denounced 3 months before expiration, extended for 1-year periods.
Provides for establishment of a mixed commission to observe execution and make recommendations. Annexes list goods to be exchanged. Supplemented by a payments agreement and an exchange of notes of the same date (next 2 documents), and by an exchange of notes of July 30 and protocols of Sept. 1 and Nov. 14, 1955.
Sources: VVS, 1955, No. 13, Art. 277.
MU, 1957, No. 10, pp. 5–7 (R, SC).
Reference: VT, 1955, No. 9, p. 23.

• 55/i/5/Yug/b

Payments agreement between the USSR and Yugoslavia

Signed Jan. 5, 1955, in Moscow.
Data on ratification, entry into force, and duration identical with those for the commercial agreement of the same date (preceding document).
Sources: VVS, 1955, No. 13, Art. 278.
MU, 1957, No. 10, pp. 7–9 (R, SC).
UNTS, 240, pp. 225–31 (R, SC), 234–37 (E, F).

• 55/i/5/Yug/c

Exchange of notes between the USSR and Yugoslavia concerning entry into force of the commercial and payment agreements of January 5, 1955

Sent Jan. 5, 1955, in Moscow.

Provides for provisional entry into force on signature, definitive on exchange of acts of ratification.
Sources: VVS, 1955, No. 13, Art. 278, p. 361.
MU, 1957, No. 10, p. 9 (R, SC).
UNTS, 240, pp. 232–33 (R, SC), 238–41 (E, F).

• 55/i/10/Yug/a

Exchange of notes between the USSR and Yugoslavia concerning flights of Yugoslav civil airplanes over territory of the Soviet Zone of Occupation of Austria

Sent Jan. 10, 1955, in Belgrade.
Approved by Yugoslavia Feb. 7, 1956. Valid until Apr. 1, 1955; renewal to be negotiated 1 month before expiration.
Source: MU, 1956, No. 82 (R, SC).

• 55/i/10/Yug/b

Exchange of notes between the USSR and Yugoslavia concerning flights of Soviet civil airplanes over Yugoslav territory

Sent Jan. 10, 1955, in Belgrade.
Approved by Yugoslavia Feb. 7, 1956.
Source: MU, 1957, No. 34.

• 55/i/24/Fin/a

Trade protocol for 1955 between the USSR and Finland

Signed Jan. 24, 1955, in Moscow.
Soviet oil products, coal, rolled ferrous metal, grain, sugar, cotton, mineral fertilizer, chemicals, automobiles, tractors and agricultural machines, industrial equipment, etc., in exchange for Finnish vessels, equipment for the lumber industry, power and mobile crane equipment, lumber, wood pulp, cellulose, cartons, paper, etc.
References: Izv., Jan. 26, 1955.
VT, 1955, No. 3, p. 26.

• 55/i/24/Fin/b

Agreement between the USSR and Finland concerning a loan to Finland

Signed Jan. 24, 1955, in Moscow.
Ratified by Finland Feb. 4, 1955; by the USSR Mar. 29, 1955. Entered into force Apr. 22, 1955, on exchange of acts of ratification in Helsinki.
Provides for a loan to Finland of 40 million gold rubles, to be used within 3 years and repaid within 10 at 2½% interest.

Sources: *VVS*, 1955, No. 12.
   UNTS, 240, pp. 243–51 (R, Finnish,
   E, F).
References: *Izv.*, Jan. 26, 1955.
   VT, 1955, No. 3, p. 26.

● 55/i/25/Rom

Agreement between the USSR and Romania concerning establishment of regular air communications

Signed Jan. 25, 1955, in Moscow.
Reference: *Izv.*, Jan. 27, 1955.

Jan. 25, 1955

See Appendix 5.

● 55/i/29/Iran

Exchange of notes between the USSR and Iran concerning border rectification

Sent Jan. 29, 1955.
Reference: Hurewitz, 2, p. 385.

● 55/ii/ /KPDR

Trade protocol for 1955 between the USSR and the Korean People's Democratic Republic

Signed during Feb. 1955, in Moscow.
Soviet machinery and equipment, tractors and agricultural machines and tools, cable products, oil products, cotton and silk materials, footwear, etc., in exchange for KPDR nonferrous metals, ferrous alloys, etc. Trade volume to increase 25 per cent over 1954.
References: *Izv.*, Mar. 3, 1955.
   VT, 1955, No. 3, p. 28; *ibid.*, No. 5, p. 4.

● 55/ii/2/India

Agreement between the USSR and India concerning Soviet assistance for establishment of a metallurgical plant in India

Signed Feb. 2, 1955, in New Delhi.
Provides for Soviet aid in establishment of a plant with an annual capacity of 1 million tons of steel. First part of the installations to be in operation by the end of 1958, remainder by the end of 1959. In connection with construction of the plant, the USSR grants India a credit, to be repaid in 12 years at 2½% interest.
References: *Izv.*, Feb. 3, 1955.
   VT, 1955, No. 3, pp. 26–27; *ibid.*, 1956, No. 10, p. 9.

● 55/ii/5/KPDR

Agreement between the USSR and the Korean People's Democratic Republic concerning scientific and technical collaboration

Signed Feb. 5, 1955.
Reference: *VT*, 1957, No. 11, p. 25.

● 55/ii/11/CPR

Trade protocol for 1955 between the USSR and the Chinese People's Republic

Signed Feb. 11, 1955, in Moscow.
Soviet equipment for ferrous metallurgy plants, machine construction, and chemical industries, etc., lathes, tractors, oil, transportation equipment, etc., in exchange for CPR wolfram, tin, molybdenum, jute, wool, hides, soy beans, rice, plant oil, tea, citrus fruits, cork.
References: *Izv.*, Feb. 12, 1955.
   VT, 1955, No. 3, p. 27.
   SCMP, No. 987, Feb. 12–14, 1955.

● 55/ii/11/H

Agreement between the USSR and Hungary concerning establishment of regular air communications

Signed Feb. 11, 1955, in Moscow.
Reference: *Izv.*, Feb. 12, 1955.

● 55/ii/15/Iran

Agreement between the USSR and Iran concerning sale and delivery of wheat to Iran

Signed Feb. 15, 1955, in Teheran.
Provides for delivery of 10,000 tons of wheat during Feb. and Mar. 1955.
References: *Izv.*, Feb. 17, 1955.
   VT, 1955, No. 3, p. 27.

● 55/ii/17/Rom

Communiqué concerning the fifth meeting of the Soviet-Romanian commission for scientific and technical collaboration

Published Feb. 17, 1955; the meeting took place a few days earlier, in Moscow.
References: *Izv.*, Feb. 17, 1955.
   VT, 1955, No. 3, p. 27.

● 55/ii/18/Pol

Agreement between the USSR and Poland concerning establishment of regular air communications

Signed Feb. 18, 1955, in Warsaw.
Reference: *Izv.*, Feb. 19, 1955.

• 55/ii/25/Pol

Trade protocol for 1955 between the USSR and Poland

Signed Feb. 25, 1955, in Moscow.
Soviet industrial equipment, tractors, combines, automobiles, ball bearings, grain, cotton, iron, manganese, and chrome ores, oil and oil products, nonferrous metals, ferrous alloys, etc., in exchange for Polish transport and commercial vessels, railroad rolling stock, rolled ferrous metals, zinc, coal, coke, sugar, etc.
References: *Izv.*, Feb. 26, 1955.
  VT, 1955, No. 3, p. 28.

• 55/ii/26/Cz

Agreement between the USSR and Czechoslovakia concerning establishment of regular air communications

Signed Feb. 26, 1955, in Moscow.
Reference: *Izv.*, Feb. 27, 1955.

• 55/ii/26/H

Trade protocol for 1955 between the USSR and Hungary

Signed Feb. 26, 1955, in Moscow.
Soviet cotton, coke, iron ore, ferrous alloys, lumber, fertilizer, agricultural machines, industrial equipment, bearings, etc., in exchange for Hungarian sea and river vessels, railroad rolling stock, floating and gantry cranes, power and electrotechnical equipment, and agricultural goods.
References: *Izv.*, Feb. 27, 1955.
  VT, 1955, No. 3, p. 28.

• 55/iii/ /GDR

Agreement between the USSR and the German Democratic Republic concerning transfer to the GDR of art treasures from the Dresden Gallery held in the USSR

Signed during Mar. 1955.
Reference: *Dokumenty GDR*, pp. 314–16.

• 55/iii/2/Bul

Trade protocol for 1955 between the USSR and Bulgaria

Signed Mar. 2, 1955, in Moscow.
Soviet industrial equipment, tractors and agricultural machines, rolled ferrous metal, nonferrous metals, automobiles, cotton, rubber, paper, fertilizer, chemicals, etc., in exchange for Bulgarian nonferrous metal ore concentrates, tobacco, barges, and agricultural products.
References: *Izv.*, Mar. 4, 1955.
  VT, 1955, No. 3, p. 28.

• 55/iii/4/Alb

Trade protocol for 1955 between the USSR and Albania

Signed Mar. 4, 1955, in Moscow.
Soviet grain, nonferrous metals and castings, chemicals, dyes, medicines, automobiles and spare parts, etc., in exchange for Albanian tobacco, plywood, copper, bitumen, etc.
References: *VT*, 1955, No. 4, p. 28.
  Izv., Mar. 10, 1955.

• 55/iii/5/Bul

Agreement between the USSR and Bulgaria concerning air transportation of passengers, baggage, freight, and mail between Moscow and Sofia

Signed Mar. 5, 1955, in Moscow.
Reference: *Izv.*, Mar. 6, 1955, p. 4.

Mar. 7, 1955. Recognition of the Hague Conventions by the USSR

In answer to an inquiry from The Netherlands, depository of the Hague Conventions of 1899 and 1907, the Soviet Ministry of Foreign Affairs on Mar. 7, 1955, stated that the Government of the USSR recognizes the Hague Conventions and Declarations of 1899 and 1907 which were ratified by Russia, insofar as they are not in conflict with the UN Charter and if they have not been amended or superseded by subsequent international agreements to which the USSR is a party. Text of Soviet note in *Pravda*, Mar. 9, 1955; see also *MPID*, 2, p. 247.

• 55/iii/9/Rom

Trade protocol for 1955 between the USSR and Romania

Signed Mar. 9, 1955, in Moscow.
Soviet industrial equipment, automobiles, tractors, combines, rolled ferrous metal, nonferrous metals, iron ore, cotton, etc., in exchange for Romanian oil products, lumber, fishing vessels, barges, etc.

References: *Izv.*, Mar. 10, 1955.
VT, 1955, No. 4, p. 28.

Mar. 22, 1955
See Appendix 5.

● 55/iii/24/GDR

Trade protocol for 1955 between the USSR and the German Democratic Republic

Signed Mar. 24, 1955, in Moscow.
Soviet grain, cotton, ferrous and nonferrous metals, coal, coke, oil, iron, manganese, and chrome ores, automobiles, etc., in exchange for GDR sea and river vessels, wagons, metallurgical equipment for rolling, lifting and moving, forge and press, etc.
References: *Izv.*, Mar. 25, 1955.
VT, 1955, No. 6, p. 28.
Dokumenty GDR, pp. 313–14.

● 55/iii/25/Mul

Convention concerning the International Institute of Refrigeration
Signed Mar. 25, 1955, in Paris.
Ratified by the USSR July 16, 1957.
Supersedes the convention of June 21, 1920, as amended May 31, 1937 (see 24/vi/17/1920).
Reference: *VVS*, 1957, No. 16, Art. 420.

● 55/iii/31/Pl. See Appendix 5.

Apr. 10, 1955. "Asian Conference for relaxation of international tension"

This conference was held in New Delhi, Apr. 6–10, 1955, with delegates from 18 nations, including the USSR, India, the Chinese People's Republic, Japan, Burma, Pakistan, Syria, the Democratic Republic of Vietnam, the Korean People's Democratic Republic, Ceylon, Lebanon, and Jordan. For resolutions adopted at the conference, see *Pravda*, Apr. 12 and 13, 1955, and *NT*, 1955, No. 16, supplement.

● 55/iv/15/Austria/a

Joint communiqué by the USSR and Austria concerning the visit to Moscow of a delegation of the Austrian Government

Issued Apr. 15, 1955, at the end of negotiations which began Apr. 12, 1955.
Summarizes provisions of the memorandum signed Apr. 15, 1955 (next docu-

ment). In addition to agreements covered there, mentions agreement of the USSR to take a favorable view of the Austrian request for repatriation of Austrian prisoners-of-war serving sentences imposed by Soviet courts.
Sources: *Izv.*, Apr. 16, 1955.
Deklaratsii, 1957, pp. 15–16.
DSB, 32, 1955, pp. 734–35.
DIA, 1955, pp. 223–24.

● 55/iv/15/Austria/b

Memorandum concerning results of negotiations between the USSR and Austria

Signed Apr. 15, 1955, in Moscow.
Provisions include: (1) Austria to adopt and ratify a declaration of neutrality. (2) The USSR is ready to sign a State Treaty for Austria and agrees that all occupation troops shall be withdrawn from Austria after entry into force of the treaty not later than Dec. 31, 1955. The USSR is ready to guarantee Austria's neutrality and territorial integrity. (3) Austria to pay the USSR $150 million US in goods in exchange for Soviet property in Austria transferred to Austria. (4) Austria to deliver to the USSR 10 million tons of crude oil in 10 equal annual instalments, or in a shorter time, in payment for Soviet oil property in Austria transferred to Austria. (5) Austria to pay $2 million US for Soviet assets in the Danube Shipping Company in Eastern Austria. (6) A 5-year commercial treaty and a 5-year trade and payments agreement to be concluded. For the State Treaty for Austria, see 55/v/15/Austria. For agreements covering Austrian payment for Soviet property, see 55/vii/12/Austria/a and /b and 55/viii/31/Austria.
Sources: *Izv.*, May 17, 1955.
Deklaratsii, 1957, pp. 17–21.
NT, 1955, No. 22, supplement, pp. 5–7.
DSB, 32, 1955, pp. 1011–13.

● 55/iv/17/Alb

Communiqué concerning the second meeting of the Soviet-Albanian commission for scientific and technical collaboration

Published Apr. 17, 1955; the meeting took place during the 2nd half of Mar. 1955, in Tirana.
Sources: *Izv.*, Apr. 17, 1955.
VT, 1955, No. 6, p. 28.

● 55/iv/19/Cz

Communiqué concerning the seventh meeting of the Soviet-Czechoslovak commission for scientific and technical collaboration

Published Apr. 19, 1955; the meeting took place a few days earlier, in Moscow.
Sources: *Izv.*, Apr. 19, 1955.
VT, 1955, No. 6, p. 29.

● 55/iv/20/Cz

Trade protocol for 1955 between the USSR and Czechoslovakia

Signed Apr. 20, 1955, in Prague.
Soviet grains, cotton, wool, nonferrous metals, iron and manganese ores, mineral fertilizer, agricultural machines, tractors, industrial equipment, etc., in exchange for Czechoslovak diesel passenger trains, river tugs, pumps, electrostations, metallurgical equipment, equipment for the food, chemical, and light industries, oil pipes, sugar, etc.
References: *Izv.*, Apr. 21, 1955.
VT, 1955, No. 6, p. 28.

● 55/iv/22/Sweden

Trade protocol for 1955 between the USSR and Sweden

Signed Apr. 22, 1955, in Stockholm.
Soviet oil products, manganese and chrome ores, asbestos, automobiles, gasoline, etc., in exchange for Swedish vessels, industrial and power equipment, drilling lathes, high grade rolled metal, paper, etc.
References: *Izv.*, Apr. 24, 1955.
VT, 1955, No. 6, p. 29.

● 55/iv/22/Rom

Agreement between the USSR and Romania concerning aid by the USSR to Romania in regard to development of research concerning atomic nuclear physics and the use of atomic energy for the needs of the national economy

Signed Apr. 22, 1955, in Moscow.
Source: *Soglasheniia*, 1958, pp. 19–21.
Reference: *Pravda*, Apr. 30, 1955.

● 55/iv/23/Cz

Agreement between the USSR and Czechoslovakia concerning aid by the USSR

to Czechoslovakia in regard to development of research concerning atomic nuclear physics and the use of atomic energy for the needs of the national economy

Signed Apr. 23, 1955, in Moscow.
Source: *Soglasheniia*, 1958, pp. 19–21.
Reference: *Pravda*, Apr. 30, 1955.

● 55/iv/23/Pol

Agreement between the USSR and Poland concerning aid by the USSR to Poland in regard to development of research concerning atomic nuclear physics and the use of atomic energy for the needs of the national economy

Signed Apr. 23, 1955, in Moscow.
Source: *Soglasheniia*, 1958, pp. 13–15.
Reference: *Pravda*, Apr. 30, 1955.

● 55/iv/26/Pl

Exchange of notes between the USSR and the United States of America, the United Kingdom, and France concerning conclusion of a State Treaty for Austria

Sent from Apr. 5 to 26, 1955.
On Apr. 5, 1955, the 3 Western Powers issued a statement declaring their willingness to conclude the State Treaty as soon as possible. On Apr. 9 the USSR informed the 3 Powers of the Soviet plan to hold bilateral talks with Austria, and on Apr. 19 informed them of the results of the talks (see 55/iv/15/Austria/a and /b), and proposed holding a 4-Power conference in Vienna, with Austrian participation, to examine and sign the treaty. On Apr. 22 the 3 Powers in separate notes proposed a meeting of the Ambassadors of the 4 Powers in Vienna on May 2 to examine the results of the Soviet-Austrian talks and reach the necessary agreements for early signature of the treaty. On Apr. 26 the USSR in notes to the 3 Powers agreed to the proposed Ambassadors' meeting.
Source: *DSB*, 32, 1955, pp. 647–48, 733–35.

● 55/iv/27/CPR

Agreement between the USSR and the Chinese People's Republic concerning aid by the USSR to the CPR in regard to development of research concerning

atomic nuclear physics and the use of atomic energy for the needs of the national economy

Signed Apr. 27, 1955, in Moscow.
Source: *Soglasheniia*, 1958, pp. 4–6.
References: *Pravda*, Apr. 30, 1955.
  SCMP, No. 1038, Apr. 30–May 2, 1955, p. 16.

• 55/iv/27/GDR

Agreement between the USSR and the German Democratic Republic concerning use of Schoenefeld Airport

Signed Apr. 27, 1955, in Berlin.
Reference: *Dokumenty GDR*, pp. 317–18.

• 55/iv/28/GDR

Agreement between the USSR and the German Democratic Republic concerning aid by the USSR to the GDR in regard to development of research concerning atomic nuclear physics and the use of atomic energy for the needs of the national economy

Signed Apr. 28, 1955, in Moscow.
Source: *Soglasheniia*, 1958, pp. 10–12.
Reference: *Pravda*, Apr. 30, 1955.

• 55/v/3/GDR

Supplementary trade protocol for 1955 between the USSR and the German Democratic Republic

Signed May 3, 1955, in Berlin.
Increases trade under the protocol of Mar. 24, 1955.
Reference: *Dokumenty GDR*, p. 318.

• 55/v/4/Iran

Exchange of notes between the USSR and Iran constituting a trade agreement for the current year

Signed May 4, 1955, in Teheran.
Soviet cotton goods, rolled ferrous metal, cement, automobiles, agricultural machinery, chemicals, lumber, etc., in exchange for Iranian rice, cotton, wool, hides, fish products, dried fruits, oil seeds, ores, etc.
Reference: *Izv.*, May 6, 1955.

• 55/v/8/Pol

Communiqué concerning the eighth meeting of the Soviet-Polish commission for scientific and technical collaboration

Published May 8, 1955; the meeting took place in late Apr. 1955, in Warsaw.
Sources: *Izv.*, May 8, 1955.
  VT, 1955, No. 7, p. 29.

Feb. 25–May 9, 1955

See Appendix 5.

• 55/v/12/Egypt

Protocol between the USSR and Egypt concerning extension of validity of trade lists

Signed May 12, 1955, in Cairo.
Extends for 1 year the lists of goods annexed to the commercial agreement of Mar. 27, 1954 (54/iii/27/Egypt/a).
References: *Pr.*, *Izv.*, May 14, 1955.
  VT, 1955, No. 7, p. 29.

• 55/v/12/Pl

Joint communiqué concerning completion of work on the State Treaty for Austria

Issued May 12, 1955, by the Ambassadors at Vienna of the USSR, the United Kingdom, the United States of America, and France.
For the 4-Power agreement under which the Ambassadors met, see 55/iv/26/Pl.
Source: *DSB*, 32, 1955, p. 833.

• 55/v/14/Pl/a

Treaty of friendship, cooperation, and mutual assistance (Warsaw Pact)

Signed May 14, 1955, in Warsaw, by the USSR, Albania, Bulgaria, Czechoslovakia, the German Democratic Republic, Hungary, Poland, and Romania. The Chinese People's Republic was associated by a statement but was not a signatory.
Ratified by the USSR May 25, 1955; act of ratification deposited June 1, 1955. Entered into force June 4, 1955, on deposit of the last act of ratification. Duration 20 years, with extension for 10 years for those signatories which have not denounced it 1 year before expiration. In the event of conclusion of an All-European Treaty of collective security, loses validity from date of entry into force of such a treaty. On Nov. 1, 1956, Hungary announced its withdrawal (text of announcement in *DIA, 1956*, pp. 474–75).
Provides for establishment of (1) a Unified Command of the armed forces of the

signatories, and (2) a Political Consultative Committee with representatives of each signatory, with such other auxiliary organs as are necessary. For decisions taken in January 1956 with regard to the Political Consultative Committee, see 56/i/28/Pl.

Sources: *VVS*, 1955, No. 9, Art. 225.
Varshavskoe soveshchanie, pp. 136–41.
MPID, 2, pp. 169–72.
NT, 1955, No. 21, supplement, pp. 65–67.
*DUPRL, 1955, No. 30, Arts. 182, 183.
*MK, 1955, No. 60, pp. 369–74.
DIA, 1955, pp. 193–97.

References: Lachs, Manfred, "Le traité de Varsovie du 14 mai 1955," *Annuaire français de droit international*, I, 1955, pp. 120–22.
VVS, 1955, No. 8, pp. 227–32 (action on ratification); *ibid.*, Art. 198 (ratification).

• 55/v/14/Pl/b

Communiqué concerning establishment of a joint command of the armed forces of the signatories to the treaty of friendship, cooperation, and mutual assistance of May 14, 1955

Adopted May 14, 1955, in Warsaw.
Supplements the treaty (preceding document). Announces the selection of Soviet Marshal I. S. Konev to head the joint command, headquarters of the staff of which are to be established in Moscow.

Sources: *Izv.*, May 15, 1955.
Varshavskoe soveshchanie, pp. 142–43.
NT, 1955, No. 21, supplement, p. 68.
DIA, 1955, p. 198.

• 55/v/14/Pl/c

Final communiqué of the Warsaw Conference of States of the Soviet bloc

Issued May 14, 1955, at the end of a conference which began May 11, 1955. Soviet title of the conference: Warsaw Conference of European countries on safeguarding European peace and security. For participants, see the list of signatories to the Warsaw Pact (55/v/14/Pl/a).

Sources: *Pravda*, May 15, 1955.
NT, 1955, No. 21, supplement, pp. 68–70.

• 55/v/15/Austria

State Treaty for the re-establishment of an independent and democratic Austria, with two annexes and two maps

Signed May 15, 1955, in Vienna, by the USSR, the United Kingdom, the United States of America, France, and Austria. Yugoslavia acceded subsequently.
Ratified by the USSR June 11, 1955; act of ratification deposited July 5, 1955. Entered into force July 27, 1955, on deposit of acts of ratification of all signatories. Annexes: (1) Definition and list of war matériel. (2) Provisions concerning German assets in Austria (Art. 22 of the treaty), in relation to the Soviet-Austrian memorandum of Apr. 15, 1955 (55/iv/15/Austria/b). In addition, Art. 22 includes 5 lists: (1) Oil fields in Eastern Austria on which concessions are to be granted to the USSR; (2) concessions on oil exploration areas in Eastern Austria to be transferred to the USSR; (3) oil refineries in Eastern Austria, the property rights to which are to be transferred to the USSR; (4) enterprises in Eastern Austria engaged in the distribution of oil products, the property rights to which are to be transferred to the USSR; and (5) assets of the Danube Shipping Company (DDSG) in Eastern Austria to be transferred to the USSR.
Two agreements were signed on July 12, 1955, providing for compensation by Austria to the USSR for property transferred to it under the treaty.

Sources: *Pravda*, May 16, 1955.
VVS, 1955, No. 18, Art. 361.
NT, 1955, No. 22, supplement, pp. 8–22.
UNTS, 217, pp. 223–379 (R, E, F, G).
UST, 6, pp. 2408–2516 (R, E, F, G).
DSB, 32, 1955, pp. 916–32.

• 55/v/19/Argentina

Trade protocol for 1955 between the USSR and Argentina, with two annexes

Signed May 19, 1955, in Buenos Aires.
Annexes list goods to be exchanged: Soviet oil, diesel fuel, ferrous metals and metal products, lumber, machinery and equipment, etc., in exchange for Argentine wool, hides, linseed oil, meat, etc. Supplements the trade and payments agreement of Aug. 5, 1953.

Source: Spanish-language official text, Argentine Embassy, Sept. 1957.
References: *Izv.*, May 21, 1955.
VT, 1955, No. 7, pp. 13, 29.

- 55/v/20/US

Exchange of notes between the USSR and the United States of America concerning reciprocal visits of farm delegations

Sent Mar. 10 and May 19 and 20, 1955.
Sources: *DSB*, 32, 1955, pp. 932–33, 970.

- 55/v/23/Norway

Trade protocol for 1955 between the USSR and Norway

Signed May 23, 1955, in Oslo.
Soviet grains, oil products, ores, automobiles, etc., in exchange for Norwegian whale oil, herring, and aluminum.
References: *Izv.*, May 24, 1955.
VT, 1955, No. 7, p. 29.

- 55/v/24/CPR

Protocol between the USSR and the Chinese People's Republic concerning evacuation of Soviet troops from Port Arthur and transfer of its installations to the CPR

Signed May 24, 1955, by the joint Soviet-CPR military commission established by the agreement of Feb. 14, 1950 (50/ii/14/CPR/d).
References: *Izv.*, May 26, 1955.
SDD, 14, pp. 24–25.
CDSP, 7, 1955, No. 21, p. 10.
SCMP, No. 1056, May 26, 1955, p. 1.
DIA, 1955, pp. 470–71.

- 55/v/25/Pl

Exchange of notes concerning a meeting of the Heads of Government of the USSR, the United Kingdom, the United States of America, and France

Sent May 10 and 25, 1955.
On May 10, 1955, the 3 Western Powers invited the USSR to hold a meeting to remove sources of conflict between the 4 Powers. The USSR accepted on May 26, 1955. For the directive prepared at the conference, see 55/vii/23/Pl.
Sources: *Pravda*, May 27, 1955.
DSB, 32, 1955, pp. 832–33, 915.
NT, 1955, No. 22, supplement, pp. 2–4.
DIA, 1955, pp. 2–5.

- 55/v/26/US

Agreement between the USSR and the
United States of America concerning return of certain United States naval vessels (Lend-Lease settlement), with annex

Signed May 26, 1955, in Washington, D.C.
Entered into force on signature. Annex provides a blank deed of delivery and receipt. Vessels to be delivered at Kiel during July and Aug. 1955.
Sources: *UST*, 6, pp. 3825–34 (E, R).
UNTS, 270, pp. 61–70 (R, E, F).
Reference: *DSB*, 32, 1955, pp. 969–70, 1060.

- 55/v/31/KPDR

Joint communiqué by the USSR and the Korean People's Democratic Republic concerning transfer to the KPDR of Soviet shares in USSR-KPDR joint-stock companies

Published May 31, 1955.
Summarizes terms of an agreement which may have been embodied in a separate instrument. Covers companies for maritime transport and oil refining which were established "several years ago." Transfer to be paid for by the KPDR in goods over a number of years.
Sources: *Izv.*, May 31, 1955.
VT, 1955, No. 8, p. 26.

- 55/vi/2/Yug

Joint declaration by the USSR and Yugoslavia concerning normalization of relations and development of collaboration between the two States

Signed June 2, 1955, in Belgrade, at the end of negotiations which began May 27, 1955.
Defines general principles on which the 2 States are prepared to collaborate, and calls for conclusion of a number of agreements and conventions between them to regulate individual questions.
Sources: *Izv.*, June 3, 1955.
NT, 1955, No. 23, pp. 1–3.
Deklaratsii, 1957, pp. 297–302.
MU, 1956, No. 54.
DIA, 1955, pp. 267–71.

- 55/vi/9/Iran

Agreement between the USSR and Iran concerning the lease of land and other property in the port of Pehlevi

Signed June 9, 1955, in Teheran.
Reference: *MZh*, 1955, No. 7, p. 127.

● 55/vi/13/CPR

Protocol concerning the second meeting of the USSR-CPR commission for scientific and technical collaboration

Signed June 13, 1955; the commission met from June 7 to 13, 1955, in Peking.
References: *SCMP*, No. 1082, July 5–6, 1955, p. 24.
Izv., July 6, 1955.

● 55/vi/13/H

Agreement between the USSR and Hungary concerning aid by the USSR to Hungary in regard to development of research concerning atomic nuclear physics and the use of atomic energy for the needs of the national economy

Signed June 13, 1955, in Moscow.
Among other things, provides for construction in Hungary of a cyclotron of a capacity of 25 million electron volts in alpha particles. According to a note in *Soglasheniia*, 1958, p. 9, construction of the cyclotron was deferred and the date for start on the work was to be agreed upon subsequently.
Source: *Soglasheniia*, 1958, pp. 7–9.

● 55/vi/13/Pl/a

Exchange of notes concerning time and place for a meeting of the Heads of Government of the USSR, the United Kingdom, the United States of America, and France

In a note of June 6, 1955, the 3 Western Powers proposed that the meeting be held in Geneva from July 18 through July 21, 1955. The USSR accepted in a note of June 13, 1955.
Sources: *DSB*, 32, 1955, p. 989; *ibid.*, 33, 1955, pp. 20–21.

● 55/vi/13/Pl/b. See Appendix 5.

● 55/vi/17/Fin/a

Supplementary protocol between the USSR and Finland to the agreement of August 19, 1946, concerning telegraph and telephone communications

Signed June 17, 1955, in Helsinki.
Modifies tariff rates; becomes an integral part of the 1946 agreement (46/viii/19/Fin/a).
Source: *SDD*, 12, p. 142.
Reference: *Izv.*, June 19, 1955.

● 55/vi/17/Fin/b

Supplementary protocol between the USSR and Finland to the agreement of August 19, 1946, concerning postal exchange

Signed June 17, 1955, in Helsinki.
Modifies a number of technical provisions of the 1946 agreement (46/viii/19/Fin/b), of which it becomes an integral part.
Source: *SDD*, 12, pp. 144–46.
Reference: *Izv.*, June 19, 1955.

● 55/vi/22/India

Joint statement by the USSR and India concerning principles underlying relations between the two States

Signed June 22, 1955, in Moscow.
Signatories declare their adherence to the Five Principles (Panch Shila): (1) mutual respect for each other's territorial integrity and sovereignty; (2) nonaggression; (3) noninterference in each other's internal affairs for any reasons whatsoever of economic, political, or ideological character; (4) equality and mutual benefit; and (5) peaceful co-existence. Calls on all States to carry out their obligations under the Geneva Agreements (see 54/vii/21/Mul).
Sources: *Izv.*, June 23, 1955.
Deklaratsii, 1957, pp. 156–60.
NT, 1955, No. 27, supplement.
DIA, 1955, pp. 472–75.

● 55/vi/25/US

Agreement between the USSR and the United States of America defining the boundary between the United States sector of Berlin and the Soviet Zone of Occupation of Germany, with map

Signed June 25, 1955, in Berlin.
Entered into force on signature.
Sources: *UST*, 6, pp. 3781–82 (E, R).
UNTS, 270, pp. 15–18 (R, E, F).
Reference: *DSB*, 33, 1955, p. 165.

● 55/vi/28/Af

Agreement between the USSR and Afghanistan concerning goods transit

Signed June 28, 1955, in Moscow.
Ratified by the USSR Aug. 24, 1955. Entered into force Sept. 19, 1955, on exchange of acts of ratification in Kabul.
Duration 5 years; if not denounced 6

months before expiration, extended for 5 years.

Based on the treaty of friendship of Feb. 28, 1921. Disputes under the agreement to be settled in accordance with the provisions on arbitration established by the trade and payments agreement of July 17, 1950.

Sources: *VVS*, 1955, No. 17, Art. 346.
MZh, 1955, No. 9, pp. 153–54.
UNTS, 240, pp. 253–65 (R, Persian, E, F).
Reference: *Izv.*, June 29, 1955.

● 55/vii/ /Yug

Agreement between the USSR and Yugoslavia concerning settlement of claims

Signed during July 1955.
Provides for cancellation of a Yugoslav debt of $90 million.
Reference: *Int. aff.*, 1956, No. 6, p. 23.

● 55/vii/1/Burma/a

Commercial agreement between the USSR and Burma, with annexes

Signed July 1, 1955, in Rangoon.
Duration 3 years; extended to 5 years by protocol of Apr. 1, 1956 (56/iv/1/Burma/b). Includes provisions for most-favored-nation treatment in trade and navigation. Annexes list goods to be exchanged: Burmese rice products, oil cakes, nonferrous metals, tropical woods, rubber, etc., in exchange for Soviet equipment for rice-cleaning, cotton-ginning, and textile factories, hydroelectric stations, tractors and agricultural machines, automobiles, electrotechnical and signals equipment, excavators, pumps and compressors, typographic equipment, lathes and instruments, motorcycles and velocipedes, photographic and cinema equipment, newsprint, cement, rolled ferrous metals, chemicals, medicines and medical equipment, etc.
References: *Izv.*, July 3, 1955.
VT, 1955, No. 8, pp. 27–28; *ibid.*, 1957, No. 3, pp. 7–8.

● 55/vii/1/Burma/b

Trade protocol between the USSR and Burma, with related documents

Signed July 1, 1955, in Rangoon.
Provides for export by Burma during 1955 of 150 to 200 thousand tons of rice, in exchange for Soviet equipment, machinery, and other goods. Burmese purchasers to be given an opportunity to visit the USSR before placing orders; Soviet specialists to be sent to Burma. Related documents, not specifically identified in references cited, concern payments. For a three-way payment agreement to settle part of the adverse Soviet trade balance under the protocol, see 56/x/9/Pl.
References: Same as those for 55/vii/1/ Burma/a.

● 55/vii/1/GDR/a–

Treaties between the USSR and the German Democratic Republic concerning reorganization of cinema relations

Signed July 1, 1955.
Provide for transfer to the GDR of leases of 91 cinema theaters and other installations in the GDR and for more favorable conditions to the GDR for exchange of films.
Reference: *Dokumente DDR*, 3, pp. 206–207, citing
ND, July 2, 1955.

● 55/vii/2/H

Communiqué concerning the sixth meeting of the Soviet-Hungarian commission for scientific and technical collaboration

Published July 2, 1955; the meeting took place a few days earlier in Budapest.
Sources: *Izv.*, July 2, 1955.
VT, 1955, No. 8, p. 27.

● 55/vii/8/Bul

Communiqué concerning the sixth meeting of the Soviet-Bulgarian commission for scientific and technical collaboration

Published July 8, 1955; the meeting took place a few days earlier in Sofia.
Sources: *Izv.*, July 8, 1955.
VT, 1955, No. 8, pp. 28–29.

● 55/vii/8/DRV/a

Trade agreement between the USSR and the Democratic Republic of Vietnam

Signed July 8, 1955, in Moscow.
Reference: *MZh*, 1955, No. 10, p. 136.

● 55/vii/8/DRV/b

Exchange of notes between the USSR and the Democratic Republic of Vietnam

concerning establishment of a Soviet Trade Mission in the DRV

Sent July 8, 1955, in Moscow.
Reference: *MZh*, 1955, No. 10, p. 136.

July 9, 1955. Soviet accession to the International Bureau of Education

The Soviet delegate at the 18th international conference on questions of popular education announced that the USSR and Belorussian and Ukrainian SSR's had become members of the International Bureau of Education.
Reference: *MZh*, 1955, No. 8, p. 115.

• 55/vii/11/US

Exchange of notes between the USSR and the United States of America concerning the visit of a *Pravda* correspondent to Stratford, Connecticut

Sent July 9 and 11, 1955.
Source (United States note only) : *DSB*, 33, 1955, pp. 134–35.

• 55/vii/12/Austria/a

Agreement between the USSR and Austria concerning deliveries by Austria to the USSR in payment for Soviet property transferred to Austria

Signed July 12, 1955, in Moscow.
In accordance with provisions of Art. 22 of the State Treaty for Austria (55/v/15/Austria), Austria is to deliver to the USSR goods to a total value of $150 million, in 6 equal annual installments, to include metallurgical and woodworking equipment, compressors, chemical apparatus, specialized automobiles, measurement-control instruments, steel and galvanized plates, copper castings, cables, oil, nitrolac, artificial silk thread and textiles, and footwear. In a joint communiqué of July 24, 1958, it was announced that the USSR had agreed to permit Austria to substitute other goods for the 200,000 tons of oil called for annually in the agreement during the 5th and 6th years (*Pr.*, *Izv.*, July 25, 1958).
References: *Izv.*, July 13, 1955.
    VT, 1955, No. 8, p. 29.

• 55/vii/12/Austria/b

Agreement between the USSR and Austria concerning oil deliveries by Austria

to the USSR in payment for oil works and refineries transferred by the USSR to Austria

Signed July 12, 1955, in Moscow.
Provides for total deliveries of 10 million tons of crude oil, in equal annual installments for 10 years, in payment for oil property transferred to Austria under the memorandum of Apr. 15, 1955 (55/iv/15/Austria/b). In a joint communiqué of July 24, 1958, it was announced that the USSR would deliver to Austria 3,500,000 tons of Soviet oil beginning Jan. 1, 1959, at the rate of 500,000 tons annually, in compensation for half of the 1 million tons of oil delivered annually to the USSR under this agreement (*Pr.*, *Izv.*, July 25, 1958).
References: *Izv.*, July 13, 1955.
    VT, 1955, No. 8, p. 29.

• 55/vii/15/Israel

Exchange of notes between the USSR and Israel constituting an agreement on most-favored-nation treatment in regard to shipping

Sent July 15, 1955, in Moscow.
Entered into force July 15, 1955.
Sources: **KA*, No. 209, Jan. 22, 1957.
    UNTS, 226, pp. 253–56 (R, E, F).

• 55/vii/18/DRV/a

Joint communiqué by the USSR and the Democratic Republic of Vietnam concerning political and economic negotiations

Issued July 18, 1955, at the end of negotiations in Moscow which began July 12, 1955.
Covers both international questions and political, economic, and cultural relations between the 2 States. Among other things, calls for fulfillment of the decisions of the Geneva Conference in regard to Vietnam (see 54/vii/21/Mul). Mentions Soviet aid for the DRV and signing of a trade agreement (see next 2 documents).
Sources: *Pr.*, *Izv.*, July 19, 1955.
    Deklaratsii, 1957, pp. 99–103.
    NT, 1955, No. 30, supplement, pp. 2–4.
    DIA, 1955, pp. 479–82.

• 55/vii/18/DRV/b

Agreement between the USSR and the

Democratic Republic of Vietnam concerning Soviet aid to the DRV

Signed during negotiations in Moscow which ended July 18, 1955.
Calls for a Soviet gift to the DRV of 400 million rubles, to raise the living standard and re-establish the economy of the DRV, including re-establishment and construction of 25 industrial and communal enterprises.
References: Mentioned in the joint communiqué (preceding document).
MZh, 1955, No. 8, p. 52; *ibid.*, No. 10, p. 136.
Izv., July 18, 1956.
VT SSSR, pp. 206, 207.

● 55/vii/18/DRV/c

Trade agreement between the USSR and the Democratic Republic of Vietnam, with annex

Signed July 18, 1955, in Moscow.
Valid through Dec. 31, 1955. Extended to 1956 by protocol of May 5, 1956, and to 1957 by protocol of Mar. 30, 1957. Annexes list goods to be exchanged. Includes provisions for payments and prices.
References: Mentioned in the joint communiqué of the same date.
VT SSSR, pp. 206–207.

● 55/vii/23/Mul

Amendments to the schedule to the international convention for the regulation of whaling

Adopted at the seventh meeting of the International Whaling Commission, July 18–23, 1955, in Moscow.
For the convention and annexed schedule, see 46/xii/2/Mul/a and /b.
Source: *UNTS*, 252, pp. 330–33 (E, F).

● 55/vii/23/Pl

Directive of the Heads of Government of the USSR, the United Kingdom, the United States of America, and France to the Foreign Ministers

Adopted July 23, 1955, at the 8th and final plenary meeting of the Geneva Conference of Heads of Government, which began July 18, 1955.
Provisions: (1) The Heads of Government agree that the settlement of the German question and the reunification of Germany by means of free elections shall be carried out in conformity with the national interests of the German people and the interests of European security. Foreign Ministers to consider various proposals for the purpose of establishing European security, with due regard to the legitimate interests of all nations and their inherent right to individual and collective self-defense. (2) The Heads of Government agree to work together to develop an acceptable system for disarmament through the Sub-Committee of the UN Disarmament Commission. (3) The Foreign Ministers are to study measures to bring about a progressive elimination of barriers to free communications and peaceful trade between people and to bring about freer contacts and exchanges. (4) The Foreign Ministers of the 4 Powers are to meet at Geneva during Oct. 1955 to begin consideration of these questions and determine the organization of their work. For the final communiqué prepared by the Foreign Ministers, see 55/xi/16/Pl.
Sources: *DSB*, 33, 1955, pp. 176–77.
DS, IOCS, I, 29, pp. 67–68.
NT, 1955, No. 31, supplement, pp. 18–19.
DIA, 1955, pp. 48–49.

● 55/vii/27/GDR

Communiqué concerning the visit of a Soviet governmental delegation to the German Democratic Republic

Issued July 27, 1955, at the end of negotiations in Berlin which began July 24, 1955.
Concerns discussion of the results of the meeting of Heads of Government at Geneva (see the preceding document) as they affect Germany. Agreement reached on desirability of establishment of a system of collective security in Europe with the participation on an equal basis of both parts of Germany, and later of a unified Germany. No mention made of all-German elections. On the subject of German prisoners of war being held in the USSR, it was decided to continue consideration of this question. Agreement reached on "further steps towards the goal of developing and strengthening the friendly relations between the USSR and the GDR on the basis of equal rights, mutual respect for sovereignty, and noninterference in each other's affairs."
Sources: *Izv.*, July 28, 1955.
Deklaratsii, 1957, pp. 104–106.

Dokumente DDR, 3, pp. 228–31.
DIA, 1955, pp. 198–200.

• 55/vii/30/Pl. See Appendix 5.

• 55/vii/30/Yug

Exchange of notes between the USSR and Yugoslavia concerning an increase in trade during 1955

Sent July 30, 1955, in Belgrade.
Supplements the commercial agreement of Jan. 5, 1955 (55/i/5/Yug/a). Provides for a supplementary exchange of goods to a value of $12 million U.S. for each party. Modified by protocol of Nov. 14, 1955.
Source: *MU*, 1957, No. 51.
References: *Izv.*, Aug. 2, 1955.
   VT, 1955, No. 9, p. 23; *ibid.*, No. 10, p. 28; *ibid.*, 1956, No. 10, p. 4.

• 55/viii/12/Italy

Trade protocol for 1955 between the USSR and Italy

Signed Aug. 12, 1955, in Moscow.
Soviet oil, anthracite, lumber, paraffin, naphthalene, benzene, etc., in exchange for Italian cranes, staple fibers, artificial silk thread, citrus fruits, volatile oils, etc.
References: *Izv.*, Aug. 13, 1955.
   VT, 1955, No. 10, p. 28.

• 55/viii/12/MPR. See Appendix 5.

• 55/viii/14/Af

Parcel post agreement between the USSR and Afghanistan

Signed Aug. 14, 1955, in Kabul.
Reference: *Izv.*, Aug. 16, 1955.

• 55/viii/16/CPR

Convention between the USSR and the Chinese People's Republic concerning quarantine and combating parasites and diseases of agricultural plants, with two annexes

Signed Aug. 16, 1955, in Peking.
Ratified by the USSR Oct. 8, 1955; by the CPR Nov. 10, 1955. Entered into force Dec. 16, 1955, on exchange of acts of ratification in Moscow. Duration 5 years; if not denounced 1 year before expiration, extended for 5-year periods. Provides for holding conferences annually, to meet alternately in the USSR and the CPR. An-

nexes list parasites and diseases covered.
Source: *VVS*, 1956, No. 2, Art. 40.
References: *Izv.*, Oct. 9, 1955.
   VVS, 1955, No. 19 (same).

• 55/viii/16/Fin

Agreement between the USSR and Finland concerning scientific and technical collaboration

Signed Aug. 16, 1955, in Helsinki.
Entered into force on signature.
Provides for establishment of a mixed Soviet-Finnish commission to carry out measures, to meet not less than once annually, alternately in Moscow and Helsinki.
Source: *SS, 1955, No. 30 (Finnish, R).
References: *Izv.*, Aug. 17, 1955.
   VT, 1955, No. 10, p. 29.

• 55/viii/19/FRG

Exchange of letters between the USSR and the Federal Republic of Germany concerning negotiations to establish diplomatic relations

Sent June 7 and 30 and Aug. 3, 12, and 19, 1955.
Source: *DIA, 1955*, pp. 245–51.

• 55/viii/23/Greece

Trade protocol between the USSR and Greece, with two annexes

Signed Aug. 23, 1955, in Athens.
Ratified by Greece Aug. 24, 1955. Covers the period July 28, 1955, through Dec. 31, 1956. Annexes list goods to be exchanged.
Sources: *Greek official gazette, A, 1955, No. 259.
   UNTS, 233, pp. 39–47 (R, Greek, E, F).
References: *Int. aff.*, 1956, No. 5, pp. 87–88.
   MZh, 1955, No. 10, p. 137.

• 55/viii/25/GDR

Protocol between the USSR and the German Democratic Republic concerning transfer to the GDR of pictures from the Dresden Gallery

Signed Aug. 25, 1955, in Moscow.
Final protocol on transfer signed Nov. 27, 1955.
Source: *Dokumente DDR*, 4, pp. 44–47.

• 55/viii/27/Alb

Convention between the USSR and Albania concerning quarantine and com-

bating parasites and diseases of agricultural plants, with annex

Signed Aug. 27, 1955, in Tirana.
Ratified by Albania Oct. 3, 1955; by the USSR Nov. 3, 1955. Entered into force Dec. 10, 1955, on exchange of acts of ratification in Moscow. Duration 5 years; if not denounced 1 year before expiration, extended for 5-year periods. Provides for holding conferences annually, to meet alternately in the USSR and Albania.
Source: *VVS*, 1956, No. 1, Art. 1.
References: *Izv.*, Dec. 11, 1955.
    VVS, 1955, No. 23, Art. 447 (Soviet ratification).

● 55/viii/27/Af

Trade protocol for 1955 between the USSR and Afghanistan

Signed Aug. 27, 1955, in Kabul.
Soviet oil products, rolled ferrous metals, construction materials, automobiles, equipment, textiles, sugar, etc., in exchange for Afghan wool, cotton, hides, dried fruit, and oil seeds.
References: *Izv.*, Aug. 30, 1955.
    VT, 1955, No. 10, p. 29.

● 55/viii/31/Austria

Final protocol between the USSR and Austria concerning the transfer to Austria of Soviet property in Austria

Signed Aug. 31, 1955; announced in a joint communiqué of the same date (not listed separately).
Covers transfer of property of the Administration of Soviet Property in Austria (USIA), oil works and enterprises of the Soviet Oil Administration (SNU), the joint-stock company for sale of oil products (OROP), and Soviet assets in the Danube Shipping Company (DDSG) in Eastern Austria, in accordance with the memorandum of Apr. 15, 1955 (55/iv/15/Austria/b), the State Treaty for Austria of May 15, 1955, and the agreements of July 12, 1955.
References: *Izv.*, Sept. 1, 1955.
    VT, 1955, No. 10, p. 29.

● 55/viii/31/KPDR

Agreement between the USSR and the Korean People's Democratic Republic concerning transfer to the KPDR of Soviet shares in the joint-stock air transport company "SOKAO"

Signed Aug. 31, 1955; announced in a joint communiqué published Sept. 8, 1955 (not listed separately).
The company was established in 1949. Transfer to be paid for by the KPDR in goods over a number of years. With the signing of this agreement, no further USSR-KPDR joint-stock companies remain in existence.
References: *Izv.*, Sept. 8, 1955.
    VT, 1955, No. 10, p. 30.

● 55/ix/ /Egypt. See Appendix 5.

● 55/ix/ /India

Protocol between the USSR and India concerning construction of a technological institute near Bombay

Signed during Sept. 1955.
Reference: *VT*, 1956, No. 10, p. 10.

● 55/ix/1/Yug/a

Joint communiqué by the USSR and Yugoslavia concerning economic negotiations

Issued Sept. 1, 1955, in Moscow, at the end of negotiations which began Aug. 23, 1955.
Summarizes provisions of the protocol signed the same day (next document). In addition, mentions exchange of opinions on possibility of collaboration in the use of atomic energy for peaceful purposes.
Sources: *Izv.*, Sept. 2, 1955.
    VT, 1955, No. 9, supplement.
    Deklaratsii, 1957, pp. 302–304.
    DIA, 1955, pp. 272–73.

● 55/ix/1/Yug/b

Protocol between the USSR and Yugoslavia concerning economic negotiations, with two annexes

Signed Sept. 1, 1955, in Moscow.
Provisions: (1) Trade during 1956 to reach a total value of $70 million U.S. Annexes, listing goods to be exchanged, to be used as basis for trade in 1957–1958. New lists to be drawn up for 1959 and 1960. Protocol on trade to be signed not later than Jan. 1, 1956. (2) A long-term credit agreement to be signed in Jan. 1956, providing a $54 million trade credit, to be used in 1956–1958 and repaid in 10 years at 2 per cent interest (see 56/ii/4/Yug/b). (3) An agreement to be signed in Jan.

1956 providing for a loan of $30 million U.S. to Yugoslavia, to be repaid in 10 years at 2 per cent interest (see 56/ii/2/Yug/a). (4) An agreement on technical collaboration and exchange of experience to be signed in the near future (see 55/xii/19/Yug). (5) The USSR is ready to advance Yugoslavia a credit of up to $110 million for capital construction of industrial plants during 1956–1959; an agreement covering this arrangement to be drawn up shortly (see 56/i/12/Yug).
Source: *MU*, 1957, No. 9 (R, SC).
Reference: Provisions summarized in the joint communiqué (preceding document).

● 55/ix/3/Yug

Agreement between the USSR and Yugoslavia concerning air communications

Signed Sept. 3, 1955, in Moscow.
Ratified by the USSR Nov. 28, 1955; by Yugoslavia Dec. 24, 1955. Entered into force Dec. 28, 1955, on exchange of acts of ratification in Belgrade, but applied from date of signature. Valid until 6 months after denunciation.
Calls for signature of a separate agreement between the Jugoslovenski Aerotransport (JAT) and the USSR Main Administration of Civil Aviation (Aeroflot) to cover technical and commercial questions.
Sources: *VVS*, 1956, No. 2, Art. 41.
MU, 1956, No. 93 (R, SC).
UNTS, 240, pp. 267–87 (R, SC, E, F).
Reference: *Pr.*, Dec. 29, 1955.

● 55/ix/5/US

Exchange of notes between the USSR and the United States of America constituting an agreement concerning exchange of medical films, with annex

Sent Mar. 17 and Sept. 5, 1955, in Washington, D.C.
Entered into force Sept. 5, 1955. Annex lists films to be exchanged.
Source: *UST*, 6, pp. 3969–74 (E, R).
UNTS, 256, pp. 307–14 (R, E, F).
Reference: *DSB*, 33, 1955, pp. 785–86.

● 55/ix/7/Denmark

Agreement between the USSR and Denmark concerning transformation of diplomatic missions into embassies

Announced Sept. 7, 1955.
Reference: *Izv.*, Sept. 7, 1955.

● 55/ix/13/FRG/a

Final communiqué concerning results of conversations between the USSR and the Federal Republic of Germany

Issued Sept. 13, 1955, at the end of negotiations in Moscow which began Sept. 9, 1955.
Mentions exchange of letters on establishment of diplomatic relations (next document) and agreement to negotiate on trade.
Sources: *Izv.*, Sept. 14, 1955.
Deklaratsii, 1957, pp. 146–47.
DIA, 1955, pp. 251–53.

● 55/ix/13/FRG/b

Exchange of notes between the USSR and the Federal Republic of Germany concerning establishment of diplomatic relations

Sent Sept. 13, 1955, in Moscow.
Confirmed by the FRG Sept. 23, 1955; by the USSR Sept. 24, 1955. Entered into force for each party on confirmation.
For a summary of the preparatory negotiations, beginning with a Soviet note of June 7, 1955, see *Izv.*, Aug. 6 and 20, 1955.
Sources: *Izv.*, Sept. 14, 1955.
VVS, 1955, No. 23, Art. 445.
BPI, Sept. 20, 1955, pp. 17 ff.
DIA, 1955, p. 253.
Reference: *DSB*, 33, 1955, pp. 494–95.
See further Appendix 5.

● 55/ix/13/GDR

Communiqué concerning the fourth meeting of the USSR–German Democratic Republic commission for scientific and technical collaboration

Published Sept. 13, 1955; the meeting took place Sept. 3, 1955, in Berlin.
Sources: *Izv.*, Sept. 13, 1955.
VT, 1955, No. 10, p. 30.
Reference: *Dokumente DDR*, 3, pp. 242–43.

● 55/ix/19/Fin/a

Agreement between the USSR and Finland concerning renunciation by the USSR of rights to the use of the territory of Porkkala-Udd as a naval base

and the withdrawal of Soviet armed forces from the territory

Signed Sept. 19, 1955, in Moscow.
Ratified by Finland Oct. 7, 1955; by the USSR Oct. 11, 1955. Entered into force Oct. 28, 1955, on exchange of acts of ratification in Helsinki.
Provides for renunciation by the USSR of rights established under Art. 8 of the armistice agreement of Sept. 19, 1944, and confirmed under Art. 4 of the peace treaty of Feb. 10, 1947. For the protocol on transfer, see 56/i/26/Fin.
Sources: *VVS*, 1955, No. 20, Art. 390.
   NT, 1955, No. 39, supplement, pp. 5–6.
   *SS, 1955, No. 34 (Finnish, R).
   UNTS, 226, pp. 187–99 (R, Finnish, E, F).
   DIA, 1955, pp. 206–209.

• 55/ix/19/Fin/b

Protocol between the USSR and Finland concerning extension of the treaty of friendship, cooperation, and mutual assistance of April 6, 1948

Signed Sept. 19, 1955, in Moscow.
Ratified by the USSR Oct. 11, 1955. Entered into force Oct. 28, 1955, on exchange of acts of ratification in Helsinki. Extends the 1948 treaty 20 years from date of entry into force; thereafter if not denounced 1 year before expiration, extended for 5-year periods.
Sources: *VVS*, 1955, No. 20, Art. 389.
   NT, 1955, No. 39, supplement, p. 4.
   UNTS, 226, pp. 334–41 (R, Finnish, E, F).
Reference: *SDD*, 13, p. 24.

• 55/ix/20/Fin

Joint communiqué by the USSR and Finland concerning the visit to Moscow of J. K. Paasikivi, President of Finland

Issued Sept. 20, 1955, at the end of negotiations in Moscow which began Sept. 16, 1955.
Mentions agreements signed Sept. 19, 1955 (2 preceding documents).
Sources: *Pr., Izv.*, Sept. 20, 1955.
   Deklaratsii, 1957, pp. 248–51.
   NT, 1955, No. 39, supplement, pp. 3–4.

• 55/ix/20/GDR/a

Final communiqué on negotiations be-tween the USSR and the German Democratic Republic

Issued Sept. 20, 1955, at the end of negotiations in Moscow which began Sept. 17, 1955.
Mentions treaty and exchange of letters of the same date (next 2 documents). States that the USSR will give favorable consideration to the question of former German prisoners of war still in the USSR serving sentences for crimes.
Sources: *Izv.*, Sept. 21, 1955.
   Deklaratsii, 1957, pp. 106–108.
   NT, 1955, No. 39, supplement, p. 7.
   Dokumente DDR, 3, pp. 278–80.

• 55/ix/20/GDR/b

Treaty concerning relations between the USSR and the German Democratic Republic

Signed Sept. 20, 1955, in Moscow.
Ratified by the USSR and the GDR Oct. 3, 1955. Entered into force Oct. 6, 1955, on exchange of acts of ratification in Berlin. Valid until unification of Germany, or until agreement by the signatories on amendment or termination.
Provisions include: (1) The GDR stated to be free to take decisions on all questions pertaining to its domestic and foreign policy, including relations with the Federal Republic of Germany. (2) Soviet forces stationed in the GDR to remain there temporarily, subject to conditions to be defined in a supplementary agreement.
On the same day the USSR Council of Ministers announced the abolition of the post of Soviet High Commissioner in Germany, and stated that the laws, directives, orders and decisions issued by the Allied Control Council in Germany concerning reconstruction of public life on a peaceful and democratic basis were henceforth superfluous and would cease to be valid in the GDR (*Pr.*, Sept. 21, 1955).
On July 17, 1956, the annual monetary contribution made by the GDR under this treaty towards the maintenance of Soviet forces in Germany was reduced from 1600 to 800 million Marks (see 56/vii/17/GDR/a). Since the text of the treaty as published makes no reference to such a contribution, it was presumably covered under an unidentified supplementary agreement.

Sources: *VVS*, 1955, No. 23, Art. 446.
NT, 1955, No. 39, supplement, pp. 8–9.
Dokumente DDR, 3, pp. 280–83; *ibid.*,
4, pp. 48–50.
UNTS, 226, pp. 201–13 (R, G, E, F).
DIA, 1955, pp. 200–202.
*Annuaire français de droit interna-
tional*, I, 1955, pp. 742–43.
Reference: *VVS*, 1955, No. 18 (ratifica-
tion).

● 55/ix/20/GDR/c

**Exchange of letters between the USSR
and the German Democratic Republic
concerning guard and control functions
to be exercised by the GDR**

Sent Sept. 20, 1955, in Moscow.
Provides that the GDR shall exercise
guard and control functions on the borders of the GDR, on the demarcation line
between the GDR and the Federal Republic of Germany, on the outer circuit of
Greater Berlin, in Berlin, and on the lines
of communication between the FRG and
West Berlin. The GDR to exercise the
function of issuing and formalizing shipping documents for traffic on internal
waterways of the GDR, etc. Control of
the movement of the French, British, and
United States garrisons in West Berlin between the FRG and West Berlin to be
exercised temporarily, pending achieve-
ment of an appropriate agreement, by the
Command of the Soviet Army Group in
Germany. Road, rail, and air corridors
defined over which movement of military
personnel and freight of the garrisons of
the 3 Western Powers in West Berlin is
to be permitted.
On Sept. 28, 1955, the Foreign Ministers
of the United States, the United Kingdom, and France issued a statement that
(1) the agreements of Sept. 20, 1955,
leave the USSR fully responsible for carrying out its obligations under agreements and arrangements between the 3
Powers and the USSR on the subject of
Germany and Berlin; (2) the Federal Republic of Germany is the only German
Government entitled to speak for Germany in international affairs; the 3 Powers do not recognize the "East German
regime"; and (3) final determination of
the frontiers of Germany must await a
peace settlement for the whole of Germany. (Text, *DSB*, 33, 1955, pp. 559–60).
On Oct. 3, 1955, the 3 Powers sent the
USSR notes reiterating their view that the

USSR retained the responsibilities it had
assumed in matters concerning transportation and communications between the
different parts of Germany, including Berlin (text, *ibid.*, p. 616).
Sources: *Pravda*, Sept. 21, 1955.
Dokumente DDR, 3, pp. 283–84.
NT, 1955, No. 39, supplement, pp. 9–10.
DIA, 1955, pp. 202–203.

● 55/ix/23/Iceland/a

**Trade protocol for 1956 between the
USSR and Iceland**

Signed Sept. 23, 1955, in Moscow.
Soviet oil products, cement, ferrous met-
als, automobiles, etc., in exchange for
salted herring and fish fillets.
References: *Izv.*, Sept. 25, 1955.
VT, 1955, No. 12, p. 28.

● 55/ix/23/Iceland/b

**Exchange of notes between the USSR
and Iceland concerning an increase in
the trade balance limit**

Sent Sept. 23, 1955, in Moscow.
Provides for an increase of the limit to
20 million Icelandic crowns, modifying
the trade and payments agreement of Aug.
1, 1953.
Reference: *SDD*, 15, p. 63.

● 55/ix/23/Yug

**Exchange of notes between the USSR
and Yugoslavia concerning establishment of trade lists**

Sent Sept. 23, 1955.
Mentioned in and modified by protocol of
Nov. 14, 1955.

● 55/ix/25/Libya

**Joint communiqué by the USSR and
Libya concerning establishment of diplomatic relations and exchange of diplomatic missions at the level of embassies**

Published Sept. 25, 1955.
Source: *Izv.*, Sept. 25, 1955.
Reference: *MZh*, 1955, No. 11, p. 107.

● 55/ix/27/Yug/a

**Agreement between the USSR and Yugo-
slavia concerning postal and telegraph-
telephone communications**

Signed Sept. 27, 1955, in Moscow.
Ratified by Yugoslavia Feb. 7, 1956. En-
ters into force at the beginning of the 1st
quarter following approval. Valid until
6 months after denunciation.
Source: *MU*, 1957, No. 50, pp. 3–8 (SC,
R).
Reference: *Izv.*, Sept. 28, 1955.

● 55/ix/27/Yug/b

**Parcel post agreement between the USSR
and Yugoslavia**

Signed Sept. 27, 1955, in Moscow.
Enters into force at the beginning of the
1st quarter following approval. Valid
until 6 months after denunciation.
Source: *MU*, 1957, No. 50, pp. 8–14 (SC,
R).
Reference: *Izv.*, Sept. 28, 1955.

● 55/ix/28/Mul

**Protocol amending the Warsaw Conven-
tion of October 12, 1929, for the unification of certain rules concerning international air transport**

Signed Sept. 28, 1955, at The Hague.
Ratified by the USSR Feb. 9, 1957; act
of ratification deposited Mar. 25, 1957.
Source: *VVS*, 1957, No. 8, Art. 217.
References: *Ibid.*, 1956, No. 6, Art. 136.
DSB, 35, 1956, p. 128.

● 55/x/1/Lebanon

**Exchange of notes between the USSR
and Lebanon concerning trade**

Sent Oct. 1, 1955, in Beirut.
Extends for 1 year the trade lists estab-
lished by the trade and payments agree-
ment of Apr. 30, 1954.
References: *Izv.*, Oct. 4, 1955.
VT, 1955, No. 12, p. 28.

Aug. 29–Oct. 7, 1955

See Appendix 5.

● 55/x/12/Canada

**Joint communiqué by the USSR and Can-
ada concerning negotiations**

Issued Oct. 12, 1955, at the end of negotiations in Moscow which began Oct. 5,
1955.
Mentions exchange of views on disarmament; Indo-China; negotiations for conclusion of a trade agreement; exchange of
visits, both official and unofficial, includ-

ing those of governmental delegations;
exchange of information and extension of
exchanges in the fields of culture, science,
and technology.
Sources: *Izv.*, Oct. 12, 1955.
Deklaratsii, 1957, pp. 179–81.

● 55/x/17/Austria/a

**Treaty of commerce and navigation be-
tween the USSR and Austria, with annex concerning the Soviet Trade Mission in Austria**

Signed Oct. 17, 1955, in Vienna.
Ratified by the USSR Jan. 21, 1956; by
Austria Jan. 30, 1956. Entered into force
Feb. 17, 1956, on exchange of acts of
ratification in Moscow. Duration 5 years;
if not denounced 12 months before expi-
ration, valid until 12 months after de-
nunciation. Supplemented by agreements
on trade and payments (next 2 docu-
ments).
Sources: *VT*, 1955, No. 12, pp. 14–16.
VVS, 1956, No. 5, Art. 130.
BGBl, 1956, No. 193.
UNTS, 240, pp. 289–315 (R, G, E, F).
References: *Izv.*, Oct. 18, 1955.
VT, 1955, No. 12, p. 29; *ibid.*, 1956, No.
12, p. 6.

● 55/x/17/Austria/b

**Payments agreement between the USSR
and Austria**

Signed Oct. 17, 1955, in Vienna.
Entered into force on signature. Duration
5 years.
Source: *BGBl*, 1956, No. 84.
References: *Izv.*, Oct. 18, 1955.
VT, 1955, No. 12, p. 29; *ibid.*, 1956, No.
12, p. 6.

● 55/x/17/Austria/c

**Trade agreement between the USSR and
Austria, with annexes**

Signed Oct. 17, 1955, in Vienna.
Entered into force on signature. Duration
5 years.
Annexes list goods to be exchanged during the first year, to a value of 100 million
rubles each: Soviet grains, coal, asbestos,
apatite concentrate, cotton, oil pipes, ferrous alloys, industrial equipment, furs,
automobiles, etc., in exchange for Austrian power and electrotechnical equipment, motor locomotives, river tugs, equipment for the wood-working and metallurgical industries, lathes, machinery for

the light and food industries, cables, plywood, etc.
References: *Izv.*, Oct. 18, 1955.
   VT, 1955, No. 12, p. 29; *ibid.*, 1956, No.
   12, p. 6.

• 55/x/17/Pl

**Protocol concerning opening of through
rail traffic between the USSR and the
Chinese People's Republic by way of the
Mongolian People's Republic**

Signed by the USSR, the CPR, and the
MPR at a conference which met in Ulan
Bator from Sept. 20 to Oct. 17, 1955.
Reference: *SCMP*, No. 1160, Oct. 29–31,
   1955, pp. 50–51.

• 55/x/17/MPR

**Protocol between the USSR and the Mon-
golian People's Republic concerning rail
communications**

Signed by a joint USSR-MPR committee
on border railroads at a conference which
met in Ulan Bator from Sept. 20 to Oct.
17, 1955.
Reference: Same as for preceding document.

• 55/x/18/GDR

**Agreement between the USSR and the
German Democratic Republic concerning technical and commercial collaboration in the field of civil aviation**

Signed Oct. 18, 1955, in Moscow.
Reference: *Izv.*, Oct. 19, 1955.

• 55/x/19/Fin

**Agreement between the USSR and Fin-
land concerning air communications**

Signed Oct. 19, 1955, in Moscow.
Entered into force on signature.
Supplemented by a technical and com-
mercial agreement of Dec. 10, 1955.
Source: *SS, 1955, No. 32 (Finnish, R).
Reference: *Izv.*, Oct. 20, 1955.

• 55/x/31/Yemen

**Treaty of friendship between the USSR
and Yemen**

Signed Oct. 31, 1955, in Cairo.
Ratified by the USSR Feb. 25, 1956; by
Yemen Mar. 17, 1956. Entered into force
Mar. 30, 1956, on exchange of acts of
ratification in Cairo. Duration 5 years;

if not denounced 6 months before expira-
tion, extended for 5 years.
Renews the treaty of friendship of Nov.
1, 1928. Incorporates a Soviet statement
recognizing the "full and absolute inde-
pendence" of Yemen and the "full inde-
pendence and lawful sovereignty" of the
King of Yemen.
Sources: *VVS*, 1956, No. 8, Art. 184.
   MZh, 1955, No. 12, pp. 142–43.
   UNTS, 240, pp. 317–27 (R, A, E, F).
Reference: *Izv.*, Nov. 1, 1955.

• 55/xi/ /GDR

**Protocol between the USSR and the Ger-
man Democratic Republic concerning
scientific and technical collaboration**

Signed during Nov. 1955.
Reference: *VT*, 1956, No. 7, p. 9.

• 55/xi/1/Yug

**Agreement between the USSR and Yugo-
slavia concerning air communications
and reciprocal services**

Signed Nov. 1, 1955, in Belgrade.
Based on the agreement of Sept. 3, 1955.
Reference: *Pravda*, Nov. 3, 1955.

• 55/xi/3/Burma

Joint statement by the USSR and Burma

Signed Nov. 3, 1955, in Moscow.
Concerns international relations as well
as relations between the 2 States.
Sources: *Pr., Izv.*, Nov. 4, 1955.
   Deklaratsii, pp. 54–57.
   NT, 1955, No. 46, supplement.
   DIA, 1955, pp. 482–85.

• 55/xi/9/Austria

**Agreement between the USSR and Aus-
tria concerning air communications, with
annex**

Signed Nov. 9, 1955, in Vienna.
Entered into force on signature. Valid
until 12 months after denunciation.
Sources: *BGBl, 1956, No. 8.
   UNTS, 255, pp. 247–73 (R, G, E, F).
Reference: *Pravda*, Nov. 10, 1955.

• 55/xi/12/Yug

**Exchange of notes between the USSR
and Yugoslavia constituting an agreement concerning the sale and delivery**

of Soviet books and other cultural products to Yugoslavia

Sent Nov. 12, 1955, in Belgrade.
Ratified by Yugoslavia July 26, 1956. May be denounced with 2 months' notice. Provides for import between Oct. 1955 and July 1956 of materials to a value of 200 thousand rubles.
Source: *MU*, 1957, No. 66, pp. 44–57 (SC, R).

● 55/xi/14/Yug

Trade protocol between the USSR and Yugoslavia, with annex

Signed Nov. 14, 1955, in Belgrade, by the mixed Soviet-Yugoslav trade commission established under the commercial agreement of Jan. 5, 1955 (55/i/5/Yug/a). Modifies the lists established by the exchanges of notes of July 30 and Sept. 23, 1955. Annex lists measures to be taken to ensure delivery of goods.
Source: *MU*, 1957, No. 63, pp. 52–53 (SC, R).

● 55/xi/15/Norway/a

Joint communiqué by the USSR and Norway concerning diplomatic negotiations

Initialed Nov. 15, 1955, in Moscow, at the end of negotiations which began Nov. 10, 1955.
Mentions discussion of (1) measures to increase scientific and technical collaboration; (2) establishment of a mixed commission of experts to study use of the water resources of the Paatso-Joki (see 57/vi/7/Norway) ; (3) negotiations to be undertaken in the near future for an agreement on shipwreck salvage service in the Barents Sea; and (4) encouragement of cultural collaboration. Norway agrees not to support any aggressive policy and not to permit the use of Norwegian territory for foreign military bases, unless attacked or threatened with attack.
Sources: *Izv.*, Nov. 16, 1955.
Deklaratsii, 1957, pp. 220–23.
VT, 1955, No. 11, supplement.

● 55/xi/15/Norway/b

Trade protocol for the period 1956–1958 between the USSR and Norway

Signed Nov. 15, 1955, in Moscow.
Soviet grain, oil products, manganese and chrome ores, and apatite concentrate, in exchange for Norwegian whale oil, salt herring, and aluminum.
Reference: *VT*, 1955, No. 11, supplement, p. 2.

● 55/xi/15/Norway/c

Supplementary trade protocol for 1956 between the USSR and Norway

Signed Nov. 15, 1955, in Moscow.
Soviet grain, oil products, manganese and chrome ore, apatite concentrate, cotton, asbestos, rosin, naphthalene, automobiles, etc., in exchange for Norwegian whale oil, staple fiber, salt and frozen herring, aluminum, fish products, etc. Total trade volume to reach 140 million rubles.
Reference: *VT*, 1955, No. 11, supplement, p. 2.

● 55/xi/16/Pl

Final communiqué of the Foreign Ministers of the USSR, the United Kingdom, the United States of America, and France

Issued Nov. 16, 1955, at the end of a conference in Geneva which began Oct. 27, 1955.
The conference was called to carry out the directive issued by the 4 Heads of Government after their conference in Geneva in July 1955; see 55/vii/23/Pl. Communiqué mentions "frank and comprehensive discussion" of (1) European security and Germany, (2) disarmament, and (3) development of contacts between East and West. No agreement reached, except to report the results of the discussion to the Heads of Government and to recommend that future discussions of the Foreign Ministers should be settled through diplomatic channels.
On the same day the 3 Foreign Ministers of the Western Powers issued a declaration stating, "The Soviet Foreign Minister, despite the Directive of the Heads of Government, made it plain that the Soviet Government refused to agree to the reunification of Germany since that would lead to the liquidation of the East German regime. He made counter proposals which would have involved the continued division of Germany as well as the eventual dissolution of the Western security system. It is for this reason that the negotiations have failed." (Text, *DSB*, 33, 1955, p. 886.)

Sources: *DSB,* 33, 1955, p. 886.
    DIA, 1955, p. 88.

• 55/xi/16/MPR

Trade protocol for 1956 between the USSR and the Mongolian People's Republic

Signed Nov. 16, 1955, in Moscow.
Soviet tractors, agricultural machinery and tools, trucks, oil products, consumption goods, etc., in exchange for Mongolian cattle, animal fats, wool, camel's hair, and other animal products.
References: *Izv.,* Nov. 17, 1955.
    VT, 1956, No. 1, p. 28.

• 55/xi/16/Syria

Trade and payments agreement between the USSR and Syria, with two annexes

Signed Nov. 16, 1955, in Damascus.
Ratified by Syria Jan. 21, 1956; by the USSR Jan. 25, 1956. Entered into force Apr. 3, 1956, on exchange of acts of ratification in Damascus. Duration 1 year; if not denounced 3 months before expiration, extended from year to year.
Annexes list goods to be exchanged: Soviet machinery and industrial equipment, automobiles and trucks, tractors and agricultural machinery, metallurgical products, chemical goods, drugs, timber, paper, etc., in exchange for Syrian cotton, seeds, vegetable oil, fats, dried fruits, beans, tobacco, wool, hides, natural and artificial silk, etc.
Sources: *VVS,* 1956, No. 8, Art. 185.
    JR, 1956, No. 6, pp. 977–84.
    UNTS, 259, pp. 71–99 (R, A, E, F).
References: *Izv.,* Nov. 18, 1955.
    VT, 1957, No. 3, p. 3.

• 55/xi/19/Syria. See Appendix 5.

• 55/xi/26/Bul

Agreement between the USSR and Bulgaria concerning transfer to Bulgaria of Soviet shares in the Soviet-Bulgarian joint-stock mining company "Gorubso"

Signed Nov. 26, 1955, in Sofia.
To be paid for over a period of years. For establishment of a Soviet-Bulgarian joint-stock mining company, see entry under Mar. 23, 1946.
References: *Izv.,* Nov. 30, 1955.
    VT, 1956, No. 1, p. 28.

• 55/xi/27/GDR

Final protocol between the USSR and the German Democratic Republic concerning transfer to the GDR of pictures from the Dresden Gallery, with three annexes

Signed Nov. 27, 1955, in Berlin.
Source: *Dokumente DDR,* 4, p. 51 (omits annexes).

• 55/xi/29/CPR. See Appendix 5.

• 55/xi/30/KPDR

Convention between the USSR and the Korean People's Democratic Republic concerning quarantine and combating parasites and diseases of agricultural plants, with two annexes

Signed Nov. 30, 1955, in Pyongyang.
Ratified by the USSR Dec. 31, 1955; by the KPDR Jan. 4, 1956. Entered into force Jan. 27, 1956, on exchange of acts of ratification in Moscow. Duration 5 years; if not denounced 1 year before expiration, extended for 5-year periods.
Provides for holding conferences annually, meeting alternately in the USSR and the KPDR. Annexes list parasites and diseases.
Source: *VVS,* 1956, No. 3, Art. 66.
Reference: *Ibid.,* No. 2, Art. 43.

• 55/xii/ /CPR

Protocol concerning the third meeting of the USSR–Chinese People's Republic commission for scientific and technical collaboration

Signed during Dec. 1955, in Moscow.
References: *Pravda,* Jan. 5, 1956.
    SCMP, No. 1203, Jan. 9, 1956, p. 24.

• 55/xii/ /GDR

Agreement between the USSR and the German Democratic Republic concerning construction of ships and floating equipment for the USSR

Signed during Dec. 1955.
The USSR to supply materials for construction of the ships, which are to be delivered during 1957–1960.
Reference: *VT,* 1956, No. 7, p. 9.

• 55/xii/2/Fin

Trade protocol for 1956 between the USSR and Finland

Signed Dec. 2, 1955, in Moscow.
Provides for total trade of over 1 billion rubles. Soviet oil products, coal, rolled ferrous metal, fertilizer, grain, cotton, automobiles, tractors and agricultural machinery, industrial equipment, tobacco, asbestos, chemicals, etc., in exchange for Finnish ships, including ice-breakers, motor vessels, tankers, marine tugs, and trawlers, and power equipment, cranes, equipment for wood-pulping, armatures, copper wire, cable products, lumber, wood-pulp, cellulose, paper, cartons, etc.
References: *Izv.*, Dec. 3, 1955.
  VT, 1956, No. 1, pp. 18, 29.

● 55/xii/3/GDR

Trade protocol for 1956 between the USSR and the German Democratic Republic

Signed Dec. 3, 1955, in Moscow.
Soviet grains and foodstuffs, cotton, ferrous and nonferrous metals, coal and coke, iron, chrome, and manganese ores, lumber, automobiles, etc., in exchange for GDR equipment for metallurgy, lifting, and moving, river and naval vessels, railroad rolling stock, etc.
References: *Pr.*, *Izv.*, Dec. 4, 1955.
  VT, 1956, No. 1, p. 28.

● 55/xii/3/Iceland

Agreement between the USSR and Iceland concerning transformation of diplomatic missions into embassies

Announced Dec. 3, 1955.
Reference: *Pravda*, Dec. 3, 1955.

● 55/xii/6/Alb

Agreement between the USSR and Albania concerning air communications, with protocol

Signed Dec. 6, 1955, in Tirana.
Reference: *Izv.*, Dec. 8, 1955.

● 55/xii/6/Burma/a

Joint statement by the USSR and Burma concerning political relations

Signed Dec. 6, 1955, in Burma.
Covers not only relations between the 2 States but also international relations.
Sources: *Izv.*, Dec. 7, 1955.
  Deklaratsii, 1957, pp. 57–60.
  Int. aff., 1956, No. 1, pp. 256–57.
  Visit of friendship, pp. 308–11.

NT, 1955, No. 51, supplement, pp. 6–7.

● 55/xii/6/Austria. See Appendix 5.

● 55/xii/6/Burma/b

Statement on economic relations between the USSR and Burma

Probably drafted Dec. 6, 1955, in Burma; published Dec. 8, 1955.
Covers discussions concerning a program of agricultural development, construction of major irrigation works, and building of several industrial enterprises in Burma. The USSR agrees to accept rice in payment for materials and services required for fulfillment of the projects. The USSR to build and equip as a gift to the people of Burma a technical college in Rangoon; in return Burma to give the USSR a corresponding quantity of rice and other goods.
Sources: *Pravda*, Dec. 8. 1955.
  Int. aff., 1956, No. 1, pp. 257–58.
  NT, 1955, No. 51, supplement, p. 8.

● 55/xii/7/KPDR

Agreement between the USSR and the Korean People's Democratic Republic concerning air communications

Signed Dec. 7, 1955, in Pyongyang.
Supplemented by a technical agreement of Dec. 9, 1955 (next document).
Reference: *Izv.*, Dec. 8, 1955.

● 55/xii/9/KPDR

Agreement between the USSR and the Korean People's Democratic Republic concerning air transportation and service

Signed Dec. 9, 1955, in Pyongyang.
Reference: *Pravda*, Dec. 10, 1955.

● 55/xii/9/Sweden

Trade protocol for 1956 between the USSR and Sweden

Signed Dec. 9, 1955, in Moscow.
Soviet oil products, coal, ferromanganese, manganese, and chrome ores, asbestos, cotton, etc., in exchange for Swedish industrial equipment, ships, high-grade steel, viscous cellulose, staple fiber, etc.
References: *Izv.*, Dec. 10, 1956.
  VT, 1956, No. 1, pp. 17–18, 30.

● 55/xii/10/Fin

Agreement between the USSR and Fin-

land concerning technical and commercial service on air communications between Moscow and Helsinki

Signed Dec. 10, 1955, in Helsinki.
Supplements the agreement of Oct. 19, 1955, concerning air communications.
Reference: *Pravda*, Dec. 12, 1955.

● 55/xii/11/Pl

Conference of the Council for Mutual Economic Aid

Held Dec. 7–11, 1955, in Budapest, with representatives of Albania, Bulgaria, Czechoslovakia, the German Democratic Republic, Hungary, Poland, Romania, and the USSR.
Reference: *Dokumente DDR*, 3, pp. 151–52.

● 55/xii/13/India/a

Joint statement by the USSR and India concerning political relations

Signed Dec. 13, 1955, in New Delhi.
Reaffirms adherence of signatories to the Five Principles (see 55/vi/22/India), and covers other aspects of international relations.
Sources: *Izv.*, Dec. 14, 1955.
  Visit of friendship, pp. 299–305.
  Deklaratsii, 1956, pp. 160–66.
  Int. aff., 1956, No. 1, pp. 252–54.
  NT, 1955, No. 51, supplement, pp. 2–4.

● 55/xii/13/India/b

Joint communiqué by the USSR and India concerning economic relations

Issued Dec. 13, 1955, in New Delhi.
Mentions the following agreements: (1) The USSR to supply and India to purchase 1 million tons of rolled ferrous metal over 3 years, beginning in 1956; delivery dates and conditions to be determined subsequently. (2) India to purchase oil-extraction, ore-mining, and other equipment and goods; delivery dates and conditions to be determined subsequently. (3) The USSR to increase its purchases in India of raw materials and manufactured goods. (4) The 2 States to grant maximum possible facilities for importing and exporting goods. (5) Regular shipping services between the USSR and India to be established. (6) Agreements to be concluded carrying out these provisions.
Sources: *Pravda*, Dec. 14, 1955.

Deklaratsii, 1957, pp. 166–67.
Int. aff., 1956, No. 1, pp. 255–56.
NT, 1955, No. 51, supplement, p. 5.

● 55/xii/13/Rom

Agreement between the USSR and Romania concerning sale to Romania of Soviet shares in the Soviet-Romanian joint-stock oil company "Sovrompetrol"

Signed Dec. 13, 1955, in Bucharest.
To be paid for by Romania over a period of years. For the 1945 agreement establishing the company, see 45/vii/19/Rom.
References: *Izv.*, Dec. 15, 1955.
  VT, 1956, No. 1, p. 30.

● 55/xii/14/Cz

Trade protocol for 1956 between the USSR and Czechoslovakia

Signed Dec. 14, 1955, in Prague.
Soviet grain, cotton, wool, nonferrous metals, pig iron, ferrous and manganese ores, oil, mineral fertilizer, agricultural machinery, tractors, ball bearings, industrial equipment, etc., in exchange for Czech ships, diesel electrostations, electric trains, metal-working lathes, metallurgical and other equipment, sugar, etc.
References: *Izv.*, Dec. 15, 1955.
  VT, 1956, No. 1, p. 29.

● 55/xii/15/Pl. See Appendix 5.

● 55/xii/16/US

Exchange of notes between the USSR and the United States of America constituting an agreement concerning distribution within the USSR of *Amerika*, an illustrated Russian-language magazine

Sent Sept. 9 and Dec. 16, 1955, in Moscow.
Provides for distribution of a minimum of 50,000 copies of *Amerika*, and for reciprocal publication of a Soviet monthly magazine in English by the Soviet Embassy in the United States.
Source: *DSB*, 34, 1956, pp. 18–19.

● 55/xii/18/Af/a

Protocol between the USSR and Afghanistan extending the treaty of neutrality and nonaggression of June 24, 1931

Signed Dec. 18, 1955, in Kabul.
Ratified by the USSR Dec. 31, 1955; by Afghanistan June 26, 1956. Entered into

force July 25, 1956, on exchange of acts of ratification in Moscow. Extends the 1931 treaty for an additional 10 years; thereafter extended from year to year until denounced with 6 months' notice.
Sources: *VVS*, 1956, No. 16, Art. 349.
  NT, 1956, No. 1, supplement, p. 30.
  Int. aff., 1956, No. 1, pp. 260–61.
  UNTS, 259, pp. 101–109 (R, Persian, E, F).
Reference: *Izv.*, Dec. 20, 1955.

• 55/xii/18/Af/b

Joint communiqué by the USSR and Afghanistan concerning economic relations
Issued Dec. 18, 1955, in Kabul.
The USSR states its willingness to provide a long-term credit of $100 million US for aid to Afghanistan in agriculture, construction of a hydroelectric station, irrigation installations, automobile repair shops, and reconstruction of Kabul airfield. Corresponding agreements to be concluded. For a loan agreement based on this pledge, see 56/i/28/Af.
Sources: *Izv.*, Dec. 20, 1955.
  Deklaratsii, 1957, pp. 43–44.
  NT, 1956, No. 1, p. 29.
  Int. aff., 1956, No. 1, pp. 259–60.

• 55/xii/18/Af/c

Joint statement by the USSR and Afghanistan concerning political relations
Signed Dec. 18, 1955, in Kabul.
Covers both relations between the 2 States and international relations.
Sources: *Izv.*, Dec. 20, 1955.
  Deklaratsii, 1957, pp. 41–43.
  NT, 1956, No. 1, supplement, pp. 28–29.
  Int. aff., 1956, No. 1, pp. 258–59.

• 55/xii/19/Yug

Agreement between the USSR and Yugoslavia concerning scientific and technical collaboration
Signed Dec. 19, 1955, in Belgrade.
Ratified by Yugoslavia Apr. 18, 1956. Entered into force on signature. Valid until Dec. 31, 1960; if not denounced 12 months before expiration, extended for 5-year periods.
Provides for establishment of a mixed commission to meet at least twice yearly, alternately in Moscow and Belgrade. Carries out a provision of the protocol of Sept. 1, 1955 (55/ix/1/Yug/b).

Source: *MU*, 1957, No. 24 (SC, R).
References: *Izv.*, Dec. 21, 1955.
  VT, 1956, No. 1, p. 29.
  Int. aff., 1956, No. 6, p. 23.

• 55/xii/23/GDR

Agreement between the USSR and the German Democratic Republic concerning delivery of ships and other naval equipment during the period 1957–1960
Signed Dec. 23, 1955, in Berlin.
Reference: *Dokumente DDR*, 3, p. 353.

• 55/xii/23/India

Agreement between the USSR and India concerning sale to India of twenty drill rigs
Signed Dec. 23, 1955, in New Delhi.
Value of the equipment more than 2 million rupees.
Reference: *Pravda*, Dec. 25, 1955.

• 55/xii/27/CPR

Trade protocol for 1956 between the USSR and the Chinese People's Republic
Signed Dec. 27, 1955, in Moscow.
Extends the commercial agreement of Apr. 19, 1950, through Dec. 31, 1956. Soviet metal-cutting machinery, mechanical hammers, presses, steam boilers, diesels, mine-hoisting machines, boring machines, oil products, ferrous metals, cables, etc., in exchange for CPR tungsten, molybdenum, tin, mercury, antimony, wool, raw silk, etc.
References: *Izv.*, Dec. 28, 1955.
  Int. aff., 1956, No. 1, p. 125.
  SDD, 14, p. 228.
  SCMP, No. 1200, Jan. 4, 1956, pp. 34–35.
Note: According to *Int. aff., loc. cit.*, the parties agreed during negotiations to extend transit shipments of goods through their countries and considered questions of their foreign trade transport in view of the opening of regular rail communications between the USSR and the CPR via the Mongolian People's Republic. It is not clear whether or not the transit agreement was incorporated in a formal document.

• 55/xii/28/Austria

Parcel post agreement between the USSR and Austria
Signed Dec. 28, 1955, in Vienna.

Entered into force on signature.
Source: *Post- und Telegraphenverordnungsblatt*, No. 3, 9/56.

● 55/xii/31/Mul

Convention for the establishment of an International Organization of Legislative Metrology

Signed Dec. 31, 1955.
Ratified by the USSR Nov. 5, 1956.
Reference: *VVS*, 1956, No. 23, Art. 505.

● 55/xii/31/Switz

Agreement between the USSR and Switzerland concerning transformation of the Soviet diplomatic mission in Berne into an embassy

Announced Dec. 31, 1955.
Reference: *Izv.*, Dec. 31, 1955.
Note: At approximately the same time the Swiss Government agreed to represent Soviet interests in Iraq (see *Izv.*, Mar. 18, 1956).

1956

● 56/ / /Pl

Protocol concerning three-way trade and payments between the USSR, Czechoslovakia, and Finland

Signed during 1956.
Accompanied by bilateral trade protocols between the 3 States (not listed separately). Trade volume to reach a value of 32 million rubles each.
Reference: *VT SSSR*, p. 87.

● 56/i/3/Rom

Agreement between the USSR and Romania concerning technical collaboration in the field of civil aviation

Signed Jan. 3, 1956, in Moscow.
References: *Izv.*, Jan. 4, 1956.
    NT, 1956, No. 2, p. 32.

● 56/i/4/Pl

Joint communiqué concerning opening of direct rail communications between the USSR, the Chinese People's Republic, and the Mongolian People's Republic

Published Jan. 4, 1956.
Marks completion of construction provided for in agreement of Sept. 15, 1952 (52/ix/15/Pl). Summarizes results of a conference held in Ulan Bator during Sept. and Oct. 1955 (see 55/x/17/Pl).
Source: *Izv.*, Jan. 4, 1956.

● 56/i/4/CPR

Agreement between the USSR and the Chinese People's Republic concerning technical collaboration in the field of civil aviation

Signed Jan. 4, 1956, in Peking.
References: *Izv.*, Jan. 5, 1956.
    NT, 1956, No. 3, p. 32.

● 56/i/5/CPR

Communiqué concerning the third meeting of the USSR–Chinese People's Republic commission for scientific and technical collaboration

Published Jan. 5, 1956; the meeting took place during Dec. 1955, in Moscow.
Source: *Izv.*, Jan. 5, 1956.

● 56/i/6/Yug

Trade protocol for 1956 between the USSR and Yugoslavia, with two annexes

Signed Jan. 6, 1956, in Belgrade.
Ratified by Yugoslavia June 5, 1956. Provides for trade to a total value of $70 million US. Supplemented by a protocol of June 6, 1956. Annexes list goods to be exchanged.
Source: *MU*, 1957, No. 63, pp. 59–61 (SC, R).
References: *Izv.*, Jan. 7, 1956.
    VT, 1956, No. 10, p. 4.
    Int. aff., 1956, No. 4, p. 134; *ibid.*, No. 6, p. 24.

● 56/i/7/Af. See Appendix 5.

● 56/i/11/Liberia

Exchange of notes between the USSR and Liberia concerning establishment of diplomatic relations

Sent Jan. 11, 1956, in Monrovia.
Included in a joint communiqué published

Jan. 20, 1956 (not listed separately).
Source: *Izv.*, Jan. 20, 1956.

● 56/i/12/Yug

Agreement between the USSR and Yugoslavia concerning collaboration in construction of industrial enterprises in Yugoslavia

Signed Jan. 12, 1956, in Belgrade.
Based on the protocol of Sept. 1, 1955 (55/ix/1/Yug/b). Supplemented by protocol of Aug. 2, 1956.
Provides for Soviet aid in construction of a nitrogen fertilizer plant with an annual capacity of 100,000 tons of ammonia, a superphosphate plant with an annual capacity of 250,000 tons of superphosphate and 120 tons of sulphuric acid, a thermal hydroelectric station with a capacity of 100,000 kilowatts, and reconstruction of 3 mines. A credit to be granted, repayable in 10 years at 2 per cent.
In Feb. 1957 Yugoslavia declared unacceptable a Soviet proposal to postpone for 5 years use of the credits under this agreement and the agreement of Aug. 1, 1956 (56/viii/1/Pl). In Aug. 1957 a renewal of the agreement was negotiated, but in May 1958, the Soviet Government again proposed deferring use of the credit under this agreement to 1962–1969 (see *Problems of Communism*, 7, 1958, No. 4, p. 35; *Pravda, Izv.*, July 1, 1958; *CDSP*, 10, 1958, No. 26, pp. 7–10).
References: *Izv.*, Jan. 14, 1956.
VT, 1956, No. 10, p. 5.
Int. aff., 1956, No. 4, p. 134; *ibid.*, No. 6, p. 24.

● 56/i/14/Bul

Trade protocol for 1956 between the USSR and Bulgaria

Signed Jan. 14, 1956, in Moscow.
Soviet industrial equipment, tractors, combines, and other agricultural machinery, automobiles, pig iron, ferrous castings, paper, cotton, superphosphates, etc., in exchange for Bulgarian nonferrous metal ore concentrates, barges, tobacco, meat, canned vegetables, fresh and dried fruits, wine, furniture, etc.
References: *Izv.*, Jan. 15, 1956.
Int. aff., 1956, No. 4, p. 134.

● 56/i/19/GDR

Protocol between the USSR and the Ger-

man Democratic Republic concerning collaboration in the field of the chemical industry

Signed on or about Jan. 19, 1956, in Berlin.
Reference: *Izv.*, Jan. 20, 1956.

● 56/i/26/Fin

Final protocol between the USSR and Finland concerning transfer to Finland of the naval base and installations at Porkkala-Udd

Signed Jan. 26, 1956, in Helsinki.
Carries out an agreement of Sept. 19, 1955 (55/ix/19/Fin/a).
Reference: *Izv.*, Jan. 27, 1956.

● 56/i/26/KPDR

Trade protocol for 1956 between the USSR and the Korean People's Democratic Republic

Signed Jan. 26, 1956, in Moscow.
Soviet industrial equipment for construction of irrigation systems, automobiles, oil products, ferrous and nonferrous rolled metal, cable products, construction materials, mineral fertilizers, etc., in exchange for KPDR lead, nonferrous metal ores and concentrates, ferrous alloys, products of the chemical industry, fruits, furs, etc.
References: *Pr., Izv.*, Jan. 27, 1956.
VT, 1956, No. 3, p. 14.

Jan. 27, 1956

The USSR rejoins the World Health Organization.
See 46/vii/22/Mul/b.

● 56/i/28/Af/a

Agreement between the USSR and Afghanistan concerning credit and technical aid to Afghanistan

Signed Jan. 28, 1956, in Kabul.
Provides for a Soviet loan of $100 million US, to be repaid in goods over 22 years at 2 per cent, starting 8 years after utilization. To be used in development of agriculture and construction of irrigation, power, and transportation facilities.
References: *Izv.*, Feb. 1, 1956 (joint communiqué).

Pr., Feb. 28, 1956.
Int. aff., 1956, No. 11, p. 131.
CDSP, 8, 1956, No. 9, p. 35.

● 56/i/28/Af/b

Joint communiqué by the USSR and Afghanistan concerning economic relations

Issued Jan. 28, 1956.
Source: *Izv.*, Feb. 1, 1956.

● 56/i/28/Pl/a

Declaration concerning international security by the States participating in the Warsaw Treaty of May 14, 1955, of friendship, cooperation, and mutual assistance

Signed Jan. 28, 1956, in Prague, by the USSR, Albania, Bulgaria, Czechoslovakia, the German Democratic Republic, Hungary, Poland, and Romania.
Sources: *Izv.*, Jan. 29, 1956.
Deklaratsii, 1957, pp. 317–24.
NT, 1956, No. 6, pp. 33–36.

● 56/i/28/Pl/b

Final protocol of the Political Consultative Committee established by the Warsaw Treaty of May 14, 1955

Signed Jan. 28, 1956, in Prague.
Summarizes decisions reached by the Committee in its meeting on Jan. 27 and 28, 1955. Statute on unified military command approved. Proposal by the German Democratic Republic to include GDR armed forces in the unified command approved. Committee to meet as necessary, but not less than twice yearly. Two permanent organs under the Committee established in Moscow: (1) a permanent commission to handle recommendations in the field of foreign policy, and (2) a unified secretariat with representatives of all member States.
Source: *Izv.*, Jan. 29, 1956.

● 56/i/28/Yug

Agreement between the USSR and Yugoslavia concerning collaboration in regard to the development of research in the field of nuclear physics and the use of atomic energy for peaceful purposes

Signed Jan. 28, 1956, in Belgrade.
Supplemented by a protocol of Feb. 9, 1957. For a communiqué on negotiations

in Moscow at which the agreement was drafted, see *Izv.*, Jan. 4, 1956.
Source: *Soglasheniia*, 1958, pp. 22–24.
References: *Izv.*, Jan. 29, 1956.
Int. aff., 1956, No. 6, p. 24.

● 56/ii/2/Yug/a

Agreement between the USSR and Yugoslavia concerning a loan to Yugoslavia

Signed Feb. 2, 1956, in Moscow.
Ratified by Yugoslavia Mar. 8, 1956; by the USSR Mar. 29, 1956. Entered into force Apr. 17, 1956, on exchange of acts of ratification in Belgrade.
Provides for a Soviet loan of $30 million US, to be used during 1956–1958 and repaid at 2 per cent within 10 years. Based on the protocol of Sept. 1, 1955 (55/ix/1/Yug/b).
Sources: *VVS*, 1956, No. 9, Art. 192.
MU, 1956, No. 94 (SC, R).
UNTS, 259, pp. 111–23 (R, SC, E, F).
References: *Izv.*, Feb. 3, 1956.
VT, 1956, No. 10, p. 5.

● 56/ii/2/Yug/b

Agreement between the USSR and Yugoslavia concerning a trade credit to Yugoslavia

Signed Feb. 2, 1956, in Moscow.
Ratified by Yugoslavia Mar. 26, 1956; by the USSR Mar. 29, 1956. Entered into force Apr. 17, 1956, on exchange of acts of ratification in Belgrade.
Provides for a Soviet credit of $54 million US, for goods to be supplied during 1956–1958. Repayment to be at 2 per cent over 10 years, starting Jan. 1, 1959. Based on the protocol of Sept. 1, 1955.
Source: *MU*, 1957, No. 65, pp. 2–4 (SC, R).
Reference: *Izv.*, Feb. 3, 1956.

● 56/ii/3/Bul

Economic agreement for the period 1956–1959 between the USSR and Bulgaria

Signed Feb. 3, 1956, in Moscow.
Provides for a Soviet credit of 70 million rubles, to be repaid in Bulgarian goods over 10 years at 2 per cent. The USSR to provide tractors, combines, and other agricultural machinery and pedigreed cattle to a value of 300 million rubles, and technical aid.
Reference: *Izv.*, Feb. 4, 1956.

- 56/ii/3/H

Trade protocol for 1956 between the USSR and Hungary

Signed Feb. 3, 1956, in Budapest.
Soviet cotton, coke, ferrous ores and alloys, lumber, fertilizer, industrial equipment, agricultural machinery, automobiles, ball bearings, etc., in exchange for Hungarian sea and river vessels, cranes, railroad rolling stock, industrial equipment, cloth, etc.
Reference: *Izv.*, Feb. 4, 1956.

- 56/ii/7/Pol

Protocol between the USSR and Poland concerning expansion of telegraph and telephone service, radio broadcasting, and television

Signed Feb. 7, 1956, in Moscow.
Reference: *Izv.*, Feb. 8, 1956.

Feb. 7, 1956. Changes in the parcel post agreement of Oct. 1, 1947, between the USSR and Poland

See 47/x/1/Pol.

- 56/ii/8/Pol

Trade protocol for 1956 between the USSR and Poland

Signed Feb. 8, 1956, in Moscow.
Soviet iron, manganese, and chrome ores, cotton, oil and oil products, industrial equipment, ship construction plates, nonferrous metals, ferrous alloys, fertilizer, chemicals, etc., in exchange for Polish transport and commercial maritime vessels, railroad rolling stock, coal, zinc, sugar, wool and linen cloth, etc.
References: *Izv.*, Feb. 9, 1956.
    Int. aff., 1956, No. 4, p. 134.

- 56/ii/11/Alb

Trade agreement for 1956 between the USSR and Albania

Signed Feb. 11, 1956, in Moscow.
Soviet nonferrous metals, chemicals and dyes, medicines, automobiles, spare parts, etc., in exchange for Albanian oil, bitumen, copper, plywood, tobacco, etc.
Reference: *Izv.*, Feb. 12, 1956.

- 56/ii/11/Rom

Trade protocol for 1956 between the USSR and Romania

Signed Feb. 11, 1956, in Moscow.
Soviet cotton, rolled ferrous metals, iron ore, coke, nonferrous metals, industrial equipment, agricultural machinery, automobiles, etc., in exchange for Romanian oil products, fishing vessels, barges, furniture, meat, etc.
Reference: *Izv.*, Feb. 12, 1956.

Feb. 11, 1956. Agreement between the USSR and Egypt concerning collaboration in the field of atomic energy

See 56/vii/12/Egypt.

- 56/ii/24/Pl

Protocol concerning regulation of the water regime of the Pasvik-El'v river and Lake Inari, with regulations

Signed Feb. 24, 1956, in Oslo, by the USSR, Finland, and Norway.
Entered into force on signature.
Modifies the rules of Apr. 24, 1947 (47/iv/24/Fin/b), and the protocol of Apr. 29, 1954 (54/iv/29/Fin/b).
Source: *UNTS*, 243, pp. 147–67 (R, Finnish, N, E, F).
Reference: *Izv.*, Feb. 25, 1956.

- 56/ii/29/Canada/a

Commercial agreement between the USSR and Canada

Signed Feb. 29, 1956, in Ottawa.
Ratified by the USSR Apr. 28, 1956; by Canada May 9, 1956. Entered into force provisionally on signature, definitively May 26, 1956, on exchange of acts of ratification in Moscow. Duration 3 years; may be prolonged for 3 years by agreement 3 months before expiration. Supplemented by 2 exchanges of notes (next 2 items).
Sources: *VT*, 1956, No. 4, pp. 26–27.
    VVS, 1956, No. 13, Art. 278.
    UNTS, 252, pp. 165–73 (R, E), 178–81 (F).
Reference: *Izv.*, Mar. 2, 1956.

- 56/ii/29/Canada/b

Exchange of notes between the USSR and Canada concerning reservation by Canada of the right to fix values of imported goods for ordinary and special duty

Sent Feb. 29, 1956, in Ottawa.

Supplements the commercial agreement of the same date.
Source: *UNTS*, 252, pp. 174–76 (R, E), 181–82 (F).

● 56/ii/29/Canada/c

Exchange of notes between the USSR and Canada concerning Soviet purchases of wheat in Canada

Sent Feb. 29, 1956, in Ottawa.
Provides for Soviet purchases during the first 3 years of validity of the commercial agreement of the same date of a total of between 1.2 and 1.5 million metric tons of wheat.
Source: *UNTS*, 252, pp. 176–77 (R, E), 183 (F).

● 56/ii/29/KPDR

Communiqué concerning the first meeting of the USSR–Korean People's Democratic Republic commission for scientific and technical collaboration

Issued Feb. 29, 1956; the meeting took place a few days earlier, in Moscow.
Source: *Izv.*, Feb. 29, 1956.

● 56/iii/1/Af

Agreement between the USSR and Afghanistan concerning technical aid to Afghanistan

Signed Mar. 1, 1956, in Kabul.
The USSR to aid in construction of 2 hydroelectric stations, 3 automobile repair shops, a road, physical and chemical laboratories, irrigation systems, nitrogen plants, and airports, under an earlier credit of $100 million.
References: *Izv.*, Mar. 4, 1956.
VT, 1957, No. 2, p. 8.

● 56/iii/3/Fin

Communiqué concerning the first meeting of the USSR-Finland commission for scientific and technical collaboration

Published Mar. 3, 1956; the meeting took place Feb. 17–25, 1956, in Moscow.
Source: *Izv.*, Mar. 3, 1956.

● 56/iii/3/Yug

Agreement between the USSR and Yugoslavia concerning collaboration in the field of steamship service on the Danube

Signed Mar. 3, 1956, in Belgrade.

Covers service of vessels, towing, aid in sinkings, and other commercial and technical matters.
Reference: *Izv.*, Mar. 4, 1956.

● 56/iii/6/Denmark/a

Joint communiqué by the USSR and Denmark concerning political and other relations

Issued Mar. 6, 1956, in Moscow.
Covers the following points among others: (1) trade talks to be held in Copenhagen in the near future for conclusion of a trade protocol; (2) an agreement signed on saving lives in the Baltic Sea (see next document); (3) cultural ties in the fields of science, art, and education to be expanded; (4) students to be exchanged; (5) tourism to be encouraged; (6) negotiations to be held in Copenhagen in the near future to settle claims for damages resulting from the incorporation of the Baltic States into the USSR; and (7) agreement reached on desirability of exchanging parliamentary delegations.
Sources: *Izv.*, Mar. 7, 1956.
Deklaratsii, 1957, pp. 150–53.

● 56/iii/6/Denmark/b

Agreement between the USSR and Denmark concerning saving human lives in the Baltic Sea

Signed Mar. 6, 1956, in Moscow.
Entered into force Oct. 1, 1956. In accordance with Art. 3, a conference of experts was held in Copenhagen from June 7 to 14, 1956, at which a supplementary agreement was signed (56/vi/14/Denmark).
Source: **Lovtidende C, Danmarks Traktater*, 1956, p. 483.
Reference: *Izv.*, Mar. 7, 1956.

● 56/iii/8/Yemen

Trade agreement between the USSR and Yemen

Signed Mar. 8, 1956, in Cairo.
Soviet industrial and agricultural machinery, construction materials, oil, foodstuffs, in exchange for Yemenite coffee, dried fruit, hides, etc.
References: *Izv.*, Mar. 10, 1956 (joint communiqué).
VT, 1956, No. 3, p. 4.
Int. aff., 1956, No. 4, p. 135.

● 56/iii/9/Yug/a and /b

Agreements between the USSR and Yugoslavia concerning insurance and reinsurance

Signed during negotiations held Mar. 5–9, 1956, in Moscow, by the USSR Administration of Foreign Insurance (Ingosstrakh) and the Yugoslav State Insurance Organization (DOZ).
Reference: *Izv.*, Mar. 10, 1956 (communiqué).

● 56/iii/17/Sudan

Communiqué concerning exchange of diplomatic missions at the level of embassies between the USSR and the Sudan

Published Mar. 17, 1956.
For a telegram of Jan. 3, 1956, from the USSR extending recognition to the Sudan, see *Izv.*, Jan. 4, 1956.
Source: *Izv.*, Mar. 17, 1956.

● 56/iii/24/Af

Agreement between the USSR and Afghanistan concerning establishment of regular air communications

Signed Mar. 24, 1956, in Kabul.
Ratified by the USSR July 2, 1956; by Afghanistan Aug. 13, 1956. Entered into force Aug. 25, 1956, on exchange of acts of ratification in Moscow. Valid until 6 months after denunciation; notification of intention to denounce may be withdrawn, leaving the agreement in force.
Source: *VVS*, 1956, No. 18, Art. 390.
Reference: *Izv.*, Mar. 27, 1956.

● 56/iii/26/Pl

Agreement concerning establishment of an Institute for Nuclear Research

Signed Mar. 26, 1956, by the USSR, Albania, Bulgaria, the Chinese People's Republic, Czechoslovakia, the German Democratic Republic, Hungary, the Korean People's Democratic Republic, the Mongolian People's Republic, Poland, and Romania.
Work of the institute to be based on a statute, a draft of which is to be prepared for ratification by member States. The founding conference issued an invitation to the Democratic Republic of Vietnam to participate in the work of the institute; the DRV joined as of Sept. 20, 1956 (*UNTS*, 274, p. 377).

Entered into force on signature.
Sources: *Izv.*, July 12, 1956.
    UNTS, 259, pp. 125–43 (R, E, F).
Reference: *Izv.*, Mar. 27, 1956.
See further Appendix 5.

● 56/iii/31/France

Trade protocol for 1956 between the USSR and France

Signed Mar. 31, 1956, in Moscow.
Soviet anthracite, coal pitch, oil and oil products, timber, chrome and manganese ores, cotton, furs, tinned crab, etc., in exchange for French rolled ferrous metals, cork, textile raw materials, chemicals, cocoa beans, citrus fruits, etc. France to deliver dry-cargo vessels and cranes.
Source: **MOCI*, No. 1783, p. 1228.
References: *Izv.*, Apr. 1, 1956.
    Int. aff., 1956, No. 4, p. 135.

● 56/iii/31/Denmark

Agreement between the USSR and Denmark concerning air communications between Moscow and Copenhagen, with two annexes and an exchange of notes

Signed Mar. 31, 1956, in Moscow.
Entered into force on signature. Valid until 12 months after denunciation.
Source: **Lovtidende C, Danmarks Traktater*, 1956, p. 277.
UNTS, 259, pp. 169–203 (R, D, E, F).
Reference: *Izv.*, Apr. 1, 1956.

● 56/iii/31/Norway

Agreement between the USSR and Norway concerning air communications, with two annexes and an exchange of notes

Signed Mar. 31, 1956, in Moscow.
Entered into force on signature. Valid until 12 months after denunciation.
Source: *UNTS*, 259, pp. 205–37 (R, N, E, F).
Reference: *Izv.*, Apr. 1, 1956.

● 56/iii/31/Sweden

Agreement between the USSR and Sweden concerning air communications, with two annexes and two exchanges of notes

Signed Mar. 31, 1956, in Moscow.
Entered into force on signature. Valid until 12 months after denunciation. Supersedes the agreement of Oct. 25, 1946 (46/x/25/Sweden/a), with the protocol of Jan. 23, 1954.

Source: *UNTS*, 259, pp. 239–77 (R, Sw., E, F).
Reference: *Izv.*, Apr. 1, 1956.

• 56/iv/1/Burma/a

Joint declaration by the USSR and Burma

Signed Apr. 1, 1956, in Rangoon.
Provides for a gift by the USSR to Burma of a hospital, theater, and cultural and sport complex. In return, Burma to give the USSR a corresponding quantity of rice.
Sources: *Izv.*, Apr. 3, 1956.
  Deklaratsii, 1957, p. 61.

• 56/iv/1/Burma/b

Supplementary trade agreement between the USSR and Burma

Signed Apr. 1, 1956, in Rangoon.
Extends the commercial agreement of July 1, 1955 (55/vii/1/Burma/a) to 5 years.
References: *Izv.*, Apr. 3, 1956 (joint communiqué).
  VT, 1957, No. 3, p. 8.
  Int. aff., 1956, No. 7, p. 135.

• 56/iv/1/Burma/c

Long-term trade protocol between the USSR and Burma, with related documents

Signed Apr. 1, 1956, in Rangoon.
Provides for exchange of 400,000 tons of Burmese rice annually for 4 years for Soviet equipment, machinery, and technical aid.
Related documents define procedure for payments.
Reference: *Izv.*, Apr. 3, 1956.

• 56/iv/3/Sweden

Joint communiqué by the USSR and Sweden concerning political negotiations

Issued Apr. 3, 1956, in Moscow.
Mentions the following points of discussion, among others: (1) both States interested in an increase in trade; (2) negotiations to be undertaken for settlement of outstanding claims related to the incorporation of the Baltic States into the USSR; (3) measures to be taken to increase contacts in the fields of culture,

science, and education; (4) the USSR promises to provide available information on the fate of Swedish diplomat Raoul Wallenberg, who disappeared in Budapest at the end of the war; (5) each State to permit citizens of the other, with their families, to return to their own country if they wish to do so; (6) the USSR recognizes and respects the policy of Sweden of not entering into alliances in peacetime.
Sources: *Izv.*, Apr. 4, 1956.
  Deklaratsii, 1957, pp. 293–96.

• 56/iv/4/1951

Convention concerning equal remuneration for men and women workers for work of equal value (International Labour Organisation Convention No. 100)

Adopted by the General Conference of the ILO June 29, 1951, in Geneva.
Ratified by the USSR Apr. 4, 1956; act of ratification deposited Apr. 30, 1956, with effect from Apr. 30, 1957. Ratified by the Ukrainian SSR July 9, 1956; act of ratification deposited Aug. 10, 1956, with effect from Aug. 10, 1957. Act of ratification of the Belorussian SSR deposited Aug. 21, 1956, with effect from Aug. 21, 1957.
Sources: *VVS*, 1956, No. 10, Art. 202.
  UNTS, 165, pp. 303–13 (E, F).
  ILO Code, 1951, I, Art. 233 (K)–(O).
Reference: *Izv.*, May 11, 1956.

• 56/iv/6/India

Agreement between the USSR and India concerning establishment of a regular shipping service

Signed Apr. 6, 1956, in New Delhi.
Entered into force on signature. Provides for connections between the Indian ports of Bombay and Calcutta and the Black Sea ports of Odessa and Novorossiisk.
References: *Pr., Izv.*, Apr. 7, 1956.
  CDSP, 8, 1956, No. 14, p. 33.

• 56/iv/7/CPR/a

Joint communiqué by the USSR and the Chinese People's Republic concerning economic negotiations

Issued Apr. 7, 1956, following negotiations which began Apr. 6, 1956, in Peking.
Summarizes provisions of 2 agreements signed on the same day (next 2 documents).

Sources: *Izv.*, Apr. 8, 1956.
  Deklaratsii, 1957, pp. 187–89.

● 56/iv/7/CPR/b

Agreement between the USSR and the Chinese People's Republic concerning aid by the USSR in construction of fifty-five industrial enterprises

Signed Apr. 7, 1956, in Peking.
Provides for Soviet aid in construction of metallurgical, m a c h i n e - building, and chemical plants, enterprises for electrical and radio technology, a synthetic liquid fuel plant, power stations, and scientific research institutions for the aeronautical industry. An atomic reactor with a capacity of more than 6,000 kilowatts to be built, and aid extended in geological exploration. Total value of aid to be about 2.5 billion rubles; to be repaid in trade.
References: Summarized in the joint communiqué (preceding document).
  Izv., Apr. 10, 1956.
  Int. aff., 1956, No. 7, p. 135.

● 56/iv/7/CPR/c

Agreement between the USSR and the Chinese People's Republic concerning collaboration in construction of a railroad from Lanchow to Aktogai on the Turksib Railroad

Signed Apr. 7, 1956, in Peking.
Based on the agreement marked by a joint communiqué of Oct. 12, 1954 (54/x/12/CPR/g).
References: Mentioned in the joint communiqué of the same date.
  Izv., Apr. 10, 1956.
  Int. aff., 1956, No. 7, p. 135.

● 56/iv/7/Rom

Agreement between the USSR and Romania concerning cultural collaboration

Signed Apr. 7, 1956, in Moscow.
Entered into force on signature. Duration 5 years; if not denounced 6 months before expiration, extended for 5 years.
Source: *UNTS*, 259, pp. 377–89 (R, Romanian, E, F).
Reference: *Izv.*, Apr. 8, 1956.

● 56/iv/8/MPR

Joint communiqué by the USSR and the Mongolian People's Republic concerning economic relations

Signed Apr. 8, 1956, in Ulan Bator.
Mentions informal agreements concerning (1) Soviet assistance to the MPR between 1956 and 1960 in construction of housing in Ulan Bator; (2) transfer of railroad lines and equipment to the Ulan Bator Railroad Stock Company; (3) construction of industrial enterprises in the MPR with Soviet aid; and (4) a Soviet long-term credit for purchase of equipment, construction machinery, and other materials.
Sources: *Izv.*, Apr. 10, 1956.
  Deklaratsii, 1957, pp. 206–207.
  Int. aff., 1956, No. 7, p. 135.

● 56/iv/14/Rom

Protocol between the USSR and Romania concerning expansion of collaboration in the fields of telephone and telegraph communications, radio broadcasting, and television

Signed Apr. 14, 1956, in Bucharest.
Reference: *Izv.*, Apr. 14, 1956.

● 56/iv/19/Yug

Protocol between the USSR and Yugoslavia concerning execution of trade deliveries for 1955

Signed Apr. 19, 1956, in Belgrade, by the mixed commission established under the commercial agreement of Jan. 5, 1955.
Ratified by Yugoslavia June 7, 1956.
Source: *MU*, 1957, No. 63, p. 61 (SC, R).

● 56/iv/24/MPR

Agreement between the USSR and the Mongolian People's Republic concerning cultural collaboration

Signed Apr. 24, 1956, in Moscow.
Entered into force on signature. Duration 10 years; if not denounced 6 months before expiration, extended for 10 years.
Includes the fields of culture, science, literature, art, education, health, physical culture, and sport.
Source: *UNTS*, 259, pp. 297–309 (R, E, F).
References: *Izv.*, Apr. 25, 1956; *ibid.*, Dec. 17, 1957.

● 56/iv/24/1951

International plant protection convention

Signed Dec. 6, 1951, in Rome.
Soviet act of adherence deposited Apr. 24,
1956, with immediate effect. General entry
into force Apr. 3, 1952.
Supersedes the International convention
of Apr. 16, 1929, for the protection of
plants (see 35/ix/26/1929).
Source: *UNTS*, 150, pp. 67–102 (E, F, S).
Reference: *DSB*, 34, 1956, p. 1080 (Soviet
adherence).

● 56/iv/26/GDR

**Agreement between the USSR and the
German Democratic Republic concerning cultural and scientific collaboration**

Signed Apr. 26, 1956, in Moscow.
Includes the fields of culture, science, literature, and higher education. Entered
into force May 19, 1956, on exchange of
notes concerning confirmation. Duration
5 years; if not denounced 6 months before
expiration, extended for 5-year periods.
Sources: *Dokumente DDR*, 4, pp. 52–55.
UNTS, 259, pp. 279–95 (R, G, E, F).
Reference: *Izv.*, Apr. 27, 1956.

● 56/iv/26/UK

**Statement on negotiations between the
USSR and the United Kingdom, with
annex**

Signed Apr. 26, 1956, in London.
Covers questions of (1) the Near and Mid-
dle East, (2) disarmament, and (3) de-
velopment of Anglo-Soviet trade relations.
Annex is a Joint declaration on the fur-
ther development of contacts between the
USSR and the United Kingdom.
Sources: *Izv.*, Apr. 27, 1956.
Deklaratsii, 1957, pp. 74–79.
NT, 1956, No. 19, supplement, pp. 3–6.
DIA, 1956, pp. 638–42, citing
Cmd. 9753, pp. 3–6.

● 56/iv/28/Bul

**Agreement between the USSR and Bul-
garia concerning cultural collaboration**

Signed Apr. 28, 1956, in Moscow.
Entered into force on signature. Duration
5 years; if not denounced 6 months before
expiration, extended for 5 years.
Source: *UNTS*, 259, pp. 363–75 (R, B, E,
F).
Reference: *Izv.*, Apr. 29, 1956.

● 56/iv/30/SM

**Communiqué concerning establishment
of consular relations between the USSR
and San Marino**

Published Apr. 30, 1956.
Source: *Izv.*, Apr. 30, 1956.

● 56/v/3/Alb

**Agreement between the USSR and Al-
bania concerning cultural collaboration**

Signed May 3, 1956, in Moscow.
Entered into force on signature. Duration
5 years; if not denounced 6 months before
expiration, extended for 5 years.
Source: *UNTS*, 259, pp. 391–403 (R, Albanian, E, F).
Reference: *Izv.*, May 4, 1956.

Mar. 19–May 4, 1956
See Appendix 5.

● 56/v/5/DRV

**Trade protocol for 1956 between the
USSR and the Democratic Republic of
Vietnam**

Signed May 5, 1956, in Moscow.
Soviet tractors, agricultural machinery,
motor vehicles, oil products, etc., in exchange for DRV precious woods, furniture, tea, spices, citrus fruits, etc. Extends
the trade agreement of July 18, 1955 (55/
vii/18/DRV/c). Further extended by protocol of Mar. 30, 1957.
References: *Izv.*, May 6, 1956.
VT SSSR, p. 206.

● 56/v/7/Neth

**Protocol between the USSR and The
Netherlands concerning the temporary
exchange of certain paintings by Rembrandt**

Signed May 7, 1956, in Moscow.
Reference: *Pravda*, May 8, 1956.

● 56/v/11/H

**Communiqué concerning the seventh
meeting of the Soviet-Hungarian Commission for scientific and technical collaboration**

Published May 11, 1956; the meeting took
place at the end of April and the beginning of May 1956, in Moscow.

Reference: *Izv.*, May 11, 1956.

● 56/v/14/Denmark

Trade protocol for the period 1956–1958 between the USSR and Denmark

Signed May 14, 1956, in Copenhagen.
Regulates deliveries from May 15, 1956, through May 14, 1958. Soviet grains, wood, coal, oil, agricultural equipment and other machinery, etc., in exchange for Danish ships and shipping machinery and industrial equipment. Value of trade 15.5 million Danish crowns each.
Sources: *Lovtidende C, Danmarks Traktater*, 1956, p. 283.
UNTS, 271, pp. 125–33 (R, D, E, F).
References: *Izv.*, May 15, 1956.
VT, 1956, No. 7, pp. 1–2.
Int. aff., 1956, No. 7, pp. 134–35.

● 56/v/14/J/a

Convention between the USSR and Japan concerning the fisheries in the high seas of the Northwest Pacific Ocean

Signed May 14, 1956, in Moscow.
Signed by Japan ad referendum; notification of Japan's approval made June 12, 1956. Entered into force Dec. 12, 1956, together with the joint declaration of Oct. 19, 1956 (56/x/19/J/a).
Sources: *CDT*, No. 1314.
NYT, Oct. 20, 1956, p. 2.
References: *Izv.*, May 16, 1956.
Int. aff., 1956, No. 11, p. 80.

● 56/v/14/J/b

Agreement between the USSR and Japan concerning cooperation for the rescue of persons in distress at sea, with exchange of notes

Signed May 14, 1956, in Moscow.
Signed by Japan ad referendum; notification of Japan's approval made June 12, 1956. Entered into force Dec. 12, 1956, together with the joint declaration of Oct. 19, 1956.
Sources: *CDT*, No. 1315.
NYT, Oct. 20, 1956, p. 2.
References: *Izv.*, May 16, 1956.
Int. aff., 1956, No. 11, p. 80.

● 56/v/17/Yug

Convention between the USSR and Yugoslavia concerning cultural collaboration

Signed May 17, 1956, in Moscow.
Ratified by the USSR June 6, 1956; by Yugoslavia July 3, 1956. Entered into force July 31, 1956, on exchange of acts of ratification in Belgrade. Duration 5 years; if not denounced 6 months before expiration, valid until 6 months after denunciation. Based on the joint declaration of June 2, 1955.
Sources: *VVS*, 1956, No. 16, Art. 352.
MU, 1957, No. 64 (SC, R).
UNTS, 259, pp. 145–53 (R, SC, E, F).
Reference: *Izv.*, May 18, 1956.

● 56/v/18/Cambodia

Communiqué concerning establishment of diplomatic relations between the USSR and Cambodia

Published May 18, 1956.
Source: *Izv.*, May 18, 1956.

● 56/v/19/France/a

Statement on negotiations between the USSR and France

Signed May 19, 1956, in Moscow.
Covers questions of (1) disarmament, (2) economic and technical assistance to underdeveloped countries, (3) the Near and Middle East, (4) Southeast Asia, (5) the development of Soviet-French commercial relations, and (6) cultural intercourse, among others. Negotiations to start in Paris in Sept. 1956 for a 3-year trade agreement.
Sources: *Izv.*, May 20, 1956.
Deklaratsii, 1957, pp. 262–68.
NT, 1956, No. 22, pp. 35–38.

● 56/v/19/France/b

Joint statement by the USSR and France concerning cultural intercourse

Issued May 19, 1956, in Moscow.
Calls for conclusion of an agreement on exchange of cinema films and for preparation of a draft convention on cultural collaboration. Agreement reached, on a reciprocal basis, on publication in the USSR of a French magazine in the Russian language.
Sources: *Pr., Izv.*, May 20, 1956.
Deklaratsii, 1957, pp. 269–70.
NT, 1956, No. 22, pp. 35–38.

● 56/v/20/Thailand

Communiqué concerning transformation of diplomatic missions of the USSR and Thailand into embassies

Published May 20, 1956.

Change to take effect from June 1, 1956.
Source: *Izv.*, May 20, 1956.

• 56/v/20/Yug

Communiqué concerning the first meeting of the Soviet-Yugoslav commission for scientific and technical collaboration

Published May 20, 1956; the meeting took place a few days earlier, in Moscow.
Mentions adoption of a Statute for the commission at the meeting.
Source: *Pravda*, May 20, 1956.

• 56/v/21/India

Agreement between the USSR and India concerning purchase by India of Soviet oil-drilling equipment

Signed May 21, 1956, in New Delhi.
Total value of equipment 7.4 million rupees.
Reference: *Izv.*, May 23, 1956.

• 56/v/22/Yug

Convention between the USSR and Yugoslavia concerning regulation of the question of citizenship of persons with dual citizenship

Signed May 22, 1956, in Moscow.
Ratified by the USSR June 6, 1956; by Yugoslavia July 3, 1956. Entered into force July 31, 1956, on exchange of acts of ratification in Belgrade. Expired July 31, 1957, but extended through July 31, 1958 (see 57/ix/6/Yug). Based on the joint declaration of June 2, 1955.
Sources: *VVS*, 1956, No. 16, Art. 353.
    MZh, 1956, No. 9, pp. 154–55.
    Int. aff., 1956, No. 9, pp. 157–58.
    MU, 1957, No. 63, pp. 22–24 (SC, R).
    UNTS, 259, pp. 155–67 (R, SC, E, F).
Reference: *Izv.*, May 23, 1956.

• 56/v/24/Egypt

Parcel post agreement between the USSR and Egypt

Signed May 24, 1956, in Cairo.
Entered into force July 1, 1956.
Reference: *Izv.*, May 26, 1956.

• 56/v/25/Fin

Protocol between the USSR and Finland concerning transfer to the USSR of a hydroelectric station on the Rajakoski waterfall

Signed May 25, 1956, in Helsinki.

Reference: *Izv.*, May 27, 1956.

• 56/v/25/Pl

Seventh conference of the Council for Mutual Economic Aid

Held May 18–25, 1956, in Berlin, with representatives of Albania, Bulgaria, Czechoslovakia, the German Democratic Republic, Hungary, Poland, Romania, and the USSR. Representatives of the Chinese People's Republic and Yugoslavia attended as observers.
Economic plans for the period 1956–1960 were drawn up; revised at the 8th conference (see 57/vi/22/Pl/a). Standing commissions were established in the fields of the oil and gas industry, wood and cellulose, nonferrous metals, coal, chemicals, ferrous metallurgy, electric power and use of the water power resources of the Danube, foreign trade, machine construction, agriculture, etc.
References: *BSE, 1957*, pp. 489–90.
    Dokumente DDR, 3, pp. 173–74.
    Tokareva, p. 108.
    Schenk and Lowenthal, 2, pp. 17–18.

• 56/v/25/UK

Agreement between the USSR and the United Kingdom concerning fisheries, with protocol and exchange of notes

Signed May 25, 1956, in Moscow.
Ratified by the United Kingdom Aug. 9, 1956; by the USSR Aug. 31, 1956. Entered into force Mar. 12, 1957, on exchange of acts of ratification in London. Duration 5 years; if not denounced 1 year before expiration, extended for 5-year periods.
Sources: *VVS*, 1957, No. 7, Art. 200.
    BTS, 1957, No. 36, Cmd. 148.
    UNTS, 266, pp. 209–19 (R, E, F).
    AJIL, 51, 1957, No. 3, pp. 687–89.
Reference: *Izv.*, May 26, 1956.

• 56/v/30/Alb/a

Agreement between the USSR and Albania concerning air communications and reciprocal services

Signed May 30, 1956, in Tirana.
Reference: *Pravda*, June 3, 1956.

• 56/v/30/Alb/b

Agreement between the USSR and Albania concerning technical collaboration in the field of civil aviation

Signed May 30, 1956, in Tirana.
Reference: *Pravda*, June 3, 1956.

● 56/v/30/GDR

Convention between the USSR and the German Democratic Republic concerning quarantine and protection of agricultural plants from diseases and parasites

Signed May 30, 1956, in Berlin.
Entered into force Aug. 7, 1956, on exchange of reports concerning confirmation. Duration 5 years; if not denounced 1 year before expiration, extended for 5-year periods.
Sources: *Dokumente DDR*, 4, pp. 56–60.
  UNTS, 263, pp. 143–63 (R, G, E, F).
Reference: *Izv.*, May 31, 1956.

● 56/v/30/H

Protocol between the USSR and Hungary concerning expansion of collaboration in the fields of telephone and telegraph communications, radio broadcasting, and television

Signed May 30, 1956, in Moscow.
Reference: *Izv.*, May 31, 1956.

● 56/vi/1/Cz

Agreement between the USSR and Czechoslovakia concerning cultural collaboration

Signed June 1, 1956, in Moscow.
Entered into force on signature. Duration 5 years; if not denounced 6 months before expiration, extended for 5 years.
Source: *UNTS*, 259, pp. 341–61 (R, Cz., E, F).
Reference: *Izv.*, June 2, 1956.

● 56/vi/1/Italy

Trade protocol for 1956 between the USSR and Italy

Signed June 1, 1956, in Rome.
Provides for an increase of 25 per cent over 1955. Based on the treaty of commerce and navigation of Dec. 11, 1948.
Soviet anthracite, manganese ore, benzine, pig iron, ferro-chrome, naphthalene, lumber, oil and oil products, cotton, flax, graphite electrodes, in exchange for Italian lathes and other equipment, citrus fruit, artificial fiber, cork, chemicals, sulphur, volatile oils, etc.
Reference: *Izv.*, June 3, 1956.

● 56/vi/2/Ethiopia

Joint communiqué by the USSR and Ethiopia concerning transformation of diplomatic missions into embassies

Published June 2, 1956.
Source: *Izv.*, June 2, 1956.

● 56/vi/4/1930

Convention concerning forced or compulsory labor (International Labour Organisation Convention No. 29)

Adopted by the General Conference of the ILO June 28, 1930, in Geneva; modified by the Final Articles Revision Convention, 1946 (54/iv/26/1946).
Ratified by the USSR June 4, 1956; by the Ukrainian SSR July 9, 1956. Acts of ratification of (1) the USSR deposited June 23, 1956; (2) the Ukrainian SSR deposited Aug. 10, 1956; (3) the Belorussian SSR deposited Aug. 21, 1956. Original entry into force May 1, 1932; for subsequent adherents, 12 months after registration of act of ratification. May be denounced with 1 year's notice.
Sources: *VVS*, 1956, No. 13, Art. 279.
  UNTS, 39, pp. 55–81 (E, F).
  ILO Code, 1951, I, Arts. 1208–33.
Reference: *Izv.*, June 12, 1956.

● 56/vi/4/1935

Convention concerning decrease of work hours to forty hours per week (International Labour Organisation Convention No. 47)

Adopted by the General Conference of the ILO June 22, 1935.
Ratified by the USSR June 4, 1956; act of ratification registered June 23, 1956, with effect from June 23, 1957. Ratified by the Ukrainian SSR July 9, 1956. May be denounced, after 10 years, with 1 year's notice.
Source: *VVS*, 1956, No. 13, Art. 280.
References: *Izv.*, June 12, 1956; *ibid.*, July 10, 1956.
  ILO Code, 1951, I, Arts 306 and 307.

● 56/vi/6/Yug

Protocol between the USSR and Yugoslavia concerning supplementary trade in 1956, with two annexes

Signed June 6, 1956, in Belgrade.
Ratified by Yugoslavia Aug. 8, 1956. Provides for an increase of $20 million each

over the trade level under the protocol of
Jan. 6, 1956. Annexes list goods to be ex-
changed.
Source: *MU*, 1957, No. 65, pp. 52–55
(SC, R).
References: *Izv.*, June 7, 1956.
Int. aff., 1956, No. 7, p. 135.

● 56/vi/10/Cz

**Communiqué concerning the ninth meet-
ing of the Soviet-Czechoslovak commission for scientific and technical collaboration**

Published June 10, 1956; the meeting took
place at the beginning of June 1956, in
Moscow.
Source: *Izv.*, June 10, 1956.

● 56/vi/12/Pl

**Agreement concerning collaboration in
the field of research in fish economy,
oceanology, and limnology in the western parts of the Pacific Ocean**

Signed June 12, 1956, in Peking, by the
USSR, the Chinese People's Republic, the
Democratic Republic of Vietnam, and the
Korean People's Democratic Republic.
Reference: *Izv.*, June 13, 1956.

● 56/vi/13/Pl. See Appendix 5.

● 56/vi/14/Denmark

**Agreement between the USSR and Den-
mark concerning communications between the rescue services of the USSR
and Denmark for collaboration in saving human lives in the Baltic Sea**

Signed at the end of a conference of Danish and Soviet experts held June 7 to 14,
1956, in Copenhagen.
Based on the agreement of Mar. 6, 1956
(56/iii/6/Denmark/b).
Reference: *Izv.*, June 16, 1956.

● 56/vi/14/H

**Supplementary protocol between the
USSR and Hungary to the agreement of
April 12, 1950, concerning collabora-
tion in the field of radio broadcasting**

Signed June 14, 1956, in Moscow.
References: *SDD*, 14, p. 265.
SDD, 15, p. 85.

● 56/vi/18/GDR/a

**Agreement between the USSR and the
German Democratic Republic concerning air communications**

Signed June 18, 1956, in Moscow.
Entered into force July 21, 1956, on ex-
change of notes concerning confirmation.
Valid until 12 months after denunciation.
Source: *Dokumente DDR*, 4, pp. 61–65.
Reference: *Izv.*, June 19, 1956.

● 56/vi/18/GDR/b

**Agreement between the USSR and the
German Democratic Republic concerning air transportation and servicing**

Signed June 18, 1956, in Moscow.
Reference: *Izv.*, June 23, 1956.

● 56/vi/20/Yug/a

**Joint statement by the USSR and Yugo-
slavia concerning political relations**

Signed June 20, 1956, in Moscow.
Covers both international relations and re-
lations between the 2 States, noting agree-
ments concluded between them since the
joint declaration of June 2, 1955.
Sources: *Izv.*, June 21, 1956.
Deklaratsii, 1957, pp. 304–11.
NT, 1956, No. 26, supplement, pp. 3–6.
DIA, 1956, pp. 381–86.

● 56/vi/20/Yug/b

**Exchange of notes between the USSR
and Yugoslavia concerning regularization of information services**

Sent on or about June 20, 1956, in Moscow.
Reference: *Pravda*, June 22, 1956.

● 56/vi/22/Egypt

**Joint communiqué by the USSR and
Egypt concerning political negotiations**

Issued June 22, 1956, in Cairo.
Sources: *Izv.*, June 23, 1956.
Deklaratsii, 1957, pp. 154–55.

● 56/vi/23/CPR

**Communiqué concerning the fourth
meeting of the USSR–Chinese People's
Republic commission for scientific and
technical collaboration**

Published June 23, 1956; the meeting took
place a few days earlier in Peking.
Source: *Pravda*, June 23, 1956.

• 56/vi/23/Yemen

Joint communiqué by the USSR and Yemen concerning political and economic relations

Signed June 23, 1956, in Moscow.
Mentions (1) agreement to exchange diplomatic representatives in the near future; (2) verification of trade lists; (3) agreement on deliveries of coffee to the USSR by Yemen and on Soviet commodities to Yemen; and (4) definition of basic forms of collaboration in assisting Yemen's economic development and reconstruction.
Sources: *Izv.*, June 24, 1956.
    Deklaratsii, 1957, pp. 173–75.
    NT, 1956, No. 27, pp. 35–36.
    Int. aff., 1956, No. 7, pp. 124–26.

• 56/vi/25/Syria

Joint communiqué by the USSR and Syria concerning political negotiations

Issued June 25, 1956, in Damascus.
Mentions, among other things, (1) agreement for an increase of economic collaboration and (2) desirability of conclusion of an agreement on cultural collaboration.
Sources: *Izv.*, June 26, 1956.
    Deklaratsii, 1957, pp. 240–41.

• 56/vi/27/Neth

Trade protocol for 1956 between the USSR and The Netherlands

Signed June 27, 1956, in The Hague.
Soviet lumber, grain, pig iron, cotton, automobiles, chemicals, etc., in exchange for Dutch cargo vessels, leather and rawhides, staple fiber, medicine, herring, etc. Constitutes the 2nd supplementary protocol to the trade and payments agreement of July 2, 1948.
Source: **Trb.*, 1956, No. 90.
Reference: *Int. aff.*, 1956, No. 7, p. 135.

• 56/vi/27/Pakistan

Trade agreement between the USSR and Pakistan, with two annexes

Signed June 27, 1956, in Karachi.
Enters into force on exchange of acts of ratification. Duration 1 year; if not denounced 3 months before expiration, valid until 3 months after denunciation.
Annexes list goods to be exchanged: Soviet industrial equipment, agricultural machinery, oil, timber, chemicals, etc., in ex-

change for Pakistani jute and jute products, cotton, wool, rawhides, etc.
Source: *VT*, 1956, No. 8, pp. 23–25.
References: *Izv.*, June 28, 1956 (joint communiqué).
    Int. aff., 1956, No. 7, p. 136.

• 56/vi/28/H

Agreement between the USSR and Hungary concerning scientific and cultural collaboration

Signed June 28, 1956, in Moscow.
Entered into force on signature. Duration 10 years; if not denounced 1 year before expiration, extended until 1 year after denunciation.
Source: *UNTS*, 259, pp. 405–25 (R, H, E, F).
Reference: *Izv.*, June 29, 1956.

• 56/vi/28/Lebanon

Joint communiqué by the USSR and Lebanon concerning political and economic negotiations

Issued June 28, 1956, in Beirut.
Mentions, among other things, (1) agreement to transform diplomatic missions into embassies and (2) desire for increased economic and cultural collaboration.
Sources: *Izv.*, June 29, 1956.
    Deklaratsii, 1957, pp. 204–205.

• 56/vi/28/Pl

Conference of railroad ministers

Held June 23–28, 1956, in Sofia, with representatives of Bulgaria, the Chinese People's Republic, Czechoslovakia, the German Democratic Republic, Hungary, the Korean People's Democratic Republic, the Mongolian People's Republic, Poland, Romania, and the USSR.
Agreements were reached on establishment of direct contact between railroad scientific research institutes of the participants, the holding of scientific and technical conferences, and publication of a joint technical-economic journal.
Reference: *Dokumente DDR*, 3, pp. 174–75.

• 56/vi/30/Pol

Agreement between the USSR and Poland concerning cultural collaboration

Signed June 30, 1956, in Warsaw.
Ratified by the USSR July 26, 1956; by Poland Oct. 18, 1956. Entered into force

Nov. 22, 1956, on exchange of acts of ratification in Moscow. Duration 5 years; if not denounced 6 months before expiration, extended for 5-year periods.
Provides for establishment of a mixed commission of implementation, to meet alternately in Moscow and Warsaw. For the protocol signed by the commission at its first meeting, see 57/ii/6/Pol/a.
Covers among others the fields of science, education and higher education, literature, art, music, theater, cinema, press, radio, television, sport, and tourism.
Sources: *VVS*, 1956, No. 23, Art. 509.
DUPRL, No. 16, Arts. 83, 84.
UNTS, 259, pp. 311–27 (R, P, E, F).
Reference: *Izv.*, July 1, 1956.

● 56/vii/ /UN

Agreement between the USSR and the Technical Assistance Board (TAB) under the Economic and Social Council (ECOSOC) of the United Nations concerning convertibility of currency

Negotiated during July 1956.
Provides for convertibility of up to 25 per cent of the Soviet contribution to ECOSOC. Follows an agreement during 1955 providing for partial convertibility (not listed separately).
Reference: *Int. org.*, 11, 1957, p. 623.

● 56/vii/3/Pl

Agreement between the USSR, the Chinese People's Republic, and the Korean People's Democratic Republic concerning collaboration between the shipwreck salvage services of the three States in saving human lives and aiding ships and airplanes wrecked in the waters of the Far Eastern Seas and the Pacific Ocean

Signed July 3, 1956, in Moscow.
Reference: *Izv.*, July 4, 1956.

● 56/vii/4/Alb

Communiqué concerning the third meeting of the Soviet-Albanian commission for scientific and technical collaboration

Published July 4, 1956; the meeting took place a few days earlier, in Moscow.
Source: *Pravda*, July 4, 1956.

● 56/vii/5/CPR

Agreement between the USSR and the

Chinese People's Republic concerning cultural collaboration

Signed July 5, 1956, in Moscow.
Entered into force Dec. 7, 1956, on exchange of notes in Peking concerning ratification. Duration 5 years. If not denounced 6 months before expiration, extended for successive 5-year periods.
Source: *UNTS*, 263, pp. 129–41 (R, C, E, F).
Reference: *Izv.*, July 6, 1956.

● 56/vii/6/1921/a

Convention concerning the age for admission of children to employment in agriculture (International Labour Organisation Convention No. 10)

Adopted by the General Conference of the ILO Nov. 16, 1921, in Geneva; modified by the Final Articles Revision Convention, 1946 (see 54/iv/26/1946).
Ratified by the USSR July 6, 1956; act of ratification deposited Aug. 10, 1956, with immediate effect. Ratified by the Ukrainian SSR Sept. 14, 1956; act of ratification deposited Oct. 31, 1956. Ratified by the Belorussian SSR Nov. 6, 1956; act of ratification deposited Nov. 15, 1956. May be denounced with 1 year's notice.
Original entry into force Aug. 31, 1923.
Source: *UNTS*, 38, pp. 143–49 (E, F).
References: *VVS*, 1956, No. 14, Art. 301.
Izv., Aug. 14, 1956.
ILO Code, 1951, I, Arts. 373–76.

● 56/vii/6/1921/b

Convention concerning the rights of association and combination of agricultural workers (International Labour Organisation Convention No. 11)

Adopted by the General Conference of the ILO Nov. 12, 1921, in Geneva; modified by the Final Articles Revision Convention, 1946.
Data on ratification, deposit of acts of ratification, entry into force, and denunciation identical with those for 56/vii/6/1921/a. Original entry into force May 11, 1923.
Source: *UNTS*, 38, pp. 153–59 (E, F).
References: *VVS*, 1956, No. 14, Art. 301.
Izv., Aug. 14, 1956.
ILO Code, 1951, I, Arts. 866–67.

• 56/vii/6/1921/c

Convention fixing the minimum age for the admission of young persons to employment as trimmers or stokers (International Labour Organisation Convention No. 15)

Adopted by the General Conference of the ILO Nov. 11, 1921, in Geneva; modified by the Final Articles Revision Convention, 1946.

Data on ratification, deposit of acts of ratification, entry into force, and denunciation identical with those for 56/vii/6/1921/a. Original entry into force Nov. 20, 1922.

Source: *UNTS*, 38, pp. 203–11 (E, F).

References: *VVS*, 1956, No. 14, Art. 301.
   Izv., Aug. 14, 1956.
   ILO Code, 1951, I, Arts. 1045, 1047, 1049, 1050.

• 56/vii/6/1921/d

Convention concerning the compulsory medical examination of children and young persons employed at sea (International Labour Organisation Convention No. 16)

Adopted by the General Conference of the ILO Nov. 11, 1921, in Geneva; modified by the Final Articles Revision Convention, 1946.

Data on ratification, deposit of acts of ratification, entry into force, and denunciation identical with those for 56/vii/6/1921/a. Original entry into force Nov. 20, 1922.

Source: *UNTS*, 38, pp. 217–23 (E, F).

References: *VVS*, 1956, No. 14, Art. 301.
   Izv., Aug. 14, 1956.
   ILO Code, 1951, I, Arts. 1044–46, 1048, and 1051 (c).

• 56/vii/6/1936/a

Convention concerning annual holidays with pay (International Labour Organisation Convention No. 52)

Adopted by the General Conference of the ILO June 24, 1936, in Geneva; modified by the Final Articles Revision Convention, 1946.

Ratified by (1) the USSR July 6, 1956; act of ratification deposited Aug. 10, 1956, with effect from Aug. 10, 1957; (2) the Ukrainian SSR Sept. 14, 1956, with effect from Sept. 14, 1957; (3) the Belorussian

SSR Nov. 6, 1956, with effect from Nov. 6, 1957. May be denounced with 1 year's notice. Original entry into force Sept. 22, 1939.

Source: *UNTS*, 40, pp. 137–49 (E, F).

References: *VVS*, 1956, No. 14, Art. 301.
   Izv., Aug. 14, 1956.
   ILO Code, 1951, I, Arts. 350–59.

• 56/vii/6/1936/b

Convention fixing the minimum age for the admission of children to employment at sea (International Labour Organisation Convention No. 58)

Adopted by the General Conference of the ILO Oct. 24, 1936, in Geneva; modified by the Final Articles Revision Convention, 1946.

Data on ratification, deposit of acts of ratification, and denunciation identical with those for 56/vii/6/1936/a. Original entry into force Apr. 11, 1939.

Source: *UNTS*, 40, pp. 205–13 (E, F).

References: *VVS*, 1956, No. 14, Art. 301.
   Izv., Aug. 14, 1956.
   ILO Code, 1951, I, Arts. 1044–46 and 1051 (1).

• 56/vii/6/1937/a

Convention fixing the minimum age for admission of children to industrial employment (International Labour Organisation Convention No. 59)

Adopted by the General Conference of the ILO June 22, 1937, in Geneva; modified by the Final Articles Revision Convention, 1946.

Data on ratification, deposit of acts of ratification, and denunciation identical with those for 56/vii/6/1936/a. Original entry into force Feb. 21, 1941.

Source: *UNTS*, 40, pp. 217–29 (E, F).

References: *VVS*, 1956, No. 14, Art. 301.
   Izv., Aug. 14, 1956.
   ILO Code, 1951, I, Arts. 365–70.

• 56/vii/6/1937/b

Convention concerning the age for admission of children to non-industrial employment (International Labour Organisation Convention No. 60)

Adopted by the General Conference of the ILO June 22, 1937, in Geneva; modified

by the Final Articles Revision Convention, 1946.
Data on ratification and deposit of acts of ratification identical with those for 56/vii/6/1936/a. May be denounced with 1 year's notice, 10 years after original entry into force (Dec. 29, 1950).
Source: *UNTS*, 78, pp. 181–95 (E, F).
References: *VVS*, 1956, No. 14, Art. 301.
    Izv., Aug. 14, 1956.
    ILO Code, 1951, I, Arts. 377–85.

• 56/vii/6/1946/a

Convention concerning medical examination for fitness for employment in industry of children and young persons (International Labour Organisation Convention No. 77)

Adopted by the General Conference of the ILO Oct. 9, 1946, in Montreal.
Data on ratification and deposit of acts of ratification identical with those for 56/vii/6/1936/a. May be denounced with 1 year's notice, 10 years after original entry into force (Dec. 29, 1950).
Source: *UNTS*, 78, pp. 197–211 (E, F).
References: *VVS*, 1956, No. 14, Art. 301.
    Izv., Aug. 14, 1956.
    ILO Code, 1951, I, Arts. 402–11.

• 56/vii/6/1946/b

Convention concerning medical examination of children and young persons for fitness for employment in non-industrial occupations (International Labour Organisation Convention No. 78)

Adopted by the General Conference of the ILO Oct. 9, 1946, in Montreal.
Data on ratification and deposit of acts of ratification identical with those for 56/vii/6/1936/a. May be denounced with 1 year's notice, 10 years after original entry into force (Dec. 29, 1950).
Source: *UNTS*, 78, pp. 213–25 (E, F).
References: *VVS*, 1956, No. 14, Art. 301.
    Izv., Aug. 14, 1956.
    ILO Code, 1951, I, Arts. 416–25.

• 56/vii/6/1946/c

Convention concerning the restriction of night work of children and young persons in non-industrial occupations (International Labour Organisation Convention No. 79)

Adopted by the General Conference of the ILO Oct. 9, 1946, in Montreal.
Data on ratification and deposit of acts of ratification identical with those for 56/vii/6/1936/a. May be denounced with 1 year's notice, 10 years after original entry into force (Dec. 29, 1950).
Source: *UNTS*, 78, pp. 227–41 (E, F).
References: *VVS*, 1956, No. 14, Art. 301.
    Izv., Aug. 14, 1956.
    ILO Code, 1951, I, Arts. 438–45.

• 56/vii/6/1948/a

Convention concerning freedom of association and protection of the right to organize (International Labour Organisation Convention No. 87)

Adopted by the General Conference of the ILO July 9, 1948, in San Francisco.
Data on ratification and deposit of acts of ratification identical with those for 56/vii/6/1936/a. May be denounced with 1 year's notice, 10 years after original entry into force (July 4, 1950).
Source: *UNTS*, 68, pp. 17–29 (E, F).
References: *VVS*, 1956, No. 14, Art. 301.
    Izv., Aug. 14, 1956.
    ILO Code, 1951, I, Arts. 855–65 and 868–69.

• 56/vii/6/1948/b

Convention concerning the night work of young persons employed in industry (International Labour Organisation Convention No. 90)

Adopted by the General Conference of the ILO July 10, 1948, in San Francisco.
Data on ratification and deposit of acts of ratification identical with those for 56/vii/6/1936/a. May be denounced with 1 year's notice, 10 years after original entry into force (June 12, 1951).
Constitutes a revision of ILO Convention No. 6, 1919.
Source: *UNTS*, 91, pp. 3–19 (E, F).
References: *VVS*, 1956, No. 14, Art. 301.
    Izv., Aug. 14, 1956.
    ILO Code, 1951, I, Arts. 428–35.

• 56/vii/6/1949

Convention concerning the application of the principles of the right to organize and to bargain collectively (International Labour Organisation Convention No. 98)

Adopted by the General Conference of the ILO July 1, 1949, in Geneva.
Data on ratification and deposit of acts of ratification identical with those for 56/vii/6/1936/a. May be denounced with 1 year's notice, 10 years after original entry into force (July 18, 1951).
Source: *UNTS*, 96, pp. 257–69 (E, F).
References: *VVS*, 1956, No. 14, Art. 301.
   Izv., Aug. 14, 1956.
   ILO Code, 1951, I, Arts. 870–76.

● 56/vii/6/1952

Convention concerning maternity protection (revised 1952) (International Labour Organisation Convention No. 103)

Adopted by the General Conference of the ILO June 28, 1952, in Geneva.
Ratified by the USSR July 6, 1956; act of ratification deposited Aug. 10, 1956, with effect from Aug. 10, 1957. Ratified by the Ukrainian SSR Sept. 14, 1956, with effect from Sept. 14, 1957; by the Belorussian SSR Nov. 6, 1956, with effect from Nov. 6, 1957. Original entry into force Sept. 7, 1955. May be denounced with 1 year's notice, 10 years after original entry into force (Sept. 7, 1955).
Source: *UNTS*, 214, pp. 321–37 (E, F).
References: *VVS*, 1956, No. 14, Art. 301.
   Izv., Aug. 14, 1956.

● 56/vii/7/Cambodia

Joint communiqué by the USSR and Cambodia concerning political negotiations

Signed July 7, 1956, in Moscow.
Covers relations between the 2 States as well as international relations. The USSR to build a hospital at Pnom-Penh as a gift.
Sources: *Pravda, Izv.*, July 8, 1956.
   Deklaratsii, 1957, pp. 176–78.
   NT, 1956, No. 29, pp. 35–36.
   DIA, 1956, pp. 735–37.

● 56/vii/9/US

Exchange of letters between the USSR and the United States of America constituting an agreement concerning destruction of seventy-nine Lend-Lease naval vessels

Sent March 26, Apr. 3 and 17, May 17, June 21 and 29, and July 9, 1956.
Provides for sinking in the presence of United States observers of 59 vessels in the Barents Sea and 20 vessels in the Far East.
Source: *Thirty-eighth report to Congress on Lend-Lease operations*, pp. 11–15.
Reference: *DSB*, 38, 1958, p. 570.

● 56/vii/11/Yemen

Agreement between the USSR and Yemen concerning economic collaboration

Signed July 11, 1956, in Prague.
Ratified by the USSR Sept. 24, 1956.
Reference: *VVS*, 1956, No. 20, Art. 432 (ratification).

● 56/vii/12/Egypt

Agreement between the USSR and Egypt concerning collaboration in regard to the use of atomic energy for peaceful purposes

Signed July 12, 1956, in Cairo.
Calls for conclusion of supplementary agreements and contracts concerning number and specialization of experts, length of assignment, expenses, etc.
Source: *Soglasheniia*, 1958, pp. 25–27.
References: *Izv.*, July 15, 1956.
   VT, 1957, No. 3, p. 5.
   Int. aff., 1956, No. 8, p. 46.
Note: A report from Cairo published in *Izv.*, Feb. 12, 1956, mentions Egyptian press reports of the signing of such an agreement on Feb. 11, 1956; the reports cite a TASS dispatch, which apparently was not published in the Soviet press. Presumably the Cairo reports concern the initialing of a draft of the agreement.

● 56/vii/12/KPDR

Joint communiqué by the USSR and the Korean People's Democratic Republic concerning political negotiations

Signed July 12, 1956, in Moscow.
Covers international relations as well as relations between the 2 States. Deliveries of (1) Soviet materials and equipment for reconstruction and further development of the KPDR economy and (2) food and consumer goods to be increased. An agreement on cultural collaboration to be concluded in the near future.
Sources: *Pravda, Izv.*, July 13, 1956.
   Deklaratsii, 1957, pp. 200–203.
   NT, 1956, No. 30, pp. 46–47.

● 56/vii/15/Egypt

Protocol between the USSR and Egypt concerning establishment of a Soviet Trade Mission in Egypt

Signed July 15, 1956, in Cairo.
Reference: *Int. aff.*, 1956, No. 8, p. 45.

● 56/vii/17/GDR/a

Statement concerning negotiations between the USSR and the German Democratic Republic

Signed July 17, 1956, in Moscow.
Covers international relations, particularly with regard to Germany, as well as relations between the 2 States. Following specific agreements mentioned: (1) The annual monetary contribution made by the GDR under the treaty of Sept. 20, 1955, towards maintenance of Soviet forces in Germany to be reduced from 1600 to 800 million Marks. (2) Trade deliveries during 1956 to be increased above the operating trade agreement, including the provision by the USSR of convertible currency for purchases by the GDR in the world market. (3) Agreement on a long-term credit for the GDR reaffirmed. (4) A number of measures to be instituted designed to ensure the fullest and most rational operation of GDR industrial capacities. (5) Agreement reached on construction of an atomic power plant in the GDR (see next document).
Sources: *Pravda, Izv.*, July 18, 1956.
  Deklaratsii, 1957, pp. 114–19.
  NT, 1956, No. 30, pp. 43–46.
  Dokumente DDR, 5, pp. 645–50.

● 56/vii/17/GDR/b

Agreement between the USSR and the German Democratic Republic concerning construction in the GDR of an atomic power plant

Signed July 17, 1956, in Moscow.
The USSR to assist in the designing of a plant of up to 100,000 kw capacity and to supply necessary equipment and materials.
Reference: Mentioned in the statement of the same date (preceding document).

● 56/vii/20/Nepal

Communiqué concerning establishment

of diplomatic relations between the USSR and Nepal

Published July 20, 1956.
Source: *Izv.*, July 20, 1956.

● 56/vii/21/Rom

Agreement between the USSR and Romania concerning delivery of vessels to the USSR during the period 1957–1960

Signed July 21, 1956.
Covers lake and river vessels and tugs. Plans to be supplied by the USSR; Soviet planning organization to work in Romania. Romania to furnish equipment.
Reference: *VT SSSR*, p. 138.

● 56/vii/23/France

Agreement between the USSR and France concerning exchange of films

Signed July 23, 1956, in Paris.
Reference: *Izv.*, July 24, 1956.

● 56/vii/25/CPR

Supplementary trade protocol for 1956 between the USSR and the Chinese People's Republic

Signed July 25, 1956, in Peking.
Soviet lathes, cranes, air compressors, pumps, diesels, generators, automobiles, agricultural machinery, instruments, etc., in exchange for CPR sulphur, mercury, caustic soda, calcified soda, rice, tea, woolen clothing, etc.
Reference: *Izv.*, July 27, 1956.

● 56/viii/ /1926

Convention concerning slavery

Signed Sept. 25, 1926, in Geneva; modified by a protocol of Dec. 7, 1953.
Ratified by the USSR during Aug. 1956. Act of accession of the Belorussian SSR deposited Sept. 13, 1956. Original entry into force Mar. 9, 1927. Supplemented by a convention of Sept. 7, 1956 (56/ix/7/ Mul).
Sources: *MZh*, 1956, No. 10, pp. 152–54
    (as modified in 1953).
  LNTS, 60, pp. 253–70 (E, F).
References: *DSB*, 35, 1956, p. 650.
  UNTS, 250, p. 314.

● 56/viii/1/Pl

Agreement concerning collaboration in

construction of enterprises of the aluminum industry in Yugoslavia, with exchange of notes

Signed Aug. 1, 1956, in Moscow, by the
USSR, the German Democratic Republic,
and Yugoslavia.
Ratified by Yugoslavia Sept. 25, 1956.
Under the exchange of notes, entered into
force provisionally on signature; definitively on notification by Yugoslavia of
its ratification. Supplemented by a protocol of the same date (next document).
Provides for a loan by the USSR to Yugoslavia of $175 million US, to be used dur-
ing the period 1956–1961 for construction
of an aluminum plant with an annual capacity of 50,000 tons, a hydroelectric station, and other auxiliary installations. To
be put into operation not later than 1961.
Credit to be repaid in 20 years at 2 per
cent, starting 1962. Subsequently the
USSR and the GDR agree to advance
Yugoslavia a further credit, to be determined, for construction of a second phase.
The USSR and the GDR agree to provide
materials and give technical aid. Number and conditions of work of specialists
to be determined by subsequent agreements. Time schedule for fulfillment of
obligations under the agreement covered
in a protocol of July 29, 1957. On May
27, 1958, the USSR proposed deferring
the use of credit under this agreement to
1963–1969 (*Pr.*, *Izv.*, July 1, 1958; see
also references under 56/i/12/Yug).
Source: *MU*, 1957, No. 64, pp. 3–11 (SC,
    R, G).
References: *VT*, 1956, No. 10, p. 5.
    Int. aff., 1956, No. 9, p. 122.
    NYT, Aug. 3, 1956.

• 56/viii/1/Yug

**Protocol between the USSR and Yugo-
slavia to the agreement of August 1,
1956, concerning collaboration in construction of enterprises of the aluminum
industry in Yugoslavia**

Signed Aug. 1, 1956, in Moscow.
Reference: *Int. aff.*, 1956, No. 9, p. 122.

• 56/viii/2/Austria

**Agreement between the USSR and Aus-
tria concerning exchange of films**

Signed Aug. 2, 1956, in Moscow.
Entered into force on signature.
Reference: *Izv.*, Aug. 3, 1956.

• 56/viii/2/BL

**Trade protocol for 1956 between the
USSR and the Belgium-Luxembourg
Economic Union**

Signed Aug. 2, 1956, in Brussels.
Based on the commercial agreement of
Feb. 18, 1948 (48/ii/18/BL/b). Soviet
grain, timber, cellulose, coal, apatite concentrate, pig iron, aluminum, automobiles,
diesel fuel, oil, cotton, etc., in exchange
for Belgo-Luxembourg rolled ferrous
metal, steel cables, copper wire, artificial
silk yarn, staple fiber, etc.
Source: *Informations commerciales*, Aug.
    10, 1956, No. 157.
References: *Pr.*, Aug. 5, 1956; *Izv.*, Aug.
    3, 1956.
    CDSP, 8, 1956, No. 31, p. 20.

• 56/viii/2/Yug

**Protocol between the USSR and Yugo-
slavia concerning execution of the agreement of January 12, 1956, concerning
collaboration in construction of industrial enterprises in Yugoslavia, with two
annexes**

Signed Aug. 2, 1956, in Moscow.
Annexes list enterprises to be built.
Source: *MU*, 1957, No. 65, pp. 77–79
    (SC, R).
Reference: *VT*, 1956, No. 10, p. 5.

• 56/viii/5/Bul

**Communiqué concerning an agreement
between the USSR and Bulgaria concerning technical collaboration in the
field of civil aviation**

Issued Aug. 5, 1956, in Sofia.
Source: *Pravda*, Aug. 6, 1956.

**Aug. 7, 1956. Extension of the agree-
ment of Aug. 8, 1946, between the USSR
and Denmark concerning establishment
of telegraph communications**

See 46/viii/8/Denmark.

• 56/viii/8/Rom

**Communiqué concerning the eighth
meeting of the Soviet-Romanian commission for scientific and technical collaboration**

Published Aug. 8, 1956; the meeting took
place a few days earlier, in Moscow.
Source: *Pravda*, Aug. 8, 1956.

• 56/viii/11/Uruguay/a

Treaty of commerce and navigation between the USSR and Uruguay

Signed Aug. 11, 1956, in Montevideo.
Subject to ratification. Enters into force 10 days after exchange of acts of ratification. Duration 3 years.
References: *Pravda*, Aug. 13, 1956.
   Int. aff., 1956, No. 12, p. 66.

• 56/viii/11/Uruguay/b

Trade and payments agreement between the USSR and Uruguay

Signed Aug. 11, 1956, in Montevideo.
Duration 2 years.
References: *Pravda*, Aug. 13, 1956.
   Int. aff., 1956, No. 12, p. 66.

• 56/viii/12/Indonesia

Commercial agreement between the USSR and Indonesia, with two annexes and an exchange of notes

Signed Aug. 12, 1956, in Djakarta.
Entered into force provisionally on signature; definitive entry to take place under an exchange of notes for that purpose. Valid through Aug. 12, 1957. If not denounced 3 months before expiration, extended for 1-year periods. Annexes list goods to be exchanged. Exchange of notes concerns principles for navigation in trade between the 2 States.
Source: *VT*, 1957, No. 1, pp. 30–33.
Reference: *Izv.*, Aug. 14, 1956.

• 56/viii/15/Pol

Communiqué concerning the tenth meeting of the Soviet-Polish commission for scientific and technical collaboration

Published Aug. 15, 1956; the meeting took place a few days earlier, in Warsaw.
Source: *Izv.*, Aug. 15, 1956.

• 56/viii/18/CPR

Agreement between the USSR and the Chinese People's Republic concerning joint scientific exploration of natural resources and prospects for development of productive forces in the Amur River basin

Signed Aug. 18, 1956, in Peking.
Provides for joint research during the period 1956–1960 into conditions of geology and water power to improve conditions of navigation, regulate water, build a hydroelectric station, develop fish-breeding, and other research.
References: *Pravda*, Aug. 19, 1956; *ibid.*, Sept. 3, 1956.

• 56/viii/20/Syria

Agreement between the USSR and Syria concerning cultural collaboration

Signed Aug. 20, 1956, in Damascus.
Ratified by the USSR Dec. 28, 1956; by Syria May 21, 1957. Entered into force May 30, 1957, on exchange of acts of ratification in Damascus. Duration 2 years; if not denounced 3 months before expiration, extended for 2 years.
Covers the fields of literature, science, art, general and technical secondary education, higher education, physical culture, sport, radio, and cinema.
Sources: *VVS*, 1957, No. 13, Art. 321.
   JR, No. 23, May 16, 1957, pp. 3117–18.
   UNTS, 274, pp. 105–13 (R, A, E, F).

Aug. 16–23, 1956

See Appendix 5.

• 56/viii/30/Belgium

Communiqué concerning an informal agreement between the USSR and Belgium concerning cultural exchange

Issued Aug. 30, 1956, in Moscow.
Covers exchange of art exhibits, theater performances, and solo performances. For a formal agreement on cultural collaboration, see 56/x/25/Belgium.
Reference: *Izv.*, Aug. 30, 1956.

• 56/ix/1/Ceylon

Joint communiqué by the USSR and Ceylon concerning political and economic relations

Signed Sept. 1, 1956, in Moscow.
Mentions agreement to establish diplomatic relations. Negotiations to be undertaken for conclusion of a commercial agreement and an agreement concerning economic collaboration. Steps to be taken to establish closer cultural ties. An agreement concerning economic and technical collaboration was signed Feb. 25, 1958 (text in *VVS*, 1958, No. 11, Art. 226).
Sources: *Izv.*, Sept. 4, 1956.
   Deklaratsii, 1957, pp. 271–72.

• 56/ix/4/Egypt

Trade agreement between the USSR and Egypt

Signed Sept. 4, 1956, in Cairo.
The USSR to sell 200,000 tons of wheat, import cotton, rice, etc.
References: *Pravda*, Sept. 6, 1956; *CDSP*, 8, 1956, No. 36, p. 9.

• 56/ix/5/Iran

Exchange of notes between the USSR and Iran constituting a trade agreement for the current year

Sent Sept. 5, 1956, in Teheran.
Soviet sugar, industrial equipment, automobiles, agricultural machines, metals, cotton goods, lumber, paper, chemicals, etc., in exchange for Iranian rice, wool, cotton, fish products, dried fruits, ores, raw hides, oil seeds, etc.
Reference: *Pravda*, Sept. 7, 1956.

• 56/ix/5/KPDR

Agreement between the USSR and the Korean People's Democratic Republic concerning cultural collaboration

Signed Sept. 5, 1956, in Pyongyang.
Entered into force on signature. Duration 10 years; if not denounced 6 months before expiration, extended for 10-year periods.
Source: *UNTS*, 259, pp. 329–39 (R, K, E, F).

• 56/ix/7/Mul

Supplementary convention on the abolition of slavery, the slave trade, and institutions and practices similar to slavery

Signed Sept. 7, 1956, in Geneva. The USSR and Belorussian and Ukrainian SSR's signed.
Ratified by the USSR Feb. 16, 1957; act of ratification deposited Apr. 12, 1957.
Supplements the slavery convention of Sept. 25, 1926, as modified by the protocol of Dec. 7, 1953. For Soviet adherence to the 1926 convention, see 56/viii/ /1926.
Sources: *VVS*, 1957, No. 8, Art. 224.
MZh, 1956, No. 10, pp. 154–57.
Int. aff., 1956, No. 10, pp. 156–61.
UNTS, 266, pp. 3–87 (R, C, S, E, F).
References: *Pravda*, Sept. 8, 1956.
Int. aff., 1956, No. 10, pp. 149–52.

• 56/ix/11/Indonesia

Joint statement by the USSR and Indonesia concerning political negotiations

Signed Sept. 11, 1956, in Moscow.
Covers international relations as well as relations between the 2 States. Calls for conclusion of a technical and economic agreement providing a long-term Soviet credit to Indonesia and for the supply by Indonesia of raw materials and other goods to the USSR. Delegations of students, specialists, etc. to be exchanged.
Sources: *Izv.*, Sept. 12, 1956.
Deklaratsii, 1957, pp. 168–70.
NT, 1956, No. 38, pp. 35–36.
DIA, 1956, pp. 738–40.

• 56/ix/11/Pl

Agreement between the USSR, Bulgaria, and Romania concerning collaboration in saving human life and assistance to vessels and aircraft in distress on the Black Sea

Signed Sept. 11, 1956, in Moscow.
Entered into force Apr. 1, 1957. Duration 3 years; if not denounced 6 months before expiration, extended for 1-year periods.
Source: *UNTS*, 266, pp. 221–41 (R, B, Romanian, E, F).
Reference: *Pravda*, Sept. 12, 1956.

• 56/ix/12/Indonesia

Trade agreement between the USSR and Indonesia

Signed Sept. 12, 1956, in Djakarta.
Soviet industrial and electrical equipment, motor vehicles, tractors, optical instruments, cement, etc., in exchange for Indonesian rubber, hides, coffee, cocoa, spices. Includes most-favored-nation provision on trade.
Reference: *Int. aff.*, 1956, No. 10, p. 118.

• 56/ix/14/Fin

Agreement between the USSR and Finland concerning trackage rights on Soviet railroads of freight trains of the Finnish railroads, with annex

Signed Sept. 14, 1956, in Moscow.
Entered into force Dec. 1, 1956. Valid until 6 months after denunciation. Annex gives a blank form for reporting detaching, repair, and re-attaching of freight cars.

Sources: *SS, 1956, No. 29 (Finnish, R). UNTS, 255, pp. 365–89 (R, Finnish, E, F).

• 56/ix/15/Indonesia

General agreement between the USSR and Indonesia concerning economic and technical collaboration

Signed Sept. 15, 1956, in Djakarta. Ratified by the USSR Nov. 2, 1956. Provides for a Soviet credit of $100 million for technical aid to Indonesia. The USSR to carry out prospecting and drafting work, supply equipment for Indonesian enterprises, give technical aid in building coal mines, nonferrous metal plants, building material plants, and hydroelectric power plants. Credit to be repaid in 12 annual installments, after 3 years, at 2½ per cent interest.
References: *Pr., Izv.*, Sept. 18, 1956; *CDSP*, 8, 1956, No. 38, p. 13. *Int. aff.*, 1956, No. 10, p. 118. *VVS*, 1956, No. 23, Art. 502. Allen, 1957, p. 442.

• 56/ix/18/Pol

Credit agreement between the USSR and Poland

Signed Sept. 18, 1956, in Moscow. Provides for a Soviet credit to Poland for 1956 of 100 million rubles in gold and Soviet goods, to be repaid in Polish goods in equal annual installments between 1957 and 1960.
References: *Pr., Izv.*, Sept. 23, 1956; *CDSP*, 8, 1956, No. 38, p. 13.

• 56/ix/22/GDR

Protocol between the USSR and the German Democratic Republic concerning expansion and development of telephone and telegraph communications, exchange of radio and television programs, and strengthening of scientific and technical collaboration in the field of communications

Signed Sept. 22, 1956, in Moscow. Reference: *Izv.*, Sept. 23, 1956.

Sept. 24, 1956

Exchange of notes, starting Nov. 3, 1954, between the USSR and the United States of America concerning safeguards against military uses of atomic energy. *NT*, 1956, No. 43, supplement.

• 56/ix/27/Iceland

Trade protocol for 1957–1959 between the USSR and Iceland

Signed Sept. 27, 1956, in Reykjavik. Soviet oil, wood, grain and flour, coal, cement, ferrous metals, automobiles, in exchange for Icelandic fish.
Reference: *VT*, 1957, No. 1, p. 17.

• 56/x/5/H

Communiqué concerning a loan agreement between the USSR and Hungary

Published Oct. 5, 1956. Agreement provides for a Soviet credit to Hungary of 100 million rubles, 60 million to cover Soviet deliveries (coke, lead, cotton, synthetic rubber, etc.), 40 million in convertible currency. To be repaid in Hungarian goods during the period 1960–1965 in equal annual installments, at 2 per cent.
Source: *Izv.*, Oct. 5, 1956.

• 56/x/4/Austria

Trade protocol for 1957 between the USSR and Austria, with annexes

Signed Oct. 4, 1956, in Moscow. Entered into force on signature. Based on the commercial treaty of Oct. 17, 1955 (55/x/17/Austria/a). Annexes list goods to be exchanged: Soviet grain, cotton, coal, oil pipes, oil drilling equipment, road construction and other equipment, automobiles, ferrous alloys, apatite concentrate, etc., in exchange for Austrian power, metallurgical, and wood-working equipment, locomotives, tugs, equipment for light industry, ball bearings, ferrous castings, staple fiber, etc.
References: *Izv.*, Oct. 5, 1956. *VT*, 1956, No. 12, p. 7.

• 56/x/5/Yug

Protocol concerning the second meeting of the Soviet-Yugoslav commission for scientific and technical collaboration

Signed Oct. 5, 1956. Reference: *BSE*, 1957, p. 36.

• 56/x/9/Pl

Agreement between the USSR, Czechoslovakia, and Burma concerning the use of multilateral trade accounting

Signed Oct. 9, 1956, in Rangoon. Provisions: Czechoslovakia to make par-

tial payment for goods delivered by the USSR in 1956 by delivering to Burma by Sept. 30, 1957, goods to the value of £4 million sterling, to be applied by Burma against the amount owed her by the USSR for delivery of Burmese rice under the protocol of July 1, 1955 (55/vii/1/Burma/b).
References: *Pravda*, Oct. 10, 1956.
VT SSSR, p. 87.

● 56/x/12/GDR/a

Agreement between the USSR and the German Democratic Republic concerning collaboration in the fields of radio and television

Signed Oct. 12, 1956, in Moscow.
Supplemented by a protocol concerning collaboration in the field of television (next document). Supersedes the agreement of Jan. 13, 1953.
Source: *Dokumente DDR*, 5, pp. 652–56.

● 56/x/12/GDR/b

Protocol between the USSR and the German Democratic Republic concerning collaboration in the field of television

Signed Oct. 12, 1956, in Moscow.
Supplements the agreement of the same date.
Source: *Dokumente DDR*, 5, pp. 657–58.

● 56/x/12/Norway

Agreement between the USSR and Norway concerning cultural collaboration

Signed Oct. 12, 1956, in Oslo.
Ratified by the USSR Apr. 3, 1958; by Norway Apr. 11, 1958. Entered into force June 3, 1958, on exchange of acts of ratification in Moscow. Duration 5 years; thereafter may be denounced with 6 months' notice.
Source: *VVS*, 1958, No. 11, Art. 229.
References: *Izv.*, Oct. 14, 1956.
NYT, Oct. 14, 1956.

● 56/x/13/Lebanon

Trade protocol for 1957 between the USSR and Lebanon

Signed Oct. 13, 1956, in Moscow.
Based on the trade and payments agreement of Apr. 30, 1954. Provides for a 50 per cent increase in trade over 1956, to reach a total value of 15 million Lebanese francs. Raises the trade balance

limit of the 1954 agreement to 2.5 million Lebanese pounds. Covers trade through Dec. 31, 1957.
According to the Lebanese Embassy, Mar. 18, 1958, the protocol had not been ratified by the Lebanese Parliament as of that date.
References: *Izv.*, Oct. 14, 1956.
VT, 1957, No. 3, p. 5.
SDD, 16, p. 304.

● 56/x/18/Fin

Communiqué concerning the second meeting of the Soviet-Finnish commission for scientific and technical collaboration

Published Oct. 18, 1956; the meeting took place Oct. 1–9, 1956, in Helsinki.
Source: *Izv.*, Oct. 18, 1956.

● 56/x/19/J/a

Joint declaration by the USSR and Japan concerning political relations

Signed Oct. 19, 1956, in Moscow.
Ratified by the USSR and Japan Dec. 8, 1956; entered into force Dec. 12, 1956, on exchange of acts of ratification in Tokyo. Covers the following agreements: (1) The state of war between the USSR and Japan to cease on the date of entry into force of this declaration; (2) diplomatic and consular relations between the USSR and Japan to be re-established; (3) the USSR and Japan affirm their support of the principles of the UN Charter, and undertake not to interfere directly or indirectly in each other's internal affairs; (4) the USSR to support Japan's application for membership in the UN; (5) Japanese citizens serving sentences in the USSR to be repatriated on entry into force of this declaration; (6) the USSR renounces claims to reparations from Japan, and both States renounce all claims arising in connection with the war as from Aug. 9, 1945; (7) the USSR and Japan agree to start negotiations in the immediate future for the conclusion of treaties or agreements concerning trade, merchant shipping, and other commercial relations; (8) the fisheries convention of May 14, 1956, and the agreement of the same date concerning cooperation for rescue at sea to enter into force together with this declaration; and (9) the USSR and Japan to continue their negotiations for con-

clusion of a peace treaty; the USSR agrees to transfer to Japan the Habomai Islands and the Island of Shikotan, the actual transfer to be effected after conclusion of the peace treaty.
Sources: *Pr., Izv.,* Oct. 20, 1956.
  VVS, 1956, No. 24, Art. 525.
  Deklaratsii, 1957, pp. 313–16.
  NT, 1956, No. 44, pp. 35–36.
  *CDT, No. 1316.
  DIA, 1956, pp. 747–49.
  NYT, Oct. 20, 1956.
  UNTS, 263, pp. 99–117 (R, J, E, F).

● 56/x/19/J/b
Protocol between the USSR and Japan concerning development of trade and reciprocal application of the most-favored-nation clause

Signed Oct. 19, 1956, in Moscow.
Ratified by the USSR and Japan Dec. 8, 1956; entered into force Dec. 12, 1956, on exchange of acts of ratification in Tokyo.
Sources: *Pr., Izv.,* Oct. 20, 1956.
  VVS, 1956, No. 24, Art. 526.
  NT, 1956, No. 44, p. 37.
  *CDT, No. 1317.
  UNTS, 263, pp. 119–27 (R, J, E, F).

● 56/x/19/Norway
Agreement between the USSR and Norway concerning collaboration in rescuing persons in distress and in searching for missing persons in the Barents Sea, with exchange of notes

Signed Oct. 19, 1956, in Oslo.
Entered into force Jan. 1, 1957. Duration 3 years; if not denounced 6 months before expiration, extended for 1-year periods. Exchange of notes provides for assistance by the Norwegian rescue service to Soviet vessels in distress or missing in the Norwegian Sea.
Source: *UNTS,* 257, pp. 3–19 (R, N, E, F).

● 56/x/22/Rom
Agreement between the USSR and Romania concerning transfer to Romania of Soviet shares in the Soviet-Romanian joint-stock uranium company "Sovrom Kvartsit"

Signed Oct. 22, 1956, in Bucharest.
Romania to pay for the shares over a period of several years.

References: *Pravda,* Nov. 15, 1956;
  CDSP, 8, 1956, No. 47, p. 22.
  NYT, Dec. 19, 1956.

● 56/x/24/H
Agreement between the USSR and Hungary concerning Soviet military aid in "restoring order" in Hungary

Announced Oct. 24, 1956, by Radio Budapest.
The request for Soviet aid by the Hungarian Government was based on the Warsaw Pact (55/v/14/Pl/a). For a statement by Hungary concerning its withdrawal from the Pact on Nov. 1, 1956, see *DIA, 1956,* pp. 474–75.
References (Hungarian statement of Oct. 24, 1956): Zinner, p. 409.
  DIA, 1956, p. 447.
  (Soviet reference): *Pravda,* Oct. 30, 1956.

● 56/x/25/Belgium
Agreement between the USSR and Belgium concerning cultural collaboration

Signed Oct. 25, 1956, in Moscow.
Entered into force on signature. Duration 5 years. If not denounced 6 months before expiration, extended for 5 years.
Provides for establishment of a permanent mixed commission to settle questions arising out of the agreement, to meet not less than once annually, alternately in the USSR and Belgium. Annual plans to be prepared, subject to approval by both Governments. Covers the fields of higher education, teacher training, science, technology, youth, literature, theater, music, graphic arts, radio, television, health, sport, and tourism. Based on negotiations from Aug. 9 to 30, 1956, in Moscow (*Izv.,* Aug. 30, 1956); see 56/viii/30/Belgium.
Sources: *Pr., Izv.,* Oct. 26, 1956.
  NT, 1956, No. 45, pp. 35–36.

● 56/x/26/Mul
Statute of the International Atomic Energy Agency, with annex

Signed Oct. 26, 1956, at Lake Success, New York.
Ratified by the USSR Feb. 9, 1957; act of ratification deposited Apr. 8, 1957.
Ratified by the Belorussian SSR Mar. 18, 1957; act of ratification deposited Apr. 8,

1957. Act of ratification of the Ukrainian SSR deposited July 31, 1957. Enters into force after ratification by 18 States, including at least 3 of the following: the USSR, the United Kingdom, the United States of America, Canada, and France. Annex, providing for establishment of a preparatory commission, entered into force on signature.

Sources: *Int. aff.*, 1957, No. 3, pp. 153–63.
UST, 8, pp. 1093–1224.
AJIL, Apr. 1957, pp. 466–85.
Reference: *VVS*, 1956, No. 5, Art. 97 (ratification).

● 56/x/29/US

Exchange of notes between the USSR and the United States of America concerning extension of diplomatic immunity to non-diplomatic members of embassy staffs

Sent by the USSR Oct. 29, 1956, in answer to a note from the United States earlier in 1956.
Based on a Soviet decree of Mar. 27, 1956, under which a similar agreement had been negotiated earlier in 1956 between the USSR and the United Kingdom (not listed separately).
Reference: G. Tunkin, "Some developments in international law concerning diplomatic privileges and immunities," *Int. aff.*, 1957, No. 12, p. 70.

● 56/x/30/Af

Joint communiqué by the USSR and Afghanistan concerning the visit of H. R. H. Sardar Mohammed Daoud, Prime Minister of Afghanistan, to the USSR

Signed Oct. 30, 1956, in Moscow.
Reaffirms friendly and cordial relations between the 2 States.
Sources: *Pr.*, *Izv.*, Nov. 1, 1956.
Deklaratsii, 1957, pp. 44–46.
NT, 1956, No. 46, p. 34.

Oct. 30, 1956. Declaration by the USSR concerning its readiness to review with other signatories of the Warsaw Pact of May 14, 1955, the question of the presence of Soviet troops on their territory

Agreements based on this declaration were signed with Poland Dec. 17, 1956; with the German Democratic Republic Mar. 12, 1957; with Romania Apr. 15, 1957; and with Hungary May 27, 1957.

Sources: *Pr.*, *Izv.*, Oct. 31, 1956.
DIA, 1956, pp. 465–68.
Zinner, pp. 485–92.

● 56/xi/ /India

Agreement between the USSR and India concerning a loan to India

Negotiated during Nov. 1956.
Provides for a loan of $126 million, to be repaid in 12 years at 2½ per cent, to be used for purchase of industrial equipment and machinery in the USSR. Provides the basis for the aid agreement of Nov. 9, 1957.
Reference: Allen, 1957, p. 441.

● 56/xi/ /Syria

Agreement between the USSR and Syria concerning shipment of Soviet munitions to Syria

Concluded during or shortly before Nov. 1956.
Inferred from evidence of Soviet arms shipments to Syria in Nov. and Dec. 1956.
Reference: Laqueur, pp. 252–53.

● 56/xi/2/Belgium/a

Joint communiqué by the USSR and Belgium concerning political, economic, and cultural relations

Signed Nov. 2, 1956, in Moscow, at the end of negotiations which began Oct. 26, 1956.
Covers general principles underlying the foreign policies of the 2 States. Mentions agreement to continue negotiations for conclusion of a 3-year trade agreement, and signature of protocol on air communications (next document). Belgian citizens or former citizens living in the USSR to receive favorable consideration from the USSR on applications for permission for themselves and their families to go to Belgium; Soviet citizens and members of their families who wish to go to the USSR to be allowed to do so by Belgian authorities.
Sources: *Pr.*, *Izv.*, Nov. 3, 1956.
Deklaratsii, 1957, pp. 50–53.
NT, 1956, No. 46, pp. 35–36.

● 56/xi/2/Belgium/b

Protocol between the USSR and Belgium concerning establishment of direct air communications between Moscow and Brussels

Signed on or about Nov. 2, 1956, in Moscow.
Mentioned in the joint communiqué of the same date (preceding document).

● 56/xi/5/Syria

Joint communiqué by the USSR and Syria concerning political negotiations

Published Nov. 5, 1956, following negotiations from Oct. 31 to Nov. 3, 1956, in Moscow.
Deals mainly with international relations, particularly the armed invasion of Egypt and the rebellion in Algeria.
Sources: *Pr.*, Nov. 5, 1956; *Izv.*, Nov. 6, 1956.
  Deklaratsii, 1957, pp. 241–43.
  NT, 1956, No. 47, p. 35.

● 56/xi/5/H

Exchange of notes between the USSR and Hungary concerning material aid to Hungary

Sent Nov. 5, 1956, from Budapest and Moscow.
Provides for Soviet deliveries of food and construction materials and for prompt deliveries of trade goods under the trade agreements for 1956 and the 1st quarter of 1957.
Source: *Pr., Izv.*, Nov. 6, 1956.

● 56/xi/9/MPR

Agreement between the USSR and the Mongolian People's Republic concerning non-commercial payments

Signed Nov. 9, 1956, in Moscow.
Reference: *Pravda*, Nov. 11, 1956.

● 56/xi/18/Pol

Joint statement by the USSR and Poland concerning political, economic, and military relations

Signed Nov. 18, 1956, in Moscow, by delegations which represented both the Governments of the 2 States and the Central Committees of the Communist Party of the Soviet Union and the Polish United Workers' Party.
Covers (1) international relations, particularly Egypt, the Chinese People's Republic, and Hungary; (2) political relations between the USSR and Poland, affirming the "great importance" of the Soviet declaration of Oct. 30, 1956 (see above, p. 371); (3) economic relations,

mentioning the following agreements: (a) as of Nov. 1, 1956, Poland's debt on credits advanced by the USSR in payment of coal delivered to the USSR under the agreement of Aug. 16, 1945 (45/viii/16/Pol/a), to be cancelled; (b) payments by Poland for railroad shipments, non-commercial payments, etc., to be adjusted; (c) the USSR to deliver 1.4 million tons of grain to Poland in 1957 on credit; (d) the USSR to grant Poland a long-term credit of 700 million rubles to pay for goods under an agreed list; (4) military relations, including statement of the principles defining the status of Soviet units stationed in Poland; an agreement on this subject to be concluded in the near future (see 56/xii/17/Pol); and (5) agreement on principles to govern the liberation and repatriation of Poles in places of detention in the USSR.
For an announcement of the return to the USSR of Marshal K. K. Rokossovsky shortly after the signature of this statement, see 49/xi/7/Pol.
Sources: *Pravda*, Nov. 19, 1956; *Izv.*, Nov. 20, 1956.
  NT, 1956, No. 48, pp. 37–40.
  Zinner, pp. 306–14.
  DIA, 1956, pp. 517–23.

● 56/xi/19/Mul

Protocol to the international convention for the regulation of whaling of December 2, 1946

Signed Nov. 19, 1956.
Ratified by the USSR June 12, 1957; act of ratification deposited July 3, 1957.
References: *VVS*, 1957, No. 14, Art. 348.
  DSB, 35, 1956, p. 970.
See further Appendix 5.

● 56/xi/26/India

Agreement between the USSR and India concerning technical collaboration in oil prospecting in India

Signed Nov. 26, 1956, in New Delhi.
Provides for sending 26 Soviet specialists to India during Dec. 1956 to assist prospecting operations being carried out in the Punjab.
Reference: *Pravda*, Nov. 28, 1956.

● 56/xi/28/Fin

Trade protocol for 1957 between the USSR and Finland, with annexes

Signed Nov. 28, 1956, in Moscow.

Annexes list goods to be exchanged: Soviet grain, sugar, fertilizer, oil products, solid fuel, rolled ferrous metals, ferrous alloys, cotton, automobiles, industrial equipment, tobacco, asbestos, chemicals, etc., in exchange for Finnish freight locomotives, tugs, fishing trawlers and other vessels, floating cranes, equipment for power, lifting, and moving, equipment for the wood-pulp industry, copper wire, cable products, paper and boxes, cellulose, lumber, staple fiber, etc.
References: *Pravda*, Nov. 29, 1956.
   VT, 1956, No. 12, p. 4; *ibid.*, 1957, No. 1, p. 3.

● 56/xi/30/Cz

Treaty between the USSR and Czechoslovakia concerning the regime on the Soviet-Czechoslovak border and procedure for settling border incidents, with related documents

Signed Nov. 30, 1956, in Moscow.
Ratified by the USSR Feb. 9, 1957.
Entered into force Mar. 30, 1951, on exchange of acts of ratification in Prague. Duration 5 years. If not denounced 6 months before expiration, extended for 5-year periods. Related documents comprise 4 annexed forms for personal identification and a supplementary protocol.
Sources: *Dogovor*, 1957.
   UNTS, 266, pp. 243–359 (R, Cz., E, F).
References: *Izv.*, Dec. 1, 1956.
   VVS, 1957, No. 5, Art. 98.

● 56/xii/1/MPR

Agreement between the USSR and the Mongolian People's Republic concerning air communications

Signed Dec. 1, 1956, in Moscow.
In connection with the signing of the agreement, all installations and property of the USSR Main Administration of the Civil Air Fleet in the MPR to be transferred without charge to the MPR. For a report on completion of the transfer, see *Pravda*, Apr. 23, 1957.
References: *Pravda*, Dec. 4, 1956; *CDSP*, 8, 1956, No. 49, p. 19.

● 56/xii/1/Mul

International sugar protocol, amending the agreement of October 1, 1953, for regulation of the production and marketing of sugar, with annex

Signed Dec. 1, 1956, in London; by the USSR Dec. 15, 1956.
Ratified by the USSR June 29, 1957; act of ratification deposited July 18, 1957. On signature the USSR made a declaration to the effect that its signature did not constitute recognition of the Nationalist Government of China as the legal Government of China. For the 1953 agreement, see 53/x/29/1953.
Sources: *SDD*, 16, pp. 596–608.
   TIAS, 3937.

● 56/xii/1/DRV. See Appendix 5.

● 56/xii/3/Rom/a

Statement by the USSR and Romania concerning political and economic negotiations

Signed Dec. 3, 1956, in Moscow.
Covers both international relations and relations between the 2 States. Affirms support for principles of the Soviet declaration of Oct. 30, 1956 (see above, p. 371). In the field of economic collaboration, mentions the following agreements: (1) supplementary trade deliveries to be made during 1957; the USSR to supply iron ore, metallurgical coke, tubing, etc.; (2) the USSR to loan Romania 450,000 tons of wheat during the first half of 1957 and supply 60,000 tons of fodder grain to be paid for under the trade agreement; (3) the USSR to give technical aid in building chemical works and oil refineries and supply equipment on credit; (4) payment by Romania on certain long-term credits to be postponed; (5) all questions concerning financial arrangements between the 2 States settled. With regard to military relations, the 2 States agree to consult together as necessary concerning the continued presence of Soviet military units on Romanian territory.
Sources: *Pr., Izv.*, Dec. 4, 1956.
   Deklaratsii, 1957, pp. 232–39.
   Pod znamenem, pp. 137–44.
   NT, 1956, No. 50, supplement.

● 56/xii/3/Rom/b

Protocol between the USSR and Romania concerning a Soviet credit

Signed Dec. 3, 1956.
Provides for a long-term credit of 370 million rubles, including 270 million rubles for repayment of project planning

and deliveries of equipment for the chemical and oil-refining industries. To be repaid within 10 years by deliveries of goods from enterprises being aided, in equal annual installments. Payment on all Romanian debts on credits granted from 1949 to 1956 deferred, particularly those to have been repaid in 1957–1959.
Summarized, but not specifically mentioned, in the statement of the same date (preceding document).
Reference: *VT SSSR*, p. 138.

● 56/xii/7/Fin

Agreement between the USSR and Finland concerning collaboration between rescue services in the Baltic Sea

Signed Dec. 7, 1956, in Helsinki.
Entered into force Jan. 1, 1957. Duration 3 years; if not denounced 6 months before expiration, extended until 6 months after denunciation.
Sources: *SS*, 1956, No. 35 (Finnish, R).
    UNTS, 258, pp. 89–101 (R, Finnish, E, F).
Reference: *Izv.*, Dec. 8, 1956.

● 56/xii/12/Bul

Communiqué concerning the eighth meeting of the Soviet-Bulgarian commission for scientific and technical collaboration

Published Dec. 12, 1956; the meeting took place a few days earlier, in Sofia.
Source: *Izv.*, Dec. 12, 1956.

● 56/xii/14/MPR

Trade protocol for 1957 between the USSR and the Mongolian People's Republic

Signed Dec. 14, 1956, in Moscow.
Soviet consumer's goods, medicines, tractors, agricultural machines, automobiles, machinery, oil products, rolled metals, etc., in exchange for Mongolian meat, butter, wool, skins, and other products of animal husbandry and hunting.
References: *Pr., Izv.*, Dec. 15, 1956; *CDSP*, 8, 1956, No. 50, p. 2.

● 56/xii/17/Pol

Treaty between the USSR and Poland concerning the legal status of Soviet troops temporarily stationed in Poland
Signed Dec. 17, 1956, in Warsaw.

Ratified by Poland Feb. 1, 1957; by the USSR Feb. 11, 1957. Entered into force Feb. 27, 1957, on exchange of acts of ratification in Warsaw.
Provides that number of Soviet troops in Poland and their location shall be defined by special agreements. Movements of troops and their training and maneuvers outside the base area to require Polish agreement. A special agreement to be negotiated on legal aid in regard to the prosecution of crimes and misdemeanors (see 57/x/26/Pol). Special agreements to determine the communication lines, time limits, procedure and terms of payment for transit of Soviet troops and military property as well as military shipments through Polish territory. Special agreements to determine application of tax, custom, and currency regulations in force in Poland as well as export and import provisions concerning Soviet troops stationed in Poland. A mixed Soviet-Polish commission to be established, with headquarters in Warsaw, to settle disputes which arise under the treaty.
Based on the Soviet declaration of Oct. 30, 1956, and the joint Soviet-Polish statement of Nov. 18, 1956.
Sources: *Pr., Izv.*, Dec. 18, 1956; *CDSP*, 8, 1957, No. 51, pp. 3–4.
    VVS, 1957, No. 7, Art. 192.
    DUPRL, 1957, No. 29, Arts. 127, 128.
    UNTS, 266, pp. 179–207 (R, P, E, F).
    AJIL, 52, Jan. 1958, pp. 221–27.
    NYT, Dec. 19, 1956.
    Current history, Mar. 1957, pp. 179–82.

● 56/xii/23/KPDR

Communiqué concerning the second meeting of the USSR–Korean People's Democratic Republic commission for scientific and technical collaboration

Published Dec. 23, 1956; the meeting took place a few days earlier, in Pyongyang.
Source: *Izv.*, Dec. 23, 1956.

● 56/xii/26/CPR

Communiqué concerning the fifth meeting of the USSR–Chinese People's Republic commission for scientific and technical collaboration

Published Dec. 26, 1956; the meeting ended Dec. 24, 1956, in Moscow, with the signing of a protocol.
Source: *Izv.*, Dec. 26, 1956.

1957

● 57/i/6/Pl

Communiqué concerning a meeting of representatives of the Communist and Workers' Parties and Governments of the USSR, Bulgaria, Czechoslovakia, Hungary, and Romania

Published Jan. 6, 1957; the meeting took place Jan. 1–4, 1957, in Budapest.
Concerns suppression of the anti-Communist uprising of Oct. 1956 in Hungary and events in the Middle East.
Sources: *Izv.*, Jan. 6, 1957.
  Deklaratsii, 1957, pp. 324–28.

● 57/i/7/Af

Trade protocol for 1957 and 1958 between the USSR and Afghanistan

Signed Jan. 7, 1957, in Kabul.
Based on the trade and payments agreement of July 17, 1950.
References: *Pravda*, Jan. 9, 1957.
  VT, 1957, No. 2, p. 8; *ibid.*, No. 7, p. 34.

● 57/i/7/GDR

Joint declaration by the USSR and the German Democratic Republic concerning political and economic relations

Signed Jan. 7, 1957, in Moscow.
Covers international relations as well as relations between the 2 States. Agreement reached on conclusion of (1) an agreement on stationing of Soviet troops in the GDR; (2) a consular convention; and (3) an agreement on legal assistance in civil and criminal cases. Existing quadripartite agreements on United States, British, and French air traffic over the air corridors between Berlin and Western Germany stated to be of a temporary and limited nature not impairing the sovereignty of the GDR over its air space. Soviet trade deliveries to the GDR in 1957 to be more than 30 per cent above the volume for 1956. The USSR to grant the GDR a credit of 340 million rubles in 1957 for purchase of goods.
Sources: *Pr.*, *Izv.*, Jan. 8, 1957.
  Deklaratsii, 1957, pp. 119–30.
  Pod znamenem, pp. 264–75.
  NT, 1957, No. 3, supplement, pp. 34–38.
  Dokumente DDR, 5, pp. 661–73.

● 57/i/10/Alb/a

Agreement between the USSR and Albania concerning postal and telephone and telegraph communications

Signed Jan. 10, 1957, in Moscow.
Reference: *Izv.*, Jan. 11, 1957.

● 57/i/10/Alb/b

Parcel post agreement between the USSR and Albania

Signed Jan. 10, 1957, in Moscow.
Reference: *Izv.*, Jan. 11, 1957.

● 57/i/11/Cz

Protocol concerning the tenth meeting of the Soviet-Czechoslovak commission for scientific and technical collaboration

Signed Jan. 11, 1957, in Prague.
Reference: *Izv.*, Jan. 12, 1957.

● 57/i/12/Bul

Trade protocol for 1957 between the USSR and Bulgaria

Signed Jan. 12, 1957, in Sofia.
Soviet industrial and road-building equipment, motor vehicles, pig iron, rolled ferrous metals, nonferrous metals, coke, cotton and other textile raw materials, in exchange for Bulgarian nonferrous ore concentrates, barges, tobacco, clothing, footwear, furniture, canned fruits and vegetables, fresh and dried fruits, wine, etc. Informal agreement reached on Soviet loans of wheat to Bulgaria over 3 years, starting with the 1957 harvest.
References: *Pravda*, Jan. 15, 1957;
  CDSP, 9, 1957, No. 2, p. 21.
  VT, 1957, No. 7, p. 34.

● 57/i/12/Cz

Agreement between the USSR and Czechoslovakia concerning cultural collaboration

Signed Jan. 12, 1957, in Prague.
Reference: *Izv.*, Jan. 13, 1957.

● 57/i/12/Pl

Communiqué concerning a meeting between representatives of the Communist and Workers' Parties and Governments

of the USSR, the Chinese People's Republic, and Hungary

Published Jan. 12, 1957; the meeting took place Jan. 10, 1957, in Moscow.
Participants agree to expand political, economic, and cultural contacts and general collaboration between the 3 States.
Sources: *Pr.*, *Izv.*, Jan. 12, 1957.

• 57/i/14/Cz

Trade agreement for 1957 between the USSR and Czechoslovakia

Signed Jan. 14, 1957, in Moscow.
References: *Pravda*, Jan. 15, 1957; *CDSP*, 9, 1957, No. 2, p. 21.
VT, 1957, No. 7, p. 34.

• 57/i/17/Burma

Economic agreement between the USSR and Burma, with annex
Signed Jan. 17, 1957, in Rangoon.
Ratified by the USSR Mar. 18, 1957; by Burma May 9, 1957. Entered into force June 7, 1957, on exchange of acts of ratification in Moscow.
Provides for construction of a technological institute, a hospital, a theater, and a cultural and sports center, between 1957 and 1963, in accordance with joint declarations of Dec. 6, 1955, and Apr. 1, 1956. For a contract agreement to carry out the provisions, see 57/viii/29/Burma.
Source: *VVS*, 1957, No. 15, Art. 382.
References: *Pr.*, *Izv.*, Jan. 19, 1957; *CDSP*, 9, 1957, No. 3, pp. 22–23.

• 57/i/18/CPR

Joint declaration by the USSR and the Chinese People's Republic concerning international relations

Signed Jan. 18, 1957, in Moscow.
Sources: *Pr.*, *Izv.*, Jan. 19, 1957.
Deklaratsii, 1957, pp. 189–97.
Pod znamenem, pp. 281–89.
NT, 1957, No. 4, supplement.

• 57/i/19/Greece

Trade protocol for 1957 between the USSR and Greece

Signed Jan. 19, 1957, in Moscow.
Increases the trade limit under the trade and payments agreement of July 28, 1953, from $1 million US to $2.5 million US.
Source: *Greek official gazette, A, 1957, No. 44.

References: *Izv.*, Jan. 25, 1957; *CDSP*, 9, 1957, No. 4, p. 21.
SDD, 15, p. 50.
VT, 1957, No. 7, p. 34.

• 57/i/25/Pl

Agreement concerning standardization of machine tools produced by participants in the Council of Mutual Economic Aid

Signed Jan. 25, 1957, in Prague, by the Engineering Working Group of the Council. The 5-day meeting of the Council was attended by Bulgaria, Czechoslovakia, the German Democratic Republic, Hungary, Poland, and the USSR, with observers from the Chinese People's Republic.
Reference: *NT*, 1957, No. 5, p. 32.

• 57/i/29/Cz

Joint declaration by the USSR and Czechoslovakia concerning political and economic relations

Signed Jan. 29, 1957, in Moscow.
Concerns international relations as well as relations between the 2 States. Mentions continued sale of uranium by Czechoslovakia to the USSR; the USSR to aid Czechoslovakia in construction of an atomic power plant and a nuclear physics institute.
A commission for Soviet-Czechoslovak economic collaboration was established in accordance with this declaration, although not specifically mentioned in it. See 57/v/19/Cz.
Sources: *Pr.*, *Izv.*, Jan. 30, 1957.
Deklaratsii, 1957, pp. 273–86.
Pod znamenem, pp. 290–303.
NT, 1957, No. 6, pp. 37–43.
NYT, Jan. 30, 1957, p. 14 (extracts).

• 57/ii/2/Fin

Joint communiqué by the USSR and Finland concerning political and economic relations

Signed Feb. 2, 1957, in Moscow.
Sources: *Izv.*, Feb. 3, 1957.
Deklaratsii, 1957, pp. 256–58.
NT, 1957, No. 6, pp. 47–48.

• 57/ii/4/Bul

Protocol between the USSR and Bulgaria concerning cultural collaboration in 1957

Signed Feb. 4, 1957, in Sofia, by the mixed

commission established under the agreement of Apr. 28, 1956.
A plan for cultural collaboration in 1957 was signed at the same time.
Reference: *Pravda*, Feb. 5, 1957.

● 57/ii/5/GDR. See Appendix 5.

● 57/ii/5/Norway

Supplementary trade protocol for 1957 between the USSR and Norway

Signed Feb. 5, 1957.
Reference: *BSE, 1958*, p. 35.

● 57/ii/6/Pol

Protocol between the USSR and Poland concerning cultural collaboration in 1957

Signed Feb. 6, 1957, in Moscow, by the mixed commission established under the agreement of June 30, 1956.
A plan for cultural collaboration in 1957 was signed at the same time.
Reference: *Izv.*, Feb. 7, 1957.

Feb. 7, 1957. Changes in the parcel post agreement of Oct. 1, 1947, between the USSR and Poland
See 47/x/1/Pol.

● 57/ii/9/Mul

Interim convention for protection of fur seals in the North Pacific Ocean, with annex

Signed Feb. 9, 1957, in Washington, D.C.
Ratified by the USSR Sept. 27, 1957; act of ratification deposited Oct. 14, 1957.
Entered into force Oct. 14, 1957.
Sources: *TIAS*, 3984.
   DSB, 36, 1957, pp. 377–80.
References: *Pravda*, Sept. 29, 1957.
   VVS, 1957, No. 21, Art. 522.

● 57/ii/9/Yug

Protocol between the USSR and Yugoslavia concerning collaboration between scientific organizations and institutions

Signed Feb. 9, 1957, in Moscow.
Supplements the agreement of Jan. 28, 1956, concerning collaboration in the field of nuclear physics.
References: *Izv.*, Feb. 13, 1957.
   VT, 1957, No. 7, p. 34.

● 57/ii/11/France/a

Trade agreement for the period 1957–1959 between the USSR and France, with four annexes

Signed Feb. 11, 1957, in Paris.
Valid from Jan. 1, 1957, through Dec. 31, 1959. Trade to be carried out in accordance with the agreement of July 15, 1953 (53/vii/15/France/a), which is extended through Dec. 31, 1959. Annexes list goods to be traded, and are to be supplemented and revised on signature of yearly protocols. First yearly protocol signed the same day (next document).
Source: *VT*, 1957, No. 6, pp. 33–37.
References: *Pr., Izv.*, Feb. 13, 1957; *CDSP*, 9, 1957, No. 7, p. 33.

● 57/ii/11/France/b

Trade protocol for 1957 between the USSR and France

Signed Feb. 11, 1957, in Paris.
Based on the trade agreement of the same date (preceding document). Provides for an increase of 40 per cent in trade volume over 1956, reaching a total of 600 million rubles.
Reference: *VT*, 1957, No. 6, p. 10.

Feb. 14, 1957
See Appendix 5.

● 57/ii/15/CPR

Protocol between the USSR and the Chinese People's Republic concerning extension and development of postal and electronic means of communication

Signed Feb. 15, 1957, in Peking.
Reference: *Pravda*, Feb. 16, 1957.

● 57/ii/15/Norway

Agreement between the USSR and Norway concerning the sea boundary in the Varanger Fjord

Signed Feb. 15, 1957, in Oslo.
Ratified by the USSR Mar. 28, 1957; by Norway Mar. 29, 1957. Entered into force Apr. 24, 1957, on exchange of acts of ratification in Moscow.
Provides for establishment of a mixed demarcation commission, to complete work

by May 1957. Protocol concerning border
demarcation signed Aug. 1, 1957. Final
documents signed Nov. 29, 1957.
Source: *VVS*, 1957, No. 14, Art. 344.
Reference: *Pravda*, Feb. 16, 1957.

• 57/ii/15/DRV

**Agreement between the USSR and the
Democratic Republic of Vietnam concerning cultural collaboration**

Signed Feb. 15, 1957, in Hanoi.
Entered into force June 4, 1957, on ex-
change of notes concerning ratification, in
Moscow. Duration 3 years; if not de-
nounced 6 months before expiration, ex-
tended for 3-year periods.
Source: *UNTS*, 274, pp. 115–31 (R, V, E,
F).
Reference: *Pravda*, Feb. 16, 1957.

• 57/ii/20/Bul

**Joint declaration by the USSR and Bul-
garia concerning political and economic
relations**

Signed Feb. 20, 1957, in Moscow.
Covers international relations as well as
relations between the 2 States. Calls for
conclusion of (1) a trade agreement for
the period 1958–1960 and (2) an agreement concerning construction and repair
of vessels for the USSR in Bulgarian
yards during 1958–1960 (see 57/v/18/
Bul). Mentions granting of a new long-
term Soviet credit of up to 200 million
rubles for industrial development. Bulgaria to continue supplying uranium to
the USSR.
Sources: *Izv.*, Feb. 21, 1957.
Deklaratsii, 1957, pp. 62–73.
NT, 1957, No. 9, pp. 33–37.

• 57/ii/20/GDR

**Trade agreement for 1957 between the
USSR and the German Democratic Republic**

Signed Feb. 20, 1957, in Berlin.
References: *Pravda*, Feb. 21, 1957;
CDSP, 9, 1957, No. 8, p. 37.
VT, 1957, No. 7, p. 34.

**Feb. 20, 1957. Convention concerning
citizenship of married women**

See 57/ix/6/1957.

• 57/ii/23/Alb

**Trade agreement for 1957 between the
USSR and Albania**

Signed Feb. 23, 1957, in Moscow.
References: *Izv.*, Feb. 24, 1957.
VT, 1957, No. 7, p. 34.

• 57/ii/26/GDR

**Agreement between the USSR and the
German Democratic Republic concerning regulation of financial aspects of the
production of the USSR-GDR joint-stock
uranium producing company "Vismut"**

Signed Feb. 26, 1957.
Provides for delivery of GDR uranium to
the USSR at prices calculated to cover
production costs and planned profits, in
exchange for goods. Financial aspects of
"Vismut's" operations, including taxes
and social insurance, to be subject to GDR
laws.
Reference: *Dokumente DDR*, 5, pp. 686–
87, citing *ND*, Mar. 15, 1957.

• 57/ii/26/Yug

**Trade protocol for 1957 between the
USSR and Yugoslavia**

Signed Feb. 26, 1957, in Moscow.
References: *Pravda*, Feb. 27, 1957;
CDSP, 9, 1957, No. 9, p. 25.
VT, 1957, No. 7, pp. 34–35.

• 57/ii/27/Iran

**Joint communiqué concerning work of
the mixed Soviet-Iranian commission for
demarcation and re-demarcation of the
state border**

Published Feb. 27, 1957.
For the agreement establishing the mixed
commission, see 54/xii/2/Iran/a.
Source: *Izv.*, Feb. 27, 1957.

• 57/iii/2/Rom

**Communiqué concerning the eighth
meeting of the Soviet-Romanian commission for scientific and technical collaboration**

Published Mar. 2, 1957; the meeting took
place during the 2nd half of February, in
Bucharest.
Source: *Izv.*, Mar. 2, 1957.

• 57/iii/3/Pol

Protocol of the eleventh meeting of the

Soviet-Polish commission for scientific and technical collaboration

Signed Mar. 3, 1957, in Moscow.
References: *Izv.*, Mar. 7, 1957 (communiqué).
BSE, 1958, p. 35.

• 57/iii/4/Rom

Trade agreement for 1957 between the USSR and Romania

Signed Mar. 4, 1957, in Moscow.
References: *Izv.*, Mar. 5, 1957.
VT, 1957, No. 7, p. 35.

• 57/iii/5/Pol

Treaty between the USSR and Poland concerning demarcation of the existing Soviet-Polish State frontier in the sector adjoining the Baltic Sea, with two maps

Signed Mar. 5, 1957, in Moscow.
Ratified by Poland Apr. 18, 1957; by the USSR Apr. 19, 1957. Entered into force May 4, 1957, on exchange of acts of ratification in Warsaw. Provides for establishment of a mixed demarcation commission, to complete work within 6 months from date of entry into force.
Sources: *VVS*, 1957, No. 14, Art. 345.
UNTS, 274, pp. 133–41 (R, P, E, F).
References: *Pr., Izv., Trud*, Mar. 6, 1957;
CDSP, 9, 1957, No. 10, pp. 26–27.

• 57/iii/11/DRV

Agreement between the USSR and the Democratic Republic of Vietnam concerning noncommercial payments

Signed Mar. 11, 1957, in Moscow.
References: *Izv.*, Mar. 13, 1957.
VT, 1957, No. 7, p. 35.

• 57/iii/12/GDR

Agreement between the USSR and the German Democratic Republic concerning questions connected with the temporary stationing of Soviet troops on the territory of the GDR

Signed Mar. 12, 1957, in Berlin.
Entered into force Apr. 27, 1957, on exchange of notes concerning confirmation. Based on the joint declaration of Jan. 7, 1957, and the treaty of Sept. 20, 1955 (55/ix/20/GDR/b). Supplemented by an agreement of Aug. 2, 1957, concerning legal aid.

Sources: *Izv.*, Mar. 14, 1957.
GBl DDR, 1957, I, No. 28.
Dokumente DDR, 5, pp. 677–85.
UNTS, 285, pp. 105–33 (R, G, E, F).
AJIL, 52, 1958, No. 1, pp. 210–15.

• 57/iii/14/Egypt

Trade agreement between the USSR and Egypt

Signed Mar. 14, 1957, in Cairo.
Provides for exchange of 500,000 tons of Soviet oil against Egyptian goods.
References: *Izv.*, Mar. 16, 1957.
NYT, Mar. 16, 1957, p. 8.

• 57/iii/14/GDR

Communiqué concerning regulation of financial aspects of the production of the USSR-GDR joint-stock uranium producing company, "Vismut"

Published Mar. 14, 1957.
Summarizes terms of an agreement signed a few days earlier, in Berlin.
Source: *Izv.*, Mar. 15, 1957.

• 57/iii/25/Pol

Agreement between the USSR and Poland concerning time schedules and procedures for further repatriation of persons of Polish nationality from the USSR

Signed Mar. 25, 1957, in Moscow.
Ratified by Poland May 23, 1957; by the USSR June 5, 1957. Entered into force July 10, 1957, on exchange of acts of ratification. Applications for repatriation to be filed before Oct. 1, 1958; repatriation to be concluded by Dec. 31, 1958. Based on the joint statement of Nov. 18, 1956.
Sources: *Izv.*, Mar. 26, 1957.
VVS, 1957, No. 16, Art. 418.
UNTS, 281, pp. 121–41 (R, P, E, F).
References: *Pr., Izv.*, Mar. 26, 1957.

• 57/iii/27/Pol

Agreement between the USSR and Poland concerning scientific collaboration in 1957 between the Academies of Sciences of the USSR and Poland

Signed Mar. 27, 1957, in Warsaw.
Includes the fields of physics, chemistry, technology, geology, and history.
References: *Pr., Izv.*, Mar. 29, 1957.

● 57/iii/28/H/a

Joint declaration by the USSR and Hungary concerning political and economic relations

Signed Mar. 28, 1957, in Moscow.
Section 1 constitutes a review of events following the Hungarian Revolution of Oct. 1956, and an apologia for Soviet action in suppressing the uprising. Section 2 reviews economic relations between the 2 States and mentions the following agreements: (1) Soviet deliveries in 1957 to be increased; (2) a trade agreement for 1958–1960 to be drawn up; (3) the USSR provides a credit of 750 million rubles, to be used in 1957 and repaid in 10 years, starting in 1961, at 2 per cent; (4) extension granted on repayment of Hungary's debt of over 150 million rubles under earlier agreements; (5) Hungary's debt of more than 1 billion forints for German assets and Soviet shares in Soviet-Hungarian joint-stock companies cancelled; (6) the USSR to aid Hungary in development of atomic energy; Hungary to continue to sell uranium to the USSR. Agreements to be negotiated concerning (1) questions of citizenship; (2) legal assistance in civil and criminal cases; and (3) property, pension, and inheritance rights. Section 3 deals with the presence of Soviet troops in Hungary and calls for conclusion of an agreement defining their legal status (see 57/v/27/H).
On the same day a joint statement was signed by the Communist Party of the Soviet Union and the Hungarian Socialist Workers' Party (text, *NT*, 1957, No. 14, supplement, pp. 11–15).
Sources: *Pr.*, *Izv.*, Mar. 29, 1957.
    Deklaratsii, 1957, pp. 81–98.
    NT, 1957, No. 14, supplement, pp. 3–10.

● 57/iii/28/H/b

Trade protocol for 1957 between the USSR and Hungary

Signed Mar. 28, 1957.
Reference: *BSE*, *1958*, p. 35.

● 57/iii/30/DRV

Trade protocol for 1957 between the USSR and the Democratic Republic of Vietnam

Signed Mar. 30, 1957, in Hanoi.
Extends for an additional year the trade

agreement of July 18, 1955 (55/vii/18/DRV/c).
References: *Izv.*, Mar. 31, 1957.
    VT, 1957, No. 7, p. 35.

● 57/iv/ /Bul/a

Agreement between the USSR and Bulgaria concerning conditions for sending Soviet specialists to Bulgaria and vice versa for rendering technical aid and other services

Signed shortly before Apr. 16, 1957, in Moscow.
References: *Izv.*, Apr. 16, 1957.
    VT, 1957, No. 7, p. 35.

● 57/iv/ /Bul/b

Agreement between the USSR and Bulgaria concerning conditions for technical industrial training of Bulgarian specialists and workers in the USSR and vice versa

Signed shortly before Apr. 16, 1957, in Moscow.
References: *Izv.*, Apr. 16, 1957.
    VT, 1957, No. 7, p. 35.

● 57/iv/6/J

Joint communiqué by the USSR and Japan concerning fishing in the Northwest Pacific

Prepared Apr. 6, 1957, by a joint Soviet-Japanese fishing commission, at the end of negotiations which began Feb. 15, 1957. Defines quantities and fishing zones for 1957 in the Northwest Pacific and the Sea of Okhotsk. Second meeting of the commission to be held in Moscow beginning Jan. 13, 1958.
References: *Pr.*, *Izv.*, Apr. 9, 1957.

● 57/iv/8/DRV

General conditions for delivery of goods from the USSR to the Democratic Republic of Vietnam and vice versa

Signed Apr. 8, 1957, in Hanoi.
Entered into force Jan. 1, 1957.
Reference: *VT SSSR*, p. 207.

● 57/iv/9/Pol

Trade protocol for 1957 between the USSR and Poland

Signed Apr. 9, 1957, in Moscow.
References: *Pr.*, *Izv.*, Apr. 10, 1957.

VT, 1957, No. 7, p. 35.
NYT, Apr. 10, 1957.

● 57/iv/10/Yug

Trade agreement for the period 1958–1960 between the USSR and Yugoslavia

Signed Apr. 10, 1957, in Moscow.
Based on the protocol of Sept. 1, 1955.
Quantities and types of goods to be defined in annual lists.
References: *Pr.*, *Izv.*, Apr. 11, 1957.
VT, 1957, No. 7, p. 35.

● 57/iv/11/CPR

Trade protocol for 1957 between the USSR and the Chinese People's Republic

Signed Apr. 11, 1957, in Moscow.
References: *Pr.*, *Izv.*, Apr. 12, 1957;
    CDSP, 9, 1957, No. 15, p. 18.
VT, 1957, No. 7, p. 35.

● 57/iv/11/Iran

Final documents concerning demarcation and re-demarcation of the border between the USSR and Iran

Signed Apr. 11, 1957, in Teheran.
References: *Pr.*, *Izv.*, Apr. 13, 1957.
    NYT, Apr. 12, 1957, p. 5.

● 57/iv/15/Rom

Agreement between the USSR and Romania concerning the legal status of Soviet troops temporarily stationed on Romanian territory

Signed Apr. 15, 1957, in Bucharest.
Ratified by Romania May 3, 1957; by the USSR May 17, 1957. Entered into force June 4, 1957, on exchange of acts of ratification in Moscow. Valid for duration of the presence of Soviet troops in Romania.
Sources: *Izv.*, Apr. 17, 1957.
    VVS, 1957, No. 15, Art. 381.
    UNTS, 274, pp. 143–71 (R, Romanian, E, F).

● 57/iv/16/MPR

Protocol between the USSR and the Mongolian People's Republic supplementing the agreement of June 6, 1949, concerning establishment of the Soviet-Mongolian joint-stock railroad company "Ulan-Batorskaia zheleznaia doroga"

Signed Apr. 16, 1957, in Ulan Bator.
Reference: *BSE*, *1958*, p. 36.

● 57/iv/16/Iran

Exchange of letters between the USSR and Iran concerning establishment of trade lists for 1957/1958, 1958/1959, and 1959/1960

Sent Apr. 16, 1957, in Teheran.
References: *Pr.*, *Izv.*, Apr. 18, 1957.
    VT, 1957, No. 7, p. 35.

● 57/iv/17/Alb

Joint declaration by the USSR and Albania concerning political and economic relations

Signed Apr. 17, 1957, in Moscow.
Reviews the international situation as well as relations between the 2 States. Following specific economic agreements mentioned: (1) A specified list of industrial enterprises built in Albania with Soviet aid to be transferred to Albania; Albania's debt of 348 million rubles for them to be cancelled. (2) An Albanian debt of 74 million rubles for Soviet deliveries of equipment and materials to be cancelled as of Jan. 1, 1957. (3) The USSR to aid Albania in drafting a long-term development plan. (4) The USSR to give Albania technical assistance in 1957–1958. (5) The USSR to deliver 31 million rubles' worth of wheat, rice, and vegetable oil during the first half of 1958 on credit. Following agreements to be signed: (1) a treaty of commerce and navigation; agreements concerning (2) citizenship and (3) legal aid in civil and criminal cases; and (4) a consular convention. For (2) and (4) see 57/ix/18/Alb/a and /b.
Sources: *Pr.*, *Izv.*, Apr. 18, 1957.
    Deklaratsii, 1957, pp. 25–40.
    NT, 1957, No. 17, pp. 33–38.

● 57/iv/18/Morocco

One-year trade protocol between the USSR and Morocco

Signed Apr. 18, 1957, in Rabat.
References: *Izv.*, Apr. 21, 1957.
    VT, 1957, No. 7, p. 35.

● 57/iv/22/MPR/a

Agreement between the USSR and the Mongolian People's Republic concerning air transportation and reciprocal services

Signed Apr. 22, 1957, in Ulan Bator, by

the Main Administration of the Civil Air
Fleet of the USSR and the Administra-
tion of Air Communications under the
Ministry for Affairs of the Troops of
Public Security of the MPR.
Reference: *Pravda*, Apr. 23, 1957.

● 57/iv/22/MPR/b

**Agreement between the USSR and the
Mongolian People's Republic concerning technical collaboration in the field
of civil aviation**

Signed Apr. 22, 1957, in Ulan Bator.
Reference: *Pravda*, Apr. 23, 1957.

● 57/iv/22/KPDR

**Trade protocol for 1957 between the
USSR and the Korean People's Democratic Republic**

Signed Apr. 22, 1957, in Pyongyang.
References: *Pravda*, Apr. 24, 1957.
   VT, 1957, No. 7, p. 35.

● 57/iv/25/KPDR

**Communiqué concerning signing of a
protocol between the USSR and the Korean People's Democratic Republic concerning transfer to the central Red Cross
hospital of the KPDR of property, equipment, and medicaments of the hospital
of the Red Cross Society of the USSR**

Published Apr. 25, 1957.
Reference: *BSE, 1958*, p. 36.

● 57/iv/27/Austria

**Joint communiqué by the USSR and
Austria concerning political and economic relations**

Issued Apr. 27, 1957, in Vienna.
Mentions informal agreement to increase
trade; negotiations to be undertaken not
later than autumn 1957. Austrian citizens
remaining in the USSR who wish to return to Austria to be repatriated. Cultural ties to be increased.
Sources: *Pr., Izv.*, Apr. 28, 1957.
   Deklaratsii, 1957, pp. 21–24.

● 57/iv/27/Iran

**Agreement between the USSR and Iran
concerning questions of transit**

Signed Apr. 27, 1957, in Teheran.
Ratified by the USSR Dec. 12, 1957. In
extension of Art. 10 of the treaty of commerce and navigation of Mar. 25, 1940,
both parties grant the right of free transit
through their territories for goods, without restriction as to nomenclature or
origin.
References: *Pr., Izv.*, Apr. 28, 1957.
   VVS, 1957, No. 2, Art. 630 (ratification; dates the agreement Apr. 25,
   1957).

● 57/v/5/India

**Communiqué concerning signing of an
agreement between the USSR and India
for the purchase by India of auxiliary
equipment for oil drilling**

Published May 5, 1957.
Reference: *BSE, 1958*, p. 36.

● 57/v/10/GDR

**Consular convention between the USSR
and the German Democratic Republic**

Signed May 10, 1957, in Moscow.
Ratified by the GDR Sept. 3, 1957; by the
USSR Sept. 23, 1957. Entered into force
Oct. 11, 1957, on exchange of acts of rati-
fication. Duration 5 years; if not de-
nounced 6 months before expiration, ex-
tended for 5-year periods.
Sources: *VVS*, 1957, No. 21, Art. 529.
   Dokumente DDR, 5, pp. 688–97.
   UNTS, 285, pp. 135–67 (R, G, E, F).
Reference: *Pravda*, May 11, 1957.

● 57/v/14/Iran

**Treaty between the USSR and Iran con-
cerning the regime on the Soviet-Iranian
border and procedure for settling border
disputes and incidents**

Signed May 14, 1957, in Moscow.
Ratified by the USSR Nov. 26, 1957.
References: *Pravda*, May 15, 1957.
   VVS, 1957, No. 26, Art. 607 (ratifica-
   tion).

● 57/v/15/MPR

**Joint communiqué by the USSR and the
Mongolian People's Republic concerning political and economic relations**

Signed May 15, 1957, in Moscow.
Section 1 reviews the international situation. Section 2 gives a résumé of relations
between the 2 States. Section 3 deals with
economic relations and mentions the following specific measures: (1) The USSR
to transfer to the MPR the property of the
oil-producing trust "Mongolneft'." (2)

The USSR to transfer to the MPR Soviet shares in the joint-stock company "Sovmongolmetall," to be repaid over 30 years, starting in 1962. (3) Airfields at Ulan Bator and Sain-Shande to be transferred to the MPR, together with a few planes. (4) A credit of up to 200 million rubles to be advanced to the MPR for purchase of machinery, vehicles, and pedigreed livestock, and for technical aid. (5) The USSR to pay half the cost of certain measures in the field of public health.
Sources: *Pr., Izv.,* May 17, 1957.
Deklaratsii, 1957, pp. 206–19.

● 57/v/17/KPDR

Protocol concerning the third meeting of the USSR–Korean People's Democratic Republic commission for scientific and technical collaboration

Signed May 17, 1957, in Moscow.
Reference: *Izv.,* May 21, 1957 (communiqué).

● 57/v/18/Cz

Agreement between the USSR and Czechoslovakia concerning collaboration in the field of veterinary science

Signed May 18, 1957, in Prague.
Reference: *BSE, 1958,* p. 36.

● 57/v/18/Bul

Agreement between the USSR and Bulgaria concerning delivery of ships and other naval equipment to the USSR during the period 1958–1960

Signed May 18, 1957, in Moscow.
Signed in accordance with the joint declaration of Feb. 20, 1957.
References: *Pravda,* May 22, 1957.
VT, 1957, No. 7, p. 35.

● 57/v/19/Cz

Communiqué concerning the first meeting of the Soviet-Czechoslovak commission for economic collaboration

Published May 19, 1957; the meeting took place May 15–17, 1957, in Prague.
The commission was established in accordance with the joint declaration of Jan. 29, 1957.
Source: *Pravda,* May 19, 1957.

● 57/v/19/Indonesia

Communiqué concerning political negotiations between the USSR and Indonesia

Issued May 19, 1957, in Djakarta.
Briefly reviews the principles of international relations accepted by the 2 States. The USSR affirms its support for Indonesia's claim to Western Irian. General understanding reached on increase of trade and cultural and other contacts.
Sources: *Izv.,* May 21, 1957.
Deklaratsii, 1957, pp. 171–73.

● 57/v/22/Pl

Protocol concerning an increase of the relative role of maritime transport in foreign trade and concerning organization of freight transportation on the internal waterways of the USSR, Poland, and the German Democratic Republic

Signed May 22, 1957, in Moscow, by the USSR, Poland, and the GDR.
Reference: *VT,* 1957, No. 7, p. 36.

● 57/v/25/GDR

Protocol between the USSR and the German Democratic Republic concerning collaboration between the machine-building industries of the two States

Signed May 25, 1957, in Moscow.
Accompanied by a plan of work. Based on the joint declaration of Jan. 7, 1957.
Reference: *VT,* 1957, No. 7, p. 36.

● 57/v/26/CPR

Communiqué concerning the visit of a Soviet governmental delegation to the Chinese People's Republic

Issued May 26, 1957, in Peking.
Reviews in general terms principles underlying relations between the 2 States.
Sources: *Izv.,* May 28, 1957.
Deklaratsii, 1957, pp. 198–99.

● 57/v/27/H

Agreement between the USSR and Hungary concerning the legal status of Soviet troops temporarily stationed on Hungarian territory

Signed May 27, 1957, in Budapest.
Ratified by Hungary July 13, 1957; by the USSR July 24, 1957. Entered into

force Aug. 16, 1957, on exchange of acts of ratification in Moscow. Valid for duration of the presence of Soviet troops in Hungary. Based on the joint declaration of Mar. 28, 1957. Supplemented by an agreement of Apr. 24, 1958, concerning legal aid (text in *VVS*, 1958, No. 16, Art. 283).
Sources: *VVS*, 1957, No. 17, Art. 447.
 AJIL, 52, 1958, No. 1, pp. 215–21.
References: *Izv.*, May 28, 1957.
 NYT, May 28, 1957, p. 1.

● 57/v/31/Cambodia/a

Commercial agreement between the USSR and Cambodia, with two annexes

Signed May 31, 1957, in Pnom-Penh.
Ratified by Cambodia Aug. 19, 1957; by the USSR Sept. 24, 1957. Entered into force Oct. 13, 1957 (15 days after notification of ratification, which took place Sept. 28, 1957, in Pnom-Penh). Duration 1 year; may be denounced with 3 months' notification, extended by exchange of notes 1 month before expiration, or modified by mutual consent. Annexes list goods to be exchanged, to a total value of 1 million pounds sterling each.
Source: *VVS*, 1957, No. 23, Art. 570.
Reference: *Ibid.*, No. 21, Art. 521 (ratification).

● 57/v/31/Cambodia/b

Agreement between the USSR and Cambodia concerning cultural and scientific collaboration

Signed May 31, 1957, in Pnom-Penh.
Data on ratification, entry into force, and duration identical with those for 57/v/31/Cambodia/a.
Provides that measures to be taken shall be agreed on through diplomatic channels.
Source: *VVS*, 1957, No. 23, Art. 572.

● 57/v/31/Cambodia/c

Payments agreement between the USSR and Cambodia

Signed May 31, 1957, in Pnom-Penh.
Data on ratification, entry into force, and duration identical with those for 57/v/31/ Cambodia/a.
Source: *VVS*, 1957, No. 23, Art. 571.

● 57/v/31/Cambodia/d

Agreement between the USSR and Cam-

bodia concerning construction of a hospital in Pnom-Penh

Signed May 31, 1957, in Pnom-Penh.
Reference: *BSE, 1958*, p. 36.

● 57/vi/4/Fin

Communiqué concerning the third meeting of the Soviet-Finnish commission for scientific and technical collaboration

Published June 4, 1957; the meeting took place a few days earlier, in Moscow.
Source: *Izv.*, June 4, 1957.

● 57/vi/7/GDR

Communiqué concerning the sixth meeting of the USSR–German Democratic Republic commission for scientific and technical collaboration

Published June 7, 1957; the meeting took place May 21–31, 1957, in Berlin.
Source: *Izv.*, June 7, 1957.
Reference: *Dokumente DDR*, 5, pp. 698– 99.

● 57/vi/7/Norway

Protocol between the USSR and Norway concerning joint exploitation of the hydroelectric resources of the border river Pasvik-el'v (Paatso-Joki)

Signed on or about June 7, 1957, in Moscow, by the joint commission of experts established in accordance with the joint communiqué of Nov. 15, 1955.
Reference: *Izv.*, June 11, 1957.

● 57/vi/12/Fin/a

Joint communiqué by the USSR and Finland concerning the visit of a Soviet governmental delegation to Finland

Signed June 12, 1957, in Helsinki.
Reviews the international situation, with stress on Finland's neutrality. Mentions signing of a supplementary trade protocol for 1957 (next document), and general agreement on certain measures for trade between Finland and the Leningrad area. Cultural contacts to be increased.
Sources: *Pr.*, *Izv.*, June 13, 1957.
 Deklaratsii, 1957, pp. 258–60.

● 57/vi/12/Fin/b

Supplementary trade protocol for 1957 between the USSR and Finland

Signed on or about June 12, 1957, in Helsinki.

Mentioned in the joint communiqué of the same date (preceding document).

● 57/vi/14/Austria

Agreement between the USSR and Austria concerning technical and commercial aspects of navigation on the Danube

Signed June 14, 1957, in Moscow.
Ratified by Austria Sept. 5, 1957; by the USSR Oct. 12, 1957. Entered into force Nov. 6, 1957, on exchange of acts of ratification in Vienna. Valid until 3 months before end of any calendar year in which denounced.

Sources: *VVS*, 1957, No. 26, Art. 606.
*BGBl, 1958, No. 4.
UNTS, 285, pp. 169–91 (R, G, E, F).
Reference: *Izv.*, June 15, 1957.

● 57/vi/14/Pl. See Appendix 5.

● 57/vi/18/Rom

Protocol between the USSR and Romania concerning transfer to Romania of functions and property of the special river administration for the Lower Danube

Signed June 18, 1957, in Moscow.
Reference: *BSE, 1958*, p. 37.

● 57/vi/22/Pl/a

Eighth conference of the Council for Mutual Economic Aid

Held June 18–22, 1957, in Warsaw, with representatives of all regular members of the Council and, as observers, of the Chinese People's Republic, the Korean People's Democratic Republic, and Yugoslavia.

Discussion concerned revision of the 5-year plan for 1956–1960 prepared at the 7th conference (see 56/v/25/Pl), and preparation of perspective plans for members covering 10 and 15 years. A multilateral payments agreement was signed (next document).

References: *BSE, 1958*, p. 374.
Schenk and Lowenthal, 3, pp. 19–20.

● 57/vi/22/Pl/b

Multilateral payments agreement

Signed at the 8th conference of the Council for Mutual Economic Aid held June 18–22, 1957, in Warsaw, by Albania, Bulgaria, Czechoslovakia, the German Democratic Republic, Hungary, Poland, Romania, and the USSR.

Replaces bilateral payments agreements between the signatories and the USSR.

References: *Pravda*, June 25, 1957; *CDSP*, 9, 1957, No. 25, p. 17.
Pravda, July 14, 1957; *CDSP*, 9, 1957, No. 28, pp. 10–11.

● 57/vi/25/Cz

Communiqué concerning the eleventh meeting of the Soviet-Czechoslovak commission for scientific and technical collaboration

Published June 25, 1957; the meeting took place a few days earlier, in Moscow.
Source: *Izv.*, June 25, 1957.

● 57/vi/29/Syria

Agreement between the USSR and Syria concerning establishment of radio-telegraph communications

Signed June 29, 1957, in Damascus.
Reference: *BSE, 1958*, p. 37.

● 57/vi/30/Yug

Communiqué concerning the third meeting of the Soviet-Yugoslav commission for scientific and technical collaboration

Published June 30, 1957; the meeting ended June 29, 1957, in Moscow.
Source: *Izv.*, June 30, 1957.

● 57/vii/6/Cz

Agreement between the USSR and Czechoslovakia concerning final settlement of property and financial questions arising out of the incorporation of the Transcarpathian Ukraine into the Ukrainian SSR

Signed July 6, 1957, in Moscow.
Ratified by the USSR Dec. 21, 1957; by Czechoslovakia Dec. 23, 1957. Entered into force Jan. 8, 1958, on exchange of acts of ratification in Prague. Provides for settlement of claims under the agreement of June 29, 1945.

Source: *VVS*, 1958, No. 2, Art. 26.
Reference: *VVS*, 1958, No. 1, Art. 3 (ratification).

● 57/vii/10/Yug

Exchange of notes between the USSR and Yugoslavia constituting an agreement concerning collaboration in the field of radio and television

Sent July 10, 1957, in Belgrade.
Reference: *BSE, 1958,* p. 37.

● 57/vii/13/Tunisia

Trade agreement between the USSR and Tunisia

Signed July 13, 1957, in Tunis.
Covers the period July 1, 1957, through June 30, 1958; extended if not denounced.
References: *Pravda,* July 14, 1957.
VT, 1957, No. 10, p. 41.

● 57/vii/16/Cz

Communiqué concerning the visit of a Soviet governmental and party delegation to Czechoslovakia

Signed July 16, 1957, in Prague.
Stresses collaboration between the 2 States and parties in a general survey of international and bilateral relations.
Sources: *Pr., Izv.,* July 17, 1957.
Deklaratsii, 1957, pp. 287–92.

● 57/vii/18/CPR

Communiqué concerning the sixth meeting of the USSR–Chinese People's Republic commission for scientific and technical collaboration

Published July 18, 1957; the meeting took place a few days earlier, in Peking.
Sources: *Pr., Izv.,* July 18, 1957; *CDSP,* 9, 1957, No. 29, pp. 17–18.

● 57/vii/18/Rom

Protocol between the USSR and Romania concerning transfer to Romania of full responsibility for direction of the Administration for the Lower Danube

Signed July 18, 1957.
Modifies the agreement of Dec. 5, 1953 (53/xii/5/Rom/a).
Reference: Logunov, p. 104.

● 57/vii/29/Yug

Protocol between the USSR and Yugoslavia concerning collaboration in con-

struction of enterprises of the aluminum industry in Yugoslavia

Signed July 29, 1957, in Moscow. It is possible that two protocols were signed and that the German Democratic Republic was a signatory to one.
Supplements and provides for execution of the agreements of Jan. 12 and Aug. 1, 1956.
References: *Pr., Izv.,* Aug. 2, 1957.
VT, 1957, No. 10, p. 41.
Pravda, July 1, 1958.

● 57/vii/30/Af

Joint communiqué by the USSR and Afghanistan concerning a state visit of the King of Afghanistan to the USSR

Signed July 30, 1957, in Moscow.
Stresses neutrality of Afghanistan and friendly relations between the 2 States.
Sources: *Izv.,* July 31, 1957.
Deklaratsii, 1957, pp. 46–48.

● 57/vii/31/Af

Communiqué concerning relations between the USSR and Afghanistan

Published July 31, 1957.
Mentions Soviet agreements to aid Afghanistan (1) in regard to oil prospecting in northern Afghanistan and (2) in training technical personnel for the economic development of Afghanistan. Negotiations to be started for conclusion of a treaty concerning the regime on the Soviet-Afghan state border. Agreement reached on collaboration in the use of border waterways. Mentions signing of a number of unspecified agreements.
Sources: *Pr., Izv.,* July 31, 1957; *CDSP,* 9, 1957, No. 31, p. 17.
Deklaratsii, 1957, pp. 48–49.

● 57/viii/1/Norway

Protocol concerning demarcation of the maritime boundary between the USSR and Norway

Signed Aug. 1, 1957, in Oslo, by the mixed commission established under the agreement of Feb. 15, 1957.
Reference: *Izv.,* Aug. 3, 1957 (communiqué).

● 57/viii/1/Rom

Agreement between the USSR and Ro-

mania concerning regulation of border waterways

Signed Aug. 1, 1957, in Bucharest.
References: *Izv.*, Aug. 2, 1957.
   Int. aff., 1957, No. 9, p. 147.

● 57/viii/2/GDR

Agreement between the USSR and the German Democratic Republic concerning mutual legal aid in matters connected with the temporary presence of Soviet troops on GDR territory

Signed Aug. 2, 1957, in Berlin.
Supplements the treaty of Mar. 12, 1957; duration the same.
Source: *Dokumente DDR*, 5, pp. 699–709.
References: *Int. aff.*, 1957, No. 9, p. 149.
   Pr., Izv., Aug. 3, 1957.

● 57/viii/4/Yug

Communiqué concerning a meeting of governmental and party delegations of the USSR and Yugoslavia

Published Aug. 4, 1957.
States that negotiations led to agreement on relations between the 2 States and on the international situation.
Sources: *Izv.*, Aug. 4, 1957.
   Deklaratsii, 1957, pp. 311–13.

● 57/viii/6/H

Communiqué concerning the eighth meeting of the Soviet-Hungarian commission for scientific and technical collaboration

Published Aug. 6, 1957; the meeting took place a few days earlier, in Budapest.
Source: *Izv.*, Aug. 6, 1957.

● 57/viii/6/Syria

Communiqué concerning the visit of a Syrian governmental delegation to the USSR

Signed Aug. 6, 1957, in Moscow.
Summarizes general agreements on Soviet technical aid to Syria and an increase in trade. For an agreement based on these negotiations, see 57/x/28/Syria.
Sources: *Pr., Izv.*, Aug. 7, 1957; *CDSP*,
   9, 1957, No. 32, pp. 17–18.
   Deklaratsii, 1957, pp. 243–45.

● 57/viii/11/Iran

Agreement between the USSR and Iran concerning establishment of preliminary plans for joint use of the border sectors of the Arax and Artek rivers for irrigation and the production of electricity

Signed Aug. 11, 1957, in Teheran; summarized in a joint communiqué issued Aug. 12, 1957.
Reference: *Izv.*, Aug. 13, 1957 (communiqué).

● 57/viii/13/GDR

Joint communiqué by the USSR and the German Democratic Republic concerning political and economic relations

Signed Aug. 13, 1957, in Berlin.
Covers the international situation as well as relations between the governments and parties of the 2 States. Negotiations to be undertaken for conclusion of (1) a trade agreement for the period 1958–1960 and (2) a treaty of commerce and navigation.
Sources: *Pr., Izv.*, Aug. 14, 1957.
   Deklaratsii, 1957, pp. 130–45.
   NT, 1957, No. 34, pp. 34–40.
   Dokumente DDR, 5, pp. 709–25.

● 57/viii/14/KPDR/a

Agreement between the USSR and the Korean People's Democratic Republic concerning conditions for sending Soviet specialists to the KPDR and vice versa, for technical aid and other services

Announced in a communiqué of Aug. 14, 1957; signed shortly before that date, in Moscow.
References: *Pr., Izv.*, Aug. 14, 1957 (communiqué).

● 57/viii/14/KPDR/b

Agreement between the USSR and the Korean People's Democratic Republic concerning conditions for technical production training of Soviet and KPDR specialists and workers

Data on signature and references identical with those for 57/viii/14/KPDR/a.

● 57/viii/14/KPDR/c

Protocol between the USSR and the Korean People's Democratic Republic concerning Soviet technical aid to the KPDR

for expansion of nitrogen fertilizer production

Data on signature and references identical with those for 57/viii/14/KPDR/a.

• 57/viii/23/France

Trade protocol between the USSR and France

Signed Aug. 23, 1957, in Paris.
Entered into force on signature.
Reference: French Embassy, 1957.

• 57/viii/23/Pol

Agreement between the USSR and Poland concerning exchange of students and research workers

Signed Aug. 23, 1957, in Warsaw.
Reference: *BSE, 1958*, p. 37.

• 57/viii/24/H/a

Convention between the USSR and Hungary concerning regulation of the question of citizenship of persons with dual citizenship

Signed Aug. 24, 1957, in Budapest.
Ratified by Hungary Oct. 25, 1957; by the USSR Dec. 12, 1957. Entered into force Jan. 15, 1958 (30 days after exchange of acts of ratification, which took place Dec. 16, 1957, in Moscow).
Source: *VVS*, 1958, No. 1, Art. 2.
References: *Pr., Izv.*, Aug. 25, 1957; *CDSP*, 9, 1957, No. 34, p. 15.

• 57/viii/24/H/b

Consular convention between the USSR and Hungary

Signed Aug. 24, 1957, in Budapest.
Data on ratification and entry into force identical with those for 57/viii/24/H/a. Duration 5 years; if not denounced 6 months before expiration, extended for 5-year periods.
Source: *VVS*, 1958, No. 1, Art. 1.
References: *Pr., Izv.*, Aug. 25, 1957; *CDSP*, 9, 1957, No. 34, p. 15.

• 57/viii/29/Burma

General contract agreement between the USSR and Burma

Signed Aug. 29, 1957, in Rangoon.
Provides for execution of the projects included in the economic agreement of Jan. 17, 1957.

Reference: *Pravda*, Aug. 31, 1957.

• 57/viii/31/Cz

Agreement between the USSR and Czechoslovakia concerning legal assistance in civil, family, and criminal cases

Signed Aug. 31, 1957, in Moscow.
Ratified by the USSR Dec. 21, 1957. Concluded in accordance with the joint declaration of Jan. 29, 1957.
References: *Pravda*, Sept. 1, 1957.
VVS, 1958, No. 1, Art. 4 (ratification).

• 57/ix/4/Rom/a

Consular convention between the USSR and Romania

Signed Sept. 4, 1957, in Bucharest.
Ratified by Romania Nov. 6, 1957; by the USSR Jan. 25, 1958. Entered into force Mar. 3, 1958, on exchange of acts of ratification in Moscow. Valid until 6 months after denunciation.
Source: *VVS*, 1958, No. 5, Art. 102.
References: *Pravda*, Sept. 7, 1957.
VVS, 1958, No. 3, Art. 57 (ratification).

• 57/ix/4/Rom/b

Convention between the USSR and Romania concerning regulation of the question of citizenship of persons with dual citizenship

Signed Sept. 4, 1957, in Bucharest.
Ratified by Romania Nov. 6, 1957; by the USSR Jan. 25, 1958. Entered into force Mar. 3, 1958, on exchange of acts of ratification in Moscow.
Source: *VVS*, 1958, No. 5, Art. 103.
References: *Pravda*, Sept. 7, 1957.
VVS, 1958, No. 3, Art. 57 (ratification).

• 57/ix/4/Syria

Communiqué concerning economic negotiations between the USSR and Syria

Published Sept. 4, 1957, following negotiations Aug. 28–Sept. 3, 1957, in Moscow.
Mentions discussion of collaboration in the fields of railroad and highway construction, irrigation, construction of electrostations and industrial and other installations, and geologic prospecting. An agreement on economic and technical collaboration to be prepared in Syria.

Source: *Pravda*, Sept. 4, 1957.

• 57/ix/5/Bul

Protocol concerning the ninth meeting of the Soviet-Bulgarian commission for scientific and technical collaboration

Signed Sept. 5, 1957, in Moscow.
Reference: *Pravda*, Sept. 7, 1957.

• 57/ix/6/Yug

Communiqué concerning extension of the convention of May 22, 1956, between the USSR and Yugoslavia concerning regulation of the question of citizenship of persons with dual citizenship

Published Sept. 6, 1957.
Mentions extension of the 1956 agreement through July 31, 1958.
Source: *Pravda*, Sept. 6, 1957.

• 57/ix/6/1957

Convention concerning citizenship of married women

Signed Feb. 20, 1957, in New York.
Signed by the USSR Sept. 6, 1957; ratified Aug. 28, 1958; act of ratification deposited Sept. 17, 1958. Enters into force after deposit of 6th act of ratification.
Source: *VVS*, 1958, No. 28, Art. 373.

Mar. 18–Sept. 6, 1957

See Appendix 5.

• 57/ix/18/Alb/a

Convention between the USSR and Albania concerning regulation of the question of citizenship of persons of dual citizenship

Signed Sept. 18, 1957, in Tirana.
Ratified by Albania Nov. 27, 1957; by the USSR Jan. 14, 1958. Entered into force Apr. 29, 1958, on exchange of acts of ratification in Moscow. Signed in accordance with the joint declaration of Apr. 17, 1957.
Source: *VVS*, 1958, No. 9, Art. 205.
Reference: *Pravda*, Sept. 22, 1957.

• 57/ix/18/Alb/b

Consular convention between the USSR and Albania

Signed Sept. 18, 1957, in Tirana.
Ratified by Albania Nov. 27, 1957; by the USSR Jan. 14, 1958. Entered into force Apr. 29, 1958, on exchange of acts of ratification in Moscow. Valid until 6 months after denunciation. Signed in accordance with the joint declaration of Apr. 17, 1957.
Source: *VVS*, 1958, No. 9, Art. 204.
Reference: *Pravda*, Sept. 22, 1957.

• 57/ix/27/GDR/a

Treaty of commerce and navigation between the USSR and the German Democratic Republic, with annex concerning the Soviet Trade Mission in the GDR and the GDR Trade Mission in the USSR

Signed Sept. 27, 1957, in Berlin.
Ratified by the USSR Nov. 30, 1957; by the GDR Jan. 16, 1958. Entered into force Feb. 8, 1958, on exchange of acts of ratification in Moscow. Valid until 6 months after denunciation.
Sources: *VVS*, 1958, No. 4, Art. 86.
Dokumente DDR, 5, pp. 730–38.

• 57/ix/27/GDR/b

Trade agreement for the period 1958–1960 between the USSR and the German Democratic Republic

Signed Sept. 27, 1957, in Berlin.
Provides for trade to a total value of 20 billion rubles.
Reference: *Pravda*, Sept. 29, 1957.

• 57/ix/27/GDR/c

Credit protocol for trade during 1958 between the USSR and the German Democratic Republic

Signed Sept. 27, 1957, in Berlin.
Provides for 2 credits: (1) 300 million rubles in convertible foreign currency and (2) 400 million rubles in goods, to be repaid in goods at 2 per cent over 5 years, starting Jan. 1, 1961.
References: *Pravda*, Sept. 29, 1957.
Dokumente DDR, 5, p. 728.

• 57/x/ /Yemen. See Appendix 5.

• 57/x/3/Mul/a

Universal Postal Convention, with final protocol

Adopted at the 14th Congress of the Universal Postal Union, Aug. 14–Sept. 30, 1957, in Ottawa. Signed by the USSR Oct. 3, 1957.
Supersedes the convention of July 11, 1952. The USSR also signed the agreements concerning (1) insured letters and

boxes and (2) parcel post (next 2 documents).
Reference: *VVS*, 1959, No. 9, Art. 66 (ratification).

• 57/x/3/Mul/b

Agreement of the Universal Postal Union concerning insured letters and boxes, with related documents

Signed by the USSR Oct. 3, 1957, in Ottawa.
Ratified by the USSR Feb. 27, 1959. Supersedes the agreement of July 11, 1952. Related documents: final protocol and regulations for execution.
Reference: *VVS*, 1959, No. 9, Art. 66.

• 57/x/3/Mul/c

Agreement of the Universal Postal Union concerning parcel post, with related documents

Signed by the USSR Oct. 3, 1957, in Ottawa.
Ratified by the USSR Feb. 27, 1959. Supersedes the agreement of July 11, 1952, which the USSR did not sign. Related documents: final protocol, regulations for execution, and final protocol to the regulations.
Reference: *VVS*, 1959, No. 9, Art. 66.

• 57/x/5/Cz/a

Convention between the USSR and Czechoslovakia concerning regulation of the question of citizenship of persons with dual citizenship

Signed Oct. 5, 1957, in Prague.
Ratified by the USSR Mar. 28, 1958; by Czechoslovakia June 30, 1958. Entered into force July 21, 1958, on exchange of acts of ratification in Moscow. Signed in accordance with the joint declaration of Jan. 29, 1957.
Source: *VVS*, 1958, No. 17, Art. 289.
References: *Pr.*, *Izv.*, Oct. 8, 1957.

• 57/x/5/Cz/b

Consular convention between the USSR and Czechoslovakia

Signed Oct. 5, 1957, in Prague.
Ratified by the USSR Mar. 28, 1958; by Czechoslovakia June 30, 1958. Entered into force July 21, 1958, on exchange of acts of ratification in Moscow. Duration 5 years; if not denounced 6 months before

expiration, extended for 5-year periods. Supersedes the convention of Nov. 16, 1935.
Source: *VVS*, 1958, No. 17, Art. 288.
References: *Pr.*, *Izv.*, Oct. 8, 1957.

• 57/x/5/US

Joint statement concerning negotiations between the USSR and the United States of America

Issued Oct. 5, 1957.
Mentions discussion of the Middle East, disarmament, the situation in Europe, and United States–Soviet contacts.
Source: *DSB*, 37, 1957, p. 635.

• 57/x/9/France. See Appendix 5.

• 57/x/10/Austria/a

Trade agreement for the period 1958–1960 between the USSR and Austria

Signed Oct. 10, 1957, in Vienna.
Reference: *Izv.*, Oct. 15, 1957.

• 57/x/10/Austria/b

Trade protocol for 1958 between the USSR and Austria

Signed Oct. 10, 1957, in Vienna.
Reference: *Izv.*, Oct. 15, 1957.

• 57/x/11/KPDR

Agreement between the USSR and the Korean People's Democratic Republic concerning collaboration between the Academies of Sciences of the USSR and the KPDR

Signed Oct. 11, 1957, in Moscow.
Reference: *Izv.*, Oct. 12, 1957.

• 57/x/14/KPDR

Convention between the USSR and the Korean People's Democratic Republic concerning regulation of border questions

Signed Oct. 14, 1957, in Pyongyang.
Reference: *Izv.*, Oct. 15, 1957.

• 57/x/16/Pakistan

Joint communiqué concerning commercial relations between the USSR and Pakistan

Published Oct. 16, 1957.
Summarizes the results of negotiations

held from Oct. 1 to 14, 1957, in Moscow.
Mentions signing of trade contracts and
agreement to consult on further measures
for trade.
Source: *Izv.*, Oct. 16, 1957.

● 57/x/16/Cz

**Protocol between the USSR and Czech-
oslovakia concerning cultural collaboration in 1958**

Signed Oct. 16, 1957, in Moscow.
Reference: *Izv.*, Oct. 17, 1957.

● 57/x/17/Cz

**Agreement between the USSR and Czech-
oslovakia concerning exchange of students and candidates for education in
institutions of higher education and scientific and technical institutions**

Signed Oct. 17, 1957, in Moscow.
Reference: *Izv.*, Oct. 18, 1957.

● 57/x/19/Egypt

**Agreement between the USSR and Egypt
concerning cultural collaboration**

Signed Oct. 19, 1957, in Cairo.
Ratified by Egypt Dec. 4, 1957; by the
USSR Feb. 1, 1958. Entered into force
Feb. 11, 1958, on exchange of acts of rati-
fication in Moscow. Valid until 6 months
after denunciation.
See further Appendix 5.
Source: *VVS*, 1958, No. 5, Art. 94.
References: *Izv.*, Oct. 20, 1957.
  NYT, Oct. 20, 1957, p. 42.

● 57/x/26/Pol

**Agreement between the USSR and Po-
land concerning legal assistance in cases
arising out of the temporary stationing
of Soviet troops in Poland**

Signed Oct. 26, 1957, in Warsaw.
Ratified by the USSR Mar. 8, 1958 (*VVS*,
1958, No. 6, Art. 126).
Supplements the treaty of Dec. 17, 1956.
Reference: *Izv.*, Oct. 27, 1957.

● 57/x/28/Syria

**Agreement between the USSR and Syria
concerning economic and technical collaboration**

Signed Oct. 28, 1957, in Damascus.
Ratified by Syria Nov. 6, 1957; by the
USSR Nov. 10, 1957. Entered into force

Dec. 11, 1957, on exchange of acts of rati-
fication in Moscow. Based on agreements
reached during Aug. 1957 (see 57/viii/6/
Syria).
Source: *JR*, 1957, No. 54, pp. 6816–22.
References: *Izv.*, Oct. 30, 1957.
  NYT, Oct. 28, 29, and 30, 1957.
  VVS, 1957, No. 25, Art. 599 (ratifica-
  tion).

● 57/xi/1/Yug

**Trade protocol for 1958 between the
USSR and Yugoslavia**

Signed Nov. 1, 1957, in Belgrade.
Soviet grain, coal, oil, chrome and manganese ores, ferrous alloys, cotton, machinery, etc., in exchange for Yugoslav
rolled ferrous metals, lead, zinc, cables,
cement, leather, etc. For a complaint by
Yugoslavia of non-delivery of 200,000 tons
of grain under this protocol, see *Izv.*, Oct.
16, 1958; *CDSP*, 10, 1958, No. 42, p. 12.
Reference: *Izv.*, Nov. 3, 1957.

● 57/xi/9/India

**Agreement between the USSR and India
concerning collaboration in construction
of industrial enterprises in India and a
Soviet credit to India of five hundred
million rubles**

Signed Nov. 9, 1957, in New Delhi.
Formalizes the credit agreement nego-
tiated during Nov. 1956 (see 56/xi/ /
India).
References: *Pr.*, *Izv.*, Nov. 11, 1957;
  CDSP, 9, 1957, No. 45, p. 21.

● 57/xi/19/Bul/a

**Trade agreement for the period 1958–
1960 between the USSR and Bulgaria**

Signed Nov. 19, 1957, in Moscow.
Reference: *Izv.*, Nov. 20, 1957.

● 57/xi/19/Bul/b

**Trade protocol for 1958 between the
USSR and Bulgaria**

Signed Nov. 19, 1957, in Moscow.
Reference: *Izv.*, Nov. 20, 1957.

● 57/xi/19/Bul/c

**Agreement between the USSR and Bul-
garia concerning trade for the period
1960–1970**

Signed Nov. 19, 1957, in Moscow.
Reference: *Izv.*, Nov. 20, 1957.

Nov. 1–20, 1957
See Appendix 5.

● 57/xi/22/Alb

Agreement between the USSR and Albania concerning technical and economic aid for the period 1957–1960

Signed Nov. 22, 1957, in Moscow.
Provides for a Soviet credit of 160 million rubles.
References: *Pravda*, Nov. 24, 1957.
  NYT, Nov. 24, 1957.
  East Europe, Jan. 1958, p. 56.

● 57/xi/22/Norway

Agreement between the USSR and Norway concerning measures for regulating seal-hunting and for protection of seal reserves in the Northeastern Atlantic Ocean, with annex and exchange of notes

Signed Nov. 22, 1957, in Oslo.
Ratified by Norway June 13, 1958; by the USSR June 25, 1958. Entered into force June 27, 1958, on exchange of acts of ratification in Moscow. Duration 3 years; thereafter may be denounced with effect from 18 months after receipt of notification. Annex concerns rules for seal-hunting. Exchange of notes provides for cancellation of a concessionary treaty of Apr. 26, 1926, between the USSR and a Norwegian seal-hunting corporation.
Source: *VVS*, 1958, No. 14, Art. 277.
Reference: *Izv.*, Nov. 24, 1957.

● 57/xi/28/GDR

Treaty between the USSR and the German Democratic Republic concerning legal aid in civil, family, and criminal cases

Signed Nov. 28, 1957, in Berlin.
Ratified by the USSR Mar. 28, 1958. Entered into force June 12, 1958 (1 month after exchange of acts of ratification, which took place May 12, 1958).
Source: *Dokumente DDR*, 5, pp. 742–68.
References: *Pravda*, Nov. 29, 1957;
  CDSP, 9, 1957, No. 48, p. 19.
  VVS, 1958, No. 7, Art. 138 (ratification).

● 57/xi/29/Norway

Final documents concerning demarcation of the border in the Varanger Fjord between the USSR and Norway

Signed Nov. 29, 1957, by the mixed commission established under the agreement of Feb. 15, 1957.
Reference: *Izv.*, Nov. 30, 1957.

● 57/xi/30/Bul

Protocol between the USSR and Bulgaria concerning preparation of a plan of cultural and scientific collaboration

Signed Nov. 30, 1957, in Moscow.
Reference: *Pravda*, Dec. 1, 1957.

● 57/xii/4/Cz

Convention between the USSR and Czechoslovakia concerning collaboration in the field of public health service

Signed Dec. 4, 1957, in Prague.
Duration 5 years.
Reference: *Pravda*, Dec. 5, 1957.

● 57/xii/4/Fin

Trade protocol for 1958 between the USSR and Finland

Signed Dec. 4, 1957, in Helsinki.
References: *Izv.*, Dec. 5, 1957.
  NYT, Dec. 5, 1957, p. 19.

● 57/xii/6/J/a

Treaty of commerce between the USSR and Japan, with annex concerning the Soviet Trade Mission in Japan

Signed Dec. 6, 1957, in Tokyo.
Ratified by the USSR Feb. 26, 1958; by Japan Apr. 8, 1958. Entered into force May 9, 1958, on exchange of acts of ratification in Moscow. Duration 5 years; if not denounced 6 months before expiration, valid until 6 months after denunciation. Supplemented by an agreement of June 3, 1958, concerning navigation (*NYT*, June 4, 1958).
Source: *VVS*, 1958, No. 10, Art. 216.
References: *Izv.*, Dec. 7, 1957.
  NYT, Dec. 7, 1957, p. 3.

● 57/xii/6/J/b

Trade and payments agreement between the USSR and Japan

Signed Dec. 6, 1957, in Tokyo.
Entered into force on signature. Duration 1 year.
References: *Izv.*, Dec. 7, 1957.
  NYT, Dec. 7, 1957, p. 3.

● 57/xii/7/Alb

Communiqué concerning preparation of a plan for cultural and scientific collaboration between the USSR and Albania in 1958

Published Dec. 7, 1957; the meeting of the mixed Soviet-Albanian commission for scientific and cultural collaboration took place Dec. 3–6, 1957, in Tirana.
Reference: *Izv.*, Dec. 7, 1957.

● 57/xii/9/Egypt

Joint communiqué by the USSR and Egypt concerning cultural collaboration

Issued Dec. 9, 1957, in Moscow.
Source: *Izv.*, Dec. 10, 1957.

● 57/xii/10/Cz

Agreement between the USSR and Czechoslovakia concerning collaboration between the Academies of Sciences of the USSR and Czechoslovakia

Signed Dec. 10, 1957, in Moscow.
Duration 3 years.
Reference: *Izv.*, Dec. 11, 1957.

● 57/xii/12/Bul/a

Treaty between the USSR and Bulgaria concerning legal aid in civil, family, and criminal cases

Signed Dec. 12, 1957, in Sofia.
Ratified by the USSR Mar. 15, 1958.
References: *Izv.*, Dec. 14, 1957.
  VVS, 1958, No. 6, Art. 127.

● 57/xii/12/Bul/b

Consular convention between the USSR and Bulgaria

Signed Dec. 12, 1957, in Sofia.
Ratified by Bulgaria Feb. 8, 1958; by the USSR Mar. 15, 1958. Entered into force Mar. 28, 1958, on exchange of acts of ratification in Moscow. Valid until 6 months after denunciation.
Source: *VVS*, 1958, No. 7, Art. 140.
Reference: *Izv.*, Dec. 14, 1957.

● 57/xii/12/Bul/c

Convention between the USSR and Bulgaria concerning regulation of the question of citizenship of persons with dual citizenship

Signed Dec. 12, 1957, in Sofia.
Data on ratification and entry into force identical with those for 57/xii/12/Bul/b.
Source: *VVS*, 1958, No. 7, Art. 141.
Reference: *Izv.*, Dec. 14, 1957.

● 57/xii/12/KPDR

Protocol concerning the fourth meeting of the USSR–Korean People's Democratic Republic commission for scientific and technical collaboration

Signed Dec. 12, 1957, in Pyongyang.
References: *Izv.*, Dec. 14 and 17, 1957.

● 57/xii/13/Cz/a

Trade agreement for the period 1958–1960 between the USSR and Czechoslovakia

Signed Dec. 13, 1957, in Moscow.
Reference: *Izv.*, Dec. 14, 1957.

● 57/xii/13/Cz/b

Trade protocol for 1958 between the USSR and Czechoslovakia

Signed Dec. 13, 1957, in Moscow.
Reference: *Izv.*, Dec. 14, 1957.

● 57/xii/16/MPR

Protocol concerning cultural and scientific collaboration between the USSR and the Mongolian People's Republic in 1958

Signed Dec. 16, 1957, in Moscow.
Based on the agreement of Apr. 24, 1956.
Reference: *Izv.*, Dec. 17, 1957.

● 57/xii/16/KPDR/a

Consular convention between the USSR and the Korean People's Democratic Republic

Signed Dec. 16, 1957, in Pyongyang.
Ratified by the KPDR Jan. 21, 1958; by the USSR Feb. 1, 1958. Entered into force Feb. 5, 1958, on exchange of acts of ratification in Moscow. Valid until 6 months after denunciation.
Source: *VVS*, 1958, No. 4, Art. 83.
References: *Izv.*, Dec. 18, 1957.
  NYT, Dec. 19, 1957, p. 6.

● 57/xii/16/KPDR/b

Convention between the USSR and the Korean People's Democratic Republic

concerning regulation of the question of
citizenship of persons with dual citizenship

Signed Dec. 16, 1957, in Pyongyang.
Data on ratification and entry into force
identical with those for 57/xii/16/KPDR/
a.
Source: *VVS*, 1958, No. 4, Art. 84.
References: As given for 57/xii/16/
KPDR/a.

● 57/xii/16/KPDR/c

**Treaty between the USSR and the Ko-
rean People's Democratic Republic concerning legal aid in civil, family, and
criminal cases**

Signed Dec. 16, 1957, in Pyongyang.
Ratified by the KPDR Jan. 21, 1958; by
the USSR Feb. 1, 1958. Entered into force
Mar. 5, 1958 (1 month after exchange of
acts of ratification, which took place Feb.
5, 1958, in Moscow). Duration 5 years;
if not denounced 6 months before expiration, valid until 1 year after denunciation.
Source: *VVS*, 1958, No. 5, Art. 93.
References: As given for 57/xii/16/
KPDR/a.

● 57/xii/17/MPR/a

**Treaty of commerce between the USSR
and the Mongolian People's Republic,
with annex concerning the Soviet Trade
Mission in the MPR and the MPR Trade
Mission in the USSR**

Signed Dec. 17, 1957, in Moscow.
Ratified by the MPR Feb. 12, 1958; by
the USSR Feb. 26, 1958. Entered into
force Apr. 30, 1958, on exchange of acts
of ratification in Ulan Bator. Valid until
6 months after denunciation.
Source: *VVS*, 1958, No. 9, Art. 206.
References: *Pr.*, *Izv.*, Dec. 18, 1957.

● 57/xii/17/MPR/b

**Trade agreement for the period 1958–
1960 between the USSR and the Mongolian People's Republic**

Signed Dec. 17, 1957, in Moscow.
Provides for trade to a total value of more
than 1 billion rubles.
References: *Pr.*, *Izv.*, Dec. 18, 1957.

● 57/xii/17/MPR/c

Trade protocol for 1958 between the

**USSR and the Mongolian People's Re-
public**

Signed Dec. 17, 1957, in Moscow.
References: *Pr.*, *Izv.*, Dec. 18, 1957.

● 57/xii/18/H

**Agreement between the USSR and Hun-
gary concerning economic and technical
aid**

Signed Dec. 18, 1957, in Moscow.
References: *Pr.*, *Izv.*, Dec. 19, 1957;
   CDSP, 9, 1958, No. 51, p. 23.
   Stolte, Stefan C., "Hungary and Mos-
   cow's Near East policy," *Bulletin*, 5,
   1958, No. 1, pp. 41–46.

● 57/xii/18/Norway

**Agreement between the USSR and Nor-
way concerning exploitation of the hydroelectric resources of the Pasvik-El'v
river**

Signed Dec. 18, 1957, in Oslo.
Ratified by the USSR May 5, 1958; by
Norway June 13, 1958. Entered into force
June 27, 1958, on exchange of acts of rati-
fication in Moscow.
Source: *VVS*, 1958, No. 14, Art. 278.
References: *Izv.*, Dec. 19, 1957.
   NYT, Dec. 19, 1957.

● 57/xii/19/Syria

**Trade agreement between the USSR and
Syria**

Signed Dec. 19, 1957, in Moscow.
References: *Izv.*, Dec. 20, 1957, p. 9;
   ibid., Dec. 21, 1957 (joint communiqué).
   NYT, Dec. 21, 1957, p. 3.

● 57/xii/19/UK

**Agreement between the USSR and the
United Kingdom concerning establishment of a civil air route between Moscow
and London**

Signed Dec. 19, 1957, in London.
To enter into force on agreement by exchange of notes; had not entered into
force by Aug. 1, 1958 (see *Sovetskaia
Rossiia*, Aug. 15, 1958; *CDSP*, 10, 1958,
No. 42, p. 16). A civil air agreement was
signed Mar. 24, 1959 (*NYT*, Mar. 26,
1959, p. 54).

References: *Pravda,* Dec. 25, 1957;
  CDSP, 9, 1958, No. 52, p. 26 (com-
  muniqué).
NYT, Dec. 20, 1957, p. 50.

● 57/xii/20/Cz

**Communiqué concerning the twelfth
meeting of the Soviet-Czechoslovak commission for scientific and technical collaboration**

Published Dec. 20, 1957; the meeting took
place a few days earlier in Prague.
Reference: *Izv.,* Dec. 20, 1957.

● 57/xii/21/CPR

**Agreement between the USSR and the
Chinese People's Republic concerning
the regime of commercial navigation on
border waterways and tributary streams
and lakes**

Signed Dec. 21, 1957, in Moscow.
Ratified by the CPR Mar. 18, 1958; by
the USSR Mar. 24, 1958. Entered into
force Apr. 19, 1958, on exchange of acts
of ratification in Peking.
Source: *VVS,* 1958, No. 8, Art. 179.
Reference: *Izv.,* Dec. 22, 1957.

● 57/xii/21/Rom

**Protocol concerning the ninth meeting
of the Soviet-Romanian commission for
scientific and technical collaboration**

Signed Dec. 21, 1957, in Moscow.
Reference: *Izv.,* Dec. 22, 1957.

● 57/xii/21/Sweden

**Trade protocol for 1958 between the
USSR and Sweden**

Signed Dec. 21, 1957, in Stockholm.
References: *Pr., Izv.,* Dec. 24, 1957;
  CDSP, 9, 1958, No. 51, p. 23.

● 57/xii/25/DRV

**Agreement between the USSR and the
Democratic Republic of Vietnam concerning cultural collaboration**

Signed Dec. 25, 1957, in Moscow.
Reference: *Izv.,* Dec. 26, 1957.

● 57/xii/26/Pol

Communiqué concerning the twelfth

**meeting of the Soviet-Polish commission
for scientific and technical collaboration**

Published Dec. 26, 1957; the meeting took
place a few days earlier, in Moscow.
Source: *Izv.,* Dec. 26, 1957.

● 57/xii/26/DRV/a

**Agreement between the USSR and the
Democratic Republic of Vietnam concerning establishment of telephone and
telegraph communications**

Signed Dec. 26, 1957, in Moscow.
Reference: *Izv.,* Dec. 27, 1957.

● 57/xii/26/DRV/b

**Agreement between the USSR and the
Democratic Republic of Vietnam concerning establishment of postal and parcel post communications**

Signed Dec. 26, 1957, in Moscow.
Reference: *Izv.,* Dec. 27, 1957.

● 57/xii/26/Yug

**Protocol concerning the fourth meeting
of the Soviet-Yugoslav commission for
scientific and technical collaboration**

Signed Dec. 26, 1957, in Belgrade.
Reference: *Izv.,* Dec. 27, 1957.

● 57/xii/27/GDR

**Agreement between the High Command
of the Soviet Armed Forces in the German Democratic Republic and the GDR
concerning procedure for settlement of
material claims for damages**

Signed Dec. 27, 1957, in Berlin.
Based on the agreement of Aug. 2, 1957.
Entered into force Jan. 1, 1958; valid for
the duration of the treaty of Mar. 12,
1957.
Source: *Dokumente DDR,* 5, pp. 771–75.

● 57/xii/28/France

**Trade protocol for 1958 between the
USSR and France**

Signed Dec. 28, 1957, in Moscow.
Provides for trade to a total value of about
700 million rubles.
References: *Pr., Izv.,* Dec. 29, 1957;
  CDSP, 9, 1958, No. 52, p. 26.
NYT, Dec. 29, 1957, p. 17.

• 57/xii/28/Italy/a

Trade agreement for the period 1958–1961 between the USSR and Italy

Signed Dec. 28, 1957, in Rome.
Provides for an increase in trade to a value of approximately 600 million rubles in 1961. Trade lists to be agreed annually, together with annual protocols.
References: *Pr., Izv.,* Dec. 29, 1957;
    CDSP, 9, 1958, No. 52, p. 26.
    NYT, Dec. 29, 1957, p. 17.

• 57/xii/28/Italy/b

Trade protocol for 1958 between the USSR and Italy

Signed Dec. 28, 1957, in Rome.
References: Same as those for 57/xii/28/Italy/a.

• 57/xii/28/Italy/c

Payments agreement between the USSR and Italy

Signed Dec. 28, 1957, in Rome.
References: Same as those for 57/xii/28/Italy/a.

• 57/xii/28/Pol

Treaty between the USSR and Poland concerning legal aid and legal relations in civil, family, and criminal cases

Signed Dec. 28, 1957, in Warsaw.
Ratified by the USSR Mar. 8, 1958 (*VVS,* 1958, No. 6, Art. 126).
Enters into force 30 days after exchange of acts of ratification.
Reference: *Izv.,* Dec. 29, 1957.

• 57/xii/29/Bul

Communiqué concerning the tenth meeting of the Soviet-Bulgarian commission for scientific and technical collaboration

Published Dec. 29, 1957; the meeting took place a few days earlier, in Sofia.
Source: *Izv.,* Dec. 29, 1957.

• 57/xii/30/CPR

Protocol between the USSR and the Chinese People's Republic concerning settlement of non-commercial payments

Signed Dec. 30, 1957, in Moscow.
Reference: *Izv.,* Jan. 1, 1958.

• 57/xii/31/Bul

Protocol between the USSR and Bulgaria concerning settlement of non-commercial payments

Signed Dec. 31, 1957, in Moscow.
Reference: *Izv.,* Jan. 3, 1958.

APPENDIXES

Appendix 1

UNRATIFIED TREATIES

(Including draft treaties initialed but not signed and resolutions of international conferences not officially adopted)

Mar. 1, 1922. Temporary commercial treaty between the RSFSR and Sweden

Signed in Stockholm.
Text initialed Feb. 1, 1922 (Shtein, 1925, p. 52; Korolenko, pp. 28, 133; *Biulleten' NKID*, 1922, No. 117, pp. 32–33). Rejected by the Swedish Riksdag May 31, 1922 (*MZh*, 1922, No. 9, p. 56).
Sources (cited in Dennis, p. 406) : *Nation* (N.Y.), Apr. 5, 1922.
    Soviet Russia, Apr. 15, 1922, pp. 207–208.
    Svenska Dagbladet, June 9, 1922.

Apr. 10–May 19, 1922. Genoa Conference for the economic and financial reconstruction of Europe

Attended by the RSFSR; the Soviet delegation represented also the other Soviet Republics, in accordance with a protocol of Feb. 22, 1922 (22/ii/22/Pl). No formal agreements were reached at the conference; committee reports, however, were prepared on finances, economics, and transportation and submitted to the plenary session, and a report by the First Commission recommending convocation of a later conference at The Hague was adopted by the final plenary session.[1] These 4 reports were subsequently printed in the official treaty series of the RSFSR; they are therefore included here.
The following sources have been cited in addition to *SDD RSFSR*:
(1) RSFSR, People's Commissariat of Foreign Affairs, *Materialy Genuezskoi Konferentsii. (Podgotovka, otchëty zasedanii, raboty komissii, diplomaticheskaia*

[1] The Hague Conference, which met from June 26 to July 20, 1922, ended without reaching any agreements, and has not been listed separately here. Its *Minutes and Documents* were published by the Department of Foreign Affairs of the Netherlands Government (The Hague, 1922).

perepiska i pr.). Moscow, 1922. Short title: *Materialy.*
(2) Great Britain, *Papers relating to International Economic Conference, Genoa, April–May 1922.* London, 1922 (Cmd. 1667). Short title: Cmd. 1667.
(3) *Les documents de la Conférence de Gênes, avec une introduction par Amedeo Giannini.* Rome, 1922. Short title: *Documents.*
(4) Germany, *Material über die Konferenz von Genua.* Berlin, 1922. Short title: *Material.*
(5) Canada, Delegates to the economic and financial conference, Genoa, 1922, *The Genoa Conference for the economic and financial reconstruction of Europe ...* Ottawa, 1922. Short title: Canadian report.
(6) Mills, J. Saxon, *The Genoa Conference.* N.Y. and London, n.d. Short title: Mills.
See also Fischer, pp. 318–54, and Eudin and Fisher, pp. 101–109.

———(1) Resolution on financial questions

Sources: *SDD RSFSR*, 3, pp. 95–101.
    Materialy, pp. 358–64.
    Cmd. 1667, pp. 60–65.
    Documents, pp. 134–42.
    Material, pp. 72–81 (F, G).
    Canadian report, pp. 68–72.
    Mills, pp. 361–68.

———(2) Resolution on questions of transportation, with two annexes

Sources: *SDD RSFSR*, 3, pp. 123–45.
    Materialy, pp. 379–98.
    Cmd. 1667, pp. 81–99.
    Documents, pp. 166–72 (omits the annexes).
    Material, pp. 152–77 (G, F).
    Canadian report, pp. 86–101.
    Mills, pp. 373–97.

———(3) Resolution on economic questions, with annex

Sources: *SDD RSFSR*, 3, pp. 102–16.
   Materialy, pp. 399–413.
   Cmd. 1667, pp. 69–80.
   Documents, pp. 149–65.
   Material, pp. 90–106 (G, F).
   Canadian report, pp. 76–86.
   Mills, pp. 416–32.

———(4) Resolution on political questions

Sources: *SDD RSFSR*, 3, pp. 7–8.
   Materialy, p. 432.
   Cmd. 1667, pp. 49–50.
   Documents, pp. 228–29.
   Material, pp. 66–67 (G, F).
   Canadian report, pp. 66–67.
   Mills, pp. 259–60.

May 24, 1922. Temporary commercial treaty between the RSFSR and Italy

Signed in Genoa.
Rejected by the Council of People's Commissars June 8, 1922.
References: *Le matin* (Paris), May 25, 1922 (signature); *ibid.*, May 28, 1922 (summary).
   Shtein, 1925, p. 68.
   Korolenko, p. 28.
   Fischer, p. 467.
Note: In an official Soviet statement on non-ratification of the treaty published in *Pravda* and *Izv.*, June 16, 1922, the date of the treaty is given as May 29, 1922. This erroneous date has found its way into both non-Soviet and Soviet accounts (e.g., Dennis, p. 402; *Istoriia diplomatii*, 3, p. 122, which adds the erroneous statement that it was Italy which refused to ratify the treaty, under French pressure).

July 24, 1923. Convention on the regime of the Black Sea Straits, with annex (Lausanne Convention)

Signed in Lausanne by the United Kingdom, France, Italy, Japan, Bulgaria, Greece, Romania, the Kingdom of the Serbs, Croats, and Slovenes, and Turkey. The USSR signed Aug. 14, 1923, in Constantinople.
Although the USSR did not ratify the convention, it subsequently provided information to the Turkish Government on Soviet naval forces in the Black Sea (Fischer, p. 410).
Sources: *MZh*, 1924, No. 1, pp. 186–94.
   LNTS, 28, pp. 115–37 (E, F).
   BTS, 1923, No. 16, Cmd. 1929.
   Hurewitz, 2, pp. 119–27.
   BFSP, 117, pp. 592–600 (F).
   Hudson, 2, pp. 1028–41 (E, F).

Mar. 14, 1924. General agreement between the USSR and China

Did not enter into force because the signature of the Chinese delegate was not recognized by the Chinese Government.
Sources: *CYB, 1924*, pp. 880–83.
   China Review, 6, May 1924, pp. 132–33.
References: *CYB, 1924*, p. 879 (Soviet statement on Chinese refusal to ratify; reprinted *SDFP*, 1, p. 435).
   Wei, p. 33.

July 3, 1924. Commercial treaty between the USSR and Persia

Signed in Teheran.
Not ratified by Persia.
References: *RIR*, Aug. 2, 1924, p. 67 (summary).
   Korolenko, p. 37.
   Sovremënnyi Iran, pp. 364–65.

Aug. 8, 1924. (1) General treaty between the USSR and the United Kingdom

Signed in London.
Not ratified by the United Kingdom.
Sources: *MZh*, 1924, No. 4–5, pp. 269–81.
   BPP, Russia No. 4 (1924), Cmd. 2260; extracts in
   SDFP, 1, pp. 453–57.
   Russian review, Sept. 15, 1924, pp. 114–17.
References: Korolenko, p. 38.
   Eudin and Fisher, pp. 259–62.

———(2) Treaty of commerce and navigation between the USSR and the United Kingdom, with protocol and two declarations

Signed in London.
Not ratified by the United Kingdom.
Sources: *MZh*, 1924, No. 4–5, pp. 282–91.
   *BPP, Russia No. 5 (1924), Cmd. 2261.
   Russian review, Oct. 1, 1924, pp. 134–37.

References: *Pravda*, Aug. 23, 1924.
Korolenko, p. 38.

Sept. 5, 1924. Treaty between the USSR and Hungary concerning establishment of diplomatic and consular relations

Signed in Berlin.
Was to have been ratified within 3 months of signature; because of Hungary's refusal to ratify, however, despite 2 extensions by the USSR, did not enter into force.
Source: Kliuchnikov, 3, I, p. 319 (shortened).
References: *Izv.*, Sept. 19, 1924.
Desiat' let, p. 70 (dates the treaty Sept. 12, 1924).

Nov. 27, 1925. Convention concerning measurement of vessels employed in inland navigation, with protocol of signature

Signed in Paris.
Entered into force Oct. 1, 1927. The USSR had not ratified as of July 10, 1944.
Source: *LNTS*, 67, pp. 63–89 (E, F).
Reference: *LNOJ*, Special supplement No. 193, p. 92.

June 23, 1926. Customs agreement between the USSR and Greece

Signed in Athens.
Duration 2 years. According to *Pravda*, June 17, 1928, applied throughout the period 1926–1928, but failed of ratification by the Greek Government shortly before expiration.
Sources: *Greek official gazette, Part A, No. 241, 1926.
STS, 1, pp. 319–20, citing
Martens, 3rd series, 27, pp. 510–12.
Reference: *Izv.*, July 25, 1926.

Mar. 16, 1934. Agreement between the USSR and Sweden concerning a loan by Sweden of one hundred million Swedish crowns

Signed in Stockholm.
Was to have entered into force May 1, 1934. Rejected by the Council of People's Commissars during Apr. 1934; rejection by the Swedish Riksdag was expected.
References: *Izv.*, Mar. 18, 1934.
ERSU, May 1934, p. 125.

Ostwirtschaft, Mar.–Apr. 1934, p. 44 (summary); *ibid.*, May 1934, p. 64 (Soviet non-ratification), citing *Za industrializatsiiu*, Apr. 27, 1934.

May 13, 1936. Agreement for a uniform system of maritime buoyage, with annexed regulations

Signed in Geneva.
Had not entered into force as of July 10, 1944. Soviet acceptance, under a reservation on signature, was made conditional on acceptance or application by Germany, Estonia, Finland, France, the United Kingdom, Japan, Norway, and Turkey. The USSR had not ratified as of July 10, 1944.
Source: LN Document C.261(1).M.154 (1).1936.VIII, cited in
LNOJ, Special supplement No. 193, p. 101.

June 26, 1936. Convention for suppression of the illicit traffic in dangerous drugs

Signed in Geneva.
Entered into force Oct. 26, 1939. The USSR had not ratified as of July 10, 1944. Amended by a protocol of Dec. 11, 1946 (46/xii/11/Mul).
Source: *LNTS*, 198, pp. 299–323 (E, F).
Reference: *LNOJ*, Special supplement No. 193, p. 130.

Sept. 23, 1936. Convention concerning the use of broadcasting in the cause of peace

Signed in Geneva.
The USSR had not ratified as of July 10, 1944. The USSR made the following reservation on signature: "The Delegation of the [USSR] declares that, pending the conclusion of the procedure contemplated in Art. 7 of the Convention, it considers that the right to apply reciprocal measures to a country carrying out improper transmissions against it, insofar as such a right exists under the general rules of international law and with the Conventions in force, is in no way affected by the Convention.
"The Delegation of the [USSR] declares that its Government, while prepared to apply the principles of the Convention on a basis of reciprocity to all the Contract-

ing States, is nevertheless of opinion that certain of the provisions of the Convention presuppose the existence of diplomatic relations between the Contracting Parties, particularly in connection with the verification of information and the forms of procedure proposed for the settlement of disputes. Accordingly the Government of the [USSR] is of opinion that, in order to avoid the occurrence of differences or misunderstandings between the States Parties to the Convention which do not maintain diplomatic relations with one another, the Convention should be regarded as not creating formal obligations between such States." (*LNTS*, 186, p. 317.)

For a Soviet proposal to revive the treaty in 1955, see *Int. org.*, 9, 1955, pp. 119–21.

Source: *LNTS*, 186, pp. 301–17 (E, F).
Reference: *LNOJ*, Special supplement No. 193, pp. 51–52.

Nov. 16, 1937. (1) Convention for creation of an International Criminal Court

Signed in Geneva.
Had not entered into force as of July 10, 1944. On signature the USSR stated that it would ratify only subject to the reservation that "with regard to the settlement of disputes relating to the interpretation or application" of the convention the USSR would assume "only such obligations as are incumbent on it as a Member of the League of Nations." The USSR had not ratified as of July 10, 1944.
Source: LN Document C.547(1).M.384 (1).1937.V., cited in
  LNOJ, Special supplement No. 193, p. 55.

——(2) Convention for the prevention and punishment of terrorism

Signed in Geneva.
Had not entered into force as of July 10, 1944. On signature the USSR made a statement identical with that made concerning the Convention for creation of an International Criminal Court of the same date (above). The USSR had not ratified as of July 10, 1944.
Source: LN Document C.546(1).M.383 (1).1937.V., cited in
  LNOJ, Special supplement No. 193, p. 54.

Apr. 8, 1938. General Radio Regulations (Cairo Revision, 1938), and Final Radio Protocol (Cairo Revision, 1938)

Signed in Cairo.
Annexed to the International Telecommunication Convention signed at Madrid, December 9, 1932. The USSR had not ratified as of Jan. 1, 1946 (Hudson, 8, p. 41). Estonia and Latvia, however, before their incorporation into the USSR, had done so.
Source: *USTS*, No. 948, 1940 (E, F); Soviet signatures, pp. 92, 141.

June 11, 1941. (1) Commercial agreement between the USSR and Japan

Initialed in Moscow but not signed; did not enter into force.
Duration 5 years. Provides for total trade of 30 million yen annually and for most-favored-nation treatment in regard to tariff and commercial transactions. Provisions for transit between Japan and Germany via the Trans-Siberian Railway were included, according to Dallin, 1942, p. 429.
References: *Izv.*, June 12, 1941.
  VP, 4, p. 555.
  MKh, 1941, No. 6, p. 123.

——(2) Trade and payments agreement between the USSR and Japan

Initialed in Moscow but not signed; did not enter into force.
References: As cited for (1) above.

Apr. 4, 1946. Exchange of notes between the USSR and Iran constituting an agreement concerning establishment of a mixed Soviet-Iranian oil company

Sent in Moscow.
The agreement was rejected by the Iranian Mejlis Oct. 22, 1946. See references cited under 46/iv/4/Iran.
Source: *ARSU*, Aug. 1946, p. 76, citing
  Soviet news, Apr. 9, 1946.

Aug. 9, 1946. Treaty of friendship, commerce, and navigation between the USSR and Uruguay, with annex concerning the Soviet Trade Mission in Uruguay

Signed in Moscow.
Evidently not ratified by Uruguay.
References: *Pr.*, *Izv.*, Aug. 11, 1946.
  Korolenko, p. 80.

Appendix 2

SECRET SOVIET-GERMAN MILITARY AGREEMENTS, 1921–1933

During the period 1921–1933 a number of secret military agreements were concluded between Soviet and German negotiators. Despite the continuing absence of authentic texts of any of these agreements from either side, their existence is now generally accepted by scholars. Some of the facts about them became known at the time, while others have been painstakingly dug out in recent years from a wide variety of sources, the most important being the German military and diplomatic archives captured by the Western Allies in World War II. Our knowledge of the agreements is still far from complete, but it is probably safe to say that the main lines of their content and the approximate dates of their conclusion have been established with a fair degree of accuracy.

Although they are here accepted as genuine, however,[1] the secret Soviet-German military agreements have not been included in the main text of the *Calendar* because (1) the evidence for them is frequently so fragmentary, scattered, and imprecise that it requires fairly lengthy analysis, and (2) in a number of cases the negotiators, at least on the German side, were not official representatives of the Government.

In order to present the evidence for the agreements adequately, we have listed the principal sources and secondary works dealing with them in a critical Bibliographical Survey; this is followed by a chronological List of Identified and Inferred Agreements.

BIBLIOGRAPHICAL SURVEY

The principal sources and secondary studies containing evidence on the Soviet-German secret military agreements are listed below, numbered serially from 1 to 42. Short title references have been assigned in accordance with the following key:

Short title	Number	Short title	Number
Brockdorff-Rantzau Nachlass	2.a	Helbig	27.a
Carr, *German-Soviet relations*	34	Hilger and Meyer	30
Carr, 3	35	Ipatieff	21
Castellan, *Réarmement*	37	Koestring ms.	5
Castellan, *Reichswehr*	38	Kulski	31
DGFP, C, 1	3	*Manchester Guardian*	12
Dirksen	28	Melville	13
Eudin and Fisher	41	1938 *Report*	22
EZh	18	Scheidemann	7
Freund	42	Seeckt papers	1.a
Gatzke	16	Speidel	4
Görlitz	32	Stresemann Nachlass	2.b
Hallgarten	14	Tschunke	1.d

[1] It should be noted that not all the agreements of this type which have been reported are accepted. For a group of unverified and probably spurious alleged secret Soviet-German military agreements, see Appendix 4, under dates Jan. 15, 1919; Apr. 17, 1919; July 8, 1920; Mar. 25, 1921; and Apr. 3, 1922.

A. *Source materials by German participants*

(1) Manuscripts from the Heeresarchiv, Potsdam.

> Originals in the National Archives, Washington, D.C.; microfilms at the Widener Library, Harvard, and (in part) the Hoover Institution, Stanford. Includes the following manuscript collections:

(1.a) The papers of General Hans von Seeckt.

> General von Seeckt was the principal agent in the plans to rebuild the German armed forces after World War I and the moving force on the German side in negotiating the secret military agreements during the early period (1919–25).

(1.b) The diary of General Paul Hasse (included in the Seeckt papers).

> A major source for several key events. Used by Hallgarten, but subsequently placed on the restricted list and not at present available for research.

(1.c) The papers of General Wilhelm Groener.

> General Groener was Reichswehr Minister during the later years of Soviet-German military collaboration. His papers have not yet been studied, although a biographical study has been promised (see Groener, Wilhelm, *Lebenserinnerungen*, Göttingen, 1957, p. 8).

(1.d) Fritz Tschunke, "General v. Seeckt nimmt die Verbindung zur Sowjetunion auf." Written as a letter to Friedrich von Rabenau, the biographer of Seeckt, on Feb. 13, 1939; included in the Seeckt papers. First published in *Der Monat*, Vol. 1, No. 2, Nov. 1948, pp. 48–50, and in translation in a pamphlet by Julius Epstein, "The Seeckt papers," N.Y., published by the author, 1948.

> Tschunke headed GEFU, the cover organization established in Germany to carry out economic collaboration with the Soviet Union under the secret military agreements.

(2) Documents of the German Auswärtiges Amt.

> Originals in the National Archives, Washington, D.C. In process of microfilming. The most significant for the present subject are the following:

(2.a) The Brockdorff-Rantzau Nachlass.

> Count Brockdorff-Rantzau was German Ambassador to the Soviet Union during the period 1922–28.

(2.b) The Stresemann Nachlass.

(3) United States, Department of State, *Documents on German foreign policy, 1918–1945. Series C (1933–1937). The Third Reich: first phase. Vol. 1, January 30–October 14, 1933*, Washington, D.C., 1957.

> Covers the last phase and winding up of the collaboration.

(4) Helm Speidel, "Reichswehr und Rote Armee," *Vierteljahreshefte für Zeitgeschichte*, Vol. 1, No. 1, Jan. 1953, pp. 9–45; introductory notes by Hans Rothfels.

> General Speidel played a prominent part in the field of aviation and pilot training during the later period (1927–33) of the Soviet-German military collaboration. His article is the principal source of our knowledge of this aspect of the subject, and a major source for the events of the later period as a whole.

(5) An unpublished manuscript by General Ernst Koestring, evidently written in Sept. 1948.

Cited in Castellan, *Reichswehr*, p. 41. Koestring was German military attaché in Moscow from 1931 to 1933 and from 1935 to 1941.

B. *Other German source materials*

(6) A memorandum prepared by the Junkers Werke, a German aircraft firm, in the early summer of 1926.

Presents the company's case for modification of agreements it had entered into for establishment of a factory to manufacture airplanes in Russia. A major source of information on the early phases of collaboration, although evidently never published; principal basis of the Scheidemann speech and the *Manchester Guardian* reports. The papers of the Auswärtiges Amt include a memorandum, "Denkschrift zum Fall Reichsfiskus—Junkers," June 25, 1926; cited by Gatzke, p. 584.

(7) A speech in the Reichstag, Dec. 16, 1926, by Socialist (SPD) Deputy Philipp Scheidemann, in *Verhandlungen des Reichstags, Stenographische Berichte*, Vol. 391 (Berlin, 1927), pp. 8577–86.

Based in part on the Junkers memorandum, in part on materials collected by the SPD.

(8) Statements by officials of the German Government to the Foreign Affairs Committee of the Reichstag, Feb. and Mar. 1927.

Not published, but summarized by the German press (*Vorwärts*, Mar. 30, 1927, cited in Castellan, *Réarmement*, p. 183). Freund, p. 92, cites the Stresemann Nachlass.

(9) Krupp documents produced in evidence at the Nuremberg Trial of Nazi war criminals.

Compiled by Georges Castellan in his thesis, "Choix de documents sur le Konzern Krupp et l'armement de l'Allemagne, 1918–1945," typescript, pp. 101–14 (cited in Castellan, *Reichswehr*, p. 141). Provide evidence on the manufacture of tanks in Russia.

(10) "Sowjetgranaten: Sowjetrussland als Munitionslieferant für die Reichswehr," a pamphlet published by the Parteivorstand of the SPD, Mar. 1927.

Translation in Melville, pp. 177–204. Based on materials collected by the SPD. A major source of information for the early period of collaboration.

(11) Contemporary German press references.

Full references have been compiled by Georges Castellan in the typescript ms. of his thesis, *Le réarmement clandestin du Reich, 1930–1935*, Vol. 3, pp. 86–104 (cited in Castellan, *Reichswehr*, p, 138).

C. *Studies based primarily on the German materials*

(12) The *Manchester Guardian*, Dec. 3, 1926, and the *Manchester Guardian Weekly*, Dec. 10, 1926, p. 468.

The first published disclosure of the existence of the military agreements.

(13) Melville, Cecil F., *The Russian face of Germany. An account of the secret military relations between the German and Soviet-Russian Governments*, London, 1932.

The fullest compilation of evidence from published German sources to approximately 1930.

(14) Hallgarten, George W. F., "General Hans von Seeckt and Russia, 1920–1922," *Journal of modern history*, Vol. 21, No. 1, Mar. 1949, pp. 28–34.

> Part of a longer unpublished work on Seeckt, based primarily on the Seeckt papers. Hallgarten had access to some materials (e.g., the Hasse diary) which were subsequently withdrawn from study, and his article remains the only available source for some key developments.

(15) Smith, Arthur L., "The German General Staff and Russia, 1919–1926," *Soviet studies*, Vol. 8, No. 2, Oct. 1956, pp. 125–33.

> Based on independent study of the Seeckt papers, but adds nothing of significance.

(16) Gatzke, Hans W., "Russo-German military collaboration during the Weimar Republic," *American historical review*, Vol. 63, No. 3, Apr. 1958, pp. 565–97.

> Based on independent study of the Heeresarchiv and Auswärtiges Amt papers; the most thorough study at present available of the subject as recorded in these sources, although it does not supersede Hallgarten.

D. *Soviet references, direct and indirect*

(17) A report by Viktor Kopp, Soviet representative in Germany, to Trotsky, dated Apr. 7, 1921, with marginal notes by Lenin and Menzhinsky.

> Original in the Trotsky Archive, Widener Library, Harvard. Cited by Carr, 3, p. 362; see also Carr, *German-Soviet relations*, p. 57. Outlines plans for the manufacture in Russia of German airplanes, submarines, and munitions. Lenin's approval indicated.

(18) Notice of the confirmation by the Council of People's Commissars of 3 agreements with Junkers, one providing for manufacture of airplanes and motors in Russia: *Ekonomicheskaia zhizn'*, Feb. 2, 1923, No. 3 (1253), p. 1.

(19) Editorial, "Lovi vora" [Stop thief!], *Pravda*, Dec. 16, 1926. Translation in Eudin and Fisher, pp. 208–209.

> Discounts the *Manchester Guardian* revelations as unimportant if true.

(20) Radek, Karl, "Neispovedimy puti gospodni, ili kak germanskaia sotsial-demokratiia prishla k otritsaniiu zashchity otechestva" [The unfathomable ways of the Lord, or how German Social-Democracy came to a denial of the defense of the Fatherland], *Izv.*, Dec. 16, 1926.

> Admits existence of the Junkers agreement but denies Soviet arms shipments to Germany via Stettin.

(21) Ipatieff, V. N., *The life of a chemist*, Stanford, 1946.

> Ipatieff participated on the Soviet side in the production of poison gas in Russia in collaboration with Germany. His memoirs, written after he left the Soviet Union, are the principal source of information on this phase of the collaboration. The relevant passages are reprinted in Eudin and Fisher, pp. 207–208.

(22) People's Commissariat of Justice of the USSR, *Report of court proceedings in the case of the Anti-Soviet "Bloc of Rights and Trotskyites"* . . . , Moscow, 1938.

> In the interrogation of N. N. Krestinsky and A. P. Rosengoltz, pp. 152–58 and 262–87, the facts of the secret Soviet-German military collaboration during the early 1920's are used as the basis for a freely elaborated phantasy of a Trotskyite conspiracy with Germany to conduct espionage in the USSR in return for German financial support. The trial evidence is analyzed against

the background of the ascertained facts in Castellan, *Reichswehr*, pp. 238–57.

(23) Fischer, Louis, *The Soviets in world affairs*, N.Y., 1930; 2nd ed., Princeton, 1951.

Fischer's book, while not, of course, in any sense an official Soviet work, has to some extent the value of an authoritative source, since it is based on first-hand materials, both written and oral, stemming from the leading figures in the field of Soviet foreign affairs during the period 1917–29. Fischer refers to the Junkers aircraft plant in Russia (p. 331) and to a Soviet-German agreement for "the exchange of military experience, army experts, and munitions" (p. 601), the latter reference accompanied by the laconic statement that "responsible Bolshevik statesmen have denied to the writer the existence of any such arrangement or co-operation." Fischer makes no mention of the later phases of collaboration.

E. *Intelligence reports*

(24) Polish intelligence reports, ca. 1925–33.

(25) French Army intelligence reports, ca. 1925–33.

Both remain unpublished, but have been extensively used in Castellan, *Reichswehr*. An essential addition to the German source material.

F. *German biographies and memoirs*

(26) Rabenau, Friedrich von, *Seeckt. Aus seinem Leben, 1918–1936*, Leipzig, 1941.

Based in large part on the Seeckt papers and provides some guarded allusions to the early stages of the collaboration. Continues Seeckt's autobiography, *Aus meinem Leben, 1866–1917*, Leipzig, 1941.

(27) Helbig, Herbert, "Die Moskauer Mission des Grafen Brockdorff-Rantzau," *Forschungen zur Osteuropäischen Geschichte*, Osteuropa-Institut an der Freien Universität Berlin, Historische Veröffentlichungen, Vol. 2, Berlin, 1955, pp. 286–344.

Based in large part on the unpublished Brockdorff-Rantzau Nachlass. Provides the best available account of Brockdorff-Rantzau's part in the collaboration (he was German Ambassador in Moscow from 1922 to 1928).

(27.a) Helbig, Herbert, *Die Träger der Rapallo-Politik (Veröffentlichungen des Max-Planck-Instituts für Geschichte*, 3), Göttingen, 1958. Incorporates (27) in revised form, together with a further essay, "Militärbündnis oder Neutralitätspakt," which reviews German archival evidence on the military agreements through approximately 1928.

(28) Dirksen, Herbert von, *Moskau, Tokio, London. Erinnerungen und Betrachtungen zu 20 Jahren deutscher Aussenpolitik, 1919–1939*, Stuttgart, 1949.

Von Dirksen was German Ambassador in Moscow from 1928 to 1933 and provides some useful but guarded references to the collaboration during that period.

(29) Gessler, Otto, *Reichswehrpolitik in der Weimarer Zeit*, Stuttgart, 1958.

Gessler, who was Reichswehr Minister from 1920 to 1928, knew the details of planning and carrying out the collaboration from the side of the German Government, and his account (pp. 196–201) is useful for the guarded insights it permits into that aspect of the subject. He carefully avoids, however, adding anything of significance to what was previously known about the agreements and attempts, not with entire success, to minimize their importance.

(30) Hilger, Gustav, and Alfred G. Meyer, *The incompatible allies. A memoir-history of German-Soviet relations, 1918–1941*, N.Y., 1953.

> Hilger held an official position in the German Embassy in Moscow from 1921 to 1941. His testimony is of value for the entire period of collaboration, but must be used with caution, since it is frequently inaccurate and sometimes tendentious.

(30.a) Spalcke, Karl, "Begegnungen zwischen Reichswehr und Roter Armee, ein Rückblick," *Aussenpolitik* (Stuttgart), Vol. 9, No. 8, Aug. 1958, pp. 506–13.

> Covers an aspect of the collaboration on which little information is otherwise available—the assignment of Red Army staff officers to Germany for training. The author was a liaison officer in the Reichswehr.

G. *Secondary works based on a variety of sources*

(31) [Kulski, Wladyslaw] (W. M. Knight-Patterson, pseudonym), *Germany from defeat to conquest, 1913–1933*, London, 1945.

> Based mainly on materials compiled by Melville, but useful because it puts the Soviet-German collaboration in a wider context.

(32) Görlitz, Walter, *Der deutsche Generalstab. Geschichte und Gestalt, 1657–1945*, Frankfurt am Main, 1950.

> Based on extensive research, but without citations, and excessively restrained on the Soviet-German collaboration (see the comments by Castellan, *Reichswehr*, p. 141).

(33) Blücher, Wipert von, *Deutschlands Weg nach Rapallo. Erinnerungen eines Mannes aus dem zweiten Gliede*, Wiesbaden, 1951.

(34) Carr, E. H., *German-Soviet relations between the two World Wars, 1919–1939*, Baltimore, 1951.

> Covers the early period but uses new materials, particularly from the Trotsky Archive (see No. 17, above).

(35) Carr, E. H., *The Bolshevik Revolution, 1917–1923 (A History of Soviet Russia)*, Vol. 3, London and N.Y., 1953.

> Covers (pp. 361–66, 435–37) in greater detail and with full references the same ground as *German-Soviet relations*. Noteworthy for use (p. 247) of newly published evidence from British diplomatic papers of an early attempt (October 1919) by Junkers to set up a branch aircraft factory in Russia (Woodward and Butler, ed., *Documents on British foreign policy*, 1st series, Vol. 2, pp. 44–47).

(36) Wheeler-Bennett, John W., *The nemesis of power. The German Army in politics, 1918–1945*, London, 1953.

> Covers chiefly the early period (pp. 119–42), based on published sources. Less full than Carr and somewhat uncritical, e.g., accepts an unsupported statement in Wollenberg, Erich, *The Red Army* (London, 1938), p. 238, that an otherwise unidentified German flying school at Liubertsy (about 20 km. southeast of Moscow) continued in operation until 1935.

(37) Castellan, Georges, *Le réarmement clandestin du Reich, 1930–1935, vu par le 2e. Bureau de l'État-Major Français*, Paris, 1954.

> Chapter 5 covers "Technical collaboration between the Reichswehr and the Red Army." Originally a doctor's thesis at the Sorbonne; the typescript deposited there has full references.

(38) Castellan, Georges, *Reichswehr et Armée Rouge, 1920–1939*, in Duroselle, J.-B., ed., *Les relations Germano-soviétiques de 1933 à 1939*, Paris, 1954, pp. 137–271.

(39) Castellan, Georges, "Choix de documents sur le Konzern Krupp et l'armement de l'Allemagne, 1918–1945," unpublished secondary thesis, Paris, ca. 1954.

> The 3 works of Professor Castellan constitute by far the most thorough and detailed treatment available of the subject. His achievement is the more noteworthy because he was denied access to the captured German archives (*Reichswehr*, p. 11). He has, however, made effective use of secondary studies based on them.

(40) Kochan, Lionel, *Russia and the Weimar Republic*, London 1955.

> Contains brief references only, primarily to the early period of collaboration.

(41) Eudin, X. J., and H. H. Fisher, *Soviet Russia and the West, 1920–1927. A documentary survey*, Stanford, 1957.

> Summarizes published evidence for the earlier phase of collaboration (pp. 171–75), and prints some of the relevant materials in translation (pp. 203–10).

(42) Freund, Gerald, *Unholy alliance. Russian-German relations from the Treaty of Brest-Litovsk to the Treaty of Berlin*, London, 1957.

> Covers the first phase of collaboration only; based on a wide range of materials, including independent study of the Seeckt papers and other archival materials (see the extensive bibliography, pp. 261–70). The fullest treatment of the first phase of collaboration available in English, though occasionally marred by a tendency to strain the evidence, e.g., in regard to the inferred agreements of August 1922 (see the List of Agreements, below).

H. *Works not available for study*

(43) Horst-Falkenhagen, "L'Armée Rouge et la Reichswehr . . . ," in *Documents* (Centre d'Etudes d'Offenburg, en Bade), 1946, No. 6, pp. 565–68; cited by Castellan, *Reichswehr*, p. 139.

(44) Strohm, G., "Vierzehn Jahre deutsch-sowjetische Militärallianz," *Stuttgarter Rundschau*, III, 11, 12; cited by Hilger and Meyer, p. 189.

LIST OF IDENTIFIED OR INFERRED AGREEMENTS

Date	Event or agreement	References and comments
May 1921	Contract for purchase by the RSFSR of rifles and cartridges in Germany.	Melville, pp. 104–105.
Dec. 10, 1921	Junkers submits a draft agreement for establishment of an airplane factory in Russia.	Melville, p. 69. *Manchester Guardian Weekly*, Dec. 10, 1926, p. 468.
Mar. 15, 1922	Contract between Sondergruppe R, a cover organization in the German Reichswehr Ministry for carrying out secret military agreements with the RSFSR, and Junkers for manufacture of airplanes in Russia.	Scheidemann, p. 8579. *Manchester Guardian Weekly*, Dec. 10, 1926, p. 468. Text in Castellan, *Reichswehr*, p. 153, citing *Vorwärts*.
July 29, 1922	Secret "preliminary commercial agreement" between the RSFSR and the Reichswehr.	Hallgarten, p. 32, citing the diary of General Hasse (Seeckt papers).

Date	*Event or agreement*	*References and comments*
Aug. 11, 1922	Seeckt sends a "trusted collaborator" to Moscow "to complete the military pact."[2]	Hallgarten, p. 32.
ca. 1923	Concession agreement between the RSFSR and Dr. Hugo Stolzenberg, a German chemist, for establishment of a joint-stock company, "Bersol," to manufacture poison gas in Russia.	Ipatieff, pp. 381–88, 399; extracts in Eudin and Fisher, pp. 207–208. Melville, p. 86. Hilger and Meyer, p. 194. Castellan, *Reichswehr*, p. 185.
Feb. 1923	The RSFSR ratifies agreements with Junkers providing for (1) manufacture of airplanes and motors in the RSFSR, (2) establishment of an airline between Sweden and Persia, and (3) making aerial surveys.	*EZh*, Feb. 3, 1923. See also Scheidemann, p. 8584; Castellan, *Reichswehr*, p. 157; Melville, pp. 76–77; *Manchester Guardian Weekly*, Dec. 10, 1926, p. 468.
Apr. 1923	Agreement drafted in Moscow providing for delivery of Soviet munitions to Germany to a total value of 35 million gold marks.	Helbig, p. 152.
July 1923	Agreement initialed in Berlin, revising the April agreement and providing for deliveries of Soviet munitions to a total value of 75 million marks.	Helbig, pp. 154–56.
	German technical aid to be rendered to Soviet munitions factories in Zlatoust, Tula, and Petrograd.	Hilger and Meyer, p. 145; Castellan, *Reichswehr*, p. 157.
Dec. 1923	Agreement between the USSR and the Kreber firm of Germany for supply of raw materials for the manufacture of lewisite, a poison gas.	Melville, p. 111.
ca. 1924	Agreement between the USSR and Germany for training German pilots in the USSR. Inferred from the evidence pointing to the establishment at about this time of an air center for pilot training at Lipetsk.	Speidel, p. 18. Castellan, *Reichswehr*, p. 170. N.B.: Carr, 3, p. 436, cites evidence for the presence of German pilots in Russia as early as Sept. 1922.
ca. 1925	Regular exchange started of visits between staff officers of the Red Army and the Reichswehr, presumably in accordance with an earlier agreement.	Speidel, p. 36.

[2] The substance and actual date of signature of the "military pact" are unknown, though both can be inferred with some degree of probability. Freund, p. 124, cites Speidel, p. 18, on German demands and assumes that they constitute a summary of a formal agreement signed in August 1922, although it seems clear that Speidel is summarizing the relationship as it developed over a period of years. Speidel, incidentally, denies that any treaties as such were signed. Freund also cites a statement by Gessler in 1927, from the Stresemann Nachlass, indicating that military agreements were signed in the summer of 1922 but not ratified by the Soviet Government until February 1923 (cf. the Junkers agreement, below). Freund also points to the testimony of Rosengoltz and Krestinsky at the 1938 trial indicating that an agreement was put into effect in 1923 (1938 *Report*, pp. 258, 265; Krestinsky made a point of dating the agreement to 1922, *ibid.*, p. 285). Castellan, *Reichswehr*, p. 170, dates the military agreement or agreements to 1924–25, citing the unpublished Koestring report; he further cites a Polish intelligence report of 1930 to the effect that the original agreements provided only for the manufacture of armaments, and were later modified to provide for training of officers and technicians. This seems likely to be close to the truth.

Date	Event or agreement	References and comments
Spring 1926	GEFU (Gesellschaft zur Förderung gewerblicher Unternehmungen), German cover organization for carrying out clandestine military-economic agreements with the USSR, replaced by WIKO (Wirtschaftskontor). Castellan, *Reichswehr*, p. 197, suggests that a new agreement may have been concluded.	Hilger and Meyer, p. 194. Kulski, p. 402. Scheidemann, p. 8584.
Autumn 1926	Unconfirmed French intelligence report of agreement to send 60 former German pilots to the USSR to train Soviet pilots on 3-motored Junkers planes.	Castellan, *Réarmement*, p. 185.
ca. 1927	"Deutsch-Russische Notgemeinschaft," a cover firm, established in Germany for recruitment and dispatch to the USSR of German officers, instructors, and technical experts, particularly chemists.	Melville, p. 94. Hilger and Meyer, p. 207, mention sending of German scientists to Orenburg to assist in chemical warfare experiments.
ca. 1927	Agreement (inferred) for establishment of a tank training center, "Kama," at Kazan.	Castellan, *Reichswehr*, pp. 180, 183. Speidel, p. 18. Görlitz, p. 363.
ca. 1928	Agreement (inferred) for establishment of a center for poison gas training, "Tomka," at Trotsk near Samara. The training center replaced the earlier poison gas plant, which was closed in 1928 and transferred to the Soviet Government.	Castellan, *Reichswehr*, p. 185. Speidel, p. 18. Ipatieff, p. 468.
1928	Agreement between the USSR and Krupp for technical assistance in the manufacture of high-grade steels for military and civilian use.	Hilger and Meyer, p. 207.
Apr. 1929	Draft agreement between the USSR and Krupp for manufacture of armaments in the USSR. Not ratified by Krupp.	Gatzke, pp. 590–91.
1929	The Junkers aircraft plant at Fili taken over by the Soviet Government.	Castellan, *Reichswehr*, p. 157, citing Koestring ms.
ca. 1930	Agreements (inferred) for (1) Soviet purchases of military supplies in Germany and (2) assignment of German technicians to aid Soviet industry.	Castellan, *Reichswehr*, pp. 198–200, citing French intelligence reports.
Feb. 10, 1930	Preliminary agreement between the USSR and Rheinmetall, a German firm, for manufacture of armaments in the USSR.	Gatzke, pp. 591–94. Hilger and Meyer, pp. 207–208.
Jan.–Feb., 1932	German specialists in military transport, aviation, and chemistry sent to Russia.	Castellan, *Réarmement*, p. 199, citing French intelligence reports.
May 1933	Agreements concerning continuation of chemical warfare experiments during 1933.	*DGFP*, C, 1, pp. 464–67.
Summer 1933	Agreement for closing the aviation training center at Lipetsk. Similar agreements were presumably negotiated for closing the tank and chemical warfare centers.	Speidel, pp. 42–43. Dirksen, pp. 124–25. Hilger and Meyer, p. 256. Castellan, *Reichswehr*, p. 207.

Date	Event or agreement	References and comments
Date	*Event or agreement*	*References and comments*
Aug. 22, 1933	Farewell dinner to mark closing of the tank training center at Kazan.	*DGFP*, C, 1, pp. 767–68.
Sept. 15, 1933	Date of discontinuation of the joint bases ("stations").	*DGFP*, C, 1, p. 820.
Sept. 23, 1933	Farewell dinner for the head of Zentrale Moskau (the German military headquarters staff in Moscow for carrying out the collaboration).	*Ibid*, pp. 856–62.
Sept. 28, 1933	Liquidation of German military stations in the USSR reported completed.	*Ibid.*, p. 875.

NOTE: Castellan, *Réarmement*, pp. 484–85, quotes an unconfirmed French intelligence report according to which a Soviet-German agreement for the exchange of military intelligence was concluded in 1929 and renewed on Sept. 20, 1932. The report was discounted by the French Deuxième Bureau in a report which Castellan quotes (*ibid.*) Although he himself does not accept it, his printing of the report has given it some currency, and a recent German study accepts it as "probable": [Meissner, Hans Otto] (Hans Roos, pseudonym), *Polen und Europa. Studien zur polnischen Aussenpolitik, 1931–1939*, Tübingen, 1957 (Tübinger Studien zur Geschichte und Politik), p. 51.

Appendix 3

NONGOVERNMENTAL AGREEMENTS

(Contracts, Concessions, and Other Agreements with Organizations below the Governmental Level)

Note: The number of agreements which could be included under this heading is large, the state of their documentation is often fragmentary, and their intrinsic importance in many cases is slight. We therefore list a selection only of the relevant agreements which have been identified. Dates followed by an asterisk are dates of Soviet confirmation.

Mar. 29, 1920. Agreement between Tsentrosoiuz and Italian cooperative organizations concerning commerce and trade

Signed in Copenhagen.
Duration 6 months; extended to 1 year by an agreement of Apr. 8, 1920 (*DVP*, 2, p. 763; not listed separately). Modified by an agreement of June 28, 1920 (below).
". . . the first trade agreement following the lifting of the blockade, which in its content closely approaches to the type of international agreements." (Korolenko, p. 14.)
References: Shtein, 1925, p. 34.
  DVP, 2, pp. 762–63.

Apr. 1920. Agreement between Leonid Krassin[1] and a Swedish exporters' association concerning trade

Reference: Dennis, p. 400, citing
  London *Times*, Apr. 9, 1920.

Apr. 23, 1920. Agreement between Tsentrosoiuz and a Danish firm concerning development of trade

Signed in Copenhagen.
Provides for establishment of a "Clearing House" in Copenhagen to facilitate exports from and imports to the RSFSR. Did not enter into force because of inability of the Danish firm to obtain credits which had been agreed upon (*DVP*, 2, p. 763).
Source: *DVP*, 2, pp. 629–30.

———. Agreement between Tsentrosoiuz

---

[1] Presumably representing Tsentrosoiuz.

and a Danish firm concerning development of trade between the RSFSR and other States through Danish commercial and industrial firms

Signed in Copenhagen.
Provides for efforts to hold an international conference on trade in Copenhagen in May 1920, in return for a statement of Soviet willingness to negotiate foreign claims.
Source: *DVP*, 2, pp. 630–31.

Apr. 27, 1920. Agreement between Tsentrosoiuz and an Estonian firm concerning purchase of locomotives, with annex

Signed in Copenhagen.
Did not enter into force because the United States of America did not authorize export of the locomotives (*DVP*, 2, p. 764).
Source: *DVP*, 2, pp. 631–37 (omits the annex, a photograph).

May 15, 1920. Agreement between Tsentrosoiuz and a group of Swedish firms concerning Soviet orders in Sweden, with letter

Signed in Copenhagen.
Approved by Sweden. Provides for Soviet orders to a value of 100 million Swedish crowns, against a deposit of 25 million Swedish gold crowns.
Source: *DVP*, 2, pp. 516–23.
Reference: Korolenko, pp. 14–15.

———. Agreement between Tsentrosoiuz and a Swedish firm concerning delivery of locomotives to the RSFSR

Signed in Copenhagen.
Modified by a protocol of May 21, 1920
(below).
Source: *DVP*, 2, pp. 523–28.
References: Shtein, 1925, p. 33.
    Desiat' let, p. 61 (dates the agreement
    May 14, 1920).

May 14 and 16, 1920. Exchange of letters between Tsentrosoiuz and Sweden constituting an agreement concerning exchange of trade delegations and other matters related to trade

Sent in Stockholm.
Source: *DVP*, 2, pp. 528–30.
Reference: *Ibid.*, p. 760.

May 21, 1920. Protocol between L. B. Krassin, representing Tsentrosoiuz, and G. Anderson, representing a Swedish firm, concerning modification of the agreement of May 15, 1920

Concerns an advance by Tsentrosoiuz to the Swedish firm of 7 million Swedish crowns.
Reference: *DVP*, 2, p. 760.

June 28, 1920. Agreement between Tsentrosoiuz and Italian cooperative organizations concerning commerce and trade, with supplement

Signed in Moscow.
Source: *DVP*, 2, pp. 590–92.
References: Shtein, 1925, p. 34.
    Korolenko, p. 14.

Sept. 16, 1920. Agreement between L. B. Krassin[2] and G. Anderson, representing a group of Swedish firms, concerning sale of Russian timber

Reference: *DVP*, 2, p. 760.

Oct. 20, 1920. Contract between the RSFSR and Henschel & Sohn, a German firm, for purchase of locomotive tires

Signed in Stockholm.
Source: *Soviet Russia*, Feb. 5, 1921, pp. 133–35.

May 14, 1921. Concession agreement between the Far Eastern Republic and

---

[2] Presumably representing Tsentrosoiuz.

Harry F. Sinclair, a United States citizen, concerning exploitation of oil resources in Northern Sakhalin

According to Fischer, p. 302, this agreement and the one of Jan. 7, 1922, are identical, that being the date of ratification. See further the entry under that date.
References: Fischer, p. 302.
    Heymann, pp. 307–308.

Sept. 1921. Agreement between the Revolutionary Council of the Siberian Armies in the RSFSR and Sinkiang concerning border security and eradication of White forces

Source and reference: A. N. Blokhina, "Novye dokumenty iz istorii sovetskokitaiskikh otnoshenii," *Voprosy istorii*, 1957, No. 3, pp. 146–48.

Nov. 11, 1921. Concession agreement concerning establishment of a mixed Soviet-German trade and transportation company for trade with Persia

Confirmed by the RSFSR Mar. 1923 (*EZh*, Mar. 22, 1923).
References: *MP RSFSR, 1922*, p. 61.
    Hilger and Meyer, p. 178.
    EZh, Sept. 23, 1922.

Jan. 1922. Concession agreement between the RSFSR and the Friedrich Krupp firm of Germany for establishment in the RSFSR of a factory and experimental station for tractors and agricultural machinery

Reference: Carr, 3, p. 368, citing a note by Lenin of Jan. 23, 1922, in the Trotsky Archive.
Note: Possibly concerns the original Krupp concession proposal submitted in Jan. 1922. See entry under Jan. 16, 1923.

Jan. 7, 1922. Concession agreement between the Far Eastern Republic and the Sinclair Exploration Company, a United States firm, concerning prospecting for oil on Sakhalin

Under a companion agreement of the same date (not listed separately), to enter into force Jan. 7, 1923. Both agreements confirmed by the RSFSR Jan. 22, 1923. Duration for prospecting 5 years, for exploitation 31 years.

On Apr. 29, 1924, the Sinclair Company declared itself unable to proceed with operations under the agreement because of the Japanese occupation of Sakhalin, and asked to be released from the agreement. The case was brought for trial before a Moscow court later in 1924; the court declared the agreements null and void.
References: *EZh*, Jan. 28, 1923.
> Hwang, pp. 67–69, citing
> *Journal de Génève*, Jan. 27, 1925.
> *RIR*, Jan. 5, 1924, p. 4.
Note: See also the entry under May 14, 1921, above.

Sept. 9, 1922. Concession agreement between the RSFSR and the Russo-Asiatic United Society, a British firm ("Krassin-Urquhart agreement")

Signed in Berlin.
Duration 99 years. Rejected by the Council of People's Commissars of the RSFSR under a decree of Oct. 7, 1922 (*SU*, 1922, I, No. 62, Art. 806).
References: *EZh*, Oct. 7, 1922.
> Gerschuni, pp. 106–14.
> Liberman, pp. 159–64.
> Rubinshtein, pp. 377–78.

Sept. 22, 1922. Contract between the Azneft oil syndicate and the International Barnsdall Corporation, a United States firm, for drilling and exploitation of oil wells in the Baku region

Confirmed by the RSFSR during 1922.
Duration 15 years.
References: *Russian review*, Feb. 15, 1924, p. 238.
> *Sovetskaia Rossiia i kapitalisticheskii mir*, p. 644.

Oct. 9, 1922. Agreement between the NKVT[3] and Otto Wolf, a German firm, for establishment of the Russo-German Trading Company, "Russgertorg"

Confirmed by the RSFSR Oct. 19, 1922.
Abrogated early in 1924.
References: *EZh*, Oct. 26, 1922; *ibid.*, Jan. 27, 1924.
> *EIK*, pp. 576, 889–900.
> Fischer, pp. 580–81.
> Hilger and Meyer, pp. 172–73.

---

[3] People's Commissariat of Foreign Trade of the RSFSR.

1923. Concession agreement between the USSR and Harry F. Sinclair, a United States citizen, concerning exploitation of oil resources in the Baku area

Invalidated in 1924.
Reference: Heymann, p. 308.

Jan. 1923.* Agreement between the RSFSR and the Jewish Colonization Society, "EKO," concerning re-establishment of agricultural enterprises in Jewish colonies in the RSFSR and restoration of Jewish technical and agricultural schools

Valid to Jan. 1926, subject to renewal.
References: *EZh*, Jan. 27, 1923.
> *Russian review*, Mar. 1, 1924, p. 255.

Jan. 16, 1923.* Concession agreement between the RSFSR and the Friedrich Krupp firm of Germany for establishment of the Manych agricultural concession in the Don region

History (as given in *EZh*, Jan. 19, 1923): The original proposal was submitted to the Concessions Committee of the People's Commissariat of Agriculture Jan. 12, 1922. Confirmed by the RSFSR Mar. 21, 1922, and signed by both parties Mar. 23, 1922. In view of the delay of Krupp to begin work under the concession, however, the Soviet trade representative in Germany, B. S. Stomon'iakov, requested a final decision by Dec. 1, 1922. In Dec. 1922, Krupp stated that a company entitled "Kruppsche Landkonzession Manytsch GmbH" was to be formed with capital from Krupp and an English company. The revised agreement was ratified by the RSFSR Jan. 16, 1923.
Modified in Aug. 1927 to permit substitution of sheep-breeding for grain-raising (*SUR*, Sept. 1927, p. 129).
Note: Hilger and Meyer, p. 172, deny that the Krupp concession was a cover for secret Soviet-German military collaboration. Castellan, *Reichswehr*, pp. 158–59, however, cites evidence from the Krupp trial at Nuremberg indicating that the real purpose of the concession was the development of tanks.

Feb. 1923.* Concession agreement between the RSFSR and a Norwegian firm

for seal hunting in Russian territorial waters

References: *EZh*, Mar. 1, 1923.
Russian review, Mar. 1, 1924, p. 264.

———.* **Concession agreements between the RSFSR and the Junkers aircraft firm of Germany for (1) manufacture of airplanes and motors in the RSFSR, (2) establishment of an air line Sweden–Persia, and (3) production by Junkers of aerial surveys**

Reference: *EZh*, Feb. 2, 1923.
Note: See also Appendix 2.

Mar. 1923.* Concession agreement between the People's Commissariat of Agriculture of the RSFSR and "Joint," an American organization, for reproduction and distribution among the peasants of improved types of agricultural plants

Reference: *EZh*, Mar. 10, 1923.

Mar. 20, 1923.* Concession agreement between the RSFSR and SKF, a Swedish firm, for manufacture of ball-bearings in the RSFSR

References: *EZh*, Mar. 22, 1923.
EIK, pp. 878–82.

May 5, 1923. Concession agreements between the RSFSR and the Gesellschaft Wirtschaftsverkehr Osten of Germany concerning (1) construction of a section of the railroad between Mga and Rybinsk and (2) exploitation of timber resources in the area

Confirmed by the USSR Sept. 11, 1923.
References: *EZh*, May 9, Sept. 18, and Oct. 27, 1923.
Russian review, Oct. 15, 1923, p. 78;
ibid., Nov. 1, 1923, p. 82.

May 8, 1923. Concession agreement between the NKVT and "Wostwag," a German firm, concerning export from and import to the RSFSR

Valid to Jan. 1, 1924. Extended in 1924.
Expired in 1927, but renewed for 2 years.
References: *EZh*, May 10, 1923.
Russian review, Dec. 15, 1923, p. 162.

SUR, Sept. 1927, p. 128.
Hwang, p. 21.

May 22, 1923. Concession agreement between the Main Fishing Administration of the RSFSR and Christian Christensen, Jr., a Norwegian citizen, concerning whale hunting

Duration 15 years.
References: *EZh*, May 24, 1923.
Russian review, Apr. 1, 1924, p. 302.

May 31, 1923. Agreement between the RSFSR and Japanese fishing organizations concerning fishing rights in the Far East

Fulfillment of the fishermen's obligations under the agreement guaranteed by the Japanese Government.
References: *EZh*, July 3, 1923.
RIR, Jan. 5, 1924, p. 5.

June 19, 1923.* Concession agreement with the German Volga Agricultural Credit Bank for restoration of agriculture in the Autonomous German Volga Commune

Duration 36 years.
References: *EZh*, June 21, 1923.
Russian review, Mar. 1, 1924.

July 16, 1923. Trade agreement with the Reichskreditgesellschaft, a German firm

Provides for delivery of 350,000 tons of Soviet grain in exchange for manufactured goods.
Reference: *RIR*, Jan. 5, 1924, p. 5.

Aug. 10, 1923. Agreement between the Administration of State Fishing Enterprises of the People's Commissariat of Supplies of the RSFSR and Martyn Lianozov concerning transfer of rights in fishing property on the Caspian Sea to the RSFSR

Included as a supplement to Protocol 2 to the Soviet-Persian agreement of Oct. 1, 1927, concerning fisheries in the southern part of the Caspian Sea (27/x/1/Persia/b).
Source: *SDD*, 5, pp. 80–81 (extracts).
Reference: Hurewitz, 1, p. 150 (background).

Oct. 25, 1923. Concession agreement between the USSR and Charles Smith, a United States citizen, representing the Far Eastern Exploration Company, concerning exploration for gold in Siberia ("Kharga gold concession")

Confirmed by the USSR. Entered into force on signature. Valid to Jan. 1, 1925. In Mar. 1924 the Soviet Government authorized transfer of the concession to the Far Eastern Prospecting Company, a United States corporation.
Source: *Russian review*, Feb. 15, 1924, pp. 235–37.
References: *EZh*, Oct. 28, 1923.
Russian review, Oct. 1, 1924, p. 128.

Dec. 1923.* Concession agreement between the USSR and an Italian-Belgian mining company concerning prospecting for and exploitation of oil and gas resources in Georgia

Term of exploration 3 years, of exploitation 30 years.
References: *EZh*, Dec. 13, 1923.
Russian review, Feb. 15, 1924, pp. 234–35.

Dec. 1923.⁴ Agreement between the Soviet Trade Mission in Germany and German representatives concerning credit for Soviet orders in Germany ("Grain agreement")

Provides for an advance of German credit to finance Soviet orders with German industrial firms.
Reference: Hilger and Meyer, p. 184.

1924. Agreement between the Soviet oil syndicate, with the participation of the Soviet Trade Mission in Italy, and Italian negotiators for export of oil products to Italy during 1924

Provides for exports to a total value of 50 million lire.
Reference: *Russian review*, July 15, 1924, p. 31.

Sept. 1924. Agreement between the All-Russian Oil Syndicate and a German firm concerning delivery of Soviet benzine and petroleum products to Germany

Provides for exports to a total value of 15 million Marks for benzine, 30 to 40 million Marks for other petroleum products.
Reference: *Russian review*, Oct. 15, 1924, p. 160.

Feb. 27, 1925. Contract between Neftesindikat and trading organizations in Canton for the sale of Soviet oil products in South China

Reference: *VT SSSR*, p. 24.

Apr. 1925. Concession agreement with an Italian-Belgian company for exploration of oil resources in the Shirak steppe in Georgia

Duration 30 years.
Reference: *Russian review*, June 1, 1925, p. 239.

Apr. 30, 1925. Concession agreement between the USSR and the Lena Goldfields Company, a British firm, concerning mining and related activities in Eastern Siberia, the Urals, and the Altai district

Ratified by the company approximately 3 months after signature; confirmed by the USSR and entered into force Nov. 14, 1925. On Sept. 2, 1930, an arbitration court in London found the Soviet Government guilty of breach of contract and awarded the company £12,965,000. For an agreement to settle the claim, see below under date 1934.
References: *Russian review*, June 15, 1925, pp. 249–51.
EIK, pp. 581–84.
ERSU, Oct. 1, 1930, pp. 379–83.
Hwang, p. 21.

June 12, 1925. Concession agreement with Harriman & Company, a United States firm, establishing the Chiaturi Manganese Concession in the Transcaucasian Republic ("Harriman concession")

Duration 20 years. Supplemented by an agreement ratified by the USSR June 28, 1927 (below). Annulled July 1928 (Hwang, p. 82).
References: *EIK*, pp. 584–85.
ERSU, Dec. 1, 1927, p. 8.
Russian review, June 1, 1925, p. 239; *ibid.*, July 15, 1925, pp. 294–95.
Liberman, pp. 149–50.

---

⁴ Approximate date.

Oct. 12, 1925. Agreement between the Soviet State Bank and a group of German banks concerning short-term credits for the USSR

Signed in Berlin.

Provides for a credit of 75 million Marks, which taken together with the Soviet trade credit, is to enable the USSR to buy goods in Germany on credit to a value of 100 million gold Marks.

References: *Izv.*, Oct. 6, 1925.
  Hilger and Meyer, pp. 184–85.
  Rubinshtein, p. 531.
  SDFP, 2, pp. 59–60.

Dec. 14, 1925. Three concession agreements with Japanese firms for exploitation of coal and petroleum resources on Northern Sakhalin

Duration 45 years. Annulled by the Soviet-Japanese agreement of Mar. 30, 1944 (44/iii/30/J/a).

References: *ERSU*, Nov. 1, 1927, p. 9;
  ibid., Sept. 1, 1930, p. 354.
  Russian review, Jan. 15, 1926, pp. 22–23.

Apr. 26, 1926. Concession agreement between the USSR and a Norwegian organization concerning seal-hunting in the Northeastern Atlantic

Mentioned in and abrogated by the Soviet-Norwegian agreement of Nov. 22, 1957.

July 1926. Credit agreement between the USSR and a group of German banks

Provides for a credit to the USSR of 300 million Marks. Preceded by an agreement on interest rates negotiated June 26, 1926 (not listed separately).

References: Fischer, pp. 698–705.
  Izv., June 27 and 29, 1926.
  Hilger and Meyer, p. 186 (dates the agreement Feb. 1926. For negotiations at this time, see Fischer, *loc. cit.*).

Dec. 21, 1926. Agreement between the Soviet oil syndicate and Standard Oil Company of New York for purchase of Soviet kerosene and construction of a refining plant in Batum

References: *ERSU*, May 1, 1927, p. 1.
  SUR, May 1927, p. 88.

1927. Contract between the USSR and Col. Hugh L. Cooper, a United States citizen, to act as consulting engineer in construction of the Dnieper electric power plant

Reference: *SUR*, Apr. 1927, p. 1.

Feb. 9, 1927. General conditions for delivery of products of the machine and apparatus industry from Germany to the USSR

Issued by the Soviet Trade Mission in Germany, following negotiations with the Verein Deutscher Maschinenbauanstalten. Superseded by the agreement of Mar. 20, 1935 (below).

References: *Ostwirtschaft*, Feb. 1935, p. 41.
  STS, 1, p. 326.

Note: The "General conditions" are mentioned in Art. 7 of the agreement of June 15, 1932, between the Soviet Trade Mission in Germany and German industrialists (below). In some versions of the agreement of Apr. 14, 1931 (below), however, reference is made to a similar document dated Nov. 9, 1927 (e.g., *SUR*, May 1931, p. 115); other versions (e.g., *Ostwirtschaft*, Apr. 1931, p. 54), give the date as Feb. 9, 1927. The weight of evidence favors that as the correct date.

Feb. 18, 1927. Concession agreement with a Japanese firm for exploitation of oil and natural gas resources on the eastern shore of Northern Sakhalin

Reference: *ERSU*, Mar. 15, 1927, p. 2.

Apr. 2, 1927. Concession agreement with a Japanese syndicate for exploitation of timber resources in the Far Eastern Region

Duration 6 years.

References: *ERSU*, May 1, 1927, p. 1.
  SUR, Mar. 1927, p. 55; *ibid.*, Mar. 1928, p. 46.

June 28, 1927.* Supplementary concession agreement between the USSR and the Georgian Manganese Company (Harriman interests) for operation of the Chiaturi manganese concession

References: *SUR*, Sept. 1927, p. 128;
  ibid., Oct. 1928, p. 154.

July 1927.* Concession agreement with a Japanese firm concerning gold mining in the Okhotsk area

Reference: *SUR*, Mar. 1928, p. 46.

Aug. 21, 1927. Preliminary financial agreement between the Soviet and Chinese administrations of the Chinese Eastern Railway

References: *Mezhdunarodnoe pravo*, 1928, No. 1, pp. 127–31 (summary).
North China Herald, Aug. 27, 1927 (cited in Degras, p. 128).

Jan. 1, 1928.[5] Agreement between the Soviet oil syndicate and the Spanish oil monopoly concerning export of Soviet oil to Spain during 1928

Reference: *SUR*, Feb. 1928, p. 31.

Mar. 20, 1928. Agreement with Chang Tso-lin concerning finances of the Chinese Eastern Railway

Reference: London *Times*, Mar. 28, 1928 (cited in Degras, p. 128).

Nov. 3, 1928. Concession agreements with Japanese fishing interests

Extended for 5 years by exchange of notes sent Mar. 30, 1944 (44/iii/30/J/c).

Feb. 27, 1929. Agreement between the Russian Oil Products Company, representing the Soviet oil syndicate, and the Anglo-American Company, representing a British-American oil combine (Deterding interests), for export of Soviet oil

Signed in London.
References: *ERSU*, Mar. 15, 1929, p. 110.
Heymann, p. 312.

Dec. 17, 1930. Contract between the Soviet oil exporting organization and the Petrofina Company of France for export of Soviet gasoline

Provides for export of 300,000 tons annually for 2 years. At approximately the same time, (1) an agreement was reached between the Soviet organization and a group of French oil concerns for export of Soviet crude oil and gasoline and (2) existing contracts with several French companies for import of Soviet lubricating oils were renewed.
Reference: *ERSU*, Jan. 15, 1931, p. 47.

Apr. 1931. Contract for supply of Soviet fuel oil to the French Navy

Reference: *ERSU*, June 1, 1931, p. 257.

Apr. 14, 1931. Trade and credit agreement between the Soviet Trade Mission in Germany and the Russland-Ausschuss der Deutschen Wirtschaft ("Pyatakov agreement")

Signed in Berlin.
Modified by agreements of June 15 and Aug. 14, 1931; superseded by agreement of June 15, 1932 (below).
Sources: *Izv.*, Apr. 21, 1931.
SUR, May 1931, p. 115.
Ostwirtschaft, Apr. 1931, p. 54.
STS, 2, p. 31.
References: *SDFP*, 2, pp. 490–92 (summary).
Hilger and Meyer, p. 242.

Apr. 28, 1931.[6] Agreement between the USSR and Metropolitan-Vickers Electrical Co., Ltd., of the United Kingdom, concerning technical assistance in the manufacture of equipment and machinery

Reference: *SUR*, May 1931, p. 118.

June 15, 1931. Agreement between the Soviet Trade Mission in Germany and representatives of German industry concerning conditions of payment for orders concluded under the agreement of April 14, 1931

Modified by an agreement of Aug. 14, 1931 (below).
Source: *Ostwirtschaft*, June 1931, pp. 99–100.

Aug. 14, 1931. Agreement between the Soviet Trade Mission in Germany and representatives of German industry modifying the agreement of June 15, 1931, concerning conditions of payment

---

[5] Date of entry into force.

[6] Date of announcement.

Signed in Berlin.
Source: *Ostwirtschaft*, Aug. 1931, p. 130.

1932. Contract between the All-Union Combine for Export of Petroleum and Petroleum Products and the Italian Navy for export of Soviet oil

Modified in 1935. Renewed by and mentioned in a secret protocol of Feb. 7, 1939 (39/ii/7/Italy/b).

——. **Contract with a representative of French oil interests for export of Soviet oil products to France**

Duration 5 years.
Reference: *ERSU*, Nov. 15, 1932, p. 402.

May 1932. Agreement between railroad authorities of the USSR and Turkey concerning establishment of direct rail connections

Reference: *Izv.*, May 28, 1932.

May 3, 1932. Agreement between the Soviet Trade Mission in Germany and the German Reichsbank concerning use of the Reichsmark in all Soviet-German trade and establishment of a legal exchange rate

Entered into force May 7, 1932. Extended through 1934 by a protocol of Mar. 20, 1934 (34/iii/20/Ger).
Reference: *VVerz.*, p. 353.

June 15, 1932. Agreement between the Soviet Trade Mission in Germany and the Russland-Ausschuss der Deutschen Wirtschaft concerning trade and payments, with annex

Signed in Berlin.
Entered into force on signature. Valid through May 31, 1933. Supersedes the agreement of Apr. 14, 1931. Annex concerns specific terms of payment, and itself has an annex concerning acceptance of shipments.
Sources: *SDTD*, 1, pp. 279–81 (omits the annex).
    QR, July–Sept. 1932, pp. 24–29.
    Ostwirtschaft, June 1932, pp. 95–97.
    STS, 2, pp. 53–54 (omits the annex).

Sept. 27, 1932. Agreement between Soiuznefteksport and a representative of Japanese interests concerning export of Soviet gasoline to Japan

Duration 5 years.
Reference: *ERSU*, Nov. 15, 1932, p. 402.

Nov. 17, 1932. Agreement between the Soviet Trade Mission in Germany and the Russland-Ausschuss der Deutschen Wirtschaft concerning a reduction in minimum discount rates, with two annexes

Source: *Ostwirtschaft*, Nov. 1932, p. 178.

Feb. 25, 1933. Credit agreement between the USSR and German banks, with exchange of notes

Signed in Berlin.
Entered into force on signature.
Reference: *VVerz.*, p. 388.
Note: Hilger and Meyer, p. 283, mention a credit grant to the USSR of 140 million Reichsmarks in Mar. 1933; not listed separately.

1934. Agreement for settlement of the claim of the Lena Goldfields Company against the USSR

Signed in Moscow.
Provides for payment by the USSR of £3 million over 20 years.
Reference: *ERSU*, Dec. 1934, p. 280.

——. **Agreement concerning establishment of a mixed Soviet-Italian company, "Irtrans," for goods transit to Iran**

Extended through June 30, 1936, under an agreement of June 15, 1935 (see note to 35/vi/15/Italy).
Reference: *Ostwirtschaft*, June–July 1935, p. 99.

Jan. 7, 1934. Agreement between the Afghan National Bank of Kabul and the United Import and Export Company of Moscow concerning sale and delivery of sugar to Afghanistan

Signed in Moscow.
Source: *STS*, 2, pp. 89–90, citing
    Deutsches Handelsarchiv, 88, Nov. 15, 1934, p. 384.

Sept. 4, 1934. Agreement between the Amur State River Steamship Company of the USSR and the Harbin Shipping Company of Manchukuo concerning improvement of the waterways of the Amur River and other border rivers and lakes

Signed at Hei-ho.
Entered into force on signature. Duration 2 years; thereafter until 3 months after denunciation. Terminated by a Soviet note of May 14, 1937 (Degras, p. 199, citing *Japan chronicle*, Apr. 14, 1938).
Sources: China, *Bulletin of the Ministry of Foreign Affairs* (in Chinese), 7, Sept. 1934, p. 159.
  STS, 2, p. 110, citing
    Japan-Manchukuo Yearbook, 1936, pp. 751–52.
References: *Izv.*, Sept. 5, 1934.
  ERSU, Oct. 1934, p. 198.

Dec. 25, 1934. Agreement between local Soviet authorities in Siberia and Japanese authorities in Manchuria concerning regulations to govern navigation on border waterways

Reference: Degras, p. 196, citing
  Japan chronicle, Jan. 3, 1935, p. 16.

Mar. 20, 1935. Agreement between the Soviet Trade Mission in Germany and the Russland-Ausschuss der Deutschen Wirtschaft concerning general conditions for delivery from Germany to the USSR, with two annexes

Signed in Berlin.
Supersedes the "General conditions" of Feb. 9, 1927. Superseded by the "General conditions" of Dec. 12, 1939 (below).
Source: *Ostwirtschaft*, Apr.–May 1935, pp. 64–68.

——. Agreement between the Soviet Trade Mission in Germany and the Russland-Ausschuss der Deutschen Wirtschaft concerning arbitration courts in commercial cases

Signed in Berlin.
Superseded by the agreement of Dec. 12, 1939 (below).
Source: *Ostwirtschaft*, Apr.–May 1935, p. 68.
Reference: *DSB*, 12, 1945, p. 893.

May 1935. Trade agreement between Sovsintorg and the Sinkiang trading organization "Tuchangunsy"

Provides for exchange of goods to a value of 22 million rubles each. Sovsintorg to deliver to Sinkiang during 2 years equipment for highway construction, electrostation construction, leather industry, and other goods on credit. "Tuchangunsy" to repay credit during 5 years following establishment of the industries for which Soviet equipment was provided by deliveries of wool, cattle, gut, furs, etc. Supplemented by agreement of July 1, 1936. For a loan agreement with Sinkiang at about the same time, see 35/v/16/Sinkiang.
Reference: *VT SSSR*, p. 31.

June 14, 1935. Agreement between the Soviet Trade Mission in Germany and the Russland-Ausschuss der Deutschen Wirtschaft concerning conditions of payment for orders placed under the credit agreement of April 9, 1935

Covers "supplementary orders" within the framework of the credit of 200 million Reichsmarks established under the Apr. 9 agreement (35/iv/9/Ger/b).
Source: *Ostwirtschaft*, June–July 1935, pp. 93–94.

Nov. 27, 1935. Agreement between the Soviet Trade Mission in Germany and the Russland-Ausschuss der Deutschen Wirtschaft concerning guarantees for trade deliveries under the agreement of June 14, 1935

Provides that by agreement between the 2 parties a security guarantee for orders to the amount of 10 percent of the value of the order can be obtained in the form of a letter of credit from one of the major German banks, or any other German bank acceptable to the Soviet Trade Mission.
Source: *Ostwirtschaft*, Dec. 1935, p. 186.

Apr. 26, 1936. General agreement between Sovafgantorg and the National Bank of Afghanistan

Reference: Teplinski, p. 21.

May 5, 1936. Contract between the USSR and Afghanistan for the purchase of Soviet tractors

Reference: Teplinski, p. 21.

May 20, 1936. Agreement between the Bank for Foreign Trade of the USSR and the National Bank of Afghanistan concerning correspondent (*korrespondentskie*) relations

Reference: Teplinski, p. 21.

May 25, 1936. Trade agreement between the Soviet Trade Mission in Afghanistan and the National Bank of Afghanistan

Signed in Kabul.
Entered into force June 1, 1936. Duration 3 years.
Source: *STS*, 2, p. 164 (summary), citing *Statesman* (Calcutta), June 3, 1936.
Reference: Degras, p. 190, citing London *Times*, June 11, 1936 (gives no date for the agreement; Degras dates it May 15, 1936).

July 1, 1936. Trade agreement between Sovsintorg and the Sinkiang trading organization "Tuchangunsy"

Provides for delivery of goods to a value of 8,760,000 rubles each under the agreement of May 1935 (above).
Reference: *VT SSSR*, p. 31.

Sept. 18, 1936. Contract between the Soviet Trade Mission in Japan and the Matsuo Dockyard company of Japan concerning construction of three steamships for the USSR

According to *Pravda*, Jan. 21, 1941, the Japanese firm informed the Soviet Trade Mission on Mar. 12, 1938, that it was abrogating the contract. Under an agreement signed in Jan. 1941 (not listed separately), a settlement of the Soviet claim was negotiated.
References: *Pravda, loc. cit.*
MKh, 1941, No. 2, p. 97.

Oct. 10, 1936. Agreement with a Japanese firm concerning oil prospecting on North Sakhalin

Extends for 5 years the period authorized for exploration under the agreement of Dec. 14, 1925 (above).
Reference: *Ostwirtschaft*, Oct. 1936, p. 144.

May 24, 1939. Trade protocol between Eksportkhleb and the Committee for Trade with the USSR of The Netherlands

Duration indefinite; may be denounced with 3 months' notice. Preceded by earlier, unidentified agreements.
Reference: Korolenko, p. 94.

Aug. 11, 1939. Agreement between the Union of Workers in the Oil Industry of the USSR and a Japanese concessionary oil company on North Sakhalin concerning conditions of work

Signed in Moscow.
Reference: *MKh*, Sept. 1939, No. 9, pp. 245–46.

Dec. 12, 1939. General conditions for deliveries from Germany to the USSR

Signed in Berlin by the Soviet Trade Mission in Germany and the Russland-Ausschuss der Deutschen Wirtschaft.
Replaces the agreement of Mar. 20, 1935 (above).
Source: *Ostwirtschaft*, Dec. 1939, pp. 153–57.

———. Agreement between the Soviet Trade Mission in Germany and the Russland-Ausschuss der Deutschen Wirtschaft concerning arbitration courts in commercial cases

Signed in Berlin.
Supersedes the agreement of Mar. 20, 1935 (above).
Source: *Ostwirtschaft*, Dec. 1939, pp. 157–58.
Reference: *DSB*, 12, 1945, p. 893, citing *VT*, 1940, No. 1, p. 42.

———. Final protocol between the Soviet Trade Mission in Germany and the Russland-Ausschuss der Deutschen Wirtschaft

Signed in Berlin.
Provides commentaries on the "General conditions" and the arbitration agreement of the same date.
Source: *Ostwirtschaft*, Dec. 1939, p. 158.

Apr. 10, 1941. Agreement between the USSR and Germany concerning supply of oil to Germany

Reference: Dallin, 1942, p. 424, citing Deutsches Nachrichtenbüro.

Sept. 1945. Contract for the delivery of Soviet locomotives and oil to Poland

Reference: Dolina, 1, p. 82.

Nov. 1945. Contract for the delivery of Soviet locomotives and oil to Poland

Reference: Dolina, 1, p. 82.

Nov. 30, 1945. Decision by the Allied Control Council for Germany concerning establishment of three corridors for air travel between Berlin and Western Germany

Modified by Soviet action Mar. 30, 1948, as part of the blockade of West Berlin.
References: *Germany, 1947–1949,* pp. 215–16 (Soviet note of Sept. 18, 1948, with commentary).
DGO, p. 310 (statement by British Foreign Secretary Bevin in June 1948).

1946. Trade agreements between Soviet foreign trade organizations and Communist Chinese firms and enterprises on the Liaotung Peninsula

Reference: *VT SSSR,* p. 38.

Dec. 21, 1946. Trade agreement between Eksportkhleb and "Tunsin," a trading company in the Northeast Provinces of China

References: *VT SSSR,* p. 37.
Kapitsa, p. 343.

Jan. 25, 1947. Agreement between the Soviet corporation "Pechenga-Nikel' " and the Finnish corporation "Imatra-Voima" concerning restoration by "Pechenga-Nikel' " of the electrostation at Jäniskoski and the control dam at Niskakoski

Mentioned in Art. 3 of a Soviet-Finnish agreement of Feb. 3, 1947 (47/ii/3/Fin/b).

Feb. 19, 1947. Agreement between the Soviet Military Administration in Germany and Norway concerning development of trade between the Soviet Zone of Occupation of Germany and Norway

Signed in Berlin.
Entered into force on signature. Extended by exchange of notes sent Dec. 29, 1947 (below).
Source: *UNTS,* 30, pp. 293–302.

July 1947. Timber contract between the USSR and the United Kingdom

Reference: *SIA, 1947–1948,* p. 102.

Nov. 10, 1947. Agreement between the Soviet Military Administration in Germany and the Belgium-Luxembourg Economic Union concerning payments

Source: *UNTS,* 18, pp. 299–308.

Dec. 29, 1947. Exchange of notes between the Soviet Military Administration in Germany and Norway constituting an agreement extending and modifying the trade agreement of February 19, 1947

Signed in Berlin.
Entered into force on signature.
Source: *UNTS,* 30, pp. 302–11.

July 21, 1948. Trade agreement between the Soviet Zone of Occupation of Germany and Czechoslovakia

Reference: *NT,* 1948, No. 31, p. 32.

Feb. 15, 1949. Trade contract between Eksportkhleb and the Norwegian State Grain Monopoly

Reference: Korolenko, p. 87.

Sept. 1949. Trade agreements between (1) Dal'intorg and Eksportkhleb and (2) "Company for the Foreign Trade of Northern China"

Provide for deliveries of goods to a value of 31 million rubles each. The first such agreements to be signed.
Reference: *VT SSSR,* p. 38.

1951. Agreement for the export of Soviet wheat to the United Kingdom in 1952

Reference: *SIA, 1952,* p. 182.

May 7, 1952. Trade contract between Eksportkhleb and the Norwegian State Grain Monopoly

Reference: Korolenko, p. 87.

Apr. 29, 1953. Trade contract between Eksportkhleb and the Norwegian State Grain Monopoly

Reference: Korolenko, p. 87.

Sept. 6, 1955. Barter contracts between the USSR and Egypt

Signed in Cairo.
Provide for export by the USSR of 500,000 tons of oil, by Egypt of 60,000 tons of cotton. Based on the trade agreement of Mar. 27, 1954.
References: *Izv.*, Sept. 9, 1955.
   VT, 1955, No. 10, p. 30.

Sept. 20, 1955. Agreement between the USSR and Air India International Corporation concerning commercial collaboration in the transportation of passengers and freight by air

Reference: *Izv.*, Sept. 21, 1955.

Nov. 18, 1955. Contracts between the USSR and Burma for delivery of Soviet industrial equipment, machinery, and other goods

Signed in Moscow by the Burmese Government purchasing mission and Soviet foreign trade organizations.
Total value of goods to be delivered over 20 million rubles. Concluded under the trade agreement of July 1, 1955.
Reference: *NT*, 1955, No. 48, p. 32.

Nov. 19, 1955. Agreement between the USSR and British European Airways Corporation concerning commercial collaboration in the field of civil aviation

Reference: *Izv.*, Nov. 20, 1955.

Dec. 1955. Agreement between Intourist and a Greek travel agency concerning exchange of tourists

Reference: *Int. aff.*, 1956, No. 5, p. 88.

Jan. 27, 1956. Agreement between the USSR and Swiss Air Lines concerning commercial collaboration in the field of civil aviation

References: *Izv.*, Jan. 28 and Mar. 18, 1956.

Mar. 2, 1956. Agreement between Mashinoeksport and Dresser Industries, a United States firm, concerning sale to Dresser Industries of the right to manufacture Soviet-designed turbodrills for oil and gas wells

Signed in Moscow.
References: *Izv.*, Mar. 3, 1956, p. 4.
   NT, 1956, No. 11, p. 32.

Mar. 31, 1956. Agreement between the USSR and the Scandinavian aviation concern "SAS" concerning service and commercial collaboration in the field of civil aviation

Supplements the 3 agreements of the same date with the Scandinavian States (text, p. 351).
References: *Izv.*, Apr. 1, 1956, and Dec. 21, 1957.
   CDSP, 9, 1958, No. 51, p. 23.

Apr. 1956. Trade contract between the USSR and Egypt

Based on the trade agreement of Mar. 27, 1954. Provides for trade to a total value of £1 million Egyptian.
Reference: *Int. aff.*, 1956, No. 8, p. 45.

Apr. 5, 1956. Contract between the USSR and India concerning delivery of metallurgical equipment

Provides for delivery to India of 60,000 tons of metal frames for a metallurgical factory in Bilhai.
Reference: *BSE, 1957*, p. 34.

Apr. 18, 1956.[7] Agreement between the USSR and the Belgian aviation company "Sabena" concerning commercial collaboration in the field of civil aviation

Reference: *Izv.*, Apr. 18, 1956.

May 11, 1956.[7] Agreement between Intourist and "MISR," an Egyptian tourist agency, concerning exchange of tourists

Signed in Cairo.
Reference: *Izv.*, May 11, 1956.

---

[7] Date of published reference.

June 1956. Contracts between (1) Tekhnoeksport and Tekhnopromeksport and (2) the Ministries of Public Works and of Mining and Industry of Afghanistan for prospecting and construction in Afghanistan by Soviet specialists

Signed in Kabul.
Based on the loan agreement of Jan. 28, 1956.
Reference: *Izv.*, June 26, 1956.

June 7, 1956. Trade agreement between Tsentrosoiuz and a Japanese cooperative

Signed in Moscow.
Provides for exchange of Soviet timber and Japanese textiles.
Reference: *Izv.*, June 8, 1956.

June 18, 1956. Trade agreement between Tsentrosoiuz and the Central Union of Agricultural Cooperatives of Poland, "Peasant Mutual Aid"

Signed in Moscow.
Soviet motorcycles, bicycles, watches, and cameras in exchange for Polish sewing machines and woolen and cotton fabrics.
Reference: *Izv.*, June 19, 1956.

July 1956. Contract between Soviet organizations and the Ministry of Public Works of Afghanistan concerning provision of equipment and assignment of Soviet specialists to carry out prospecting work for a road Charikar–Dushi

Signed in Kabul.
Reference: *Pravda*, July 6, 1956.

———. Contract between Soviet and Afghan organizations concerning provision of equipment and assignment of Soviet specialists to give technical aid in the construction of three oil bases

Signed in Kabul.
Reference: *Pravda*, July 6, 1956.

———. Contract between Soviet and Afghan organizations concerning assignment of Soviet specialists to instruct Afghan personnel in the use of a grain combine

Signed in Kabul.
The combine is to be built in Kabul with funds advanced under the credit agreement of May 24, 1954.
Reference: *Izv.*, July 25, 1956.

Aug. 4, 1956. Trade agreement between Tsentrosoiuz and the Scottish Cooperative Association

Soviet grain in exchange for Scottish woolen goods.
Reference: *Izv.*, Aug. 5, 1956.

Aug. 13, 1956. Trade agreement between cooperative organizations of the USSR and Denmark

Reference: *BSE, 1957*, p. 36.

Aug. 24, 1956. Agreement between the USSR and Pan-American Airways concerning commercial collaboration in the field of civil aviation

Signed in Moscow.
References: *Pr.*, *Izv.*, Aug. 25, 1956.
    CDSP, 8, 1956, No. 34, p. 12.

Sept. 1956. Trade agreement between Tsentrosoiuz and cooperatives of the German Democratic Republic

Signed in Leipzig.
Soviet foodstuffs and beverages in exchange for textiles and other goods.
Reference: *Pravda*, Sept. 15, 1956.

Sept. 29, 1956. Contract between the USSR and Egypt concerning delivery of two hundred thousand tons of wheat to Egypt

Signed in Cairo.
Reference: *Izv.*, Sept. 30, 1956.

Nov. 1, 1956. Agreement between the USSR and the Afghan aviation company "Da ariani khavai sherkat" concerning commercial collaboration and reciprocal services in the field of civil aviation

Reference: *Izv.*, Nov. 2, 1956.

Nov. 20, 1956. Contract between Tekhnoeksport and a Burmese corporation concerning assignment of Soviet technicians to Burma

Purpose to carry out exploratory work and planning of irrigation equipment, mechanization of agriculture, study and classification of soils, organization of machine-tractor stations, etc.
Reference: *Izv.*, Nov. 22, 1956.

Nov. 26, 1956. Contract for the delivery of Soviet wheat to Egypt

Reference: Embassy of the United Arab Republic, 1958.

Jan. 28, 1957. Act concerning transfer to Iran of the USSR's rights in the mixed Soviet-Iranian company "Kevir-Khourian"

Signed in Teheran.
References: *NT*, 1957, No. 6, p. 33.
Izv., July 29, 1956.

Feb. 15, 1957. Contract for the delivery of Soviet wheat to Egypt

Reference: Embassy of the United Arab Republic, 1958.

Feb. 27, 1957. Contract between Vostokintorg and the Ministry of Communications of Afghanistan concerning provision during 1957 of equipment for interurban telephone lines in Afghanistan

Signed in Kabul.
References: *Izv.*, Mar. 2, 1957.
VT, 1957, No. 7, p. 35.

Apr. 1957. Trade agreement between Tsentrosoiuz and the Danish cooperative union

Signed in Copenhagen.
Soviet grain in exchange for Danish consumer goods.
Reference: *Izv.*, Apr. 24, 1957.

June 13, 1957. Trade contract between Tsentrosoiuz and a Japanese cooperative trading company

Signed in Moscow.

Coal from Sakhalin and timber in exchange for Japanese textiles and other goods.
References: *Izv.*, June 14, 1957.
VT, 1957, No. 7, p. 36.

July 1957. Agreement between Mashinoimport and a group of French industrial firms concerning delivery of electric locomotives to the USSR

Signed in Moscow.
References: *Izv.*, July 13, 1957.
CDSP, 9, 1957, No. 28, p. 20.

Oct. 1957. Trade contracts between the USSR and Pakistan

Mentioned in the joint communiqué of Oct. 16, 1957 (57/x/16/Pakistan).

Oct. 28, 1957. Agreement between (1) the Soviet-Danube State Navigation Company of the USSR and (2) Bavarian Lloyd and the "Josef Wallner" corporation of the Federal Republic of Germany concerning reciprocal tug service on the Danube, aid in accidents, representation of ships in Danube ports, and commercial collaboration

Signed in Bonn.
Reference: *Izv.*, Oct. 29, 1957.

Nov. 1957. Agreement between Intourist and "Bunvanit," a Thailand organization, concerning exchange of tourists

Signed in Bangkok.
Reference: *Izv.*, Nov. 21, 1957.

Nov. 26, 1957. Agreement between the USSR and Egypt concerning delivery of 100,000 tons of wheat to Egypt

Reference: *BSE, 1958*, p. 245.

Appendix 4

UNVERIFIED TREATIES

Dec. 22, 1917. Alleged convention between Russia and Germany concerning Poland

Signed at Brest-Litovsk.
Source: *TRP*, pp. 11–12, based on *Glos narodu* (Cracow), June 18, 1918, as translated in the British *Daily review of the foreign press, neutral press supplement*, July 5, 1918. *TRP*, p. 11, gives the following additional information: A summary of this document, corresponding to the text translated from *Glos narodu*, was published in the *Gazette de Lausanne* of May 12, 1918. The existence of the convention was denied by the Russian Government (*NYT*, July 2, 1918), and by the Austrian Government and the German Minister at Berne (*Christian Science Monitor*, Aug. 3, 1918). The *Daily review of the foreign press, neutral press supplement* for July 12, 1918, refers to the announcement in *Novaia zhizn'* for May 4, 1918, of the discovery by the Cheka of a secret organization for the fabrication of forged documents such as this alleged convention, and to a statement by the *Russische Nachrichten* (Berne) providing an alibi for 7 of the persons alleged to have signed the convention on the Russian side and denying the existence of the 2 others. *TRP, loc. cit.*, adds that anti-Bolshevik papers in Russia which printed the convention were suppressed for publishing false statements.
Further information can be found in the *Confidential press review* published by G. H. Q., A. E. F., June 29, 1918, pp. 6–7, citing the *Journal des debats*, June 28, 1918.
Not accepted as genuine.

Jan. 5, 1919. Alleged secret treaty of recognition, mutual assistance, and collaboration between the RSFSR and the German Soviet Republic

References: Miliukov, pp. 137–38, citing
London *Daily Chronicle*, Apr. 5, 1919 (based on an "absolutely reliable

source" reported by the Geneva correspondent of the paper).
STS, 1, pp. 137–38.
Not accepted as genuine.

Apr. 1919. Alleged secret military alliance between the RSFSR, the Ukrainian SSR, and the Hungarian Soviet Republic

Sources: Miliukov, p. 168, citing
London *Times*, Apr. 24, 1919, and
Berliner Tageblatt, late March, 1919.
STS, 1, p. 381.

Apr. 17, 1919. Alleged secret military agreement between the RSFSR and Germany

Reference: Cited in the alleged secret military convention of Apr. 3, 1922 (below). Validity denied by the German Embassy, 1958. Not accepted as genuine. For evidence on secret military agreements between the Soviet and German Governments, see Appendix 2.

July 8, 1920. Alleged secret agreement between the RSFSR and Germany concerning political, economic, and military relations

Source: *STS*, 1, pp. 381–82, citing
"G. Grant Smith, from Budapest, Sept. 10, 1920" (a Department of State dispatch?).
Validity denied by the German Embassy, 1958. Not accepted as genuine.

Nov. 1920. Alleged political agreement between the RSFSR and Turkey

References: *Current history*, 13, Dec. 1920, p. 67, citing
British and French governmental publications (unspecified) of Nov. 23, 1920;
NYT, Nov. 25, 1920;
Associated Press dispatch from Constantinople, Nov. 23, 1920, based on a "private source."

Mar. 25, 1921. Alleged secret military agreement between the RSFSR and Germany

Reference: Mentioned in the alleged secret military agreement of Apr. 3, 1922 (below).
Validity denied by the German Embassy, 1958. Not accepted as genuine.

Apr. 3, 1922. Alleged secret military agreement between the RSFSR and Germany

Sources: *STS*, 1, p. 383, citing
"C. B. Gary, from Constantinople, Feb. 28, 1928" (a Department of State dispatch?);
London *Times*, May 6, 1922; and
L'éclair, May 11, 1922.
Described by the German Embassy, 1958, as a "falsification, the origin of which can be proved in Riga." Not accepted as genuine. In some details, however, notably (1) the provision in Art. 6 for German aid to Soviet munitions factories in Tula, Samara, and Petrograd, and (2) the provision in Art. 8 for establishment of German airplane, poison gas, and gun factories in Russia, possibly reflects authentic information about the secret Soviet-German military agreements which were actually negotiated at about this time (see Appendix 2).

1925. General commercial agreement between the USSR and Sinkiang

See note to 24/x/ /Sinkiang.

Mar. 19, 1925. Agreement between the USSR and Hungary concerning exchange of political prisoners

Reference: *Soviet Union Yearbook, 1930*, p. 61; no source cited.

Sept. 1925. Agreement between the USSR and the Mongolian People's Republic concerning construction of a railroad between Urga and Chita

Reportedly supplemented by agreements providing for the eventual extension of the railroad towards Kalgan and Uliassutai.
References: *CYB, 1926–27*, p. 800 (summary, based on press reports).
Wu, p. 170.
Eudin and North, p. 257.

June 1926. Agreement between the USSR and the Mongolian People's Republic concerning navigation by Soviet vessels on Mongolian rivers

References: Degras, p. 129, citing
London *Times*, June 15, 1926.
STS, 1, p. 320 (same; misdated July 1926).

Mar. 1930. Agreement between the USSR and Japan concerning exchange of military officers to be attached to army units

Reference: Degras, p. 153, citing
Manchester Guardian, Mar. 22, 1930.

Dec. 1931. Agreement between the Armenian SSR and Greece concerning repatriation of Armenian citizens

Reference: Degras, p. 150, citing
Messager d'Athènes, Dec. 12, 1931.

Jan. 1, 1936. Treaty of mutual assistance between the USSR and Sinkiang

References: *Great Britain and the East*, 46, Apr. 16, 1936, p. 515 (summary, based on reports by "recent travellers" through Sinkiang); reprinted in
Moslem World, 26, Oct. 1936, pp. 414–15, and
STS, 2, pp. 154–55.
Note: Whiting, p. 77, states that "references to such a treaty abound in the Japanese archives" but that "no credible Chinese or Russian source has been found to substantiate these reports," while "a forged treaty apparently was circulated by Japanese agents at the time."

——. Military agreement between the USSR and Sinkiang

Mentioned in the treaty of mutual assistance of the same date (above).

Jan. 25, 1936. Trade agreement for 1936 between the USSR and Turkey

Signed in Ankara.
Establishes trade contingents for the first 6 months of 1936.
Reference: *Ostwirtschaft*, Jan. 1936, p. 8.

Jan. 11, 1939. Trade agreement between the USSR and Estonia

Signed in Moscow.

Reference: Simmons, *USSR*, p. 126; no source cited.
Note: Soviet-Estonian trade in 1939 was carried out under the agreement of Feb. 26, 1938, until its replacement by that of Sept. 28, 1939. In view of the lack of verification from either Soviet or Estonian sources, not accepted as genuine.

Dec. 1939. Protocol between the USSR and Romania concerning restoration of railroad traffic between Romania and occupied Poland

Reference: Degras, p. 230, citing
Le temps, Dec. 5, 1939.

1940. Agreement between the USSR and China concerning a Soviet loan to China of fifty million dollars

Reference: McLane, p. 129, citing
Contemporary China, No. 1, May 25, 1941.

June 16, 1940. Agreement between the USSR and China concerning a Soviet credit for purchase of supplies

References: Beloff, 2, p. 317.
McLane, p. 130.

July 1940. Agreement between the USSR and Finland concerning military use of Finnish railroads

Reference: *NYT*, July 27, 1940 (mentions "Finnish concessions to Russia which became effective last week" concerning shipments to Hangö Base).

June 18, 1944. Agreement between the USSR and Czechoslovakia concerning printing Czechoslovak currency in the USSR for use of civilian authorities and the Red Army

Reference: *OSS chronology*, 2, p. 206.

June 30, 1944. Agreement between the USSR and Czechoslovakia concerning appointment of a delegate to liberated territory

Reference: *OSS chronology*, 2, p. 208.

Nov. 18, 1944. Agreement between the USSR and the French Provisional Government concerning liberated Soviet citizens

Reference: *OSS chronology*, 2, p. 240.

Dec. 12, 1944. Agreement between the USSR and Romania concerning execution of economic provisions of the armistice agreement

Reference: *OSS chronology*, 2, p. 246.

Aug. 22, 1947. Long-term trade agreement between the USSR and Bulgaria

Reference: Dellin, *Bulgaria*, p. 409.
Note: Possibly confused with the trade and payments agreement of July 5, 1947.

——. Three-way clearing agreement between the USSR, Yugoslavia, and Bulgaria

Reference: Dellin, *Bulgaria*, p. 409.
Note: A Yugoslav-Bulgarian protocol concerning three-way clearing arrangements between the USSR, Yugoslavia, and Bulgaria was signed on this date (text, *UNTS*, 111, pp. 241–47). Although the protocol called for participation of the State Bank of the USSR in transfer of funds from one account to another, the USSR was not directly a party to the protocol.

1949. Two secret agreements between the USSR and the Chinese Communist regime ("Harbin" and "Moscow" agreements)

Reference: *DSB*, 22, 1950, p. 218.

July 26, 1949. Agreement between the USSR and Poland concerning relations between the Polish administration and the Soviet High Command

Reference: Halecki, *Poland*, p. 539.

May 1950. Secret agreement between the USSR and Czechoslovakia concerning Russification of the Czechoslovak Army

Reference: For reports of actions which would imply the existence of such an agreement, see *SIA, 1949–1950*, p. 240.

Dec. 29, 1953. Trade agreement between the USSR and Iran

Signed in Teheran.
Reference: Laqueur, p. 207.
Note: Trade relations between the USSR
and Iran for 1953 were determined by the
exchange of notes of June 10, 1953, as
modified by the later exchange of Sept. 3,
1953. This was followed by a similar exchange on June 17, 1954, setting conditions for trade in 1954. If valid, therefore,
this agreement presumably covered supplementary trade.

**Spring 1956. Agreement between the
USSR and Syria concerning shipment of
Soviet munitions to Syria**

Value of munitions allegedly estimated at
$30 million.
Reference: Laqueur, pp. 272–73.

**Aug. 1956. Agreement between the
USSR and Afghanistan concerning a
Soviet loan to Afghanistan of twenty-
five million dollars**

References: Allen, 1957, p. 438, citing
        London *Times*, Sept. 27, 1956;
        NYT, Oct. 28, 1956; and
        Middle East journal, Winter, 1957,
        pp. 71–72.

Appendix 5

ADDENDA

- 18/v/4/Ukraine

Cease-fire agreement between the Military Commands of the RSFSR and of Germany and the Ukraine

Signed May 4, 1918, in Korenovo.
Entered into force May 5, 1918.
Sources: *TUP*, pp. 151–52.
    STS, 1, pp. 22–23.
Note: The text cited is from the British *Daily review of the foreign press*, May 9, 1918, based on a Soviet radio broadcast of May 6, 1918. No published Russian text of the agreement has been traced, but its validity is indicated by several authentic documents. (1) *DVP*, 1, p. 281, publishes a note from Chicherin, the Soviet Commissar of Foreign Affairs, dated May 4, 1918, broadcast to the German Minister of Foreign Affairs, with a copy to the representative of the RSFSR, expressing the willingness of the RSFSR to conclude a peace treaty with the Ukrainian Central Rada. (2) On May 4, 1918, V. A. Antonov-Ovseenko, the commander of the Soviet forces in the Ukraine, sent a radio message from the Kremlin to the Soviet Governments of the Ukraine and the Donets Workers' Republic in which he declared "the cessation by me of military operations" against the German-Ukrainian troops, and offered his resignation (text in Antonov-Ovseenko, V. A., *Zapiski o grazhdanskoi voine*, Moscow, 1928, Vol. 2, pp. 294–95). To this Lenin and Trotsky added a directive to local Soviet military commanders instructing them to propose an immediate armistice with German and Ukrainian forces (*ibid.*). (3) See also the draft of a telegram from Lenin to the Soviet peace delegation at Kursk, dated May 6, 1918, stating that the delegation's policy "must be to do everything possible to hasten armistice and peace, paying for it, of course, with new concessions" (*Leninskii sbornik*, 11, p. 74).

- 19/i/15/Fin

Agreement between the RSFSR and Finland concerning conditions of trade

Signed Jan. 15, 1919, in Petrograd; for Finland by the Finnish Temporary Economic Committee in Petrograd.
Provides for (1) freeing Finnish citizens in the RSFSR arrested for other than general criminal offences; (2) repatriation of Finnish citizens who wish to leave the RSFSR; and (3) granting to Finnish citizens in the RSFSR equal rights with other foreigners in respect to forced labor, requisitions, confiscation, taxes, and military collections. Russian citizens in Finland to be granted similar rights.
Source: *DVP*, 2, pp. 29–30.

- 20/i/30/Lat

Secret armistice treaty between the RSFSR and Latvia, with two supplementary articles and a protocol

Signed Jan. 30, 1920, in Moscow.
Provides for cessation of hostilities on Feb. 1, 1920; thereafter military operations may be resumed only after 2 months' notice. Mixed control commissions to be established to supervise execution of the treaty, to begin work after its publication. (N.B.: The treaty was never published during the existence of Latvia as a State.) Modified by a supplementary treaty of Feb. 1, 1920.
Source: *DVP*, 2, pp. 333–39.
Reference: *FRUS*, 1920, III, p. 646.

- 20/ii/1/Lat

Secret supplementary armistice treaty between the RSFSR and Latvia

Signed Feb. 1, 1920, presumably in Moscow.
Supplements the secret armistice treaty of Jan. 30, 1920. Provides that the demarcation line between the armies of the RSFSR and Latvia shall be that occupied at noon on Feb. 1, 1920. All articles of the secret armistice treaty of Jan. 30, 1920, except that concerning the demarcation line, to be included in a future open armistice treaty (see 20/viii/11/Lat).
Source: *DVP*, 2, pp. 338–39.

• 20/iii/31/Est

Treaty between the RSFSR and Estonia concerning delivery of goods from Sweden to the RSFSR

Signed Mar. 31, 1920.
Entered into force Jan. 1, 1921.
Source: *DVP*, 2, pp. 430–32.

• 20/iv/20/Belgium/b

Agreement between the RSFSR and the Ukrainian SSR on the one hand and Belgium on the other concerning repatriation of military and civilian personnel

Signed Apr. 20, 1920, in Copenhagen; on behalf of Belgium by the French consul.
Source: *DVP*, 2, pp. 468–70.

• 20/iv/27/Italy/b

Exchange of notes between the RSFSR and Italy concerning appointment of representatives to supervise repatriation

Sent Apr. 27, 1920, in Copenhagen.
Supplements the agreement of the same date.
Source: *DVP*, 2, p. 487.

• 20/iv/27/Italy/c

Exchange of notes between the RSFSR and Italy concerning conditions for repatriation

Sent Apr. 27, 1920, in Copenhagen.
Concerns (1) interpretation of Art. 4 of the agreement of the same date under which persons sentenced for serious crimes are excluded from repatriation, and (2) an Italian proposal to exchange Italian products for Soviet grain, to be sent with those being repatriated.
Source: *DVP*, 2, pp. 487–89.

• 20/v/14/FER

Telegram extending recognition by the RSFSR to the Far Eastern Republic

Sent May 14, 1920.
Sources: Kliuchnikov, 3, I, p. 24.
  Eudin and North, p. 210.

• 20/vii/7/UK

Exchange of notes between the RSFSR and the United Kingdom concerning completion of repatriation

Sent June 30 and July 7, 1920.
Completion of repatriation of British citizens from Russia under the agreement of Feb. 12, 1920, was made a condition for conclusion of a Soviet-British trade treaty in the British note of June 30. The condition was accepted in the Soviet note of July 7.
References: *Soviet Russia*, Jan. 1, 1921, p. 21.
  Degras, p. 11, citing
  London *Times*, July 15, 1920.

• 20/vii/10/Lith

Protocol between the RSFSR and Lithuania concerning conditions for exchange of hostages and civilian prisoners

Signed July 10, 1920.
Supplements the agreement of Nov. 19, 1919 (19/xi/19/Lith). Confirms list of persons to be exchanged and provides for application in regard to their property of provisions of the treaty of June 30, 1920, concerning re-evacuation of refugees.
Reference: *DVP*, 2, p. 745.

• 21/ii/26/Persia (Continuation)

On Mar. 3, 1959, the Iranian Foreign Minister announced that Iran was denouncing Articles 5 and 6 of the treaty, which gave the Soviet Union the right to move troops into Iran if hostile forces should enter that country with the aim of threatening or attacking the Soviet Union's southern borders. On Mar. 15, 1959, *Pravda* published an article by S. A. Golunski asserting that the treaty remained fully operative despite Iran's action. See the *NYT*, Mar. 16, 1959. Golunski's article is translated in *CDSP*, Vol. 11, No. 11, pp. 24–25.

• 21/xii/27/Pr

Agreement between the RSFSR and the Italian Red Cross concerning famine relief

Signed Dec. 27, 1921.
Reference: *MP RSFSR, 1922*, p. 27.

• 23/ii/20/MPR

Economic agreement between the RSFSR and the Mongolian People's Republic

Signed during 1923, according to Meshcheriakov, pp. 49–50, 152; non-Soviet sources give the date of signature as Feb. 20, 1923, in Moscow.

With regard to the content of the agreement, Meshcheriakov says only that it was a trade agreement, concluded on equal terms. Chinese sources, cited below, provide a summary of a secret economic agreement which may well be the same document. Korostovetz, p. 333, presumably basing his account on Chinese sources, lists the following provisions: (1) Land, forests, mineral resources, rivers, and seas in the MPR to be nationalized; private property in these areas forbidden, and the property of the princes to be sequestrated. Unclaimed lands, the nomads' pastures, to be distributed among poor Mongols and Russians for use. (2) Russian specialists to be given control of prospecting for natural resources and developing trade and industry in the MPR. Mines to be developed by Russian companies using Mongolian laborers. (3) Russian troops to remain in the MPR with the agreement of the MPR Government. (4) Foreigners not to be granted extraterritoriality, but a Russian representative to sit on the MPR court, with the right of veto in cases involving Russians. (5) The Hutuktu (Mongolian religious leader) to retain his title but take no part in the government. The highest organ of government to be the National Assembly, with a Cabinet of Ministers as the executive.

References: Meshcheriakov, *loc. cit.*
  Korostovetz, *loc. cit.*
  Ho Han-Wên, *A history of Sino-Russian relations* (in Chinese), pp. 300–301.
  Wu, pp. 168–69, citing
    Lin Kuei-Han, *The past and future of Outer Mongolia* (in Chinese).

● 23/xii/4/Rom

Agreement between the USSR and Romania concerning establishment of mixed commissions to settle navigation disputes on the Dniester River

Negotiated Dec. 4, 1923.
Reference: *RIR*, Jan. 5, 1924, p. 6.

● 23/xii/8/Cz

Agreement between the USSR and Czechoslovakia concerning import of agricultural machinery for Czechoslovak settlers in the Crimea, the Ukraine, and the Caucasus

Signed Dec. 8, 1923.
Ratified by the USSR.
References: *Russian review*, Apr. 1, 1924, p. 301 (summary; does not give date).
  RIR, Jan. 5, 1924, p. 6.
Note: Degras, p. 78, dates the agreement Nov. 8, 1923, citing *Russian review, loc. cit.*

● 25/iv/4/J

Joint announcement by the USSR and Japan concerning surrender of Northern Sakhalin to the USSR

Issued Apr. 4, 1925, in Aleksandrovsk.
Source: *Russian review*, May 15, 1925, p. 219.

● 26/ii/1/Af

Protocol between the USSR and Afghanistan concerning removal of Soviet troops from the island Urta-Tugai in the Amu-Darya River, entry of Afghan troops to the island, and establishment of a mixed commission to determine ownership of the island

Signed Feb. 1, 1926, in Kabul.
For a protocol signed by the mixed commission giving the island to Afghanistan, see 26/viii/18/Af.
Reference: Teplinski, p. 15.

● 26/viii/18/Af

Protocol between the USSR and Afghanistan concerning transfer of the island Urta-Tugai to Afghanistan

Signed Aug. 18, 1926, in Kabul, by the mixed commission established under the protocol of Feb. 1, 1926.
On the same date Afghanistan assured the USSR by note that it would not permit the island to be used as a base for attacks on the USSR.
Reference: Teplinski, p. 15.

● 28/vi/ /Af

Agreement between the USSR and Afghanistan concerning transformation of diplomatic missions into embassies

Negotiated during June 1928.
Reference: Teplinski, p. 17.

- 29/ / /MPR

Agreement between the USSR and the Mongolian People's Republic concerning basic principles of relations between the two States

Signed during 1929.
Meshcheriakov, p. 59, gives no details concerning the agreement but states, "the agreement . . . played an important role in raising the economy and culture of the [MPR] and in eliminating difficulties connected with the reorganization of foreign trade."
Reference: Meshcheriakov, *loc. cit.*

- 30/vi/28/MPR

Convention between the USSR and the Mongolian People's Republic concerning execution of judicial decisions in certain categories of civil cases

Signed June 28, 1930.
Mentioned in an exchange of notes of Aug. 25, 1958, between the USSR and the MPR, as being superseded by the treaty of the same date concerning reciprocal legal aid in civil, family and marriage, and criminal cases (*VVS*, 1958, No. 35, Art. 424, p. 956).

- 32/iii/12/Norway

Trade agreement between the USSR and Norway

Signed Mar. 12, 1932, in Oslo.
References: *STS*, 2, p. 48, citing
London *Times*, Mar. 14, 1932.

- 32/iv/3/Af/a

Agreement between the USSR and Afghanistan concerning postal communications

Signed Apr. 3, 1932, in Kabul.
Extended by exchange of notes dated July 3, 1937.
References: Teplinski, p. 20.
ERSU, May 15, 1932, p. 238.

- 32/iv/3/Af/b

Agreement between the USSR and Afghanistan concerning telegraph and radio-telegraph communications

Signed Apr. 3, 1932, in Kabul.

Extended by exchange of notes dated July 3, 1937.
Reference: Teplinski, p. 20.

- 33/xi/14/Af

Exchange of notes between the USSR and Afghanistan concerning maintenance of friendly relations

Sent Nov. 14, 1933, from Kabul, and Nov. 14, 1933, from Moscow, on the occasion of the enthronement of Mohammed Zafir.
References: *Izv.*, Nov. 18, 1933.
SUR, Dec. 1933, p. 268.

- 33/xii/30/Lat

Agreement between the USSR and Latvia concerning introduction of direct fares on railroads

Signed Dec. 30, 1933.
Entered into force Feb. 1, 1934.
Reference: *Ostwirtschaft*, Jan. 1934, p. 6.

- 34/iii/20/Ger

Economic protocol between the USSR and Germany

Signed Mar. 20, 1934, in Berlin (but cf. the *Izv.* reference cited below).
Extends through 1934 (1) existing agreements with regard to "current business" and credit periods, and (2) the agreement of May 3, 1932 (see Appendix 3), on use of the Reichsmark in German-Soviet trade.
References: *Izv.*, Mar. 28, 1934 (dates the protocol Mar. 26, 1934).
Ostwirtschaft, Mar.–Apr. 1934, pp. 37–38.
STS, 2, p. 97, citing
Frankfurter Zeitung, Mar. 28, 1934.

- 35/xi/15/Mul

Convention for the export of timber

Signed Nov. 15, 1935, in Copenhagen, by the USSR, Austria, Czechoslovakia, Finland, Poland, Romania, Sweden, and Yugoslavia.
Reference: *Ostwirtschaft*, Dec. 1935, p. 188.

- 36/ii/ /Iran

Agreements between the USSR and Iran

concerning direct rail transportation of passengers and freight

Negotiated during Feb. 1936, in Tabriz.
Reference: *Ostwirtschaft*, Feb. 1936, p. 26.

- 37/ii/3/Spain

Act of transfer of the Spanish gold reserve to the USSR

Signed Feb. 3, 1937.
Provides for transfer of about 500 tons of gold which was deposited in the USSR early in 1937. For an agreement on transfer of the gold, see 36/x/ /Spain.
Reference: *Pravda*, Apr. 5, 1957.
Note: *Pravda, loc. cit.*, mentions in addition a credit of $85 million granted the Spanish Republican Government by the USSR; presumably formalized in an agreement, but not otherwise identified, and not listed separately.

- 37/vii/3/Af

Exchange of notes between the USSR and Afghanistan extending the agreements of April 3, 1932, concerning postal, telegraph, and radio-telegraph communications

Sent July 3, 1937, in Kabul.
Reference: Teplinski, p. 20.

- 38/ix/1/Ger

Agreement between the USSR and Germany extending to Austria the provisions of the trade and clearing agreement of March 1, 1938

Signed Sept. 1, 1938, in Berlin.
Entered into force on signature.
Reference: *Ostwirtschaft*, Sept. 1938, p. 124.

- 39/x/11/UK

Barter agreement between the USSR and the United Kingdom

Signed Oct. 11, 1939, in London.
Reference: London *Times*, Oct. 12, 1939.

Nov. 1, 1939. Decree concerning agreement by the USSR to accept the request of the National Assembly of Western Ukraine for incorporation into the USSR

Source: *Pravda*, Nov. 4, 1939.

Nov. 2, 1939. Agreement between the USSR and the National Assembly of Western Belorussia concerning incorporation of Western Belorussia into the USSR

Reference: *Pravda*, Nov. 4, 1939.

- 40/ix/ /Sweden

Agreement between the USSR and Sweden concerning repatriation of persons of Swedish origin from Estonia

Concluded shortly before Sept. 7, 1940, in Moscow.
Reference: Schechtman, pp. 400–401, citing
Deutsche Allgemeine Zeitung, Sept. 7, 1940.

- 41/viii/ /France

Agreement between the USSR and the Free French movement concerning establishment of direct contact and exchange of unofficial representatives

Negotiated during Aug. 1941 in London and Ankara.
Reference: Tsybina, pp. 123–24.

- 41/viii/2/US/b

Exchange of notes between the USSR and the United States of America concerning economic aid to strengthen the USSR in its struggle against armed aggression

Sent Aug. 2, 1941, in Washington, D.C.
Sources: *NYT*, Aug. 5, 1941.
ARSU, 4, Oct.–Nov. 1941, pp. 56–58.

- 41/ix/28/Pol

Exchange of notes between the USSR and the Polish Government-in-Exile concerning establishment of a mixed commission to supervise the welfare of Polish citizens freed from Soviet prisons and labor camps

Sent Aug. 22 and Sept. 28, 1941, in Moscow.
Reference: Rozek, p. 69, citing
Official Polish documents.

- 41/x/16/Af

Exchange of notes between the USSR and Afghanistan concerning expulsion of Italians and Germans from Afghanistan

Sent Oct. 11, 1941, from Moscow and Oct. 16, 1941, from Kabul.
Reference: Teplinski, p. 23.

● 42/iii/18/Pol

Agreement between the USSR and the Polish Government-in-Exile concerning evacuation of part of the Polish Army to Iran

Negotiated orally Mar. 18, 1942.
Reference: Rozek, p. 111, citing
    Official Polish documents.

● 42/vii/31/Pol

Agreement between the USSR and the Polish Government-in-Exile concerning evacuation of the remainder of the Polish Army to the Middle East

Negotiated July 31, 1942.
Reference: Rozek, p. 112, citing
    Kot, Stanislaw, *Listy z Rosji do Generala Sikorskiego* (London, 1956), p. 40.

● 42/x/13/Lux

Agreement between the USSR and the Luxembourg Government-in-Exile concerning establishment of diplomatic relations

Signed Oct. 13, 1942, in London.
References: *Izv.*, Oct. 17, 1942.
    SDD, 11, p. 37.

● 42/xii/ /France

Agreement between the USSR and Fighting France concerning establishment of a French air squadron in the USSR

Negotiated toward the end of 1942.
Reference: Tsybina, p. 124.

● 43/xii/31/US

Exchange of letters between the USSR and the United States of America concerning exchange in the fields of radio and motion pictures

Sent by the United States during Oct. 1943 and by the USSR Dec. 31, 1943.
Eventually led to agreement for publication of *Amerika*, a Russian-language magazine published by the Department of State for distribution in the USSR.

Reference: Simmons, 1951, pp. 245–46.

● 44/ii/2/US

Agreement between the USSR and the United States of America concerning provision of facilities in Siberia for operation of American bombers

In answer to a request by President Roosevelt during the Teheran Conference (Dec. 1943), Stalin on Feb. 2, 1944, agreed to the proposal.
Reference: Deane, 1951, p. 20.

● 44/ix/ /Pl

Agreement between the USSR and the United Kingdom and the United States of America concerning aerial support for the Polish insurgents in Warsaw

Negotiated during the second half of Sept. 1944.
Reference: Rozek, p. 255, citing
    Official Polish documents.

● 44/ix/9/Iraq (continuation)

Soviet-Iraq relations were interrupted in Nov. 1954 when Iraq closed its legation, and were suspended with Iraq's decision on Jan. 3, 1955, to break off diplomatic relations with the USSR completely (Laqueur, p. 203). They were resumed in 1958 (see the *NYT*, July 31, 1958, for appointment of a Soviet Ambassador to Iraq).

● 44/x/18/US

Agreement between the USSR and the United States of America concerning establishment of air bases in Siberia for American bombers in return for shipment to the USSR of American military and other supplies

Negotiated on or about Oct. 18, 1944, in Moscow.
Reference: Deane, 1951, pp. 22–26.

Feb. 27, 1945. Soviet demand for the reorganization of the Romanian Government

Complied with by King Michael under Soviet pressure on Feb. 28, 1945.
References: Byrnes, p. 51.
    Roberts, pp. 263–73.

- 45/iii/31/Cz

Joint communiqué by the USSR and Czechoslovakia concerning the visit of Czechoslovak President Benes to Moscow

Issued Mar. 31, 1945, at the end of negotiations which began Mar. 17, 1945.
Reaffirms friendly relations established under the treaty of Dec. 12, 1943.
Source: *Izv.*, Apr. 1, 1945.

- 45/iv/2/Brazil

Exchange of notes between the USSR and Brazil concerning establishment of diplomatic and consular relations

Sent Apr. 2, 1945, in Washington, D.C.
On Oct. 20, 1947, Brazil broke off diplomatic relations with the USSR (text of notes by Brazil and the USSR in *DIA, 1947–1948*, pp. 781–85).
Sources: *Izv.*, Apr. 4, 1945.
VT, 1945, No. 4–5, p. 41.
VPSS VP, 3, pp. 157–59.
Reference: *SDD*, 11, p. 197.

- 45/v/23/Pl

Agreement between the High Commands of the Armies of the USSR, the United Kingdom, and the United States of America concerning arrest of members of the Dönitz regime in Germany and members of the German General Staff

Negotiated May 23, 1945.
Reference: *NT*, 1945, No. 1, p. 31.

- 45/vi/23/Mul

Temporary agreement concerning the functions of the Preparatory Commission of the United Nations

Signed June 23, 1945, in San Francisco.
Text: *Pravda*, June 25, 1945.

- 45/vii/14/China

Joint communiqué concerning negotiations between the USSR and China

Published July 14, 1945.
Mentions negotiations held recently in Moscow for improvement of relations between the 2 States. For a protocol based on the negotiations, see 45/viii/14/China/g (p. 192 above).
Source: *Pravda*, July 14, 1945.

- 45/viii/27/US

Agreement between the USSR and the United States of America concerning policy in China

Negotiated orally Aug. 27, 1945, in Moscow.
Provisions: The USSR agrees to issue a public statement expressing support of the Open Door policy in China, including Manchuria, equal opportunity for trade and commerce in China, and freedom from discrimination for all free countries. The United States undertakes to have a similar statement issued by China.
Reference: *U.S. relations with China*, p. 119.

- 46/i/8/Pl

Communiqué concerning work of the Allied Tripartite Commission for settlement of the Romanian problem

Published Jan. 8, 1946.
Accompanied by a statement by Romania affirming its compliance with the relevant decisions of the Moscow Conference of Foreign Ministers (see 45/xii/27/(5)).
Reference: *NT*, 1946, No. 2, p. 32.

- 46/iii/8/Pl

Three-Power communiqué concerning distribution of the German merchant fleet

Published Mar. 8, 1946.
Summarizes decisions taken by the USSR, the United Kingdom, and the United States of America on the basis of recommendations of the Three-Power commission set up under an agreement reached at the Potsdam Conference (see 45/xii/7/Pl).
Source: *Pravda*, Mar. 8, 1946.

- 46/vii/25/Cz/b

Joint communiqué concerning negotiations between the USSR and Czechoslovakia

Published July 25, 1946.
Mentions discussion of questions arising from termination of the war and from Soviet-Czechoslovak agreements concerning military collaboration.
Reference: *NT*, 1946, No. 15, p. 30.

• 46/ix/25/Pl

Four-Power declaration concerning the question of the Italian colonies

Published Sept. 25, 1946, in Paris, by the USSR, the United Kingdom, the United States of America, and France.
Source: *Izv.*, Sept. 27, 1946.

• 46/x/21/Pl

Communiqué concerning results of the work of the Five-Power Telecommunication Conference

Issued Oct. 21, 1946.
The conference, attended by the USSR, the United Kingdom, the United States of America, France, and China, was held Sept. 28–Oct. 21, 1946, in Moscow.
Source: *Pravda*, Oct. 23, 1946.

• 47/iv/15/US

Agreement between the USSR and the United States of America to begin negotiations for a Lend-Lease settlement

Announced Apr. 15, 1947.
Reference: *Izv.*, Apr. 15, 1947.

• 47/x/13/Pl/a

Agreement concerning Eastern European rail transportation of passengers and luggage

Signed Oct. 13, 1947, in Belgrade, by the USSR, Bulgaria, and, presumably, Hungary, Poland, and Romania.
Superseded by the agreement of Dec. 22, 1948 (below). Confirmed by Bulgaria Aug. 18, 1948; repealed by Bulgaria Jan. 14, 1950.
Reference: Sipkov, p. 264, citing
    DV, No. 186, Aug. 10, 1948, and No. 13, Jan. 17, 1950.

• 47/x/13/Pl/b

Agreement concerning transport of goods by rail in direct international communication

Signed Oct. 13, 1947, in Belgrade, by the USSR, Bulgaria, and, presumably, Hungary, Poland, and Romania.
Data on confirmation and repeal by Bulgaria identical with those for 47/x/13/Pl/a; reference the same.

• 47/xi/16/Fin

Joint communiqué concerning negotiations between the USSR and Finland

Published Nov. 16, 1947.
No indication given of subjects discussed at the negotiations, held Nov. 4–13, 1947, in Moscow.
Source: *Izv.*, Nov. 16, 1947.

• 48/i/6/Bul

Agreement between the USSR and Bulgaria concerning transformation of diplomatic missions into embassies

Announced Jan. 6, 1948.
Reference: *NT*, 1948, No. 3, p. 31.

• 48/iii/   /Italy

Exchange of notes between the USSR and Italy concerning negotiations for conclusion of agreements on reparations and trade

Sent before Mar. 30, 1948.
Reference: *NT*, 1948, No. 15, p. 31.

• 48/iii/1/H

Agreement between the USSR and Hungary concerning transformation of diplomatic missions into embassies

Announced Mar. 1, 1948.
Reference: *NT*, 1948, No. 11, p. 31.

• 48/v/13/Pol

Trade protocol for 1948 between the USSR and Poland

Signed May 13, 1948.
Provides for total value of trade of $220 million.
Reference: Dolina 1, p. 84.

• 48/xii/22/Pl/a

Agreement concerning transportation of passengers and luggage by rail in direct international communications

Signed Dec. 22, 1948, in Warsaw, by the USSR, Bulgaria, and other unidentified States, presumably including Albania, Czechoslovakia, Hungary, Poland, and Romania. Approved by Bulgaria Jan. 14, 1950.
Reference: Sipkov, pp. 264–65, citing
    DV, Jan. 17, 1950, No. 13.

• 48/xii/22/Pl/b

Agreement concerning transport of goods by rail in international communication

Signed Dec. 22, 1948, in Warsaw, by the USSR, Bulgaria, and other unidentified States, presumably including Albania, Czechoslovakia, Hungary, Poland, and Romania.
Supersedes the agreement of Oct. 13, 1947.
Approved by Bulgaria Jan. 14, 1950.
Reference: As for 48/xii/22/Pl/a.

• 49/i/10/Norway

Trade protocol for 1949 between the USSR and Norway

Signed Jan. 10, 1949.
Reference: *Recent trade agreements*, p. 8.

• 49/ii/24/MPR

Agreement between the USSR and the Mongolian People's Republic concerning organization of geologic prospecting for oil and of industrial exploitation of MPR oil reserves

Signed Feb. 24, 1949, in Moscow.
Reference: Meshcheriakov, pp. 98, 153.

• 49/iii/12/MPR

Agreement between the USSR and the Mongolian People's Republic concerning establishment of a USSR-MPR joint-stock company, "Sovmongolmetall," for prospecting for, extracting, and preparing useful minerals

Signed Mar. 12, 1949, in Ulan Bator.
For a decision to transfer the Soviet share in the company, amounting to 40 million rubles, to the MPR, see 57/v/15/MPR.
Reference: Meshcheriakov, pp. 97–98, 153.

• 49/vi/6/MPR/b

Agreement between the USSR and the Mongolian People's Republic concerning a Soviet loan

Signed June 6, 1949, presumably in Ulan Bator.
Loan to be used to cover the MPR's capital investment in the USSR-MPR joint-stock company "Ulan-Batorskaia zheleznaia doroga."
Reference: Meshcheriakov, p. 153.

• 49/viii/4/Pl

Resolution of the First International Congress of Plant Pathology, Entomology, and Plant Protection

Signed Aug. 4, 1949, in Bucharest, by the USSR, Albania, Bulgaria, Czechoslovakia, Hungary, Poland, and Romania, at the end of a congress which began July 25, 1949.
Provides that (1) each signatory shall establish government offices as independent agencies under its Ministry of Agriculture to enforce quarantine and combat plant diseases, in accordance with Soviet methods; (2) scientific research shall be carried out on the basis of the agricultural-biological teachings of Vil'iams, Michurin, and Lysenko; and (3) congresses are to be called at intervals of 1 or 2 years; a permanent organizational bureau is to be established to carry on business between congresses.
Source: *MK*, June 29, 1950, No. 93 (R, H), cited in
Sipkov, p. 273.

• 49/xii/9/MPR/b

Trade protocol for 1950 between the USSR and the Mongolian People's Republic

Signed Dec. 9, 1949, presumably in Moscow.
Reference: Meshcheriakov, pp. 88, 153.

• 50/x/28/MPR

Trade protocol for 1951 between the USSR and the Mongolian People's Republic

Signed Oct. 28, 1950, in Moscow.
Reference: Meshcheriakov, p. 153.

• 50/xi/1/MPR

Protocol between the USSR and the Mongolian People's Republic concerning the joint-stock company "Ulan-Batorskaia zheleznaia doroga"

Signed Nov. 1, 1950, in Moscow.
Supplements the agreement of June 6, 1949.
Reference: Meshcheriakov, p. 153.

• 50/xii/6/Pl/a   (50/ / /Pl continued)

Agreement concerning transportation of freight by rail in direct international communication

Signed Dec. 6, 1950, in Warsaw. Entered into force Nov. 1, 1951. Supplemented and revised July 10, 1951, in Budapest; July 31, 1953, in Moscow (see 53/vii/31/Pl); and July 30, 1955, in Berlin. Duration indefinite. May be denounced with 6 months' notice.
Additional reference: Sipkov, p. 265.

● 50/xii/6/Pl/b

Agreement concerning transportation of passengers by rail in direct international communications

Signed Dec. 6, 1950, in Warsaw, by the USSR, Albania, Bulgaria, Czechoslovakia, the German Democratic Republic, Hungary, Poland, and Romania.
Data on entry into force, revision, and additional signatories evidently identical with those for 50/xii/6/Pl/a (above).
Reference: Sipkov, pp. 265–66.

● 51/iv/14/Pl

Agreement concerning three-way trade between the USSR, Poland, and Finland

Signed Apr. 14, 1951.
Provides for settlement of part of Finland's claim against the USSR by Polish deliveries to Finland.
Reference: Dolina, 3, p. 176.

July 10, 1951. Revision of the conventions concerning transportation of (1) freight and (2) passengers in direct international communication

See 50/xii/6/Pl/a, above.

● 51/xii/17/Pl

Protocol concerning three-way trade between the USSR, Poland, and Finland

Signed Dec. 17, 1951.
Accompanied by a Polish-Finnish trade protocol for 1952 providing for deliveries by each party to a value of approximately $13 million. Presumably a similar Soviet-Finnish protocol was also signed (not listed separately).
Reference: Dolina, 3, p. 160.

● 51/xii/21/MPR

Agreement between the USSR and the Mongolian People's Republic concerning conditions for paying Soviet specialists sent to the MPR to render technical aid

Signed Dec. 21, 1951, in Ulan Bator.
Reference: Meshcheriakov, p. 153.

● 51/xii/26/MPR

Trade protocol for 1952 between the USSR and the Mongolian People's Republic

Signed Dec. 26, 1951, in Moscow.
Reference: Meshcheriakov, p. 154.

● 51/xii/29/MPR

Agreement between the USSR and the Mongolian People's Republic concerning conditions of trade deliveries

Signed Dec. 29, 1951.
Mentioned in Korolenko, p. 109, as still valid as of Nov. 25, 1953.
Note: Meshcheriakov, p. 88, mentions the signing by the Ministries of Foreign Trade of the USSR and the MPR in 1950 of general conditions for trade delivery. If this was a valid separate agreement, it was presumably superseded by the present agreement.

● 52/ / /Pol

Trade protocol for 1952 between the USSR and Poland

Signed during 1952.
Provides for a 20 per cent increase over 1951.
Reference: Dolina, 3, p. 147.

● 52/ / /Pl

Protocol concerning three-way trade and payments between the USSR, Czechoslovakia, and Finland

Concluded during 1952.
Accompanied by bilateral trade protocols between the 3 States (not listed separately).
For terms and reference, see 50/vi/ /Pl.

● 52/vi/13/MPR

Protocol between the USSR and the Mon-

golian People's Republic concerning Soviet technical aid to the MPR

Signed June 13, 1952, in Moscow.
Covers construction of a coal mine in the Nalaikha region, preparation of a general plan for the city of Ulan Bator, and planning of an automobile repair shop and a circus in Ulan Bator.
Reference: Meshcheriakov, p. 154.

● 53/i/ /Bul

Trade agreement between the USSR and Bulgaria for the period 1953–1955

Signed in Jan. 1953.
Reference: *Osteuropa-Recht,* Vol. 1, No. 2, Dec. 1955, p. 118, citing *Der Aussenhandel,* Berlin, 1952.

● 53/ii/23/MPR

Trade protocol for 1953 between the USSR and the Mongolian People's Republic

Signed Feb. 23, 1953, in Moscow.
Reference: Meshcheriakov, p. 154.

● 53/iv/8/MPR/a

Protocol between the USSR and the Mongolian People's Republic concerning an increase in capitalization of the joint-stock company "Ulan-Batorskaia zheleznaia doroga"

Signed Apr. 8, 1953, in Ulan Bator.
Supplements the agreement of Sept. 15, 1952 (52/ix/15/Pl).
Reference: Meshcheriakov, p. 154.

● 53/iv/8/MPR/b

Agreement between the USSR and the Mongolian People's Republic concerning a Soviet loan

Signed Apr. 8, 1953, in Ulan Bator.
Loan to be used to cover the MPR share in the increased capitalization of the joint-stock company "Ulan-Batorskaia zheleznaia doroga."
Reference: Meshcheriakov, p. 154.

● 53/vii/2/Norway

Informal agreement between the USSR and Norway concerning care of the graves of Soviet citizens killed in Norway during the war

Negotiated shortly before July 2, 1953, by a mixed commission established in Jan. 1952.
Reference: *Izv.,* July 3, 1953.

● 53/vii/31/Pl, continued

Revised July 30, 1955. See 55/vii/30/Pl, below.

● 53/xii/ /Israel

Trade agreement between the USSR and Israel

Concluded in Dec. 1953.
Provides for shipment of Soviet oil to Israel. Cancelled by the USSR after the invasion by Israel of the Suez Peninsula in Oct.–Nov. 1956.
References: Laqueur, p. 204, citing A statement by Moshe Sharett in the Israeli Knesset, Sept. 1, 1954.
Ibid., pp. 242, 271.

● 54/i/6/US

Agreement between the USSR and the United States of America concerning procedure for talks on atomic energy

Negotiated orally Jan. 6, 1954, in Moscow. Follows a proposal by President Eisenhower on Dec. 8, 1953, and a Soviet statement of Dec. 21, 1953.
Reference: *Pravda,* Jan. 7, 1954.

● 54/i/16/Austria

Exchange of notes between the USSR and Austria concerning preparation of a state treaty for Austria

Sent Jan. 5, 1954, from Vienna and Jan. 16, 1954, from Moscow.
Reference: *Pravda,* Jan. 18, 1954 (summary).

● 54/ii/6/Fin, continued

In Mar. 1959 the USSR agreed to a request by Finland to permit repayment of the loan in commodity deliveries during 1959 (*Int. aff.,* No. 6, 1959, p. 101).

● 54/v/29/CPR

Agreement between the USSR and the Chinese People's Republic concerning distribution of Soviet films in the CPR

Signed May 29, 1954, in Peking.
Reference: *Verträge der Volksrepublik China*, p. 21.

● 54/vi/15/Pl

Tenth meeting of the Danube Commission

Held June 8–15, 1954, in Budapest, with representatives of the 6 member States.
Source: *PDK*, 10 (R, F).

May 13–June 22, 1954. Meetings of the United Nations Subcommittee on Disarmament

Held in London.
The Subcommittee, with representatives of the USSR, the United Kingdom, the United States of America, Canada, and France, was established under a resolution of the UN Disarmament Commission of Apr. 19, 1954 (text in *DSB*, 30, 1954, p. 687), in accordance with a resolution by the General Assembly of the UN dated Nov. 28, 1953 (text, *ibid.*, 29, 1953, p. 838). Although no agreements were reached during its 1954 meetings, the Subcommittee submitted a report to the Committee on June 22, 1954 (text, *ibid.*, 31, 1954, pp. 177–83).
Reference: *Int. org.*, 9, 1955, pp. 158–59.

● 54/vi/25/Pl

Meeting of the Council for Mutual Economic Aid

Held June 24 and 25, 1954, in Moscow.
Discussed questions of industry, agriculture, and foreign trade.
Reference: *Pravda*, June 26, 1954.

● 54/vii/ /Pol

Agreement between the USSR and Poland concerning Soviet commercial transit through Poland

Signed during July 1954.
Modifies transit rates under the agreement of Nov. 23, 1945.
Reference: Dolina, 3, p. 148.

● 54/vii/28/Uruguay/b

Trade agreement between the USSR and Uruguay

Signed July 28, 1954, in Montevideo.
Possibly not a formalized agreement but simply agreed lists of commodities to be traded: Soviet oil and oil products, lumber, newsprint, coal, chemicals, agricultural machines, industrial equipment, and metallurgical products, in exchange for Uruguayan meat and canned meat, wool, and rawhides.
Reference: *Pravda*, Aug. 1, 1954.

● 54/x/28/GDR

Communiqué concerning the third meeting of the Soviet-GDR commission for scientific and technical collaboration

Published Oct. 28, 1954; the meeting took place a few days earlier, in Moscow.
Sources: *Izv.*, Oct. 28, 1954.
  VT, 1954, No. 12, p. 42.

● 54/xi/3/Cz

Agreement between the USSR and Czechoslovakia concerning noncommercial payments

Signed Nov. 3, 1954, in Moscow.
Reference: *Izv.*, Nov. 5, 1954.

● 54/xii/ /Af

Agreement between the USSR and Afghanistan concerning showing Soviet films in Afghanistan

Signed during Dec. 1954, in Kabul.
Duration 6 months, with automatic extension for 6 months if not denounced. A similar agreement was signed in 1953 (not listed separately).
Reference: *Izv.*, Dec. 17, 1954.

● 54/xii/15/Pl

Eleventh meeting of the Danube Commission

Held Dec. 8–15, 1954, in Budapest, with representatives of the 6 member States. The meeting approved the budget and plan of work for the Commission for 1955.
Source: *PDK*, 11 (R, F).

Jan. 25, 1955. Soviet decree ending the state of war between the USSR and Germany

Sources: *Pravda*, Jan. 26, 1955.
  DIA, 1955, pp. 244–45, citing *Soviet news*, June 8, 1955.

Mar. 22, 1955. Communiqué by the Ministry of Foreign Affairs of the USSR

concerning plans for conclusion of a treaty of friendship, collaboration, and mutual aid

Published following a conference in Moscow of Albania, Bulgaria, Czechoslovakia, the German Democratic Republic, Hungary, Poland, Romania, and the USSR, with the participation of the Chinese People's Republic. For the treaty (the Warsaw Pact), see 55/v/15/Pl/a.
Source: *Pravda*, Mar. 22, 1955.

● 55/iii/31/Pl

Agreement concerning three-way trade between the USSR, Poland, and Finland

Signed Mar. 31, 1955.
Provides for settlement of a Polish export surplus of $13 million, under a Polish-Finnish trade agreement of Dec. 21, 1954.
Reference: Dolina, 3, p. 161.

Feb. 25–May 9, 1955. Meetings of the United Nations Subcommittee on Disarmament

Held in London, with representatives of the USSR, the United Kingdom, the United States of America, Canada, and France, following a procedural meeting in New York on Dec. 8, 1954 (not listed separately).
No agreements were reached. Texts of documents submitted to the Subcommission are given in *DSB*, 32, 1955, pp. 892–905.

● 55/vi/13/Pl/b

Twelfth meeting of the Danube Commission

Held June 8–13, 1955, in Budapest, with representatives of the 6 member States.
Source: *PDK*, 12 (R, F).

● 55/vii/30/Pl

Agreement concerning transportation of freight by rail in direct international communication

Signed July 30, 1955, in Berlin.
Revises the agreement of Dec. 6, 1950 (above, p. 267, under number 50/ / / Pl), as revised July 10, 1951, and July 31, 1953. Entered into force Jan. 1, 1956. Duration indefinite; may be denounced with 6 months' notice.
Sources (cited in Sipkov, p. 266):

Archiv für Eisenbahnwesen, Frankfurt/Main, Vol. 67, No. 2, II, pp. 239–99.
Haustein-Pschirrer, *Internationales Eisenbahnrecht, Quellensammlung*, Frankfurt/Main, Vol. 1, 1956, pp. 431 ff. (F, G).

● 55/viii/12/MPR

Agreement between the USSR and the Mongolian People's Republic concerning technical aid and credit

Signed Aug. 12, 1955, in Moscow.
Provides for construction of industrial and communal enterprises.
Reference: Meshcheriakov, p. 154.

● 55/ix/ /Egypt

Agreement between the USSR and Egypt concerning shipment of Czechoslovak munitions to Egypt

Negotiated during Sept. 1955.
Ostensibly a contract agreement between Egypt and Czechoslovakia providing for exchange of Czechoslovak heavy arms for Egyptian cotton and rice; an underlying agreement between the USSR and Egypt, however, is highly probable. Laqueur, p. 227, cites statements by Egyptian Premier Nasser during July and Aug. 1956 indicating that the public designation of Czechoslovakia as the formal agent in the agreement was "merely a matter of convenience."
Reference: Laqueur, pp. 211–22.

● 55/ix/13/FRG/b, continued

On Sept. 15, 1955, FRG Chancellor Konrad Adenauer sent Soviet Premier N. A. Bulganin a note stating that (1) the establishment of diplomatic relations between the FRG and the USSR does not constitute a recognition by the FRG of existing territorial arrangements; the definitive settlement of the question of Germany's boundaries will be determined in the peace treaty, and (2) the establishment of diplomatic relations does not alter the FRG's legal position in regard to its claim to speak for the German people in international relations, and in regard to the political relations in those German territories which now lie outside its effective exercise of authority. In reply a TASS communiqué of Sept. 15, 1955, stated that (1) the FRG and the German Democratic

Republic are regarded by the USSR as two parts of Germany; (2) the question of the German boundaries was settled by the Potsdam Agreement; and (3) the FRG exercises jurisdiction over those territories under its control.
Sources: *Pravda*, Sept. 16, 1955 (TASS communiqué).
Rönnefarth-Euler, p. 506.

Aug. 29–Oct. 7, 1955. Meetings of the United Nations Subcommittee on Disarmament

Held in New York, with representatives of the 5 member States.
No agreements were reached.
Reference: *Int. org.*, 10, 1956, pp. 143–48.

• 55/xi/19/Syria

Agreement between the USSR and Syria concerning transformation of diplomatic missions into embassies

Announced Nov. 19, 1955.
Reference: *Pravda*, Nov. 19, 1955.

• 55/xi/29/CPR

Agreement between the USSR and the Chinese People's Republic concerning reciprocal acquisition of copyright on films

Signed Nov. 29, 1955, in Peking.
Reference: *Verträge der Volksrepublik China*, p. 21.

• 55/xii/6/Austria

Exchange of notes between the USSR and Austria concerning Austrian neutrality

Sent Nov. 14, 1955, from Vienna and Dec. 6, 1955, from Moscow. Similar exchanges took place between Austria and the United Kingdom, the United States of America, and France.
The Austrian note incorporates the text of a law concerning Austrian neutrality passed by the Austrian Parliament Oct. 26, 1955. In their replies the 4 States, all signers of the State Treaty for Austria (55/v/15/Austria), recognized "the perpetual neutrality of Austria" as defined in the Austrian note.
Sources: *Pravda*, Dec. 7, 1955.
   DSB, 33, 1955, pp. 1011–12.
   DIA, 1955, p. 239.

• 55/xii/15/Pl

Thirteenth meeting of the Danube Commission

Held Dec. 7–15, 1955, in Budapest, with representatives of the 6 member States. The meeting approved the budget and plan of work for the Commission for 1956.
Source: *PDK*, 13 (R, F).

• 56/i/7/Af

Trade protocol between the USSR and Afghanistan

Signed Jan. 7, 1956, in Kabul.
Provides for increase in trade during 1957–58. Soviet automobiles and equipment, oil products, ferrous metals, in exchange for Afghan cotton, wool, raw hides, dried fruits, and oil seeds.
Reference: *NYT*, Jan. 9, 1957.

• 56/iii/26/Pl, continued

The statute of the Institute, together with a Table of Personnel, was signed at Dubna, USSR, on Sept. 23, 1956, by the 12 member States. Its provisions are summarized in M. M. Lebedenko, "Ustav Ob"edinënnogo Institut Yadernykh Issledovanii," *Sovetskoe gosudarstvo i pravo*, 1957, No. 2, pp. 116–18.

Mar. 19–May 4, 1956. Meetings of the United Nations Subcommittee on Disarmament

Held in London, with representatives of the 5 member States.
No agreements were reached. A selection of documents submitted to the Subcommittee is given in *DIA, 1956*, pp. 552–75.
References: *Int. org.*, 10, 1956, pp. 429–34.
   Rönnefarth-Euler, pp. 516–20.

• 56/vi/13/Pl

Fourteenth meeting of the Danube Commission

Held June 7–13, 1956, in Budapest, with representatives of the 6 member States and of the European Economic Commission.
Source: *PDK*, 14 (R, F).

Aug. 16–23, 1956. Conference to con-

sider a proposal to internationalize the Suez Canal

Held in London by 22 States, including the USSR.
The conference decided to send to Egypt a mission composed of representatives of 5 States (not including the USSR) to present its proposals. The USSR did not support this decision, nor did it attend the continuation of the conference, held in London Sept. 19–21 and Oct. 1–5, 1956.
References: *BSE, 1957*, pp. 296–97.
  Laqueur, pp. 233–34.

● 56/xi/19/Mul, continued

Entered into force May 4, 1959.
Source: *VVS*, 1959, No. 25, Art. 135.

● 56/xii/1/DRV

Agreement between the USSR and the Democratic Republic of Vietnam concerning a Soviet credit

Signed Dec. 1, 1956.
Provides for a credit of 30 million rubles.
Reference: *VT SSSR*, p. 207.

● 57/ii/5/GDR

Protocol between the USSR and the German Democratic Republic concerning establishment of a permanent commission of historians of the USSR and the GDR

Signed Feb. 5, 1957, in Moscow.
Reference: *Izv.*, Feb. 6, 1957.

Feb. 14, 1957. Act concerning transfer by the USSR to the Mongolian People's Republic of telegraph and telephone equipment and installations built by the USSR on the territory of the MPR

Signed in Ulan Bator.
Reference: Meshcheriakov, p. 154.

● 57/vi/14/Pl

Fifteenth meeting of the Danube Commission

Held June 5–14, 1957, in Budapest, with representatives of the 6 member States, the European Economic Commission, as an observer, and Austria and the Federal Republic of Germany, as experts.
The meeting adopted a plan of work for 1957 and considered a draft budget for 1957.

Source: *PDK*, 15 (R, F).

Mar. 18–Sept. 6, 1957. Meetings of the United Nations Subcommittee on Disarmament

Held in London, with representatives of the 5 member States.
No agreements were reached.
References: *Int. org.*, 11, 1957, pp. 659–61.
  DSB, 37, 1957, pp. 631–35, 667–73.
  Rönnefarth-Euler, p. 520.

● 57/x/ /Yemen

Agreement between the USSR and Yemen concerning transformation of diplomatic missions into embassies

Negotiated during Oct. 1957.
Reference: *NYT*, Oct. 11, 1957.

● 57/x/9/France

Plan for cultural collaboration in 1958 between the USSR and France

Prepared at a conference held Sept. 30–Oct. 9, 1957, in Paris.
The conference also decided to establish a mixed commission to supervise cultural and scientific ties between the USSR and France.
Reference: *Pravda*, Oct. 10, 1957.

● 57/x/19/Egypt, continued

By a subsequent exchange of notes, which the USSR ratified June 22, 1959, extended to both sections of the United Arab Republic.
Reference: *VVS*, 1959, No. 25, Art. 139.

Nov. 1–20, 1957. Negotiations between the USSR and Egypt

Held in Moscow.
An informal agreement was reached on Soviet technical and economic aid to Egypt, later formalized in an agreement concerning economic and technical collaboration signed Jan. 29, 1958 (*Pr., Izv.*, Jan. 30, 1958). Laqueur, p. 272, mentions an agreement concluded in Nov. 1957 for a Soviet loan to Egypt of 700 million rubles; the 1958 agreement included a 12-year loan.
Reference: *BSE, 1958*, p. 245.

LIST OF ABBREVIATIONS
INDEX BY COUNTRIES
SHORT TITLE LIST

LIST OF ABBREVIATIONS

ABBREVIATIONS USED IN SERIAL NUMBERS

(Names of States not listed here are not abbreviated)

Af—Afghanistan
AH—Austria-Hungary
Alb—Albania
Arm—Armenia
Az—Azerbaidzhan
Bash—Bashkiria
BL—Belgium-Luxembourg Economic Union
BSSR—Belorussian SSR
Bukh—Bukhara
Bul—Bulgaria
CP—Central Powers
CPR—Chinese People's Republic
CR—Costa Rica
DR—Dominican Republic
DRV—Democratic Republic of Vietnam
Est—Estonia
FER—Far Eastern Republic
Fin—Finland
FRG—Federal Republic of Germany
FSWR—Finnish Socialist Workers' Republic
GDR—German Democratic Republic
Ger—Germany
GrDR—Georgian Democratic Republic
GrSSR—Georgian SSR
H—Hungary
Hei—Heilungkiang
J—Japan

Kh—Khorezm
KPDR—Korean People's Democratic Republic
Lat—Latvia
Lith—Lithuania
Lux—Luxembourg
MPR—Mongolian People's Republic
Mul—Multilateral
Neth—The Netherlands
NK—North Korea
NZ—New Zealand
Pl—Plurilateral
Pol—Poland
Pr—Private
Rom—Romania
SA—Union of South Africa
SM—San Marino
Switz—Switzerland
T—Turkey
TT—Tannu Tuva
UK—United Kingdom of Great Britain and Northern Ireland
UN—United Nations
US—United States of America
VC—Vatican City
Yug—Yugoslavia

LANGUAGE ABBREVIATIONS

A—Arabic
B—Bulgarian
C—Chinese
Cz—Czech
D—Danish
E—English
F—French
G—German

H—Hungarian
I—Italian
J—Japanese
K—Korean
Lat.—Latvian
Lith.—Lithuanian
M—Mongolian
N—Norwegian

P—Polish
Per.—Persian
R—Russian
S—Spanish
SC—Serbo-Croat
T—Turkish
U—Ukrainian
V—Vietnamese

SHORT TITLE LIST

AD—Annuaire diplomatique du Commissariat du Peuple pour les Affaires Étrangères. Moscow, Edition du Commissariat du Peuple pour les Affaires Étrangères, issued annually, 1925–35.

AJIL—American Journal of International Law. Washington, D.C., quarterly.

Allen, 1952—Allen, David Edwards, Jr., "The Soviet Union and the Spanish Civil War." Ph.D. thesis, Stanford, 1952.

Allen, 1957—Allen, Robert Loring, "The Soviet and East European foreign credit program," *American Slavic and East European Review,* Vol. 16, No. 4, Dec. 1957, pp. 433–49.

Alvarez del Vayo—Alvarez del Vayo, J., *The last optimist.* N.Y., Viking, 1950.

Anders—Anders, Lt. Gen. W., *An Army in exile. The story of the Second Polish Corps.* London, Macmillan, 1949.

AQSU—American Quarterly on the Soviet Union. N.Y.

ARSU—American Review on the Soviet Union. N.Y.

Axis in defeat—U.S., Department of State, *The Axis in defeat. A collection of documents on American policy toward Germany and Japan.* Washington, D.C. [1945].

Babaiants—Babaiants, A. A., *Mezhdunarodnye otnosheniia i vneshniaia politika SSSR, 1939–1941. Dokumenty i materialy.* Moscow, 1948.

Batsell—Batsell, Walter R., *Soviet rule in Russia.* N.Y., Macmillan, 1929.

Beloff—Beloff, Max, *The foreign policy of Soviet Russia, 1929–1941.* Issued under the auspices of the Royal Institute of International Affairs. London, Oxford University Press, 2 vols., 1947–49.

BFSP—British and foreign state papers. London, H.M.S.O.

BGBl—Bundesgesetzblatt. Vienna.

BL—Bollettino di legislazione doganale e commerciale. Rome.

BO—Buletinul oficial. Bucharest.

BPI—Bulletin des Presse- und Informationsamtes der Bundesregierung. Bonn.

BPP—British Parliamentary papers. London.

BSE, 1957—Vvedenskii, B. A., ed., *Yezhegodnik Bol'shoi Sovetskoi Entsiklopedii, 1957.* [Moscow], Gosudarstvennoe nauchnoe izdatel'stvo "Bol'shaia Sovetskaia Entsiklopediia" [1957].

BSE, 1958—Idem, Moscow-Leningrad, 1958.

BTS—Treaty series. London.

Bulletin—Bulletin of the Institute for the Study of the USSR. Munich, monthly.

Byrnes—Byrnes, James F., *Speaking frankly.* N.Y., Harper, 1947.

Carr, 3—Carr, E. H., *The Bolshevik Revolution, 1917–1923. (A history of Soviet Russia).* Vol. 3, London, Macmillan, 1953.

CDSP—Current digest of the Soviet press. N.Y., weekly.

CDT—Collection des traités. Tokyo, Ministry of Foreign Affairs.

Chen—Chen, Yin Ching, ed., *Treaties and agreements between the Republic of China and other Powers, 1929–1954, together with certain international documents affecting the interests of the Republic of China.* Washington, D.C., Sino-American Publishing Service, 1957.

Cheng—Cheng Tien-fang, *A history of Soviet-Chinese relations.* Washington, D.C., Public Affairs Press, 1957.

Childs—Childs, James Rives, *Perso-Russian treaties and notes of 1828–1931.* Teheran, 1934–35 (typescript copy in the Library of Congress, Washington, D.C.).

Churchill, 5—Churchill, Sir Winston Spenser, *The Second World War.* Vol. 5, *Closing the ring.* Boston, Houghton Mifflin, 1951.

Churchill, 6—*Ibid.* Vol. 6, *Triumph and tragedy.* Boston, Houghton Mifflin, 1953.

Clay—Clay, Lucius D., *Decision in Germany.* Garden City, N.Y., Doubleday, 1950.

Cmd.—Command paper. London, H.M.S.O.

Correspondence—*Correspondence between the Chairman of the Council of Ministers of the U.S.S.R. and the Presidents of the U.S.A. and the Prime Ministers of Great Britain during the Great Patriotic War of 1941–1945.* Moscow, 1957.
CTS—Canada, *Treaty series.* Ottawa.
Current background—U.S. Consulate General in Hong Kong, *Current background.* Weekly.
Current history—N.Y., monthly.
CYB—*The China Year Book.* London, Routledge, annual, 1912–39.

DAFR—*Documents on American foreign relations.* Boston, World Peace Foundation, annual, 1939–54.
Dallin, 1942—Dallin, David J., *Soviet Russia's foreign policy, 1939–1942.* New Haven, Yale University Press, 1942.
Deane, 1947—Deane, John R., *The strange alliance. The story of our efforts at wartime co-operation with Russia.* N.Y., Viking, 1947.
Deane, 1951—Deane, John R., "Negotiating on military assistance, 1943–1945," in Raymond Dennett and Joseph E. Johnson, eds., *Negotiating with the Russians.* Boston, World Peace Foundation, 1951, pp. 3–28.
Decade of American foreign policy—U.S., Senate Committee on Foreign Relations, *A decade of American foreign policy. Basic documents, 1941–1949.* Washington, D.C., 1950.
Dedijer—Dedijer, Vladimir, *Tito.* N.Y., Simon and Schuster, 1953.
Degras—Degras, Jane, *Calendar of Soviet documents on foreign policy.* London, Royal Institute of International Affairs, 1948.
Deklaratsii, 1957—*Deklaratsii, zaiavleniia i kommiunike Sovetskogo Pravitel'stva s pravitel'stvami inostrannykh gosudarstv, 1954–1957 gg.* Moscow, Gosudarstvennoe izdatel'stvo politicheskoi literatury, 1957.
Dellin, *Bulgaria*—Dellin, L. E. D., ed., *Bulgaria.* N.Y., Praeger, for the Mid-European Studies Center, 1957.
Dennis—Dennis, Alfred L. P., *The foreign policies of Soviet Russia.* N.Y., Dutton, 1924.
Desiat' let—*Desiat' let Sovetskoi diplomatii (akty i dokumenty).* Moscow, Izdanie Litizdata Narkomindela, 1927.
Dewar—Dewar, Margaret, *Soviet trade with Eastern Europe, 1945–1949.* London, Royal Institute of International Affairs, 1951.
DGFP—U.S., Department of State, *Documents on German foreign policy.*
DGO—Ruhm von Oppen, Beate, ed., *Documents on Germany under occupation, 1945–1954.* Issued under the auspices of the Royal Institute on International Affairs. London, Oxford University Press, 1955.
DIA—*Documents on international affairs.* Annual, issued under the auspices of the Royal Institute of International Affairs. London, Oxford University Press, in progress.
Dogovor, 1957—*Dogovor mezhdu Soiuzom Sovetskikh Sotsialisticheskikh Respublik i Chekhoslovatskoi Respublikoi o rezhime sovetsko-chekhoslovatskoi granitsy i o poriadke uregulirovaniia pogranichnykh intsidentov.* Moscow, Verkhovnyi Sovet SSSR, 1957.
Dokumente DDR—*Dokumente zur Aussenpolitik der Regierung der Deutschen Demokratischen Republik.* In progress. Berlin, Rütten & Loening, 1954–.
Dokumenty GDR—*Dokumenty o vneshnei politike pravitel'stva G.D.R.* Moscow, 1956.
Dolina, 1—Dolina, Józef, "Poland's foreign trade agreements," Part I, *Polish review,* Vol. 1, No. 4, Autumn 1956, pp. 80–91.
Dolina, 3—*Idem*, Part II, *ibid.*, Vol. 3, No. 1-2, Winter-Spring 1958, pp. 147–76.
DR—*Deutscher Reichsanzeiger.* Berlin.
DSB—U.S., *Department of State Bulletin.* Washington, D.C., weekly.
DSCS, 52—U.S., Department of State, *United Nations Conference on Food and Agriculture. Hot Springs, Virginia, May 18–June 3, 1943. Final Act and section reports.* Washington, D.C., 1943 (Department of State, Conference Series, 52).
DSCS, 53—U.S., Department of State, *First session of the Council of the United Nations Relief and Rehabilitation Administration. Selected documents.* Washington, D.C., 1944 (Department of State, Conference Series, 53).

DSCS, 55—U.S., Department of State, *United Nations Monetary and Financial Conference. Bretton Woods, New Hampshire, July 1 to July 22, 1944. Final Act and related documents.* Washington, D.C., 1944 (Department of State, Conference Series, 55).

DSCS, 56—U.S., Department of State, *Dumbarton Oaks documents on international organization.* Washington, D.C., 1944 (Department of State, Conference Series, 56).

DSCS, 60—U.S., Department of State, *Dumbarton Oaks documents on international organization, together with chart and questions and answers.* Washington, D.C., 1944 (Department of State, Conference Series, 60).

DSCS, 79—U.S., Department of State, *Moscow meeting of Foreign Ministers, December 16–26, 1945. Report by James F. Byrnes, Secretary of State, and Soviet-Anglo-American communiqué.* Washington, D.C., 1946 (Department of State, Conference Series, 79).

DSCS, 91—U.S., Department of State, *International Health Conference, New York, N.Y., June 19 to July 22, 1946. Report of the United States Delegation, including the Final Act and related documents.* Washington, D.C., 1947 (Department of State, Conference Series, 91).

DSCS, 93—U.S., Department of State, *Third Session of the Council of Foreign Ministers, New York City, November 4 to December 12, 1946.* Washington, D.C., 1947 (Department of State, Conference Series, 93).

DSCS, 98—U.S., Department of State, *Moscow meeting of the Council of Foreign Ministers, March 10–April 24, 1947. Address by the Secretary of State.* Washington, D.C., 1947 (Department of State, Conference Series, 98).

DSCS, 103—U.S., Department of State, *Paris Peace Conference, 1946. Selected documents.* Washington, D.C., 1947 (Department of State, Conference Series, 103).

DSES, 22—U.S., Department of State, *Soviet supply protocols.* Washington, D.C., 1948 (Department of State, European Series, 22).

DSES, 24—U.S., Department of State, *Making the peace treaties, 1941–1947.* Washington, D.C., 1947 (Department of State, European Series, 24).

DS GFPS, 15—U.S., Department of State, *Postwar foreign policy preparation, 1939–1945.* Washington, D.C., 1949 (Department of State, General Foreign Policy Series, 15).

DS, IOCS, 1.3—U.S., Department of State, *Proceedings and documents of the United Nations Monetary and Financial Conference, Bretton Woods, New Hampshire, July 1–22, 1944.* Washington, D.C., 2 vols., 1948 (Department of State, International Organization and Conference Series, 1.3).

DS, IOCS, 1.4—U.S., Department of State, *International Telecommunications Conferences, Atlantic City, New Jersey, May–October 1947.* Washington, D.C., 1948 (Department of State, International Organization and Conference Series, 1.4).

DS, IOCS, 1.6—U.S., Department of State, *International Conference on Safety of Life at Sea. London, April 23–June 10, 1948. Report of the United States Delegations, including Final Act and related documents.* Washington, D.C., 1948 (Department of State, International Organization and Conference Series, 1.6).

DS, IOCS, 1.26—U.S., Department of State, *Foreign Ministers Meeting. Berlin discussions, January 25–February 18, 1954.* Washington, D.C., 1954 (Department of State, International Organization and Conference Series, 1.26).

DS, IOCS, II, 4—U.S., Department of State, *The Korean problem at the Geneva Conference, April 26–June 15, 1954.* Washington, D.C., 1954 (Department of State, International Organization and Conference Series, II, 4).

DSP—U.S., Department of State, *Documents and state papers.*

DUPRL—*Dziennik ustaw Polskiej Rzeczypospolitej Ludowej.* Warsaw.

Durdenevskii and Krylov—Durdenevskii, V. N., and S. B. Krylov, eds., *Organizatsiia Ob"edinënnykh Natsii. Sbornik dokumentov, otnosiashchikhsia k sozdaniiu i deiatel'nosti.* Moscow, Gosudarstvennoe izdatel'stvo yuridicheskoi literatury, 1956.

DURP—*Dziennik ustaw Rzeczypospolitej Polskiej.* Warsaw.

Düstur—Turkish collection of laws and decrees.

DV—*Durzhaven vestnik.* Bulgarian official law gazette.

DVP—Ministerstvo Inostrannykh Del SSSR, *Dokumenty vneshnei politiki SSSR.* Moscow, Gosudarstvennoe izdatel'stvo politicheskoi literatury, 1957–; in progress.

EAS—U.S., Department of State, *Executive agreement series.* Washington, D.C.

East Europe—N.Y., monthly. Published by the Free Europe Committee.

EB—*Encyclopædia Britannica,* ed. of 1956.

Economic treaties—Mid-European Studies Center, Mid-European Law Project, *Economic treaties and agreements of the Soviet Bloc in Eastern Europe, 1945–1951.* 2d ed., N.Y., Mid-European Studies Center, 1952.

EIK—Troianovskii, A., L. Yurovskii, and M. Kaufman, eds., *Eksport, import i kontsessii Soiuza S.S.R.* Moscow, Izdanie Gosudarstvennoi Kontory Ob"iavlenii "Dvigatel'," n.d. (ca. 1925). Text in Russian, German, French, and English.

ELV—Estonia, Ministry of Foreign Affairs, *Eesti Lepingud Välisriikdega.* Tallinn.

ERSU—Amtorg Trading Corporation, Information Department, N.Y., *Economic review of the Soviet Union. A semi-monthly survey of Soviet economic developments and of trade between the United States and the Soviet Union.*

Eudin and Fisher—Eudin, X. J., and Harold H. Fisher, in collaboration with Rosemary Brown Jones, *Soviet Russia and the West, 1920–1927. A documentary survey.* Stanford, Stanford University Press, 1957.

Eudin and North—Eudin, X. J., and Robert C. North, *Soviet Russia and the East, 1920–1927. A documentary survey.* Stanford, Stanford University Press, 1957.

EZh—*Ekonomicheskaia zhizn'.* Moscow, semi-weekly.

FAO Fisheries bulletin—United Nations, *Food and Agriculture Organization Fisheries Bulletin.*

Feis—Feis, Herbert, *Churchill, Roosevelt, Stalin: the war they waged and the peace they sought.* Princeton, Princeton University Press, 1957.

Feis, *The China tangle*—Feis, Herbert, *The China tangle.* Princeton, Princeton University Press, 1953.

Fischer—Fischer, Louis, *The Soviets in world affairs. A history of relations between the Soviet Union and the rest of the world.* 2 vols., London, Cape, 1930; 2d ed., Princeton, Princeton University Press, 1951.

Fisher—Fisher, Harold H., *The famine in Soviet Russia, 1919–1923; the operations of the American Relief Administration.* N.Y., Macmillan, 1927.

Die Friedensverhandlungen in Brest-Litowsk—*Die Friedensverhandlungen in Brest-Litowsk und der Friede mit Russland. Authentische Berichte.* Leipzig, Meiner, 1918. (Deutscher Geschichtskalender, 33. Jg., 2.)

Friters—Friters, G. M., *Outer Mongolia and its international position.* Issued under the auspices of the International Secretariat, Institute of Pacific Relations. Baltimore, Johns Hopkins University Press, 1949.

FRUS—U.S., Department of State, *Foreign relations of the United States.*

FRUS, CMY—U.S., Department of State, *Foreign relations of the United States. Diplomatic papers. The conferences at Malta and Yalta, 1945.* Washington, D.C., 1955.

FRUS, SU, 1933–1939—U.S., Department of State, *Foreign relations of the United States. Diplomatic papers. The Soviet Union, 1933–1939.* Washington, D.C., 1952.

GBl DDR—*Gesetzblatt der Deutschen Demokratischen Republik.* Berlin.

Genkin—Genkin, D. M., ed., *Pravovye voprosy vneshnei torgovli SSSR s yevropeiskimi stranami narodnoi demokratii.* Moscow, Vneshtorg, 1955.

Germany, 1947–1949—U.S., Department of State, *Germany, 1947–1949. The story in documents.* Washington, D.C., 1950.

Gerschuni—Gerschuni, G., *Die Konzessionspolitik Sowjetrusslands.* Berlin, Prager, 1927.

God bor'by—RSFSR, Narodnyi Komissariat po Prodovol'stviiu, *God bor'by s golodom. Uchastie Narodnogo Komissariata po Prodovol'stviiu v dele pomoshchi golodaiushchim.* Moscow, 1922.

Halecki, *Poland*—Halecki, Oscar, ed., *Poland.* N.Y., Praeger, for the Mid-European Studies Center, 1957.

H. C. Deb.—*Parliamentary debates* (Hansard), House of Commons. London, H.M.S.O.

Heymann—Heymann, Hans, Jr., "Oil in Soviet-Western relations in the interwar years." *American Slavic and East European Review,* Vol. 7, No. 4, 1948, pp. 303–16.

Hiebert—Hiebert, P. C., and Orie O. Miller, *Feeding the hungry; Russia famine, 1919–1925; American Mennonite relief operations under the auspices of Mennonite Central Committee.* Scottdale, Pa., Mennonite Central Committee, 1929.
Highlights—U.S., Library of Congress, Mid-European Law Project, *Highlights of current legislation and activities in Mid-Europe.* Washington, D.C., monthly.
Hilger and Meyer—Hilger, Gustav, and Alfred G. Meyer, *The incompatible allies. A memoir-history of German-Soviet relations, 1918–1941.* N.Y., Macmillan, 1953.
Ho Han-wen, *A history of Sino-Russian relations*—Ho Han-wen, *Chung-O Wai-Chiao Shih.* Shanghai, 1935.
Hoeffding—Hoeffding, W., "German trade with the Soviet Union," *Slavonic and East European Review*, London, Vol. 14, 1935–36, pp. 473–94.
Hoffmann, *War diaries*—Hoffmann, Max, *War diaries and other papers.* 2 vols., London, Secker, 1929.
Hsin-hua Yueh-pao—Peiping.
Hudson—Hudson, Manley O., ed., *International legislation. A collection of the texts of multipartite international instruments of general interest.* 9 vols., N.Y., Carnegie Endowment for International Peace, 1931–50.
Hurewitz—Hurewitz, J. C., *Diplomacy in the Near and Middle East; a documentary record.* 2 vols., Princeton, Van Nostrand, 1956.
Hwang—Hwang Jen, *Le régime des concessions en Russie Soviétique.* Paris, Gamber, 1929.

ILO Code, 1951—International Labour Office, *The International Labour Code, 1951.* Geneva, 2 vols., 1952.
Informations commerciales—Periodical published by the Office Belge du Commerce Extérieur.
Int. aff.—*International affairs.* Moscow, monthly.
International Telecommunication Convention, 1947—International Telecommunication Union, *Final Acts of the International Telecommunication and Radio Conferences, Atlantic City, 1947.* Atlantic City, N.J., 1947. (Includes French and English texts of the International Telecommunication Convention, Radio Regulations, and Recommendations and Resolutions adopted by the Conference, each paged separately).
Int. org.—*International organization.* N.Y., quarterly.
Istoriia diplomatii—Potëmkin, V. P., ed., *Istoriia diplomatii.* Moscow, 3 vols., OGIZ, 1941–45.
Istoriia sovetskoi konstitutsii—*Istoriia sovetskoi konstitutsii (v dokumentakh), 1917–1956.* Moscow, Gosudarstvennoe izdatel'stvo yuridicheskoi literatury, 1957.
Itogy bor'by—RSFSR, Tsentral'naia Komissiia pomoshchi golodaiushchim, *Itogi bor'by s golodom v 1921–22 gg.; sbornik statei i otchëtov.* Moscow, Ts. K. Pomgol, 1922.
Itogi peregovorov—*Itogi peregovorov mezhdu sovetskim pravitel'stvom i pravitel'stvennoi delegatsiei Germanskoi Demokraticheskoi Respubliki.* Moscow, 1953.
Izv.—*Izvestiia.* Moscow, daily.

JO—*Journal officiel.* Paris.
JR—*al-Jaridah al-Rasmiyyah.* Official Syrian gazette.

KA—*Kitvei Amana.* Official Israeli treaty series.
Kamenev, *Bor'ba za mir*—Kamenev, L. B., *Bor'ba za mir. (Otchët o mirnykh peregovorakh v Breste). S prilozheniem dogovora o peremirii, germanskikh i russkikh uslovii mira, deklaratsii i etnograficheskoi, politicheskoi i voennoi karty predlozhennoi germantsami granitsy.* Petrograd, 1918.
Kanunlarimiz—Official Turkish treaty collection.
Kapitsa—Kapitsa, M. S., *Sovetsko-kitaiskie otnosheniia v 1931–1945 gg.* Moscow, Gospolitizdat, 1956.
Keilin—Keilin, A. D., *Sovetskoe morskoe pravo.* Moscow, Vodtransizdat, 1954.
Kennan, 2—Kennan, George F., *Soviet-American relations, 1917–1920.* Vol. 2, *The decision to intervene.* Princeton, Princeton University Press, 1958.
Kliuchnikov—Kliuchnikov, Yu. V., and A. Sabanin, eds., *Mezhdunarodnaia politika*

noveishego vremeni v dogovorakh, notakh i deklaratsiakh. Moscow, 3 vols., Izdanie Litizdata NKID, 1925–29.
Korea—U.S., Department of State, Office of Public Affairs, *Foreign affairs background summary. Korea.* Washington, D.C., 1947.
Korolenko—Korolenko, A. S., *Torgovye dogovory i soglasheniia SSSR s inostrannymi gosudarstvami.* Moscow, Vneshtorgizdat, 1953.
Korostovetz—Korostovetz, I. J., *Von Cinggis Khan sur Sowjetrepublik.* Berlin, de Gryler, 1926.
Korovin, 1925—Korovin, Ye. A., *Mezhdunarodnoe pravo perekhodnogo vremeni.* Moscow, Gos. izd., 1925.
Krasnaia kniga—R.S.F.S.R., Narodnyi Komissariat Inostrannykh Del, *Krasnaia kniga. Sbornik diplomaticheskikh dokumentov o russko-pol'skikh otnosheniiakh s 1918 po 1920 g.* Moscow, Gos. izd., 1920.
Krasnaia letopis'—Leningrad, quarterly.

Laqueur—Laqueur, Walter Z., *The Soviet Union and the Middle East.* N.Y., Praeger, 1959.
Lattimore, *Pivot of Asia*—Lattimore, Owen, *Pivot of Asia; Sinkiang and the inner Asian frontiers of China and Russia.* Boston, Little, Brown, 1950.
Leahy—Leahy, Adm. William D., *I was there; the personal story of the Chief of Staff to Presidents Roosevelt and Truman, based on his notes and diary made at the time.* N.Y., Whittlesey House, 1950.
Leiss and Dennett—Leiss, Amelia C., in cooperation with Raymond Dennett, ed., *European peace treaties after World War II. Negotiations and texts of treaties with Italy, Bulgaria, Hungary, Rumania, and Finland.* N.Y., World Peace Foundation, 1954.
Lenin, *Soch.*—Lenin, V. I., *Sobranie sochinenii.* Moscow, Gos. izd., 1920–27.
Leninskii sbornik, 11—Institut Lenina pri Ts. K.V.K.P. (b.), *Leninskii sbornik,* No. 11. Moscow-Leningrad, 1929.
Liberman—Liberman, Simon, *Building Lenin's Russia.* Chicago, University of Chicago Press, 1945.
Liubimov—Liubimov, N. N., "Vneshniaia torgovlia SSSR posle vtoroi mirovoi voiny," *Istoricheskie zapiski,* Vol. 50, 1955, pp. 3–45.
Livre rouge—R.S.F.S.R., Narodnyi Komissariat Inostrannykh Del, *Livre rouge. Recueil des documents diplomatiques relatifs aux relations entre la Russie et la Pologne, 1918–1920.* Moscow, Gos. izd., 1920. (French translation of *Krasnaia kniga,* above.)
LNOJ—League of Nations Official Journal. Geneva.
LNTS—League of Nations, *Treaty Series. Treaties and international engagements registered with the Secretariat of the League of Nations.* Lausanne, 205 vols.
Logunov—Logunov, V. D., *Sovremënnyi mezhdunarodno-pravovoi rezhim Dunaia.* Moscow, Izdatel'stvo Institut Mezhdunarodnykh Otnoshenii, 1958.
LRR—Bilmanis, Alfred, comp., *Latvian-Russian relations.* Washington, D.C., Latvian Legation, 1944.
LS—Lietuvos sutartys su svetimomis valstybemis / Recueil des traités conclus par la Lithanie avec les pays étrangers. Kaunas, Vol. 1, 1930.
LT—La législation turque; lois promulgées par la Grande Assemblée Nationale de Turquie. Istanbul.

Marshall, 1947—Marshall, George C., *The London meeting of the Council of Foreign Ministers, November 25–December 16, 1947.* Washington, D.C., Department of State, 1947.
Martens—Triepel, Henrich, comp., *Nouveau recueil général des traités et autres actes relatifs aux rapports du droit international.* Leipzig.
Mazour—Mazour, Anatole, *Finland between East and West.* Princeton, Van Nostrand, 1956.
MB—Moniteur Belge. Brussels.
McLane—McLane, Charles B., *Soviet policy and the Chinese Communists, 1931–1946.* N.Y., Columbia University Press, 1958.
Memorial—Official journal of the Grand Duchy of Luxembourg.

Meshcheriakov—Meshcheriakov, M. V., *Ocherk ekonomicheskogo sotrudnichestva Sovetskogo Soiuza i Mongol'skoi Narodnoi Respubliki.* Moscow, Vneshtorgizdat, 1959.
Miliukov—Miliukov, Paul, *Bolshevism: An international danger.* London, Allen and Unwin, 1920.
Mirnyi dogovor—Mirnyi dogovor mezhdu Rossiei s odnoi storony i Germaniei, Avstro-Vengriei, Bolgariei i Turtsiei s drugoi. Moscow, 1918.
Mirnyi dogovor mezhdu Rossiei i Gruziei—Moscow, Tipografiia "Prodput," 1920.
Mirnyi dogovor mezhdu Rossiei i Latviei—Mirnyi dogovor mezhdu Rossiei i Latviei / Meera lihgums starp Latwiju un Kreewiju. N.p., n.d.
Mirnyi dogovor mezhdu Ukrainoi i Litvoi—Khar'kov, 6-ia Sovetskaia Tipografiia, 1921.
MK—Magyar Kozlony, Hivatalos Lap. Budapest. Official Hungarian collection of laws.
MKh—Mirovoe khoziaistvo i mirovaia politika. Moscow, monthly.
MO—Monitorul Oficial. Bucharest. Romanian law collection.
MOCI—Moniteur officiel du commerce et de l'industrie. Paris.
Moore—Moore, Harriet L., *Soviet Far Eastern policy, 1931–45.* Princeton, Princeton University Press, 1945.
Mosely, 1950—Mosely, Philip E., "Dismemberment of Germany," *Foreign Affairs,* Vol. 28, 1950, pp. 487–98; "The occupation of Germany," *ibid.,* pp. 580–604.
Mosely, 1951—Mosely, Philip E., "Some Soviet techniques of negotiation," in Raymond Dennett and Joseph E. Johnson, eds., *Negotiating with the Russians,* Boston, World Peace Foundation, 1951, pp. 271–303.
MP, 1930—Sabanin, A. V., ed., *Mezhdunarodnaia politika v 1930 g.* Moscow, Izd. Narkomindel, 1932.
MPID—Mezhdunarodnoe pravo v izbrannykh dokumentakh. Moscow, 2 vols., Institut Mezhdunarodnykh Otnoshenii, 1957.
MP RSFSR, 1922—R.S.F.S.R., Narodnyi Komissariat po Inostrannym Delam, *Mezhdunarodnaia politika RSFSR v 1922 g. Otchët Narodnogo Komissariata po Inostrannym Delam.* Moscow, 1923.
MU—Medunarodni ugovori Federativne Narodne Republike Jugoslavije. Belgrade.
MZh—Mezhdunarodnaia zhizn'. Moscow, monthly.

Navasardian—Navasardian, Vahan, *Bolshevism yev Dashnaktzoutioun.* Cairo, Houssaper, 1949.
NCNA—New China News Agency. Peking.
ND—Neues Deutschland. Berlin, daily.
Norins, *Gateway to Asia*—Norins, M. R., *Gateway to Asia: Sinkiang.* N.Y., John Day, 1944.
NSR—Sontag, Raymond J., and James S. Beddie, eds., *Nazi-Soviet relations, 1939–1941. Documents from the Archives of the German Foreign Office.* Washington, D.C., Department of State, 1948.
NT—New times. Moscow, monthly.
NYT—New York Times. N.Y., daily.

Obrazovanie SSSR—Genkina, E. B., ed., *Obrazovanie SSSR. Sbornik dokumentov, 1917–1924.* Moscow, Izdatel'stvo Akademii Nauk SSSR, 1949.
OSS chronology—U.S., Office of Strategic Services, Research and Analysis Branch, *Chronology of principal events relating to the USSR.* Washington, D.C., 2 vols., 1945.
Ostwirtschaft—Berlin, semi-monthly.
OT—Országos Törvénytár. Budapest.

Parfenov—Parfenov, P. S., *Bor'ba za Dal'nii Vostok, 1920–1922.* Leningrad, "Priboi," 1928.
PC—People's China. Peiping.
PDK—Protokoly Dunaiskoi Komissii / Procès-verbaux de la Commission du Danube. Galatz and Budapest, 1951–; in progress.
Pipes, *Formation of the Soviet Union*—Pipes, Richard E., *Formation of the Soviet Union; communism and nationalism, 1917–1923.* Cambridge, Harvard University Press, 1954.

Pod znamenem—*Pod znamenem proletarskogo internatsionalizma. Sbornik materialov.* Moscow, Gospolitizdat, 1957.
Polish White Book—Poland, Ministry for Foreign Affairs, *Official documents concerning Polish-German and Polish-Soviet relations, 1933–39.* London, Hutchinson, n.d.
Pr.—*Pravda.* Moscow, daily.
Problems of Communism—Washington, D.C., quarterly.
PV—Bruns, Viktor, ed., *Politische Verträge. Eine Sammlung von Urkunden / Traités politiques. Recueil de documents.* Berlin, Carl Heymanns, 1942.

QR—USSR Chamber of Commerce, *Quarterly review.* Moscow.

Radio regulations, 1947—See *International Telecommunications Convention, 1947.*
RDT—*Recueil des traités.* Tokyo, Ministry of Foreign Affairs.
Recent trade agreements—U.S., Department of State, Division of Research for Europe, Office of Intelligence Research, *List of most recent trade agreements between OEEC countries and countries of Eastern Europe (revised).* (DRE Information Paper EER-73, May 3, 1950.)
Records of an inspection tour in Sinkiang—Feng Yu-chen, *Hsin-Chiang Shih-Ch'a Chi.* Shanghai, 1934.
Reference material on the Sino-Soviet conference—*Chung-O Hui-i Ts'an K'ao Wen-chien.* Peking, Ministry for Foreign Affairs, n.d.
RG—*Resmî Gazete.* Official Turkish gazette.
RGBl—*Reichsgesetzblatt.* Berlin.
RIR—*Russian information and review.* London, published by the Information Department of the Russian Trade Delegation.
RMBl—*Reichsministerialblatt.* Berlin.
RO—*Recueil officiel des lois et ordonnances de la Confédération Suisse.*
Roberts—Roberts, Henry L., *Rumania: political problems of an agrarian state.* New Haven, Yale University Press, 1951.
Rönnefarth-Euler—Rönnefarth, Helmuth K. G., and Heinrich Euler, eds., *Konferenzen und Verträge. Vertrags-Ploetz, ein Handbuch geschichtlich bedeutsamer Zusammenkünfte und Vereinbarungen. Teil II, 4. Band: Neueste Zeit, 1914–1959.* 2d ed., Würzburg, A. G. Ploetz, 1959.
Roumania at the Peace Conference—Paris, 1946.
Rozek—Rozek, Edward J., *Allied wartime diplomacy. A pattern in Poland.* N.Y., Wiley, 1958.
RSFSR i GDR—R.S.F.S.R., Narodnyi Kommissariat Inostrannykh Del, *Rossiiskaia Sotsialisticheskaia Federativnaia Sovetskaia Respublika i Gruzinskaia Demokraticheskaia Respublika: ikh vzaimootnosheniia. Sostavleno po ofitsial'nym materialam Narodnogo Komissariata Inostrannykh Del Rossiisskoi Sotsialisticheskoi Respubliki.* Moscow, Gos. izd., 1921.
RT—*Rüigi Teataja.* Official Estonian state gazette.
Rubinshtein—Rubinshtein, N. L., *Vneshniaia politika Sovetskogo gosudarstva v 1921–1925 godakh.* Moscow, Gos. izd. polit. lit., 1953.
Russian review—N.Y., monthly.

Sabanin, 1929—Sabanin, A. V., ed., *Mezhdunarodnaia politika v 1929 godu. Dogovory, deklaratsii i diplomaticheskaia perepiska.* Moscow, Izdanie Narkomindela, 1931.
Sabanin, 1930—*Ibid.,* . . . *v 1930 godu.* Moscow, 1932.
Schechtman—Schechtman, Joseph B., *European population transfers, 1939–1945.* N.Y., Oxford University Press, 1946. (Studies of the Institute of World Affairs.)
Schenk and Lowenthal, 1–3—Schenk, Fritz, and Richard Lowenthal, "Politics and planning in the Soviet empire," *New Leader*, N.Y., Vol. 42, Nos. 1–3, Jan. 5, 12, and 19, 1959.
Schmidt—Schmidt, Dana Adams, *Anatomy of a satellite.* Boston, Little, Brown, 1952.
SCMP—*Survey of the China Mainland Press.* Hong Kong, U.S. Consulate General.
Scott—Scott, James Brown, ed., *The Hague Conventions and Declarations of 1899 and 1907, accompanied by tables of signatures, ratifications and adhesions of the various*

powers and texts of reservations. N.Y., Oxford University Press, 1915. (Carnegie Endowment for International Peace, Division of International Law.)

SDD—USSR, Ministerstvo Inostrannykh Del, *Sbornik deistvuiushchikh dogovorov soglashenii i konventsii, zakliuchënnykh SSSR s inostrannymi gosudarstvami.* Moscow, Gos. izd. polit. lit., 1924–; in progress.

SDD RSFSR—RSFSR, Narodnyi Komissariat po Inostrannym Delam, *Sbornik deistvuiushchikh dogovor, soglashenii i konventsii, zakliuchënnykh R.S.F.S.R. s inostrannymi gosudarstvami.* Moscow, 5 vols., 1921–23.

SDFP—Degras, Jane, ed., *Soviet documents on foreign policy.* London, Oxford University Press, 3 vols., 1951–53. Issued under the auspices of the Royal Institute of International Affairs.

SDTD—USSR, Narodnyi Komissariat po Inostrannym Delam, *Sbornik deistvuiushchikh torgovykh dogovor i inykh khoziaistvennykh soglashenii SSSR, zakliuchënnykh s inostrannymi gosudarstvami. Vypusk 1* . . . Moscow, Izdanie NKID, 1935 (only one number has been identified).

Seidl—Seidl, A., ed., *Die Beziehungen zwischen Deutschland und der Sowjetunion, 1939–1941. Dokumente des Auswärtigen Amtes.* Tübingen, Laupp'sche Buchhandlung, 1949.

SFP PW—Rothstein, Andrew, tr., *Soviet foreign policy during the Patriotic War; documents and materials.* London, Hutchinson, 2 vols., 1944–45.

Sherwood—Sherwood, Robert E., *Roosevelt and Hopkins. An intimate history.* N.Y., Harper, 1948.

Shishkin—Shishkin, S. N., *Grazhdanskaia voina na Dal'nem Vostoke, 1918–1922 gg.* Moscow, Voennoe izdatel'stvo Ministerstva Oborony Soiuza SSSR, 1957.

Shtein, 1923—Shtein, B. Ye., *Torgovaia politika i torgovye dogovory Sovetskoi Rossii, 1917–1922 gg.* Moscow-Petrograd, 1923.

Shtein, 1925—Shtein, B. Ye., *Vneshniaia torgovaia politika SSSR.* Moscow-Leningrad, Tsentral'noe upravlenie pechati VSNKh, 1925.

SIA—*Survey of international affairs.* London, Oxford University Press. Issued annually under the auspices of the Royal Institute of International Affairs.

SIA, ABR—McNeill, William Hardy, *Survey of international affairs, 1939–1946. America, Britain, and Russia. Their co-operation and conflict, 1941–1946.* London, Oxford University Press, 1953.

SIA, FPCGA—Balfour, Michael, and John Mair, *Survey of international affairs, 1939–1946. Four-Power control in Germany and Austria, 1945–1946.* London, Oxford University Press, 1956.

SIA, HE—Toynbee, Arnold, and Veronica M. Toynbee, eds., *Survey of international affairs, 1939–1946. Hitler's Europe.* London, Oxford University Press, 1954.

SIA, RE—Toynbee, Arnold, and Veronica M. Toynbee, eds., *Survey of international affairs, 1939–1946. The realignment of Europe.* London, Oxford University Press, 1955.

SIA, WN—Toynbee, Arnold, and Veronica M. Toynbee, eds., *Survey of international affairs, 1939–1946. The war and the neutrals.* London, Oxford University Press, 1956.

Simmons, 1951—Simmons, Ernest J., "Negotiating on cultural exchange, 1947," in Raymond Dennett and Joseph E. Johnson, eds., *Negotiating with the Russians,* Boston, World Peace Foundation, 1951, pp. 239–69.

Simmons, *USSR*—Simmons, Ernest J., ed., *U.S.S.R., a concise handbook.* Ithaca, N.Y., Cornell University Press, 1947.

Sino-Soviet treaty—*The Sino-Soviet treaty and agreements, signed in Moscow on February 14, 1950.* Peiping, Foreign Languages Press, 1951.

Sipkov—Sipkov, Dr. Ivan, "The Soviet Union treaties and agreements with Bulgaria, 1944–1958," supplement to *Highlights of current legislation and activities in Mid-Europe,* Vol. 7, Nos. 5 and 6, May and June, 1959.

Smirnov—Smirnov, V. P., *Turtsiia. Ekonomika i vneshniaia torgovlia.* Moscow, Vneshtorgizdat, 1956.

Sö—*Sveriges överenskommelser med främmande makter.* Official Swedish treaty series.

Soglasheniia, 1958—*Soglasheniia o sotrudnichestve i pomoshchi v oblasti mirnogo*

ispol'-zovaniia atomnoi energii, zakliuchënnye Sovetskim Soiuzom s drugimi stranami. Moscow, Atomizdat, 1958.
Sovetskaia Rossiia i kapitalisticheskii mir—USSR, Akademiia nauk SSSR, Institut Istorii, *Sovetskaia Rossiia i kapitalisticheskii mir v 1917–1923 gg.* Moscow, Gos. izd. polit. lit., 1957.
Sovetskii Soiuz i koreiskii vopros—USSR, Ministerstvo po Inostrannym Delam, *Sovetskii Soiuz i koreiskii vopros (dokumenty).* Moscow, 1948.
Soviet Russia—N.Y., irregular.
Soviet Union and the Berlin Question, The—USSR, Ministry of Foreign Affairs, *The Soviet Union and the Berlin Question (documents).* Moscow, 1948.
Soviet Union's economic invasion of Sinkiang, The—*Su-lieh Tui Sinkiang Chih Ch'ingchi Ch'in-lüeh.* Taipei, Ministry of Foreign Affairs, 1950.
Sovremënnyi Iran—USSR, Akademiia nauk, Institut Vostokovedeniia, *Sovremënnyi Iran. Spravochnik.* Moscow, Izdatel'stvo Akademii Nauk SSSR, 1957.
SP—*Sobranie postanovlenii i rasporiazhenii pravitel'stva Soiuza Sovetskikh Respublik.* Moscow.
SS—*Sopimussarja.* Official Finnish treaty series.
SSSkS—*Sylloge synthekon, symbaseon kai symphonion.* Official Greek treaty series.
Stalin, *Soch.*—Stalin, J. V., *Sochineniia.* Moscow, 1946–; in progress.
STS—Shapiro, Leonard, ed., *Soviet treaty series. A collection of bilateral agreements and conventions, etc., concluded between the Soviet Union and foreign Powers.* Washington, D.C., Georgetown University Press, 2 vols., 1950–55.
SU—*Sobranie uzakonenii i rasporiazhenii rabochego i krest'ianskogo pravitel'stva RSFSR.* Moscow.
SUR—*Soviet Union review.* Washington, D.C., published by the Soviet Union Information Bureau.
Svoboda Rossii—Moscow, daily.
SZ—*Sobranie zakonov i rasporiazhenii raboche-krest'ianskogo pravitel'stva Soiuza Sovetskikh Sotsialisticheskikh Respublik.* Moscow.
SZ, 1938–1956—*Sbornik zakonov SSSR i ukazov prezidiuma Verkhovnogo Soveta SSSR (1938–Iiul' 1956 gg.).* Moscow, Gos. izd. yur. lit., 1956.
SZN—*Sbírka zákonu i narizení statu československého.* Official Czechoslovak collection of laws.

TA—*Treaties and agreements with and concerning China, 1919–1929.* Washington, D.C., Carnegie Endowment for International Peace, 1929.
TC—*Trattati e convenzioni.* Official Italian treaty series.
Teplinski—Teplinski, L. B., "Sovetsko-Afganskie otnosheniia za sorok let sushchestvovaniia nezavisimogo Afganistana," in *Nezavisimyi Afganistan. 40 let nezavisimosti, sbornik statei.* Moscow, Izdatel'stvo vostochnoi literatury, 1958, pp. 5–38. (Akademiia nauk SSSR, Institut Vostokovedeniia.)
Texts of the Finland "peace"—U.S., Department of State, *Texts of the Finland "peace."* Washington, D.C., 1918.
Thirty-eighth report to Congress on Lend-Lease operations—Washington, D.C., President's Office, 1958.
TIAS—U.S., *Treaties and other international acts series.* Washington, D.C.
Tokareva—Tokareva, P. A., "Mezhdunarodnaia ekonomicheskaia organizatsiia novogo tipa," *Sovetskoe gosudarstvo i pravo,* 1959, No. 2, pp. 104–11.
Trb—*Tractatenbladen.* Official Dutch treaty source.
Trial of Japanese war criminals—U.S., Department of State, *Trial of Japanese war criminals. Documents . . .* Washington, D.C., 1946.
Trial of war criminals—U.S., Department of State, *Trial of war criminals. Documents.* Washington, D.C., 1945.
TRP—U.S., Department of State, *Texts of the Russian "peace."* Washington, D.C., 1918.
Tsybina—Tsybina, K., "The German question and wartime Franco-Soviet relations (1941–1945)," *International affairs,* Moscow, No. 4, 1959, pp. 122–28.

TUP—U.S., Department of State, *Texts of the Ukraine "peace."* Washington, D.C., 1918.
Twentieth report to Congress on Lend-Lease operations—Washington, D.C., President's Office, 1945.

United Nations documents—*United Nations documents, 1941–1945.* London and N.Y., Royal Institute of International Affairs, 1946.
United States and Italy—U.S., Department of State, *United States and Italy, 1936–1946.* Washington, D.C., 1946.
UNTS—United Nations *Treaty Series. Treaties and international agreements registered or filed and recorded with the Secretariat of the United Nations.* N.Y., 1946–; in progress.
UST—*United States treaties and other international agreements.* Washington, D.C.

Varshavskoe soveshchanie — *Varshavskoe soveshchanie yevropeiskikh gosudarstv po obespecheniiu mira i bezopasnosti v Yevrope.* Moscow, Gospolitizdat, 1955.
Verträge der Volksrepublik China—*Die Verträge der Volksrepublik China mit anderen Staaten. Bearbeitet im Institut für Asienkunde, Hamburg.* Frankfurt/Main and Berlin, Metzner, 1957.
Visit of friendship—Bulganin, N.A., and N.S. Khrushchev, *Visit of friendship to India, Burma and Afghanistan. Speeches and official documents. November–December 1955.* Moscow, Foreign languages publishing house, 1956.
Visti VUTsIK—Official Ukrainian collection of laws.
VP—*Vneshniaia politika SSSR. Sbornik dokumentov.* Moscow, Vysshaia partiinaia shkola pri TsK VKP(b), 5 vols., 1944–47.
VPSR—Chicherin, G. V., *Vneshniaia politika sovetskoi Rossii za dva goda.* Moscow, Gos. izd., 1920.
VPSS—*Vneshniaia politika Sovetskogo Soiuza. Dokumenty i materialy.* Moscow, Gos. izd. polit. lit., 8 vols., 1945–50.
VPSS VP—*Vneshniaia politika Sovetskogo Soiuza v period Otechestvennoi Voiny.* Moscow, OGIZ, Gos. izd. polit. lit., 3 vols., 1946–48.
Vratzian—Vratzian, *Haiaisani Hanrabedoutioun.* Paris, Navarre, 1928.
VT—*Vneshniaia torgovlia.* Moscow, monthly.
VT SSSR—*Vneshniaia torgovlia SSSR.* Moscow, Vneshtorgizdat, 1958.
VV—*Valdibas Vestnesis.* Latvian official gazette.
VVerz—*Vertrags-Verzeichnis seit 1920. Stand Oktober 1941.* Berlin, n.d.
VVS—*Vedomosti verkhovnogo soveta.* Moscow.
VŽ—*Vyriausbyés Žinios.* Lithuanian official gazette.

Wei—Wei, Henry, *China and Soviet Russia.* Princeton, Van Nostrand, 1956.
Whiting—Whiting, Allen S., and General Sheng Shi-Ts'ai, *Sinkiang: pawn or pivot?* East Lansing, Michigan State University Press, 1958.
Wu—Wu, Aitchen K., *China and the Soviet Union.* N.Y., John Day, 1950.

Yugoslav White Book—Federal People's Republic of Yugoslavia, Ministry of Foreign Affairs, *White Book on aggressive activities by the governments of the USSR, Poland, Czechoslovakia, Hungary, Rumania, Bulgaria and Albania towards Yugoslavia.* Belgrade, 1951.

Zhizn' natsional'nostei—Moscow, monthly.
Zhukov *et al.*—Zhukov, Ye. M., *et al.*, eds., *Mezhdunarodnye otnosheniia na Dal'nem Vostoke (1840–1949).* 2d ed., Moscow, Gos. izd. polit. lit., 1956.
Zinner—Zinner, Paul E., ed., *National Communism and popular revolt in Eastern Europe.* N.Y., Columbia University Press, 1956.
ZO—*Zahraniční Obchod.* Prague, organ of the Czechoslovak Ministry of Foreign Trade.
ZT—*Zbior Traktatow handlowych Rzeczpospolitej Polskiej.* Warsaw, Ministry for Foreign Affairs.

INDEX

TABLE OF INDEX HEADINGS

Afghanistan,[1,6] bilateral
Three-way
Unverified
Albania,[2] bilateral
Four-way
Argentina, bilateral
Armenia, bilateral
Armenian SSR,[3] bilateral
Australia, bilateral
Austria, bilateral
(including Austria-Hungary[4])
Azerbaidzhan SSR,[3] bilateral
Bashkiria, bilateral
Belgium,[1] bilateral
Belgium-Luxembourg Economic Union,[1] bilateral
Belorussian SSR,[3] bilateral
Bolivia, bilateral
Brazil, bilateral
Bukhara (People's) Soviet Republic,[3] bilateral
Bulgaria,[2,4] bilateral
Three- and four-way
Unverified
Burma,[1] bilateral
Three-way
Cambodia, bilateral
Canada,[5] bilateral
Three-way
Ceylon, bilateral
Chile, bilateral
China,[1,5] bilateral
Unratified
Unverified
(See also Heilungkiang; Sinkiang)
Chinese People's Republic,[2] bilateral
Three-way
Unverified
Colombia, bilateral
Costa Rica, bilateral
Cuba, bilateral
Czechoslovakia,[1,2,6] bilateral
Three-way
Unverified
Danzig,[6] see Poland, bilateral
Denmark,[1] bilateral
Four-way
Dominican Republic, bilateral
Ecuador, bilateral
Egypt,[1] bilateral
Estonia,[1,6] bilateral
Three- and four-way
Unverified
Ethiopia, bilateral
Far Eastern Republic,[3] bilateral
Finland,[1,6] bilateral
Three-way
Unverified
Finnish Democratic Republic, bilateral
Finnish Socialist Workers' Republic, bilateral

France,[1,5] bilateral
Unverified
Georgian Democratic Republic, bilateral
Georgian SSR,[3] bilateral
Germany,[1,4] bilateral
Secret military agreements
Three-way
Unverified
Germany, Federal Republic,[1] bilateral
Germany, Soviet Republic, unverified
German Democratic Republic,[1,2] bilateral
Three-way
Greece,[1] bilateral
Unratified
Unverified
Guatemala, bilateral
Heilungkiang, bilateral
Hejaz, bilateral
Hungary,[2] bilateral
Three-way
Unratified
Unverified
Hungarian Soviet Republic, unverified
Iceland, bilateral
India,[1] bilateral
Indonesia, bilateral
Iran,[1,6] bilateral
Three-way
Unratified
Unverified
Iraq, bilateral
Israel, bilateral
Italy,[1] bilateral
Unratified
Japan,[1] bilateral
Three-way
Unratified
Unverified
Khorezm Soviet People's Republic,[3] bilateral
Korean People's Democratic Republic,[2] bilateral
Three-way
Latvia,[6] bilateral
Three- and four-way
Lebanon, bilateral
Liberia, bilateral
Libya, bilateral
Liechtenstein, see Switzerland, bilateral
Lithuania, bilateral
Luxembourg, bilateral
(See also Belgium-Luxembourg Economic Union)
Manchukuo,[1] bilateral
Three-way
Mexico, bilateral
Mongolian People's Republic,[2] bilateral
Three-way
Unverified

Morocco, bilateral
Multilateral: International agreements and conferences
League of Nations
United Nations
Unratified
Nepal, bilateral
Netherlands,[1] bilateral
New Zealand, bilateral
Nicaragua, bilateral
Nongovernmental
Norway,[1] bilateral
Three-way
Pakistan,[1] bilateral
Persia—see Iran
Plurilateral: Central Powers
Great Power agreements and conferences
Internal Soviet treaties
Nonaggression agreements
Soviet bloc agreements and conferences
Poland,[2,6] bilateral
Three-way
Unverified
Private organizations
Romania,[2,6] bilateral
Three- and four-way
Unverified
San Marino, bilateral
Sinkiang,[1] bilateral
Unverified
Slovakia, bilateral
Spain,[1] bilateral
Sweden,[1] bilateral
Four-way
Unratified
Switzerland,[1] bilateral
Four-way
Sudan, bilateral
Syria, bilateral
Unverified
Tannu Tuva, bilateral
Thailand,[1] bilateral
Tunisia, bilateral
Turkey,[1,4,6] bilateral
Unverified
Ukraine, bilateral
Ukrainian SSR,[3] bilateral
Union of South Africa, bilateral
United Kingdom,[1,5] bilateral
Three-way
Unratified
United States of America,[1,5] bilateral
Uruguay, bilateral
Unratified
Vatican City, bilateral
Venezuela, bilateral
Vietnam, Democratic Republic of,[2] bilateral
Yemen, bilateral
Yugoslavia,[2,6] bilateral
Three-way

[1] See also Nongovernmental agreements. [2] See also Plurilateral, Soviet bloc agreements and conferences. [3] See also Plurilateral, internal Soviet treaties. [4] See also Plurilateral, Central Powers. [5] See also Plurilateral, Great Power agreements and conferences. [6] See also Plurilateral, Nonaggression agreements.

461

AFGHANISTAN, bilateral

Apr. 21 and May 27, 1919. Exchange of letters concerning reciprocal recognition. 8
Sept. 13, 1920. Provisional treaty. 12
Feb. 28, 1921. Treaty of friendship. 17
Feb. 1, 1926. Protocol concerning removal of Soviet troops from the island Urta-Tugai in the Amu-Darya River, entry of Afghan troops to the island, and establishment of a mixed commission to determine ownership of the island. 433
Aug. 18, 1926. Protocol concerning transfer of the island Urta-Tugai to Afghanistan. 433
Aug. 31, 1926. Treaty of neutrality and non-aggression, with final protocol. 57
Nov. 28, 1927. Agreement concerning the airline Kabul-Tashkent. 63
June 1928. Agreement concerning transformation of diplomatic missions into embassies. 433
Oct. 15, 17, and 19, 1929. Exchange of telegrams concerning recognition of a new regime in Afghanistan. 72
June 24, 1931. Treaty of neutrality and non-aggression. 78
Apr. 3, 1932. Agreement concerning postal communications. 434
Apr. 3, 1932. Agreement concerning telegraph and radio-telegraph communications. 434
Sept. 13, 1932. Exchange of notes constituting an agreement concerning settlement of border incidents. 83
Nov. 14, 1933. Exchange of notes concerning maintenance of friendly relations. 434
May 6, 1935. Agreement concerning the campaign against locusts. 102
Mar. 29, 1936. Protocol extending the treaty of neutrality and nonaggression of June 24, 1931. 110
July 3, 1937. Exchange of notes extending the agreements of April 3, 1932, concerning postal, telegraph, and radio-telegraph communications. 435
May 26, 1938. Agreement concerning the campaign against parasites and diseases of the cotton plant. 121
July 27, 1940. Trade agreement. 137
Oct. 11 and 16, 1941. Exchange of notes concerning expulsion of Italians and Germans from Afghanistan. 435
June 13, 1946. Agreement concerning demarcation of the border, with protocol. 213
June 13, 1946. Exchange of notes concerning demarcation of a sector of the border. 213
June 13, 1946. Exchange of notes concerning use of water from the Kushka River. 213
Apr. 13, 1947. Agreement concerning establishment of radio-telegraph communications. 231
Sept. 29, 1948. Protocol concerning demarcation of the border, with maps and annexes. 253

July 17, 1950. Trade and payments agreement. 276
Sept. 1952. Agreement concerning showing Soviet films in Afghanistan. 290
Dec. 24, 1953. Trade protocol for 1954. 305
Jan. 27, 1954. Credit agreement. 306
May 24, 1954. Credit agreement. 313
Oct. 5, 1954. Agreement concerning Soviet credit and technical aid for paving the streets of Kabul and vicinity. 316
Nov. 28, 1954. Trade protocol for 1955. 319
Dec. 1954. Agreement concerning showing Soviet films in Afghanistan. 442
June 28, 1955. Agreement concerning goods transit. 330
Aug. 14, 1955. Parcel post agreement. 334
Aug. 27, 1955. Trade protocol for 1955. 335
Dec. 18, 1955. Protocol extending the treaty of neutrality and nonaggression of June 24, 1931. 344
Dec. 18, 1955. Joint communiqué concerning economic relations. 345
Dec. 18, 1955. Joint statement concerning political relations. 345
Jan. 7, 1956. Trade protocol. 444
Jan. 28, 1956. Agreement concerning credit and technical aid to Afghanistan. 347
Jan. 28, 1956. Joint communiqué concerning economic relations. 348
Mar. 1, 1956. Agreement concerning technical aid to Afghanistan. 350
Mar. 24, 1956. Agreement concerning establishment of regular air communications. 351
Oct. 30, 1956. Joint communiqué concerning the visit of H. R. H. Sardar Mohammed Daoud, Prime Minister of Afghanistan, to the USSR. 371
Jan. 7, 1957. Trade protocol for 1957 and 1958. 375
July 30, 1957. Joint communiqué concerning a state visit of the King of Afghanistan to the USSR. 386
July 31, 1957. Communiqué concerning relations between the USSR and Afghanistan. 386

AFGHANISTAN, three-way

June 30, 1947. Documents concerning the border mark at the junction of the borders of the USSR, Afghanistan, and Iran (USSR, Afghanistan, Iran). 233

AFGHANISTAN, unverified

Aug. 1956. Agreement concerning a Soviet loan of twenty-five million dollars. 430

Afghanistan. See also Nongovernmental agreements.

ALBANIA, bilateral

July 4 and Sept. 4, 1924. Exchange of notes concerning establishment of diplomatic relations. 47

Sept. 17, 1934. Exchange of notes concerning establishment of diplomatic relations. 97

Nov. 10, 1945. Exchange of notes concerning establishment of diplomatic relations. 201

July 26, 1947. Joint communiqué concerning economic and cultural relations. 235

July 26, 1947. Credit agreement. 235

Dec. 15, 1947. Agreement concerning training of Albanian citizens in civic institutions of higher learning in the USSR and their maintenance. 241

Sept. 3, 1948. Trade agreement. 252

Sept. 3, 1948. Agreement concerning a Soviet trade credit for Albania. 252

Apr. 10, 1949. Joint communiqué concerning economic relations. 258

Apr. 10, 1949. Agreement concerning delivery of industrial equipment to Albania on credit. 258

Apr. 10, 1949. Trade protocol for 1949. 258

June 27, 1950. Agreement concerning collaboration in the field of radio broadcasting, with supplementary protocol. 275

Jan. 16, 1951. Protocol supplementing the agreement of December 15, 1947, concerning training of Albanian citizens in the USSR. 279

Feb. 17, 1951. Agreement concerning delivery to Albania on credit of industrial equipment during the period 1951–1955, together with technical assistance to Albania. 280

Feb. 17, 1951. Trade agreement for 1951. 280

Apr. 19, 1952. Agreement concerning conditions of trade deliveries. 286

Apr. 19, 1952. Agreement concerning scientific and technical collaboration. 286

July 5, 1952. Agreement concerning training of Albanian citizens in civic institutions of higher education in the USSR. 288

Apr. 8, 1953. Trade protocol for 1953. 295

Aug. 3, 1953. Verbal agreement concerning transformation of diplomatic missions into embassies. 299

Nov. 10, 1953. Joint communiqué concerning a meeting of the Soviet-Albanian commission for scientific and technical collaboration. 303

Mar. 6, 1954. Trade protocol for 1954. 308

Mar. 4, 1955. Trade protocol for 1955. 324

Apr. 17, 1955. Communiqué concerning the second meeting of the Soviet-Albanian commission for scientific and technical collaboration. 325

Aug. 27, 1955. Convention concerning quarantine and combating parasites and diseases of agricultural plants, with annex. 334

Dec. 6, 1955. Agreement concerning air communications, with protocol. 343

Feb. 11, 1956. Trade agreement for 1956. 349

May 3, 1956. Agreement concerning cultural collaboration. 354

May 30, 1956. Agreement concerning air communications and reciprocal services. 356

May 30, 1956. Agreement concerning technical collaboration in the field of civil aviation. 356

July 4, 1956. Communiqué concerning the third meeting of the Soviet-Albanian commission for scientific and technical collaboration. 360

Jan. 10, 1957. Agreement concerning postal and telephone and telegraph communications. 375

Jan. 10, 1957. Parcel post agreement. 375

Feb. 23, 1957. Trade agreement for 1957. 378

Apr. 17, 1957. Joint declaration concerning political and economic relations. 381

Sept. 18, 1957. Convention concerning regulation of the question of citizenship of persons of dual citizenship. 389

Sept. 18, 1957. Consular convention. 389

Nov. 22, 1957. Agreement concerning technical and economic aid for the period 1957–1960. 392

Dec. 7, 1957. Communiqué concerning preparation of a plan for cultural and scientific collaboration in 1958. 393

ALBANIA, four-way

Aug. 20, 1952. Agreement concerning establishment of a regular steamship line between the Black Sea ports of the USSR, Bulgaria, and Romania, and the ports of Albania, with two annexes (USSR, Albania, Bulgaria, Romania). 290

Albania. See also Plurilateral, Soviet bloc agreements and conferences.

ARGENTINA, bilateral

June 5, 1946. Exchange of notes concerning establishment of diplomatic, consular, and commercial relations. 212

Aug. 5, 1953. Trade and payments agreement, with two annexes. 299

Aug. 15, 1954. Exchange of notes concerning extension of the validity of the annexes to the trade and payments agreement of August 5, 1953. 315

Sept. 3, 1954. Exchange of notes constituting an agreement on the exchange of motion pictures. 316

May 19, 1955. Trade protocol for 1955, with two annexes. 328

ARMENIA, bilateral

Aug. 10, 1920. Military agreement. 12

Dec. 2, 1920. Agreement concerning recognition of the independence of Armenia. 16

ARMENIAN SSR, bilateral

Sept. 30, 1921. Agreement concerning financial matters. 24

Armenian SSR. See also Plurilateral, internal Soviet treaties.

AUSTRALIA, bilateral

Oct. 10, 1942. Exchange of notes concerning establishment of diplomatic relations. 152
July 15, 1947. Exchange of notes concerning transformation of diplomatic mission into embassies. 234

AUSTRIA, bilateral (including Austria-Hungary)

Jan. 31, 1918. Agreement concerning repatriation of civilians. 2
Feb. 10, 1918. Protocol and supplement to the agreement of January 31, 1918, concerning repatriation of civilians. 2
Feb. 13, 1918. Agreement concerning treatment of prisoners of war. 2
Feb. 14, 1918. Agreement concerning temporary rules for postal, telegraph, and railroad communications, with final protocol. 3
Mar. 3, 1918. Treaty concerning political and legal matters, supplementing the peace treaty between the RSFSR and the Central Powers. 4
June 3, 1918. Agreement concerning repatriation of prisoners of war. 5
July 5, 1920. Agreement concerning repatriation of prisoners of war and interned civilians. 11
Jan. 17, 1921. Agreement concerning redemption of treasury bills deposited with the Austro-Hungarian Bank in favor of the Ukrainian State. 16
Dec. 7, 1921. Temporary agreement concerning future relations. 27
Dec. 7, 1921. Agreement extending the agreement of July 5, 1920, concerning repatriation of prisoners of war and interned civilians. 27
July 28, 1923. Agreement concerning embassy buildings. 40
Sept. 8, 1923. Exchange of notes extending to the USSR the temporary agreement of December 7, 1921, concerning future relations. 40
Feb. 25 and 26, 1924. Exchange of notes concerning recognition of the USSR de jure. 41
Sept. 19, 1924. Agreement concerning legal assistance in civil cases. 48
Apr. 6, 1927. Exchange of notes concerning suspension of Art. 8 of the agreement of September 19, 1924, concerning legal assistance in civil cases. 59

Apr. 26, 1927. Exchange of notes concerning reciprocal registration of trade-marks. 60
July 16, 1927. Agreement concerning execution of the agreement of July 28, 1923, concerning embassy buildings. 61
Apr. 29, 1945. Announcement of recognition by the USSR of the Provisional Government of Austria. 176
Oct. 20 and 24, 1945. Exchange of notes concerning re-establishment of diplomatic relations. 200
July 16, 1946. Communication concerning Soviet claims on German assets in Austria. 215
June 9 and 12, 1953. Verbal agreement concerning transformation of diplomatic missions into embassies. 296
July 17, 1953. Agreement concerning transfer to Austria of assets of the hydroelectric station at Ybbs-Persenbeug. 297
July 30, 1953. Exchange of notes concerning occupation costs. 298
Jan. 5 and 16, 1954. Exchange of notes concerning preparation of a state treaty for Austria. 441
Apr. 15, 1955. Joint communiqué concerning the visit to Moscow of a delegation of the Austrian Government. 325
Apr. 15, 1955. Memorandum concerning results of negotiations. 325
May 15, 1955. State Treaty for the re-establishment of an independent and democratic Austria, with two annexes and two maps. 328
July 12, 1955. Agreement concerning deliveries by Austria to the USSR in payment for Soviet property transferred to Austria. 332
July 12, 1955. Agreement concerning oil deliveries by Austria to the USSR in payment for oil works and refineries transferred by the USSR to Austria. 332
Aug. 31, 1955. Final protocol concerning the transfer to Austria of Soviet property in Austria. 335
Oct. 17, 1955. Treaty of commerce and navigation, with annex concerning the Soviet Trade Mission in Austria. 339
Oct. 17, 1955. Payments agreement. 339
Oct. 17, 1955. Trade agreement, with annexes. 339
Nov. 9, 1955. Agreement concerning air communications, with annex. 340
Nov. 14 and Dec. 6, 1955. Exchange of notes concerning Austrian neutrality. 444
Dec. 28, 1955. Parcel post agreement. 345
Aug. 2, 1956. Agreement concerning exchange of films. 365
Oct. 4, 1956. Trade protocol for 1957, with annexes. 368
Apr. 27, 1957. Joint communiqué concerning political and economic relations. 382
June 14, 1957. Agreement concerning technical and commercial aspects of navigation on the Danube. 385

Oct. 10, 1957. Trade agreement for the period 1958–1960. 390
Oct. 10, 1957. Trade protocol for 1958. 390

Austria-Hungary. See also Plurilateral, Central Powers.

AZERBAIDZHAN SSR, bilateral

Sept. 30, 1920. Treaty of military and economic alliance. 14
Sept. 30, 1920. Agreement concerning coordination of food policies. 14
Sept. 30, 1920. Agreement concerning unification of the administration of posts, telegraph, telephone, and radio-telegraph. 14
Sept. 30, 1920. Agreement concerning financial matters. 14
Sept. 30, 1920. Agreement concerning foreign trade. 14
Sept. 30, 1920. Agreement concerning conduct of a unified economic policy. 14

Azerbaidzhan SSR. See also Plurilateral, internal Soviet treaties.

BASHKIRIA, bilateral

Mar. 23, 1919. Agreement concerning establishment of the Autonomous Bashkir Republic within the RSFSR. 7

BELGIUM, bilateral

Apr. 20, 1920. Agreement concerning political relations. 9
Apr. 20, 1920. Agreement concerning repatriation of military and civilian personnel. 432
July 12, 1935. Exchange of notes concerning establishment of diplomatic relations. 104
Apr. 16, 1938. Parcel post agreement. 121
Apr. 4, 1941. Trade and payments agreement. 143
Aug. 7, 1941. Agreement concerning re-establishment of diplomatic relations. 145
Dec. 26, 1942, and Jan. 21, 1943. Exchange of notes concerning reorganization of diplomatic missions into embassies. 153.
Mar. 13, 1945. Agreement concerning repatriation of citizens displaced as a result of the war. 174
Nov. 27, 1945, and Apr. 18, May 3 and 11, 1946. Exchange of notes concerning execution of judicial instructions. 212
Feb. 12 and June 28, 1951. Exchange of notes concerning tariff duties and weight categories under the parcel post agreement of April 16, 1938. 282
Nov. 21, 1951, and Feb. 5, 1952. Exchange of notes concerning an alteration in tax rates under the parcel post agreement of April 16, 1938. 284
Aug. 26 and Sept. 11, 1953. Exchange of

notes modifying the parcel post agreement of April 16, 1938. 301
Aug. 30, 1956. Communiqué concerning an informal agreement concerning cultural exchange. 366
Oct. 25, 1956. Agreement concerning cultural collaboration. 370
Nov. 2, 1956. Joint communiqué concerning political, economic, and cultural relations. 371
Nov. 2, 1956. Protocol concerning establishment of direct air communications between Moscow and Brussels. 371

Belgium. See also Nongovernmental agreements.

BELGIUM-LUXEMBOURG ECONOMIC UNION, bilateral

Sept. 5, 1935. Temporary commercial treaty. 106
Nov. 5, 1937. Exchange of notes extending and modifying the temporary commercial treaty of September 5, 1935. 119
Aug. 21 and Oct. 1, 1939. Exchange of notes extending the temporary commercial treaty of September 5, 1935. 130
Feb. 18, 1948. Exchange of notes concerning application of the active provisions of the temporary commercial treaty of Sept. 5, 1935. 244
Feb. 18, 1948. Commercial agreement, with two annexes. 244
Feb. 18, 1948. Payments agreement. 245
Nov. 14, 1950. Trade protocol. 278
Jan. 30, 1954. Trade protocol for 1954. 306
Aug. 2, 1956. Trade protocol for 1956. 365

Belgium-Luxembourg Economic Union. See also Nongovernmental agreements.

BELORUSSIAN SSR, bilateral

Jan. 16, 1921. Military-economic alliance. 16
July 26, 1921. Agreement concerning financial matters. 22
Jan. 19, 1922. Agreement concerning entry of the Belorussian SSR into the Federal Committee on Agricultural Affairs. 28
Nov. 2, 1939. Agreement concerning incorporation of Western Belorussia into the USSR. 435

Belorussian SSR. See also Plurilateral, internal Soviet treaties.

BOLIVIA, bilateral

Apr. 18, 1945. Exchange of notes concerning establishment of diplomatic and consular relations. 176

BRAZIL, bilateral

Apr. 2, 1945. Exchange of notes concerning

establishment of diplomatic and consular relations. 437

BUKHARA SOVIET REPUBLIC (and Bukhara People's Soviet Republic), bilateral

Nov. 1920. Temporary military-political agreement. 15
Mar. 4, 1921. Treaty of alliance. 19
Mar. 4, 1921. Economic agreement. 19
Aug. 9, 1922. Economic agreement. 34
May 31, 1923. Customs agreement, with supplementary protocol. 39

Bukhara People's Soviet Republic. See also Plurilateral, internal Soviet treaties.

BULGARIA, bilateral

Feb. 11, 1918. Agreement concerning repatriation of civilians, with protocol and supplementary protocol. 2
Feb. 14, 1918. Agreement concerning postal, telegraph, and maritime service, with supplementary protocol. 3
Mar. 3, 1918. Treaty concerning political and legal matters, supplementing the peace treaty between the RSFSR and the Central Powers. 4
July 23, 1934. Exchange of telegrams concerning establishment of diplomatic relations. 95
July 23, 1934. Protocol concerning non-interference in internal affairs. 96
July 10, 1935. Parcel post agreement. 104
Dec. 11, 1939. Convention concerning establishment of air communications between Moscow and Sofia. 132
Jan. 5, 1940. Treaty of commerce and navigation, with annex concerning the Soviet Trade Mission in Bulgaria. 133
Jan. 5, 1940. Agreement concerning trade and payments during 1940. 133
Sept. 6 and 9, 1944. Cease-fire agreement. 163
Oct. 11, 1944. Agreement concerning preliminary conditions for an armistice. 166
Oct. 28, 1944. Armistice agreement. 167
Dec. 30, 1944. Agreement concerning handing over to Bulgaria of eleven individuals accused as war criminals. 169
Mar. 14, 1945. Trade agreement, with five annexes. 175
Aug. 14, 1945. Exchange of notes concerning re-establishment of diplomatic relations. 193
Dec. 15, 1945. Supplementary trade agreement. 202
Mar. 23, 1946. Bulgarian law establishing a Soviet-Bulgarian mining company. 208
Apr. 27, 1946. Trade agreement for 1946. 211
Apr. 27, 1946 (approximate date). Protocol concerning completion of Soviet deliveries

under the trade agreement of March 14, 1945. 211
Feb. 10, 1947. Treaty of peace, with six annexes. 226
July 5, 1947. Trade and payments agreement. 233
Aug. 23, 1947. Agreement concerning deliveries of industrial equipment to Bulgaria on credit. 236
Nov. 15, 1947. Agreement concerning training of Bulgarian citizens in civic institutions of higher learning in the USSR and their maintenance. 238
Dec. 17, 1947. Agreement concerning establishment of postal and telephone-telegraph communications, with final protocol. 241
Dec. 17, 1947. Parcel post agreement. 241
Jan. 6, 1948. Agreement concerning transformation of diplomatic missions into embassies. 438
Jan. 10, 1948. Two protocols concerning regulation of certain questions connected with the transfer of former German assets in Bulgaria to Soviet possession. 243
Mar. 18, 1948. Treaty of friendship, cooperation, and mutual assistance. 246
Apr. 1, 1948. Treaty of commerce and navigation, with annex concerning the Soviet Trade Mission in Bulgaria. 247
Apr. 1, 1948. Trade agreement for 1948. 247
Aug. 9, 1948. Credit agreement. 251
May 28, 1949. Bulgarian law establishing a Soviet-Bulgarian civil aviation company. 259
Dec. 1949. Agreement concerning direct rail communications. 264
Feb. 18, 1950. Agreement concerning scientific and technical collaboration. 271
Feb. 18, 1950. Trade protocol for 1950. 271
May 20 and 24, 1950. Exchange of notes concerning execution of letters rogatory. 274
Aug. 25, 1950. Convention concerning quarantine of agricultural plants and their protection from parasites and diseases. 277
Mar. 14, 1951. Trade protocol for 1951. 280
Apr. 10, 1951. Agreement concerning scientific research on the biology of commercial fishes of the Black Sea and exchange of experience on the technique of fishing. 281
Feb. 9, 1952. Trade protocol for 1952. 285
Mar. 7, 1952. Agreement concerning training of Bulgarian citizens in civic institutions of higher learning in the USSR. 285
June 16, 1952. Agreement concerning conditions of trade deliveries. 287
Jan. 1953. Trade agreement for the period 1953–1955. 441
Mar. 31, 1953. Trade protocol for 1953. 294
Aug. 27 and Sept. 17, 1953. Exchange of notes modifying the parcel post agreement of December 17, 1947. 301
Jan. 17, 1954. Communiqué concerning the fourth meeting of the Soviet-Bulgarian commission for scientific and technical collaboration. 305

Feb. 11, 1954. Trade protocol for 1954. 307

June 7, 1954. Trade agreement for the period 1955–1957. 313

Sept. 30, 1954. Communiqué concerning the fifth meeting of the Soviet-Bulgarian commission for scientific and technical collaboration. 316

Oct. 9, 1954. Agreement concerning transfer and sale to Bulgaria of Soviet shares in Soviet-Bulgarian joint-stock companies. 317

Mar. 2, 1955. Trade protocol for 1955. 324

Mar. 5, 1955. Agreement concerning air transportation of passengers, baggage, freight, and mail between Moscow and Sofia. 324

July 8, 1955. Communiqué concerning the sixth meeting of the Soviet-Bulgarian commission for scientific and technical collaboration. 331

Nov. 26, 1955. Agreement concerning transfer to Bulgaria of Soviet shares in the Soviet-Bulgarian joint-stock mining company "Gorubso." 342

Jan. 14, 1956. Trade protocol for 1956. 347

Feb. 3, 1956. Economic agreement for the period 1956–1959. 348

Apr. 28, 1956. Agreement concerning cultural collaboration. 354

Aug. 5, 1956. Communiqué concerning an agreement concerning technical collaboration in the field of civil aviation. 365

Dec. 12, 1956. Communiqué concerning the eighth meeting of the Soviet-Bulgarian commission for scientific and technical collaboration. 374

Jan. 12, 1957. Trade protocol for 1957. 375

Feb. 4, 1957. Protocol concerning cultural collaboration in 1957. 377

Feb. 20, 1957. Joint declaration concerning political and economic relations. 378

Apr. 1957. Agreement concerning conditions for sending Soviet specialists to Bulgaria and vice versa for rendering technical aid and other services. 380

Apr. 1957. Agreement concerning conditions for technical industrial training of Bulgarian specialists and workers in the USSR and vice versa. 380

May 18, 1957. Agreement concerning delivery of ships and other naval equipment to the USSR during the period 1958–1960. 383

Sept. 5, 1957. Protocol concerning the ninth meeting of the Soviet-Bulgarian commission for scientific and technical collaboration. 389

Nov. 19, 1957. Trade agreement for the period 1958–1960. 391

Nov. 19, 1957. Trade protocol for 1958. 391

Nov. 19, 1957. Agreement concerning trade for the period 1960–1970. 391

Nov. 30, 1957. Protocol concerning preparation of a plan of cultural and scientific collaboration. 392

Dec. 12, 1957. Treaty concerning legal aid in civil, family, and criminal cases. 393

Dec. 12, 1957. Consular convention. 393

Dec. 12, 1957. Convention concerning regulation of the question of citizenship of persons with dual citizenship. 393

Dec. 29, 1957. Communiqué concerning the tenth meeting of the Soviet-Bulgarian commission for scientific and technical collaboration. 396

Dec. 31, 1957. Protocol concerning settlement of noncommercial payments. 396

BULGARIA, three- and four-way

Aug. 20, 1952. Agreement concerning establishment of a regular steamship line between the Black Sea ports of the USSR, Bulgaria, and Romania, and the ports of Albania, with two annexes (USSR, Bulgaria, Albania, Romania). 290

Sept. 11, 1956. Agreement concerning collaboration in saving human life and assistance to vessels and aircraft in distress on the Black Sea (USSR, Bulgaria, Romania). 367

BULGARIA, unverified

Aug. 22, 1947. Long-term trade agreement. 429

Aug. 22, 1947. Three-way clearing agreement. 429

Bulgaria. See also Plurilateral, Central Powers; Plurilateral, Soviet bloc treaties and conferences.

BURMA, bilateral

Feb. 18, 1948. Exchange of notes concerning establishment of diplomatic and consular relations. 245

July 1, 1955. Commercial agreement, with annexes. 331

July 1, 1955. Trade protocol, with related documents. 331

Nov. 3, 1955. Joint statement. 340

Dec. 6, 1955. Joint statement concerning political relations. 343

Dec. 6, 1955 (approximate date). Statement on economic relations. 343

Apr. 1, 1956. Joint declaration. 352

Apr. 1, 1956. Supplementary trade agreement. 352

Apr. 1, 1956. Long-term trade protocol, with related documents. 352

Jan. 17, 1957. Economic agreement, with annex. 376

Aug. 29, 1957. General contract agreement. 388

BURMA, three-way

Oct. 9, 1956. Agreement concerning the use of multilateral trade accounting (USSR, Burma, Czechoslovakia). 368

Burma. See also Nongovernmental agreements.

CAMBODIA, bilateral

May 18, 1956. Communiqué concerning establishment of diplomatic relations. 355
July 7, 1956. Joint communiqué concerning political negotiations. 363
May 31, 1957. Commercial agreement, with two annexes. 384
May 31, 1957. Agreement concerning cultural and scientific collaboration. 384
May 31, 1957. Payments agreement. 384
May 31, 1957. Agreement concerning construction of a hospital in Pnom-Penh. 384

CANADA, bilateral

Mar. 24, 1924. Exchange of notes concerning recognition of the USSR de jure. 42
Feb. 5, 1942. Agreement concerning establishment of consular relations. 149
June 12, 1942. Agreement concerning establishment of diplomatic relations. 150
Sept. 8, 1942. Credit agreement. 151
Nov. 17, 1943. Exchange of notes concerning reorganization of diplomatic missions into embassies. 157
Feb. 11, 1944. Agreement concerning principles relating to the provision by Canada of military supplies for the USSR. 158
Sept. 29, 1950. Exchange of notes constituting an agreement concerning payment by the USSR for supplies delivered by Canada in 1945–1946. 277
Oct. 12, 1955. Joint communiqué concerning negotiations. 339
Feb. 29, 1956. Commercial agreement. 349
Feb. 29, 1956. Exchange of notes concerning reservation by Canada of the right to fix values of imported goods for ordinary and special duty. 349
Feb. 29, 1956. Exchange of notes concerning Soviet purchases of wheat in Canada. 350

CANADA, three-way

Oct. 8, 1944. Protocol to the armistice agreement with Finland concerning compensation to Canada for nickel mines in former Finnish territory (USSR, Canada, United Kingdom). 165
Sept. 29, 1947. Protocol concerning modification in the method of payment by the USSR to Canada under the protocol of October 8, 1944, to the armistice agreement with Finland (USSR, Canada, United Kingdom). 237

Canada. See also Plurilateral, Great Power agreements and conferences.

CEYLON, bilateral

Sept. 1, 1956. Joint communiqué concerning political and economic relations. 360

CHILE, bilateral

Dec. 11, 1944. Exchange of notes concerning establishment of diplomatic and consular relations. 168

CHINA, bilateral

Mar. 1918. Border agreement. 3
Jan. 6, 1921. Agreement concerning the disarming and evacuation of White Russian troops. 16
May 31, 1924. Agreement concerning general principles for the settlement of problems, with seven declarations and an exchange of notes. 43
May 31, 1924. Agreement concerning provisional management of the Chinese Eastern Railway, 43
May 31, 1924. Exchange of notes concerning establishment of diplomatic relations. 43
Sept. 20, 1924. Agreement concerning mutual rights and privileges. 48
Jan. 24, 1926. Agreement concerning settlement of the dispute over the Chinese Eastern Railway. 54
Dec. 3, 1929. Protocol concerning settlement of the conflict over the Chinese Eastern Railway. 72
Dec. 22, 1929. Protocol concerning settlement of the conflict over the Chinese Eastern Railway. 73
Dec. 12, 1932. Exchange of notes concerning re-establishment of diplomatic and consular relations. 86
Nov. 20, 1936. Parcel post agreement. 113
Aug. 21, 1937. Treaty of nonaggression. 118
May 1938. Agreement concerning two loans to China each of fifty million dollars. 121
June 16, 1939. Commercial treaty, with annex concerning the Soviet Trade Mission in China. 125
June 16, 1939. Exchange of notes supplementing the commercial treaty of June 16, 1939. 126
July 10, 1939 (approximate date). Agreement concerning a loan to China of 150 million dollars. 126
Sept. 9, 1939. Agreement concerning establishment of regular air communications between Alma-Ata and Hami. 127
July 27, 1940 (approximate date). Trade agreement. 137
Dec. 11, 1940 (approximate date). Trade agreement. 141
Jan. 3, 1941. Trade agreement. 141
Jan. 12, 1941. Trade agreement. 142
Feb. 16, 1944. Agreement concerning the purchase by China of the Wu-su Hsien oil field installations and equipment from the USSR. 159
July 14, 1945. Joint communiqué concerning negotiations. 437
Aug. 14, 1945. Treaty of friendship and alliance. 191
Aug. 14, 1945. Exchange of notes concerning relations. 191

Aug. 14, 1945. Exchange of notes concerning Outer Mongolia. 191

Aug. 14, 1945. Agreement concerning the port of Dairen, with protocol. 191

Aug. 14, 1945. Agreement concerning Port Arthur, with annex and map. 192

Aug. 14, 1945. Agreement concerning relations between the Soviet commander-in-chief and the Chinese administration following the entry of Soviet forces into the territory of the Three Eastern Provinces in connection with the war against Japan, with annexed protocol. 192

Aug. 14, 1945. Protocol concerning evacuation of Soviet forces from Chinese territory after the capitulation of Japan. 192

Aug. 14, 1945. Agreement concerning the Chinese Changchun Railway. 192

Nov. 1945. Informal agreement concerning a delay in evacuation of Soviet troops from Manchuria. 201

Nov. 27, 1945. Agreement concerning withdrawal of Chinese Communist forces from Changchun and Mukden and their occupation by Chinese Nationalist forces. 201

Mar. 23, 1946. Announcement concerning withdrawal of Soviet forces from Manchuria, except Port Arthur and Dairen. 208

May 1949. Agreement concerning civil aviation. 259

CHINA, unratified

Mar. 14, 1924. General agreement. 400

CHINA, unverified

1940. Agreement concerning a Soviet loan to China of fifty million dollars. 429

June 16, 1940. Agreement concerning a Soviet credit for purchase of supplies. 429

China. See also Nongovernmental agreements; Plurilateral, Great Power agreements and conferences.

CHINESE PEOPLE'S REPUBLIC, bilateral

Oct. 1 and 2, 1949. Exchange of telegrams concerning establishment of diplomatic relations. 263

Feb. 7, 1950. Agreement concerning exchange of mail and parcel post. 268

Feb. 7, 1950. Agreement concerning establishment of telephone and telegraph communications, with protocol. 268

Feb. 14, 1950. Joint communiqué concerning conclusion of political and economic treaties and agreements. 269

Feb. 14, 1950. Treaty of friendship, alliance, and mutual assistance. 269

Feb. 14, 1950. Exchange of notes concerning political relations. 269

Feb. 14, 1950. Agreement concerning the Chinese Changchun Railway, Port Arthur, and Dairen. 269

Feb. 14, 1950. Credit agreement. 270

Feb. 14, 1950. Exchange of notes concerning transfer to the CPR of industrial and commercial enterprises and other property acquired by Soviet organizations from Japanese owners in 1945. 270

Feb. 14, 1950. Exchange of notes concerning transfer to the CPR of Soviet buildings in the military compound of Peking, with map and annex. 270

Mar. 27, 1950. Agreement concerning establishment of a Soviet-CPR joint-stock oil company, "Sovkitneft." 272

Mar. 27, 1950. Agreement concerning establishment of a Soviet-CPR joint-stock company for production of nonferrous metals, "Sovkitmetall." 272

Mar. 27, 1950. Agreement concerning establishment of a Soviet-CPR joint-stock civil aviation company, "SKOGA." 272

Mar. 27, 1950. Agreement concerning working conditions of Soviet specialists sent to the CPR as instructors and advisers in Chinese organizations. 272

Apr. 19, 1950. Commercial agreement, with two annexes. 273

Apr. 19, 1950. Trade agreement for 1950. 273

Apr. 19, 1950. Protocol concerning delivery by the USSR of equipment and goods under the credit agreement of February 14, 1950. 273

July 20, 1950. Protocol concerning transfer to the CPR of Soviet buildings in the military compound of Peking. 276

Aug. 7, 1950. Agreement concerning measures for the transfer to the CPR of industrial and commercial properties acquired by Soviet organizations from Japanese owners in 1945. 276

Aug. 28, 1950. Agreement concerning completion of the transfer to the CPR of industrial and commercial properties acquired by Soviet organizations from Japanese owners in 1945, with related documents. 277

Oct. 25, 1950. Agreement concerning working conditions for Soviet specialists sent to the CPR to give technical assistance in the installation and operation of Soviet equipment. 278

Jan. 2, 1951. Agreement concerning navigation procedure on the border rivers Amur, Ussuri, Argun, and Sungacha and on Lake Hanka, and the establishment of conditions for navigation on these waterways. 279

Jan. 16, 1951. Agreement concerning direct rail communications. 279

Mar. 14, 1951. Agreement concerning direct rail communications, with related documents. 280

June 15, 1951. Trade protocol for 1951. 281

June 15, 1951. Protocol concerning delivery

by the USSR of equipment and goods under the credit agreement of February 14, 1950. 281

July 28, 1951. Agreement concerning establishment of a USSR-CPR joint-stock company for ship building and repair, "Sovkitsudostroi." 282

Dec. 6, 1951. Agreement concerning technical training of CPR specialists in the USSR. 283

Apr. 12, 1952. Trade protocol for 1952. 286

Apr. 12, 1952. Protocol concerning delivery by the USSR of equipment and goods under the credit agreement of February 14, 1950. 286

Mar. 29, 1952. Agreement concerning conditions of trade deliveries. 285

Aug. 9, 1952. Agreement concerning training of CPR citizens in civic institutions of higher education in the USSR. 289

Aug. 9, 1952. Exchange of notes concerning training of CPR citizens in the USSR. 290

Sept. 15, 1952. Joint communiqué on negotiations. 290

Sept. 15, 1952. Joint communiqué concerning transfer of the Chinese Changchun Railway to the CPR. 290

Sept. 15, 1952. Exchange of notes concerning extension of the stay of Soviet troops in Port Arthur. 290

Sept. 21, 1952. Trade agreement. 291

Dec. 31, 1952. Protocol concerning transfer to the CPR of the Chinese Changchun Railway. 292

Dec. 31, 1952. Documents concerning transfer of assets and operations of the Soviet Foreign Insurance Administration in Northeast China (Manchuria) to the China People's Insurance Company. 292

Mar. 21, 1953. Trade protocol for 1953. 294

Mar. 21, 1953. Protocol concerning delivery by the USSR of equipment and goods under the credit agreement of February 14, 1950. 294

Mar. 21, 1953. Agreement concerning aid to the CPR in enlarging electro-stations already in operation and construction of new ones. 294

Summer, 1953. Agreement concerning Soviet material and technical aid. 296

Aug. 26 and Oct. 31, 1953. Exchange of notes modifying the parcel post agreement of February 7, 1950. 303

Jan. 23, 1954. Trade protocol for 1954. 306

Jan. 23, 1954. Protocol concerning delivery by the USSR of equipment and goods under the credit agreement of February 14, 1950. 306

May 29, 1954. Agreement concerning distribution of films in the CPR. 441

Aug. 21, 1954. Agreement concerning collaboration in the field of radio broadcasting. 315

Oct. 12, 1954. Communiqué on negotiations. 317

Oct. 12, 1954. Joint declaration concerning Soviet-CPR relations and the international situation. 317

Oct. 12, 1954. Joint declaration concerning relations with Japan. 317

Oct. 12, 1954. Joint communiqué concerning withdrawal of Soviet troops from the naval base at Port Arthur and transfer of the naval base to the CPR. 317

Oct. 12, 1954. Joint communiqué concerning transfer to the CPR of Soviet shares in Soviet-CPR joint-stock companies. 317

Oct. 12, 1954. Agreement concerning scientific and technical collaboration. 318

Oct. 12, 1954. Joint communiqué concerning construction of a railroad, Lanchow–Urumchi–Alma-Ata, and the organization of direct communications. 318

Oct. 12, 1954. Credit agreement. 318

Oct. 12, 1954. Protocol concerning Soviet technical aid. 318

Dec. 28, 1954. Protocol concerning the first meeting of the USSR–Chinese People's Republic commission for scientific and technical collaboration. 321

Dec. 30, 1954. Agreement concerning establishment of regular air communications. 321

Dec. 30, 1954. Protocol concerning termination of the USSR-CPR joint-stock civil aviation company and transfer of Soviet shares in the company to the CPR. 321

Dec. 30, 1954. Protocol concerning termination of the USSR-CPR joint-stock company for nonferrous and rare metals and transfer of Soviet shares in the company to the CPR. 321

Dec. 31, 1954. Protocol concerning termination of the USSR-CPR joint-stock oil company and transfer of Soviet shares in the company to the CPR. 321

Dec. 31, 1954. Protocol concerning termination of the USSR-CPR joint-stock company for shipbuilding and repair and transfer of Soviet shares in the company to the CPR. 321

Feb. 11, 1955. Trade protocol for 1955. 323

Apr. 27, 1955. Agreement concerning aid by the USSR to the CPR in regard to development of research concerning atomic nuclear physics and the use of atomic energy for the needs of the national economy. 326

May 24, 1955. Protocol concerning evacuation of Soviet troops from Port Arthur and transfer of its installations to the CPR. 329

June 13, 1955. Protocol concerning the second meeting of the USSR-CPR commission for scientific and technical collaboration. 330

Aug. 16, 1955. Convention concerning quarantine and combating parasites and diseases of agricultural plants, with two annexes. 334

Nov. 29, 1955. Agreement concerning reciprocal acquisition of copyright on films. 444

Dec. 1955. Protocol concerning the third meeting of the USSR-Chinese People's Republic commission for scientific and technical collaboration. 342

Dec. 27, 1955. Trade protocol for 1956. 345

Jan. 4, 1956. Agreement concerning technical collaboration in the field of civil aviation. 346

Jan. 5, 1956. Communiqué concerning the third meeting of the USSR–Chinese People's Republic commission for scientific and technical collaboration. 346

Apr. 7, 1956. Joint communiqué concerning economic negotiations. 352

Apr. 7, 1956. Agreement concerning aid by the USSR in construction of fifty-five industrial enterprises. 353

Apr. 7, 1956. Agreement concerning collaboration in construction of a railroad from Lanchow to Aktogai on the Turksib Railroad. 353

June 23, 1956. Communiqué concerning the fourth meeting of the USSR–Chinese People's Republic commission for scientific and technical collaboration. 358

July 5, 1956. Agreement concerning cultural collaboration. 360

July 25, 1956. Supplementary trade protocol for 1956. 364

Aug. 18, 1956. Agreement concerning joint scientific exploration of natural resources and prospects for development of productive forces in the Amur River basin. 366

Dec. 26, 1956. Communiqué concerning the fifth meeting of the USSR–Chinese People's Republic commission for scientific and technical collaboration. 374

Jan. 18, 1957. Joint declaration concerning international relations. 376

Feb. 15, 1957. Protocol concerning extension and development of postal and electronic means of communication. 377

Apr. 11, 1957. Trade protocol for 1957. 381

May 26, 1957. Communiqué concerning the visit of a Soviet governmental delegation to the Chinese People's Republic. 383

July 18, 1957. Communiqué concerning the sixth meeting of the USSR–Chinese People's Republic commission for scientific and technical collaboration. 386

Dec. 21, 1957. Agreement concerning the regime of commercial navigation on border waterways and tributary streams and lakes. 395

Dec. 30, 1957. Protocol concerning settlement of non-commercial payments. 396

CHINESE PEOPLE'S REPUBLIC, three-way

Sept. 15, 1952. Agreement concerning construction of a railroad from Tsinin to Ulan-Bator and establishment of direct rail communications (USSR, CPR, Mongolian People's Republic). 291

Sept. 21, 1952. Trade and payments agreement, with two annexes (USSR, CPR, Finland). 291

Oct. 12, 1954. Joint communiqué concerning construction of a railroad from Tsinin to Ulan-Bator and the organization of direct communications (USSR, CPR, Mongolian People's Republic). 318

Oct. 17, 1955. Protocol concerning opening of through rail traffic between the USSR and the CPR by way of the Mongolian People's Republic (USSR, CPR, MPR). 340

Jan. 4, 1956. Joint communiqué concerning opening of direct rail communications (USSR, CPR, Mongolian People's Republic). 346

July 3, 1956. Agreement concerning collaboration in saving human lives and aiding ships and airplanes wrecked in the waters of the Far Eastern Seas and the Pacific Ocean (USSR, CPR, Korean People's Democratic Republic). 360

Jan. 12, 1957. Communiqué concerning a meeting between representatives of the Communist and Workers' Parties and Governments (USSR, CPR, Hungary). 375

CHINESE COMMUNIST REGIME, unverified

1949. Secret agreements ("Harbin" and "Moscow" agreements). 429

Chinese People's Republic. See also Plurilateral, Soviet bloc agreements and conferences.

COLOMBIA, bilateral

June 25, 1935. Exchange of notes concerning establishment of diplomatic relations. 103

Feb. 3 and 4, 1943. Exchange of notes concerning exchange of ambassadors. 153

COSTA RICA, bilateral

May 8, 1944. Exchange of notes concerning establishment of diplomatic and consular relations. 160

CUBA, bilateral

Oct. 5, 1942. Exchange of notes concerning establishment of diplomatic and consular relations. 152

CZECHOSLOVAKIA, bilateral

June 5, 1922. Temporary treaty concerning trade and commerce and the maintenance of neutrality. 32

June 6, 1922. Temporary treaty concerning trade and commerce and the maintenance of neutrality (with the Ukrainian SSR). 32

Dec. 8, 1923. Agreement concerning import of agricultural machinery for Czechoslovak settlers in the Crimea, the Ukraine, and the Caucasus. 433

June 9, 1934. Exchange of notes concerning establishment of diplomatic relations. 95

Dec. 7, 1934. Exchange of notes concerning Czechoslovakia's adherence to the Franco-Soviet protocol of December 5, 1934, concerning conclusion of an Eastern Pact. 98

Mar. 25, 1935. Treaty of commerce and navigation, with annex and final protocol. 100

Mar. 25, 1935. Agreement concerning reciprocal protection of rights to industrial property, with final protocol. 100

May 16, 1935. Treaty of mutual assistance, with protocol of signature. 102

May 16, 1935. Agreement concerning establishment of regular air service between Moscow and Prague. 102

June 3, 1935. Credit agreement. 103

June 8, 1935. Parcel post agreement. 103

June 11, 1935. Communiqué concerning negotiations. 103

Nov. 16, 1935. Consular convention, with final protocol. 107

July 18, 1941. Agreement concerning resumption of diplomatic relations and mutual aid in the war against Germany. 144

Sept. 27, 1941. Military agreement. 147

Jan. 22, 1942. Agreement concerning a loan for maintenance of a Czech brigade in Soviet territory. 148

Sept. 28, 1942. Exchange of notes concerning reorganization of diplomatic missions into embassies. 151

May 28, 1943. Agreement concerning a grant of funds, materials, and services for maintenance of the Czech Brigade on Soviet territory for the duration of the war. 154

Dec. 12, 1943. Treaty of friendship, mutual assistance, and postwar collaboration, with protocol. 158

May 8, 1944. Agreement concerning relations between the Soviet High Command and Czechoslovak administrative authorities after the entry of Soviet troops into Czechoslovak territory. 160

Mar. 31, 1945. Joint communiqué concerning the visit of Czechoslovak President Beneš to Moscow. 437

June 29, 1945. Treaty concerning the incorporation of Sub-Carpathian Ruthenia (Transcarpathian Ukraine) into the Ukrainian SSR, with protocol and map. 181

Sept. 8, 1945. Preliminary trade agreement. 196

Oct. 22, 1945. Agreement concerning establishment of mail and telephone-telegraph communications, with final protocol. 200

1946. Agreement concerning direct railroad freight communications. 205

Apr. 12, 1946. Trade agreement, with protocols. 210

Apr. 12, 1946. Protocol concerning settlement of unfinished accounts remaining from prewar trade operations. 210

July 10, 1946. Agreement concerning choice of citizenship and resettlement. 214

July 25, 1946. Agreement concerning establishment of air services, with protocol. 216

July 25, 1946. Joint communiqué concerning negotiations. 437

Oct. 25, 1946. Informal agreement modifying the agreement of July 10, 1946, concerning choice of citizenship and resettlement. 220

July 12, 1947. Joint communiqué concerning trade relations. 234

Nov. 28, 1947. Convention concerning quarantine of agricultural plants and their protection from parasites and diseases. 239

Dec. 11, 1947. Treaty of commerce and navigation, with annex concerning the Soviet Trade Mission in Czechoslovakia. 240

Dec. 11, 1947. Trade and payments agreement. 240

Dec. 11, 1947. Agreement concerning a short-term credit for Czechoslovakia. 240

Dec. 11, 1947. Agreement concerning scientific and technical collaboration. 240

Feb. 9, 1948. Agreement concerning general conditions of deliveries from Czechoslovakia to the USSR, with protocol. 244

June 11, 1948. Agreement concerning training of Czechoslovak citizens in civic institutions of higher education in the USSR and their maintenance. 249

Dec. 15, 1948. Joint communiqué concerning economic relations. 255

Feb. 22, 1950. Trade protocol for 1950. 271

Feb. 22, 1950. Agreement concerning technical training of Czechoslovak specialists in the USSR. 271

Nov. 3, 1950. Five-year economic agreement. 278

Nov. 29, 1950. Protocol concerning working conditions for Soviet specialists sent to Czechoslovakia to give technical assistance. 278

Mar. 13, 1951. Protocol concerning supplementary commodity deliveries during 1951. 280

Mar. 14, 1951. Protocol concerning general conditions of deliveries. 280

Aug. 8, 1951. Parcel post agreement, with protocol. 282

Aug. 8, 1951. Changes in the agreement of Oct. 22, 1945, concerning establishment of mail and telephone-telegraph communications. 283

Apr. 5, 1952. Trade agreement. 285

Apr. 5, 1952. Agreement concerning general conditions of deliveries. 285

Apr. 11, 1952. Agreement concerning training of Czechoslovak citizens in civic institutions of higher learning in the USSR. 286

Feb. 1953. Long-term trade agreement. 293

June 16, 1953. Agreement supplementing the convention of November 28, 1947, concerning quarantine of agricultural plants. 296

Jan. 8, 1954. Joint communiqué concerning the fifth meeting of the Soviet-Czechoslovak commission for scientific and technical collaboration. 305

Apr. 15, 1954. Trade protocol for 1954. 310

May 5, 1954. Communiqué concerning the sixth meeting of the Soviet-Czechoslovak commission for scientific and technical collaboration. 312

Nov. 3, 1954. Agreement concerning non-commercial payments. 442

Feb. 26, 1955. Agreement concerning establishment of regular air communications. 324

Apr. 19, 1955. Communiqué concerning the seventh meeting of the Soviet-Czechoslovak commission for scientific and technical collaboration. 326

Apr. 20, 1955. Trade protocol for 1955. 326

Apr. 23, 1955. Agreement concerning aid by the USSR to Czechoslovakia in regard to development of research concerning atomic nuclear physics and the use of atomic energy for the needs of the national economy. 326

Dec. 14, 1955. Trade protocol for 1956. 344

June 1, 1956. Agreement concerning cultural collaboration. 357

June 10, 1956. Communiqué concerning the ninth meeting of the Soviet-Czechoslovak commission for scientific and technical collaboration. 358

Nov. 30, 1956. Treaty concerning the regime on the border and procedure for settling border incidents, with related documents. 373

Jan. 11, 1957. Protocol concerning the tenth meeting of the Soviet-Czechoslovak commission for scientific and technical collaboration. 375

Jan. 12, 1957. Agreement concerning cultural collaboration. 375

Jan. 14, 1957. Trade agreement for 1957. 376

Jan. 29, 1957. Joint declaration concerning political and economic relations. 376

May 18, 1957. Agreement concerning collaboration in the field of veterinary science. 383

May 19, 1957. Communiqué concerning the first meeting of the Soviet-Czechoslovak commission for economic collaboration. 383

June 25, 1957. Communiqué concerning the eleventh meeting of the Soviet-Czechoslovak commission for scientific and technical collaboration. 385

July 6, 1957. Agreement concerning final settlement of property and financial questions arising out of the incorporation of the Transcarpathian Ukraine into the Ukrainian SSR. 385

July 16, 1957. Communiqué concerning the visit of a Soviet governmental and party delegation to Czechoslovakia. 386

Aug. 31, 1957. Agreement concerning legal assistance in civil, family, and criminal cases. 388

Oct. 5, 1957. Convention concerning regulation of the question of citizenship of persons with dual citizenship. 390

Oct. 5, 1957. Consular convention. 390

Oct. 16, 1957. Protocol concerning cultural collaboration in 1958. 391

Oct. 17, 1957. Agreement concerning exchange of students and candidates for education in institutions of higher education and scientific and technical institutions. 391

Dec. 4, 1957. Convention concerning collaboration in the field of public health service. 392

Dec. 10, 1957. Agreement concerning collaboration between the Academies of Sciences of the USSR and Czechoslovakia. 393

Dec. 13, 1957. Trade agreement for the period 1958–1960. 393

Dec. 13, 1957. Trade protocol for 1958. 393

Dec. 20, 1957. Communiqué concerning the twelfth meeting of the Soviet-Czechoslovak commission for scientific and technical collaboration. 395

CZECHOSLOVAKIA, three-way
(Cz—Czechoslovakia ; F—Finland)

June 29, 1949. Trade and payments agreement (USSR, Cz, F). 261

1950. Trade and payments protocol (USSR, Cz, F). 274

1951. Trade and payments protocol (USSR, Cz, F). 279

1952. Trade and payments protocol (USSR, Cz, F). 440

1953. Trade and payments protocol (USSR, Cz, F). 293

1954. Trade and payments protocol (USSR, Cz, F). 305

1955. Trade and payments protocol (USSR, Cz, F). 321

1956. Trade and payments protocol (USSR, Cz, F). 346

Oct. 9, 1956. Agreement concerning the use of multilateral trade accounting (USSR, Cz, Burma). 368

CZECHOSLOVAKIA, unverified

June 18, 1944. Agreement concerning printing Czechoslovak currency in the USSR for use of civilian authorities and the Red Army. 429

June 30, 1944. Agreement concerning appointment of a delegate to liberated territory. 429

May 1950. Secret agreement concerning Russification of the Czechoslovak Army. 429

Czechoslovakia. See also Nongovernmental agreements; Plurilateral, Soviet bloc agreements and conferences; Plurilateral, Nonaggression agreements.

DANZIG. See Plurilateral, Nonaggression agreements; Poland, bilateral.

DENMARK, bilateral

Sept. 21, 1918. Trade and credit agreement. 7
Dec. 18, 1919. Agreement concerning repatriation. 8
Apr. 23, 1923. Preliminary agreement concerning political and economic relations, with protocol and declaration concerning claims. 38
June 18, 1924. Note extending recognition de jure to the USSR. 43
June 18, 1924. Exchange of notes constituting an agreement on commerce and navigation, with declaration concerning claims. 44
Dec. 13, 1924, and June 23 and 29, 1925. Exchange of notes constituting an agreement concerning reciprocal recognition of tonnage measurement certificates. 51
Dec. 23, 1927. Exchange of notes concerning reciprocal registration of trade-marks. 64
Jan. 24, 1929. Exchange of notes extending the agreement of June 29, 1925, concerning reciprocal recognition of tonnage measurement certificates. 68
June 11, 1934. Trade agreement. 95
June 17, 1935. Trade agreement for 1935. 103
June 29, 1936. Parcel post agreement. 112
July 7, 1936. Trade agreement. 112
July 22, 1936. Agreement modifying the trade agreement of July 7, 1936. 112
Nov. 30, 1938. Exchange of notes concerning payment for goods supplied to the USSR during 1937. 122
Sept. 18, 1940. Trade and payments agreement. 139
May 21, 1941. Trade protocol. 144
Apr. 18 and 23, 1944. Exchange of notes concerning establishment of diplomatic relations. 160
May 10 and 16, 1945. Exchange of notes concerning re-establishment of diplomatic relations. 178
Mar. 3, 1946. Announcement of beginning of evacuation of Soviet military units from the island of Bornholm. 208
July 8, 1946. Commercial agreement. 214
July 8, 1946. Trade protocol. 214
Aug. 8, 1946. Agreement concerning establishment of telegraph communications, with annex. 217

Aug. 17, 1946. Treaty of commerce and navigation, with annex concerning the Soviet Trade Mission in Denmark. 217
Aug. 17, 1946. Protocol concerning temporary principles of arbitration. 217
July 8, 1948. Protocol modifying and extending the commercial agreement of July 8, 1946, and extending the arbitration protocol of August 17, 1946. 250
July 8, 1948. Trade protocol. 250
July 17, 1953. Trade protocol, with two annexes. 297
Sept. 7, 1955. Agreement concerning transformation of diplomatic missions into embassies. 336
Mar. 6, 1956. Joint communiqué concerning political and other relations. 350
Mar. 6, 1956. Agreement concerning saving human lives in the Baltic Sea. 350
Mar. 31, 1956. Agreement concerning air communications between Moscow and Copenhagen, with two annexes and an exchange of notes. 351
May 14, 1956. Trade protocol for the period 1956–1958. 355
June 14, 1956. Agreement concerning communications between the rescue services of the USSR and Denmark for collaboration in saving human lives in the Baltic Sea. 358

DENMARK, four-way

Aug. 9, 1918. Agreement concerning exchange of civilian and military personnel (RSFSR, Denmark, Sweden, Switzerland). 6

Denmark. See also Nongovernmental agreements.

DOMINICAN REPUBLIC, bilateral

Mar. 7 and 8, 1945. Exchange of notes concerning establishment of diplomatic and consular relations. 174

ECUADOR, bilateral

June 12 and 16, 1945. Exchange of notes concerning establishment of diplomatic and consular relations. 180

EGYPT, bilateral

July 6 and 26, 1943. Exchange of notes concerning establishment of diplomatic relations. 154
Mar. 3, 1948. Trade agreement. 245
Mar. 3, 1948. Protocol concerning commercial relations. 246
Feb. 23, 1952. Barter agreement. 285
Aug. 18, 1953. Payments agreement. 299
Mar. 23, 1954. Agreement concerning transformation of diplomatic missions into embassies. 308

Mar. 27, 1954. Commercial agreement, with two annexes. 309

Mar. 27, 1954. Exchange of notes concerning transportation of trade shipments. 309

Mar. 27, 1954. Exchange of notes concerning Soviet trade representatives in Egypt. 309

May 12, 1955. Protocol concerning extension of validity of trade lists. 327

Sept. 1955. Agreement concerning shipment of Czechoslovak munitions to Egypt. 443

May 24, 1956. Parcel post agreement. 356

June 22, 1956. Joint communiqué concerning political negotiations. 358

July 12, 1956. Agreement concerning collaboration in regard to the use of atomic energy for peaceful purposes. 363

July 15, 1956. Protocol concerning establishment of a Soviet Trade Mission in Egypt. 364

Sept. 4, 1956. Trade agreement. 367

Mar. 14, 1957. Trade agreement. 379

Oct. 19, 1957. Agreement concerning cultural collaboration. 391

Nov. 1–20, 1957. Negotiations. 445

Dec. 9, 1957. Joint communiqué concerning cultural collaboration. 393

Egypt. See also Nongovernmental agreements.

ESTONIA, bilateral

Nov. 19, 1919. Agreement concerning exchange of hostages and civilian prisoners. 8

Dec. 31, 1919. Treaty concerning suspension of hostilities. 8

Feb. 2, 1920. Peace treaty, with annexes and supplementary articles. 8

Mar. 31, 1920. Treaty concerning delivery of goods from Sweden to the RSFSR. 432

Apr. 6, 1920. Agreement concerning procedure for choice of citizenship. 9

Aug. 19, 1920. Agreement concerning repatriation of prisoners of war, refugees, hostages, and others. 12

Sept. 17, 1920. Convention concerning direct rail communications for passengers and freight. 13

Sept. 17, 1920. Protocol of a conference for conclusion of a convention concerning direct rail communications for passengers and freight. 13

Sept. 17, 1920. Agreement concerning movement of through trains. 13

Sept. 17, 1920. Regulations concerning the transportation of passengers and their baggage and freight in direct rail communications. 13

Sept. 17, 1920. Agreement concerning direct rail communications and the exchange of freight cars. 13

Dec. 2, 1920, and Jan. 25, 1921. Temporary postal agreement. 17

Mar. 16, 1921. Temporary agreement concerning telegraph communications. 19

Nov. 25, 1921. Treaty concerning future relations. 26

Nov. 25, 1921. Agreement concerning procedure for choosing Estonian or Ukrainian citizenship, with annex. 26

May 9, 1922. Treaty concerning rafting timber. 31

May 27, 1922. Supplementary protocol to the treaty of November 25, 1921, concerning future relations. 32

June 25, 1922. Sanitary convention. 33

Feb. 17, 1923. Supplementary protocol to the treaty of November 25, 1921, concerning future relations. 37

July 5, 1923. Convention concerning direct rail communications for passengers and freight. 39

July 5, 1923. Protocol concerning rail communications. 39

July 5, 1923. Protocol concerning rail communications. 39

June 27, 1924. Convention concerning postal communications, with final protocol and supplementary protocol. 45

June 27, 1924. Convention concerning telephone communications, with final protocol and supplementary protocol. 45

June 27, 1924. Convention concerning telegraph and radio-telegraph communications, with final protocol and supplementary protocol. 45

June 27, 1924. Agreement concerning exchange of postal money orders, with final protocol. 46

June 27, 1924. Regulations concerning exchange of postal money orders. 46

Mar. 4, 1926. Exchange of notes constituting a provisional agreement concerning reciprocal recognition of tonnage measurement certificates. 55

Aug. 8, 1927. Agreement concerning procedure for settlement of border disputes, with protocol. 61

Mar. 3, 1928. Agreement concerning reciprocal protection of trade and commercial marks. 65

May 17, 1929. Commercial treaty, with final protocol. 70

May 17, 1929. Exchange of notes concerning most-favored-nation regime in trade treaties. 70

May 17, 1929. Exchange of notes concerning certificates of origin of goods. 70

Jan. 20, 1930. Agreement concerning legal aid in civil cases, with final protocol. 73

Dec. 22, 1930, and Jan. 8, 1931. Exchange of notes modifying the agreement of January 20, 1930, concerning legal aid in civil cases. 76

Oct. 22, 1931. Protocol modifying the protocol to the agreement of August 8, 1927, concerning procedure for settlement of border disputes. 79

Apr. 22, 1932. Agreement concerning direct freight shipments to and from Leningrad and transit through Estonia. 82

May 4, 1932. Treaty concerning nonaggression and the peaceful settlement of disputes. 82
June 16, 1932. Convention concerning conciliation procedure. 83
Apr. 4, 1934. Protocol extending the treaty of May 4, 1932, concerning nonaggression and the peaceful settlement of disputes. 93
July 30, 1934. Communiqué concerning political negotiations. 96
Oct. 31, 1934. Trade agreement. 97
Oct. 28, 1936. Exchange of notes concerning repair of border markers. 113
Feb. 26, 1938. Trade agreement for 1938. 120
Sept. 28, 1939. Pact of mutual assistance. 128
Sept. 28, 1939. Trade agreement. 128
June 16, 1940. Soviet ultimatum demanding formation of a new government in Estonia and the entrance of Soviet troops into major cities. 136

ESTONIA, three- and four-way

Mar. 30, 1922. Final protocol concerning economic problems and the consolidation of peace in Eastern Europe (RSFSR, Estonia, Latvia, Poland). 30
Aug. 19, 1925. Agreement defining areas subject to control under the convention of August 19, 1925, concerning suppression of the contraband traffic in alcoholic products (USSR, Estonia, Finland). 52
Oct. 29, 1925. Convention concerning through passenger and freight communications by rail, with related documents (USSR, Estonia, Latvia). 53
Apr. 22, 1926. Protocol defining state borders under the agreement of August 19, 1925, supplementary to the convention of the same date concerning suppression of the contraband traffic in alcoholic products, with final protocol (USSR, Estonia, Finland). 56
Apr. 21, 1933. Agreement abrogating the convention of October 29, 1925, concerning through passenger and freight communications by rail, and the annexed regulations (USSR, Estonia, Latvia). 86

ESTONIA, unverified

Jan. 11, 1939. Trade agreement. 428

Estonia. See also Nongovernmental agreements; Plurilateral, Nonaggression agreements.

ETHIOPIA, bilateral

Apr. 21, 1943. Exchange of notes concerning establishment of diplomatic relations. 154
June 2, 1956. Joint communiqué concerning transformation of diplomatic missions into embassies. 357

FAR EASTERN REPUBLIC, bilateral

May 14, 1920. Telegram extending recognition to the Far Eastern Republic. 10
Nov. 15, 1920. Agreement concerning establishment of zoological farm reservations in the region of Lake Baikal. 15
Nov. 30, 1920. Convention concerning direct rail communications. 15
Nov. 30, 1920. Convention concerning conditions of navigation on internal border waterways. 15
Dec. 15 and 30, 1920. Treaty concerning boundaries. 16
Sept. 20, 1922. Agreement concerning passport matters. 35

Far Eastern Republic. See also Plurilateral, internal Soviet treaties.

FINLAND, bilateral

July 29, 1918. Agreement concerning liberation and exchange of citizens arrested for political reasons. 6
Jan. 15, 1919. Agreement concerning conditions of trade. 431
Aug. 13, 1920. Armistice agreement. 12
Oct. 14, 1920. Peace treaty, with note, five declarations, and an annex (Treaty of Dorpat). 15
Aug. 23, 1921. Agreement concerning establishment of border trading posts. 22
Sept. 7, 1921. Temporary agreement concerning transfer of railroad rolling stock. 22
Sept. 7, 1921. Temporary agreement concerning rafting timber in the Minalanioki and Tulemanioki Rivers. 24
Oct. 11, 1921. Agreement concerning rafting timber in the Repola and Porosozero volosts. 25
Oct. 31, 1921. Act regulating the functions of the Central Russian-Finnish Mixed Commission, established under Art. 37 of the peace treaty of October 14, 1920. 25
Dec. 14, 1921. Temporary agreement concerning rail transportation of passengers, baggage and freight from Finland to Russia and vice versa, via the frontier stations of Rajajoki and Valeasaari (Beloostrov). 27
Mar. 21, 1922. Agreement transferring the solution of border incidents to the Central Mixed Russo-Finnish Commission. 30
June 1, 1922. Agreement concerning measures for ensuring security of the border, with protocol. 32
June 13, 1922. Temporary agreement concerning establishment of telegraph communications. 33
June 22, 1922. Temporary agreement concerning establishment of postal communications. 33
July 7, 1922. Agreement concerning former government property. 34

Aug. 12, 1922. Agreement concerning repatriation, with three declarations. 34

Aug. 12, 1922. Agreement concerning the return of ships. 34

Sept. 20, 1922. Agreement concerning fishing regulations in the Gulf of Finland. 35

Oct. 21, 1922. Convention concerning fishing and seal hunting in territorial waters of the Arctic Ocean. 35

Oct. 28, 1922. Agreement concerning maintenance of the main channel and fishing in the border water systems. 35

Oct. 28, 1922. Convention concerning floating of timber in water courses running from the territory of Russia into the territory of Finland and vice versa. 36

Oct. 28, 1922. Agreement concerning the conditions under which the RSFSR and its citizens shall be entitled to free transit through the district of Petsamo (Pechenga). 36

Oct. 28, 1922. Convention concerning fishing and seal hunting on Lake Ladoga. 36

Jan. 2 and 4, 1923. Exchange of notes concerning consular matters. 37

Feb. 12, 14, and 21, 1923. Exchange of notes concerning exemption of certain urban property from stamp duty and all other charges on the occasion of its homologation or registration. 38

June 5, 1923. Agreement concerning navigation by Finnish merchant and cargo vessels of the Neva between Lake Ladoga and the Gulf of Finland, with protocol. 39

July 28, 1923. Agreement concerning maintenance of order in the parts of the Gulf of Finland situated outside territorial waters, the upkeep of maritime installations, and pilotage service in the Gulf. 40

July 31, 1923. Protocol modifying the convention of October 21, 1922, concerning fishing and seal hunting. 40

June 18, 1924. Convention concerning telephone communications, with final protocol. 41

June 18, 1924. Convention concerning postal communications, with supplementary protocol. 44

June 18, 1924. Convention concerning telegraph communications, with supplementary protocol and annex. 44

June 18, 1924. Convention concerning direct transportation of passengers and freight by rail. 44

June 18, 1924. Regulations concerning direct transportation of passengers and freight by rail. 45

June 18, 1924. Agreement concerning reciprocal return of archives and documents of public institutions, with protocol and annex. 45

July 12, 1924. Protocol concerning identification papers of citizens engaged in fishing and seal hunting on Lake Ladoga, with annex. 46

Feb. 20, 1925. Agreement concerning exchange of postal money orders. 50

Mar. 29, 1927. Agreement modifying the Regulations of June 18, 1924, concerning direct transportation of passengers and freight by rail. 59

Sept. 2, 1927. Exchange of notes concerning regulations for Finnish merchant and cargo vessels navigating the Neva. 61

Mar. 17, 1928. Agreement concerning regulations for Finnish merchant and cargo vessels navigating the Neva. 65

Sept. 24, 1928. Exchange of notes constituting an agreement concerning appointment of border commissioners on the Karelian Isthmus. 67

Nov. 17, 1928. Exchange of notes modifying the Regulations of June 18, 1924, concerning direct transportation of passengers and freight. 68

Apr. 13, 1929. Convention concerning customs supervision in the Gulf of Finland, with final protocol. 69

Apr. 13, 1929. Protocol amending the agreement of July 28, 1923, concerning maintenance of order in the Gulf of Finland, in accordance with the convention of April 13, 1929, concerning customs supervision in the Gulf of Finland. 69

Oct. 7, 1929. Protocol modifying the postal convention of June 18, 1924, with supplementary protocol. 72

Jan. 21, 1932. Treaty concerning nonaggression and the peaceful settlement of disputes, with protocol of signature. 81

Apr. 22, 1932. Convention concerning conciliation procedure. 82

June 17, 1932. Agreement concerning navigation in the Gulf of Finland. 83

Nov. 30, 1932. Exchange of notes concerning reciprocal recognition of trade-marks. 84

Jan. 5, 1933. Convention revising the convention of June 18, 1924, concerning direct transportation of passengers and freight by rail. 86

July 4, 1933. Convention concerning reindeer, with final protocol. 88

Oct. 15, 1933. Convention modifying the convention of October 28, 1922, concerning floating of timber in border water courses, with final protocol. 90

Apr. 7, 1934. Protocol extending the treaty of January 21, 1932, concerning nonaggression and the peaceful settlement of disputes. 93

May 25, 1934. Convention concerning fishing and seal hunting in Lake Ladoga, with protocol and two annexes. 94

Feb. 11, 1936. Protocol modifying the convention of June 18, 1924, concerning direct transportation of passengers and freight by rail. 109

Feb. 11, 1937. Communiqué concerning negotiations. 115

Apr. 11, 1938. Parcel post agreement. 120

Apr. 28, 1938. Protocol concerning demarcation of the border, with maps and protocol of border marks. 121

Dec. 23, 1938. Exchange of notes confirming documents and maps defining the state border. 123

Mar. 12, 1940. Peace treaty, with map and protocol concerning an armistice. 133

Apr. 8, 1940. Exchange of notes concerning procedure for exchange of prisoners of war. 135

Apr. 9, 1940. Act of transfer of Petsamo to Finland. 135

Apr. 19, 1940. Exchange of notes concerning establishment of temporary direct telephone and telegraph communications between Moscow and Helsinki. 135

Apr. 29, 1940. Protocol concerning demarcation of the border. 135

June 28, 1940. Commercial treaty, with annex concerning the Soviet Trade Mission in Finland. 136

June 28, 1940. Agreement concerning payments. 136

Sept. 6, 1940. Agreement concerning direct railroad freight traffic. 138

Oct. 11, 1940. Agreement concerning demilitarization of the Aaland Islands. 139

Nov. 18, 1940. Protocol concerning demarcation of the border, with maps and protocols of border marks. 140

May 10, 1941. Exchange of notes validating the protocol of November 18, 1940, concerning demarcation of the border. 144

Aug. 25–Sept. 3, 1944. Cease-fire agreement. 162

Sept. 19, 1944. Armistice agreement, with annex and two maps. 164

Dec. 16, 1944. Protocol concerning demarcation of the border in the Porkkala-Udd region, with annex, maps, and protocol of border marks. 169

Dec. 17, 1944. Agreement concerning reparations deliveries by Finland. 169

Jan. 31, 1945. Trade agreement. 170

Mar. 14, 1945. Exchange of notes concerning entry into force of the border protocol of Dec. 16, 1944, describing the border in the region of Porkkala-Udd, with annexes. 175

May 8, 1945. Trade agreement for 1945. 177

Aug. 5, 1945. Communiqué by the Allied Control Commission for Finland concerning modification of the conditions of the armistice. 188

Aug. 6, 1945. Exchange of declarations concerning re-establishment of diplomatic relations. 188

Aug. 11, 1945. Supplementary trade agreement. 190

Oct. 26, 1945. Protocol concerning the boundary in the Pechenga (Petsamo) area, with annexes and maps. 200

Dec. 31, 1945. Agreement concerning extension of the period of reparations payments and reduction of annual instalments, with protocol. 205

Feb. 19, 1946. Exchange of notes confirming the protocol of October 26, 1945, concerning the boundary in the Pechenga (Petsamo) area. 207

Apr. 24, 1946. Joint communiqué concerning negotiations. 211

Apr. 30, 1946. Trade agreement for 1946. 211

Apr. 30, 1946. Agreement concerning lease to the Soviet combine Pechenga-Nikel' of a concession for a power station on the Patso-Yoki, with protocol. 211

Aug. 19, 1946. Agreement concerning telegraph and telephone communications. 217

Aug. 19, 1946. Agreement concerning postal exchange. 217

Dec. 5, 1946. Trade and payments agreement. 222

Dec. 5, 1946. Trade protocol for 1947, with annex. 222

Feb. 3, 1947. Treaty concerning transfer to the USSR of part of the state territory of Finland in the region of the Jäniskoski hydroelectric station and the Niskakoski control dam, with annex and map. 225

Feb. 3, 1947. Agreement concerning use by the USSR of former German funds in Finland transferred to the USSR, with annex and two protocols. 225

Feb. 3, 1947. Protocol concerning establishment of a Soviet-Finnish joint-stock company for production of artificial fibers. 225

Feb. 3, 1947. Protocol concerning work of the Soviet combine Pechenga-Nikel' in Finland. 226

Feb. 10, 1947. Treaty of peace, with six annexes. 226

Apr. 24, 1947. Agreement concerning regulation of Lake Inari by means of the regulating dam at Niskakoski, with four annexes. 231

Apr. 24, 1947. Rules for regulating the water level on Lake Inari in connection with operation of the Niskakoski dam. 231

May 24, 1947. Agreement granting Finland the right of railroad transit for freight and passengers through the area of the Soviet naval base at Porkkala-Udd. 232

Oct. 14, 1947. Agreement concerning direct rail transportation of passengers and freight between Helsinki and Leningrad. 238

Nov. 16, 1947. Joint communiqué concerning negotiations. 438

Dec. 1, 1947. Treaty of commerce, with annex concerning the Soviet Trade Mission in Finland. 239

Dec. 1, 1947. Trade protocol for 1948. 239

Dec. 7, 1947. Protocol concerning demarcation of the border in the area of the Jäniskoski hydroelectric station and the Niskakoski control dam, with eight appendices. 239

Dec. 19, 1947. Agreement concerning direct rail communications, with annex. 242

Mar. 13 and 16, 1948. Exchange of notes concerning renewal of prewar treaties. 246

Apr. 6, 1948. Treaty of friendship, cooperation, and mutual assistance. 247

June 3, 1948. Decision to reduce reparations payments. 249

June 19, 1948. Convention concerning procedure for settling border disputes and incidents, with related documents. 249

Dec. 9, 1948. Treaty concerning the regime on the state border, with final protocol. 254

Dec. 17, 1948. Trade agreement for 1949. 256

June 1950. Agreement defining trade contingents for three-way trade between the USSR, Czechoslovakia, and Finland. 274

June 13, 1950. Trade agreement for the period 1951–1955. 275

June 13, 1950. Trade protocol for 1950. 275

May 29 and July 18, 1950. Exchange of notes concerning entry into force of the border protocol of Dec. 7, 1947. 276

Dec. 2, 1950. Trade protocol for 1951. 278

Dec. 21, 1951. Trade protocol for 1952. 284

Sept. 21, 1952. Trade agreement. 291

Sept. 23, 1952. Agreement concerning supplementary trade during 1952–1955. 291

Jan. 1, 1953. Changes in the agreement of Dec. 19, 1947, concerning direct railroad communications. 242

Feb. 23, 1953. Trade protocol for 1953. 293

June 1 and Aug. 26, 1953. Exchange of notes modifying the agreement of August 19, 1946, concerning postal exchange. 300

Nov. 25, 1953. Trade protocol for 1954. 303

Feb. 6, 1954. Agreement concerning a loan to Finland. 307

Apr. 29, 1954. Protocol concerning execution of the agreement of April 24, 1947, concerning regulation of Lake Inari. 311

Apr. 29, 1954. Protocol modifying the rules of April 24, 1947, for regulating the water level on Lake Inari. 311

July 17, 1954. Joint communiqué concerning negotiations. 314

July 17, 1954. Trade agreement for the period 1956–60. 314

Dec. 1, 1954. Communiqué concerning a visit to Finland of A. I. Mikoyan, Deputy Chairman of the Council of Ministers of the USSR. 319

Jan. 24, 1955. Trade protocol for 1955. 322

Jan. 24, 1955. Agreement concerning a loan to Finland. 322

June 17, 1955. Supplementary protocol to the agreement of August 19, 1946, concerning telegraph and telephone communications. 330

June 17, 1955. Supplementary protocol to the agreement of August 19, 1946, concerning postal exchange. 330

Aug. 16, 1955. Agreement concerning scientific and technical collaboration. 334

Sept. 19, 1955. Agreement concerning renunciation by the USSR of rights to the use of the territory of Porkkala-Udd as a naval base and the withdrawal of Soviet armed forces from the territory. 336

Sept. 19, 1955. Protocol concerning extension of the treaty of friendship, cooperation, and mutual assistance of April 6, 1948. 337

Sept. 20, 1955. Joint communiqué concerning the visit to Moscow of J. K. Paasikivi, President of Finland. 337

Oct. 19, 1955. Agreement concerning air communications. 340

Dec. 2, 1955. Trade protocol for 1956. 342

Dec. 10, 1955. Agreement concerning technical and commercial service on air communications between Moscow and Helsinki. 343

Jan. 26, 1956. Final protocol concerning transfer to Finland of the naval base and installations at Porkkala-Udd. 347

Mar. 3, 1956. Communiqué concerning the first meeting of the USSR-Finland commission for scientific and technical collaboration. 350

May 25, 1956. Protocol concerning transfer to the USSR of a hydroelectric station on the Rajakoski waterfall. 356

Sept. 14, 1956. Agreement concerning trackage rights on Soviet railroads of freight trains of the Finnish railroads, with annex. 367

Oct. 18, 1956. Communiqué concerning the second meeting of the Soviet-Finnish commission for scientific and technical collaboration. 369

Nov. 28, 1956. Trade protocol for 1957, with annexes. 372

Dec. 7, 1956. Agreement concerning collaboration between rescue services in the Baltic Sea. 374.

Feb. 2, 1957. Joint communiqué concerning political and economic relations. 376

June 4, 1957. Communiqué concerning the third meeting of the Soviet-Finnish commission for scientific and technical collaboration. 384

June 12, 1957. Joint communiqué concerning the visit of a Soviet governmental delegation to Finland. 384

June 12, 1957 (approximate date). Supplementary trade protocol for 1957. 384

Dec. 4, 1957. Trade protocol for 1958. 392

FINLAND, three-way

Sept. 19, 1921. Agreement concerning telegraph communications (RSRSF, Finland, Norway). 24

Aug. 19, 1925. Agreement defining areas subject to control under the convention of August 19, 1925, concerning suppression of the contraband traffic in alcoholic products (USSR, Estonia, Finland). 52

Apr. 22, 1926. Protocol defining state borders under the agreement of August 19, 1925, supplementary to the convention of the same date concerning suppression of the contraband traffic in alcoholic products, with final protocol (USSR, Estonia, Finland). 56

Oct. 26, 1945. Protocol defining the junction point of the borders of the USSR, Finland, and Norway (USSR, Norway, Finland). 200

Dec. 3, 1947. Documents concerning the frontier mark erected at Muotkavaara (Krokfjellet) (USSR, Norway, Finland). 239

June 29, 1949. Trade and payments agreement (USSR, Finland, Czechoslovakia). 261

June 29, 1949. Trade and payments agreement (USSR, Finland, Poland). 261

1950. Trade and payments protocol (USSR, Finland, Czechoslovakia). 274

1951. Trade and payments protocol (USSR, Finland, Czechoslovakia). 279

Apr. 14, 1951. Trade agreement (USSR, Finland, Poland). 440

Dec. 17, 1951. Trade protocol (USSR, Finland, Poland). 440

1952. Trade and payments protocol (USSR, Finland, Czechoslovakia). 440

Sept. 21, 1952. Trade and payments agreement, with two annexes (USSR, Finland, Chinese People's Republic). 291

1953. Trade and payments protocol (USSR, Finland, Czechoslovakia). 293

Feb. 7, 1953. Protocol concerning maintenance of the border mark erected at Muotkavaara (Krokfjellet) (USSR, Finland, Norway). 293

1954. Trade and payments protocol (USSR, Finland, Czechoslovakia). 305

1955. Trade and payments protocol (USSR, Finland, Czechoslovakia). 321

Mar. 31, 1955. Trade agreement (USSR, Finland, Poland). 443

1956. Trade and payments protocol (USSR, Finland, Czechoslovakia). 346

Feb. 24, 1956. Protocol concerning regulation of the water regime of the Pasvik-El'v river and Lake Inari, with regulations (USSR, Finland, Norway). 349

FINLAND, unverified

July 1940. Agreement concerning military use of Finnish railroads. 429

Finland. See also Nongovernmental agreements; Plurilateral, nonaggression agreements.

FINNISH DEMOCRATIC REPUBLIC, bilateral

Dec. 1, 1939. Exchange of notes concerning recognition and establishment of diplomatic relations. 132

Dec. 2, 1939. Treaty of mutual assistance and friendship. 132

FINNISH SOCIALIST WORKERS' REPUBLIC, bilateral

Mar. 1, 1918. Treaty of friendship and brotherhood. 3

FRANCE, bilateral

Apr. 20, 1920. Agreement concerning repatriation of prisoners of war and civilians, with supplementary articles, supplementary agreement, and declaration. 9

Oct. 28, 1924. Exchange of telegrams concerning establishment of diplomatic relations. 48

Nov. 29, 1932. Treaty of nonaggression. 84

Nov. 29, 1932. Convention concerning conciliation procedure. 84

Jan. 11, 1934. Temporary commercial agreement, with three protocols. 91

Dec. 5, 1934. Protocol concerning conclusion of an Eastern Pact. 98

Dec. 9, 1934. Protocol concerning commercial relations. 98

May 2, 1935. Treaty of mutual assistance, with protocol of signature. 102

May 16, 1935. Communiqué concerning negotiations. 102

Jan. 6, 1936. Agreement modifying and extending the temporary commercial agreement of January 11, 1934, with three annexes and protocol of signature. 108

Jan. 21, 1936. Agreement modifying the commercial agreement of January 6, 1936, with three annexes. 108

Feb. 4, 1936. Agreement concerning removal of import duties on Soviet products and the transit of French merchandise through the territory of the USSR. 109

Mar. 9, 1936. Parcel post agreement, with final protocol. 109

Aug. 5, 1936. Exchange of notes concerning Soviet adherence to the principle of nonintervention in the Spanish civil war. 113

Aug. 11, 1936. Agreement concerning transmission of legal and notarial documents and the execution of letters rogatory in civil and commercial matters. 113

Dec. 17, 1936. Agreement extending the temporary commercial agreement of January 11, 1934, and the supplementary agreements of January 6 and 21, 1936, with two annexes. 114

Dec. 31, 1937. Agreement extending the temporary commercial agreement of January 11, 1934, and related documents. 120

Dec. 30, 1938. Agreement extending the temporary commercial agreement of January 11, 1934, and related documents. 123

Aug. 1941. Agreement concerning establishment of direct contact and exchange of unofficial representatives. 435

Sept. 20, 1941. Exchange of notes concerning joint action in the war against Germany. 146

Sept. 27, 1941. Exchange of notes concerning recognition and mutual assistance in the war against Germany. 147

Sept. 28, 1942. Joint communiqué concerning recognition of the French National Committee as the representative of France. 151

Dec. 1942 (approximate date). Agreement concerning establishment of a French air squadron in the USSR. 436

Aug. 26, 1943. Declaration by the USSR concerning its decision to recognize the French Committee of National Liberation as the representative of the governmental interests of France, and to establish diplomatic relations with the Committee. 154

Oct. 23, 1944. Declaration concerning recognition of the French Provisional Government. 166

Dec. 10, 1944. Treaty of alliance and mutual assistance. 168

Dec. 11, 1944. Joint communiqué concerning the visit of General Charles de Gaulle to Moscow. 168

June 29, 1945. Agreement concerning treatment and repatriation of Soviet citizens under the control of French authorities and of French citizens under the control of Soviet authorities, with protocol. 181

Dec. 29, 1945. Commercial agreement, with protocol. 205

Apr. 6, 1946. Agreement concerning delivery of grain to France. 209

June 19, 1946. Treaty concerning establishment of postal and telephone-telegraph communications, with final protocol. 214

Sept. 3, 1951. Agreement concerning reciprocal trade relations and the status of the Soviet Trade Mission in France, with protocol. 283

July 15, 1953. Trade agreement, with two annexes. 297

July 15, 1953. Payments agreement. 297

Jan. 28, 1954. Supplementary trade agreement. 300

June 29, 1954. Agreement concerning establishment of regular air service between Moscow and Paris. 313

Nov. 10, 1954. Trade protocol. 319

Mar. 31, 1956. Trade protocol for 1956. 351

May 19, 1956. Statement on negotiations. 355

May 19, 1956. Joint statement concerning cultural intercourse. 355

July 23, 1956. Agreement concerning exchange of films. 364

Feb. 11, 1957. Trade agreement for the period 1957–1959, with four annexes. 377

Feb. 11, 1957. Trade protocol for 1957. 377

Aug. 23, 1957. Trade protocol. 388

Oct. 9, 1957. Plan for cultural collaboration in 1958. 445

Dec. 28, 1957. Trade protocol for 1958. 395

FRANCE, unverified

Nov. 18, 1944. Agreement concerning liberated Soviet citizens. 429

France. See also Nongovernmental agreements; Plurilateral, Great Power agreements and conferences.

GEORGIAN DEMOCRATIC REPUBLIC, bilateral

May 7, 1920. Peace treaty. 10

May 7, 1920. Secret supplement to the peace treaty. 10

May 12, 1920. Agreement concerning a border dispute between Georgia and Azerbaidzhan. 10

Nov. 14, 1920. Agreement concerning trade and transit, with secret supplement concerning storage of oil. 15

Dec. 9, 1920. Agreement concerning procedure for the choice of Georgian citizenship. 16

Dec. 16, 1920. Agreement concerning ships of the RSFSR in Georgian ports. 16

Mar. 18, 1921. Agreement concerning cessation of hostilities. 20

GEORGIAN SSR, bilateral

May 21, 1921. Treaty of alliance. 21

May 21, 1921. Agreement concerning financial matters. 21

Georgian SSR. See also Plurilateral, internal Soviet treaties.

GERMANY, bilateral

Dec. 4, 1917. Agreement concerning temporary suspension of hostilities. 1

Feb. 9, 1918. Agreement concerning repatriation of civilians, with supplementary protocol and final protocol. 2

Mar. 3, 1918. Treaty concerning political and legal matters, supplementing the peace treaty between the RSFSR and the Central Powers. 4

June 17, 1918. Armistice. 5

June 24, 1918. Protocol concerning basic principles for the exchange of able-bodied prisoners of war. 5

July 1918. Exchange of notes concerning the guard at the German embassy in Moscow. 5

July 19, 1918. Protocol concerning procedure for commercial vessels and cargoes which have fallen into the hands of the enemy. 6

Aug. 8, 1918. Agreement concerning postal, telegraph, and railroad communications. 6

Aug. 27, 1918. Treaty concerning political and territorial matters, supplementing the treaty of peace of March 3, 1918. 6

Aug. 27, 1918. Financial agreement. 6

Aug. 27, 1918. Civil law agreement. 6

Aug. 27, 1918. Exchange of notes constituting a secret military protocol to the treaty of the same date. 6

Sept. 12, 1918. Agreement concerning requisitioning in areas occupied by German troops. 7

Sept. 15, 1918. Protocol of an agreement concerning evacuation of the area occupied by German troops east of the Berezina River. 7

Oct. 10, 1918. Protocol supplementing the agreement of September 15, 1918, concerning evacuation of the area occupied by German troops east of the Berezina River. 7

Apr. 19, 1920. Agreement concerning repatriation of prisoners of war and interned civilians. 9

Apr. 23, 1920. Agreement concerning repatriation of prisoners of war. 10

July 7, 1920. Agreement concerning repatriation of prisoners of war and interned civilians. 11

Jan. 22, 1921. Agreement concerning repatriation of prisoners of war and interned civilians, supplementing the agreement of April 19, 1920, with declaration by the Central Administration for Affairs of Military and Civilian Prisoners, in Berlin. 17

Jan. 22, 1921. Agreement concerning repatriation of Red Army soldiers. 17

Apr. 23, 1921. Treaty concerning repatriation. 21

May 6, 1921. Temporary agreement concerning extension of the sphere of activity of delegations engaged in care of prisoners of war, with protocol. 21

May 6, 1921. Agreement concerning repatriation of prisoners of war and interned civilians, with protocol. 21

May 6, 17, and 25, 1921. Exchange of notes concerning courier service. 21

Dec. 10, 1921. Agreement concerning return of merchant ships. 27

Apr. 16, 1922. Treaty of Rapallo. 31

June 7, 1922. Protocol concerning reciprocal transfer of the embassies in Berlin and Petrograd. 32

Nov. 5, 1922. Agreement extending the Treaty of Rapallo of April 16, 1922, to the Union Republics. 36

Apr. 23, 1923. Agreement concerning merchant vessels which have fallen under the authority of the other party, with exchange of notes. 38

June 29, 1924. Protocol concerning settlement of the dispute over the Soviet Trade Mission in Germany, with annex. 46

Oct. 12, 1925. Treaty comprising (1) an agreement concerning conditions of residence and business and legal protection, (2) an economic agreement, (3) a railway agreement, (4) an agreement concerning navigation, (5) a fiscal agreement, (6) an agreement concerning commercial courts of arbitration, and (7) an agreement concerning legal protection of industrial property, with final protocol. 52

Oct. 12, 1925. Consular treaty, with annex and final protocol. 53

Oct. 12, 1925. Agreement concerning legal aid in civil cases. 53

Apr. 24, 1926. Treaty of neutrality and non-aggression, with exchange of notes. 56

June 7 and July 2, 1926. Exchange of notes constituting an agreement concerning courier service. 57

Aug. 31, 1926. Agreement concerning inheritance rights. 58

Dec. 21, 1928. Protocol concerning commercial and economic relations, with eight annexes. 68

Jan. 25, 1929. Convention concerning conciliation procedure. 69

Apr. 16, 1929. Exchange of notes constituting an agreement concerning reciprocal recognition of tonnage measurement certificates. 70

June 13, 1930. Joint statement concerning mutual relations. 75

Feb. 7 and Mar. 20, 1931. Exchange of notes amending the agreement of October 12, 1925, concerning legal aid in civil cases. 77

June 24, 1931. Protocol extending the treaty of neutrality and nonaggression of April 24, 1926, and the convention of January 25, 1929, concerning conciliation procedure. 78

Dec. 22, 1931. Joint statement concerning development of economic relations. 80

Dec. 22, 1931. Protocol concerning development of economic relations. 80

May 3, 1932. Agreement concerning grain. 82

May 28, 1932. Protocol concerning customs duties and reciprocal recognition of certificates of origin, with annex. 82

1933. Agreement concerning postponement of payments on the Soviet debt to Germany. 86

Mar. 20, 1934. Economic protocol. 434

Aug. 8, 1934. Trade protocol. 96

Mar. 7, 1935. Parcel post agreement, with final protocol. 100

Apr. 9, 1935. Trade agreement. 100

Apr. 9, 1935. Credit agreement. 100

Aug. 23, 1935. Exchange of notes concerning the address of the Soviet Trade Mission in Berlin. 105

Apr. 29, 1936. Agreement concerning trade and payments in 1936. 110

Dec. 24, 1936. Exchange of notes constituting a protocol extending the agreement of April 29, 1936, concerning trade and payments. 114

Nov. 15, 1937. Agreement concerning closing of German consulates in the USSR. 119

Dec. 16, 1937. Agreement extending the

deadline for payments under the protocol of December 24, 1936. 119

Mar. 1, 1938. Trade and clearing agreement. 120

Sept. 1, 1938. Agreement extending to Austria the provisions of the trade and clearing agreement of March 1, 1938. 435

Dec. 19, 1938. Exchange of notes extending the trade and clearing agreement of March 1, 1938. 122

Aug. 19, 1939. Trade and credit agreement, with three annexes and a secret final protocol. 126

Aug. 23, 1939. Treaty of nonaggression. 127

Aug. 23, 1939. Secret protocol concerning spheres of influence in Eastern Europe. 127

Aug. 26, 1939. Confidential protocol concerning the exchange rate of the Reichsmark in Soviet-German trade. 127

Sept. 18, 1939. Joint communiqué concerning military actions in Poland. 128

Sept. 22, 1939 (approximate date). Agreement concerning a demarcation line in occupied Poland. 128

Sept. 28, 1939. Friendship and border treaty, with map. 129

Sept. 28, 1939. Confidential protocol concerning transfer to the USSR or Germany of persons of German, Ukrainian, or Belorussian origin from occupied areas in Poland. 129

Sept. 28, 1939. Secret protocol concerning the division of Lithuania between Soviet and German spheres of influence. 129

Sept. 28, 1939. Secret protocol concerning suppression of resistance in occupied Poland. 129

Sept. 28, 1939. Declaration calling for an end to the war between Germany on the one hand and Great Britain and France on the other. 129

Sept. 28, 1939. Exchange of notes concerning trade. 129

Sept. 28, 1939. Exchange of notes concerning (1) railroad communications between Germany and Romania, Iran, Afghanistan, and the countries of the Far East, and (2) trade of Soviet oil for German coal and steel. 130

Oct. 4, 1939. Protocol concerning demarcation of the border in occupied Poland, with map. 130

Oct. 8, 1939. Secret exchange of notes confirming an understanding concerning procedure for the division of Lithuania. 130

Oct. 24, 1939. Agreement concerning Soviet grain exports to Germany. 131

Nov. 16, 1939. Agreement concerning repatriation of persons of German origin from the parts of Poland occupied by the USSR and of persons of Ukrainian and Belorussian origin from the parts of Poland occupied by Germany, with protocol and supplementary protocol. 131

Dec. 23, 1939. Agreement concerning establishment of regular air communications. 132

Dec. 23, 1939. Agreement concerning rail communications. 132

Dec. 31, 1939. Exchange of notes extending the trade and clearing agreement of March 1, 1938. 132

Feb. 11, 1940. Economic agreement, with a protocol and several exchanges of notes. 133

Apr. 1940. Understanding concerning maintenance of Sweden's independence. 134

Apr. 9, 1940. Agreement concerning use by Germany of a naval base on the Murman Coast. 135

June 10, 1940. Convention concerning procedure for settlement of border disputes and incidents. 135

June 12, 1940. Agreement concerning direct telephone and telegraph communications. 135

July 5, 1940 (approximate date). Agreement concerning reopening of consulates. 136

July 29, 1940. Exchange of notes concerning appointment of a diplomatic representative to negotiate the transfer of persons of German origin from Bessarabia and Northern Bukovina to Germany. 137

Aug. 31, 1940. Treaty concerning legal relations on the border, with protocol and final protocol. 137

Sept. 5, 1940. Agreement concerning transfer of persons of German origin from Bessarabia and Northern Bukovina to Germany, with protocol and supplementary protocol. 138

Oct. 1, 1940. Agreement concerning direct railroad freight communications. 139

Oct. 1, 1940. Agreement concerning border railroad communications. 139

Oct. 1, 1940. Agreement concerning direct railroad passenger communications. 139

Oct. 25, 1940. Communiqué concerning formation of a United Danube Commission, to replace the International Danube Commission and the European Danube Commission. 140

Dec. 31, 1940. Exchange of notes constituting an agreement extending the trade and clearing agreement of March 1, 1938. 141

Jan. 10, 1941. Economic agreement. 141

Jan. 10, 1941. Exchange of notes concerning payments. 141

Jan. 10, 1941. Protocol concerning termination of business activities in the Baltic States. 141

Jan. 10, 1941. Agreement concerning transfer of persons of German citizenship or national origin from the Lithuanian SSR to Germany, and of persons of Lithuanian citizenship or Lithuanian, Belorussian, or Russian national origin from those portions of Lithuania (the Memel and Suwalki areas) incorporated into Germany to the Lithuanian SSR, with supplementary protocol. 141

Jan. 10, 1941. Agreement concerning transfer of persons of German citizenship or national origin from the Latvian and Estonian SSR's to Germany, with supplementary protocol and final protocol. 141

Jan. 10, 1941. Agreement concerning property claims arising out of population transfers in the Baltic States. 141

Jan. 10, 1941. Treaty concerning the border between the Lithuanian SSR and Germany, with exchange of notes. 141

Jan. 10, 1941. Secret protocol concerning the sale by Germany to the USSR of that part of Lithuania allocated to Germany by the secret protocol of September 28, 1939. 142

Dec. 31, 1940, and Feb. 25, 1941. Exchange of notes concerning exchange of reports on the water level and ice conditions on the Memel. 142

Apr. 18, 1941. Protocol concerning fulfillment of the economic agreement of February 11, 1940, with exchange of notes. 144

Apr. 29, 1945. Instrument of surrender of German and Italian forces in Italy. 176

May 7, 1945. Act of military surrender of the German High Command. 177

May 8, 1945. Act of military surrender of the German High Command. 177

Jan. 25, 1955. Soviet decree ending the state of war between the USSR and Germany. 442

GERMANY, secret military agreements

See Appendix 2.

GERMANY, three-way

Dec. 14, 1934. Protocol concerning regulation of the export of rye and rye flour, with final protocol (USSR, Germany, Poland). 98

GERMANY, unverified

Dec. 22, 1917. Convention concerning Poland. 427

Apr. 17, 1919. Military agreement. 427

July 8, 1920. Agreement concerning political, economic, and military relations. 427

Mar. 25, 1921. Military agreement. 428

Apr. 3, 1922. Military agreement. 428

Germany. See also Nongovernmental agreements; Plurilateral, Central Powers.

GERMANY, FEDERAL REPUBLIC, bilateral

June 7 and 30 and Aug. 3, 12, and 19, 1955. Exchange of letters concerning negotiations to establish diplomatic relations. 334

Sept. 13, 1955. Final communiqué concerning results of conversations. 336

Sept. 13, 1955. Exchange of notes concerning establishment of diplomatic relations. 336

Germany, Federal Republic. See also Nongovernmental agreements.

GERMANY, SOVIET REPUBLIC, unverified

Jan. 5, 1919. Treaty of recognition, mutual assistance, and collaboration. 427

GERMAN DEMOCRATIC REPUBLIC, bilateral

Oct. 16, 1949. Establishment of diplomatic relations. 263

Nov. 11, 1949. Soviet statement concerning establishment of a Soviet Control Commission for Germany, replacing the Soviet Military Administration in Germany. 264

Nov. 19, 1949. Exchange of notes concerning establishment of a Soviet Trade Mission in Berlin. 264

Apr. 12, 1950. Trade and payments agreement for 1950. 273

May 11 and 15, 1950. Exchange of letters concerning reduction of reparations payments to the USSR. 274

May 19, 1950. Communiqué announcing transfer to the GDR of twenty-three enterprises appropriated by the USSR as reparations. 274

July 1, 1950. Agreement concerning establishment of postal communications. 275

July 1, 1950. Parcel post agreement. 275

July 1, 1950. Agreement concerning establishment of telegraph and telephone communications. 276

July 21, 1950. Supplementary trade protocol for 1950. 276

Mar. 1951. Protocol concerning general conditions of trade deliveries. 280

Mar. 16, 1951. Trade and payments agreement for 1951. 281

Sept. 27, 1951. Agreement concerning scientific and technical collaboration. 283

Sept. 27, 1951. Trade agreement for the period 1952–1955. 283

Apr. 11, 1952. Protocol concerning supplementary deliveries of commodities during 1952. 286

Apr. 29, 1952. Communiqué concerning transfer to the GDR of sixty-six joint-stock companies. 286

May 12, 1952. Agreement concerning training of GDR citizens in civic institutions of higher education in the USSR. 287

May 12, 1952. Exchange of notes concerning training of GDR citizens in the USSR. 287

July 1, 1952. Agreement concerning working conditions of Soviet specialists sent to the GDR to give technical assistance. 288

Jan. 13, 1953. Agreement concerning collaboration in the field of radio broadcasting, with supplementary protocol. 293

Apr. 26, 1953. Trade protocol for 1953. 295

Aug. 22, 1953. Joint communiqué concerning negotiations. 299

Aug. 22, 1953. Protocol concerning discontinuance of reparations payments by the GDR and other measures to alleviate the financial and economic obligations of the GDR arising out of the war. 300

Aug. 22, 1953. Verbal agreement concerning transformation of diplomatic missions into embassies. 300

Dec. 1, 1953. Protocol concerning procedure for transfer to the GDR of thirty-three Soviet industrial enterprises in the GDR, with annex. 304

Dec. 31, 1953. Communiqué concerning completion of the transfer to the GDR of thirty-three industrial enterprises in the GDR. 305

Feb. 13, 1954. Trade protocol for 1954. 307

Feb. 15, 1954. Protocol concerning completion of the transfer to the GDR of thirty-three Soviet enterprises in the GDR. 307

Mar. 25, 1954. Declaration concerning relations between the USSR and the GDR. 308

Apr. 30, 1954. Protocol concerning transfer to the GDR of the film archive of "Soveksportfilm" in the GDR, with list. 311

June 22, 1954. Supplementary trade protocol for 1954. 313

Sept. 20, 1954. Agreement concerning non-commercial payments. 316

Oct. 5, 1954. Agreement concerning establishment of consulates. 317

Oct. 28, 1954. Communiqué concerning the third meeting of the Soviet-GDR commission for scientific and technical collaboration. 442

Mar. 1955. Agreement concerning transfer to the GDR of art treasures from the Dresden Gallery held in the USSR. 324

Mar. 24, 1955. Trade protocol for 1955. 325

Apr. 27, 1955. Agreement concerning use of Schoenefeld Airport. 327

Apr. 28, 1955. Agreement concerning aid by the USSR to the GDR in regard to development of research concerning atomic nuclear physics and the use of atomic energy for the needs of the national economy. 327

Mar. 3, 1955. Supplementary trade protocol for 1955. 327

July 1, 1955. Treaties concerning reorganization of cinema relations. 331

July 27, 1955. Communiqué concerning the visit of a Soviet governmental delegation to the GDR. 333

Aug. 25, 1955. Protocol concerning transfer to the GDR of pictures from the Dresden Gallery. 334

Sept. 13, 1955. Communiqué concerning the fourth meeting of the USSR-GDR commission for scientific and technical collaboration. 336

Sept. 20, 1955. Final communiqué on negotiations. 337

Sept. 20, 1955. Treaty concerning mutual relations. 337

Sept. 20, 1955. Exchange of letters concerning guard and control functions to be exercised by the GDR. 338

Oct. 18, 1955. Agreement concerning technical and commercial collaboration in the field of civil aviation. 340

Nov. 1955. Protocol concerning scientific and technical collaboration. 340

Nov. 27, 1955. Final protocol concerning transfer to the GDR of pictures from the Dresden Gallery, with three annexes. 342

Dec. 1955. Agreement concerning construction of ships and floating equipment for the USSR. 342

Dec. 3, 1955. Trade protocol for 1956. 343

Dec. 23, 1955. Agreement concerning delivery of ships and other naval equipment during the period 1957–1960. 345

Jan. 19, 1956 (approximate date). Protocol concerning collaboration in the field of the chemical industry. 347

Apr. 26, 1956. Agreement concerning cultural and scientific collaboration. 354

May 30, 1956. Convention concerning quarantine and protection of agricultural plants from diseases and parasites. 357

June 18, 1956. Agreement concerning air communications. 358

June 18, 1956. Agreement concerning air transportation and servicing. 358

July 17, 1956. Statement concerning negotiations. 364

July 17, 1956. Agreement concerning construction in the GDR of an atomic power plant. 364

Sept. 22, 1956. Protocol concerning expansion and development of telephone and telegraph communications, exchange of radio and television programs, and strengthening of scientific and technical collaboration in the field of communications. 368

Oct. 12, 1956. Agreement concerning collaboration in the fields of radio and television. 369

Oct. 12, 1956. Protocol concerning collaboration in the field of television. 369

Jan. 7, 1957. Joint declaration concerning political and economic relations. 375

Feb. 5, 1957. Protocol concerning establishment of a permanent commission of historians of the USSR and the GDR. 445

Feb. 20, 1957. Trade agreement for 1957. 378

Feb. 26, 1957. Agreement concerning regulation of financial aspects of the production of the USSR-GDR joint-stock uranium producing company "Vismut." 378

Mar. 12, 1957. Agreement concerning questions connected with the temporary stationing of Soviet troops on the territory of the GDR. 379

Mar. 14, 1957. Communiqué concerning regulation of financial aspects of the production of the USSR-GDR joint-stock uranium producing company, "Vismut." 379

May 10, 1957. Consular convention. 382

May 25, 1957. Protocol concerning collaboration between the machine-building industries of the two States. 383

June 7, 1957. Communiqué concerning the sixth meeting of the USSR-GDR commission for scientific and technical collaboration. 384

Aug. 2, 1957. Agreement concerning mutual legal aid in matters connected with the temporary presence of Soviet troops on GDR territory. 387

Aug. 13, 1957. Joint communiqué concerning political and economic relations. 387

Sept. 27, 1957. Treaty of commerce and navigation, with annex concerning the Soviet Trade Mission in the GDR and the GDR Trade Mission in the USSR. 389

Sept. 27, 1957. Trade agreement for the period 1958–1960. 389

Sept. 27, 1957. Credit protocol for trade during 1958. 389

Nov. 28, 1957. Treaty concerning legal aid in civil, family, and criminal cases. 392

Dec. 27, 1957. Agreement concerning procedure for settlement of material claims for damages. 395

GERMAN DEMOCRATIC REPUBLIC, three-way

Aug. 1, 1956. Agreement concerning collaboration in construction of enterprises of the aluminum industry in Yugoslavia, with exchange of notes (USSR, GDR, Yugoslavia). 364

May 22, 1957. Protocol concerning an increase of the relative role of maritime transport in foreign trade and concerning organization of freight transportation on internal waterways (USSR, GDR, Poland). 383

German Democratic Republic. See also Nongovernmental agreements; Plurilateral, Soviet bloc agreements and conferences.

GREECE, bilateral

Mar. 8, 1924. Exchange of notes concerning recognition of the USSR de jure. 41

June 11, 1929. Convention of commerce and navigation. 71

July 14 and 17, 1931. Exchange of notes constituting an agreement concerning reciprocal recognition of trade and commercial marks. 78

Apr. 22, 1933. Agreement concerning reciprocal abolition of consular visas on bills of health of merchant ships. 86

June 8, 1934. Trade and clearing agreement. 95

Sept. 8, 1933. Trade and clearing agreement, with three exchanges of notes. 89

July 13, 1934. Agreement concerning consular fees on passports. 95

Mar. 5, 1935. Trade and clearing agreement. 100

Jan. 11, 1936. Trade and clearing agreement. 108

Feb. 27, 1937. Trade and clearing agreement. 115

Apr. 18, 1938. Agreement extending the trade and clearing agreement of February 27, 1937. 121

Aug. 5, 1941. Agreement concerning establishment of diplomatic relations. 145

Apr. 14, 1943. Exchange of notes concerning reorganization of diplomatic missions into embassies. 153

July 28, 1953. Trade and payments agreement, with two annexes. 298

Sept. 2, 1954. Exchange of notes constituting a trade agreement, with two annexes. 315

Aug. 23, 1955. Trade protocol, with two annexes. 334

Jan. 19, 1957. Trade protocol for 1957. 376

GREECE, unratified

June 23, 1926. Customs agreement. 401

GREECE, unverified

Dec. 1931. Agreement concerning repatriation of Armenian citizens. 428

Greece. See also Nongovernmental agreements.

GUATEMALA, bilateral

Apr. 19, 1945. Exchange of notes concerning establishment of diplomatic relations. 176

HEILUNGKIANG, bilateral

Oct. 2, 1920. Agreement concerning border trade. 14

Mar. 7, 1921. Agreement concerning direct rail communications between the Chinese Eastern Railway and Chita Railway. 19

HEJAZ, bilateral

Aug. 6, 1924. Agreement concerning establishment of diplomatic and economic relations. 47

Feb. 16 and 19, 1926. Exchange of notes concerning recognition and establishment of diplomatic relations. 55

Apr. 3, 5, and 19, 1927. Exchange of notes

concerning recognition and maintenance of diplomatic relations. 60

HUNGARY, bilateral

May 21, 1920. Agreement concerning repatriation of prisoners of war and civilians. 10

July 28, 1921. Agreement concerning exchange of prisoners of war and interned civilians. 22

Oct. 3, 1921. Protocol concerning exchange of prisoners of war through the mediation of Latvia and the International Red Cross. 24

Feb. 4, 1934. Exchange of notes concerning establishment of diplomatic relations. 92

Feb. 6, 1934 (approximate date). Protocol concerning establishment of a Soviet legation in Budapest. 92

Sept. 23, 1939 (approximate date). Agreement concerning resumption of diplomatic relations. 128

Sept. 3, 1940. Treaty of commerce and navigation, with protocol and two annexes. 138

Sept. 3, 1940. Exchange of notes concerning date of entry into force of the treaty of commerce and navigation of September 3, 1940. 138

Sept. 3, 1940. Trade and payments agreement, with two annexes. 138

Mar. 2, 1941 (approximate date). Agreement concerning telegraph communications. 143

Mar. 2, 1941 (approximate date). Agreement concerning railroad communications. 143

Jan. 20, 1945. Armistice agreement, with annex. 170

June 15, 1945. Agreement concerning payment of reparations by Hungary, with annexes. 180

Aug. 21, 1945. Temporary agreement concerning organization of postal and telephone-telegraph communications. 194

Aug. 27, 1945. Agreement concerning economic collaboration. 194

Aug. 27, 1945. Trade agreement. 194

Sept. 25, 1945. Exchange of notes concerning re-establishment of diplomatic relations. 198

Mar. 29, 1946. Agreement concerning establishment of a Soviet-Hungarian joint-stock civil aviation company. 208

Mar. 29, 1946. Agreement concerning establishment of a Soviet-Hungarian joint-stock navigation company. 209

Apr. 8, 1946. Agreement concerning establishment of a Soviet-Hungarian joint-stock company for exploration and extraction of oil and gas, refinement of oil, and sale of oil products. 209

Apr. 8, 1946. Agreement concerning establishment of a Soviet-Hungarian joint-stock company for bauxite-aluminum. 209

Apr. 18, 1946. Joint communiqué concerning

extension from six to eight years of the term of payment of reparations by Hungary. 210

May 4, 1946. Hungarian decree promulgating the statute of a Soviet-Hungarian civil aviation company. 209

May 4, 1946. Hungarian decree promulgating the statute of a Soviet-Hungarian navigation company. 209

July 23, 1946. Hungarian decree promulgating the statutes of the Soviet-Hungarian crude oil company "Maszovol." 209

July 25, 1946. Hungarian decrees promulgating the statutes of (1) the Soviet-Hungarian crude oil company "Molaj," and (2) the Soviet-Hungarian bauxite-aluminum company "Danube Valley Aluminum Industry." 209–10

Aug. 6, 1946. Hungarian decree promulgating the statutes of the Soviet-Hungarian bauxite-aluminum company "Magyar Bauxitbanya." 210

Feb. 10, 1947. Treaty of peace, with six annexes. 227

Apr. 12, 1947. Hungarian decrees exempting Soviet-Hungarian joint-stock companies from taxes and duties. 209–10, 231

July 15, 1947. Treaty of commerce and navigation, with annex concerning the Soviet Trade Mission in Hungary. 234

July 15, 1947. Trade and payments agreement, with two annexes. 234

July 15, 1947. Final protocol, concerning financial payments, to the trade agreement of August 27, 1945. 235

Sept. 15, 1947. Agreement concerning direct rail communications. 236

Sept. 22, 1947. Agreement concerning establishment of postal and telephone-telegraph communications, with final protocol. 236

Sept. 22, 1947. Parcel post agreement. 237

Dec. 9, 1947. Communiqué concerning negotiations on economic matters. 239

Dec. 9, 1947. Secret protocol concerning conversion of the Soviet-Hungarian joint-stock companies into Soviet monopolies. 240

Dec. 9, 1947. Secret protocol concerning payment by Hungary to the USSR of a Soviet claim based on debts of Hungarian nationals to German nationals. 240

Dec. 9, 1947. Secret protocol authorizing transfer to the USSR of former German assets in Hungary without assuming their liabilities. 240

Dec. 9, 1947. Exchange of notes. 240

Feb. 18, 1948. Treaty of friendship, collaboration and mutual assistance. 245

Mar. 1, 1948. Agreement concerning transformation of diplomatic missions into embassies. 438

June 5 and 7, 1948. Exchange of notes concerning reduction in reparations payments by Hungary. 249

Aug. 31, 1948. Hungarian decree promulgating the statute of the Soviet-Hungarian bauxite-aluminum company "Aluminum ore-mines and industry." 210

Oct. 2, 1948. Trade protocol. 253

Oct. 2, 1948. Protocol modifying and extending the trade and payments agreement of July 15, 1947. 253

Oct. 28, 1948. Agreement concerning training of Hungarian citizens in civic institutions of higher education in the USSR and their support. 254

July 26, 1949. Agreement concerning scientific and technical collaboration. 261

July 30, 1949. Protocol concerning redemarcation of the state border, with related documents. 261

Jan. 21, 1950. Hungarian decrees promulgating the statutes of (1) the Soviet-Hungarian Bauxite-Aluminum Company and (2) the Soviet-Hungarian Oil Company. 268

Feb. 24, 1950. Treaty concerning the regime on the state border, with final protocol. 271

Feb. 24, 1950. Convention concerning procedure for settling border disputes and incidents, with related documents. 271

Mar. 1, 1950. Trade protocol for 1950. 272

Mar. 1, 1950. Agreement concerning technical production work by Hungarian specialists in the USSR. 272

Apr. 12, 1950. Agreement concerning collaboration in the field of radio broadcasting, with supplementary protocol. 273

June 9, 1950. Convention concerning measures for preventing floods and regulating the water system on the border in the area of the Tisza River, with two annexes. 274

July 13, 1950. Convention concerning quarantine of agricultural plants and their protection from parasites and diseases. 276

Mar. 19, 1951. Trade protocol for 1951. 281

Mar. 19, 1951. Protocol concerning working conditions for Soviet specialists sent to Hungary to give technical assistance. 281

Jan. 23, 1952. Trade agreement for the period 1952–1955. 284

Jan. 23, 1952. Agreement concerning delivery of industrial equipment and technical assistance to Hungary. 284

May 19, 1952. Agreement concerning training of Hungarian citizens in civic institutions of higher education in the USSR. 287

June 30, 1952. Agreement concerning conditions of trade deliveries. 288

Sept. 30, 1952. Agreement concerning transfer to Hungary of sixty-nine Soviet enterprises in Hungary. 291

Mar. 24, 1953. Trade protocol for 1953. 294

June 16 and Aug. 27, 1953. Exchange of notes modifying the parcel post agreement of September 22, 1947. 300

Aug. 28, 1953. Protocol concerning preparation and exchange of radio programs. 301

Apr. 7, 1954. Trade protocol for 1954. 310

May 9, 1954. Communiqué concerning the fifth meeting of the Soviet-Hungarian commission for scientific and technical collaboration. 312

Nov. 6, 1954. Agreement concerning transfer and sale to Hungary of Soviet shares in Soviet-Hungarian joint-stock companies. 319

Feb. 11, 1955. Agreement concerning establishment of regular air communications. 323

Feb. 26, 1955. Trade protocol for 1955. 324

June 13, 1955. Agreement concerning aid by the USSR to Hungary in regard to development of research concerning atomic nuclear physics and the use of atomic energy for the needs of the national economy. 330

July 2, 1955. Communiqué concerning the sixth meeting of the Soviet-Hungarian commission for scientific and technical collaboration. 331

Feb. 3, 1956. Trade protocol for 1956. 349

May 11, 1956. Communiqué concerning the seventh meeting of the Soviet-Hungarian Commission for scientific and technical collaboration. 354

May 30, 1956. Protocol concerning expansion of collaboration in the fields of telephone and telegraph communications, radio broadcasting, and television. 357

June 14, 1956. Supplementary protocol to the agreement of April 12, 1950, concerning collaboration in the field of radio broadcasting. 358

June 28, 1956. Agreement concerning scientific and cultural collaboration. 359

Oct. 5, 1956. Communiqué concerning a loan agreement. 368

Oct. 24, 1956. Agreement concerning Soviet military aid in "restoring order" in Hungary. 370

Nov. 5, 1956. Exchange of notes concerning material aid to Hungary. 370

Mar. 28, 1957. Joint declaration concerning political and economic relations. 380

Mar. 28, 1957. Trade protocol for 1957. 380

May 27, 1957. Agreement concerning the legal status of Soviet troops temporarily stationed on Hungarian territory. 383

Aug. 6, 1957. Communiqué concerning the eighth meeting of the Soviet-Hungarian commission for scientific and technical collaboration. 387

Aug. 24, 1957. Convention concerning regulation of the question of citizenship of persons with dual citizenship. 388

Aug. 24, 1957. Consular convention. 388

Dec. 18, 1957. Agreement concerning economic and technical aid. 394

HUNGARY, three-way

Jan. 12, 1957. Communiqué concerning a meeting between representatives of the Communist and Workers' Parties and Governments (USSR, Hungary, Chinese People's Republic). 375

HUNGARY, unratified

Sept. 5, 1924. Treaty concerning establishment of diplomatic and consular relations. 401

HUNGARY, unverified

Mar. 19, 1925. Agreement concerning exchange of political prisoners. 428

Hungary. See also Plurilateral, Soviet bloc treaties and conferences.

HUNGARIAN SOVIET REPUBLIC, unverified

Apr. 1919. Military alliance. 427

ICELAND, bilateral

June 22 and 24, 1926. Exchange of notes concerning recognition of the USSR *de jure* and establishment of diplomatic relations. 57
May 25, 1927. Exchange of notes concerning the regime of most-favored-nation in trade relations. 60
July 27, Sept. 21, and Oct. 4, 1943. Exchange of telegrams concerning establishment of diplomatic relations. 155
Aug. 1, 1953. Trade and payments agreement, with two annexes. 298
Jan. 30 and Feb. 5, 1954. Exchange of notes modifying the trade and payments agreement of August 1, 1953. 307
June 19, 1954. Trade protocol. 313
Sept. 23, 1955. Trade protocol for 1956. 338
Sept. 23, 1955. Exchange of notes concerning an increase in the trade balance limit. 338
Dec. 3, 1955. Agreement concerning transformation of diplomatic missions into embassies. 343
Sept. 27, 1956. Trade protocol for 1957–1959. 368

INDIA, bilateral

Apr. 2 and 4, 1947. Exchange of notes concerning establishment of diplomatic relations. 231
Dec. 2, 1953. Commercial agreement, with two annexes. 304
Dec. 2, 1953. Exchange of notes concerning the Soviet Trade Mission in India. 304
Dec. 23, 1954. Exchange of notes concerning trade. 321
Feb. 2, 1955. Agreement concerning Soviet assistance for establishment of a metallurgical plant in India. 323
June 22, 1955. Joint statement concerning principles underlying relations between the two States. 330
Sept. 1955. Protocol concerning construction of a technological institute near Bombay. 335
Dec. 13, 1955. Joint statement concerning political relations. 344
Dec. 13, 1955. Joint communiqué concerning economic relations. 344
Dec. 23, 1955. Agreement concerning sale to India of twenty drill rigs. 345
Apr. 6, 1956. Agreement concerning establishment of a regular shipping service. 352
May 21, 1956. Agreement concerning purchase by India of Soviet oil-drilling equipment. 356
Nov. 1956. Agreement concerning a loan to India. 371
Nov. 26, 1956. Agreement concerning technical collaboration in oil prospecting in India. 372
May 5, 1957. Communiqué concerning signing of an agreement for the purchase by India of auxiliary equipment for oil drilling. 382
Nov. 9, 1957. Agreement concerning collaboration in construction of industrial enterprises in India and a Soviet credit to India of five hundred million rubles. 391
India. See also Nongovernmental agreements.

INDONESIA, bilateral

May 22, 1948. Exchange of notes concerning establishment of consular relations. 248
Jan. 26 and Feb. 3, 1950. Exchange of telegrams concerning recognition and establishment of diplomatic relations. 268
Nov. 30 and Dec. 17, 1953. Exchange of notes concerning establishment of embassies in Moscow and Djakarta. 304
Aug. 12, 1956. Commercial agreement, with two annexes and an exchange of notes. 366
Sept. 11, 1956. Joint statement concerning political negotiations. 367
Sept. 12, 1956. Trade agreement. 367
Sept. 15, 1956. General agreement concerning economic and technical collaboration. 368
May 19, 1957. Communiqué concerning political negotiations. 383

IRAN (PERSIA), bilateral

May 20, 1920. Exchange of notes concerning sending a Persian diplomatic mission to Moscow. 10
Feb. 26, 1921. Treaty of friendship. 18, 432
Oct. 1, 1921. Temporary railroad agreement. 24
Dec. 12, 1921. Exchange of notes concerning Arts. 3, 5, 6, 13, and 20 of the treaty of friendship of February 26, 1921. 27
Spring, 1922. Agreement concerning lease of fishing vessels for the spring season. 29
Spring, 1922. Temporary agreement con-

cerning the water supply to the Tejen region. 30

Apr. 25, 1923. Postal convention, with declaration. 38

Apr. 27, 1923. Telegraph convention, with declaration. 38

Oct. 7, 1924. Protocol concerning official language and entry into force of the postal convention of April 25, 1923, and the telegraph convention of April 27, 1923. 48

Feb. 20, 1926. Agreement concerning use of border rivers and waters from the river Geri-Rud (Tejen) to the Caspian Sea. 55

Aug. 14, 1927. Exchange of notes concerning establishment of the position of border commissioners. 61

Oct. 1, 1927. Treaty of nonaggression and neutrality, with two protocols and an exchange of notes. 61

Oct. 1, 1927. Agreement concerning exploitation of fisheries on the southern shore of the Caspian Sea, with related documents. 61

Oct. 1, 1927. Exchange of notes concerning Port Pehlevi. 62

Oct. 1, 1927. Customs convention, with final protocol, exchange of notes, and three lists. 62

Oct. 1, 1927. Exchange of notes constituting a temporary trade agreement, with related documents. 62

Nov. 23, 1927. Protocol concerning establishment of a link between the airlines of the USSR and those of Persia. 63

Jan. 31, 1928. Protocol concerning amendment of the Persian text of the second protocol to the agreement of October 1, 1927, concerning exploitation of fisheries on the southern shore of the Caspian Sea. 65

May 10 and 18, 1928. Exchange of notes abrogating the customs convention of October 1, 1927. 66

May 31, 1928. Convention concerning border crossing by inhabitants of border regions, with annex and supplementary protocol. 66

Aug. 14, 1928. Exchange of notes concerning establishment of the position of border commissioners. 67

Oct. 15 and Nov. 20, 1928. Exchange of notes concerning border commissioners. 68

Mar. 10, 1929. Customs convention, with supplementary protocol. 69

Aug. 2, 1929. Parcel post agreement, with supplementary protocol. 71

Oct. 27, 1931. Convention concerning settlement, commerce, and navigation, with related documents. 29

Dec. 11, 1933. Exchange of notes concerning settlement of commercial disputes. 91

May 30, 1935. Exchange of notes concerning transfer to Iran of lighthouses situated on the Iranian coast of the Caspian Sea. 102

Aug. 27, 1935. Treaty concerning settlement, commerce, and navigation, with related documents. 105

Aug. 27, 1935. Convention concerning the campaign against locusts in border districts. 105

Aug. 27, 1935. Convention concerning the campaign against plant diseases and parasites. 105

Aug. 27, 1935. Veterinary sanitary convention, with three annexes. 105

Aug. 27, 1935. Exchange of notes concerning entry into force of railroad conventions for direct and transit communications. 106

Aug. 27, 1935. Agreement concerning loading and unloading in Iranian ports of the Caspian Sea. 106

Feb. 1936. Agreements concerning direct rail transportation of passengers and freight. 434

Aug. 3, 1936. Exchange of notes concerning confirmation of the third annex of the veterinary sanitary convention of August 27, 1935. 113

Aug. 4 and 9, 1937. Exchange of notes concerning transfer to Iran of the floating lighthouse "Ashur-Ade." 118

Mar. 25, 1940. Treaty of commerce and navigation. 134

Mar. 25, 1940. Exchange of notes concerning nationals of third States employed on the Caspian Sea. 134

Mar. 25, 1940. Exchange of notes concerning reciprocal protection of trade-marks. 134

Mar. 25, 1940. Exchange of notes concerning representation of Soviet commercial organizations in Iranian courts. 134

Mar. 25, 1940. Exchange of notes concerning procedure for registration of passports of employees of the Soviet Trade Mission in Iran. 134

Mar. 25, 1940. Exchange of notes concerning technical conditions for railroad freight transportation and payment for reciprocal services. 134

Sept. 13, 1940. Agreement concerning railroad communications. 139

Sept. 13, 1940. Regulations for conferences concerned with railroad communications. 139

Sept. 13, 1940. Border railroad agreement, with thirteen annexes. 139

Aug. 25, 26, 28, and 30, and Sept. 1, 6, and 8, 1941. Exchange of notes concerning entry of Soviet troops into Iran. 146

Mar. 18, 1943. Payments agreement. 153

Oct. 3, 1945. Protocol supplementing the convention of August 27, 1935, concerning the campaign against plant diseases and parasites. 199

Mar. 6, 1946. Joint communiqué concerning negotiations on matters of common interest. 207

Mar. 24, 1946. Informal understanding concerning withdrawal of Soviet troops from Iran. 208

Apr. 4, 1946. Joint communiqué concerning negotiations. 209

Nov. 4, 1950. Exchange of letters constituting an agreement for the renewal of trade on the basis of the treaty of commerce and navigation of March 25, 1940, with annex. 278

May 1952. Trade agreement. 287

June 10, 1953. Exchange of notes constituting a trade agreement for the current year. 296

Aug. 10, 1953. Agreement concerning convocation in Teheran of a mixed Soviet-Iranian commission to settle disagreements on financial, border, and other questions. 299

Sept. 3, 1953. Exchange of notes concerning an increase in trade for the current year. 301

June 17, 1954. Exchange of notes concerning trade for the current year. 313

Dec. 2, 1954. Agreement concerning settlement of border and financial questions, with related documents. 320

Dec. 2, 1954. Exchange of notes concerning a payment by the USSR to Iran. 320

Dec. 2, 1954. Exchange of notes concerning a border rectification. 320

Jan. 29, 1955. Exchange of notes concerning border rectification. 323

Feb. 15, 1955. Agreement concerning sale and delivery of wheat to Iran. 323

May 4, 1955. Exchange of notes constituting a trade agreement for the current year. 327

June 9, 1955. Agreement concerning the lease of land and other property in the port of Pehlevi. 329

Sept. 5, 1956. Exchange of notes constituting a trade agreement for the current year. 367

Feb. 27, 1957. Joint communiqué concerning work of the mixed commission for demarcation and redemarcation of the state border. 378

Apr. 11, 1957. Final documents concerning demarcation and re-demarcation of the border. 381

Apr. 16, 1957. Exchange of letters concerning establishment of trade lists for 1957/1958, 1958/1959, and 1959/1960. 381

Apr. 27, 1957. Agreement concerning questions of transit. 382

May 14, 1957. Treaty concerning the regime on the border and procedure for settling border disputes and incidents. 382

Aug. 11, 1957. Agreement concerning establishment of preliminary plans for joint use of the border sectors of the Arax and Artek rivers for irrigation and the production of electricity. 387

IRAN, three-way

Jan. 29, 1942. Treaty of alliance, with three annexes (USSR, Iran, United Kingdom). 148

June 30, 1947. Documents concerning the border mark at the junction of the borders of the USSR, Afghanistan, and Iran (USSR, Iran, Afghanistan). 233

IRAN, unratified

July 3, 1924. Commercial treaty. 400

Apr. 4, 1946. Exchange of notes constituting an agreement concerning establishment of a mixed Soviet-Iranian oil company. 402

IRAN, unverified

Dec. 29, 1953. Trade agreement. 429

Iran. See also Nongovernmental agreements; Plurilateral, Nonaggression agreements.

IRAQ, bilateral

May 16, 1941. Exchange of notes concerning establishment of diplomatic, commercial, and consular relations. 144

Aug. 25 and Sept. 9, 1944. Exchange of telegrams concerning establishment of diplomatic relations. 163, 436

ISRAEL, bilateral

May 15 and 18, 1948. Exchange of telegrams concerning recognition of Israel by the USSR. 248

May 24 and 26, 1948. Exchange of telegrams concerning establishment of diplomatic missions in Moscow and Tel Aviv. 248

July 6 and 15, 1953. Exchange of notes concerning re-establishment of diplomatic relations. 297

Dec. 1953. Trade agreement. 441

Apr. 29 and May 13, 1954. Exchange of notes concerning transformation of diplomatic missions into embassies. 312

July 15, 1955. Exchange of notes constituting an agreement on most-favored-nation treatment in regard to shipping. 332

ITALY, bilateral

Apr. 27, 1920. Agreement concerning exchange of prisoners of war and interned civilians. 10

Apr. 27, 1920. Exchange of notes concerning appointment of representatives to supervise repatriation. 432

Apr. 27, 1920. Exchange of notes concerning conditions for repatriation. 432

Dec. 26, 1921. Preliminary agreement concerning political and economic matters, with declaration concerning recognition of claims. 28

Dec. 26, 1921. Preliminary agreement concerning political and economic matters, with declaration concerning recognition of claims (with the Ukrainian SSR). 28

June 22, 1922. Exchange of notes concerning extension of the preliminary agreement of Dec. 26, 1921. 33

Feb. 7, 1924. Treaty of commerce and navigation, with annex and final protocol. 40

Feb. 7, 1924. Customs agreement, with five annexes. 41

Feb. 7 and 13, 1924. Exchange of notes concerning recognition of the USSR *de jure*. 41.

June 16 and 25, 1925. Exchange of notes concerning import and export of samples. 51

June 19, 1926, and June 15, 1927. Exchange of notes concerning reciprocal registration of trade-marks. 61

Mar. 21, 1930. Exchange of notes constituting an agreement concerning exemption of certificates of origin from consular visas. 73

July 26, 1930. Exchange of notes concerning immunity of property belonging to a foreign State. 75

Aug. 2, 1930. Credit agreement, with three annexes. 75

Apr. 27, 1931. Credit agreement, with two annexes. 77

June 2, 1931. Exchange of notes modifying the agreement of March 21, 1930, concerning certificates of origin. 78

Sept. 11, 1931. Exchange of notes concerning entry into force of the agreement of March 21, 1930, concerning certificates of origin. 79

Aug. 7, Sept. 20, and Oct. 23, 1932. Exchange of notes modifying the agreement of March 21, 1930, concerning certificates of origin. 84

May 6, 1933. Customs convention, with final protocol. 86

May 6, 1933. Credit agreement, with two annexes. 87

June 10, 1933. Exchange of notes concerning provisional entry into force of the customs convention of May 6, 1933. 87

Sept. 2, 1933. Treaty of friendship, nonaggression and neutrality. 89

Dec. 5, 1933. Protocol extending existing economic and commercial agreements through December 31, 1934. 91

Dec. 31, 1934. Protocol extending existing economic and commercial agreements. 99

June 15, 1935. Credit agreement, with two annexes. 103

Nov. 20, 1937. Agreement concerning closing of Italian consulates in the USSR. 119

Feb. 7, 1939. Trade and payments agreement. 123

Feb. 7, 1939. Secret protocols supplementing the trade and payments agreement of February 7, 1939. 123

Feb. 7, 1939. Exchange of notes concerning commercial transactions between Italian firms and Soviet economic organizations. 123

Sept. 3, 1943. Armistice agreement. 154

Sept. 29, 1943. Instrument of surrender (Additional conditions of the armistice with Italy). 155

Nov. 9, 1943. Protocol concerning modifications in the text of the instrument of surrender of September 29, 1943. 156

Mar. 7 and 11, 1944. Exchange of notes concerning establishment of diplomatic relations. 159

Oct. 25, 1944. Declaration concerning establishment of full diplomatic relations. 167

Feb. 10, 1947. Treaty of peace, with seventeen annexes. 227

Mar. 1948. Exchange of notes concerning negotiations for conclusion of agreements on reparations and trade. 438

Nov. 6, 1948. Preliminary agreement concerning reparations deliveries by Italy. 254

Dec. 11, 1948. Joint communiqué concerning economic relations. 254

Dec. 11, 1948. Agreement concerning reparations payments by Italy, with annex. 255

Dec. 11, 1948. Trade agreement, with four annexes. 255

Dec. 11, 1948. Payments agreement. 255

Dec. 11, 1948. Treaty of commerce and navigation, with annex concerning the Soviet Trade Mission in Italy and protocol. 255

Mar. 11, 1952. Trade protocol for 1952, with two annexes. 285

Oct. 27, 1953. Trade protocol, with exchange of notes. 302

Aug. 12, 1955. Trade protocol for 1955. 334

June 1, 1956. Trade protocol for 1956. 357

Dec. 28, 1957. Trade agreement for the period 1958–1961. 396

Dec. 28, 1957. Trade protocol for 1958. 396

Dec. 28, 1957. Payments agreement. 396

ITALY, unratified

May 24, 1922. Temporary commercial treaty. 400

Italy. See also Nongovernmental agreements.

JAPAN, bilateral

Apr. 29, 1920. Armistice agreement. 10

June 15, 1920. Supplementary armistice agreement. 11

July 15, 1920. Armistice agreement. 12

July 16, 1920. Joint declaration concerning establishment of a buffer State and associated matters. 12

Sept. 24, 1920. Agreement concerning establishment of a neutral zone south of the river Iman after withdrawal of Japanese forces from Khabarovsk. 13

Oct. 24, 1922. Agreement concerning evacuation of Vladivostok by Japanese troops. 35

Apr. 6, 1924. Temporary agreement concerning fisheries. 42

Jan. 20, 1925. Convention concerning general principles of mutual relations. 49

Jan. 20, 1925. Protocol concerning governmental diplomatic property, debts owed by Japan to the former Russian Government, evacuation of Japanese troops from Northern Sakhalin, and agreements with third parties. 49

Jan. 20, 1925. Protocol concerning concessions in Northern Sakhalin. 49

Jan. 20, 1925. Declaration by the USSR disavowing responsibility for conclusion of the Treaty of Portsmouth between Russia and Japan of September 5, 1905. 49

Jan. 20, 1925. Exchange of notes concerning Japanese industrial operations in Northern Sakhalin. 50

Jan. 20, 1925. Note expressing the regret of the USSR to Japan for the Nikolaevsk incident of 1920. 50

Jan. 20, 1925. Protocol of signature to the convention of January 20, 1925. 50

Apr. 4, 1925. Joint announcement concerning surrender of Northern Sakhalin to the USSR. 433

1926. Exchange of notes concerning consular relations. 54

Jan. 23, 1928. Fishery convention, with related documents. 65

Aug. 17, 1929. Exchange of notes constituting an agreement concerning reciprocal recognition of tonnage measurement certificates. 72

Apr. 24, 1931. Agreement concerning a provisional rate for payments by Japanese firms for lease of fishing lots. 77

Nov. 23, 1931. Parcel post agreement. 80

Nov. 23, 1931. Regulations for execution of the parcel post agreement of November 23, 1931. 80

Aug. 13, 1932. Provisional agreement concerning fisheries. 83

June 3, 1933. Exchange of notes concerning negotiations between the USSR and Manchukuo for the sale of the Chinese Eastern Railway. 87

Mar. 23, 1935. Exchange of notes concerning guarantee of payments by Manchukuo to the USSR for the Chinese Eastern Railway. 100

May 25, 1936. Protocol extending the fishery convention of January 23, 1928. 111

Dec. 28, 1936. Protocol extending the fishery convention of January 23, 1928. 114

July 2, 1937. Agreement concerning withdrawal of military forces from the Amur River islands. 116

Dec. 29, 1937. Protocol extending the fishery convention of January 23, 1928. 120

Aug. 10, 1938. Agreement concerning settlement of the dispute on the Soviet-Manchurian border. 122

Apr. 2, 1939. Protocol extending the fishery convention of January 23, 1928. 124

Apr. 2, 1939. Exchange of notes concerning auction of fishery lots. 125

Sept. 15, 1939 (approximate date). Armistice agreement on behalf of the Mongolian People's Republic and Manchukuo. 127

Nov. 19, 1939. Agreement concerning establishment of a mixed commission for demarcation of the border between the Mongolian People's Republic and Manchukuo. 132

Dec. 31, 1939. Agreement concerning payment of the final installment due the USSR from Manchukuo for the Chinese Eastern Railway and settlement of claims. 132

Dec. 31, 1939. Protocol extending the fishery convention of January 23, 1928. 133

Dec. 31, 1939. Exchange of notes concerning fishery lots. 133

June 9, 1940. Agreement concerning the border between Manchukuo and the Mongolian People's Republic. 135

July 18, 1940. Agreement concerning the boundary between Manchukuo and the Mongolian People's Republic. 135

Jan. 20, 1941. Protocol extending the fishery convention of January 23, 1928. 142

Jan. 20, 1941. Exchange of notes concerning auction of fishery lots. 142

Jan. 20, 1941 (approximate date). Agreement concerning establishment of a mixed commission to prepare a new fishery convention. 142

Apr. 13, 1941. Pact of neutrality. 143

Apr. 13, 1941. Joint declaration pledging respect for the territorial integrity and inviolability of Manchukuo and the Mongolian People's Republic. 144

Mar. 20, 1942. Protocol extending the fishery convention of January 23, 1928. 149

Mar. 20, 1942. Exchange of notes concerning fishery lots. 149

Mar. 25, 1943. Protocol extending the fishery convention of January 23, 1928. 153

Mar. 25, 1943. Exchange of notes concerning fishery lots. 153

Mar. 10, 1944. Agreement concerning procedure for transfer to the Soviet Government of the property of Japanese oil and coal concessions in North Sakhalin. 159

Mar. 30, 1944. Protocol concerning transfer to the USSR of Japanese oil and coal concessions in North Sakhalin, with annex. 159

Mar. 30, 1944. Protocol extending the fishery convention of January 23, 1928. 159

Mar. 30, 1944. Exchange of notes concerning fishery lots. 160

Mar. 30, 1944. Exchange of notes concerning closing of consulates. 160

Aug. 8, 1945. Declaration calling for Japanese surrender. 189

Aug. 10 and 11, 1945. Exchange of notes concerning surrender by Japan. 190

Aug. 14, 1945. Exchange of communications concerning surrender by Japan. 193

Sept. 2, 1945. Instrument of surrender by Japan. 196

Dec. 19, 1946. Agreement concerning repatriation of Japanese prisoners of war and civilians from the USSR and from territories under Soviet control, as well as Korean nationals from Japan to Soviet-occupied North Korea, with two annexes. 224

Nov. 19, 1953. Joint communiqué concerning negotiations between (1) the Red Cross and Red Crescent Societies of the USSR and (2) the Red Cross Society of Japan concerning repatriation of Japanese prisoners of war and civilians from the USSR. 303

May 14, 1956. Convention concerning the fisheries in the high seas of the Northwest Pacific Ocean. 355

May 14, 1956. Agreement concerning cooperation for the rescue of persons in distress at sea, with exchange of notes. 355

Oct. 19, 1956. Joint declaration concerning political relations. 369

Oct. 19, 1956. Protocol concerning development of trade and reciprocal application of the most-favored-nation clause. 370

Apr. 6, 1957. Joint communiqué concerning fishing in the Northwest Pacific. 380

Dec. 6, 1957. Treaty of commerce, with annex concerning the Soviet Trade Mission in Japan. 392

Dec. 6, 1957. Trade and payments agreement. 392

JAPAN, three-way

Mar. 23, 1935. Protocol concerning payments to be made by Manchukuo to the USSR for the Chinese Eastern Railway (USSR, Japan, Manchukuo). 100

JAPAN, unratified

June 11, 1941. Commercial agreement. 402

June 11, 1941. Trade and payments agreement. 402

JAPAN, unverified

Mar. 1930. Agreement concerning exchange of military officers to be attached to army units. 428

Japan. See also Nongovernmental agreements.

KHOREZM SOVIET PEOPLE'S REPUBLIC, bilateral

Sept. 13, 1920. Treaty of alliance. 13

Sept. 13, 1920. Economic agreement. 13

June 29, 1922. Economic agreement. 33

Khorezm Soviet People's Republic. See also Plurilateral, internal Soviet treaties.

KOREAN PEOPLE'S DEMOCRATIC REPUBLIC (including North Korea), bilateral

Aug. 4, 1948. Agreement concerning training of North Korean students in civic institutions of higher education in the USSR and their maintenance, with protocol. 251

Sept. 10 and 18, 1948. Exchange of notes concerning withdrawal of Soviet troops from Korea. 253

Oct. 8 and 12, 1948. Exchange of notes concerning establishment of diplomatic and commercial relations. 253

Mar. 17, 1949 (approximate date). Joint communiqué concerning economic relations. 257

Mar. 17, 1949. Agreement concerning economic and cultural collaboration. 257

Mar. 17, 1949. Trade and payments agreement. 258

Mar. 17, 1949. Agreement concerning a Soviet credit. 258

Mar. 17, 1949. Agreement concerning Soviet technical aid. 258

Oct. 5, 1950. Agreement concerning conditions of trade deliveries. 277

May 6, 1952. Agreement concerning training of KPDR citizens in civic institutions of higher education in the USSR. 287

Sept. 19, 1953. Joint communiqué concerning conversations. 302

Mar. 15, 1954. Trade protocol for 1954. 308

Dec. 28, 1954. Agreement concerning exchange of mail and parcel post. 321

Dec. 28, 1954. Agreement concerning establishment of telephone and telegraph communications. 321

Feb. 1955. Trade protocol for 1955. 323

Feb. 5, 1955. Agreement concerning scientific and technical collaboration. 323

May 31, 1955. Joint communiqué concerning transfer to the KPDR of Soviet shares in USSR-KPDR joint-stock companies. 329

Aug. 31, 1955. Agreement concerning transfer to the KPDR of Soviet shares in the joint-stock air transport company "SO-KAO." 335

Nov. 30, 1955. Convention concerning quarantine and combating parasites and diseases of agricultural plants, with two annexes. 342

Dec. 7, 1955. Agreement concerning air communications. 343

Dec. 9, 1955. Agreement concerning air transportation and service. 343

Jan. 26, 1956. Trade protocol for 1956. 347

Feb. 29, 1956. Communiqué concerning the first meeting of the USSR-KPDR commission for scientific and technical collaboration. 350

July 12, 1956. Joint communiqué concerning political negotiations. 363

Sept. 5, 1956. Agreement concerning cultural collaboration. 367

Dec. 23, 1956. Communiqué concerning the second meeting of the USSR-KPDR commission for scientific and technical collaboration. 274

Apr. 22, 1957. Trade protocol for 1957. 382

Apr. 25, 1957. Communiqué concerning signing of a protocol concerning transfer to the central Red Cross hospital of the KPDR of property, equipment, and medicaments of the hospital of the Red Cross Society of the USSR. 382

May 17, 1957. Protocol concerning the third meeting of the USSR-KPDR commission for scientific and technical collaboration. 382

Aug. 14, 1957 (approximate date). Agreement concerning conditions for sending Soviet specialists to the KPDR and vice versa, for technical aid and other services. 387

Aug. 14, 1957 (approximate date). Agreement concerning conditions for technical production training of Soviet and KPDR specialists and workers. 387

Aug. 14, 1957 (approximate date). Protocol concerning Soviet technical aid to the KPDR for expansion of nitrogen fertilizer production. 387

Oct. 11, 1957. Agreement concerning collaboration between the Academies of Sciences of the USSR and the KPDR. 390

Oct. 14, 1957. Convention concerning regulation of border questions. 390

Dec. 12, 1957. Protocol concerning the fourth meeting of the USSR-KPDR commission for scientific and technical collaboration. 393

Dec. 16, 1957. Consular convention. 393

Dec. 16, 1957. Convention concerning regulation of the question of citizenship of persons with dual citizenship. 393

Dec. 16, 1957. Treaty concerning legal aid in civil, family, and criminal cases. 394

KOREAN PEOPLE'S DEMOCRATIC REPUBLIC, three-way

July 3, 1956. Agreement concerning collaboration in saving human lives and aiding ships and airplanes wrecked in the waters of the Far Eastern Seas and the Pacific Ocean (USSR, KPDR, Chinese People's Republic). 360

Korean People's Democratic Republic. See also Plurilateral, Soviet bloc agreements and conferences.

LATVIA, bilateral

Nov. 19, 1919. Agreement concerning exchange of hostages and civilian prisoners. 8

Jan. 30, 1920. Secret armistice treaty, with two supplementary articles and a protocol. 431

Feb. 1, 1920. Secret supplementary armistice treaty. 431

June 12, 1920. Treaty concerning re-evacuation of refuges. 11

Aug. 11, 1920. Peace treaty. 12

Nov. 16, 1920. Agreement concerning repatriation of prisoners of war. 15

Feb. 26, 1921. Convention concerning direct rail communications for passengers and freight. 18

Feb. 26, 1921. Protocol of a conference for conclusion of a convention concerning direct rail communications for passengers and freight. 18

Feb. 26, 1921. Regulations concerning transportation of passengers and their baggage and freight in direct rail communications. 18

Feb. 26, 1921. Agreement concerning direct rail communications and the use of freight cars, with annex. 18

Mar. 3, 1921. Temporary agreement concerning postal and telegraph communications. 19

June 12, 1921. Provisional agreement concerning transportation of passengers, baggage and freight between the railroads of Latvia and the rail network Orël-Vitebsk. 21

July 22, 1921. Agreement concerning procedure for choice of citizenship. 22

Aug. 3, 1921. Treaty concerning future relations, with annex. 22

Aug. 3, 1921. Convention concerning repatriation of Latvian refugees from the Ukrainian SSR. 22

Nov. 6, 1921. Agreement concerning repatriation. 26

Nov. 6, 1921. Agreement concerning export and destruction of property. 26

Dec. 23, 1921. Temporary agreement concerning parcel post. 28

Aug. 16, 1922. Protocol of an agreement concerning exchange of arrested and imprisoned persons. 35

Nov. 10, 1922. Protocol concerning responsibility for requisitions and military actions on Ukrainian territory before July 26, 1922. 37

Mar. 19, 1925. Exchange of declarations concerning reciprocal recognition of tonnage measurement certificates. 50

July 19, 1926. Agreement concerning consideration and settlement of border disputes, with protocol. 57

June 2, 1927. Agreement concerning legal aid in civil cases. 60

June 2, 1927. Commercial treaty, with final protocol. 60

June 2, 1927. Customs convention, with related documents. 61

Oct. 10, 1927. Convention concerning arbitration tribunals in commercial and civil cases, with final protocol. 63

May 18, 1928. Protocol concerning amendments in the Latvian text of the convention of October 10, 1927, concerning arbitration tribunals. 66

Dec. 17, 1930, and Jan. 14, 1931. Exchange of notes modifying the agreement of June 2, 1927, concerning legal aid in civil cases. 76

Feb. 5, 1932. Treaty of nonaggression. 81

June 18, 1932. Convention concerning conciliation procedure. 83

Dec. 4, 1933. Treaty of commerce, with final protocol. 91

Dec. 4, 1933. Economic agreement, with final protocol. 91

Dec. 30, 1933. Agreement concerning introduction of direct fares on railroads. 434

Apr. 4, 1934. Protocol extending the nonaggression treaty of February 5, 1932. 93

Aug. 3, 1934. Communiqué concerning political negotiations. 96

Apr. 9, 1937. Exchange of notes constituting an agreement concerning repair and restoration of boundary marks. 115

June 18, 1937. Communiqué concerning negotiations. 116

June 21, 1937. Protocol modifying the economic agreement of December 4, 1933. 116

Feb. 11, 1939. Trade agreement for 1939. 123

Oct. 5, 1939. Pact of mutual assistance. 130

Oct. 18, 1939. Trade agreement for 1939–1940, with protocol. 131

Oct. 23, 1939. Agreement concerning establishment of Soviet military bases in Latvia. 131

June 16, 1940. Soviet ultimatum demanding formation of a new government in Latvia and the entrance of Soviet troops into major cities in Latvia. 136

LATVIA, three- and four-way

Mar. 30, 1922. Final protocol concerning economic problems and the consolidation of peace in Eastern Europe (RSFSR, Latvia, Estonia, Poland). 30

June 24, 1922. Sanitary convention (RSFSR, Latvia, Belorussian SSR, Ukrainian SSR). 33

Oct. 29, 1925. Convention concerning through passenger and freight communications by rail, with related documents (USSR, Latvia, Estonia). 53

Apr. 21, 1933. Agreement abrogating the convention of October 29, 1925, concerning through passenger and freight communications by rail, and the annexed regulations (USSR, Latvia, Estonia). 86

Latvia. See also Plurilateral, nonaggression agreements.

LEBANON, bilateral

July 31 and Aug. 3, 1944. Exchange of telegrams concerning establishment of diplomatic relations. 162

Apr. 30, 1954. Trade and payments agreement, with two annexes. 311

Apr. 30, 1954. Exchange of notes concerning the value of trade between the two States. 311

Apr. 30, 1954. Exchange of notes concerning the Soviet Trade Mission in Lebanon. 312

Oct. 1, 1955. Exchange of notes concerning trade. 339

June 28, 1956. Joint communiqué concerning political and economic negotiations. 359

Oct. 13, 1956. Trade protocol for 1957. 369

LIBERIA, bilateral

Jan. 11, 1956. Exchange of notes concerning establishment of diplomatic relations. 346

LIBYA, bilateral

Sept. 25, 1955. Joint communiqué concerning establishment of diplomatic relations and exchange of diplomatic missions at the level of embassies. 338

LITHUANIA, bilateral

Nov. 19, 1919. Agreement concerning exchange of hostages and civilian prisoners. 8

Mar. 10, 1920. Protocol concerning conditions for exchange of hostages and civilian prisoners. 9

June 30, 1920. Treaty concerning re-evacuation of refugees. 11

July 10, 1920. Protocol concerning conditions for exchange of hostages and civilian prisoners. 432

July 12, 1920. Peace treaty. 11

July 14, 1920. Exchange of notes concerning the passage of Soviet troops through Lithuanian territory. 12

Sept. 25, 1920. Agreement concerning legal guarantees. 13

Jan. 28, 1921. Agreement concerning procedure for choosing Lithuanian citizenship. 17

Jan. 28, 1921. Agreement concerning provisional regulations for transportation of Lithuanian refugees on their re-evacuation from the Ukrainian SSR. 17

Feb. 14, 1921. Peace treaty. 17

Feb. 14, 1921. Treaty concerning re-evacuation of refugees. 17

June 28, 1921. Agreement concerning procedure for choice of Lithuanian citizenship, with annex. 21

Apr. 5, 1922. Agreement concerning temporary rules for the transportation by rail of the property of persons choosing Lithuanian citizenship. 31

Apr. 5, 1922. Supplementary treaty to the peace treaty of February 14, 1921, with supplementary protocol. 31

Sept. 28, 1926. Treaty of nonaggression, with two exchanges of notes. 58

Sept. 24, 1928. Exchange of notes constituting a trade agreement. 67

May 17 and 19, 1930. Exchange of notes concerning reciprocal recognition of trade-marks. 74

May 6, 1931. Protocol extending for five years the treaty of nonaggression of September 28, 1926. 78

Aug. 29, 1931. Protocol concerning the legal status of the Soviet Trade Mission in Lithuania, with two exchanges of notes. 79

July 5, 1933. Convention concerning the definition of aggression, with annex. 88

Apr. 4, 1934. Protocol extending the treaty of nonaggression of September 28, 1926. 93

Mar. 23, 1935. Trade protocol for 1935. 100

Jan. 15, 1936. Trade agreement for 1936. 108

Jan. 23, 1937. Trade agreement for 1937. 115

Dec. 23, 1937. Trade agreement for 1938. 120

Feb. 14, 1939. Trade agreement for 1939. 124

Oct. 10, 1939. Treaty concerning mutual assistance and the transfer of the city of Vilna and Vilna Province to Lithuania, with map. 130

Oct. 15, 1939. Trade agreement for 1939–1940. 131

Oct. 27, 1939. Protocol concerning redefinition of the border as the result of the transfer to Lithuania of the city and province of Vilna, with map. 131

June 14 and 15, 1940. Soviet ultimatum demanding formation of a new government in Lithuania and the entrance of Soviet troops into major cities in Lithuania. 136

Lithuania. See also Plurilateral, nonaggression agreements.

LUXEMBOURG, bilateral (see also Belgium-Luxembourg Economic Union)

Aug. 26, 1935. Exchange of notes concerning establishment of diplomatic relations. 105

Oct. 13, 1942. Agreement concerning establishment of diplomatic relations. 436

MANCHUKUO, bilateral

Mar. 23, 1935. Agreement concerning transfer to Manchukuo of the rights of the USSR to the Chinese Eastern Railway, with final protocol. 100

MANCHUKUO, three-way

Mar. 23, 1935. Protocol concerning payments to be made by Manchukuo to the USSR for the Chinese Eastern Railway

Manchukuo. See also Nongovernmental agreements; Japan, bilateral.

MANCHURIA (Communist regime), bilateral

July 30, 1949 (approximate date). Trade agreement. 261

MEXICO, bilateral

Aug. 4, 1924. Declaration (aide-mémoire) concerning recognition of the USSR de jure. 46

Nov. 10 and 12, 1942. Exchange of notes concerning re-establishment of diplomatic relations. 152

June 7 and 14, 1943. Exchange of notes concerning reorganization of diplomatic missions into embassies. 154

MONGOLIAN PEOPLE'S REPUBLIC (including Mongolia), bilateral

July–Aug. 10, 1921. Exchange of telegrams concerning Soviet military aid. 22

Oct. 17 and 28, 1921. Exchange of notes concerning Soviet military aid to wipe out resistance in western Mongolia. 25

Nov. 5, 1921. Agreement concerning establishment of friendly relations. 26

May 31, 1922. Protocol concerning ownership of various property. 32

Feb. 20, 1923. Economic agreement. 432

Oct. 3, 1924. Agreement concerning telegraph communications, with supplementary protocol. 48

Feb. 22, 1927. Protocol extending and modifying the agreement of October 3, 1924, concerning telegraph communications. 59

1929. Agreement concerning basic principles of relations between the two States. 434

May 20, 1930. Agreement concerning questions of citizenship. 74

June 1930. Agreement concerning sanitation. 74

June 1930. Agreement concerning eradication of animal diseases. 74

June 1930. Agreement concerning border crossing. 74

June 28, 1930. Convention concerning execution of judicial decisions in certain categories of civil cases. 434

Feb. 28, 1931. Exchange of notes constituting an agreement concerning questions relating to extradition of criminals. 76

Apr. 16, 1931 (date of entry into force).

Agreement concerning execution of judgments in civil cases. 77

Nov. 27, 1934. Gentlemen's agreement concerning mutual aid in case of attack by a third party. 98

Dec. 1, 1934. Trade agreement. 98

Dec. 1, 1934. Agreement concerning payments. 98

Dec. 1, 1934, (possible date). Agreement concerning currency exchange rates. 98

Dec. 1, 1934 (possible date). Agreement concerning mixed Soviet-Mongolian companies. 98

Mar. 12, 1936. Protocol of mutual assistance. 109

Apr. 24, 1937. Agreement concerning questions of citizenship. 115

July 22, 1941. Agreement concerning compensation to the USSR for expenditures for the maintenance and education of Mongolian citizens in educational institutions of the USSR. 145

Oct. 10, 1944. Agreement concerning exchange of mail and packages. 166

Feb. 27, 1946. Treaty of friendship and mutual assistance. 207

Feb. 27, 1946. Agreement concerning economic and cultural collaboration. 207

May 12, 1948. Agreement concerning training of Mongolian citizens in civic institutions of higher learning in the USSR and their maintenance. 248

Feb. 24, 1949. Agreement concerning organization of geologic prospecting for oil and of industrial exploitation of MPR oil reserves. 439

Mar. 12, 1949. Agreement concerning establishment of a USSR-MPR joint-stock company, "Sovmongolmetall," for prospecting for, extracting, and preparing useful minerals. 439

June 6, 1949. Agreement concerning establishment of a Soviet-Mongolian joint-stock railroad company, "Ulan-Batorskaia zheleznaia doroga." 260

June 6, 1949. Agreement concerning a Soviet loan. 439

Dec. 9, 1949. Trade agreement for the period 1950–1954. 265

Dec. 9, 1949. Trade protocol for 1950. 439

Apr. 1950. Agreement concerning transformation of diplomatic missions into embassies. 273

Oct. 28, 1950. Trade protocol for 1951. 439

Nov. 1, 1950. Protocol concerning the joint-stock company "Ulan-Batorskaia zheleznaia doroga." 439

Dec. 21, 1951. Agreement concerning conditions for paying Soviet specialists sent to the MPR to render technical aid. 440

Dec. 26, 1951. Trade protocol for 1952. 440

Dec. 29, 1951. Agreement concerning conditions of trade deliveries. 440

Apr. 30, 1952. Agreement concerning training of Mongolian citizens in civic institutions of higher education in the USSR. 286

June 13, 1952. Protocol concerning Soviet technical aid to the MPR. 440

Feb. 23, 1953. Trade protocol for 1953. 441

Apr. 8, 1953. Protocol concerning an increase in capitalization of the joint-stock company "Ulan-Batorskaia zheleznaia doroga." 441

Apr. 8, 1953. Agreement concerning a Soviet loan. 441

Sept. 11, 1953. Agreement concerning collaboration in the field of radio broadcasting. 301

Dec. 26, 1953. Trade protocol for 1954. 305

Nov. 19, 1954. Trade agreement for the period 1955–1957. 319

Nov. 19, 1954. Trade protocol for 1955. 319

Aug. 12, 1955. Agreement concerning technical aid and credit. 443

Oct. 17, 1955. Protocol concerning rail communications. 340

Nov. 16, 1955. Trade protocol for 1956. 342

Apr. 8, 1956. Joint communiqué concerning economic relations. 353

Apr. 24, 1956. Agreement concerning cultural collaboration. 353

Nov. 9, 1956. Agreement concerning non-commercial payments. 372

Dec. 1, 1956. Agreement concerning air communications. 373

Dec. 14, 1956. Trade protocol for 1957. 374

Feb. 14, 1957. Act concerning transfer by the USSR to the MPR of telegraph and telephone equipment and installations built by the USSR on the territory of the MPR. 445

Apr. 16, 1957. Protocol supplementing the agreement of June 6, 1949, concerning establishment of the Soviet-Mongolian joint-stock railroad company "Ulan-Batorskaia zheleznaia doroga." 381

Apr. 22, 1957. Agreement concerning air transportation and reciprocal services. 381

Apr. 22, 1957. Agreement concerning technical collaboration in the field of civil aviation. 382

May 15, 1957. Joint communiqué concerning political and economic relations. 382

Dec. 16, 1957. Protocol concerning cultural and scientific collaboration in 1958. 393

Dec. 17, 1957. Treaty of commerce, with annex concerning the Soviet Trade Mission in the MPR and the MPR Trade Mission in the USSR. 394

Dec. 17, 1957. Trade agreement for the period 1958–1960. 394

Dec. 17, 1957. Trade protocol for 1958. 394

MONGOLIAN PEOPLE'S REPUBLIC, three-way

(CPR—Chinese People's Republic)

Sept. 15, 1952. Agreement concerning construction of a railroad from Tsinin to

Ulan-Bator and establishment of direct rail communications (USSR, MPR, CPR). 291

Oct. 12, 1954. Joint communiqué concerning construction of a railroad from Tsinin to Ulan-Bator and the organization of direct communications (USSR, MPR, CPR). 318

Oct. 17, 1955. Protocol concerning opening of through rail traffic between the USSR and the Chinese People's Republic by way of the MPR (USSR, MPR, CPR). 340

Jan. 4, 1956. Joint communiqué concerning opening of direct rail communications (USSR, MPR, CPR). 346

MONGOLIAN PEOPLE'S REPUBLIC, unverified

Sept. 1925. Agreement concerning construction of a railroad between Urga and Chita. 428

June 1926. Agreement concerning navigation by Soviet vessels on Mongolian rivers. 428

Mongolian People's Republic. See also Plurilateral, Soviet bloc treaties and conferences; Japan, bilateral.

MOROCCO, bilateral

Apr. 18, 1957. One-year trade protocol. 381

MUKDEN GOVERNMENT (Government of the Three Autonomous Eastern Provinces), see China.

MULTILATERAL, international agreements and conferences

Note: Entries are in chronological order by original date of signature. Where the date of Soviet accession differs, it is shown in parentheses.

May 20, 1875 (July 21, 1925). International Metric Convention, with Statute. 51

July 22, 1875 (Apr. 11, 1925). International Telegraph Convention. 50

Mar. 14, 1884 (Feb. 2, 1926). International convention concerning protection of underwater telegraph cables, with declaration and final protocol. 55

July 5, 1890 (Dec. 21, 1935). Convention concerning establishment of an International Union for the Publication of Customs Tariffs, with Regulations and protocol of signature. 107

Dec. 21, 1904 (June 4, 1918; June 16, 1925). Hague Convention concerning the exemption of hospital ships from port and other dues. 5, 50

June 7, 1905 (Apr. 4, 1936). Convention concerning establishment of a permanent International Institute of Agriculture. 110

July 6, 1906 (June 4, 1918; June 16, 1925). Geneva Convention for the amelioration of the condition of sick and wounded soldiers in the field. 5, 51

Oct. 18, 1907 (June 4, 1918; June 16, 1925). Hague Convention for the adaptation to maritime warfare of the principles of the Geneva Convention of July 6, 1906. 5, 51

Dec. 9, 1907 (Oct. 27, 1925). International agreement concerning establishment of an International Office of Public Health, with Statute. 53

Oct. 11, 1909 (Dec. 29, 1925). Convention on the international circulation of automobiles. 54

May 9, 1910 (July 8, 1935; May 14, 1949). Agreement for suppression of the circulation of obscene publications. 104, 259

Sept. 23, 1910 (Feb. 2, 1926). Convention for unification of certain rules concerning collisions between vessels at sea. 55

Sept. 23, 1910 (Feb. 2, 1926). Convention for unification of rules concerning assistance and salvage at sea. 55

July 7, 1911 (Feb. 2, 1926). Convention concerning protection of fur seals. 55

Jan. 17, 1912 (Oct. 27, 1925). International sanitary convention, with two annexes and protocol. 53

Feb. 9, 1920 (Feb. 27, 1935). Treaty concerning the Archipelago of Spitsbergen, with annex. 100

Apr. 20, 1921 (Apr. 7, 1935). Declaration recognizing the right to a flag of states having no seacoast. 100

Sept. 30, 1921 (Dec. 18, 1947). International convention for suppression of the traffic in women and children. 242

Oct. 6, 1921 (June 16, 1925). International convention introducing changes into the International Metric Convention signed May 20, 1875, in Paris, and the Statute annexed to it. 51

Nov. 11, 1921 (July 6, 1956). Convention fixing the minimum age for the admission of young persons to employment as trimmers or stokers (International Labour Organisation Convention No. 15). 361

Nov. 11, 1921 (July 6, 1956). Convention concerning the compulsory medical examination of children and young persons employed at sea (International Labour Organisation Convention No. 16). 361

Nov. 12, 1921 (July 6, 1956). Convention concerning the rights of association and combination of agricultural workers (International Labour Organisation Convention No. 11). 360

Nov. 16, 1921 (July 6, 1956). Convention concerning the age for admission of children to employment in agriculture (International Labour Organisation Convention No. 10). 360

Sept. 12, 1923 (July 8, 1935). International convention for suppression of the circulation of and traffic in obscene publications. 104

Jan. 25, 1924 (Oct. 20, 1927). International agreement for the creation at Paris of an international office for dealing with contagious diseases of animals, with Statute. 63

Aug. 28, 1924. Universal Postal Convention, with related documents. 47

Aug. 28, 1924. Agreement of the Universal Postal Union concerning insured letters and boxes, with related documents. 47

Aug. 28, 1924. Agreement of the Universal Postal Union concerning money orders, with related documents. 47

Feb. 19, 1925 (Oct. 31, 1935). International opium convention, with annex and protocol. 106

Feb. 19, 1925 (Oct. 31, 1935). Final Act of the Second International Opium Conference. 107

June 17, 1925 (Dec. 2, 1927). Protocol concerning prohibition of the use in war of asphyxiating, poisonous or other gases, and of bacteriological methods of warfare. 64

Aug. 19, 1925. Convention concerning suppression of the contraband traffic in alcoholic products, with final protocol. 52

Oct. 29, 1925. International Service Regulations annexed to the International Telegraph Convention of July 22, 1875, as revised at Paris, October 29, 1925. 53

Dec. 31, 1925 (Feb. 9, 1929). Baltic Geodetic Convention. 69

Apr. 21, 1926 (Apr. 4, 1936). Protocol modifying the convention of June 7, 1905, concerning establishment of a permanent International Institute of Agriculture. 46

Apr. 24, 1926. International convention concerning motor traffic, with six annexes. 56

June 21, 1926. International sanitary convention, with annex and protocol of signature. 56

Sept. 25, 1926 (Aug. 1956). Convention concerning slavery. 364

Oct. 29, 1927. Convention for the creation at Paris of an International Office of Chemistry, with Regulations. 63

Aug. 27, 1928. General Treaty for renunciation of war as an instrument of national policy (Kellogg-Briand Pact; Treaty of Paris). 67

Sept. 22, 1928 (Oct. 8, 1929). Protocol concerning changes and additions to the International Service Regulations annexed to the International Telegraph Convention of 1875, as revised 1925 in Paris. 72

Nov. 22, 1928. Convention concerning international exhibitions, with protocol and protocol of signature. 68

Apr. 16, 1929 (Sept. 26, 1935). International convention for the protection of plants, with annex. 106

Apr. 20, 1929. International convention for suppression of counterfeiting currency, with protocol. 70

May 31, 1929. International convention for the safety of life at sea, with regulations. 70

May 31, 1929. Final Act of the International Conference on Safety of Life at Sea. 71

June 28, 1929. Universal Postal Convention, with related documents. 71

June 28, 1929. Agreement of the Universal Postal Union concerning insured letters and boxes, with related documents. 71

July 27, 1929 (Aug. 25, 1931). Geneva Convention for the amelioration of the condition of the wounded and sick in armies in the field. 79

Oct. 12, 1929. Convention for the unification of certain rules concerning international air transport, with supplementary protocol. 72

Oct. 12, 1929. Final protocol of the Second International Conference on private law affecting air questions. 72

June 7, 1930 (Nov. 25, 1936). Convention providing a uniform law for bills of exchange and promissory notes, with two annexes and a protocol. 114

June 7, 1930 (Nov. 25, 1936). Convention concerning settlement of certain conflicts of laws in connection with bills of exchange and promissory notes, with protocol. 114

June 7, 1930 (Nov. 25, 1936). Convention concerning stamp laws in connection with bills of exchange and promissory notes, with protocol. 114

June 28, 1930 (June 4, 1956). Convention concerning forced or compulsory labor (International Labour Organisation Convention No. 29). 357

July 5, 1930. International Load Line Convention, with final protocol and four annexes. 75

July 5, 1930. Final Act of the international conference on load lines. 75

Aug. 1, 1930. Convention concerning anti-diphtheria serum. 75

Oct. 23, 1930 (Apr. 27, 1931). Agreement concerning manned lightships not on their stations, with regulations. 77

Oct. 23, 1930 (Apr. 27, 1931). Agreement concerning maritime signals, with regulations. 77

Mar. 28, 1931 (Sept. 6, 1935). Agreement concerning procedure in case of undischarged or lost triptychs. 106

Mar. 30, 1931 (July 23, 1935). Convention concerning taxation of foreign motor vehicles, with annex and protocol. 104

Mar. 30, 1931 (Jan. 23, 1936). Convention concerning unification of road signals, with annex and three tables. 108

July 13, 1931 (Oct. 31, 1935). Convention for limiting the manufacture and regulating the distribution of narcotic drugs, with protocol of signature. 107

July 13, 1931 (Oct. 31, 1935). Final Act of the conference to study a draft convention for limiting the manufacture and regulating the distribution of narcotic drugs. 107

Dec. 9, 1932. International Telecommunication Convention, with annex. 85

Dec. 9, 1932. General radio regulations annexed to the International Telecommunication Convention, with fourteen annexes and final protocol. 85

Dec. 9, 1932. Additional radio regulations annexed to the International Telecommunication Convention. 85

Dec. 9, 1932. Additional protocol to the acts of the International Radiotelegraph Conference of Madrid signed by the Governments of the European Region, with annex. 85

Dec. 10, 1932. Telegraph regulations annexed to the International Telecommunication Convention, with two annexes and final protocol. 85

Dec. 10, 1932. Telephone regulations annexed to the International Telecommunication Convention, with annex. 85

June 19, 1933. European Broadcasting Convention, with final protocol. 87

June 19, 1933. Lucerne Plan for the allocation of radio broadcasting frequencies. 87

Aug. 25, 1933. Final Act of the Conference of Wheat Importing and Exporting Countries, with related documents. 89

Oct. 11, 1933 (Dec. 18, 1947). International convention for suppression of the traffic in women of full age. 242

Mar. 20, 1934. Universal Postal Convention, with related documents. 92

Mar. 20, 1934. Agreement of the Universal Postal Union concerning insured letters and boxes, with related documents. 93

July 25, 1934. International convention for protection against dengue fever. 96

Nov. 23, 1934. Revision of the convention of June 21, 1920, concerning establishment of an International Institute of Refrigeration. 97

Dec. 22, 1934. Agreement for dispensing with bills of health. 99

Dec. 22, 1934. Agreement for dispensing with consular visas on bills of health. 99

Feb. 20, 1935. International convention for the campaign against contagious diseases of animals, with declaration. 99

Feb. 20, 1935. International convention concerning the transit of animals, meat, and other products of animal origin, with annex. 99

Feb. 20, 1935. International convention concerning export and import of animal products, other than meat, meat preparations, fresh animal products, milk, and milk products, with annex. 99

June 22, 1935 (June 4, 1956). Convention concerning decrease of work hours to forty hours per week (International Labour Organisation Convention No. 47). 357

Nov. 15, 1935. Convention for the export of timber. 434

June 22, 1936. Protocol concerning renewal of the Baltic Geodetic Convention of December 31, 1925. 111

June 24, 1936 (July 6, 1956). Convention concerning annual holidays with pay (International Labour Organisation Convention No. 52). 117

June 26, 1936. Procès-verbal to alter the latest date of issue of the annual statement of the estimated world requirement of dangerous drugs. 361

July 20, 1936. Convention concerning the regime of the Black Sea Straits, with four annexes and a protocol (Montreux Convention). 112

Oct. 24, 1936 (July 6, 1956). Convention fixing the minimum age for employment at sea (International Labour Organisation Convention No. 58). 361

Nov. 6, 1936 (Feb. 3, 1937). Rules of submarine warfare. 115

May 6, 1937. Agreement concerning regulation of the production and marketing of sugar, with protocol. 116

June 8, 1937 (Nov. 25, 1946). International agreement for the regulation of whaling. 221

June 22, 1937 (July 6, 1956). Convention fixing the minimum age for admission of children to industrial employment (International Labour Organisation Convention No. 59). 361

June 22, 1937 (July 6, 1956). Convention concerning the age for admission of children to non-industrial employment (International Labour Organisation Convention No. 60). 361

Sept. 14, 1937. Agreement concerning piracy by submarines in the Mediterranean, with two annexes and a map (Nyon Arrangement). 118

Sept. 17, 1937. Agreement concerning attacks by aircraft and surface vessels on merchant ships in the Mediterranean. 118

June 24, 1938 (Nov. 25, 1946). Protocol amending the international agreement of June 8, 1937, for the regulation of whaling. 221

May 23, 1939. Universal Postal Convention, with related documents. 125

July 22, 1942. Protocol providing for entry into force and extension of the agreement of May 6, 1937, concerning regulation of the production and marketing of sugar. 150

Aug. 31, 1944. Protocol extending the agreement of May 6, 1937, concerning regulation of the production and marketing of sugar. 162

Aug. 31, 1945. Protocol extending the

agreement of May 6, 1937, concerning regulation of the production and marketing of sugar. 195

Sept. 27, 1945. Agreement concerning establishment of a European Central Inland Transport Organization, with protocol. 198

Sept. 27, 1945. Protocol concerning transfer from the Provisional Organization for European Inland Transport to the European Central Inland Transport Organization. 198

Nov. 26, 1945 (Nov. 25, 1946). Protocol for the regulation of whaling during the 1946–1947 season. 221

Aug. 30, 1946. Protocol extending the agreement of May 6, 1937, concerning regulation of the production and marketing of sugar. 218

Oct. 2, 1946 (Apr. 26, 1954). Final Articles Revision Convention, 1946, of the International Labour Organisation, with annex. 310

Oct. 9, 1946 (July 6, 1956). Convention concerning medical examination for fitness for employment in industry of children and young persons (International Labour Organisation Convention No. 77). 362

Oct. 9, 1946 (July 6, 1956). Convention concerning medical examination of children and young persons for fitness for employment in non-industrial occupations (International Labour Organisation Convention No. 78). 362

Oct. 9, 1946 (July 6, 1956). Convention concerning the restriction of night work of children and young persons in nonindustrial occupations (International Labour Organisation Convention No. 79). 362

July 29–Oct. 15, 1946. Conference to consider the draft peace treaties with Finland, Romania, Hungary, Bulgaria, and Italy. 219

Dec. 2, 1946. International convention for the regulation of whaling. 222

Dec. 2, 1946. Schedule annexed to the international convention for the regulation of whaling. 222

Dec. 2, 1946. Final Act of the International Whaling Conference, with annex and addendum. 222

Dec. 2, 1946. Protocol for the regulation of whaling during the 1947–1948 season. 222

Dec. 11, 1946. Protocol amending the agreements, conventions, and protocols on narcotic drugs concluded at The Hague on January 23, 1912; at Geneva on February 11, 1925, February 19, 1925, and July 13, 1931; at Bangkok on November 27, 1931; and at Geneva on June 26, 1936, with annex. 223

Feb. 10, 1947. Treaty of peace with Bulgaria, with six annexes. 226

Feb. 10, 1947. Treaty of peace with Finland, with six annexes. 226

Feb. 10, 1947. Treaty of peace with Hungary, with six annexes. 227

Feb. 10, 1947. Treaty of peace with Italy, with seventeen annexes. 227

Feb. 10, 1947. Treaty of peace with Romania, with six annexes. 228

Mar. 3, 1947. Supplementary protocol concerning entry into force of the whaling protocol of November 26, 1945. 229

July 5, 1947. Universal Postal Convention, with related documents. 233

July 5, 1947. Agreement concerning insured letters and boxes, with final protocol. 233

Sept. 27, 1947. Report on the proceedings of the International High Frequency Broadcasting Conference. 237

Oct. 2, 1947. International Telecommunication Convention, with related documents. 237

Oct. 2, 1947. Radio regulations annexed to the International Telecommunication Convention, with related documents. 238

Oct. 11, 1947 (Apr. 2, 1948). Convention of the World Meteorological Organization, with two annexes and a protocol. 247

Nov. 12, 1947 (Dec. 18, 1947). Protocol to amend the convention for suppression of the circulation of and traffic in obscene publications of September 12, 1923, with annex. 242

Nov. 12, 1947 (Dec. 18, 1947). Protocol to amend the convention for suppression of the traffic in women and children of September 30, 1921, and the convention for suppression of the traffic in women of full age of October 11, 1933, with annex. 242

June 10, 1948 (Apr. 19, 1954). Final Act of the International Conference on Safety of Life at Sea, with related documents. 310

June 10, 1948 (May 10, 1954). International convention for the safety of life at sea, 1948, with regulations and annex. 312

June 10, 1948 (July 14, 1954). Regulations for preventing collisions at sea. 313

July 9, 1948 (July 6, 1956). Convention concerning freedom of association and protection of the right to organize (International Labour Organisation Convention No. 87). 362

July 10, 1948 (July 6, 1956). Convention concerning the night work of young persons employed in industry (International Labour Organisation Convention No. 90). 362

Sept. 15, 1948. European broadcasting convention, with related documents. 252

Sept. 15, 1948. Copenhagen Plan for distribution of frequencies between the broadcasting stations of the European Broadcasting Area. 253

Nov. 19, 1948. Protocol bringing under international control drugs outside the scope of the convention of July 13, 1931, for limiting the manufacture and regulating the distribution of narcotic drugs, as amended by the protocol of December 11, 1946. 254

Dec. 9, 1948 (Dec. 16, 1949). Convention on the prevention and punishment of the crime of genocide. 266

Feb. 8, 1949 (Apr. 10, 1958). International convention for the Northwest Atlantic fisheries. 257

May 4, 1949 (May 14, 1949). Protocol amending the agreement for suppression of the circulation of obscene publications signed May 4, 1910, in Paris, with annex. 259

June 7, 1949. Amendments to the schedule to the international convention for the regulation of whaling. 260

July 1, 1949 (July 6, 1956). Convention concerning the application of the principles of the right to organize and to bargain collectively (International Labour Organisation Convention No. 98). 362

Aug. 5, 1949. Telegraph regulations (Paris revision, 1949), with three annexes and final protocol. 262

Aug. 12, 1949. Final Act of the diplomatic conference for revision of the Geneva Conventions, with eleven resolutions. 262

Aug. 12, 1949 (Dec. 12, 1949). Geneva Convention for the amelioration of the condition of the wounded and sick in armed forces in the field, with two annexes. 265

Aug. 12, 1949 (Dec. 12, 1949). Geneva Convention for the amelioration of the condition of wounded, sick, and shipwrecked members of armed forces at sea, with annex. 265

Aug. 12, 1949 (Dec. 12, 1949). Geneva Convention concerning the treatment of prisoners of war, with five annexes. 265

Aug. 12, 1949 (Dec. 12, 1949). Geneva Convention concerning the protection of civilian persons in time of war, with three annexes. 266

Dec. 16, 1949 (Aug. 27, 1954). Protocol modifying the Convention of July 5, 1890, concerning creation of an International Union for the Publication of Customs Tariffs, the Regulations for execution of the convention, and the protocol of signature. 315

Mar. 21, 1950 (Aug. 11, 1954). Convention for suppression of the traffic in persons and of the exploitation of the prostitution of others, with final protocol. 315

July 21, 1950. Amendments to the schedule to the international convention for the regulation of whaling. 276

June 29, 1951 (Apr. 4, 1956). Convention concerning equal remuneration for men and women workers for work of equal value (International Labour Organisation Convention No. 100). 352

July 30, 1951. Amendments to the schedule to the international convention for the regulation of whaling. 282

Sept. 4–8, 1951. Conference for the conclusion and signature of a treaty of peace with Japan. 283

Dec. 6, 1951 (Apr. 24, 1956). International plant protection convention. 353

June 6, 1952. Amendments to the schedule to the international convention for the regulation of whaling. 287

June 28, 1952 (July 6, 1956). Convention concerning maternity protection (revised 1952) (International Labour Organisation Convention No. 103). 363

July 11, 1952. Universal Postal Convention, with related documents. 288

July 11, 1952. Agreement of the Universal Postal Union concerning insured letters and boxes, with related documents. 289

Dec. 22, 1952. International Telecommunication Convention, with related documents. 291

Mar. 31, 1953. Convention on the political rights of women. 295

June 26, 1953. Amendments to the schedule to the international convention for the regulation of whaling. 296

Oct. 1, 1953 (Oct. 29, 1953). International agreement for regulation of the production and marketing of sugar (International sugar agreement). 303

May 12, 1954 (Aug. 11, 1954). International convention for prevention of pollution of the sea by oil. 315

May 12, 1954. Final Act of the international conference on pollution of the sea by oil, with related documents. 312

May 14, 1954. Convention for protection of cultural property in the event of armed conflict, with regulations and protocol. 312

July 21, 1954. Final declaration of the Geneva Conference on the problem of restoring peace in Indo-China. 314

July 23, 1954. Amendments to the schedule to the international convention for the regulation of whaling. 314

Mar. 7, 1955. Recognition of the Hague Conventions. 324

Mar. 25, 1955. Convention concerning the International Institute of Refrigeration. 325

July 23, 1955. Amendments to the schedule to the international convention for the regulation of whaling. 333

Sept. 28, 1955. Protocol amending the Warsaw Convention of October 12, 1929, for the unification of certain rules concerning international air transport. 339

Dec. 31, 1955. Convention for the establishment of an International Organization of Legislative Metrology. 346

Sept. 7, 1956. Supplementary convention on the abolition of slavery, the slave trade, and institutions and practices similar to slavery. 367

Nov. 19, 1956. Protocol to the international convention for the regulation of whaling of December 2, 1946. 372

Dec. 1, 1956. International sugar protocol, amending the agreement of October 1, 1953, for regulation of the production and marketing of sugar, with annex. 373

Feb. 9, 1957. Interim convention for protection of fur seals in the North Pacific Ocean, with annex. 377

Feb. 20, 1957 (Sept. 6, 1957). Convention concerning citizenship of married women. 389

Oct. 3, 1957. Universal Postal Convention, with final protocol. 389

Oct. 3, 1957. Agreement of the Universal Postal Union concerning insured letters and boxes, with related documents. 390

Oct. 3, 1957. Agreement of the Universal Postal Union concerning parcel post, with related documents. 390

MULTILATERAL, League of Nations

June 4 and 7, 1934. Exchange of telegrams concerning Soviet accession to an embargo on arms shipments to Bolivia and Paraguay. 95

Sept. 15, 1934. Documents concerning entry of the USSR into the League of Nations. 97

Sept. 18, 1934. Resolution concerning entry of the USSR into the League of Nations. 97

MULTILATERAL, United Nations

Sept. 24, 1941. Inter-Allied agreement concerning rehabilitation principles. 147

Jan. 1, 1942. Declaration of the United Nations. 148

Dec. 17, 1942. Joint declaration concerning extermination of the Jewish population of Europe by Hitlerite forces. 152

Jan. 5, 1943. Inter-Allied declaration condemning acts of dispossession committed in territories under enemy occupation or control. 153

June 3, 1943. Final Act of the UN conference on food and agriculture, with declaration, resolutions, and recommendations. 154

Sept. 3, 1943. Armistice agreement with Italy. 154

Sept. 29, 1943. Instrument of surrender of Italy (Additional conditions of the armistice with Italy). 155

Nov. 9, 1943. Agreement establishing UNRRA. 156

July 22, 1944. Final Act of the UN Monetary and Financial Conference, with three annexes. 161

Sept. 19, 1944. Armistice agreement with Finland, with annex and two maps. 164

Oct. 28, 1944. Armistice agreement with Bulgaria. 167

Jan. 1, 1945. Armistice agreement with Hungary, with annex. 170

June 23, 1945. Temporary agreement concerning the functions of the Preparatory Commission of the UN. 437

June 26, 1945. Charter of the UN. 180

June 26, 1945. Statute of the International Court of Justice. 181

June 26, 1945. Interim arrangements of the UN. 181

Sept. 2, 1945. Instrument of surrender by Japan. 196

Nov. 16, 1945 (Apr. 21, 1954). Constitution of UNESCO. 310

Jan. 17, 1946. Provisional rules of procedure of the Security Council of the UN. 205

Feb. 13, 1946. Financial regulations of the UN. 181

Feb. 13, 1946 (Sept. 22, 1953). Convention concerning privileges and immunities of the UN. 302

July 22, 1946. Final Act of the International Health Conference for establishment of an international health organization. 215

July 22, 1946. Constitution of the World Health Organization. 215

July 22, 1946. Arrangement establishing an Interim Commission of the World Health Organization. 216

July 22, 1946. Protocol concerning the Office Internationale d'Hygiène Publique, with annex. 216

Dec. 11, 1946. Financial regulations of the UN. 181

Dec. 14, 1946. UN regulations concerning registration and publication of treaties. 181

Apr. 23, 1947. Rules of procedure of the Trusteeship Council of the UN. 181

July 4, 1947. Agreement between the UN and the Universal Postal Union. 233, 288

Aug. 14, 1947. Agreement between the UN and the International Telecommunication Union. 236

Nov. 17, 1947. Rules of procedure of the General Assembly of the UN. 181

Nov. 20, 1947. Provisional financial regulations of the UN. 181

May 13, 1948. Staff rules of the UN. 181

July 24, 1948. World Health Organization Regulations No. 1, concerning nomenclature with respect to diseases and causes of death. 215

Sept. 27, 1948. Agreement transferring residual assets of UNRRA to the UN. 157

June 30, 1949. Supplementary regulations to World Health Organization Regulations No. 1. 215

July 15, 1953. Admission of the USSR to the UN Technical Assistance Program. 297

June 25, 1953 (Oct. 7, 1954). Instrument for the amendment of the constitution of the International Labour Organisation. 317

Oct. 12, 1954. Letter from the USSR recognizing an agreement between Italy and

Yugoslavia of October 5, 1954, concerning division of the territory of Trieste. 318

July 9, 1955. Soviet accession to the International Bureau of Education. 332

July 1956. Agreement between the USSR and the Technical Assistance Board (TAB) under the Economic and Social Council (ECOSOC) of the UN concerning convertibility of currency. 360

Oct. 26, 1956. Statute of the International Atomic Energy Agency, with annex. 370

UN. See also Plurilateral, Great Power agreements and conferences. For meetings of the UN Subcommittee on Disarmament, see Multilateral, Great Power agreements and conferences. For conventions of the International Labour Organisation, see Multilateral, international agreements and conferences.

MULTILATERAL, unratified

Apr. 10–May 19, 1922. Genoa Conference for the economic and financial reconstruction of Europe. 399

July 24, 1923. Convention on the regime of the Black Sea Straits, with annex (Lausanne Convention). 400

Nov. 27, 1925. Convention concerning measurement of vessels employed in inland navigation, with protocol of signature. 401

May 13, 1936. Agreement for a uniform system of maritime buoyage, with annexed regulations. 401

June 26, 1936. Convention for suppression of the illicit traffic in dangerous drugs. 401

Sept. 23, 1936. Convention concerning the use of broadcasting in the cause of peace. 401

Nov. 16, 1937. Convention for creation of an International Criminal Court. 402

Nov. 16, 1937. Convention for the prevention and punishment of terrorism. 402

Apr. 8, 1938. General Radio Regulations (Cairo Revision, 1938), and Final Radio Protocol (Cairo Revision, 1938). 402

NEPAL, bilateral

July 20, 1956. Communiqué concerning establishment of diplomatic relations. 364

NETHERLANDS, bilateral

July 10, 1942. Agreement concerning establishment of diplomatic relations. 150

Oct. 22 and Nov. 4, 1942. Oral agreement concerning reorganization of diplomatic missions into embassies. 152

Oct. 1945. Exchange of notes concerning establishment of a Soviet Trade Mission in The Netherlands. 199

July 2, 1948. Trade and payments agreement, with two annexes. 250

Apr. 28, 1954. Trade protocol for 1954. 311

May 7, 1956. Protocol concerning the temporary exchange of certain paintings by Rembrandt. 354

June 27, 1956. Trade protocol for 1956. 359

Netherlands. See also Nongovernmental agreements.

NEW ZEALAND, bilateral

Apr. 13, 1944. Exchange of notes concerning establishment of diplomatic relations. 160

NICARAGUA, bilateral

Nov. 10 and Dec. 12, 1944. Exchange of notes concerning establishment of diplomatic and consular relations. 169

NONGOVERNMENTAL AGREEMENTS (indexed by partner and title)

Aerotransport, 134, 220
Afghanistan, 421, 425, 426
Afghanistan aviation company, 425
Afghanistan National Bank, 420, 421, 422
Air India International Corporation, 424
Allied Control Council for Germany, 423
Anderson, G., 414
Anglo-American Oil Company, 419
Belgian firm, 424
Belgium-Luxembourg Economic Union, 423
British European Airways Corporation, 424
British firms, 415, 417, 424
Bunvanit, 426
Burma, 424
Burmese firm, 425
Canton, trading organizations in, 417
Chang Tso-lin, 419
Chiaturi Manganese Concession, 417, 418
China, Company for the Foreign Trade of Northern, 423
Chinese Eastern Railway, 419
Chinese firms, Communist, 423
Christensen, Christian, 416
Cooper, Col. Hugh L., 418
Czechoslovakia, 423
Danish cooperatives, 425, 426
Danish firms, 413
Deterding interests, 419
Dresser Industries, 424
Egypt, 424, 425, 426
Egyptian firm, 424
EKO, 415
Estonian firm, 413
Finnish firm, 423
French firms, 419, 420, 426
French Navy, 419
Georgian Manganese Company, 418

German banks, 418, 420
German Democratic Republic cooperatives, 425
German firms, 414, 416, 417, 418, 419, 420, 421, 422
German Reichsbank, 420
German Volga Agricultural Credit Bank, 416
Germany, 422
Germany, Allied Control Council for, 423
Germany, Federal Republic, firms, 426
Gesellschaft Wirtschaftsverkehr Osten, 416
Grain agreement, 417
Greek firm, 424
Harbin Shipping Company, 421
Harriman & Company, 417, 418
Henschel & Sohn, 414
Imatra-Voima, 423
India, 424
Indian firms, 424
International Barnsdall Corporation, 415
Iran, 426
Irtrans, 420
Italian-Belgian mining company, 417
Italian cooperatives, 413, 414
Italian firms, 417, 420
Italian Navy, 420
Japanese authorities in Manchuria, 421
Japanese cooperatives, 425, 426
Japanese firms, 416, 418, 419, 420, 422
Jewish Colonization Society, 415
"Joint," 416
Junkers, 416
Kevin-Khourian, 426
Kharga gold concession, 417
Krassin-Urquhart agreement, 415
Krupp, 414, 415
Lena Goldfields Company, 417, 420
Lianozov, Martyn, 416
Manchukuo firm, 421
Manych concession, 415
Matsuo dockyards firm, 422
Metropolitan-Vickers Electric Co., Ltd., 419
Mga-Rybinsk concession, 416
MISR, 424
Netherlands, The, Committee for Trade with the USSR, 422
Norway, 423
Norwegian firms, 416, 418
Norwegian State Grain Monopoly, 423, 424
Pakistan, 426
Pan-American Airways, 425
Petrofina Company, 419
Poland, 423
Polish cooperatives, 425
Pyatakov agreement, 419
Reichskreditgesellschaft, 416
Russgertorg, 415
Russland-Ausschuss der Deutschen Wirtschaft, 419, 420, 421, 422
Russo-Asiatic United Society, 415
Sabena, 424
SAS, 424
Scottish cooperatives, 425
Shirak steppe concession, 417
Sinclair, Harry F., 414

Sinkiang, 414
Sinkiang firms, 421, 422
SKF, 416
Smith, Charles, 417
Spanish oil monopoly, 419
Standard Oil Company of New York, 418
Sweden, 414
Swedish firms, 220, 413, 414, 416
Swiss Air Lines, 424
Thailand tourist organization, 426
Tuchangunsy, 421, 422
Tunsin, 423
Turkey, 420
United Kingdom, 423
United States firms, 414, 415, 416, 417, 418, 424, 425
Verein Deutscher Maschinenbauanstalten, 418
Wolf, Otto, 415
Wostwag, 416

NORTH KOREA, *see* Korean People's Democratic Republic.

NORWAY, bilateral

Sept. 2, 1921. Temporary agreement concerning political and economic relations. 22
Nov. 15, 1922. Agreement concerning conditions of a loan offered by Norway to the RSFSR. 37
Feb. 15 and Mar. 10, 1924. Exchange of notes concerning recognition of the USSR *de jure* 41
Dec. 15, 1925. Treaty of commerce and navigation, with final protocol. 54
Apr. 9, 1926. Declaration concerning reciprocal recognition of tonnage measurement certificates. 55
June 9 and Oct. 26, 1927, and Jan. 16, 1928. Exchange of notes concerning mutual notification in the case of nationals of either country being arrested in the other. 64
Feb. 24, 1928. Convention concerning reciprocal protection of industrial property rights, with final protocol. 65
Mar. 12, 1932. Trade agreement. 434
May 29, 1933 Trade agreement for 1933. 87
May 19, 1934. Trade agreement. 94
Apr. 10, 1941. Trade and payments agreement. 143
Aug. 5, 1941. Exchange of notes concerning re-establishment of diplomatic relations. 145
Aug. 1, 1942. Exchange of notes concerning reorganization of diplomatic missions into embassies. 151
May 16, 1944. Agreement concerning civil administration and jurisdiction in Norwegian territory after its liberation by Allied expeditionary forces. 161
1945. Agreement concerning establishment of a mixed Soviet-Norwegian commission to investigate living and working condi-

tions of Soviet citizens in German captivity in Norway. 169

Dec. 27, 1946 Trade and payments agreement. 224

Dec. 27, 1946. Trade protocol for 1947. 224

Feb. 11, 1947. Agreement concerning establishment of telegraph and telephone communications. 228

Feb. 11, 1947. Parcel post agreement, with final protocol. 229

Dec. 18, 1947. Final protocol of the mixed Soviet-Norwegian border commission, with related documents, constituting an agreement for demarcation of the state border. 241

Dec. 22, 1947. Informal agreement concerning trade in 1948. 242

Jan. 6, 1948. Trade protocol for 1948. 243

Apr. 28, 1948. Communiqué and protocol concerning work of a mixed Soviet-Norwegian commission to investigate living and working conditions of Soviet citizens in German captivity in Norway. 248

Jan. 10, 1949. Trade protocol for 1949. 439

May 23, 1949. Exchange of notes concerning approval and entry into force of the border protocol of December 18, 1947. 259

Dec. 29, 1949. Treaty concerning the regime on the state border and procedure for settling border disputes and incidents, with related documents. 267

July 2, 1953 (approximate date). Informal agreement concerning care of the graves of Soviet citizens killed in Norway during the war. 441

Aug 26 and Sept. 7, 1953. Exchange of notes modifying the parcel post agreement of February 11, 1947. 301

Jan. 25, 1954. Trade protocol for 1954. 306

May 23, 1955. Trade protocol for 1955. 329

Nov. 15, 1955. Joint communiqué concerning diplomatic negotiations. 341

Nov. 15, 1955. Trade protocol for the period 1956–1958. 341

Nov. 15, 1955. Supplementary trade protocol for 1956. 341

Mar. 31, 1956 Agreement concerning air communications, with two annexes and an exchange of notes. 351

Oct. 12, 1956. Agreement concerning cultural collaboration. 369

Oct. 19, 1956. Agreement concerning collaboration in rescuing persons in distress and in searching for missing persons in the Barents Sea, with exchange of notes. 370

Feb. 5, 1957. Supplementary trade protocol for 1957. 377

Feb. 15, 1957. Agreement concerning the sea boundary in the Varanger Fjord. 377

June 7, 1957 (approximate date). Protocol concerning joint exploitation of the hydroelectric resources of the border river Pasvik-El'v (Paatso-Joki). 384

Aug 1, 1957. Protocol concerning demarcation of the maritime boundary. 386

Nov. 22, 1957. Agreement concerning measures for regulating seal-hunting and for protection of seal reserves in the Northeastern Atlantic Ocean, with annex and exchange of notes. 392

Nov. 29, 1957. Final documents concerning demarcation of the border in the Varanger Fjord. 392

Dec. 18, 1957. Agreement concerning exploitation of the hydroelectric resources of the Pasvik-El'v river. 394

NORWAY, three-way

Sept. 19, 1921. Agreement concerning telegraph communications (RSFSR, Norway, Finland). 24

Oct. 26, 1945. Protocol defining the junction point of the borders of the USSR, Finland, and Norway (USSR, Norway, Finland) 200

Dec. 3, 1947. Documents concerning the frontier mark erected at Muotkavaara (Krokfjellet) (USSR, Norway, Finland). 239

Feb. 7, 1953. Protocol concerning maintenance of the border mark erected at Muotkavaara (Krokfjellet) (USSR, Norway, Finland). 293

Feb. 24, 1956. Protocol concerning regulation of the water regime of the Pasvik-El'v river and Lake Inari, with regulations (USSR, Norway, Finland). 349

Norway. See also Nongovernmental agreements.

PAKISTAN, bilateral

Apr. 27 and May 1, 1948. Exchange of notes concerning establishment of diplomatic relations. 248

June 27, 1956. Trade agreement, with two annexes. 359

Oct 16, 1957. Joint communiqué concerning commercial relations. 390

Pakistan. See also Nongovernmental agreements.

PERSIA, see Iran.

PLURILATERAL, Central Powers (Germany, Austria-Hungary, Bulgaria, and Turkey)

Dec. 5, 1917. Agreement concerning temporary suspension of hostilities. 1

Dec. 15, 1917. Armistice. 1

Dec. 15, 1917. Supplement to the armistice of December 15, 1917. 2

Feb. 7, 1918. Agreement concerning repatriation of wounded and sick prisoners of war. 2

Mar 3, 1918. Peace treaty, with five appendixes (Treaty of Brest-Litovsk). 3

PLURILATERAL, Great Power agreements and conferences

Abbreviations: CFM—Council of Foreign Ministers. EAC — European Advisory Commission. FEC—Far Eastern Commission. SCAP—Supreme Commander of the Allied Powers. SHAEF—Supreme Headquarters, Allied Expeditionary Force.

Aug. 2, 1941 (Sept. 24, 1941). Atlantic Charter (USSR, UK, USA). 146

Oct. 1, 1941. Confidential protocol concerning provision of military and other supplies for the USSR, with three annexes (First Lend-Lease Protocol) (USSR, UK, USA). 147

May 29 and July 7, 1942. Exchange of notes concerning approval of the proposed Second Lend-Lease Protocol (USSR, UK, USA). 150

Oct 6, 1942. Protocol concerning provision of military and other supplies for the USSR, with three annexes (Second Lend-Lease Protocol) (USSR, UK, USA). 152

Sept. 3, 1943. Armistice agreement with Italy (USSR, UK, USA, Italy). 154

Sept. 29, 1943. Instrument of surrender of Italy (Additional conditions of the armistice with Italy) (USSR, UK, USA, Italy). 155

Oct. 13, 1943. Joint declaration recognizing Italy as a co-belligerent (USSR, UK, USA). 155

Oct. 19, 1943. Protocol concerning provision of military and other supplies for the USSR, with annexes (Third Lend-Lease Protocol) (USSR, Canada, UK, USA). 155

Oct. 30, 1943. Joint communiqué concerning the conference of Foreign Ministers in Moscow (USSR, UK, USA). 155

Oct 30, 1943. Declaration on general security (USSR, China, UK, USA). 156

Oct. 30, 1943. Declaration concerning Italy (USSR, UK, USA). 156

Oct. 30, 1943. Declaration concerning Austria (USSR, UK, USA). 156

Oct. 30, 1943. Declaration concerning German atrocities (USSR, UK, USA). 156

Nov. 1, 1943. Protocol concerning establishment of a European Advisory Commission (USSR, UK, USA). 156

Nov. 9, 1943. Protocol concerning modification in the text of the instrument of surrender by Italy of September 29, 1943 (Allied High Command, Italy). 156

Dec 1, 1943. Declaration concerning coordinated action in the war against Germany and postwar cooperation (USSR, UK, USA). 157

Dec. 1, 1943. Declaration concerning Iran (USSR, UK, USA). 157

Dec. 1, 1943. Military conclusions of the Teheran Conference (USSR, UK, USA). 157

Dec. 1, 1943. Agreement concerning transfer of Italian naval vessels to the USSR (USSR, UK, USA). 157

Dec. 1, 1943. Understanding concerning the postwar boundaries of Poland (USSR, UK, USA). 158

Jan. 1944. Agreement concerning appointment of Soviet and French representatives as observers on the Allied Control Commission for Italy (USSR, France, UK, USA). 158

Feb. 23, 1944. Joint declaration concerning purchase of gold from countries not constituting part of the United Nations (USSR, UK, USA). 159

May 13, 1944. Joint statement addressed to Hungary, Romania, Bulgaria, and Finland, urging their withdrawal from collaboration with Germany (USSR, UK, USA). 161

July 25, 1944. Agreement concerning an Instrument of Unconditional Surrender by Germany (USSR, UK, USA; EAC). 162

Aug. 11, 1944. Agreement concerning preliminary unofficial negotiations for establishment of an international organization for maintenance of peace and security (USSR, UK, USA). 162

Sept. 1944. Agreement concerning aerial support for the Polish insurgents in Warsaw (USSR, UK, USA). 436

Sept. 12, 1944. Protocol of agreement concerning occupation zones in Germany and the administration of Greater Berlin, with two maps (USSR, UK, USA; EAC). 163

Sept. 12, 1944. Armistice agreement with Romania, with annex (USSR, UK, USA, Romania). 163

Sept. 12, 1944. Protocol to the armistice agreement with Romania (USSR, UK, USA). 164

Sept. 19, 1944. Armistice agreement with Finland (USSR, UK, Finland). 164

Sept. 28, 1944. Joint statement concerning conversations on an international peace and security organization (USSR, UK, USA). 165

Oct. 7, 1944. Proposals for establishment of a general international security organization (USSR, China, UK, USA). 165

Oct. 9, 1944. Statement by the participating governments in the conversations on an international peace and security organization (USSR, China, UK, USA). 166

Oct. 28, 1944. Armistice agreement with Bulgaria (USSR, UK, Bulgaria). 167

Oct. 28, 1944. Protocol to the armistice agreement with Bulgaria (USSR, UK, USA). 167

Nov. 11, 1944. Joint communiqué concerning an invitation to the French Provisional Government to become a member of the European Advisory Commission (USSR, UK, USA). 167

Nov. 14, 1944. Agreement modifying the protocol of September 12, 1944, concerning occupation zones in Germany and the administration of Greater Berlin, with map (USSR, UK, USA; EAC). 167

Nov. 14, 1944. Agreement concerning control machinery in Germany (USSR, UK, USA; EAC). 168

Jan. 20, 1945. Armistice agreement with Hungary (USSR, UK, USA, Hungary). 170

Jan. 20, 1945. Protocol to the armistice agreement with Hungary (USSR, UK, USA). 170

Feb. 9, 1945. Oral agreement concerning formation of a Yugoslav Government (USSR, UK, USA). 170

Feb. 11, 1945. Report of the Crimea Conference (USSR, UK, USA). 171

Feb. 11, 1945. Protocol of the proceedings of the Crimea Conference (USSR, UK, USA). 172

Feb. 11, 1945. Protocol concerning reparations in kind from Germany (USSR, UK, USA). 172

Feb. 11, 1945. Secret agreement concerning entry of the USSR into the war against Japan (USSR, UK, USA). 173

Apr. 17, 1945. Protocol concerning provision of military and other supplies to the USSR, with annexes (Fourth Lend-Lease Protocol) (USSR, Canada, UK, USA). 175

May 1, 1945. Agreement modifying the agreement of November 14, 1944, concerning control machinery in Germany to provide for inclusion of the French Provisional Government in the Control Council (USSR, France, UK, USA; EAC). 176

May 1, 1945. Protocol concerning inclusion of the French Provisional Government as a signatory to the Instrument of Unconditional Surrender by Germany (USSR, France, UK, USA; EAC). 177

Apr. 25–May 6, 1945. Exchange of messages concerning military operations in Czechoslovakia (USSR, SHAEF). 177

May 23, 1945. Agreement concerning arrest of members of the Dönitz regime in Germany and members of the German General Staff (USSR, UK, USA). 437

May 31, 1945. Informal agreement concerning establishment of a Control Council for Germany (USSR, France, UK, USA). 178

June 5, 1945. Declaration concerning the defeat of Germany and the assumption of supreme authority with respect to Germany (USSR, France, UK, USA). 179

June 5, 1945. Statement concerning zones of occupation in Germany (USSR, France, UK, USA). 179

June 5, 1945. Statement concerning consultation with the governments of other nations in connection with the exercise of supreme authority with respect to Germany (USSR, France, UK, USA). 179

June 5, 1945. Statement concerning control machinery in Germany (USSR, France, UK, USA). 179

June 7, 1945. Statement concerning voting procedure in the Security Council (USSR, China, UK, USA). 180

June 12, 1945. Statement concerning an invitation to Polish leaders to come to Moscow for a conference on the formation of a Provisional Polish Government of National Unity (USSR, UK, USA). 180

June 29, 1945. Oral agreement on the entry of American and British troops into Berlin (USSR, UK, USA). 182

July 4, 1945. Agreement concerning control machinery in Austria (USSR, France, UK, USA; EAC). 182

July 7, 1945. Agreement concerning establishment of a Four-Power governing body (Kommandatura) in Berlin (USSR, UK, USA). 182

July 9, 1945. Agreement concerning zones of occupation in Austria and administration of the city of Vienna, with two maps (USSR, France, UK, USA; EAC). 183

July 18 and 20, 1945. Agreement on establishment of a Council of Foreign Ministers (USSR, UK, USA). 185

July 21, 1945. Statement concerning the Polish Provisional Government of National Unity (USSR, UK, USA). 186

July 21 and 25, 1945. Agreement concerning military collaboration in the Far East (USSR, UK, USA). 188

July 25, 1945. Agreement concerning certain additional requirements to be imposed on Germany (USSR, France, UK, USA; EAC). 184

July 26, 1945. Agreement concerning changes in the occupation zones in Germany and the administration of Greater Berlin, with map (USSR, France, UK, USA; EAC). 184

July 26, 1945. Protocol concerning military conditions for the occupation of Vienna (USSR, France, UK, USA; EAC). 184

July 19 and 30, 1945. Agreement concerning the political and economic principles to govern the treatment of Germany in the initial control period (USSR, UK, USA). 185

July 30 and 31, 1945. Agreement concerning the western border of Poland (USSR, UK, USA). 186

July 31, 1945. Statement concerning common policy for establishing the conditions of lasting peace in Europe (USSR, UK, USA). 187

July 31, 1945. Agreement concerning revision of procedure of the Allied Control Commissions in Romania, Bulgaria, and Hungary, with annex (USSR, UK, USA). 187

July 31, 1945. Agreement concerning the inclusion of a representative of France on the Allied Reparations Commission (USSR, UK, USA). 188

July 29 and Aug. 1, 1945. Agreement concerning principles to govern distribution of the German Navy and merchant marine (USSR, UK, USA). 186

July 30 and Aug. 1, 1945. Agreement concerning reparations from Germany (USSR, UK, USA). 185

Aug. 1, 1945. Agreement concerning transfer to the USSR of the city of Koenigsberg and the adjacent area (USSR, UK, USA). 186

Aug. 1, 1945. Agreement to examine a proposal by the USSR concerning extension of the authority of the Austrian Provisional Government to all of Austria (USSR, UK, USA). 186

Aug. 1, 1945. Agreement not to exact reparations from Austria (USSR, UK, USA). 186

Aug. 1, 1945. Agreement concerning removal of Germans from Poland, Czechoslovakia, and Hungary (USSR, UK, USA). 187

Aug. 1, 1945. Agreement concerning establishment of two bilateral commissions to investigate questions arising from the removal of oil equipment in Romania (USSR, UK, USA). 187

Aug. 1, 1945. Agreement concerning withdrawal of troops from Teheran (USSR, UK, USA). 187

Aug. 1, 1945. Agreement that the Zone of Tangier is to remain international (USSR, UK, USA). 187

Aug. 1, 1945. Agreement concerning revision of the Montreux Convention on the Black Sea Straits (USSR, UK, USA). 187

Aug. 1, 1945. Agreement concerning directives to military commanders on the Allied Control Council for Germany (USSR, UK, USA). 188

Aug. 1, 1945. Communiqué concerning the Three-Power Conference at Berlin (Potsdam communiqué) (USSR, UK, USA). 184

Aug. 1, 1945. Protocol of the Three-Power Conference at Berlin, with two annexes (Potsdam protocol) (USSR, UK, USA). 184

Aug. 8, 1945. Agreement concerning prosecution and punishment of the major war criminals of the European Axis (USSR, France, UK, USA). 189

Aug. 8, 1945. Charter of the International Military Tribunal (USSR, France, UK, USA). 189

Aug. 10, 1945. Organization plan of the Allied Control Council for Germany (USSR, France, UK, USA). 190

Aug. 11, 1945. Exchange of notes concerning surrender by Japan (USSR, UK, USA, China, Japan). 190

Aug. 14, 1945. Exchange of communications concerning surrender by Japan (USSR, UK, USA, China, Japan). 193

Aug. 15, 1945. General Order No. 1 concerning surrender of Japanese forces (SCAP). 193

Aug. 29, 1945. Joint communiqué listing major war criminals to be tried by the International Military Tribunal (USSR, France, UK, USA). 194

Aug. 30, 1945. Proclamation concerning establishment of the Control Council for Germany (USSR, France, UK, USA). 195

Aug. 31, 1945. Final Act of the conference concerning re-establishment of the international regime in Tangier (USSR, France, UK, USA). 195

Sept. 2, 1945. Instrument of surrender by Japan (USSR, UK, USA, China, Japan). 196

Sept. 29, 1945. Agreement on establishment of a Far Eastern Advisory Commission (USSR, China, UK, USA). 198

Sept. 11–Oct. 2, 1945. First meeting of the CFM (USSR, China, France, UK, USA). 199

Dec. 7, 1945. Recommendation on distribution of the German merchant fleet (USSR, UK, USA). 202

Dec. 27, 1945. Communiqué concerning a meeting of the Foreign Ministers (USSR, UK, USA). 202

Dec. 27, 1945. Agreement concerning preparation of peace treaties with Italy, Romania, Bulgaria, Hungary, and Finland (USSR, UK, USA). 202

Dec. 27, 1945. Agreement concerning establishment of a Far Eastern Commission and an Allied Council for Japan (USSR, UK, USA). 203

Dec. 27, 1945. Agreement concerning establishment of a provisional Korean government (USSR, UK, USA). 204

Dec. 27, 1945. Agreement concerning policy in China (USSR, UK, USA). 204

Dec. 27, 1945. Agreement concerning policy in Romania (USSR, UK, USA). 204

Dec. 27, 1945. Agreement concerning policy in Bulgaria (USSR, UK, USA). 204

Dec. 27, 1945. Agreement concerning establishment by the United Nations of a commission for the control of atomic energy (USSR, UK, USA). 204

Jan. 8, 1946. Communiqué concerning work of the Allied Tripartite Commission for settlement of the Romanian problem (USSR, UK, USA). 437

Jan. 19, 1946. Proclamation concerning establishment of an International Military Tribunal for the Far East (SCAP). 205

Jan. 19, 1946. Charter of the International Military Tribunal for the Far East (SCAP). 205

Jan. 22, 1946. Joint communiqué concerning disposal of the German Navy (USSR, UK, USA). 206

Feb. 28, 1946. Joint communiqué concerning appointment of a commission of experts to prepare a report on the Italy-Yugoslavia boundary (USSR, France, UK, USA; CFM Deputies). 207

Mar. 8, 1946. Three-Power communiqué concerning distribution of the German merchant fleet (USSR, UK, USA). 437

Apr. 26, 1946. Order amending the Charter of the International Military Tribunal for the Far East (SCAP). 211

Apr. 25–May 16, 1946. Second meeting of the CFM (first half) (USSR, France, UK, USA). 212

June 28, 1946. Agreement concerning machinery of control in Austria, with annex (USSR, France, UK, USA). 214

June 15–July 12, 1946. Second meeting of the CFM (second half) (USSR, France, UK, USA). 215

Sept. 25, 1946. Four-Power declaration concerning the question of the Italian colonies (USSR, France, UK, USA). 438

Oct. 21, 1946. Communiqué concerning results of the work of the Five-Power Telecommunication Conference (USSR, China, France, UK, USA). 438

Sept. 28–Oct. 31, 1946. Preliminary Telecommunication Conference (USSR, China, France, UK, USA). 221

Nov. 4–Dec. 12, 1946. Third meeting of the CFM (USSR, France, UK, USA). 223

Dec. 12, 1946. Protocol concerning appointment of a governor for the Free Territory of Trieste. 224

Dec. 19, 1946. Agreement concerning repatriation of Japanese prisoners of war and civilians from the USSR and from territories under Soviet control, as well as Korean nationals from Japan to Soviet-occupied North Korea, with two annexes (USSR, SCAP). 224

Feb. 10, 1947. Protocol concerning establishment of a Four-Power Naval Commission, disposal of excess units of the Italian fleet, and return by the USSR of warships on loan, with annex (USSR, France, UK, USA). 228

Feb. 25, 1947. Decree of the Allied Control Council for Germany concerning abolition of the State of Prussia (USSR, France, UK, USA; CFM). 229

Jan. 14–Feb. 25, 1947. Conference of Foreign Ministers' Deputies to consider preparation of a peace treaty with Germany and hear the views of other countries (USSR, France, UK, USA). 229

Mar. 10–Apr. 24, 1947. Fourth meeting of the CFM (USSR, France, UK, USA). 231

June 19, 1947. Directive concerning basic post-surrender policy for Japan (FEC). 233

June 19 and 22, 1947. Exchange of notes concerning convocation of a conference to discuss plans for American aid to Europe (USSR, France, UK). 233

June 27–July 2, 1947. Conference to consider plans for American aid to Europe (USSR, France, UK). 233

Nov. 25–Dec. 15, 1947. Fifth meeting of the CFM (USSR, France, UK, USA). 241

Feb. 20–May 6, 1948. Conference of the Deputy Foreign Ministers (USSR, France, UK, USA). 248

Aug. 30, 1948. Four-Power directive on implementation of general principles for ending the Berlin crisis (USSR, France, UK, USA). 252

May 4, 1949. Agreement concerning removal of restrictions on communications, transportation, and trade between Berlin and the Eastern and Western Zones of Germany (USSR, France, UK, USA). 259

May 23–June 20, 1949. Communiqué concerning the sixth meeting of the CFM (USSR, France, UK, USA). 260

July 26, 1949. Agreement concerning procedure for quadripartite consultation among the Occupying Powers in Germany (USSR, France, UK, USA). 261

Feb. 8–Dec. 15, 1949. Negotiations by the Deputy Foreign Ministers on a draft treaty for Austria (USSR, France, UK, USA). 266

Jan. 9–Dec. 15, 1950. Meetings of the Deputy Foreign Ministers to negotiate a draft treaty for Austria (USSR, France, UK, USA). 279

Mar. 5–June 21, 1951. Meeting of the Deputy Foreign Ministers to draw up an agenda for the CFM (USSR, France, UK, USA). 282

Feb. 18, 1954. Four-Power communiqué concerning a meeting of the Foreign Ministers (USSR, France, UK, USA). 308

May 13–June 22, 1954. Meetings of the UN Subcommittee on Disarmament (USSR, Canada, France, UK, USA). 442

Apr. 5–26, 1955. Exchange of notes concerning conclusion of a State Treaty for Austria (USSR, France, UK, USA). 326

Feb. 25–May 9, 1955. Meetings of the UN Subcommittee on Disarmament (USSR, Canada, France, UK, USA). 443

May 12, 1955. Joint communiqué concerning completion of work on the State Treaty for Austria (USSR, France, UK, USA). 327

May 15, 1955. State Treaty for the re-establishment of an independent and democratic Austria, with two annexes and two maps (USSR, France, UK, USA, Austria, Yugoslavia). 328

May 10 and 25, 1955. Exchange of notes concerning a meeting of the Heads of Government (USSR, France, UK, USA). 329

June 13, 1955. Exchange of notes concerning time and place for a meeting of the

Heads of Government (USSR, France, UK, USA). 330

July 23, 1955. Directive of the Heads of Government to the Foreign Ministers (USSR, France, UK, USA). 333

Aug. 29–Oct. 7, 1955. Meetings of the UN Subcommittee on Disarmament (USSR, Canada, France, UK, USA). 444

Nov. 16, 1955. Final communiqué of the Foreign Ministers (USSR, France, UK, USA). 341

Mar. 19–May 4, 1956. Meetings of the UN Subcommittee on Disarmament (USSR, Canada, France, UK, USA). 444

Mar. 18–Sept. 6, 1957. Meetings of the UN Subcommittee on Disarmament (USSR, Canada, France, UK, USA). 445

PLURILATERAL, internal Soviet treaties

June 1, 1919. Decree concerning unification of the RSFSR and the Ukrainian, Latvian, Lithuanian, and Belorussian SSR's. 8

Apr. 16, 1921. Agreement concerning administration of railroad communications in the Transcaucasus (RSFSR, Armenian SSR, Azerbaidzhan SSR, Georgian SSR). 20

Sept. 21, 1921. Agreement concerning administration of the Amu-Darya flotilla (RSFSR, Bukhara and Khorezm People's Soviet Republics). 24

Feb. 22, 1922. Protocol concerning transfer to the RSFSR of the representation of the various republics to the European Economic Conference, with declaration (RSFSR, Armenian SSR, Azerbaidzhan SSR, Belorussian SSR, Bukhara People's Soviet Republic, Georgian SSR, Far Eastern Republic, Ukrainian SSR, Khorezm Soviet Republic). 29

Mar. 12, 1922. Treaty of alliance establishing the Federative Union of Socialist Soviet Republics of the Transcaucasus (Armenian, Azerbaidzhan, and Georgian SSR's). 30

Apr. 11, 1922. Agreement concerning financial relations, with two annexes (RSFSR, Armenian, Azerbaidzhan, and Georgian SSR's). 31

May 24, 1922. Agreement concerning unification of the administrations of posts, telegraph, telephone, and radio-telegraph (RSFSR, Armenian, Azerbaidzhan, and Georgian SSR's). 32

Dec. 30, 1922. Treaty concerning establishment of the USSR (RSFSR, Ukrainian and Belorussian SSR's, and Transcaucasian SFSR, including the Armenian, Azerbaidzhan, and Georgian SSR's). 37

Apr. 30, 1923. Agreement concerning administration of the Amu-Darya flotilla (RSFSR, Bukhara and Khorezm People's Soviet Republics). 38

PLURILATERAL, nonaggression agreements

Feb. 9, 1929. Protocol concerning entry into force of the General Treaty of August 27, 1928, for renunciation of war as an instrument of national policy (Litvinov Protocol) (USSR, Danzig, Estonia, Latvia, Lithuania, Persia, Poland, Romania). 69

July 3, 1933. Convention concerning the definition of aggression, with annex and protocol of signature (USSR, Afghanistan, Estonia, Finland, Latvia, Persia, Poland, Romania, Turkey). 88

July 4, 1933. Convention concerning the definition of aggression, with annex (USSR, Czechoslovakia, Romania, Turkey, Yugoslavia). 88

PLURILATERAL, Soviet bloc agreements and conferences

Abbreviations:
A—Albania
B—Bulgaria
CPR—Chinese People's Republic
Cz—Czechoslovakia
DRV—Democratic Republic of Vietnam
GDR—German Democratic Republic
H—Hungary
KPDR—Korean People's Democratic Republic
MPR—Mongolian People's Republic
P—Poland
R—Romania
Y—Yugoslavia

Oct. 13, 1947. Agreement concerning Eastern European rail transportation of passengers and luggage (USSR, B, . . .). 438

Oct. 13, 1947. Agreement concerning transport of goods by rail in direct international communication (USSR, B, . . .). 438

June 24, 1948. Statement concerning the decisions of the London Conference on Germany (USSR, A, B, Cz, H, P, R, Y). 249

Aug. 18, 1948. Convention concerning the regime of navigation on the Danube, with two annexes and a supplementary protocol (USSR, Ukrainian SSR, B, Cz, H, R, Y). 251

Dec. 22, 1948. Agreement concerning transportation of passengers and luggage by rail in direct international communications (USSR, B, . . .). 438

Dec. 22, 1948. Agreement concerning transport of goods by rail in international communication (USSR, B, . . .). 439

Jan. 24, 1949. Secret protocol concerning establishment of the Council of Mutual Economic Aid (USSR, B, Cz, H, P, R. A and GDR joined later). 256

Jan. 25, 1949. Communiqué announcing establishment of the Council of Mutual Economic Aid (USSR, B, Cz, H, P, R). 256

Aug. 4, 1949. Resolution of the First International Congress of Plant Pathology, Entomology, and Plant Protection (USSR, A, B, Cz, H, P, R). 439

Aug. 25–27, 1949. Meeting of the Council of Mutual Economic Aid (USSR, A, B, Cz, H, P, R). 262

Nov. 12–17, 1949. First meeting of the Danube Commission (USSR, B, Cz, H, R, Y). 264

Mar. 23–27, 1950. Second meeting of the Danube Commission (USSR, B, Cz, H, R, Y). 272

Oct. 20, 1950. Joint declaration concerning the remilitarization of Western Germany (USSR, A, B, Cz, GDR, H, P, R). 277

Dec. 6, 1950. Agreement concerning transportation of passengers by rail in direct international communications (USSR, A, B, Cz, GDR, H, P, R). 267, 440

Dec. 6, 1950. Agreement concerning transportation of freight by rail in direct international communications (USSR, A, B, Cz, GDR, H, P, R). 440

Dec. 10–15, 1950. Third meeting of the Danube Commission (USSR, B, Cz, H, R, Y). 279

May 23–June 3, 1951. Fourth meeting of the Danube Commission (USSR, B, Cz, H, R, Y). 281

Dec. 10–19, 1951. Fifth meeting of the Danube Commission (USSR, B, Cz, H, R, Y). 284

June 23–July 1, 1952. Sixth meeting of the Danube Commission (USSR, B, Cz, H, R, Y). 288

Aug. 1952. Military conference (USSR, B, CPR, Cz, H, P, R). 289

Dec. 15–26, 1952. Seventh meeting of the Danube Commission (USSR, B, Cz, H, R, Y). 292

June 26–July 3, 1953. Eighth meeting of the Danube Commission (USSR, B, Cz, H, R, Y). 297

July 31, 1953. Agreement concerning international freight communications (USSR, A, B, CPR, Cz, GDR, H, KPDR, MPR, P, R. DRV joined later). 298

Dec. 9–17, 1953. Ninth meeting of the Danube Commission (USSR, B, Cz, H, R, Y). 305

Jan. 1954. Agreement concerning through goods and passenger railroad traffic (USSR, CPR, . . .). 305

Mar. 26–27, 1954. Meeting of the Council for Mutual Economic Aid (USSR, A, B, Cz, GDR, H, P, R). 309

June 8–15, 1954. Tenth meeting of the Danube Commission (USSR, B, Cz, H, R, Y). 442

June 24–25, 1954. Meeting of the Council for Mutual Economic Aid (USSR, A, B, Cz, GDR, H, P, R). 442

Dec. 2, 1954. Joint declaration concerning policies of the Western Powers in regard to Germany (USSR, A, B, Cz, GDR, H, P, R). 320

Dec. 8–15, 1954. Eleventh meeting of the Danube Commission (USSR, B, Cz, H, R, Y). 442

Jan. 1955. Amendments to the United Transit Tariff (USSR, A, B, CPR, Cz, GDR, H, KPDR, MPR, P, R). 321

Mar. 22, 1955. Communiqué concerning plans for conclusion of a treaty of friendship, collaboration, and mutual aid (USSR, A, B, CPR, Cz, GDR, H, P, R). 442

May 14, 1955. Treaty of friendship, cooperation, and mutual assistance (Warsaw Pact) (USSR, A, B, Cz, GDR, H, P, R; CPR associated). 327

May 14, 1955. Communiqué concerning establishment of a joint command of the armed forces of the signatories to the treaty of friendship, cooperation, and mutual assistance of May 14, 1955 (USSR, A, B, Cz, GDR, H, P, R). 328

May 14, 1955. Final communiqué of the Warsaw Conference of States of the Soviet bloc (USSR, A, B, Cz, GDR, H, P, R). 328

June 8–13, 1955. Twelfth meeting of the Danube Commission (USSR, B, Cz, H, R, Y). 443

July 30, 1955. Agreement concerning transportation of freight by rail in direct international communication (USSR, A, B, CPR, Cz, DRV, GDR, H, KPDR, MPR, P, R). 443

Dec. 7–11, 1955. Conference of the Council for Mutual Economic Aid (USSR, A, B, Cz, GDR, H, P, R). 344

Dec. 7–15, 1955. Thirteenth meeting of the Danube Commission (USSR, B, Cz, H, R, Y). 444

Jan. 28, 1956. Declaration concerning international security (USSR, A, B, Cz, GDR, H, P, R). 348

Jan. 28, 1956. Final protocol of the Political Consultative Committee established by the Warsaw Treaty of May 14, 1955 (USSR, A, B, Cz, GDR, H, P, R). 348

Mar. 26, 1956. Agreement concerning establishment of an Institute for Nuclear Research (USSR, A, B, CPR, Cz, GDR, H, KPDR, MPR, P, R. DRV joined later). 351

May 18–25, 1956. Seventh conference of the Council for Mutual Economic Aid (USSR, A, B, Cz, GDR, H, P, R; as observers, CPR, Y). 356

June 7–13, 1956. Fourteenth meeting of the Danube Commission (USSR, B, Cz, H, R, Y). 444

June 23–28, 1956. Conference of railroad ministers (USSR, B, CPR, Cz, GDR, H, KPDR, MPR, P, R). 359

Jan. 6, 1957. Communiqué concerning a meeting of representatives of Communist and Workers' Parties and Governments

(USSR, B, CPR, Cz, GDR, H, KPDR, MPR, P, R). 359

Jan. 25, 1957. Agreement concerning standardization of machine tools produced by participants in the Council for Mutual Economic Aid (USSR, B, Cz, GDR, H, P; CPR as observer). 376

June 5–14, 1957. Fifteenth meeting of the Danube Commission (USSR, B, Cz, H, R, Y, Austria, Federal Republic of Germany). 445

June 18–22, 1957. Eighth conference of the Council for Mutual Economic Aid, (USSR, A, B, Cz, GDR, H, P, R; as observers, CPR, KPDR, Y). 385

June 22, 1957. Multilateral payments agreement (USSR, A, B, Cz, GDR, H, P, R). 385

POLAND, bilateral

Nov. 2, 1919. Agreement concerning the final solution of the question of Polish hostages in the RSFSR. 8

Nov. 9, 1919. Agreement concerning exchange of civilian prisoners. 8

Oct. 5, 1920. Agreement (procès-verbal) to conclude an armistice not later than October 8, 1920. 14

Oct. 12, 1920. Agreement concerning preliminary conditions of peace, with two annexes (Preliminary peace treaty). 14

Oct. 12, 1920. Armistice agreement. 15

Feb. 24, 1921. Protocol concerning extension of the armistice agreement of October 12, 1920. 18

Feb. 24, 1921. Protocol concerning establishment of a mixed border commission. 18

Feb. 24, 1921. Agreement concerning repatriation, with supplementary protocol. 18

Mar. 18, 1921. Peace treaty, with five annexes. 20

June 1, 1921. Protocol concerning instructions for arbitration commissions to deal with border incidents. 21

Oct. 7, 1921. Agreement concerning the expulsion from Poland of the "Russian Political Committee" headed by Boris Savinkov. 25

Nov. 27, 1921. Temporary agreement concerning railroad traffic between Stolbce and Negoreloe. 26

Dec. 17, 1921. Temporary agreement concerning rail transportation between Szepietovka and Zdolbunowo. 27

Jan. 24, 1922. Protocol supplementing the agreement of June 1, 1921, concerning instructions for arbitration commissions to deal with border incidents. 29

June 19, 1922. Temporary agreement concerning rail transportation between Volochisk and Podvolochisk. 33

July 4, 1922. Regulations on the settlement of border disputes. 34

Oct. 1922. Temporary agreement concerning border railroad traffic. 35

Feb. 7, 1923. Sanitary convention. 37

May 24, 1923. Postal and telegraph convention, with final protocol and supplementary protocol. 39

Apr. 24, 1924. Convention concerning direct rail transportation of passengers and freight, with supplementary protocol and two annexes. 42

Apr. 24, 1924 (presumable date). Regulations concerning direct transportation of passengers and baggage. 42

Apr. 24, 1924 (presumable date). Amendments and additions to the International Berne Convention on the transportation of goods by rail. 42

July 18, 1924. Consular convention with two supplementary protocols and exchange of notes. 46

July 31, 1924. General final protocol of the Mixed Soviet-Polish Border Demarcation Commission, with annexes. 46

Aug. 3, 1925. Agreement concerning settlement of border disputes. 51

Dec. 27, 1927. Protocol concerning exchange of political prisoners. 64

Apr. 10, 1932. Agreement concerning legal relations in the border zone, with related documents. 81

July 25, 1932. Treaty of nonaggression, with two protocols of signature. 83

Aug. 3, 1932. Protocol concerning exchange of political prisoners. 83

Nov. 23, 1932. Convention concerning conciliation procedure. 84

June 3, 1933. Convention concerning procedure for investigating and settling border incidents and disputes, with final protocol and protocol of signature. 87

June 3, 1933. Protocol concerning appointment of representatives for border affairs. 87

June 19, 1933. Convention concerning floating timber in border rivers, with final protocol. 88

July 9, 1933. Protocol concerning floating timber on the border canal during the spring floods. 89

Sept. 18 and Oct. 9, 1933. Exchange of notes constituting a temporary customs agreement, with list of duty reductions. 90

Feb. 6, 1934. Communiqué concerning negotiations. 92

May 5, 1934. Protocol extending the treaty of nonaggression of July 25, 1932, with final protocol. 94

June 22, 1934. Exchange of notes constituting a temporary customs agreement, with list of duty reductions. 95

July 26, 1934. Protocol modifying certain provisions of the convention of April 24, 1924, concerning direct rail transportation, with final protocol. 96

July 26, 1934 (presumable date). Regulations concerning crossing the border by railroad, postal, and other employees and their stay in the territory of the other party, with two annexes. 96

Sept. 10, 1934. Exchange of notes reaffirming existing treaties, on the occasion of the entry of the USSR into the League of Nations. 96

Dec. 1, 1934. Exchange of notes constituting a temporary customs agreement. 98

Mar. 3, 1936. Exchange of notes constituting a temporary customs agreement, with list of duty reductions. 189

Mar. 31, 1936. Exchange of notes constituting an agreement concerning reciprocal recognition of tonnage measurement certificates. 110

Mar. 31, 1936. Exchange of notes constituting an agreement concerning most-favored-nation treatment with regard to dues paid by merchant ships. 110

June 14, 1936. Agreement concerning the legal status of the Soviet Trade Mission in Poland, with final protocol. 111

Nov. 12 and 13, 1936. Exchange of notes concerning Soviet representatives for border affairs. 113

Feb. 23, 1937. Exchange of notes concerning extension to Danzig of the agreements of March 31, 1936, concerning reciprocal recognition of tonnage measurement certificates and dues paid by merchant ships. 115

Dec. 15, 1937. Exchange of notes constituting a temporary customs agreement, with list of duty reductions. 119

Nov. 26, 1938. Joint communiqué concerning diplomatic and commercial relations. 122

Dec. 21, 1938. Statement concerning commercial negotiations. 122

Feb. 19, 1939. Commercial treaty, with final protocol, supplementary protocol, and two annexes. 124

Feb. 19, 1939. Clearing agreement. 124

Feb. 19, 1939. Trade agreement. 124

Feb. 19, 1939. Exchange of notes concerning temporary entry into force of the commercial treaty of February 19, 1939, with protocol. 124

Feb. 19, 1939. Exchange of notes concerning exchange of acts of ratification of the commercial treaty of February 19, 1939, and the agreement of June 14, 1936, concerning the legal status of the Soviet Trade Mission in Poland. 124

Sept. 17, 1939. Note abrogating existing treaties between the USSR and Poland. 128

July 30, 1941. Agreement concerning resumption of diplomatic relations and mutual aid in the war against Germany, with secret protocol. 145

July 30, 1941. Protocol concerning an amnesty for Polish citizens imprisoned in the USSR. 145

Aug. 14, 1941. Agreement concerning formation of a Polish army in the USSR. 146

Aug. 22 and Sept. 28, 1941. Exchange of notes concerning establishment of a mixed commission to supervise the welfare of Polish citizens freed from Soviet prisons and labor camps. 435

Dec. 4, 1941. Joint declaration of friendship and mutual aid. 148

Dec. 31, 1941. Agreement concerning a loan to Poland for assistance to Polish citizens in the USSR. 148

Jan. 22, 1942. Agreement concerning a loan to Poland for maintenance of the Polish Army in Soviet territory. 148

Mar. 18, 1942. Agreement concerning evacuation of part of the Polish Army to Iran. 436

July 31, 1942. Agreement concerning evacuation of the remainder of the Polish Army to the Middle East. 436

July 26, 1944. Agreement concerning relations between the Soviet High Command and Polish administrative authorities after the entry of Soviet troops into Polish territory. 162

Sept. 9, 1944. Agreement concerning evacuation of Ukrainian population from Polish territory and Polish population from the territory of the Ukrainian SSR. 163

Sept. 9, 1944. Agreement concerning evacuation of Belorussian population from Polish territory and Polish population from the territory of the Belorussian SSR. 163

Sept. 22, 1944. Agreement concerning evacuation of Lithuanian population from Polish territory and Polish population from the territory of the Lithuanian SSR. 164

Oct. 20, 1944. Economic agreement. 166

Jan. 2 and 5, 1945. Exchange of letters concerning establishment of diplomatic relations. 169

Apr. 21, 1945. Treaty of friendship, mutual assistance, and postwar collaboration. 176

July 6, 1945. Agreement concerning the right to relinquish Soviet citizenship on the part of persons of Polish and Jewish nationality [sic] living in the USSR and their removal into Poland, and the right to relinquish Polish citizenship on the part of persons of Russian, Ukrainian, Belorussian, Ruthenian, and Lithuanian nationality living in Polish territory and their removal into the USSR, with protocol. 182

July 7, 1945. Treaty of commerce and navigation, with annex concerning the Soviet Trade Mission in Poland. 182

July 7, 1945. Trade protocol. 183

July 11, 1945. Agreement concerning changes in the administration of Polish railroads. 183

Aug. 16, 1945. Agreement concerning reparations for damages caused by the German occupation. 193

Aug. 16, 1945. Treaty concerning the state border, with map. 194

Nov. 23, 1945. Agreement concerning establishment of direct rail communications. 201

Feb. 8, 1946. Agreement concerning grain deliveries to Poland. 206

Mar. 1946. Agreement concerning organization of air communications. 207

Mar. 20, 1946. Agreement concerning establishment of postal and telephone and telegraph communications, with final protocol. 207

Apr. 12, 1946. Trade agreement. 210

May 27, 1946. Joint communiqué concerning negotiations. 212

Mar. 5, 1947. Joint communiqué concerning political and economic negotiations. 229

Mar. 5, 1947. Agreement on a loan to Poland. 230

Mar. 5, 1947. Agreement concerning settlement of reciprocal financial obligations outstanding on January 1, 1947, and the establishment of principles for financial payments in the future. 230

Mar. 5, 1947. Agreement concerning reduction of Polish coal deliveries to the USSR. 230

Mar. 5, 1947. Agreement concerning transfer to Poland of railroad rolling stock seized by the USSR as war booty. 230

Mar. 5, 1947. Agreement concerning scientific and technical collaboration in the field of industrial production. 230

Mar. 5, 1947. Agreement concerning provision to Poland of armaments and military equipment on credit. 230

Apr. 30, 1947. Protocol concerning demarcation of the state border, with maps and related documents. 232

May 6, 1947. Protocol concerning completion of the evacuation of Ukrainian citizens from Polish territory to the Ukrainian SSR and of Polish citizens from the Ukrainian SSR to Poland. 232

Aug. 1947 (approximate date). Agreement concerning supplementary delivery of grain to Poland. 235

Aug. 4, 1947. Trade agreement. 235

Oct. 1, 1947. Parcel post agreement. 237

Jan. 26, 1948. Joint communiqué concerning economic negotiations. 243

Jan. 26, 1948. Long-term trade agreement. 243

Jan. 26, 1948. Agreement concerning delivery of Soviet industrial equipment to Poland on credit. 244

Apr. 8, 1948. Convention concerning quarantine of agricultural plants and their protection from parasites and diseases. 247

May 13, 1948. Trade protocol for 1948. 438

May 28, 1948. Agreement concerning training of Polish citizens in civic institutions of higher learning in the USSR and their maintenance. 248

July 8, 1948. Treaty concerning the regime on the state border, with final protocol. 250

July 8, 1948. Convention concerning procedure for settling border disputes and incidents, with related documents. 250

Jan. 15, 1949. Trade protocol for 1949. 256

Oct. 10, 1949. Modifications in the agreement of Mar. 20, 1946, concerning postal and telephone-telegraph communications. 263

Oct. 22, 1949. Agreement concerning collaboration in the field of radio broadcasting. 263

Nov. 7, 1949. Agreement concerning transfer of Soviet Marshal K. K. Rokossovsky to the Polish Army. 264

Jan. 25, 1950. Trade protocol for 1950. 268

Jan. 25, 1950. Protocol concerning working conditions for Soviet specialists sent to Poland to give technical assistance, with annex. 268

Jan. 25, 1950. Agreement concerning technical training of Polish specialists in the USSR. 268

June 29, 1950. Trade agreement for the period 1953–1958. 275

June 29, 1950. Trade protocol for the period 1951–1952. 275

June 29, 1950. Agreement concerning delivery of industrial equipment to Poland on credit during the period 1951–1958. 275

Feb. 15, 1951. Treaty concerning exchange of territories, with protocol, two annexes, and a map. 279

Mar. 9, 1951. Trade protocol for 1951. 280

Oct. 23, 1951. Documents concerning demarcation of the state border. 283.

Dec. 8, 1951. Protocol concerning amendment of the treaty concerning the regime on the Soviet-Polish state border and the convention concerning procedure for settling border disputes and incidents, both of July 8, 1948, in accordance with the provisions of the treaty concerning exchange of territories of February 15, 1951. 284

1952. Trade protocol for 1952. 440

Feb. 29, 1952. Agreement concerning conditions of trade deliveries. 285

Apr. 5, 1952. Agreement concerning construction of a Palace of Culture and Science in Warsaw. 285

May 19, 1952. Agreement concerning training of Polish citizens in civic institutions of higher education in the USSR. 287

Apr. 22, 1953. Trade protocol for 1953. 295

Sept. 5, 1953. Protocol concerning preparation and exchange of radio programs. 301

Aug. 26 and Sept. 17, 1953. Exchange of notes modifying the parcel post agreement of October 1, 1947. 302.

Nov. 1953. Protocol concerning termination of coal deliveries by Poland to the USSR at special prices. 303

Nov. 5, 1953. Communiqué concerning a

meeting of the Soviet-Polish commission for scientific and technical collaboration. 303

Feb. 11, 1954. Trade protocol for 1954. 307

July 1954. Agreement concerning Soviet commercial transit through Poland. 442

Sept. 18, 1954. Communiqué concerning the seventh meeting of the Soviet-Polish commission for scientific and technical collaboration. 310

Feb. 18, 1955. Agreement concerning establishment of regular air communications. 323

Feb. 25, 1955. Trade protocol for 1955. 324

Apr. 23, 1955. Agreement concerning aid by the USSR to Poland in regard to development of research concerning atomic nuclear physics and the use of atomic energy for the needs of the national economy. 326

May 8, 1955. Communiqué concerning the eighth meeting of the Soviet-Polish commission for scientific and technical collaboration. 327

Feb. 7, 1956. Protocol concerning expansion of telegraph and telephone service, radio broadcasting, and television. 349

Feb. 8, 1956. Trade protocol for 1956. 349

June 30, 1956. Agreement concerning cultural collaboration. 359

Aug. 15, 1956. Communiqué concerning the tenth meeting of the Soviet-Polish commission for scientific and technical collaboration. 366

Sept. 18, 1956. Credit agreement. 368

Nov. 18, 1956. Joint statement concerning political, economic, and military relations. 372

Dec. 17, 1956. Treaty concerning the legal status of Soviet troops temporarily stationed in Poland. 374

Feb. 6, 1957. Protocol concerning cultural collaboration in 1957. 377

Mar. 3, 1957. Protocol of the eleventh meeting of the Soviet-Polish commission for scientific and technical collaboration. 378

Mar. 5, 1957. Treaty concerning demarcation of the existing State frontier in the sector adjoining the Baltic Sea, with two maps. 379

Mar. 25, 1957. Agreement concerning time schedules and procedures for further repatriation of persons of Polish nationality from the USSR. 379

Mar. 27, 1957. Agreement concerning scientific collaboration in 1957 between the Academies of Sciences of the USSR and Poland. 379

Apr. 9, 1957. Trade protocol for 1957. 380

Aug. 23, 1957. Agreement concerning exchange of students and research workers. 388

Oct. 26, 1957. Agreement concerning legal assistance in cases arising out of the temporary stationing of Soviet troops in Poland. 391

Dec. 26, 1957. Communiqué concerning the twelfth meeting of the Soviet-Polish commission for scientific and technical collaboration. 395

Dec. 28, 1957. Treaty concerning legal aid and legal relations in civil, family, and criminal cases. 396

POLAND, three-way

Dec. 14, 1934. Protocol concerning regulation of the export of rye and rye flour, with final protocol (USSR, Poland, Germany). 98

June 29, 1949. Trade and payments agreement (USSR, Poland, Finland). 261

Apr. 14, 1951. Trade agreement (USSR, Poland, Finland). 440

Dec. 17, 1951. Trade protocol (USSR, Poland, Finland). 440

Mar. 31, 1955. Trade agreement (USSR, Poland, Finland). 443

May 22, 1957. Protocol concerning an increase of the relative role of maritime transport in foreign trade and concerning organization of freight transportation on internal waterways (USSR, Poland, German Democratic Republic). 383

POLAND, four-way

Mar. 30, 1922. Final protocol concerning economic problems and the consolidation of peace in Eastern Europe (USSR, Poland, Estonia, Latvia). 30

POLAND, unverified

July 26, 1949. Agreement concerning relations between the Polish administration and the Soviet High Command. 429

Poland. See also Nongovernmental agreements; Plurilateral, Soviet bloc agreements and conferences; Plurilateral, non-aggression agreements.

PRIVATE ORGANIZATIONS

Aug. 20, 1921. Agreement between the RSFSR and the American Relief Administration concerning procedure for famine relief. 22

Aug. 27, 1921. Agreement between the RSFSR and Fridtjof Nansen, High Commissioner of the Geneva Conference for Aid to the Famine Victims in Russia, concerning famine relief, with annex (Chicherin-Nansen agreement). 22

Aug. 27, 1921. Supplementary agreement between the RSFSR and Fridtjof Nansen concerning famine relief operations of the International Russian Relief Executive. 22

Aug. 29, 1921. Agreement between the RS-

FSR and the German Red Cross concerning medical aid to famine victims. 22

Sept. 16, 1921. Agreement between the RSFSR and representatives of the Society of Friends (Quakers) concerning famine relief. 24

Oct. 1, 1921. Agreement between the RSFSR and the Ukrainian SSR on the one hand and the American Mennonite Relief on the other concerning famine relief, with annex. 24

Oct. 18, 1921. Agreement between the RSFSR and the International Trade Union Alliance concerning famine relief. 25

Oct. 19, 1921. Agreement between the RSFSR and the American Relief Administration concerning food remittances. 25

Oct. 20, 1921. Agreement between the Ukrainian SSR and the American Mennonite Relief concerning famine relief, with annex. 25

Oct. 20, 1921. Agreement between the Ukrainian SSR and Holland Mennonite Relief concerning famine relief. 25

Nov. 8, 1921. Agreement between the RSFSR and a group of Swedish trade and industrial enterprises concerning famine relief. 26

Nov. 14, 1921. Agreement between the RSFSR and Fridtjof Nansen concerning relief parcels. 26

Dec. 25, 1921. Agreement between the RSFSR and Fridtjof Nansen concerning a loan from Norway for famine relief. 28

Dec. 27, 1921. Agreement between the RSFSR and the Italian Red Cross concerning famine relief. 432

Dec. 30, 1921. Agreement between the RSFSR and the American Relief Administration concerning famine relief to adults. 28

Dec. 30, 1921. Agreement between the RSFSR and the American Relief Administration concerning purchase by the RSFSR of food supplies and seed in America for famine relief. 28

Dec. 31, 1921. Agreement between the Ukrainian SSR and Fridtjof Nansen concerning famine relief. 28

Jan. 10, 1922. Agreement between the Ukrainian SSR and the American Relief Administration concerning provision of food for famine relief. 28

Feb. 1, 1922. Agreement between the Ukrainian SSR and the American Relief Administration concerning purchase of food and seed for famine relief. 29

Feb. 13, 1922. Agreement between the RSFSR and the Central Committee of the organization "Pro Russia" under the Italian Socialist Party concerning famine relief. 29

Feb. 27, 1922. Agreement between the RSFSR and the Lithuanian Red Cross concerning food parcels for famine relief. 29

Mar. 1922. Agreement between the RSFSR and the Student Friendship Fund concerning provision of food for students. 30

Mar. 16, 1922. Agreement between the RSFSR and the French Red Cross concerning famine relief. 30

Apr. 20, 1922. Agreement between the Ukrainian Red Cross and the Nansen Commission. 31

June 18, 1922. Agreement between the RSFSR and Fridtjof Nansen concerning relief parcels to Russian professors. 32

Aug. 1922. Exchange of letters between the RSFSR and the American Relief Administration, acting for the American Mennonite Relief, concerning validation of an undated agreement between the RSFSR and the American Mennonite Relief concerning aid for agricultural reconstruction. 34

Oct. 26, 1922. Agreement between the RSFSR and the American Relief Administration concerning clothing remittances. 35

Dec. 11, 1922. Agreement between the RSFSR and the American Jewish Joint Distribution Committee concerning aid for agricultural and other reconstruction. 37

June 15, 1923. Agreement between the RSFSR and the American Relief Administration concerning termination of the ARA's operations. 39

May 28, 1924. Agreement between the USSR and the American Mennonite Relief concerning aid for agricultural reconstruction. 42

ROMANIA, bilateral

Mar. 5 and 9, 1918. Agreement concerning political and military matters. 4

Mar. 5 and 9, 1918. Protocol concerning exchange of prisoners. 4

Mar. 9, 1918. Protocol concerning the return of Russian soldiers in Romania. 4

Mar. 9, 1918. Protocol concerning evacuation by Romania of the Akkerman district and a general political amnesty for Romanian political emigrants and deserters. 5

Nov. 20, 1923. Regulations concerning measures to prevent and settle conflicts which might arise along the Dniester River. 40

Dec. 4, 1923. Agreement concerning establishment of mixed commissions to settle navigation disputes on the Dniester River. 433

June 9, 1934. Exchange of notes concerning establishment of diplomatic relations. 95

June 9, 1934. Exchange of notes constituting an agreement concerning non-interference in each other's internal affairs. 95

Feb. 8, 1935. Agreement concerning establishment of direct rail communications. 99

Feb. 8, 1935. Agreement concerning reconstruction of a railroad bridge across the Dniester. 99

Feb. 17, 1936. Payments agreement, with protocol. 109

June 26, 27, and 28, 1940. Exchange of notes constituting an agreement concerning cession to the USSR of Bessarabia and Eastern Bukovina, with map. 136

Feb. 26, 1941. Treaty of commerce and navigation, with annex concerning the Soviet Trade Mission in Romania. 143

Feb. 26, 1941. Trade and payments agreement. 143

Aug. 23, 1944. Conditions for an armistice. 162

Sept. 12, 1944. Armistice agreement, with annex. 163

Jan. 16, 1945. Reparations agreement. 169

Feb. 27 and 28, 1945. Soviet demand for the reorganization of the Romanian Government. 436

Mar. 8 and 9, 1945. Exchange of notes concerning establishment of Romanian administration in Transylvania. 174

May 8, 1945. Agreement concerning ecomomic collaboration. 178

May 8, 1945. Protocol concerning the content and form of organization of the collaboration of Romania and the USSR in certain fields of the Romanian economy. 178

May 8, 1945. Trade agreement, with two annexes. 178

May 8, 1945. Protocol concerning liquidation of the balance of the account of the State Bank of the USSR in the Romanian National Bank. 178

July 17, 1945. Agreement concerning establishment of a joint-stock Soviet-Romanian company for exploration, extraction, refining, and marketing of oil and oil products, "Sovrompetrol," with three annexes. 183

July 19, 1945. Agreement concerning establishment of a joint-stock Soviet-Romanian navigation company, "Sovromtransport," with protocol and annex. 183

Aug. 6, 1945. Exchange of declaration concerning re-establishment of diplomatic relations. 188

Aug. 8, 1945. Agreement concerning establishment of a Soviet-Romanian joint-stock civil aviation company, "T. A. R. S." 189

Aug. 15, 1945. Agreement concerning establishment of a joint-stock Soviet-Romanian bank, "Sovrombank," in Bucharest. 193

Aug. 20 and 24, 1945. Exchange of notes concerning reorganization of diplomatic missions into embassies. 194

Sept. 13, 1945. Agreement concerning deliveries of grain to Romania. 197

Sept. 13, 1945. Agreement concerning substitution of other goods for grain in reparation deliveries, and deferment of part of the grain delivery until the following harvest year. 197

Sept. 13, 1945. Agreement concerning a reduction in deliveries by Romania of food and fodder for use of the Soviet troops in Romania and of material and financial payments as required by the Allied High Command in Romania. 197

Sept. 13, 1945. Agreement concerning a reduction of Romania's indebtedness under the armistice agreement of September 12, 1944. 197

Sept. 13, 1945. Agreement concerning transportation. 197

Sept. 13, 1945. Agreement concerning repatriation. 197

Sept. 13, 1945. Agreement concerning collaboration in the fields of culture and education. 198

Feb. 15, 1946. Payments agreement. 206

Feb. 15, 1946. Protocol concerning the most-favored-nation principle. 206

Mar. 20, 1946. Agreement concerning establishment of a Soviet - Romanian joint-stock lumber company, "Sovromles." 208

Apr. 15, 1946 (approximate date). Agreement concerning extension from six to eight years of the term of payment of reparations by Romania. 210

Feb. 10, 1947. Treaty of peace, with six annexes. 228

Feb. 20, 1947. Treaty of commerce and navigation, with annex concerning the Soviet Trade Mission in Romania. 229

Feb. 20, 1947. Trade and payments agreement for 1947. 229

June 12, 1947. Agreement concerning direct rail communications. 232

Dec. 15, 1947. Agreement concerning training of Romanian citizens in civic institutions of higher learning in the USSR and their maintenance. 241

Feb. 4, 1948. Treaty of friendship, collaboration and mutual assistance. 244

Feb. 4, 1948. Protocol concerning demarcation of the border, with two maps. 244

Feb. 18, 1948. Trade and payments agreement for 1948. 245

Feb. 18, 1948. Supplementary protocol concerning the Soviet-Romanian joint-stock lumber company. 245

Feb. 18, 1948. Supplementary protocol concerning the Soviet-Romanian joint-stock civil aviation company. 245

June 4 and 7, 1948. Exchange of notes concerning reduction in reparations payments by Romania. 249

Aug. 20, 1948. Agreement concerning establishment of postal and telephone-telegraph communications. 252

Aug. 20, 1948. Parcel post agreement. 252

Jan. 24, 1949. Agreement concerning technical aid to Romania. 257

Jan. 24, 1949. Trade and payments agreement for 1949, with two annexes. 257

Mar. 9, 1949. Romanian decree establishing the "Sovromgaz" company. 257

Apr. 27, 1949. Agreement concerning collaboration in the field of radio broadcasting. 258

Aug. 20, 1949. Romanian decrees establishing the Soviet-Romanian joint-stock companies "Sovrommetal," "Sovromsig" (insurance), "Sovromcarbune" (coal), "Sovromconstructio," "Sovromchim" (chemicals), "Sovromtractor." 262

Sept. 27, 1949. Protocol concerning demarcation of the state border, with related documents. 263

Nov. 25, 1949. Treaty concerning the regime on the state border, with final protocol. 264

Nov. 25, 1949. Convention concerning procedure for settling border disputes and incidents, with related documents. 264

Feb. 17, 1950. Agreement concerning scientific and technical collaboration. 270

Feb. 17, 1950. Trade and payments agreement for 1950. 270

May 27, 1950. Convention concerning quarantine of agricultural plants and their protection from parasites and diseases. 274

Sept. 26, 1950. Protocol concerning working conditions for Soviet specialists sent to Romania to give technical assistance. 277

Mar. 15, 1951. Trade and payments agreement for 1951. 280

Aug. 24, 1951. Long-term agreement concerning delivery of industrial equipment and technical aid to Romania and development of trade. 282

Jan. 7, 1952. Protocol modifying the parcel post agreement of August 20, 1948. 284

Mar. 20, 1952. Agreement concerning training of Romanian citizens in civic institutions of higher education in the USSR. 285

June 25, 1952. Agreement concerning conditions of trade deliveries. 288

Dec. 25, 1952. Convention concerning measures for prevention of floods and regulation of the water level on the River Prut, with two annexes. 292

Aug. 17, 1953. Protocol concerning preparation and exchange of radio programs. 299

Aug. 26 and Sept. 10, 1953. Exchange of notes modifying the parcel post agreement of August 20, 1948. 301

Dec. 5, 1953. Agreement concerning a special river administration for the mouth of the Danube, with protocol. 304

Dec. 5, 1953. Exchange of notes concerning transfer to the special river administration for the mouth of the Danube of property necessary for maintenance of conditions for navigation on the Danube. 304

Mar. 31, 1954. Trade protocol for 1954. 309

Mar. 31, 1954. Agreement concerning transfer and sale to Romania of Soviet shares in Soviet-Romanian joint-stock companies. 309

Mar. 31, 1954. Credit agreement. 310

July 10, 1954. Communiqué concerning the fourth meeting of the Soviet-Romanian commission for scientific and technical collaboration. 313

Sept. 18, 1954. Agreement concerning transfer and sale to Romania of Soviet shares in Soviet-Romanian joint-stock companies. 316

Jan. 25, 1955. Agreement concerning establishment of regular air communications. 323

Feb. 17, 1955. Communiqué concerning the fifth meeting of the Soviet-Romanian commission for scientific and technical collaboration. 323

Mar. 9, 1955. Trade protocol for 1955. 324

Apr. 22, 1955. Agreement concerning aid by the USSR to Romania in regard to development of research concerning atomic nuclear physics and the use of atomic energy for the needs of the national economy. 326

Dec. 13, 1955. Agreement concerning sale to Romania of Soviet shares in the Soviet-Romanian joint-stock oil company "Sovrompetrol." 344

Jan. 3, 1956. Agreement concerning technical collaboration in the field of civil aviation. 346

Feb. 11, 1956. Trade protocol for 1956. 349

Apr. 7, 1956. Agreement concerning cultural collaboration. 353

Apr. 14, 1956. Protocol concerning expansion of collaboration in the fields of telephone and telegraph communications, radio broadcasting, and television. 353

July 21, 1956. Agreement concerning delivery of vessels to the USSR during the period 1957–1960. 364

Aug. 8, 1956. Communiqué concerning the eighth meeting of the Soviet-Romanian commission for scientific and technical collaboration. 365

Oct. 22, 1956. Agreement concerning transfer to Romania of Soviet shares in the Soviet-Romanian joint-stock uranium company "Sovrom Kvartsit." 370

Dec. 3, 1956. Statement concerning political and economic negotiations. 373

Dec. 3, 1956. Protocol concerning a Soviet credit. 373

Mar. 2, 1957. Communiqué concerning the eighth meeting of the Soviet-Romanian commission for scientific and technical collaboration. 378

Mar. 4, 1957. Trade agreement for 1957. 379

Apr. 15, 1957. Agreement concerning the legal status of Soviet troops temporarily stationed on Romanian territory. 381

June 18, 1957. Protocol concerning transfer to Romania of functions and property of the special river administration for the Lower Danube. 385

July 18, 1957. Protocol concerning transfer to Romania of full responsibility for direction of the Administration for the Lower Danube. 386

Aug. 1, 1957. Agreement concerning regulation of border waterways. 386

Sept. 4, 1957. Consular convention. 388

Sept. 4, 1957. Convention concerning regulation of the question of citizenship of persons with dual citizenship. 388

Dec. 21, 1957. Protocol concerning the ninth meeting of the Soviet-Romanian commission for scientific and technical collaboration. 395

ROMANIA, three- and four-way

Aug. 20, 1952. Agreement concerning establishment of a regular steamship line between the Black Sea ports of the USSR, Bulgaria, and Romania, and the ports of Albania, with two annexes (USSR, Romania, Albania, Bulgaria). 290

Sept. 11, 1956. Agreement concerning collaboration in saving human life and assistance to vessels and aircraft in distress on the Black Sea (USSR, Romania, Bulgaria). 367

ROMANIA, unverified

Dec. 1939. Protocol concerning restoration of railroad traffic between Romania and occupied Poland. 429

Dec. 12, 1944. Agreement concerning execution of economic provisions of the armistice agreement. 429

Romania. See also Plurilateral, nonaggression agreements; Plurilateral, Soviet bloc agreements and conferences.

SAN MARINO, bilateral

Apr. 30, 1956. Communiqué concerning establishment of consular relations. 354

SINKIANG, bilateral

May 27, 1920. Agreement concerning border trade and the return of Russian soldiers and refugees (Ili protocol). 11

Oct. 1924. Exchange of notes concerning consulates. 48

Oct. 1, 1931. Provisional trade agreement, with four annexes. 79

May 16, 1935. Loan agreement. 102

Nov. 26, 1940. Agreement concerning prospecting, exploration, and exploitation of tin mines and associated minerals. 140

SINKIANG, unverified

1925. General commercial agreement. 428

Jan. 1, 1936. Treaty of mutual assistance. 428

Jan. 1, 1936. Military agreement. 428

Sinkiang. See also Nongovernmental agreements.

SLOVAKIA, bilateral

Dec. 6, 1940. Treaty of commerce and navigation, with annex concerning the Soviet Trade Mission in the Slovak Republic. 140

Dec. 6, 1940. Trade and payments agreement. 140

SPAIN, bilateral

July 28, 1933. Exchange of telegrams concerning establishment of diplomatic relations. 89

Oct. 1936. Agreement concerning transfer of part of the Spanish gold reserve to the Soviet State Bank. 113

Feb. 3, 1937. Act of transfer of the Spanish gold reserve to the USSR. 435

Spain. See also Nongovernmental agreements.

SWEDEN, bilateral

June 1, 1918. Trade agreement. 5

Oct. 28, 1918. Trade agreement. 7

Oct. 31, 1918. Agreement supplementing the trade agreement of October 28, 1918. 7

Mar. 15, 1924. Commercial agreement. 41

Mar. 15, 1924. Declaration concerning claims. 42

Mar. 15 and 18, 1924. Exchange of notes concerning recognition of the USSR *de jure*. 42

Sept. 12, 1924. Agreement concerning exchange of parcel post and insured letters. 47

July 21, 1926. Exchange of notes concerning reciprocal protection of trade-marks. 57

Feb. 2, 1927. Exchange of notes constituting an agreement on rights and immunities of consuls. 59

Oct. 9, 1927. Convention concerning the legal status of the Soviet Trade Mission in Sweden, with final protocol. 63

Apr. 1940. Agreement concerning regular air communications during the summer of 1940. 134

Sept. 1940. Agreement concerning repatriation of persons of Swedish origin from Estonia. 435

Sept. 7, 1940. Trade and payments agreement. 138

Sept. 7, 1940. Agreement concerning an arbitration court. 138

Sept. 7, 1940. Trade agreement for 1940–1941. 139

Sept. 7, 1940. Credit agreement, with protocol. 139

May 30, 1941. Agreement concerning settlement of property claims relating to the Baltic States. 144

Nov. 4, 1941. Protocol concerning regulation of questions concerning trade under wartime conditions. 147

Oct. 7, 1946. Protocol modifying and extending the trade and payments agreement of September 7, 1940, with two lists. 218

Oct. 7, 1946. Credit agreement, with annex, list, and protocol. 218

Oct. 7, 1946. Exchange of notes concerning an increase in trade. 219

Oct. 7, 1946. Exchange of notes concerning prices for goods purchased in Sweden by the USSR. 219

Oct. 7, 1946. Informal agreement concerning settlement of certain property claims arising out of the war. 219

Oct. 25, 1946. Agreement concerning establishment of regular air communications. 220

Oct. 25, 1946. Protocol concerning flights using air facilities in Finland.

Nov. 5, 1946. Parcel post agreement. 221

Dec. 10, 1946. Exchange of notes concerning entry into force of the trade protocol of Oct. 7, 1946. 222

Jan. 30, 1947. Agreement concerning general conditions for delivery of goods to the USSR, with annex. 225

Dec. 31, 1947. Trade protocol for 1948. 243

Apr. 2, 1949. Trade protocol for 1949. 258

Apr. 9, 1953. Trade protocol for 1953. 295

June 29 and Aug. 26, 1953. Exchange of notes modifying the parcel post agreement of November 5, 1946. 300

Jan. 23, 1954. Protocol modifying the agreement of October 25, 1946, concerning establishment of regular air communications. 306

Feb. 2, 1954. Trade protocol for 1954. 307

Sept. 29, 1954. Agreement concerning cooperation for rescue in the Baltic Sea. 316

Nov. 24 and Dec. 4, 1954. Exchange of notes modifying the parcel post agreement of November 5, 1946. 320

Apr. 22, 1955. Trade protocol for 1955. 326

Dec. 9, 1955. Trade protocol for 1956. 343

Mar. 31, 1956. Agreement concerning air communications, with two annexes and two exchanges of notes. 351

Apr. 3, 1956. Joint communiqué concerning political negotiations. 352

Dec. 21, 1957. Trade protocol for 1958. 395

SWEDEN, four-way

Aug. 9, 1918. Agreement concerning exchange of civilian and military personnel (RSFSR, Sweden, Denmark, Switzerland). 6

SWEDEN, unratified

Mar. 1, 1922. Temporary commercial treaty. 399

Mar. 16, 1934. Agreement concerning a loan by Sweden of one hundred million Swedish crowns. 401

Sweden. See also Nongovernmental agreements.

SWITZERLAND, bilateral

Apr. 14, 1927. Exchange of notes concerning settlement of the dispute over the assassination of V. V. Vorovsky. 60

Feb. 24, 1941. Trade agreement. 142

Sept. 10, 1945. Final procès-verbal of the commission to examine the living conditions of Soviet citizens who had escaped from German captivity and taken refuge in Switzerland. 196

Mar. 18, 1946. Exchange of notes concerning re-establishment of diplomatic relations. 207

Mar. 17, 1948. Commercial treaty. 243

Mar. 17, 1948. Agreement concerning the Soviet Trade Mission in Switzerland. 246

Mar. 17, 1948. Trade agreement, with annexes. 246

SWITZERLAND, four-way

Aug. 9, 1918. Agreement concerning exchange of civilian and military personnel (RSFSR, Switzerland, Sweden, Denmark). 6

Switzerland. See also Nongovernmental agreements.

SUDAN, bilateral

Mar. 17, 1956. Communiqué concerning exchange of diplomatic missions at the level of embassies. 351

SYRIA, bilateral

July 21 and 22, 1944. Exchange of telegrams concerning establishment of diplomatic relations. 162

Nov. 16, 1955. Trade and payments agreement, with two annexes. 342

Nov. 19, 1955. Agreement concerning transformation of diplomatic missions into embassies. 444

June 25, 1956. Joint communiqué concerning political negotiations. 359

Aug. 20, 1956. Agreement concerning cultural collaboration. 366

Nov. 1956 (approximate date). Agreement concerning shipment of Soviet munitions to Syria. 371

Nov. 5, 1956. Joint communiqué concerning political negotiations. 372

June 29, 1957. Agreement concerning establishment of radio-telegraph communications. 385

Aug. 6, 1957. Communiqué concerning the

visit of a Syrian governmental delegation to the USSR. 387

Sept. 4, 1957. Communiqué concerning economic negotiations. 388

Oct. 28, 1957. Agreement concerning economic and technical collaboration. 391

Dec. 19, 1957. Trade agreement. 394

SYRIA, unverified

Spring 1956. Agreement concerning shipment of Soviet munitions to Syria. 430

TANNU-TUVA, bilateral

Aug. 1926. Treaty of friendship. 57

THAILAND, bilateral

Mar. 12, 1941. Exchange of notes concerning establishment of diplomatic, consular, and commercial relations. 143

Dec. 28 and 31, 1946. Exchange of notes concerning re-establishment of diplomatic relations. 225

May 20, 1956. Communiqué concerning transformation of diplomatic missions into embassies. 355

Thailand. See also Nongovernmental agreements.

TUNISIA, bilateral

July 13, 1957. Trade agreement. 386

TURKEY, bilateral

Dec. 18, 1917. Armistice. 2

Dec. 18, 1917. Act concerning demarcation lines. 2

Feb. 14, 1918. Agreement concerning temporary regulation of postal, telegraph, and maritime service. 3

Mar. 3, 1918. Treaty concerning political and legal matters, supplementing the peace treaty between the RSFSR and the Central Powers. 4

Apr. 26 and June 2, 1920. Exchange of notes concerning establishment of diplomatic relations. 11

Mar. 16, 1921. Treaty of friendship, with three annexes. 20

Mar. 28, 1921. Convention concerning repatriation of military and civilian prisoners. 20

Sept. 17, 1921. Convention concerning repatriation of military and civilian prisoners. 24

Oct. 13, 1921. Treaty of friendship. 25

Jan. 21, 1922. Treaty of friendship. 29

Mar. 20, 1922. Convention concerning the use by citizens of both countries of pastures lying on the opposite side of the border, with three annexes. 30

Mar. 20, 1922. Convention concerning cross-ing the border by inhabitants of border regions. 30

July 9, 1922. Postal-telegraph convention. 34

July 9, 1922. Railroad convention. 34

Dec. 17, 1925. Treaty of friendship and neutrality, with three protocols. 54

May 31, 1926. Protocol concerning establishment of a one-year limit for persons wishing to exercise the right to change their citizenship by moving from one country to the other. 56

June 29, 1926. Protocol concerning exchange of acts of ratification of the treaty of friendship and neutrality of December 17, 1925. 57

Nov. 14, 1926. Joint communiqué concerning strengthening of political relations. 58

Jan. 8, 1927. Convention concerning use of water from border rivers and streams. 58

Jan. 8, 1927. Protocol concerning construction of a dam for the Sardarabad Canal, with annex. 58

Mar. 11, 1927. Treaty of commerce and navigation, with annex and final protocol. 59

Nov. 17 and Dec. 14, 1927. Exchange of notes modifying and extending the convention of March 20, 1922, concerning border crossing. 64

Sept. 18 and Dec. 15, 1927. Exchange of notes modifying and extending the convention of March 20, 1922, concerning the use of pastures. 64

May 17, 1928. Protocol extending the convention of March 20, 1922, concerning the use of pastures. 65

Aug. 6, 1928. Convention concerning use of pastures across the border by citizens of both states, with three annexes. 66

Aug. 6, 1928. Convention concerning prevention of the spread of animal diseases across the border between the Georgian SSR and Turkey, with protocol and four annexes. 66

Aug. 6, 1928. Convention concerning border crossing by inhabitants of border zones. 66

Aug. 6, 1928. Convention concerning procedure for consideration and settlement of border disputes, with protocol. 67

Dec. 23, 1928. Protocol concerning exchange of acts of ratification of the railroad convention of July 9, 1922. 68

Dec. 17, 1929. Protocol extending the treaty of friendship and neutrality of December 17, 1925 (Karakhan Protocol). 73

July 28, 1930. Protocol concerning exchange of acts of ratification of the protocol of December 17, 1929, extending the treaty of friendship and neutrality of December 17, 1925. 75

Oct. 3, 1930. Joint communiqué reaffirming friendship. 75

Nov. 25 and Dec. 25, 1930. Exchange of

notes concerning provisions for visits of warships. 76

Mar. 7, 1931. Protocol concerning naval armament in the Black Sea, with protocol of signature. 76

Mar. 16, 1931. Treaty of commerce and navigation, with final protocol. 77

June 13, 1931. Agreement concerning direct rail communications. 78

Oct. 30, 1931. Communiqué concerning negotiations. 80

Oct. 30, 1931. Protocol extending the treaty of friendship and neutrality of December 17, 1925, and related protocols. 80

Apr. 17, 1932. Trade agreement. 81

May 8, 1932. Informal agreement concerning a Soviet long-term credit to Turkey of eight million dollars. 82

Oct. 10, 1932. Protocol extending for six months the convention of August 6, 1928, concerning procedure for consideration and settlement of border disputes. 84

Mar. 28, 1933. Protocol extending for an additional six months the convention of August 6, 1928, concerning procedure for consideration and settlement of border disputes. 86

Oct. 3, 1933. Barter agreement. 90

Nov. 29, 1933. Protocol extending for an additional six months the convention of August 6, 1928, concerning procedure for consideration and settlement of border disputes. 91

Jan. 21, 1934. Protocol concerning realization of a credit of eight million dollars, with supplementary protocol and annex. 92

Apr. 12, 1934. Protocol extending for an additional six months the convention of August 6, 1928, concerning procedure for consideration and settlement of border disputes. 93

June 20, 1934. Trade agreement. 95

Oct. 6, 1934. Protocol extending for an additional six months the convention of August 6, 1928, concerning procedure for consideration and settlement of border disputes. 97

June 24, 1935. Trade agreement. 103

Nov. 7, 1935. Protocol extending the treaty of friendship and neutrality of December 17, 1925, and related protocols. 107

Apr. 11 and 16, 1936. Exchange of notes concerning negotiations for a revision of the Lausanne Convention on the Black Sea Straits. 110

June 9, 1936. Exchange of notes extending the convention of August 6, 1928, concerning procedure for consideration and settlement of border disputes. 111

Oct. 20, 1936. Agreement modifying the railroad convention of July 9, 1922. 113

July 15, 1937. Convention concerning procedure for considering and settling border incidents and disputes, with final protocol. 116

July 15, 1937. Protocol concerning appointment of border commissioners. 117

July 15, 1937. Protocol concerning border contact points. 117

July 15, 1937. Exchange of notes constituting an agreement concerning restitution for damages caused by border incidents and disputes. 117

July 15, 1937. Exchange of notes concerning use of water from border rivers and streams. 117

July 16, 1937. Communiqué concerning negotiations. 117

Oct. 8, 1937. Treaty of commerce and navigation, with final protocol. 118

Oct. 8, 1937. Exchange of notes concerning tax assessment of the Soviet Trade Mission in Turkey. 118

Oct. 8, 1937. Trade and clearing agreement, with three annexes and an exchange of notes. 119

Mar. 31, 1938. Exchange of notes concerning branches of the Soviet Trade Mission in Turkey. 120

May 18, 1938. Exchange of notes modifying annex 1 of the trade and clearing agreement of October 8, 1937. 121

June 5, 1939. Exchange of notes extending the treaty of friendship and neutrality of December 17, 1925. 125

June 5, 1939. Agreement modifying the railroad convention of July 9, 1922, with protocol. 125

July 5, 1939. Exchange of notes modifying the protocol of July 15, 1937, concerning appointment of border commissioners. 126

Oct. 18, 1939. Statement on negotiations. 131

Mar. 25, 1941. Joint statement concerning neutrality. 143

May 30 and July 17, 1953. Exchange of notes concerning Soviet claims on Turkish territory and regulation of the Black Sea Straits. 298

Sept. 15, 1953. Agreement concerning irrigation of the Igdir plain, with three protocols. 301

TURKEY, unverified

Nov. 1920. Political agreement. 427

Jan. 25, 1936. Trade agreement for 1936. 428

Turkey. See also Nongovernmental agreements; Plurilateral, Central Powers; Plurilateral, Nonaggression agreements.

UKRAINE, bilateral

May 4, 1918. Cease-fire agreement. 430

June 12, 1918. Armistice. 5

UKRAINIAN SSR, bilateral

Dec. 28, 1920. Treaty of workers' and peasants' alliance, with supplementary decree and five annexes. 16

Ukrainian SSR. See also Plurilateral, internal Soviet treaties.

UNION OF SOUTH AFRICA, bilateral

Feb. 21, 1942. Agreement concerning establishment of consular relations. 149

UNITED KINGDOM, bilateral

Feb. 12, 1920. Agreement concerning exchange of military and civilian prisoners, with two annexes and two lists of names. 9

June 30 and July 7, 1920. Exchange of notes concerning completion of repatriation. 432

Mar. 16, 1921. Trade agreement, with declaration concerning recognition of claims. 20

Aug. 16, 1921. Agreement concerning the Anglo-Russian submarine cable. 22

Dec. 1 and 6, 1921. Exchange of notes concerning cable rates. 27

July 3, 1922. Exchange of notes concerning extension of the trade agreement of March 16, 1921, to Canada. 33

Feb. 2 and 8, 1924. Exchange of notes concerning recognition of the USSR *de jure* and the settlement of outstanding questions. 41

Oct. 3, 1929. Protocol concerning procedure for settlement of outstanding questions. 72

Dec. 20 and 21, 1929. Exchange of notes on the occasion of the resumption of diplomatic relations. 73

Apr. 16, 1930. Temporary commercial agreement, with related documents. 74

May 22, 1930. Temporary agreement concerning regulation of the fisheries in waters contiguous to the northern coasts of the USSR, with two protocols. 74

Dec. 1, 1930, and Jan. 19, 1931. Exchange of notes extending the temporary commercial agreement of April 16, 1930, to certain British colonies. 76

Feb. 16, 1934. Temporary commercial agreement, with annex concerning balance of payments. 92

Apr. 19, 1934. Parcel post convention. 94

Apr. 19, 1934. Regulations concerning parcel post. 94

Apr. 19 and May 28, 1934. Exchange of notes concerning interpretation of Articles 3 and 33 of the parcel post convention of April 19, 1934. 94

Jan. 21 and Mar. 9 and 11, 1935. Exchange of notes concerning the Russian text of the parcel post convention of April 19, 1934. 100

July 28, 1936. Exchange of notes constituting an agreement on trade credits, with annex. 112

July 14, 1937. Exchange of notes concern-

ing reciprocal notification of arrests and imprisonments. 116

July 17, 1937. Agreement providing for limitation of naval armament and exchange of information concerning naval construction, with protocol of signature. 117

Nov. 12 and 19, 1937. Exchange of notes concerning the Russian text of the naval agreement of July 17, 1937. 119

July 6, 1938. Protocol modifying the agreement of July 17, 1937, providing for limitation of naval armament and exchange of information concerning naval construction. 121

Oct. 11, 1939. Barter agreement. 435

July 12, 1941. Agreement concerning joint action in the war against Germany, with protocol. 144

Aug. 16, 1941. Agreement concerning mutual deliveries, credit, and methods of payment. 146

Sept. 7, 1941. Agreement regulating methods of payment and exchange. 146

May 26, 1942. Treaty concerning alliance in the war against Germany and collaboration and mutual assistance after the war. 149

June 12, 1942. Joint communiqué concerning the visit of the Soviet Commissar of Foreign Affairs to London. 150

June 22, 1942. Exchange of letters constituting an agreement concerning ships' expenses and freights, with memorandum. 150

June 27, 1942. Agreement concerning financing of British military deliveries and other aid. 150

Aug. 17, 1942. Joint communiqué concerning a conference. 151

Sept. 30, 1942. Exchange of notes concerning exchange of information on military weapons. 151

May 5 and 18, 1944. Informal agreement concerning a temporary division of the Balkans into operational spheres of influence. 161

Sept. 19, 1944. Protocol to the armistice agreement with Finland. 164

Sept. 23, 1944. Agreement concerning establishment of direct radio-telephone service. 165

Oct. 9, 1944. Informal agreement concerning spheres of influence in the Balkans. 166

Oct. 21, 1944. Joint communiqué concerning political negotiations. 166

Feb. 11, 1945. Agreement concerning repatriation of liberated Soviet citizens in the United Kingdom, with two annexes. 173

Feb. 11, 1945. Exchange of notes concerning the status of liberated Soviet citizens in the United Kingdom. 173

Feb. 11, 1945. Agreement concerning treatment and repatriation of Soviet citizens liberated by forces operating under British command, and of British citizens liberated by forces operating under Soviet command. 173

Feb. 11, 1945. Exchange of notes modifying the agreement of the same date concerning treatment and repatriation of liberated Soviet and British citizens. 174

Sept. 11–Oct. 2, 1945. Exchange of notes concerning the time of withdrawal of Allied troops from Iran. 199

Apr. 19 and July 9, 1946. Exchange of notes modifying the agreement of September 23, 1944, concerning establishment of direct radio-telephone service. 214

July 24, Aug. 17, and Sept. 7, 1946. Exchange of notes concerning entry into force of the agreement of September 23, 1944, concerning establishment of direct radio-telephone service, as modified by an exchange of notes of April 19 and July 9, 1946. 218

Mar. 24, 1947. Negotiations. 230

Dec. 27, 1947. Protocol of agreement on questions of trade and finance, with annex and two schedules. 243

Dec. 27, 1947. Exchange of notes constituting a payments agreement. 243

Feb. 17 and Mar. 19, 1953. Exchange of communications concerning release of British civilians interned in North Korea. 293

Mar. 18 and 24, 1953. Agreement concerning convocation of a conference on air safety. 294

June 24, 1953. Exchange of notes extending for one year the temporary fisheries agreement of May 22, 1930. 296

Apr. 26, 1956. Statement on negotiations, with annex. 354

May 25, 1956. Agreement concerning fisheries, with protocol and exchange of notes. 356

Dec. 19, 1957. Agreement concerning establishment of a civil air route between Moscow and London. 394

UNITED KINGDOM, three-way

Jan. 29, 1942. Treaty of alliance, with three annexes (USSR, UK, Iran). 148

Oct. 8, 1944. Protocol to the armistice agreement with Finland concerning compensation to Canada for nickel mines in former Finnish territory (USSR, UK, Canada). 165

Sept. 29, 1947. Protocol concerning modification in the method of payment by the USSR to Canada under the protocol of October 8, 1944, to the armistice agreement with Finland (USSR, UK, Canada). 237

UNITED KINGDOM, unratified

Aug. 8, 1924. General treaty. 400

Aug. 8, 1924. Treaty of commerce and navigation, with protocol and two declarations. 400

United Kingdom. See also Nongovernmental agreements; Plurilateral, Great Power agreements and conferences.

UNITED STATES, bilateral

Nov. 15, 1933. Gentlemen's agreement concerning a payment to the United States on pre-Soviet Russian debts. 90

Nov. 16, 1933. Exchange of notes concerning establishment of diplomatic relations, with related documents. 90

July 13, 1935. Exchange of notes constituting a commercial agreement. 104

July 11 and 15, 1935. Exchange of notes concerning purchases to be made by the USSR in the United States during the coming year. 104

Nov. 22, 1935. Exchange of notes concerning execution of letters rogatory, with annex. 107

July 11, 1936. Exchange of notes extending the commercial agreement of July 13, 1935. 112

July 9 and 13, 1936. Exchange of notes concerning purchases to be made by the USSR in the United States during the coming year. 112

Jan. 7, 1937. Exchange of notes concerning claims in regard to debts and nationalized property. 115

Aug. 4, 1937. Exchange of notes constituting a commercial agreement. 117

Aug. 4, 1937. Exchange of notes concerning exemption from excise tax of coal, coke, and coal or coke briquettes imported into the United States from the USSR. 118

Aug. 2 and 5, 1937. Exchange of notes concerning purchases to be made by the USSR in the United States during the coming year. 118

Aug. 2 and 4, 1938. Exchange of notes concerning purchases to be made by the USSR in the United States during the coming year. 122

Aug. 5, 1938. Exchange of notes extending the commercial agreement of August 4, 1937, for one year. 122

Aug. 5, 1938. Exchange of notes concerning exemption from excise tax of coal, coke, and coal or coke briquettes imported into the U.S. from the USSR. 122

Feb. 25, 1939. Parcel post agreement. 124

Feb. 25, 1939. Regulations for execution of the parcel post agreement of February 25, 1939. 124

Aug. 2, 1939. Exchange of notes extending the commercial agreement of August 4, 1937, for one year. 126

Aug. 2, 1939. Exchange of notes concerning purchases to be made by the USSR in the United States during the coming year. 126

Aug. 2, 1939. Exchange of notes concerning exemption from excise tax of coal, coke, and coal or coke briquettes imported into the United States from the USSR. 126

Aug. 6, 1940. Exchange of notes extending the commercial agreement of August 4, 1937, for an additional year. 137

Aug. 6, 1940. Exchange of notes concerning purchases to be made by the USSR in the United States during the coming year. 137

Aug. 6, 1940. Exchange of notes concerning exemption from excise tax of coal, coke, and coal or coke briquettes imported into the United States from the USSR. 137

Sept. 27, and Nov. 5, 1940. Agreement concerning opening of a United States consulate in Vladivostok. 140

Aug. 2, 1941. Exchange of notes extending the commercial agreement of August 4, 1937, for one year. 145

Aug. 2, 1941. Exchange of notes concerning economic aid to strengthen the USSR in its struggle against armed aggression. 435

Oct. 30 and Nov. 4, 1941. Exchange of notes concerning conditions for Lend-Lease shipments. 147

Nov. 6 and 14, 1941. Exchange of letters concerning organizational forms of cooperation between the Red Cross societies of the two States. 147

Feb. 13, 18, and 23, 1942. Exchange of communications concerning the grant to the USSR of an additional one billion dollars' Lend-Lease aid and methods of delivery. 149

June 11, 1942. Agreement concerning principles applicable to mutual aid in the conduct of the war against aggression, with exchange of notes (Lend-Lease agreement). 149

July 31, 1942. Exchange of notes extending the commercial agreement of August 4, 1937. 151

Sept. 1, 1943. Exchange of notes concerning modification of shipments under the Third Lend-Lease Protocol. 154

Oct. and Dec. 31, 1943. Exchange of letters concerning exchange in the fields of radio and motion pictures. 436

1944. Agreement concerning distribution in the USSR of *Amerika,* a Russian-language magazine published in the United States. 158

Dec. 1943 and Feb. 2, 1944. Agreement concerning provision of facilities in Siberia for operation of American bombers. 436

June and July 1944. Informal agreement concerning an exchange of views of technical experts on questions of the coordination of technical measures in the field of international civil aviation. 161

Oct. 18, 1944 (approximate date). Agreement concerning establishment of air bases in Siberia for American bombers in return for shipment to the USSR of American military and other supplies. 436

Feb. 8, 1945. Oral agreement concerning use of air bases in Soviet territory. 170

Feb. 11, 1945. Agreement concerning treatment and repatriation of Soviet citizens liberated by forces operating under American command, and of American citizens liberated by forces operating under Soviet command. 174

Feb. 10 and 11, 1945. Exchange of notes concerning voting procedure in the General Assembly of the United Nations. 174

May 26–June 6, 1945. Negotiations. 179

June 14 and 16, 1945. Exchange of telegrams concerning entry of United States troops into Berlin and Vienna and withdrawal of United States forces in Germany to the zonal boundary. 180

Aug. 11 and 12, 1945. Exchange of communications concerning conditions for surrender by Japan. 190

Aug. 27, 1945. Agreement concerning policy in China. 437

Aug. 15, 16, 17, 22, 26 and 30, 1945. Exchange of communications concerning conditions of surrender of Japanese armed forces. 195

Sept. 17, 1945. Agreement concerning boundary changes between the Soviet and American zones of occupation in Germany. 198

Oct. 15, 1945. Agreement concerning disposition of Lend-Lease supplies in inventory or procurement in the United States, with two schedules. 200

Nov. 1 and 7, 1945. Exchange of communications concerning withdrawal of Soviet and American troops from Czechoslovakia. 201

Feb. 5, 1946. Joint communiqué concerning military administration in Korea. 206

Feb. 5, 1946. Joint communiqué concerning establishment of a Joint Commission for Korea. 206

Apr. 18, 1946. Communiqué concerning political reconstruction in Korea. 210

Apr. 23, 1946. Exchange of notes concerning an increase in the circulation of *Amerika* in the USSR. 210

May 24, 1946. Agreement concerning organization of commercial radio teletype communication channels. 212

Aug. 7 and 19, 1946. Exchange of notes concerning revision of the regime of the Black Sea Straits established by the Montreux Convention of July 20, 1936. 218

Apr. 15, 1947. Agreement to begin negotiations for a Lend-Lease settlement. 438

Apr. 8 and 19, and May 2, 7, and 12, 1947. Exchange of notes concerning resumption of the work of the Joint Commission for Korea. 232

June 16, 1947. Agreement concerning opening of an American consular office in Leningrad. 232

Aug. 11 and 23, 1947. Exchange of notes concerning work of the Joint Commission for Korea. 236

Jan. 1948. Informal agreement concerning the return of eight Lend-Lease vessels. 243

Sept. 27, 1949. Agreement concerning return of Lend-Lease vessels, wtih annex. 263

Mar. 21, 1951. Soviet note concerning a Lend-Lease settlement. 281

June 27, 1951. Interview concerning the possibility of a truce in Korea, 282

Sept. 11–Dec. 26, 1953. Exchange of notes concerning return of Lend-Lease naval craft. 305

Jan. 6, 1954. Agreement concerning procedure for talks on atomic energy. 441

Mar. 26, 1954. Agreement concerning return to the United States of thirty-eight small naval craft received by the USSR under Lend-Lease, with annex. 308

Dec. 22, 1954. Agreement concerning return of twenty-seven Lend-Lease naval craft, with annex. 320

Mar. 10, May 19 and 20, 1955. Exchange of notes concerning reciprocal visits of farm delegations. 329

May 26, 1955. Agreement concerning return of certain United States naval vessels (Lend-Lease settlement), with annex. 329

June 25, 1955. Agreement defining the boundary between the United States sector of Berlin and the Soviet Zone of Occupation of Germany, with map. 330

July 9 and 11, 1955. Exchange of notes concerning the visit of a *Pravda* correspondent to Stratford, Connecticut. 332

Mar. 17 and Sept. 5, 1955. Exchange of notes constituting an agreement concerning exchange of medical films, with annex. 336

Sept. 9 and Dec. 16, 1955. Exchange of notes constituting an agreement concerning distribution within the USSR of *Amerika,* an illustrated Russian-language magazine. 344

Mar. 26–July 9, 1956. Exchange of letters constituting an agreement concerning destruction of seventy-nine Lend-Lease naval vessels. 361

Oct. 29, 1956. Exchange of notes concerning extension of diplomatic immunity to non-diplomatic members of embassy staffs. 371

Oct. 5, 1957. Joint statement concerning negotiations. 390

United States. See also Nongovernmental agreements; Plurilateral, Great Power agreements and conferences.

URUGUAY, bilateral

Aug. 21 and 22, 1926. Exchange of tele-grams concerning recognition of the USSR *de jure* and establishment of diplomatic relations. 57

Aug. 11 and 13, 1933. Exchange of telegrams concerning establishment of permanent diplomatic missions. 89

May 1935. Trade agreement. 102

Jan. 27, 1943. Exchange of notes concerning re-establishment of diplomatic and commercial relations. 153

July 28, 1954. Payments agreement. 315

July 28, 1954. Trade agreement. 442

Aug. 11, 1956. Treaty of commerce and navigation. 366

Aug. 11, 1956. Trade and payments agreement. 366

URUGUAY, unratified

Aug. 9, 1946. Treaty of friendship, commerce, and navigation, with annex concerning the Soviet Trade Mission in Uruguay. 402

VATICAN CITY, bilateral

Mar. 12, 1922. Agreement concerning famine relief. 30

VENEZUELA, bilateral

Mar. 14, 1945. Exchange of notes concerning establishment of diplomatic and consular relations. 175

VIETNAM, DEMOCRATIC REPUBLIC OF, bilateral

Jan. 14 and 30, 1950. Exchange of notes concerning establishment of diplomatic relations. 268

July 8, 1955. Trade agreement. 331

July 8, 1955. Exchange of notes concerning establishment of a Soviet Trade Mission in the DRV. 331

July 18, 1955. Joint communiqué concerning political and economic negotiations. 332

July 18, 1955. Agreement concerning Soviet aid to the DRV. 332

July 18, 1955. Trade agreement, with annex. 333

May 5, 1956. Trade protocol for 1956. 354

Dec. 1, 1956. Agreement concerning a Soviet credit. 445

Feb. 15, 1957. Agreement concerning cultural collaboration. 378

Mar. 11, 1957. Agreement concerning non-commercial payments. 379

Mar. 30, 1957. Trade protocol for 1957. 380

Apr. 8, 1957. General conditions for delivery of goods. 380

Dec. 25, 1957. Agreement concerning cultural collaboration. 395

Dec. 26, 1957. Agreement concerning establishment of telephone and telegraph communications. 395

Dec. 26, 1957. Agreement concerning establishment of postal and parcel post communications. 395

Democratic Republic of Vietnam. See also Plurilateral, Soviet bloc agreements and conferences.

YEMEN, bilateral

Nov. 1, 1928. Treaty of friendship and commerce (Treaty of Sanaa). 67
Feb. 1939. Exchange of notes extending the treaty of friendship and commerce of November 1, 1928. 123
Oct. 31, 1955. Treaty of friendship. 340
Mar. 8, 1956. Trade agreement. 350
June 23, 1956. Joint communiqué concerning political and economic relations. 359
July 11, 1956. Agreement concerning economic collaboration. 363
Oct. 1957. Agreement concerning transformation of diplomatic missions into embassies. 445

YUGOSLAVIA, bilateral

May 11, 1940. Treaty of commerce and navigation, with supplementary protocol concerning the Soviet Trade Mission in Yugoslavia and the Temporary Yugoslav Trade Mission in the USSR. 135
May 11, 1940. Agreement concerning trade and payments for 1940–1941. 135
June 25, 1940 (approximate date). Agreement concerning establishment of diplomatic relations. 136
Apr. 5, 1941. Treaty of friendship and non-aggression. 143
Sept. 14, 1942. Exchange of notes concerning reorganization of diplomatic missions into embassies. 151
Sept. 28, 1944. Press communiqué concerning an agreement concerning joint military operations in Yugoslavia. 165
Sept. 28, 1944 (probable date). Agreement concerning a Soviet loan. 165
Nov. 25, 1944. Joint communiqué concerning establishment of a unified Yugoslav Government. 168
Apr. 11, 1945. Treaty of friendship, mutual assistance, and postwar collaboration. 175
Apr. 13, 1945. Trade agreement, with protocol. 175
Nov. 13, 1945. Agreement concerning conditions of work of Soviet experts assigned to Yugoslavia. 201
Nov. 30, 1945. Agreement concerning deliveries of petroleum products. 201
Apr. 26, 1946. Agreement concerning delivery of grain and pulse to Yugoslavia. 211
June 8, 1946. Joint communiqué concerning negotiations. 213
June 8, 1946. Trade agreement. 213
June 8, 1946. Agreement concerning economic collaboration. 213
Feb. 4, 1947. Agreement concerning estab-

lishment of a Soviet-Yugoslav joint-stock Danube steamship company, "Juspad," with five annexes. 226
Feb. 4, 1947. Agreement concerning establishment of a Soviet-Yugoslav joint-stock civil aviation company, "Justa," with four annexes. 226
July 5, 1947. Trade and payments agreement, with protocol. 234
July 5, 1947. Agreement concerning reciprocal provision of funds for maintenance of diplomatic missions and other non-commercial payments. 234
July 25, 1947. Agreement concerning deliveries of industrial equipment to Yugoslavia on credit, with two annexes. 235
July 25, 1947. Trade agreement. 235
Aug. 23, 1947. Agreement concerning the sale to Yugoslavia of railroad rolling stock, with three annexes and a protocol. 236
Dec. 15, 1947. Agreement concerning training of Yugoslav citizens in civic institutions of higher learning in the USSR and their maintenance. 241
Feb. 12, 1948. Joint statement concerning mutual consultation on questions of foreign policy. 244
Dec. 27, 1948. Trade protocol for 1949, with three annexes. 256
Aug. 31, 1949. Protocol concerning liquidation of the Soviet-Yugoslav joint-stock Danube steamship company "Juspad" and the Soviet-Yugoslav joint-stock civil aviation company "Justa," with four annexes. 262
June 14, 1953. Agreement concerning resumption of diplomatic relations. 296
Oct. 1, 1954. Barter agreement, with annexes. 316
Jan. 5, 1955. Commercial agreement, with two annexes. 322
Jan. 5, 1955. Payments agreement. 322
Jan. 5, 1955. Exchange of notes concerning entry into force of the commercial and payment agreements of January 5, 1955. 322
Jan. 10, 1955. Exchange of notes concerning flights of Yugoslav civil airplanes over territory of the Soviet Zone of Occupation of Austria. 322
Jan. 10, 1955. Exchange of notes concerning flights of Soviet civil airplanes over Yugoslav territory. 322
June 2, 1955. Joint declaration concerning normalization of relations and development of collaboration between the two States. 329
July 1955. Agreement concerning settlement of claims. 331
July 30, 1955. Exchange of notes concerning an increase in trade during 1955. 334
Sept. 1, 1955. Joint communiqué concerning economic negotiations. 335
Sept. 1, 1955. Protocol concerning economic negotiations, with two annexes. 335

Sept. 3, 1955. Agreement concerning air communications. 336

Sept. 23, 1955. Exchange of notes concerning establishment of trade lists. 338

Sept. 27, 1955. Agreement concerning postal and telegraph-telephone communications. 338

Sept. 27, 1955. Parcel post agreement. 339

Nov. 1, 1955. Agreement concerning air communications and reciprocal services. 340

Nov. 12, 1955. Exchange of notes constituting an agreement concerning the sale and delivery of Soviet books and other cultural products to Yugoslavia. 340

Nov. 14, 1955. Trade protocol, with annex. 341

Dec. 19, 1955. Agreement concerning scientific and technical collaboration. 345

Jan. 6, 1956. Trade protocol for 1956, with two annexes. 346

Jan. 12, 1956. Agreement concerning collaboration in construction of industrial enterprises in Yugoslavia. 347

Jan. 28, 1956. Agreement concerning collaboration in regard to the development of research in the field of nuclear physics and the use of atomic energy for peaceful purposes. 348

Feb. 2, 1956. Agreement concerning a loan to Yugoslavia. 348

Feb. 6, 1956. Agreement concerning a trade credit to Yugoslavia. 348

Mar. 3, 1956. Agreement concerning collaboration in the field of steamship service on the Danube. 350

Mar. 9, 1956. Agreements concerning insurance and reinsurance. 351

Apr. 19, 1956. Protocol concerning execution of trade deliveries for 1955. 353

May 17, 1956. Convention concerning cultural collaboration. 355

May 20, 1956. Communiqué concerning the first meeting of the Soviet-Yugoslav commission for scientific and technical collaboration. 356

May 22, 1956. Convention concerning regulation of the question of citizenship of persons with dual citizenship. 356

June 6, 1956. Protocol concerning supplementary trade in 1956, with two annexes. 357

June 20, 1956. Joint statement concerning political relations. 358

June 20, 1956 (approximate date). Exchange of notes concerning regularization of information services. 358

Aug. 1, 1956. Protocol to the agreement of August 1, 1956, concerning collaboration in construction of enterprises of the aluminum industry in Yugoslavia. 365

Aug. 2, 1956. Protocol concerning execution of the agreement of January 12, 1956, concerning collaboration in construction of industrial enterprises in Yugoslavia, with two annexes. 365

Oct. 5, 1956. Protocol concerning the second meeting of the Soviet-Yugoslav commission for scientific and technical collaboration. 368

Feb. 9, 1957. Protocol concerning collaboration between scientific organizations and institutions. 377

Feb. 26, 1957. Trade protocol for 1957. 378

Apr. 10, 1957. Trade agreement for the period 1958–1960. 381

June 30, 1957. Communiqué concerning the third meeting of the Soviet-Yugoslav commission for scientific and technical collaboration. 385

July 10, 1957. Exchange of notes constituting an agreement concerning collaboration in the field of radio and television. 386

July 29, 1957. Protocol concerning collaboration in construction of enterprises of the aluminum industry in Yugoslavia. 386

Aug. 4, 1957. Communiqué concerning a meeting of governmental and party delegations. 387

Sept. 6, 1957. Communiqué concerning extension of the convention of May 22, 1956, concerning regulation of the question of citizenship of persons with dual citizenship. 389

Nov. 1, 1957. Trade protocol for 1958. 391

Dec. 26, 1957. Protocol concerning the fourth meeting of the Soviet-Yugoslav commission for scientific and technical collaboration. 395

YUGOSLAVIA, three-way

Aug. 1, 1956. Agreement concerning collaboration in construction of enterprises of the aluminum industry in Yugoslavia, with exchange of notes (USSR, Yugoslavia, German Democratic Republic). 364

Yugoslavia. See also Plurilateral, Nonaggression agreements; Plurilateral, Soviet bloc agreements and conferences.